tenth edition
PHYSICAL EDUCATION
FOR ELEMENTARY
SCHOOL CHILDREN

Glenn Kirchner
Simon Fraser University

Graham J. Fishburne
University of Alberta

Boston, Massachusetts   Burr Ridge, Illinois   Dubuque, Iowa
Madison, Wisconsin   New York, New York   San Francisco, California   St. Louis, Missouri

WCB/McGraw-Hill

A Division of The **McGraw·Hill** *Companies*

TITLE: PHYSICAL EDUCATION FOR ELEMENTARY SCHOOL CHILDREN

 Recycled/acid free paper

5678910 QPH QPH 0654321
Library of Congress Catalog Number: 97–20122

Cover and interior designer: Elise Lansdon
Cover photo: Glenn Kirchner

ISBN 0–697–29486–2

Editorial director: *Kevin T. Kane*
Publisher: *Edward E. Bartell*
Sponsoring editor: *Vicki Malinee*
Developmental editor: *Theresa Grutz/Shirley R. Oberbroeckling*
Marketing manager: *Pamela S. Cooper*
Senior project manager: *Kay J. Brimeyer*
Production supervisor: *Laura Fuller*
Designer: *Katherine Farmer*
Photo research coordinator: *John C. Leland*
Art editor: *Jodi K. Banowetz*
Compositor: *Shepherd, Inc.*
Typeface: *10/12 Minion Regular*
Printer: *Quebecor/Hawkins*

Library of Congress Cataloging-in-Publication Data

Kirchner, Glenn.
     Physical education for elementary school children/Glenn
Kirchner, Graham J. Fishburne.—10th ed.
        p. cm.
     Includes bibliographical references and index.
     ISBN 0–697–29486–2
     1. Physical education for children. 2. Physical education for
children—United States—Curricula. I. Fishburne, Graham J. II. Title.
GV443.K57 1997
372.86–dc21   97–20122
                                     (CIP)

http://www.mhhe.com

To the memory of my brother, Harold.
He did a lot of things in his lifetime,
and he did them very well.
Glenn Kirchner

This one's for you Jack.
To David (Jack) Harper-Tarr, my role model,
mentor, and physical educator.
Graham J. Fishburne

Brief Contents

BRIEF CONTENTS

PART 7

Gymnastic and Movement Activities

PART 8

Dance and Movement Activities

CONTENTS

PART 5

Provision for Special Needs and Programs 261

PART 6

Game and Movement Activities 311

PART 7

**Gymnastic
and Movement
Activities   497**
....

PART 8

Dance and Movement Activities 605
· ·

PREFACE

THE AIM OF THIS TEXTBOOK

This textbook has been written and designed to serve a dual purpose. The primary aim is teacher development. The content material will help students develop into effective teachers of physical education. Students will learn developmentally appropriate teaching strategies for physical education, and they will acquire knowledge and skills in the areas of classroom management, discipline, evaluation, and many other areas of effective teaching. This teacher education knowledge forms a sound foundation for teaching any subject area or age group. The textbook's second aim is to provide teachers with a rich resource of games, dances, gymnastic, and movement activities that are developmentally appropriate for elementary school children. There is not only an explanation of how to teach each activity, but a description of the activity, complete with rules and often a photograph or line drawing. The textbook presents over 500 games, dances, and gymnastic stunts and tumbling activities—one of the most comprehensive listings currently available.

THE TENTH EDITION

This edition blends theory, research findings, and sound pedagogical knowledge related to child development into practical ideas for the generalist classroom teacher. The book continues to serve as a university and college textbook and as an excellent resource for administrators, school boards, curriculum developers, and educational consultants, in addition to elementary school teachers.

The tenth edition of *Physical Education for Elementary School Children* will serve as a learning tool for teacher development and a lifetime resource for teaching physical education.

AIDS

The changes and new material in this tenth edition of *Physical Education for Elementary School Children* have been made primarily to facilitate student learning. While we have retained the content of the previous edition, we have added new material, reorganized some of the chapters, added one new chapter, and rewritten various areas of the text. Throughout the text we have included more headings and highlighted major points for ease of understanding. Four major changes have been made to facilitate student learning.

Key Concepts

To help students recognize important ideas, key concepts are identified in each chapter. These concepts are listed at the start of each chapter, and are highlighted at appropriate points in the text.

Key Objectives

At the beginning of each chapter, a list of key learning objectives is outlined. This list identifies for the student what knowledge should be gained from the chapter.

Summary Review

At the conclusion to each chapter, a brief summary review helps students identify major points and issues.

Individual and Group Projects

To help solidify and reinforce chapter content, a selection of individual and group projects is provided at the end of each chapter. These projects have been designed to provide students with problem-solving opportunities, the solutions of which require an understanding of chapter content. The small-group projects permit students to work together in a cooperative learning environment. Students can help each other learn the concepts and skills as they strive to achieve a common goal.

TENTH EDITION CONTENT CHANGES

Additional changes in the tenth edition reflect contemporary concerns in physical education, health and wellness, and education in general.

Classroom Management

Clearly, it is vital that all teachers develop effective classroom management skills. The discussions of classroom management, student misbehavior, and discipline have been expanded in the tenth edition. The latest models of behavior management have been included, together with a variety of practical techniques to improve classroom control and to handle student misbehavior. Practical teaching suggestions are provided to help teachers develop their skills and knowledge in this important area.

Student Progress and Teacher Effectiveness

All fields of education have a concern for evaluation and accountability. At no other time in the history of education has there been a greater need for instruments and methods to provide information on student progress and teacher effectiveness. In the tenth edition, we have added to the checklists, instruments, methods, and techniques outlined in earlier editions. For example, a variety of checklists have been added to assist in the assessment of a child's development in fundamental motor skills. Use of these checklists will provide the teacher with diagnostic and evaluative information. Also, to assist the teacher, several checklists are included to assess teacher effectiveness. For example, an observational checklist for the evaluation of teaching is provided to help teachers "self-reflect" and improve on their teaching. Other checklists and techniques have been included to help improve classroom control and to handle student misbehavior. These checklists and techniques are practical and easy to use, and they can be readily applied to the teaching situation.

Photographic Models

Two other major changes in the tenth edition are new photographs and the move to a full-color text. We strongly believe not only that "a picture is worth a thousand words" but that a picture provides a visual model for the reader. The photographs provide visions of real teaching situations, and help translate ideas and activities into practical teaching demonstrations. The tenth edition contains all-new color photographs. The move to a full-color text is to facilitate readability and learning. The use of color provides opportunities to highlight various features of the text and to provide a visually appealing image.

Technology

Numerous opportunities exist to utilize technology with physical education. For example, newsgroups and web sites on the Internet, CD-ROM, and various computer software programs offer exciting opportunities to expand and improve the quality of a physical education program. Ideas to employ such technology have been included in several chapters within the text. Also, a new appendix (D) reviews such technology and offers suggestions on how to use it to enhance the physical education program. Specific ideas are forwarded for each of the thirty chapters in the text, and a resource list is provided.

OVERVIEW OF THE TENTH EDITION

The following overview explains the philosophy, direction, and organization and content of the text.

Philosophy

The changes and new material in the tenth edition of *Physical Education for Elementary School Children* reflect our continuing emphasis on a developmentally based curriculum. Each chapter continues to accommodate the three developmental levels established in previous editions. **Level I** represents the beginning phase of acquiring game, dance, gymnastic, and movement concepts and skills that children pass through in the early primary years. As children move into **Level II,** they begin to show an increased proficiency in all fundamental and manipulative skills, coupled with an improved ability to perform more coordinated movement patterns with greater speed and accuracy. Developmental **Level III** is a period of refinement in all game, dance, and gymnastic activities. Because children at each chronological age can vary as much as four or five years in physical maturity and have markedly different physical education experiences, the three developmental levels are considered to be "signposts" along a continuum of concept and motor skill development. To accommodate these basic differences, each activity area in this book allows the teacher to choose activities from the most appropriate level for each child or group of children.

Direction

The major theme carried throughout this text is the health-related benefits of a quality program of physical education. Development of an "active lifestyle" is essential for all children if they are to benefit from a program of physical education. Bridging school, community, and home lives is crucial. Ideas to achieve this, and to monitor and encourage involvement in physical activity, are included throughout the text. The concern for health and wellness through the development of an active lifestyle fits with contemporary trends and the current view of the important role of physical education in a childs life. The historic "1996 Surgeon General's Report on Physical Activity and Health" identified very clearly the need for quality programs of physical education. These current trends, supported by our major professional associations (AAHPERD and CAHPERD), are consistent throughout North America and are now being endorsed by the international community.

Organization and Content

The textbook is organized to reflect our belief in the sequential progress of teacher development. It is divided into eight separate but interconnected parts.

Part I

Part 1 consists of four chapters that provide the foundation for teaching children physical education. Before commencing teaching, it is first necessary to understand the aim, goals, and objectives of the program, and to be familiar with the meaning and purpose of the curriculum. This is accomplished in chapter 1. It is also essential that the teacher have a sound understanding of how children grow, develop, and learn. Chapter 2 deals with children's growth and development, and chapter 3 provides the basis for learning motor skills. Finally, the teacher must also be familiar with effective teaching strategies and techniques, to ensure that all children will acquire the desired skills and knowledge. Chapter 4 covers teaching strategies and techniques. This chapter also addresses ways to motivate children and discusses methods and suggestions to deal with discipline and behavior problems.

Part 2

Part 2 consists of two chapters. Chapter 5 introduces the movement concepts and skills that provide a framework for introducing children to movement activities and experiences. One of this book's features is the way in which a discussion of Laban's movement concepts and skills has been integrated into every game, dance, and gymnastic activity. This integration allows the teacher to select and emphasize structured skills, movement concepts, or both, according to the developmental level, interest, and background of the children in each class. Chapter 6 provides a full description of the locomotor, nonlocomotor, and manipulative skills that children develop. Checklists to monitor and assess development of these fundamental skills are provided.

Part 3

Health, wellness, and active living are covered in Part 3. Chapter 7 deals with the human body, how it functions, and the importance of nutrition and a healthy lifestyle. Chapter 8 provides guidance in the assessment and improvement of physical fitness. This is an extremely important chapter, in light of recent national concerns about decreasing levels of physical fitness among the elementary school population. The information contained in Part 3 provides a comprehensive view of the link between health and physical activity, reinforcing the important role of elementary school physical education in a child's life.

Part 4

Part 4 consists of four chapters designed to offer guidance in developing the physical education curriculum to meet individual needs. Chapter 9 provides a step-by-step analysis of the planning process involved in creating a quality program of physical education. This chapter illustrates how to plan a yearly program, units of instruction, and daily lesson plans. Chapter 10 deals with the organization of personnel, facilities, and equipment to meet the needs of the teaching situation. The legal responsibilities of the teacher are covered here. Organization decisions also impact on class management, and so this important area is also discussed. Once these decisions are made, it is essential that the planning,

organizational, and teaching decisions are assessed and evaluated. Chapter 11 provides advice on selecting appropriate evaluative methods and techniques. A variety of instruments and checklists are provided to assist in the assessment and evaluation process. For example, portfolios and journal writing are presented as additional forms of assessment to help the teacher build a profile of each child's growth and development in physical education.

In addition to the regular physical education curriculum, most schools offer a variety of extraclass programs. Chapter 12 covers this important area and explains how to design and supervise intramural and interschool sports programs.

Part 5

Special considerations or arrangements have to be made to accommodate children with disabilities, and to accommodate physical education when normal facilities or equipment is unavailable. The three chapters of part 5 deal with these special considerations. Chapter 13 provides advice and guidance on integrating children with special needs into the regular physical education program. A comprehensive review of some of the most common disabilities is provided, together with teaching suggestions and methods of assessment. Ideas on integrating children with disabilities into regular instructional and extraclass programs are presented throughout the text.

A new feature of the tenth edition is the inclusion of a separate chapter (14) dedicated to the important area of using the medium of physical activity to teach academic concepts and skills. In addition to this separate chapter, ideas and suggestions to teach and/or enhance academic skills and concepts through physical education activities can be found throughout the text.

Chapter 15 provides suggestions and guidance on adapting physical education activities to the classroom.

Part 6

Part 6 commences with an important introduction highlighting how games and movement activities should be introduced and taught to children. This is followed by chapter 16, which covers locomotor and manipulative games for each of the three developmental levels. Chapter 17 is dedicated to cooperative games and learning activities and the elements that make up a cooperative game. The cooperative games chapter has been expanded in the tenth edition to include many new games created by children from all parts of the world. Chapters 18 through 23 provide instruction on how to teach the major games of soccer, hockey, football, volleyball, basketball, and softball. A suggested sequence for presenting motor skills, practice activities, lead-up games, and evaluative techniques is included. Chapter 24 covers track and field and cross-country activities. Over 225 games and game activities are included in these chapters, providing a valuable resource for teachers.

PREFACE

Part 7

Part 7 covers gymnastic and movement activities appropriate for elementary-school-age children. Chapter 25 deals with stunts, tumbling, and movement skills. Introducing small equipment into the teaching situation is considered in chapter 26, where stunts and manipulative skills with small equipment are covered. Chapter 27 considers large apparatus gymnastic activities. Over 240 gymnastic stunts and movement skills are included in these chapters, again providing a valuable resource for teachers.

Part 8

Dance and movement activities are introduced in Part 8. Chapter 28 provides guidance on introducing children to rhythmic and movement activities. The teaching of traditional and contemporary dances, in the form of square dances, line dances, and folk dances, is introduced in chapter 29. As a teacher resource, over 50 dances are included in this part of the text. Chapter 30 is the final chapter and provides guidance on teaching children creative dance activities.

Appendixes

Four Appendixes are included to provide supplementary content and resource information.

Appendix A provides a description of five videotapes that have been made to complement the contents of the text. Four tapes cover the teaching of games, gymnastics, folk dances, and creative dance activities. Each videotape describes class management techniques, organization of content, and teaching strategies. The fifth videotape provides a comprehensive and graphic display of how the heart and circulatory system operate.

Appendix B is a resource section that describes how to make inexpensive physical education equipment.

Appendix C is a resource section that lists apparatus, equipment, and supply companies.

Appendix D explains how to use technology to enhance the physical education program. A brief review of the Internet and the World Wide Web is provided, together with a short glossary of terms. Ideas for using technology are included for each of the text's thirty chapters.

Glossary of Terms

An expanded glossary of terms is provided at the end of the book.

ADDITIONAL INFORMATION

Throughout this book, the pronouns *she* and *her* are generally used when referring to the teacher, for the sake of simplicity and consistency. Likewise, the pronouns *he* and *his* are often used to describe the student, although feminine pronouns are used to refer to female students in the illustrations. The use of the word *gender* has also been widely used throughout this text.

ANCILLARIES

Revised *Instructor's Manual* accompanying this text provides a summary outline for each chapter, along with teaching suggestions and evaluative techniques. The manual offers an overview of each chapter and acquaints the instructor with the audiovisual resources that are available.

Yearly Programs, Units, and Daily Lesson Plans have been revised and expanded by Glenn Kirchner and Graham Fishburne.

MICROTEST III testing program has new and improved test items. It is available in IBM and Macintosh.

Set of Overhead *Transparencies* is also provided for adopters of this edition.

Videotapes have been produced by the authors to illustrate the content and the strategies used to teach game, gymnastic, dance, and health-related fitness activities to elementary school children. Each videotape is accompanied by a user manual, which includes brief descriptions of each scene and its approximate location on the videotape.

FitSolve II is fitness assessment software available for IBM compatible and MAC computers.

ACKNOWLEDGMENTS

The writers of this book are deeply indebted to the many teachers and children from many schools in the United States, Canada, and numerous other countries for their generous support. We are particularly grateful to Mrs. Deirdre DeGagne and Mr. Brian Rosell of Sandy Hill Elementary, Abbotsford, B.C., for their great ideas and generous support.

We wish to express our gratitude to the teachers and students of the following schools for their outstanding contributions to this book:

Mrs. D. Fishburne, and the students of Idylwylde Elementary School, Edmonton, Alberta

Mrs. M. Greene, Briarwood Elementary School, Prarie, Kansas

Mr. Norm Lindburg, and the students of Parksville Elementary School, Parksville, B.C.

Mr. M. McComb, and the students of Village Park Elementary School, Comox, B.C.

Mr. H. Peason, and the students of Ferry Pass Elementary School, Pensacola, Florida

Ms. Andrea Roland, and the students of Glacier Park Elementary School, Courtney, B.C.

Ms. J. Simmons, and the students of N. B. Cook
Elementary School, Pensacola, Florida
Ms. Gail Teague, and the students of Haskel
Elementary School, Northridge, California

The extensive changes found in chapter 13 are due to the excellent suggestions made by Dr. M. Miller, St. Bonaventure University.

We would also like to express our thanks to Dr. Carol Conkell, *Western Carolina University;* Dr. Leon Greene, *University of Kansas,* Dr. Jenifer Romack, *California State University,* Northridge, and Jeanne Kentel, *University of Alberta,* for their generous assistance.

The following boys and girls were helpful in posing for various skills and movement activities for this tenth edition. To each our special thanks for their patience and proficiencies:

Michelle Baynton, Reghan Blake, Brian Buchan, John Buchan, Chris, Kristine, and Rob Caughell, Jacquelyn Duke, Rebecca Fishburne, Vanessa Fuller, Shannon MacGillivray, Claire McWilliam, Lexi Jones-Maartmen, Will Maartmen, Bradley Tomblin, and James Tomblin

We also wish to extend our thanks to all the teachers and children who were part of Dr. Kirchner's International Games Project. Their games, drawings, and photographs provide a wonderful international representation to the games section of this book.

We would also like to express our gratitude to the individuals who reviewed earlier editions of this text, and in particular to the reviewers of this edition:

Sharon Mathis, *Benedictine College*
Carol Haussermann, *Dana College*
Carolyn R. Prettyman, *Trinity Bible College*
Rolayne Wilson, *Utah State University*
Dr. Ellen Campbell, *University of Central Oklahoma*
Dwan Bridges, *California State University-Los Angeles*
Rip Marsten, *University of Northern Iowa*

The following individual's responses to a survey provided useful feedback that helped improve this edition:

Dr. Jane Beougher, *Capital University*
Charman Humphrey, *Alabama A&M University*
John Kuchinsky, *Bucks County Community College*
Dr. Sandra Slabik, *Alvernia College*
Tim Carney, *Glenville State College*
Joy I. Butler, *Plymouth State College of New Hampshire*
Dr. Larry Goodrich, *North Central Bible College*
Donna Cucunato, *Chapman University*
Randall L. Tenney, *West Virginia Wesleyan College*
Bertha Landes, *Philadelphia College of the Bible*
Dr. Gerald E. Hampton, *Graceland College*
John B. Gratton, *Bee County College*
Rufus R. Hackney, *Francis Marion University*
Eddie Bedford, *Eastern Michigan University*
Gina Barton, *Cornerstone College*
Susie Myers, *Kansas City, Kansas Community College*
Darlene Bullock, *Slippery Rock University*
Josey Templeton, *Citadel Military College of South Carolina*

P A R T 1

Physical Education and the Growing Child

To be an effective teacher of children, one must have a thorough understanding of child development, learning theories, and the most effective teaching strategies available. It is also vital to have a thorough understanding of the role physical education plays in the health and well-being of a growing child. Part 1 is designed to provide teachers with such knowledge—to give them a basic understanding of the meaning and purpose of physical education and of how to effectively teach children so they will grow, learn, and develop to their full potential. Chapter 1 presents a brief history of physical education and explains its content, aim, goals, and objectives. The major growth and developmental changes in children are considered in chapter 2. Chapter 3 demonstrates how children learn motor skills and identifies the changes that occur during this process. Chapter 4 provides a review of teaching strategies and techniques, and demonstrates their effective use when teaching physical education. Part 1 provides the strong foundation for teaching elementary school children physical education.

Elementary School Physical Education

KEY CONCEPTS

1.1 A physical education program makes a significant contribution to a child's development

1.2 Physically educated individuals have active lifestyles

1.3 Outlining the aim, goals, and objectives provides an understanding of the learning outcomes associated with a quality physical education program

1.4 The physical education curriculum should foster activity independence in children

1.5 The physical education curriculum should be developmentally appropriate for all children

KEY OBJECTIVES

After completing this chapter you will be able to:

1. Understand the rationale for including physical education in the elementary school curriculum
2. Write the aim, goals, and objectives of elementary school physical education
3. Understand the need for a developmentally appropriate program of physical education for elementary school children
4. Understand that optimum growth and development are dependent on appropriate and consistent forms of physical exercise
5. Understand the need for a program that ensures equal opportunity for all learners
6. Understand that external social, political, and economic factors affect the nature and direction of elementary school physical education programs
7. Understand the historical development of physical education
8. Understand how contemporary trends, such as new instructional strategies, and changes in society affect the nature and direction of physical education

The process of developing an elementary school physical education curriculum must begin with a clear statement of the curriculum's general aim, goals, and objectives before discussing appropriate content and teaching strategies. This chapter will deal with this first important step. It will provide a statement of beliefs that is used as a foundation from which the general aim, goals, and objectives of physical education are derived. The stated goals are used in this book as a basis for the book's organization, the inclusion and emphasis of certain teaching strategies, and the diversity of activities provided in the resource sections.

STATEMENT OF BELIEFS

The following statement of beliefs is based on several sources of information. First, general statements about the nature and role of education are derived from a set of philosophical tenets concerning life and education. They are not the result of science or surveys; rather, they are the end products of critical thinking about the way we see ourselves in society. Second, other statements relating to why and how children learn are based on a body of knowledge that includes many disciplines. Third, some statements about teaching, children, and physical education are based, in part, on intuition and experience. Taken collectively, the following beliefs provide a basis for the general aim, goals, and objectives of elementary school physical education. In turn, these will act as guidelines for the programs and strategies provided in the following chapters of this book.

About Education and Teaching

1. Education should be a process through which all students are able to reach their greatest potential.
2. Teaching is an art and a science of helping children reach their greatest potential.

The first statement means that all children must be treated as equal, participating members of society. From this perspective, the second belief implies that teachers should use all of the scientific knowledge available about how and why children learn, as well as their own ingenuity and common sense, to guide children to realize their greatest potential. In addition, all teaching must be done within a democratic environment that recognizes the worth and integrity of every child.

About the Child

1. All children are unique individuals who learn according to their own level of ability and style of learning.
2. All children are capable of making their own decisions; however, a child must learn to do so in a gradual and systematic way.

Because children of similar age vary greatly in maturity and ability, we must provide variety in the learning tasks and the time available to complete them. Because children differ in their styles of learning, a variety of activities must

Figure I.I Every child is a unique individual.

be offered within each lesson and throughout the curriculum, and a variety of teaching methods and approaches will be necessary to accommodate the unique individual needs of each child. Because children are rational individuals, we must provide many experiences, in a graduated way, to allow each child opportunities to learn how to make correct and effective decisions. Our task, then, is to help each child become a self-directed and independent learner who will constantly seek new challenges (figure 1.1).

About Physical Education

1. Physical education has a unique, but not exclusive, role to play in the education of children. In order to ensure the health and well-being of children over the entire life span, we need to teach each child to develop and maintain an *active lifestyle.* An active lifestyle requires, among other things, competencies, knowledge, desire, and fitness. Physical education's role, then, is not only to enhance children's physical fitness, but to teach children a variety of motor skills, knowledge, and other competencies that will provide the foundation for the development of an active lifestyle.
2. Physical education, through its activities and experiences, can and *must* contribute to the shared goals of education, such as enhancing self-direction, self-esteem, and cooperative behavior.
3. Physical education should be an enjoyable and satisfying experience for every child.

C O N C E P T

I.I *A Physical Education Program Makes a Significant Contribution to a Child's Development*

The first belief sets a priority for physical education. Whatever else we profess to do, we must provide experiences that will enhance children's levels of health and fitness, and we must teach them concepts and motor skills inherent in a wide selection of physical activities. As we perform these tasks, we can also contribute to other goals of the elementary school curriculum through the way we structure the environment and through the teaching styles and techniques we choose to use. Finally, to make physical education an enjoyable and satisfying experience, we must provide opportunities for *all* children to reap success every time they are involved in a movement experience. Physical education must be an enjoyable and satisfying experience for all children.

THE HISTORICAL DEVELOPMENT OF PHYSICAL EDUCATION

A study of the history of education reveals that physical education has always been present but has been regarded with varying degrees of importance. In the classical age of Greece, the idea of harmony of body and mind was emphasized in the education of Greek citizens. This concept of unity and balance involved the harmonious development of the mental, physical, and spiritual aspects of the human personality. Consequently, physical education was considered an integral component of the educational program, with similar purposes but unique contributions. Plato expressed this idea in his writings and in his participation in physical exercise. Although strength and physical prowess were important, Greek ideals embraced more than mere strength alone; for example, they included the grace and beauty of movement and various moral expectations. Indeed, the Greek legacy of sport festivals celebrating the magnificence of movement is the basis of the modern Olympic Games. During the classical Greek period, where mind and body were considered in a balanced view and where physical activity was valued, there was intellectual and cultural development rarely equaled in the generations that followed. The balanced view, however, gave way to a military focus on physical strength and fitness, with the warlike Spartans emphasizing the physical training of the body for military purposes. A military emphasis has been recorded in virtually every civilization since. One major exception was the emphasis on aesthetics in the Middle Ages, which stressed the spiritual to the complete neglect of the physical and social aspects of human development.

From the period of the Enlightenment to the twentieth century, education primarily emphasized intellectual development. Physical education expressed in terms of natural play or organized activities, such as gymnastics and games, was emphasized by such writers as Locke, Rousseau, and Spencer. The purposes of such programs, however, were conceived in terms of training the body in order to enhance intellectual development. Although such connections were made between the mental and the physical, the "mind–body" distinction was still firmly in place. Only in the twentieth century has the philosophy of education begun a return to the Greek ideal of balance and harmony between mind and body.

Since the beginning of the twentieth century there have been profound changes in the philosophy, content, and methods of teaching at all levels in the public school. These changes toward "education for democratic living" did not happen by chance. New theories of learning, such as those presented by Thorndike and Gestalt psychology, produced significant changes in the way children were taught. Dewey and his disciples interpreted the nature of learning chiefly in terms of their social philosophy. The combined influences of philosophers, economists, and educators provided the impetus and rationale for the transition toward a liberal or general education for all citizens.

Physical education underwent profound changes in the nature of its activities and its methods of teaching. At the turn of the century, rigid gymnastic programs were still strongly emphasized, although games were beginning to be accepted as a valid part of elementary and secondary school physical education programs. The influence of Dewey, particularly in the 1930s and 1940s, created major changes in the philosophy of education and thereby influenced both the teaching and the content of physical education. Gymnastics were almost eliminated, and games were given a predominant role. Because the educational emphasis was on "learning by doing" and children were allowed to determine their own needs and interests, play through games was considered to be a strong contributor to social adjustment. Only minor emphasis was placed on skill and physical development.

During the period from the early 1940s and until the late 1960s, physical education programs underwent substantial change. Increased attention was given to the professional preparation of specialists in physical education as well as classroom teachers. Various state laws and educational certification requirements upgraded both the caliber of physical education teaching and its perceived degree of importance in the schools. Extensive research in such areas as growth and development, motor learning, and physical performance restored the rationale for a balanced program of physical activities for all levels of public and private education. For reasons of national survival, a special emphasis was still placed on physical fitness.

The past thirty years have seen further changes in the content and teaching of physical education. Again, these changes reflect philosophy, economic needs, and new knowledge regarding children's growth and development. Trends in automation and urbanization throughout the Western world have presented physical educators with new challenges. Programs in harmony with contemporary philosophies of education have been designed to develop within each child the knowledge, skill, health, fitness, and positive attitude that will enable them to participate in wholesome recreational activities throughout life. To accommodate this, elementary school physical education programs have shifted from group-paced instruction toward more individualized programs and toward teaching techniques that emphasize self-direction through exploratory and problem-solving methods.

CONTEMPORARY PHYSICAL EDUCATION

The move toward a concern for the individual has been reflected by two major thrusts in recent years. The first is the move toward a developmentally appropriate physical education program, in which the activities, teaching methods, practices, and so on, are designed to meet the developmental needs of the individual child. The child's current level of development determines the starting point for the physical education teacher. The second major thrust has been a decrease in the emphasis on physical fitness for military purposes and an increase in individual health. Because of burgeoning health care costs, governments struggle to meet society's health care needs. Improving the health of people through the development of active and healthy lifestyles is one of the major aims of today's educational systems. This view is reflected in the role physical education is now playing in public health. The development of active lifestyles is one of the major driving forces behind current physical education programs (figure 1.2). However, although the development of active lifestyles through developmentally appropriate activities is the desired outcome of contemporary physical education programs, achieving this will not be easy.

C O N C E P T

1.2 *Physically Educated Individuals Have Active Lifestyles*

There are approximately 80,000 elementary schools in the United States, teaching 31 million children. Schools vary in size from rural one-room schools to large urban schools of more than 1,000 children. Physical education facilities also vary from large gymnasia and outdoor playgrounds to multistory inner-city schools without gymnasia or adequate playground facilities. According to the National Children and Youth Fitness studies (1983, 1985), the status of physical education throughout the United States is relatively low. These studies indicate that a surprising 97 per-

Figure 1.2 Children learn an active lifestyle.

cent of all children in grades 1 through 4 participate in a physical education program 3.1 times per week. However, only 36.4 percent of the children in the first four grades, 18.4 percent in the fifth grade, and 27.4 percent in the sixth grade participate in daily physical education. It was also found that 37.2 percent of first through fourth grades, 48.4 percent of fifth grades, and 42 percent of sixth grades are scheduled for only one or two classes per week. With respect to time allotments, the average class period is 33.4 minutes for grades 1 through 4 and 90 minutes per week for fifth- and sixth-grade children. Such dismal statistics led Congress in 1987 to pass resolutions (Senate Resolution 43 / House Resolution 97) encouraging states to require daily physical education for all children in grades K through 12. Daily physical education is also advocated by the American Alliance for Health, Physical Education, Recreation and Dance (AAHPERD), which recommends that elementary school children should have, as a minimum, a daily physical education program of 30 minutes a day for a total of 150 minutes per week. Similar recommendations have been endorsed by the Canadian Association for Health, Physical Education, Recreation and Dance (CAHPERD) and by the International Council for Health, Physical Education, and Recreation (ICHPER).

The continuing trend toward inactivity and weight gain among children is alarming. The decline in fitness and activity as children progress through school has been well documented (Fishburne 1996). For example, from six to sixteen years of age, children's level of physical activity declines approximately 50 percent, and a 1995 report published in the American Medical Association's *Archives of Pediatrics and Adolescent Medicine* indicated that the number of school-age children who are overweight has doubled over the past thirty years, with the largest increases in the last ten years. Concern for the health and fitness of American children is reflected in the call, from many professional associations and government agencies, for quality programs of daily physical education. The design of such programs requires clear statements to identify their general aim, goals, and objectives.

GENERAL AIM, GOALS, AND OBJECTIVES OF PHYSICAL EDUCATION

An educational aim is a statement that identifies the expectation that should result from the overall educational experience. For example, "the aim of the elementary school science curriculum is to. . . ." Once the general aim has been identified, specific goal statements need to be established that specify the goals that must be achieved in order to meet the aim. Finally, goal statements can be broken down into even more specific statements outlining the learning objectives that need to be met in order to ensure that goals are realized. Because objectives describe in greater detail the specific content of goals, these statements play an important role in the teaching/learning process. For example, both unit plan objectives and lesson plan objectives are essential components in a teacher's planning because these statements describe the specific content to be covered and the desired learning outcomes. The book of unit plans and lesson plans that accompanies this text describes in detail the process of translating goal statements into clearly stated unit and lesson plan learning objectives. The organizational makeup of aim, goals, and objectives is a commonly accepted framework for identifying educational outcomes.

C O N C E P T

1.3 *Outlining the Aim, Goals, and Objectives Provides an Understanding of the Learning Outcomes Associated with a Quality Physical Education Program*

The Aim of Physical Education

It can be said that the aim of physical education is to produce physically educated individuals. However, this statement alone is not very helpful to a teacher, because it does not identify what characteristics constitute a physically educated individual. To help clarify this position, in 1992 the National Association for Physical Education and Sport (NASPE) published a nationally endorsed guide on the desired outcomes of quality physical education programs. Their definition of a physically educated person is based on ten goal statements that fall under the headings *Has, Is, Participates, Knows,* and *Values.*

NASPE Definition of a Physically Educated Person
A Physically Educated Person:

HAS *learned skills necessary to perform a variety of physical activities*

1. *The learner will develop body, spatial, and temporal awareness.*
2. *The learner will develop locomotor, manipulative, and nonlocomotor skills.*
3. *The learner will combine locomotor, nonlocomotor, and manipulative skills in movement, dance, games, and sports.*

IS *physically fit*

PARTICIPATES *regularly in physical activity*

4. *The learner will understand the benefits of regular physical activity and will enhance personal fitness.*

KNOWS *the implications and benefits of involvement in physical activities*

5. *The learner will be a knowledgeable consumer in the areas of health and fitness.*
6. *The learner will develop listening skills and safety awareness.*
7. *The learner will understand the general function and structure of the body.*
8. *The learner will understand, appreciate, and apply rules, regulations, strategies, and etiquette for movement, dance, games, and sports.*
9. *The learner will appreciate the aesthetic and creative qualities of movement.*

VALUES *physical activity and its contributions to a healthful lifestyle*

10. *The learner will develop self-confidence and interpersonal skills.*

National Standards for Physical Education

To provide guidance in the design of a physical education curriculum that will achieve the outcomes associated with a quality physical education program, NASPE produced a second publication, *Moving into the Future: National Standards for Physical Education* (1995). This document provides a guide to physical education content and assessment. Content standards (goals of the curriculum) and performance standards (benchmarks) are identified for grades K through 2, 4, 6, 8, 10, and 12. Content standards specify "what students should know and be able to do"; performance standards specify "how good is good enough." Performance standards indicate the levels of achievement that students are expected to attain in the content standards. Performance benchmarks (see chapter 11) are used to describe behavior that indicates progress toward a performance standard. The NASPE performance standards and suggested assessment techniques, together with numerous other methods used to evaluate physical education, can be found in chapter 11. The NASPE (1995) content standards are similar to goal statements identified by other professional groups concerned with quality physical education programs. The content standards (goals) identified in the NASPE (1995) standards document are included in the physical education goals that follow.

The Goals of Physical Education

We present the following goal statements to further clarify the goals that lead to quality programs of physical education and to provide a framework for the selection and emphasis of activities used in this book, and for the inclusion of numerous teaching methods and techniques.

Physical Fitness and Well-Being

Goal: *To help each child develop and maintain an optimum level of health and well-being and to acquire the knowledge, attitude, and ability to maintain this state of well-being throughout life*

Prior to 1980, physical fitness was broadly defined as having sufficient strength and energy to meet daily life activities. However, virtually every physical fitness test that was used measured motor fitness performance, which is an individual's ability to perform motor tasks involving such factors as agility and power. In most instances, physical fitness was also looked upon as an end in itself, rather than a process of understanding and achieving a positive state of health. The publication of AAHPERD's *Health Related Fitness Test* (1980) and its revised edition, *Physical Best Test* (1989), redefined physical fitness in terms of health rather than motor performance. Physical fitness is more broadly defined as "a physical state of well-being that allows people to (1) perform daily activities with vigor, (2) reduce their risk of health problems related to lack of exercise, and (3) establish a fitness base for participation in a variety of physical activities."

This change toward understanding and maintaining a positive state of well-being is also reflected in the report *Healthy People 2000: National Health Promotion and Disease Prevention Objectives.* This document was released in 1991 by the U.S. Department of Health and Human Services and outlines realistic health objectives to be achieved by the year 2000. These objectives were established by representatives from more than three hundred national organizations. The major focus of this report is on health as represented by a high quality of life and a sense of well-being. Such a focus has major implications for physical education programs. Because the interpretation of health-related fitness now includes strength, cardiorespiratory endurance, flexibility, and body composition, these components must be stressed in the program and, of course, on an individual basis. Programs must be designed to help children understand how

Figure 1.3   Children learn to appreciate and enjoy wellness.

their bodies function, the effects of exercise, and how to create one's own physical fitness program. If children are to leave elementary school with a positive and sustained interest in maintaining a healthy lifestyle, the physical education program must be taught in a way that helps them learn to appreciate and enjoy wellness (figure 1.3). The developmental approach that is emphasized in this book provides content and strategies that can accomplish this goal.

Growth and Development

Goal: *To provide opportunities for children to participate in activities that will enhance their own level of physical growth and development*

All children are born with certain inherited characteristics that determine their approximate height, weight, and general physique. Such environmental factors as proper nutrition, amount of sleep, exposure to disease, and general parental care also affect the child's growth and development. In addition, substantial evidence has shown that normal growth and development of bone as well as connective and muscle tissue occur only when a child receives adequate and continuous exercise throughout the growing period. Regular exercise, for example, increases bone width and mineralization (Rarick 1973). Similarly, lack of exercise can severely limit the potential growth of other bodily systems and organs.

There is growing evidence of the important role physical education can play in the prevention of coronary heart disease. Although heart disease is usually manifest in adulthood, it has been suggested that it is frequently of pediatric origin. Indeed, autopsy studies have revealed fatty streaks in the aortas of children younger than three years in age (Armstrong and Bray 1986). The buildup of fatty streaks in the inner lining of the arterial wall is the first step toward coronary heart problems. Childhood would therefore appear to be the appropriate time to commence the fight against cardiovascular heart disease. For many adults, the coronary heart risk factors of physical inactivity and poor diet may have their roots in the habits, attitudes, and interest levels established in early school experiences. It is well documented that regular vigorous physical activity is associated with low incidence of coronary heart disease in adult life. Participation in developmentally appropriate physical activity as a child will increase the likelihood of participation as an adult. Clearly, the elementary school physical education program offers the potential to influence development over the total life span.

Body Management and Useful Physical Skills

Goal: *To provide opportunities to help children develop effective body management and useful physical skills*

All the movements used in everyday activities, such as the locomotor and nonlocomotor skills of walking, dodging, and stopping, and the movement skills and concepts of transfer of weight and moving with a change of speed and direction are useful physical skills. Some of these skills help children control their bodies while moving on or over an apparatus or through space. Other skills are used in combination with one or more locomotor and movement skills to form the complex skills and movement patterns involved in sports, gymnastics, and dance activities. Regardless of their nature and type, skills are usually learned through a systematic program of instruction.

Poorly developed motor abilities such as hand-eye coordination, balance, and finger dexterity will severely limit success in performing most physical skills. Children need to develop their motor abilities to their fullest potential. Since environmental experiences influence the development of basic motor abilities, the physical education program has an important role to play in fostering both motor skill and motor ability development (Fishburne 1990). With well-developed motor abilities, a person has the prerequisite foundation for the acquisition of motor skills.

The values of efficient and skillful movements, particularly in sports and dance, are many. Children who demonstrate ease and grace of movement are usually both physically fit and well adjusted among their peers. Furthermore, a child who displays a skill in an activity, such as basketball or swimming, not only experiences a great deal of enjoyment through participation but usually pursues the activity for many years. Adults should understand this lesson well, for we generally participate in activities in which we show a

reasonable degree of skill; rarely do we actively pursue or enjoy a sport that we cannot master at least in part.

Understanding and Appreciating Human Movement

Goal: *To help children understand and appreciate the knowledge and concepts related to effective and efficient movement*

The intent of this goal is to help children understand the components of each skill they learn and how the laws and principles of gravity and motion affect their performance. Knowledge of Laban's movement concepts and skills expands children's movement vocabulary and helps them design, perform, and appreciate unique movement sequences. In addition, a knowledge of game skills and rules, of dance steps and patterns, and of gymnastic movements and safety skills helps all learners execute each movement with ease, efficiency, and an appreciation of the efforts and intricacies involved in human movement.

Active Lifestyle

Goal: *To help each child develop and acquire the knowledge, skills, attitude, ability, and desire to maintain an active lifestyle*

One of the major goals of elementary school physical education is to educate children toward the development of an active lifestyle. Children must achieve what Armstrong (1989) terms "activity independence." That is, they must be active as part of their normal lifestyles rather than only when a teacher offers instruction. In a way, the physical education teacher should have an easy task. When they enter school, most children possess a reasonably high level of physical fitness, an interest in the joy of moving, a desire to move, and abundant energy and enthusiasm. In fact, many children have difficulty sitting still! Children have a natural penchant for movement—they will run to the gymnasium. A teacher's task, then, is to maintain this natural interest and motivation as the child progresses through school.

C O N C E P T

1.4 The Physical Education Curriculum Should Foster Activity Independence in Children

Sadly, statistics too frequently reveal that students' fitness and activity levels deteriorate as they progress through school; this is more true for girls than for boys. Clearly, the social influences of watching television, diet, inactivity, and the lack of good role models outside of school play an influencing part. Schools cannot make all the changes in isolation from these other factors. However, the physical education program can play an important role in providing a child with an appropriate environment where the child

Figure 1.4   Joy of movement may be the key to excellence.

develops the necessary prerequisites for an active lifestyle. To participate in physical endeavors, children will need to acquire skills. Without skills, there will be little success. Without success, there will be little motivation. Without motivation, there will be little interest, and without interest an attitude commensurate with inactivity will develop. Skills alone will likely not be sufficient to maintain an active lifestyle. Knowledge, a prerequisite degree of fitness (necessary to achieve success), and a desire to achieve will all be necessary. A child will need to be physically educated (the aim of the program) in order to support an active lifestyle. Further, the influences outside of school must foster and support the education within the school. This latter point has implications for parental and community involvement, assessment and reporting procedures, developmentally appropriate activities, and instructional methods that promote "transfer." Each of these areas is covered in this text.

Enjoyment through Play

Goal: *To provide opportunities for children to experience enjoyable play experiences*

The meaning of enjoyment goes far beyond "having fun" or "being amused" in playing a game or performing a dance movement. Enjoyment, as used in this goal, relates to the intrinsic value of the activity to the child. If the child truly enjoys what she is doing, this enjoyment often becomes her main reason for continuous participation in the activity, as well as her motivation to seek higher levels of performance. Joy of movement might be the key to excellence—a goal we want all learners to achieve (figure 1.4). Therefore, this goal should be given a high priority in the physical education program.

Fostering Intellectual Growth

Goal: *To provide opportunities to help children develop their intellectual competency*

The intellectual growth of a young child involves the cognitive skills of acquiring, ordering, and communicating knowledge and ideas. It also involves the ability to communicate one's ideas and feelings in a creative way and through a variety of modes of expression. Although the physical education program should be predominantly physical, it should encourage the acquisition of vocabulary and concepts as well as exercise the thinking process of every child. For example, in gymnastics and dance activities, when children plan a movement sequence, they are required to understand movement terms and concepts and to mentally join together a series of movements that answer a movement challenge efficiently, safely, and creatively. In a similar manner, creative and cooperative game activities provide an effective medium in which young children exercise their thinking processes in active and inventive ways.

Physical activities can also be an effective means to teach a variety of academic skills and concepts. Simple games like Steal the Bacon (p. 336) and Hot Spot (p. 325) can be used to teach addition, subtraction, sets, and many other mathematical concepts. Gymnastic movements can be effective examples for explaining balance, force, and geometrical shapes. Physical education can provide a rich source of activities through which academic skills and concepts can be taught or reinforced in an exciting, effective, and enjoyable way.

Personal and Social Development

Goal: *To provide opportunities for children to develop positive personal and social development*

Five-year-old children enter school with certain feelings and attitudes about themselves, their parents, and the people who have affected their lives in various ways. In terms of enhancing personal and social development, physical education provides an effective environment in which each child can learn to behave in a variety of social settings. Through small- and large-group activities, such as games, dance, and aquatic activities, primary children begin to learn to test their tolerance and perseverance and to explore alternatives in a nonthreatening environment. As children progress through this type of program, they begin to learn the meaning of patience, honesty, fair play, and team loyalty—valuable lessons for the future citizens of a democratic society.

Self-Image

Goal: *To provide opportunities for every child to develop a positive self-image*

Self-image is essentially a child's feelings about himself. Children develop feelings about their intellectual abilities, popularity among peers, and ability to perform physical activities. If they are reasonably successful in each of these dimensions, children normally have positive feelings about their personal worth. A child who has positive feelings is generally eager to attempt new challenges. However, children who constantly experience failure in any of these areas normally have a very low opinion of themselves. Too often this leads to withdrawal or other forms of undesirable behavior. Classroom teachers must clearly understand the implications of such children's problems in learning tasks and in getting along with classmates.

The physical education environment can either foster or impede the development of a child's positive self-image. If the activities are presented so that each child, regardless of physical ability, can achieve a measure of success, the child's self-image is enhanced. One need only see a young child perform a successful roll or swim her first few strokes to observe the joy of success and the eagerness to try again. On the other hand, a child who is repeatedly required to attempt movement skills beyond her capabilities generally develops a negative attitude.

Because self-image is one of the most important factors in learning motor skills, physical education activities must be presented in such a way that every child achieves some success. New methods and techniques described in later chapters can assist teachers in providing this type of program for all children.

Creative Talents

Goal: *To provide opportunities for all children to develop their own creative talents*

Contemporary public education stresses the development of creativity at all levels. Creativity, however, is a difficult concept to define. A work of art, such as a painting, sculpture, or musical score, is creative in that it is unique in composition, color, or form. In physical education, creativity is defined in terms of the way in which a movement or series of movements is performed or by the degree of inventiveness of a movement.

According to Gladys Andrews and her colleagues, creativity is what one thinks, feels, sees, and expresses in terms of oneself and in one's own way (Andrews, Saurborn, and Schneider 1960). Because every child has the potential to be creative, the physical education program should provide numerous opportunities for each child to explore and express creativity through movement (figure 1.5).

FACTORS INFLUENCING THE NATURE AND DIRECTION OF PHYSICAL EDUCATION

During the past three decades, the elementary physical education curriculum has been profoundly influenced by the changing philosophy of elementary education, by new federal

Figure 1.5 Every child has the potential to be creative.

and state laws and regulations, and by new developments in the content and teaching strategies of physical education. The selected major trends discussed in the following paragraphs illustrate how these factors are shaping the future elementary physical education curriculum.

Individualized and Personalized Instructional Programs

Perhaps one of the most significant trends affecting every subject area in the elementary school curriculum is the shift toward individualized and personalized instruction. This form of teaching creates an environment for successful personal encounter, fostering the free and open expression of ideas, facts, and feelings. It is an environment in which learning activities integrate the personal interests of the students with the goals of the school. In physical education, this means we no longer teach according to our own predetermined goals, exclusively choose the types of physical activities for the program, or use only a formal method of instruction. Rather, we shift from group-paced instruction toward a process of teaching that is a shared enterprise between the learner and the teacher.

Movement Education

Just prior to the Second World War, Rudolph Laban, an Austrian dance teacher, moved to England and brought a new way of analyzing all forms of human movement. During the war, English primary teachers, most of whom had little or no training in physical education, began to use Laban's movement analysis and more problem-solving methods in their physical education programs. Gradually this new analysis of movement, coupled with more exploratory methods, became known as the Movement Education approach. During the past thirty-five years, Movement Education as a curriculum model has received mixed reviews. Some proponents have used Movement Education as the structure on which all movement concepts and skills are taught (Graham, Holt-Hale, and Parker 1993; Logsdon 1984; Wall and Murray 1994). There has been some success with the model in the primary grades; however, very few intermediate programs have successfully adopted Movement Education as an all-inclusive approach to teaching physical education.

One of the most significant trends has been the integration of Laban's movement concepts and skills with all content areas of the elementary school physical education program. At times, particularly during early primary years, the Movement Education approach is used exclusively as the curriculum model. As children grow older, the physical education program still emphasizes the basic movement concepts in a way that is complementary to acquiring individual and team game skills, gymnastic movements, and many folk dance movement patterns. Creative dance programs throughout every grade in the elementary school use Laban's four elements of movement as a basic structure to teach creative movement activities. The contemporary developmental model, which is emphasized throughout this book, is an example of how the Movement Education approach has been integrated into new and exciting elementary school physical education curriculum models.

Integration of Subjects

A feature of this textbook is a demonstration of the way physical education can be used to enhance and teach academic concepts and skills. Clearly, it is efficient use of children's learning time if a teacher is able to promote learning connections between the content of different subject areas. Also, use of the sensory experiences of movement in combination with the sensory experiences of vision and hearing provides a basis for greater understanding, since this caters to the variety of learning styles found among children. Hence, contemporary trends promote the integration of subject areas. Physical education can be used in two unique ways to foster subject area integration. One way is to enhance or reinforce academic concepts and skills—to reinforce academic concepts from other subject areas while children are working to achieve physical education learning outcomes. For example, if the game Boundary Ball (p. 341) is being played in order to develop children's foot-eye coordination, at the same time the mathematical concepts of addition and subtraction can be reinforced through the scoring system associated with this game. It is also possible to use the physical education medium in a second way: using movement activities to teach academic concepts and skills. For example, cooperative group learning, another feature that is emphasized throughout this text, is recognized as a powerful and educationally proven way to teach children (Johnson and Johnson 1991). Through cooperative group activities, mathematical concepts of sets, division, addition, and subtraction, and so on can all be taught as children move and organize themselves into various groupings (figure 1.6).

Figure 1.6 Children learn academic concepts through movement experiences.

In addition to the chapter on subject area integration, academic concepts and skills that can be taught and enhanced through physical education activities are identified throughout this textbook. Further, the accompanying text on designing yearly programs, units, and daily lesson plans demonstrates how to plan for the integration of other subject areas.

Multicultural Society

Most of the early American immigrants were white Anglo-Saxon Protestants. The remaining early settlers were of African, Hispanic, or Asian origin. As the public educational system became established, it attempted to assimilate all students into a single new culture. The resulting mix became known as the "melting pot" and has unfairly forced students to accept a white-dominated, Anglo-Saxon culture, regardless of their own heritage. During the past thirty-five years, there has been a positive shift toward a multicultural or pluralistic society. Today the United States is rapidly changing from a white majority society to a society with a large population of Middle Easterners, South Asians, Hispanics, African Americans, and Native Americans.

Multicultural education emphasizes the need to accept and respect the rights and cultural heritage of all people. It also recognizes that ethnic diversity enriches everyone's life.

For example, physical education has played an important role in teaching games and dances from other countries. This trend will continue to stress a very broad-based multicultural program of physical activities at all levels of the public school system. These programs will be found not just in schools where there is a major shift in the cultural background of their school population but in all schools regardless of the initial makeup of their population.

National Physical Fitness Programs

In 1953 Dr. Hans Kraus released the results of his physical fitness survey, which showed the level of physical fitness of American children to be far lower than that of European children. The resulting impact of this study created a wave of interest in physical fitness throughout North America, in primary- to university-level programs. Within a few years, the federal government created the President's Council on Physical Fitness, which in turn had a major effect on the elementary and secondary physical education programs in North America. The council's Physical Fitness Test and recommended programs were adopted by numerous school districts from New York to California. Other organizations, such as the American Alliance for Health, Physical Education, Recreation and Dance (AAHPERD) and several state departments of education, also produced their own physical fitness tests and special programs to raise the level of physical fitness of elementary and secondary school children. Although other trends and programs, such as lifetime sports and Movement Education, have changed the nature and direction of elementary school physical education, the emphasis on physical fitness that was started in 1953 is still felt today. The contemporary trend toward human wellness and active living is, in many respects, a continuation of this trend, but with a major change in the meaning of physical fitness toward more health-related aspects.

Human Wellness and Positive Lifestyle

During the past few years, many elementary physical fitness programs have incorporated more health-related aspects of human wellness. The excessive number of either overweight or undernourished children has created a need for programs that help children assess their eating habits and plan effective weight-control programs. Problems relating to stress management and alcohol and drug addiction have also prompted the physical education profession to redefine and emphasize new aspects of physical fitness. For example, AAHPERD's *Physical Best Fitness Test Manual* emphasizes cardiorespiratory function; body composition (leanness/fatness); and abdominal, arm and shoulder girdle, and low-back-hamstring muscular skeletal function (AAHPERD 1989). This direction toward an emphasis on a positive state of well-being, which is further supported by the *Healthy People 2000* document, has created a need for programs that help children understand how their bodies work, how they can monitor body changes, and how they can design personal fitness programs for improving and maintaining optimum levels of health.

Active Living

Health-related concerns have prompted a move toward an "active living" concept. This thrust has been seen throughout North America. U.S. documents such as *Healthy People 2000* and findings stemming from the monumental research work of Sallis and McKenzie (1991) highlight the need to develop programs that promote active living. Similar support is seen in Canada through the Canadian Association for Health, Physical Education, Recreation and Dance's foundation document *Physical Education 2000* (CAHPERD 1992) and through their coordination of a program entitled "The Canadian Active Living Challenge." The idea is that if children are engaged in developmentally appropriate activities throughout their school years, then their natural interest in movement will be nurtured and developed from childhood through to adulthood. The active living concept is important because there is overwhelming evidence that exercise of the appropriate type, intensity, frequency, and duration will improve all health-related aspects of children's physical fitness. Further, apart from the obvious benefits of physical and motor development, there is also evidence that regular physical activity has beneficial effects on mental health, including decreased anxiety and depression, a more positive mood, and elevated self-esteem. Clearly, fostering and maintaining a physically active lifestyle throughout the entire life span is deemed desirable from a health point of view. *This important trend toward active living is a major theme throughout this book.*

Equal Opportunity for All Children

Two laws that have dramatically affected all aspects of physical education are the Educational Amendment Act of 1972 (Title IX) and Section 504 of the Rehabilitation Act of 1973. A definition of each law follows, along with a brief explanation of the implications of these laws for teachers of elementary school children.

The Educational Amendment Act of 1972 (Title IX)

Title IX of this act states that "no person in the United States shall, on the basis of sex, be excluded from participation in, be denied the benefits of, or be subjected to discrimination under any education program or activity receiving federal financial assistance" (AAHPERD 1976). This law requires all schools to provide equal opportunities to girls and boys within the instructional and extracurricular program. This includes such aspects as facilities, time allotment, and equal employment of the teaching staff. This law, however, allows students to be grouped by ability and is applied without regard to gender. It also allows students to be separated by gender within the instructional program when this is deemed appropriate.

The most significant result of this act is that virtually all elementary physical education classes are now coeducational. As a result, this law has provided an opportunity for much greater social interaction among boys and girls. In addition, it has placed sport participation into a more natural lifetime environment. As a consequence of this law, AAHPERD has published an extensive guide describing a variety of methods and techniques for implementing the basic requirements of Title IX.

Section 504 of the Rehabilitation Act of 1973 (Public Law 93-112)

This law states that "no otherwise qualified handicapped individual shall, solely by reason of his handicap, be excluded from participation in, be denied the benefits of, or be subject to discrimination under any program or activity receiving federal financial assistance." This law requires schools to provide equal opportunities for any child with a disability to participate in all programs offered by the school. This law has been interpreted to include the regular instructional program, intramurals, and interschool athletics. The act has required schools to provide (1) special access to buildings for special needs children, (2) appropriate transportation, (3) appropriate curricular adjustments, and (4) appropriate adaptations in activities. The latter would include changes in rules and regulations, special ramps, and adjustments to playing equipment (figure 1.7).

The Individuals with Disabilities Education Act of 1990 (Public Law 101-476)

Since the early seventies there have been a number of public laws dealing with equal opportunities for all people. In 1975 the Education for All Handicapped Children Act (Public Law 94-142) was passed, and this was followed in 1983 and 1985 with new acts to help assure that all schoolchildren with disabilities are treated with respect and dignity and are provided with equal opportunities. In 1990 the Individuals with Disabilities Education Act (Public Law 101-476), known by the acronym *IDEA,* was passed to provide services to individuals with a broader range of disabilities and covering a wider age span. Under present legislation, children are included from birth and require *individual family service plans (IFSPs)* before school age and *individual education plans (IEPs)* when they enter school. The IEP is discussed in detail in chapter 13.

Figure 1.7 A child with a disability can participate in a regular physical education program through developmentally appropriate activities.

Other Public Laws

The general implications of laws dealing with negligence have helped teachers improve the general care and safety of the children within their care. In very direct ways, such laws help teachers focus on the key points of teaching, on the quality of facilities and equipment, and on the general supervision of children. In a similar way, the laws dealing with children with disabilities have forced teachers and administrators to adjust facilities and modify teaching strategies to allow these children greater access to and participation in the physical education program.

Research Findings and Platform Statements

Other factors directly affecting the nature and direction of elementary physical education programs have resulted from research findings and statements by influential individuals or groups interested in the education and welfare of children. Numerous studies, for example, have been conducted to determine the effects of exercise on such factors as bone and muscle growth, perceptual-motor efficiency, and academic achievement. Two outstanding publications provide a comprehensive summary of research findings relating to children and physical activity. *Physical Activity and Well-Being* (1986) is written by leading researchers in the fields of health and physical education and is published by AAHPERD. *Children and Exercise XI* (1985), published by Human Kinetics Publishers, provides similar information. The investigations cited in these two publications clearly indicate that young children must receive appropriate daily exercise to ensure that their bodies grow and develop in a normal, functional manner.

Long-term studies, such as the Vanves program (Albinson and Andrews 1976), in which one-third of the school day was devoted to physical education, have shown dramatically that children with strong, healthy bodies tend to do very well academically. These studies do not imply, however, that increases in strength, endurance, or motor coordination increase a child's intelligence. They simply demonstrate that physically fit children who possess good motor control do well academically. These investigations also show that strong, robust children can meet everyday personal and social pressures and challenges with relative ease.

The American Medical Association (AMA) and numerous other influential organizations have issued statements supporting the importance of daily physical education for children and youths. Such support has encouraged state and local officials to construct playing fields and facilities for physical education and athletic programs.

Public and private organizations have also influenced the direction and emphasis of instructional and extraclass programs. For example, the efforts of the President's Council on Physical Fitness and Sports, the AMA, and many other organizations have encouraged and supported physical education programs emphasizing physical fitness, intramural activities, or specific types of interschool competitive athletics. With respect to the latter, the publication *Guidelines for Children's Sports,* prepared by the American Alliance for Health, Physical Education, Recreation and Dance and approved by the American Academy of Pediatrics, has had a major impact on all forms of children's athletics.

The collective influence of these factors and trends has required teachers to add new objectives to the elementary physical education program. This influence has also required teachers to set new priorities and to place renewed emphasis on key objectives of the program. This is *not* an undesirable situation, because schools, being a mirror of society, must constantly adapt to legitimate trends and influences.

TOWARD A DEVELOPMENTALLY BASED PHYSICAL EDUCATION CURRICULUM

The term *developmentally appropriate* has been used for many years in the field of early childhood education. In 1987 the National Association for the Education of Young Children (NAEYC) provided an official definition of developmentally appropriate practice (Bredekamp 1987). NAEYC defines "developmentally appropriate" programs as

> those which are based on knowledge of what is age-appropriate for the group of children served as well as information about what is individually appropriate (i.e., the needs and interests of individual children within the program). (Bredekamp 1992, p. 31)

If children are to grow and develop to their full potential, they must be provided with the most conducive learning environments. Unfortunately this is not always the case,

and many children experience failure and frustration in a physical education setting. Designing a curriculum around developmentally appropriate practices provides the necessary focus to ensure that all children experience success and develop to their full potential.

C O N C E P T

1.5 *The Physical Education Curriculum Should Be Developmentally Appropriate for All Children*

A developmentally based curriculum is based on several important factors. First, every child passes through a series of developmental stages. For example, in the process of learning to throw a ball, every child progresses through an initial and somewhat jerky stage, to a more focused second stage, to a final automatic step in which the movement is performed smoothly and effortlessly. A second important factor is that although the majority of children follow similar sequences of motor development and arrive at developmental points at approximately the same age level, the rate of motor development varies; hence the rate of development is not age-dependent. Children pass through each developmental stage according to their own level of maturity and ability, rather than according to chronological age or grade level. Although it is impossible for a classroom teacher to individualize a program for each child, it is possible to use new organizational techniques, new content areas, and new teaching strategies to allow children within any given learning experience in physical education to develop and learn according to their own levels of interest, ability, and previous experience.

Social, emotional, cognitive, and psychomotor development must all be understood if developmentally appropriate programs are to be achieved. All of these developmental areas are highlighted in this text.

Summary Review

The health and well-being of children is of vital importance. Educational environments must provide learning opportunities that enable all children to develop to their full potential. A quality program of physical education can make a significant contribution to a child's overall development. In addition, the foundation provided through physical education can have a significant impact on involvement in physical activity over the entire life span. Hence, physical education plays a vital role in the development of active lifestyles and thus plays a crucial role in children's health and well-being. Further:

1. Contemporary physical education is based on developmentally appropriate teaching.
2. A physically educated person has an active lifestyle.

3. *All* children are special and have needs that must be met through developmentally appropriate activities.
4. Outlining the aim, goals, and objectives provides an understanding of the learning outcomes associated with a quality physical education program.
5. Physical education contributes to a child's development in a multitude of ways and is an essential subject area in the elementary school curriculum.

INDIVIDUAL *and* **GROUP** **PROJECTS**

1. Discuss five major influences a quality program of physical education can have on child development.
2. Discuss the implications for physical education of the contemporary emphasis on health-related aspects of human wellness.
3. Discuss the importance and implications of the Individuals with Disabilities Education Act of 1990 (Public Law 101-476) for physical education.
4. Compare the aim, goals, and objectives of your local and state physical education curriculum guides with those identified in this chapter.

SELECTED READINGS

AAHPERD. 1980. *Personalized learning in physical education.* Reston, VA: AAHPERD.

————. 1993. *Physical Best program.* Reston, VA: AAHPERD.

Albinson, J. G., and G. Andrews. 1976. *Child in sport and physical activity.* Baltimore: University Park Press.

Andrews, G., J. Saurborn, and E. Schneider. 1960. *Physical education for today's boys and girls.* Boston: Allyn & Bacon.

Armstrong, N. 1989. Children are fit but not active! *Education and Health* 7 (2): 28–32.

Armstrong, N., and S. Bray. 1986. The role of the physical education teacher in coronary prevention. In *Trends and Developments in Physical Education,* ed. B. Wright and G. Donald, 346–52. London: E. & F. N. Spon.

Bennett, W. J. 1986. *First lessons: A report on elementary education in America.* Washington, DC: GPO.

Bredekamp, S. 1987. *Developmentally appropriate practice in early childhood programs servicing children from birth through age 8.* Washington, DC: NAEYC.

————. 1992. What is "developmentally appropriate" and why is it important? *Journal of Physical Education, Recreation and Dance* (August): 31–32.

CAHPERD. 1992. *Physical education 2000.* Gloucester, Ontario: CAHPERD.

COPEC. 1992. *Developmentally appropriate physical education practices for children.* A statement of the Council on Physical Education for Children.

Cratty, R. J. 1967. *Movement behavior and motor learning.* 2d ed. Philadelphia: Lea & Febiger.

Fishburne, G. J. 1990. Motor and physical development during early childhood. In *Teaching health and physical education in the early childhood classroom,* ed. L. Read. Edmonton: Alberta Teachers' Association.

————. 1994. Teaching and enhancing academic concepts and skills through physical education. In *Proceedings of the Tenth Commonwealth and International Scientific Congress,* ed. F. Bell and G. Van Gyn. Victoria, BC: University of Victoria.

————. 1996. The need for and value of quality programmes of physical education. *Canadian Administrator* 35, 6–11.

Fishburne, G. J., and I. R. Haslam. 1992. Critical issues in elementary school education: Integration and the curriculum. In *Sport and Physical Activity,* ed. T. Williams, L. Almond, and A. Sparkes, 132–37. London: E. & F. N. Spon.

Gallahue, D. L. 1993. *Developmental physical education for today's children.* Dubuque, IA: Brown & Benchmark.

Graham, G., S. A. Holt-Hale, and M. Parker. 1993. *Children moving.* 3d ed. Mountain View, CA: Mayfield.

Haywood, K. M. 1991. The role of physical education in the development of active lifestyles. *Research Quarterly for Exercise and Sport* 62 (2): 151–56.

Healthy people 2000: National health promotion and disease prevention objectives. 1991. Washington, DC: DHHS, Public Health Service.

Hellison, D. R. 1985. *Goals and strategies for teaching physical education.* Champaign, IL: Human Kinetics.

Humphrey, J. H. 1990. *Integration of physical education in the elementary school curriculum.* Springfield, IL: Charles C. Thomas.

Jewett, A. E., and L. L. Bain. 1985. *The curriculum process in physical education.* Dubuque, IA: Wm. C. Brown.

Johansen, J. H., H. W. Collins, and J. A. Johnson. 1990. *American education: An introduction to teaching.* 6th ed. Dubuque, IA: Wm. C. Brown.

Johnson, D. W., and R. T. Johnson. 1991. *Learning together and alone.* Englewood Cliffs, NJ: Prentice Hall.

Johnson, M. 1987. *The body in the mind: The bodily basis of meaning.* Chicago: University of Chicago Press.

Kline, M. 1977. *Why the professor can't teach: Mathematics and the dilemma of university education.* New York: Academic Press.

Lindsey, R., B. J. Jones, and A. V. Whitley. 1989. *Fitness for the health of it.* Dubuque, IA: Wm. C. Brown.

Logsdon, R. J. 1984. *Physical education for children: A focus on the teaching process.* 2d ed. Philadelphia: Lea & Febiger.

Morris, D. G. S., and J. Stiehl. 1985. *Physical education: From intent to action.* Columbus, OH: Merrill.

NASPE. 1992. *Outcomes of quality physical education programs.* Reston, VA: NASPE/AAHPERD.

————. 1995. *Moving into the future: National standards for physical education.* St. Louis: Mosby.

Rarick, G. L. 1973. *Physical activity and human growth and development.* New York: Academic Press.

Sallis, J. F., and T. L. McKenzie. 1991. Physical education's role in public health. *Research Quarterly for Exercise and Sport* 62 (2): 124–34.

Steinhaus, A. H. 1966. Your muscles see more than your eyes. *Journal of Health, Physical Education, and Recreation* (September): 38–40.

Thomas, J. R., A. M. Lee, and K. T. Thomas. 1988. *Physical education for children: Concepts into practice.* Champaign, IL: Human Kinetics.

U.S. Department of Health and Human Services. 1985. Summary of findings from National Children and Youth Fitness Study. *Journal of Physical Education, Recreation and Dance* 56 (1): 1–48.

————. 1987. Summary of findings from National Children and Youth Fitness Study II. *Journal of Physical Education, Recreation and Dance* 58 (1): 1–48.

Wall, J., and N. Murray. 1994. *Children and movement: Physical education in the elementary school,* 2d ed. Dubuque, IA: Wm. C. Brown.

Werner, P. H., and E. G. Burton. 1979. *Learning through movement: Teaching cognitive content through physical activities.* St. Louis: Mosby.

CHAPTER 2

Children and Activity

KEY CONCEPTS

2.1 To understand motor development, it is necessary to understand basic terminology

2.2 Knowledge of children's growth and development forms the foundation for effective teaching at the elementary-age level

2.3 Body composition is affected by genetic and environmental factors, but it is especially influenced by diet and exercise

2.4 The environment in which a child is placed can facilitate or delay motor development

2.5 Effective teachers learn to embed declarative knowledge into their instructional practices (procedural knowledge)

2.6 A sensitive time in human development is when a child is unusually receptive to environmental influences

KEY OBJECTIVES

After completing this chapter you will be able to:

1. Understand the basic terminology associated with children's growth and development
2. Understand children's physical growth and development
3. Understand motor ability development and identify the stages of motor skill development
4. Understand children's personal and social development
5. Identify and understand developmental differences between children in early childhood, middle childhood, and late childhood
6. Understand how knowledge of children's growth and development is vital when planning a quality program of elementary school physical education
7. Understand how knowledge of children's growth and development forms the foundation for effective teaching at the elementary-age level

ontemporary education focuses on helping children develop to their full potential. Not only do we want children to grow and develop during their school years, we also want them to develop the habits, skills, and knowledge required for an active lifestyle outside of school hours and beyond the school years. As teachers of physical education, we must understand children's growth and developmental stages in order to choose appropriate activities and movement experiences that will foster optimum development. For example, a cursory knowledge of bone growth during childhood clearly indicates that strong bones are developed when they are subjected to stress. Much of children's natural play activity, such as climbing and swinging on equipment, involves weight-bearing activities that put stress on bones, which in turn causes the bones to grow and to become strong and healthy. However, research also shows that *excessive* weight-bearing activities can seriously impair bone development. Current trends show an increase in overuse injuries among children. Clearly, children who engage in developmentally inappropriate activities risk serious injury. Severe blows to the body can also have harmful effects on correct bone and tissue development. Hence, games like full-contact football are not appropriate for elementary school children. Teachers and parents of elementary school children should be aware of the potential harm of certain types of activity and oppose the adoption of such activities for this age level.

However, physiological changes are not the sole criterion for selecting activities or teaching methods. Psychological changes involving self-image and attention span, as well as motivation and sociological changes relating to peer group importance, also have significant implications for the physical education program.

Children's growth and development forms the foundation for effective teaching at the elementary age level. This chapter summarizes the important physical, psychological, and social changes children experience as they move through three levels of development, and discusses the important implications of these changes for physical education programs.

Human development

The purpose of any educational environment is to create the most conducive situation for optimum learning and development. This will allow students to develop to their true potential. Children develop and grow in unique ways, so it is imperative that the individuals who structure children's learning environments be knowledgeable about the developmental level of the students for whom the learning experience is intended. To provide developmentally appropriate activities, teachers of physical education must be cognizant of human development.

Studying human development is an extremely complex undertaking. As Bower (1979), a developmental psychologist, aptly stated:

> We enter this world small and helpless, with few capacities and few behaviors. Within two decades, however, we have the full range of human skills at our disposal, for whatever purposes we desire. Within another two decades the inexorable decline in powers and skills through aging begins, and will continue until death. The human adult is the lord of creation, the most successful organism ever evolved. Yet no other primate—indeed no other mammal—is as dependent as we are at birth. How does anything as helpless as a human baby become something as competent as an adult? (p. 3)

Development is a difficult area to study, due to the interaction of nature and nurture. Whatever area of development

is considered, be it intellectual, social, or physical, the same problem is always encountered: What part does nature play and what is the influence of nurture? Teasing out the precise benefits of environmental influence (nurture) is difficult due to the complex interaction that constantly occurs with heredity (nature). As difficult as the problem may seem, some headway has been made through systematic observation, experimentation, and careful analysis of human behavior. Some of the major developmental findings in the physical and motor domain are described in the sections that follow. However, before undertaking a review of children's physical and motor development, it will be helpful to clarify several terms.

Definition of terms

Developmentalists have gained some insights through first defining the terms under study. Defining terms such as *skill* and *ability*, for example, can be an extremely valuable start to gaining an understanding of child development.

C O N C E P T

2.1 *To Understand Motor Development, It Is Necessary to Understand Basic Terminology*

The following terms have been identified and agreed on by most developmental psychologists.

GROWTH: *A quantitative increase in size. In terms of physical growth, quantitative changes in body mass. For example, an increase in the size of the calf muscle would represent growth.*

MATURATION: *The physical and behavioral changes that are primarily a product of an innate process of growth rather than a result of direct experiences with the environment. For example, as a baby grows (matures) there is a natural progress toward walking. Maturation is a qualitative advancement toward maturity.*

DEVELOPMENT: *A continuous process of change. Development can occur in the form of quantitative and/or qualitative change. For example, a young child develops language and speech through the interaction of growth, maturation, and learning opportunities.*

MOTOR DEVELOPMENT: *A continuous process of change in the motor area. That is, as children grow, mature, and learn, both quantitative and qualitative changes occur in their motor proficiency. For example, a young child will develop proficiency in catching a small ball through the interaction of growth, maturation, and learning opportunities. Motor development involves such a process of change.*

MOTOR TASK: *A specific movement activity. For example, the motor task might be to throw a ball at a target.*

MOTOR PERFORMANCE: *The actual movement performance that occurs when an attempt is made to complete a motor task—for example, hitting the center of a target with a ball.*

MOTOR LEARNING: *The term* motor *refers to movement. Hence, motor learning deals with aspects of learning involving body movement. Improving motor performance through practice would constitute motor learning. Hence, improving catching performance through practice would be classified as motor learning.*

MOTOR LEARNING *and* **MOTOR PERFORMANCE:** *Performance can be thought of as observable behavior. Learning, on the other hand, is an internal phenomenon that cannot be observed directly. Learning is inferred from performance. If permanent changes in motor performance occur over trials (practices), it is suggested that learning has occurred. However, all that is observable is performance. This is reflected in definitions of motor learning. For example, Magill (1993) defines motor learning as "a change in the capability of a person to perform a skill that must be inferred from a relatively permanent improvement in performance as a result of practice or experience" (p. 44). As can be seen, Magill's definition of motor learning relies on observable motor performance, since learning can only be inferred from performance.*

MOTOR BEHAVIOR: *This is a general term that is often used when both learning and performance of movement are to be addressed. For example, it is possible to observe a child's motor behavior.*

MOTOR SKILL *and* MOTOR ABILITY: *The terms* skill *and* ability *are often used in the educational setting. Sometimes these terms are used interchangeably, with little regard for any real differences between them. However, careful examination of the differences between skill and ability can be extremely helpful to a teacher of young children.*

MOTOR SKILL: *The degree of proficiency in performing a motor task. Skill is task oriented and is judged on a continuum from poor (unskillful) to excellent (highly skilled). For example, a child who performs the motor task of catching a small ball would perform observable behavior. When a judgment of proficiency is assigned to this motor performance, this refers to the level of skill exhibited.*

MOTOR ABILITY: *Fleishman (1964) has suggested that motor skills depend on motor abilities. Individuals bring with them to each situation a set of underlying traits (abilities), which are utilized when making a motor performance. For example, the level of proficiency (skill) exhibited when catching a small ball will depend on motor abilities such as hand-eye coordination, finger dexterity, wrist-finger speed, and arm-hand steadiness.*

Now that these terms have been defined, it is appropriate to move to the significance of these defined areas in terms of children's motor and physical development. Understanding developmental changes of elementary-school-age children will provide a foundation from which developmentally appropriate activities and strategies of teaching can be determined.

C O N C E P T

2.2 Knowledge of Children's Growth and Development Forms the Foundation for Effective Teaching at the Elementary-Age Level

PHYSICAL GROWTH AND DEVELOPMENT

Young children experience significant changes as they grow and develop. For example, they experience changes in height and weight and in other areas of body composition. Knowledge of children's physical growth and development is essential if a developmentally appropriate program of physical education is to be realized.

Height and Weight

Two of the most common measures of a child's growth pattern are height and weight. In figures 2.1 and 2.2, the average heights of girls and boys are plotted according to age and expressed in percentiles to show relative position for children within any particular age level. To illustrate, a nine-year-old boy whose height is 51.2 inches is at the 25th percentile on

CHAPTER 2

Figure 2.1 Girls' height by age and expressed in percentiles. The central line represents the mean, or 50th centile. The two lines above and below it represent the 75th and 25th centiles (i.e., 25 percent of the cross-sectional sample fell below the lower line and 25 percent fell above the upper line). Other centile lines are also provided. (From David L. Gallahue, *Understanding Motor Development,* 2d edition, Copyright © 1989 by Benchmark Press, Inc. Reprinted by permission of Wm. C. Brown Communications, Inc., Dubuque, IA. All Rights Reserved.)

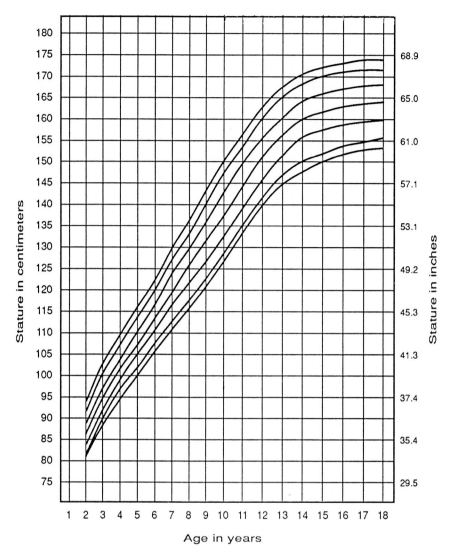

Figure 2.2 Boys' height by age and expressed in percentiles. (From David L. Gallahue, *Understanding Motor Development,* 2d edition, Copyright © 1989 by Benchmark Press, Inc. Reprinted by permission of Wm. C. Brown Communications, Inc., Dubuque, IA. All Rights Reserved.)

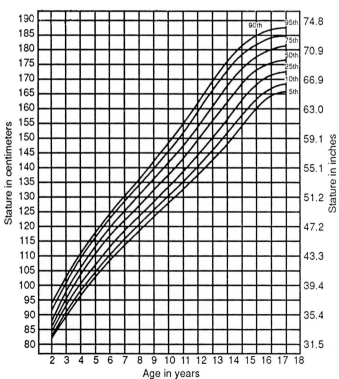

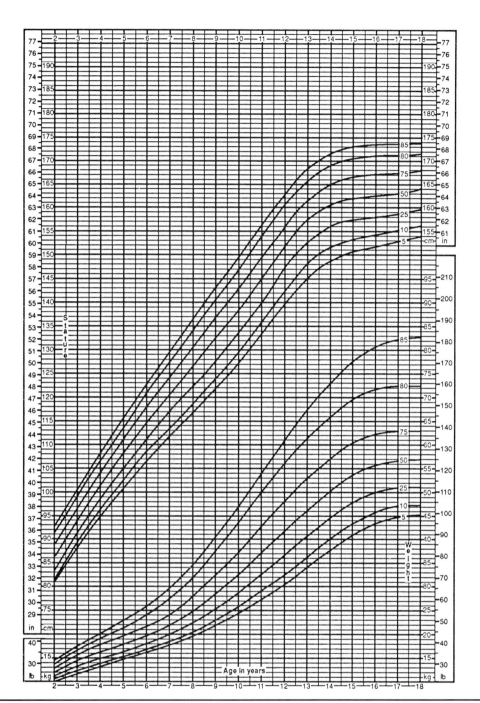

Figure 2.3 Girls' weight by age. (Reprinted with permission of Ross Laboratories, Columbus, OH 43216, from NCHS Growth Charts, © 1986 Ross Laboratories. Adapted from: Hamill PVV, Drizd TA, Johnson CL, Reed RB, Roche AF, Moore WM, *Physical Growth: National Center for Health Statistics Percentiles.* AM J CLIN NUTR 32:607–629, 1979. Data from the National Center for Health Statistics [NCHS], Hyattsville, Maryland.)

the chart. This means that 75 percent of all nine-year-olds are taller than he is and 25 percent are shorter.

The first period of rapid growth for both sexes occurs during infancy. During the early primary period (approximately ages five to seven), there is a time of steady growth of about 2 to 3 inches per year. At around nine years for girls and eleven years for boys, the adolescent growth spurt begins. Most girls reach their peak of this growing period by age twelve or thirteen, whereas most boys reach their maximum gains by age fourteen or fifteen. Boys' height gain is much greater than girls' by the time both have reached early adolescence.

The average gains in weight, which appear in figures 2.3 and 2.4, show a relatively steady increase until they reach a peak for girls at age twelve and for boys at age fourteen. It should also be noted that the peak in weight is about six to eight months behind the peaking of height for both sexes. Height-weight charts provide estimates of

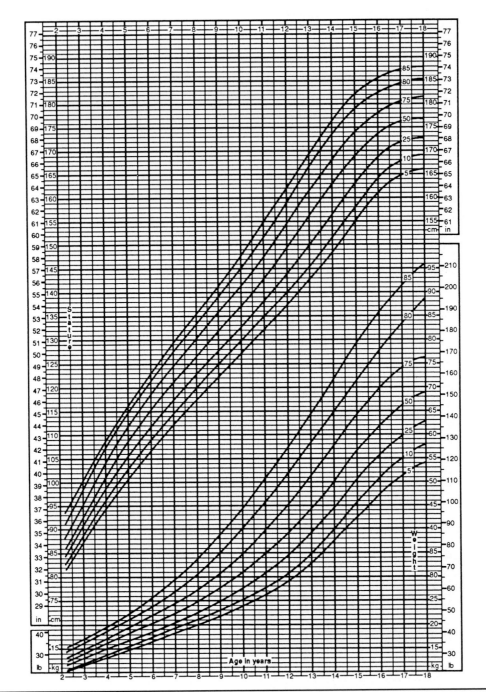

Figure 2.4 Boys' weight by age. (Reprinted with permission of Ross Laboratories, Columbus, OH 43216, from NCHS Growth Charts, © 1986 Ross Laboratories. Adapted from: Hamill PVV, Drizd TA, Johnson CL, Reed RB, Roche AF, Moore WM, *Physical Growth: National Center for Health Statistics Percentiles*. AM J CLIN NUTR 32:607–629, 1979. Data from the National Center for Health Statistics [NCHS], Hyattsville, Maryland.)

"ideal" weight for age and gender. A person is considered *overweight* (or *underweight*) if they weigh 10 to 20 percent above (or below) their ideal weight. A person weighing 20 to 50 percent above ideal weight is classified as *obese;* those more than 50 percent above ideal weight are classified as *super-obese.* However, one problem with interpreting age-

height charts is that weight values give no indication of how fat children are at any given age. For example, a child might weigh within an acceptable range yet still carry a high percentage of body fat. Similarly, a child with relatively heavy bones and strong muscle development might be classified as overweight even though she might be carrying a low percentage of body fat. To obtain more information about children's growth as it relates to weight, we are now beginning to use a measure of body leanness/fatness measured by a simple estimate of body composition, which will be described in the next section.

The period of steady and fairly even growth of boys and girls during the latter part of early childhood (five to seven years) and partially through middle childhood (eight to nine years) provides a stable period to acquire and improve many basic locomotor and manipulative skills. There are negligible differences between the sexes in weight and height until the beginning of the adolescent growth spurt, so it is appropriate to combine girls and boys for instruction in physical education. Further, during this period of time, there is no reason to expect either boys or girls to show a superior performance in using motor skills. If they do, such performance levels may be attributed to the relative time devoted to practice and playing physical activities rather than to any inherent physiological differences between boys and girls.

Body Composition

Body composition is the proportionate amount of total body mass that is lean (bone, muscle, organs, and tissues) or fat (adipose tissue). The total amount of body fat in any individual cannot be directly measured. Fairly reliable and valid estimates of an individual's proportionate body fat can be obtained, however, by placing a caliper over a fold of skin and underlying fat tissue. Since approximately 50 percent of the fat stored in the body is in a layer just below the skin, skinfold measurements, such as those now used in the AAHPERD Fitness Test (see chapter 8), are considered fairly accurate indicators of a child's proportionate amount of fat. In terms of body composition, males are considered obese with a proportionate level of fat of 25 percent or more, and females are considered obese with 30 percent or more.

However, a few important points should be noted when evaluating the body composition of elementary school children. Some children who look overweight might not register a high level of body fat when measured with skinfold calipers. Conversely, a child might look thin but register a high percentage of body fat. Many young children, particularly those who have not reached puberty, have not developed a high percentage of muscle mass and, hence, record a higher percentage of body fat than expected. The overfat child is usually (but not always) overweight, and the overweight child is usually (but not always) overfat.

Health Hazards of Obesity

It is currently estimated that somewhere between 20 and 35 percent of elementary-school-age children have excessive proportions of fatty tissue to lean body mass, or what

is commonly called obesity. As noted in chapter 1, recent surveys suggest that the incidence of obesity among children is rising. Such surveys have prompted some medical practitioners to claim that it is a form of child abuse to allow young children to become obese.

The health-related implications associated with obesity are significant. For example, the chances of developing diabetes, hypercholesterolemia, hypertension, and respiratory and orthopedic problems are all greater for an obese person than for a person of "normal" weight. In fact, everything from flat feet to cancer is more likely in obese people. Obese children are more likely to become obese adults and therefore will be at greater risk of stroke, heart disease, cardiac enlargement, congestive heart failure, osteoarthritis, gall bladder disease, and the many other ailments and diseases cited. It is imperative that elementary school physical education programs address this problem.

Dieting to Lose Weight

It has been suggested that overeating in young children is quite rare (Mayer 1968) and that, rather, inactivity is the common characteristic of obese children. Reducing caloric intake without exercising can result in the loss of lean body tissue as well as fat weight. Further, a reduction of caloric intake to the level of 1,000 calories per day can temporarily slow down or even arrest growth. Obviously, a combination of diet and activity is needed for the most effective approach to combating obesity. As Haywood (1993) states:

> Increasing the number of calories expended through increased activity permits a child to reduce weight while maintaining a safe level of caloric intake. Exercise, then, plays an important role in weight reduction at any age, but particularly in children. (p. 276)

The Role of Nature in Obesity

The role of genetics in obesity is unclear because it is difficult to separate the effects of nature and nurture. Separating eating and exercise habits from genetic influences is difficult, but so far current research has identified only a limited influence of genetic inheritance (Haywood 1993). For example, only about 5 percent of the obese population suffer from metabolic disturbances that predispose them to accumulate fat (Lindsey, Jones, and Whitley 1989). Also, genetic inheritance appears to affect internal fat more than the subcutaneous fat just below the skin.

CONCEPT

2.3 *Body Composition is Affected by Genetic and Environmental Factors, but It Is Especially Influenced by Diet and Exercise*

The Role of Nurture in Obesity

It should be remembered that although children cannot alter their genetic makeup, they can control their diet and activity levels. As Parizkova (1977) suggests, inactivity probably does not result from obesity but precedes it. However, once the child is overweight, it is difficult to reinstitute activity into the child's life. The challenge teachers face is to break the unfortunate cycle obese children find themselves in. Due to their obese condition these children must exert relatively greater effort when engaged in activity. This is likely to reduce their pleasure in the activity, which in turn will lead to a reduction in effort. Hence, they burn fewer excess calories and remain overweight.

The Role of Physical Education in Proper Weight Control and Body Composition

It is unlikely that physical education programs alone will be able to address the issue of obesity in children. Integration of other subject areas, which is a feature of this text, is one avenue of opportunity to help stress the need to combine a correct nutritional diet with regular physical activity. Integrating health curriculum topics of nutrition and healthy eating habits with physical education offers a valuable educational opportunity. However, without parental support, even this combined approach may not be sufficient. Intervention techniques to help alleviate obesity are usually tied to continued participation by the child and family support—hence the need for an active lifestyle both in and outside of school. Unfortunately, children who are overweight or obese have difficulty performing virtually all motor skills. In addition, as noted above, overweight children normally display early fatigue. Poor motor skill proficiency combined with early fatigue results in little accomplishment, which in turn results in a lack of pleasure. These effects contribute to a decrease in participation in all forms of physical activity. A sound nutritional diet helps decrease the percent body fat, but without daily vigorous physical activity, overweight children continue to be overweight or become obese as they enter adolescence and adulthood. A major challenge for teachers of physical education programs is to develop activities that help each overweight and obese child, on an individual basis, to begin to become more physically active and to maintain this lifestyle throughout the life span. One instrument teachers might find useful is the observation system developed by McKenzie et al. (1991) for assessing children's eating and physical activity behaviors. Understanding children's eating and physical activity patterns facilitates the development of individual educational plans (see IEPs in chapter 13, p. 267) and provides baseline data for individual goal setting activities (see goal setting in chapter 4, p. 80).

Health Hazards of Being Too Thin

There are also health hazards associated with excessive thinness. Anorexia nervosa afflicts more than 280,000 Americans, especially females, between the ages of twelve and twenty-five. Approximately 1 out of every 100 adolescent girls might be affected. Sufferers of anorexia nervosa are committed to self-starvation in a pursuit of excessive thinness. Anorexia nervosa patients often lose as much as 50 percent of their normal body weight and, as a result, more than 15 percent of them will die (Lindsey, Jones, and Whitley 1989). Another compulsive behavior hazardous to health is bulimia. Bulimics eat excessively and then induce vomiting and/or take large quantities of laxatives in order to rid their body of the excessive food. Although bulimics might maintain normal weight, the health hazards associated with such unnatural behavior include intestinal bleeding, stomach rupture, and death. Both anorexia nervosa and bulimia are difficult to diagnose because victims usually deny or attempt to hide these eating disorder behaviors. Treatment is complicated and involves psychological counseling and nutritional therapy. Medical advice must be sought if a child exhibits excessive thinness. A comprehensive program of school physical education and health in the elementary years is the foundation all children need. Monitoring and educating children as they progress through their school years is essential for their healthy development.

Physique

Physique refers to body build, which is a composite of body proportion and body characteristics. We normally use three body somatotypes (Sheldon, Dupertuis, and McDermott 1954) to describe general physiques. A tall and relatively thin, or Ichabod Crane–like, person is classified as an *ectomorph*. A more proportionate and muscular-looking person is known as a *mesomorph*. Finally, a person who is round in contour with a tendency toward fatness and obesity has an *endomorphic* physique.

There appears to be little relationship between the three somatotypes and body type and strength during early, middle, and late childhood. Performance in locomotor or manipulative skills is also largely unaffected by body physique, except in unusually tall or excessively obese children.

Body Proportion

Changes occur in both body form and proportion as a child moves from birth to adulthood. A child is not a miniature adult who merely gains in height each year. Body proportions change as the child grows. As the infant's body begins to grow and develop, dramatic proportional changes take place in the size of various parts of the body. For example, the head changes from being one-quarter of the body length

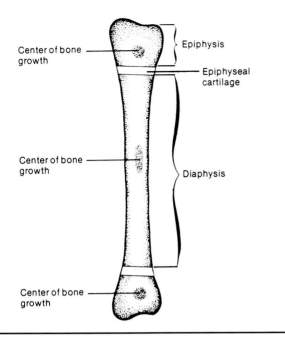

Center of bone growth — Epiphysis

— Epiphyseal cartilage

Center of bone growth

— Diaphysis

Center of bone growth

Figure 2.5 Growth of long bones.

It should be noted that research has shown that bones attain their greatest mass and strength through appropriate weight-bearing activities. This probably accounts for the natural propensity of children to climb and swing during their normal play activities.

Because the bones of an elementary school child are relatively soft and flexible, they normally can absorb many jars or blows without fracturing. However, severe blows, such as those experienced in contact football, and excessive weight bearing on any joint should be avoided. The ends of the bones and other connecting tissues around the joints are extremely supple, though, so children can bend and stretch all parts of their body farther than even the most fit adult.

Boys and girls from age five to approximately eleven show a steady increase in bone growth. During this period the bone structure is still relatively weak and flexible. As a child reaches puberty, bone growth appears to be more rapid; this is quite evident with eleven- and twelve-year-old girls.

Bones have many functions, some of which are not obvious. In addition to providing the shape and form of the body, support and protection for internal organs, and limbs for locomotion and movement, they perform many other vital bodily functions. For example, bones provide a site for blood formation, are a basic component of the body's immune system, and provide a dynamic reservoir for calcium and phosphate (Bailey et al. 1986). The body uses the calcium and phosphate reservoir to supply the nerves, heart, and muscles, and the metabolic pathways. Bones go through a process of deposit and withdrawal. The development and maintenance of strong healthy bones is necessary to provide the mineralization (calcium and phosphate) reservoir and to keep the reservoir in balance with the withdrawal demands made by the body. The most efficient way to develop strong and healthy bones is through physical activity.

When the calcium and phosphate withdrawal is greater than the mineralization deposit, osteoporosis can occur. This is the most common skeletal disorder in North America and is the result of progressive bone loss. Over 25 million Americans suffer from osteoporosis. Further, approximately one-half of all postmenopausal women over the age of fifty will experience a bone fracture related to osteoporosis (Craig 1996). A suggested remedy and prevention for osteoporosis is the intake of calcium supplements. However, epidemiologic evidence does not support the hypothesis that larger intakes of calcium are associated with increased bone density or the decreased incidence of fractures (Martin and Houston 1987). The research evidence suggests that regular physical activity is probably the most effective way to maintain the mineralization reservoir. According to Martin and Houston (1987),

> Regular physical activity, started early in childhood, can increase the peak bone mass of early adulthood, delay the onset of bone loss and reduce the rate of loss. (p. 591)

at birth to being approximately one-sixth at age six and one-eighth at maturity. Legs increase in length five times, and the trunk three times, from birth to maturity. During early childhood, the center of gravity for girls and boys is near the umbilicus, so young children have some difficulty keeping their balance when catching balls or while performing balance movements on small and large apparatus. As children mature, their center of gravity lowers to the pelvic area, giving them a greater stability for all motor activities.

As boys and girls reach the beginning of puberty, they start to show proportionate differences in the width of their shoulders and hips. Girls begin to increase in hip width relatively more than in shoulder width. Boys do not show any increase in shoulder width over hip width until around age ten. As both sexes reach adolescence, boys develop greater shoulder width than girls and proportionately longer legs, giving them an advantage in activities involving forceful arm actions and running speed.

SKELETAL GROWTH AND DEVELOPMENT

The bones of an elementary school child undergo continuous change in length, width, and general composition. The long bones, such as the humerus (upper arm) and femur (upper leg), have one center of growth in the middle of the long shaft of the bone (the diaphysis) and one or more centers at each end of the bone (the epiphysis) (figure 2.5). Growth occurs from the center of the bone toward the ends and from the ends toward the center. When these centers merge into a solid bone, bone maturation is complete.

In other words, regular physical activity is probably more beneficial to the integrity of bone development and maintenance than the intake of milk or other calcium supplements. Parents and teachers encourage children to drink milk for bone growth, but regular physical activity is of equal or greater importance to the integrity of bone development.

Children should be denied neither milk nor regular physical activity. It should also be remembered that the movement experiences children undertake must include careful, but necessary, weight-bearing activities. The teacher cannot rely on "recess" to provide these opportunities but must structure an environment that will provide developmentally appropriate activities for optimum bone development.

Maturation

Certain changes, relatively independent of environmental influence, take place as growth proceeds. For example, there are changes in a child's motor performance as growth proceeds. At approximately four months of age a baby can sit with support. At seven months the infant can sit alone. Creeping, climbing, and eventually standing occur as the child matures and is able to increase control over voluntary movements. Such development is predictable:

> Since all human life is subject to this same basic process it is logical to believe that characteristics subject to the maturational process will be broadly predictable in all normal children. (Hottinger 1980, p. 15)

Phylogenetic and Ontogenetic Behavior

Two terms used to differentiate automatic maturational skills from those developed through a learning environment are *phylogenetic* and *ontogenetic*. Phylogenetic skills are movements that occur in a predictable sequence and develop somewhat automatically. Examples are grasping, walking, and running. Ontogenetic behaviors are learned skills that do not appear automatically through maturation. Examples are swimming, skating, and bicycling. Although maturation is assumed to account for phylogenetic skill acquisition, current views do not dismiss environmental influences on maturational changes.

Motor Milestones

Since maturational changes are predictable, motor milestones have been identified and are used as developmental checks to establish whether a child is proceeding along the normal path of development. For example, if an infant is not walking at twenty months of age, there will be some concern regarding the child's motor development. For the interested reader, a comprehensive list of motor milestones can be found in Espenschade and Eckert (1980) and Haywood (1993). In addition to motor milestones, there are two other areas of development that need to be considered if a developmentally appropriate program of physical education is to be realized.

Cephalocaudal and Proximodistal Development

Some growth tends to proceed from the head toward the feet, or in a "cephalocaudal" direction. Both growth and motor function follow this pattern. The nervous system develops from the brain downward. Hence, the child gains control of the head before gaining control of the trunk. Control of the legs follows control of the trunk. Hence, based on this knowledge of development, the sequencing of the motor milestones mentioned earlier can be understood.

Other growth tends to proceed from the center of the body to the periphery, or in a "proximodistal" direction. Again, both growth and function follow this pattern. Motor control proceeds from the trunk to arms and then to hands and fingers. Also, control proceeds from the hips to legs, then to feet and toes. Further, there will be control of gross muscle movements before fine muscle movement.

Evidence of proximodistal development is seen in kindergarten children who cannot perform the fine motor task of tying a shoelace. Apart from the cognitive aspects involved in this task, many children have difficulty due to a lack of finger dexterity—this motor ability has not yet fully developed. To solve the problem, some teachers demand that children wear slip-on or easy-to-fasten shoes when they attend school. This might solve the teacher's problem, but it might not be in the best interest of child development to mainly provide gross motor tasks and ignore practice of fine manipulative abilities. Because there is evidence of sensitive periods or times in development when a child needs to experience certain activities, a full range of experiences should be provided.

THE DEVELOPMENT OF MOVEMENT, BODY, SPATIAL, AND RHYTHMIC AWARENESS

As children develop, they gain a better awareness of what their bodies can do, how to move more effectively, and how to make appropriate responses. Children develop a better sense of overall awareness. Four important areas that contribute to this overall awareness are movement, body, spatial, and rhythmic awareness. As these areas of awareness develop, the child becomes more proficient in all aspects of human movement. Indeed, the importance of developing both body awareness and spatial awareness is seen in Laban's view of Movement Education, where these types of awareness are two of the four elements used to classify movement (see chapter 5). Following are brief descriptions of the development of the four types of awareness identified above.

Movement Awareness

Movement awareness involves effectively monitoring, interpreting, and correctly responding to sensory experiences. The body receives information through its five senses (vision, touch, hearing, smell, and taste). Perception, using memory of past experiences, interprets this sensory information so that decisions and responses can be made. Another sensory modality, which is often referred to as the "sixth sense," is kinesthetic awareness. Unlike many of the other senses that receive information from outside the body, the kinesthetic sensory system receives information from the vestibular (balance) mechanism (inner ear), tendons, joints, muscles, and other internal areas. This information is combined with information from the other senses (especially vision) to provide feedback on movement and body position (movement awareness). Hence, movement awareness improves as children learn and develop more effective ways of interpreting and processing sensory-perceptual information.

Body Awareness

Body awareness, or body knowledge, involves correctly identifying body parts and their relationship to each other. Body awareness also includes a knowledge of the capabilities and limitations of body parts, and how to execute movements efficiently. Environmental experiences contribute to the development of body awareness. For example, when children first enter elementary school, they are able to identify approximately 50 percent of their body parts correctly. By the time they leave elementary school, they should have achieved 100 percent accuracy. An extension of body awareness is *directional awareness.* Although many children can correctly identify the left and right sides of their body by the time they enter elementary school, this knowledge of laterality is not usually fully developed until around seven years of age.

Spatial Awareness

Spatial awareness is the ability to recognize and respond to objects in three-dimensional space. It is the sense of the location of one's body in relation to the environment. It has been suggested that knowledge of the spatial environment and of the body is the information necessary for the formulation of a plan of action (see motor program, p. 46, chapter 3). *Visual awareness* is obviously involved in the development of spatial awareness. Depth and distance perception, form discrimination, and visual-motor coordination all contribute to spatial awareness. To demonstrate spatial awareness differences between early, middle, and late childhood, Williams (1973) had children watch a ball projected into the air by a machine, with the instruction to move quickly to the spot where they could catch the ball when it came down. Although the children could see the ball's initial flight path, a large canvas roof prevented continuous

vision of the ball's flight. All of the children moved in the correct direction, but the younger children (grades 1, 2, and 3) had a mean error of 22 feet in projecting the correct landing spot of the ball. The older children (grades 4, 5, and 6) had a mean error of only 2.5 feet. Although the younger children moved in the correct direction, they not only made a large error in estimating the landing spot of the ball, they arrived far too late to catch it. Improvement was seen by the fourth-graders, who were very good in locating the anticipated landing position but took a long time to make the judgment. In fact, they too would not have reached the correct position in time to meet the landing ball. The fifth-graders were a little less accurate than the fourth-graders but moved quickly in order to be in position when the ball landed. The sixth-graders were both quick and accurate in their projected estimations. Although the older children (grades 4 to 6) all knew where the ball was going to land, the fourth-graders could not use that information as quickly as the sixth-graders. From this study and others it has been demonstrated that complex spatial awareness involving perceptual anticipation of rapidly moving objects with locomotor movements and manipulative responses are not well developed in children until late childhood. Hence, a teacher should not expect children of eight years and younger to be capable of catching a well-hit fly ball or correctly monitoring the flight path of a soccer ball as it travels through the air.

Rhythmic Awareness

All movements involve spatial-temporal characteristics. That is, movements occur in space within a time structure. *Temporal awareness* refers to a well-developed sense of time. A child who has a well-developed sense of time can perform movements in a rhythmic, coordinated manner. As Gabbard, LeBlanc, and Lowey (1994) state:

> Rhythmic awareness is a basic component of all coordinated movement, and it plays an important role in the everyday lives of children. (p. 26)

A related awareness is *auditory awareness,* which involves auditory discrimination, sound localization, and temporal and auditory perception. The ability to perceive and discriminate among variations in sounds presented in time is a vital part of rhythmic awareness. Rhythmic activities using lummi sticks, or folk dances such as tinikling (see chapter 29, p. 660) require a discrimination of tempo, order, emphasis, and underlying beat.

Numerous studies have demonstrated changes in rhythmic awareness between older and younger children. Children in early and middle childhood often experience more difficulty in rhythmic awareness compared to children in late childhood. There is also some evidence that young boys experience more difficulty with rhythmic timing activities compared with girls of the same age. However, more research on gender differences is needed before generalizations can be made. Clearly, children need to be exposed to rhythmic activities and provided with experiences that foster auditory awareness. Chapter 28 deals with the development and teaching of rhythmic awareness.

MUSCULAR GROWTH AND DEVELOPMENT

Prior to birth, the muscles of the developing embryo increase in the number of muscle cells (hyperplasia) and in the size of each cell (hypertrophy). After birth, hyperplasia continues for a brief period; however, thereafter muscle growth is activated only by an increase in the size of the muscle fibers. With respect to school-age children, an initial rapid growth in muscle tissue occurs between ages five and six. However, from ages seven to eleven or twelve, the growth of muscle mass is relatively gradual and continuous. By age twelve, the average child has nearly double the amount of muscle tissue he had at age six. Experts in the field of growth and development indicate that increases in the size and strength of muscles, particularly in children in grades 3 to 5, make this a period of restlessness for most children. As with all other systems of the human body, muscle tissue must be exercised if its full potential is to be reached.

The majority of physical fitness norms show that boys are slightly stronger than girls between five and twelve years of age. This difference, particularly prior to puberty, is not the result of an inherent difference in muscular systems but normally is due to social factors—boys tend to participate in vigorous activities, whereas girls lean toward less active and less physically demanding activities. However, this tendency clearly is being reduced by social and cultural changes, along with the current policy of giving equal time to both sexes in all publicly supported sport and physical activity programs. With the onset of puberty, however, boys begin to show significant increases in muscle mass and strength, and physiological changes in girls create proportionately less muscle mass and more fatty tissue. These changes, coupled with other structural changes in both sexes, produce a major difference in the strength of girls and boys as they enter adolescence.

CARDIORESPIRATORY GROWTH AND DEVELOPMENT

The heart is a special kind of muscle, but it grows and develops in the same way as skeletal muscle tissue. The growth of the heart muscle and lungs is almost proportional to the growth of bones and muscles throughout the elementary school years. At age six, boys and girls have an average heart rate of about ninety beats per minute. Girls' heart rates are two to three beats higher at this age than boys'.

Respiration rate for both sexes is approximately twenty breaths per minute. Thus, easy fatigue and rapid recovery are characteristic of this age.

At age twelve, boys' heart rates drop to about seventy and girls' to around seventy-two. Respiration rate is between fifteen and twenty breaths per minute. Children between nine and twelve have more cardiorespiratory endurance, although girls with early signs of puberty may tire sooner. Maximum heart rate, which is the fastest the heart beats during heavy exercise, is around 212 beats per minute for six-year-old children. This maximum rate declines slightly to around 205 beats for both sexes by the time they reach early adolescence.

FACTORS AFFECTING GROWTH AND DEVELOPMENT

Every child's growth and developmental process is determined by two interdependent factors: heredity and the environment. Heredity sets the limits on growth, physique, and ultimate performance. Environmental factors, such as nutrition and exercise, also play important roles in this developmental process. The following four environmental factors are particularly important in determining whether children will reach their potential.

Nutrition

One of the most important environmental factors affecting growth is nutrition. During periods of rapid growth, the body must have sufficient quantities of proteins, carbohydrates, fats, water, minerals, and vitamins. Without sufficient quantities of these basic elements, the growing child will not reach maximum height. Chronic malnutrition can also cause delay in puberty and serious diseases such as rickets and scurvy. Furthermore, children who suffer from chronic malnutrition during infancy and early childhood might not resume a normal growth and developmental pattern once an adequate diet is provided.

Exercise

As stated earlier, scientific evidence indicates that exercise is necessary during the formative years for normal bone growth. Therefore, an active lifestyle will be necessary for the development of strong bones and muscles. It has also been shown that long periods of inactivity cause some decalcification of bones (Albinson and Andrews 1976). The result of this demineralization is weaker and brittler bone, which is more susceptible to fractures and other injuries. On the other hand, regular physical activity increases bone mineralization and density, which makes the bone more resistant to stress and trauma. It has also been established that an appropriate dose of daily physical activity increases muscle mass. Exercise causes the muscle fiber to increase in size but it does not increase the number of muscle cells. Regular exercise also decreases the amount of body fat. However, in some cases, particularly with long-term exercise programs, a child will lose body fat but will not lose weight, due to a proportionate increase in muscle tissue.

Geography and Climate

Several physical environmental factors, such as climate, geographical location, and altitude, seem to affect normal growth patterns. Short, stocky physiques are more common in cold climates and tall, thin physiques are prevalent in hot climates, for example. Other related factors, such as diet, types of exercise, and genetic inheritance, can have overriding influences. Nevertheless, the trend is common throughout the world. Children who are raised in high altitudes, such as in the Himalayas, have proportionately smaller bodies and slower growth rates than children who live at lower altitudes. This might be due to an insufficient supply of oxygen, which is needed for normal growth and development. At high altitudes, two other factors—a colder climate and poor nutrition—might combine with altitude to simultaneously affect normal growth patterns.

MOTOR ABILITY DEVELOPMENT

Children improve their motor skills through practice. Frequently they are faced with new motor tasks they have never before performed, yet they can often turn to the new task and produce a fairly satisfactory motor performance. How can children perform motor skills that have never been specifically practiced? One view to explain such "transfer" effects is the idea of a general motor ability. Just as psychologists have searched to measure and define a general intellectual ability (IQ), there has been a drive to isolate a similar correlate in the motor domain. Two of the main proponents who have attempted to isolate and define motor ability are Fleishman (1954) and Guilford (1958). Guilford postulated a matrix of psychomotor abilities. Fleishman's work indicated that a general motor ability could not be found; instead, four categories of motor abilities were identified. His position is that individuals bring with them to each situation a set of underlying motor abilities that largely determine the level of proficiency at which a skill will be performed.

To explain transfer effects, it is only necessary to present one of the four categories here, namely the category of fine manipulative abilities. This category consists of four basic motor abilities: arm-hand steadiness, wrist-finger speed, finger dexterity, and manual dexterity. Consider now the two dissimilar motor tasks of catching a small ball and typing, as shown in figures 2.6 and 2.7. If the four motor abilities in the category of fine manipulative abilities are not

Figure 2.6 A child uses fine manipulative abilities to catch a small ball.

Figure 2.7 A child uses fine manipulative abilities to type.

| **TABLE 2.1** | **Stages of Motor Skill Development** |

Babyhood (Age One Month through Second Year)	Early Childhood (Ages Three to Seven)	Middle Childhood (Ages Eight to Nine)	Late Childhood (Ages Ten to Twelve)
Stage 1: Rudimentary Skills Rudimentary skills—sit, crawl, creep, stand, walk	**Stage 2: Fundamental Movement Skills** Basic locomotor skills— walk, run, leap, jump, hop Combined locomotor skills—skip, slide, stop, and dodge Basic nonlocomotor skills—bend, stretch, twist, turn, push, pull, swing Basic manipulation skills— throw, catch, strike	**Stage 3: Refined Movement Skills** Combination and refinement of one or more fundamental skills—run and jump, slide and stop, land and roll, catch and throw, dribble and kick	**Stage 4: Specific Sport, Dance, or Specialized Skills** Advanced and refined versions of sports, dance, or other specialized skills—running long jump, football pass, Scottish sword dance, hand spring

developed to a high degree in the performer, then a poorly skilled performance will result when each of the motor tasks is attempted. The same underlying motor abilities necessary for performing a sport skill are needed to perform many other skills well outside the realm of sport.

In essence, then, a performer who has well-developed motor abilities has many of the prerequisites for performing all motor skills. Transfer effects can now be explained, since a performer who has well-developed motor abilities can turn to a novel motor task and use the developed abilities to make an adequate motor performance. Obviously, the cognitive aspects and precise nuances associated with each unique motor skill will affect the performance too, but the basic motor abilities will be of primary importance.

Fleishman (1964) also found important changes in the development of motor abilities. He stated that motor abilities are themselves the "product of learning and develop at different rates, mainly during childhood and adolescence" (p. 9). Since there are sensitive times early in life for developing motor abilities, it is imperative that a rich environment occurs in the elementary school years to ensure that children develop to their maximum potential. Elementary school teachers must provide opportunities for children to develop their underlying motor abilities. Having children involved in a great variety of movement activities, with lots of opportunity for practice, will ensure that each child has the chance to develop to her or his full potential. Providing experiences mainly in gross motor activities and limiting opportunities to develop motor abilities through fine motor tasks (e.g., tying shoelaces) might not be in the best interests of the child, and yet attempting motor tasks that provide little or no success can result in frustration. Thus, a variety of different motor tasks of varying levels of difficulty (developmentally appropriate) must be provided to ensure success. Threading ropes of various thicknesses through holes of various sizes is one way of controlling the level of difficulty for the development of fine manipulative abilities.

When children practice these motor skills, they are contributing to the development of their motor abilities. The period from early childhood to adolescence should be a time of continuing to refine basic motor skills, while at the same time developing underlying motor abilities to their full potential. Once a solid foundation of basic motor abilities has been established, there exists the opportunity to transfer such abilities to new situations in order to perform and learn new motor skills with some ease.

CONCEPT

2.4 *The Environment in Which a Child Is Placed Can Facilitate or Delay Motor Development*

Returning once more to the four motor abilities that make up the category of fine manipulative abilities, the teacher must realize that when movement experiences are used to develop these fine manipulative abilities, it is not for the sole purpose of learning sport skills. As mentioned earlier, the same motor abilities used to catch a small ball are needed to perform many other motor skills well outside the realm of sport. For example, typing, handwriting, drawing and drafting, playing a musical instrument, and sewing all require fine manipulative motor abilities. This is why the curriculum area is termed "physical education" and not merely "sports education." The aim of a developmentally appropriate program of physical education is to develop physically educated children.

MOTOR SKILL DEVELOPMENT

The development of motor skills, from birth to late childhood, follows an orderly sequence through four overlapping age ranges, as illustrated in table 2.1.

Figure 2.8 A child begins to develop basic manipulative skills.

Stage 1: Babyhood or Infancy

The first stage, known as babyhood or infancy, begins about one month after birth and lasts to the end of the second year. During this period, a child displays reflex responses and then proceeds to the rudimentary skills of sitting, crawling, creeping, climbing, standing, and walking.

Stage 2: Early Childhood

The next stage, known as early childhood, continues from age three to approximately the seventh year. During this period, a child develops the fundamental motor skills—the basic motor skills that allow humans to move purposefully and efficiently and that form the building blocks for more complex motor skills in later phases of development. Fundamental motor skills can be classified into three general groups: locomotor, nonlocomotor, and manipulative skills. Although chapter 6 is devoted to a full explanation of these three kinds of skills and their stages of development, the following descriptions are provided here for clarity.

Locomotor Skills

Locomotor skills are the basic motor skills necessary for moving through space and from one place to another. They include running, jumping, leaping, hopping, skipping, sliding, dodging, and stopping.

Nonlocomotor Skills

Nonlocomotor skills involve movements that do not require transportation of the body through space or from place to place. They include swinging, twisting, bending, turning, and stretching.

Manipulative Skills

Manipulative skills involve control of objects, usually with the hands or feet (figure 2.8). Three classifications of manipulative skills have been forwarded: *receptive, propulsive,* and *retentive.* Receptive manipulative skills are receiving skills

Figure 2.9 A child begins to develop complex combinations of movements.

and include catching and trapping. Propulsive manipulative skills exert force on objects and include throwing, kicking, and striking. Retentive manipulative skills maintain control over an object while one is moving and include dribbling a basketball, hockey puck/ball, or soccer ball.

Stage 3: Middle Childhood

As children move into middle childhood, they begin to show greater ease and efficiency in performing fundamental motor skills and develop more complex combinations of locomotor, nonlocomotor, and manipulative skill patterns (figure 2.9). During third and fourth grades, increases in physical size and strength, coupled with improved perceptual and cognitive development, contribute to a child's ability to perform more coordinated movement patterns with greater speed and accuracy.

Stage 4: Late Childhood

During late childhood, the more specific movement skills required of games, dance, and gymnastics begin to show some refinement. In game activities like soccer, fifth- and sixth-graders learn to dribble with changing speeds as well as to add feints and other tactics necessary for moving a ball through a variety of complex game situations. Similarly, dance and gymnastic skills become more fluid and creative as the performers acquire greater skill and understanding of the finer aspects of a movement or sequence of movements (figure 2.10). As children move into adolescence, they

Figure 2.10   A child becomes more fluid and creative.

Figure 2.11   These children need to explore many types of activities.

continue to refine these more specialized game, dance, and gymnastic skills to acquire new skills that are more related to their social and future leisure activities.

These four developmental stages, coupled with the tremendous individual differences existing at each grade level, have a direct bearing on a teacher's choice of activities, the way in which these activities are taught, and the learning expectations of every child. The early childhood program should be a time for acquiring minimal form in the fundamental and manipulative skills (see chapter 6). This program should emphasize exposure to these movement concepts and skills and include numerous opportunities for experimenting with different ways of moving and manipulating balls, bats, and a variety of other small equipment. It is clearly not a time for refinement or specialization.

As children enter middle childhood, they become interested in improving specific motor skills; therefore, they devote more time and energy to acquiring these skills. They also are keenly interested in playing more organized and challenging games. Teachers of these children not only should show them how to improve their performances and provide interesting and challenging game and dance activities, but they should also provide opportunities for exploration and creative expression regardless of the nature of the activity. Children in this age range enjoy competition, but they also like cooperative activities that provide avenues for positive interpersonal relationships.

Late childhood is essentially a continuation of the previous stage, characterized by a keener interest in improving performance. Differences in physiological maturity, particularly for girls who have entered puberty, present some problems with respect to activity interests and gender preferences in playing or performing some activities. These

problems can be dealt with by using more individualized teaching strategies, as suggested in later chapters.

PERSONAL AND SOCIAL DEVELOPMENT

The personal and social characteristics of children, as well as their physical growth and motor development, must be considered when planning a physical education program. This section describes some of the more common personal and social characteristics of children in early childhood (three to seven years), middle childhood (eight to nine years), and late childhood (ten to twelve years).

Early Childhood (Five to Seven Years)

Five- and six-year-old children are quite egocentric; hence, they enjoy playing by themselves or with one or two other children. They have boundless curiosity and enthusiasm, but they tire easily. These children need to explore many types of physical activities and challenges (figure 2.11)—but without pressure and with generous praise for their accomplishments. As they enter grade 2, they become much more cooperative and they display an interest in all types of physical activity, although for relatively short periods of time. Teachers find that seven-year-olds seek adult approval much more than they did just a year earlier.

Middle Childhood (Eight to Nine Years)

As children enter middle childhood, their interests shift toward more group activities and group success (figure 2.12). They show a keen interest in more complex game

Figure 2.12 Children's interests shift toward more group activities.

Figure 2.13 A period of transition and differentiation in interests and abilities.

and dance activities and a willingness to practice to improve their individual skills. Although these children seem to display a great deal of group or team loyalty, they tend toward adult-supervised activities. It is very important that teachers provide challenging activities *with many opportunities for each child to be successful.* Middle childhood is a period when children begin to test their abilities in a group setting. If a child fails at all challenges, her self-image will reach a very low ebb, and it is doubtful that she will continue to be interested in physical activities. Therefore, it is important that instructors provide children with a strong base for coping with the failures that everyone experiences during a lifetime.

Late Childhood (Ten to Twelve Years)

Physical maturation influences the social and psychological development of children ten to twelve years old, creating a period of transition and differentiation in the interests and behavior of both boys and girls (Arnold 1968) (figure 2.13). Both sexes enjoy highly complex team games and, like the previous age range, are willing to practice for long periods to improve their playing ability. They have an intense need

to become responsible for their own actions, so they enjoy planning, organizing, and supervising their own activities—which has major implications for daily instructional, intramural, and interschool programs.

Boys tend to be less concerned with dress and appearance, are keenly interested in vigorous competitive sports, and show a strong concern about their peers' opinions and a great deal of confidence in adults. Hero worship, particularly of well-known athletes, is the rule rather than the exception.

Girls' attitudes toward active participation in all types of vigorous physical activities are changing. More girls are now participating in organized intramural and interschool team sports. Community clubs for gymnastics, swimming, and soccer are also experiencing a major increase in the number of girls wishing to participate in their sports programs. Although this is a significant trend, girls of this age level still become increasingly concerned with their personal femininity and tend toward less vigorous activities. They are keenly interested in current fad dances, however, and will participate in this type of activity with great vigor.

No magic line separates one age from another; teachers of grades 5 and 6 are aware of the tremendous diversity in the psychological characteristics of these children. However, as with the younger age range, some basic considerations should be made when planning a physical education program for children in the intermediate grades (see p. 191).

COGNITIVE DEVELOPMENT

For many years, physical education has been justified as enhancing the physical fitness of children and teaching them a variety of physical activities. These objectives are still the cornerstone of most physical education programs; however, the shift toward a more developmental approach now requires a greater emphasis on cognitive development. The basic philosophy of the developmental approach is to teach children the underlying concepts and principles of health and movement. When they understand their bodies' functions, the principles of exercise, and body mechanics, they learn to appreciate the importance of maintaining optimum levels of well-being and to engage in and enjoy a variety of physical activities. A conscious effort has been made throughout this text to provide the basic knowledge and important concepts for each content area of the program.

According to contemporary views of cognitive development, *meaningful learning* should be the goal of all teachers (Lefrançois 1994). Meaningful learning involves relating new material to existing cognitive structures. One way of relating concepts and skills to existing cognitive structures is to seek connections between different subject areas. Hence, subject area integration (described in chapter 1, p. 12) is a feature of this textbook. For many years, classroom teachers have recognized the value of using the medium of movement to teach a variety of academic skills and concepts. For example, the use of the game Foxes and Squirrels (p. 323) to reinforce the concept of mathematical sets or the modification of Steal the Bacon (p. 336) to teach addition and subtraction is not new to classroom teachers. The premise of using physical activities to enhance academic concepts and skills is based on three important factors. First, children have a greater chance of learning an academic skill when they are actively involved in the learning. Games and other exciting movement activities that also emphasize an academic skill can accomplish this task. Second, children learn through a variety of experiences. Some learn best through auditory modes; others through visual modes; and others through an active and enjoyable game, dance, or gymnastic activity. Third, to learn and retain an academic concept, a child must practice it many times through different media. Since meaningful learning can be advanced through subject area integration, an entire chapter (chapter 14) is devoted to this topic, and numerous examples and suggestions are provided throughout this text.

KNOWLEDGE DEVELOPMENT

As children develop more knowledge about a topic, they usually have corresponding improvement in performance. That is, as the knowledge base improves, performance improves. Indeed, Haywood (1993) suggests, "Children undoubtedly have a smaller base of knowledge than adults because they have had fewer experiences" (p. 294). Hence, through knowledge development, performance increases can be expected. However, before considering the development of knowledge it is necessary to identify the different types of knowledge base. Although many types of knowledge base have been postulated (e.g., Chi 1981), the major two are termed *declarative* and *procedural*.

> *Declarative knowledge* is knowing factual information. It is knowing what to do. *Procedural knowledge* is knowing how to do something and doing it in accordance with specific rules. (Haywood 1993)

Effective teaching involves the development of both knowledge bases. For example, when children are taught mathematics, their declarative and procedural knowledge bases are both developed. Children learn mathematical concepts and strategies (declarative knowledge—knowing what to do), in addition to being given practice opportunities to apply these concepts and strategies to specific problems (procedural knowledge—knowing how to solve a mathematical problem). Indeed, this textbook is designed on the same premise. It is designed to help teachers develop their knowledge bases. That is, learning the textbook content (declarative knowledge) assists teachers as the content becomes embedded in their instructional teaching practices (procedural knowledge).

C O N C E P T

2.5 *Effective Teachers Learn to Embed Declarative Knowledge into Their Instructional Practices (Procedural Knowledge)*

In the same way, children need to develop both declarative and procedural knowledge in the area of physical education. According to Chi (1981), declarative knowledge is acquired first to provide a foundation for procedural knowledge. Young children often lack declarative knowledge in physical activity settings. As Haywood (1993, p. 295) states, "They typically are novices who must learn game rules, goals, and strategies before they can exhibit procedural knowledge and make appropriate decisions as to which action to perform." Although the precise interaction between declarative and procedural knowledge in the learning phase is unknown at this time, the important point is that both types of knowledge require development (Fishburne 1996). As a result, teachers will need to design instructional practices that facilitate the development of these two types of knowledge. Chapter 3 provides examples and further clarification on this topic.

SENSITIVE TIMES DURING DEVELOPMENT

It was stated earlier that children should receive opportunities to develop their motor abilities during their elementary years because this might be a sensitive or critical time for motor ability development. Although research studies have not identified the precise timing associated with sensitive periods, the research does indicate that the early years of life are a crucial time. The sensitive time frame applies to many areas of development:

> Although the research does not strongly support remediation of cognitive deficiencies through

perceptual-motor activities, there are indications that sensitive periods for perceptual development exist. It is important that individuals have experience moving in their environments during these periods. Perceptual deficiencies that result from lack of experience could later manifest themselves in both motor and cognitive performance. (Haywood 1993, p. 230)

Indeed, it has been shown that the development of neuronal connections during brain development is susceptible to environmental influence. It would appear that a lack of correct exposure and usage at sensitive times might impair brain development. Many researchers (e.g., Fifkova 1967; Weisel and Hubel 1963) have demonstrated the lack of structural brain development, and the consequent diminishment of function, resulting from a lack of appropriate activity. According to Sperry (1965):

> Many elements deeper in the brain centers must discharge only in very special activities, and, if these activities are not exercised—especially during maturational stages when the neurons seem to be particularly dependent on use—the neuron types involved may regress, leaving profound functional deficiencies in the integrative machinery. (p. 201)

Stated simply, these researchers suggest that children should experience rich environmental situations in order to ensure optimum brain development.

Adipose tissue (fat cells) is another important area of development that appears to be influenced during sensitive times. Fat cells grow both in number (*hyperplasia*) and in size (*hypertrophy*). However, evidence suggests that after puberty the number of fat cells becomes set and that only the size of individual fat cells can change after this time (Gabbard 1992). Hence, before puberty is the sensitive time for developing the number of fat cells. Clearly, providing children with regular physical activity and a correct nutritional diet during elementary school years is vital. Neglect at this age can result in an abundant number of fat cells that will be with the child for the rest of his or her life.

C O N C E P T

2.6 A Sensitive Time in Human Development Is When a Child is Unusually Receptive to Environmental Influences

Many other areas of development might be programmed to develop at certain times and require particular environmental experiences. Although much research remains to be done in the area of sensitive time frames, the one common feature of all studies conducted thus far is the finding that sensitive times appear early in life and certainly not after

puberty. The years spent in elementary school are crucial years for children. Experiences here can determine the limits of future potential.

IMPLICATIONS FOR THE PHYSICAL EDUCATION PROGRAM

The choice of an activity, as well as the manner in which children are motivated to learn, must be based on the characteristics and needs of children within each level of development. The previous discussion on growth and development has provided a general understanding of elementary school children. Through a period of seven years, these children undergo major physiological, psychomotor, cognitive, personal, and social changes. The major changes and their implications for the physical education program are summarized in tables 2.2, 2.3, and 2.4. We have grouped developmental changes into three levels—early, middle, and late childhood—as guidelines to help teachers plan developmentally appropriate activities and teaching strategies to meet the needs and interests of each age group.

Summary Review

Knowledge of children's growth and development is vital when planning developmentally appropriate programs of elementary school physical education. This knowledge also forms the foundation for effective teaching at the elementary age level. Furthermore:

1. There are potential health hazards associated with being too thin or being overweight.
2. Body composition is affected by genetic and environmental factors. Physical activity and diet play a significant role in weight control and health.
3. The environment in which a child is placed can facilitate or delay motor development.
4. There are sensitive times in human development. Correct environmental influences during sensitive times are essential for optimum development.
5. Failure to capitalize on sensitive times could result in permanent effects that are irreversible.
6. During their elementary school years, children acquire fundamental skills that are the foundation for more complex motor skills.
7. Developmental differences among children in early childhood, middle childhood, and late childhood influence teaching and planning decisions.
8. Movement education concepts can be identified to correspond with the development of movement awareness.

CHAPTER 2

 **2.2**   Developmental Level I (Early Childhood, Five to Seven Years)

Characteristics	Implications for the Physical Education Program

Physical Growth and Development

Height and weight gains moderate and steady.	Provide daily vigorous activity, particularly running, climbing, and swimming, with frequent rest intervals. Discourage long periods of inactivity. Encourage recess and period breaks throughout the school day that incorporate vigorous and total body movement.
Heart and breathing rates relatively high.	Attend to postural development; early detection of structural anomalies is important. Children of this age have relatively small bodies; hence, consider the relative size of supplies and equipment.
Steady growth in strength and muscular endurance. Both sexes maintain high level of flexibility.	Expect the same level of performance from both sexes.

Motor Skill Development

Hand-eye coordination shows steady improvement.	Provide for manipulation (catching, throwing, kicking, etc.) of balls of various sizes. Initial instruction should include relatively low speeds of throwing with short distances. Gradually increase speed, use of small objects, and distance as skill develops.
Reaction time is slow but shows persistent increase throughout this stage. Locomotor and manipulative skills show continuous improvement. Static and dynamic balance skill shows steady improvement.	Encourage participation in numerous activities involving a change of speed, direction, and level. Provide opportunities to practice balance and agility movements on small and large apparatus.
Rhythmic and dance skills show increase in quality and complexity of movement.	Provide a variety of rhythmic, folk, and creative dance activities.

Cognitive Development

Gradual increase in attention span.	Provide a large variety of activities within the instructional period. Initiate games for the individual and for small groups. Keep them simple in purpose, rules, and directions.
Extremely creative.	Provide material and content that foster creative interests and movements (creative dance and movement education).
Enjoy rhythm and music.	Provide various forms of dance experiences, including singing games and creative dance.
Keen desire to repeat activities they know and perform well. Curious—want to know how things work.	Allow children to choose activities, such as playing the same game each recess period. In dance and gymnastic activities, chronic interest in one activity is characteristic. With patience, children soon run the course and move on to other challenges. Your challenge is to provide more interesting and challenging activities.
Can work with simple movement concepts.	Take time to answer questions and explain reasons for activities whenever the opportunities arise.

Personal and Social Development

Individualistic but show a need for adult approval. Enjoy working in small groups.	In one respect, five- to seven-year-olds are basically individualistic. Therefore, provide numerous individual activities for all children regardless of ability. Children of this age level also need adult approval.
General lack of fear and an extremely high spirit of adventure. Little concern for the opposite sex during early grades.	Encourage the spirit of adventure (climbing, testing one's own ability with other children). At the same time, develop within each child concern for personal safety and a general awareness and concern for the safety of others. Extensively use the Movement Education approach with gymnastic activities.
Very sensitive to feeling and criticism of adults. Egocentric.	Provide frequent and generous praise and encouragement to all children. Provide situations in which children learn to take turns, to share equipment, and to win and lose gracefully.

TABLE 2.3 Developmental Level II (Middle Childhood, Eight to Nine Years)

Characteristics	Implications for the Physical Education Program
Physical Growth and Development	
Height and weight gains continue to be moderate and steady.	Continue to provide daily vigorous physical activities.
Girls begin to show early signs of puberty.	
Heart and lungs continue to develop at a slow and steady rate.	Continue to give close attention to postural development, particularly to girls who begin early growth spurt.
Early signs of poor posture.	Use simple postural screening tests.
Steady growth in strength.	
Slight decrease in flexibility, especially in boys.	Provide activities that enhance flexibility.
Motor Skill Development	
Eye-hand coordination continues to improve, along with major improvements in manipulative skills.	Introduce basic sports skills and lead-up games.
General improvement in reaction time.	Stress form rather than speed, distance, or accuracy.
General improvement in balance skills.	Provide more complex balance and agility skills with small and large apparatus.
General improvement in rhythmic and dance skills.	Provide more complex rhythmic and folk dance activities.
Cognitive Development	
Continued increase in attention span.	Continue to provide a variety of more complex activities, which require closer attention and cooperative behavior.
Continue to be very curious, particularly about their own abilities.	Teach the mechanical principles relating to performing movement skills. Encourage children to invent their own games and movement sequences.
General movement toward more group activities.	Continue to provide challenging tasks on apparatus and on the playing field. Stress personal and group safety throughout this age range.
Beginning to show interest in ways and means of improving personal fitness.	
Personal and Social Development	
Continued high spirit of adventure.	Plan game, dance, and gymnastic activities that boys and girls can participate in together. When "fierce" antagonism and/or major differences in skill levels exist, particularly in combative activities and ball games, separate the sexes.
Gradual trend of mutual antagonism toward the opposite sex.	
Lack of discrimination on the basis of race, color, or religion.	Take care in the methods and techniques used to choose teams, leaders, and various social groupings. The essential teaching characteristic should be fairness to all children.
Accept just punishment for self and for group.	Do not punish a whole group for the wrongdoings of one child. Children recognize inconsistencies in degrees of punishment; therefore, be consistent and fair with the type and amount of discipline and punishment. Because of the "social awareness" and inherent fairness of children, stress group control through self-discipline.
Display honesty, team loyalty, and strong group identity.	

Developmental Level III (Late Childhood, Ten to Twelve Years)

Characteristics	Implications for the Physical Education Program
Physical Growth and Development	
Rapid height and weight gains after beginning of puberty. Girls normally reach puberty between ten and twelve years, whereas boys begin approximately two years later. Marked differences in height and weight gains occur in grades 5 and 6.	Continue to provide vigorous activities, emphasizing strength and endurance for longer periods of time. Although girls, particularly those who have reached the early stages of puberty, may show a general disinterest in vigorous activities, remember that normal growth and development depend on vigorous and continuous activity.
Heart and lungs increase in size and capacity proportionate to height and weight gains.	Postural development for this age group is a particular problem. The problem has been intensified by excessive viewing of television and video games, and general sedentary living. Therefore, observe sitting and walking postures of students, and plan activities for general posture development. Give special attention to girls who have reached puberty and tend toward sloping shoulders to compensate for height and chest development.
Muscle strength increases with boys and girls; differences in strength between boys and girls during this age level may be due to the type of activities in which they participate rather than to inherent structural or physiological changes within each sex.	
Flexibility decreases, with boys showing greater losses than girls.	Continue to provide activities that enhance flexibility.
Motor Skill Development	
Muscle coordination continues to improve in both sexes.	Provide more highly organized and competitive individual and team sports. If there is a marked difference in level of skill between boys and girls, separate them when playing team games to allow both sexes to develop according to their own level of skill and interest.
Boys and girls begin to show major differences in level of skill in team sport activities.	Both sexes, however, require extensive practice in the refinement of throwing, catching, and kicking skills. Separate and solid unit construction is appropriate, particularly in the upper grades. Provide more complex challenges in small and large apparatus activities. Provide more socially based folk and square dance activities.
Cognitive Development	
Marked increase in attention span.	Provide more complex and challenging activities. This applies to individual and team games where allowance is made for extensive practice in learning skills, rules, and complex team strategy. Similarly, with dance and gymnastic activities, allow time for developing complex and creative movements.
General increase in intellectual curiosity.	Teach concepts and principles of movement related to the physical and motor skills the children are learning. Through the application of the problem-solving method, test and challenge a child's intellectual ability through movement tasks.
Genuine interest in knowing about the human body and how to improve health and performance.	
Curiosity leading to tendency to constantly ask questions and challenge reasons for studying or performing activities.	Provide good reason and rationale for your decisions.
	Encourage open discussion and debate whenever possible.
Personal and Social Development	
Increased control of emotions in individual and group situations	Select activities commensurate with the emotional development of each age group. Outbreaks of emotions in tense game situations are normal and, in some situations, desirable. Make provision for each child to experience leadership roles.
Girls tend to be more self-conscious in the presence of boys as well as when performing within their own sex grouping.	The essence of good teaching should be the development of self-direction on the part of each child. Independence is a natural tendency for this age group and must be provided for both in methods and appropriate activities. Teacher-directed approaches should not be completely abandoned but should be blended with other approaches that call for greater freedom and responsibility on the part of the learner. Pay special attention to the kinds of groupings that provide for identification as well as foster team cooperation and loyalty.
General increase toward independence and peer group identity.	
Major differences in attitude toward opposite sex as well as toward different types of activities. Boys and girls alike, particularly during upper grades, show a lack of sympathy and understanding toward each other. Boys tend toward more rough team sports, increased concern for physique and skill, and a dominant interest in competition. Girls begin to show concern for personal appearance and activities involving graceful and creative movements.	Make provisions within the instructional and extraclass program for children to participate in both individual sex and mixed group activities. Allow extensive opportunities for boys and girls to plan and direct activities. The latter not only contributes to the development of cooperation, leadership, and team loyalty, but also allows children to develop other important social traits and personal friendships.
Social acceptance is more peer-centered than adult-centered.	Use discretion when asking girls (particularly fifth- and sixth-graders) to demonstrate skills or movements in a mixed setting. Although girls are normally more graceful than boys in gymnastic-type movements, they tend to be embarrassed when asked to demonstrate. The reverse, however, is generally true with ball skills, where girls are usually less proficient than boys. Develop an understanding and appreciation for the differences that exist between boys and girls of this age level.

INDIVIDUAL *and* GROUP PROJECTS

1. Request permission from a local elementary school to measure the heights and weights of one class of children. Discuss average heights, weights, ranges, and differences among boys and girls in the selected class.
2. Debate whether boys and girls in physical education should be segregated in grades 4 through 6.
3. Interview a general medical practitioner or specialist in pediatrics about her or his concerns for physical activity of elementary-age schoolchildren and report to the class the essential points of your interview.
4. Interview elementary-age children to obtain a profile of their physical activity patterns. Share your findings with the class.
5. Visit a school during lunch hour to observe the types and quantities of food children bring for lunch. Share your findings with the class.
6. List three areas of human development that can be positively influenced through a quality program of physical education.
7. Form cooperative groups to create ideas to motivate and help children who are severely overweight. Report group ideas to other class members.

SELECTED READINGS

Albinson, J., and G. Andrews. 1976. *Child in sport and physical activity.* Baltimore: University Park Press.

Arnold, P. J. 1968. *Education, physical education and personality development.* London: Heinemann Educational Books.

Bailey, D. A., A. D. Martin, C. S. Houston, and J. L. Howie. 1986. Physical activity, nutrition, bone density, and osteoporosis. *Australian Journal of Science and Medicine in Sport* 18 (3): 3–8.

Bower, T. G. R. 1979. *Human development.* San Francisco: W. H. Freeman.

Chi, M. T. H. 1981. Knowledge development and memory performance. In *Intelligence and learning*, ed. M. P. Friedman, J. P. Das, and N. O'Connor, 221–29. New York: Plenum.

Corbin, C. 1980. *A textbook of motor development.* 2d ed. Dubuque, IA: Wm. C. Brown.

Craig, G. 1996. *Human development.* Englewood Cliffs, NJ: Prentice Hall.

Espenschade, A. S., and H. D. Eckert. 1980. *Motor development.* Columbus, OH: Charles E. Merrill.

Fifkova, E. 1967. The influence of unilateral visual deprivation on optic centers. *Brain Research* 6:763–66.

Fishburne, G. J. 1983. Explaining the mystery of movement. *Elements: A Journal for Elementary Education* 15 (1): 18–21.

———. 1988. Sensitive periods during brain development: Implications for the development of motor abilities. In *Proceedings for the 1986 ICHPER World Conference,* ed. D. McNair, 170–88. London: Foresee Enterprise.

———. 1996. "The need for and value of quality programmes of physical education." *Canadian Administrator* 35: 6–11.

Fleishman, E. A. 1954. A dimensional analysis of motor abilities. *Journal of Experimental Psychology* 48: 437–54.

———. 1964. *The structure and measurement of physical fitness.* Englewood Cliffs, NJ: Prentice Hall.

———. 1967. Individual differences and motor learning. In *Learning and individual differences,* ed. R. M. Gagne. Columbus, OH: Charles E. Merrill.

Gabbard, C. 1992. *Lifelong motor development.* Dubuque, IA: Wm. C. Brown.

Gabbard, C., B. LeBlanc, and S. Lowy. 1994. *Physical education for children.* 2d ed. Englewood Cliffs, NJ: Prentice Hall.

Guilford, J. P. 1958. A system of psychomotor abilities. *American Journal of Psychology* 71: 164–74.

Haywood, K. 1993. *Life span motor development.* Champaign, IL: Human Kinetics.

Hottinger, W. 1980. Importance of studying motor development. In *A textbook of motor development,* ed. C. B. Corbin. Dubuque, IA: Wm. C. Brown.

Krus, P. H., R. H. Bruininks, and G. Robertson. 1981. Structure of motor abilities in children. *Perceptual and Motor Skills* 52: 119–29.

Lefrançois, G. R. 1994. *Psychology for teaching.* Belmont, CA: Wadsworth.

Lindsey, R., B. J. Jones, and A. V. Whitley. 1989. *Fitness for the health of it.* Dubuque, IA: Wm. C. Brown.

Magill, R. A. 1993. *Motor learning concepts and applications.* Dubuque, IA: Brown & Benchmark.

Martin, A. D., and C. S. Houston. 1987. Osteoporosis, calcium and physical activity. *Canadian Medical Association Journal* 136: 587–93.

Mayer, J. 1968. *Overweight: Causes, cost, and control.* Englewood Cliffs, NJ.: Prentice Hall.

McKenzie, T. L., et al. 1991. BEACHES: An observational system for assessing children's eating and physical activity behaviors and associated events. *Journal of Applied Behavior Analysis* 24:141–51.

Parizkova, J. 1977. *Body fat and physical fitness.* The Hague, Netherlands: Martinus Nijhoff.

Rarick, G. 1973. *Physical activity: Human growth and development.* New York: Academic Press.

Roberton, M., and L. Halverson. 1984. *Developing children—Their changing movement.* Philadelphia: Lea & Febiger.

Sheldon, W. H., C. W. Dupertuis, and F. McDermott. 1954. *Atlas of man: A guide for somatotyping the adult male at all ages.* New York: Harper & Row.

Sperry, R. W. 1965. Embryogenesis of behavioral nerve nets. In *Organogenesis,* ed. R. L. Dehaan and H. Ursprung. New York: Holt, Rinehart & Winston.

Wiesel, T. N., and D. H. Hubel. 1963. The effects of visual deprivation on morphology and physiology of cells in the cat's lateral geniculate body. *Journal of Neurophysiology* 26:978–93.

CHAPTER 3

Learning Motor Skills

KEY CONCEPTS

3.1 Competency in human movement is tied to motor skill acquisition

3.2 Motor skill development is influenced by growth, maturation, and learning

3.3 When a child is learning a motor skill, three distinct phases of learning can be observed

3.4 During the process of learning a motor skill, several changes occur at different points in time

3.5 Theories of motor learning provide a basis for organizing the most effective learning environments for motor skill acquisition

3.6 Several principles of learning motor skills have been identified and provide a framework for creating effective learning environments

3.7 Observations of changes in basic motor skill development can benefit from knowledge of the laws of motion and the principles of balance, force, and leverage

3.8 Applying basic mechanical principles to movements of the body provides an understanding for effective instruction

3.9 Basic laws of motion apply to human movement and provide an understanding for creating effective learning environments

KEY OBJECTIVES

After completing this chapter you will be able to:

1. Understand and identify three different phases of learning that occur during the acquisition of motor skills
2. Identify the changes that occur during the process of learning a motor skill
3. Identify, based on sound principles of motor learning, the most appropriate and effective learning environments for motor skill acquisition
4. Apply the basic mechanical principles of balance to children's movement activities

5. Understand Newton's laws of motion and apply these laws to children's movement activities
6. Understand the principles of force and apply these principles to children's movement activities
7. Understand the principles of mechanical leverage and apply these principles to children's movement activities

I f children are to successfully participate in physical endeavors, they must possess the requisite motor skills. Hence, one of the fundamental objectives in physical education is to teach a variety of game, dance, and gymnastic skills to children of all age levels in the elementary school. Our challenge is to teach motor skills and concepts to children of varying physical maturity, interests, and abilities. To do this effectively and safely, we must understand *when* it is appropriate to introduce a motor skill and *how* it should be taught. In the past few decades, researchers in this area have produced a body of knowledge that can help us understand the nature of motor learning and the process of acquiring motor skills and movement concepts.

This chapter will briefly cover several important areas related to learning motor skills. It will summarize the current theories of motor learning that provide a framework on which to build a series of working concepts and principles related to teaching motor skills. The remaining sections include information about the stages of motor skill development, the phases of learning a motor skill, and the concepts related to the mechanics of movement, as well as some general guidelines for teaching motor skills and concepts. The concepts and principles presented in this chapter are fundamental to all future chapters dealing with teaching game, dance, and gymnastic activities.

DEVELOPING AN ACTIVE LIFESTYLE

To enjoy an active lifestyle, children need to be competent in movement. As Denny (1996) states, "the more competency in movement a person has acquired, the more confident and capable he/she will feel when trying other physical activities" (p. 34). Competency is tied to skill acquisition. Denny makes the obvious but important point that nonswimmers rarely go boating, canoeing, waterskiing, or whitewater rafting. Likewise, a person with poorly developed rhythmic awareness seldom joins an aerobics class, a dance group, or a marching band or tries rhythmic gymnastics. And a person with poor hand-eye coordination is unlikely to join a tennis, badminton, or squash club; in fact, this person will find it difficult to succeed in most sports or even to enjoy the successes associated with playing a game of Frisbee or a simple game of catch. It is vital, therefore, that children acquire motor skills. Hence, one of the major goals of all physical education programs is to promote motor skill acquisition.

3.1 *Competency in Human Movement Is Tied to Motor Skill Acquisition*

UNDERSTANDING THE TERMINOLOGY

Because physical education programs are designed to promote motor learning, it is important to consider what is currently known about this area. *Motor learning* and *motor skill* were initially defined in chapter 2. In this chapter these terms will be expanded upon and dealt with in more detail. Motor skill was defined as the degree of proficiency with which a person performs a motor task, where "performance" is viewed as the single execution of a movement or sequence of movements and "proficiency" refers to the level

of performance at any given time. *Motor skill,* then, as used throughout this book, denotes any muscular activity, under voluntary control of the brain, that is directed toward a specific objective. This includes all voluntary muscle movements—from the large gross motor movements, such as running and jumping, to fine motor movements, such as the creative finger-flicking movements in an interpretive dance sequence. This definition also includes static balance positions, since they involve voluntary contractions of skeletal muscles.

C O N C E P T

3.2 *Motor Skill Development Is Influenced by Growth, Maturation, and Learning*

The term *motor skill development* was also introduced in chapter 2 and refers to a change in the proficiency and form of a motor skill as a result of growth, maturation, and learning (Stallings 1973). This term is further clarified by Kathleen Haywood (1993), who states that motor skill development is

> the sequential, continuous age-related process whereby an individual progresses from simple, unorganized, and unskilled movements to the achievement of highly organized, complex motor skills and finally to the adjustment of skills that accompanies aging. (p. 7)

The latter part of this statement implies that motor skill development continues throughout the life span.

Although growth and maturation influence the acquisition of motor skills, learning plays a significant role. Learning is an internal phenomenon that cannot be observed directly; it can only be inferred from observation of a person's performance. Motor learning, then, as defined in chapter 2, is a change in a person's capability to perform a skill, and this must be inferred from observing a relatively permanent improvement in motor performance that is a result of practice or experience.

Figure 3.1 With practice, riding a bicycle becomes automatic.

THE PROCESS OF LEARNING A MOTOR SKILL

If you can remember when you first learned a particular skill, such as riding a bicycle, your memories will provide you with a basis for understanding the process of learning any motor skill. When you first got on your two-wheel bicycle (three-wheelers don't count) without training wheels, your parent or friend held the bicycle upright while you sat on the seat. Your initial attempts were chaotic and clumsy—you were thinking, "How do I do this?" "What happens when this occurs?" and so on. Gradually you learned to stay upright, but you still were concerned about how to stop or judge your position in relation to your "proficient" friends, who were circling and dodging around your bicycle. With practice you gradually became one of the gang, because you reached a phase of riding in which you did not worry about the actual process of riding; it had become automatic (figure 3.1). Your concerns were now about other things, such as playing bicycle hockey or another complex activity involving a high level of proficiency in all aspects of maneuvering a bicycle in and around objects and eluding very tricky opponents.

3.3 *When a Child Is Learning a Motor Skill, Three Distinct Phases of Learning Can Be Observed*

This scenario illustrates a three-stage model of motor learning. These three stages were first identified by Paul Fitts and Michael Posner (1967) who labeled them the *initial, intermediate,* and *autonomous* phases of learning. This three-stage model will now be discussed, along with suggestions and implications for teaching motor skills to children in the primary and intermediate grades.

Initial Phase

The initial phase of learning is often called the "cognitive" phase because it involves *thinking* about a skill as much as it does trying to perform it. For example, when first introduced to dribbling a soccer ball, a child thinks about virtually every part of the skill, then tries to perform it. Consequently, her movements are somewhat jerky, inaccurate, and inconsistent. Although the child knows the ball should be "pushed," she usually kicks and chases it in the early stages. Unless she is allowed to experiment with various ways of moving the ball with her feet, and then receives gradual and specific assistance from the teacher, she might stay at this phase for a long time.

The following are implications for the teacher during this phase of motor skill acquisition:

1. Introduce each skill with clear, simple, and short explanations.
2. Allow the learner to practice the skill by herself. During this initial phase, encourage the child to experiment with a variety of ways of dribbling the ball.
3. Help the child concentrate on one or two main parts of the skill—contacting the ball with both feet, then the sides of both feet, and so on.
4. Provide continuous and positive feedback throughout the beginning phase of this skill.
5. As the child begins to understand how to perform the skill, gradually place more stress on form. This phase does not include accuracy, distance, or speed.
6. Use practice activities and low-organization games that are simple, cooperative, and fun and that require few participants and very few rules.

Intermediate Phase

The second phase in acquiring a motor skill is often called the "associative" or "intermediate" phase and represents a gradual shift from the concentrated thinking and hit-or-miss activities of the initial phase to a more focused effort to refine the skill. As the learner shifts into this phase, he should possess a clear mental picture of the skill so he is not consciously thinking about isolated elements of the movement. Also, many of the basic fundamentals of the skill should have been acquired. For example, while dribbling the ball, the child can detect some of his own errors, such as leaning too far forward, using one foot too often, or not looking up while dribbling. This is the time for teachers to make keen observations so they can give helpful suggestions to improve and refine the skill performance.

This is a very important phase of acquiring any motor skill. Consequently, the following guidelines should be adhered to throughout this phase of motor skill development.

1. Provide numerous practice activities that require increased levels of skill performance.
2. Provide appropriate coaching hints and suggestions throughout practice activities and lead-up games.
3. Gradually increase the rate until the skill is performed at the speed required in the mature form of the activity. This applies to learning game, dance, or gymnastic motor skills.
4. Stress short practice sessions with frequent breaks, rather than long practice sessions with fewer breaks.
5. Stress practice sessions and lead-up activities that are performed with small groups and require maximum participation.
6. Stress practicing the correct form until it is learned or even overlearned. Once a smooth and efficient form has been achieved, begin to emphasize other factors—speed and accuracy.
7. Consider individual differences in the rate and level of ability within and among children of the same chronological age.

Automatic Phase

After the learner has completed numerous practice sessions and performed the skill in a variety of settings, she enters the automatic phase. Now she performs the motor skill in a way that feels and looks like it is an automatic or habitual movement. In the case of the soccer player, she now can move the ball with short pushes of her feet, giving the impression of a smooth, almost effortless movement of the ball. When this phase is reached, the child no longer needs to concentrate mentally on the various components of the skill or on how she is executing each one at any given moment in the game. She now concentrates on her offensive or defensive playing skills, separately or in concert with dribbling the ball. As with all game, dance, and gymnastic skills, this phase is not considered the final, advanced, or terminal phase. If it were, there would be no room for improvement. The automatic phase, thus, always allows time and room for more practice and experience to enhance and fine-tune the motor skill. Most elementary school children reach this phase with the majority of funda-

mental skills. However, in terms of the specialized skills of game, dance, and gymnastic activities, few children have advanced beyond the minimum level of the automatic phase of motor skill development.

The following are the implications of this phase of motor skill development for the teacher and learner.

1. Provide practice sessions that enhance form, style, and accuracy.
2. Provide more qualified coaching techniques, including better skill analysis and effective motivational devices.
3. When learners reach plateaus, encourage them to experiment with new ideas or a change of pace. Doggedly continuing without improvement or satisfaction can lead to regressive skill performance.
4. Provide greater variety and more intensity in practice sessions, in lead-up activities, and in official sport, dance, or gymnastic contests.

In summary, it is obvious that the three phases of motor skill development are not sharply defined, but instead are stages along a continuum of acquiring and retaining a motor skill. Hence, the suggestions made within each phase of motor skill learning should be used as guidelines for teaching. Other factors, such as the characteristics and maturity levels of children, also have significant effects on how or when a child can and will learn a motor skill. In addition to these factors, if teachers are to provide developmentally appropriate activities and teaching situations, they need to understand the following changes that occur during the process of motor learning.

C O N C E P T

3.4 *During the Process of Learning a Motor Skill, Several Changes Occur at Different Points in Time*

CHANGES DURING THE PROCESS OF LEARNING A MOTOR SKILL

Several changes occur at different points in time as the child begins to learn a motor skill. As children move from the initial and intermediate phases of learning toward the automatic phase, they begin to understand what to do and how the motor skill should be performed. They get better at detecting errors in performance and correcting their motor actions. They learn where to direct their attention. They also become more efficient at performing the motor skill, producing smooth coordinated movements that do not waste energy. What follows is a brief description of these changes. The teacher's job is to provide children with opportunities to gain the necessary practice and experience to get to the automatic phase of motor learning, and understanding the changes that occur during the process of learning a motor skill will help achieve this goal.

Changes in Knowledge

In chapter 2 we identified two important areas of children's knowledge development: declarative knowledge and procedural knowledge. In terms of motor skill acquisition, *declarative knowledge* refers to "knowing what to do" and *procedural knowledge* refers to "knowing how to perform the motor skill."

It has been well established that experts have more declarative and procedural knowledge than novices, so these two major knowledge bases clearly are subject to change (French and Thomas 1987). Indeed, there is a constant interaction between both knowledge bases as motor performance improves. The performer's level of knowledge about what to do and how the motor skill can be performed changes during motor learning. In the initial stage of learning, a child will need to know what to do (early or cognitive phase), in addition to knowing how to perform the motor skill. For example, when learning to throw a ball for distance, a child will need to know the effect of gravity and that throwing at an angle of approximately 45 degrees will be the most effective strategy. This will be a new piece of knowledge the child adds as he acquires the motor skill. Without this declarative knowledge the child might attempt to throw the ball at an ineffective angle and thus develop an ineffective pattern. As motor learning progresses, appropriate declarative knowledge becomes embedded into procedural knowledge. That is, as the automatic stage of learning to throw for distance is approached, the child will throw at the 45-degree angle without consciously thinking about gravity or this particular strategy. The child has learned to incorporate this declarative knowledge into the motor skill performance of throwing for distance. Hence, changes in knowledge occur as motor learning progresses. Further, practice and experience can now be viewed as the interaction of declarative knowledge (knowing what to do) with procedural knowledge (knowing how to perform the skill).

The goal of the teacher, then, is to get children to embed appropriate declarative knowledge into their procedural knowledge (figure 3.2). Teachers will not only need to provide children with opportunities to practice motor skills, but at the same time they will need to help them understand what knowledge is important to perform the skill effectively (Fishburne 1996). Background information, such as the 45-degree throwing angle (declarative knowledge), together with information about how to perform the motor skill (procedural knowledge), needs to be provided.

Changes in Error Detection and Correction

As learners move toward the highly skilled automatic phase of learning, their capability to detect errors and make appropriate corrections will improve. Throughout

Figure 3.2 Children develop both declarative and procedural knowledge.

all stages of motor skill development, children should be taught to detect errors in motor performance, correctly identify appropriate corrections, and carry out the error corrections to improve performance. To achieve this, a teacher must provide children with guidance and accurate feedback on performance. This can be achieved through a variety of teaching methods, ranging from direct instruction to discovery learning (see chapter 4). In the example of learning to throw a ball for distance, guided discovery can be used to pose questions to the child, such as "What happens if you throw the ball straight and parallel with the ground?" and "What happens when you throw the ball very high into the sky?". Once these questions have been answered, the following challenge can be given: "Now try to find the best throwing angle between sky and ground that will result in the farthest distance you can throw." Once this knowledge (declarative) is acquired, the child will be in a position to detect errors and offer solutions to improve performance.

A similar form of error detection and correction will need to be applied to the actual throwing movement (procedural knowledge). For example, feedback from a checklist on throwing movement pattern (see chapter 6) can be provided through direct instruction to enable the child to gain an understanding of errors in this area of performance. When completing the checklist, the teacher might notice the child is not extending his arm fully behind him at the start of the throw. Pointing this out will help the child realize the error and provide a solution to correct it. This procedural knowledge will help the child detect and correct errors in the throwing movement; that is, he learns to know how to perform the motor skill correctly.

Changes in Coordination

Performing a motor skill requires muscles and limbs to work together in a coordinated manner. Throwing a ball, for example, requires various muscles and limbs to work together in one smoothly coordinated movement. In the initial stages of learning, limb movements tend to be locked, with each limb operating somewhat independently. This may account for some of the jerkiness associated with first attempts at a new motor skill. Limb segments need to be flexible to adapt as needed toward a smooth coordinated movement. Getting children to "feel" the sensation of the movement is an important characteristic in motor learning. Children who have motor learning disabilities (see chapter 13) frequently exhibit very stiff movements, as they tend to have difficulty relaxing their muscles and limbs. Getting these children to concentrate on feeling the sensation of the actual movement is a worthwhile endeavor. Manually moving their limbs through the movement pattern to ensure correct limb movement and coordination is a helpful strategy. Also, as the skill improves, the energy expended to perform the movement decreases. Young children tire easily, but as their skills improve they will experience energy savings that will allow for more continuous movement.

Changes in Visual Attention

In the initial and intermediate phases of learning a motor skill, a child will not know what cues are the most important for performing the skill. Highly skilled performers who have reached the automatic phase of learning are able to select the most appropriate cues in the environment to help produce the desired performance. During motor learning, the teacher might need to point out areas that require the child's attention. For example, if the teacher is trying to develop a child's mature throwing pattern and a right-handed child who is learning to throw for distance puts her right foot forward during the throwing action, the teacher could point out that the opposite (left) foot needs to be placed forward during the throwing action. Getting the child to visually attend to the correct foot action will provide the appropriate cue to ensure that the child is performing the correct foot movement. By helping a child to identify the correct things to attend to, the teacher will be assisting in the motor learning process (figure 3.3).

THEORIES OF MOTOR LEARNING

A theory of learning is a theoretical assumption about how individuals learn. In physical education, the theory must provide a reasonable basis for understanding motor learning and also provide a list of learning principles that can be applied to the teaching and learning of physical activities. Although there is a history of motor learning (Schmidt 1991), only the most recent theories will be reviewed here. Contemporary theories involve the concepts of a motor program and a schema to explain motor learning, and it is these two areas that will be addressed.

Figure 3.3   Visually attending to correct cues.

C O N C E P T

3.5 Theories of Motor Learning Provide a Basis for Organizing the Most Effective Learning Environments for Motor Skill Acquisition

Motor Program Theory

The concept of a motor program was forwarded to explain the accuracy and consistency of movement that occurs when a skill has been learned to the automatic level. For example, once the skill of walking has been learned, it can be consistently performed with accuracy and with minimum conscious thought. It is as if a computer program inside the brain were automatically "running off" the motor responses each time the skill is performed. The concept of the motor program is seen as being analogous to a computer program in the brain. When initiated, the motor program automatically sets off all the movements necessary to run off the motor skill with minimum conscious intervention. In the initial phase of learning, the motor program does not exist and thus needs to be developed. With practice and experience the motor program is constantly refined. When the learner reaches the automatic phase of learning, the motor program will have been developed to a point where it can now automatically produce the desired motor skill. Motor program theory views motor learning as the creation and reorganization of motor programs as motor skills improve toward the automatic phase of learning. The key implication for the physical education teacher is the need to provide children with opportunities for many practices to encourage development of well-organized motor programs. Developing effective motor programs that can run almost unconsciously will free processing space in the brain for other use.

Figure 3.4 Generalizable motor program.

Since the children will run the motor programs without much conscious thought, they will be free to concentrate on other important aspects, such as strategies and tactics.

Generalizable Motor Program Theory

Unfortunately, the motor program concept cannot account for all aspects of motor learning. For example, a performer is often capable of performing well-learned skills in a variety of situations, even though these skills were not learned in previous situations. To explain this, there would have to be motor programs that had never been learned or practiced. An attempt to explain some of the transfer effects of motor skills to new situations has been made through the theory of a generalizable motor program.

To illustrate, a person's written signature can be made with a pen between teeth or toes, or the fingers of the non-dominant hand. In all cases the signatures will be remarkably similar; that is, consistency and accuracy will be maintained. It is believed that, regardless of where the pen is held, a common motor program for the motor skill of written signature is responsible for the similarity in responses among tasks. However, it is also possible to write one's signature much larger than normal (see figure 3.4). For this to occur, significant changes to the motor program would be needed, since it would involve more than merely running off the same (computerized) motor program. The fact that

we are able to write a large signature resembling the smaller, "normal" one, led to the development of the concept of a generalizable motor program—a motor program that can be adjusted somewhat to meet the needs of a changing environment. (It should be noted that timing is rather inflexible in a motor program, which is why we speed up our hand movement when we write a much larger signature. The generalizable motor program attempts to run off the movement from beginning to end in a constant amount of time, regardless of the size of the movement.)

Even with this degree of flexibility built into it, the motor program concept still cannot explain the large variety of transfer effects noted in skilled performances. Also, the number of motor programs that would need to be stored to accommodate the infinite variety of motor skill responses would strain the limits of human memory. The concept of a schema was therefore invoked to address both storage problems and the infinite variety of motor skills human beings are capable of performing.

Schema Theory

Schema theory addresses the fact that people can successfully perform novel motor skill responses. That is, they can make skillful responses that they have not made before in exactly the same way. In chapter 2, it was suggested that calling on well-developed motor abilities will account for some of the transfer effects. In addition to these effects, generalizable motor programs and schemas will also play a part in transfer of learning.

According to Schmidt (1991), a schema is a rule or set of rules that is used to provide an individual with a basis for making a decision. A schema is developed by abstracting key pieces of information from experiences, then combining them into a rule. To illustrate, a child's initial contact with an animal, such as the family's pet cat, provides an initial schema. With experience, the child enlarges his concept of the cat to include size, speed, and habits the animal exhibits. Gradually, through extended experience, the child learns that there are smaller, larger, fatter, noisier cats and begins to form an ever-expanding schema for this class of animal. The same idea is believed to hold true in motor learning. Take, for example, the class of movements that would fall under "overhand throw pattern." Whenever overhand throws are made, the performer begins to abstract different pieces of information about each throwing response (figure 3.5). Through continuous and varied experiences, the performer constructs and develops a schema that will allow her to successfully carry out a variety of movements involving the overhand throw pattern. The response requirements to perform a novel overhand throw are synthesized and generated from the motor response schema. A well-developed schema will allow correct motor responses to be generated, whereas a poorly developed schema will probably result in the production of an incorrect response.

CHAPTER 3

Figure 3.5 A child learns to throw a ball.

In soccer, for example, the ball does not always remain on the ground—it can arrive in the air and from a variety of angles. A young child who does not have a well-developed motor response schema for dealing with this class of movement responses (controlling the ball with the upper body) will not be in a position to generate an appropriate motor response. Instead, the child might try to create a response from other motor schemas he already possesses. In all likelihood the child will use his hands to control the ball, even when there is no immediate danger of injury. When a soccer ball is bouncing over the heads of a group of players, hands frequently go out to control the ball (figure 3.6). Adults often chastise children for breaking the soccer rule of "no handball," when in fact the children may be aware of the rule (declarative knowledge) yet not be in a position to offer a more appropriate motor response (procedural knowledge) because they have not yet developed the appropriate response schema. This is one reason why playing the full game of soccer or basketball is inappropriate for elementary-age children. Instead, developmentally appropriate activities such as practice activities, lead-up games, and small-sided games (e.g., three versus three) are needed, where schema development can be nurtured. Further, it will be necessary to provide a variety of practices within each class of movements. For example, if teaching the skill of passing in basketball, rather than have the children stand the same distance apart for the practice activity, vary the distance between the children. Or if teaching a child to throw a ball at a target, vary the distances and the angles from the target (figure 3.7). That is, not only should the children practice throwing from a variety of distances directly in front and in line with the

Figure 3.6 Hand reaction to a ball in the air.

target, they should also practice throwing from a variety of distances from either side of the target.

Based on the aforementioned theories of motor learning, teachers will need to design developmentally appropriate practices to ensure the development of well-organized motor programs and richly developed motor response schemas. If this is accomplished, children will be able to react to a wide range of novel movement situations with a high level of success.

GENERAL GUIDELINES

Theories of learning are just theories; that is, they are assumptions about how individuals learn. Nevertheless, the theories discussed in this text provide a basis for organizing content, developing styles of teaching, and using various types of evaluative techniques. Further knowledge of the benefits associated with different practice schedules will also aid the instructional process. In addition, an understanding of the stages of motor skill development, coupled with the knowledge of how children pass through a three-phased sequence to acquire a motor skill, provides a basis on which to effectively teach children a variety of physical activities.

It is inherent in this principle that the teacher must foster in children a desire to learn motor skills. Learning generally takes place if children experience immediate satisfaction, if they see the necessity of building strong, healthy bodies, or if they value the skill as something they can use during leisure activities. Learning can also occur out of fear or because of an extrinsic reward, such as a star or check mark put beside one's name.

Implications for Physical Education

1. Select activities appropriate to the child's interests, needs, and capacities.
2. Stress the intrinsic value of the activity.
3. Present activities so that each child achieves a degree of success.

Principle of Practice

Research in motor learning strongly suggests that practice is necessary for the acquisition of a motor skill. The child must practice the skill correctly until it becomes automatic. Once a child has learned to swim, several months can elapse without practice, and he will still be able to swim. In general, the more the skill is practiced, the longer the time before it is lost. When a skill is practiced incorrectly, however, it will not lead to improvement and might even lead to regression.

Implications for Physical Education

1. Select skills appropriate to the group's interests and maturation level.
2. Stress proper form while the skill is being learned. After the skill has been learned, stress other factors, such as speed and distance.
3. Repeat drill activities after several months to ensure retention.

Principle of Distributed Practice

A motor skill is usually performed more effectively with distributed practice periods than with massed practice periods. However, in terms of learning, as measured by degree of retention of the skill, research indicates little difference between distributed and massed practice schedules. Since a greater number of massed practices can occur in a fixed time frame (single lesson), teachers can plan sessions that have little rest between practice trials. However, a teacher's judgment is crucial here. Young children tend to tire easily and recover quite quickly, so breaks between practice trials will be necessary and some form of distributed practice will be needed. Further, since performance might be higher during distributed practice, this could have corresponding effects on motivation. So not only is it important to consider the time between practice trials; it is important to consider the overall length of the practice period. As a general rule, a short period of intense effort and attention is better than a halfhearted longer period.

Figure 3.7 Schema development requires variety in practice.

In a similar way, the following principles of learning motor skills provide a general understanding of the important factors that affect the way we teach and how children should learn motor skills.

C O N C E P T

3.6 Several Principles of Learning Motor Skills Have Been Identified and Provide a Framework for Creating Effective Learning Environments

Principle of Interest

Any skill, whether it is climbing a rope or throwing a softball, is acquired more efficiently if the child has a motive for learning it. A child's attitude toward learning a skill determines, for the most part, the amount and kind of learning.

This principle generally applies to all age levels and virtually all skills, but there are times, depending on the interest of the children and the amount of effort required, when the practice period might be longer or shorter than normally considered wise. For example, if children are permitted to practice a forward roll until they become dizzy and fatigued, the practice period is too long and too strenuous, regardless of student interest. Self-testing activities for any age group should have variation so that no part of the body is overworked.

A teacher working with fifth- and sixth-grade children in an activity like volleyball lead-up games might find that the students remain interested and enthusiastic for ten or fifteen minutes or even longer. As long as interest is high and skill development is fostered, it is not only permissible but desirable to extend the practice period. On the other hand, when the children are indifferent and are not attaining the skill, a change in the lead-up activity or a shorter practice period is suggested.

Implications for Physical Education

1. Adjust the length of the practice period and the spacing of rest periods to the material being taught and to the children's developmental needs.
2. Change an activity whenever the children show fatigue, boredom, and poor skill development.

Principle of Variable Practice

Practice sessions can be organized in blocked or variable schedules. In a blocked schedule, the same motor task is practiced repeatedly. For example, if teaching two gymnastic stunts, a blocked practice would have children complete their practice trials for the first stunt before engaging in practices of the second stunt. In a variable practice schedule, the learner would mix practices between the two stunts. Intuitively, the blocked practice schedule might be considered most effective, because this form of practice allows the learner to concentrate on only one task at a time. But numerous studies have shown that although blocked practices do produce superior motor performances at the time of practice (in the lesson), variable practice creates superior learning when measured in terms of skill retention between lessons. It might be thought that when two tasks are to be learned together, as in variable practice, they would "interfere" with each other. However, rather than "interfere," it has been suggested that when the "context" for the practice (type of schedule) causes the learner to really concentrate on differences between motor tasks, then superior learning occurs. Hence the term *context interference* is sometimes used to explain the superior learning associated with variable practice schedules (figure 3.8). Although a variable practice schedule has been shown to benefit motor skill learning, a teacher's own judgment as to the best form of practice schedule is also very important. During variable practices, motor performance is frequently lower, as the

Figure 3.8 Variable practice for superior retention of motor skills.

learner concentrates to sort out motor response differences between tasks, so there can be a drop in motivation. This could easily happen in the initial phase of learning. Changing to a blocked practice will likely heighten performance and may produce a corresponding rise in motivation.

Implications for Physical Education

1. Start children off with blocked practices and quickly move to a variable practice schedule.
2. Variable practices usually result in better retention, and they play a major role in developing schemas.
3. If children begin to lose motivation due to slow progress while practicing in a variable practice situation, move to a blocked practice schedule.

Principle of Skill Specificity

A child's ability to acquire a particular skill depends on the child's unique characteristics. A child might excel in one skill but be awkward in others that require about the same maturity and physical effort. A nine-year-old girl might be able to throw, catch, and hit a softball with ease and accuracy but still show a subpar performance in kicking a ball. As discussed in chapter 2, there does not appear to be a general motor ability; instead, many abilities need to be developed. If different motor abilities are needed to perform two motor skills, then vast differences in performance can occur.

This principle of skill specificity also applies to children who have reached the same psychological and physiological maturity level. After a single demonstration of a skill, one child might be able to perform it in its entirety, whereas another child might need more demonstration and practice to perform even a part of the skill. Differences in schema development will obviously play a part here, in addition to other differences in information-processing capacities between children. Hence, developmentally appropriate activities will need to be provided in order to accommodate children's preferred learning styles and differences in their existing knowledge bases.

Implications for Physical Education

1. Provide varied activities at all grade levels.
2. Allow for individual differences in the standards of performance.
3. Allow for variations in the speed at which different children acquire the same skill.
4. Develop standards based on the individual's level and rate of development rather than on the class average.

Principle of Whole-Part Learning

According to Knapp (1967), material is learned in the *whole method,* by going through it completely again and again. In the *part method,* the material is divided into portions, which are practiced; eventually the parts are joined as a whole. In physical education, it is difficult to define what is the whole and what is a part of the skill or game. Recognizing this difficulty, the available evidence indicates that the whole method is usually superior to the part method in teaching motor skills.

A teacher must decide whether to teach a movement in its entirety or to break it into parts. The choice depends, first, on the complexity of the skill and, second, on the learner's amount and speed of skill development. For example, a teacher demonstrates to her third-grade class a one-foot hop-skipping skill using a single rope. The children then attempt to do the skill in its entirety; this is practice through the whole method. If only a few children learn the skill after repeated attempts, however, it would be better to break down the skill into simpler movements. The children could do a one-foot hop over a long rope turned by two people, then attempt the one-foot hop with a single rope, using a half swing. Finally, with a full turn of the rope, the hopping movement could be integrated into the rhythmic turning of the rope.

Implications for Physical Education

1. Use the whole method whenever the skill involves a single functional movement.
2. It may be desirable to break complex skills into smaller parts. Complexity depends on the skill as well as the learner's ability.
3. Generally, the rate and amount of learning indicate the effectiveness of the method used.

Principle of Transfer

Transfer in physical education can be defined as the effect of the practice of one motor task on the learning or performance of a second, closely related task. Underlying this principle is the assumption that a learner will take advantage of what a new situation has in common with a previous experience. Clearly, many factors account for transfer effects. Similar motor abilities, well-developed motor

schemas, generalizable motor programs, and existing procedural and declarative knowledge bases will all influence the degree of transfer achieved. This is reflected in current research indicating that transfer depends on the degree of resemblance between skills.

Implications for Physical Education

Proponents of the Movement Education approach have said that Movement Education has a strong carryover to other skill learning, but no firm evidence indicates a common motor skill transfer factor among all skills. There are, however, many other reasons for incorporating the Movement Education approach. One important reason is that in Movement Education there is a carryover of a positive attitude to other activities. Also, individualized instruction, which is a major feature of the Movement Education approach, will contribute to the development of all the major factors highlighted above that influence transfer effects.

Principle of Skill Improvement

A child does not always learn every physical skill in the same way. Too many factors affect the learning curve, including the complexity of the skill, the child's motivation and physical ability, and the adequacy of instruction.

Generally speaking, the initial phase of learning is usually quite rapid, perhaps due to the child's enthusiasm for a new activity and the fact that the child learns the easy parts first, using previously acquired skills. As practice continues, though, progress slows down gradually, to a period of almost no overt improvement. These learning "plateaus" have been given numerous explanations, such as lack of motivation, failure to learn a prerequisite skill, and improper instruction. However, even when no obvious improvement in skill performance is visible, consolidation can be occurring in memory reorganization and in neuronal connections in the brain. Keeping children motivated through this consolidation period is obviously important. After consolidation, with proper analysis and correction, an increase in skill attainment should result.

Implications for Physical Education

1. Recognize children's individual differences in the learning curve for the same activity.
2. After a new skill is introduced, allow sufficient practice time for mastery.
3. Provide positive reinforcement and encouraging feedback to motivate children through learning plateaus.
4. Be aware of physiological limitations that hinder or prevent additional improvement.

Principle of Feedback

Feedback is defined as the information a learner receives from internal or external sources (Drowatzky 1975). Such information, whether it comes from an internal "feeling" about a movement or from an observation made by the teacher, is used to direct or redirect the learner toward a goal. Feedback acts as a positive motivator as well as a strong reinforcer of behavior. However, it should be emphasized that it is not necessary for a teacher to provide feedback on every practice trial. Indeed, providing feedback after every practice has been found to be not as beneficial to learning as providing feedback on an intermittent basis. This is probably due to the learners becoming dependent on the teacher for identifying the errors and possible corrections. When children are provided with appropriate instruction for error detection and correction, spacing feedback will cause them to solve problems themselves. Learning to problem solve is a desirable educational goal, because it encourages children to take responsibility for their own learning. Giving guidance and accurate feedback on an intermittent basis provides the necessary reinforcement for continued success. Since it is not possible to provide feedback to each child after every practice trial, the teacher can share feedback time and observations of performance among children, knowing that this form of intermittent feedback is both effective and reinforcing.

Implications for Physical Education

Feedback is an indispensable aspect of learning any cognitive, affective, or psychomotor skill or concept. Virtually all learning involves a form of internal feedback through the visual, auditory, or kinesthetic senses. The following guidelines apply more generally to external feedback methods and techniques.

1. Structure the teaching situation to allow time for the learner to practice alone as well as while being observed by the teacher or a classmate.
2. When observing and guiding a performer, make sure the performer has a clear understanding of the goal, and do not set the goal too high for the performer.
3. Provide guidance or teaching cues while the student is performing a motor skill. Assistance, such as auditory clues or touching (spot belts, etc.), as the performer is executing a movement is a very effective form of feedback.
4. Terminal feedback techniques using videotape or individual photographic sequences should be commonplace in elementary school physical education programs.
5. Provide feedback on an intermittent basis, not after every single practice trial.

Feedback is a very important component of teaching and learning. Further aspects of feedback are considered in chapter 4, where teaching styles, motivational strategies, and other effective teaching techniques are discussed.

Older teaching methods were based on the premise that the teacher is the sole authority on what is correct and desirable for children. Children were expected to learn, regardless of their limitations and interests or the inadequacies of the learning situation. Contemporary education has replaced these concepts with principles of learning that are based on tested thinking and experimentation.

All principles of learning are applicable to physical education. Those stated in this chapter, however, are extremely important for selecting physical activities, choosing appropriate methods, and understanding how motor skills are learned. When these principles are considered in relation to the goals of the physical education program and the characteristics of the learner, the scope and direction of the program and the way it should be taught should become abundantly clear.

APPLYING MECHANICAL PRINCIPLES

Basic laws, concepts, and principles affect all movements of the body. The laws of gravity, for example, affect balance and the adjustment of position while moving. In addition, mechanical principles can also be used to understand and determine the most effective and efficient movement patterns. The human body is a living machine; it converts food into energy and expends the energy in movement. If the human body is kept in optimum condition and is moved in accordance with the principles of force and motion, expenditure of energy will be proportionate to the task, but if movement is contrary to the laws of motion and force, too much energy will be expended and maximum results will not be achieved.

CONCEPT

3.7 *Observations of Changes in Basic Motor Skill Development Can Benefit from Knowledge of the Laws of Motion and the Principles of Balance, Force, and Leverage*

It is difficult for teachers who have not studied kinesiology (the science of human movement) to understand all the important mechanical principles of human movement. They should, however, understand the following important concepts and principles concerning balance, force, motion, and leverage (declarative knowledge) and be able to apply them (procedural knowledge) when teaching motor skills and movement patterns.

Balance

Balance, or stability, is the ability of the body to maintain a stationary position or to perform purposeful movements while resisting the force of gravity (figure 3.9). Our first consideration, then, is the law of gravity, which is the natural force that pulls everything toward the center of the earth. Most important to balance is the fact that gravitational pull always occurs through the center of the weight or mass of an object. On the human body, the center of gravity is the point

Figure 3.9　A child resists the force of gravity.

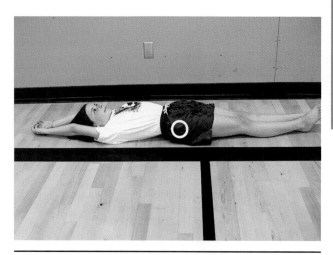

Figure 3.10　The center of gravity (*circle*) is in the middle of the body weight.

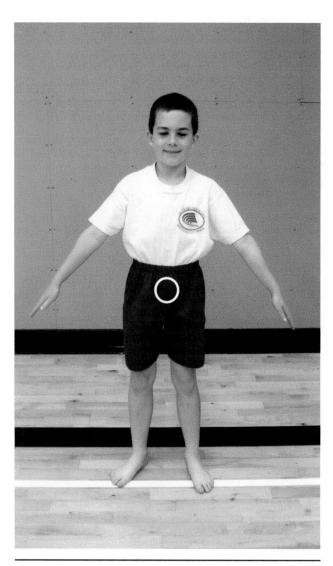

Figure 3.11　The center of gravity is in the middle of the hips.

around which the weight is distributed equally in all directions. The human body is in balance when all forces acting on it equal zero. The child in figure 3.10 is lying on his back with all his muscles in a state of relaxation. His body is not resisting gravity; therefore, the center of gravity is the point in the middle of his body weight, indicated by the circle.

In figure 3.11, the center of gravity is in the middle of the hips. The child is maintaining a state of equilibrium, or balance, through the tension he is applying to his antigravitational muscles (the large muscles of the trunk and legs). When the boy raises his arms, as illustrated in figure 3.12, his center of gravity also rises. If the boy relaxes those muscles, he will fall to the ground, obeying the law of gravity.

C O N C E P T

3.8 *Applying Basic Mechanical Principles to Movements of the Body Provides an Understanding for Effective Instruction*

The basic principles and concepts relating to balance are important in understanding all stationary and movement skills. When attempting to hold a *static* balance position, a child is concerned with keeping her center of gravity in a stable position. When she is moving, her center of gravity is an important factor in retaining *dynamic balance,* or equilibrium. The ability of the child to maintain stability or

Figure 3.12 The center of gravity rises when the arms are elevated.

balance while in a static position or in motion is governed by the following principles of balance.

Principles of Balance

1. *The wider or broader the base of support, the more stable the body.* This principle is extremely important in many game, dance, and gymnastic skills. For example, in figure 3.13 the hands and head of the child performing a headstand form a wide triangle, or broad base of support. The center of gravity is located through the hips and head and midpoint between the hands. By comparison, the child's hands in figure 3.14 are almost in line with the shoulders, thus greatly reducing the base of support. Teachers will observe that a child performing a headstand this latter way will not hold the position very long, because even a slight movement will cause him to fall sideways, backward, or forward, which can result in a severe strain on the neck muscles, as well as a hard thud.
2. *The lower the center of gravity, the greater the stability.* The child in figure 3.15 has assumed the same position as in figure 3.13 but has kept his knees bent, thus dropping the center of gravity closer to his base of support. This example shows that a wide base of support, coupled with a low center of gravity, helps in

Figure 3.13 A wide base of support increases stability.

the performance of numerous balance stunts. In sports, a stable position is often required when meeting an oncoming force, such as a large ball. A large utility ball thrown with force could knock a young child off balance if he is standing upright with his feet close together, as in figure 3.16. He has a narrow base of support and a high center of gravity. However, in figure 3.17, his legs are spread and his knees are bent, giving him a wider base of support and a lower center of gravity.

3. *The nearer the center of gravity to the middle of the base of support, the greater the stability.* Gravity was defined as the natural force that pulls everything toward the center of the earth. The *line of gravity* is an imaginary straight line that extends through the center of gravity directly down to the center of the earth. In skills requiring a very stable base, the child spreads her arms and legs, lowers her body, and makes sure the line of gravity is near the center of the base of support. The

Figure 3.14 A narrow base of support reduces stability.

Figure 3.16 A narrow base of support and a high center of gravity do not provide stability when meeting an oncoming force.

Figure 3.15 A wide base of support and a low center of gravity increase stability.

Figure 3.17 A wide base of support and a low center of gravity increase stability when meeting an oncoming force.

CHAPTER 3

Figure 3.18 When the line of gravity is near the center of the base of support, greater stability is achieved.

child balancing on her hands and knees in figure 3.18 illustrates this important principle. The wide base is low to the ground, and the line of gravity passes downward through the middle of her body.

There are numerous skills in game, sport, and dance activities, though, where an unstable base of support is necessary to perform the skill correctly. The principles of balance still apply. Sometimes one must deliberately shift the center of gravity to an unstable position in order to move quickly. When the line of gravity reaches a point outside the base of support, the individual falls in that direction. This happens when we walk or run; we shift our weight forward in order to move. The sprinter in a crouched starting position leans forward considerably, shifting his center of gravity forward (figure 3.19). He then raises his hips higher than his shoulders to further increase the "unstable" position toward the direction in which he intends to move and to place the strong hip muscles in a position to contract effectively.

Other examples of skills requiring an unstable base of support are listed in table 3.1. The three principles of balance described previously are normally taught to elementary school children in the science curriculum. It is hoped the illustrations provided will encourage teachers to use the medium of physical education to further clarify these principles through the child's own movement patterns. In addition,

Figure 3.19 A sprinter shifts his center of gravity (*circle*) to an unstable position for a quick start.

TABLE 3.1 Skills Requiring an Unstable Base of Support

Activity	Skill	Page
Soccer	Dribbling (fig. 18.11)	379
Track and field	Sprint start (fig. 24.2)	481
Track and field	Hop, step, and jump (fig. 24.14)	487
Gymnastics	Backward roll (fig. 25.19)	509
Gymnastics	Cartwheel (fig. 25.29)	513
Rope jumping	Two-foot basic (fig. 26.7)	556
Juggling	Three bags (fig. 26.59)	576
Gymnastics	Straddle vault (fig. 27.33)	594
Dance	Tinikling (fig. 29.15)	661

if the following concepts are also explained to children in a meaningful way through the use of their own bodies, they will understand the mechanical advantages of the principles and apply them in sports, games, and other daily activities.

Concepts Relating to Balance

1. To achieve the greatest stability, assume a wide base of support, be low to the ground, and have the line of gravity running through the middle of your base of support.
2. To receive a heavy force or a fast-moving object, widen your base of support in line with the direction of the oncoming force.
3. To apply a forceful movement, widen your base of support in line with the direction of the force.
4. To lift or carry a heavy object, keep the object close to your body.
5. To stop quickly, bend your knees and lean away from the direction in which you are moving.

In game, dance, and gymnastic activities there are many skills that illustrate the application of one or more of

TABLE 3.2   Skills Requiring a Stable Base of Support

Activity	Skill	Page	Principle		
			Wide Base of Support	Lower Center of Gravity	Center of Gravity to Middle of Base of Support
Soccer	Volley kick (fig. 18.4)	376	Partial	X	X
Soccer	Heading (fig. 18.12)	379	Partial	X	X
Field hockey	Scoop shot (fig. 19.7)	400	X	X	X
Touch football	Forward pass (fig. 20.1)	410	X		X
Volleyball	Bumping (fig. 21.2)	426	Partial	X	X
Basketball	Pivoting (fig. 22.12)	447	Partial	X	X
Softball	Batting (fig. 23.11)	466	Partial		X
Track and field	Standing long jump (fig. 24.7)	483	X	X	X
Gymnastics	Turk stand (fig. 25.82)	530	No	X	X
Gymnastics	Squat on one leg (fig. 27.8)	584	No	X	X

these principles. Table 3.2 provides a few examples for each activity. Note that the principles of balance might apply mainly to the initial position of each skill.

C O N C E P T

3.9 Basic Laws of Motion Apply to Human Movement and Provide an Understanding for Creating Effective Learning Environments

Motion

Motion is any form of movement that is produced by a force exerted by a push or pull. In the human body, motion is produced by muscular contraction. All movements of the human body, whether they change position, slow down, or start another object in motion, are directly influenced by three laws discovered by Sir Isaac Newton in the seventeenth century. These three laws explain how, where, and why the body moves, as well as how to project or receive an object.

Law of Inertia

LAW OF INERTIA: *An object at rest will remain in a state of rest, and an object in motion will remain in motion at the same speed and direction, unless acted upon by a force.*

Inertia is directly proportional to the size or mass of the object and its velocity. This means that the greater an object's mass and velocity, the more difficult it is to change its direction or motion. The force that changes an object's motion or direction could be gravity, wind, another object, the contraction of muscles, and so forth.

Understanding this law is extremely important when performing physical movements. For example, a ball thrown toward a target moves in a straight line and at uniform speed until a force, such as gravity or wind, causes it to change direction (figure 3.20). Thus, a child must learn

to adjust to or compensate for these forces in all throwing and striking activities.

Another example for understanding and overcoming the effects of the law of inertia is dribbling a soccer ball. The ball will not move until it receives an external force—from the foot. A force starts the ball moving (overcoming mass); however, as long as the ball is kept in motion, the effect of inertia is minimal. Performing continuous sit-ups and maintaining a steady running or swimming pace are also good examples of overcoming the effects of inertia.

Law of Acceleration

LAW OF ACCELERATION: *When an object is acted upon by a force, it will move in the direction of that force. The resulting change of speed (acceleration) of the object will be directly proportional to the force acting on it and inversely proportional to the object's mass.*

To illustrate this second law, consider a volleyball player executing a serve. In a high "floating" serve (figure 3.21a), the force exerted behind the ball is relatively gentle, producing a slow acceleration. A more forceful serve (figure 3.21b) is hit behind the ball, causing a rapid acceleration. In this case, the acceleration is directly proportional to the force. If a player makes the same forceful hit with a tennis ball, the ball's acceleration will be greater because its mass is much less than that of a volleyball. Acceleration in this example is inversely proportional to the mass of the ball.

Law of Action-Reaction

LAW OF ACTION-REACTION: *For every action there is an equal and opposite reaction.*

Tug-of-war (figure 3.22) can be used to illustrate this law to elementary school children. The distance that team A moves backward is equal to the distance that team B is forced to move forward. When swimming, a child moves forward by

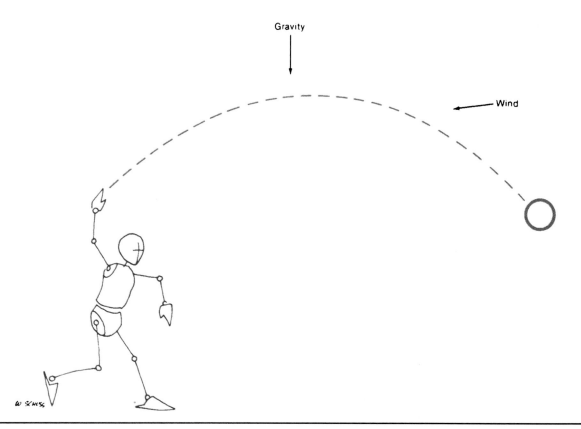

Figure 3.20 Throwing a ball with a high arc allows for the effects of gravity and wind.

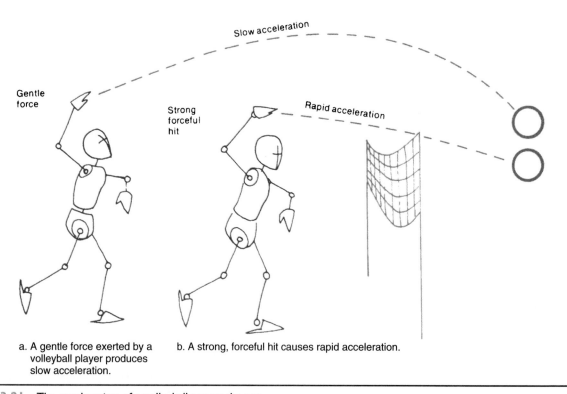

a. A gentle force exerted by a volleyball player produces slow acceleration.

b. A strong, forceful hit causes rapid acceleration.

Figure 3.21 The acceleration of a volleyball across the net is directly proportional to the force exerted behind the ball.

Figure 3.22 Tug-of-war illustrates that every action creates an equal, opposite reaction.

a. Hard road provides a stable surface.

b. Grass field gives, thus reducing force.

c. Soft sand or mud gives even more, with a much greater decrease in force.

Figure 3.23 Law of action-reaction. The force that propels a runner forward is a result of the action-reaction between his feet and the surface on which he is running.

pushing backward against the resistance of the water. The water is pushing the child forward with a force equal to the force that she is exerting in her backward body movements.

Although this principle is relatively hard to explain to children, and at times to adults, it applies to all movements directed away from a hard surface. For example, when a child jumps up to tip a basketball, the floor pushes back with a force equal to the force the child exerts downward through his feet. There is an equal and opposite reaction. Also, to receive the maximum reaction force, the surface against which the force is exerted must be stable. For instance, a hard surface (figure 3.23a) allows a runner to push off with maximum thrust because of the equal and opposite reaction between the foot and the hard surface, but on grass (figure 3.23b), soft mud, or sand (figure 3.23c) the surface gives and thus decreases the force that propels the runner forward.

Types of Motion

Linear motion is the movement of a body or an object as a whole in a straight line with uniform speed. An example is the human body being carried by another object such as a car or skis. In this type of motion, the body takes on the same motion as the object carrying it. The human body can also move in a linear pathway, as in a walking or running movement; this, however, is a pathway of movement resulting from the rotary action of the legs at the hip joints.

Rotary motion is a movement that traces an arc or circle around an axis or a fixed point. As the radius of the circle becomes smaller, the rotary speed increases. For example, in the first phase of a forward roll, the radius is large because the legs and trunk are partially extended (figure 3.24a). As the performer tucks and rolls, she decreases the radius (figure 3.24b). When the roll is completed, the leg and trunk are extended, thus lengthening the radius and slowing the forward motion (figure 3.24c).

Virtually all physical skills involve a combination of linear and rotary motions. Movements normally begin with a rotary action of the body, then transfer to linear speed. In running, the rotary action of the legs at the hip joints is converted into linear speed to move the body forward. Similarly, as the ball leaves the thrower's hand, it is converted from the rotary motion of the arm and shoulder into a linear motion. As the ball travels through the air, the motion begins to change into a curvilinear motion because of gravity and air resistance. Curvilinear motion follows a curved pathway, rather than the true arc or circle of rotary motion.

Concepts Relating to Motion

1. Once a human being or an object is in motion, it will continue in motion unless stopped by a force.
2. Once a human being or an object is in motion, less force is required to maintain its speed and direction.
3. The heavier the object, the more force required to move it.
4. The heavier the object and the faster it is moving, the more force required to stop its motion.
5. When an object moves, another object moves in the opposite direction.
6. When performing rotary movements, shortening the radius of the rotation increases speed, and lengthening the radius decreases speed.
7. When performing linear movements, lengthening the radius increases linear speed, shortening the radius decreases linear speed.

Force

According to K. F. Wells (1955), force can be felt and its effect can be seen and measured, but force itself, like the wind, is invisible. Force is the effect one body has on another. This can be the movement of one body by another, such as a child throwing a ball, hitting a softball, or volleying a ball. Force can also be the stopping of one body by another, such as the tackler stopping the ball carrier. Finally, force can be resistance against movements, such as that used in isometric exercises or when a wrestler in a defensive position attempts to prevent his opponent from moving him. Force, then, is the push or pull exerted against something.

Teachers should understand several principles relating to the production, direction, and absorption of force to help children execute movement skills with ease, efficiency, and safety.

Production of Force

The total effective force of a movement is the sum of all forces produced by the muscle groups when applied in the same direction and in proper sequence. The jump-reach

a. Large radius as legs are extended, producing slow rotary speed

b. As legs move to a tuck position, this creates a short radius and produces a fast speed

c. As legs and trunk are extended, this creates a large radius and produces a slow speed

Figure 3.24 Rotary motion during a forward roll.

Figure 3.25   Production of force in a jump-reach stunt.

TABLE 3.3		Production, Direction, and Absorption of Force			
Sport	**Skill**	**Page**	**Production of Force**	**Direction of Force**	**Absorption of Force**
Soccer	Kicking	375	Fig. 18.1(a)	Fig. 18.1(b)	—
Soccer	Throw-in	380	Fig. 18.13(b)	Fig. 18.13(c)	—
Field hockey	Scoop shot	400	Fig. 19.7(a)	Fig. 19.7(b)	—
Volleyball	Bumping	426	Fig. 21.2(a)	Fig. 21.2(b)	—
Basketball	Layup shot	446	Fig. 22.10(a)	Fig. 22.10(b)	—
Track and field	Long jump	483	Fig. 24.8(a)	Fig. 24.8(b)	Fig. 24.8(c)
Gymnastics	Kip	528	Fig. 25.75(a)	Fig. 25.78(b,c)	Fig. 25.78(c)
Gymnastics	Headspring	527	Fig. 25.74(a)	Fig. 25.77(b)	Fig. 25.77(c)
Gymnastics	Squat vault	593	Fig. 27.30(a)	Fig. 27.30(b,c)	Fig. 27.30(d)

stunt illustrates this principle, as well as related factors that must be considered when executing any forceful movement.

Any muscular action that is intended to move the body weight must have a firm base of action (stability). In figure 3.25a, the child's legs are spread reasonably apart and his knees are bent to lower his center of gravity. Strong muscles exert more than weak ones, and the flexed-knee position allows the boy to begin his jump by contracting his thigh muscles, the strongest muscles of the body. As stated earlier, the total effective force of a movement is the sum of all forces produced by the muscle groups in the same direc-

tion. This means that the jump should be executed in a continuous movement, beginning with the extension of the legs, then stretching upward (figure 3.25b), and finally fully extending the body (figure 3.25c).

Achieving maximum results in any forceful movement requires continuity of flow from one part through another and the timing of each muscle group contraction. One only needs to swing a softball bat forward to understand the importance of continuity and the cumulative effect of a properly executed forceful action. Refer to table 3.3 for other examples.

Figure 3.26   The center of gravity (*circle*) is too high and too far back to gain maximum force.

Figure 3.27   Shifting the center of gravity lower and in the direction of the intended action increases force potential.

Direction of Force

To initiate a forceful movement, the force should be directed through the center of the body weight in the direction intended. In the jumping procedure illustrated in figure 3.25, the weight of the body is directly over and midway between the feet. To make a forward movement, the force should be applied through the center of the weight and in the direction in which it is intended to go. In figure 3.26, the center of gravity is too high and too far back to gain maximum force. By bending and leaning forward (figure 3.27), the child shifts the weight forward in the direction of the intended forceful action.

Perhaps one of the most important areas of concern is the application of force when lifting heavy objects. "Lift with the legs and not the back" is the overriding principle. The child in figure 3.28 is attempting to lift the box, but his center of gravity is too high and too far away from the box. When he applies force, it will be upward and backward, decreasing the maximum forces that could have been applied in an upward direction. He is also in a vulnerable position, because too much strain might be placed on his back muscles. The potential force of the leg muscles in assisting the upward movement is almost negligible here. However, in figure 3.29, the child has moved his center of gravity closer to the box and lower by flexing his legs. A

Figure 3.28   The center of gravity (*circle*) is too high and too far away from the box to gain maximum force. (Also vulnerable to back strain.)

Figure 3.29 Shifting the center of gravity (*circle*) lower and closer to the object increases force potential.

forceful movement can now be made by extending the weight upward. Refer to table 3.3 for other examples.

Absorption of Force

When it is necessary to absorb the impact of a forceful movement or object, the shock should be spread over as large an area or as long a distance, or both, as possible. This principle applies when receiving a blow, landing from a fall, or catching or trapping a ball. The essential point is to gradually decrease the force of the movement or object. In figures 3.30b and 3.30c, the gymnast has landed, flexing his knees to absorb part of the downward and forward momentum and using the remaining forward momentum to execute the forward roll. He has gradually and systematically dissipated the forward momentum.

Other examples of gradually spreading the shock of a forceful movement are catching an oncoming ball with arms extended forward, then recoiling the arms; or rolling after falling on a ball when playing football. Refer to table 3.3 for other examples.

Concepts Relating to Force

1. The more fully each working muscle group is stretched, the greater the force that can be supplied.
2. Pushing or pulling an object should be done through the center of the weight of the object and in the direction in which the object is to move.

a

b

c

Figure 3.30 Absorption of force. This gymnast executes a forward roll to absorb the force of landing from a stunt.

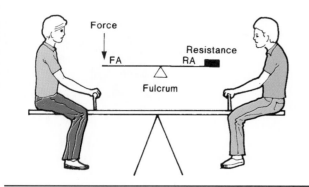

Figure 3.31   Example A: first-class lever.

3. Maximum force is achieved when each body part is involved in sequential order. The sequence for a throwing action would be trunk rotation, shoulder, upper arm, lower arm, hand, and fingers. The sequence for kicking action would be hip, upper leg, lower leg, and foot.
4. When individual body parts (such as arms or legs) or implements (such as bats or paddles) are used, they should be completely extended at the moment they make contact with the object to be propelled. The longest extension of the arm creates the greatest force.
5. When receiving or absorbing the force of an object, the largest possible area and distance (recoiling) should be used to absorb force.
6. When landing from a jump, each joint should give (bend) to gradually absorb the force.
7. Once maximum force has been applied in throwing, striking, and kicking movements, the movement should continue in a follow-through action to ensure that maximum force has been applied and to allow for a gradual reduction in force.
8. Force is increased by using more muscles and by increasing the speed of the movement.

Leverage

All movement of the body, whether a simple bending of the arm or the rapid running action of the legs, is made possible through a system of levers. A lever, as shown in figure 3.31, is a rigid bar that turns around a fixed point (axis or fulcrum) when a force is applied to overcome resistance. The functions of a lever are (1) to gain mechanical advantage to increase speed and distance and (2) to reduce the effort necessary to overcome resistance. There are three types of levers, classified according to the location of the fulcrum and the point at which force and resistance are applied.

First-Class Lever

A first-class lever has the *fulcrum* between the force and the resistance. The distance between the force and fulcrum is the *force arm* (FA), and the distance between the resistance and the fulcrum is the *resistance arm* (RA). In the seesaw in

figure 3.31, the length of the force arm and the resistance arm are equal and the two children weigh the same. In this example, there is no mechanical advantage to either the force arm or the resistance arm, since both are an equal distance from the fulcrum. In figure 3.32, the force arm (FA) is longer than the resistance arm (RA); therefore, this first-class lever favors force and the doghouse is easily moved. In figure 3.33, the resistance arm (RA) is longer, so this lever favors speed and range of movement.

Second-Class Lever

In a second-class lever, the resistance is located between the fulcrum and the force (figure 3.34). This type of lever has a longer force arm, so it produces force at the expense of speed and range of movement. Children should remember that, when lifting a wheelbarrow or prying up a heavy object with a plank, the longer the force arm, the less force required to move the object.

Third-Class Lever

In a third-class lever, the force is between the fulcrum and the resistance. Because this type of lever has a longer resistance arm, it produces speed and range of movement at the expense of force. Most levers of the human body are third-class levers; the bones act as lever arms, the joints as fulcrums, and the muscles as force. In figure 3.35, the elbow joint, where the movement occurs, is the fulcrum. The radius bone in the lower arm acts as the lever, and the bicep muscle (in this case, the point of insertion at the top of the forearm) acts as the force. The resistance is the lower arm that is moved, as well as any additional weight such as a ball or heavy object.

Most game, dance, and gymnastic movements involve the sequential action of many levers. For example, as an individual begins to swing a softball bat, the speed and force of the movement starts in the body, then transfers the built-up force and speed through the bat to the coming ball.

Concepts Relating to Levers

1. The longer the force arm, the greater the force produced.
2. The longer the resistance arm at the moment of release, the faster the action.
3. The mechanical advantage of any lever is the ratio between the length of the force arm (from fulcrum to force) to the length of the resistance arm (from fulcrum to resistance).
4. Levers are used in the production and absorption of force.

Practical Implications for Motor Performance

1. When throwing a ball, a straight arm at the moment of release produces the fastest thrown ball. When the arm is straightened, the fulcrum moves from the elbow to the shoulder joint, thus extending the length of both the force arm and the resistance arm. Hence, both force and speed of movement are increased.

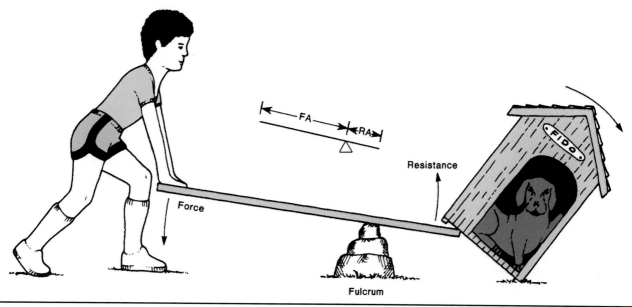

Figure 3.32   Example B: first-class lever.

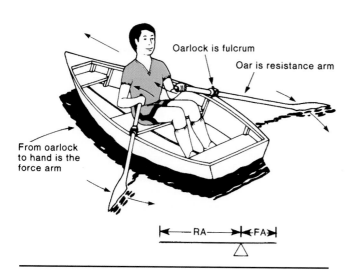

Figure 3.33   Example C: first-class lever.

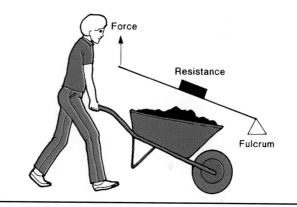

Figure 3.34   Second-class lever.

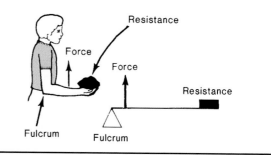

Figure 3.35   Third-class lever.

2. When kicking a ball, straightening the leg for a full-extension follow-through will produce the strongest kicking action. When the leg is straightened, the fulcrum moves from the knee to the hip joint, thus extending the length of both the force arm and the resistance arm. Hence, both force and speed of movement are increased.

3. Similarly, when implements (bats or racquets) are used, they act as an extension of the lower arm at the moment of contact to propel the object (ball or bird) back in the fastest possible action. The implement increases the length of the force and resistance arms.

The concepts and principles related to balance, motion, force, and leverage are important considerations when teaching virtually any skill or movement pattern.

Children should learn these concepts and principles (declarative knowledge) through their own performances and through the teacher's explaining the basic concepts in a meaningful way. Then as motor learning progresses, this declarative knowledge becomes embedded into the procedural knowledge associated with performing the most effective motor skills.

CHAPTER 3

Summary Review

Because the pursuit of an active lifestyle depends on specific competencies, learning motor skills is a crucial component of all physical education programs. Individual motor skill development is dependent upon the interaction between genetically inherited attributes and environmental influences. Established principles of motor learning provide the guidelines and foundations for these environmental influences. The challenge facing teachers is to tailor instructional activities to individual capabilities and characteristics:

> Optimal motor skill development is likely related to the degree that practice opportunities and insightful instruction are matched to individual capability and potential. Although it is both complex and time-consuming to individualize motor development goals and instruction in most institutional settings, findings from motor development research at various stages of the life span point in this direction. . . . Our task remains to find ways of using our knowledge to foster optimal motor development in every individual. (Haywood 1993, p. 331)

INDIVIDUAL *and* **GROUP** **PROJECTS**

1. Choose a novel motor skill to teach a colleague. Videotape your teaching. Review the video in order to
   a. identify the three phases of motor learning
   b. identify the type and frequency of feedback provided by the teacher
   c. identify the changes that occurred during the process of learning the motor skill. For example, note changes in coordination, visual attention, and error detection
   d. identify the questions raised by the learner during the three phases of motor learning and ascertain whether the knowledge provided (declarative) become embedded in the learner's performances (procedural knowledge)

2. Using the "whole" method of teaching, teach a colleague the motor skill of juggling three balls. Teach another colleague to juggle using the "part" method of teaching. Videotape both teaching situations. Then
   a. analyze the videotapes to discover which teaching method was most effective
   b. interview your colleagues to receive feedback regarding the methods of instruction

3. Observe an elementary school physical education lesson or view one of the videotapes that accompany this textbook. Identify and consider
   a. which principles of motor learning are being followed
   b. what form of practice schedule is being followed (blocked or variable)
   c. whether the practices will be effective for schema development
   d. the translation of declarative knowledge into procedural knowledge
   e. what mechanical principles or laws of motion apply to the activities being taught

Selected Readings

Denny, C. 1996. Physical activity or physical education. *CAHPERD Journal* 62 (1): 34.

Drowatzky, J. 1975. *Motor learning: Principles and practices.* Minneapolis: Burgess.

Fishburne, G. J. (1996). The need for and value of quality programmes of physical education. *Canadian Administrator* 35 (6): 6–11.

Fitts, P. M., and M. I Posner. 1967. *Human performance.* Belmont, CA: Brooks/Cole.

French, K. E., and J. R. Thomas. 1987. The relation of knowledge development to children's basketball performance. *Journal of Sport Psychology* 9: 15–32.

Haywood, K. M. 1993. *Life span motor development.* Champaign, IL: Human Kinetics.

Keogh, J., and D. Sugden. 1985. *Motor skill development.* New York: Macmillan.

Knapp, B. 1967. *Skill in sports.* London: Routledge & Kegan Paul.

Magill, R. A. 1993. *Motor learning concepts and applications.* 4th ed. Dubuque, IA: Wm. C. Brown.

Schmidt, R. A. 1976. The schema as a solution to some persistent problems in motor learning theory. In *Motor control: Issues and trends,* ed. G. E. Stelmach, 41–65. New York: Academic Press.

———. 1977. Schema theory: Implication for movement education. *Motor Skills: Theory into Practice* 2: 36–48.

———. 1991. *Motor learning and performance.* Champaign, IL: Human Kinetics.

Stallings, L. M. 1973. *Motor skill development and learning.* Dubuque, IA: Wm. C. Brown.

Wells, K. F. 1955. *Kinesiology.* Philadelphia: Saunders.

Using Teaching Strategies and Techniques

KEY CONCEPTS

4.1 Effective teachers utilize a wide variety of teaching strategies to meet the individual needs of all students under their tutorship and care

4.2 Different teaching styles promote different types of learning

4.3 Effective teachers utilize many different teaching methods

4.4 Research has identified several key teaching behaviors associated with effective teaching

4.5 Effective teachers are enthusiastic and motivate their students

4.6 Adjusting the rules, space, number of participants, and amount or type of equipment to promote student success is an effective teaching strategy

4.7 Goal setting helps promote higher achievement and enhances motivation

4.8 Cooperative learning is an effective way of teaching children in small groups

4.9 Maintaining discipline is necessary to ensure that children stay focused and spend time on-task.

4.10 Children should be held responsible for their behavior; written contracts between child and teacher can help promote positive behavior

KEY OBJECTIVES

After completing this chapter you will be able to:

1. Identify different styles and methods of teaching
2. Understand the strengths and weaknesses of different styles and methods of teaching
3. Identify key teaching behaviors for effective instruction
4. Understand the importance of maintaining discipline
5. Improve classroom control through knowledge of techniques to both handle misbehavior and facilitate good behavior
6. Understand a variety of behavior management models designed to facilitate and maintain appropriate student behavior
7. Improve student learning through motivational techniques that foster intrinsic motivation

CHAPTER 4

he first three chapters of this text identified the need for and basis of quality programs of physical education. It is clear that educational environments that facilitate correct child development are essential if all children are to develop to their optimum potential. Indeed, if all children are to develop and maintain active healthy lifestyles over the entire life span, then they must be educated toward this goal. Hence, a full understanding of how children grow, learn, and develop is vital knowledge for all teachers. Of equal importance is knowledge of teaching strategies and techniques that will best facilitate this growth and development. Teachers need to know the strengths and weaknesses of different teaching styles and methods. They also need to know and be able to create the key teaching behaviors that will result in effective instruction.

The essential duties of the teacher of physical education, as with all subjects, are to provide learning tasks that are within each child's reach (developmentally appropriate) and to give continuous encouragement and assistance throughout the learning process. However, it is clear that the many skills and movement concepts of physical education cannot be learned through one teaching model, strategy, or method. Each new learning situation must be tailored to the varying degrees of interest, individual learning styles, and skill found in a class of twenty-five or more young learners. There is no ideal style of teaching, no single set of concepts or learning principles, and no best motivational technique that will guarantee success for all children in all situations. It is essential, therefore, that a teacher be familiar with a variety of teaching strategies and techniques, and know when to apply these techniques and strategies. This chapter is designed to help the teacher develop effective styles of teaching, sound motivational techniques, and effective ways of creating good classroom control and positive student behavior.

EFFECTIVE TEACHING

A little boy tells his friend
"I taught my dog to whistle"
With an ear up to the dog's face, the friend responds
"I don't hear him whistling"
The first boy responds
"I said I taught him, I didn't say he learned it"

—*Anonymous*

Although it is difficult to precisely define effective teaching, no one can deny that effective teaching is intimately linked to learning. An effective teacher is a communicator whose primary goal is to enable students to learn. A teacher, then, must be cognizant of the most effective teaching strategies, techniques, and behaviors that will facilitate student learning.

TEACHING STRATEGIES

The word *teaching* finds its root in the Greek language and means "to show, point out, direct, or guide." The word *strategy* also derives from Greek, coming from the word *strategia*, which means "the art or science of devising or employing plans to reach a goal." Hence, *teaching strategies* are the ways we devise and employ plans to show, direct, or guide learners. Teachers must be familiar with a variety of teaching strategies in order to accommodate different teaching situations and children's unique styles of learning.

Learning Style

Students receive and process information in very different ways. Each student will have a preferred style of learning. Knowledge about learning styles can help teachers become more effective in their teaching practices and to realize that no one teaching method or strategy suits all learners. For example, some students excel with highly structured, teacher-directed instructional methods, while others prefer unstructured informal settings. Some prefer visual stimuli to model, whereas others might prefer the tactile experience involved in active participation. Some prefer to learn within an individual setting, whereas others might prefer the shared learning experience found working with partners or in small groups. There is no limit to the types of preference; each student has a personal and unique learning style.

Schools do not cater very well to students' unique learning styles; this might account for some of the individual differences in performance and achievement levels found among children in typical schools. Unfortunately, identifying each student's preferred learning style is difficult. In fact, the preferred style may change depending on context and/or subject area. However, even though the teacher might not have an accurate assessment of each child's preferred learning style, just knowing that there will be differences in learning styles in any group of children should be sufficient reason to include variety in lesson planning. By giving attention to learning styles, teachers can learn to modify and vary their teaching strategies and understand why some students learn better than others.

Figure 4.1 The learner, not the subject, is the center of the curriculum in an individualized instructional program.

The broad goals of physical education, the characteristics of children, and the knowledge of how and why children learn through the medium of physical activities have significantly changed the teaching strategies employed in physical education. Teaching is no longer considered a simplistic form of cohort instruction (AAHPERD 1976), with the teacher teaching the same material to all children in the same way. Differences in each child's maturation, potential ability, learning style, and interests require educators to design and employ teaching strategies that cater to more individualized and personalized forms of learning.

C O N C E P T

4.1 *Effective Teachers Utilize a Wide Variety of Teaching Strategies to Meet the Individual Needs of All Students Under Their Tutorship and Care*

Individualized Learning

Individualized learning is based on the premise that teaching should be adapted to the unique abilities and special needs of the learner. This places the learner, not the subject, at the center of the curriculum and teaching (figure 4.1). It must be understood that a teacher who provides individual assistance to one or more children in a class of thirty or more is applying a technique and is in no way teaching an individualized instructional program.

Individualized learning occurs only when there is a sequential plan for every child, including a diagnosis of the

child's potential ability and a teaching prescription to develop that potential. True individualization is possible when there is a ratio of one teacher to one child. However, for groups of two or more children with varying degrees of ability, rarely is a true individualized instructional program ever achieved. Efforts to improve individualized learning have been seen in the area of special needs, where individual educational plans (IEP) are required for students with disabilities (see chapter 13).

The term *individualized instruction* in physical education refers to a process that adjusts the learning to the student. Such a program usually takes two approaches. The first is to vary the time it takes the child to achieve a specific movement task. For example, we can ask three children with varying levels of ability to walk across a narrow balance beam, allowing each child to complete the task in her own time. However, when the task is structured, and the child does not possess the ability to accomplish it regardless of the time given her, this is an exercise in futility. The second approach is to vary the task and, if necessary, the time. Allowing each child to cross the length of the balance beam in any way possible would be varying the task. If a teacher can vary the task, she can provide an individualized program.

Personalized Learning

Personalized learning is a version of individualized learning in which the student's involvement with others in the learning environment is used or emphasized. This might involve the learner in a guider-learner relationship with the teacher, or it might involve learner with learner in a shared experience characterized by mutual trust and respect. The benefits of this form of shared experience can be seen in the *cooperative learning* strategy outlined later in this chapter and expanded upon in chapter 17. Personalizing the learning process enhances the dignity and self-image of each child and creates a learning atmosphere that increases each child's learning efficiency.

Elementary school teachers can individualize and personalize their teaching in several ways. The following section on styles of teaching describes methods that allow the task to be varied and that provide a learning environment that encourages children to share their ideas and creative talents. These approaches also allow all children to progress at their own rate and level of ability, to feel at ease, and to experience success with the task at hand.

STYLES OF TEACHING

A review of contemporary books in elementary school physical education indicates that there is no general agreement as to what constitutes an approach, a style, a model, or a method of teaching. In this text, an *approach,* a *model,* and

CHAPTER 4

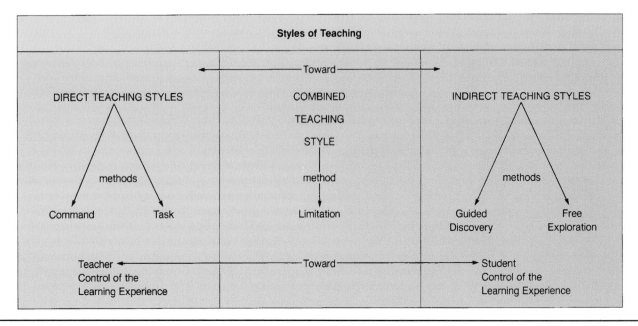

Figure 4.2   Three general teaching styles.

a *style* of teaching are all considered to be the same thing. They are, in essence, general ways of guiding and controlling the learning experiences of children. Various styles (Mosston and Ashworth 1994) and models (Joyce and Weil 1996) of teaching have been forwarded, each offering particular approaches to guide the teaching/learning process.

A *method of teaching* is a way of teaching that considers and emphasizes particular "aspects of learning" that are unique to the method. Each teaching method can be identified as falling under one of three general teaching styles (see figure 4.2) derived from Mosston's original spectrum of teaching styles (see Mosston and Ashworth 1994). Before presenting the teaching methods that fall under these three styles, it is necessary to first consider the merits of each style. Which teaching style is the most effective, and when should it be employed? The answer depends, in part, on how one views learning. Different teaching styles promote different forms of learning.

Observational Learning

One of the most influential ways of learning is through observation. According to Bandura (1977), much of what we learn is through **modeling.** Indeed, the powerful influence of the role model has been well established in the research literature, with studies dating back as far as the 1930s and 1940s (Arends 1988). Bandura's research confirmed earlier findings, and in 1977 Bandura concluded that "most human behavior is learned observationally through modeling: from observing others one forms an idea of how new behaviors are performed, and on later occasions this coded information serves as a guide for action" (p. 22). Arends (1988) asserts that "demonstration

is usually the practical strategy for teachers to use in promoting learning through modeling" (p. 368). However, Arends goes on to caution that the "demonstrations must be carefully planned and executed" (p. 368) for, as Bandura (1977) notes, the demonstration must be structured so the learner will "attend to, and perceive accurately, the significant features of the modeled behavior" (p. 24). Arends summarizes three key principles that have been identified by research on modeling:

1. Effective demonstrations require careful attention from teachers to ensure that all behaviors being demonstrated are accurately modeled.
2. Conditions must enable learners to clearly perceive what is going on.
3. Explanation and discussions during demonstrations enhance later student performance.

Clearly, role model demonstrations can be a powerful influence on learning. Teaching styles that promote demonstration and modeling offer effective ways of learning.

Constructivist Views of Learning

Constructivist approach is a general term for discovery-oriented approaches to teaching (Borich 1996). The constructivist approach is based on the premise that learners should build (construct) knowledge for themselves. One criticism of the role model demonstration is the view that demonstrations do not promote "insightful" learning. The demonstration provides the "answer" or "solution" to the problem. Hence children do not solve the problem for themselves but merely copy the solution provided by the teacher (demonstrator). Contemporary views on learning promote a constructivist approach that emphasizes discovery learning, where children are encouraged to create their own solutions to problems and gain insights for themselves. This is believed to be more meaningful to the child because self-discovery promotes stronger connections with prior learning and fosters creativity. Clearly, teaching styles that promote discovery learning offer exciting learning opportunities. The Movement Education approach advocated through Laban's principles (see chapter 1, p. 11) promotes the constructivist views of learning. Chapter 5 provides a comprehensive overview of the movement concepts and skills that form the basis of the Movement Education approach.

The merits of the constructivist approach are obvious, yet the outcomes are not always achieved in the school setting. The teacher might refrain from offering a demonstration (solution), but the child rarely operates in isolation and constantly views other children's performances (demonstrations). Observational learning occurs throughout the physical education lesson. An added problem is that the three principles of observational learning identified above by Arends are not always present. Children often view "incorrect" demonstrations and use these as the models for their learning.

Another problem facing the constructivist approach is motor skill specificity. The principle of skill specificity was identified in chapter 3 (p. 50) and states that many physical activities require specific motor skills. It is quite possible that children might not create (construct) the specific motor skill during their discovery learning opportunities. If children are to develop and maintain an active lifestyle, they need to develop the required competencies. As stated in chapter 3, a child who cannot swim will not go swimming and is unlikely to go whitewater rafting or even boating. The biomechanically efficient swimming strokes of front crawl and breast stroke (specific motor skills) are most effectively taught through demonstration and direct instruction. It is much more difficult to teach these specific strokes through discovery learning approaches. Children need to develop a wide repertoire of motor skills and well-developed schemas. As stated above, direct methods of teaching have been shown to be most effective in motor skill acquisition.

Modeling versus Constructivism

Some educators advocate the merits of constructivism over modeling, while others offer the opposite point of view. We believe that both views of learning offer strengths that should be capitalized upon and can be accommodated in the physical education setting. We advocate "modeling *and* constructivism." At times, teachers will stress the direct style of teaching; in other situations, the nature of learning will require the more exploratory methods of the combined or indirect teaching styles. Therefore all three teaching styles, ranging from direct to free discovery, are presented here.

TABLE 4.1   **Command Method**

Aspects of Learning	Teacher	Learner
Sets objectives	X	
Chooses content	X	
Chooses methods	X	
Chooses evaluation	X	

C O N C E P T

4.2 Different Teaching Styles Promote Different Types of Learning

These three general approaches are based on the amount of freedom or choice given to the students in a particular learning task. Each style, described in the following paragraphs, emphasizes one or more methods when teaching movement concepts or skills or when fostering the development of positive behavioral traits. The teaching methods differ on the basis of decision making. In the direct methods, teacher decisions dominate, whereas in the indirect methods students make their own decisions about many aspects of their learning. The three teaching styles and accompanying methods can be considered to lie on a continuum, with the direct teaching style at one end and the indirect style at the other.

DIRECT TEACHING STYLE

Direct styles of teaching are classified as teacher-centered because of the way the teacher handles various aspects of the learning process. As stated above, research has demonstrated that direct methods of teaching are among the most effective ways of teaching specific skills. Two of the most common teaching methods associated with the direct teaching style are the *command* and *task* methods. In the command and task methods, teachers decide what objectives are to be accomplished, what the content will be, how children should perform, and how the children's performance should be evaluated. The characteristics and general applications of each method are described here.

Command Method

The primary characteristic of the command method of teaching, as described by Mosston (see Mosston and Ashworth 1994), is that the teacher makes all the decisions in the learning episode (see table 4.1). For example, the teacher arranges the class in lines or in a circle, chooses the activity (such as teaching the forward roll), and prescribes how and where each child will practice the movement. Use

CHAPTER 4

Figure 4.3 This teacher is using a direct method to teach a defensive skill in basketball. The choice of the activity and how it is performed are controlled by the teacher.

of the command method can also be illustrated in teaching a defensive skill in basketball (figure 4.3).

1. *Class organization:* The class is scattered or arranged in a semicircle formation so each child can view the demonstration. The essential aspect is that all children watch a demonstration (model) and then practice the skill.
2. *Choice of activity:* In this example, the children are restricted to practicing a defensive basketball skill. The choice is the teacher's.

Student participation in choosing the activity and how it should be practiced is limited in this method. However, it is the most effective and efficient way to teach a specific movement skill, a safety procedure, or the rules of a game. When the general level of skill is low, such as for heading in soccer or performing a headstand in gymnastics, the command method is appropriate for illustrating, clarifying, and practicing various aspects of a skill or movement. This method can also be used to regain control and direction when class discipline is low.

Task Method

The task method is very similar to the command method of teaching in several important aspects. The teacher sets the objectives, chooses what should be learned, and evaluates the amount and quality of learning by an individual or a group of learners. An important change for the learner is that the learning task can be graduated from beginner to advanced levels of performance for each skill. This method also provides for variations in the time different learners need to acquire the same skill (see table 4.2). An example would be to establish a basketball skill circuit involving dribbling, passing, and shooting skills. All skills would first be explained and demonstrated (modeled), and then students would attempt each task according to their own level

TABLE 4.2 Task Method

Aspects of Learning	Teacher	Learner
Sets objectives	X	
Chooses content	X	
Chooses methods		X
Chooses evaluation	X	

Figure 4.4 Completing a basketball task at a station.

of ability (figure 4.4). Task cards would be used by each student to record scores at each station. This method of teaching recognizes individual differences in levels of ability and in rates of learning motor skills and yet provides for maximum participation. Finally, this way of teaching allows partners to work together, observing and evaluating each other's skill performance.

COMBINED TEACHING STYLE

The combined teaching style combines elements of the direct and indirect styles of teaching. It offers an opportunity, within certain limitations, for students to create and discover solutions to the tasks (problems) set. Due to the limitations associated with the combined teaching style, the teaching method linked to this style is named the limitation method of teaching.

Limitation Method

In the limitation method of teaching, the choice of activity or how it is performed is limited in some way by the teacher. But children are also given some freedom to perform the movement or task in their own way, and at their own pace (see table 4.3). For example, a teacher might pose the challenge for children to create a gymnastic movement sequence that involves two balance positions with the limitation that three body parts must touch the floor in one balance position and two body parts must touch the floor in

TABLE 4.3	Combined Teaching Style	
Aspects of Learning	**Teacher**	**Learner**
Sets objectives	X	
Chooses content	X	X
Chooses methods	X	X
Chooses evaluation	X	X

Figure 4.6   "How many different ways can you balance over the hoop?"

Figure 4.5   Combined teaching style. "Can you balance on three parts of your body?"

the other. The children are directed (limited) in the number of body parts touching the floor in each balance, but they are free to create their own balance creations and to choose which body parts touch the floor. Another example would be allowing variations in leg positions when performing a forward roll. Although the child is limited to the forward roll, some freedom of interpretation is provided by the challenge the teacher poses, such as "Practice the forward roll and see how many variations in leg positions you can make." This freedom is a basic characteristic of the combined style of teaching. Figure 4.5 illustrates this freedom of interpretation.

The combined teaching style has the greatest application and value in virtually all areas of the physical education program. For example, when teaching dance, an early childhood teacher might use the command method initially to teach a skip or gallop step. Once the step has been learned, the limitation method can be applied by providing musical accompaniment and allowing the children to move in any direction to create individual or pair patterns. The single limitation might be that the children use a skipping movement.

The following are a few of the more obvious advantages of this style of teaching:

1. It allows the teacher to give some direction without restricting the children's free or creative expressions.
2. The freedom of interpretation allows for children's physical differences and varying interests.

3. Through a careful choice of activities, the teacher using this method can develop all aspects of movement, avoiding the potential for "one-sided" development in children who are left solely to their own self-discovery.
4. Analysis and correction of movement by the teacher is simplified because children can be limited to practicing one type of movement.

One problem that virtually all teachers must overcome when using this style of teaching is the problem of shifting from *directing* children to perform a movement to *guiding* them through suggestions and challenging questions (figure 4.6). Although each teacher develops her own technique of asking questions, the following phrases and words have proved quite successful:

Can you make a . . . ?
Can you discover a new . . . ?
Can you add to this by . . . ?
Can you find another way of . . . ?
Can you add a different way to . . . ?
Can you vary your . . . ?
Can you improve on the . . . ?
Could you move from . . . ?
Could you shift . . . ?
Could you change . . . ?
Try to add on to . . .
Try to vary . . .
How many different ways . . . ?
Are you able to . . . ?
See if you can . . .
Attempt to do . . .
Is it possible to . . . ?
Discover a new way to . . .

Avoid the words *I want you to do.* . . . The key words should stimulate a creative interpretation of a task or challenge. Once you have posed the question, it is usually necessary to give a command to start. Probably the most common, and informal, beginning is "Off!" or "Away you go!"

Children react extremely well to this type of cue. Other expressions are "And begin!" or "Start!"

4.3 *Effective Teachers Utilize Many Different Teaching Methods*

INDIRECT TEACHING STYLE

An indirect teaching style is an approach that allows children degrees of freedom in the choice of an activity, how it should be performed or practiced, and, at times, how it should be evaluated. This style includes methods of teaching that require the teacher to shift from being a director of the learning experience to being a guide or facilitator (table 4.4). The following methods also dramatically change the role of the learners; they become increasingly more responsible, creative, and self-directed through the application of these methods.

Guided Discovery Method

The guided discovery method involves a sequential series of challenges and observations that lead toward an understanding of predetermined objectives. Consider, for example, a third-grade teacher who is teaching a three-week

gymnastic unit. The main objective of lesson 3 is to teach children that a stable balance position depends on a wide and low base of support. His first challenge, as shown in figure 4.7, is "Can you balance on one foot?" From this point on, the teacher would observe the class, then present another challenge that would clarify the meaning of these fundamental principles of balance.

In this method of teaching, children are encouraged to use their creative powers to answer each movement challenge. This method allows all children to move at their own rates and levels of ability and understanding, it allows the teacher to use his knowledge and observational skills in a continuous process of guiding each learner toward a predetermined objective (table 4.5).

Free Exploration Method

The free exploration method is what Mosston called the "divergent style" (see Mosston and Ashworth 1994). This method shifts to the learner the major responsibility for the learning task and how it should be performed. The teacher simply sets the stage by presenting a general direction or challenge, such as "Use small equipment" or "Work on flow." The use and ultimate success of this method depend on a gradual shift from direct to indirect methods of teaching. Through this process, children gradually learn to be self-directed learners who show care and concern for their own safety as well as for the other children in the class.

TABLE 4.4 Indirect Teaching Style

Aspects of Learning	Teacher	Learner
Sets objectives	X	
Chooses content	X	X
Chooses method		X
Chooses evaluation	X	X

TABLE 4.5 Guided Discovery Method

Aspects of Learning	Teacher	Learner
Sets objectives		X
Chooses content		X
Chooses methods		X
Chooses evaluation	X	X

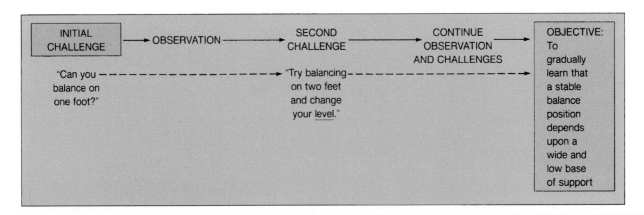

Figure 4.7 Guided discovery method.

TECHNIQUES OF EFFECTIVE TEACHING

A review of effective teaching practices in physical education has identified several key teaching behaviors. These key behaviors have been shown to exist regardless of context. They form the basis for effective instructional practices and provide a valuable framework for teaching physical education activities to elementary school children.

4.4 *Research Has Identified Several Key Teaching Behaviors Associated With EffectiveTeaching*

Structure the Lesson

Structuring refers to helping children organize where the lesson content fits into their learning experiences. Too often in physical education we see children leave the gymnasium or class without understanding why they had to do a particular activity. Structuring involves clearly explaining to children why the content of the lesson is being covered and where this fits into their learning experiences. Reminding children of what was covered in the last physical education lesson and how it relates to the current lesson provides structure. In the same way, providing connections between the current physical education lesson content and what is to come in future lessons also provides structure and builds a meaningful connection. Meaningfulness is defined in terms of the relationship between new learning and existing cognitive structure (knowledge). *Meaningful learning* involves relating new material to existing structure. Some teachers use what are called *advance organizers* to provide this form of structure. An advance organizer is introductory information given to increase the ease with which new material, given at a later date, can be understood and learned. Advance organizers make explicit the connection between prior knowledge and the lesson to be presented. Effective physical education teachers provide structure in their instructional strategies in order to achieve meaningful learning.

Explaining why practice is necessary, why a particular practice has been scheduled, and how that practice connects with the next activity helps make the connecting "links" for the child. Without this structure, children often do not understand the reason for practicing physical activities. A child's community play outside of school usually consists of playing the game, not sequentially practicing skills, and most children see their sports heroes only on television or at the ball park, when their role models are playing the game; rarely do they see the hours of practice that precede the actual event. Hence, children do not make the natural connection between practice and performing; too frequently the teacher hears, "When are we going to play the game?" Apart from pointing out the connection, a school field trip

to a professional sport team's practice can be worthwhile. Once children understand the reason and need for practice, future lessons involving practice activities become more understandable and meaningful to the children. Planning and organizing children's learning experiences through structured connections is an essential component of effective teaching. As the old adage says, "Transfer should be sought and taught."

In addition to making connections for students, there is a need for classroom structure and routine, which establishes an environment in which students learn how the teacher will manage the class. Classroom structure and routine involve organizing equipment and facilities, establishing routine procedures, and setting codes of behavior, as well as teaching students when to ask questions, telling them how much talking and independent behavior is permissible, and acquainting them with many other day-to-day operational procedures. Once children understand and appreciate the teacher's format of teaching and his fair and consistent ways of handling routine procedures, an ongoing positive rapport between students and teacher is assured, along with effective and efficient use of the instructional time. If a teacher can establish the following structure and basic routine procedures within the first month of the school year, he will have begun the process of effective class management.

1. Procedure for changing and entering the gymnasium or playing area
2. Procedure for getting out and returning equipment (class and extra class time)
3. Procedures for establishing a safe environment
4. Procedure for handling accidents
5. Method of stopping children in order to give instructions (whistle, hand signal, etc.)
6. General form of teaching, including the lesson format, the procedure for children to ask questions, and the use of teaching formations
7. Method of selecting leaders and monitors
8. Ways in which praise and punishment are used
9. Method of integrating children with disabilities into the program

Teachers should check for student understanding. It cannot be assumed that when instructions are given verbally all children will clearly understand the information. Developing effective questioning strategies, covered later in this chapter, is an important consideration when checking for student understanding. Task cards involving both written instructions and diagrams will help supplement verbal instructions, as will demonstrations and modeling.

Provide Variety within Each Lesson

Instructional variety is the variability or flexibility of delivery during a lesson. Variety has been linked to student attention; if students don't attend to practices and instructions, little learning is likely to occur. Studies have also shown that there is less disruptive behavior when more varied activities and materials are used. It should be remembered that variety does not mean constantly changing, without regard for learning. Teachers need to plan for variety with learning in mind. As mentioned earlier in this chapter, variety is an essential component in the instructional process to accommodate children's personal and unique learning styles. The following suggestions will help teachers plan for variety with units and lessons.

1. Use stations to set up a variety of activities. For example, if teaching basketball skills, passing activities can take place in one station, dribbling in another, shooting in a third, a two-versus-two game in a fourth, a creative basketball game in a fifth, and a variation involving a passing and shooting practice in the sixth.
2. Bring out a selection of equipment. For example, provide children with a variety of sizes and colors of balls when teaching throwing and catching skills. In general, children learn faster when they choose the size and color of the ball.
3. During creative dance activities, use props such as scarves, ribbons, and wands. Provide a variety of music to match the themes being taught.

Monitor Time On-Task

Time on-task is the amount of learning time devoted to the task. As soon as a teacher has established his format and procedures for effective class management, he can begin to develop a teaching strategy that will keep his students on-task. This includes planning well-organized and appropriate units and lessons, using good observational practices, and applying effective motivational techniques. Time on-task (engagement) is a very important learning variable. It should be noted that the teacher might be task oriented but the child might be disengaged. A teacher must monitor for engagement and plan to achieve maximum time on-task. The following general guidelines are important in maintaining a task-oriented atmosphere.

1. Develop lessons that are adaptable to individual levels of ability and interest (developmentally appropriate).
2. Provide opportunities for every child to experience and learn how to develop self-directed techniques.
3. Develop an effective observational plan that includes observation of specific types of behavior or skills and a procedure to carry this out and record the information.
4. Develop an ability to allow for changes in pace and content within a lesson while still moving toward the main objectives.
5. Develop the knowledge and skills necessary to apply the appropriate type and amount of feedback to individuals and groups of students.

6. Try to eliminate lineups to use equipment. Careful planning and organization will help minimize waiting. For example, provide each child with his own equipment (e.g., a ball each), and organize gymnastic stations so that equipment is not laid out in a straight line. Using star shapes and other creative designs where children can have multiple entries onto, through, and around the gymnastic apparatus will allow all the children to work at the same time. Teachers should also reflect on their organizational time to determine the most efficient practices for getting children started as quickly as possible. These practices will assist in getting children engaged in the learning process.

Provide for Success in Each Learning Task

Success rate is the rate at which a child understands and correctly completes activities. In physical education it is quite common to see a teacher move on to the next practice before a child has correctly completed the first activity. The teacher must organize and plan instruction that will yield moderate to high success rates for all children. A connection has been established between success and intrinsic motivation. Without intrinsic motivation there is little chance that children will develop active lifestyles over the entire life span. Student success is a vital component in effective teaching. Observing and monitoring children's progress is very important, since achieving success is not only essential for motivation and learning, but has been linked to higher-level problem solving and critical thinking. The following guidelines will help teachers organize successful experiences for all children.

1. Set up a variety of stations where children can work on activities designed for their level of development. Children can be organized on the basis of ability level (developmental standing) to maximize their success rate. Planning developmentally appropriate activities to match children's ability levels with the activities they are engaged in will assist in providing success.
2. Once children experience success, they should be challenged to be creative, to problem-solve, and to go beyond their current levels of performance. For example, in gymnastics, after a child completes a gymnastic stunt such as the backward roll, she might be issued the challenge to see how many different variations in leg movement she can achieve. Or when a child has practiced several individual gymnastic stunts, he can be challenged to create a sequence that includes all of the individual stunts.

Use Student Ideas and Contributions

Apart from involving children in their own learning experiences, using students' ideas and contributions places the lesson content within the context of their world, within their own "lived experience." They become part of the learning enterprise, have a degree of ownership, and are motivated because they contribute to the learning endeavor. When the student's own ideas are used, the content material becomes connected to their previous learning experiences, thus contributing toward more meaningful learning. Thus, whenever possible, a teacher should strive to incorporate student ideas and contributions into the lesson. A teacher will find the creative dance activities in chapter 30 and the creative and cooperative games described in chapter 17 helpful, because these activities involve using student ideas and contributions in an effective way. The following suggestions will also be of help.

1. Try to understand and incorporate the student's point of view. As human beings, we normally see each situation from our own perspective. For example, when we teach a dance skill, such as the waltz step, we tend to see it as a motor skill that is performed in three-quarter rhythm and as a dance skill that children enjoy when they pair off to dance. A child who is shy, who is from a culture where girls and boys don't dance together, or who particularly dislikes dance, has a different perspective on the dance activity. The essential point is to try to find out the different attitudes of the children in the class, then adjust to cope with some of the more important ones.

2. Teachers should work to understand and improve their listening skills. The preceding guidelines are primarily designed to improve a teacher's ability to communicate knowledge, skills, and attitudes to the learner. Of equal, if not more, importance in the learning process is the ability to receive messages from students. Few people are good listeners, though—particularly when it comes to taking seriously what children want to say or reading their many important nonverbal messages. The following are some ways of improving such receiving skills:

    a. Paraphrase or restate what a child has said and include hidden messages or feelings you may have detected.

    b. Use effective nonverbal listening gestures, such as looking directly at the student, leaning slightly forward, and showing you are attentive by not doing something else as you listen.

    c. Try to understand and adjust your own feelings since they might affect how you interpret the student's message.

    d. Try to be open, honest, and consistent with all students regardless of their skill level, or color, or any other social or interpersonal characteristic.

Communicate Effectively

Effective communication is one of the most important skills a teacher must understand and use. In every learning situation, effective communication between the teacher and a

Figure 4.8 A two-way process of exchanging knowledge, skills, ideas, and feelings.

student or group of students is a continuous, two-way process of exchanging knowledge, skills, ideas, and feelings (figure 4.8). The teacher's task is to be able to communicate what is to be learned, how it should be learned, and what quality of performance is expected from each student. For example, when teaching the class how to dribble a basketball, the teacher must communicate to every child how the skill is to be performed. This might involve verbally pointing out the main parts of the skill as each student dribbles the ball. At this stage in the process, the learners must be able to ask questions, seek clarification, and express their feelings verbally or nonverbally about what is to be learned. As this process continues, the teacher must be able to draw on effective communication skills and strategies and to keep all children on-task and striving toward their highest level of achievement. To accomplish this goal, the teacher needs to develop a set of guidelines she can use to help her communicate with every child in the class. If the following guidelines are adhered to, effective communication between the teacher and her class can be reasonably assured.

1. Use such pronouns as *I*, *my*, and *mine* to establish personal ownership of what you are going to say. When the teacher says, "I think you need to . . ." rather than "Wouldn't it be better if . . . ," the suggestions are coming from her and she is being open and honest about what she wants to say.

2. Use positive rather than negative reinforcement. If a child performs a structured skill, such as a forward roll, one-hand overthrow, or schottische step, stress the positive aspects of the performance. For example, if a child throws a softball with the one-hand overhand throw and steps forward with the foot on the same side as the throwing arm, begin by emphasizing the correct aspects, such as, "You had good trunk rotation and the ball started from a good throwing position. Keep in mind the opposite foot should come forward with your throwing arm to give you the correct and best throwing action. Try it again and try to get the opposite leg moving with your throwing arm."

Figure 4.9 Use facial expressions or body movements to express ideas and feelings.

3. Be aware of and use nonverbal cues effectively. Nonverbal communication is the use of facial expressions, body alignment, and movement to express a variety of ideas and feelings (figure 4.9). People use many different types of nonverbal communicative expressions but may or may not be aware they are using them. For example, if a teacher praises a student for performing a headstand and at the same moment does not look at the child, or makes a physical movement that communicates insincerity, the child will read the "action message" with more meaning than the empty words. Each teacher should try to discover what negative nonverbal signals she uses and consciously curtail them. When verbal instruction or praise is accompanied by a smile, nod, or positive body gesture, such as clasping two hands together and shaking them in a victory salute, a more positive and effective signal is conveyed.

Develop an Effective Questioning Strategy

A vital component in teaching is asking questions. An average of 100 to 150 questions per class hour are asked in the typical elementary school classroom. In fact, it has been suggested that 80 percent of all school time is devoted to questions and answers. Of these questions, 70 to 80 percent would be considered low-level questions requiring a simple recall of facts, while only 20 to 30 percent require the higher-level thought processes of clarifying, expanding, generalizing, and making inferences. For example, a low-level question would be to ask an upper-elementary-age child a simple basketball game rule, whereas a higher-level question would be to ask for an appropriate strategy for scoring a basket against a certain defensive setup. Teachers need to consider carefully how they phrase their questions, because different questions can elicit different kinds of responses.

TABLE 4.6	Desirable Qualities of an Effective Teacher

1. Enthusiasm
2. Sense of humor
3. Desire for learning
4. Health and wellness
5. Nonverbal qualities
6. Role model

Further, effective questioning strategies involve checking for understanding, as mentioned previously in the discussion of structuring the lesson. Also, as noted earlier in this chapter, different teaching styles demand different kinds of questions. In addition to the kind of question posed, consideration should be given to eliciting student responses. The following guidelines will help the teacher organize effective question-and-answer interactions with children.

1. Probing is related to encouraging students to elaborate upon an answer. Probing can be accomplished through asking more questions, waiting longer than usual for responses, and/or using nonverbal signals. Probing questions can be used to clarify, reframe, and redirect new responses. Helping a child to clarify a response will encourage the child to respond to questions in the future.

2. Teachers generally overestimate the time they think they wait for a response. Teachers frequently wait for only one second or less before providing the answer or moving on to a different student for a response. Research indicates that a wait time of at least three seconds is more effective, resulting in longer responses, higher-level responses (not just a repeat of content), an increase in the number of unsolicited responses, more questions from students, and an increase in student confidence when answering questions. During indirect instruction, where questions may require thinking through and evaluating alternatives, up to fifteen seconds in wait time may be appropriate.

3. There is also value in waiting after an initial response to the question is received. Staying with the same child and waiting again for at least three seconds tends to produce further responses. Nonverbal movements from the teacher, such as head nodding and smiling, will also encourage a child to continue responding.

Demonstrate Positive Personal Characteristics

The personal qualities of effective teachers have been described by numerous authorities and apply to physical education as well as any other subject. Some of the most important qualities are presented here and are summarized in table 4.6. Although the list of qualities is incomplete, if a

Figure 4.10 The teacher's genuine enthusiasm for the value of physical education is the most critical factor in making physical education a true educational experience.

teacher possesses these qualities, there is more than a reasonable chance that the physical education period will be enjoyable and educational.

1. *Enthusiasm:* The teacher's genuine enthusiasm for the value of physical education is one of the most critical factors in making this subject a true educational experience (figure 4.10).

2. *Sense of humor:* A teacher should possess a sense of humor. Teaching is very hard work, but it is also a very rewarding profession. The ability to laugh at one's own inadequacies and "gentle" errors is vital for the maintenance of personal well-being and perspective in the day-to-day task of teaching. This is particularly important to classroom teachers who work long hours in confined quarters with children who are extremely demanding of one's patience and understanding.

3. *Desire for learning:* A teacher should want to acquire more competence in teaching physical education. Classroom teachers are normally required to take one or two professional courses in physical education. This, of course, is inadequate preparation for teaching all the areas of this subject, so it is necessary for teachers to gain new skills and insights through additional courses, texts, films, and other in-service media. Probably of equal importance is that the teacher "have the courage to be imperfect and enjoy it." No teacher can be an expert in every subject. What is more important is the courage to try new ideas and teaching methods, however insecure one might feel. A child's attitude toward a teacher is not based entirely on the teacher's overall competence; it is also based on the very simple premise that the child and the teacher are jointly engaged in the search for knowledge and

understanding, with a mutual respect for each other's abilities and efforts. When children know the teacher is trying something new for their benefit, they, in turn, will respond in a mature and understanding way.

4. *Health and wellness:* A teacher should possess an optimum level of health. Teachers obviously need to maintain good physical and mental health. Otherwise, the pressure of teaching becomes too demanding, with serious consequences to both teacher and student. Because physical education is physically demanding, a teacher who lacks strength and stamina will tend to neglect this area of the curriculum, with a loss to both the teacher and the class. New teaching methods do not require a high level of motor skill on the part of the teacher. They do, however, require physical effort and enthusiasm.

5. *Nonverbal qualities:* In addition to enthusiasm and a sense of humor, there are nonverbal signals such as body movement, facial expression, gestures, and eye contact—all are part of a teacher's personal characteristics. Open expressions of warmth, sensitivity, and empathy are also part of a teacher's style of teaching. Personal characteristics cannot be overemphasized in effective teaching. These characteristics, in conjunction with other key teaching behaviors, interact to produce the child's learning environment.

6. *Role model:* The teacher plays a vital role in a child's learning environment, and being a good role model to children is very important. The powerful influence of *observational learning* has already been mentioned. Children need the most appropriate role models to observe and learn from. A teacher who is an effective role model for students displays several important characteristics. One of the most crucial of these is the teacher's genuine interest in the subject. Since an elementary school teacher is often required to teach seven or eight different subject areas, it is unrealistic to expect the teacher to be a specialist in every one of them. However, the teacher must show the children that he considers physical education to be an equally important subject by planning for and teaching well-organized and exciting lessons. In addition, wherever possible, he should participate in the activities with genuine enthusiasm (figure 4.11). The following guidelines will help develop the essential characteristics and competencies of an effective role model for young children.

a. Attempt to be fair and consistent with all children.
b. Display a sense of confidence and competence in your ability as a teacher.
c. Never use your authority to belittle students or display other forms of aggressive behavior to your students.
d. Communicate your expectations clearly and concisely.

Figure 4.11   An effective role model.

    e. Communicate to children that you personally and professionally enjoy teaching them.
    f. Dress appropriately for physical education and physical activity. Set the dress code through role modeling, not just through rules.
    g. Whenever appropriate, personally demonstrate activities and actively participate in physical activities with the children.

C O N C E P T

4.5 *Effective Teachers Are Enthusiastic and Motivate Their Students*

Adjust the Learning Environment

One of the challenges facing teachers is to adjust the teaching environment to meet the developmental levels of the children. An effective teacher adjusts the learning environment to support successful completion of the activities. Four environmental variables under the teacher's control are these:

1. Rules
2. Space
3. Number of participants
4. Amount or type of equipment

One or more of these four variables can be adjusted to engender students' success. For example, when children are involved in relay games, they easily can become more excited at the prospect of "winning" the relay "race" than in the sense of accomplishment in completing the activity. Changing the number of participants in each team (variable 3) ensures that teams will be finishing at different times, so children can concentrate on the activities rather than on who "wins." This also enables children who are at a lower level of development to participate with far less anxiety, knowing they will not be letting their team down in a race to be first. It might be necessary to adjust some of the other variables too. Providing a choice of equipment, such as

large-diameter hoops in addition to smaller ones, allows the overweight child to pass through the hoop of his choice and achieve success and not embarrassment. Adjusting environmental variables to accommodate the full range of developmental levels in the class of students is essential if success is to be achieved and students' motivation maintained.

    In a similar way, these four variables can be adjusted to create challenges to more gifted students. For example, shortening the distance (space: variable 2) between cones offers a greater challenge for the basketball, soccer ball, or hockey puck dribble; changing the rules (variable 1) in a basketball-type game to require five consecutive passes before a shot can be made offers a greater challenge for the more skillful players. An effective teacher observes her students, continually adjusting rules, space, number of participants, and equipment to ensure success and challenges that are developmentally appropriate for her children.

C O N C E P T

4.6 *Adjusting the Rules, Space, Number of Participants, and Amount or Type of Equipment to Promote Student Success Is an Effective Teaching Strategy*

MOTIVATIONAL TECHNIQUES

One of the premises of good teaching is that the amount a child learns depends on the frequency, intensity, and variation of the learning task. We know the importance of practice activities in learning a motor skill. We also understand how important it is for a child to be actively involved in the learning task and the importance of learning the skill or concept in and through different situations. However, even when all three of these learning factors are present, a child might still not learn or retain the concept or motor skill. This might be due to inherent physical or intellectual limitations, immaturity, or inconsistent motor skill development. It also might be due to a lack of motivation; that is, the child might not have a personal desire to achieve the goal. Our task is to find effective ways of helping each child set higher goals and stay on the task until the goal has been reached. Four types of motivational techniques can be used to accomplish this task. As described in the next paragraphs, each has strengths and weaknesses.

Goal Setting

Studies have shown that when children set attainable goals, they usually achieve more than when the teacher simply instructs the child to "try the best you can." This is especially so if a child is personally involved in the goal setting. Externally controlled goals have been shown to weaken intrinsic motivation, whereas self-determined goals have been shown to enhance it. Involving children in goal-setting decisions motivates them because they now have a personal responsibility to try to achieve the goals they set for themselves. Personal activity log (PAL) books that act as a child's personal journal are introduced and described under methods of assessment in chapter 11. Individual goal-setting activities can be accomplished through the use of these personal journals. Success in meeting personal goals can be monitored and recorded in the PAL journal.

4.7 *Goal Setting Helps Promote Higher Achievement and Enhances Motivation*

Cooperative Learning

Placing children in group situations where competition between children is replaced with the goal of learning together in a cooperative environment can have positive effects on both learning and motivation. Research studies have demonstrated that cooperative learning techniques lead to superior academic achievement, high motivation, and enhancement of social skills. To be effective, cooperative learning must include two elements: a group goal and individual accountability. For example, the group goal might be to produce a gymnastic sequence of balances. Individual accountability could involve each child choosing one piece of gymnastic equipment to include in the apparatus setup, or each child could be responsible for contributing one particular gymnastic stunt to the sequence. Individual accountability is required to ensure that all children play a part in the cooperative learning activity.

Studies have shown positive effects when both group goals and individual accountability are present in cooperative learning activities. Small groups of approximately four children of mixed ability level work particularly well. A developmental mix of one high performer (developmental level III), two average performers (developmental level II), and one child who is progressing at developmental level I, has been suggested as the ideal combination for cooperative learning activities. Positive results from cooperative learning have been found to include improved self-esteem, better intergroup relations, acceptance of children with special needs, positive attitudes toward school, and ability to work cooperatively. Another interesting finding is that even when problems are not correctly solved, motivation remains high among the cooperative group members. This is frequently not the case in more competitive situations.

Due to the many positive benefits associated with cooperative learning, leaders in education are promoting this teaching strategy. We believe that cooperative learning techniques offer exciting possibilities for teachers of physical education. Hence a comprehensive introduction to cooperative learning is presented in chapter 17 together with cooperative game activities for children. These ideas will help teachers establish cooperation among children

Figure 4.12 Intrinsic motivation—pleasure derived from the activity.

while achieving many other learning outcomes. It should be noted that planning cooperative learning activities will also contribute to instructional variety and the use of student ideas: two key teaching behaviors and two areas that help keep children motivated.

4.8 *Cooperative Learning Is an Effective Way of Teaching Children in Small Groups*

Intrinsic Motivation

Intrinsic motivation is motivation internally perceived by the learner that keeps the learner moving toward the goal. This might be the sheer pleasure the child derives from the game or dance activity (figure 4.12). It might also be an increased feeling of pride and self-confidence with each successful trial or movement activity. The child participates in the activity because she wants to and without external pressure.

Authorities on intrinsic motivation suggest enjoyment is a key ingredient of intrinsic motivation (e.g., Deci 1975; Deci and Ryan 1985). They also state that enjoyment of an activity is based on feelings of competency arising from involvement in the activity. Stated simply, this means that if intrinsic motivation is to be fostered and nurtured, children must develop competencies and these competencies must be nurtured through developmentally appropriate activities that will generate success. Children and youth frequently cite the following motives for participation in sports and physical activities:

1. Having fun
2. Participating in skill improvement
3. Winning or competition
4. Being with friends (affiliation)

It is clear that enjoyment and skill improvement are important characteristics for involvement (active participation). Indeed, Weiss (1993) states that children must have enjoyable experiences as an integral part of their involvement in sports and physical activities in order to sustain continued activity. She quite correctly states that we must "turn children on" to physical activity by making it enjoyable. Then, because they have intrinsic motivation to be involved in physical activity, children will continue to be active.

The following suggestions can help teachers create situations within which each child can be intrinsically motivated to participate, enjoy, and retain the required skill or concept.

1. Select activities that are challenging, yet allow each child to reap some immediate success. Good curriculum design will guarantee the proper selection of activities. Create a daily teaching situation within which children find the activities challenging, enjoyable, and successful. All three factors are critical.
2. Show enthusiasm toward the activity. This can be done in many ways, such as participating in the game activity, talking positively about the activity, and indicating where you feel improvement in the class performance and playing skill has occurred.
3. Provide for maximum participation within every learning task. You can keep students' interest as long as they are active and enjoying what they are doing. Playing basketball is fun, but not if one is watching from the sidelines. As a general guideline, increase the number of game situations (two games playing crosscourt) or decrease the number of players (to three or four per team, to provide for more movement and ball contact) in each game situation.
4. Make practice activities and lead-up games as close to a game situation as possible. Boring drills or slow, dull lead-up games do not motivate young children. Numerous suggestions are provided in later chapters for applying the inventive or creative games approach to game activities.
5. Provide praise and positive corrections rather than scorn or negative criticism. Praise is the strongest form of reinforcement. Be honest; that is, give praise for positive achievement. Do not praise or tell a student that his performance has improved when it has not—

particularly in front of other children. Also, when praising a child, recognize the personality of the child. Some children love to be praised in front of peers, whereas others prefer that your comments be made quietly and away from earshot of their peers.
6. Ensure that activities are developmentally appropriate for each child. Change rules or other conditions to ensure that children achieve success and enjoyment.
7. Combine enjoyment with skill and concept acquisition. It is quite easy to create an entertaining environment in physical education that contributes little to skill or concept development. Remember that intrinsic motivation is tied to competency. Children can experience fun and enjoyment in physical activities yet gain little in terms of skills or new knowledge that will help them maintain an active lifestyle. An effective teacher accomplishes both enjoyment *and* skill and concept development.

Intrinsic motivation is what we seek to instill in all children. Good curriculum design, effective organization, and generous adherence to the suggestions given will help develop learners who are intrinsically motivated toward physical activities.

Extrinsic Motivation

Extrinsic motivation refers to activities or behavior external to the learner that encourages the learner to act in a particular way. Badges or awards for certain standards of performance would be considered extrinsic motivators. This form of motivation is not as desirable as the child's intrinsic motivation for performing an act or movement. If children are to develop active lifestyles that are to be continued over the entire life span, then intrinsic motivation will be essential. It is unlikely that extrinsic motivators will be available later in life or able to maintain this desirable outcome. However, extrinsic motivators are very useful when the child or class is not personally motivated. Extrinsic motivational techniques offer very powerful ways of shaping and controlling children's behavior, and they should be thought of as effective techniques to *start* the process—a process that will foster, encourage, and nurture intrinsic motivation.

Achievement charts and points for performance have been used in education for generations. Achievement charts for such activities as gymnastics and physical fitness have several inherent problems that must be addressed. If such charts are solely based on "how much and how high," the lower achiever is guaranteed to be a failure. Such charts should be designed on the basis of individual improvement. On this basis, physically ungifted children who try as hard as they can are capable of receiving the same recognition as any other average or highly skilled performer in the class, even though their performance level is much lower. Closely related to the design and application of achievement charts are various applications of point and award systems. For

Figure 4.13   Peer recognition—a form of extrinsic motivation.

example, in intramural activities, awarding points only to the winners of events or games is a mistake. Certainly, do reward winners for their efforts. However, rewarding other qualities, such as participation, sportsmanship, and special effort, will open doors heretofore not available to the less-gifted athlete.

There are many philosophical differences with respect to grading in elementary physical education programs. Some schools prefer pass/fail, whereas others insist on letter grades or no grades at all. If the school district's policy is to have a grading system, the solution is to attempt to design a process that is fair to all children and based on individual improvement. Wherever possible, such a system should include cumulative records and valid descriptions of the child's performance in the various activities of the physical education program (see chapter 11 for suggestions). Too often, grades are based on fitness scores or simple skill tests.

Regarding the use of peer recognition, help children understand the inherent worth of all children (figure 4.13). This is particularly important for children with disabilities, who are equal participants in the instructional and extra-class programs. If we can guide children to recognize each other's strengths and limitations and to praise and encourage all class members, extrinsic motivation of this nature is to be highly valued.

MAINTAINING DISCIPLINE

One of the most common concerns of both experienced and new teachers is how to maintain *discipline*. When asked to define this term, however, some describe discipline as a general method of control over the class, whereas others interpret discipline as a way of handling problem cases. In its broadest meaning, discipline is a process of helping children

adjust to the school environment and develop acceptable self-control (Harrison 1983). This can involve organizational decisions in addition to appropriate teaching strategies. Hence discipline is often discussed under the wider category of classroom management. However, we believe that maintaining discipline involves specific teaching strategies and techniques, and so it is appropriate to address this topic here. The organizational decisions that impact on discipline and classroom management are covered in chapter 10, where classroom organization is discussed. This section on maintaining discipline describes some of the more common types of discipline problems, their potential causes, and ways of alleviating the problems or preventing them from arising.

4.9 *Maintaining Discipline Is Necessary to Ensure That Children Stay Focused and Spend Time On-Task*

Causes of Misbehavior

Most discipline problems can be traced to the teacher, the learner, or the learning task. A behavior problem arising from something the teacher has created usually is the result of being unfair or inconsistent or displaying a general lack of enthusiasm or genuine concern for children. A second, closely related source centers on the nature of the learning task. In this case, the motor task, dance, or game might be too easy or too hard or simply played too long. The result is usually one or more undesirable behavior problems. The third cause, which seems to give teachers the most concern, is the misbehavior of children. The underlying reason for a child's misbehavior may be traced to problems at home, to poor interpersonal relations with peers, or to an ignorance of rules or codes of conduct. Regardless of the cause, a child will normally misbehave through the ways described in the next section.

Types of Discipline Problems

The following types of discipline problems occur in virtually every grade in the elementary school. Teachers are concerned with all these behavioral problems. Due to the potential risk in such areas as gymnastics and competitive game activities, teachers must be aware of the following behaviors:

1. *Talking:* The most common example of this type of behavior is the child who talks to peers while you are explaining or demonstrating something. Another example is one or more children talking too loud or too much—or both—while engaged in a physical activity.
2. *Not paying attention:* This type of behavior takes many forms, such as looking at something else, daydreaming, or bothering another child while you are explaining something.

TABLE 4.7 Techniques to Improve Classroom Control

1. Be a role model—set a good example of self-control and concern for others.
2. Be consistent—establish reasonable rules of conduct and stay with them.
3. Be fair to all children—don't pick on one or two, and don't have classroom pets.
4. Be a good teacher and not a pal.
5. Treat every child as an individual and with respect. All children should be valued for their true worth and dignity.
6. Change your instructional program when there are significant increases in behavioral problems.
7. Attempt to display a friendly and firm attitude in daily experiences with children.
8. Be prepared with planned strategies to deal with behavior problems. A teacher who is not well prepared usually "reacts" to situations, and this may not produce the desired outcome.
9. Take a deep breath and try to remain calm when dealing with classroom control problems. Emotional responses should be avoided, since they often are not linked to planned strategies and can result in both teacher and students being upset after the interaction.
10. Carefully plan teaching situations. Excellent teaching does not usually occur fortuitously. Well-planned lessons that are interesting and enjoyable engage children. Effective classroom management involves planning.

TABLE 4.8 Techniques to Handle Student Misbehavior

1. Get a complete profile on the child.
2. Use nonverbal cues to complement verbal explanations.
3. Plan for and use a time-out area.
4. Make students accountable for their behavior—written contracts often produce desirable changes in behavior.
5. Loss of privilege can be used successfully as an extrinsic motivator to change student behavior.

Techniques to Handle Misbehavior

Experienced teachers are aware of the fact that, no matter how hard they try to be good teachers—to plan and teach appropriate activities—inevitably there will be a discipline problem to solve. There is no single answer to any problem arising from the various types of behavior problems described earlier. A number of acceptable practices and suggestions that can be used to deal with individuals or groups who have displayed unacceptable behavior are presented below and appear in summarized form in table 4.8.

1. *Student profile:* Always try to consider the whole child, including behavior in other classes, as well as available information about the home environment. If the child has a consistent pattern and type of misbehavior, such as attention getting, the solution is to try to find the cause. Also, when there are similar problems with other teachers, check with them to make sure you are all reasonably consistent in your approach to this child's misbehavior.
2. *Nonverbal communication:* If an individual or a group of children is displaying unacceptable behavior, display an "aggressive waiting stance." This stance should appear to be "quietly aggressive"—for example, frowning, shaking your head, and generally giving the appearance that you disapprove of their behavior. This is a powerful form of nonverbal communication that adds to the verbal explanation that the behavior is unacceptable. When different modes of communication are in unison, more effective communication occurs. By all means, do not yell at them or try to compete by blowing your whistle louder or harder. Sometimes a serious move toward the trouble spot is sufficient to eliminate the problem. If it is solved, quickly move on to another part of the lesson, rather than giving the troublemakers more time than they deserve. Nonverbal signals are powerful forms of communication. An effective teacher can point a finger, nod her head at a disruptive student, pause and make eye contact, or move closer to the student, and cause a change in student behavior without having to stop the flow of her teaching.

3. *Attention seeking:* The most common form of attention seeking is showing off or bothering other classmates.
4. *Dishonesty:* The major problems here relate to violating rules in games, cheating on tests, stealing other students' or school property, and lying to you or classmates.
5. *Overaggressive behavior:* Many physical activities require the learner to be aggressive—but in a positive sense, as in "steal a base" or "leap higher to tap the ball." The type of aggressive behavior to be concerned about is fighting, bullying, or doing something that may injure another student.
6. *Defiance:* In this type of behavior, the child openly refuses to obey rules or directions. It is poor behavior and can lead to injury or harm to other members of the class.

Techniques to Improve Classroom Control

According to Joyce Harrison, the key to good classroom control comes from an understanding of the worth of each child. In addition, all students need the guidance and security that is provided only by well-defined rules of expected behavior, coupled with the knowledge that the teacher cares enough about these rules to enforce them consistently (Harrison 1983). The best preventive measure is an appropriate curriculum taught through effective teaching styles and techniques. Beyond this, the suggestions presented in table 4.7 will help in the day-to-day challenge of teaching and dealing with classroom control.

3. *Time-out:* If a child is displaying misbehavior and will not heed your advice, remove him from the activity. This means you should have a location all the children know as the place one goes when one is being disciplined. This can be a bench in the gymnasium or a spot on the sideline of the playing field that is in sight of, yet away from, the area where children are performing: If the child is a potential hazard, he is away from other children, and, by being located in a known spot, he is always under observation.

4. *Student Accountability:* Arrange to meet after class with the child who has displayed a discipline problem. At noon or after school, both of you have had a chance to calm down. Individual conferences provide more time to find out what the cause may be and to solve it in a calm atmosphere. It also provides time to develop a better understanding of the child and the problem and, equally important, to build a greater friendship and trust. In addition to holding a student responsible for her work, she should also be held responsible for her behavior. A student returning from a misbehavior time-out should make some form of contract with the teacher to prevent a repeat of the misbehavior; she should not be allowed to just return. This form of goal setting provides added motivation for the child to meet socially acceptable standards of behavior. Within this written contract the teacher can add reinforcers. That is, privileges can be built into the contract to help *reinforce* the desired behavior. Once the contract is made and the child returns to class, let her know that you start from zero again. Constantly reminding a child of past mistakes will not help, and it certainly will not improve your rapport with her.

5. *Loss of privilege:* One type of acceptable punishment for misbehavior is a loss of privilege. For example, if a child cheats or misbehaves in an intramural game, he can be denied the privilege of playing for a reasonable number of games. However, loss of privilege should not include denial of other subject areas. A child should not be denied art, for example, for poor behavior in physical education. Nor should a child be denied physical education for poor behavior in other subject areas. Note: Corporal punishment is banned in virtually all school districts.

A few unacceptable practices have been used in the past but are rarely used in contemporary school programs. These are (1) ridiculing children, (2) punishing the group for the misbehavior of one child, (3) having the children perform calisthenics or other exercise as a form of punishment, (4) forcing an apology, and (5) lowering a grade because of misbehavior. Care should be taken not to revert to these techniques, regardless of the pressures of the day.

TABLE 4.9 Models of Behavior Management

1. Behavior modification: Teacher controlled. Based on stimulus-response theory and the views of B. F. Skinner.
2. Assertive discipline: Teacher controlled. Similar to the behavior modification model.
3. Reality therapy: Teacher and student control. Based on the views of William Glasser (1987). Students are responsible for the choices they make. Teacher empowers students to make appropriate choices.
4. Consistency management and cooperative discipline (CMCD): Teacher and student control. A research-based model that uses cooperative learning techniques to agree on rules and procedures for appropriate behavior.

C O N C E P T

4.10 Children Should Be Held Responsible for Their Behavior; Written Contracts Between Child and Teacher Can Help Promote Positive Behavior

Behavior Management Models

A number of behavior management models have been developed for use with schoolchildren. These models offer particular viewpoints on the most effective and desirable ways of shaping and controlling children's behavior. Some are based on sound theoretical viewpoints, while others are based on research support. It is not possible to cover all such models here. The following models, identified in table 4.9, are presented because they are among the most commonly accepted models in use (Freiberg and Driscoll 1996). They also represent the variety of views on behavior management. The choice of behavior management model will be based on personal and school philosophy. Some teachers prefer to use techniques that are a combination of models.

The first two models emphasize teacher control; the other two favor control shared between teacher and students. The teacher-control models emphasize behavior modification. The latter two models favor cooperation and emphasize cooperative learning. This is especially true of the fourth model, consistency management and cooperative discipline, which has produced positive results in research studies. The benefits of cooperative learning, mentioned earlier in this chapter and expanded upon in chapter 17, are again seen in the success of this model.

Behavior Modification

When you use a behavior modification technique, you analyze the observed behaviors of your students and design ways to change or maintain them. The teacher's role in a behavior modification system is to control or shape student behavior. This is accomplished through reinforcing desired behaviors by using rewards and extinguishing undesirable behavior by ignoring or punishing. For example, a teacher might reward her class for good behavior with a free choice of activities in a games lesson. She might also deny the "fun game" at the end of the lesson because of unacceptable behavior. This model is based on teacher control.

Assertive Discipline

This model is based on the view that no child has the right to disrupt (violate the rights of) other students or the teacher. It is based on prescribed consequences for misbehavior. Students are told what constitutes acceptable and unacceptable behavior. They are then informed of the procedure for documenting unacceptable behavior and the ensuing consequences. The rules and limits are clearly explained to students. For example, the first misbehavior might result in the student's name being recorded on the board or in the teacher's assertive discipline notebook. A second misbehavior by the same student would result in a check mark placed next to the name. A third would result in a further check mark, and so on. The recording of a name and each number of check marks would have a particular consequence attached to it. For example, three check marks might warrant a visit to the principal's office. The degree of severity of the consequence would match the number of check marks. Some teachers build extrinsic motivators into this model to reinforce desirable behavior. For example, check marks could be given to a category entitled "excellent behavior by all students in the lesson today." When 50 such check marks are reached, the class is given a privilege or reward (e.g., pizza day). The use of "rewards" and "consequences" in this model has similarities to the behavior modification model.

Reality Therapy

Reality therapy is based on Glasser's (1987) view that children are responsible for their actions. It emphasizes the current situation (reality) and helps children understand that what they do in the classroom, gymnasium, or field area is *their* choice. There is no set plan to this approach. The teacher takes the role of facilitator and works with the children to facilitate the opportunity for children to make appropriate choices. Student control rather than teacher control is the emphasis. Democratic and cooperative decision making among students results in their choices and ensuing behavior. Student responsibility is the major emphasis.

Consistency Management and Cooperative Discipline (CMCD)

The CMCD model is a research-based model that has similarities to the reality therapy model in that it is based on shared responsibility between teacher and students (Stein and Huang 1995). The teacher joins with the students in a flexible but consistent learning environment to cooperatively establish the rules and procedures for the physical education setting. Through cooperative learning techniques (see chapter 17) the class works toward a shared understanding of the rules, procedures, and disciplinary consequences for appropriate and inappropriate behavior in physical education.

Summary Review

A variety of teaching strategies and techniques can be used to create an effective learning environment where all children experience success at their own level of development. For example, utilizing different styles and methods of instruction caters to children's unique styles of learning. Further, an effective teacher demonstrates key teaching behaviors, exhibits desirable teaching qualities, is able to motivate students, and maintains discipline throughout instructional activities. Table 4.10 summarizes these points.

INDIVIDUAL *and* **GROUP** **PROJECTS**

1. Microteaching: In small groups each student chooses a motor skill, simple dance, or game to teach. Each student then chooses a particular teaching method. The task is to teach the selected topic in ten minutes, via the chosen teaching method, to the other group members. Videotape *and* audiotape each student teaching the selected topic.

   Audiotape: Count the number of questions involved in ten minutes of teaching. Time the wait response time before teacher responds to questions. Check for probing. Count the number of lower- and higher-order questions. Analyze tape for clarity and effective communication.

   Videotape: Analyze the tape for demonstrations, modeling, and any observational learning (e.g., students learning from other students). View the tape with sound muted to analyze nonverbal cues. Compare videotape recordings of different teaching methods and analyze the strengths and weaknesses of the methods. Share the findings with the other groups.

2. Visit a school and observe a physical education lesson. Identify the methods used to maintain discipline and promote appropriate behavior. Identify the methods used to motivate students. Identify the extrinsic and intrinsic motivators. Check for smooth transitions between activities, student engagement in the activities and time on-task. Share your findings with the rest of the class.

TABLE 4.10   Requirements for Effective Teaching

1. Use a system of rules that allows students to carry out learning tasks with a minimum of direction.
2. Use a standard signal to get students' attention.
3. Do not begin speaking to a group of students until all students are paying attention.
4. Use a variety of teaching strategies and techniques, adapting instruction to meet learning needs.
5. Use a mixture of high- and low-order questions.
6. Direct questions to many different students.
7. Use probing techniques, such as rephrasing, giving clues, or asking a new question to help students give improved responses when their answers are incorrect or only partially correct.
8. Wait for a minimum of three seconds after posing a question before giving the answer or redirecting the question.
9. Use advance organizers to build a connection (structure) between current knowledge and new knowledge.
10. Utilize student ideas to facilitate meaningful learning.
11. Plan smooth transitions from one activity to another, thus minimizing disruptions and maximizing time on-task.
12. Be knowledgeable about strategies and techniques to motivate students.
13. Create learning environments that promote skill and concept development while maintaining an element of fun and enjoyment.
14. Adjust the instructional environment to create successful experiences for all children regardless of developmental level.
15. Provide evidence of caring, accepting, and valuing students.
16. Be clear in presentations to individual students and groups of students.
17. Respond accurately to both the obvious and the subtle meanings, feelings, and experiences of children.
18. Use praise to reward outstanding work as well as to encourage students who are not always able to do outstanding work.
19. Use mild criticism on occasion to communicate expectations to more able students.
20. Accept and integrate student-initiated interaction such as questions, comments, or other contributions.
21. Optimize learning time. Students should be actively involved and productively engaged in learning tasks.
22. Use a system of rules that allows students to carry out learning tasks with a minimum of direction.
23. Handle disruptive situations in a low-key manner (nonverbal messages such as eye contact and proximity).
24. Move around the instructional area to monitor students, and to check for understanding.
25. Deal with misbehavior problems efficiently and consistently.
26. Follow a plan (model) to reinforce and maintain acceptable student behavior.

SELECTED READINGS

AAHPERD. 1976. *Personalized learning in physical education.* Reston, VA: AAHPERD.

Arends, R. I. 1988. *Learning to teach.* New York: Random House.

Bandura, A. 1977. *Social learning theory.* Englewood Cliffs, NJ: Prentice Hall.

Bellon, J. J., E. C. Bellon, and M. A. Blank. 1992. *Teaching from a research knowledge base.* New York: Macmillan.

Borich, G. D. 1996. *Effective teaching methods.* New York: Macmillan.

Deci, E. L. 1975. *Intrinsic motivation.* New York: Plenum.

Deci, E. L., and A. Ryan. 1985. *Intrinsic motivation and self-determination in human behavior.* New York: Plenum.

Eggen, P. D., and D. P. Kauchak. 1996. *Strategies for teachers.* Boston: Allyn & Bacon.

Freiberg, H. J., and A. Driscoll. 1996. *Universal teaching strategies.* Boston: Allyn & Bacon.

Freiberg, H. J., T. A. Stein, and S. Huang. 1995. Effects of classroom management intervention on student achievement in inner-city elementary schools. *Educational Research and Evaluation* 1: 36–66.

Gallahue, D. L. 1993. *Developmental physical education for today's children.* New York: Macmillan.

Glasser, W. 1987 . *Control theory in the classroom.* New York: Harper & Row.

Harrison, J. M. 1983. *Instructional strategies for physical education.* Dubuque, IA: Wm. C. Brown.

Heitmann, H. M., and M. E. Kneer. 1976. *Physical education instructional techniques: An individualized humanistic approach.* Englewood Cliffs, NJ: Prentice Hall.

Johansen, J. H., H. W. Collins, and J. A. Johnson. 1990. *American education: An introduction to teaching.* Dubuque, IA: Wm. C. Brown.

Joyce, B., and M. Weil. 1996. *Models of teaching.* Boston: Allyn & Bacon.

Lefrançois, G. R. 1994. *Psychology for teaching.* Belmont, CA: Wadsworth.

Mosston, M., and S. Ashworth. 1994. *Teaching physical education.* 4th ed. New York: Macmillan.

Reiser, R. A., and W. Dick. 1996. *Instructional planning.* Boston: Allyn & Bacon.

Siedentop, D. 1983. *Developing teaching skills in physical education.* 2d ed. Palo Alto, CA: Mayfield.

Weiss, M. R. 1993. Children's participation in physical activity: Are we having fun yet? *Pediatric Exercise Science* 5: 205–9.

P A R T 2

The Nature and Analysis of Movement

PART 2 is designed to provide teachers with a basic understanding of the movement concepts and skills associated with Movement Education and to provide an understanding of the development of children's fundamental motor skills. Chapter 5 describes and illustrates the basic movement concepts and skills appropriate for children in the primary and intermediate grades. The four elements of Laban's classification of movement are described, and practical examples are presented to illustrate how these four elements form the basis of Movement Education. These examples help illustrate how to teach physical education through a Movement Education approach. Chapter 6 covers locomotor, nonlocomotor, and manipulative skills, and their corresponding movement patterns. Because these fundamental motor skills form the basis of most motor behavior, it is important for teachers to understand how these skills develop. Checklists are provided for diagnostic purposes, to enable teachers to conduct developmental assessments of children's fundamental movement patterns.

Movement Concepts and Skills

KEY CONCEPTS

5.1 All movement can be classified and analyzed through Laban's movement concepts and skills

5.2 Laban's movement concepts and skills are grouped under the four elements of body awareness, space awareness, qualities, and relationships

5.3 Movement Education is based on Laban's classification of movement

5.4 *Body awareness* refers to what the body can do

5.5 *Space awareness* refers to where the body moves

5.6 *Qualities* refers to how the body moves

5.7 *Relationships* refers to whom and what the body relates to

KEY OBJECTIVES

After completing this chapter you will be able to:

1. Understand the meaning of Movement Education
2. Understand Laban's system of analyzing movement
3. Identify and understand the four elements of body awareness, space awareness, qualities, and relationships
4. Understand how these four elements relate to the movement concepts and skills associated with Movement Education
5. Apply movement concepts and skills to all forms of human movement
6. Organize and teach movement concepts and skills in a lesson format

Contemporary education is characterized more than ever by an inquiring approach to learning. Through a process that might include guided experience, experimentation, observation, and selection, children make many important discoveries for themselves. The teacher uses concrete materials and visual aids, where suitable and available, to link abstract thought to the real world. In the interest of promoting understanding rather than isolated memorization, the teacher classifies ideas to help children learn to link information to meaningful concepts. At the same time, children learn the skills of classification and analysis. In selecting subject matter, the teacher pays greater attention than ever before to children's intellectual development and to the enormous range of skill and maturity among individuals in any primary or intermediate class.

The developmental model, which is stressed throughout this book, is based on these principles. This approach incorporates the movement concepts and skills of Movement Education into every aspect of game, dance, and gymnastic activities. Each of the movement concepts and skills is described in this chapter, followed by suggestions to guide primary and intermediate teachers when they introduce these concepts.

TABLE 5.1 Movement Concepts and Skills

Body Awareness (What the Body Can Do)	Space Awareness (Where the Body Moves)	Qualities (How the Body Moves)	Relationships (to Whom and to What the Body Relates)
Shapes the body can make	Personal and general space	Speed of moving	To people
Balance on parts of the body	Direction and pathways of moving	Force of moving	To objects
Transfer of weight from one part of the body to another	Levels of moving	Bound and flow movements	

MOVEMENT CONCEPTS AND SKILLS

Rudolph Laban (1974) introduced a classification system that allows all movement to be identified and analyzed. Whether a creative dance movement, a forward roll in gymnastics, or a layup move in basketball, all can be analyzed through Laban's movement classification system.

CONCEPT

5.1 *All Movement Can Be Classified and Analyzed Through Laban's Movement Concepts and Skills*

His classification of movement is based on a number of movement concepts and skills, which are identified in table 5.1. The movement concepts and skills are grouped under the four elements of body awareness, space awareness, qualities, and relationships. *Body awareness* refers to what the body can do—the shapes it can make, the way it balances, and the transfer of weight from one part of the body to another. *Space awareness* refers to the spatial aspects of movement, as well as the skills related to moving in different directions, levels, and pathways. *Qualities* refers to how the body can move; this includes skills involving speed, force, and flow of movement. *Relationships* refers to the connection between the body and other performers or between the body and small and large apparatus.

CONCEPT

5.2 *Laban's Movement Concepts and Skills Are Grouped Under the Four Elements of Body Awareness, Space Awareness, Qualities, and Relationships*

The four elements underlying Laban's classification of movement form the basis of Movement Education. These four elements of Movement Education are briefly described in the following pages. Under each element, references are also provided to other chapters that present expanded definitions, illustrations, sample challenges, and lesson plans. Two videotapes described in appendix A were also produced by one of the authors (Kirchner) to explain and illustrate the four elements of Movement Education. *Videotape No. 1: Teaching Gymnastic Activities* describes each of the four elements and demonstrates how to teach gymnastics through a Movement Education approach. This videotape also demonstrates how to teach gymnastic activities through a more traditional teaching approach. Finally, the videotape describes how to combine both approaches and provides a demonstration to show how gymnastic activities can be taught when Movement Education is integrated with a traditional teaching approach. *Videotape No. 4: Teaching Creative Dance* uses the four elements of Movement Education as the basic framework for developing a creative dance lesson (see figure 5.1).

CONCEPT

5.3 *Movement Education is Based on Laban's Classification of Movement*

BODY AWARENESS

Body awareness, or what the body can do, is the way in which the body or parts of it can be controlled, moved, or balanced on. This involves three subelements: the *shapes* the body can make, the *balance* positions the body can take, and the way the body can *transfer* weight from one part to

Figure 5.1 Using movement concepts and skills to teach a creative dance lesson.

another. The shapes the body can make will be described and illustrated, followed by a progressive addition of balance, or weight bearing, and transfer of weight.

5.4 Body Awareness *Refers to What the Body Can Do*

Shapes the Body Can Make

The human body is capable of forming an infinite variety of shapes. Three basic types form the framework on which children learn how to bend, stretch, and twist their bodies.

Stretched and Curled Shapes

A stretched shape (figure 5.2) is an extension of the whole body or a part of it in various directions. For example, children can stretch upward, to the side, or through their legs. A curled shape (figure 5.3) results from an action that flexes or bends the body or a part of it. Assisting children to find or discover what stretched and curled shapes their bodies are capable of making should start from the familiar and simple, then gradually shift to the more complex. Once a child has developed a "movement vocabulary," which is simply knowing what shapes the body can make, greater freedom should be permitted. However, attempting a variety of shapes without concern for form hinders both physical and intellectual development. Progression in shape or combinations of shapes involves thought, repetition, and constant attention on the part of the teacher and child.

Wide and Narrow Shapes

Wide and narrow shapes, like curled and stretched ones, are contrasting shapes. A wide shape requires the legs and/or arms to be away from the trunk (figure 5.4). In contrast, the arms or legs must be extended close together or in a thin line with the trunk to form a narrow shape (figure 5.5).

Figure 5.2 Stretched shapes.

Figure 5.3 Curled shapes.

Figure 5.4   Wide shapes.

Figure 5.6   Twisting away from a stable base.

Figure 5.5   Narrow shapes.

Figure 5.7   Twisted shape in the air.

Twisted Shapes

A twisted shape can be performed in two ways. One can hold a part of the body in a fixed or stabilized position, such as on the floor or apparatus, then turn the body or any part of it away from the fixed base. In figure 5.6 the body is stabilized by two feet restricting the degree of twisting away from this stationary base. A twisted shape can also be made when the body is in flight. In this case, as illustrated in figure 5.7, one part of the body is held in a fixed position while the other part turns away from the fixed part, producing a

twisted shape. Although it could be argued that the latter is a "turn" (usually defined as a rotation of the body coupled with a loss of a fixed contact), with young children the synonymous use of *twist* and *turn* is quite acceptable at this stage of development. Later the meaning can be refined. Once a child has developed an understanding of what

Figure 5.8 Balance, or weight bearing, on different parts of the body.

Figure 5.9 Transfer while in contact with a surface.

shapes the body can make, new challenges should lead to more interesting and complex forms.

References to Activities Stressing Shapes

1. Suggested progression, photographic illustrations, and combinations with structured skills, chapter 25, p. 542
2. Making shapes of letters and spelling words with parts of the body, chapter 25, p. 543
3. Combined with beanbag activities, chapter 26, p. 555
4. Combined with wand activities, chapter 26, p. 570
5. Combined with balance beam activities, chapter 27, p. 585
6. Combined with rope climbing activities, chapter 27, p. 590
7. Combined with vaulting box activities, chapter 27, p. 595
8. Matching and contrasting shapes, chapter 25, p. 546

Balance, or Weight Bearing

A second important aspect of body awareness is balancing, or "maintaining the weight" on different parts of the body. For example, a child can balance on one foot or any number of body parts, including the head positioned as in a headstand. (See figure 5.8.)

References to Activities Stressing Balance, or Weight Bearing

1. Suggested progression, photographic illustrations, and combinations with structured skills, chapter 25, p. 543
2. Sample lesson plan with balance as the main theme, chapter 25, p. 549
3. Challenge involving weight bearing and individual ropes, chapter 26, p. 565
4. Challenge involving balance and vaulting box, chapter 27, p. 595

Figure 5.10 Transfer from one body surface to another.

5. Challenge involving balance and horizontal bar, chapter 27, p. 597

Transfer of Body Weight

The third aspect of body awareness is the transfer of weight from one part of the body to another, while in contact with a surface such as the floor or parts of apparatus (figure 5.9). Sliding on the feet or seat is an exception. Transference of weight can take place from one foot to another, as in walking. It can take place with a variety of steplike actions, using various permutations of the feet or the hands and feet. It can also take place when one body surface receives the body weight from an adjacent part, as in a forward rolling action (figure 5.10). Flight is also a form of transfer of weight that requires the body to be propelled off the floor or apparatus and to remain off the ground for a period of time. For example, the body can leap off the floor from one or both feet, and it can land on one or both feet (figure 5.11). The

Figure 5.11 Transfer through flight.

body can be thrust into the air from the feet, with the weight received by the hands as in the Cat Spring or jumping onto a rope or vaulting box.

Even when it is in the air, the body has shape. It can be stretched long and thin or spread in a number of directions. The positions and actions of the limbs in flight also alter the shape of the body. Furthermore, the body can perform complete or various degrees of revolution in midair.

Finally, attention must be given to landing. The body weight can be brought back to the floor by one or both feet or hands. The depth of landing or the degree of body resilience can also vary. All landings, however, require "give," or flexion, of the leg joints, especially the knees. When jumping, children should be encouraged to make a deep landing, which brings them into a full knee-bend position. This allows them to continue to absorb the momentum of the fall and the shock of impact by rolling.

References to Activities Stressing Transfer of Weight

1. Suggested progression, photographic illustrations, and combinations with structured skills, chapter 25, p. 542
2. Sample lesson plan with transfer of weight (flight) as main theme, chapter 30, p. 675
3. Sample dance lesson with transfer of weight as the main theme, chapter 29, p. 628
4. Challenge involving transfer of weight and beanbag activities, chapter 26, p. 555
5. Challenge involving transfer of weight and balance bench activities, chapter 27, p. 582
6. Challenge involving transfer of weight and climbing frame activities, chapter 27, p. 602

SPACE AWARENESS: WHERE THE BODY MOVES

Space awareness is one element of movement that includes concepts relating to general and personal space, direction, pathways, and levels.

5.5 Space Awareness *Refers to Where the Body Moves.*

General and Personal Space

All space that a child or group of children can use is divisible into two types. General space is the total space that can be used by one child or a group of children. In figure 5.12, the gymnasium floor constitutes the general space the child can use when performing a series of movement skills. Personal, or limited, space is the immediate space a child can use around her. The top of the vaulting box constitutes the personal space available to the child when performing a series of balance skills. As the child moves off the top of the box, she enters the general space.

References to Activities Stressing General and Personal Space

1. Definition and photographic illustrations, chapter 25, p. 545
2. Sample lesson plan with general space as the subtheme, chapter 30, p. 673
3. See tables 16.1 and 16.2 for a list of games stressing general and personal space, chapter 16, pp. 321, 333

Direction

Direction includes moving forward, backward, sideways, diagonally, and up and down.

References to Activities Stressing Direction

1. Definition and photographic illustrations, chapter 25, p. 546
2. Challenge involving change of direction and beanbags, chapter 26, p. 555
3. Challenge involving change of direction and individual ropes, chapter 26, p. 565
4. Challenge involving change of direction and musical accompaniment, chapter 28, p. 611
5. Challenge involving change of direction, musical accompaniment, and individual ropes, chapter 28, p. 613
6. Direction as an element in creative folk dance activities, chapter 29, p. 627
7. Sample lesson plan with change of direction as the main theme, chapter 29, p. 629
8. See tables 16.1 and 16.2, for a list of games stressing change of direction, chapter 16, pp. 321, 333

Pathways

Pathways are the patterns a child or an object makes when moving on or off the floor. The child in figure 5.12 might leap off the box, travel in a curve followed by a straight pathway, and end in a zigzag pathway.

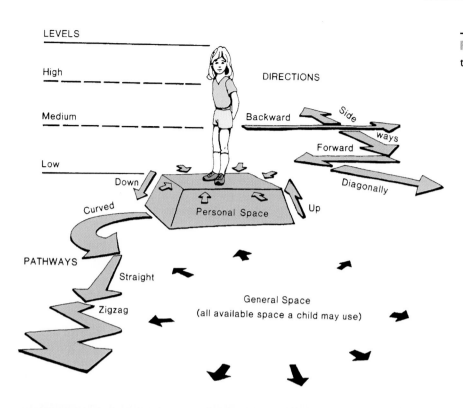

Figure 5.12 Space awareness: where the body moves.

Figure 5.13 Low to the floor.

References to Activities Stressing Pathways

1. Sample lesson plan with pathway as a subtheme, chapter 30, p. 673
2. Pathway as an element in creative folk dance activities, chapter 29, p. 629

Levels

Level refers to the location of the body or body parts in relation to the floor or apparatus. In figure 5.12, the child is high in relation to the top of the box. In figure 5.13, movement is low to the floor; in figure 5.14, movement is at a medium level; and, in figure 5.15, movement is at a high level. Level also involves the relation of one part of the body to another. High movements are those per-

Figure 5.14 Medium level.

formed above the shoulders; medium movements, between the shoulders and knees; and low movements, from the knees to the toes.

References to Activities Stressing Levels

1. Challenge involving levels, shapes, and wands, chapter 26, p. 570
2. Challenge involving levels and the climbing frame, chapter 27, p. 603

Figure 5.15   High level.

QUALITIES: HOW THE BODY MOVES

Qualities (the third element of Movement Education) or effort, includes concepts that describe how the body moves from one position to another. Speed, force, and flow of movement are concepts described within this element.

C O N C E P T

5.6 Qualities *Refers to How the Body Moves*

Speed

Speed is the rate of a movement. In figure 5.16, the child runs toward a traffic cone, leaps over it, lands, and slowly rolls across the mat to dissipate the forward momentum.

References to Activities Stressing Speed

1. Definition and photographic illustrations of quick and slow, chapter 25, p. 544
2. Speed as a subtheme of a lesson, chapter 25, p. 549
3. Speed combined with structured skills, chapter 25, p. 549
4. Challenge with speed, pathways, and traffic cones, chapter 26, p. 574

5. Challenge with speed and benches, chapter 27, p. 585
6. Sample lesson plan with speed as the subtheme, chapter 30, p. 673

Force

Force is the effort or tension involved in a movement. A child leaping over a traffic cone, as in figure 5.16, performs a strong thrusting action to gain enough height and distance to clear the obstacle. In dance, however, a child might shift her arms lightly from one side to the other to describe something light or gentle (figure 5.17).

References to Activities Stressing Force

1. Definition and photographic illustrations, chapter 25, p. 544
2. Challenge involving force and an individual rope, chapter 26, p. 565
3. Sample lesson plan with strong and light as main theme, chapter 30, p. 675

Flow

Flow is how a movement or a number of movements are linked in a purposeful action. Bound flow occurs when a series of movements is stopped, with the balance maintained, then continued to another static movement. For example, a child performing a tumbling routine shifts from a roll to a shoulder stand and holds this balance position momentarily before lowering her legs and trunk in preparation for another roll (figure 5.18). Movements that proceed smoothly from one to another are described as free flow. This is illustrated in movements that are difficult to stop, such as running, leaping, and landing. Once a child begins to perform the forward roll, there should be a smooth, uninterrupted flow of movements throughout the rolling action.

References to Activities Stressing Flow

1. Definition and photographic illustrations, chapter 25, p. 544
2. Challenge involving flow, hoops, and musical accompaniment, chapter 28, p. 567
3. Challenge involving flow, transfer of weight, and wands, chapter 26, p. 570

RELATIONSHIPS: TO WHOM AND TO WHAT THE BODY RELATES

The fourth element of movement involves the relationship of an individual or a group to other performers or objects. A relationship to an object is described as the position of a performer relative to an apparatus. For example, in figure 5.19,

Figure 5.16   Qualities: how the body moves.

Figure 5.17   Light or gentle force.

the child on the left side begins outside the turret, moves around and then over, and stops on the top surface. He is positioned near the apparatus. As he moves toward the other turret, he travels under the beam.

Concepts describing the manner in which performers relate to each other represent another dimension of relationships. The two performers in figure 5.19 are performing matching shapes, with the child on the right turret leading her partner. As they continue their sequence, they will "meet" and "part."

C   O   N   C   E   P   T

5.7 Relationships *Refers to Whom and What the Body Relates to*

References to Activities Stressing Relationships to People

1. Description and photographic illustrations of relationship to individuals and to groups, chapter 25, p. 546
2. Challenge involving relationship to partner, individual ropes, and force, chapter 26, p. 566
3. Challenge involving partners and shape, chapter 25, p. 546
4. Challenge involving matching and contrasting shapes and wands, chapter 26, p. 570
5. Challenge involving matching and contrasting shapes and balance benches, chapter 27, p. 585
6. Challenge involving relationship of two people and a musical accompaniment, chapter 28, p. 610

References to Activities Stressing Relationships to Equipment and Apparatus

1. Description and photographic illustrations of relationship to equipment, chapter 25, p. 547
2. Challenge involving partners and balancing on a vaulting box, chapter 27, p. 595
3. Challenge involving matching sequences and traffic cones, chapter 26, p. 574

a   b   c

Figure 5.18   **Bound flow.**

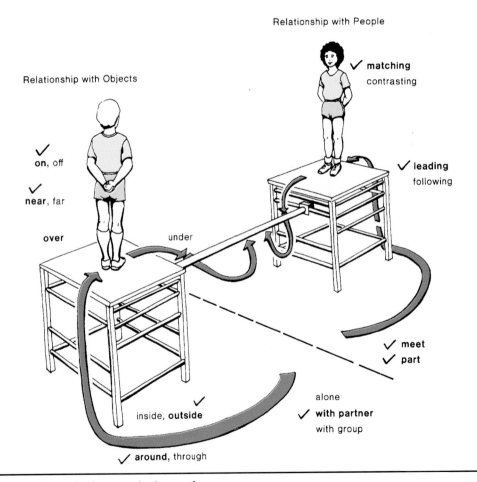

Figure 5.19   Relationship with objects and other performers.

SUGGESTED TEACHING PROCEDURE

Success in teaching movement concepts and skills depends on creating an atmosphere in which children can work safely and independently and on the teacher's ability to introduce skills and movement ideas in a systematic, progressive way. One must remember that the contemporary approach to teaching game, dance, and gymnastic activities stresses the importance of the direct method, which requires the teacher to plan what and how each skill is to be performed. In this method of teaching, emphasis is given to following orders rather than to encouraging children to think for themselves or produce creative movements. Hence, the shift from a predominantly formal, teacher-directed situation to an informal atmosphere in which the learner assumes responsibility for learning is a tremendous challenge for both teacher and class. However, the rewards inherent in this transition are worth the patience and effort required of the teacher and, of course, the children under his charge.

It is vital, therefore, that the initial lessons, particularly for children beyond level I, be more concerned with establishing the "atmosphere for learning" than with the teaching of introductory movement skills and ideas. The latter will come much more rapidly and effectively when children learn to work independently at their own rate and according to their own ability.

The four elements (body awareness, space awareness, qualities, and relationships) are introduced sequentially in chapter 25 ("Stunts, Tumbling, and Movement Skills"). A sample lesson and unit plan are also provided as a format for developing individual lessons and extended themes. Once a teacher acquires the basic movement vocabulary, she will in turn develop variations in the suggested procedure. Additional sample lesson plans, using one or more movement concepts and skills, are provided in the dance and game resource sections.

Summary Review

Movement can be identified and classified through a number of unique movement concepts and skills; namely: body awareness, space awareness, qualities, and relationships. These movement concepts and skills form the basis of Movement Education and provide a framework for teaching all game, gymnastic, and dance activities.

INDIVIDUAL *and* **GROUP** PROJECTS

1. Plan to teach a group of early childhood children a game activity through a Movement Education approach. Now plan to teach the same game activity learning objectives through a more traditional teaching approach. Contrast the two lesson plan approaches, highlighting strengths and weaknesses of both.
2. Debate the strengths and weaknesses of Movement Education as an approach to teaching physical education.
3. Research Rudolph Laban's ideas and views through his original publications and debate whether Laban considered his movement classification and analysis as a basis for teaching all areas of school physical education.

SELECTED READINGS

Graham, G., S. A. Holt-Hale, and M. Parker. 1993. *Children moving.* 3d ed. Mountain View, CA: Mayfield.

Kirchner, G., J. Cunningham, and E. Warrell. 1978. *Introduction to movement education.* 2d ed. Dubuque, IA: Wm. C. Brown.

Laban, R. 1974. *Modern educational dance.* Boston: Plays Inc.

Laban, R., and F. C. Lawrence. 1974. *Effort.* Boston: Plays Inc.

Laban, R., and L. Ullmann. 1975. *The mastery of movement.* 3d ed. Boston: Plays Inc.

Logsdon, et al. 1984. *Physical education for children: A focus on the learning process.* 2d ed. Philadelphia: Lea & Febiger.

Morrison, R. 1969. *A movement approach to educational gymnastics.* London: J. M. Dent & Sons.

Wall, J., and N. Murray. 1994. *Children and movement: Physical education in the elementary school.* 2d ed. Dubuque, IA: Wm. C. Brown.

KEY OBJECTIVES

After completing this chapter you will be able to:

1. Identify and understand the fundamental motor skills that children need to acquire during their elementary school years
2. Identify locomotor, nonlocomotor, and manipulative skills
3. Understand and apply basic mechanical principles to all fundamental motor skills
4. Apply movement concepts and skills to all fundamental motor skills
5. Identify mature and immature fundamental movement patterns
6. Identify important points to stress when teaching fundamental motor skills
7. Understand that, due to sensitive times during development, mature fundamental movement patterns should be developed during the elementary school years

The motor skills described in this chapter are termed *fundamental* because they are the important building blocks for more specialized sport, dance, and gymnastic activities. By the time children reach school age, they have acquired some proficiency in such motor skills as running and dodging, as well as a few basic throwing, catching, and hitting skills. However, such factors as lack of physical and mental maturity and lack of opportunities to learn and practice these basic movements leave many primary-age children with low levels of proficiency in these prerequisite motor skills. Because these basic locomotor, nonlocomotor, and manipulative skills are prerequisites for advanced sport, gymnastic, and dance movement patterns, they should be learned in a systematic and progressive manner in developmental levels I and II. Once children can perform these motor skills with ease and efficiency, they have the confidence and ability to learn more advanced skills and movement patterns.

In this chapter, under each basic skill are descriptions and illustrations, as well as important mechanical principles and points to stress when teaching these fundamental motor skills. Observational methods to analyze fundamental movement patterns are provided, and lists of suggested activities accompany each basic motor skill to provide further guidance and ideas for teaching. To demonstrate how movement concepts and skills apply to each fundamental motor skill, examples are provided for each of the four basic elements of body awareness, space awareness, qualities, and relationships. Locomotor skills, such as walking, running, and hopping, are individual skills used to move the body through space by shifting from one base of support to another. The skills of skipping, stopping, and dodging are traditionally placed in this category; however, they are essentially a combination of locomotor and nonlocomotor movements. Nonlocomotor skills consist of movements of the body where one or more parts of the body maintain contact with the floor or apparatus while other parts of the body move in different directions, pathways, and levels. Manipulative skills, such as throwing, catching, and striking, are combined movement patterns involving one or more locomotor or nonlocomotor skills combined with other movement skills and concepts. The teaching strategies and methods of organization that are used to teach these skills are presented in other chapters.

FUNDAMENTAL MOTOR SKILLS AND MOVEMENT PATTERNS

Simple manipulative, locomotor, and nonlocomotor movement patterns are acquired during infancy. Such movement patterns not only are the foundation for developing everyday utilitarian and safety skills, they are the building blocks for all specialized skills involved in game, dance, and gymnastic activities. The simple movement patterns developed during infancy undergo further development and refinement during childhood, when a multitude of basic skills are added to the movement repertoire. The basic motor patterns that are learned first are continuously modified and combined into patterns of increasingly greater specificity and complexity.

C O N C E P T

6.1 *Fundamental Motor Skills Provide the Foundation for more Specialized Sport, Dance, and Gymnastic Activities*

The natural process of growth and maturation, coupled with the untutored experiences that result from imitation, trial and error, and freedom of movement, contribute to the development of basic motor patterns. This process is important, but unless it is supplemented with specific nur-

turing opportunities, the child can fail to progress to optimum levels of development. That is, without the correct nurturing environment, children can fall far short of producing what might be considered optimum motor skill development. Hence, the elementary school physical education program plays a significant role in the development of children's basic fundamental motor skills and their accompanying movement patterns.

Mature Patterns of Movement

Mature merely means fully developed and does not relate to adult status. Mature motor patterns are skill-related rather than age-related. Indeed, there are many adults who do not exhibit mature movement patterns in some of the fundamental motor skills. This is especially true for the overhand throwing pattern. Unfortunately, if the mature throwing pattern is not in place by the end of adolescence, it might never be acquired (Wickstrom 1983). Hence, the childhood years appear to be a *sensitive period* for the development of this fundamental motor pattern. As stated in chapter 2, although motor skill development is subject to change over the entire life span, the elementary school years are considered a crucial time for determining optimum development. This can be witnessed at a beginners badminton class for adults. Often there are some participants who experience difficulty in striking the shuttlecock with the racket on the initial serve to commence the game or first practice, and miss with great regularity. Because physical movement is public and failure does not engender excitement or satisfaction, these adults quickly retire from participating in the game of badminton. At first sight, it might be assumed that such adults exhibit poor hand-eye coordination, which results in their repeated failure to strike the shuttlecock with the racket head. However, these adults rarely find themselves unable to grasp a door handle or place food in their mouths. One of the principles of motor skill development identified in chapter 3 needs to be considered here, and that is the principle of skill specificity. These adults lack hand-eye coordination with an extended implement. Although they might be able to successfully strike a ball or shuttlecock with their hand, due to principles of specificity this coordination is insufficient for success with an extended implement. It is very probable that these unfortunate adults were never introduced to sequentially planned, multiple practices with a variety of different lengths and types of rackets when they were in their elementary years. As adults, they are likely to experience slow progress in developing the mature striking sidearm movement pattern with an extended racket. The sensitive time to develop the mature pattern for this manipulative skill occurs much earlier in life. Although we prefer to consider motor skill acquisition in terms of developmentally appropriate activities rather than age-related levels of expectancy, due to sensitive times in development teachers should strive to have children develop the mature movement patterns associated with fundamental motor skills by the end of middle childhood.

CONCEPT

6.2 *Fundamental Motor Skills Require the Development of Mature Movement Patterns*

Developmental Levels and Movement Patterns

To help teachers identify both mature movement patterns and the developmental changes that occur as a child progresses toward the mature form, we have provided detailed descriptions, illustrations, and, for a large number of fundamental motor skills, developmental assessment checklists. Assessment of the developmental sequences associated with fundamental motor skill acquisition is useful for the purposes of evaluation, identification of developmental progress, and diagnostic assessment to facilitate individualized remediation. For teachers who have ample time to guide students individually in the improvement of their motor behavior, extensive and detailed information is of great practical value. However, for teachers who have contact with a large number of different children each week, extensive individual evaluation of specific motor skills is extremely difficult. Since they

will have little time available for giving individual and detailed analysis, gross information is often more practical. Hence, the checklists contained in this chapter may include more detail than is practically useful for some teachers; these teachers will need to adjust these checklists to provide more gross assessment of children's fundamental motor skill development. The checklists indicate either a description of the mature movement pattern or the developmental sequence that usually occurs leading up to the mature form. In the latter instance, three developmental sequence levels of initial, elementary, and mature are identified. Further checklists and detailed descriptions and analyses of other movement patterns can be found in several sources, including Gabbard (1996), Haywood (1993), and Wickstrom (1983).

CONCEPT

6.3 *Fundamental Movement Patterns Can Be Classified Using Three General Levels of Development: Initial, Elementary, and Mature*

LOCOMOTOR SKILLS

Nine locomotor skills are described and illustrated in this section. The discussion of each skill includes the mechanical principles involved in its proper execution, things to stress, applications of movement concepts and skills, and suggested activities. The first five locomotor skills described—walking, running, leaping, jumping, and hopping—represent the skeleton on which the child begins to develop complex movement skills. Although skipping, sliding (or galloping), stopping, and dodging combine several of the first five skills, they will be described as separate locomotor skills.

CONCEPT

6.4 *Locomotor Skills Are the Basic Motor Skills Necessary for Moving through Space and from Place to Place*

Walking

Walking is the transfer of weight from one foot to the other while moving forward or backward. In a natural and rhythmic walking action, the body is erect and the eyes focus forward. The heel of the stepping foot strikes the ground (figure 6.1a), and the weight of the body is transferred through the ball of the foot, then off the toes. At that moment, the heel of the free-swinging leg touches the ground, and the knee of that leg bends, allowing it to absorb the shock of the weight transferred to this leg (figure 6.1b). In a walking movement, one foot is always in contact with the ground, and the arms swing freely in opposition to the feet (figure 6.1c).

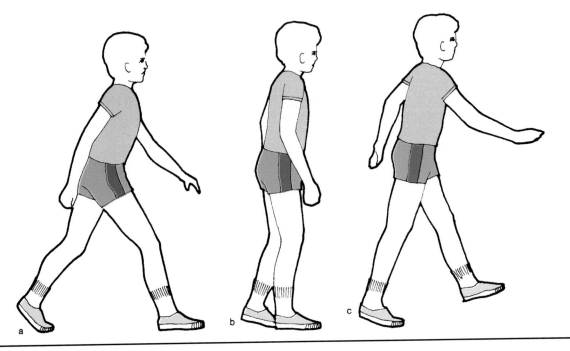

Figure 6.1 Walking.

Applying Mechanical Principles

1. *Balance:* Walking has been described as a continuous process of losing and gaining balance. Hence, the inner edges of the feet should move along a straight line to allow the center of gravity to shift directly over the base of support. This also prevents unnecessary swaying movements.
2. *Production of force:* The total effectiveness of a movement is the sum of all the forces, so properly synchronized leg and arm movements are essential.
3. *Direction of force:* The force initiated from the back leg should be directed forward and upward through the center of the body weight. If the direction of force is too vertical, the walk will be bouncy and inefficient. If the force is primarily horizontal, the walk will be a shuffle.
4. *Absorption of force:* The force should be gradually dissipated by transferring weight from the heels through the ball of the foot toward the toes.
5. *Momentum:* The forward motion initiated by the backward thrust of the leg is directed forward through the trunk. An unchecked forward movement would carry the trunk beyond the forward base of support too quickly, resulting in a forward fall or a shift to running. To counteract this, the front leg momentarily restrains the forward motion of the trunk, allowing a smooth transfer of weight as the back leg begins to move forward.

Things to Stress

1. Keep the body straight, head up, look straight ahead, and move in a relaxed manner.
2. Swing arms freely and naturally, but not too far.

3. Point toes straight ahead and take easy strides to avoid excessive up-and-down and jerky movements.

Applying Movement Concepts and Skills

1. *Body awareness:* Walking in different ways by changing use of body parts, varying size of step, and transferring weight to different parts of the foot
2. *Space awareness:* Walking in different directions and pathways with a change in level
3. *Qualities:* Walking with changes in speed and force and showing bound and flow forms of walking
4. *Relationships:* Walking with a partner, showing relationships such as side-by-side, near and far, and slow and fast

Walking Activities

1. Walk informally about the room in an easy, relaxed, natural way.
2. Same as activity 1, but walk in a circle.
3. Same as activity 2, but change direction.
4. Walk in different ways—short or long steps, fast or slow, hard or soft, high or low.
5. Change speed. Start slowly, walk at a moderate pace, then walk briskly, walk moderately again, walk slowly, then stop.
6. Walk on the heels of the feet, using exaggerated arm movements.
7. Walk on tiptoes.
8. Walk slowly for balance (use two, three, or four beats per measure).
9. Walk sideways by crossing one foot in front of the other.
10. Do pantomimes of a "happy" or "sad" walk, of carrying a heavy or light load, of a toddler or of an

Figure 6.2 Running.

adult walking with a cane, of walking through mud or wet concrete.

11. Combine walking with other locomotor skills. Begin with a walk, shift to a run, then shift back to a walk. Repeat with another locomotor skill, such as a skip or slide.
12. Gradually lower and raise the body while walking.
13. Change arm positions and movements while walking (e.g., hands swinging forward and backward above the shoulders).
14. Walk on painted lines, balance benches, planks, and other available apparatus.
15. Walk in step with a partner. Begin walking together slowly, then increase speed, change direction, or use other locomotor movements.

Walking skills can be enhanced through the application of the elements of rhythm described in chapter 28. Most of the activities in this list can be performed in time to a musical accompaniment. Rhythmic activities teach children to walk in time to an underlying beat, to change direction on an accented beat, and to develop walking sequences according to measures and phrases of music.

Many of the singing games and folk dance activities listed in chapter 29 (see table 29.1, p. 631) stress walking as a main locomotor skill. Through these simple dances children learn to walk in time to a musical accompaniment and to walk with grace and ease of movement.

Running

Running is the transfer of weight from one foot to the other with a momentary loss of contact with the ground by both feet (figure 6.2). In a slow run, such as jogging, the body leans slightly forward; arms, bent at the elbows, swing forward and backward from the shoulders and move in opposition to the leg movements. The knees are bent and the heel of the foot contacts the ground, followed by a shift of the body weight through the ball, then off the toes, of the foot. As the speed of the run increases, so does the forward lean and arm action. In a fast run, the ball of the foot touches the ground first. A developmental assessment checklist for running is provided in table 6.1

Applying Mechanical Principles

1. *Inertia:* Overcoming inertia is most difficult at the takeoff and decreases as the child gains speed. Therefore, take off from a crouched position to gain maximum speed in the shortest period of time; this allows maximum force to be exerted in a horizontal direction.
2. *Momentum:* Any increase in momentum is directly proportional to the force producing it. In running, the greater the power of the backward leg drive, the greater the forward acceleration.
3. *Direction of force:* In running, the body should lean forward about 20 degrees from vertical. This slight forward lean keeps the center of gravity ahead of the forward foot as it contacts the ground and allows the backward extension of the leg to propel the body in a nearly horizontal direction, producing the greatest forward speed and minimizing the inefficient upward movements of the body. To avoid lateral movements of the body, which restrict forward momentum, move the knees directly forward and upward and swing the arms forward and backward.

TABLE 6.1   Developmental Assessment of Running Pattern

	Good	Fair	Needs Work
Arm Action			
1. Elbows bent at 90 degrees			
2. Arm action in opposition to leg action			
3. Arms do not cross midline of body			
4. Arms swing in direction of movement			
Leg Action			
1. Weight on soles of feet			
2. Feet and knees point straight ahead			
3. High knee lift (especially when running fast)			
4. Heel of rear foot near buttock			
5. Relaxed stride (not overreaching)			
6. Center of gravity over support foot (no extended lean forward or backward)			
Trunk Action			
1. Slight lean forward as speed increases—otherwise upright			

4. *Absorption of force:* In long-distance running, the heel of the foot touches the ground first, and the force is gradually dissipated through the outer edge of the foot toward the toe. In sprinting, the ball of the foot contacts the ground first. This permits the force to be absorbed by slightly flexed hips, knees, and ankles.

5. *Levers:* By shortening the lever arm, the speed of a movement is increased. Bending the knees and elbows shortens the lever arms to increase running speed.

Things to Stress

1. In jogging, run in a relaxed and rhythmical manner, with a slight forward body lean; gently swing the arms with elbows bent and land lightly on the heels.

2. In fast running, increase knee and elbow flexion, swing arms forward and backward, and land on the balls of the feet.

3. In all types of running, breathe naturally; never hold your breath.

Applying Movement Concepts and Skills

1. *Body awareness:* Running in different ways by changing the use of body parts, varying length of stride, and transferring weight to different parts of the foot

2. *Space awareness:* Running in different directions and pathways with a change in level

3. *Qualities:* Running with a change of speed and force

4. *Relationships:* Running with a partner, showing matching form, speed, and changes in direction and level; running with, on, or around small equipment and large apparatus

Running Activities

1. Run informally around the gymnasium.
2. Run with short or long steps.
3. Run with a high knee lift.

4. Run backward and sideward.
5. Change speed—begin slowly, run at a moderate speed, then run fast.
6. Run on the heels or on tiptoe.
7. Run and change directions.
8. Run and keep in time with a partner.
9. Combine running with other locomotor skills—run, walk, run, slide, and so on.
10. Run around obstacles, such as other children, chairs, or beanbags.
11. Do pantomime running—run like a tall person, a dog, an elephant.
12. Run and jump rope on each step or alternate steps.

Many of the games listed in table 16.1 (p. 321) and table 16.2 (p. 333) stress running as the major locomotor skill. These games also help children learn to run at different speeds, change direction, and combine running with one or more locomotor or manipulative skills.

Leaping

Leaping, like running, is the transfer of weight from one foot to the other. The toe of the takeoff foot leaves the floor last, whereas the ball of the landing foot contacts the floor first (figure 6.3). In leaping, however, contact with the ground is lost for a longer period than in running, and greater height and distance are achieved. Also, a leap is usually preceded by a few running steps to achieve a maximum lift through the air.

Applying Mechanical Principles

Leaping is essentially the same as running, and the same mechanical principles apply. In addition, the following principles are important in producing a maximum leap.

1. *Momentum:* Momentum is directly proportional to the force applied, so the performer should take several

Figure 6.3 Leaping.

running steps before leaping. The increased momentum gained in the run produces a higher and farther leap.

2. *Direction of force:* The height of the leap is directly proportional to the angle of takeoff, as well as to the backward force of the takeoff leg. To gain maximum height, increase the angle of takeoff and exaggerate the forward and upward movement of the arms.

Things to Stress

1. To gain maximum height, stretch upward with the hands and forward with the lead foot.
2. Execute a short and fast run before leaping.
3. To absorb the shock, flex the knee as soon as the ball of the foot touches the ground.

Applying Movement Concepts and Skills

1. *Body awareness:* Showing different ways to move arms in the leaping action, and changing the length of stride
2. *Space awareness:* Changing direction and level of leap
3. *Qualities:* Changing speed and force of leap
4. *Relationships:* Leaping alone or with a partner, through space, over small equipment, or carrying small equipment

Leaping Activities

1. Run a few steps, then leap. Alternate the takeoff foot.
2. Leap for height and distance.
3. Hop in place a few times, then leap forward or sideward.
4. Leap in different directions.
5. Combine leaping with other locomotor skills—run, leap, walk, and so on.
6. Leap over obstacles—rope, beanbag, hoop.

7. Perform a series of consecutive leaps without breaking stride.
8. Leap without using arms.
9. Leap while holding on to small equipment such as hoops or individual ropes.

Jumping

Jumping is the transfer of weight from one foot or both feet to both feet (figure 6.4). For example, a running long jump begins with a one-foot takeoff and ends with a two-foot landing action. Other jumping movements, such as the standing long jump or the jump-reach, start and land with two feet. The developmental sequence for the standing long jump is shown in figure 6.5 and a developmental assessment checklist is provided in table 6.2.

Applying Mechanical Principles

There are two types of jumping movements: one for height, such as the vertical or high jump, and the other for distance, such as the standing or running long jump. The basic mechanical principles for leaping also apply to jumping movements; the following principles are specific to jumping:

1. *Jumping for distance:* To gain the greatest distance, the jumper should take off with the greatest forward speed and upward thrust. The running long jump requires maximum speed prior to takeoff; the standing long jump requires a maximum forward and upward swing of the arms. The angle of takeoff should be about 45 degrees. As the jumper begins to descend, the arms and body are brought forward, with the knees bent and the feet parallel. The resulting forward momentum prevents the body from falling back on

a. Long jump   b. High jump   c. Jump-reach

Figure 6.4 Jumping.

a. Initial Pattern

b. Elementary Pattern

c. Mature Pattern

Figure 6.5 Developmental sequence for standing long jump.

landing and allows the forward momentum to gradually dissipate through the flexed knees and forward arm movements.

2. *Jumping for height:* Maximum height depends on several important factors. The angle of takeoff must be as close to vertical as possible. The hips, knees, and ankles should be flexed in the starting position to permit maximum force to be directed upward by the forceful extension of the strong leg muscles. Additional height is also attained by forward and upward movement of the arms.

3. *Production of force:* To gain maximum height or distance, the movement must be smooth and synchronized—the sum of all forces.

Things to Stress

1. To gain maximum height or distance, make a few preliminary swings of the arms, then a ballistic but synchronized movement of the various segments of the body through the proper angle of movement.

2. To gain maximum force, flex the ankles and knees prior to initiating the movement.

3. To absorb shock, land on the toes and flex the knees.

TABLE 6.2   Developmental Assessment of Standing Long Jump Pattern

	Good	Fair	Needs Work

Prior to Takeoff
1. Arms swing backward and upward
2. Forward lean of trunk
3. Hips, knees, and ankles flexed approximately 90 degrees

Takeoff
1. Hip, knees, and ankles increase flexion as arms swing downward
2. Arms swing downward and upward
3. Trunk continues to lean forward
4. Heels rise off the floor as arms swing upward
5. Takeoff angle is approximately 45 degrees
6. Hips, knees, and ankles straighten to cause body to straighten
7. Arms extend upward over head in line with body

Flight
1. During flight, lower legs bend with heels moving toward buttocks
2. Hips bend bringing thighs close to trunk
3. Lower legs extend forward for landing position
4. Arms and trunk move forward for landing

Landing
1. Arms and trunk continue to move forward and downward
2. Legs move forward with trunk close to thighs
3. Knees bend on contact with floor, bringing thighs close to trunk while body continues to move forward and downward

Applying Movement Concepts and Skills

1. *Body awareness:* Changing position of arm during vertical and horizontal jumping movements; changing length and height of jump
2. *Space awareness:* Changing direction, pathways, and levels of jumping
3. *Qualities:* Changing speed and force of jumping movements and moving in time to rhythmic accompaniment
4. *Relationships:* Jumping alone or with a partner through space and onto or over small equipment

Jumping Activities

1. Jump with feet together and gradually spread legs with each jump.
2. Jump forward, sideward, and backward.
3. Begin jumping from a crouched position and gradually increase the height of each jump.
4. Jump over small equipment, such as ropes, beanbags, and hoops.
5. Jump up and mark the wall with chalked fingertips.
6. Combine jumping with other locomotor or nonlocomotor skills—run, twist, turn, stretch, and so on.
7. Jump rope activities. See chapter 26 for individual and long rope jumping skills.
8. Jump from various heights—from a box, bench, or other apparatus. Combine this jumping activity with a roll to allow for a gradual dissipation of force.
9. Jump with a partner—with or without a skipping rope.
10. Jump in time to a musical accompaniment (see chapter 28).
11. Pantomime jumping skills in sports (jump shot), dance (seven jumps), and gymnastics (two-foot takeoff).

Hopping

Hopping is the transfer of weight from one foot to the same foot. In the upward phase, the toe leaves the floor last; on the way down, the toe contacts the floor first, then the weight gradually shifts to the ball and heel of the foot (figure 6.6). Throughout this movement, the arms help maintain balance and assist in the upward movement. A developmental assessment checklist for hopping is provided in table 6.3

Applying Mechanical Principles

1. *Balance:* The hop is performed on one leg, so the body should lean slightly in the direction of the jumping leg, allowing the center of gravity to shift slightly away from the midline of the body.
2. *Force:* For maximum height, the angle of takeoff should be as close to vertical as possible. Additional height is gained by moving both arms upward simultaneously.

Things to Stress

1. To gain maximum height, swing arms backward, then vigorously forward and upward.

2. To apply force in the right direction, lean slightly toward the support leg to allow the force to be directed through the body's center of gravity.
3. To absorb shock, land first on the toes, then on the ball of the foot while gradually bending the knee.

Applying Movement Concepts and Skills

1. *Body awareness:* Changing use of different parts of body and hopping in different ways (short, medium, and long hop)
2. *Space awareness:* Changing directions, levels, and pathways
3. *Qualities:* Changing speed and force of hopping movement in time to a rhythmic accompaniment
4. *Relationships:* Hopping with a partner while matching movements, directions, and pathways

Hopping Activities

1. Hop in place. Clear the floor on the first hop, then gradually increase the height of each successive hop.
2. Hop forward, sideward, and backward.
3. Hop in place and make a quarter turn on each hop.
4. Hop in place to a 4/4 rhythm. Perform different positions in the air on ascent, such as right leg forward, arms sideward or overhead.
5. Hop several times on one foot, then switch to the other foot without losing rhythm.

a   b   c

Figure 6.6   Hopping.

TABLE 6.3   **Developmental Assessment of Hopping Pattern**

	Good	Fair	Needs Work
Initial Level			
1. Nonhopping leg, knee raised vertically			
2. Hopping leg pulled up from floor, producing only momentary flight in an upward direction			
3. Arm action is bilateral and not helpful (i.e., one arm up and one arm down) to vertical lift			
4. Body remains straight and upright			
Elementary Level			
1. Slight forward lean of body on takeoff			
2. Nonhopping knee is raised, but leg is tucked behind with heels closer to buttocks			
3. Arm action is still bilateral, which hinders vertical height			
4. Some horizontal movement achieved with each hop			
Mature Level			
1. Nonhopping leg is tucked fully behind supporting leg			
2. Forward lean of body promotes horizontal movement			
3. Hopping-leg knee is bent and then fully extended at takeoff to generate vertical and horizontal lift			
4. Arms act together in an upward motion at takeoff and with each hop to add vertical lift			
5. Nonhopping-leg knee is raised during upward flight to add to vertical lift			
6. Entire hopping action is coordinated into a rhythmic movement			

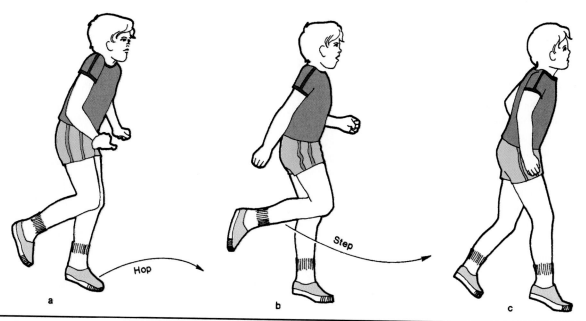

Figure 6.7 Skipping.

6. Combine hopping with other locomotor skills—run, hop, skip.
7. Hop over floor lines or small equipment such as beanbags or ropes.
8. Hop in time with a partner.
9. Hop and change level of body from high to medium to low.
10. Hop in place or on the move and keep changing arm position.

Skipping

A skip is a combination of a long step and a short hop, alternating the lead foot after each hop. In figure 6.7, the child hops on the left foot and swings the right leg forward, stepping on the ball of the right foot. The next sequence would involve a hop on the right foot, followed by a step on the left foot.

Applying Mechanical Principles

Because skipping combines a step and a hop, the mechanical principles that apply to these skills also apply to the skip. The following additional principles are important.

1. *Balance:* The base of support is narrow and alternately shifts from one foot to the other, so the arms should extend sideward to help maintain balance.
2. *Force:* The extension of the leg on the hop produces the upward movement, so the angle of takeoff should be nearly vertical. An exaggerated forward lean on the hop causes too much forward movement and makes it difficult for the child to freely swing the opposite leg forward.

Things to Stress

1. Step and hop on the same foot.
2. Because dance style and rhythm are normally emphasized more than distance or height, keep the length of the step and the height of the hop relatively short and small, and maintain smoothness.

Applying Movement Concepts and Skills

1. *Body awareness:* Changing use of different parts of the body while skipping in different ways; making shapes and varying length and height of skipping action
2. *Space awareness:* Changing direction, level, and pathways, moving in small and large spaces
3. *Qualities:* Changing to quick and slow, strong or light, and bound and flowing movements
4. *Relationships:* Moving with a partner or small group, matching, contrasting, or performing movements with or around other objects

Skipping Activities

1. Skip forward, backward, in a circle, or in different directions.
2. Cross hands with a partner and skip together, or skip in other dance positions.
3. Skip four long steps forward, then four short steps backward.
4. Skip four steps beginning with the right foot, then four steps beginning with the left foot.
5. Skip diagonally right for three steps (right–left–right) and bring feet together on the fourth count. Repeat to left.
6. Combine a skip with other locomotor skills—run, skip, walk.

7. Skip and change directions on the step phase of the movement.
8. Combine a skip with other body movements, such as change arm movements, snap fingers, or clap in time to musical accompaniment (see chapter 28 for additional ideas).
9. Skip and change body position from high to medium to low.

Use the list of singing games and folk dances listed in chapter 29 (table 29.1, p. 631) to teach children to skip in time to a musical accompaniment and to combine skipping skills with other locomotor and nonlocomotor movements.

Sliding (Galloping)

A slide combines a step and a short leap and can be performed in a forward, sideward, or backward direction. When the direction is forward or backward, the slide is called a *gallop;* when sideways, it is known as a *slide.* The movement is performed by stepping with one foot, then sliding with the other foot. The weight is transferred from the lead foot to the back foot. Once the sliding or galloping action begins, the lead foot is always the same foot (figure 6.8).

Applying Mechanical Principles

Sliding employs many of the mechanical principles listed under walking, running, and leaping. Of these, the following are important for the proper execution of the slide.

1. *Balance:* The center of gravity should be kept within the base of support. When moving to the side, the body should not lean too far, or the center of gravity will fall outside of the body. Similarly, when moving forward, the angle of takeoff for the leap should be close to vertical.
2. *Force:* Forward or sideward momentum is generated by the forceful action of the leap. In dance and sport activities, control rather than height is normally desired. Therefore, the force is controlled or adjusted by the extension of the back leg movement.

Things to Stress

1. Encourage movement in a variety of directions.
2. Emphasize light, smooth actions rather than long, forceful leaps followed by a heavy sliding movement of the following foot.

Applying Movement Concepts and Skills

1. *Body awareness:* Changing use of different parts of the body while sliding or galloping; making shapes and varying the length and height of the stepping action

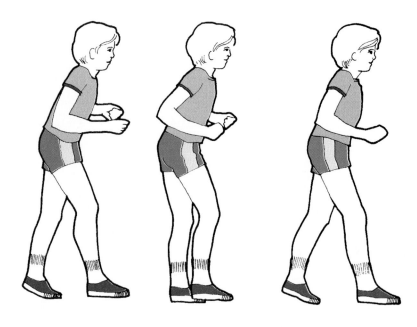

Figure 6.8   Sliding (galloping).

2. *Space awareness:* Changing direction, level, and pathways, and moving in small and large spaces
3. *Qualities:* Changing to quick and slow, strong and light movements
4. *Relationships:* Moving in groups of two or more persons, matching, contrasting, or performing movements with or around small objects

Sliding Activities

1. In a circle or line formation, slide forward, backward, and sideward.
2. Slide four steps to the right, make a half turn, then slide four steps to the left.
3. With partners, slide four steps right, then four steps left.
4. Slide and vary the height of the leap.
5. Slide with the left foot forward, stop, then slide with the right foot forward.
6. Slide in different directions.
7. Combine the slide with other locomotor movements—run, slide, skip.
8. Slide and gallop, changing levels and other body movements.
9. Pantomime sport skills that require a sliding action.
10. Develop sliding routines for partners or small groups.

Use the list of singing games and folk dances listed in chapter 29 (table 29.1, p. 631) to teach children to slide in time to a musical accompaniment and to combine sliding skills with other locomotor and nonlocomotor movements.

Stopping

Two basic types of stopping action are used in many sports and daily activities. In the forward stride stop (figure 6.9),

Figure 6.9 Stopping.

the runner simultaneously bends the knees and leans backward while moving the arms sideward. In the skip stop, the performer takes a step and a hop, which allows him to shift upward and lean backward to slow down his forward movement; he then lands in a stride position with the weight over the balls of the feet.

Applying Mechanical Principles

1. *Absorption of force:* Initiating a preliminary skip and landing in a stride position with knees bent spreads the force over a maximum distance.
2. *Balance:* Landing in a stride position with knees bent and trunk leaning backward provides a low, stable base of support.

Thing to Stress

1. Land with feet apart (stride or parallel) and bend the knees as contact is made.
2. Lean backward from the waist and away from the direction of the movement.
3. Keep your head up.

Applying Movement Concepts and Skills

1. *Body awareness:* Changing different parts of the body and landing in different ways; making shapes in the air before landing; making a sequence of run, jump, land, and roll
2. *Space awareness:* Changing direction in flight, land, and roll
3. *Qualities:* Showing landing movements that vary from light and gentle to forceful and heavy
4. *Relationships:* Moving with a partner, showing matching run, jump, land, and roll, in varying heights, speeds, and over small equipment

Stopping Activities

1. Run forward and stop when the whistle blows.
2. Select a line or spot on the floor. Run and stop with front foot on the line.

3. Run forward, sideward, and diagonally and stop when the whistle blows.
4. With a partner, follow the leader with back player stopping when leader stops. Run side-by-side with one player calling "Stop."
5. Run, jump over small equipment, and stop.
6. Repeat activities 1 to 5 using a skip stop.
7. Repeat activities 1 to 5 backward.

Dodging

Dodging is a quick shifting of one part or all parts of the body away from a stationary or moving object. A dodge is normally executed after a momentary stop by bending the knees and then thrusting the body vigorously toward the side. One or both feet may leave the ground as a performer executes a dodging movement (figure 6.10).

Applying Mechanical Principles

1. *Balance:* Dodging requires a quick shift in position, so the center of gravity should be low and close to the center of the base of support just before the shift is made.
2. *Production of force:* To gain maximum force, the knees should be flexed to allow a maximum extension of the powerful muscles of the legs.
3. *Direction of force:* By keeping the body relatively low, the force can be directed through the body in a sideward direction. If the player is standing erect, the direction of force is upward and only slightly toward the side.

Things to Stress

1. Keep the body low, with the weight over both feet and the arms to the side.
2. Always lean in the direction of the dodge.
3. Once a dodging movement is made, keep low and shift the center of gravity toward the middle of the body in order to prepare for another movement.

Applying Movement Concepts and Skills

1. *Body awareness:* Changing the position of different parts of the body while dodging; developing sequences involving other locomotor movements with dodging (e.g., run, dodge, slide)
2. *Space awareness:* Changing direction and pathways before and after a dodging movement
3. *Qualities:* Changing to quick and slow movements before, during, and after a dodging action
4. *Relationships:* Traveling and dodging around other players or objects; in partners, repeat movements around small and large objects

Dodging Activities

1. Run, stop, move right, then move left.
2. Run to a partner, stop, and change direction.
3. Run around obstacles—beanbags, balls, chairs.

Figure 6.10 Dodging.

4. Bounce or dribble a ball, stop, and change direction on command.
5. Bounce or dribble a ball around obstacles.
6. See table 16.1 (p. 321) and table 16.2 (p. 333) for lists of games that stress dodging.
7. Combine dodging with other locomotor skills—slide, stop, dodge, run.

NONLOCOMOTOR SKILLS

Nonlocomotor, or axial, movements (swing, bend and stretch, twist and turn, push and pull) are performed from a relatively stable base of support. These movements are usually performed while standing, kneeling, sitting, or lying down; however, they can be combined with locomotor skills.

CONCEPT

6.5 Nonlocomotor Skills Involve Movements That Do Not Require Transportation of the Body through Space or from Place to Place

Swinging

A swing is a pendular or circular movement of the body or its parts around a stationary center (figure 6.11).

Applying Mechanical Principles

The following principles apply to the swinging movements of parts of the body while the body as a whole maintains a stationary standing or sitting position.

1. *Lever:* In movements of the arm, the hand has greater speed when the elbow is kept straight. Similarly, the foot has greater speed when the knee is kept straight.
2. *Momentum:* The momentum of any part of a supported body can be transferred to the rest of the body. For example, swinging an arm sideward and

Figure 6.11 Swinging.

upward moves the whole body in those directions. This transfer takes place only when the body is in contact with a supporting surface.

3. *Gravity:* The movement of a pendulum is caused by the force of gravity. As the pendulum swings downward, its speed increases; as it swings upward, its speed decreases until it stops at the top of the swing. The speed of pendular movement is not increased by body weight; it is increased only by the application of additional muscular force.

Things to Stress

1. Keep swinging movements relaxed, smooth, and rhythmic.
2. Keep swinging movements equal on both sides; hence, do not apply additional muscular force to one side.
3. Dismount swinging bars, rings, or swings at the top of the swing.

Applying Movement Concepts and Skills

1. *Body awareness:* Using different parts of the body to initiate and perform swinging actions; combining body shapes with different swinging movements
2. *Space awareness:* Performing swinging movements while moving and changing directions and pathways
3. *Qualities:* Changing swinging movements from quick to slow, strong to light, and combinations of both
4. *Relationships:* Swinging with light scarves, hoops, or wands; developing sequences with partner, with equipment and while traveling and stopping

Swinging Activities

1. Swing arms forward and backward and from side to side.
2. Swing arms overhead, forward and backward, and sideward.

Figure 6.12 Bending.

3. Lie on back and swing arms and legs.
4. Repeat activity 1 with legs.
5. Swing head forward and backward and from side to side.
6. Ask the children how many parts of the body can swing or sway from standing or sitting positions. Allow them to experiment.
7. Swing or sway parts of the body in pantomime. Tell the children to sway like a tree, swing like a windshield wiper, and so on. Change tempo with each pantomime movement.
8. Swing arms or legs with moderate speed, then shift to slower or faster speeds.
9. Stand on a box, step, or other apparatus and swing the leg.
10. Grasp chinning bar and swing body forward and backward. Flex arm and repeat.
11. Swing on a rope and release it at different points on the forward and backward swing. Note that the top of the backswing is the best point at which to release a rope.
12. Combine swinging with other locomotor skills such as a jump or slide.
13. Hang from a bar or rings, then swing.

Bending and Stretching

A bend is a flexing movement around one or more joints (figure 6.12). A stretch is an extension of one or more joints of the body (figure 6.13). A light or gentle stretch moves the joint partially through its range of movement. A strong forceful stretch, such as a stretch upward and backward, requires maximum extension through many joints.

Things to Stress

1. To increase flexibility, bend in a slow and sustained manner.
2. Encourage children to find, test, and extend different parts of the body that bend. Also, use such terms as *tuck, curl,* and *coil* in place of *bend* or *flex.*
3. Initial stretching movements should be light and gentle; discourage ballistic movements.
4. Encourage children to stretch through the full range of movement.

Figure 6.13 Stretching.

5. Where possible, combine stretching and bending movements.
6. Encourage stretching movements from a variety of positions and in a variety of ways.

Applying Movement Concepts and Skills

1. *Body awareness:* Balancing on different parts of the body and seeing how many different parts and ways to bend and stretch; making matching curved and stretched shapes with a partner; using individual ropes, wands, or hoops, designing sequences that involve stretch and curved shapes
2. *Space awareness:* Bending and stretching in different directions, levels, and pathways
3. *Qualities:* Changing from bending and stretching movements with quick and slow and strong and light movements
4. *Relationships:* Developing sequences with partners showing matching and contrasting bending and stretching movements; adding speed, force, and small equipment to the sequence

Bending and Stretching Activities

1. Imitate things that bend—tree, snake, dog, ostrich, giraffe, and so on.
2. Bend one part of the body while keeping another part straight.
3. Combine bending with other locomotor or nonlocomotor movements—bend while stretching, swinging, or jumping.
4. Run and jump, and bend one or more parts while in the air.

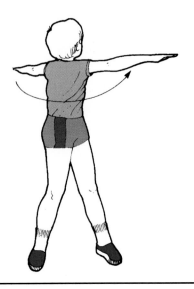

Figure 6.14 Twisting.

Figure 6.15 Turning.

5. Stand and stretch trunk, then arms, wrists, and fingers in a slow upward movement. Repeat and move in other directions.
6. Repeat activity 5 from a front or back lying position.
7. Slowly stretch in one direction and then slowly curl back to the starting position. Repeat and move quickly back to the curled position.
8. Run, jump, and stretch, then land and bend.
9. Stretch one arm slowly and bend it back rapidly; reverse movement. Do the same with other parts of the body.
10. Bend one part of the body (arms) while stretching another (legs).
11. Stand on a box or step with toes touching near the edge. Keep legs straight and bend forward and down; try to extend the fingers beyond the toes.
12. Pantomime sport movements that require strong sustained stretching movements.
13. Stretch while holding individual ropes, wands, or hoops.

Twisting and Turning

A twist is a rotation of parts of the body around the body's own axis (figure 6.14). Twisting movements usually occur at the neck, shoulders, spine, hips, ankles, and wrists. A turn is a partial or total rotation of the body, accompanied by a shift in the base of support (figure 6.15). A pivot to one side illustrates a turning movement involving a partial rotation and a shift in the base of support. A jump followed by a full rotation in the air illustrates a total rotation and a complete change in the base of support.

Things to Stress

1. A twisting movement can take place on or off the ground.
2. The range of the twisting action is determined by the type of joint (hinge joint, ball-and-socket joint, etc.).

3. Keep the part of the body around which the twisting action occurs stable.
4. To increase the speed of a turn, pull the legs and arms close to the body.
5. In activities requiring a quick change of direction, keep the body weight low and the feet about shoulder-width apart.

Applying Movement Concepts and Skills

1. *Body awareness:* Finding out how many different parts of the body one can twist and turn on; using individual ropes, wands, and hoops, designing sequences involving twisting and turning
2. *Space awareness:* Designing sequences involving twisting and turning in different directions, levels, and pathways
3. *Qualities:* Performing twisting and turning movements quickly and slowly and strongly and lightly
4. *Relationships:* Developing sequences with a partner showing twisting and turning movements that involve changes in direction, level, and speed

Twisting and Turning Activities

1. Twist to pantomime movements—trees and wind.
2. Combine twisting with other locomotor skills—walk, stop, leap, and jump.
3. Twist part of the upper body one way while twisting part of the lower body the opposite way.
4. With a partner, make up twisting routines—together and against each other's body parts.
5. Pantomime athletic and mechanical movements that involve twisting.
6. Turn the body a quarter, half, or full turn to the right, then to the left.
7. Turn the body to music.

Figure 6.16   Pushing.

Figure 6.17   Pulling.

8. Turn to pantomime movements—tops, doors, sport skills.
9. Combine twisting and turning movements.
10. Face a partner and pivot toward and away from each other.
11. Begin a turn with arms outstretched, then quickly draw in the arms as the turn is made. Repeat with the legs or legs and arms.
12. Combine turning movements with a walk, run, jump, skip, or slide.
13. Combine a turn with small equipment such as individual ropes, hoops, wands, and traffic cones.
14. With a partner, make up sequences involving twisting and turning movements. Perform these standing, walking, and from different positions.

Pushing and Pulling

Pushing is directing a force or object away from the base of support, such as pushing a door open or pushing against an imaginary object with hands or feet (figure 6.16). Pulling is directing a force or object toward the body (figure 6.17). A pulling action is normally initiated by the hands and arms; however, other parts of the body, such as the foot, knee, or trunk, can also initiate a pulling movement.

Things to Stress

1. For movements requiring excessive force, lower the body to direct the force through the center of the body's weight.
2. Start strong pushing movements with a wide base of support.
3. Keep the back straight during strenuous pushing movements.
4. When lifting or pulling heavy objects, start with a wide base of support, bent knees, and straight back, and pull the object upward toward the body.

5. Keep the pulling action smooth; use a controlled sequence of muscular contractions rather than rigid, ballistic-type movements.

Applying Movement Concepts and Skills

1. *Body awareness:* Finding out how many different parts of the body with which one can push and pull; finding out how many different positions the body can be in, such as lying on the back or side and pushing and pulling with different parts of the body
2. *Space awareness:* Designing sequences involving pushing and pulling in different directions, pathways, and levels
3. *Qualities:* Performing pushing and pulling sequences involving quick and slow and strong and light movements
4. *Relationships:* Developing individual or partner sequences showing pushing and pulling and involving one or more elements of body awareness, qualities, and space awareness

Pushing and Pulling Activities

1. Pull in pantomime—pull a wagon or row a boat.
2. Pull objects of varying weights and sizes toward the body. Start with light objects and progress to heavier ones, gradually adjusting the base of support and angle of pull as the weight increases.
3. Use different parts of the body to pull an object, such as a leg, the trunk, or head.
4. Repeat activity 3 but from different positions, such as lying on your back and pulling an object toward your body with the lower leg.
5. Pull an object with different rates of speed—begin pulling slowly, then gradually increase speed.
6. Play tug-of-war with two players. Play as usual, beginning in a standing position; then vary the starting position, and begin by kneeling, lying on one side and the back, and so on.

7. Repeat with four or more players.
8. Push in pantomime—push a box or a wheelbarrow.
9. Push objects of various weights and sizes. Begin with small objects and gradually increase weight and size.
10. Push objects with the hands, feet, and back.
11. Do partner activities—from a standing position, one partner assumes a good base of support and the other attempts to push the other backward. Experiment in various positions with different parts of the body. For example, have both partners face each other on the floor and push their legs or arms against each other. From a back-to-back position, one partner pulls the other over her head.
12. Balance on one foot and push a box against a wall or partner. Try the same movements, but balance on two feet. Repeat the movements, lowering the body and widening the base of support.
13. Pantomime sport skills that require a pushing action.
14. Perform five or six calisthenic exercises or stunts that require a pushing action.

MANIPULATIVE SKILLS

The fundamental manipulative skills of throwing, catching, and striking are the foundation of all major individual and team sport activities. These skills involve controlling objects with the hands or feet and can be classified under three headings: receptive, propulsive, or retentive. These terms refer, respectively, to skills that involve receiving an object, exerting force on an object, or retaining control of an object while the person or object is moving. These fundamental skills should be taught to primary-age children in a systematic manner using a direct and limitation method of teaching and through a variety of running, tag, simple team, and creative game activities. As children progress to the intermediate grades, these fundamental skills form the foundation for the development of more specialized skills, which are identified and organized sequentially within each major sport in part 5 of the text. Thus, the following skills should be acquired by girls and boys before they reach developmental level III.

C O N C E P T

6.6 *Manipulative Skills Involve Control of Objects, Usually with the Hands or Feet*

Throwing

Throwing is classified as a propulsive manipulative skill because force must be exerted on an object. Children in developmental levels I and II often begin with a two-hand underhand throw. They progress to a one-hand underhand throw, and finally tackle the one-hand overhand throw.

C O N C E P T

6.7 *Propulsive Manipulative Skills Are Movement Skills That Exert Force on Objects*

Two-Hand Underhand Throw

The child begins with her back straight, feet about shoulder-width apart, and knees slightly bent. Arms are straight, and the ball is held with the fingers of both hands (figure 6.18a). Keep the back straight, then swing the arms forward and upward, and straighten the knees (figure 6.18b). Release the ball off the fingers and follow through in the direction of the ball (figure 6.18c).

Applying Mechanical Principles   The following mechanical principles apply to all three basic throwing skills.

1. *Momentum:* The momentum of any part of the body can be transferred to the ball. To apply this principle, rotate the body toward the side while shifting the weight to the back foot. Bring back the throwing arm as far as possible. If the forward swinging action is smooth, maximum force will be transferred to the ball as it leaves the hands.
2. *Speed:* Greater speed can be gained by increasing the distance over which the force is applied. This is particularly important in the one-hand underhand and overhand throws. The straighter the arm in the forward throwing movement, the greater the force that is generated and the greater the speed of the ball.

Things to Stress
1. Use a large ball (beach ball or 8 ½-to-12-inch utility ball) with young children, particularly five- and six-year-olds.
2. Begin a throw with legs far enough apart to provide a good base of support.
3. Rotate the body in the same direction as the ball during the preparatory movement.
4. Keep arms straight on the forward swing, and follow through after the ball has been released.

Applying Movement Concepts and Skills
1. *Body awareness:* Finding different positions and ways of throwing a ball with two hands
2. *Space awareness:* Finding different directions, levels, and distances the ball can be thrown
3. *Qualities:* Experimenting with throwing a ball with different speeds and forces
4. *Relationships:* Throwing a ball to a partner, changing ways of throwing and from different levels and distances

Throwing Activities
1. Use large balls (beach balls, playballs) and large targets (walls, lines on floor, colorful targets painted on plywood). Have children begin by throwing a few feet from the target, then gradually increase the distance.

a   b   c

Figure 6.18   Two-hand underhand throw.

2. Throw and catch with a partner.
3. Have children experiment with different ways of throwing a two-hand side throw (from either side, while kneeling, or while lying on back).
4. Play simple throwing games. Refer to "Classroom Games" (in chapter 15), "Incorporating the Inventive Games Approach" (p. 315), and chapter 16 (table 16.1, p. 321, and table 16.2, p. 333).

One-Hand Underhand Throw

For this throw, the child stands facing the target with legs slightly apart and weight evenly distributed on both feet. He holds the ball in front of his body with both hands slightly under the ball (figure 6.19a). His right hand swings down and back as his body twists to the right and his weight shifts to his right foot. As his right arm swings forward, he steps forward onto his left foot and releases the ball off the fingertips (figure 6.19b).

Things to Stress

1. Use a large ball (beach or utility ball).
2. Begin with a wide base of support and extend the arms far enough in the initial backswing.
3. Make a smooth forward swing, and follow through after the ball is released.

Applying Movement Concepts and Skills

1. *Body awareness:* Finding different positions and ways of throwing a one-hand underhand throw
2. *Space awareness:* Finding different directions, levels, and distances the ball can be thrown
3. *Qualities:* Experimenting with throwing a ball with different force and speed

4. *Relationships:* Throw a ball to a target or partner, changing the way of throwing from different levels and distances

Throwing Activities

1. Adapt two-hand side throw activities to the one-hand underhand throw.
2. Adapt two-hand side throw activities using a beanbag or fleece ball.
3. Roll a ball toward a target or partner.
4. Throw various-size balls into the air and catch them on the volley or after one bounce.
5. Repeat activities 2 to 4 using your other hand.
6. Run, change direction, and throw at a target.
7. Run, stop, turn, and throw at a target.
8. Make up games for individuals or partners that require a one-hand underhand throw.

One-Hand Overhand Throw

The player begins with her left foot forward and her body weight evenly distributed over both feet. She holds the ball with both hands in front of her body. In the first part of the backswing, she raises her upper arm and flexes her wrist so the hand points backward. At this point, her left side faces the direction of the throw; her left arm extends forward; and her weight is on the rear foot (figure 6.20a). In a simultaneous movement, her upper arm lifts up and forward and her left arm moves down and back as her weight shifts to the front foot. The ball is released off the fingertips. The follow-through should be in a downward direction, ending with the palm of the throwing hand facing the ground (figure 6.20b). The developmental sequence for acquiring the overhand throw is illustrated in figure 6.21. A developmental assessment checklist for the overhand throw is provided in table 6.4

a   b

Figure 6.19   One-hand underhand throw.

a   b

Figure 6.20   One-hand overhand throw.

Things to Stress

1. Hold the ball with fingertips and thumb.
2. Raise upper arm and forearm well above the shoulder on the backward swing.
3. Keep elbow away from the body on the forward throwing action.
4. Snap the wrist and release the ball off the fingertips.
5. Follow through after the ball is released and take a step on the right foot (right-handed thrower).

a. Initial Pattern

b. Elementary Pattern "A"

c. Elementary Pattern "B"

d. Mature Pattern

Figure 6.21   Developmental sequence for overhand throw.

Applying Movement Concepts and Skills

1. *Body awareness:* Finding different positions and ways of throwing a one-hand overhand throw
2. *Space awareness:* Finding different directions and levels in which the ball can be thrown
3. *Qualities:* Experimenting with throwing the ball with varying force and speed
4. *Relationships:* Throwing the ball at different targets or to a partner, changing ways of throwing from different levels and distances

Throwing Activities

1. Adapt the two-hand and one-hand underhand activities to the one-hand overhand throw.
2. Refer to practice activities and lead-up games in chapter 22 ("Basketball Activities").
3. Refer to practice activities and lead-up games in chapter 23 ("Softball Activities").

4. Play simple throwing games listed in chapter 16 (table 16.1, p. 321, and table 16.2, p. 333).

Catching

Catching is classified as a receptive manipulative skill, because it involves receiving an object. It is one of the more difficult skills for early primary school children. The child must learn to focus on an oncoming object, to move into a correct catching position, and to decide whether to use an underhand or overhand catch. All of these movements take a lot of practice; hence, young children show a great deal of inconsistency with this skill. Using large balls, such as balloons and fleece balls, and throwing from short distances can help build confidence and skill during the initial stages of learning to catch. As skill improves, introduce smaller balls and increase other aspects such as catching a ball from different levels and at different rates of speed. This variability in practice helps develop a rich schema for catching. These points should be kept in mind when teaching the following catching skills.

C O N C E P T

6.8 *Receptive Manipulative Skills are Receiving Skills*

Two-Hand Underhand and Overhand Catches

Use the two-hand underhand catch when the ball approaches below the waist. The player stands with feet about shoulder-width apart, elbows bent, and fingers pointing down. As the ball approaches, the player steps forward, extends her arms, and brings her hands close together (figure 6.22a). The ball is caught with the tips of the fingers and thumbs. The pinkies (baby fingers) should be close together when the ball is caught (figure 6.22b). As the ball is caught, the hands recoil toward the body to soften the force (figure 6.22c). The developmental sequence for acquiring the two-hand underhand catch is illustrated in figure 6.23. A developmental assessment checklist for underhand catching is provided in table 6.5.

When the ball approaches above the waist, the two-hand overhand catch should be used. The elbows are bent and held high, and the fingers and thumbs are spread (figure 6.24a). As the ball approaches, the arms extend forward and up. The ball should be caught with the tips of the fingers and thumbs; the thumbs are close together (figure 6.24b). As the ball is caught, the hands recoil toward the body to deaden the force of the oncoming ball.

Applying Mechanical Principles

1. *Center of gravity:* The body should be kept in line with the ball. The legs should be comfortably spread or in a stride position to provide a firm base of support. With the underhand catch, a slightly crouched position lowers the center of gravity, providing an even firmer base of support.

CHAPTER 6

TABLE 6.4   Developmental Assessment of Overhand Throwing Pattern

	Good	Fair	Needs Work

Backswing Action
1. Ball held (and thrown) with fingers—not in palm of hand _____
2. Legs apart, with left leg (right-handed thrower) and left side toward the target _____
3. Weight on back foot _____
4. Throwing arm extended at side with elbow slightly flexed _____
5. Throwing elbow pointing away from target with ball held in a palm-up position _____
6. Throwing-arm wrist in hyperextended (cocked) position _____

Throwing Action
1. Weight is transferred to front foot _____
2. Hips and trunk rotate to face the target _____
3. Throwing arm elbow leads the rest of the arm as it turns toward the target _____
4. Power comes from straightening the elbow and extending the arm quickly _____
5. Throwing wrist snaps as the arm is extended, as if to throw the hand with the ball _____
6. As the throwing arm extends, both the front knee and the back knee bend slightly _____

Follow-Through
1. The throwing arm continues the forward motion after the ball is released and then moves down and back _____
2. Back leg steps forward to establish new base of support _____
3. Trunk bends slightly at the hips as body moves forward _____

2. *Absorption of force:* To absorb the impact of the oncoming ball, the force should be spread over as large an area as possible or as long a distance as possible, or both. Catch the ball with the arms extended and the fingers spread and cupped, then recoil the arms toward the body to provide the greatest surface and distance for absorbing the force.

Things to Stress
1. Move into a "ready" position, where the body is in line with the oncoming ball.
2. Meet the ball with cupped hands and slightly bent elbows, then recoil the arms back toward the body.
3. Keep feet in a comfortable stride position; for low catches, bend the knees and lean forward in the direction of the oncoming ball.

Applying Movement Concepts and Skills
1. *Body awareness:* Finding different positions and ways to catch a ball
2. *Space awareness:* Exploring different ways of receiving a ball or other small and large objects—on rebound from floor or wall

3. *Qualities:* Exploring ways of receiving balls, beanbags, and other light objects that are thrown with different speeds and force
4. *Relationships:* Explore throwing and catching with a partner, changing height, distance, and speed of throw

Catching Activities
1. See the activities lists for one- and two-hand throws.
2. Throw and catch objects of different sizes (large utility balls, Nerf and tennis balls, beanbags, etc.) from a short distance, then gradually increase the distance between players.
3. Throw and catch a large ball over a net or string tied between two chairs.
4. Throw and catch a ball thrown under the string or through a hoop held off the ground by a third player.
5. Play simple throwing and catching games listed in chapter 16 (table 16.1, p. 321, and table 16.2, p. 333).

Striking

Striking is classified as a propulsive manipulative skill, because force is applied to propel an object. Two basic types

a. Arms extended, hands close together

b. Pinkies close together

c. Hands recoil toward the body

Figure 6.22   Two-hand underhand catch.

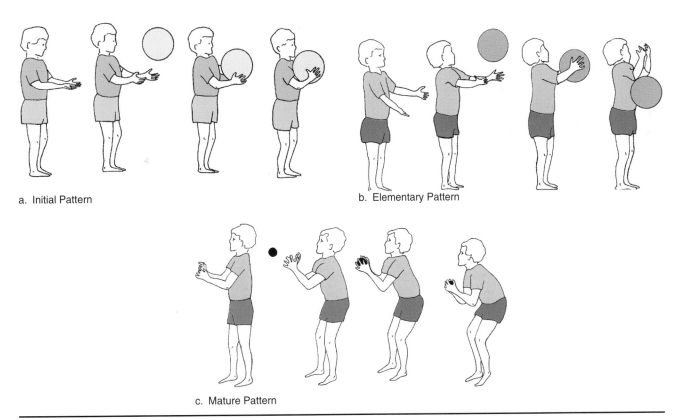

a. Initial Pattern

b. Elementary Pattern

c. Mature Pattern

Figure 6.23   Developmental sequence for two-hand underhand catch.

TABLE 6.5	Developmental Assessment of Catching Pattern		
	Good	**Fair**	**Needs Work**

Initial Level

1. Often an avoidance reaction, with head turning away from the ball as it approaches and hands being raised to protect face
2. Arms extended straight in front of body
3. Hands are held palms-upward, fingers extended and tense
4. Limited movement until contact is made
5. Body is used to "trap" the ball, or arms are used to "scoop" the ball with fingers playing minor role

Elementary Level

1. Avoidance reaction is limited, but eyes may close on contact with the ball
2. Arms held at sides with forearms extended at 90 degrees
3. Hands held with palms upward
4. Fingers attempt to "squeeze" the ball, with limited success
5. Arms still dominate in trapping the ball—minimum finger movement

Mature Level

1. Arms held relaxed at sides with forearms held up and in front of body
2. Arms adjust to the flight of the ball
3. Arms give upon ball contact to absorb the force of the ball
4. No avoidance reaction
5. Thumbs and fingers held in mirror image position with palms slightly up and little fingers touching
6. Upon ball contact, fingers grasp the ball in a well-coordinated movement

a   b

Figure 6.24   Two-hand overhand catch.

a   b

Figure 6.25   Hitting the ball with an underhand striking action.

of striking skills are used in individual, partner, and group games: hitting a ball with the hand or foot, and hitting an object with a bat, racket, or other implement. The basic skills within each of these general areas are described in this section. The more sport-specific manipulative skills are detailed in chapters 18 to 24.

Striking with the Hand

When striking a ball with the hand or fist, the player stands in line with the oncoming ball. The feet are in a stride position, with the weight on the back foot. If the ball is hit with an underhand striking action (figure 6.25a), the striking arm extends straight back, then forcefully moves forward to contact the ball when it is opposite the front foot (figure 6.25b). The hand of the striking arm is held firm as the ball is contacted. Follow-through is forceful in the direction of the hit. When a ball is hit with a two-hand overhand striking action, the elbows are bent slightly, the fingers are spread apart, and the thumbs face each other. As the ball drops, the body and arms extend upward and slightly forward, and the ball is hit with "stiff" fingers. Follow-through is an upward and forward motion in the direction of the ball (figure 6.26).

Dribbling is classified as a retentive manipulative skill, because it involves retaining control over an object while

moving. When dribbling with the hands, the striking action is downward. The body leans forward slightly and the knees are bent. The wrist of the dribbling hand is flexed, with the fingers cupped and spread (figure 6.27). The forearm extends downward and the ball is "pushed" toward the ground. As the ball rebounds, the fingers, wrist, and arm "ride" back with it. The developmental sequence for acquiring the movement pattern for striking a ball with the hand is illustrated in figure 6.28. A developmental assessment checklist for striking a ball with the hand is provided in table 6.6.

C O N C E P T

6.9 *Retentive Manipulative Skills are Motor Skills that Maintain Control Over an Object While the Person or Object is Moving*

Applying Mechanical Principles

1. *Stability:* In all striking skills, the legs should be comfortably spread to provide a wide, stable base of support from which to hit the ball. Standing with the knees slightly bent also lowers the center of gravity, further increasing stability.

2. *Action-reaction:* Every action causes an equal and opposite reaction. When a player begins to swing his arm

Figure 6.26 Hitting the ball with a two-hand overhand striking action.

toward the oncoming ball, he is building up force. If he maintains a steady forward momentum at the moment of contact, the ball will recoil with an equal force.

3. *Production of force:* Hitting a ball is basically the transfer of rotary force to linear force. More force can be gained by increasing the distance of the backswing and by cocking the wrist at the top of the backswing. Additional force is also gained by extending the arms as the bat is moved toward the ball.

4. *Direction of force:* The direction in which an object moves is determined by the direction in which the force is applied. If the force is applied in line with the ball's center of gravity, the ball travels in a straight line, but if the bat hits the ball above or below its center of gravity, the ball travels in a rotary motion, losing distance and speed.

5. *Inertia:* An object has its greatest inertia when it is not moving. Once dribbling begins, it should be continued by easy, sequential pushing actions. Each time the ball comes to rest, more force must be applied to overcome the initial inertia.

Figure 6.27 Dribbling with the hand.

a. Initial Patttern

b. Elementary Patttern

c. Mature Patttern

Figure 6.28 Developmental sequence for striking a ball with the hand (dribbling).

TABLE 6.6	Developmental Assessment of Striking a Ball with the Hand (Dribbling)		
	Good	**Fair**	**Needs Work**

Initial Level

1. Ball is hit rather than pushed _____
2. Fingers of hitting hand are together _____
3. Fingers of hitting hand tend to be hyperextended (bent upward) _____
4. Wrist action produces a "slapping" (hitting) action _____
5. Limited elbow extension, forearm quickly moves up for next hit _____
6. Eye-hand coordination poor, hence variation in hand contact, direction of hit, and timing of hit _____
7. Trunk and head bent over ball, with eyes on the ball, and chin close to chest _____

Elementary Level

1. Reduction in hitting action, but ball is still "patted" through wrist movement _____
2. Pushing action begins to develop, but hand contact is not consistent _____
3. Eye contact is still on the ball, but head is raised a little higher as distance between chin and chest increases _____
4. Elbow is extended to allow arm to move downward after ball contact, but arm does not completely straighten _____
5. Hand returns to horizontal positioning to await ball return _____
6. Eye-hand coordination improves to decrease variation in hand contact, direction of hit, and timing _____

Mature Level

1. Ball is pushed toward the floor _____
2. Fingers of hitting hand remain in contact with ball for a long time as elbow starts to almost fully extend the arm pointing downward _____
3. Arm stays extended and, after ball makes contact with floor, starts to move up with the ball to a final horizontal position _____
4. Recontact with the ball occurs about two-thirds of way up on the rebound, and fingers spread just before contact _____
5. Hand rides up with the ball to a horizontal level and then pushes the ball downward again _____
6. Hand remains in unbroken contact with the ball on the upward and then downward push _____
7. Fingers conform to ball's shape on contact, and palm of hand makes contact at the peak of the rebound _____
8. Slight knee bend and trunk flexion (forward bend), but head remains high with good separation between chin and chest _____

Things to Stress

1. Keep your eye on the ball.
2. Get in line with the ball.
3. Strike and follow through.
4. When dribbling, push the ball and ride back with the rebound.

Applying Movement Concepts and Skills

1. *Body awareness:* Exploring different ways of hitting a light object, such as a balloon or Nerf ball; using different parts of the body to hit an object, and hitting the object from different positions and while moving
2. *Space awareness:* Exploring ways of hitting objects in space—high and far, short and down, etc.
3. *Qualities:* Varying the force and speed of hitting small and large balls
4. *Relationships:* Exploring different ways of hitting a balloon or fleece ball back and forth to a partner

Striking Activities

1. Strike a balloon with the hand or the elbow, then with different parts of the body.
2. Repeat activity 1 with either hand and with both hands.
3. Strike balls of various sizes toward a target or to a partner.
4. Attempt to strike a balloon or light Nerf ball into the air three or more times.
5. Make up a sequence of striking, throwing, and catching a balloon or ball.

6. Run, change direction, then strike a Nerf ball toward a target.
7. Strike a ball into the air, perform a stunt, then catch the returning ball.
8. Make up a game for one person or partners that requires a strike.

Adapt games from the following chapters that stress striking skills with one or two hands.

Chapter 15: "Adapting Physical Education Activities to the Classroom"
Chapter 16: "Locomotor and Manipulative Games"
Chapter 17: "Cooperative Games and Learning Activities"
Chapter 21: "Volleyball Activities"

Play simple striking games listed in chapter 16 (table 16.1, p. 321, and table 16.2, p. 333).

Striking with the Feet

Most kicking games played in elementary school involve kicking a stationary or moving ball with the top or side of the instep. Just before the ball is kicked, the nonkicking foot is even with the ball, the head and trunk lean forward slightly, and the kicking leg is well back with the knee slightly bent. The eyes are focused on the ball, and the arms are extended outward with the left arm (right-foot kick) leading toward the direction of the kick. The kicking leg is then brought downward and forward, and the top of the instep contacts the ball. The kicking leg continues forward and slightly upward (figure 6.29). The developmental sequence for acquiring the movement pattern for kicking a ball is illustrated in figure 6.30. A developmental assessment checklist for kicking a ball is provided in table 6.7.

Many kicking games also involve a controlled striking or dribbling action of both feet (figure 6.31). In this type of striking action, the body is bent slightly forward with the head over the ball. The ball is moved with short, controlled pushes.

Applying Mechanical Principles   The mechanical principles listed above under "Striking with the Hand" also apply to "Striking with the Feet." The following principles also apply to kicking a ball.

1. *Acceleration:* A ball that is kicked moves in the direction in which the force is applied, and the resulting change of speed is directly proportional to the force acting on it. It is important that the force applied by the kicking foot be directly behind the ball and moving in the direction in which the ball is intended to move.
2. *Increasing linear velocity:* Kicking a ball involves the conversion of angular velocity to linear velocity. Linear velocity can be increased by taking more steps prior to the kick or by extending the lower leg more to create a longer lever and, thus, more force when the ball is contacted.

Figure 6.29   Kicking.

Things to Stress

1. Never kick with the toes.
2. Bend the knee prior to kicking, and follow through in the direction of the kick.
3. When dribbling, push the ball and maintain a steady, rhythmical dribbling action.

Applying Movement Concepts and Skills   Adapt the movement ideas listed above in the section "Striking with the Hand."

Kicking Activities

1. Adapt the striking activities listed under "Striking with the Hand" to kicking or dribbling.
2. Adapt the practice activities and lead-up games provided in the following chapters to kicking or dribbling a ball:
   Chapter 18: "Soccer Activities"
   Chapter 20: "Flag or Touch Football Activities"
3. Play simple kicking games listed in chapter 16 (table 16.1, p. 321, and table 16.2, p. 333)

Striking with an Implement

When performing underarm striking with a racket or paddle, the player stands with feet comfortably apart, knees

a. Initial Pattern

b. Elementary Pattern

c. Mature Pattern

Figure 6.30 Developmental sequence for striking a ball with the foot (kicking).

Figure 6.31 Dribbling with the feet.

TABLE 6.7 Developmental Assessment of Kicking Pattern

	Good	Fair	Needs Work

Preparation Phase
1. Kicker takes at least two preliminary steps
2. Arms move in opposition to legs
3. Kicker steps into the kicking action
4. Nonkicking foot is placed to the side of the ball, pointing toward the target direction, and is slightly bent
5. Kicking leg is extended backward with knee slightly bent and foot near buttocks
6. Left arm (right-footed kick) raised and pointing in target direction
7. Trunk leans slightly backward

Kicking Action
1. Ankle and knee extend forward as kicking leg swings toward the ball
2. Left arm (right-footed kick) continues to extend forward in direction of the kick
3. Right arm (right-footed kick) extends backward
4. Trunk bends forward at hip during ball contact
5. Foot makes contact with the ball on tops of toes (toes down) and instep, slightly under the center of the ball

Follow-Through
1. Leg extends along the line of the intended flight
2. Support leg extends so kicker is on sole of foot or might even leave the ground momentarily

Figure 6.32   Striking a lightweight object with an implement (underhand).

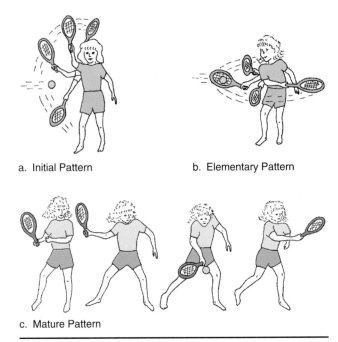

a. Initial Pattern   b. Elementary Pattern

c. Mature Pattern

Figure 6.33   Developmental sequence for striking a ball with a racket (sidearm).

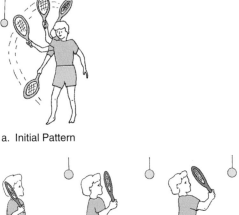

a. Initial Pattern

b. Elementary Pattern

c. Mature Pattern

Figure 6.34   Developmental sequence for striking a ball with a racket (overarm).

slightly bent, and elbow flexed and away from the body. Young children begin with lightweight objects such as balloons or sponge balls (figure 6.32). The striking action for these objects involves light elbow and wrist movements. The developmental sequences for acquiring the movement patterns to strike a ball sidearm and overarm are illustrated in figures 6.33 and 6.34, respectively. A developmental assessment checklist for striking a ball with a racket sidearm is provided in table 6.8 and a checklist for overarm is given in table 6.9. As a teaching progression, it is easier for children to hit a stationary object rather than one that is moving. Suspending the object to be hit (e.g., ball or shuttlecock) on a string provides an easier target. Adjustment of string length provides the correct practice height for different children and for practicing underarm, sidearm, and overarm striking.

When striking a ball with a bat, the right-handed player stands with feet parallel, about shoulder-width apart. His left side faces the pitcher. He grips the bat comfortably, shifting it to the back of his head about shoulder high. His arms, bent at the elbows, are held away from his body. As the ball leaves the pitcher's hand, the batter shifts his weight to his rear foot, then swings the bat forward as he shifts his weight to his front foot. He keeps a firm grip on the bat as the ball is hit. After the ball is hit (figure 6.35), the bat continues to swing around the left shoulder. As a

TABLE 6.8 Developmental Assessment of Striking an Object with a Racket (Sidearm)

	Good	Fair	Needs Work

Initial Level
1. Body faces the target
2. Arms only are swung
3. Racket is held with a tight grip
4. Racket is swung in a vertical plane with a chopping action
5. No foot action is involved in the movement
6. No trunk action is involved in the movement

Elementary Level
1. Body faces the target
2. Arms only are swung
3. Racket is swung in a horizontal plane
4. No foot action is involved in the movement
5. Limited trunk rotation

Mature Level
1. Left side of body turned toward object to be hit (right-handed striker)
2. Legs apart, stepping with left leg into the striking action
3. Racket held with a "shake hands" grip
4. Right wrist extended back in "cocked" position
5. Right elbow lags behind during the striking action
6. Trunk turns with the arm striking action, to produce added power
7. On contact, right wrist is snapped forward
8. Right arm continues to follow through in the direction of the flight path

TABLE 6.9 Developmental Assessment of Striking an Object with a Racket (Overarm)

	Good	Fair	Needs Work

Initial Level
1. No movement of trunk
2. Elbow stays bent at approximately 90 degrees throughout swing
3. Arm and racket swing together
4. Hand grip is tight in a power grip
5. Contact with object (ball) is low on the racket head
6. Body position faces front

Elementary Level
1. Minimal trunk rotation
2. Nonstriking side of body turned slightly toward target
3. Slight backswing, but elbow remains bent at approximately 90 degrees
4. Elbow leads racket on forward swing
5. Striking wrist is extended slightly during forward swing and straightens on racket contact with the object (ball)
6. Contact with object (ball) is in the middle of racket head
7. Elbow is extended on contact but does not fully straighten on follow-through

Mature Level
1. Nonstriking side of body is turned toward target
2. Trunk rotates to frontal position during arm swing
3. Hand grip is a "shake hands" grip
4. Long backswing, and then racket lags behind the arm during the forward swing
5. Striking wrist is extended back in cocked position during forward swing
6. Contact with object (ball) is high on the racket head
7. Striking wrist is snapped forward during object (ball) contact
8. Arm is fully extended during follow-through in an upward extension and direction

Figure 6.35 Batting.

starting progression, either suspend a ball on a string or place a ball on a cone or batting tee. Again, care should be taken to adjust the height of the batting tee, size of cone, or length of string to ensure that the ball is at the correct height for the size of child attempting the strike.

Applying Mechanical Principles The mechanical principles listed under "Striking with the Hand" apply to "Striking with an Implement."

Applying Movement Concepts and Skills Adapt the movement ideas listed under "Striking with the Hand."

Things to Stress
1. Keep your eye on the ball.
2. Start with feet spread apart and knees slightly flexed.
3. Maintain a firm grip through the forward swing and follow-through.

Striking Activities
1. Adapt striking activities listed under "Striking with the Hand" to striking with an implement.
2. Play simple striking games listed in chapter 16 (table 16.1, p. 321, and table 16.2, p. 333)
3. Adapt the practice activities and lead-up games provided in the following chapters to batting an object.
   Chapter 19: "Hockey Activities"
   Chapter 23: "Softball Activities"

In the primary grades, the fundamental skills of throwing, catching, and striking should be facilitated through an informal exploratory approach, with the teacher providing direct instruction where needed. Emphasis should be on exploring different ways of performing each manipulative skill. Gradually, teachers should stress throwing, kicking, or hitting a ball for distance or speed. Accuracy should be of secondary concern during initial learning. The game activities provided in chapters 16 and 17 stress an informal and enjoyable environment for acquiring these fundamental manipulative skills. Equally stressed in each of these chapters is the generous application of exploratory teaching methods and techniques.

SPECIALIZED SKILLS AND MOVEMENTS

Specialized skills are the more complex skills and movements unique to individual and team sports, folk dance, and gymnastic activities. These specialized skills and movements require a high level of speed and accuracy (procedural knowledge). In addition, each sport requires a knowledge of rules and an understanding of complex offensive and defensive playing strategies (declarative knowledge). Hence, proficiency in each sport requires extensive practice to develop specialized skills and knowledge. Whenever possible, the specialized skills and movements should be learned through realistic practice activities and lead-up games, as well as by playing the game or mini-game according to its rules and regulations. Chapters 18 through 24 include descriptions of specialized skills, ideas by which to assess them, and a suggested sequence for acquiring these skills through a variety of appropriate activities. Although the emphasis within each of these chapters is on acquiring and refining skills and improving playing ability, there is also a discussion of exploratory methods and modified games to cope with individual differences in the levels of ability, needs, and interests of upper elementary school children. Videotape No. 1 (see appendix A) provides practical examples and guidance in teaching both fundamental and specialized sports skills.

The basic skills of traditional gymnastic activities are classified as balance, vaulting, climbing, and agility skills. These skills are organized within each category according to their difficulty. Chapter 25 ("Stunts, Tumbling, and Movement Skills") includes stunts and tumbling skills appropriate for developmental levels I to III and describes how the movement concepts and skills of body awareness, space awareness, qualities, and relationships can be integrated with the more traditional approach to teaching fundamental and specialized gymnastic skills. Chapters 26 and 27 follow a similar pattern, combining the traditional and movement education approaches to teaching specialized gymnastic skills and concepts with small equipment and large apparatus. Videotape No. 2 (see appendix A) provides practical examples and guidance in teaching both fundamental and specialized gymnastic skills through traditional and Movement Education approaches.

The specialized skills and movement patterns required in folk and square dance activities are quite different from those involved in gymnastics and individual or team sports. In folk dances, an increased complexity of skill is required in such steps as the waltz or polka. Perhaps more important, however, is the complexity of the dance, style, and finesse of each dancer or group of performers. Because of this, the scope and sequence of the dances provided in chapter 29 are simple guidelines. Teachers should view the suggested level for each dance activity as a very rough guideline and select dance activities according to the class's background in dance and the children's level of interest in folk and square dance activities. Videotape No. 3 (see appendix A) provides practical examples and guidance for teaching the specialized skills and movement patterns involved in folk dance.

Creative dance activities do not involve specialized skills, nor does this form of activity adhere to a scope and sequence of skill development. The suggested ideas in chapter 30 provide a basis for teaching this type of activity to children in primary and intermediate grades. Videotape No. 4 (see appendix A) provides practical examples and guidance in teaching creative dance activities.

Summary Review

It is essential that young children develop fundamental motor skills during their elementary years. Because there are sensitive times during development, children need to develop during their early years the mature movement patterns associated with fundamental motor skills. It is more difficult to change these fundamental movement patterns in adulthood. These fundamental skills form the foundation for more complex skills. Without this foundation, success in many sport, gymnastic, and dance activities will be unlikely. Children should be exposed to a whole variety of game, dance, and gymnastic activities to ensure optimum development of fundamental motor patterns.

INDIVIDUAL *and* **GROUP** PROJECTS

1. Photograph or videotape children performing a standing long jump, catching a ball, and throwing a ball. Using the developmental assessment checklists, identify the children's levels of motor skill development.
2. After completing project I above, select a child who has an immature movement pattern in one or more of the fundamental motor skills tested, and design a series of movement experiences to aid the child in his or her development toward the mature movement patterns.
3. Choose two locomotor, nonlocomotor, and manipulative skills (six in total) and debate how knowledge of mechanical principles can be applied to help teach each of these fundamental motor skills.
4. Discuss, in groups, what distinguishes walking from running, hopping from jumping, skipping from sliding, and sidearm striking from overhead striking.

Selected Readings

Corbin, C. R. 1980. *A textbook of motor development.* 2d ed. Dubuque, IA: Wm. C. Brown.

Gabbard, C. 1996. *Lifelong motor development.* Dubuque, IA: Brown & Benchmark.

Gallahue, D. L. 1989. *Understanding motor development: Infants, children, adolescents.* 2d ed. Indianapolis: Benchmark.

Graham, G. S., S. A. Holt-Hale, and M. Parker. 1993. *Children moving.* 3d ed. Mountain View, CA: Mayfield.

Hammett, C. T. 1992. *Movement activities for early childhood.* Champaign, IL: Human Kinetics.

Haywood, K. M. 1993. *Life span motor development.* Champaign, IL: Human Kinetics.

Keogh, J., and D. Sugden. 1985. *Motor skill development.* New York: Macmillan.

Pica, R. 1991. *Early elementary children moving and learning.* Champaign, IL: Human Kinetics.

Roberton, M. A., and L. E. Halverson. 1984. *Developing children— Their changing movement.* Philadelphia: Lea & Febiger.

Wickstrom, R. L. 1983. *Fundamental movement patterns.* Philadelphia: Lea & Febiger.

Health, Wellness, and Active Living

One of the main themes featured throughout this text is the health-related benefits associated with active living. In addition to lowering the risk of chronic diseases, physical activity is also known to benefit many other physical, social, psychological, emotional, and cognitive areas. Hence, physical activity plays a key role in maintaining a healthy lifestyle and contributes to human wellness. **PART 3** of this text is designed to provide teachers with a basic understanding of the human body and to establish the contribution physical education makes to human wellness. Chapter 7 provides background information related to wellness and the structure and function of the skeletal, muscular, and cardiovascular systems. Chapter 8 explains how to assess and improve health-related physical fitness.

Chapter 7
Learning about the Human Body and Wellness

Chapter 8
Assessing and Improving Physical Fitness

CHAPTER 7

Learning about the Human Body and Wellness

KEY CONCEPTS

7.1 *Wellness* refers to the achievement of the highest level of health possible in each of several key areas

7.2 Although heart attacks usually occur in adulthood, the cause is often the lifestyle established much earlier in life

7.3 Lifestyle factors that are basically under the control of the individual account for the majority of health problems suffered by people today

7.4 Health promotion seeks to maintain or improve behaviors, attitudes, and values related to the development of a healthy lifestyle

7.5 Regular exercise of weight-bearing joints, maintenance of muscular strength and flexibility, and an adequate supply of calcium and minerals through a nutritionally balanced diet is the key to maintaining healthy bones

7.6 The primary category of physical activity known to improve cardiovascular fitness is aerobic exercise

7.7 A physically active lifestyle is the key to improved cardiovascular health

7.8 Optimum physical fitness and a healthy lifestyle cannot be achieved without a nutritionally balanced diet

7.9 Two vital components of human wellness are effective stress management and the avoidance of substance abuse

KEY OBJECTIVES

After completing this chapter you will be able to:

1. Identify the health and wellness benefits associated with quality programs of physical education
2. Identify and understand the skeletal and muscular systems of the human body
3. Identify and understand the cardiorespiratory system of the human body
4. Measure human heart rate and understand what factors affect heart rate
5. Understand what constitutes a nutritional diet
6. Identify the four major food groups and know minimum daily servings for elementary school children
7. Identify the meaning of a balanced diet and know how to plan for a balanced diet
8. Identify the basic causes of stress in society and suggest ways in which physical education can help reduce levels of stress
9. Identify the types and effects of substance abuse that occur in society and suggest means of helping children develop a positive lifestyle that is free of illicit drugs and substances that are detrimental to human health and wellness
10. Identify the dangers of exposure to sunlight and suggest ways to monitor and control exposure to sunlight

n 1980, the Public Health Service of the U.S. Department of Health and Human Resources established a set of health objectives for the nation. The objectives included health protection (seat belt legislation, fluoridation, etc.), preventive health (immunization, disease control, etc.), and health promotion (physical fitness, nutrition, etc.). Many of the goals set under health protection have been met. For example, numerous states now have effective laws relating to wearing seat belts and pollution control. However, the goals associated with health promotion and health prevention have proven more difficult to attain. In 1990 the Public Health Service released a new document entitled *Healthy People 2000: National Health Promotion and Disease Prevention Objectives.* This document outlines a national strategy for significantly improving the health of the nation. The aim is to realize a number of specific health objectives by the year 2000. More than three hundred objectives have been identified, under three major headings: health promotion, health protection, and preventive services. Although all three categories are important, health promotion is particularly important—for, as Williams (1993) notes, unless personal health promotional practices occur, health protection and preventive services will not succeed. The health promotion category focuses on eight major areas, five of which are most relevant to school physical education programs: physical fitness and exercise, nutrition, mental health, smoking and health, and misuse of alcohol and drugs. Health promotion practices are seen as involving lifestyle factors that are basically under the control of the individual.

To meet the objectives of health promotion, our profession has developed the concept of human wellness to include fitness, nutrition, stress management, and the avoidance of all forms of substance abuse. Human wellness, however, is not simply the absence of disease; it is viewed as a positive healthy lifestyle. The human wellness concept requires every individual to be responsible for setting their own lifestyle goals in a self-directed manner. This means embarking on a lifelong program of reaching and maintaining optimum levels of health and fitness, good nutrition, effective stress management, and an avoidance of tobacco and substance abuse.

The physical education program can play an effective role in laying the foundation for each child to develop her or his own healthy lifestyle. If we preach to children, we will accomplish little in terms of developing long-term health-related goals. However, if we can provide programs that allow children to discover how their bodies work and how to develop their own fitness programs, there is a reasonable chance they will want to continue the programs indefinitely. Toward this goal, the material in this chapter should be used to help children understand how the human body works. Knowledge and concepts about bones, muscles, nutrition, stress management, smoking and health, and substance abuse can be taught in a variety of ways. At times, there are "teachable moments" when facts about how a muscle works or about ways to control stress can be covered individually. At other times it is appropriate to meet with the children for a few minutes at the end of a physical education lesson to discuss the link between these health-related topics and a child's active lifestyle. The next chapter, "Assessing and Improving Physical Fitness," will provide additional knowledge about levels of fitness and individualized ways to use this information to maintain an optimum level of fitness throughout life.

HEALTH AND WELLNESS

The term *health* has evolved over time. Initially, it referred to the absence of disease or infirmity. However, the term was expanded in the 1940s, when the World Health Organization (1947) defined health as the state of complete physical, mental, and social well-being. This definition remained prominent into the 1960s, until critics argued that health is not a "state" of well-being but an ever-changing dimension of life. It was also argued that emotional, spiritual, and environmental health contribute to quality of life. The term *health* was seen to include many different components and aspects of human life. Eventually, the term *wellness* was introduced; wellness is seen as the achievement of the highest level of health in several key areas (see table 7.1). Today, the terms *health* and *wellness* are often used interchangeably

to mean the dynamic, ever-changing process involved in achieving the highest level of health in a variety of key areas.

C O N C E P T

7.1 Wellness *Refers to the Achievement of the Highest Level of Health Possible in Each of Several Key Areas*

Health Treatment

North Americans suffer from a variety of chronic diseases that require health treatment. However, the most common health problem is cardiovascular disease. Cardiovascular diseases (CVDs) are the leading cause of death in the United States today and account for more than 42 percent of all deaths. This is almost three times the number of deaths

TABLE 7.1 Six Key Dimensions of Health

1. Physical health
2. Social health
3. Mental health
4. Emotional health
5. Environmental health
6. Spiritual health

caused by cancer and more than the total number of deaths caused by all other diseases combined (Donatelle and Davis 1996). The statistics are similar for Canada, where approximately 40 percent of adult deaths are related to cardiovascular diseases. In the United States, every 34 seconds a person dies of CVD, accounting for approximately 1 million deaths per year. In addition, many people suffer from CVD problems; of the current U.S. population of about 255 million people, 60 million people suffer from the effects of CVD. Family members and relatives suffer pain, anxiety, fear, disruptions in work and home life, and in general a diminished quality of life. The American Heart Association (1995a) has estimated that if all forms of major CVD were eliminated, total life expectancy would rise by nearly ten years. By comparison, if all forms of cancer were eliminated, the gain would be three years (American Cancer Society 1995). In addition to life expectancy, the quality of life for a vast number of people would be improved. Although it is neither possible nor morally correct to place a monetary value on human life, the cost of health care related to CVD in the United States was estimated by the American Heart Association (1995b) to be in excess of $137 billion per year. The cost of CVD in terms of both human suffering and monetary cost to society makes prevention of CVD a high priority. Educating children early in life is a major step toward CVD prevention.

CONCEPT

7.2 ***Although Heart Attacks Usually Occur in Adulthood, the Cause Is Often the Lifestyle Established Much Earlier in Life***

Health Prevention

CVD is only one of many chronic diseases that are preventable. The American Medical Association has suggested that 90 percent of the health problems in the United States are, to a high degree, preventable (Williams 1993). The AMA stresses personal health decisions as the key to preventing disease and suggests that simple lifestyle changes could prevent as many as nine major chronic diseases (coronary heart disease, stroke, diabetes, chronic obstructive pulmonary disease, lung cancer, breast cancer, cervical cancer, colorectal cancer, and chronic liver disease). Prescribed changes include eating a healthier diet, reducing body fat, controlling high blood pressure, stopping smoking, moderating alcoholic consumption, becoming physically active, and using available screening techniques for early detection of cancer. Such practices would contribute to disease prevention.

CONCEPT

7.3 ***Lifestyle Factors That Are Basically under the Control of the Individual Account for the Majority of Health Problems Suffered by People Today***

Health Promotion

Health promotion seeks to maintain or improve behaviors, attitudes, and values related to the development of a healthy lifestyle. Physical education has a major role to play in health promotion. Providing children with a quality program of physical education will help them develop the necessary behaviors, attitudes, and values that contribute to the development and maintenance of active lifestyles. An active lifestyle does not guarantee protection against all chronic diseases and health problems, but it may delay the onset of such diseases or reduce the severity of disabling symptoms, thus enabling children to have a high quality of life throughout their entire life spans. Health promotion, especially in the form of active living, is vital if the appalling statistics cited earlier are to be changed.

CONCEPT

7.4 ***Health Promotion Seeks to Maintain or Improve Behaviors, Attitudes, and Values Related to the Development of a Healthy Lifestyle***

THE HUMAN BODY AND WELLNESS

To obtain optimum functioning and optimal health, it is imperative that children understand how the human body functions and how to look after it. A brief description of the skeletal, muscular, and cardiovascular systems is presented here to provide a basic understanding of body function. Sections on nutrition, stress management, substance abuse, and exposure to sunlight offer guidance on looking after the human body.

Skeletal System

The human skeleton consists of 208 bones that work together with the muscles and connective tissues to move the body, to support it, and to protect the internal organs (figure 7.1). Bones are divided into two broad groups, known as axial and appendicular bones. *Axial bones* consist of the skull, spine, and ribs and provide the basic structure to which the *appendicular bones,* the bones of the arms and legs, are attached.

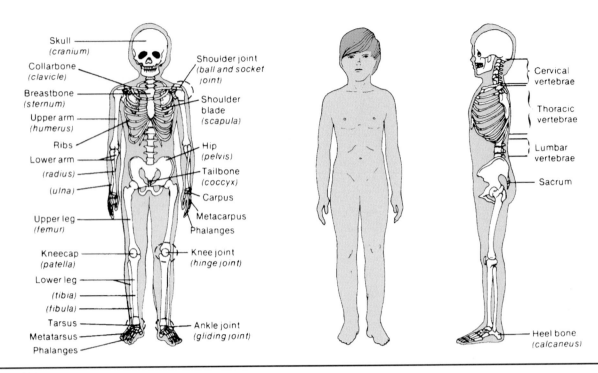

Figure 7.1   The human skeleton.

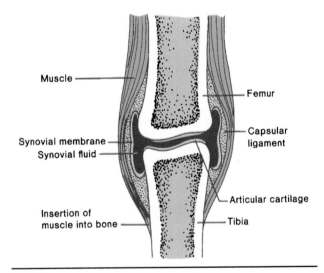

Figure 7.2   Bones forming the knee joint.

A joint is a meeting point between bones. For example, the knee joint (figure 7.2) is a hinge joint that allows the leg to flex and extend. The shoulder and hip joints are ball-and-socket joints, which allow rotary movements in several directions. The ankle and thumb joints are saddle joints, which permit movement in two directions but without rotation.

The ends of the bones forming a joint, such as the knee joint, are covered with a smooth protective layer of cartilage that acts like a shock absorber between the bone surfaces. The space between the bones in a joint is filled with a lubricating fluid known as synovial fluid. This fluid works like the oil in an engine; it reduces friction between the moving parts. These joints have strong, nonelastic stabilizing ligaments that bind the joint together.

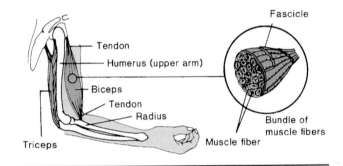

Figure 7.3   Muscle fibers enclosed by the fascicle.

Muscular System

The muscular system of the human body represents about 35 to 45 percent of the total body weight. It consists of 650 muscles that are grouped in three categories according to their structure and function. Involuntary, or smooth, muscles (about 30) form the muscle portion of the internal organs and function automatically, rather than under the direct control of the brain. The cardiac, or heart, muscle performs its unique function under the involuntary control of the brain. The voluntary, or skeletal, muscles (about 620) are attached to the bones and are directly controlled by the brain. Both types of muscles, however, operate in the same general way by contracting and relaxing their muscle fibers.

In physical education, we are concerned mainly with the skeletal muscles, although all muscles are indirectly affected through movement. A skeletal muscle is composed of bundles of muscle fibers enclosed in a sheath of fibrous tissue called the fascicle (figure 7.3). At the end of the mus-

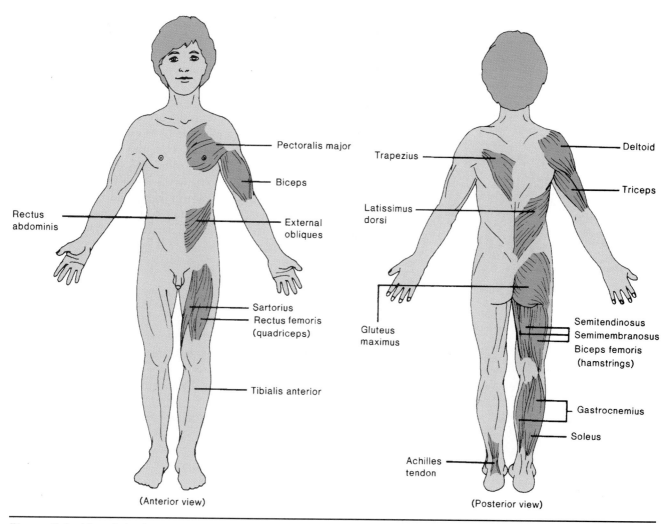

Pectoralis major

Biceps

Rectus abdominis

External obliques

Sartorius
Rectus femoris (quadriceps)

Tibialis anterior

(Anterior view)

Trapezius

Latissimus dorsi

Gluteus maximus

Deltoid

Triceps

Semitendinosus
Semimembranosus
Biceps femoris (hamstrings)

Gastrocnemius

Soleus

Achilles tendon

(Posterior view)

Figure 7.4 Main skeletal muscles.

cle is a noncontracting fibrous tissue called a tendon. The tendon normally is attached to a bone or ligament. When a nerve impulse is received by a muscle, the fibers contract, causing the muscle to become shorter and thicker. As illustrated in figure 7.3, when the arm is flexed, the biceps become shorter and thicker. Since muscle fibers can only contract, the antagonist (or opposing) tricep muscles relax as the biceps flex. When the arm is extended, the triceps contract and the biceps relax. Figure 7.4 will help you locate the main skeletal muscles. The muscles of the anterior view and posterior view are arranged in pairs. As one (hamstrings) contracts, the antagonist (quadriceps) gradually relaxes to give a smooth and controlled movement. Throughout any movement, however, the antagonist muscle never completely relaxes. The feeling of firmness of a relaxed antagonist muscle is known as muscle tone. When muscle groups, such as the hamstrings and quadriceps or abdominal and lower back muscles, are exercised vigorously and routinely, they show firm muscle tone and good posture.

C O N C E P T

7.5 *Regular Exercise of Weight-Bearing Joints, Maintenance of Muscular Strength and Flexibility, and an Adequate Supply of Calcium and Minerals through a Nutritionally Balanced Diet Is the Key to Maintaining Healthy Bones*

Cardiorespiratory System

The cardiorespiratory system is primarily made up of the heart, arteries and veins, and lungs (figure 7.5). Blood carrying oxygen and other nutrients leaves the heart through the aorta, which branches into smaller vessels called arteries. Arteries keep branching and getting smaller until they reach every part of the body. The ends of the smallest arteries branch out into a tiny network of vessels called capillaries. Capillary walls are so thin that oxygen and nutrients pass through to the surrounding tissue cells, while carbon dioxide and other waste products move into the capillaries.

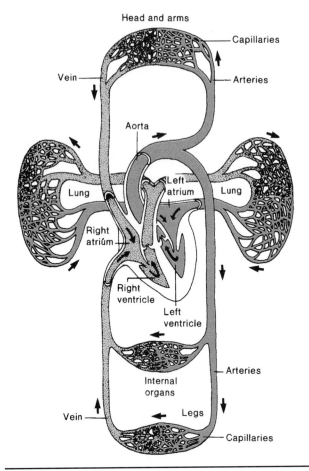

Figure 7.5 Blood flow through the body.

The capillaries then join small veins, becoming bigger until they reach the upper right chamber of the heart. Blood moves down into the lower chamber (right ventricle) and is pumped through the pulmonary artery into the lungs. In the lungs, carbon dioxide is released through the capillary wall into the lung cavity's air sac (figure 7.6). At the same moment as this is occurring, oxygen is being moved from the air sac to the capillary to be transported by the blood to the upper left chamber (left atrium) of the heart. During exhalation, the carbon dioxide is moved out of the lungs, through the bronchioles, to the larger bronchi, and finally out through the trachea (windpipe). The oxygen-rich blood that has been transported to the heart is pumped out from the lower left chamber (left ventricle) of the heart through the large aorta to begin the cycle again.

Respiration Rate

Respiration, a chemical process that occurs in every living cell of the body, involves the absorption of oxygen, the release of energy, and the elimination of carbon dioxide. The exchange of these gases in the lungs is the breathing part of respiration. Breathing in is caused by the contraction of the muscular diaphragm, moving it downward (figure 7.7a), and the contraction of the rib muscles, pulling them upward and outward. After the lungs expand and fill with air, the diaphragm and rib muscles relax, allowing the diaphragm to move upward and the ribs to move closer together (figure 7.7b), thus forcing air out of the lungs.

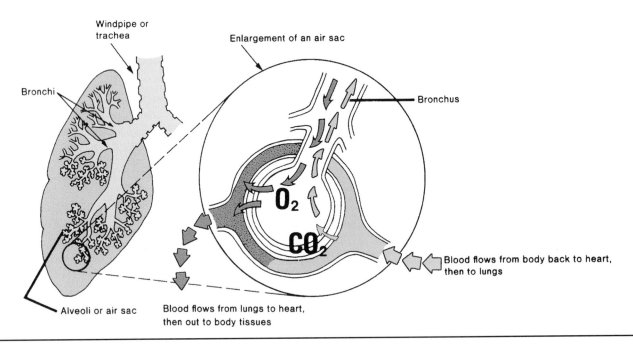

Figure 7.6 Circulation of blood through the lungs.

A normal breathing cycle occurs about twelve to sixteen times per minute. However, during vigorous exercise, the demand for oxygen increases in the body tissues, particularly in the muscle cells. In an individual who is in good physical condition, the increased breathing rate increases the supply of oxygen to the muscle cells. When oxygen is supplied to the muscle cells and body tissues during a steady state of breathing, the energy that is produced with sufficient oxygen supply is termed aerobic. Thus *aerobic exercise* is activity when the cardiorespiratory system is able to meet the demands of the body's muscles and tissues with an adequate supply of oxygen. When exercise is too strenuous, the muscle cells cannot get enough oxygen from the lungs and they begin to produce energy without oxygen; such *anaerobic exercise* can last for a few minutes. During anaerobic exercise, the cells build up an oxygen debt that must be paid back during the recovery or rest period.

C O N C E P T

7.6 *The Primary Category of Physical Activity Known to Improve Cardiovascular Fitness Is Aerobic Exercise*

Pumping Action of the Heart

The pumping action, or cycle, of the heart is actually a series of very rapid contractions, like squeezes, beginning in the upper chambers and moving in a wavelike action down through the lower chambers (figure 7.8). The cycle includes the following three steps.

> *Step 1:* The heart relaxes. While the heart is relaxed, the valves between the upper and lower chambers are open so blood flows into the upper chamber and down into the lower chamber.
>
> *Step 2:* The upper chambers contract, forcing more blood into the lower chambers.
>
> *Step 3:* The thick-walled ventricles contract, causing the valves between the upper and lower chambers to close and the valve in the aorta and pulmonary artery to open, allowing the blood to flow to the lungs and then to the rest of the body. (The heart relaxes again to begin the next cycle.)

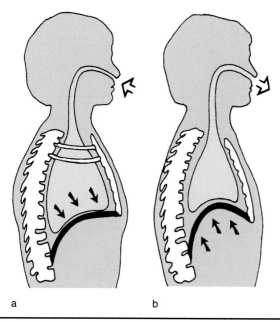

Figure 7.7 Expansion and contraction of the diaphragm during breathing.

a   b

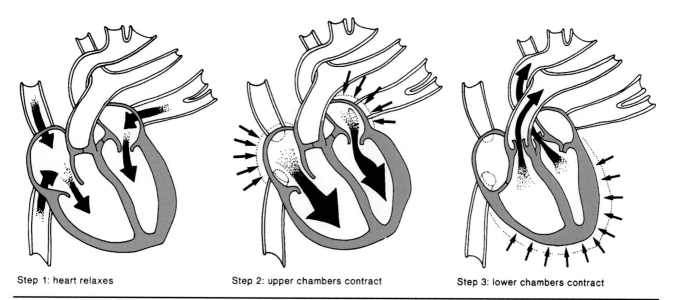

Step 1: heart relaxes   Step 2: upper chambers contract   Step 3: lower chambers contract

Figure 7.8 Pumping cycle of the heart.

CHAPTER 7

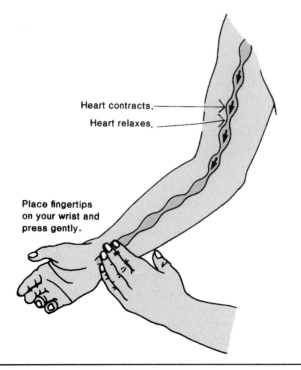

Heart contracts.
Heart relaxes.

Place fingertips
on your wrist and
press gently.

Figure 7.9   Measuring heart rate.

How to Measure Heart Rate

First: Resting heart rate is the number of heartbeats per
minute while the person is in a quiet resting state.
The best time to take this measure is just before
getting out of bed in the morning. In a school
situation, have the children take their heart rate in
class before going to their physical education class.
If this procedure is not possible, have the children
take their heart rate after they are sitting down and
before they begin to participate in physical activity.

Second: Show children how to place their fingertips
gently on the artery on the wrist near the base of the
thumb (figure 7.9).

Third: Tell the class they will count their heart rate for
ten seconds. You will say "Ready," wait a second or
two, then say "Count." At the tenth second, say
"Stop" and "Record your score."

Fourth: Each child records the number of heartbeats.
Then tell them to multiply their number by six to
give them their heart rate for one minute.

Fifth: Arrange the children in pairs and have them take
each other's heart rate. This is to check how accurate
the students were in taking their own heart rates.

Resting and Maximum Heart Rate

The best method of determining whether cardiorespiratory
endurance is being improved is by monitoring the person's
heart rate before and after exercise. Maximum heart rate,
obtained during very strenuous exercise, would reach about

TABLE 7.2   Cardiorespiratory
Endurance

Heart Rate

220	**Maximum Heart Rate**
200	
190	
180	**Target heart rate zone** (This is between 70 and 85
170	percent of a child's maximum heart rate.)
160	
150	
140	
130	
120	
110	
100	
90	
80	**Resting Heart Rate Zone**
70	
60	

220 beats per minute (table 7.2). To improve their cardiorespiratory endurance, children must increase their
heart rate to about 160 to 190 beats per minute for about
ten to fifteen minutes per day. This training zone heart rate
is approximately 70 to 85 percent of an individual's maximum rate. It would be used, therefore, as a very general
guideline. Hence, children who have difficulty performing
an exercise, such as running or swimming, for a short period of time should adjust their training zone downward to
130 beats per minute or less. The training zone can be
increased to higher levels as the individual gradually
improves his or her cardiorespiratory endurance.

How Heart Rate Is Affected

The following cardiovascular activities can be used to illustrate how the heart and circulatory system are affected by a
variety of physical and psychological activities.

Experiment 1: Comparative Heart Rates   Have children measure each other's heart rates. Group the results
according to age and gender. Compare the heart rates of
various children in the class, and compare children's with
teachers' heart rates. Make further comparisons with parents, grandparents, high school athletes, and so on.

Experiment 2: Heart Rate Recovery   The children
record their resting heart rate, then run in place for three
minutes. Immediately after running, they take their pulse and
record it in the appropriate column (see table 7.3). Retake
and record heart rates after resting two, four, and six minutes. Use test results to discuss individual students' recovery
rates and how their cardiovascular fitness can be improved.

TABLE 7.3 Heart Rate Recovery

Activity	Rate 15 secs	Rate 1 min
Resting heart rate		× 4 =
Immediately after running on the spot, as fast as possible, for 3 minutes		× 4 =
After 2 minutes		× 4 =
After 4 minutes		× 4 =
After 6 minutes		× 4 =

TABLE 7.4 Effects of Different Activities

Physical Activity	Resting Rate	Activity Rate	Difference
Resting heart rate	_____	....	....
3 minutes tic-tac-toe	....	_____	_____
Rest and record	_____	....	....
3 minutes playing catch	....	_____	_____
Rest and record	_____	....	....
3 minutes of rope skipping (or run in place)	....	_____	_____
Rest and record	_____	....	....

Experiment 3: Effects of Different Activities Divide the class into partners. Partners rotate to each of the three activities listed in table 7.4. Partners cannot start any activity, however, until their heart rates have resumed the resting heart rate. Repeat the experiment at a later date, but change the three activities.

Experiment 4: Excitement and Fear Divide the class into partners. One partner repeats the rhyme "Peter Piper . . ." twelve times as fast as possible while the other partner attempts to distract her in a funny manner (makes faces, counts out loud, maybe tickles). Heart rate is measured before and after. Use this experiment to discuss the effects of stress and excitement on cardiovascular fitness (table 7.5). Also, design similar experiments involving stressful situations.

TABLE 7.5 Excitement and Fear

Resting heart rate (take for 15 secs × 4) =	
Heart rate after repeating rhyme (take for 15 secs × 4) =	

Repeat the following rhyme 12 times:
   "Peter Piper picked a peck of pickled peppers. How many
   pecks of pickled peppers did Peter Piper pick?"

C O N C E P T

7.7 *A Physically Active Lifestyle Is the Key to Improved Cardiovascular Health*

NUTRITION AND WELLNESS

Human wellness, defined in terms of health-related components, must include a concern for the type and amount of food we eat. A well-planned and properly executed exercise program for young children can fail simply because the children lack the basic nutrients or sufficient calories, or because they are overweight or obese. These factors, along with high-pressure advertising tactics and questionable diet programs, make it imperative that children understand what constitutes a nutritionally sound diet. The following sections explain what foods must be included in a balanced diet and how to maintain proper weight, and they list a few suggested activities for helping children build and maintain a nutritionally balanced diet.

Balanced Diet

The human body uses more than fifty nutrients to keep its life processes operating effectively and efficiently. These essential nutrients are found in the six general food classes listed in table 7.6. They provide the necessary foods for building and repairing body tissues, supplying energy for daily life activities, and regulating body processes.

The task for parents and teachers is to translate knowledge of the nutritional value of various food classes into a balanced daily diet for each child within their care. The U.S. Department of Agriculture designed the food guide pyramid to help people of different ages and lifestyles plan nutritionally balanced diets (figure 7.10). The key to this simple grouping of foods is recognizing that all foods except fats, oils, and sweets have a high nutritional value. Thus, a balanced diet includes food from all levels of the pyramid. Our task is to teach children to understand the food groups and to consciously select at least the minimum number of servings from each food group each day of their lives. The notes on the right side of the pyramid describe the types of foods and their basic functions.

Weight Control

Diet planning based on the food guide pyramid helps every person, regardless of age, receive the essential nutrients. However, the amount of food consumed within each of these groups should depend upon age, body structure, metabolism, and daily activities. In addition, the amount and type of food consumed by each member of the family is strongly influenced by the family's cultural and ethnic back-

ground. For example, in our multicultural society, children from Hispanic and Asian families eat balanced diets but might not appear to follow the typical selection of food from the food groups. Similarly, strict vegetarians combine rice, grains, and legumes to create the required proteins and select other nutrients to complete a balanced diet that is free of meats, eggs, and milk products.

If we take all of the above factors into account, and the child's weight is within the recommended range for his age and height, the caloric intake is correct. On the other hand, if a child gains excessive weight, he is consuming more calories than he needs. Consequently, his body is converting the excessive food into fat. Taking off excessive body fat and maintaining the proper weight for one's age and lifestyle require a reduction in daily calorie intake and an increased participation in a regular exercise program. One without the other is not an effective and long-term weight control program. Reducing the amount of food one eats to the point where the body draws on its own stored fat is the first effective part of a weight reduction program.

The daily servings in table 7.7 illustrate how a child who needs to lose body fat would choose foods from the food guide pyramid. It is important to note that table 7.7 can be used by individuals with strong ethnic eating habits or vegetarians in planning their own balanced diets. Further information on serving sizes, snacking, nutrients, and food choices for good health can be found in *Physical Best and Nutrition,* an AAHPERD (1996) guide to nutrition education.

When the dietary program is combined with a regular and systematic exercise program, more body fat is used and muscle tone is improved to prevent flabbiness as weight is

TABLE 7.6	Essential Nutrients of a Balanced Diet

Food Class	Function
Protein	Builds and repairs body tissues and provides energy
Carbohydrates	Supply energy and fiber for digestion and elimination
Fats	Supply energy
Minerals (21 essential minerals including calcium, iron, phosphorus, and sodium)	Build and repair body tissues and regulate essential processes
Vitamins (including A, B-complex, C, D, E, and K)	Regulate body processes
Water	Builds and repairs body tissues and regulates essential processes

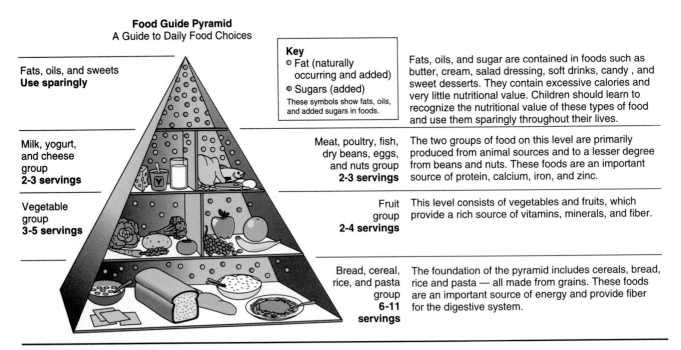

Food Guide Pyramid
A Guide to Daily Food Choices

Key
○ Fat (naturally occurring and added)
◎ Sugars (added)
These symbols show fats, oils, and added sugars in foods.

Fats, oils, and sweets
Use sparingly

Milk, yogurt, and cheese group
2-3 servings

Vegetable group
3-5 servings

Meat, poultry, fish, dry beans, eggs, and nuts group
2-3 servings

Fruit group
2-4 servings

Bread, cereal, rice, and pasta group
6-11 servings

Fats, oils, and sugar are contained in foods such as butter, cream, salad dressing, soft drinks, candy , and sweet desserts. They contain excessive calories and very little nutritional value. Children should learn to recognize the nutritional value of these types of food and use them sparingly throughout their lives.

The two groups of food on this level are primarily produced from animal sources and to a lesser degree from beans and nuts. These foods are an important source of protein, calcium, iron, and zinc.

This level consists of vegetables and fruits, which provide a rich source of vitamins, minerals, and fiber.

The foundation of the pyramid includes cereals, bread, rice and pasta — all made from grains. These foods are an important source of energy and provide fiber for the digestive system.

Figure 7.10   Food guide pyramid.

TABLE 7.7 Minimum Daily Servings for Elementary School Children

Food Group	Number of Servings	Sample Serving Size
Meat, nuts	2	2 ounces of lean meat 2 ounces of beans
Milk	3	1 cup of skim milk 1 cup nonfat yogurt
Bread and cereal	6	1/2 cup cooked pasta 1 slice whole wheat bread
Fruit and vegetables	4	1 orange 2 ounces carrots

lost. The end result is a lower percentage of body fat and a general improvement in all body systems.

Teaching Suggestions

Experts in the field of nutrition have clearly indicated that optimum physical fitness and a positive lifestyle cannot be achieved without a balanced diet. However, what a child eats might depend on the nutritional style of her parents or friends or the availability and cost of food. We have also learned that preaching to children about what and how much they should eat is usually unproductive. Instead, a proven effective approach for leading children toward a positive nutritional lifestyle is the implementation of activities that allow children to investigate and relate nutritional information to their own immediate needs and lifestyles. The following activities and suggestions will help children understand what constitutes a balanced diet and how to maintain proper weight control throughout their lives.

Bulletin Board

The bulletin board can be used to display children's growth charts, energy demands of various physical activities, or comparative nutritional values of various foods.

Measuring Body Fat

Measure each child's body fat with skinfold calipers. This test is included in the AAHPERD Physical Best test (AAHPERD 1993), along with norms for elementary school children. Inexpensive skinfold calipers can be purchased through several companies listed in appendix C.

Basic Four Food Groups

Use a chart similar to the one shown in table 7.7 and have children make displays, workbooks, or catalogs with pictures of foods from magazines and newspapers.

Daily Food Intake

Use a "Minimum Number of Daily Servings Chart" to have children keep daily records of their food consumption. For older students, include an analysis of their caloric intake and their consumption of junk foods.

Weight Control Programs

Develop a weight control program for all children in the class. Record each child's height and weight. Design daily food and exercise diaries to allow them to see how many calories were used, stored, or needed to meet their daily life activities. This type of activity can lead to effective weight-reducing programs and provide information to parents and health officials concerning children who may need medical attention. Note: The children's diaries can be included in their portfolios (see chapter 11) to provide information on individual growth and development.

Special Diets and Food Fallacies

There are numerous questions to raise about food fads, diet pills, and food fallacies. The following questions might provoke interesting class discussions or lead to more extensive individual or group projects:

1. What are three popular fad diets?
2. Should we take vitamin and mineral supplements?
3. Do vegetarians eat a balanced diet?
4. Do fast-food restaurants serve nutritionally valuable foods?
5. Are there special diets for athletes?
6. What happens to the body if we fast for more than three days?

Many outstanding nutrition books and related audiovisual materials suitable for primary and intermediate children are listed in the selected readings at the end of this chapter.

CONCEPT

7.8 *Optimum Physical Fitness and a Healthy Lifestyle Cannot Be Achieved without a Nutritionally Balanced Diet*

STRESS MANAGEMENT

The rapid social-economic changes in our society have affected children, youths, and adults, regardless of whether they live in cities or rural areas. Problems related to family breakups, poor interpersonal relations, and school grades are a few of the problems that are currently causing serious stress and anxiety for elementary school children.

Stress is the body's response to any demand made on it, an attempt to maintain a state of equilibrium (Corbin and Lindsey 1994). A person who is under stress might have a variety of physiological responses, depending on the problem that is causing the tension or anxiety and the individual's ability to cope with the situation. In most instances, a stressful situation increases the heart rate, blood pressure, and muscle tension. These responses are the body's natural preparations for an activity that might require an extra effort. As soon as the special response has been met, the stress response fades and the body returns to its normal state. If the stress response remains for prolonged periods of time, it leads to serious health problems such as high blood pressure and severe depression.

The term *stress management* denotes methods for reducing high levels of stress. The following guidelines will help teachers understand and cope with children who may be suffering from excessive tension.

1. Develop a learning environment in which children feel comfortable in your presence and have a sense of trust in you and your judgment.
2. Watch for major changes in each student's general behavior. If you observe serious problems, such as excessive aggressive behavior or withdrawal, attempt to find out the cause.
3. Teach children to recognize and cope with stressful situations. This involves learning about coping with learning tasks, interpersonal relations, and their own strengths and weaknesses.
4. Provide effective ways to help children cope with stress. This includes teaching children proper breathing techniques, methods of relaxation, and tension-relief techniques through wholesome physical activities.

SUBSTANCE ABUSE

The term *substance abuse* refers to the use and effects of alcohol, tobacco, and illegal drugs. According to one article (Kraus 1988), substance abuse is one of the three most popular forms of adult leisure in the United States. In fact, Americans consume 60 percent of the world's illicit mind-altering substances. Although consumption of these substances is predominantly in the adult and older teen populations, there are dangerous signs that a growing number of elementary school children have experimented with or become users of these substances. Parents, educators, and other leaders in our society look to the schools to help educate children about the effects of these substances on health. Although teaching about substance abuse is normally done through health or science courses, there are

special "teaching moments" when the adverse effects of alcohol, tobacco, and illicit drugs can be covered effectively in a physical education class. With this in mind, the following key points should be emphasized.

1. The use of alcohol and tobacco prevents performers from reaching their greatest potential.
2. Virtually all drugs possess a high potential for addiction. Initially these drugs are taken because they produce a sense of well-being. However, their continued use leads to dependency and increased levels of stress.
3. Choosing a lifestyle that involves a dedication to keeping fit and adhering to positive health habits contributes to a productive and happy life.

C O N C E P T

7.9 Two Vital Components of Human Wellness Are Effective Stress Management and the Avoidance of Substance Abuse

EXPOSURE TO EXCESSIVE SUNLIGHT

Many local weather reports now include an ultraviolet index indicating the intensity of the sun's rays. If the index is high on days when children will be outdoors for prolonged periods (sport days, school camping trips, etc.), they should be encouraged to wear protective clothing, such as hats and long-sleeve shirts, or use sunscreen lotions.

Summary Review

Human wellness is the ongoing dynamic process of being healthy in a variety of key areas or dimensions. Quality programs of physical education contribute to wellness by promoting fitness, a nutritionally balanced diet, stress management, and the avoidance of all forms of substance abuse. The health promotion practices fostered through physical education are lifestyle practices that are basically under the control of the individual. Children need to develop the healthy lifestyle practices of active living (procedural knowledge). To do this effectively, they will need to acquire the declarative knowledge associated with health and wellness. Hence, they need to learn how the human body functions and to understand what is required to attain the highest levels of human wellness.

INDIVIDUAL *and* **GROUP** PROJECTS

1. In small groups, identify the health and wellness benefits associated with a quality program of physical education. Share and compare findings with other groups.
2. In pairs, take turns pointing to various bones in the body while the partner attempts to name each major bone. Repeat the procedure with one partner first naming the bone while the other partner attempts to identify its location in the body.
3. Repeat the procedures in activity 2 above, substituting major muscles for bones.
4. In pairs, measure resting heart rates. Perform the same physical activity together for 2 minutes (e.g., stepping up and down on a gymnastic bench) and again measure heart rates. Over the next 15 minutes, repeat measuring heart rates every 3 minutes. Draw a graph to plot the rise in heart rate from rest to exercise, and the recovery rate over 15 minutes. Share and compare the graphs to identify individual differences in heart rates and recovery rates. Discuss possible reasons for individual differences.
5. Each student makes a detailed list of food consumed over the past 24 hours. Based on the four food groups, identify whether the food consumed provided a nutritionally balanced diet.

SELECTED READINGS

AAHPERD. 1986. *Physical activity and well-being.* Reston, VA: AAHPERD.

————. 1993. *Physical Best instructor's guide.* Reston, VA: AAHPERD.

————. 1996. *Physical Best and nutrition: An AAHPERD guide to nutrition education.* Reston, VA: AAHPERD.

American Cancer Society. 1995. *Cancer facts and figures—1994.* Atlanta: American Cancer Society.

American Heart Association. 1995a. *Heart and stroke facts 1995.* Dallas: American Heart Association.

American Heart Association. 1995b. *Heart and stroke facts: 1995 statistical supplement.* Dallas: American Heart Association.

Bailey, C. 1984. *The fit or fat target diet.* Boston: Houghton Mifflin.

Corbin, C. B., and R. Lindsey. 1994. *Concepts of physical fitness with laboratories.* 8th ed. Dubuque, IA: Brown & Benchmark.

Donatelle, R. J., and L. G. Davis. 1996. *Access to health.* 4th ed. Boston: Allyn & Bacon.

Greensberg, J. S., and H. S. D. Telljohann. 1992. *Your personal stress profile.* Dubuque, IA: Wm. C. Brown.

Healthy people 2000: National health promotion and disease prevention objectives. 1990. Washington, DC: DHHS, Public Health Service.

Kraus, R. G. 1988. Changing Views of Tomorrow's Leisure. JOPERD (August).

Kuntzleman, C. T. 1990a. *Fitness discovery activities.* Reston, VA: AAHPERD.

————. 1990b. *Instructor's guide for feeling good.* Reston, VA: AAHPERD.

Maione, J. 1989. *Kids weigh to fitness.* Reston, VA: AAHPERD.

McGlynn, G. 1990. *Dynamics of fitness: A practical approach.* Dubuque, IA: Wm. C. Brown.

McIntosh, M. 1990. *Lifetime aerobics.* Dubuque, IA: Wm. C. Brown.

Mullen, K. D., R. J. McDermott, R. S. Gold, and P. A. Belcastro. 1996. *Connections for health.* 4th ed. Dubuque, IA: Brown & Benchmark.

Williams, M. 1993. *Lifetime fitness and wellness.* 2d ed. Dubuque, IA: Brown & Benchmark.

World Health Organization. 1947. Constitution of the World Health Organization. *Chronicles of the World Health Organization,* Geneva, Switzerland: WHO.

Assessing and Improving Physical Fitness

KEY CONCEPTS

8.1 To understand physical fitness, it is necessary to understand the basic health-related components of physical fitness

8.2 Health-related components of physical fitness include muscular strength, muscular endurance, cardiorespiratory endurance, flexibility, and body composition

8.3 *Aerobic endurance* refers to performing movement activities at moderate to high intensity levels over an extended period of time

8.4 Body composition is the relative percentage of body fat compared to other body tissues (bone, muscle, internal organs, etc.)

8.5 Flexibility is the degree of ease and range of motion of the joints in the human body

8.6 Muscular strength and endurance is the amount of force that a muscle or group of muscles can exert and endure over an extended period of time

8.7 Following the three principles of exercise (overload, progression, and specificity) leads to improved physical fitness

8.8 A number of conditioning exercises are potentially harmful to the human body, particularly to muscles, tendons, and ligaments, and should be avoided

KEY OBJECTIVES

After completing this chapter you will be able to:

1. Understand the health benefits associated with physical fitness
2. Understand how health-related physical fitness is related to active living
3. Understand how the development of health-related physical fitness is the foundation of a quality program of elementary school physical education
4. Understand the basic components of physical fitness
5. Assess children's physical fitness
6. Understand how to improve children's physical fitness
7. Establish specialized and remedial programs for children with low levels of fitness
8. Help all children understand and improve their own physical fitness
9. Identify exercises and activities that are potentially harmful for elementary-school-aged children

As discussed in earlier chapters, it has been estimated that almost one-third of children today are overweight or obese. It has also been estimated that over 80 percent of these children are destined to become obese adults (Gabbard 1996). The proportion of children in the United States who are overweight has increased more than 50 percent over the past two decades. To compound the problem, substantial evidence indicates that children who are unfit and obese show early warning signs of coronary heart disease, high blood pressure, and high cholesterol levels (Binkhorst, Kemper, and Soris 1985; Williams et al. 1992). Hence, cardiovascular disease and obesity are the two primary medical concerns associated with children's health.

One of the leading causes of obesity and cardiovascular disease is a lack of physical activity, so children need to be active and fit. Unfortunately, according to the most recent National Children and Youth Fitness Study, the general level of health and fitness of elementary school children has not improved over the past several years. Further, there is evidence that levels of fitness and activity participation decline as children progress through their school years and into adulthood. Such a trend must be reversed; it is vital that children both achieve and maintain appropriate levels of health-related fitness. Since there is mounting evidence that diet and physical activity lifestyles are learned early in life, there is strong support for early intervention and prevention programs for young children—programs that focus on health-related aspects of physical fitness.

It is relatively easy to create positive dietary habits and exercise patterns during the first seven or eight years of life. As children move into puberty and beyond, it becomes increasingly more difficult to change their health habits and routines. Our challenge is to help children develop an active and positive lifestyle from kindergarten on, through each grade in the elementary school. Positive results are possible. Long-term reduction of body fatness in children has been achieved by educating children and their parents about body composition, physical activity, and diet (Epstein, Valoski, and McCurly 1990). Once children are personally convinced that exercise is important to their well-being, there is a good chance that physical activity will become a permanent part of their daily lives. It also appears that, once their lifestyles move in this direction, children will begin to modify their diet and other health factors to complement this positive and healthy way of living.

The first two sections of this chapter describe ways of assessing and improving the main components of health-related physical fitness. The next section provides information on how children in the primary and intermediate grades can improve their physical fitness and explains how test results are interpreted and used to help children improve their level of physical fitness.

PHYSICAL FITNESS

Since the original Kraus physical fitness survey in 1953, the physical education profession has attempted to define and assess the physical fitness of children, youths, and adults. Although the definition of physical fitness that accompanied each test battery stressed individuals' ability to function according to their own mental, emotional, social, and physical potential, virtually every state and national physical fitness test produced from 1957 to 1978 measured motor fitness components such as strength, muscular endurance, speed, and power. In 1980, with the Health Related Physical Fitness Test developed by AAH-PERD, a major change in the philosophy and direction of elementary and secondary school physical fitness programs was established. AAHPERD defines physical fitness as "a physical state of well-being that allows people to: perform daily activities with vigor, reduce their risk of health problems related to lack of exercise, and establish a fitness base for participation in a variety of physical activities" (AAHPERD 1988a).

Many elementary education teachers would agree with this definition and would say they contribute to one or more of these general areas of fitness in the classroom. There is general agreement in physical education that physical fitness is just one aspect of total fitness. However, the AAHPERD definition gives little guidance as to what aspects of fitness should be stressed in the physical education program. So we describe a physically fit child as one who possesses adequate strength and endurance to carry out daily activities without undue fatigue and still has energy to enjoy leisure activities and to meet emergencies. This definition, as it applies to each child, must be interpreted on the basis of genetic structure, which sets the optimum level of physical fitness the child is capable of reaching. One must also consider the child's nutritional status and other personal health habits that will determine the potential level of improvement the child is capable of reaching.

CONCEPT

8.1 To Understand Physical Fitness, It Is Necessary to Understand the Basic Health-Related Components of Physical Fitness

PHYSICAL FITNESS AND HEALTH

Research has indicated that a lack of physical activity contributes to heart disease in a cause-and-effect relationship, with sedentary individuals almost twice as likely to develop heart disease compared to the most active persons (Gabbard 1996). Research has also indicated a strong and consistent relationship between physical fitness levels and mortality due to all causes. That is, regardless of parent history, smoking, cholesterol level, cardiovascular disease, cancer, or diabetes, etc., when comparing least fit to most fit, the chance of early death has been shown to be almost five times greater for people with low fitness levels compared to individuals who have a high level of physical fitness.

It should be noted that the chance of early death can be reduced with moderate levels of physical activity. Unfortunately, current trends show a steady decline in exercise participation with age, and it has been reported that approximately 30 percent of adults live sedentary lives. The environmental pressure toward inactivity is fostered by the modern demand for "labor-saving" devices (electronic remote controls, motorized lawn mowers, etc.), coupled with the continuous trend toward sedentary computer and television viewing. Indeed, for the majority of people, work, education, and leisure activity are tied to sedentary computer interaction. The influence of the computer in school education is on an upward spiral, with the Internet playing an ever increasing role in children's lives. Given these environmental pressures, it is absolutely vital that children not only understand the health-related benefits of physical fitness, but also know how to maintain and improve their own physical fitness.

COMPONENTS OF PHYSICAL FITNESS

Although there are differing opinions about which basic components of physical fitness should be measured, the contemporary view is that a health-related test battery should measure muscular strength, muscular endurance, cardiorespiratory endurance, flexibility, and body composition. A low score on a test battery containing the majority of these health-related components would indicate that the child does not possess the strength and vitality to carry out everyday activities and respond to emergencies. It can also reveal not only a lack of exercise but a possible nutritional need or congenital or temporary illness that could be the cause of low physical fitness.

The following definitions of each component of health-related fitness are generally agreed upon by members of the physical education profession.

Muscular Strength

MUSCULAR STRENGTH is the amount of force that a muscle or group of muscles can exert.

The importance of developing and maintaining muscular strength cannot be overemphasized. Without sufficient muscular strength, the other components of physical fitness cannot be developed to their full potential.

Muscular Endurance

MUSCULAR ENDURANCE is the ability of the muscles to continue to function over a long period of time.

Muscular endurance is primarily dependent upon the strength and physiological condition of the muscle groups involved in the movement.

CONCEPT

8.2 Health-Related Components of Physical Fitness Include Muscular Strength, Muscular Endurance, Cardiorespiratory Endurance, Flexibility, and Body Composition

Cardiovascular Endurance

CARDIOVASCULAR ENDURANCE is the efficiency of the heart, blood vessels, and lungs while the individual is performing a continuous aerobic movement over a period of time.

Cardiovascular endurance is the combined ability of the circulatory and respiratory systems to supply oxygen and nutrients to the muscles, coupled with the ability of the muscles to utilize fuel.

Flexibility

FLEXIBILITY is the range and ease of movement of a joint.

The amount of flexibility depends upon the structure and nature of the joint(s) involved, the nature of the ligaments surrounding the joint, and the extensibility of the muscles connected to the joint. Although flexibility appears to be more a specific quality related to one or more joints in a particular movement, in elementary school programs it is considered to be a general quality. A child with a relatively high degree of flexibility can absorb an oncoming force or blow through a wider range of movement. Flexibility, or suppleness of movements, is also a prerequisite for performing many gymnastic and creative dance movements.

CHAPTER 8

Body Composition

***BODY COMPOSITION** is the relative percentage of fat compared to other tissues (bone, muscle, internal organs) of the body.*

While a certain amount of body fat is deemed essential for good health, extra body fat is not seen as conducive to health-related fitness. It is possible to obtain estimates of percent body fat through measurements taken with skinfold calipers. Mathematical equations are then used to calculate the ratio of body fat to lean tissue. However, charts are also available to indicate the accepted healthy standards of skinfold thickness, measured in millimeters and based on gender and age. Such charts also indicate the skinfold thickness associated with obesity. Two of the areas identified for skinfold measurement are triceps and calf. These areas can be measured easily and are highly correlated with total body fat (Cooper Institute for Aerobics Research 1994). When the two skinfold measurements (triceps and calf) are added together, the acceptable "healthy fitness zone" range for girls of all ages is 17 to 32 millimeters, and for boys of all ages it is 10 to 25 millimeters. Children who score higher than this should engage in physical activity and nutritional eating programs to reduce their body weight and bring their overall percent body fat to a more acceptable level. The optimal range for boys is 10 to 20 millimeters, and for girls it is 17 to 25 millimeters. Children who score very low (below 8 millimeters for boys and below 13 millimeters for girls) should be identified as being very lean. These children might be naturally lean, or they might have poor nutritional habits or be suffering from an eating disorder.

Another measure associated with body composition is body mass index (BMI). To calculate BMI, it is necessary to determine, in the metric system, measures of height and weight. The formula is this:

$$BMI = \frac{Body\ weight\ in\ kilograms}{(Height\ in\ meters)^2}$$

A BMI range of 20 to 25 is considered acceptable. However, the optimal range is 21.3 to 22.1 for females and 21.9 to 22.4 for males (Williams 1993). The American Dietetic Association classifies a BMI greater than 30 as obese. However, the BMI is not the recommended procedure for determining body composition, because it does not estimate the percent body fat. The BMI includes bone and muscle in its calculation, and so it merely provides an indication of the appropriateness of a child's weight relative to height. For those children found to be too heavy for their height, a skinfold test is recommended to determine if the weight is due to excess fat.

METHODS OF ASSESSING PHYSICAL FITNESS

As indicated earlier, although the emphasis today is on health-related items, most fitness tests in the past emphasized the assessment of skill-related items. These early fitness tests were often "norm-referenced" to allow teachers to compare children's performances with "expected" standards based on the "normal" population. Standards of excellence or substandard performance were often identified in terms of children falling above or below certain percentiles. The emphasis was on comparing one child's performance with that of other children. Criterion-referenced fitness tests also compare a child's performance to a set standard, but here the standard represents mastery or an acceptable level of fitness. There is no emphasis on comparing one child's performance with another child's performance. If the child reaches the mastery level (set standard), then the child is successful, regardless of other children's performances. However, care needs to be taken when using criterion-referenced testing. Some fitness tests provide awards for excellence, in the form of badges, for attaining certain criterion levels of performance. These extrinsic motivators spur many children on to achieve high levels of performance, but these same extrinsic motivators can also have a negative impact on those children who soon realize that they will never attain the high criterion standards. Such children soon lose interest because the set standard is clearly not developmentally appropriate for their level of development.

Today, criterion-referenced health standards form the basis of health-related physical fitness tests (Cooper Institute for Aerobics Research 1994). In an attempt to keep all children motivated, many of these new tests identify "minimum" health standards as the criteria that all children must strive toward. Instead of extrinsic motivators (e.g., badges), individual goal-setting techniques (see chapter 4) provide the intrinsic motivation to improve and/or maintain minimum levels of health-related fitness. Self-improvement, rather than improvement in order to outperform other children, becomes the focus of the fitness testing.

AAHPERD's Health-Related Physical Fitness Test

To reflect the move toward health-related components of physical fitness, AAHPERD designed and produced the health-related physical fitness test (AAHPERD 1988a). This test is known as the Physical Best test and is recommended for use in elementary and secondary schools. Since its inception, this fitness test has been adopted widely and used in many school settings. The general premise underlying health-related fitness tests such as the Physical Best test is that students who meet the health fitness standards of each test item possess sufficient cardiorespiratory fitness, endurance, strength, and suppleness to meet the demands of their daily activities. In 1993, AAPHERD entered into a partnership with the Cooper Institute for Aerobics Research and adopted their fitness test instrument, the FITNESSGRAM, as the physical fitness assessment component of the Physical Best test. One of the strengths of the FITNESSGRAM is its identification of "healthy fitness zones." Students are compared not to each other, but to these health fitness standards. This emphasis follows the Physical Best philosophy. AAHPERD now produces the educational material to supplement and support the Physical Best test, while the Cooper Institute provides the assessment instrument. Both the original Physical Best (1988b) test battery items and the FITNESSGRAM test items (Cooper Institute 1994) are discussed and presented here, since both sets of test items are currently in use. The AAHPERD (1988) health-related Physical Best test items are as follows:

Test No. 1: Aerobic Endurance: One-Mile Run/Walk

Purpose: To measure the ability to perform large muscle activity of moderate to high intensity over an extended period of time.

Testing area: A track or any other flat surface area. Mark off an appropriate area such as a 75 × 35 yard rectangle. This would require eight laps for a one-mile run/walk.

Equipment: Stopwatch.

Description: Students are instructed to move at their fastest pace around the one-mile course. They are permitted to run, walk, or perform combinations of both movements throughout the one-mile distance.

Scoring: Measured in minutes and seconds.

Optional tests: Any similar test item that lasts six minutes or longer and where acceptable national standards can be substituted for this one-mile run/walk test. Examples are a one-half-mile run/walk for primary children or a nine-minute run or walk for older children.

C O N C E P T

8.3 Aerobic Endurance *Refers to Performing Movement Activities at Moderate to High Intensity Levels over an Extended Period of Time*

Test No. 2: Body Composition: Triceps and Calf Skinfolds

Purpose: To measure the degree of body fatness.

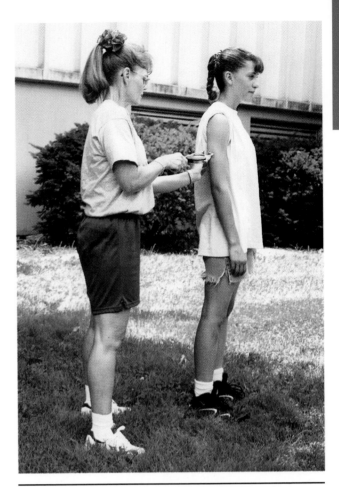

Figure 8.1   Skinfold test—triceps.

Testing area: This test should be conducted away from the main activity area of the class (in a locker room or behind a screen). No other students should be allowed to observe the child being measured.

Equipment: Skinfold calipers; low-cost plastic calipers are acceptable.

Description: The triceps skinfold is measured on the back of the arm, halfway between the elbow and the shoulder. As the student stands erect with the arm relaxed, grasp the skinfold vertically between your thumb and index finger and approximately 1/2 inch (12 mm) above the midpoint. While holding the skinfold, place the jaws of the caliper about 1/2 inch (12 mm) below the index finger (figure 8.1) and allow the caliper to exert its full tension for 2 seconds before taking a reading. The calf skinfold is measured on the inside of the right lower leg at the point of the greatest calf girth (figure 8.2). Follow the same procedure for the triceps skinfold.

Figure 8.3   Sit-and-reach.

Figure 8.2   Skinfold test—calf.

Scoring: Read the scale to the nearest 1.0 mm. Take three separate readings for each skinfold test and record the middle score for each site.
Optional test: Subscapular skinfold.

C O N C E P T

8.4 *Body Composition Is the Relative Percentage of Body Fat Compared to Other Body Tissues (Bone, Muscle, Internal Organs, etc.)*

Test No. 3: Flexibility: Sit-and-Reach

Purpose: To evaluate the flexibility (range of motion) of the lower back and hamstring muscles (figure 8.3).
Testing area: Any available regular instructional area.
Equipment: Sit-and-reach box or measuring stick substitute.
Description: Students are permitted to warm up by a slow stretching of the lower back and hamstring muscles prior to taking this test. The student sits with the knees fully extended, feet about shoulder-width apart, feet flat against the board, with one

hand on top of the other, palms down. In one steady movement, the student reaches forward, sliding the fingertips as far forward as possible and holding this position momentarily. Four trials are allowed, with the fourth trial held for at least one second.
Scoring: Each student is permitted four trials. The score is the most distant point reached on the fourth trial.
Optional tests: None.

C O N C E P T

8.5 *Flexibility Is the Degree of Ease and Range of Motion of the Joints in the Human Body*

Test No. 4: Muscular Strength and Endurance: Modified Sit-Ups

Purpose: To evaluate abdominal muscular strength and endurance.
Testing area: Mats or any other comfortable surface area.
Equipment: Mats and stopwatch.
Description: The performer lies on her back with knees bent, feet on the floor, and arms crossed and held against the chest, with hands on opposite shoulders and the chin tucked to the chest (figure 8.4). Her feet are held down on the floor throughout the exercise. Keeping the elbows against her chest, the performer raises up and touches her elbows to her thighs, then returns until her midback makes contact with the testing surface.
Scoring: Number of sit-ups in sixty seconds; students are permitted to rest between sit-ups.
Optional tests: None.

Figure 8.4   Modified sit-ups.

a   b

Figure 8.5   Pull-ups.

C O N C E P T

8.6 *Muscular Strength and Endurance Is the Amount of Force That a Muscle or Group of Muscles Can Exert and Endure over an Extended Period of Time*

Test No. 5: Upper Body Strength and Endurance: Pull-Ups

> *Purpose:* To measure arm and shoulder girdle strength and endurance.
>
> *Testing area:* A variety of testing areas suitable to mount or construct a horizontal bar.
>
> *Equipment:* Suitable pull-up bar, such as a bar across a doorway, hanging bar, or horizontal ladder.
>
> *Description:* The student assumes a hanging position with an overhand grip (palms facing forward). The feet should not touch the floor. The student raises her body up until her chin is over the bar, then returns to a complete hanging position (figure 8.5). The student may take as much time as she desires to complete as many pull-ups as she can.
>
> *Scoring:* Total number of correctly completed pull-ups.
>
> *Optional tests:* None.
>
> *Alternate test of upper body strength and endurance*

Note: This test is recommended for use with students who scored zero on the pull-up test. It is not an optional test; it is an adjunct to the pull-up test.

> *Equipment:* Modified pull-up apparatus (see appendix B for detailed plans for constructing this apparatus).
>
> *Description:* The student lies under the bar, back straight and grasping the bar with a forward grip (figure 8.6). The bar is set one to two inches above the student's outstretched arms. An elastic band is placed on a peg seven to eight inches below the bar. The student keeps his body straight and raises up until his chin rises above the elastic band, then returns to the starting position.

Figure 8.6   Modified pull-ups.

Scoring: Total number of correctly completed pull-ups; there is no time limit, but the action should be continuous.

The Prudential FITNESSGRAM: Physical Best (1993)

As stated above, since 1993 AAHPERD has endorsed the Prudential FITNESSGRAM as the assessment portion of the Physical Best test. This test was developed by the Cooper Institute for Aerobics Research and consists of a series of simple tests that are very similar in nature to the original AAHPERD (1988a) fitness test. The test items are designed to measure three health-related fitness areas: aerobic capacity; muscle strength, endurance, and flexibility; and body composition. The test items in the FITNESSGRAM are briefly described below.

Note: Where more than one test item is offered, teachers have the choice of selecting the item they prefer.

Aerobic Capacity

The one-mile run/walk test, similar to test no. 1 in the 1988 Physical Best test, is used to assess aerobic capacity. An alternative to the mile run is the PACER (Progressive Aerobic Cardiovascular Endurance Run), which consists of a 20-meter shuttle run that can be performed indoors. (This test item is often less daunting to children compared to a mile run!) The objective is to run back and forth across the 20-meter distance within a specified time. The test is progressive and starts out with a time that all children can successfully master. The time is then gradually decreased.

Body Composition

Body composition is assessed in the same manner as in test no. 2 in the original Physical Best test (1988), using skinfold calipers on the triceps and calf. The alternative test is calculation of body mass index (described earlier).

Flexibility

Flexibility is measured with the back-saver sit-and-reach. The back-saver sit-and-reach differs from the typical two-hand sit-and-reach, test no. 3 shown in figure 8.3, in that it is performed with one knee bent and raised while the other remains fully extended (see figure 8.7). The bent knee helps reduce possible strain on the lower back and is recommended over the two-hand sit-and-reach technique. Measurements are taken for both right and left legs fully extended.

Abdominal Strength

Abdominal strength is assessed through the curl-up test. This is similar to test no. 4, modified sit-ups, in the original Physical Best (1988) test, with some noted differences. In the curl-up test, performers lie on their backs, knees bent at a 140-degree angle, with the hands placed palms down on

Figure 8.7   Back-saver sit-and-reach

Figure 8.8   Curl-ups.

the mat next to the hips. The objective is to sit up and slide the hands along the mat (toward the feet) to a specified position (figure 8.8). Students perform these curl-ups to a cadence of one curl-up every three seconds.

Note: The feet remain unsupported compared to modified sit-ups (figure 8.4), reducing possible strain to the lower back.

Upper Body Strength

The test item for upper body strength is the push-up, which is also done to a cadence of one push-up every three seconds. A successful push-up is counted when the arms are bent to a 90-degree angle (figure 8.9). The push-up replaces the pull-up (test no. 5) in the original Physical Best test. However, one of the alternate FITNESSGRAM tests is the pull-up. Others are the flexed-arm hang and the modified pull-up.

Note: With children, the push-up provides more opportunities for success compared to the pull-up and the flexed-arm hang.

Figure 8.9   Push-ups: Arms bent to a 90-degree angle.

Figure 8.10   Trunk lift.

Trunk Extensor Strength and Flexibility

The trunk lift is used as the test item for this area of fitness. Performers lie flat on their stomachs with hands at their sides. The objective is to raise the head and upper body six to twelve inches off the floor using the muscles of the back. The raised position must be held until measurements are verified (figure 8.10).

Preferred Test Items

As noted already, the FITNESSGRAM test items are somewhat similar to the original Physical Best (1988) test items. Although the test items assess similar health-related components of physical fitness, the FITNESSGRAM back-saver sit-and-reach test (figure 8.7) and the curl-up test (figure 8.8) are recommended over the original (1988) test no. 3 (sit-and-reach) and test no. 4 (modified sit-ups), because they have a lower risk of injury.

FITNESSGRAM Computer Software

After children complete the FITNESSGRAM test items, their scores are entered into a computer, and the FITNESS-

GRAM software program generates a personalized, printed report for each participant. This diagnostic information can be used to help children establish realistic personal goals for health-related fitness and to motivate children toward an active lifestyle.

Motivating Children through Goal Setting

The FITNESSGRAM report provides healthy fitness zone standards for a variety of test items for girls and boys who are between five and eighteen years of age. Color-coded areas on the FITNESSGRAM report signify healthy fitness zones in the three major areas of health-related fitness—aerobic capacity; muscle strength, endurance, and flexibility; and body composition. Individual test scores are identified under the headings "Needs improvement," "Good," and "Better." Based on the child's individual test performance, the report makes several recommendations to improve or maintain performance (see figure 8.11). The emphasis is on physical activity rather than on achieving high levels of fitness performance. Whereas developing children's physical fitness is very important, it is the establishment of the habits of an active lifestyle that will produce a lifetime of health.

The most important factor in determining a child's fitness goals is to assess his or her initial level of physical fitness. If a child's level of fitness is very low, the child has an opportunity to make very large gains. However, children who meet the standard for their age can make only small gains, even with a daily rigorous exercise program. Hence, the FITNESSGRAM does not reward children for achieving a certain level of fitness performance, but instead, in conjunction with AAHPERD's Physical Best program, AAHPERD and the Cooper Institute for Aerobics Research (1995) have developed a recognition system called "You Stay Active." This recognition system identifies numerous events that a child can participate in and be recognized for. A child can be recognized for participating in regular physical activity or for achieving an individual fitness goal. One of the You Stay Active goal-setting contracts is illustrated in Table 8.1. Here the child identifies daily personal activity goals on a weekly basis. This personal contract is very similar in nature to the personal activity log (PAL) described in chapter 11. Also, the You Stay Active ideas to promote regular physical activity are similar to those expressed in the Canadian Active Living Challenge, a school and community resource produced through CAHPERD (1993) to promote active living among children and youth.

Class and School Overviews

In addition to creating individual reports on health-related fitness, the FITNESSGRAM software is also designed to produce a statistical overview of class or school results. For schools lacking computer access, a hand-scored version of the test, complete with an easy-to-use scoring guide, is available. However, class and school overviews are available

CHAPTER 8

The Prudential FITNESSGRAM®

COMMITTED TO HEALTH RELATED FITNESS

Developed by The Cooper Institute for Aerobics Research
Endorsed by The American Alliance for Health, Physical Education, Recreation and Dance

Jane Jogger
FITNESSGRAM Elem. Sch.
FITNESSGRAM Test District
Instructor: Bridgman
Grade: 06   *Period:* 04   *Age:* 12

Test Date	Height	Weight
MO - YR	FT - IN	LBS
09-96	4 - 06	98
09-97	4 - 08	100

AEROBIC CAPACITY
HEALTHY FITNESS ZONE

One Mile

Needs Improvement	Good		Better
***			
***			

12 : 00   9 : 00

VO_{2max} *Indicates ability to use oxygen. Expressed as ml of oxygen per kg body weight per minute. Healthy Fitness Zone = 35 + for girls & 42 + for boys.*

	Current	Past
min : sec	9 : 00	10 : 15
ml/kg/min	45	43

MUSCLE STRENGTH, ENDURANCE & FLEXIBILITY
HEALTHY FITNESS ZONE

The Curl-up (Abdominal)

Needs Improvement	Good	Better
******************************		
******************************		

18   32

# performed	
27	23

Push-up (Upper Body)

Needs Improvement	Good	Better
***************		
***************		

7   15

# performed	
5	5

Trunk Lift (Trunk Extension)

Needs Improvement	Good	Better
**		
**		

9   12

The test of flexibility is optional. If given, it is scored pass or fail and is performed on the right and left.
Test given: Back Saver Sit and Reach

inches	
12	12

Right	P
Left	F

BODY COMPOSITION
HEALTHY FITNESS ZONE

Percent Body Fat

Needs Improvement	Good	Better
*****************		
*****************		

32   17

% fat	
33	33

Jane, your aerobic capacity was very good. Try to maintain your fitness by doing 20 - 30 minutes of vigorous activity at least 3 or 4 times each week.

Improve your upper body strength by doing push-ups against the wall, push-ups, horizontal ladder and other climbing activities.

Improve your flexibility by doing slow stretches and holding the stretch 20-30 seconds.

To improve your body composition remember to do some aerobic activity each day and follow a balanced nutritional program eating more fruits and vegetables and fewer fats and sugars. Improvement on this item would most likely improve your scores on other test items.

To parent or guardian: *The Prudential FITNESSGRAM is a valuable tool in assessing a young person's fitness level. The area of the bar highlighted in yellow indicates the "healthy fitness zone." All children should strive to maintain levels of fitness within the "healthy fitness zone" or above. By maintaining a healthy fitness level for these areas of fitness your child may have a reduced risk for developing heart disease, obesity or low back pain. Some children may have personal interest that require higher levels of fitness (eg. athletes).*
Recommended activities for improving fitness are based on each individual's test performance. Ask your child to demonstrate each test item for you. Some teachers may stop the test when performance equals the upper limit of the "healthy fitness zone" rather than requiring a maximal effort.
Developing good exercise habits is important to maintaining lifelong health. You can help your son or daughter develop these habits by encouraging regular participation in physical activity.
© 1994 The Cooper Institute for Aerobics Research

FITNESSGRAM.

Sponsored by
The Prudential
Insurance Company
of America

Figure 8.11   FITNESSGRAM report.

TABLE 8.1   You Stay Active: Activity Goals Contract

	Activity I Plan to Do	Person Who Will Be Active With Me	I Did the Following Activity	I Was Unable to Do the Activity Because
Monday				
Tuesday				
Wednesday				
Thursday				
Friday				
Saturday				
Sunday				
Week of_____ Student's Initials_____ Parent's Initials_____				

only through the computer software. With the initial purchase of Prudential FITNESSGRAM report forms, schools receive a complimentary copy of the computer software. The FITNESSGRAM is appropriate for use with students in grades K through 12. For further details contact:

> The Prudential FITNESSGRAM
> 12330 Preston Road
> Dallas, TX 75230
> 1-800-635-7050

Computer Software and Physical Fitness

A number of software programs are available to track students' fitness and wellness. A software program similar to FITNESSGRAM is the wellness profile system FITNESS TRACKER by Espiritu and McAlister (1992), which is published by Brown & Benchmark. This program provides a written printout to show how each individual child is progressing along the path toward fitness and health. In addition to health-related fitness components, this program will store and track all school health-related data. Other computer software to monitor and track health-related fitness components is available through AAHPERD and other organizations. Table 8.2 provides a brief review of some of the physical fitness programs available on computer software.

Hundreds of computer software programs are produced each year, and skills are needed for selecting appropriate software. Teachers who are contemplating using computer software might wish to consult Harrison et al. (1996), which provides a comprehensive review of basic considerations when selecting software. They also discuss several uses of the computer as a physical education program aid.

Physical Best and Individuals with Disabilities

The philosophy behind the Physical Best fitness test is that the test is recommended for use by all populations, including those with disabilities. Instead of norms, the criterion level necessary for good health is stated for each test item. The emphasis is on the individual, with each student striving for a "physical best." This philosophy promotes the concepts of least restrictive environment and inclusion. A handbook has been produced by AAHPERD (1995) to assist teachers with inclusion in fitness programs. It contains alternative items for fitness testing to enable all participants to be included in fitness and education programs. A comprehensive list of fitness standards for students with various disabilities is also provided. Further ideas on adapting equipment and activities to enable all children to be included in fitness programs can be found in Claudine Sherrill's (1997) specialized text on adapted physical activity.

Physical Fitness Tests for Special Populations

In addition to the Physical Best, a number of other fitness tests have been developed to assess children with disabilities. For example, Winnick and Short (1985) developed a physical fitness test that can be administered to nonimpaired, sensory impaired, and orthopedically impaired students. Those with cerebral palsy or spinal neuromuscular conditions are included within this last category. Norms are provided for individuals with sensory, auditory, cerebral palsy, and spinal neuromuscular conditions. There are numerous tests available that have been designed or modified for the appropriate developmental level associated with specific disabilities. Reviews of these tests can be found in Sherrill 1997, Dunn and Fait 1989, and Gabbard, LeBlanc, and Lowy 1994.

METHODS OF IMPROVING PHYSICAL FITNESS

The first part of this section deals with three important principles of exercise that apply to every type of physical fitness activity. The next part discusses ways to help children understand and improve their physical fitness. This is followed by a discussion of exercises and activities appropriate for developmental levels I, II, and III, and includes a description of how game, dance, and gymnastic activities can be modified and integrated into regular physical education programs.

Principles of Exercise

The activities and special programs in this chapter are designed to improve the health-related components of physical fitness. Individuals who adhere to the following

TABLE 8.2   Physical Fitness Programs and Software Packages

Program Developer/ Sponsor	Grades	Test Items	Printouts	Norm- or Criterion-Referenced	Computers	Motivation Awards	Cost	Other/
Prudential FITNESSGRAM (1993) Cooper Institute for Aerobics Research, 12330 Preston Rd., Dallas, TX 75230 (214) 701-8001 The Prudential Insurance Company of America	K-12 and College	1-mile walk/run curl-ups pull-ups, flexed-arm hang, or push-ups sit-and-reach or shoulder stretch skinfold or BMI trunk extensor	Student report card with fitness profile Individualized exercise prescription Cumulative record of test results Statistics—student; class; school Award qualifiers Group summaries	Criterion-based	Apple IIe IBM Macintosh Non-computer version Electronic scanning capability Toll-free technical support Extensive documentation	Get Fit and Fit for Life Awards—complete activity program I'm Fit Award—meet criteria on 4/5 items or 5/6 items SMARTCHOICE Award—perform assessment and do activities at school, home, community	Manual and software free with order of 200 FIT-NESSGRAM cards, $22	Teaching Strategies book, $21.95
Chrysler Fund AAU Physical Fitness Program (1989) Poplar Building Bloomington, IN 47405 (812) 855-2059 Chrysler Corporation Fund	K-12	1/4–1-mile endurance run sit-ups pull-ups or flexed-arm hang sit-and-reach *Optional* (1 required) standing long jump isometric or modified push-up sprints isometric leg squat shuttle run	Individual fitness reports Group profiles Record keeping No prescriptive information	Criterion- and norm-referenced	Apple IBM Phone number for assistance	Outstanding Achievement Certificate—above 80th percentile for 4 + 1 optional items Attainment certificate 45th–80th percentiles for 4 + 1 optional items Participation certificate 0–45th percentiles	$15 0–599 certificates, $8 shipping	Instructional/ motivational video (rental or purchase) Instructors manual Activity card file *Test-Tips* newsletter Letter to parents (available in Spanish)
President's Council on Physical Fitness and Sports Fit America Fitness Management President's Challenge Poplars Research Center, 400 E. 7th St., Bloomington, IN 47405 (812) 855-8946 For program information— PCPFS 450 5th St., NW, Suite 7103 Washington, D.C. 20001	Ages 6–17	1-mile run/walk curl-ups pull-ups or flexed-arm hang V-sit or sit-and-reach shuttle run *Optional* 2-mile run/walk skinfolds standing broad jump	Individual student profiles—scores, percentiles Class composites Top 25 scores for any or all events No exercise prescription Must be ordered List of students about 85th percentile Statistics and data management with transfer to other programs	Presidential—norm-referenced National—criterion-referenced	Apple IBM Limited documentation Card reader Phone number for assistance	Presidential Physical Fitness Award—85th percentile on all 5 items National Physical Fitness Award—50th–84th percentile on all 5 items (test available for students with physical disabilities) State Champion Award—schools with highest percent of students above 85 percent Presidential Sports Award—recognizes participation in specific sport or activity	Disk and limited documentation $85	
Dino*Fit™ Software System. ARA/Human Factors 15312 Spencerville Court (301) 384-0800	Ages 6–18	Cognitive, affective, fitness test options	Individual profiles, class profiles Class average profile Class roster Awards list for Physical Best or Fit America	Both	IBM Apple Allows configuration to various fitness tests or customized testing Phone number		None	

Sources: Stroot, Sandra and Bumgartner, Shan. (1989, August). Fitness Assessment—Putting Computers to Work. *Journal of Physical Education, Recreation and Dance*, 44–49. Brochures from each organization listed above.

TABLE 8.3   Exercise Zones

Training Zone	Cardiorespiratory Endurance	Strength	Flexibility
Excessive zone	Runs 10-minute mile first day—feels sick after run and very tired and sore next day	20 curl-ups	Sit-and-reach to 30 cm
Target zone (60–85% of maximum effort)	Runs one mile each day and by end of fifth day runs mile in 10 minutes—feels good each day	10 curl-ups	Sit-and-reach to 13 cm
	Threshold Level		
Normal zone	Runs one mile in 12 minutes	7 curl-ups	No exercise
Inactivity zone	No activity beyond getting up, going to school, coming home, etc.	No exercise	No exercise

principles of exercise while they participate in vigorous physical activities will improve their cardiorespiratory endurance, strength, and flexibility. As children learn to understand and apply these important principles of exercise, they develop the foundation for continuous participation in physical activity.

Principle 1: Overload

The exercise activity should require an overload performance. The systems of the body constantly adapt to a daily routine. For example, if we are inactive, our muscles become smaller (atrophy) and lose strength; our breathing becomes less efficient because we do not force the expansion of the lungs, thus closing off areas of lung tissue where exchange of oxygen and carbon dioxide would otherwise take place. To become stronger or to improve cardiorespiratory efficiency, the performer must increase the intensity (how hard), duration (how long), or frequency (how often) of an activity in accordance with a target zone that sets optimum limits for each individual and for each component of physical fitness. For example, to improve cardiorespiratory endurance, the exercise should result in raising the heart rate to 70 to 85 percent of the maximum for a sustained period of time (see chapter 7). The maximum heart rate for elementary-age children is approximately 210 to 220 beats per minute. Hence, to improve their cardiorespiratory endurance, their heart rate should be raised to approximately 160 beats per minute during exercise. Table 8.3 illustrates the overload principle. Under the strength category, if a child performs seven curl-ups (intensity) in one minute (duration) each day (frequency) without causing any "overload" effort, she will not increase her strength. Her exercise is below the threshold level. If she begins to perform ten curl-ups each day, without undue strain, she is moving into the target zone and begins to improve her level of strength. If she were to shift immediately to twenty curl-ups each day, she would feel extremely sore and tired, having reached into the excessive zone. Between ten and twenty curl-ups is her optimum training limit. This limit is found by gradually increasing the number of repeti-

tions so there can be an overload performance without excessive soreness and fatigue. The principle of overload applies to all components of physical fitness.

Principle 2: Progression

Exercise or activity should provide for progression. This principle is closely associated with principle 1. Any planned exercise program must begin with what is comfortable for or within the tolerance level of the child. From there, the program should gradually overload the muscles to increase strength or the demands on the heart and lungs.

Principle 3: Specificity

The principle of specificity described in chapter 3 also applies to developing the components of physical fitness. Simply stated, to increase strength, exercises must be of a strength-building nature such as pull-ups or weight lifting. However, such exercises might be of little value for improving cardiovascular fitness or flexibility; therefore, other exercises must be included for these parts of the program. Specificity of exercise also applies to each part of the body. For example, curl-ups increase the strength of the abdominal muscles but have no effect on the strength of the arm and shoulder girdle muscles. The implication of this principle is to develop a balanced physical fitness program that will improve cardiorespiratory endurance, strength, and flexibility.

C O N C E P T

8.7 *Following the Three Principles of Exercise (Overload, Progression, and Specificity) Leads to Improved Physical Fitness*

Helping Children Understand and Improve Their Physical Fitness

The following example of a twelve-year-old girl will illustrate how to use Physical Best's FITNESSGRAM guidelines for setting goals to determine a reasonable target. Note that the FITNESSGRAM "healthy fitness zone" standards for twelve-year-old girls were identified earlier in figure 8.11.

In our sample case, twelve-year-old Olga Kalish is tested initially during the first week of school in September. Her score on the one-mile run/walk is 14 minutes. This is a fairly poor performance (the established healthy fitness zone is 9–12 minutes), indicating a need to improve her cardiorespiratory endurance. Olga needs to decrease her time by 2 to 5 minutes to be in the healthy fitness zone. At this point, other factors, such as how many physical education classes she has each week and whether she is encouraged by her parents and friends to participate in after-school physical activities, must be considered. Her diet, amount of sleep, and level of stress are also very important considerations when setting this anticipated level of improvement in physical fitness. The next item, skinfold, is 27 mm (the established standard is 17–32 mm), so she is not carrying excess fat for her age and gender. Similarly, her score of 11 inches on the sit-and-reach test (the minimum pass standard is 10 inches) and 10.5 inches on the trunk lift (the healthy fitness range is 9 to 12 inches) shows she has a good range of motion (flexibility); hence, she needs few extra stretching activities beyond what she is getting in her regular physical education classes. Her scores of 3 on the push-up test and 10 on the curl-up test clearly indicate a very low level of strength and endurance of the abdominal and arm and shoulder girdle regions (the established standards suggest minimums of 7 and 18, respectively). These low scores suggest a goal-setting figure of five to ten repetitions for curl-ups and one to two for push-ups.

Teachers should use the suggested increases provided as general guidelines only. To provide motivation while upper body strength is being developed, a modified push-up with knees touching the floor can be done, or a standing push-up against the wall can be used. The standing push-up is particularly useful because the degree of difficulty can be easily adjusted. As the child's upper body strength improves, the feet can be placed farther away from the wall to increase the degree of body lean or inclination, which in turn requires greater strength to complete the standing push-up.

Goal-setting techniques can be used to foster motivation and interest. For example, a "challenge contract" could be used (see AAHPERD's You Stay Active 1995 resource), or children could do goal-setting activities using a personal activity log (PAL) as described in chapter 11. As the child improves, new goals can be created to keep the child moving to higher levels of health-related physical fitness. Further ideas on fitness programming and how to change children's exercise habits can be found in the *FITNESSGRAM Test Administration Manual* (Cooper Institute 1994).

Exercises and Activities for Developmental Level I

The emphasis of early primary physical education programs should be on exploratory activities in games, dance, and gymnastics. This is a time when children have an opportunity to explore how their bodies work, how to perform a variety of activities, and how to act and react in small- and large-group settings. It is also a time when they form attitudes about themselves and toward physical activities. The following activities can effectively contribute to a child's level of fitness in an enjoyable and positive way. Suggestions are provided to show how to modify these activities to enhance one or more elements of health-related physical fitness.

Game Activities

Game activities, such as running, tag, and simple team games, have a minimal effect on improving strength and flexibility. These activities can, however, contribute to cardiorespiratory endurance if the following guidelines are followed.

1. Include rules or modifications that require all children to be moving.
2. Do not eliminate any player from the game.
3. Change the method of moving to enhance the strength and endurance of different parts of the body.

The following games are effective contributors to cardiorespiratory endurance; suggested modifications are included with each game description:

Simple Tag, p. 323
Automobiles, p. 323
Traffic Lights, p. 323
Dribble Tag, p. 326
Crab Soccer, p. 329

The creative games approach can be used to design games that enhance cardiorespiratory endurance. For example, posing challenges that require constant movement, moving on all fours, or piggybacking another player meet this goal.

Dance Activities

Dance activities are an enjoyable and integral part of the primary physical education program. With the exception of rhythmics and creative dance, dance activities are low contributors to cardiovascular endurance, strength, and flexibility. The rhythmic activities described in chapter 28 can be used to enhance cardiorespiratory endurance, whereas creative dance activities, described in chapter 30, can be used to increase flexibility and strength. The following suggestions illustrate how to use rhythmic activities to enhance physical fitness.

1. Stress rhythmic activities that involve long routines and require running, jumping, hopping, and sliding.
2. Stress rhythmic activities involving rope-skipping skills, as well as those that use the rope on the floor for a variety of rhythmic jumping routines.

Gymnastic Activities

Many of the gymnastic activities in the primary program can effectively contribute to strength, flexibility, and, at

TABLE 8.4 Activities for Health-Related Physical Fitness

	Muscular Strength		Muscular Endurance		Flexibility		Posture		Cardiovascular Fitness	
Area of Contribution	High	Low	High	Low	High	Low	High	Low	High	Low
Game Activities										
Relays	X		X			X	X			X
Tag games	X		X			X		X	X	
Simple team games	X		X			X		X	X	
Individual and team games	X		X			X		X	X	
Dance Activities										
Fundamental skills		X		X	X		X			X
Singing games		X		X		X		X		X
Folk dances		X		X		X	X			X
Creative rhythms		X		X	X		X			X
Rhythmics		X	X			X		X		X
Gymnastic Activities										
Conditioning exercises	X		X		X		X		X	
Vaulting box	X		X		X			X	X	
Balance beam		X		X	X		X			X
Rope skipping	X		X		X		X		X	
Horizontal bar	X		X		X		X		X	
Climbing rope	X		X		X		X		X	
Stunts and tumbling	X		X		X		X		X	
Swedish gym	X		X		X		X			X
Climbing cube	X		X		X		X			X
Overhead ladder	X		X		X		X			X
Agility apparatus	X		X		X		X			X

times, cardiorespiratory endurance. Activities that use the climbing ropes, overhead ladder, and outdoor climbing apparatus are very strong contributors to the strength and endurance of arm and shoulder muscles. Stunts, such as the Crab Walk, Forward Roll, and Wring the Dishrag, enhance a child's flexibility. When teachers use the Movement Education approach in the medium of gymnastics, they can design challenges to enhance one or more health-related components of physical fitness. For example, movement challenges that require the child to stretch in a variety of ways enhance range of motion of one or more joints. In a similar way, challenges that stress weight bearing and transfer of weight can be presented so that strength is required in one or more movements involved in the sequence.

Children in the early primary grades enjoy freedom of movement and opportunities to explore different ways of moving and performing game, dance, and gymnastic skills. The previous examples listed in this section illustrate how teachers can modify these activities to enhance physical fitness goals. The more structured activities provided in the next section can be used, at times, with some success with children in developmental level I. However, teachers should modify these activities to cope with the unique characteristics of children in the early primary grades.

Exercises and Activities for Developmental Levels II and III

Those who teach children eight years and older face the multiple tasks of providing vigorous physical activities, teaching a wide variety of motor skills, and providing experiences that foster intellectual and social development. No single activity can accomplish all these goals. Furthermore, no single activity can contribute to all of the basic components of health-related fitness described earlier. Table 8.4 shows how various activities contribute to these basic elements.

Let us assume we have tested a fifth-grade class in September and found results similar to those shown in table 8.5. This class needs activities that will increase the strength and endurance of the arm and shoulder girdle and the abdominal muscles. Both boys and girls tend to be overweight, as shown by the high percent body fat. During the first few months of the school year, pleasant weather and student interests indicate that an outdoor activity would be the most suitable choice. The teacher had decided to begin with a four-week unit on soccer activities, but table 8.4 indicates that soccer, as a team game, is a low contributor to strength. Recognizing this inherent weakness of soccer and

TABLE 8.5 Average Class Scores on FITNESSGRAM

Test Item	Component	Girls	Healthy Fitness[a] Zone	Boys	Healthy Fitness[a] Zone
Age		10		10	
One-mile run	Aerobic endurance	12.1	9.5–12.5 mins	11.1	9–11.5 mins
Skinfold (triceps and calf)	Body composition	33%[b]	12–32%	26%[b]	10–25%
Sit-and-reach (back-saver)	Flexibility	9 in.	9 in.	8 in.	8 in.
Curl-up	Abdominal strength and endurance	10[b]	12–26	11[b]	12–24
Push-up	Upper body strength and endurance	3[b]	7–15	6[b]	7–20

[a]*FITNESSGRAM Test Administration Manual.* 1994. Cooper Institute for Aerobics Research, 12330 Preston Road, Dallas, TX.
[b]Value is outside the healthy fitness zone

the need for activities involving strength, the teacher emphasizes pregame warm-up exercises that develop strength in the arm and shoulder girdle and abdominal and leg muscles. Because of the many overweight children, the teacher emphasizes diet and weight control during her health education program.

Other units of instruction involving game, dance, and gymnastic activities should be analyzed for their potential contribution to health-related fitness (table 8.4). Once the inherent limitations of each activity are known, supplemental activities can be included to meet the special needs of the individual child or the class. The following activities can be used to supplement regular game, dance, or gymnastic lessons or for special programs to enhance one or more components of health-related physical fitness.

Warm-Up Activities

Conditioning, or calisthenic, exercises have traditionally been used as a warm-up activity. The fundamental purposes of these exercises are to develop physical fitness and to prepare the body for the main activities of the lesson. Normally the warm-up begins with a moderate to vigorous activity, such as running around the gymnasium, rope skipping, or playing a simple tag game, followed by stretching exercises for flexibility, arm and shoulder girdle, trunk, and legs. The warm-up period usually lasts about three to five minutes, though this varies.

The following suggestions can make the conditioning exercises effective and enjoyable:

1. Demonstrate the exercise, then have the class perform it slowly so each child can learn the correct form and cadence.

2. Each exercise should be performed in a steady fashion rather than in quick or ballistic-like motions.

3. Instruct children not to hold their breath during an exercise, but to breathe normally.

4. Once the children know the exercise, let them do the repetitions at their own rates. This is particularly important for flexibility exercises, given the variation in children's body structures and potential ranges of movement.

5. Add variations to each exercise. For example, "trunk bending forward and backward" can be changed on each forward movement by such directions as "through the legs," "to the left side," or "with right foot in front."

6. Change the basic set of exercises on alternate days.

7. Perform exercises to a musical accompaniment. This becomes a "health hustle." Select music with a good 4/4 beat (see chapter 28) and adjust the tempo to the class's level of physical fitness.

The exercises described in the following pages are grouped in terms of exercises for flexibility (group 1), arm and shoulder girdle (group 2), trunk (group 3), and legs (group 4). References to other activities, such as gymnastic stunts and rhythmic skills, are provided within each group.

A typical warm-up activity begins with a general vigorous activity to increase the cardiorespiratory circulation, followed by one or two exercises from each group. The following sample routine illustrates how exercises are selected to complement the main emphasis of the lesson. Once the exercise is demonstrated by a teacher or class leader, the children should perform the exercise at their own speed for the designated period of time.

Lesson Emphasis

Routine No. 1: The general situation involves a fourth-grade class participating in a thirty-minute lesson. The main emphasis of the lesson is dribbling the ball with the right and left hand and passing it while on the move.

Performing the "same daily dozen" exercise routine for weeks or months leads to boredom and other class management problems. Hence, change the set of exercises every two weeks, allow children to substitute appropriate exercises from each category, or design a series of color-coded task cards containing a set of warm-up exercises that the children can select and perform according to their own levels of physical fitness.

P R A C T I C E   A C T I V I T I E S

Sample Routine: Game Lessons

Exercise Number	Name of Exercise	Group	Page	Time
	General vigorous activity–running		481	2 minutes
1	Walk and arm swing	1	170	30 seconds
2	Push-ups	2	173	30 seconds
3	Curl-ups	3	174	30 seconds
4	Alternate leg kneel	4	176	30 seconds
5	Knee to nose touch	3	176	30 seconds

General Vigorous Activities

The following general vigorous activities are used to increase cardiorespiratory circulation.

Running   Begin slowly then increase speed, exaggerate knee lift, and include other tasks such as "run with hands behind neck," "run with hands at sides." Add additional challenges, such as changes in direction and level, and substitute hopping, jumping, or other locomotor skills for running.

Rope Jumping   See page 555. Stress different steps performed in a stationary position, as well as while traveling around the gymnasium or outdoor play area.

Rhythmic Activities   See page 607. In order to have children begin a vigorous rhythmic warm-up, introduce rhythmic activities in a previous lesson. Once children understand how to develop sequences or routines, the teacher need only say, "Make up a routine that has a run, hop, change of direction," then play a tape with a bouncy tune and a fast tempo.

Vigorous Game Activities   Game or tag activities that require all children to keep moving are enjoyable and

acceptable vigorous warm-up activities. Following are some examples:

> Number game: On signal all children begin to run (or any other locomotor movement called by the teacher). As they are running, the teacher calls out a number, such as three—all must immediately form groups of threes. The game should move very quickly, to improve the children's cardiorespiratory endurance.

Simple Tag, p. 323
Traffic Lights, p. 323

Group 1 Exercises: Flexibility

Flexibility or stretching exercises are movements that slowly stretch the muscles to an extended position, which is then held for a few seconds before returning to the starting position. The purpose of these exercises is to prepare the muscles for more intensive and complex movements, to prevent injuries, and to increase the range of motion around the joints (figures 8.12 to 8.19).

Basic Guidelines for Stretching Exercises   The following guidelines should be adhered to when performing stretching exercises.

1. Participate in a general warm-up activity, such as running or rope jumping, before performing any stretching exercises.
2. Perform slow, static stretching rather than ballistic stretching (stretching with a vigorous force of momentum).
3. Learn to stretch muscles just beyond their normal length but not to the point of pain.
4. Begin stretching muscles in the small joints of the extremities, then progress toward the trunk.

Stunts Stressing Flexibility
Wring the Dishrag (arm and shoulder), p. 516
Back Roller (arm and shoulder), p. 505
Camel Walk (arm and shoulder), p. 515
Crab Walk (arm and shoulder), p. 517
Rabbit Jump (arm and shoulder), p. 518
Measuring Worm (upper and lower back and legs), p. 519
Circle Roll (upper and lower back and hamstrings), p. 519
Scale Stand (quadriceps and hamstrings), p. 530
Single-Leg Balance (quadriceps and hamstrings), p. 530
Rear Support (arm and shoulder and trunk), p. 531
Walking Down Wall (quadriceps and abdominals), p. 534
The Bridge (quadriceps and abdominals), p. 534
Back Touch (quadriceps and abdominals), p. 568
Thread the Needle (upper and lower back), p. 530
Twist Away (arm and shoulder girdle), p. 569

Figure 8.12 Walk and arm swing. Begin walking on the spot or around the instructional area. Swing arms forward and backward and gradually increase the height of the forward and backward swing.

Variations:

1. Walk and swing both arms over head.
2. Repeat (1) to top of swing then rotate one arm, then both arms, toward the right and left.
3. Walk forward and simulate a crawl-stroke swimming action of the arms. Repeat with backstroke action.
4. Walk, clasp hands overhead, then bend alternately toward the right, back, and left side.
5. Walk forward turning head and trunk to right and left sides.
6. Walk and alternately bend trunk toward right side, backward, then left side.
7. Walk with exaggerated high-knee rise. Add hands above head, stretched sideways, or held behind the head.
8. Walk with long stride movement.
9. Walk with extended right leg crossing in front of left, then extended left leg in front of right.
10. Slide toward the left side with a slow extended shift of the left leg followed by a slow follow-up movement of the right leg.

Figure 8.13 Shoulder pull. Extend right hand backward and upward and left hand behind head and downward to grasp hands, hold, pull gently, and release. Reverse hands and repeat movement.

Variation:

Grasp a skipping rope, hold with upper hand, and reach backward and upward with lower hand, hold, and release.

Figure 8.14 Arm and shoulder stretch. Extend arms behind back and grasp hands. Rotate elbows inward, then raise backward and upward.

Figure 8.15 Side trunk stretch. Begin in a cross-legged position, back straight, right arm extended overhead, and left arm reaching as far as possible toward the right. Reverse arms and repeat to opposite side.
Variation:
Repeat exercise from a kneeling or standing position.

Figure 8.16 Trunk twister. Start in a sitting position with right leg extended and left leg bent and crossed over the right leg. The left hand is resting on the floor, and the right arm is resting on the side of the left leg. Simultaneously push against the leg with the right arm and turn the trunk as far as possible toward the left side. Reverse positions and repeat exercise.

a

b

Figure 8.17 Lower back stretch. Begin in a back lying position with knees bent, legs and trunk extended upward, and

head and arms on the floor (*a*). Relax , hold legs behind the knees, and pull thighs to chest. (*b*). Hold for a few seconds

Figure 8.18   Hip and thigh stretch. Begin with back straight, right knee flexed, and left knee and toe resting on the floor. Keeping both hands resting on the right knee, press the hips forward and downward.

Figure 8.19   Back-saver hamstring stretch. Sit with one foot against the wall, one knee bent with foot close to buttocks. Clasp hands behind back and bend forward, keeping lower back as straight as possible. Allow the bent knee to move to the side to allow the trunk to move forward. Stretch and hold for a few seconds. Reverse the positions of the legs and repeat the exercise.

Group 2 Exercises: Arm and shoulder girdle muscles

The exercises in this group are designed to exercise the strength and endurance of the arm and shoulder girdle muscles. (See figures 8.20 to 8.24.)

Stunts Contributing to Arm and Shoulder Girdle Strength and Endurance

Wring the Dishrag (arm and shoulder girdle flexibility), p. 516

Figure 8.20   Arm rotators. Stand with feet together, back straight, and arms extended sideways, with palms facing forward. Rotate arms forward, upward, and backward in a circular movement. Gradually increase the size of the circle and change direction of arm movement after three or four rotations.

Variations:

1. Swing each arm in the opposite direction.
2. Begin with arms at sides. Alternately swing arms overhead and back to side position.
3. Bend forward and move arms in a breaststroke or crawl action.
4. Swing both arms to the same side or cross them in front.

Figure 8.21   Push-ups. Begin in a front-lying position, with hands approximately shoulder-width apart, fingers pointing forward, and chin a few inches off the floor. Extend arms, keeping the back of the legs straight.

Variations:

1. Rest weight on knees and perform knee push-ups.
2. Instead of lowering the body straight down, lower it to one side.
3. Move hands close together, then farther apart.
4. Repeat original exercise with one leg off the floor.

Figure 8.22   Pull-ups. One partner assumes a back-lying position, with arms up. The other partner stands with feet on opposite sides of partner's shoulders and extends arms down. Both lock hands. The standing partner holds her arms straight while the lower partner pulls her body up.

Figure 8.23   Side stretch. Lie on left hip and extend both legs. Place right hand on the hip. Place left hand on the ground and extend left arm, raising the body, keeping the left hand and foot on the floor until the legs and trunk form a straight line. Repeat on opposite side.

Variations:

1. When legs and trunk are straight, stretch top arm and leg forward, then backward.
2. From variation 1, raise top leg upward.
3. From variation 1, place top hand on floor, then twist body toward the ceiling and back.

Figure 8.24   Crab kick. Begin in a crab walk position. Raise left leg up and point toe toward the ceiling.
Variations:
1. From toe-pointing position, twist right leg to the left side.
2. From toe-pointing position, bend arms and lower shoulders a few inches, then return to starting position.
3. Repeat with right leg raised.

Figure 8.25   Curl ups. Begin by lying on back, with hands at sides. Knees should be partly flexed, with heels resting on mat. Raise the trunk about 30 degrees, then return to starting position.
Variations:
1. Sit up, turning body toward the right. Repeat toward the left.
2. Sit up and wrap arms around knees, then return to starting position.
3. Sit up with arms crossed on chest.

Centipede (arm and shoulder girdle strength and endurance), p. 524
Lame Puppy Walk (arm and shoulder girdle strength and endurance), p. 516
Crab Walk (abdominal strength and endurance), p. 517
Rabbit Jump (arm and shoulder girdle strength and endurance), p. 518
Measuring Worm (arm and shoulder girdle strength and endurance), p. 519
Puppy Dog Walk (arm and shoulder girdle strength and endurance), p. 515
Frog Stand (arm and shoulder girdle strength and endurance), p. 533
Pig Walk (arm and shoulder girdle strength and endurance), p. 521
Chinese Get-Up (arm and shoulder girdle strength and endurance), p. 517
Handstand (arm and shoulder girdle strength and endurance), p. 535
Forward Drop (arm and shoulder girdle strength and endurance), p. 523

Figure 8.26   Floor bicycle pump. Sit in a partial back lying position with heels and hands resting on the floor. Lift the right leg slightly off the floor, bend right knee, and move right heel close to buttock. Return to starting position and repeat with the left leg.

Group 3 Exercises: Trunk

The exercises in this group are designed to improve the strength and endurance of abdominals and of upper and lower back muscles. Warm-up programs should include one or more exercises for each set of muscle groups. (See figures 8.25 to 8.30.)

Stunts Contributing to Trunk Strength and Endurance

Backward Roll (abdominal strength and endurance), p. 509
Rear Support (abdominal strength and endurance), p. 531
V-Sit (abdominal strength and endurance), p. 534

Figure 8.29 Head and arm raisers. Begin by lying face down, with forehead resting on back of hands. Keeping head in line with body, raise hands, head, and elbows about two inches. Then, keeping hands and head in same position, raise elbows as high as possible.
Variations:

1. Repeat to the two-inch position, then stretch one arm sideways, forward, and back to the starting position.
2. Keep chest on the floor and raise one or both extended legs upward.

Figure 8.27 Reverse curl. Lie on the back with knees bent, feet flat on the floor, and arms placed at the sides with palms down. Raise the knees upward until they are just over the shoulders, then return to the starting position.

Figure 8.30 Cat stretcher. Begin in a partially crouched position. Stretch back upward, hold at the highest point for a few seconds, then return to the starting position.
Variations:
From original position, dip chin to floor and raise right leg upward. Repeat with left leg.

Figure 8.28 Trunk stretcher. Begin in a stride-standing position, with hands fully extended over head and knees slightly bent. Bend forward and reach toward the floor with fingertips. Return to original position.
Variations:

1. Repeat original exercise to opposite side.
2. Repeat original exercise and touch right hand to left toe, then repeat to opposite side.
3. Repeat original exercise and grasp left ankle and gently pull body downward. Repeat to opposite ankle.

a   b

Figure 8.31   Knee-to-nose touch. Begin in a partially crouched position, right knee on the floor and left knee touching the chest. Simultaneously raise head up and extend left leg backward to a horizontal position. Then balance on left knee and repeat the exercise.

Figure 8.33   Jumping jack. Stand with both legs together and arms at sides. Simultaneously jump to a straddle position and clap hands over head.
Variations:
1. Cross legs instead of bringing feet together.
2. Shift legs to a forward and backward stride position. Jump and alternately move the arms and legs in a forward and backward direction.

Figure 8.32   Treadmill. Lie facedown. Push up off the floor with arms in an elevated push-up position. Keep one leg extended and draw the other leg forward until the knee is under the chest. Reverse leg positions in a continuous and simultaneous motion.
Variations:
1. Begin with both legs together. Draw both legs forward and backward.
2. From variation 1, keep legs together and shift feet toward the right and left sides.

a   b

Group 4 Exercises: Legs

The exercises in this group are designed to increase strength and endurance of the hip and leg muscles (figures 8.31 to 8.34).

Stunts Contributing to Leg Strength and Endurance

Jackknife (strength and power), p. 524
Turk Stand (strength and balance), p. 530
Heel Click (strength and power), p. 524
Rocking Chair (strength and endurance), p. 517

Figure 8.34   Alternate leg kneel. Begin in a standing position with arms at sides and feet together. Step forward with the right foot until the upper and lower leg is at ninety degrees and touch the left knee to the floor. Return to the starting position and repeat movement to the opposite side.

Potentially Harmful Exercises

Some conditioning exercises are potentially harmful to the body, particularly to the muscles, tendons, and ligaments. The following exercises are potentially hazardous, especially when performed in unison in a class warm-up or group fitness routine. Young children with immature bone structure might be able to perform some of these activities without much harm; however, from a long-term perspective, it is important to eliminate these exercises from the children's repertoire so they will not use them in the future when their bodies are fully developed.

Neck Circling

From a standing or sitting position, the head is rotated in circular fashion. This can damage the cervical artery and nerves and can depress the discs in the cervical region.

Substitute exercise: Neck stretch

Leg Lifts

From a back lying position, straight legs are raised and lowered. This movement is a hip-flexor strengthening exercise; that is, it strengthens the iliopsoas muscles, which attach to the lumbar vertebrae, ilium, and upper femur; hence, when executed, leg lifts tilt the pelvis forward, arching the body and promoting hyperextension of the lower back. The same problem is encountered with the straight-leg sit-up; therefore this exercise should be avoided.

8.8 A Number of Conditioning Exercises are Potentially Harmful to the Human Body, Particularly to Muscles, Tendons, and Ligaments, and Should Be Avoided

Toe Touch

From a standing position with legs straight, the child bends forward and places hands on the floor. When this movement is performed, particularly in a ballistic way, it can cause lower back strain and hyperextension of the knee, stretching the ligaments and capsule of the joint.

Substitute exercise: Sitting stretch

Back Arch

The subject begins by lying facedown with hands under shoulders, then raises the body up and arches the head back. This exercise stretches the abdominal muscles, which are usually too weak in young children to act as strong antagonistic muscles, resulting in hyperextension of the lower back. It can also damage the nerves of the neck and the intervertebral discs.

Bicycle

Body weight rests on the head, shoulders, and elbows, and the hands are placed under the hips. When the bicycle action is performed, the movement causes hyperflexion of the upper back and neck (kyphosis). It can also cause excessive stretching of the ligaments and nerves in this body region. The "plough," which moves legs from this position upward and over the head, causing the same hyperflexion, should also be avoided.

Substitute exercise: Knee-to-chest

Hurdle Stretch

The subject sits on the floor with the left leg extended forward and the thigh of the right leg stretched to the side; the knee is bent and stretched toward the rear. She then bends her trunk and reaches toward the left foot. This exercise places a heavy stress on the knee of the extended leg and a strain in the groin. It also places heavy stress on the cartilage of the bent knee.

Substitute exercise: Lateral straddle stretch

Knee Bends

This exercise begins in a standing position, legs together and arms extended forward. The back is kept straight and the subject squats until the upper and lower leg touch each other.

Avoid repeated and excessive knee bends (more than 90 degrees). The knee joints of young children are still maturing and thus permit a wide range of movement. To be on the cautious side, and to develop a long-term attitude, permit half knee bends for all children. Occasional full knee-bending activities, performed in stunts, animal walks, and some movement challenges, are not considered harmful.

Substitute exercise: Wall seat

Sit-Up with Hands behind Neck

This exercise begins in a back lying position, hands grasped behind the head, knees bent, and feet flat on the floor. The upper body is pulled forward to touch the knees. As the person pulls upward and forward, the hands pull on the neck, placing it in a hyperflexion position, which stretches the ligaments and places excess pressure on the intervertebral discs.

Substitute exercise: Curl-ups

TABLE 8.6   Circuit Training Program for Increasing Strength and Endurance

Exercise	Page	Maximum Number	Training Dose No. 1 (1/4 Dose)	Jan. 15	Jan. 16	Jan. 17	Etc.
1. Jumping jacks (legs)	176	16	4				
2. Push-ups (arms and shoulders)	173	8	2				
3. Head and arm raiser (trunk)	175	6	2				
4. Treadmill	176	20	5				
5. Curl-ups (trunk)	174	11	3				

OTHER TYPES OF EXERCISE PROGRAMS AND ACTIVITIES

Performing the same warm-up exercises day after day can be very boring for children. The following exercise programs and activities should be used throughout the school year to provide variety and to cope with individual differences in interest and levels of physical fitness. Modifications can be made to each program to contribute to the unit and lesson emphasis.

Circuit Training

Circuit training involves the repetition of one or more exercises as many times as possible within a time limit. A simple circuit would be doing six push-ups, ten curl-ups, and eighteen toe touches within two minutes. The number and type of exercises are optional and the variations unlimited.

This type of conditioning exercise program has many advantages, particularly for teachers in self-contained classrooms. In the first place, circuit training allows for individual differences. The number of repetitions of each exercise is determined by each child, not by the most physically fit child in the class, and one of the most important administrative advantages is the time limit. The teacher determines how much time he wants to devote to circuit training, then tailors a program to the needs of his class.

The following example is provided to show how to develop a circuit for each member of the class.

Step 1: Determine how much time you want to spend on the circuit. Time might range from six to ten minutes; our example is ten minutes.

Step 2: Select appropriate exercises. Let us assume that the teacher has administered a physical fitness test and has noted that the majority of students show low strength and endurance in the arm and shoulder girdle (pull-ups), abdominal muscles (curl-ups), and leg muscles (1-mile run). The circuit

training program, thus, should contain exercises that improve these weaknesses. The five exercises listed in table 8.6 would meet these needs.

Step 3: Determine the maximum number of repetitions for each exercise. This is the first day involving exercise. Start with the first exercise, jumping jacks. All children attempt to do the exercise as many times as they can in one minute. Record the number of repetitions under the "maximum number" column in table 8.6. Let us assume that this is the chart of a fifth-grade girl who has performed sixteen jumping jack repetitions. Immediately following this test, let the children rest for one minute. Next, have them do as many push-ups as possible in one minute. Let them rest for one minute, and continue the procedure to the fifth exercise.

Step 4: Set the training dose. The training dose (see table 8.6) is the number of repetitions the child performs when she starts the circuit program. It might be one-quarter, one-half, or three-quarters of the maximum number. As a suggestion, start with one-quarter of the maximum number as the child's first training dose. Place these numbers in the "Training Dose No. 1" column. Now the child is ready to perform the circuit without any rest between each exercise. In other words, she must try to complete the following three laps of exercises in ten minutes.

Step 5: Attempt to complete the circuit. Each child has ten minutes to complete the circuit. Let us assume that this girl has completed one lap in three minutes. Now, without rest, she starts her second lap. This lap takes her three and one-half minutes, leaving three and one-half minutes to complete the third lap. She immediately starts her third lap and gets to the second exercise, the push-ups, when the whistle blows. Record her results under the appropriate date. She completed two laps and was on exercise 2 of the third lap, so "3-2" would be recorded under the date and opposite push-ups.

Step 6: Continue step 5 until the child performs three laps within the time limit. Then increase each exercise by one repetition. Our girl would now do five jumping jacks, three push-ups, three head raisers, six treadmills, and four curl-ups.

Lap 1	Lap 2	Lap 3
4 jumping jacks	4 jumping jacks	4 jumping jacks
2 push-ups	2 push-ups	2 push-ups
2 head raisers	2 head raisers	2 head raisers
5 treadmills	5 treadmills	5 treadmills
3 curl-ups	3 curl-ups	3 curl-ups

The length of time devoted to a circuit-training program depends foremost on the physical fitness needs of the class. If the class scored low on the physical fitness test, it would be wise to require a daily circuit for five to six weeks. The teacher might also design a ten-minute circuit for use in the classroom on those days when her class does not have access to the gymnasium. In this case, she should consider student interest and change the exercises in the circuit each month.

There is a wonderful opportunity here to help the child who scores extremely low on the physical fitness test. First, attempt to determine the reasons for the low fitness, such as obesity or chronic lack of exercise. Design a circuit for the child to do at home. This might involve drawing stick figures to explain the exercises and sending a short note to the parents or interviewing them. Also, the child should set goals for himself in his personal activity log (PAL) as explained in chapter 11. The results can be tremendous if the teacher shows an interest, making periodic checks with the child and the parents.

Obstacle Course

An obstacle course is an arrangement of small equipment and large apparatus designed to improve one or more of the components of physical fitness. Commercial obstacle courses normally include apparatus to climb, balance on, vault over, and crawl through. This type of apparatus is basically for use outdoors and normally is permanently anchored to the ground. Homemade obstacle courses using the natural building materials of a region have become very popular in many elementary schools. They are generally built by parents and usually have a theme, such as a western fort or outpost, space travel, or a jungle trek.

Portable obstacle courses can be made with the equipment and apparatus available in the school. These courses have several advantages: They can be arranged in a variety of patterns, and they can be located in a gymnasium or on the playground. The illustrated portable obstacle course requires a minimum amount of small and large apparatus used in an imaginative and constructive way.

Portable Obstacle Course

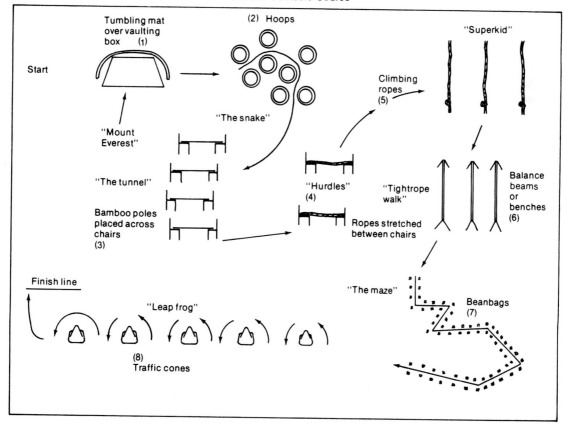

Each child tries to complete the course as quickly as possible. The items along this obstacle course contribute to physical fitness in the following ways:

1. *Mount Everest:* Climbing improves strength and power.
2. *The snake:* Running through the hoops, placing alternate feet in them, improves agility.
3. *The tunnel:* Crawling through a tunnel improves the strength and endurance of the arm and shoulder girdle.
4. *Hurdles:* Jumping over hurdles improves leg power.
5. *Superkid:* Climbing the rope as high as possible improves the strength of the arm and shoulder girdle.
6. *Tightrope walk:* Walking across a balance bench improves balance.
7. *The maze:* Hopping through a beanbag course improves the strength and power of the legs.
8. *Leapfrog:* Straddle-jumping over traffic cones (or milk cartons) improves the power of the legs.

Assign one child to start at each station, to provide maximum participation and avoid confusion and collisions. On the signal "Go," each child tackles the task at his station, then continues through the obstacle course until completing all eight tasks. If possible, duplicate stations 2, 7, and 8 so that two students can begin at each of these stations.

Children thoroughly enjoy indoor and outdoor obstacle courses. Once the students understand the basic purpose of an obstacle course, they should have an opportunity to plan their own. Their designs are usually very imaginative and more demanding than the teacher-designed course.

Jogging

A jog is an easy or relaxed run that does not unduly fatigue the runner. Jogging is one of the most effective and enjoyable means of improving muscular and cardiovascular endurance. If taught correctly, elementary children—including first-graders—can participate in jogging activities in the gymnasium, on the playing field, or in a cross-country setting.

The proper form is like that of a distance runner: body erect and relaxed, and arms swinging in an easy manner. The heel of the foot contacts the ground, then rocks forward to a gentle push off the front of the foot.

Before introducing jogging, the teacher should present it to young children as a recreational activity. Jogging should not be seen as a prerequisite to competitive cross-country running; rather, it should be seen as an activity in which children can experience enjoyment and success as they increase the distance they can run without undue fatigue or strain. This means that children should set their own goals (see the activity log in chapter 11) and that other activities should be interspersed with jogging, since young children might become bored with the same jogging pace and such tracks as "around the gymnasium" or "around the outside of the playing field."

The basic approach used to teach children to jog is to have them begin with a series of stretching exercises, then a walk. When they feel ready, they begin to jog as far as they can without feeling overfatigued or out of breath. Once the children learn to pace themselves to a jog-walk-jog pattern, they will gradually increase their jogging distance as they decrease the walking distance.

After a few days of basic jog-walk-jog activities, introduce the "scout's pace." Have each child jog 110 yards, walk 55 yards, jog 110 yards, continuing the pattern as long as possible. The distances can be adjusted to the child's or the class's ability and condition.

As soon as most of the children can jog a reasonable distance, such as a mile, introduce other jogging activities into the program, such as "hash running" (p. 491), orienteering (p. 492), or a 100-mile club, all of which involve enjoyable recreational jogging. The 100-mile club is a program in which each child keeps his own jogging "log" or record sheet. He might receive a certificate when he reaches 100 miles; however, if the jogging program has been introduced correctly, the child should find that completing 100 miles is valuable in itself and he has little need for a badge or certificate.

Rope Jumping

The individual rope-jumping steps described in chapter 26 can be incorporated into an excellent program for enhancing cardiorespiratory fitness. The following procedure will help develop a rope-jumping program for upper primary or intermediate grades.

1. Set a time limit for rope jumping (duration). This program will last ten minutes.
2. Allow each child to choose three or four steps that can be performed on each turn of the rope (example: two-foot basic, running, one-foot hop, or cross-arm step).
3. Set a heart rate training zone between 160 and 190 beats per minute.
4. Before starting the rope-jumping session, have the class perform a series of stretching exercises.
5. For the ten-minute rope-jumping program, all children begin jumping rope to a cadence of 80 jumps per minute. (Use a record with a 4/4 beat and adjust the speed to 80 beats per minute.) Each child tries to jump to the pace for ten minutes. If a child stops, say at four and one-half minutes, he should immediately take his heart rate. At the ten-minute mark, have all remaining children take their heart rate. If half of the students' heart rates are less than 160 beats, increase the cadence to 90 beats and instruct each child to include more difficult and demanding steps (intensity).
6. On successive days, each child tries to keep up to the cadence as long as possible. As children improve, they will continue longer and add more demanding steps. Continue adjusting the cadence upward until all children are performing within the target zone.

Aerobic Dancing

Aerobic dancing involves moving rhythmically through a series of movement patterns. It may include simple dance steps, nonlocomotor movements, or combined movements involving small equipment such as ropes, wands, or hoops. The musical accompaniment for aerobic dance routines is normally a bouncy, even, 4/4 rhythm. Most popular rock and roll, disco, marching, folk dance, and country western music can be used with equal success.

The success of an aerobic dance program for elementary school children will depend on their ability to keep in time to a musical accompaniment. Teachers should review chapter 28, "Rhythmic and Movement Activities," before designing aerobic routines. Once children understand what even rhythm and accent mean and can design their own rhythmic sequences, they are very close to performing aerobic dance routines.

The following teaching suggestions and sample routines will provide a start toward developing a variety of beneficial cardiorespiratory routines that are thoroughly enjoyed by children in grades 2 through 6. In addition, there are numerous commercial aerobic programs involving written exercises and accompanying records or tapes. Teachers should consult local record stores and talk to local fitness class instructors for additional ideas relating to types of exercises and appropriate music for elementary school children.

Teaching Suggestions

1. Design movement patterns that involve 4, 8, or 16 counts. Stress changing the movement on the first beat of each measure.
2. Teach children a basic aerobic dance vocabulary. The following are some useful cue words.
   a. *Bounce:* Perform small jumps on both feet.
   b. *Clap:* Jump in place, clap hands, and move elbows back, then forward to clap again.
   c. *Jog:* Running with a high knee lift. "Hand jive"—jog and cross and uncross hands in front at a low level. "Wild"—jog and shake hands overhead. "Wiper"—jog and move hands in front like a windshield wiper.
   d. *Kick:* Step on right foot and kick left foot about waist high.
   e. *Leroy Brown:* A variation of jumping jacks that involves feet together and bounce twice while keeping hands at shoulders, then feet astride, bounce twice, and simultaneously raise hands overhead and back to shoulders.

3. Design several aerobic routines involving different steps, exercises, and lengths of time. Change routines when children show boredom or when performance levels dictate more intensity and duration for the children's increased fitness level.

Figure 8.35 Jump with feet together.

4. Use simple dance steps such as walk, run, jump, hop, slide, and skip.
5. Encourage children to design their own aerobic dance routines and to lead the class through their routines.
6. As soon as the children know a few routines and feel at ease, introduce aerobic dance routines involving small equipment such as individual ropes, elastic bands, or hoops.

Sample Aerobic Dance Routine

The following aerobic dance routine uses two, four, or eight counts for each movement.

A. Jog.
   1. Jog eight steps forward (high knee lift).
   2. Jog eight steps backward (high knee lift).
   3. Hand jive eight steps forward (cross and uncross hands while jogging).
   4. Hand jive eight times backward (cross and uncross hands while jogging).

B. Jump and swing.
   1. Jump with feet together (count 1; figure 8.35).
   2. Jump onto left foot and simultaneously lift right foot off floor and swing arms forward and upward (count 2; figure 8.36).
   3. Jump with feet together (count 3; figure 8.35).
   4. Jump on right foot and swing arms forward and upward (count 4).
   5. Repeat movements 1–4 three times.

Figure 8.36 Jump onto left foot.

Figure 8.37 Jump with feet together.

C. Jump and lunge.
   1. Begin with elbows out, fingers on shoulders and feet together. Jump with feet together (count 1; figure 8.37).
   2. Jump to a right lunge (count 2; figure 8.38).
   3. Jump with both feet together (count 3).
   4. Jump to a left lunge (count 4).
   5. Repeat movements 1–4 three times.

D. Elbow knee jump.
   1. Begin with hands clasped behind head. Jump and lift right knee to left elbow (count 1).
   2. Jump and lift left knee to right elbow (count 2; figure 8.39).
   3. Repeat movements 1–2 sixteen times.

E. Leroy Brown (modified jumping jack).
   1. Begin with feet together and fingertips touching shoulders. Jump twice with hands on shoulders (counts 1 and 2; figure 8.40).
   2. Jump to stride, rebound in this position, and simultaneously raise hands over head (counts 3 and 4).
   3. Repeat movements 1–2 times.

Repeat the entire sequence of exercises one or more times, depending on each individual's level of cardiorespiratory endurance.

Figure 8.38 Right lunge.

Figure 8.39 Jump and lift left knee to right elbow.

Figure 8.40 Jump with hands on shoulders.

F. Cool-down.
   1. Slow jog on spot (16 counts).
   2. Walk slowly around gymnasium for one minute.

Other Cardiorespiratory Activities

If the following activities are performed on a continuous basis, they will provide a positive cumulative effect on the child's cardiovascular system.

1. Cross-country running or skiing
2. Distance walking at a brisk rate
3. Bicycling
4. Swimming
5. Rhythmic exercises (chapter 28)
6. Step aerobics

The above examples are individual fitness activities conducted within existing physical education programs. A few school districts have expanded their cardiorespiratory fitness programs to include other important related factors, such as drug education and nutrition. The Sunflower Project[1] in Shawnee Mission, Kansas, is a good example of this type of program. This district initiated a broad-based program for every member of the family. It began with a daily aerobics program before school for family members. Recess became a twenty-minute fitness program for all children, and eventually a special aerobic fitness program was organized for teachers after school.

Summary Review

One of the major goals of the physical education program is to help all children develop an active lifestyle. Teaching children the health-related benefits of physical activity is an important piece of declarative knowledge. However, knowing that an active lifestyle is important is insufficient knowledge in itself; children must also develop the procedural knowledge to monitor and improve their own physical fitness. Physical activity must become an integral part of children's daily lives. This chapter provides guidance in the assessment of health-related physical fitness and offers ideas to motivate children toward developing lifelong fitness.

[1]Contact the Instructional Program Center, 6649 Lamar Street, Shawnee Mission, KA 66202, for additional information.

INDIVIDUAL *and* **GROUP** **PROJECTS**

1. In small groups, based on the body locations identified for fitness testing, practice measuring each other's body fat with skinfold calipers.

2. In small groups, using the back-saver sit-and-reach technique, assess individual flexibility. The sit-and-reach evaluates range of motion primarily for the lower back and hamstring. Design three methods of assessing other areas of flexibility (avoid potentially harmful movement activities).

3. In small groups, design an intervention program to improve the physical fitness of a group of overweight children. Compare group designs, discussing the strengths and weaknesses of each intervention program.

4. Table 8.6 in the text provides an example of a circuit training program for increasing strength and endurance. In small groups, design a circuit training program to improve primarily the strength and endurance of the lower body (legs). Design another circuit to improve the strength and endurance of the upper body (arms, shoulders, and trunk muscles). Compare designs among groups, discussing the strengths and weaknesses of the circuits.

SELECTED READINGS

AAHPERD. 1988a. *AAHPERD technical manual, Health Related Physical Fitness Test.* Reston, VA: AAHPERD.

———. 1988b. *Physical Best manual.* Reston, VA: AAHPERD.

———. 1976. *AAHPERD youth fitness test manual.* Rev. ed. Reston, VA: AAHPERD.

AAHPERD and Cooper Institute for Aerobics Research. 1995. *You Stay Active.* Reston, VA: AAHPERD.

Binkhorst, R. A., H. C. G. Kemper, and W. H. M. Soris. 1985. *Children and exercise.* Champaign, IL: Human Kinetics.

Blair, S. N. 1993. C. H. McCloy Research Lecture: Physical activity, physical fitness, and health. *Research Quarterly for Exercise and Sport* 64 (4): 365–76.

CAHPERD. 1993. *The Canadian Active Living Challenge.* Gloucester, Ontario: CAHPERD.

Cooper Institute for Aerobics Research. 1993. *Prudential FITNESSGRAM.* 12330 Preston Rd., Dallas, TX 75230

Cooper Institute for Aerobics Research. 1994. *FITNESSGRAM Test Administration Manual.* Dallas: Cooper Institute for Aerobics Research.

Corbin, C. B., and R. Lindsey. 1996. *Physical fitness concepts.* Dubuque, IA: Brown & Benchmark.

——— 1991. *Concepts of physical fitness with laboratories.* 7th ed. Dubuque, IA: Wm. C. Brown.

de Vries, H. A., and T. J. Housh. 1994. *Physiology of Exercise.* Madison, WI: Brown & Benchmark.

Donatelle, R. J., and L. G. Davis. 1996. *Access to health.* 4th ed. Boston: Allyn & Bacon.

Dunn, J., and H. Fait. 1989. *Special physical education.* Dubuque, IA: Brown & Benchmark.

Epstein, L. H., A. Valoski, and J. McCurly. 1990. Ten-year follow-up of behavioral family-based treatment for obese children. *Journal of the American Medical Association* 264: 2519–24.

Espiritu J. K., and C. McAlister. 1992. *FITNESS TRACKER: Wellness profile system.* Dubuque, IA: Brown & Benchmark.

Foster, E. R., K. Hartinger, and K. A. Smith. 1990. *Fitness fun.* Champaign, IL: Human Kinetics.

Gabbard, C. 1996. *Lifelong motor development.* Dubuque, IA: Brown & Benchmark.

Gabbard, C., B. LeBlanc, and S. Lowy. 1994. *Physical education for children.* Englewood Cliffs, NJ: Prentice Hall.

Golding, L. A., C. R. Meyers, and W. E. Sinning. 1989. *Y's ways to physical fitness.* 3d ed. Champaign, IL: Human Kinetics.

Harrison, J. M., C. L. Blakemore, M. M. Buck, and T. L. Pellett. 1996. *Instructional strategies for secondary school physical education.* 4th ed. Dubuque, IA: Brown & Benchmark.

Kalish, S. 1996. *Your child's fitness.* Champaign, IL: Human Kinetics.

Kuntzleman, C. 1990a. *Fitness discovery activities.* Reston, VA: AAHPERD.

———. 1990b. *Instructor's guide for feeling good.* Reston, VA: AAHPERD.

Kuntzleman, C., and G. McGlynn. 1991. *Aerobics with fun.* Reston, VA: AAHPERD.

———. 1984. *Fitness for children.* Spring Arbor, MI: Fitness Finders.

McGlynn, G. 1990. *Dynamics of fitness: A practical approach.* Dubuque, IA: Wm. C. Brown.

Mullen, K. D., R. J. McDermott, R. S. Gold, and P. A. Belcastro. 1996. *Connections for health,* 4th ed. Dubuque, IA: Brown & Benchmark.

Scicchitano, J. 1989. *Super star fitness.* Durham, NC: Great Activities.

Sherrill, C. 1997. *Adapted physical activity, Recreation and sport.* 5th ed. Dubuque, IA: Brown & Benchmark.

Steen, D. 1982. *Aerobic fun for kids.* Toronto: Fitzhenry & Whiteside.

Stewart, G. W. 1982. *Everybody's fitness book.* Santa Barbara, CA: 3 S Publishers.

Stewart, G. W., and R. A. Faulkner. 1984. *Bend and stretch: Suppleness and strength exercises.* Santa Barbara, CA: 3 S Publishers.

Williams, D. P., S. B. Going, T. G. Lohman, D. W. Harsha, L. S. Webber, and G. S. Bereson. 1992. Body fatness and the risk of elevated blood pressure, total cholesterol and serum lipoprotein ratios in children and youth. *American Journal of Public Health* 82: 358–63.

Williams, M. 1993. *Lifetime fitness and wellness.* 2d ed. Dubuque, IA: Brown & Benchmark.

Winnick, J., and F. Short. 1985. *Physical fitness testing of the disabled: Project UNIQUE.* Champaign, IL: Human Kinetics.

PART 4

Developing a Physical Education Curriculum

The contemporary definition of an elementary school curriculum includes all the experiences of children for which the school accepts responsibility. In physical education, this encompasses all the learning experiences related to the physical activities provided in the regular instructional period and out of class. The school or teacher can organize the physical education curriculum in several ways. The fundamental purpose of organization is to provide an effective way to choose activities, develop teaching strategies, and provide experiences that best meet the goals of the program.

Contemporary educational practices, such as individualized teaching strategies, team teaching, cooperative learning, and concept development, directly affect the nature and structure of the physical education program. Teachers must also consider the unique characteristics and needs of children within each grade of the elementary school when selecting the length, type, and nature of each instructional unit. In addition, such federal laws as PL 93-112 (1973), PL 94-142 (1975), and PL 101-476 (1990) require that equal opportunities be provided for all children with physical, psychological, or social disabilities. Each of these factors is considered when planning the elementary school physical education curriculum.

The process of developing a physical education curriculum is outlined in the chart below. To accomplish the broad goals of elementary education, the physical education curriculum is divided into two types of programs: the instructional program and the co-curricular program. The instructional program is the central core within which children acquire knowledge, skills, and understandings related to human movement. The co-curricular program offers educational opportunities, outside the regular physical education class, that are designed to complement the instructional program. The process of developing the instructional and the co-curricular program is the focus of PART 4.

Chapter 9 describes how to develop a yearly, unit, and daily instructional program. Chapter 10 deals with organizational decisions for effective instruction. This chapter covers class management, ways of organizing children and other personnel (assistants), and standards relating to facilities, equipment, and supplies. This chapter also deals with providing a safe environment for children, teachers' legal responsibilities, and the implications of recent laws for elementary physical education programs. Chapter 11 describes the process of selecting appropriate evaluative techniques and methods. A variety of observational techniques and evaluative procedures are identified. Chapter 12 considers the design and development of the co-curricular program.

Process of Curriculum Development

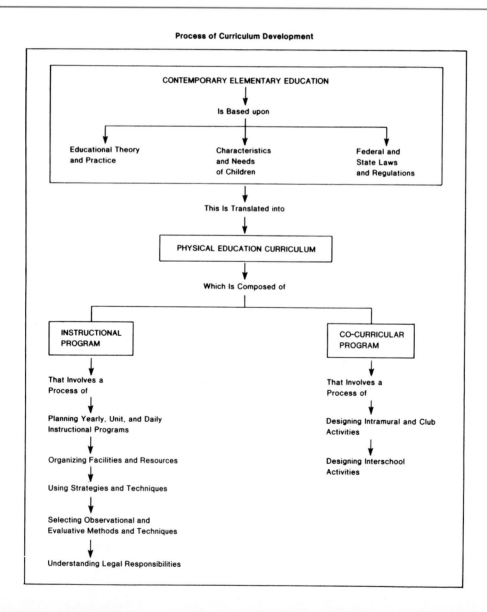

CHAPTER 9

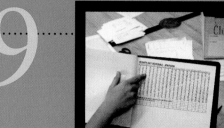

Planning a Physical Education Curriculum

KEY CONCEPTS

9.1 The traditional teaching model stresses formal teaching strategies and norm-based progress for all children

9.2 The Movement Education model is based on Laban's classification of movement and includes the four elements of body awareness, space awareness, qualities, and relationships

9.3 The developmental curriculum model incorporates the strengths of both the traditional model and the Movement Education model

9.4 The developmental model is based on activities appropriate to a child's level of development, regardless of age or grade level

9.5 Learning descriptors provide a guide to a child's developmental level as the child moves along a continuum toward full maturity

9.6 Developing a yearly program of physical education requires careful planning that includes decision making regarding demands that arise before, during, and after teaching

9.7 The multiple, modified, and solid types of instructional units offer alternative ways of organizing teaching of the physical education curriculum

9.8 A lesson plan should include these three essential parts: set, body, and closure

KEY OBJECTIVES

After completing this chapter you will be able to:

1. Identify three different curriculum models and state their strengths and weaknesses
2. Identify and understand developmental differences between early, middle, and late childhood
3. Identify developmentally appropriate physical education activities for the three levels associated with the developmental model
4. Develop a yearly program of physical education
5. Identify three types of instructional unit and state the strengths and weaknesses of each
6. Develop instructional teaching units for physical education
7. Develop lesson plans that are appropriate for elementary school physical education
8. Plan for student and program evaluation

The instructional program is more than the physical activities that are taught to the class. Rather, it is the total experience of activities, methods, and teaching strategies.

The activities themselves serve two basic functions. First, through the activities the children develop their motor abilities and they learn fundamental locomotor and nonlocomotor skills and the specialized and basic movement skills and concepts involved in games, dance, and other organized activities. Developing motor abilities and mastering these skills, in turn, helps children maintain an optimum level of physical fitness, move their bodies easily and efficiently, and express themselves creatively. Second, physical activities provide a medium within which children learn many intangible, yet important, lessons of life. They learn, for example, to share experiences, to give and take, and to control their emotions under a variety of cooperative and competitive situations.

This chapter describes some types of activities and outlines the process of developing yearly, unit, and daily lessons. Sample programs are provided as guidelines to help teachers develop their own programs—which must always be based on the teachers' stated goals and teaching competence, the characteristics and needs of children, and the available time, facilities, and equipment.

TYPES OF CURRICULUM MODELS

An elementary school curriculum includes all of the children's experiences for which the school accepts responsibility. In physical education, this encompasses all learning experiences related to physical activities in both the regular instructional period and the intramural and interschool programs. This discussion is limited to the learning experiences that are part of the regular instructional program. The physical education curriculum can take several forms. The fundamental purpose of a curriculum model is to provide an effective means of choosing activities, developing teaching strategies, and providing experiences that meet the objectives of the instructional program.

A review of current elementary school physical education programs and contemporary guides and textbooks indicates that there are about four types of curriculum models. There are variations within and between each model as well as a strong tendency toward one particular type of curriculum. Three of the most common types are described in this section. Although each type of curriculum model can be found throughout Canada and the United States, the developmental model is one of the more prevalent and is stressed throughout this book.

Traditional Model

The traditional model, as outlined in table 9.1, is the oldest type of elementary school physical education curriculum. It is an activity-based program that includes separate content areas of game, dance, gymnastic, and physical fitness activities. A percentage of instructional time is allocated to each activity area according to grade level. The primary-level curriculum stresses informal participation in low-organization activities such as running and tag games, singing games, and a variety of stunts and tumbling activities. The general teacher-centered approach to this type of

curriculum model is continued in the intermediate grades. However, as outlined in table 9.1, emphasis in each content area shifts to developing more specialized skills. Both primary and intermediate programs stress formal teaching strategies and norm-based progress, particularly in game, gymnastic, and physical fitness activities.

9.1 *The Traditional Teaching Model Stresses Formal Teaching Strategies and Norm-Based Progress for All Children*

Movement Education Model

The Movement Education model, originally proposed by Rudolph Laban (see Laban and Ullman 1960), is based on an analysis of movement that is different from that of the traditional model. The Movement Education model bases the elementary school physical education program on Laban's movement classification system, which involves these four elements: body awareness, space awareness, qualities, and relationships. These four elements represent four content areas of the curriculum. The central idea of this program is that children learn how their bodies move through a variety of mediums such as games, gymnastics, and dance. The individualized, child-centered approach teaches children to learn new movement concepts and skills according to their own rate and level of development. The teacher's role is that of a guide or facilitator rather than a director of the learning experience. As such, teaching strategies stress exploratory methods and techniques. Although physical fitness is listed under both levels in table 9.1, fitness development is not a separate unit or theme; it is integrated into each theme and, thus, is seen as a means to moving effectively and efficiently rather than as an end in itself.

TABLE 9.1	Types of Curriculum Models	
Traditional Model	**Movement Education Model**	**Developmental Model**
Primary Level		
Games	**Games**	**Games**
Basic game skills	Body awareness	Basic game skills
Running, tag, and simple team games	Space awareness	Locomotor and nonlocomotor skills
	Qualities	Simple team and creative games
	Relationships	Movement Education concepts and skills
Dance	**Dance**	**Dance**
Locomotor and nonlocomotor skills	Body awareness	Locomotor and nonlocomotor skills
Singing games, folk dance	Space awareness	Rhythmics, singing games, and folk dance
Creative dance	Qualities	Creative dance stressing Movement
	Relationships	Education concepts and skills
Gymnastics	**Gymnastics**	**Gymnastics**
Stunts and tumbling	Body awareness	Stunts and tumbling
Small equipment	Space awareness	Small equipment
Some large apparatus	Qualities	Large apparatus
	Relationships	Movement Education concepts and skills
Fitness	**Fitness**	**Fitness**
Increase and maintain level of physical fitness	Integrated into Movement Education program	Understanding and development of individualized approaches to health-related fitness
Intermediate Level		
Games	**Games**	**Games**
Low organization games	Body awareness	Low organization and creative games
Sport skills and games	Space awareness	Sports skills and team sports
Knowledge of rules and playing strategies	Qualities	Knowledge of rules and playing strategies
	Relationships	Movement Education concepts and skills
Dance	**Dance**	**Dance**
Rhythmics	Body awareness	Rhythmics
Folk and square dance	Space awareness	Folk and square dance
Creative dance	Qualities	Creative dance—emphasis on on Movement
	Relationships	Education concept and skills
Gymnastics	**Gymnastics**	**Gymnastics**
Stunts and tumbling	Body awareness	Stunts and tumbling
Small equipment	Space awareness	Small equipment
Large apparatus	Qualities	Large apparatus
	Relationships	Movement Education concepts and skills
Fitness	**Fitness**	**Fitness**
Increase and maintain level of physical fitness	Integrated into Movement Education program	Understanding and development of individualized approaches to health-related fitness

C O N C E P T

9.2 *The Movement Education Model Is Based on Laban's Classification of Movement and Includes the Four Elements of Body Awareness, Space Awareness, Qualities, and Relationships*

Developmental Model

The developmental model is essentially an eclectic approach that uses a developmental sequence of acquiring movement concepts and motor skills according to each child's level of ability, interest, and maturity. The program is based on a philosophy of education that emphasizes the development of each child's human potential through a personalized and humanistic learning environment. It draws on knowledge of how children grow and develop, of theories of learning motor skills, and of important social and cultural factors related to the types of activities children enjoy. In addition, the model considers the long-term concepts and skills children will need to meet the challenges of an exciting future.

CONCEPT

9.3 The Developmental Curriculum Model Incorporates the Strengths of Both the Traditional Model and the Movement Education Model

In table 9.1, the content outlined under the developmental model shows that this approach includes the game, dance, and gymnastic activities of the traditional model, as well as the basic movement concepts and skills of Movement Education. The developmental model also emphasizes creative and exploratory methods and the acquisition of knowledge and skills that will help children learn how the human body works and how to maintain a high level of health and fitness throughout life. It is truly a child-centered program.

CONCEPT

9.4 The Developmental Model is Based on Activities Appropriate to a Child's Level of Development, Regardless of Age or Grade Level

PROGRAM EMPHASIS

The developmental approach to curriculum development rests on the premise that each child learns concepts and motor skills according to her own rate and level of development. This process-based, rather than product-based, curriculum views each child as progressing through stages of development according to her own time clock. A stage of development is not a rigid set of standard academic, motor, and social skills that a child must acquire before advancing to the next stage. Rather, developmental stages are approximate time periods from early through late childhood in which children acquire psychomotor, cognitive, and affective concepts, skills, and understandings. In this text, three general levels of development are used as a rough guide for designing appropriate physical education programs.

In tables 9.2, 9.3, and 9.4, the term *learning descriptor* is used rather than *outcomes*. If the teacher were to state what she wants every child to accomplish within each of these developmental periods, she would violate the premise of this curriculum design. Learning descriptors must be considered as signposts along a child's path of development. Such words as *performs, shows,* and *demonstrates* are used to stress that there are no rigid boundary lines between stages

of development. Also, because of a variety of contemporary educational factors—such as previous physical education experiences, number of physical education periods per week, and available equipment and facilities—a standard grade-level approach would be inappropriate. Each level of development, however, provides a general framework on which each teacher can plan a physical education program.

CONCEPT

9.5 Learning Descriptors Provide a Guide to a Child's Developmental Level as the Child Moves along a Continuum toward Full Maturity

LEVEL I: EARLY CHILDHOOD

The characteristics and needs of children in the early primary grades have a very strong influence on the selection of appropriate physical activities. For example, children's physical immaturity, short attention span, and lack of experience in the content areas indicate that a broad exposure to all types of game, dance, and gymnastic activities is required. This is a time for children to explore and discover how their bodies work, so emphasis should be placed on movement concepts and fundamental skills. These considerations are reflected in the percentage of time allocated for activities in table 9.5. During the first and second year of a child's school life, attention is given to creative and exploratory ways of learning the skills involved in game and gymnastic activities. Exposure to a variety of activities fosters movement awareness and helps to establish the movement patterns associated with basic locomotor, non-locomotor, and manipulative skills. Dance activities should also take a strong creative approach as early primary children learn rhythmic skills, singing games, and creative movements. The range in the suggested percentage of time for each activity allows each teacher to develop a curriculum that meets the level of maturity and ability of the children in his care.

LEVEL II: MIDDLE CHILDHOOD

Level II is the important transitional period in a physical education program. According to table 9.5, there is a slight reduction in the time devoted to movement concepts and skills and fundamental skills. As children progress through this age range, they develop an understanding of how their bodies work, they learn more complex skills and strategies, and they become more group oriented. This period of time should reflect participation in group activities, and children should be given many opportunities to increase their level of skill and understanding in a wide variety of physical activities. It is also a time to use creative and exploratory teaching strategies to enhance children's creative expressions in games, gymnastics, and dance.

TABLE 9.2 Learning Descriptors for Developmental Level I

Psychomotor Domain	Cognitive Domain	Affective Domain
Performs locomotor skills of walking, running, jumping, hopping, sliding, and skipping individually or in a simple sequence	Knows the names and locations of the main parts of the body	Shows joy and excitement for movement experiences
Performs nonlocomotor skills of swinging, bending, stretching, twisting, turning, pushing, pulling, individually or in simple sequences	Can identify and name simple movements such as run, twist, and catch	Accepts different abilities of others
Moves through general space in a safe and controlled manner	Shows ability to describe simple movements	Accepts responsibility for own efforts
Performs a run, jump, land, and roll	Understands meaning and importance of strength and endurance	Demonstrates willingness to play and share ideas, space, and equipment with others
Performs simple movement sequence	Understands difference between personal and general space	Shows willingness to listen to directions and simple explanations
Moves through personal and general space changing speed and direction	Knows names and meanings of directions, levels, and pathways of moving	Shows willingness to assume responsibility for one's own safety
Executes simple sequences using small equipment and large apparatus	Knows names and meanings of quick and slow, strong and light, and flow	Demonstrates a willingness to create games or other movement sequences with others
Performs a variety of simple balance and agility stunts	Knows names and meanings of weight bearing, shapes, and balance	Shows willingness to stay on-task until the activity is completed
Shows ability to roll a ball with both hands	Understands meaning of simple relationships of self to others and to objects	Demonstrates understanding and tolerance toward classmates who have physical or mental disabilities
Performs two-hand underhand throws with control and accuracy	Shows ability to create and explain simple movement sequences	Demonstrates understanding and tolerance toward classmates who may have different skin color
Performs one-hand underhand and overhand throw with minimum skill and accuracy	Understands meaning of safety of self and others	
Executes a one-hand dribble with either hand	Shows ability to understand simple rules of games and contests	
Shows ability to catch a ball using a two-hand underhand catch	Knows the meaning of sharing, cheating, and other social behaviors	
Shows limited ability to catch a ball using a two-hand overhand catch	Understands meaning of rhythm	
Executes a stationary kick with dominant foot	Knows how to plan simple dance sequences	
Performs a simple dribble using both feet		
Shows basic ability to stop a moving ball with one foot		
Shows ability to play simple running, tag, and team games		
Performs simple striking actions with arm or small implement		
Shows ability to perform locomotor and nonlocomotor movements in time to simple rhythmic accompaniment		
Performs singing games and simple folk dances		
Performs simple pantomime movements		
Shows ability to respond to a variety of stimuli such as stories and poems		

LEVEL III: LATE CHILDHOOD

As children move from the latter part of level II to level III, they begin to refine many fundamental motor skills and become fairly proficient at performing the more complex skills of sports, dance, and gymnastics. This is reflected in table 9.6, where there is a significant increase in time devoted to sport activities. However, these children still enjoy running, tag, and individual and cooperative games. Although less time is allotted for dance activities within each intermediate grade, the proportionate percentage of time for this area supports its value.

There is a slight reduction in time allotments for gymnastic activities from grade 4 through grade 6. The major change with this program, however, is the shift toward more artistic types of gymnastic movements and a decrease in the emphasis on Laban's movement concepts and skills. There is, though, a good argument for blending these two approaches in order to cope with varying levels of interest and ability and to provide a program that fosters creative expression. Videotape No. 2 (see appendix A) provides guidance on the blending of gymnastic approaches.

Table 9.5 provided 12 to 20 percent of time for special interest activities in level III. This time allotment can be

CHAPTER 9

TABLE 9.3 Learning Descriptors for Developmental Level II

Psychomotor Domain	Cognitive Domain	Affective Domain
Demonstrates a mature form in all locomotor and nonlocomotor movements	Shows a basic understanding of principles of gravity and force	Continues to show joy and excitement for movement experiences
Adjusts locomotor and nonlocomotor movements to varying rhythm and tempo	Demonstrates increased ability to invent and describe movement sequences for gymnastics and dance	Displays open willingness to work with others who possess different abilities and interests
Performs simple movement sequences involving two or more elements of body awareness, qualities, space awareness, and relationships	Possesses an understanding of major components of physical fitness and how to improve and maintain optimum levels of health-related fitness	Shows increased willingness to work in small and large groups
Shows ability to repeat and improve quality of movement sequences	Shows ability to understand simple team strategies in low-organization games and modified team sports	Shows willingness to assume responsibility for one's own safety as well as for the general safety of the class
Performs a variety of stunts and tumbling skills	Demonstrates a reasonable understanding of sharing, cheating, and other social behavior	Demonstrates willingness to stay on-task for long periods of time
Shows ability to develop movement sequences involving small and large apparatus		Shows a continuous support to work with others of lesser ability
Executes simple movement sequences with a partner and using small and large apparatus		Reveals tolerance toward others of different race and cultural backgrounds
Performs a variety of individual and long rope jumping skills		Demonstrates a willingness to participate in group discussions and abide by the groups's decisions on rules and regulation
Shows improved form, speed, and accuracy with underhand and overhand throw		
Demonstrates increased skill in two-hand underhand and overhand catch		
Performs one-hand dribble with either hand with a change in level, speed, and direction		
Shows ability to kick a stationary and moving ball with increased power and accuracy		
Dribbles ball with both feet with a change of direction and speed		
Shows ability to stop a moving ball with feet, legs, and body		
Performs striking actions with large instruments, such as bats and hockey sticks, with increased control and proficiency		
Plays more complex running tag and lead-up games to major team sports		
Performs movement sequences involving locomotor and nonlocomotor movements and in combination with different rhythm patterns		
Performs folk dances with increased skill and style		
Performs creative dance movements with increased skill and expression		

used for such programs as swimming or for other special outdoor pursuits that are popular and important to unique geographical areas of North America. These might include cross-country skiing, canoeing, and orienteering programs. Many educators have stressed the importance of including a basic drown-proofing swimming unit as part of all elementary physical education programs. If local budgets can afford such programs, local recreational agencies, such as the YMCA or Red Cross, can provide this program on a contractual basis. Finally, this unscheduled time allotment can be devoted to special interests in any of the main categories or to introduce new activities, such as rhythmic gymnastics or European handball, into the curriculum.

The relative percentage of time suggested for each activity area in table 9.5 provides a very rough guideline as to what types of activities should be taught at various developmental levels. Table 9.6 goes one step further by providing an overview of the specific activities recommended for each level. This table will be used extensively in the next section, which discusses planning a yearly program.

TABLE 9.4 Learning Descriptors for Developmental Level III

Psychomotor Domain	Cognitive Domain	Affective Domain
Performs complex movement sequences involving four elements of movement	Shows mature understanding of principles of gravity, force, and motion	Continues to show the same joy and excitement for movement experiences as previous levels
Shows increased ability to repeat and improve quality of movement sequences	Demonstrates increased ability to invent and describe movement sequences for gymnastics and dance	Displays a mature and open willingness to work with others who possess different abilities and interests
Executes a wide variety of stunts and tumbling skills and movement patterns in combination with one or more elements of movement	Plans more complex game strategies for individual and team sports	Shows willingness to develop into a self-directed human being
Performs a wide variety of gymnastic skills and movements using small equipment and large apparatus in combination with one or more elements of movement	Understands the factors affecting performance such as body type, conditioning, and training methods	Shows mature ways and means of working with children with special needs
Performs motor skills and movement patterns with good mechanics and efficacy of performance	Shows understanding and ability to discriminate between a poor and good performance in game, dance, and gymnastic activities	Shows a mature tolerance toward others of different races and cultural backgrounds
Performs basic sport skills and movement patterns with increased proficiency	Demonstrates an increased knowledge of health-related fitness and how to design individual programs to improve and maintain one's own physical fitness	Demonstrates a mature understanding and manner in dealing with safety of self and others
Applies concepts and skills of Movement Education while playing individual and team sports	Understands the basic principles of exercise and how to apply them in an exercise program	Shows an appreciation for the ideas and physical abilities of others
Demonstrates increased defensive and offensive playing strategies in individual and team sports	Demonstrates a mature understanding of acceptable social behavior	Displays a mature attitude toward criticisms by the teacher and fellow students
Executes track and field skills with increased style and performance		Shows a positive attitude toward cooperative and competitive attitudes of others
Applies effective spotting techniques in stunts, tumbling, and other gymnastic activities		Displays an active and positive attitude toward learning new types of physical activity
Demonstrates increased style and form in folk, square, and social dance activities		Shows an attitude and direction toward activities that are intrinsically motivating
Performs expressive dance sequences using numerous types of stimuli with increased creativity and form		Demonstrates a positive attitude toward game, dance, and other movement activities from other countries
		Demonstrates an increased willingness to participate in group discussions and to abide by majority rule

TABLE 9.5 Percentage of Time for Activities

Type of Activity	Suggested Yearly Percentage of Time		
	Level I	Level II	Level III
Movement Education skills and concepts	15–25	10–20	10–15
Locomotor and nonlocomotor skills	15–20	5–10	2–5
Game activities	20–25	20–35	30–40
Dance activities	20–25	20–25	15–20
Gymnastic activities	20–30	20–25	15–20
Physical fitness activities	5–15	10–15	15–20
Special interest activities	5–20	5–20	12–20

TABLE 9.6   Physical Education Activities

	Chapter	Level I	Level II	Level III	Page
Physical Fitness Activities					
Posture activities	13	───	───	──▶	282
Conditioning exercises	8	───	───	──▶	169
Circuit training	8		───	──▶	178
Obstacle course	8		───	──▶	179
Rope jumping	26			──▶	555
Jogging	8		───	──▶	180
Aerobic dancing	8			──▶	181
Movement Education					
Body awareness	25	───	───	──▶	542
Space awareness	25	───	───	──▶	545
Qualities	25	───	───	──▶	544
Relationships	25	───	───	──▶	546
Locomotor Activities	6	───	───	──▶	105
Nonlocomotor Activities	6	───	───	──▶	116
Game Activities					
Basic game skills	6	───	──▶		120
Running, tag, and simple team games	16	───	───	──▶	321
Individual and partner games	16	───	───	──▶	321
Cooperative games	17		───	──▶	357
Classroom games	15	───	───	──▶	302
Soccer activities	18		───	──▶	372
Hockey activities	19		───	──▶	396
Football activities	20			──▶	408
Volleyball activities	21		───	──▶	424
Basketball activities	22		───	──▶	440
Softball activities	23		───	──▶	458
Track and field activities	24		───	──▶	478
Gymnastic Activities					
Stunts and tumbling skills	25	───	───	──▶	504
Movement skills	25	───	───	──▶	542
Pyramid building	25			──▶	503
Beanbag activities	26	───	───	──▶	552
Individual and long rope activities	26	───	───	──▶	555
Hoop activities	26	───	───	──▶	566
Wand activities	26	───	───	──▶	567
Parachute activities	26	───	───	──▶	570
Indian clubs, traffic cones	26	───	───	──▶	574
Juggling activities	26		───	──▶	575
Balance beam and benches	27	───	───	──▶	581
Climbing ropes	27	───	───	──▶	586
Springboard, vaulting box	27		───	──▶	590
Horizontal bar, ladder, stall bars	27	───	───	──▶	596
Agility apparatus	27	───	───	──▶	602
Outdoor apparatus	27	───	───	──▶	603
Dance Activities					
Elements of rhythm	28	───	───	──▶	608
Rhythm activities	28	───	───	──▶	612
Singing games	29	───	──▶		624
Folk dance	29		───	──▶	630
Creative dance	30	───	───	──▶	670

DEVELOPING A YEARLY PROGRAM

In most elementary schools in the United States and Canada, the classroom teacher has the primary responsibility for planning the yearly physical education program. Her task is to translate her goals, and those expressed by school officials and parents, into a broad-based activity program that meets the needs and interests of the children.

If every class were assigned thirty to forty-five minutes a day for physical education; if the interests and abilities of each class were equal, or at least similar; and if all facilities, equipment, and supplies were available for any activity selected, then a basic program with specific percentages of time allocated for specific activities would be suggested for each class. This ideal situation simply does not exist in elementary schools in the United States and Canada. There are, for example, local cultural factors to consider, such as a large local population of German- or Spanish-speaking families who might wish certain dances or game activities taught to their children. The climate also has a direct bearing on the selection of activities and when they are taught. Also, as mentioned earlier, the teacher's background and competence in physical education directly affect the nature and direction of every aspect of the program. School conditions, such as time allotments, class size, and available equipment and facilities must also be given consideration before beginning the first step in planning a yearly program. Once these are considered, the following five-step plan provides a framework on which the classroom teacher can develop her own program.[1]

C O N C E P T

9.6 Developing a Yearly Program of Physical Education Requires Careful Planning that Includes Decision Making Regarding Demands That Arise before, during, and after Teaching

---

Step 1: Establish the Aim and Goals of the Program

The basic aim and goals of an elementary physical education program discussed in chapter 1 can be used as a starting point for the classroom teacher. It is likely that the aim of producing "physically educated individuals" will be common to all programs of physical education. However, the particular goals established to achieve this aim might differ slightly between particular programs. The goals identified

in chapter 1 can be modified, or others can be added, to reflect the philosophy or curriculum goals of the local school district, or the wishes of parents and school officials. The developmental curriculum described earlier used Bloom's (1976) three domains of learning (psychomotor, cognitive, and affective) to outline the learning descriptors for the three developmental levels in the elementary school physical education program. These three domains are also used below as a framework to provide an example of basic goals of a physical education curriculum.

Psychomotor Domain

1. To enhance physical growth and development through the provision of a quality daily physical education program
2. To help each child develop and maintain an optimum level of health-related fitness
3. To help children develop a wide variety of physical skills that can and will be used to achieve long-term enjoyment through wholesome and recreational activities

Cognitive Domain

1. To help each child understand how the human body works, the ways of learning skills and movement concepts, and the basic principles and mechanics of movement
2. To develop children's knowledge and understanding of a wide variety of game, dance, gymnastic, and body management principles, concepts, and strategies
3. To provide opportunities for all children to enhance their innate creative talents
4. To provide opportunities to enhance academic concepts and skills through the medium of physical activity

Affective Domain

1. To develop within each child a feeling of joy and excitement through movement
2. To enhance each child's positive self-image
3. To develop within each child a willingness to listen to and accept the ideas and opinions of others
4. To develop each child's conscious feeling for the safety and protection of self and other classmates
5. To develop each child's understanding of and appreciation for differences in ethnic and cultural backgrounds, in abilities, and in disabilities

Step 2: Select General Activity Areas

Selecting and allocating a percentage of time to game, dance, and gymnastic activities is a difficult task for the classroom teacher. In the first place, classes are usually organized according to age rather than ability. Ability in physical education, as with other subject areas, varies immensely within any age level. For example, a class of second-graders, ranging in

---

[1] The five-step process in developing a yearly physical education curriculum is explained in detail in Kirchner and Fishburne (1998). Blank copies of all the program planning sheets and worksheets identified in this chapter, together with a number of other important planning sheets, are provided in this supplemental text.

TABLE 9.7 Yearly Program Planning Sheet: Ms. Green's Third-Grade Class

Activities	Chapter	Value		Student Interest		Safety Risk		Teacher Competence		Facilities	Equipment	No. of Lessons
		High	Low	High	Low	High	Low	High	Low			
Game Activities												
Unit 1: Ball Skills (hand-eye)	16	X		X			X	X		Adequate	Class sets of balls	15
Unit 2: Ball skills (foot-eye)	16	X		X			X	X		Adequate	Class sets of balls	15
Unit 3: Cooperative games	17	X		X			X	X		Adequate	Class sets of balls	10
Unit 4: Ball skills	18	X		X			X	X		Adequate	Class sets of balls	15
												55 lessons
Gymnastic Activities												
Unit 1: Gymnastics	25–27	X		X		X			X	Adequate	Small equipment sufficient	15
Unit 2: Gymnastics	25–27	X		X		X			X	Adequate	Large equipment limited	15
Unit 3: Gymnastics	25–27	X		X		X			X	Adequate	Large equipment limited	15
Unit 4: Gymnastics	25–27	X		X		X			X	Adequate	Large equipment limited	10
												55 lessons
Dance Activities												
Unit 1: Rhythmics	28	X			X	X		X		Adequate	Tapes	5
Unit 2: Creative folk dance	29	X			X	X		X		Adequate	Tapes	10
Unit 3: Folk dance	29	X			X	X		X		Adequate	Tapes	15
Unit 4: Creative folk dance	30	X			X	X		X		Adequate	Tapes and instruction	15
												45 lessons
Other Activities	Reserved 25 lessons for extras											25 lessons

↑ In terms of your stated goals.

↑ In terms of class's needs and interests.

↑ Consider class's age in relation to nature and activity.

↑ Consider teaching skills and experiences in each activity.

↑ Consider quality and quantity of facilities and equipment: Describe situation for each unit.

↑ Attempt to provide a balanced program of activities.

Note: Physical fitness and movement concepts and skills have been incorporated into each respective unit of instruction.

age from late six to early eight, can vary as much as five years in physiological maturity. In addition, differences occur in prior experience of children, teacher competence in each activity area, and available facilities and equipment. The following teaching situation illustrates how this important step in selecting appropriate activities can be accomplished.

This example illustrates how Ms. Green, a third-grade teacher, used the "Yearly Program Planning Sheet" shown in table 9.7 to develop a balanced program of activities. Her teaching situation included 180 teaching days, each having a thirty-minute physical education class with access to indoor and outdoor facilities.

		Suggested Percentage	Total Percentage	Number of Days
180 days of instruction	Games	20	30	54
30-minute lessons	Dance	25	25	45
5 lessons/week or 36 weeks of instruction (180 ÷ 5)	Gymnastics	30	30	54
	Movement concepts	⑩		
	Fitness (stress in each area)	5	5	9
	Nonscheduled	10	10	18
			100%	180 days

TABLE 9.8 Worksheet A (from Table 9.5)

Ms. Green's first decision was to allocate a percentage of time to one or more of the activity areas outlined in table 9.5. Based on the recommended percentages of time, Ms. Green recorded the suggested division of time on Worksheet A, illustrated in table 9.8. She then adjusted the suggested percentage of time to meet her own unique situation. Because she planned to emphasize the Movement Education concepts and skills in her gymnastic program, Ms. Green decided to take the 10 percent allocated for Movement Education concepts and use it to increase her game activities (see Table 9.8, "Worksheet A"). She felt that the 30 percent allocation of time for gymnastics would be adequate time to handle the Movement Education concepts and skills in her gymnastic program. The 5 percent for physical fitness activities, she decided, would be represented in the warm-up activities for all lessons within each content area. The remaining 10 percent was reserved for other activities.

According to Ms. Green's checks and written comments in table 9.7, she has made a preliminary selection of activities and indicated where problems might arise. For example, she was concerned about the high level of risk in gymnastic activities and her general low level of competence to teach these activities using the Movement Education approach. Consequently, she would need to participate in in-service programs and perhaps eliminate the higher-risk large-apparatus activities she felt unsure about teaching. She also saw the importance of creative dance activities but noted her class's low interest in these activities. This lack of interest will require a review of more creative and appropriate teaching strategies for this activity. After reviewing the teaching and administrative considerations, she decided to teach four units within each activity area.

The "Yearly Program Planning Sheet" (table 9.7) provides a means of allocating the available instructional time to appropriate activities. It does *not*, however, indicate what should be emphasized within each activity area or the month of the year when these activities should be taught. Table 9.9 is used to accomplish this task. Ms. Green has decided to block the activities according to the way she had

planned her original units, that is, in blocks of one, two, or three weeks. She started the program with the first games unit, then followed a general pattern of alternating activities until the end of April. With the five remaining weeks, sufficient school funds were available for a two-week swimming program that would be handled by a local YMCA. After taking a course in orienteering in March, she decided to try out a few ideas during the first week in May. The activities of the last two weeks were chosen by the children.

The format illustrated in this general outline is perhaps the easiest way to organize the full year's program of activities. However, other factors—such as climate, age of children, and available facilities—might indicate other patterns of organizing the program. The various types of units are discussed under the next step in the process of developing a physical education curriculum.

Step 3: Develop Instructional Units

An instructional unit is one segment of the yearly program, which normally emphasizes one type of activity and lasts for a set period of time. Because it is unlikely that a single lesson of gymnastics, for example, will achieve all the desired learning outcomes in that area, several sequentially planned lessons will be necessary. This grouping of several lessons, usually connected by an underlying theme, is known as an instructional unit. Instructional units require careful planning if learning outcomes are to be realized. Although there is no standard format for a unit plan, it usually contains the following seven items:

A. Objectives
B. Sequential list of concepts and skills to be learned
C. Selection of activities
D. Organization and teaching strategies
E. Equipment and facilities
F. Evaluation
G. Resources

A clarification of each item is provided below, along with suggestions to help each teacher construct his own unit plans.

TABLE 9.9 General Outline of a Yearly Program (Level II)

September Week		February Week	
1	Unit 1: game skills (hand-eye)	20	Unit 8: dance—creative folk
2	Unit 1: game skills (hand-eye)	21	Unit 9: gymnastics—level 3 (Movement Education)
3	Unit 1: game skills (hand-eye)	22	Unit 9: gymnastics—level 3 (Movement Education)
4	Unit 2: gymnastics—level 1 (Movement Education)	23	Unit 9: gymnastics—level 3 (Movement Education)
October **Week**		**March** **Week**	
5	Unit 2: gymnastics—level 1 (Movement Education)	24	Unit 10: dance—creative
6	Unit 2: gymnastics—level 1 (Movement Education)	25	Unit 10: dance—creative
7	Unit 3: rhythmics	26	Unit 10: dance—creative
8	Unit 4: cooperative games	27	Unit 11: games—ball skills
9	Unit 4: cooperative games		
November **Week**		**April** **Week**	
10	Unit 5: folk dance	28	Unit 11: games—ball skills
11	Unit 5: folk dance	29	Unit 11: games—ball skills
12	Unit 5: folk dance	30	Unit 12: gymnastics—level 4 (Movement Education)
13	Unit 6: gymnastics—level 2 (Movement Education)	31	Unit 12: gymnastics—level 4 (Movement Education)
December **Week**		**May** **Week**	
14	Unit 6: gymnastics—level 2 (Movement Education)	32	Unit 13: orienteering
15	Unit 6: gymnastics—level 2 (Movement Education)	33	Unit 14: swimming
		34	Unit 14: swimming
January **Week**		35	Unit 15: track and field
16	Unit 7: games (foot-eye)	**June** **Week**	
17	Unit 7: games (foot-eye)	36	Unit 16: softball
18	Unit 7: games (foot-eye)		
19	Unit 8: dance—creative folk		

A. Objectives

The objectives of a unit are normally expressed in terms of general objectives, then broken down into learning descriptors. For example, a fifteen-lesson soccer unit for a fifth-grade class might have the following general objectives:

1. To teach children to play soccer
2. To teach children to appreciate the rules and strategies of soccer
3. To provide for positive interpersonal relations
4. To enhance leadership qualities, fair play, and sportsmanship

Although these objectives are global and sometimes difficult to evaluate, they are extremely important guidelines for selecting activities, for developing teaching strategies, and for dealing with other related parts of an instructional unit.

Once the general objectives for a unit are established, a list of learning descriptors must be stated. The level III descriptors are outlined in table 9.4 on page 193. For example, in the soccer unit cited, the learning descriptors would be as follows:

1. Shows how to kick a stationary and moving ball with the instep and side of foot

2. Possesses the ability to trap a ball with the chest, leg, shin, and foot
3. Performs dribble and pass with reasonable accuracy
4. Shows how to head a ball with reasonable accuracy
5. Demonstrates positional play and team strategy
6. Understands own level of ability prior to and after a unit of soccer
7. Shows mature tolerance toward others with different levels of ability
8. Demonstrates willingness to participate in team discussions and to abide by majority rule

These learning descriptors provide guideposts for the teacher to follow. They can tell the direction a child in each level should be moving, but they cannot demand that she reach the signpost at a certain time or restrict her if her level of maturity and ability demand higher levels of performance and achievement.

B. Sequential List of Concepts and Skills

Learning outcomes help identify the skills and concepts for each unit of instruction. The previous soccer unit can be used to illustrate the sequential listing of introductory skills, rules, and strategies. After referring to the "Suggested Sequence of

Presenting Soccer Skills and Rules" (chapter 18, table 18.1), the teacher would make the following tentative list:

1. Instep kick
2. Heading
3. Corner and penalty kicks
4. Pass and trap
5. Throw in
6. Positional play

After administering a skill test and observing the children play a few lead-up games, the teacher would be able to properly sequence the selected activities to meet the general level of interest and ability of her class.

C. Selection of Activities

The activities for a unit are the medium through which the general objectives are accomplished. In the soccer unit, appropriate activities would include these:

1. A list of practice activities, p. 381
2. A list of lead-up games, p. 387
3. Rules and regulations of soccer, p. 389

D. Organization and Teaching Strategies

This part of the instructional unit outlines the various organizational techniques and teaching strategies used throughout the unit. The fifth-grade teacher of the soccer unit might outline the methods and techniques she will use throughout the unit as follows:

Organization
Modified unit (see "Types of Instructional Unit" below)
Station work
Rotational team or group leaders
Reduce size of outdoor instructional area and mark out grids for station work
Improvise: size and type of balls, location and number of goals, number of players, change rules

Teaching Strategies
Stress progression from individual to partner to group activities
Stress balance between structured drills and lead-up games with inventive activities
Stress individual progress and self-evaluation
Use direct methods of teaching for skill acquisition and indirect methods for creative and inventive play

E. Equipment and Facilities

The success of any instructional unit depends on having adequate facilities and sufficient equipment for all participants. In the games program, balls and related small equipment should be procured for each games unit. Balls of various sizes and improvised equipment should be acceptable in schools with budget limitations, and should be used in all schools to accommodate children with special needs. Gymnastic units involving a large number of small and larger

equipment might require the use of "pooled" apparatus or a revamping of the gymnastic units of instruction to cope with limitations in the type and number of apparatus, and again, to accommodate children of all developmental levels. Finally, dance units normally require tedious hours of selecting and taping musical accompaniments. If all teachers in a school agree on a standardized procedure of storing tapes, tapes can be shared, saving many hours of work for each teacher. Improvised instruments (see appendix B) can also be used in most creative dance programs.

F. Evaluation

To determine whether the unit objectives have been realized, some form of assessment will be necessary. Formative and summative evaluative procedures should be established for every instructional unit. An explanation of these evaluative procedures, together with a description of appropriate subjective and objective evaluative instruments, is provided in chapter 11.

G. Resources

Two basic types of resources should be listed in each unit plan: (1) written materials, such as textbooks, individual activity units, and other printed materials, and (2) audiovisual materials, such as films, videotapes, or demonstration charts. It is wise to include order forms for films and tapes to confirm their availability before the instructional unit begins.

This type of instructional plan is appropriate for most structured activities within game, dance, and gymnastic programs. Instructional units involving creative dance or the Movement Education approach in gymnastics must be adapted to meet the unique conditions of a theme approach to sequencing as well as to methods of evaluation.

Types of Instructional Unit

Selecting the appropriate type of instructional unit is one of the most important tasks within step 3. Following are three basic types of units that can be used in the primary and intermediate grades. Each teacher should select the unit that most readily meets the needs of his class and is in harmony with his basic teaching approach.

C O N C E P T

9.7 The Multiple, Modified, and Solid Types of Instructional Units offer Alternative Ways of Organizing Teaching of the Physical Education Curriculum

Multiple Teaching Unit

The multiple teaching unit is actually two or three units taught concurrently throughout the year. In other words, game, dance, and gymnastic activities are taught on alternate days for an indefinite period (see table 9.10). Kindergarten activities might include games on Monday, gymnastics

TABLE 9.10   Sample Weekly Plan for Level I (Multiple Unit)

Monday *Game Skills*	Tuesday *Floor Stunts*	Wednesday *Rhythmic Activities*	Thursday *Singing Games*	Friday *Classroom Games*

Bouncing practice activities
1. Bounce and catch
2. Bounce several times
3. Bounce to partner
	Camel walk,
	  elevator, tightrope
	  walk
		Pantomime animal
		  walks, such as
		  bears, lions, dogs,
		  and horses
			"London Bridge"	"Ringmaster"

TABLE 9.11   Dance Unit for Level II (Modified Unit)

	Monday	Tuesday	Wednesday	Thursday	Friday
1st Week	*Introduce:* "Paw Paw Patch"	*Review:* "Paw Paw Patch" *Introduce:* "Bleking"	*Games:* Stunts Relay Pinch-oh	*Review:* "Bleking" "Skip to My Lou"	*Review:* "Paw Paw Patch" "Bleking" "Skip to My Lou"
2nd Week	*Review:* "Skip to My Lou" *Introduce:* "Pease Porridge Hot"	*Review:* "Pease Porridge Hot" "Skip to My Lou"	*Gymnastics:* Stunts Balance beam Rope skipping	*Review:* "Bleking" "Pease Porridge Hot"	*Review:* "Skip to My Lou" *Introduce:* Jiffy Mixer
3rd Week	*Review:* Jiffy Mixer *Introduce:* "Shoo Fly"	*Review:* Jiffy Mixer "Shoo Fly"	*Review:* Games or stunts	*Review:* "Paw Paw Patch" "Bleking" "Skip to My Lou"	*Review:* "Pease Porridge Hot" "Skip to My Lou" Jiffy Mixer

on Tuesday, dance on Wednesday, and singing games (representing dance) on Thursday to start the second rotation. In this case, the rotation system has been modified by having similar activities two days in a row.

Advantages of this approach are its variety of activities and its flexibility; therefore, it can be used in kindergarten and first-grade classes to cope with the short attention spans of five- and six-year-olds. The facilities and equipment available may determine whether this method can be adopted. Whatever the reasons for selecting the multiple unit, the teacher should make sure that game, dance, and gymnastic activities are given the appropriate amount of emphasis.

Modified Teaching Unit

The modified teaching unit is a block of time allocated primarily for the instruction of one type of activity. For example, dance might be emphasized 90 percent of the time during a three- or four-week period, while the remaining 10 percent might be devoted to game and gymnastic activities. Table 9.11 exemplifies a third-grade class with a thirty-minute physical education period scheduled every day in the gymnasium. During the first week of the unit, dance activities are taught on Monday, Tuesday,

Thursday, and Friday. Wednesday is set aside for gymnastics or outdoor games.

This method provides both continuity and variety. For example, "Paw Paw Patch" is introduced on Monday and repeated on Tuesday so that the basic skills and dance patterns are learned. Later in the Tuesday lesson, "Bleking" is introduced. To provide variety, Wednesday is set aside for vigorous running and tag games, which could be played in the gymnasium or outdoors. The remaining two days are devoted to dance activities. This pattern continues throughout the second and third weeks.

The modified block, unlike the multiple unit, provides continuity in learning skills and has certain desirable instructional features. It permits the teacher to plan one type of activity for an extended period, rather than three different types each week. Furthermore, planning a one-year program is much easier using the modified unit than the multiple approach.

Solid Teaching Unit

A solid teaching unit is an extended period of instruction—from one to several weeks—devoted exclusively to one type of activity. Its value lies in its continuity, as there is no disruption in the type of skill development. Perhaps the solid

TABLE 9.12	**Softball Unit for Level III (Solid Block Approach)**				
	Monday (40 min.)	**Tuesday (15 min.)**	**Wednesday (40 min.)**	**Thursday (15 min.)**	**Friday (40 min.)**
1st week	*Explain:* Underhand throw (pitching) *Practice:* Zigzag passing *Lead-up:* Center ball	*Practice:* Throwing *Lead-up:* Shuttle throw	*Explain:* Bunting *Practice:* Swing at four *Lead-up:* Twenty-one softball	*Review:* Shuttle throw Twenty-one	*Explain:* Grounders *Practice:* Zigzag passing *Lead-up:* Bat ball

Note: Continue the above pattern during the second, third, and fourth weeks.

TABLE 9.13	**Structure of a Lesson**			
Entry Activity	**Part 1** *Introductory Activity (Set)*		**Part 2** *Skill Development (Body)*	**Part 3** *Closure*
	Stress vigorous warm-up activities Standard for all types of physical education lessons		**Games:** Stress acquisition of skills and concepts through individual and partner activities and group games **Gymnastics:** Stress acquisition of stunts and movement skills and concepts through individual, partner, and small equipment activities and large apparatus **Dance:** Stress acquisition of skills and movement ideas and concepts through individual, partner, and group activities	Stress key points

unit has its greatest application in team teaching, where the most qualified teacher is used to maximum effectiveness. However, fifth- and sixth-grade teachers who are responsible for their own physical education programs might find this type of unit applicable in teaching activities that are of great interest to their students.

Refer to table 9.12, in which a solid four-week unit of softball has been organized for a sixth-grade class. Note that the physical education period is scheduled for forty minutes on Monday, Wednesday, and Friday but for only fifteen minutes on Tuesday and Thursday. New skills are explained and demonstrated, drills are practiced, and lead-up games are played during the longer periods. The shorter periods are just long enough for a short drill and possibly a lead-up game.

It is suggested that the first week be planned in detail. After four or five days of instruction, the teacher might note that certain skills require additional concentration, or that students are ready for more advanced skills and lead-up games. The remaining three weeks should be planned around the skill level and interests of the class.

It is possible to use both modified and solid units during the year. Early fall and spring activities are particularly adaptable to the solid unit, while the modified unit might be the only feasible approach for activities requiring the use of indoor facilities.

Step 4: Develop Flexible Lesson Plans

The next important phase in curriculum design is to plan and execute a series of lesson plans for each unit. This is one of the most important aspects of teaching. Good lesson plans set the direction and tone, establish the main focus, minimize confusion and loss of time, and help keep the teacher and class on track throughout each part of the lesson.

A physical education lesson plan should be considered a flexible guideline that includes brief notes and suggestions relating to objectives, equipment, content, organizational procedures, and teaching cues. The lesson plan for teaching game, dance, or gymnastic activities normally contains three parts, as shown in table 9.13. The general progression within each content area is to begin with a warm-up session. This time can be used to explain what is to occur in the current lesson and how this relates to the last class, and perhaps what will happen in the subsequent class. This part of the lesson is termed "set" and provides an opportunity for "structure," one of the key teaching behaviors described in chapter 4. Note that, to save time and maximize student participation in activity, setting up the lesson (set) can begin in the classroom before moving to the activity area. The lesson progresses from a warm-up session (set) to the main "body" of the lesson, which is part 2. Here, the main skill and/or concept is developed. The final part of the lesson, part 3, is designed to bring "closure," which provides the opportunity to check for children's understanding of the concepts and skills being taught (evaluation). Since all lessons should end with a cool-down time, closure may involve a review of the key points of the lesson during this time. Hence, the lesson plan format is often termed "set–body–closure" to represent these three distinct parts. The sample lesson plan in table 9.14 will help each teacher develop her own lesson format.

C O N C E P T

9.8 *A Lesson Plan Should Include these Three Essential Parts: Set, Body, and Closure*

Entry Activities

In table 9.14, the three minutes allocated for entry activities is the time children normally take to come into the gymnasium, change, and wait for the lesson to begin. Although the changing procedures vary from school to school and from grade to grade, a definite procedure should be established in order to use this time effectively. If children change and enter the gymnasium in a somewhat staggered fashion, establish a routine that will reward the quick changer. In this sample lesson, the teacher places four containers of balls and small equipment in the four corners of the gymnasium. As soon as a child enters the gymnasium, she is allowed to get a ball and practice kicking it from a stationary position toward the wall. When all the children have arrived, the teacher instructs them to put the balls back in the containers and then either sit in their station places or line up in their teams. The lesson is now ready to begin.

Part 1: Introductory Activities (Set)

Introductory activities, or what has been known as the warm-up period, serve three general purposes. The first is to provide an opportunity to "set up" the lesson. Providing children with an understanding of what is to occur in the lesson, and why, allows children to make connections between existing knowledge and what is to come (advance organizer). The second purpose is to provide an activity that involves all children in vigorous movement for the first three to five minutes of the lesson. Finally, the third purpose is to include in these activities movements or skills that will be stressed in the remaining parts of the lesson. In a sense, it is "catching two birds with one net." In the sample lesson, requiring children to roll the ball, then to run and jump over it, contributes to general vigorous movement. Rolling the ball and learning to judge its speed and position

when jumping over it, also provides opportunities to improve foot-eye coordination, which is part of the unit and lesson emphasis. Usually teachers can plan activities that contribute to both purposes. However, there are times when the teacher wants to introduce a change of pace, such as a vigorous lead-up game, a physical fitness circuit, or rope skipping, which might contribute only to the physical fitness purpose and not directly to the main theme of the lesson. This situation should be encouraged.

Part 2: Skill Development (Body)

The second part of the lesson establishes its focus and direction. Once the first lesson has been taught, the second and all remaining lessons normally begin with a quick review of the key point or skills introduced in the preceding lesson. Following this, new skills are introduced and practiced individually, then with a partner, and finally in small groups. This is the usual teaching progression. However, the exact way a particular skill, game, or movement idea is taught to children will depend on their age and ability, and the particular style of teaching. If children are being taught a specific sport skill, they are normally introduced to the skill by an explanation and demonstration of the key components of the movement. This is followed by individual practice drills that progress to partner and group drill activities. The latter phase of part 2 normally includes one or more lead-up or modified games. Gymnastic lessons follow a similar pattern, beginning with the introduction of individual movement concepts or skills on the floor or mats followed by practice with small equipment before moving to large apparatus. Dance lessons also begin with individual movements, then progress to partner and group dance activities.

The sample lesson plan in table 9.14 illustrates the use of the direct teaching style. Each skill is explained and demonstrated, followed with individual and partner practice. The teacher could have used more exploratory methods, particularly with this first-grade class. Her choices, in this case, could have been based on the general maturity or background of the class. However, she changed her style toward the end of part 2.

Part 3: Closure

This short session at the end of the lesson has a twofold purpose. First, it is a time to review the key points of the lesson or to stress a valuable concept that arose during the lesson. The second purpose is to provide a quiet time to allow children to "settle down" before returning to the classroom.

Variations in Lesson Plans

The lesson plan example illustrated in table 9.14 was based on a thirty-minute physical education period; however, in many schools, particularly for the primary grades, the period might last only fifteen to twenty minutes. Since it may not be possible to cover three main parts of a lesson in such a short period, the lesson can begin on one day and continue on the next without any major loss in the continuity of

 **ABLE 9.14**   Unit No. 2: Ball Skills—Foot-Eye

Grade 1

Lesson No. 3: Kicking a moving ball

Objectives: To learn how to kick a moving ball

To learn how to roll and gain possession of the ball

To learn to follow a few simple rules of the game

To learn to stay on-task until the practice activity or game is completed

Equipment: Class set of 8½-inch utility balls or old volleyballs

Content	Organization/Cues	Lesson Evaluation
Entry Activity (3 Minutes)	Place balls and small equipment in four containers Get ball and no equipment	Children used equipment and balls—next time balls only
Part 1: Introductory Activities: Set (3 to 5 Minutes) Roll and jump over a ball	Roll and jump over as many as possible Repeat with change of direction	Stress safety practices in future lessons
Part 2: Skill Development: Body (10 to 15 Minutes) *Review:* Kicking Stationary ball *Introduce:* Kick moving ball Gaining possession Kick toward target Partner and kicking game	Toward wall and kick rebound Roll, chase, kick Roll, chase, kick to wall Repeat above with partner Make up game—partners and two goals Add to game—must kick while ball is rolling	Check key teaching points Too difficult—make challenge for individual and small equipment
Part 3: Closure (2 Minutes) Discuss ball contact on foot and staying on-task		

learning. The previous lesson will be used to illustrate such a modification. As shown in figure 9.1, part 1 and the first half of part 2 were covered in the twenty-five-minute instructional period on Monday. The second part of the lesson took longer than the teacher had expected. Thus, on Tuesday, the lesson started with a five-minute introductory activity warm-up, then moved directly to partners making up a game. As this second lesson had five minutes remaining, the teacher added two more variations to the challenge before moving to part three: closure. Note, however, that even though the single lesson was split over two days, some form of closure and introduction (set) occurred on both days to ensure continuity in learning.

Regardless of the time available during the first five or six lessons, a considerable amount must be devoted to skill development. As the children acquire skill and movement understanding, more time can be devoted to group activities. The best guideline for determining the emphasis of the lesson plan is the children's progress. If the skill level appears to be quite low, continue to emphasize practice activities. If there is marked improvement, increase the difficulty of individual and partner activities and give more time and emphasis to group activities.

The amount of detail that a teacher records on his lesson plan depends, of course, on his professional background and experience. Beginning teachers tend to write down more detail. Abbreviated notes under each of the main parts of the lesson usually suffice for the more experienced teacher.

Step 5: Conduct Student and Program Evaluations

The final step in curriculum development is assessing student progress and the success of each part of the physical education program. Evaluation, as discussed in chapter 11, is an ongoing process of determining whether program, unit, or lesson plan objectives are being met. Teachers should use formative

CHAPTER 9

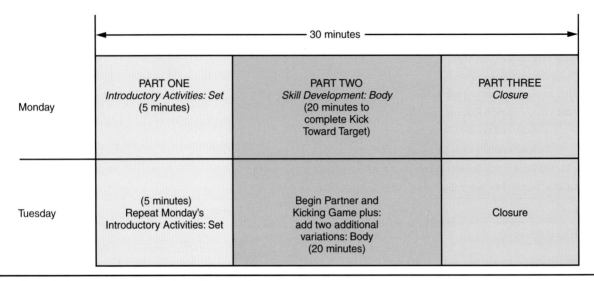

Figure 9.1   A three-part instructional unit for two class periods.

techniques throughout the yearly program and make appropriate adjustments in content and teaching strategies according to these objective and subjective assessments.

The evaluation of the instructional program that occurs at the end of the year can take many forms. For example, the "Physical Education Program Evaluation Form" (chapter 11, table 11.6) can be modified to accommodate individual school or district programs. Other methods, such as using external evaluative teams, can be very effective in assessing the total program. The important consideration of the latter type of evaluation is to use the findings to meet revealed deficiencies and, where indicated, to enrich program offerings.

Summary Review

The instructional process consists basically of three distinct areas, each characterized by different demands on the teacher: before teaching, during teaching, and after teaching. To ensure effective instruction, each area requires careful planning and decision making. Initially, a teacher must identify the local conditions and teaching situation. Once the school conditions have been identified—such as class size, children with special needs, type and availability of facilities and equipment, etc.—a five-step plan can be followed to assist in the design of the yearly program. The five-step plan provides a framework for designing quality programs of physical education that meet the needs of the local conditions and teaching situation. The five steps are as follows:

1. Establish the aim and goals of the program
2. Select general activity areas
3. Develop instructional units
4. Develop flexible lesson plans
5. Conduct student and program evaluations

Another important teaching decision that must occur during the planning process, is deciding on a teaching approach that will meet the aim, goals, and objectives of the program. Three of the most popular curriculum models are traditional, Movement Education, and developmental. The developmental model is favored because it encompasses strengths of both the traditional approach and the Movement Education approach. Further, this model is based on developmentally appropriate activities for children that engender success, and this is a sound principle of effective teaching.

INDIVIDUAL *and* **GROUP** PROJECTS

1. In small groups, assuming early childhood developmental level I children, design three lesson plans—one for each of the game, dance, and gymnastic areas. Compare group lesson plans, identifying strengths and weaknesses.
2. Assuming late childhood developmental level III children, repeat the activities described above in number 1.
3. In small groups, identify the strengths and weaknesses of the three popular curriculum models: traditional, Movement Education, and developmental. Share ideas among groups.
4. Individually or in small groups, visit local schools to determine what types of instructional unit design (solid, modified, multiple) are being used with different curriculum subject areas. As a class, share and debate findings.

SELECTED READINGS

Bloom, B. S. 1976. *Human characteristics and school learning.* New York: McGraw-Hill.

Borich, G. D. 1996. *Effective teaching methods.* New York: Macmillan.

Eggen, P. D., and D. P. Kauchak. 1996. *Strategies for teachers.* Boston: Allyn & Bacon.

Freiberg, H. J., and A. Driscoll. 1996. *Universal teaching strategies.* Boston: Allyn & Bacon.

Gabbard, C., E. Leblanc, and S. Lowy. 1994. *Physical education for children: Building the foundation.* Englewood Cliffs, NJ: Prentice Hall.

Gallahue, D. L. 1993. *Developmental physical education for today's children.* 2d ed. Dubuque, IA: Brown & Benchmark.

Graham, G., S. A. Holt-Hale, and M. Parker. 1987. *Children moving.* 2d ed. Palo Alto, CA: Mayfield.

Harrison, J. M., C. L. Blakemore, M. M. Buck, and T. L. Pellet. 1996. *Instructional strategies for secondary school physical education.* 4th ed. Dubuque, IA: Wm. C. Brown.

Jewett, A. E., and L. L. Bain. 1985. *The curriculum process in physical education.* Dubuque, IA: Wm. C. Brown.

Kirchner, G., and G. J. Fishburne. 1998. *Developing yearly programs, units, and daily lesson plans for physical education for elementary school children.* 10th ed. Dubuque, IA: Brown & Benchmark.

Laban, R., and L. Ullman. 1960. *The mastery of movement.* London: Macdonald & Evans.

Lefrançois, G. R. 1994. *Psychology for teaching.* Belmont, CA: Wadsworth.

Logsdon, B. J., et al. 1977. *Physical education for children: A focus on the teaching process.* Philadelphia: Lea & Febiger.

Mosston, M., and S. Ashworth. 1994. *Teaching physical education.* 4th ed. New York: Macmillan.

Pangrazi, R. P., and V. P. Dauer. 1995. *Dynamic physical education for elementary school children.* New York: Macmillan.

Reiser, R. A., and W. Dick. 1996. *Instructional planning.* Boston: Allyn & Bacon.

Siedentop, D., C. Mand, and A. Taggart. 1986. *Physical education and curriculum strategies for grades 5–12.* Palo Alto, CA: Mayfield.

Wall, J., and N. Murray. 1994. *Children and movement.* 2d ed. Dubuque, IA: Wm. C. Brown.

KEY CONCEPTS

10.1 Physical education should be provided on a daily basis to all elementary school children

10.2 Parent and student assistance enhances the scope and quality of elementary school physical education programs

10.3 Effective program planning requires an understanding of each child's health status

10.4 Teachers act *in loco parentis* (that is, in the place of the parent) in all aspects of the elementary school program

10.5 Effective class management ensures a positive and safe learning environment

10.6 Grouping of children should be done without showing favoritism or portraying any child as inadequate

10.7 Understanding her legal responsibilities helps the teacher maintain a safe learning environment

10.8 Adequate facilities, equipment, and supplies are prerequisite to a well-balanced physical education program

10.9 Playgrounds should be planned collaboratively by architects, landscape designers, educators, parents, and children

KEY OBJECTIVES

After completing this chapter you should be able to:

1. Develop policies and procedures relating to the operational components of the physical education program
2. Design and apply effective class management skills and techniques
3. Organize and manage the apparatus, equipment, and supplies required in an elementary school physical education program
4. Understand the design and application of adventure and creative playgrounds
5. Understand the basic legal terminology
6. Maintain a safe learning environment for all scheduled physical activities

The quality of any physical education program depends primarily on the philosophy and competence of the teacher. Both philosophy and competence are reflected in the way the teacher manages her class and in the way she uses available space and equipment. This chapter provides some ideas and suggestions relating to general class management. It also provides information related to maintaining and effectively using available facilities, equipment, and supplies.

ORGANIZATIONAL DETAILS

Once the physical education program has been designed and teaching responsibilities have been assigned to the teaching staff, a number of other important organizational details must be completed. Policies and procedures should be established for the following areas before any instructional program begins.

Class Size

Class size in physical education normally should not exceed the regular number of children in each respective classroom. Generally speaking, assigning two classes to one physical education class is educationally unsound and can create an extremely unsafe teaching environment. In addition, it is very difficult to individualize and provide developmentally appropriate activities in large classes. A few acceptable exceptions to this rule are discussed later in this chapter. Also, if two or more children with severe disabilities are enrolled in a physical education class, extra assistance is warranted.

Time Allotment

The recommended amount of time for physical education varies from a minimum of 20 minutes to one hour per day. The most common figure is 150 minutes per week, which translates into daily 30-minute classes. In the intermediate grades, the 150 minutes may be arranged into three 50-minute classes per week to provide for showering and longer periods of instruction. However, the 150 minutes per week does not include recess, supervised free play, or other intramural or interschool activities.

CONCEPT

10.1 *Physical Education Should Be Provided on a Daily Basis to All Elementary School Children*

Scheduling

The problems of scheduling physical education vary from school to school. If the principal and staff are cooperative, it is wise to devise the schedule for all physical education classes before scheduling other classes. This is not favoritism; it simply permits the most appropriate scheduling of a limited number of physical education facilities. Whenever there are limited facilities for the number of classes, equal access should be given to all classes. In previous years, the upper elementary grades were normally scheduled indoors or outdoors first, leaving only what time remained to early childhood classes. The same general procedure was also used to schedule specialist help if it was available. Today all classes, regardless of grade level, must be given equal access to facilities and specialist assistance.

When there is adequate staff, facilities, and equipment to provide for daily physical education, class schedules can be devised with relative ease. Teachers' individual preferences regarding when their classes should have physical education can be accommodated, because there is no evidence to support claims that physical education is more effective at a specific time in the instructional day. However, when facilities and equipment are limited or other special programs have to be offered at a certain time, more "give and take" is required, as is a creative approach to timetabling. A few alternatives are described below to illustrate how daily physical education can be provided in spite of limited facilities and equipment or schedule conflicts with other special programs (Bell 1990).

Perhaps one of the simplest methods of providing daily physical education for all children is combining two classes into one. As a general rule, classes should be combined by grade level. However, exceptions to this rule can be made for such activities as physical fitness programs, where several classes could meet at the same time in the gymnasium or outdoors and participate in a general exercise program. The use of alternate facilities, particularly in regions where gymnasiums are used because of cold and inclement weather, is another option. Many schools have used the lunchroom, empty classrooms, hallways, and, at times, the library. Community facilities, such as recreational centers, swimming pools, ice rinks, and church halls, have also been used to help provide quality daily physical education programs. Another method, known as "back to back" timetabling, is used in situations where a school employs a physical education specialist and a music specialist. In this example, the timetables of the classroom teacher and the two specialists are coordinated to facilitate the maximum use of all three teachers. For example, when the classroom teacher's class is receiving instruction in physical education or music, the classroom teacher is assigned preparation time or scheduled to teach another class.

Figure 10.1   Effective use of paraprofessional assistance.

Paraprofessional Assistance

The term *paraprofessional* denotes a wide variety of voluntary or paid assistants who have special qualifications but normally do not possess a teaching certificate (figure 10.1). A few of the more common types of paraprofessionals used in the elementary physical education program are described in the following paragraphs.

Teaching Assistants

State and local school districts vary with respect to the certification requirements and types of duties that can legally be assigned to a teaching assistant. Normally a teaching assistant completes a special program in a community college and may be assigned to assist regular teachers or to supervise recess, noon-hour, and intramural activities. This type of teaching assistance and supervisory help has been very popular in virtually all school districts that have hired these paraprofessionals.

Contracted Recreational Specialists

During the past few years, the trend toward contracting local recreational specialists in such activities as swimming, skiing, and skating has grown in a number of geographical areas. Perhaps the most popular program has been contracting with local YMCA or recreational centers to teach a basic or survival swimming program to a particular grade. In most cases, these specialists' philosophy and instructional approach to teaching young children is similar to the school's. These factors should, however, be checked before entering into a contractual agreement with any nonschool agency.

C O N C E P T

10.2 *Parent and Student Assistance Enhances the Scope and Quality of Elementary School Physical Education Programs*

Volunteer Assistance Programs

Under the umbrella term *volunteer assistance* are many interested and talented parents and neighbors who donate their time and talent to the elementary physical education program. For example, in the city of Nanaimo on Vancouver Island, more than 700 parents have volunteered their time to help teach, supervise, and administer physical fitness tests. Special in-service sessions are given to these volunteers to prepare them for specific tasks in each school. This program has been in operation for several years and not only has enhanced the quality of the physical education offerings but has created a positive relationship between parents and school officials.

Student Assistance

Two types of student assistance programs appear to be emerging in a large number of school districts. The first uses high school students to assist classroom teachers in the regular instructional program or as supervisors and assistant coaches in the extra-class program. Many teenagers who have worked in this program have received excellent references from principals, teachers, and parents. This early practical experience has also proven a positive method of recruiting mature, talented, and enthusiastic young men and women into the teaching profession.

The second type of student assistance program uses upper-grade students to help classroom teachers and to act as coaches, managers, and referees in the intramural program. Studies of these programs seem to indicate that older children work exceptionally well with kindergarten and first-grade children. Fifth- and sixth-graders, who are not always highly skilled but enjoy working with lower-grade children, can develop a strong rapport with young children. In numerous cases, through this program, the younger children develop motor skills as well as demonstrate a very positive self-image and a respect and an appreciation for their older "idols." It is a program that should be encouraged in virtually every elementary school.

EFFECTIVE CLASS MANAGEMENT

In education, the term *instruction* refers to the amount of time devoted to the objectives of a lesson or learning experience. It includes time spent explaining the expected learning outcomes to the class, assessing levels of ability, using a variety of motivational methods and techniques, providing practice and other learning activities, and evaluating the progress of students and the effectiveness of the instructional program. *Management* refers to those activities that are used to ensure optimum use of instructional time, facilities, and equipment. Management includes the operational skills and techniques that are used to organize the learning environment, to get attention, to move students from station to station, and to obtain and return apparatus and equipment (figure 10.2). The essential operational health policies and programs described below contribute to a healthy and safe learning environment. And the management skills and techniques that follow are the requisite skills and strategies for ensuring that maximum time is devoted to the instructional objectives of the lesson.

Medical and Health Policies and Practices

There are several health services and practices, such as periodic medical examinations, emergency care procedures, and a variety of screening tests, that are provided in most public school health programs. A few of the more common programs, policies, and practices are described below.

10.3 *Effective Program Planning Requires an Understanding of Each Child's Health Status*

Health Status Assessment

The variety of current programs designed to assess the health status of children include medical examinations and visual and hearing screening tests. The most common is a required medical examination for every child entering public school. This is normally performed by the family physician; for families with financial limitations, this service is performed by public health clinics. Visual and auditory screening assessments are normally administered periodically by the school nurse, or whenever the classroom teacher observes major changes in a child's vision or hearing. The use of physical fitness and posture tests, such as those described in chapters 8 and 13, can help teachers identify potential fitness and postural problems that should be referred to the school nurse for follow-up discussions with the parents. Other records, such as height and weight charts, also provide important information about a child's general growth and development (see chapter 2).

Figure 10.2 When equipment is properly stored, children can more easily retrieve it for quick and quiet setup.

The results of each child's medical examination and other health status information should be kept on file and be readily available to the classroom teacher. Teachers should review these files to be aware of any potential health problems that may require special consideration with respect to participation in various physical activities. For example, a child who has epilepsy might not be permitted to participate on climbing apparatus, or a child with a severe allergy to dust might be prevented from using tumbling mats but allowed to participate in other gymnastic activities, such as rope skipping, balance beam, and climbing rope activities. When a child's limitations are known and discussed by parents, teachers, and medical personnel, the child is able to participate to the best of his or her abilities in the widest range of physical activities.

10.4 *Teachers Act in Loco Parentis, (That Is, in the Place of the Parent) in All Aspects of the Elementary School Program*

Emergency Care

Whether at home or in school, elementary school children can become sick or injured. As teachers, we act *in loco parentis*, in the place of the parent. By law, we must provide a safe environment, teach physical skills in an educationally sound and safe manner, and provide emergency care whenever it is considered wise and prudent to do so. Regardless of how well teachers organize, teach, and supervise physical education activities, accidents will occur. To ensure that proper procedures are followed, school districts have developed written policies and procedures for assisting a child who has become ill or has had an accident. Because teachers are responsible for administering emergency first aid, they should possess an up-to-date first aid certificate and be qualified to administer

CPR (cardiopulmonary resuscitation). There should be first aid equipment and supplies available in the classroom and in the gymnasium, and there should be a procedure that is followed when an accident occurs. The procedure should be similar to the following.

1. *Administer first aid to the injured child.* If the teacher is alone with a class in the gymnasium or outdoors when the injury occurs, what action she should take will depend upon the seriousness of the injury. If there is life-threatening bleeding, the teacher must administer immediate first aid. In this situation, she would normally tell a responsible child to get the school nurse, the principal, or another teacher as quickly as possible. If the injury is not life threatening, the teacher should not move the child but should send for the nurse by sending a child or using a nearby teacher or custodian. Whenever a teacher is in doubt about the seriousness of the injury, and medical personnel are not available, it is wise to not move the injured child until medical personnel arrive on the scene. Whenever in doubt, be cautious to avoid aggravating the injury.
2. *Notify the child's parents or guardian as soon as possible after you have administered emergency care to the child.* School policies normally require the office to keep up-to-date phone numbers where parents or guardians can be reached. These policies should also clearly state how and to whom the child should be released after an injury has occurred, when the child is still on school premises.
3. *Complete an accident report form similar to the one shown in figure 10.3.* This form should be completed as soon as possible after the injured child has been taken care of. The teacher should provide copies to the principal and superintendent, and keep one for her own records. Accident reports can help prevent future injuries; teachers can check similar injuries with other teachers to note whether the accidents occurred because of the age and ability of the children, the element of risk involved, or the method or technique that was used to teach the activity. If a general trend begins to be revealed, teachers can institute changes to prevent future accidents. Accident report forms should also be periodically reviewed by administrators, teachers, and medical personnel to ensure that they are in harmony with current emergency policies and practices.

Student Accident Report Form

Name of injured student: ____________ Phone: ____________

Age: ________ Address: ____________

P.E. class: ____________ ____________

Homeroom: ____________ ____________

School: ____________

Date of accident: ________ A.M. P.M. ____________
(time) (day) (month)

Place of accident: ____________

Date reported: ____________

Location and description of accident: ____________

Nature of injury: ____________

Condition of environment: ____________

Supervising person: ____________

Type of activity: ____________

First-aid treatment: ____________

Where taken: ____________

Parents contacted: yes ☐ no ☐ Time: ____________

School nurse contacted: yes ☐ no ☐ Time: ____________

Witnesses: (1) ____________
(2) ____________
(3) ____________

Signature ____________

Date ____________

White copy: Superintendent's office
Pink copy: Principal's office
Green copy: Teacher's copy

Figure 10.3 Student accident report form

Student Excuses

Excuses for not participating in physical education range from permanent waivers because of chronic health conditions to temporary waivers because of colds or other illnesses. It is imperative that the principal, the school nurse, and the teacher establish policies covering problems encountered in this area. The following situations should be included in the policies:

1. A temporary excuse should be authorized by the school nurse.
2. The school nurse should authorize children to return to physical activity after any illness.
3. Children with disabilities should be encouraged to participate in physical education classes. The amount and type of participation should be indicated by the parents and/or family physician.
4. On the recommendation of the teacher, a child may be excused from participation in a physical education class because of a detectable illness or injury.

Attire

Elementary school children usually are not required to wear special uniforms for physical education. The time required to change in relation to the time available, particularly for five-, six-, and seven-year-olds, does not justify a complete change. However, tennis shoes should be worn for games and some dance activities. For gymnastic activities, the teacher should seriously consider letting the children participate in bare feet if the floor is clean and free of hazards. Bare feet assist in balance activities and encourage freedom of movement. However, this should be a gradual process to allow the children to get used to running, balancing, jumping, and landing on their bare feet. If the children enjoy participating in gymnastic activities with bare feet and there are no adverse effects (plantar warts or excessive bruising), continue the practice. Students should not be allowed to participate in physical activities wearing socks without shoes. Socks are very slippery on the floor and approaches, and can lead to accidents or injuries.

With respect to jewelry, a good policy is to have children remove all jewelry and place it in a safety box stored in the teacher's office. Pockets should also be emptied and, where appropriate, contents stored with the jewelry. Finally, all heavy clothing that would restrict a child's movements should be removed, or gymnasium shorts and T-shirts should be required to ensure safe and effective participation in physical activities.

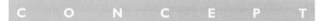

C O N C E P T

10.5 *Effective Class Management Ensures a Positive and Safe Learning Environment*

Class Management Skills and Techniques

One of the most important aspects of good teaching is to develop, in the early stages of the school year, a clear and simple set of management skills and procedures. These include a list of voice and hand signals to start and stop the class, techniques for organizing the class into groups, procedures for obtaining and returning apparatus and equipment, and techniques for controlling noise and undesirable behavior. When children understand the management strategies and know that they are carried out in a fair and consistent manner, they will be more likely to react positively toward the teacher and the learning environment.

Voice and Hand Signals

Teachers should develop a set of voice commands and hand signals to start and stop the class, to gain immediate attention, to warn or caution, and for a variety of other purposes. In general, a teacher should create and maintain a learning environment in which his normal speaking voice is sufficient for students to hear. A voice command combined with raising one hand overhead should be sufficient to gain the class's attention. There are exceptions to this general

Figure 10.4 Section places.

rule, such as when the class is spread out over a large playing field and you want to stop them for additional instruction. In this case, a short blow of the whistle is certainly in order. Clear and effective voice and hand signals need to be practiced on a regular basis. A class that learns to listen and react quickly to the teacher's commands and signals gives them more time on-task and more freedom to move within a safe and relaxed learning environment.

Assigning Section Places or Squad Positions

Early childhood teachers arrange children into small and somewhat permanent working groups called "section places" (figure 10.4). In the middle and late childhood grades, "squads" or "teams" are used for the same purpose. At the beginning of the school year or at the start of each new unit, children are usually arranged into four groups, assigned a place to sit, with the teacher delegating students to be section place leaders and allowing each group to choose their own leader and group name. Once established, a simple command or gentle request, such as "Section places," signals the children to stop what they are doing and immediately return to their positions in the section place. This is a very important routine procedure that aids in the instructional process of any lesson. It is also an effective way of redirecting children if they become off-task or if an emergency arises.

Organizing Facilities and Equipment

In the initial planning of a physical education program, the teacher designs each unit of instruction on the basis of available time, facilities, and equipment. Such planning provides information that allows her to plan to use teaching methods and techniques that are appropriate for the available equipment and supplies. For example, a gymnasium equipped with one or two mats, a balance bench, and one climbing rope is inadequate for teaching stations and an extensive use of limitation and indirect methods of instruction. Let us assume that the facilities and equipment planning has been done in the process of designing a physical

Figure 10.5 Controlling the instructional space.

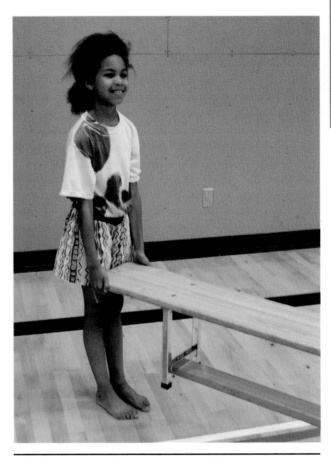

Figure 10.6 Lift with the legs.

education program. What is of concern here is the day-to-day management of facilities to ensure that the teacher's and students' time and effort are devoted primarily to instructional aspects of the lesson.

When a gymnasium or playing field is too large for effective instruction, the teacher should reduce instructional space—for instance, by placing traffic cones around one corner of the instructional area before the lesson begins and instructing students to stay within this area (figure 10.5). Placing supplies and equipment in three or four boxes or bags and locating them at the corners of the instructional area also sets the stage for an immediate and time-saving start to each lesson. Assigning monitors to accomplish these tasks gives the teacher more time for other important aspects of the lesson.

Gathering and Returning Apparatus and Equipment

Responsibility for getting out and putting away apparatus and equipment should be delegated to the children. Squad leaders are normally given the task of obtaining balls and small equipment from nearby bins or the storage room. When large apparatus, such as balance benches or large mats, are used, children as young as five and six should be taught how to "lift with the legs" (figure 10.6) and carry the apparatus with care and safety (see chapter 3). When children are asked to get hoops, wands, or other pieces of equipment that are noisy, it is a wise procedure to have children practice getting and returning this equipment. Practice in moving classroom furniture and equipment safely and with a minimum of noise (see "Classroom Games" in chapter 15) prepares children to move gymnastic apparatus in the same manner. With practice and a little patience on the part of the teacher, children soon learn to move equipment without making excessive noise. Hence, it is imperative that the teacher establish a level of noise that

he and his class will accept. It should be noted that various studies have shown that the noise level established at the beginning of the school year usually prevails throughout the school year. Repeating this process over and over until the noise level is acceptable is time well spent. Children and teachers alike enjoy a learning atmosphere that is fun and challenging and free of excessive and abusive noise.

Establishing Class Rules

Developing a set of rules for physical education is, in essence, establishing guidelines for acceptable behavior. The following set of rules is an example of what should be covered and how the rules should be stated.

> WEAR proper gymnasium clothes and remove jewelry.
> LISTEN to and abide by voice and hand signals.
> MOVE with care and concern for yourself and other students.
> USE apparatus and equipment in a safe and sensible manner.
> RESPECT the rights of other students.

A few key points should be kept in mind when designing a set of class rules. Rules should cover observable behavior and be written in a positive manner. Limit the number of rules to five or six and take time to discuss the importance of each rule with your class. As you progress through a unit

Figure 10.7 Before the lesson begins.

of instruction, take time to remind the class about one or two rules and occasionally compliment individual students or the whole class when you notice positive behavior. Posting class rules provides a visual reminder to complement the verbal instruction.

Using Time before a Lesson Starts

Normally children change into physical education uniforms, or at least into tennis shoes, and begin the lesson when everyone is present. The following procedure has been adopted in numerous schools and has proved to be extremely effective in using the time before the lesson officially begins. Although the type of activity and the time available vary from class to class, this procedure can be applied to every physical education lesson, whether in the gymnasium or on the playing field.

Each child should constructively use the free time before the lesson begins (figure 10.7). Thus, for children who enter the gymnasium or go out on the playing field early, provide an opportunity to exercise or to practice a skill or movement pattern while they wait for the lesson to begin. This might involve a personal task card that indicates the area of physical fitness that needs to be improved upon and a list of exercises to perform.

The procedure varies slightly with different types of instructional units. In a game-type lesson, a variety of balls is made available when the children enter the instructional area. A few instructions are given, such as "Practice bouncing and catching by yourself or with a partner as soon as you come into the gymnasium." In a gymnastic unit, a variety of small equipment—hoops, beanbags, skipping ropes—is placed on the floor. As the children enter the gymnasium, they are instructed to choose equipment and practice any skill they learned in the previous lesson or to

explore a movement of their choice. Practice with large apparatus, such as climbing ropes, vaulting box, or springboard, should be avoided during the free practice time. Free practice activities prior to a dance lesson could involve ball or other small equipment activities, rather than practice of a specific dance step or movement pattern.

The following suggestions show how this procedure can be used effectively even in the first few lessons. Tell the children how and where to change their clothing. Tell them that after they have changed, they can practice one or more of the following activities:

1. *Balls:* Choose a ball and practice bouncing it (or throwing and catching it, jumping over it, or playing catch with a partner).
2. *Beanbags:* Same as activity 1.
3. *Hoop:* Place a hoop on the floor and practice jumping over it, jumping in and out of it, or hopping around it.
4. *Skills:* As skills are taught, indicate one or two that can be practiced during this free practice time.

Children in the upper elementary grades have acquired many gymnastic skills, so you need only require that the children practice one or more of them as they enter the gymnasium:

1. *Balance stunts:* Have students practice a handstand, cartwheel, one-foot balance, and so on.
2. *Balls:* Have students practice bouncing and change of direction (bounce, throw into air, and make a full turn of body before bouncing again).
3. *Partners:* Do not suggest free practice with partners until the class has demonstrated its ability to work independently in this type of atmosphere.

Managing a Lesson

Several studies have shown that teachers devote as much as 30 to 50 percent of class time to management skills and strategies (Stewart 1977). Clearly, this is far too much. Spending no more than 5 percent of class time managing a lesson should be the goal of a well-organized teacher. When the following management skills and strategies are adhered to, maximum time can be devoted to instructional activities.

Keep the Lesson Focused and Flowing. A teacher might plan a lesson that includes all the appropriate content and instructional strategies yet still loses focus or lacks flow. This can be caused by several factors. Momentum of the lesson is commonly broken when a student interrupts in class or a message is brought in from another teacher. For disruptive influences, such as one or two children misbehaving, teachers should have a set routine to follow to handle the problem without losing the flow of the lesson. For example, have a set location—such as the stage, or the side or corner of the playing field—where you direct disruptive students to wait until you are ready to talk to them. Messages of a nonemergency nature can usually be handled quickly and without losing the flow of the lesson. However, stopping the class to answer messages will usually result in a loss of momentum and students will soon disengage from the task . This is often the start of disruptive behavior. Other factors that can hinder the focus and flow of the lesson include taking too much time to explain and demonstrate a skill or activity, or prolonging a practice activity or lead-up game beyond its usefulness.

Keep Students Active and On-Task. During any lesson the teacher uses a variety of instructional methods and techniques to teach motor skills or game strategies or to stress elements of personal and social behavior. For example, selecting the command method, choosing a child to demonstrate a skill, and stressing cooperative learning techniques during a practice activity are all parts of the instructional aspect of teaching.

Teachers also use several complementary management skills and techniques to ensure that every student is actively participating and on-task throughout the lesson. To illustrate: When a softball activity involves throwing and catching, and there are not enough softballs for every pair of players, use other balls, such as small utility balls or old tennis balls. When children are forced to wait in line for any type of physical activity, they will quickly become bored and begin to misbehave.

Whenever space and equipment are available, divide the class into the *smallest manageable groups* possible. If you are teaching a third-grade class dribbling and passing skills outdoors with adequate space and enough balls for every two children, pair off the children and use the maximum space that will allow you to teach while keeping good class control and a safe learning environment. Two lines of children with only two dribbling at a time is a misuse of valuable teaching time. The management policy of organizing children into the smallest manageable groups applies to teaching all physical activities. Eliminate lineups when using small equipment or large apparatus by reducing the number of students waiting to perform or adopting the use of task cards and station work (see below).

Another closely related management skill involves the setup and use of large apparatus. As noted earlier, young children can and should be taught to fetch and return large apparatus safely and efficiently. It takes time and energy to set up large apparatus, such as large mats, benches, and vaulting boxes, so develop a policy to achieve a maximally useful arrangement of apparatus. Constantly rearranging apparatus during a lesson or over a series of lessons can negatively affect the flow and direction of the lesson. If the box, mats, and benches are arranged to emphasize "flight and change of direction" for lessons 1 to 3, try to use the same arrangement for at least one or two lessons, then slightly rearrange apparatus for lesson 3. Slight rearrangements of apparatus often help keep children on-task and in focus, while major rearrangements often result in loss of momentum and structure (see chapter 4). Finally, when children shift from station to station during a lesson, develop a set routine for stopping, dismounting, and moving from one apparatus to the next.

INDIVIDUALIZED TEACHING PATTERNS

The following two individualized teaching patterns allow the teacher to set challenges to meet the level of ability and interest of each member of the class. Task or challenge cards are extremely helpful to beginning teachers, since they can be prepared prior to each lesson. Once the class is working on its tasks, the teacher can move about the instructional area, providing assistance and encouragement where needed. The second teaching pattern, known as station work, not only allows for a variety of individualized teaching patterns, but also is an effective way to use all available equipment. This contributes to the key teaching behavior of instructional variety (see chapter 4).

Task Challenge Cards

Task, or challenge, cards are an enjoyable way of individualizing game, dance, and gymnastic activities. The value of this technique is that the teacher can prepare a series of tasks, varying from simple to complex movement challenges, to adapt to the differences in ability in a class of thirty or more children. The examples provided in figure 10.8 illustrate how this technique can be applied to game, dance, and gymnastic activities.

Several examples of the application of tasks or challenges are found in later chapters. Refer specifically to chapters 16 and 25 for additional ideas.

Station Work

Station work involves the establishment of a number of practice areas within the available instructional space. Students work at one assigned area for a set period of time, then rotate to the next station. Five or six children are assigned to a station for a few minutes to practice the preassigned skill, as shown in figure 10.9. When the whistle blows, each group rotates clockwise to the next station. This basic form of station work can be used to teach all game, rhythmic, and gymnastic activities. It is also particularly useful in developing physical fitness stations in the gymnasium or outdoors. Combining station work with task cards is an excellent way to individualize the tasks for each child, and it provides valuable time for the teacher to move freely to stations where special help or praise may be needed.

Challenge Cards

Inventive Games
(Partner Activities)
Make up a game with your partner that
includes one ball, a bounce, and a catch.

Gymnastics
(Individual Sequences)
Make up a sequence that includes a stretch, a
curl, and a change of direction.

Dance
(Rhythmic Activities: Group Work)
In your group of four, develop a routine that
includes clapping, walking, hopping, and two
changes in direction. (Music: ''Pluma Blanca'')

Figure 10.8 Challenge cards.

Figure 10.9 Station work.

TEACHING FORMATIONS

The basic formations for organizing physical education activities are the *circle, line,* and *shuttle.* These patterns, shown in table 10.1, are used to divide classes into smaller groups for relays, team games, and practice exercises. Once learned, the patterns can be formed quickly and in an orderly manner at a simple command by the teacher. They save valuable practice and play time, eliminate confusion, and minimize the potential for accidents.

Often the selection of a formation is determined by the activity itself. Running and tag games require specific formations, and many folk dances begin with the children in a circle or line. Such activities as warm-up exercises, apparatus activities, and low-organization games can be performed from a variety of formations. However, two basic principles should be applied when selecting a formation: Each squad should be aligned so that all members can see the performer, and the activities of one squad should not interfere with those of another.

CONCEPT

10.6 *Grouping of Children Should Be Done without Showing Favoritism or Portraying Any Child as Inadequate*

GROUPING PROCEDURES

In physical education classes, children are grouped into squads according to their age, height, ability, or another criterion. The criterion depends upon the activity and the performance levels of the class. For example, a third-grade teacher who wishes to organize the children into four teams for a relay could (1) arrange them into groups of two girls and two boys: (2) assign the children numbers 1 through 4; (3) have four captains choose their own teams; (4) randomly assign every child a number, and select teams by pulling numbers out of a hat; and so on. Because the third method is commonly used to organize equal teams, as well as to foster leadership and team loyalty, it is explained here in detail.

The teacher selects four captains. To preclude favoritism, gender preferences, and emotional and social problems stemming from the order in which children are selected, the captains should meet with the teacher before class or, if in the gymnasium, away from the rest of the class. The teacher would explain the rules, then have the four teams selected in the following manner. As illustrated in table 10.2, captain A is awarded first choice; B, second; C, third; and D, fourth. The captains are told that if, for example, the first choice is a girl, then the second choice must be a boy, and that their selections must alternate girl/boy until

TABLE 10.1   Teaching Formations

Formation	Explanation	Uses
Circle *Teacher or Leader*	Children may form a circle by following the teacher as she walks around in a circle. Other methods include all joining hands and forming a circle, or having the class take positions on a circle printed on the floor or play area.	Simple games Warm-up exercises Circle relays Teaching simple stunts Teaching basic dance steps Teaching throwing and kicking skills Marching Mimetics
Line *Teacher or Leader*	Place one child for each line desired equidistant apart, then signal the class to line up behind these children. The first child in each line may move out in front of his line or shift to the side as illustrated.	Relays Simple games Marching Teaching stunts on floor or mats Roll taking Teaching basic skills
Fan *Teacher or Leader*	The fan formation is used for small group activities. Arrange children in a line facing their leader, then have them join hands and form a half circle.	Throwing and kicking drills Relays Mimetics Simple floor stunts Teaching dance skills
Shuttle *Teacher or Leader*	Arrange children in two, three, or more equal lines, then separate lines the distance required for the activity. Player 1 performs the skill, then shifts to the rear of the opposite line; player 2 performs and shifts to the rear of the opposite line, etc.	Throwing and kicking drills Relays Tumbling activities from opposite ends of mat Activities requiring close observation by teacher
Zigzag *Teacher or Leader*	Arrange class or squads into two equal lines, with partners facing each other. Player 1 passes to 2, 2 passes to 3, 3 passes to 4, until the last player is reached.	Throwing, catching, and kicking skills
Scattered *Teacher or Leader*	Allow children to find a spot in the play area. Have each child reach out with her arms to see if she can touch another person. Require the children who can touch others to shift until they are free of obstructions.	Warm-up exercises Mimetics Tag games Simple floor stunts Creative activities

TABLE 10.2 Order of Team Selection by Captains

Round No.	Captain A	Captain B	Captain C	Captain D
1	1st choice	2nd choice	3rd choice	4th choice
2	8th choice	7th choice	6th choice	5th choice
3	9th choice	10th choice	11th choice	12th choice
4	16th choice	15th choice	14th choice	13th choice
5	17th choice	etc.		

the last child is chosen. Let us assume that captain D selected a boy in round 1 and that, as in table 10.2, captain D also has the next selection; D must now select a girl. (Note that the entire selection process occurs without the other students witnessing the order of choice.) After the choices are made by the captains, the names are organized alphabetically and only then is the class told of the teams.

Other methods of organizing children into squads should be used throughout the year to provide opportunities for children to work with different groups, as both leaders and followers. The method chosen will depend on the activity, the space, and the age of the children. Following are some methods for selecting squad members:

1. Skill tests based on observation of skill ability
2. Counting off in twos, fives, or whatever other number of teams is desired
3. Arranging the class in a circle, then dividing the circle into the desired number of segments (squads)
4. Birth dates; for example:
   Team 1: Children born January through March
   Team 2: Children born April through June
   Team 3: Children born July through September
   Team 4: Children born October through December
5. Drawing numbers or colored cards from a hat

Once children can effectively move into squads (teams, groups, section places, units), such groupings can be highly profitable to both the students and the teacher. From the teacher's point of view, the children can be organized quickly according to a particular criterion selected either by the teacher or by the class and teacher jointly.

The duties of the elected or assigned leader should include the following:

1. Maintain order and general control of the squad
2. Check routine procedures such as attendance, uniforms, and tardiness
3. Assist the teacher in daily planning and lesson organizing
4. Set an example of leadership

From a purely organizational standpoint, the inherent value of squads cannot be overemphasized. Also, it is important to let every child have an opportunity to experience a leadership role at least once during each instructional

unit. Whatever grouping procedure is used, it should never portray any child as inadequate or show favoritism toward any group of children because of race, ethnic, or other social reasons.

10.7 Understanding Her Legal Responsibilities Helps the Teacher Maintain a Safe Learning Environment

LEGAL RESPONSIBILITIES

In virtually every school situation, the teacher acts *in loco parentis*—that is, in the place of the parent. The definition of a reasonably careful parent comes from a famous English case in 1893 (*Williams v. Eady*) that states:

> as to the law on the subject there should be no doubt; and it was correctly laid down by the learned judge, that the schoolmaster was bound to take such care of his boys as a careful father would take of his boys, and there could not be a better definition of the duty of a schoolmaster. (CAHPER 1978)

This definition of a reasonably careful parent has become the standard definition of the schoolteacher's duty of care. A teacher, whether in the classroom or gymnasium, on the playground or on a class trip, should act in a reasonable and responsible manner with respect to the welfare and safety of the children in her care. Reasonable behavior of an elementary school teacher is interpreted by the courts on the basis of what one would expect of a person with ordinary intelligence, ordinary perception, ordinary memory (Koehler 1987), and specified academic and professional credentials.

The important professional implication of the previous paragraph is that the teacher should select and teach only those physical activities that he feels competent to teach, in order to prevent any serious injury to the children in his care. This does not mean that teachers should eliminate virtually every game, gymnastic, or dance activity that has the slightest element of risk. Children need to learn how to climb, fall, and roll correctly in order to learn to move with ease and competence in a variety of life's activities. This is a part of a child's education that is expected to be learned in physical education. With this in mind, the following hypo-

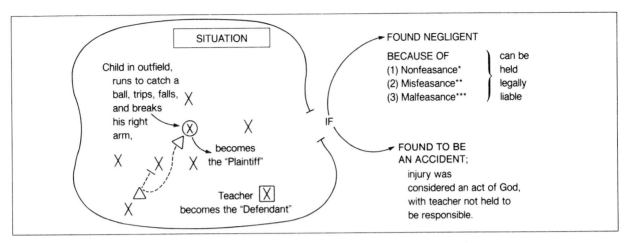

*Nonfeasance is failing to do what is required, such as failing to teach proper landing skills in gymnastics.

**Misfeasance is doing something incorrectly, such as moving an injured student improperly.

***Malfeasance is doing something illegal, such as administering medical advice.

Figure 10.10   Understanding legal liability.

thetical situation will help you understand the meaning of legal liability.

The hypothetical situation involves fifth-graders participating in a physical education class (figure 10.10). After several practice activities, the teacher arranges the class into two teams to play a full game of softball. A fly ball is hit into the field, and a fielder runs to catch it but trips and falls, breaking his arm. This child, William Brown, and his parents become the plaintiffs. The plaintiffs can initiate, through a civil court, a legal action charging the teacher and/or school board with an act of negligence. The teacher, Ms. Buchan, and her school board become the defendants.

If the plaintiff takes this action to court, the case is based on the assumption that a tort, in this case an action resulting in injury, has been committed. If the defendant is found to be legally responsible for the injury, she and/or her school board can be held liable and can be forced to pay compensation to the plaintiff. The following description of the various types of negligence will be followed by suggestions for preventing such acts from occurring within the various parts of the physical education program.

ELEMENTS OF NEGLIGENCE

As stated earlier, negligence is the failure to act as a reasonably careful parent would act under the circumstances involved in the specific situation. A teacher, principal, or school board may be held liable if the following four elements of negligence are proven.

Established Duty

This duty involves an obligation that has grown out of a special relationship between the teacher and the student. It requires the teacher to (1) anticipate foreseeable risk in an activity, (2) take reasonable steps to prevent injuries, (3) provide a warning relating to any risk that is inherent in the task or activity, (4) provide aid to the injured student, and (5) prevent an increase in the severity of the injury.

Breach of Duty

In breach of duty, a teacher fails to conform to his required duties. There are two general areas in which this can occur. The first is a situation in which the teacher fails to do something that should have been done (an act of omission). Normally, in this case, a teacher fails to teach an activity according to an acceptable progression or fails to provide equipment or apparatus that is safe to use. The second area of breach of duty is a situation in which the teacher does something that is not supposed to be done (an act of commission). Examples of this type of breach of duty would be allowing a player to continue playing a game after severely injuring her leg, striking a student for not performing a movement correctly, or failing to allow players to drink water during practice.

Injury

With respect to every potential negligent act, the injury must have occurred while the student was under the care and safety of the teacher. To illustrate, if a student runs after a soccer ball, trips and falls on a broken bottle, and cuts himself, an obvious injury has occurred. For another example, suppose that a teacher permits a student to use a broken vaulting box and, in the process of leaping over it, the student sustains no injury. In the latter case, even though the elements under "established duty" or "breach of duty" were not adhered to, there are no grounds for civil tort action, because no injury has occurred.

Proximate Cause

Proximate cause is a situation in which the teacher's behavior is the main factor in an injury to the student. The following case illustrates how the court interpreted the relationship of the teacher's presence and behavior and the cause of the injury.

Gard v. Board of School Trustees of Duncan (1946)

An eleven-year-old boy was injured in the eye by another player's stick while playing in a pickup grass hockey game after school on the school grounds. At the time of the injury, there was general supervision of the playground by teachers, but there was no special supervision of the game. The teacher in charge of grass hockey had given the children permission to play, but she was not able to supervise the game immediately because she first had to attend a staff meeting. It was also noted that both boys had previously played about five scheduled games under the teacher's supervision and that the rules had been clearly explained to them (CAPHER 1978). The court applied the classic "reasonably careful parent" test to the facts of this case and ruled there was no breach of duty of care owed to the student. In this case, the absence of the teacher was not judged to be the main cause of the injury.

TYPES OF NEGLIGENCE

As stated previously, negligence is an individual's failure to act as a reasonably careful parent would act under the circumstances of any particular situation. To be held liable for a negligent act, the elements of established duty, breach of duty, injury, and proximate cause must be proven. Proven negligence is due to one of the following types of negligent behavior on the part of the defendant.

Malfeasance

Malfeasance is an unlawful act. With respect to teaching, it occurs when a teacher does something that is illegal and usually results in an injury or adverse effect on the student. Examples of malfeasance would be using unauthorized corporal punishment, failing to spot children while they perform a difficult vault, or discriminating against a child on the basis of nationality, race, or religious beliefs.

Misfeasance

Misfeasance is improperly performing a lawful act. In this instance, the teacher adheres to the law and/or established procedures but does not perform his duties according to an established standard of conduct. The resulting effect of the teacher's performance usually results in injury or psychological harm to the student. One of the most common forms of misfeasance relates to the teacher administering improper first aid treatment to an injury that results in

further damage or permanent disability. Other types of misfeasance involve improper spotting techniques and violations of safety codes and regulations.

Nonfeasance

Nonfeasance is failing to perform a required act. In this instance, the teacher knows the proper procedures to follow but fails to perform them. It is essentially an act of omission. In the misfeasance example in which the teacher administers improper first aid treatment, injury results from subpar performance. In nonfeasance, the teacher knows what first aid procedure should be applied to an injured student but fails to apply it.

Contributory and Comparative Negligence

Contributory negligence is the failure of an injured party to exercise due care for his or her own good and welfare (Koehler 1987). In several states, the courts normally hold that a person who is contributory negligent cannot recover damages (Delon 1977). During the past few years, this aspect of the law has gradually changed in many states. A more reasonable legal doctrine, called comparative negligence, has begun to replace contributory negligence (Ware 1958). Under comparative negligence, plaintiffs may collect compensation based on a percentage of their negligence. Comparative negligence, therefore, is more reasonable, logical, and fair to the plaintiff and the defendant.

Act of God

An act of God is considered to be a situation that is completely unexpected and due to forces beyond the control of the defendant (teacher or supervisor). An example of an act of God would be a strong and sudden wind blowing a branch off a tree, which strikes and injures a child playing on the school grounds. In a legal case, if the injury is ruled to be caused by an act of God, negligence cannot be charged against the defendant (teacher, supervisor, or principal).

AREAS IN WHICH NEGLIGENCE MIGHT OCCUR

Five general areas in the physical education program might give rise to a legal action. Each of these areas will be discussed, along with a set of guidelines that will help maintain an educationally sound and safe learning environment.

Instructional Program

The instructional program is probably the most vulnerable area for teachers, particularly for activities that involve an element of risk. According to many legal experts, proper instruction should include using an acceptable teaching procedure to teach students (1) how to perform the activity, (2) how to use equipment and apparatus, (3) how to apply proper safety precautions, and (4) the amount of risk inherent in the activity (Appendzeller 1970). The teacher should also be able to foresee and prevent malicious conduct by any child under her care. The class must adhere to a standard of conduct that includes respect and consideration for the safety of every class member. This is usually stated by the teacher (and, better yet, agreed on by the pupils) in the form of "rules of conduct" that the children must follow. When one child's malicious behavior causes injury to another, the "case" against the teacher would depend on an evaluation of the teacher's ability and the situation, and a thorough investigation of the incident.

Because the instructional program is one of the most common areas in which potential cases of negligence occur, the following guidelines should be adhered to.

1. Use an approved written curriculum, arrange activities into sequential units of instruction, and follow written lesson plans.
2. Use acceptable teaching methods and techniques for the age, ability, and maturity levels of the class.
3. Provide effective safety precautions. For example, lifeguards, mats, jumping pits, and protective headgear should be provided according to the specifications outlined by the school board. Where spotting techniques are used, teachers should provide this service according to the policy of the school district. When students are used as spotters, they must be taught the proper methods before being permitted to spot a fellow student.
4. Explain to students that the decision to perform any activity that has an inherent risk rests with the student. No student should be required to perform a movement that she is afraid of or thinks may cause physical harm.
5. Activities taught off campus by school personnel should be thoroughly planned, documented, and agreed on by the principal and/or school board.
6. Develop in students an attitude of self-discipline and a consideration for the safety of other members of the class.
7. Require students to wear appropriate clothing and footwear and to remove watches and jewelry.

Supervision

The general policy followed in public school situations is that all activities under the jurisdiction of the school must be supervised. The degree of supervision within a school varies according to the type of activity. During a regular instructional class, the teacher must be present at all times and perform his duties carefully. This ensures that the class is following established rules and regulations and that high-risk activities are taught properly and closely supervised or spotted by the teacher. During recess, noon-hour, and

after-school or school-sponsored events, general supervision policies require the teacher or other person appointed by the school district to be present in the general area in which the activity is taking place. The person in charge of the general supervision is primarily concerned with maintaining a safe environment and ensuring that children follow established rules.

More successful liability cases have been brought against physical education teachers concerning supervision than concerning any other area of a teacher's responsibilities (CAHPER 1978). The following guidelines will help you maintain a safe and properly supervised physical education environment.

1. List the rules and regulations and insist that all students adhere to them while under your supervision.
2. Be present at all delegated supervisory activities. When forced to leave the area because of a student injury or another legitimate reason, make sure another qualified person assumes your supervisory activities. If you cannot get a qualified substitute, it might be wise and prudent to cancel the activity.
3. Use safe, tested, and school-approved apparatus and equipment.
4. Establish a standard procedure for checking out and returning equipment and supplies.

Facilities and Equipment

Quality and safety standards for all facilities and equipment are normally established by the school district. Each teacher, however, should routinely inspect instructional equipment and areas for problems such as broken glass, nails, holes, or defective equipment. Also, activities that require running and other general vigorous movements should be played in areas that are clear of obstructions such as gymnastic apparatus, chairs, or other movable equipment. Adequate safety zones should also be provided around the perimeter of playing areas, particularly where they border walls or potentially hazardous obstructions.

The following guidelines will help you keep your facilities and equipment in good working order and prevent unnecessary accidents.

1. Routinely check all facilities and equipment before using them. When you find something that is too hazardous to use or needs to be repaired, refrain from using it and write a memo to the principal.
2. Purchase equipment according to quality and safety standards established by the school board or other appropriate agencies.
3. List the rules and regulations for locker and shower rooms. These should include codes of behavior, traffic patterns, and time limits and should be strictly enforced.
4. Limit the use of outdoor apparatus according to weather conditions.

Equipment and Supply Checklist

Equipment / Supplies	Quantity	Good	Poor	Comments	Date
Equipment					
Example No. 1					
Vaulting Box					
(1) Surface Condition		x		small tear	
(2) Section Locks		x		stable	
(3) Wood Surface		x		clear	
List other equipment, such as climbing ropes and wall apparatus in a similar format.					
Supplies					
Example No. 2					
Hoops – 36"	22	19	3	3 destroyed	
Hoops – 42"	24	24	0	complete set	
List other supplies such as individual ropes, balls, and bats in a similar format.					

Date inventory completed_____

Teacher's signature_____

Original submitted to the principal on_____

Copy of original filed_____

Figure 10.11 Sample equipment and supply checklist form.

The responsibility for checking, maintaining, and ordering equipment and supplies may be delegated to the physical education specialist or to a classroom teacher. Some school districts have their own form and a standard procedure for checking inventory and submitting the completed form to the principal. This checklist should itemize all equipment and supplies, describe their condition, and indicate what should be repaired or replaced. If a school district does not have a standard checklist form, the sample form in figure 10.11 can be modified to suit local school conditions. Teachers should refer to the standard list of equipment and supplies when designing their own checklist. A well-designed form, similar to the one shown in figure 10.11, can help maintain a safe teaching environment and assist teachers in ordering needed equipment and supplies.

Transportation

The transportation of students from school to off-campus locations involves school vehicles, commercial vehicles, or private cars. The most sensible and prudent choice is to use school buses or commercial vehicles. Commercial vehicles must adhere to strict safety standards, as well as possess adequate liability coverage. If teachers use their own vehicles or parents' vehicles, the school board should provide insurance riders to cover the car owner and the children in the car owner's care.

The following guidelines will help ensure safe transportation for students to and from school-sponsored activities.

1. Prepare detailed travel plans and have them approved by the principal or another appropriate school administrator.
2. Hire licensed drivers and school-approved commercial vehicles.
3. If teachers or parents use their vehicles to transport students, obtain adequate liability coverage to cover potential lawsuits.
4. Require all travelers to be properly seated and to use seat belts. Do not use vehicles such as vans without seats, open bed trucks, or vehicles that do not meet adequate maintenance and safety standards.
5. Prior to embarking on any official school trip, check the vehicle for such items as safe tires, working lights, extra keys, and emergency equipment, such as fire extinguisher, blankets, and a first aid kit.
6. Establish a standard procedure for seating travelers, loading and unloading equipment, and administering emergency care.

LIABILITY INSURANCE

Who should purchase liability insurance varies from district to district. Policies are normally held by local school districts, teacher associations, or individual teachers. Since the costs incurred in this area of responsibility are high, each teacher should consult with local school officials regarding the extent of liability coverage. If no policy exists to cover teaching responsibilities, particularly in the area of physical education, a personal policy is warranted.

C O N C E P T

10.8 *Adequate Facilities, Equipment, and Supplies Are Prerequisite to a Well-Balanced Physical Education Program*

FACILITIES, EQUIPMENT, AND SUPPLIES

One of the most important considerations in the development of a comprehensive physical education program is the adequacy of facilities, equipment, and supplies. National standards regarding the size of the school property, outdoor play areas, gymnasium, and swimming pools provide guidelines for local districts and individual schools (Athletic Institute 1979). Beyond this point, however, it is the local community's responsibility, along with each school within its jurisdiction, to provide the facilities, equipment, and supplies required to meet the goals of the program. The following sections provide basic coverage of these important considerations.

Outdoor Facilities

Elementary schools normally have three types of play areas. The first, an open area, is designated for team games and track and field activities. A second facility, a hard surface area, is used for team games such as volleyball and basketball, as well as for many other activities such as four-square and hopscotch. Many schools also have a third area set aside for large playground apparatus (figure 10.12).

Open Area

Since the open area is used for running, tag games, and team sports such as soccer, softball, and track and field, it should be a flat, grassy area. If there is not an adequate water supply, the surface might have to be dirt or another composition. Regardless of the type of surface, there should be good drainage and no hazardous objects (such as automobiles, overhead wires, or other obstructions) on or near the playing area. Chalk lines, rather than sticks or permanent and protruding marks, should be used to mark playground lines. A safety zone should also be provided around the marked-off playing areas.

Figure 10.12 Example of large playground apparatus.

Figure 10.13 Example of a hard surface area.

Hard Surface Area

The hard surface area normally is located near the school and used for a variety of activities (figure 10.13). Part of this area usually has permanently marked-off courts for basketball and volleyball. The remaining surface area normally is covered with hopscotch, four-square, and other game patterns.

Playgrounds

Teachers who are serious about helping children become self-directing individuals capable of expressing themselves creatively must not only practice creative teaching strategies but also see that the physical environment stimulates creativity. In many schools, a boxlike gymnasium and a flat playing field constitute the physical education facilities. Playground equipment normally includes swings, slides, and unattractive steel climbing apparatus encased in concrete and surrounded by asphalt, concrete, or sand. Although these apparatus may be easy to keep tidy, they are unimaginative and lack educational value.

CHAPTER 10

10.9 *Playgrounds Should Be Planned Collaboratively by Architects, Landscape Designers, Educators, Parents, and Children*

The following nine criteria (Ledermann and Trachsel 1968) for creative playgrounds provide guidelines for evaluating existing playground facilities and constructing new ones.

1. Playgrounds must be designed and equipped with their play function foremost in mind. The playground should not be designed purely from the landscape gardener's aesthetic conception or the educator's concern for children's play habits and needs. It must serve the play characteristics of children and, at the same time, be aesthetic in the selection and arrangement of apparatus, pathways, and greenery.

2. Architects, landscape designers, and educators must work together to produce good solutions to playground problems. Architects, landscape designers, and educators tend to visualize the creative playground from their own points of view. Architects inject their bias toward artistic creations; landscape gardeners are more concerned with tree and flower arrangements than with children's play activities; and educators often see the creative playground as an extension of the classroom. Each specialist must recognize the contributions of the others, so that the overall playground plan is seen as a cooperative effort.

3. The playground is not meant for passive entertainment. It must encourage active, spontaneous, and creative play. The creative playground should not be a simple collection of commercial equipment, old cars, or concrete tunnels arranged in parallel rows. The apparatus, whether natural or commercial, should be selected and arranged to stimulate the child's imagination and enhance continuous exploration.

4. Half-finished components and materials for play are more valuable than mechanical equipment. Most playgrounds are dominated by inflexible apparatus such as slides, swings, and a variety of rotary-type equipment. It is not suggested that slides and swings be removed, but consideration should be given to including more creative and, if possible, natural equipment such as large tree roots or other materials that are available in the local area.

5. Playground design and equipment must conform to the typical games of the age group for which the playground is intended. In most cases, creative playgrounds are first seen as an addition to the primary school playground area. Children of ages five to eight thoroughly enjoy playing on and around a creative playground. Intermediate children appear to be more sophisticated; however, experience shows that children of this age level are equally interested in using creative equipment. Thus, plans should consider the full age range in the elementary school.

6. The playground design must reflect the functions and movements of different games. This involves the total play area of the school. For example, an elementary school playground serves both primary and intermediate children. Consequently, the creative playground area should be away from the main ball game areas. If the school is near an area with trees, a ravine, or any type of natural area, the creative playground should be put near this site. Of course, safety must be considered; natural areas that are potentially hazardous should not be considered desirable locations.

7. Games of fantasy should not be overlooked. Some children enjoy playing by themselves. Therefore, the creative playground, particularly for children in the primary grades, should provide small individual areas on or near apparatus where children can absorb themselves in fantasy or other forms of self-expression.

8. Architects and landscape designers should "play" a little while designing the creative playground. The specialists should observe children at play and attempt to visualize the potential area through "the eyes of a child." The designer who does this would not build a square sandbox, place a slide in the middle of an area with slopes and contours, or place equipment in straight lines. Relevance, too, is important. A creative playground near a coast should be representative of the area, with "ships" and "trees"—natural or synthetic—in the general play area. Similar themes for the South and Midwest should be present in the creative playground.

9. Interested groups of people should cooperate in designing, equipping, and maintaining a playground. The majority of creative playgrounds that have been constructed in Canada and the United States are the results of cooperative parent-teacher groups that wished to do something for local schoolchildren. Initially, such projects were undertaken because of the lack of tax money to construct this type of outdoor facility. This cooperative action has given the parents an understanding of the value and purpose of such playgrounds and has also significantly reduced the amount of vandalism, as parents and children consider these jointly built facilities community property, and not just for use during school hours.

Indoor Facilities

Physical education can be taught in several locations within a typical elementary school. In geographical areas where there is a need for an indoor facility, gymnasia are normally designed as multipurpose facilities for assemblies, cafeteria lunches, and physical education. In most instances, a single multipurpose room is not sufficient for all classes on a daily

Figure 10.14   Example of a gymnasium.

basis or even two or three times per week. Other events, such as assemblies, plays, and concerts, too often take precedence over physical education. As a consequence, other areas of the school, such as the classroom, library, and hallway, can be used for limited game, dance, gymnastic, and fitness activities. The creative use of each type of indoor facility provides the teacher with several important options for her instructional program.

Gymnasium

The location, size, and special features of the multipurpose room or gymnasium should be determined by the philosophy and activities of the physical education program (figure 10.14). Often, incorrect planning results in inadequate court dimensions, low ceilings, and avoidable hazards or obstructions. To help eliminate mistakes in the planning and construction of future elementary school gymnasia, national leaders in the field of health and physical education have developed a guide, *Planning Facilities for Athletics, Physical Education and Recreation* (Athletic Institute 1979). Included in this guide are standard recommendations for floor construction, playing space, storage facilities, and numerous other aspects of a well-planned gymnasium. For the planning of new facilities, this publication is a basic reference for nationally acceptable standards of gymnasium construction.

However, some recommendations relating to floor dimensions, placement of equipment, and general safety apply to any gymnasium or multipurpose room that is used for physical education. The following suggestions will help you organize an indoor facility for maximum use and optimum safety:

1. Maintain gymnasium temperature between 60 and 65 degrees.

2. Paint permanent boundary lines on the floor for activities held most often. Use a different color of lines for each—black for basketball, red for volleyball, and green for a large center circle.
3. Provide adequate safety margins for all games. The standard dimensions for a basketball area for elementary school children are 74 by 42 feet. If the facility is only 70 by 40 feet, the actual court dimensions should be 67 by 37 feet to provide a minimum 3-foot safety zone around the court.
4. Remove all equipment that is not being used during the physical education class.
5. Request that any hazardous fixtures, such as floor-level heating ducts and lighting fixtures, be covered with protective screens.
6. Establish a standard procedure for obtaining and returning equipment to the storage room.

Classroom

In many elementary schools throughout North America, the only available space indoors for physical education is the classroom. Although this is inadequate, some minor furniture adjustments can make the classroom suitable for a variety of physical activities (see chapter 15). By shifting movable desks and tables, one area of the classroom can be made free of obstructions. Since most lighting and window fixtures in the classroom are not screened, do not permit activities for which these would be hazards. Adjustable and movable bars can be placed in doorways, mats can be used for tumbling activities, and chairs and four-by-four-inch beams can be used for balance activities.

Library, Hallway, and Other Locations

The importance of daily physical education has been recognized by parents, teachers, physicians, and related professional organizations. As a consequence, efforts are being made in many schools throughout North America to use other large areas of the school in addition to the gymnasium for a variety of physical activities. The primary purpose of the library is obviously to store and use written and audiovisual resources. However, carpeted library floors are a very desirable surface for gymnastic and creative dance activities. Creative scheduling, coupled with the use of chairs and tables, can provide an adequate teaching area, particularly for lower elementary children. Discussions with the principal and the librarian can often lead to opening this room to physical education when it is not being used for library purposes.

In a similar way, the hallway can be used for some game activities such as shufflecurl, hopscotch, and four-square. This area can also be used for a variety of fitness activities and, to a lesser extent, some gymnastic activities. The main problem in using the hallway relates to disturbing adjacent classrooms. Once again, working with teachers in nearby classrooms or creative scheduling can lead to a more open use of the hallway. For example, if teachers in adjacent rooms can schedule the gymnasium and library for the same time, the hallway will become a place another teacher can use with a little more freedom and with a slightly higher acceptable noise level of her class.

Basic Equipment and Supplies

The term *physical education equipment* refers to permanent apparatus such as balance beams and outdoor play apparatus. Generally speaking, these materials last from five to twenty years, even with repeated use. Supplies, on the other hand, are expendable items such as balls, whistles, and tapes. These items last one to two years. Teachers should list the proper equipment for their grade level and, where budgets are limited, suggest how to make various types of equipment. (See appendix B for diagrams of inexpensive equipment. See appendix C for a list of commercial manufacturers and distributors of equipment and supplies.)

The type of physical education program, the geographic area, and economic conditions, among other things, determine the type of equipment a school will buy. The following suggestions will help you order the proper type and size of equipment and supplies.

Recommended Playground Equipment

Climbing apparatus: climbing cubes, etc.
Horizontal bar: "chinning" or "turning bar" at three levels—48, 54, and 64 inches—all 5 feet wide
Horizontal ladder: 6½ feet high, length optional
Balance beam: 8 to 12 feet long, three levels—18, 24, or 48 inches with alternate surface of 4 inches and 2 inches
Tetherball standards: minimum of three
Basketball standards: minimum of two; 8 feet high (heavy duty construction)
Parachutes: two
Volleyball standards: minimum of two with adjustable height
Softball backboards: minimum of two
Soccer goalposts: minimum of two
Creative playground apparatus
Track and field equipment: long-jump pit, high-jump pit and standards, hurdles
Tug-of-war rope

Optional and Homemade Equipment

Automobile tires: suspended on rope or chain, with bottom of line 12 to 14 inches off ground
Movable barrows and kegs
Movable planks: 8 to 12 feet long, with planed edges
Sawhorses: different heights
Concrete sewer pipes: arranged in units of three or four
Obstacle courses: permanent or portable; type and construction should complement the climate and geographic area

Recommended Indoor Equipment

Climbing ropes: 6 to 8 on a sliding track; 1¼ to 1½-inch hemp rope
Tumbling mats: minimum of four; light synthetic material; sizes are optional, although 4 × 7 foot mats are easy to handle and store
Individual mats: 18 × 36 inches; minimum of forty, or one per child
Record player (three speeds)
Tape recorder
Dance drum
Balance beam: 1 to 4 feet high, depending on general use, and approximately 10 feet long
Balance benches: reversible for optional use (2-inch and 4-inch sides), plus hook attachment on one end
Horizontal bar: see appendix B
Scooters: 12 × 12 inches with four casters
Volleyball net and standards: adjustable heights
Basketball standards: adjustable heights
Vaulting box: see appendix B
Set of jumping boxes: see appendix B
Springboard or mini-tramp
Sawhorses: minimum of six
Hockey nets: two
Cargo nets
Supply cart
Climbing frame

Recommended Supplies

The number of items listed here is a suggested minimum based on a maximum of thirty children using the supplies during one physical education period. If two or more classes meet at the same time, double or triple the number.

Supplies	Minimum Number
Game supplies	
Ball inflater with gauge	1
Balloons	60–100
Beachballs, 12- and 16-inch	6 of each
Braids (cloth)	30
Beanbags, 6-inch, assorted colors	40–60
Basketball (junior size)	30
Basketball (standard size)	30
Basketball net	6–8
Cageball, 24-inch	5–10
Clipboards	4
Colored armbands	2 sets of 15
Deck tennis rings	10–15
Earthball	2
Eyeglass protectors	6–8
Field hockey sticks	30–40
Field hockey balls	30
Fleece balls	40
Football (junior size,)	10–15
Football kicking tee	2

Supplies	Minimum Number
Frisbee	15–20
Gymnasium scooters	30
Hoops, 36- and 42-inch	30–40
Horseshoe sets	4–6
Indian clubs or bowling pins	24–30
Jacks	60
Juggling scarfs	90
Juggling bags	90
Line marker	1
Measuring tape (50 feet)	1
Nerf balls	20–30
Plastic tape (1-, 1½-, and 2-inch)	2 rolls of each
Paddles (tennis, etc.)	30
Scoops	30–40
Softballs	10–15
Softball bases	8–10
Softball gloves	10–15
Softball bats	10–15
Softball mask and body protector	2 of each
Softball batting tee	3–4
Sponge or tennis balls	40–50
Soccer balls (rubber)	30
Stopwatches	6
Tote bags	10–15
Traffic cones	10–15
Tetherball sets	6–8
Track and field equipment (batons, crossbars, starters, etc.)	
Utility balls, 6½-, 8½- and 10½-inch	10 of each
Volleyballs	30
Volleyball nets	4–6
Whistles	6–8
Yardsticks	6–8

Dance supplies

Audiotapes (see part 8)	
Dance drums	6–8
Lummi sticks	60–80
Percussion instruments (castanets, tambourines, bells, etc.)	4 of each
Records (see part 8)	
Tinikling poles	12–16

Gymnastic supplies

Blocks (4 inches × 4 inches × 1 foot)	15–20
Individual ropes (⅜ = inch sash, nylon, or plastic; 6, 7, 7½, and 8 feet)	10 of each
Long ropes (⅜-inch sash, nylon, or plastic; 13, 14, and 15 feet)	3 of each
Wands (10 each at 3, 3½, 4, and 4½ feet)	1 set of 40

Testing and first aid supplies

Skinfold calipers (plastic)	3–5
Sit-and-reach boxes	3
Blankets	2
First aid kit	2

Optional and homemade supplies

Automobile tires	6–8
Assorted small barrels (for dance drums)	
Broom handles	10–15
Shuffleboard supplies	3 sets
Stilts	10–20 pairs
Targets (various sizes)	
Tool chest (saw, hammer, etc.)	1
Walking board	1
Walking cans	60

Care and Maintenance of Equipment and Supplies

Because equipment and supplies represent a large expenditure of money, they should be stored, used, and maintained in an effective and prudent manner. The following suggestions should be incorporated into each school's policies and procedures for handling equipment and supplies.

1. All apparatus, equipment, and supplies should be permanently marked with a number and school identification.
2. Each school should establish a set of rules and procedures for handing out and returning equipment and supplies.
3. All apparatus, equipment, and supplies should be checked before they are issued. Broken equipment should not be issued; it should be repaired as soon as possible and returned to the storage room. Worn-out equipment should be discarded, as it leads to poor skill development and potential accidents.
4. Inflate all balls to the recommended pressure. Place a chart near the ball inflator and adhere strictly to the recommended pressure for each inflated ball. Store balls partially inflated during the off-season.
5. Store all materials according to recommended standards.
6. Design your equipment room to permit easy and efficient access to all materials.
7. Each school should make a complete inventory of all physical education materials at the beginning and end of each season. Records of how well items like rubber volleyballs, mats, and skipping ropes perform will aid in future replacement or purchase policies.
8. When ordering materials, always write out the specifications, such as brand name, size, and required options. If materials are ordered through a central purchasing department, it is extremely important to state the specifications and add "or its equivalent." The latter will guarantee the purchase of a quality item rather than a cheaper, but inferior, second- or third-choice item.

CHAPTER 10

Construction of Inexpensive Equipment and Supplies

Equipment and supplies should be purchased from commercial firms whenever possible. Normally school districts have clear-cut purchasing policies that each school must adhere to. If not, the principal and teaching staff should develop a purchasing plan to secure new equipment and supplies and to provide funds to replace and maintain existing inventory.

If local funds are not available, some equipment can be constructed by interested parents. Appendix B contains examples of locally constructed equipment and supplies. It is strongly recommended that all such homemade equipment be constructed with the best available materials. Furthermore, such equipment should be checked by school maintenance personnel for quality construction and safety before it is used in the program.

Summary Review

Effective teaching is dependent upon how well a teacher organizes her class, time, and available facilities and equipment. This chapter has outlined each of these areas and provided suggestions to create a safe and efficient learning environment. Teachers who create and implement policies and practices relating to management skills and strategies, can devote maximum time and effort to instructional activities.

INDIVIDUAL *and* **GROUP** **PROJECTS**

1. Suppose that a new school has just been completed with a large (100 × 100 foot) blacktop area located near the school building. Design the permanent markings (for hopscotch, etc.) that you would like painted on this area.
2. Review the accident form (figure 10.2) and suggest possible additions to cope with children with special needs.
3. In small groups, create a set of class rules for activities held away from school (field trips, etc.).
4. Observe a physical education class and record the number of minutes that are devoted to management skills and strategies.
5. In groups of two or three, design an adventure playground using any material that is free or very inexpensive (e.g., a donated large tractor tire) and available in your geographical area.
6. In groups of three or four, review the supplies and equipment shown in appendix B, then design two new items to add to this list.

SELECTED READINGS

AAHPERD. 1976. *Complying with Title IX of Education Amendments of 1972 in physical education and high school sports programs.* Washington, DC: AAHPERD.

Alberta Education, Curriculum Branch. 1992. *Better safe than sorry: Safety guidelines for elementary and secondary school physical education.* Learning Resources Distributing Center, 12360: 142 Street, Edmonton, Alberta, Canada, T5L 4X9.

Appendzeller, H. 1970. *From the gym to the injury.* Charlottesville, VA: Michie Company Law Publishing.

Arnold, D. E. (1983). *Legal considerations in the administration of public school physical education and athletics programs.* Springfield, IL: Charles C. Thomas.

Athletic Institute. 1979. *Planning facilities for athletics, physical education and recreation.* Rev. ed. Reston, VA: AAHPERD.

Bailey, J. A., and D. L. Matthews, 1984. *Law and liability in athletics, physical education and recreation.* Boston: Allyn & Bacon.

Brown, R. 1977. Tort liability as a form of social control over violence in sports. Unpublished paper, Faculty of Law, University of Windsor, Ontario.

Brunt, R. T. 1969. Tortious liability of Canadian physical education and recreation practitioners. Master's thesis, University of Alberta.

Bruya, L. D., ed. 1988. *Play spaces for children: A new beginning.* Reston, VA: AAHPERD

CAHPER. 1978. *Legal liability in physical education.* Vanier, Ontario: CAHPER.

Clement, A. 1985. *Law in sport and physical education.* Dubuque, IA: Brown & Benchmark.

Della-Giustina, D. E., and C. P. Yost. 1991. *Teaching safety in the elementary school.* Reston, VA: AAHPERD.

Delon, F. G. 1977. Tort liability, *Yearbook of school law.* Shannon v. Addison Trial, 339 N.E., 2d 372.

Ellis, M., and A. B. Neilson. 1980. *Play things.* Willowdale, Ontario: John Degill.

Federal Register. 1977. Vol. 42, 23 August 1977 (part 2), p. 42480.

Hall, T. 1984. *Inexpensive movement material.* Bryon, CA: Front Row Experience.

Kaiser, R. A. 1986. *Liability and the law in recreation, parks and sports.* Englewood Cliffs, NJ: Prentice Hall.

Koehler, R. W. 1987. *Law, sport activity and right management.* Champaign, IL: Stipes.

Ledermann, A., and A. Trachsel. 1968. *Creative playgrounds and recreation centers.* 2d ed. New York: Praeger.

Levin, J., and J. F. Nolan. 1996. *Principles of classroom management.* Boston: Allyn & Bacon.

Moore, R. E., S. M. Goltsman, and D. S. Iacofano, eds. 1987. *Play for all guidelines: Planning, design and management of outdoor play settings for all children.* Berkeley, CA: MIG Communications.

Selby, R. 1977. What's wrong (and right!) with coed physical education classes: Secondary school physical educators' views on Title IX implementation. *Physical Educator* 29:60.

Stillwell, J. L. 1987. *Making and using creative play equipment.* Champaign, IL: Human Kinetics.

U.S. Consumer Product Safety Commission. *1986. A handbook for public playground safety.* Vols. 1–2. Washington, DC: U.S. Consumer Product Safety Commission.

Ware, M. 1958. Is the teacher liable? *National Education Association Journal* 47:603.

Werner, P. H., and R. A. Simmons. 1990. *Homemade play equipment for children.* Reston, VA: AAHPERD.

CHAPTER 1

Selecting Evaluative Methods and Techniques

K E Y   O B J E C T I V E S

After completing this chapter you will be able to:

1. Understand the importance of observation and evaluation in physical education
2. Assess and evaluate student performance in physical education through subjective and objective measuring devices
3. Evaluate a physical education program
4. Use a physical activity log (PAL) book to assist in the evaluation of a child's active lifestyle
5. Understand the benefits of portfolio assessment in physical education and know how to use portfolios in the evaluation and reporting process
6. Identify the benchmark levels of expectancy in elementary school physical education for children in kindergarten and grades 2, 4, and 6
7. Understand appropriate methods of reporting and grading a child's progress in physical education
8. Assess the effectiveness of your own teaching

K E Y   C O N C E P T S

11.1 Evaluation is an important factor in physical education, essential to curriculum, unit, and daily lesson planning

11.2 Formative evaluation is used within a lesson or unit to assess children's progress; summative evaluation occurs at the end of a unit or program to provide an indication of the total achievements of individuals or groups of children

11.3 Norm-referenced tests permit comparison of a child's score with performance standards for children of similar age and gender who represent the normal population

11.4 Criterion-referenced tests enable comparison of an individual's score with a mastery level of performance

11.5 Observational techniques, such as group time sampling and event, duration, and interval recording, allow for assessment of how well the instructional program is meeting its stated goals

11.6 Benchmarks describe developmentally appropriate behaviors representative of progress toward achieving the goals and objectives of a quality physical education program

11.7 A number of methods and techniques, such as checklists and rating scales, can be used effectively to evaluate student progress

11.8 Student journals, such as personal activity log (PAL) books, can be used effectively in both student evaluation and goal-setting activities

11.9 Portfolios offer the potential to portray growth and development regarding a variety of learning outcomes that are difficult to assess using traditional methods

11.10 Systematic evaluation of the physical education program is essential and requires careful planning and self-reflection by the teacher

valuation is essential to all phases of the physical education program. A teacher uses the techniques of observation to assess the strengths and weaknesses of his daily lessons in order to make appropriate changes in his teaching strategies. He also uses a variety of objective and subjective evaluational tools to assess performance, motivate children, and communicate information to parents and interested citizens. Teachers, therefore, must be knowledgeable and skilled in this important area of assessment and evaluation.

To assist teachers with assessment and evaluation, NASPE (1995) has produced guidelines for assessment of physical education goals and objectives. They suggest a number of teacher-friendly assessment techniques appropriate for evaluating student achievement. This chapter reviews these assessment techniques, together with numerous other evaluative tools and procedures related to student and program development, and presents ideas about monitoring and promoting active living.

ASSESSMENT AND EVALUATION

According to Sherrill (1993), evaluation is "the continuous process of determining student gain and program effectiveness" (p. 12), whereas assessment "refers to data collection, interpretation, and decision making" (p. 155). However, federal law uses the term *evaluation* to include all the functions of assessment. Hence, *assessment* and *evaluation* can be considered synonyms, even though experts often claim that *assessment* is a broader term. Both terms are used throughout this text.

MEANING OF EVALUATION

Contemporary education favors a "reflective practice" approach to teaching (e.g., see Hellison and Templin 1991). Just as there is an emphasis today on providing individual children with developmentally appropriate experiences, there is an equally important need to reflect on the effectiveness of our teaching practices. Evaluation is an important aspect of the physical education program.

Because effective teaching is related to student learning, assessment of student progress is vital. Authentic assessment procedures should be chosen to compare a child's performance to expected competencies—what the child should know and be able to do (NASPE 1995). In addition to monitoring and reporting student progress, evaluation of both teaching practices and the effectiveness of the overall physical education program will be required. Self-reflection is one of the hallmarks of an effective teacher.

Evaluation in physical education is a process of determining whether the goals of an individual, a group, or a program are being reached. It is an ongoing process of measuring the effectiveness of a teaching strategy, the level of skill development of an individual child or a class, and the efficacy of a unit of instruction or a total program. Its purpose can be to evaluate progress, to motivate a child, or to provide effective ways of reporting a child's progress to parents.

C O N C E P T

11.1 *Evaluation Is an Important Factor in Physical Education, Essential to Curriculum, Unit, and Daily Lesson Planning*

Formative and Summative Evaluation

Two types of evaluation are used in the physical education program. Formative evaluation is used within each lesson to assess the progress each child is making toward the goals of the lesson. It is a process of dividing the lesson into smaller units of learning, then evaluating each student's progress in these subparts as the lesson proceeds. With this type of assessment, the teacher can determine how much has been learned and what problem areas have arisen, and she can then make consequent changes to the learning task or teaching strategy, or she can redirect the learner to another activity. The second type of evaluation, summative evaluation, occurs at the end of an instructional activity—for example, at the completion of a unit or yearly program. The results of this form of evaluation normally produce a cumulative score for determining the achievement of each child or the whole class. This form of evaluation assesses individual levels of achievement, compares individuals or groups, establishes standards of performance, or provides a basis for establishing a grading system.

C O N C E P T

11.2 *Formative Evaluation Is Used within a Lesson or Unit to Assess Children's Progress; Summative Evaluation Occurs at the End of a Unit or Program to Provide an Indication of the Total Achievements of Individuals or Groups of Children*

Norm-Referenced and Criterion-Referenced Tests

The contemporary goals of elementary school physical education stress improving physical fitness and well-being, enhancing skill development, fostering good interpersonal relations, and developing positive attitudes toward physical activity as a desirable part of a healthy lifestyle. The implication of these goals is that formative and summative evaluations of student progress must include techniques that measure both quantitative and qualitative aspects of the child's development. Quantitative aspects are usually measured by "norm-referenced" testing, which is used in many standardized tests of physical fitness and skill development. For example, the standardized test batteries used in

AAHPERD's Physical Best test and the Canada Fitness Test represent norm-referenced testing. Qualitative aspects, such as the quality and form of a child's movement in dance or gymnastics, are often measured by "criterion-referenced" techniques. Both types of evaluative measures will be discussed in the following paragraphs.

Norm-Referenced Tests

Norm-referenced assessment of a child's fitness and skill development has been used in elementary physical education programs for decades. The physical fitness test developed by AAHPERD (1989) is an excellent example of a standardized norm-referenced test battery. The physical fitness and posture tests described in chapters 8 and 13, respectively, provide objective measures of a child's posture and fitness in a variety of motor and health-related areas. Children are assessed and compared with a standard of what is considered normal for their age and gender. These objective test batteries are used to assess individual levels of fitness and to prescribe remedial programs where warranted.

In a similar way, standardized and teacher-made skill tests have been used to measure levels of skill development. The American Alliance for Health, Physical Education, Recreation and Dance has produced a number of standardized test batteries with accompanying norms for boys and girls, ages ten to eighteen. A series of manuals covering such sports as basketball, football, softball, and volleyball can be purchased from AAHPERD Publications, Dept. V, P.O. Box 704, 44 Industrial Park Circle, Waldorf, MD 20601. The skill tests described in part 6 of this text are examples of teacher-made tests. Generally they are product-type (quantitative) tests that measure the number of successive trials, speed of performance, or distance covered.

Each test, whether standard or homemade, should have the following characteristics:

1. Each item in the test battery should accurately measure one important skill (for example, an underhand catch).
2. The test battery should be inexpensive and easy to administer and should yield scores that can be totaled.
3. Each test item should accurately measure the skills and movements of the activity. A dribbling test item in basketball or soccer should include such factors as speed, change of direction, and ball control.
4. Each item in the battery should distinguish between low and high levels of ability. If all children score eight or ten points out of a possible ten on an accuracy test—throwing at a large target from ten feet away—the test would be of little value. The results would indicate that either the distance was too short or the target too large.

C O N C E P T

11.3 *Norm-Referenced Tests Permit Comparison of a Child's Score with Performance Standards for Children of Similar Age and Gender Who Represent the Normal Population*

Criterion-Referenced Tests

A criterion-referenced assessment evaluates an individual's quality of performance (Morris and Stiehl 1985). For instance, criterion-referenced fitness testing evaluates the child's quality of performance compared to the criterion level of fitness needed to maintain a healthy lifestyle. Criterion-referenced testing of skill acquisition is usually an evaluation of the quality of a child's performance compared to the criterion level associated with a fully developed skill or movement pattern. Table 11.1 is an example of this type of assessment. The table provides a description of a child's performance of fundamental locomotor, nonlocomotor, and manipulative skills at the beginning of the school year. In this example, each skill is subjectively rated as initial, intermediate, or automatic; these categories refer to the three stages of motor learning described in chapter 3. In the "Correction Indicated" column, comments are written to help the teacher plan activities to correct the child's weaknesses. This type of evaluation sheet can also be developed for specific sport skills and gymnastic activities and is especially useful in explaining a child's level of performance to parents and in pointing out corrective measures that can be undertaken at home.

C O N C E P T

11.4 *Criterion-Referenced Tests Enable Comparison of an Individual's Score with a Mastery Level of Performance*

Feedback and Learning

Assessment of a child's performance is essential if correct feedback is to be provided in the learning process. Because the learner requires specific information on what needs to be changed or corrected, the teacher will need to gather appropriate information. Two important sources of feedback that are needed for error detection and correction are *knowledge of results* and *knowledge of performance*. Knowledge of results is information associated with the outcome of the movement, whereas knowledge of performance is information related to the correct movement pattern during execution of the skill. Unfortunately, there is a tendency to observe the outcome of the performance more than the movement pattern itself. For example, when a child throws a ball, the tendency is to watch the flight path of the ball to determine the distance thrown (knowledge of result). However, in order to provide useful feedback to the child to correct or improve performance, changes in the child's movement throwing pattern may be required. Hence, to obtain knowledge of performance, the teacher needs to concentrate on observing the movement pattern during the throw, and not follow the ball flight (outcome). This information (knowledge of performance) can then be used to provide feedback to the child to help correct and improve performance.

A teacher must be cognizant of assessment techniques that help provide both knowledge of results and knowledge

TABLE 11.1   Subjective Rating of Performance in Fundamental Skills

Name: Jim Adams
Date: September 1998

| Name of Skill | Developmental Sequence | | | Correction Indicated |
	Initial Stage	Intermediate Stage	Automatic Stage	
Walking			X	Toes inward
Running			X	Toes inward
Skipping	X			
Leaping	X			
Jumping		X		
Sliding	X			Changes lead foot
Hopping	X			
Swinging and swaying		X		
Rising and falling		X		
Pushing and pulling		X		
Bending and stretching		X		
Striking and dodging		X		

of performance. Knowledge of results often occurs naturally for children, since their vision can provide this information in most situations. However, the teacher should always strive to ensure that this form of corrective feedback information is available as quickly as possible after the child performs the skill. For example, when children are throwing for distance, colorful markers can be used to indicate distance thrown on each trial. This alleviates the child's uncertainty or having to wait for a tape measure, and provides instant feedback of knowledge of results. Markers can also be used and adjusted by the children in personal goal setting (see chapter 4).

To help provide knowledge of performance, a large number of criterion-referenced checklists, to assess children's development in fundamental locomotor and manipulative skills, are provided in chapter 6. These checklists provide specific details on the movement patterns associated with these fundamental skills. Not only are the checklists helpful for the purpose of corrective feedback, they provide a valuable tool for evaluating and reporting children's level of development in these important areas.

EVALUATING THE TEACHING PROCESS

Evaluation of the teaching process is an ongoing observational assessment of how well the instructional program is meeting its stated goals (figure 11.1). Once the lesson has begun, the teacher must be continuously aware of a series of interrelated instructional and learning factors. For example, he needs to know whether the content is appropriate, whether the children are keeping on-task and for how long,

Figure 11.1   Evaluation involves observational assessment.

and whether he is providing sufficient guidance and encouragement to all students in the class. Four contemporary systematic observational methods have proven to be effective, reliable, and valid. The following methods—event recording, duration recording, interval recording, and group time sampling—can be used by classroom teachers with slight modifications to cope with the realities of specific teaching situations and the maturity and observational skills of student helpers.

Event Recording

Event recording is defined as recording the number of times an event occurs within a given time period. One of the first and most important tasks is to define accurately what is to

TABLE 11.2   Activity Chart

Date _____

	| Minutes					
	1 2 3 4 5 6	7 8 9 10 11 12	13 14 15 16 17 18	19 20 21 22 23 24	25 26 27	28 29 30
Stop	X X X X X X		X X X X X X		X X X	X X X
Moving		X X X X X X		X X X X X X		
Parts of Lesson	Changing and waiting for class to begin	Introductory activity	Skill development	Skill development	Skill development	Closure

be observed. To illustrate: A second-grade teacher wants to know if the children are physically active during her gymnastic unit. She is using a Movement Education approach and wants to know how much movement occurs during her thirty-minute lesson. A student in the sixth grade is available to observe and record according to the activity chart in table 11.2. The student is taught how to use a stopwatch and when to place an *X* for "Stop" (meaning the whole class is sitting or standing and listening to the teacher) or for "Moving" (meaning the children are engaged in any form of movement). The student then records her observation at intervals of one minute throughout the lesson. Daily observations following this procedure could be made by the sixth-grade student or another volunteer helper, or the teacher could videotape each session and do her own observation.

This example is only a simple quantitative observation of one aspect of the lesson. Nevertheless, table 11.2 shows that the teacher is talking too much and the children are not getting sufficient exercise. For example, after the children changed into their exercise clothing, the introductory activity kept all children moving, but during the second part of the lesson the teacher talked too long (minutes 13–18 and 25–30). After reviewing this chart, she made a decision to keep her comments and instructions shorter to give the children more time to practice their sequences.

Event recording is one of the easiest and most useful methods of observing skills, events, or behavior characteristics. It is essentially a quantitative measurement that can be used as a basis of assessing one or more parts of a lesson or program.

Duration Recording

Duration recording is recording the length of time a student or group of children participates in a given activity. In event recording, the information revealed only two types of activity the whole class was engaged in (stopping and moving). With duration recording, the teacher can measure the length of time a child stays on a given task. This is important information because time on-task is one of the key

behaviors associated with effective teaching (see chapter 4). Let's use the same class and activity as in the previous example. The teacher wants to determine whether her tasks involving individual sequences are too easy or too hard for the children. She uses four sixth-grade children to observe four children chosen at random.

	Task Number			
Student	**1**	**2**	**3**	**4**
Michelle Leblanc	1.35	0.30	0.32	2.46
Ruben Katz	2.40	0.16	0.23	2.40
Juan Gonzales	2.00	0.10	0.26	1.55
Souka Tan	2.15	0.18	0.24	2.30

The results shown in the chart indicate that the first and fourth movement tasks are sufficiently challenging and interesting to keep the children engaged for a relatively long period of time. Tasks 2 and 3 are too easy, so each child gave each task proportionately less time. The teacher then changes tasks 2 and 3 to make them more challenging and, thus, more enjoyable and interesting to this particular group of children. Duration recording has many useful applications in observing and measuring practice sessions, behavior, and equipment utilization. It is suggested that each teacher design his own form(s) to assess one or more aspects of his own teaching or to assess the specific motor skills or behavior patterns of his students.

Interval Recording

Interval recording is a sequential method of observing behavior for a short period of time (e.g., ten seconds) followed by a short recording period (e.g., fifteen seconds). During the fifteen-second recording interval, the recorder describes the behavior that occurred during the preceding ten seconds. This type of method is good for observing individual movement patterns or specific behavior characteristics. This method requires quick and precise judgments, so it

CHAPTER 11

cannot easily be administered by student helpers. Without adult assistance, interval recording has limited application to the typical elementary physical education program.

Group Time Sampling

Group time sampling is a variation of interval recording. In this method, the observer scans the whole group (usually from left to right) for a short time period (e.g., ten seconds). During this scanning period, the observer quickly counts the number of children engaged in a particular behavior category, such as talking, participating, or misbehaving. Once again, this is a difficult task for fifth- or sixth-grade helpers, so it is of limited use to a classroom teacher. Teachers can use modified scanning techniques, though, to assess general class behavior and whether certain activities or challenges are appropriate for the children. For example, in virtually every lesson the teacher constantly checks the safety of the equipment, the tone of the class, the noise level, and the effort the children are making—throughout the lesson and from different vantage points. To illustrate this process, let us assume that figure 11.2 represents a soccer lesson. The lesson emphasis is dribbling and passing the ball. The first observation is made from a corner of the field a few minutes after the children begin dribbling the ball within the instructional area. As the teacher quickly scans from left to right, she makes a mental note of spacing, colliding, and individual effort. If the pace and tone of the class appear satisfactory, she begins observing the main focus points of the lesson. As the lesson progresses, she periodically scans the class from a variety of vantage points and makes appropriate adjustments to alleviate any problem areas.

C O N C E P T

11.5 *Observational Techniques, Such as Group Time Sampling and Event, Duration, and Interval Recording, Allow for Assessment of How Well the Instructional Program Is Meeting Its Stated Goals*

Lesson Focus Observations

Within each lesson, observations should be limited to one or two key skills or movement patterns that are considered the main focus of the lesson. In the previous example, dribbling and passing the ball was the main emphasis of the lesson. The almost universal question that arises is, What and whom do I observe within my class of thirty children? The answer to this question is based on the teacher's knowledge of the activity and the potential level of ability of each child in the class. For example, teaching dribbling and passing requires a basic understanding of mechanical principles, progression of skill development, and alternate teaching strategies for enhancing the development of these skills. The teacher must also have a reasonable idea of each child's level of maturity, interest, and motivation. With this general background information, the

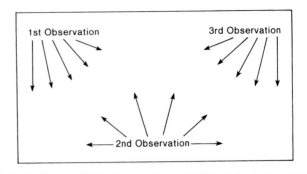

Figure 11.2   Group time sampling—soccer.

teacher assesses the child's or group's performance and, where indicated, changes the task or teaching technique to improve performance. Most classroom teachers, however, do not possess this background information and often feel frustrated when they try to apply observational skills in a productive manner. The following guidelines will help teachers use their observational skills according to their own general background in physical education.

1. Before the lesson begins, select one or two *key focus points*, and, where appropriate, assist individual children or change the direction of the whole class. For example, the two key focus points in dribbling and passing are keeping the ball close to the feet while dribbling and passing the ball with either foot. As the lesson progresses, the teacher is satisfied with the children's ability to keep the ball close; however, she notes that most children pass the ball with their right foot only. She stops the class (while they are practicing with partners) and stipulates that every second pass must be with the left foot. As a teacher's observational skills and competence in an activity improve, she gradually increases the number of key focus points.
2. Make the observation very brief.
3. If the observation is for the benefit of the whole class, make sure each child has a clear view of the performance.
4. Limit the number of observations for the class's benefit to a few demonstrations.
5. When choosing an individual or a group to perform, do not always select the best performers. Every child, regardless of ability, has something to offer and something to gain when demonstrating a skill or movement idea to peers.
6. When observing a demonstration, provide constructive comments and praise. A child gains from positive, not negative, criticism.
7. When children are asked to observe a performance, specify one or two aspects for them to comment on. Children, like teachers, learn to observe (figure 11.3). Ask them to observe one or two aspects, such as which foot was used to trap the ball or the number of times a player used his right or left foot to pass the ball.

Figure 11.3   Observational skills can be developed and improved.

Figure 11.4   Children observing and sharing.

Observational skills are not restricted to teachers; they are equally important to every child in the class. A child who can observe another child's performance might gain insight into her own performance, acquire another idea, or learn to appreciate the individual characteristics of other children, whether in performing the same skill or in answering a movement challenge in a creative way (figure 11.4).

EVALUATING STUDENT PROGRESS

The stated goals and objectives of elementary physical education determine the various types of evaluative tools that are used in the program. These goals and objectives indicate a need to evaluate progress in a wide variety of motor skills. Appropriate testing instruments should also be available to measure changes in levels of physical fitness. Knowledge tests relating to movement concepts and skills in game, dance, and gymnastic activities assess children's declarative knowledge and are required for upper elementary school children. Some form of evaluation is required to assess the changes in interpersonal skills and social behavior at all levels of the elementary physical education program.

In chapter 9, a set of learning descriptors for the psychomotor, cognitive, and affective domains was listed for each developmental level. These learning descriptors are to be considered signposts along a child's path of develop-

ment. They also provide a rough guideline of what children within each developmental level should be expected to perform, show, or demonstrate. As stated in chapter 1, in 1992 the National Association for Sport and Physical Education (NASPE), an AAHPERD association, produced a similar set of learning descriptors, which they identified as "benchmarks." In 1995, NASPE published national standards for physical education, which also included these performance benchmarks. The benchmarks are seen as developmentally appropriate behaviors representative of progress toward achieving the goals and objectives of a quality program of physical education. These developmentally appropriate behaviors, however, are tied to chronological age—since the benchmarks are listed by grade level and are produced for kindergarten and grades 2, 4, 6, 8, 10, and 12. According to NASPE, these time periods were chosen to suggest when assessment might occur and to indicate what might be assessed in these time periods. Specifically, they consider whether the child

HAS *learned skills necessary to perform a variety of physical activities*

IS *physically fit*

DOES *participate regularly in physical activity*

KNOWS *the implications of and the benefits from involvement in physical activities*

VALUES *physical activity and its contributions to a healthful lifestyle.*

The NASPE benchmarks for kindergarten and grades 2, 4, and 6 are provided here as additional reference points that teachers can use as guidelines for developing appropriate evaluative instruments for children within each developmental level.

Examples of Benchmarks—Kindergarten

As a result of participating in a quality physical education program it is reasonable to expect that the student will be able to:

HAS	K	1.	Travel, in different ways, in a large group without bumping into others or falling.
HAS	K	2.	Travel, in forward and sideways directions, and change direction quickly in response to a signal.
HAS	K	3.	Demonstrate clear contrasts between slow and fast speeds while traveling.
HAS	K	4.	Distinguish between straight, curved, and zigzag pathways while traveling in various ways.
HAS	K	5.	Make both large and small body shapes while traveling.
HAS	K	6.	Travel, demonstrating a variety of relationships with objects, (e.g. over, under, behind, alongside, through).
HAS	K	7.	Place a variety of body parts into high, middle, and low levels.
HAS	K	8.	Without falling, walk forward and sideways the length of a bench.
HAS	K	9.	Roll sideways (right or left) without hesitating or stopping.
HAS	K	10.	Toss a ball and catch it before it bounces twice.
HAS	K	11.	Demonstrate the difference between an overhand and underhand throw.
HAS	K	12.	Kick a stationary ball, using a smooth, continuous running approach prior to the kick.
HAS	K	13.	Continuously jump a swinging rope held by others.
HAS	K	14.	Form round, narrow, wide, and twisted body shapes alone and with a partner.
HAS	K	15.	Walk and run using a mature motor pattern.
IS	K	16.	Sustain moderate physical activity.
DOES	K	17.	Participate daily in vigorous physical activity.
KNOWS	K	18.	Identify selected body parts, skills, and movement concepts.
KNOWS	K	19.	Recognize that skill development requires practice.
KNOWS	K	20.	Recognize that physical activity is good for personal well-being.
KNOWS	K	21.	State guidelines and behaviors for the safe use of equipment and apparatus.
KNOWS	K	22.	Identify feelings that result from participation in physical activities.
KNOWS	K	23.	Enjoy participation alone and with others.
KNOWS	K	24.	Look forward to physical education lessons.

Examples of Benchmarks—Second Grade

As a result of participating in a quality physical education program it is reasonable to expect that the student will be able to:

HAS	2	1.	Travel in a backward direction and change direction quickly, and safely, without falling.
HAS	2	2.	Travel, changing speeds and directions, in response to a variety of rhythms.
HAS	2	3.	Combine various traveling patterns in time to the music.
HAS	2	4.	Jump and land using a combination of one and two foot take-offs and landings.
HAS	2	5.	Demonstrate skills of chasing, fleeing, and dodging to avoid or catch others.
HAS	2	6.	Roll smoothly in a forward direction without stopping or hesitating.
HAS	2	7.	Balance, demonstrating momentary stillness, in symmetrical and asymmetrical shapes on a variety of body parts.
HAS	2	8.	Move feet into a high level by placing the weight on the hands and landing with control.
HAS	2	9.	Use the inside or instep of the foot to kick a slowly rolling ball into the air or along the ground.
HAS	2	10.	Throw a ball hard demonstrating an overhand technique, a side orientation, and opposition.
HAS	2	11.	Catch, using properly positioned hands, a gently thrown ball.
HAS	2	12.	Continuously dribble a ball, using the hands or feet, without losing control.
HAS	2	13.	Use at least three different body parts to strike a ball toward a target.
HAS	2	14.	Strike a ball repeatedly with a paddle.
HAS	2	15.	Consistently strike a ball with a bat from a tee or cone, using a correct grip and side orientation.
HAS	2	16.	Repeatedly jump a self-turned rope.
HAS	2	17.	Combine shapes, levels, and pathways into simple sequence.
HAS	2	18.	Skip, hop, gallop, and slide using mature motor patterns.
IS	2	19.	Move each joint through a full range of motion.
IS	2	20.	Manage own body weight while hanging and climbing.
DOES	2	21.	Demonstrate safety while participating in physical activity.
DOES	2	22.	Participate in a wide variety of activities that involve locomotion, nonlocomotion, and the manipulation of various objects.
KNOWS	2	23.	Recognize similar movement concepts in a variety of skills.
KNOWS	2	24.	Identify appropriate behaviors for participating with others in physical activity.
KNOWS	2	25.	Identify changes in the body during physical activity.
KNOWS	2	26.	State reasons for safe and controlled movements.
KNOWS	2	27.	Appreciate the benefits that accompany cooperation and sharing.
KNOWS	2	28.	Accept the feelings resulting from challenges, successes, and failures in physical activity.
KNOWS	2	29.	Be considerate of others in physical activity settings.

Examples of Benchmarks—Fourth Grade

As a result of participating in a quality physical education program it is reasonable to expect that the student will be able to:

HAS	4	1.	While traveling, avoid or catch an individual or object.
HAS	4	2.	Leap, leading with either foot.
HAS	4	3.	Roll, in a backward direction, without hesitating or stopping.
HAS	4	4.	Transfer weight, from feet to hands, at fast and slow speeds using large extensions (e.g., mulekick, handstand, cartwheel.)
HAS	4	5.	Hand dribble and foot dribble a ball and maintain control while traveling within a group.
HAS	4	6.	Strike a softly thrown, lightweight ball back to a partner using a variety of body parts, and combinations of body parts (e.g., the bump volley as in volleyball, the thigh as in soccer.
HAS	4	7.	Consistently strike a softly thrown ball with a bat or paddle demonstrating an appropriate grip, side to the target and swing plane.
HAS	4	8.	Develop patterns and combinations of movements into repeatable sequences.
HAS	4	9.	Without hesitating, travel into and out of a rope turned by others.
HAS	4	10.	Balance, with control, on a variety of moving objects S(e.g., balance boards, skates, scooters).
HAS	4	11.	Jump and land for height, and jump and land for distance using a mature motor pattern.
HAS	4	12.	Throw, catch, and kick using mature motor patterns.
HAS	4	13.	Demonstrate competence in basic swimming strokes and survival skills in, on, and around the water.
IS	4	14.	Maintain continuous aerobic activity for a specified time.
IS	4	15.	Maintain appropriate body alignment during activity (e.g., lift, carry, push, pull).
IS	4	16.	Support, lift, and control body weight in a variety of activities.
DOES	4	17.	Regularly participate in physical activity for the purpose of improving skillful performance and physical fitness.
KNOWS	4	18.	Distinguish between compliance and noncompliance with game rules and fair play.
KNOWS	4	19.	Select and categorize specialized equipment used for participation in a variety of activities.
KNOWS	4	20.	Recognize fundamental components and strategies used in simple games and activities.
KNOWS	4	21.	Identify ways movement concepts can be used to refine movement skills.
KNOWS	4	22.	Identify activities that contribute to personal feelings of joy.
KNOWS	4	23.	Describe essential elements of mature movement patterns.
KNOWS	4	24.	Describe healthful benefits that result from regular and appropriate participation in physical activity.
KNOWS	4	25.	Analyze potential risks associated with physical activities.
KNOWS	4	26.	Design games, gymnastics, and dance sequences that are personally interesting.
VALUES	4	27.	Appreciate differences and similarities in others' physical activity.
VALUES	4	28.	Respect persons from different backgrounds and the cultural significance they attribute to various games, dances, and physical activities.
VALUES	4	29.	Enjoy feelings resulting from involvement in physical activity.
VALUES	4	30.	Celebrate personal successes and achievements and those of others.

Examples of Benchmarks—Sixth Grade

As a result of participating in a quality physical education program it is reasonable to expect that the student will be able to:

HAS	6	1.	Throw a variety of objects demonstrating both accuracy and distance (e.g., Frisbees, deck tennis rings, footballs).
HAS	6	2.	Continuously strike a ball to a wall, or a partner, with a paddle using forehand and backhand strokes.
HAS	6	3.	Consistently strike a ball, using a golf club or a hockey stick, so that it travels in an intended direction and height.
HAS	6	4.	Design and perform gymnastics and dance sequences that combine traveling, rolling, balancing, and weight transfer into smooth, flowing sequences with intentional changes in direction, speed, and flow.
HAS	6	5.	Hand dribble and foot dribble while preventing an opponent from stealing the ball.
HAS	6	6.	In a small group keep an object continuously in the air without catching it (e.g., ball, foot bag).
HAS	6	7.	Consistently throw and catch a ball while guarded by opponents.
HAS	6	8.	Design and play small group games that involve cooperating with others to keep an object away from opponents (basic offensive and defensive strategy) (e.g., by throwing, kicking, and/or dribbling a ball).
HAS	6	9.	Design and refine a routine, combining various jump rope movements to music, so that it can be repeated without error.
HAS	6	10.	Leap, roll, balance, transfer weight, bat, volley, hand and foot dribble, and strike a ball with a paddle, using mature motor patterns.
HAS	6	11.	Demonstrate proficiency in front, back, and side swimming strokes.
HAS	6	12.	Participate in vigorous activity for a sustained period of time while maintaining a target heart rate.
IS	6	13.	Recover from vigorous physical activity in an appropriate length of time.
IS	6	14.	Monitor heart rate before, during, and after activity.
IS	6	15.	Correctly demonstrate activities designed to improve and maintain muscular strength and endurance, flexibility, and cardiorespiratory functioning.
DOES	6	16.	Participate in games, sports, dance, and outdoor pursuits, both in and outside of school, based on individual interests and capabilities.

Examples of Benchmarks—Sixth Grade *Continued*

KNOWS	6	17.	Recognize that idealized images of the human body and performance, as presented by the media, may not be appropriate to imitate.
KNOWS	6	18.	Recognize that time and effort are prerequisites for skill improvement and fitness benefits.
KNOWS	6	19.	Recognize the role of games, sports, and dance in getting to know and understand others of like and different cultures.
KNOWS	6	20.	Identify opportunities in the school and community for regular participation in physical activity.
KNOWS	6	21.	Identify principles of training and conditioning for physical activity.
KNOWS	6	22.	Identify proper warm-up, conditioning, and cool-down techniques and the reasons for using them.
KNOWS	6	23.	Identify benefits resulting from participation in different forms of physical activities.
KNOWS	6	24.	Detect, analyze, and correct errors in personal movement patterns.
KNOWS	6	25.	Describe ways to use the body and movement activities to communicate ideas and feelings.
VALUES	6	26.	Accept and respect the decisions made by game officials, whether they are students, teachers, or officials outside of school.
VALUES	6	27.	Seek out, participate with, and show respect for persons of like and different skill levels.
VALUES	6	28.	Choose to exercise at home for personal enjoyment and benefit.

From NASPE Benchmarks for kindergarten, grade two, grade four, and grade six. Reprinted from *Outcomes of Quality Physical Education Programs* with the permission of the National Association for Sport and Physical Education, 1900 Association Drive, Reston, VA 22091.

TABLE 11.3　Locomotor Skill Checklist

1st Check ___(date)___ 2nd Check ___(date)___ 3rd Check ___(date)___ Correct Form (C) Incorrect (I)	**Walk**			**Run**			**Leap**			**Jump**			**Hop**			**Skip**			**Slide**			**Stop**			**Dodge**		
	1st check	2nd check	3rd check	1st check	2nd check	3rd check	1st check	2nd check	3rd check	1st check	2nd check	3rd check	1st check	2nd check	3rd check	1st check	2nd check	3rd check	1st check	2nd check	3rd check	1st check	2nd check	3rd check	1st check	2nd check	3rd check
Student 1. _____																											
2. _____																											
3. _____																											
4. _____																											
5. _____																											
6. _____																											
7. _____																											

C O N C E P T

11.6 *Benchmarks Describe Developmentally Appropriate Behaviors Representative of Progress toward Achieving the Goals and Objectives of a Quality Physical Education Program*

Motor Skills

In most elementary school physical education programs, the majority of instructional time is devoted to learning motor skills. As children mature both physically and in motor skill performance, the emphasis, particularly in the upper elementary grades, shifts to acquiring advanced motor skills and movement patterns in game, dance, and gymnastic activities. The following sample testing instruments are used in the primary and intermediate grades.

Checklists

Children in the primary grades do not perform reliably on most standardized or teacher-made motor skill tests. A more appropriate way to test is to develop your own checklist and rating scales. The checklist in table 11.3 illustrates how a teacher can use a formative evaluation to determine whether a child can perform each of the important fundamental loco-motor skills. If this form is used in the first part of the school year, it generally indicates the locomotor skills that need to be stressed in the physical education program. The fact that it

TABLE 11.4 Manipulative Skills

Rating Scale (See Stages of Skill Development) 0 Cannot Perform 1 Initial Stage 2 Intermediate Stage 3 Automatic Stage	One-Hand Underhand Throw			One-Hand Overhand Throw			One-Hand Underhand Catch			Two-Hand Overhand Catch			Striking with Hand			Striking with an Implement			Kicking a Ball			Dribbling a Ball		
	1st check	2nd check	3rd check	1st check	2nd check	3rd check	1st check	2nd check	3rd check	1st check	2nd check	3rd check	1st check	2nd check	3rd check	1st check	2nd check	3rd check	1st check	2nd check	3rd check	1st check	2nd check	3rd check
Name 1. _____																								
2. _____																								
3. _____																								
4. _____																								
5. _____																								
6. _____																								
7. _____																								

does not distinguish among good, average, and poor levels of performance is the main limitation of this checklist. However, rating scales can provide this type of information.

Rating Scales

A rating scale is an instrument that measures the degree or level of performance of a skill or movement pattern. Table 11.4 uses the three phases of motor learning described in chapter 3. Because this scale is intended for early and late primary grades, some children are not able to perform at the minimum "initial level." Hence, a zero rating has been added.

The value of rating scales is that they can give each teacher an overview of the skills that need greater attention. They also provide general guidelines to help each child acquire the important manipulative skills according to his own level of skill and ability. Rating scales are also used in the intermediate grades to assess game skills, as well as dance and gymnastic movement skills and patterns.

Checklists and rating scales are valuable tools for teachers in the primary and intermediate grades. The following suggestions will help teachers design and use these instruments.

1. In designing checklists and rating scales, limit each observation to one skill or concept.
2. Try to understand the key aspect of each skill being assessed. This means reading about the skill, checking videotapes that describe the execution of the skill, or seeking help from physical education specialists.
3. Keep the skill as simple as possible until you gain greater knowledge of the skills and movement patterns involved in the specific activity.

4. Observe each child performing the specific movement several times before making an assessment.
5. Record observations for every child under the same conditions and in the same sequence. For example, when two skills are being observed, all children should be rated on the first skill before any child on the list is assessed on the second skill.

Skill Tests

As children move through the upper primary and into the intermediate grades, there is an increased need to measure performance levels in a wide variety of game skills. There are a few standardized skill tests produced by AAHPERD (1989); however, most skill tests used to assess game, gymnastic, and dance skills are developed by local school districts and individual teachers.

Table 11.5 is an example of a teacher-made battery test for measuring throwing and catching skills; it is simple, inexpensive, and easy to administer. Each test item can be modified to meet the skill levels of several grades. The first four tests measure form and accuracy; the fifth measures distance.

Test 1: Underhand catch. The teacher stands twenty feet from the child and throws consecutively ten balls, which the child must catch with an underhand catch. One point is awarded for each successful catch.

Test 2: Overhand catch. Repeat test 1, but require an overhand catch.

Test 3: One-hand underhand throw. The child stands fifteen feet from a wastepaper basket and attempts

TABLE 11.5 **Objective Skill Test**

	Throwing and Catching Skills						
Name of Student	Test 1: Underhand Catch	Test 2: Overhand Catch	Test 3: One-hand Underhand Throw	Test 4: Two-hand Chest Throw	Test 5: Throw for Distance	Total	Grade
1. John Smith	7	5	6	5	8	31	B
2. Mary Able	6	4	5	5	5	25	C
3.							
4.							

to throw ten softballs into it. The underhand throw must be used. One point is awarded for each successful throw.

Test 4: Two-hand chest throw. Repeat test 3, but with a two-hand chest throw and a larger utility ball.

Test 5: Throw for distance. The child throws a softball three times. The three distances are added together and divided by three and recorded against a linear scale of 1 to 10. For example, distances of 0 to 10 feet might receive a score of 1, 11 to 20 feet might receive a 2, and so on, up to 91 to 100 feet, which would receive a 10. This scale can be adjusted to meet the developmental level of the children being tested. The important criterion is that test number 5, for distance, be measured under the same weighting as all other tests. In this example, each test is scored "out of 10." This helps eliminate bias between test items. If the distance throw were not scaled down to fit a weighting of 10, then a child who throws the ball a long distance would be awarded a high grade regardless of her performance on the other four test items.

A teacher-made skill test should be devised so that the individual scores can be totaled to provide a means of ranking children, and it should indicate where additional emphasis should be placed in the selection of practice activities and lead-up games. Several sample teacher-made tests are provided in part 6 of this text.

Movement Education Concepts and Skills

When teaching Movement Education concepts and skills, there is no common standard by which to judge progress. The essential purpose of these concepts and skills is to help children use their bodies in a variety of ways on and off apparatus—each movement task should produce different shapes and movement patterns for each child, so performance is an individualized matter and must be evaluated on that basis. The Sequence of Development chart illustrates how a simple checklist can be used to evaluate a child's understanding of a movement challenge and the quality of her performance.

Student	Sequence of Development				
	Stretch	Curl	Twisted	Flow	
				Smooth	Jerky
Jill Wells	✓	✓			✓
Paul Martinez	✓		✓	✓	

The movement challenge evaluated with this chart was to make up a sequence that included stretched, curled, and twisted shapes. According to the chart, Jill Wells included a stretch and a curl but no twisted shape. The teacher also judged her sequence to be somewhat jerky. Paul Martinez's sequence included a stretch and a twist but lacked a curled shape. Nevertheless, he moved smoothly from one shape to the other.

The sample criterion-type evaluations of these two students emphasize the developmental aspect of movement. As teachers become more experienced with this form of evaluation, they can expand it to include other concepts and skills, as well as additional items that describe the quality of the movement. Finally, developmental assessment can and should be made jointly by the teacher and the child. Children progress at their own rate and according to their individual potential, so the teacher's assessment is based on whether a child is sufficiently challenged and is continually improving her ability to produce more difficult shapes and movements. Progress, then, is as much concerned with the quality of movement as with the individuality and variety of movements the child performs.

C O N C E P T

11.7 *A Number of Methods and Techniques, Such as Checklists and Rating Scales, Can Be Used Effectively to Evaluate Student Progress*

Physical Fitness

The AAHPERD Physical Best fitness test is an excellent example of a health-related fitness test designed for elementary-age schoolchildren. The test items include measures of cardiovascular endurance (aerobic capacity), body composition, muscle strength, endurance, and flexibility. This test can be easily administered in the elementary school setting and is described in chapter 8.

Personal Activity Log (PAL)

The contemporary move toward promoting active living requires changes to many of the traditional approaches physical education has taken in the past. The move to a developmentally appropriate approach is one positive change that will provide children with the necessary background to enjoy an active lifestyle. However, even with quality daily physical education, there will be a need to foster children's transfer of their healthy activity to their world outside of school. The physical education curricula will need to be integrated into the child's life outside of school if the goal of "activity independence" outlined in chapter 1 is to be achieved. In line with a reflective practice approach to teaching has been a move toward understanding children's individual needs by encouraging children to keep personal journals. Through journals, children can express their own personal needs, desires, aspirations, feelings, experiences, and so on, reflecting their "lived experiences." Reviewing journal entries will be part of a teacher's reflective practices; the journals will help the teacher reflect on the congruency between children's needs and his own teaching practices. As a result, the teacher should be in a better position to plan developmentally appropriate activities.

A personal activity log (PAL) can be arranged for each child; as the acronym suggests, this journal is the child's "pal." Children can use their PAL not only to express their own lived experiences, but also for goal setting and planning activities that are commensurate with their own environments outside of school. As noted in chapter 4, goal setting usually produces superior performance over merely telling a child, "Try the best you can." This is especially true if children are personally involved in the goal setting. For example, a child who enjoys riding a bicycle might set the personal goal of cycling twice around a local park on Saturday. The parent of the child can then become involved in monitoring this activity and signing the log book to state that permission to pursue the activity was granted and that indeed the goal was achieved. The child's PAL thus serves many purposes; not only does it cater to the child's home and local commu-

nity activities, it provides an avenue for getting parents involved in monitoring and taking an interest in the child's active lifestyle. A similar idea to the PAL has been developed by AAHPERD in its new You Stay Active recognition system, which is designed to promote regular participation in physical activity. A goal-setting contract, illustrated in table 8.1 in chapter 8, promotes regular participation in physical activities that are endorsed by parents.

Traditionally, homework is not usually assigned in physical education. Through the child's PAL, homework becomes a natural part of the link between school activities and community and home life. Further, this homework activity is designed by the child; hence, children learn to take responsibility for their own learning. The children's PAL activities can also be linked back to school and integrated with physical education and other areas of curricula. In the example cited above, cycling can be discussed and integrated with fitness and health curricula in terms of aerobic fitness, balance, strength, and endurance. Cycling might also be linked to social studies through discussion of events such as international bike races (such as the Tour de France). Orienteering skills of map reading and planning routes that are considered safe for cycling might be linked to community cycle paths. Language arts activities could include writing stories about cycling trips or cycling holidays, and research projects could involve studying the history surrounding the invention and development of the bicycle. Research projects linked to the science curriculum might include studying the mechanical principles that allow the bicycle to convert human movement into movement speed that far exceeds the capability of a human, or studying the engineering designs that have resulted in differences between the mountain bike and the racing bicycle. Linking bicycling with the mechanical principles of balance, motion, force, and leverage, outlined in chapter 3, will help increase the child's (declarative) knowledge base in this area.

Clearly, teacher direction and planning will be required to assist children with their PALs. As noted in chapter 4, setting realistic goals that are achievable to ensure success is essential for motivation. Also, parental permission is essential before any of the planned activities occur outside of the school setting. Further, younger children, children with disabilities, and others who experience difficulty in writing will have problems responding through journal writing. Modifications might be necessary because these children will require help in filling out their PALs.

Many teachers do not plan for daily physical education because the gymnasium or other specified physical education area is not always available. Rather than lose the opportunity of daily physical education, classroom activities can be arranged (see chapter 15). Classroom time can also be set aside on a regular basis for children to work on their PALs. This time can also be used for planning and monitoring an active lifestyle, and for planning group, cooperative, and individual projects that integrate PAL content with schoolwork. The time could also be used for assessment and acquisition of other areas of declarative knowledge associated with physical education.

11.8 Student Journals, such as Personal Activity Log (PAL) Books, Can Be Used Effectively in Both Student Evaluation and Goal-Setting Activities

Knowledge

One objective of physical education is to acquire a knowledge and understanding of physical activities and their contribution to physical and mental health. When children know the team positions, rules, and strategy of a game, there is less chance of misunderstandings and misbehavior. Furthermore, as indicated in chapter 3, declarative knowledge of the rules of a team sport, the verses in a singing game, or the parts of a complex gymnastic skill enhances motor learning.

In the primary grades, verbal questions are used to teach simple rules and verses in singing games and to stimulate creative thought through interpretive movements. Written tests can be used in the upper grades in all phases of the physical education program. But written tests are rarely used in physical education, where the major emphasis is usually assessment of procedural knowledge and not declarative. Written tests offer the opportunity to address this imbalance, and children who do not possess well-developed procedural knowledge skills but are still knowledgeable in terms of declarative knowledge will likely benefit from written tests. Further, research has shown that when people are told that the material they are learning in class will form part of the content for later written testing, greater retention and achievement scores usually occur. Planning for written testing of declarative knowledge would appear to be an effective teaching strategy. The choice of true/false, multiple-choice, or short-answer tests depends on the teacher and the capabilities of her students. Regardless of the type of test chosen, care should be taken to pose questions that are clear and appropriate to the physical activity.

Social Development

The traits denoted by the term *social development* do not lend themselves readily to either subjective or objective measurement. For example, the ability to get along with others, team loyalty, and sportsmanship cannot be measured accurately by a rating scale, an anecdotal record, or even an expert's judgment. Nevertheless, these are extremely important qualities that we profess to develop within the physical education program. Consequently, an attempt, however meager, should be made to evaluate the development of these qualities. Some of the more practical techniques follow.

Teacher Observations

Probably the most common technique for assessing individual social growth is the daily observation a teacher makes while the children are playing in a structured situation or during free-play activities. The teacher might notice behavioral problems, such as cheating and poor sportsmanship, for instance. The manner of coping with adjustment problems varies—from changing the method of instruction to completely changing the activities.

Interview

A personal interview between the teacher and the child and/or parent is another technique used to gain a better understanding of a child's general behavior. Usually, specific adjustment problems are discussed with the child or, when appropriate, the parent to determine the reasons behind certain behavioral problems. The teacher should take care, however, not to lecture, but to win the child's confidence and show genuine concern for the child. When a child respects and trusts the teacher, chances are he will gain an understanding of his problem and make appropriate changes.

Sociogram

The sociogram is a technique used to study the relationships within a group. By posing such key questions as "With whom would you like to practice catching skills during recess?" or "Who would you like to have on your team?" it is possible to identify children who appear to be well adjusted within the group and those who are isolated and rejected. To obtain the best results from this technique, it is wise to keep the following procedures in mind when asking students such questions (Kozman, Cassidy, and Jackson 1967):

1. Make sure the situation for which students are asked to make choices is a real one.
2. Use the choices to group students according to their preferences.
3. Make sure the atmosphere is informal and friendly.
4. Let the students understand that their answers will be confidential.
5. Give no clues to the student about how to choose.

The results of the sociogram can help identify children who need assistance. By drawing circles on a sheet of paper to represent each child and lines between children as the answers dictate, it becomes quite clear who are the popular children and the rejected children in a particular social group. By a simple regrouping, the shy and retiring child can be brought into a more favorable group without making the reasons for such a change obvious. Furthermore, undesirable group situations can also indicate the need to vary the methods of class organization, selection of team captains, and type of group activities.

ASSESSMENT OF CHILDREN WITH SPECIAL NEEDS

If a child is working on an individualized educational program (IEP) (an example is provided in figure 13.2 in chapter 13), then evaluation techniques and methods must be chosen that best reflect the goals and objectives outlined in the IEP. However, there are many kinds of disabilities (see chapter 13), so often it is difficult to find authentic assessment techniques, and to identify appropriate performance standards, that are suitable for children with special needs. Authentic assessment involves techniques and methods that reflect "real-life" situations and not contrived testing situations (NASPE 1995). The evaluative techniques and methods outlined in this chapter offer examples of authentic assessment techniques. Most of these methods and techniques can be used effectively with all children. However, specific disabilities might require specialized knowledge of expected student competencies and appropriate assessment procedures. A number of validated tests and procedures have been designed to assess student competencies related to specific disabilities. For example, chapter 8 outlined a selection of fitness tests that have been designed to assess fitness levels of children with various disabilities. There are a number of texts that address developmentally appropriate physical education for children with specific disabilities. Teachers will find the Sherrill (1997), Dunn and Fait (1989), and Jansma and French (1994) texts particularly useful as resources for both identifying student competencies and developing appropriate techniques and methods for evaluating children with special needs.

GRADING AND REPORTING

The purpose of grading in physical education is the same as in all other subjects—to report the child's progress. Although the majority of elementary school report cards require only an *S* or *U*, or *P* or *F*, additional information relating to skill performance, physical fitness, and social adjustment should be available in the form of a cumulative record. When a parent asks, "How is my child doing in physical education?" and the answer is, "She is well adjusted in her group" or "She is doing fairly well in physical skills," very little insight has been gained and the parent might come away with an unfavorable impression of the program.

To overcome the weakness of the pass/fail grading and reporting system, many schools require a cumulative record in physical education. This is particularly true in districts where children are given physical fitness tests in the fall and spring. After the spring test has been given, the physical fitness scores are reported to parents or passed on to the next grade to assist the new teacher in setting reasonable limits for the child. Additional information about skill performance in rhythmic, game, and gymnastic activities should

be recorded in the cumulative record. The child's evaluation should then be based on her improvement rather than on how she ranks with others in the class. However, improvement alone is not the only consideration. Due to known sensitive times in development (see chapter 2), certain minimum levels of achievement should be in place as the child progresses through the elementary years. The "mature" form of fundamental motor patterns (automatic phase) associated with basic motor skills of running, jumping, throwing, catching, and kicking (see chapter 6) can be expected to be in place by middle childhood. If a child is reaching the upper grades of elementary school, yet is still exhibiting "immature" movement patterns in these basic movement tasks (early or associative phases), then individualized practices should be scheduled to help the child move along on the skill/learning continuum. As the child reaches adolescence and beyond, it will become increasingly more difficult to change these fundamental motor patterns. The checklists cited earlier, together with the NASPE benchmarks and the fundamental motor pattern checklists provided in chapter 6, will be helpful to teachers in both monitoring and reporting motor development to parents, administrators, and policy makers.

Portfolio Assessment

Traditionally portfolios have been used in subject areas other than physical education, yet they can be a useful assessment tool. Portfolios have the potential to portray growth and development about a variety of student outcomes that are difficult to assess using traditional methods. Portfolios are more than a collection of folders containing examples of children's work. They are a purposeful collection of student work that shows both progress and achievement in given areas. What to include in a portfolio is a matter of teacher (and often student) choice. Children's involvement in the process provides an opportunity for ownership in their own educational process. Portfolios in physical education can include a variety of materials, including videotaped recordings of student accomplishments. A videotape of dance or gymnastic performances, for example, might capture the essence of the child's accomplishment better than many other forms of assessment and evaluation. It would also be possible in small classes to videotape before and after shots of a given locomotor or manipulative skill. A visual record of motor development would add substantially to other forms of assessment. A computer disk for each child, which might contain journal entries and other forms of declarative knowledge gained through the physical education program, could also be included in the portfolio. Adding the child's personal activity log (PAL) to the portfolio would offer further evidence of student progress. In addition, if the developmentally appropriate activities covered in physical education have been integrated into other areas of the school curriculum, then a variety of student work to represent these connections and topics could be gathered to include in the portfolio. Sharing these accomplishments with both the child and the parent can offer a unique insight into the child's achievement and progress. A portfolio is not meant to replace other forms of assessment and evaluation; it merely offers the opportunity to purposefully gather various forms of evidence to display both progress and achievement, adding another dimension to the evaluation process.

C O N C E P T

11.9 Portfolios Offer the Potential to Portray Growth and Development Regarding a Variety of Learning Outcomes That Are Difficult to Assess Using Traditional Techniques

EVALUATING THE PROGRAM

The physical education program in its broadest form includes all the organized experiences, the facilities, and the teachers involved in teaching and supervisory roles. Evaluative techniques for measuring all these factors are simply not available. Even if they were, the time element alone would prohibit extensive assessments. There are, however, periodic evaluations teachers should make about program content, daily lessons, facilities, equipment, and their own effectiveness. Most of the following suggestions apply to each teacher; however, joint evaluative programs, involving the principal, supervisors, or other teachers, should be encouraged for providing greater expertise and support to areas of the program where improvement or redirection is indicated.

Program Content

The content of a physical education curriculum can be effectively and formally evaluated by external organizations, such as state department of instruction or an official accrediting agency. Such evaluations normally use highly refined evaluative instruments and include many items of a physical education program. Another way of evaluating the program content is for each classroom teacher to develop his own self-appraisal scale that covers key elements in his instructional program. The sample scale shown in table 11.6 will help the teacher judge how well he is meeting a particular goal or providing a particular service to his students.

Daily Lesson

Perhaps the most important evaluation procedure that teachers make is the ongoing assessment of each physical education lesson. If the following areas are checked routinely, teachers can gauge whether the objectives of the lesson are being reached and where specific changes in content and teaching strategies are needed.

Because the time available for physical education is usually quite short, each lesson must be planned carefully to encourage maximum participation. The teacher should, therefore, assess the following:

1. The time children take to change and enter the gymnasium
2. The amount of time devoted to explaining and demonstrating skills (most teachers spend so much time explaining that they allow too little time for practice)
3. The time available for each child to practice each skill or movement

Effective Routine Procedures

Many unnecessary problems and much waste of time can be avoided when children know what is expected of them in the gymnasium. Simple routine procedures should be established and followed from the first lesson. These should include the following:

1. Arrangement of apparatus—who should be responsible
2. Rotation procedure—moving from one piece of equipment or apparatus to another
3. Carrying and putting away equipment and apparatus

Sufficient Challenge to Children

When teachers are continually confronted with disciplinary problems, the reason could be lack of challenge in the tasks they give children. The teacher should constantly observe the amount of concentration and effort the children are giving to the task. These are some specific things to look for:

1. After you have introduced a new skill, game, or challenge, is there a demonstration of general boredom or a general rise in noise?
2. Are various children moving away from their assigned working area to be with friends or to irritate other children?
3. Is there a marked increase in irrelevant questions and comments by the children?

Individual Observation and Guidance

In any learning situation, each child needs some guidance and encouragement, regardless of ability. Too often, the outstanding performer is selected for demonstrations and praise, while the low achiever, who really needs attention and encouragement, is neglected. Hence, the teacher should also

1. Observe, correct, and encourage as many children as possible
2. Select many different children for demonstrations
3. Record important and successful techniques that will assist in future lessons

Facilities and Equipment

Most school districts have established policies for the allocation of funds for physical education. Normally each school receives an annual equipment and supplies grant

TABLE 11.6 Physical Education Program Evaluation Form

Program Area	Excellent Compliance	Adequate Compliance	Needs Improvement
1. Objectives of the program are clearly stated.			
2. Objectives of the program are used as a guideline for selecting and emphasizing program content.			
3. The written curriculum is an up-to-date program that provides adequate scope and sequence for each grade level.			
4. The curriculum contains a variety of activities appropriate for children in the primary or intermediate grades.			
5. Provision is made for periodic revisions of the physical education curriculum.			
6. Program content reflects a consideration of the needs and interests of both sexes.			
7. Program content reflects a consideration of children with special needs.			
8. Provisions are made to integrate program content of physical education with other subject areas in the elementary school curriculum.			
9. Time allotments for physical education meet school district, state, or national standards.			
10. Provisions are made for student involvement in the selection of activities.			
11. Provisions are made for the involvement of parents and interested citizens in the selection of activities.			
12. Children are required to have a physical examination by a qualified physician on a scheduled basis. The actual schedule is a written policy of the school.			
13. An up-to-date professional physical education library is available within the district.			
14. Flexible plans are followed with respect to the nature and length of instructional units.			
15. An evaluation of the program content is made on a yearly schedule by the classroom teacher and/or other school personnel.			

based on the number of children in the school. Teachers should refer to the list of suggested equipment and supplies in chapter 10 as a basic guideline. It is extremely valuable for each school district to establish its own recommended list so teachers have a reasonable idea of the quantity and quality of equipment they can expect to receive.

Facilities and equipment should also be inspected prior to and during each lesson for the following:

1. Safety of playing space and equipment.
2. Appropriateness of space and equipment. For example, if the instructional space is too large for good control,

reduce its size using markers or another device. If balls, bats, or other equipment or apparatus are too small or too large for the learners, make immediate and appropriate adjustments. Finally, is there equipment in the gymnasium or outdoor playing area that is not recommended for use in the elementary school program? Serious consideration should be given to such apparatus as merry-go-rounds, swings with steel or wooden seats, and such gymnastic equipment as the trampoline and mini-tramp. The latter two pieces of equipment are desirable for upper elementary, provided competent teachers are present to teach skills on them.

CHAPTER 11

3. Adequate supply of equipment. If the number of balls or other pieces of small equipment is insufficient for the number of children, introduce techniques like station work to provide for maximum participation.

Teacher Effectiveness

All teachers should appraise their teaching to determine how they can improve their effectiveness in the classroom and gymnasium. Although it is often perceived as stressful, evaluation of one's teaching should be viewed as a positive experience that is designed to promote growth and learning. A plan of action should be undertaken to systematically evaluate the effectiveness of the instructional process. Since research has identified several key teaching behaviors with effective teaching (see chapter 4), methods and techniques to assess these teaching behaviors must be sought. Many of the evaluative techniques and methods described earlier, such as group time sampling and event recording, can be applied to the teacher. A colleague or volunteer can observe classes to systematically record various aspects of the teaching situation. For example, time spent helping individual students (time on-task), the number of student successes, the type and frequency of feedback given to students, and time spent on transitions between activities can all be easily monitored through observational techniques. Two other methods that are very effective ways of identifying key teaching behaviors are audiotaping and videotaping of lessons.

Audiotape Analysis

Analysis of audiotape reveals the effectiveness of verbal communication. Checks for "wait time" between question and student response, probing for higher-level responses, number and types of questions posed, use of repeated words such as *okay,* use of slang words such as *gonna, gotta,* etc., can easily be identified through audiotaping. Voice level, variation, pacing, and clarity of pronunciation can all be checked through playback analysis of the audiotaped lesson.

Videotape Analysis

Videotaping offers a powerful method of self-evaluation. Although it can be intimidating at first, teachers find it very instructive to view their own teaching (figure 11.5). A whole variety of areas and behaviors can be analyzed during playback. For example, use of nonverbal communication, proximity to students, use of student ideas, providing instructional variety, structuring the lesson, teacher enthusiasm, and a concern for children's safety can all be monitored through videotape playback analysis. To assist in videotape analysis, a checklist is provided in table 11.7. The checklist is organized under the three major elements: set, body, and closure. These elements provide a focus for observations during the analysis.

Figure 11.5 Teachers find it very instructive to analyze videotaped lessons.

Professional Development and Lifelong Learning

The field of physical education is changing extensively, in both content and methods of instruction, and teachers should assess whether they are as up-to-date in this area as they are in other subjects. Consideration should be given to the following areas:

1. New developments in health-related physical fitness tests, movement education, and cooperative and creative games
2. New textbooks in the general field of physical education and specialized texts in game, dance, and gymnastic activities
3. New developments in audiovisual materials for physical education (films, filmstrips, and videotapes)
4. New developments in equipment and apparatus, particularly the new agility apparatus
5. Related research in motor learning, teaching academic concepts through movement, perceptual motor development, and physical education
6. New program developments, particularly programs supported by federal and state funds

Information and general assistance in these areas can be secured from state and local district supervisors of physical education. Numerous national organizations, such as the American Alliance for Health, Physical Education, Recreation and Dance (AAHPERD), the Office of Education, and the Athletic Institute, provide information on request.

C O N C E P T

11.10 *Systematic Evaluation of the Physical Education Program Is Essential and Requires Careful Planning and Self-Reflection by the Teacher*

Evaluation should be an ongoing process of assessing whether goals are being achieved. Adequate program evaluation pri-

TABLE 11.7   Observation Checklist for the Evaluation of Teaching

Observation	+	–	0	Notes

Instructional Set

Introduced content _____
Stated objectives clearly _____
Explained usefulness of skill or concept _____
Related lesson to previous and next lesson _____
Established positive mood _____
Exhibited enthusiasm _____
Motivated students to learn _____

Body of Lesson

Communicated effectively _____
Two-way communication maintained _____
Clarified and defined new terms _____
Controlled amount of content _____
Emphasized major points _____
Used demonstrations, visual examples, or illustrations _____
Summarized periodically _____
Used student ideas _____
Used questioning techniques _____
Accepted student responses _____
Probed students for higher-level responses to questions _____
Responded to student feedback _____
Changed stimuli and provided instructional variety _____
Encouraged student–student interaction _____
Managed time effectively _____
Maintained eye contact with students _____
Maintained effective organization _____
Maintained high time-on-task for children _____
Used nonverbal communication (body language) effectively _____
Provided effective feedback for both learning and motivation _____

Instructional Closure

Summarized major points _____
Related points to instructional set _____
Checked for student understanding _____
Provided sense of achievement _____
Monitored student progress (assessment) _____

Assessment of Success in Helping Students meet Instructional Objectives

Strengths	Weaknesses
a.	a.
b.	b.
c.	c.
d.	d.

Were the activities developmentally appropriate for all children?   Yes ___   No ___
Did all children experience success?   Yes ___   No ___

Goals for Improvement

a.
b.
c.
d.

---

marily involves the day-to-day assessment of each lesson in order to make modifications in activities and methods of instruction. Contemporary programs also include student evaluation of the program. Although the children cannot always see the value of and reason for all activities, they can provide valuable assistance with respect to their needs and interests. Provision should be made for children to participate actively in program evaluation. When children are respected for their contributions, they, in turn, will generally provide the effort and enthusiasm to make the program a success.

Summary Review

Education reform has created a desire for nationwide education standards. Indeed, the demand for educational standards was written into federal law in 1994 in the Goals 2000: Educate America Act. Rather than create a national curriculum or an approved course of study to meet this demand, the preference has been toward establishing student competencies. Student competencies refer to what students should "know and be able to do," and this is being addressed in all areas of education today. What students should know and be able to do relates to the content standards of the program (curriculum goals and objectives). Performance standards indicate the level of achievement that students are expected to attain in the content standards. Performance standards are inextricably tied to issues of evaluation and assessment. Hence, appropriate methods and techniques to evaluate student progress, the teaching process, and the quality of the physical education program as a whole must be sought. Further, appropriate methods for reporting evaluation and assessment of these areas need to be established.

Because there are a variety of observational techniques and methods to choose from, careful decision making is required when evaluating a child's experiences in physical education. The types of evaluative techniques and methods chosen must be authentic in nature—that is, assessment should reflect the "lived experiences" of children, and not reflect contrived testing conditions. The evaluative techniques and methods discussed in this chapter reflect performance-based authentic assessment procedures that can be used effectively in the physical education setting.

INDIVIDUAL and GROUP PROJECTS

1. In small groups, design observation forms for
   a. event recording
   b. duration recording
   c. interval recording
   d. group time sampling
   Share the newly created observation forms with other groups, discussing strengths and weaknesses.
2. In small groups, administer a standardized physical fitness test (e.g., the Physical Best test) to each group member. Discuss the limitations of standardized tests.
3. Design a personal activity log (PAL) book appropriate for children in a local elementary school class.
4. Individually or in small groups, design an evaluation form appropriate for assessing creative dance experiences. Discuss the strengths and weaknesses of the newly created assessment procedure.
5. In small groups, discuss what should be included in a physical education portfolio. Debate the most appropriate ways of sharing the portfolio with (a) parents, (b) school district officials, and (c) the child.

SELECTED READINGS

AAHPERD. 1989. *Physical Best instructor's guide.* Reston, VA: AAHPERD.

Baumgartner, T. A., and A. S. Jackson. 1987. *Measurement for evaluation in physical education and exercise science.* 3d ed. Dubuque, IA: Wm. C. Brown.

Darst, P. W., V. H. Mancini, and D. B. Zakrajsek. 1988. *Systematic observation Instrumentation for physical education.* 2d ed. Champaign, IL: Human Kinetics.

Dunn, J., and H. Fait. 1989. *Special physical education.* Dubuque, IA: Brown & Benchmark.

Hellison, D. R., and T. J. Templin. 1991. *A reflective approach to teaching physical education.* Champaign, IL: Human Kinetics.

Jansma, P., and R. French. 1994. *Special physical education.* Englewood Cliffs, NJ: Prentice Hall.

Kirkendall, D. R., J. J. Gruber, and R. E. Johnson. 1987. *Measurement and evaluation for physical educators.* 2d ed. Dubuque, IA: Wm. C. Brown.

Kozman, H. C., R. Cassidy, and C. O. Jackson. 1967. *Methods in physical education.* 4th ed. Dubuque, IA: Wm. C. Brown.

Morris, D. G. S., and J. Stiehl. 1985. *Physical education: From intent to action.* Columbus, OH: Charles E. Merrill.

NASPE. 1992. *Outcomes of quality physical education programs.* Reston, VA: NASPE/AAHPERD.

———. 1995. *Moving into the future: National standards for physical education.* St. Louis: Mosby.

Safrit, M. J. 1990. *Introduction to measurement in physical education and exercise science.* 2d ed. St. Louis: Times Mirror/Mosby.

Sherrill, C. 1997. *Adapted physical activity, recreation and sport.* 5th ed. Dubuque, IA: Brown & Benchmark.

Siedentop, D. 1983. *Developing teaching skills in physical education.* 2d ed. Palo Alto, CA: Mayfield.

Designing Extraclass Programs

KEY CONCEPTS

12.1 All children, including children with special needs, should be free to participate in extraclass programs

12.2 Intramural activities should be planned and organized by students, with teachers acting as advisors

12.3 Selection of tournaments should be based on equal competition and maximum participation

12.4 Point and award systems should encourage maximum participation, leadership, and sportsmanship

12.5 Interschool leagues and events should not adversely affect the scope and quality of the instructional and intramural programs

KEY OBJECTIVES

After completing this chapter, you should be able to:

1. Understand the nature, scope, and objectives of the intramural and interschool physical education programs
2. Plan, organize, and supervise intramural and interschool programs
3. Integrate children with special needs into the extraclass programs

The extraclass program is an extension of the regular instructional program. Its purposes are to provide opportunities for all children to practice the skills they have learned in their physical education classes, to develop leadership and followership skills, and to enhance personal and social interests through a wide variety of competitive and noncompetitive activities. This is also a program in which students participate on a voluntary basis, where they take on the major responsibility of planning, organizing, and running their own program of activities. The teacher starts the process, then gradually shifts to the role of helpful guide.

To develop a well-balanced extraclass program, teachers should understand the methods of organizing for competition, when to offer activities, the types of tournaments children enjoy, and special programs such as play days and interschool activities. These topics, along with guidelines and sample programs, are included in this chapter.

CHAPTER 12

INTRAMURAL PROGRAM

The contemporary intramural program in the elementary school should be considered a logical extension of the regular instructional program. As such, it should include all children from kindergarten through grade 6. Students participate in this program on a voluntary basis and play a variety of games and activities learned in the instructional program. However, the main emphasis of this program should be on playing for fun as well as to experience positive social interactions with fellow students. The following guidelines will provide a basis for developing a student-centered intramural program.

Guidelines

1. All children, including those with special needs, should be free to participate in the program.
2. Girls and boys in the primary and intermediate grades should have equal access to the facilities and activities of the program.
3. Once the intramural program has been established, students should assume responsibility for planning, organizing, and running their own activities.
4. Since this is a voluntary program, parental consent should be obtained before students are permitted to participate. This is particularly important for after-school activities.
5. Where facilities and time permit, competition should emphasize continuous participation rather than sudden-death or rapid-elimination tournaments.
6. Noncompetitive and cooperative activities should be included in the intramural program.
7. Award systems should emphasize group effort and participation on an equal basis with fair competition.

Time Schedules for Participation

The time scheduled for intramural activities usually depends on the nature of the school population and the available facilities. Before school can be an effective time, particularly in districts where many parents work or children arrive early by bus. The most popular time, of course, is the noon hour; this provides an opportunity for participation by virtually all children. There is, however, a general trend to hold intramural activities after school. In urban areas where many parents work and community recreational facilities are lim-

ited, the school playground or gymnasium is used for many after-school intramural and club activities.

Supervision of Program

The success of any intramural program depends on support, encouragement, and effective supervision from teachers, parents, or other adult supervisory staff. The adults' role in this program should be to help children organize themselves and their activities. Through this process, children take on more responsibility for planning and operating their program, while teachers gradually shift from directing the program to the role of interested advisor and supervisor of facilities and student-run activities.

Methods of Grouping Children

Because intramural activities should be voluntary, the procedure used to group children for competition is paramount. Perhaps the success of these programs ultimately depends on equal competition and adequate provision for participation by all children. This must be considered in selecting the method of organization for upper elementary grades, as well as the nature and extent of adult supervision. The following methods are currently being used in elementary schools.

Grade and Homeroom

Organizing teams by homeroom appears to be the most popular method. Sixth-graders competing against sixth-graders is generally fair competition; sixth-graders matched against fifth-graders is generally unfair. Therefore, in team sports, such as volleyball and track, use homerooms within the same grade when possible; otherwise competition could be unequal and the children could become disinterested.

Classification Index

By the time children reach the fifth and sixth grades, age alone is an unfair assessment of physical growth and maturation. Another method should be used to arrange these players into groups of approximate physical maturation and ability. A classification index can be used to put children into groups according to both size and age. To illustrate, let us suppose that sixty fifth- and sixth-grade children register for an after-school intramural basketball tournament. The four examples give an idea of how to divide the sixty players into two leagues of three teams each, with ten players on a team. Assuming that about half of the children had a score of 196 or less, use this score as the dividing line between the two leagues. The actual dividing line, of course, depends on the maturity of the children.

Player No.		Score
1. 10×10 (age) + 70 (weight)	=	170
2. 10×11 (age) + 86 (weight)	=	196
3. 10×11 (age) + 92 (weight)	=	202
4. 10×12 (age) + 123 (weight)	=	243

Teacher's Choice

Competition in team and individual sports is often more dependent on skill and desire than on age, height, and weight. Thus, it may be desirable to organize teams and leagues according to the level of skill needed for each intramural activity. However, this method is dependent primarily on the teacher's assessment of the child's performance.

To illustrate, let us assume that, at the end of a four-week instructional unit in volleyball, three sixth-grade classes wish to have a volleyball tournament after school. Ten boys and ten girls from each class register for the tournament. Since the children are not playing for their homerooms, the intramural director has asked each homeroom teacher to rate the class members as either A or B players and to divide the class into two approximately equal groups. The intramural director could then place all A players in one league and all B players in another. If only one league is desired, the director would place an equal number of A and B players on each team.

Date of Birth

If the school has an average of three classes per grade, the children's birth dates can be the most even and effective way of dividing the whole school into three or more groups. These groups can become permanent from year to year. Subgroups can be organized into leagues on the basis of ability, age, or any other criterion.

To illustrate, assume we have a school of 540 children in grades 1 through 6, with three classes in each grade. The intramural program needs four basic groups. Divide the calendar year into four equal parts and assign the children in the following manner.

Group 1: January 1 to March 31 (approximately 135 children)

Group 2: April 1 to June 30 (approximately 135 children)

Group 3: July 1 to September 30 (approximately 135 children)

Group 4: October 1 to December 31 (approximately 135 children)

Any number of groups can be obtained simply by dividing the calendar year into the desired number of units. It is important to let each group select its own name. Such themes as Indian tribes, colors, and professional sports teams are very popular with elementary school children.

Administrative Organization

The type of administrative organization that a school decides to use depends on its size and the interest of the students. The house system (figure 12.1) provides for maximum student leadership and effective communication to all children.

Children should be elected to the House Council by their own house members. All other committees can be assigned responsibilities by the House Council, and the committee members can be elected, or appointed by the House Council. The roles of the Games and Rules Committee and the Schedule Committee are obvious; the Primary Leaders Committee organizes older children who wish to help primary children. These older students can play a very important role in organizing informal and noncompetitive activities for the boys and girls in the first three grades, such as beanbag bowling, skill instruction during the noon hour, and beanbag basket shooting.

CONCEPT

12.3 *Selection of Tournaments Should Be Based on Equal Competition and Maximum Participation*

Types of Tournaments

There are numerous ways teams or individuals can compete. The type of tournament selected depends on the activity, the space available, the time, and the number of competitors. An Olympic meet plan is the only feasible type of tournament for track, swimming, and gymnastic activities. Single or double elimination and round-robin tournaments may be used for a variety of team and individual sports. Ladder tournaments are very useful for individual activities that can be played during instruction time, the noon hour, or after school. However, careful consideration should be given to the strengths and weaknesses of the following tournaments on the basis of available time, space, and number of competitors.

Olympic Meet Plan

The Olympic meet tournament is used for contests that include a number of separate events, such as swimming, gymnastics, and track and field activities. The winners of each event are awarded points, with an aggregate individual and team champion determined on the basis of points. In

INTRAMURAL HOUSE SYSTEM

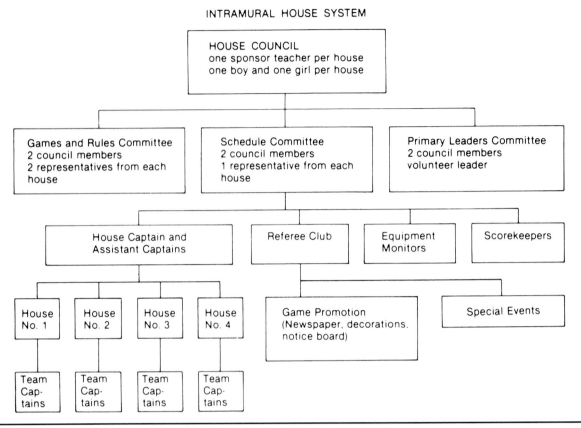

Figure 12.1 Intramural house system.

keeping with the idea of wide participation, first- to sixth- or seventh-place winners are awarded points. In an all-school track meet, for instance, the first six places in a fifty-yard dash might be awarded 10, 9, 8, 7, 6, and 5 points, respectively. To encourage participation, relay and tug-of-war contests might be awarded a higher number of points than individual events.

Single Elimination Tournament

The elimination tournament is the easiest to organize and the quickest for determining a winner. Its use, therefore, depends on there being a large number of teams, limited facilities, and a minimum number of days to complete the tournament. Two examples of single elimination tournaments are shown in figure 12.2.

In the first round of tournament A, the odd-numbered teams played the even-numbered, which eliminated teams 2, 3, 6, and 8 from competition. In the second round, team 4 beat team 1, and team 7 beat team 5. Teams 4 and 7 competed in the last round, and team 4 won the tournament. In tournament B, three teams were given a "bye" in the first round, because there was an odd number of teams.

The single elimination tournament does not require any byes when there is an even number of teams, providing it equals any power of two (2, 4, 8, 16, etc.). With an odd number of teams, or those even-numbered teams not equaling a power of two, it is necessary to give one or more

teams a bye in the first round; the number of byes required for specific numbers of teams follows.

Number of Teams	Numbers of Byes	Number of Games
3	1	2
4	0	3
5	3	4
6	2	5
7	1	6
8	0	7
9	7	8
10	6	9
11	5	10
12	4	11

In the single elimination tournament, the number of games required to complete a tournament is always one less than the number of teams.

Double Elimination Tournament

In a single elimination tournament, once a team loses a game, it is eliminated from all further competition. It is also quite possible for the second-best team in a league to be defeated in the first round. Since the purpose of intramurals is to provide maximum activity for all competitors, a *consolation bracket* can be added to any single elimination tournament. The added bracket, as shown in figure 12.3, assures each team at least two games.

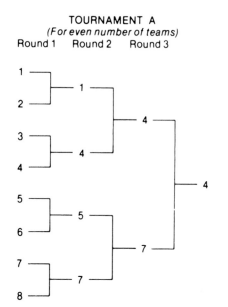

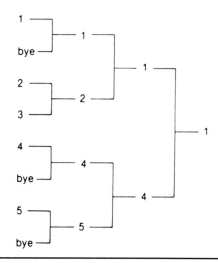

Figure 12.2 Single elimination tournaments.

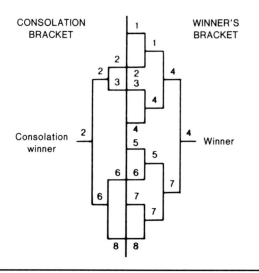

Figure 12.3 Double elimination tournament.

Round-Robin Tournament

In a round-robin tournament, each team plays every other team in the league. If time and facilities permit, this is the most desirable type of competition for team and individual sports. The winner is the player or team that wins the most games. Following is the procedure for organizing a round-robin tournament:

1. Determine the number of games to be played by applying the formula $n(n-1) \div 2$ (n equals the number of teams). For example, six teams would require $6(6-1) \div 2$, or 15, games.
2. Give each team a number and arrange the teams in two columns. For round 1:
   1 plays 6
   2 plays 5
   3 plays 4

3. Keep team number 1 constant and rotate all other teams one place in a counterclockwise direction until fifteen games have been scheduled.

Round 1	Round 2	Round 3	Round 4	Round 5
1 vs. 6	1 vs. 5	1 vs. 4	1 vs. 3	1 vs. 2
2 vs. 5	6 vs. 4	5 vs. 3	4 vs. 2	3 vs. 6
3 vs. 4	2 vs. 3	6 vs. 2	5 vs. 6	4 vs. 5

4. With an odd number of teams, use *bye* in place of a number and follow the same procedure. This example is for five teams, with each bye indicating the team will not play.

1 vs. bye	1 vs. 5	1 vs. 4	1 vs. 3	1 vs. 2
2 vs. 5	bye vs. 4	5 vs. 3	4 vs. 2	3 vs. bye
3 vs. 4	2 vs. 3	bye vs. 2	5 vs. bye	4 vs. 5

Ladder Tournament

A ladder tournament is a continuous competition limited only by the space and time available. Each player or team is placed (arbitrarily, by chance, or by the results of prior competition) on a ladder. The object is to climb to the top of the ladder and remain there until the end of the tournament. This type of competition is primarily used with individual activities during the instructional period, at the noon hour, or after school.

To illustrate how this type of extended tournament can be used: A noon-hour tetherball tournament was offered to all children in grades 4 through 6. On the first day, seven children signed up for the tournament. Their names were put into a hat, drawn out, and placed on the ladder (figure 12.4), from the top down. The ladder was made from tongue depressors placed on cup hooks. The rules were explained and posted next to the ladder, then the children were allowed to challenge one another. The next day,

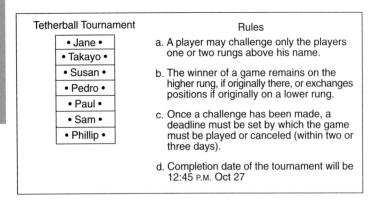

Figure 12.4 Ladder tournament.

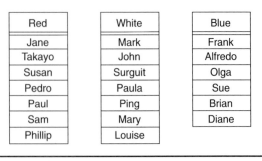

Figure 12.5 Multiple ladder tournament.

thirteen more children wanted to join the tournament, so the teacher simply added two more ladders and gave them a color identification. After placing the new players on the ladders (figure 12.5), she explained to the whole group how players on each ladder may challenge any player one or two rungs above on their own ladder or on either of the other two ladders. This new multiple-ladder tournament allowed children to shift back and forth to find other players with similar levels of playing ability.

Pyramid Tournament

The pyramid tournament (figure 12.6), is basically a variation of the ladder tournament. The main difference is that there are always several players sharing the lowest rung, rather than just one player. There are also more opportunities to play a greater number of different players or teams. This factor is increased when the king or crown variation (figure 12.7) is added to a single tournament.

The following procedures illustrate how an eight-team pyramid tournament operates:

1. Construct a pyramid as shown in figure 12.6.
2. Establish a set of rules similar to the ladder tournament.

In this eight-team tournament, all teams begin by challenging any other team. To illustrate, team 7 beat team 5, and so advances to the lowest row. Similarly, teams 3, 1, and 4 have won their first games. A team on the lowest row may challenge any team on that row only. Winners move up to the next row. If the row immediately above is filled, winners of the lower row simply wait for a space. When all teams are on the pyramid, challenges are made to teams in the row above. The winning team takes the highest position.

The king or crown variation provides many more opportunities to challenge horizontally and vertically. In this example, player number 3 from tournament A has moved to the top of her ladder, then challenged player 9 from tournament B. Player number 9 wins and becomes the

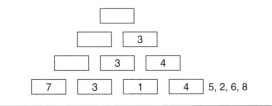

Figure 12.6 Pyramid tournament.

first player to reach tournament C. Players from tournament A or B may challenge any player on the opposite side and on the same level. To illustrate, while player number 3 was playing player 9, player 7 from tournament A was playing number 12 from tournament B. Player 7 wins and moves over and takes player 9's position as he, in turn, moves up to tournament C.

C O N C E P T

12.4 *Point and Award Systems Should Encourage Maximum Participation, Leadership, and Sportsmanship*

Point and Award Systems

Intramural point and award systems are designed to increase participation and to show appreciation for such things as performance, sportsmanship, and leadership. The following suggestions and guidelines will help you develop a point and award system that will encourage informal participation as well as minimize the importance of winning.

Point Systems

Any point system that places an excessive emphasis on participation tends to place too much pressure on team or house members simply to show up for a game or an event. Similarly, a point system that recognizes only the athletically gifted performers disinterests virtually all other children. The following example provides a balance that reflects participation and achievement.

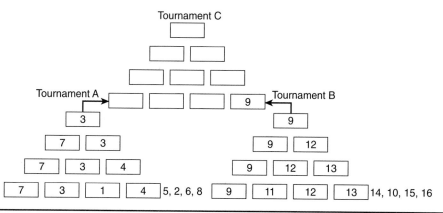

Figure 12.7 King tournament.

		Place in Tournament or Event				
	Participation	1st	2nd	3rd	4th	5th
Team sports	10 points	15	10	8	7	6
Individual sports	5 points	5	4	3	2	1
Olympic meets:						
Individual events	1 point	5	4	3	2	1
Team events	3 points	10	9	8	7	6

This example should be used only as a guideline. Each school should design its own point value system for the various competitive events. Whatever system is decided on should be easy for children to tabulate. The system should also give more weight to activities involving a large number of participants and to those extending over a long period of time.

Award Systems

Ideally, participation in an intramural program should be based on intrinsic values such as enjoyment and friendship. Hence, when presenting awards in the form of cups, ribbons, or other visual recognitions, consideration should be given to the following areas.

1. All awards should reflect the goals of the intramural program. Major awards should represent performance, sportsmanship, leadership, and participation. Special service awards to managers, particularly those who are physically disabled, should be a priority item in any intramural program.
2. Awards should be well earned, rather than a meaningless gesture.
3. Awards should be inexpensive. Exceptions should be perpetual awards, such as the aggregate trophy that is won each year by a classroom or house. These are initially quite expensive; however, yearly winners

normally require only a simple and inexpensive inscription on the base plate.
4. Intramural awards should be presented at the end of the school year during the school assembly when all other academic and achievement awards are presented to deserving students.

Officiating Intramural Activities

One of the most important factors of any intramural program is the development and performance of student officials. Whether officials are chosen by the intramural director or through the student referees' club, the following suggestions will help contribute to a successful program.

1. Encourage children who have demonstrated good leadership qualities, fair play, and an interest in officiating to join the referees' club. Although age is not a major consideration, fifth- and sixth-graders tend to command more respect from their peers.
2. A high level of skill should not be a major requirement; thus, disabled children, wherever possible, should be encouraged to become referees, timekeepers, or scorekeepers.
3. The intramural director or an interested staff member should provide special instructions for all officials. This should be done on a weekly basis.
4. A staff member should be present during all competitive events to provide encouragement and support to student officials. Officials' decisions should be respected by all participants and supported by the supervising teacher. If a performer or a team has a legitimate complaint, it should be directed to the referees' club or committee for resolution.
5. All officials should be given recognition for their efforts. This can be accomplished by naming the officials over the loudspeaker, by awarding points to the referee's homeroom or house, or by creating service awards.

TABLE 12.1   Primary Intramural Activities

Activity	Page	Activity	Page
Simple Team Games		**Individual Activities**	
Squirrel in the Forest (level I)	320	Hopscotch (level I)	329
Simple Tag (level 1)	323	Marbles (levels I–III)	330
Beanbag Basket (level I)	328	Beanbag Basket (level I)	328
Two Square (level I)	326	Tetherball (levels I and II)	331
Roll Ball (level I)	325	Jacks (level I)	331
Progressive Dodgeball (level II)	337		
Crab Soccer (level II)	329	**Gymnastic Activities**	
Barnyard Golf (level II)	338	Rope jumping (levels I–III)	555
		Parachute activities (levels I–III)	570
Cooperative Games		Hoop activities (level I)	566
Doubles Hopscotch (level I)	358		
Perpetual Motion Machine (level I)	358	**Dance Activities**	
Recycled Snake Skins (level II)	360	Rhythmic activities (levels I–III)	612
Twister (level II)	361	Singing games (level I)	624
Modified Musical Chairs (level II)	361	Folk dances (levels II–III)	630
Co-op Tag (level I)	362		

Types of Intramural Activities

The intramural activities that children enjoy generally are the activities they have learned in the regular instructional program. Because participation is voluntary, children should be allowed to choose their activities, as well as the type and length of each tournament. The activities listed in tables 12.1 and 12.2 have proven very popular in intramural programs for primary (grades K–3) and intermediate (grades 4–6) children. Activities selected for any program should be modified to meet the uniqueness of each school.

Primary Intramural Activities

The main emphasis of primary intramural activities should be to develop skills in an enjoyable and informal atmosphere (figure 12.8). Through the assistance of boys and girls in the upper grades, younger children can acquire new skills in addition to a positive attitude toward physical activities

The following outline of a one-year program of activities reflects instructional program emphases as well as the unique interests of primary children. For example, parachute activities were introduced to the first and second grades in September. The children enjoyed the parachute games so much that they requested more parachute games during their scheduled noon hour in September. The same thing occurred with third-graders when they were introduced to sideline soccer in early September. Two new activities, not taught in the regular instructional periods, were introduced to primary children during the intramural program. Volunteer helpers (fifth- and sixth-graders) taught groups of children in the second and third grades to play Double Hopscotch and Japanese Marbles.

The activities listed under each two-month time schedule follow a similar pattern. Teachers should monitor the interests of children month by month and make adjustments in playing time or, where necessary, delete unpopular activities in favor of newfound interests.

Yearly Program—Primary

September–October
Parachute Games
Double Hopscotch
Japanese Marbles
Sideline Soccer

November–December
Chair Bowling
Crab Soccer
Checkers
Indoor Obstacle Meet

January–Febuary
Two Square
Califonia Kickball
Gymnorama
Rope Skipping (Partners)

March–April
Beanbag Golf
Cross-Country
Softball (modified)
Folk Dance

May–June
Paper Airplane Contest
Hopscotch
Novelty Track Meet

Intermediate Intramural Activities

The main emphasis of intramural activities for the upper elementary grades is on fun, practicing skills, positive social interaction, and competition (figure 12.9). Older children enjoy competing with their peers, just as their older brothers and sisters do in high school. The task for elementary school teachers is to develop a program that has equal competition for all activities, equal playing time for all who wish to play, and, whenever possible, round-robin tournaments to ensure maximum participation of all players and teams. The principles outlined here are reflected in table 12.2. Although interest shifts to more team games, there should be opportunities for individual and dual activities such as sidewalk tennis, kite flying, and slow-motion bicycle racing. Also, the majority of activities outlined in this program should be played as coeducational activities.

Figure 12.8   In an enjoyable and informal atmosphere.

Figure 12.9   Fun, skill, and social interaction.

TABLE 12.2	Intermediate Intramural Activities

Activity	Page	Activity	Page
Tournament-Type Activities		***Other Games***	
Basketball Games		Shufflecurl	350
Sideline Basketball	453	Tetherball	331
Twenty-One	453	Frisbee	352
Bucket Ball	452	Beanbag Basket	328
Tennis Games		***Special One-Day Events***	
Deck Tennis	350	Cross-country meet	491
Paddleball	351	Track and field meet	489
		Novelty track meet	490
Field and Floor Hockey Games		Orienteering day	492
Line Field Hockey	403	Punt for distance tournament	414
Seven-Player Hockey	404	Frisbee tournament	352
		Juggling contests	575
Football Games		Hash running day	491
One-Down Football	417		
European Handball	348	***Cooperative Game Activities***	
Punt Back	417	Juggle a Number	361
		Cross-Over Blanket Volleyball	362
Soccer Games		Nine-Person Skip	362
California Kickball	346	Modified Muscial Chairs	361
Four Goal Soccer	389	One-Hole Parachute Golf	572
Seven-Player Soccer	389	Tug-o-Peace	361
		Co-op Tag	362
Softball Games			
Five Hundred	472	***Gymnastic Activities***	
		Rope jumping	555
Volleyball Games		Parachute activities	570
Newcomb	433	Pyramid activities	540
Blind Newcomb	433		
Four-Way Volleyball	434	***Dance Activities***	
Goodminton	349	Folk dances	630
Sideline Volleyball	434		
Paddle-Handball Games			
Paddleball	351		

Play Days

Basketball Play Day

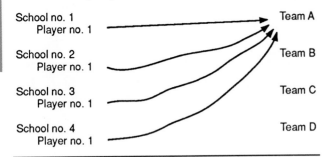

Figure 12.10 Play days.

Yearly Program—Intermediate

September–October	*March–April*
Sideline Soccer	Softball
Group Rope Skipping	Kite Flying
Sidewalk Tennis	Square Dance
Cross Country	Cross Country
November–December	*May–June*
Floor Hockey	Goodminton
Volleyball	Paper Airplanes
Punt for Distance	Flying Contest
Checkers	Track Meet
	Frisbee

January–Febuary
Juggling Contest
Gymnorama
Shufflecurl
Basketball

Club Activities

Club activities should be considered part of the intramural program. Teachers might find a group of children interested in continuing an activity learned in the instructional program that does not lend itself to competition, such as yoga, jogging, or folk dance. Other activities that cannot be offered in the regular instructional program, such as skiing or canoeing, can also be organized as a club activity.

The basic responsibility of the teaching staff is to provide the initial organization. Obviously, if a teacher is interested in sponsoring a skiing or canoeing club, the children will gain by the teacher's efforts and talents. However, club activities can and should reach out into the community for parents and other interested citizens to assist in activities that are beyond the financial, facility, and staff limitations of the school.

SPECIAL PROGRAMS

Throughout the year, a variety of special activities lasting from one hour to the whole day have become part of most

Sports Days

Basketball Sports Day

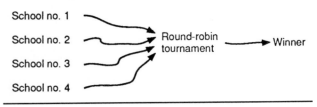

Figure 12.11 Sports days.

extraclass programs. The following activities, which vary in time span, require a lot of planning and volunteer help if they are to be successful.

Play Days

A play day involves children from two or more schools playing together on the same teams. Consider, for example, a basketball play day involving four schools as illustrated in figure 12.10. Player number 1 from each school is assigned to team A. Player number 2 from each school is assigned to team B, player number 3 to team C, and player number 4 to team D. Player 5 for each school goes to team A, and so on until all children are assigned to a team. Schools lose their identity in this type of competitive event, thus reducing the need to "win for one's school." The emphasis of this type of activity shifts from excessive competition to fun and making new friends from other schools.

Sports Days

Sports days are similar to play days, except that the teams represent their own schools. For example, each school enters one basketball team in a round-robin tournament, as illustrated in figure 12.11. Because one school is eventually declared the winner in sports day events, there is more emphasis on competition and maintaining one's school identity. However, because these are one-day events, the emphasis on winning can be minimized if more effort is given to meeting new friends and sharing ideas about each other's neighborhood, intramural program, or other items of interest to girls and boys of this level.

Field Days

A field day normally involves one school inviting two or more neighboring schools to participate in one activity for an afternoon. A track and field day could involve three schools on a Friday afternoon. Participants from each school participate in activities without keeping an aggregate school score. This type of field day emphasizes fun and meeting new friends. The cooperative games and activities listed in chapter 17 are particularly suited to field days of this type.

12.5 *Interschool Leagues and Events Should Not Adversely Affect the Scope and Quality of the Instructional and Intramural Programs*

INTERSCHOOL SPORTS PROGRAM

One of the most longlasting and controversial issues in elementary physical education is the desirability of interschool competition. Proponents of interschool sports programs can present numerous facts and opinions to support their argument. However, medical authorities and professional organizations have generally opposed highly organized sports for children below the ninth grade because of the possibility that these will have adverse physical and psychological effects on such young children. This point of view was formalized in the 1968 AAHPERD publication *Desirable Athletic Competition for Children of Elementary School Age.* Most elementary schools have adhered to the guidelines contained in this publication.

A set of guidelines titled *Guidelines for Children's Sports* (AAHPERD 1979) applies to children thirteen years of age and younger who wish to participate in sports. The intent of this publication is to "encourage and promote the greatest amount of participation in sports under conditions that are safe and enjoyable for children." According to the authors of this book, the philosophy of "child first, winning second" is easy to endorse for most adults but more difficult to practice in the heat of the game. The experts who wrote this set of guidelines believe that, in order to practice the philosophy of putting a child's welfare first and winning second, teachers, coaches, and parents must agree to implement the Bill of Rights for Young Athletes (AAHPERD 1979).

Many of these rights are now being realized through broad-based intramural and extramural or interschool programs. When developing an extramural program of activities, the following points should be incorporated into the operating policies of participating schools.

1. Interschool leagues or events should not interfere with the ongoing instructional or intramural program.
2. Boys and girls should have equal access to the interschool program.
3. Adverse parent or community pressure should not be allowed to interfere with the philosophy and general management of the interschool program.
4. All forms of competition should be minimized, with emphasis placed on participation rather than on winning. Play days and sports days should be given higher priority than organized leagues between schools.
5. Adequate facilities, equipment, and supervision must be available.
6. Interschool activities should usually take place after school. Evening and weekend competition between schools should not be permitted.
7. The health, safety, and general welfare of girls and boys competing in interschool events should be stringently protected. This means medical examinations prior to competition, safe transportation to and from events, and safe facilities and equipment.

Summary Review

The extraclass program includes intramurals, clubs, field and sports days, and tournaments and other types of competition between schools. This program is based upon voluntary participation and provides an opportunity for all children to practice skills learned in physical education classes as well as to develop personal and social skills and interests. To provide this type of program, teachers need to understand methods of organizing for competition, types of appropriate tournaments and award systems, and the nature and scope of the interschool physical activity program.

Bill of Rights for Young Athletes

1. Right to participate in sports
2. Right to participate at a level commensurate with each child's maturity and ability
3. Right to have qualified adult leadership
4. Right to play as a child and not as an adult
5. Right to share in the leadership and decision making of their sport participation
6. Right to participate in safe and healthy environments
7. Right to proper preparation for participation in sports
8. Right to an equal opportunity to strive for success
9. Right to be treated with dignity
10. Right to have fun in sports

INDIVIDUAL *and* **GROUP** **PROJECTS**

1. Describe various ways children with special needs can be integrated into intramural and interschool programs.
2. Prepare a list of intramural activities under each type of tournament.
3. Construct a six-team single elimination tournament and a five-team round-robin tournament.
4. In groups of two or three, show how a team sport can be modified to include children with special needs.
5. In groups of three or four, design a sports day that emphasizes cooperative games and events.

Selected Readings

AAHPERD. 1979. *Guidelines for children's sports.* Reston, VA: AAHPERD.

Calgary Board of Education. 1980. *Intramurals in the elementary school.* Calgary, Alberta: Board of Education.

Micheli, L. J. 1990. *Sportswise: An essential guide for young athletes, parents, and coaches.* Boston: Houghton Mifflin.

Orlick, T., and C. Botterill. 1975. *Every kid can win.* Chicago: Nelson-Hall.

Smoll, F., et al. 1988. *Children in sport.* 3d ed. Champaign, IL: Human Kinetics.

Turner, L. F., and M. A. Turner. 1989. *Alternative sports and games for the new physical education.* Needham Heights, MA: Ginn Press.

Weiss, M., and D. Gould. 1986. *Sports for children and youth.* Champaign, IL: Human Kinetics.

Provision for Special Needs and Programs

The special needs and interests of all children must be met in the instructional and extraclass programs. Chapter 13 describes how children with special needs can be integrated effectively both into the regular instructional program and into a variety of intramural and interschool activities. Chapter 14 describes how academic concepts and skills can be taught through a variety of physical activities. The last chapter in PART 5 covers ways to use the classroom to teach game, dance, gymnastic, and fitness activities.

Integrating Children with Special Needs

KEY CONCEPTS

13.1 Children with special needs can be effectively integrated into regular physical education programs

13.2 The least restrictive environment is an individualized approach to teaching children with special needs

13.3 The physical education program is an effective medium through which children with mild or moderate mental disabilities can improve their physical, personal, and social skills

13.4 Good posture is correct alignment of the body while moving, standing, or holding a variety of positions

KEY OBJECTIVES

After completing this chapter you should be able to:

1. Understand the legal basis for integrating children with special needs into the instructional and extraclass physical education program

2. Understand the various types of physical, cognitive, and emotional disabilities that children might possess in a regular physical education class

3. Provide for children with special needs in the regular physical education program

4. Know where to obtain additional resource information from local specialists and national organizations

O ne of the major challenges facing public education programs is inclusion. Originally called mainstreaming, *inclusion* is an educational fact of life that most elementary school teachers will have to deal with at some time during their career.

In the early 1970s more than 1.75 million children were excluded from public education because they exhibited various psychological and physical disabilities. Further, more than one-half of the estimated 8 million children with disabilities in the United States were not receiving appropriate educational services. Recognizing this, the federal government passed two laws that substantially affected the educational opportunities of children with disabilities. Public Law 93-112 (the Rehabilitation Act of 1973, Sec. 504) made it increasingly difficult for children with disabilities to be denied an education or excluded from educational institutions receiving federal monies. Subsequently, pressure applied by parents, courts, and legislation resulted in the passage of Public Law 94-142 (the Education for All Handicapped Children Act) in 1975, which was enacted in 1978. This law, recognized as landmark legislation, entitles school-age children with disabilities to free and appropriate public education in the least restrictive environment. Important to our profession is the fact that adapted physical education is written into the law as a required direct service. According to Public Law 94-142, physical therapy does not legally substitute for physical education services.

Throughout the 1970s and 1980s, students classified as mildly handicapped (learning disabled, educable mentally retarded, socially and emotionally disturbed) began to be integrated into the regular classrooms. Prior to that time, a dual physical education system existed—adapted physical education programs for the "handicapped" children and regular physical education programs for "normal" children. Today, children with disabilities who in earlier decades would have received adapted physical education in approved special education schools, inside or outside of their home school district, are taught by elementary school physical education teachers. Today, children who attend separate adapted physical education programs are mostly preschool children with multiple disabilities, children with severe autism and pervasive developmental delays, or children with such severe social and emotional difficulties that the public school district is not yet ready to address their educational needs.

The implications of Public Law 93-112 and Public Law 94-142 for the elementary school physical education program are basically that all children must be integrated into instructional and extraclass programs and that individualized teaching strategies and activity areas should be used in order to more successfully address the special needs of children with disabilities. This chapter provides a general overview of federal and state laws related to children with disabilities, a basic description of the various types of disabilities common to public school inclusion, teaching suggestions, and ideas illustrating how children with special needs can be integrated into the regular physical education program.

TERMINOLOGY

The 1975 Public Law 94-142—the Education for All Handicapped Children Act—which covered students five to twenty-one years of age, was followed in 1986 with PL 99-457, the Education for the Handicapped Act, which extended the mandate and services to children below five years of age. An additional amendment resulted in the 1990 passage of PL 101-476, which renamed the 1986 law as the Individuals with Disabilities Education Act (IDEA). These changes reflect both the philosophy of providing "inclusive" education for all children from birth to adulthood and concerns about labeling children as "handicapped." Unfortunately, all terms can suffer the problem of becoming a label or stereotype. Adoption of the global term *disability* offers some improvement, but even this term presents problems. A child who suffers from asthma or a visual impairment, for example, is unlikely to gain from being labeled as having a "disability." A variety of terms, including *handicap, disability,* and *special needs,* are used throughout this text, since these terms have been identified in the education literature and refer to certain characteristics and conditions. Given the potential for "labeling" effects, the following are two important points teachers need to remember:

1. Care and sensitivity are required at all times to ensure that *all* children, regardless of skill, ability, or any other characteristic, are treated with dignity and respect.
2. Every child is, in fact, "special," and each child has unique "needs."

3. As educators, teachers must ensure that developmentally appropriate activities are provided for all children in an inclusive environment.

LEGAL BASIS FOR INTEGRATING CHILDREN WITH DISABILITIES

CONCEPT

13.1 *Children with Special Needs Can Be Effectively Integrated into Regular Physical Education Programs*

Prior to 1971, the responsibility for educating children with special needs lay primarily with state and local governments. This was done with a dual educational system (special versus regular education) serving two types of students (special versus regular). There were few quality physical education programs for students with special needs, and those that did exist primarily served individuals classified as mentally retarded. For others with special needs, physical education was not made available. With increased parent pressure, the federal government passed landmark legislation to more fully equate the civil and educational rights of children with disabilities. As a result, the following two federal laws have brought the child with disabilities into the mainstream of public education (in today's terminology, these laws mandate *inclusion*).

Rehabilitation Act of 1973

Section 504 of the Rehabilitation Act of 1973 (PL 93-112) and the reauthorized PL 99-057 of 1986 state that "No otherwise qualified handicapped individual . . . shall, solely by reason of his handicap, be excluded from participation in, be denied the benefits of, or be subjected to discrimination under any program or activity receiving Federal financial assistance." The implication of this section is that children with disabilities are to be provided equal opportunity to participate in regular instructional physical education classes, as well as in intramural and interschool programs. Participation in these programs is based on the premise of "the least restrictive setting." The intention of this definition is not to change the basic way teachers instruct students but to modify teaching strategies and equipment to cope with children who display a variety of disabilities in the regular instructional program (figure 13.1).

Education for All Handicapped Children Act of 1975

Of all the federal laws enacted, PL 94-142 is the most important to physical education. This law was first enacted in 1975 and has been reauthorized three times. This law now affects the nature and direction of physical education programs in the following areas:

C O N C E P T

13.2 *The Least Restrictive Environment Is an Individualized Approach to Teaching Children with Special Needs*

1. Students will be educated in the "least restrictive environment." "Least restrictive environment" is explained on the basis of a cascade of educational placements that should be available within a school district. Accordingly, the least restrictive environment for each student is determined on an individual basis and based on the environment in which the student will gain the most in terms of physical, mental, and social development. The six levels of placement shown in table 13.1 illustrate the variety of environments that should be made available to children with disabilities.

   The "least restrictive environment" also varies according to the type of disability and the curriculum content and teaching strategies the teacher uses. For example, for a student in a wheelchair, a regular instructional unit of soccer or flag football would be the most restrictive environment. However, the same child in a gymnastic unit could participate partially or be fully integrated with some special assistance. The same child placed in a swimming class taught with exploratory teaching strategies would be in a least

Figure 13.1 Planning a physical education program to meet the unique needs of exceptional children is more readily achieved by the combined efforts of physicians, teachers, and parents.

TABLE 13.1   Placement Cascade for Children with a Disability

Level 1	Full integration in regular physical education classes
Level 2	Full integration, with class size limited (e.g., one child with a disability to fifteen children without a disability)
Level 3	Full integration, with opportunities for children with a disability to have special assistance with an aide as a resource person
Level 4	Partial integration, with children with a disability assigned a number of days per week in regular physical education classes and a number of days per week in separate, adaptive classes
Level 5	Full time in separate, adaptive physical education classes
Level 6	Full time in separate physical education in special schools for children with a disability

restrictive environment. The essential point is to continually evaluate the teaching unit and teaching strategies used, then place students with disabilities into the best situations in which they can develop according to their needs, interests, and levels of ability.

2. Students between the ages of three and twenty-one will receive educational services. According to this age-level designation, all elementary schools must provide appropriate physical education programs for children with disabilities based on the levels outlined in table 13.1.

3. Each student will have a specially developed plan called an individualized education program (IEP). This plan must be developed in a meeting with parents, teachers, local administrators, and, where appropriate, the student for whom the plan is intended. The written plan for each child must contain the following (PL 101-475, Sec. 1401 [20]):

   a. A statement of the child's present levels of educational performance
   b. A statement of annual goals, including short-term instructional objectives
   c. A statement of the specific educational and related services to be provided to the child and the extent to which the child will be able to participate in regular educational programs
   d. A statement of the needed transition services for students beginning no later than age 16 and annually thereafter (and, when determined appropriate for the individual, beginning at age 14 or younger), including, when appropriate, a statement of interagency responsibilities or linkages (or both) before the student leaves the school setting
   e. The projected date for initiation, and the anticipated duration, of such services
   f. Appropriate objective criteria and evaluation procedures and schedules for determining, on at least an annual basis, whether instructional objectives are being achieved.

Figure 13.2, a sample IEP form from the Seattle Public Schools, illustrates how each child's program is assessed, incorporated into a short- and long-term program, and evaluated on the basis of established criteria of expected performance. This type of record keeping helps all personnel concerned with the child's development, monitor her progress and, where necessary, make appropriate changes in level of placement, equipment, or teaching strategies.

4. Federal funds will be available to state educational agencies and local educational agencies. The average yearly cost of educating students with disabilities is approximately $1,000 more than the cost of educating nondisabled children. Part of this extra funding is provided by federal grants awarded to state education agencies. However, these monies must be spent only

for the excess cost of special education over the average student costs in regular education. Generally speaking, state and local governments raise about $800 for each child with a disability, and the federal government contributes the remaining $200 per student.

5. Physical education is identified as a direct service. Public Law 94-142 clarifies the definition of special physical education as follows: "If specially designed physical education is prescribed in a child's individualized education program, the public agency responsible for the education of that child shall provide the service directly, or make arrangements for it to be provided through other public or private programs." This definition allows separate or segregated classes of special physical education to be part of physical education rather than part of a separate adapted physical education program (figure 13.3). In this interpretation, "specially designed physical education" does not have to be a full-time placement in a separate class; rather, it can be part of the cascade of placements that was outlined in table 13.1.

Regular Education Initiative and Inclusion

Prior to the late 1980s, most school-age children having a special education classification were sent to special (segregated) education schools either inside or outside of the home school district. Several factors have resulted in a significant change, including the fact that the majority of these children, unless classified as suffering from severe and profound multiple disabilities, are attending the public school in their home district. In some states, children with severe disabilities, regardless of school age, are partially or fully integrated across all classes in the public school.

To comprehend today's regular education initiative, it is important that elementary school teachers understand why increasingly more public school districts are keeping special education children in regular school programs instead of placing them in separate special education programs. The most significant factor in the drive toward inclusion is parents' increasing awareness of their children's educational rights as well as their own rights as parents of children with disabilities. Second, the weak economy has forced educational administrators at the state level to significantly reduce the amount of money to support special programs that were commonly found outside the public school district. Hence, public education must provide, as best as possible, the appropriate educational staff and programs necessary to successfully address the educational needs of children with special needs. Finally, the parent awareness movement has become so strong that it is of paramount importance that elementary school physical education teachers do the best they can to involve every child in developmentally appropriate and nonrestrictive learning experiences.

STUDENT SERVICES DEPARTMENT
Individualized Education Program (IEP)
SPECIAL EDUCATION

The Seattle Public Schools

Purpose of Meeting	☐ Initial IEP ☐ Annual Review ☐ Develop Exit/Transition Plan ☐ _____

STUDENT: _____   GRADE: _____ UNIT: _____   IEP CONFERENCE DATE: _____

SCHOOL: _____   BIRTHDATE: _____   IEP PROJECTED REVIEW DATE: _____

IEP RESPONSIBLE EDUCATOR: _____   STUDENT ID NO.: _____   MOST CURRENT ASSESSMENT DATE: _____

I. SUMMARY OF PRESENT LEVELS OF PERFORMANCE/SUMMARY OF IEP COMMITTEE MEETING
Description of scholastic, physical and adjustment levels

Wide Range Achievement Test-R	Reading		Spelling		Arithmetic		Slosson Oral Reading Test	
Date: _____ Level: _____	Raw Score	Grade Rating	Raw Score	Grade Rating	Raw Score	Grade Rating	Date: _____	Raw Score / Grade Level
Date: _____ Level: _____	_____	_____	_____	_____	_____	_____	Date: _____	_____

Woodcock-Johnson Psycho-Educational Battery	Reading _____ Standard Score / Grade Rating	Math _____ Standard Score / Grade Rating	Written Language _____ Standard Score / Grade Rating
Date: _____			

____ ____ ____ ____ ____ ____ ____ ____ ____

II. ANNUAL GOALS AND SHORT-TERM OBJECTIVES

STUDENT: _____

ANNUAL GOAL

A minimum of one objective is to be written for each grading period. Example: **4** if quarters, **3** if trimesters.

SHORT-TERM OBJECTIVES	Date Initiated	Date Completed

- Each goal statement, related to an assessed deficit area, contains a *measurable* unit of achievement for a school year.
- Each objective states WHO will be doing WHAT and HOW to determine if the objective has been completed (evaluation criteria).

COMPLIANCE

Figure 13.2   Seattle Public Schools IEP form.

STUDENT: _____

☐ Check if this is an initial placement.

IEP Responsible
Educator: _____

III. PROPOSED EDUCATIONAL PROGRAM AND RELATED SERVICES

	Minutes per Week	Projected Starting Date	Anticipated Duration*

More ← **RESTRICTIVE** → Less

Level of Special Education Service
(Please check one only)

Description/Areas of Service

☐ 1. Regular Program w/Itinerant Service

☐ 2. Special Education Resource Service

☐ 3. Self-Contained Special Education Service

☐ 4. Specialized Self-Contained Service

☐ 5. Non-District Placement
(requires program supervisor approval)

All non-selected placement options were considered and rejected, at this time, as being too restrictive or for the reasons indicated under "Less Restrictive Environment."

Career/Vocational Education (14 years or older)

☐ Regular Program (list minutes under reg. ed.) Describe: _____

☐ Special Program—Describe: _____ Service Provider: _____

☐ No Vocational Education: Parent Preference ☐ Other _____

Related Services
Services required
for the student
to benefit from
special education.

Service Provider: _____   Speech/Lang. ☐   — — — —

Service Provider: _____   OT ☐   — — — —

Service Provider: _____   PT ☐   — — — —

Service Provider: _____   _____ ☐   — — — —

Service Provider: _____   _____ ☐   — — — —

Service Provider: _____   _____ ☐   — — — —

Evaluation for Service
Recommended (Attach referral)

◄ Total Special Education
Minutes per Week

Physical Education Program   Regular Program ☐   Special Program ☐

Less Restrictive Environment

Extent of participation in Regular Education (This is the maximum possible for this student):

◄ Total Regular Education
Minutes per Week

◄ Total Minutes per Week

Statement of non-academic and extracurricular activities:

Home School: Is student attending school he/she would usually attend if not handicapped? ☐ Yes ☐ No if no, state reason(s):

Less Restrictive Placement rejected for the following reasons: ☐ academic level ☐ behavioral concerns ☐ unique needs
☐ failure to succeed in less restrictive setting ☐ Other _____

Comments (Other tests, information or factors used in making placement decision):

Extended School Year (ESY) Status:

Eligibility for Extended School Year
services is determined based on one
or more of the following criteria:

Your child will be:	Referred for ESY services	Will be considered at a later date
a) regression/recoupment	☐	☐
b) behavioral regression/recoupment	☐	☐
c) physical/medical	☐	☐
d) new student	☐	☐
e) unexpected growth spurt	☐	☐
f) unique needs	☐	☐

(Rev. 08/89)   **COMPLIANCE**

Figure 13.2   (Continued)

STUDENT: _____

IV. GRADUATION STATUS (High School Students Only)

Number of current High School credits _____ . Projected date of High School Completion ____ / ____ .
Comments:

V. ALTERNATIVE DISCIPLINARY PROCEDURES REQUIRED ☐ Yes ☐ No

If yes, document specific agreements (principal or designee must be present). If more space is needed use comments section.

_____

_____

_____

VI. IEP COMMITTEE MEMBERS

We agree the listed programs and related services are necessary to provide an appropriate education in the least restrictive environment for this student.

Present Yes No	Agree Yes No	Name (print or type)	Signature	Position*

*Program Specialists and Supervisors are team members but may not be present at all meetings.

_____   _____
SIGNATURE OF PRINCIPAL   DATE

Comments: _____

_____

_____

_____

_____

_____

_____

VII. PARENTS RIGHTS/AGREEMENT (Copy of Summary of Safeguards and Due Process Procedures on back of form).

I have had the opportunity to participate in the development of this individualized education program. I give my permission for my child/ward to participate in the services and placement listed; this permission can be revoked. I understand that I have the right to request a hearing regarding the identification, evaluation, or educational placement of my child/ward. I also understand that school records will not be released to non-school personnel without my permission. I have received a copy of the Summary of Safeguards and Due Process Procedures and understand my rights and responsibilities in connection with these procedures.

If not parent, please check position below

_____   ☐ Legal Guardian   ☐ Surrogate Parent   _____
SIGNATURE OF PARENT   ☐ Adult Acting as Parent   ☐ Adult Student   DATE

(Rev. 08/89)   **COMPLIANCE**

Figure 13.2 (*Continued*)

CHAPTER 13

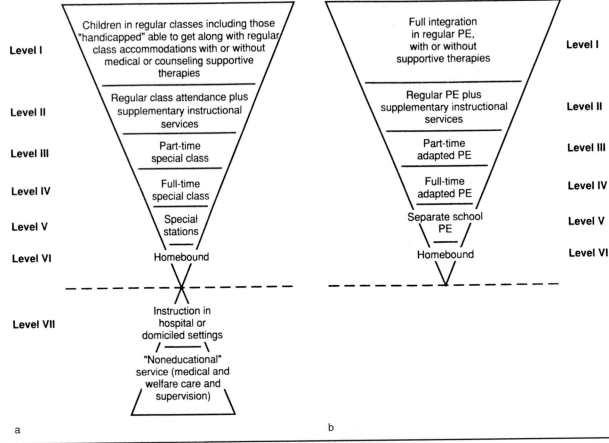

a

Level I	Children in regular classes including those "handicapped" able to get along with regular class accommodations with or without medical or counseling supportive therapies
Level II	Regular class attendance plus supplementary instructional services
Level III	Part-time special class
Level IV	Full-time special class
Level V	Special stations
Level VI	Homebound
Level VII	Instruction in hospital or domiciled settings
	"Noneducational" service (medical and welfare care and supervision)

b

Full integration in regular PE, with or without supportive therapies	Level I
Regular PE plus supplementary instructional services	Level II
Part-time adapted PE	Level III
Full-time adapted PE	Level IV
Separate school PE	Level V
Homebound	Level VI

Figure 13.3　(*a*) Deno's cascade system of special education services. (*b*) Sherrill's cascade system of adapted physical education services. Levels I, II, and III utilize adapted physical educators as resource room or consultant teachers.

INTEGRATING CHILDREN WITH SPECIAL NEEDS INTO THE REGULAR PHYSICAL EDUCATION PROGRAM

Federal legislation specifies that each child with a disability must be afforded the opportunity to participate in the regular physical education program available to other children, unless (1) the child is enrolled full-time in a separate facility or (2) the child needs specially designed physical education, as prescribed in the child's individualized education program (IEP). As described earlier in this chapter, this stipulation brought about the placement of children with disabilities into the least restrictive environment (figure 13.4). This is a process where children with disabilities are constantly evaluated, then placed into a new least restrictive environment according to their developmental level. It is also a process in which the teacher adjusts organizational patterns, teaching strategies, and equipment in order to meet the goals and aspirations of fully able students and children with disabilities within a regular class setting. Several teaching strategies described earlier in this text are expanded in the following pages to illustrate how children with disabilities can be integrated effectively into instructional and extraclass activities.

Figure 13.4　In the least restrictive environment.

Station Work

Stations are particularly useful when attempting to individualize the instructional program for a variety of physical activities (see chapter 10). To illustrate this technique, suppose that a fourth-grade teacher is teaching a gymnastic unit. Three children in his class have moderate limitations—

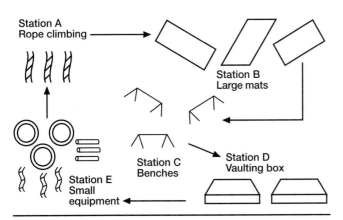

Figure 13.5   Station work.

heart, sight, and partial spasticity—and cannot participate in vaulting or rope-climbing activities. The teacher organizes the class into six groups (see figure 13.5), with the three children with moderate disabilities designated as group 4 and assigned to station C along with group 3. All children practice the assigned skills at their stations until it is time to rotate. When the groups rotate, group 3 moves to the vaulting box while groups 4 and 5 shift to small equipment. The teacher has demonstrated his ability to integrate the three exceptional children according to their limitations and without drastically changing the content or emphasis of his gymnastic program.

The organizational structure of station work is particularly effective for teaching physical fitness activities using circuit training and obstacle courses (see chapter 8). Stations can also be adopted when teaching a variety of game activities.

Task Cards

Task cards, described in chapter 10, can be predesigned to accommodate a variety of exceptional children. Using the previous station work example, all children, with the exception of the three children with disabilities, could choose cards representing three levels of performance (levels 1, 2, and 3). Special task cards could be designed for children with moderate blindness, heart defect, or movement impairments to accommodate their expected levels of performance. For a child whose reading level is low, task cards could include photographs or drawings with several words identifying the action to be performed or solved. Although task cards present various limitations when working with children who have severe mental disabilities or are totally blind, numerous applications of the task card technique can accommodate the exceptional child in virtually every area of the physical education program.

Peer Tutors

Studies of the most accommodating teaching and participation effects for various children with special needs who

Figure 13.6   Providing developmentally appropriate activities is vital for all children.

require great amounts of assistance emphasize the use of peer tutors. This strategy is especially helpful for children who have extreme difficulty following directions or whose functional mobility and manipulation are very limited. Teachers who have used a peer tutor strategy report that it enables them to pay more attention to the entire class as well as to the special child; this strategy also fosters less dependence on the teacher. The key to successful peer tutoring is to select mature students, use them on a consistent basis, and rotate them with other tutors so everyone has optimal active learning time. In addition, it is important to train the peer tutors before class time.

TYPES OF DISABILITIES

In physical education, as in all subjects, it is first necessary to understand the various types of physical, mental, social, and emotional disabilities in order to provide developmentally appropriate activities. A few of the more common disabilities are described below. Once they are understood, it is possible, within the broad range of physical activities and instructional strategies, to provide for the needs of these children (figure 13.6).

Disabilities that Affect Learning

This section covers congenital conditions and disabilities that directly relate to mild and moderate learning difficulties with or without social or emotional disturbances. Classifications in this category are described below.

Mental Disability

The term *mental disability* denotes various degrees of intellectual ability. Although each state has its own classification system, the most commonly used and accepted system is the intelligence quotient (IQ). Students can be classified by IQ along the following scale of mental disability:

> Mild (IQ of 50 to about 70)
> Moderate (IQ of 40 to 49)
> Severe (IQ of 25 to 39)
> Profound (IQ of 25 or less)

In terms of the public school system, students who possess a mild or moderate mental disability are classified as being educable and must be integrated into the regular academic and physical education program. In the United States, there are approximately 4 million such children mainstreamed into the public educational system.

C O N C E P T

13.3 *The Physical Education Program Is an Effective Medium Through Which Children with Mild or Moderate Mental Disabilities Can Improve Their Physical, Personal and Social Skills*

Children who are classified as having mild mental disabilities show deficiencies in intellectual and motor development. Academically, these children find it difficult to understand and follow directions, to remember facts and figures, and to be creative. They also lack motivation and might be hesitant to attempt new challenges for fear of failure and ridicule from other children. The problems associated with intellectual development also influence the child's physical and motor development. These children are generally overweight and well behind in all aspects of motor development. Some of the more pertinent reasons for this lack of motor development are the child's low motivation toward physical activity, few opportunities to participate in appropriate and meaningful activities, and professionals' disinterest and inability to modify programs and instructional approaches to meet the needs of children with mental disabilities.

Down Syndrome

Approximately 10 percent of all persons with a mental disability are born with a chromosomal abnormality that results in Down syndrome. This syndrome is the most recognizable disability among individuals with intellectual

limitations. Although no two persons with Down syndrome are the same (Sherrill 1997), the chromosomal abnormality does cause similar physical appearances. However, while many Down syndrome children appear obese, obesity is not a typical genetic feature of this syndrome; it is rather more closely linked to poor diet and lack of exercise. What is important for elementary school teachers to recognize is that many of these children might have congenital heart disorders. Consequently, it is imperative for the teacher to review the child's medical record prior to the child's participation in physical education. Depending on the nature of the heart condition, physical restrictions might or might not be advised. However, for legal protection, physical education teachers should have on file current health records indicating what types of activity the child can participate in without undue stress or physical harm.

Another important related disability that might be overlooked is an orthopedic condition called atlantoaxial instability, which occurs in approximately 17 percent of all children with Down syndrome. *Atlantoaxial* refers to the joint between the first two cervical vertebrae. The ligaments and muscles surrounding the joint are lax, allowing the vertebrae to slip out of alignment. A forceful forward or backward bending of the neck, which might occur in gymnastic activities or other sport events, can dislocate the vertebrae, causing damage to the spinal cord (Sherrill 1997).

Since atlantoaxial instability can be detected only by X ray, it is recommended that teachers of children with Down syndrome request the school nurse or parent to provide evidence that this condition is not present in the child. It should be noted that X rays are required for persons with Down syndrome to participate in Special Olympics. If the child is an active participant in these activities, check with local Special Olympics officials to see if X rays have been taken. If medical clearance is not available, the teacher should not allow the child to participate in the above-mentioned activities until X rays are taken.

The physical education program can be a very beneficial medium through which children with mild and moderate mental disabilities can improve their motor proficiency and personal and social skills. It can also be one of the most effective media for improving the child's self-image. The following suggestions relating to these two levels of mental disability provide general guidelines for integrating these children into the regular physical education program.

1. Confer with speech, special education, and other specialists to determine each child's level of physical, social, and academic ability and to obtain suggestions related to appropriate instructional and management techniques.
2. Constantly remind these students to follow the basic safety rules, and teach students without disabilities to be especially aware of students with mental disabilities.
3. Teach regular children to understand and assist children with mental disabilities.

4. Emphasize the elements of fun and success in all activities taught to these children.

5. Activities taught to children with mental disabilities should be the same as those taught in the regular physical education program but modified to cope with each child's level of physical and intellectual ability.

6. Help students focus on one skill at a time, and provide extra demonstrations, physically assist students in performing the movement, and offer extra verbal cues.

7. When a student is being taught a movement or skill, name the key points to help the student develop a movement vocabulary.

8. Provide frequent verbal praise as children progress toward the acquisition of a skill or movement.

9. Provide a physical fitness program that recognizes the unique characteristics and needs of children with mental disabilities.

10. When using the problem-solving method, select tasks that are short and have simple solutions, and repeat the same verbal challenges as the child attempts to answer the movement problem.

Learning Disability

Children classified as having learning disabilities constitute the greatest percentage of exceptional children in today's public schools (approximately 40 percent). Twice as many boys as girls are given this classification. In the past two decades, there has been considerable debate and discussion about the definition of learning disabilities. For some parents and educators, the term *learning disability* refers to any problem with learning (Dunn and Fait 1989). For others, the term designates a specific brain dysfunction caused by injury or infection. The following definition from the Individuals with Disabilities Education Act of 1990, Sec. 1401, consolidates these concepts into the unified definition of specific learning disabilities (SLDs) that is used as a standard in public schools:

> [A specific learning disability is] a disorder in one or more of the basic psychological processes involved in understanding or in using language, spoken or written, which disorder may manifest itself in an imperfect ability to listen, think, speak, read, write, spell, or do mathematical calculations. Such disorders include such conditions as perceptual disabilities, brain injury, minimal brain dysfunction, dyslexia, and developmental aphasia. Such a term does not include children who have learning problems which are primarily the result of visual, hearing, or motor disabilities, of mental retardation, of emotional disturbance, or of environmental, cultural, or economic disadvantage.

Since there is still a general lack of understanding among specialists in medicine, psychology, and education, children who exhibit learning disabilities are often misunderstood.

Too often, teachers classify these children as lazy, slow, mentally disabled, or possessing behavioral problems (Horvat 1990). This false impression is due to the misleading nature of this disorder's outward manifestations. For example, children with a learning disability might act disinterested because they might have a short attention span. Clumsiness and an inability to stay on-task are often mistaken for behavioral problems or boredom, and hyperactivity is often interpreted as signs of a troublemaker. With these factors in mind, teachers should consider the following suggestions when developing physical education programs for these children.

1. Children with learning disabilities learn best in a learning environment that is structured and routine. Structuring a relatively stable environment allows children to develop a sense of security. Once the children feel comfortable and confident, they acquire motor skills and concepts more rapidly and with a more positive attitude.

2. Children with learning disabilities might be socially immature and, hence, initially might be afraid to engage in small- and large-group activities. Follow a social-sequence format that begins with children practicing or playing alone and progresses to two students working in a parallel way without interaction, then to playing together with small and then gradually larger groups.

3. Learning disabilities manifest themselves in a variety of ways, so teachers should consult with a specialist to understand the nature of the child's learning disability and obtain advice on how to best cope with it in a regular physical education class.

4. Children with learning disabilities learn academic concepts and skills more effectively through a variety of physical activities than through traditional instructional methods. Teachers should provide numerous physical activities that can also be used to teach or reinforce academic concepts and skills taught in language arts, mathematics, or other subject areas.

Behavior Disorders

It is not uncommon for physical education teachers to encounter students who have behavior difficulties. Conservative estimates indicate that 2 percent or more of school-age children have emotional disabilities. This means that more than a million children in North America have severe behavior disorders that affect their ability to learn and influence the general learning environment of all children in elementary school physical education. Quite often, especially at the beginning of the school year or when changes in a routine occur, addressing behavior problems becomes the first priority, and initiatives to improve physical fitness and motor performance become secondary. For any teacher, this can be the most difficult task and greatest challenge. The important thing is getting and keeping students' attention so

CHAPTER 13

learning can occur. As long as a student remains noncompliant with the general class management routines and rules established at the beginning of the school year, motor learning will be difficult.

According to Public Law 94-142, the Education for All Handicapped Children Act, behavior disorders are conditions exhibiting over a long period of time, to a marked degree, and adversely affecting educational performance, one or more of the following characteristics (*Federal Register*, 23 August 1977, p. 42478):

1. An inability to learn that cannot be explained by intellectual, sensory, or health factors
2. An inability to build or maintain satisfactory interpersonal relationships with peers and teachers
3. Inappropriate types of behavior or feelings under normal circumstances
4. A general pervasive mood of unhappiness or depression
5. A tendency to develop physical symptoms or fears associated with personal or school problems

In regular physical education programs, teachers will observe children with mild mental disabilities exhibiting overaggression, direct noncompliance with general rules and basic management routines, and extreme impulsiveness to the point of causing constant interruption and interference with the entire learning process. Any one or combination of these behaviors often results in poor interpersonal skills, ineffective teaching, and less than optimal learning opportunities. The following strategies will help teachers become aware of ways to appropriately address behavior disorders to maintain a healthy teaching and learning atmosphere.

1. It is important for the teacher to gain as much information as possible about the child's general behavior. This can be done by talking to other teachers, parents, or any other professional having direct contact with the student. Also, review the child's educational folder to gather information that may help with setting appropriate goals and expectations.
2. Examine the developmental appropriateness of the learning activities presented in class. Many behavior difficulties occur when class content is either too easy or too difficult.
3. Review the student's medical history. The student might be recovering from a head injury; aggressive behaviors are inherent in post-traumatic recovery periods for some head injuries. The student might be receiving medication that has side effects (e.g., dizziness, aggression, and headaches). This is particularly true for children with seizure disorders that are controlled by medication.
4. Develop an effective method of handling each type of disorder. For example, establish a basic procedure to follow with overaggressive children; use a specific instructional technique to enhance the interpersonal relationships of extremely shy or withdrawn children.

5. Avoid techniques that can weaken appropriate behavior responses. Avoid the use of punishments such as denial, extra exercise, or angry facial expressions.
6. Inform students without emotional disabilities of the nature of the child's behavior disorder and how to cope with it. Teachers should use wise counsel when explaining what type of behavior might be exhibited by a child with emotional disabilities when certain factors become present. The key point is to indicate when and where it is wise to interact with students who are displaying unacceptable emotional behavior and when to avoid them.

Perceptual-Motor Deficiencies

Throughout the 1960s and 1970s there was a growing awareness of the importance of perceptual-motor development to academic achievement, particularly in such areas as reading, writing, and drawing skills. In 1959, Delacato presented a theory known as neurological organization, which assumed that every individual progresses sequentially through a series of motor skills. He argued that children with perceptual-motor deficiencies missed specific developmental steps along this continuum.

Another theory, proposed by Kephart, holds that a child progresses through a sequence of learning stages (1960). Kephart's proposed program for slow learners was based on levels of generalization through which a child is taught. Because the ability to read is based on previously acquired perceptual-motor skills, such as directionality and laterality, these skills are emphasized for children with learning disabilities.

The general conclusion drawn from these investigators is that inadequate preschool motor development could lead to serious perceptual-motor problems. A child who does not possess the prerequisite perceptual-motor skills might have serious difficulties in learning to read, write, and perform other academic skills. Hence, over the years a large number of children classified as having learning disabilities and mental retardation were placed in perceptual-motor training programs. It was believed that providing gross motor tasks, such as balance beam walking, would help improve their reading skills. Numerous research studies indicate there is not sufficient evidence to substantiate these claims. Teachers considering the use of perceptual-motor training to aid specific academic performance must carefully consider the evidence. Perceptual-motor training programs can improve performance of the activities worked on, but there is at best only a weak transfer of perceptual-motor training to academic performance.

All movement is perceptual in nature, so the regular physical education program is already providing a variety of activities necessary to enhance perceptual-motor performance. More specifically, a physical education teacher possessing the competence to provide specific perceptual-motor training to a child experiencing serious perceptual-motor deficiencies might provide supplemental activities in addition to the regular physical education program or refer the student to a trained specialist.

Symptoms of Perceptual-Motor Deficiencies

Perceptual-motor competency is a composite of a number of specific motor skills and movement patterns. The following characteristic symptoms are commonly observed in the primary school, particularly in kindergarten and first grade:

1. Body image
   a. Inability to identify and locate body parts, such as the right and left hand, knee, or elbow
   b. Inability to move parts of the body as directed by the teacher, such as raising the right arm or raising the left arm and the left foot
   c. Inability to imitate movements performed by the teacher or another performer

2. Balance
   a. Inability to maintain static balance, such as standing on one foot or standing with the arms folded and eyes closed
   b. Inability to maintain balance while moving, such as walking forward or backward in a straight line
   c. Inability to maintain balance while in flight, as in a simple run, jump, and land or a jump off a low box or balance bench

3. Spatial awareness
   a. Inability to move parts of the body in specified directions, such as crossing the right arm over the left side of the body
   b. Inability to move the body through space, such as moving forward, backward, up, down, and around
   c. Inability to move through space without bumping into objects or other children in the general pathway of movement

4. Hand-eye and foot-eye coordination
   a. Inability to throw a ball into the air and catch it after one bounce
   b. Inability to perform basic locomotor skills, such as running, hopping, jumping, or galloping
   c. Inability to kick a stationary or moving ball
   d. Inability to move to rhythm, such as performing rhythmic hand or foot tapping or walking to rhythmic accompaniment

Guidelines

Once the decision has been made to pursue a perceptual-motor training program in the regular physical education class or in a supplemental remedial program, and the previously mentioned research findings have been taken into consideration, the following guidelines can be applied to help incorporate various types of perceptual-motor activities.

1. A child who is suspected of possessing serious perceptual-motor deficiencies should be referred to competent specialists.

2. The choice of all physical activities should be commensurate with the child's developmental level.
3. Application of individualized instructional techniques, particularly the limitation method, is imperative in coping with individual differences in levels of ability and rate of development.
4. Every movement task that is presented should allow each child to achieve a measure of success.
5. The primary physical education program should stress the following types of activities.
   a. Balance activities—floor work, with small equipment, and on large apparatus
   b. Locomotor skills—moving in different directions, changing speed, and moving to a rhythmic accompaniment
   c. Body awareness—activities and movement challenges stressing shapes (form) and the movement of different parts (unilateral and bilateral movements)
   d. Manipulative activities—stressing hand-eye and foot-eye coordination (ball-handling skills involving throwing, catching, and kicking) and a variety of manipulative skills using beanbags, hoops, and other small equipment

Sensory Impairments

Sensory impairment are conditions in which one or more of the five senses are diminished in their function (Dunn and Fait 1989). From an educational point of view, loss of sight or hearing results in major problems for the learner and teacher. Hence, this section will discuss only visual and auditory disabilities.

Visual Impairment

The term *visual impairment* denotes a range of legal blindness from being partially sighted to being totally blind. Visual impairment is a serious loss or absence of vision that cannot be corrected by medical procedures or with corrective eyeglasses. Such impairments vary from child to child and, at times, within each child. For example, a child might gradually lose his sight due to a degenerative disease. Another child might become partially or totally blind after she has had a serious illness or an accident. In other cases, vision can fluctuate from time to time over the school year.

The following guidelines will help teachers integrate students with visual impairments into the regular physical education program.

1. Consult the school nurse and parents of children who have visual disabilities. The teacher's knowledge of each child's deficiency can provide a general guideline for the type of activity and degree of participation appropriate for the child.
2. Refer to the school nurse for further examination any child who chronically demonstrates one or more of the following symptoms:
   a. Excessive squinting

b. Constant leaning toward or moving close for demonstrations

c. Inattentiveness and a general lack of interest

d. Extremely low level of skill—children with visual impairments generally show poor catching skills, even with a large utility ball

3. Too often, partially sighted children shy away from vigorous physical activities and thus tend to be overweight and generally uncoordinated. Whenever possible, provide a little extra encouragement and praise when these children participate in physical activities.

4. Blind children usually have developed extremely good memories. When teaching physical education, reinforce this strength and increase the child's self-esteem by asking the blind child to review instructions given in previous lessons (Sherrill 1997).

5. Partially sighted children often say they can see more than they actually do, in order to act like other children. Teachers should recognize this characteristic and give subtle assistance and encouragement whenever possible.

6. Determine what each partially sighted child is capable of doing in physical education. Within the child's limitations, modify rules and provide special boundary markers, sound sources, peer helpers, and other considerations to help integrate the child into each appropriate physical activity.

7. Provide a safe learning environment for visually impaired children. The first step is to check with parents and other specialists to determine what precautions should be taken, such as ensuring that the child wears protective eyeglasses or limiting the child's performance on certain apparatus.

8. Use the following instructional and management suggestions to help integrate children with visual impairments into the regular physical education class.

a. Use peers to guide children with visual impairments to the locker room, showers, and toilets.

b. Provide an "anchor" student—a classmate the child with visual impairments will sit next to every time they come into the instructional area.

c. Use bright colored objects to encourage children to use their residual vision. For instance, use yellow balls when outside on the grass and blue balls when playing on an orange gymnasium floor.

d. Use tactile and auditory boundaries. For example, mark playing areas with cones, mark floor boundaries with tape, play tape recorders next to the target to mark its location, (basket or goalpost), and have teammates clap or wear wristbells to indicate their locations.

Hearing Impairment

In PL 94-142, both deaf and hard of hearing are included in the definition of hearing impairment. Deafness is defined as an impairment so severe that the student is prevented from

Figure 13.7 Paraprofessional aides can help children integrate.

acquiring linguistic information, even with the use of a hearing aid. On the other hand, an individual who is hard of hearing can, with the assistance of a hearing aid, have sufficient hearing to process linguistic information (Horvat 1990). Approximately a million school-age children in the United States have a hearing impairment and are currently enrolled in regular physical education programs. Of this group, approximately one in every twenty-five has a hearing impairment that requires extensive special education services. The following general guidelines will help the classroom teacher integrate the child with a moderate or mild hearing impairment into a regular physical education class.

1. If a child with a hearing loss is in your class, check with his parents on the type of oral, manual, or combined method of communication that is preferred.

2. When giving directions to a deaf child, face in her direction. This is particularly important when writing on a chalkboard. Write the directions first, then face the class and verbally clarify your directions.

3. When giving specific directions to a deaf child, position yourself so the child can see you.

4. If a child is wearing a hearing aid, do not raise your voice when speaking to the child. Also, discuss with the parent and child when the hearing aid will be worn. Rain, wind, mud, sand, or excessive noise might dictate the removal of the hearing aid.

5. When teaching outdoors, try to position yourself so the deaf child does not face the sun.

6. Always permit children with hearing losses to move freely about the instructional space in order to be within seeing or hearing range.

7. Change methods of gaining class attention from audio cues (whistles, yells, and hand claps) to visual cues (raised arms to stop, rolling wrists to continue, and pointing to destinations).

8. Use paraprofessional aides or peer tutors to repeat directions and to give additional demonstrations (see figure 13.7). Each class will normally have one or two students without disabilities who like to help children with visual or hearing impairments. These peers usually learn enough sign language to communicate reasonably well with their partners who have hearing impairments.

Neurological Disorders

The two most common neurological disorders found among elementary school children are seizures (epilepsy) and cerebral palsy. Both affect a child's level of performance in many physical activities. The following definitions, lists of characteristics, and guidelines will help teachers determine appropriate adjustments within the physical education program.

Seizure Disorders (Epilepsy)

Epilepsy is a condition of recurring seizures that is initiated by abnormal electrical discharges in the brain. Seizures affect approximately 3 percent of the general population and can be inherited or caused by traumatic brain injury (e.g., from car or bicycle accidents) or by an infection such as meningitis. It is not unusual for individuals with cerebral palsy to have seizure disorders. Depending on the type of seizure, a loss of consciousness and bladder control may occur. Elementary school children who have a seizure disorder that is controlled through medication may often experience side effects. Teachers should check with the school nurse or parent to determine the nature of the seizure disorder, the type of medication, and any physical restrictions that should be noted. Table 13.2 describes the main types of seizures that teachers should be able to recognize and apply appropriate first aid measures for.

The successful medical control of seizure disorders permits the majority of children with these conditions to participate on a restriction-free basis in most or all activities. Adhere to the following suggestions for children with seizure disorders who participate in a regular physical education program.

1. A child who has a series of seizures throughout the school year while receiving medication should not be permitted on large apparatus such as climbing ropes and climbing frames.
2. Adhere to an appropriate procedure for managing a seizure in a large-group situation.
3. Review the type of seizure medication a child is receiving and know the side effects.
4. It is possible for a child who has a seizure history to not have a seizure for several years but then suddenly experience one. A recurrence can happen during a growth spurt, and the medication must then be adjusted.
5. Teachers should explain, within the limits of the class's understanding, the nature of the disorder and what should be done when a child has a seizure.

Cerebral Palsy

Cerebral palsy is a neurological impairment caused by damage to the motor areas of the brain. The majority of such damage occurs before or just after birth. Other causes include trauma, infection, and anoxia (lack of oxygen). Many children with cerebral palsy are unable to perform appropriate motor skills because of an interfering reflex behavior that is typically observed in early infancy. The persistence of these primitive reflexes makes it difficult to perform simple neuromuscular skills. In addition, abnormal muscle tone (too high or too low) and skeletal deformities resulting from muscle imbalances all interfere with movement. In cases where both legs are affected, the child wears braces to walk. In extreme cases, mobility is by way of a wheelchair where the hands or, if the hands are affected, the feet are used to propel the wheels. The following guidelines will help teachers make the appropriate adjustments to integrate these children into the regular physical education program.

1. Even though independence is the goal of all children with special needs, develop a peer tutoring strategy to assist these children with mobility.
2. Review the child's medical file and discuss the child's limitations with the school nurse and a parent.
3. Consult with the school district's occupational therapist for ideas about how to provide the most appropriate activities for the child.
4. Most children with cerebral palsy love movement and enjoy participating in physical education. As these students generally ambulate very slowly, modify the distance they have to travel. For ball activities, a suspended ball can be used to practice throwing, catching, and kicking skills—without the need to retrieve the ball.

Nutritional Disorders

The common nutritional disorders associated with obesity, anorexia nervosa, and bulimia were discussed in chapter 2. The eating disorders anorexia nervosa and bulimia are more prevalent among teenagers and hence generally need to be dealt with by high school teachers. Obesity, however, needs to be considered at all age levels.

Obesity

The criteria for obesity depend upon the assessment approach used. Two of the most common assessment approaches are skinfold caliper measurements and height-weight standards based on age and gender. Based on skinfold caliper measurements to determine percent body fat, obesity is body fat greater than 25 percent for males and greater than 30 percent for females. Based on height and weight tables, the traditional criterion for overweight is being 10 to 20 percent above ideal weight for gender and age. The criterion for obesity is being 20 percent above ideal weight; people who weigh more than 50 percent over the ideal weight are classified as super-obese. The height-weight guidelines are not as accurate as skinfold measures, but they are easy to understand and apply.

Approximately one out of every five (20 percent of) elementary school children can be considered obese. This statistic is cause for concern itself, but of equal concern is the upward trend in obesity levels. Studies over the last thirty years show a continuous increase in obesity levels,

TABLE 13.2 Seizures: Recognition and First Aid

Seizure Type	Characteristics	First Aid
Convulsive Generalized tonic-clonic (also called grand mal)	Sudden cry, fall, rigidity, followed by muscle jerks, shallow breathing or temporarily suspended breathing, bluish skin, possible loss of bladder or bowel control, usually lasts a couple of minutes followed by normal breathing. There may be fatigue, followed by a return to full consciousness.	Look for medical identification. Protect from nearby hazards. Loosen ties or shirt collars. Protect head from injury. Turn on side to keep airway clear. Reassure when consciousness returns. If single seizure lasted less than five minutes, ask if hospital evaluation is wanted. If multiple seizures, or if more than five minutes, take to the emergency room.
Nonconvulsive Absence (also called petit mal)	A blank stare, beginning and ending abruptly, most common in young students. May be accompanied by rapid blinking, chewing movements of the mouth. Students may be unaware of what's going on during the seizure but quickly return to full awareness once it has stopped. May result in learning difficulties if not recognized and treated.	No first aid necessary, but medical evaluation should be recommended.
Simple partial (also called Jacksonian)	Jerking begins in one area of body, arm, leg, or face and cannot be stopped by patient, but patient stays awake and aware. Jerking may proceed to involve hand, then arm and sometimes spreads to whole body and becomes a convulsive seizure.	No first aid necessary unless seizure becomes convulsive, then first aid as above.
Simple partial (also called sensory)	Preoccupied or blank expression. Student experiences a distorted environment. May see or hear things that are not there, may feel unexplained fear, sadness, anger, or joy. May have nausea, experience odd smells, and have a generally "funny" feeling in the stomach.	No action needed other than reassurance and emotional support.
Complex partial (also called psychomotor or temporal lobe)	Usually starts with blank stare, followed by chewing, followed by random activity. Students appear unaware of surroundings, may seem dazed and mumble. Unresponsive. Actions clumsy and not directed. May pick at clothing, pick up objects, try to take clothes off. May run and appear afraid. May struggle or flail at restraint. Once pattern is established, same set of actions usually occurs with each seizure. Lasts a few minutes, but postseizure confusion can last substantially longer. No memory of what happened during seizure period.	Speak calmly and reassuringly to patient and others. Guide gently away from obvious hazards. Stay with student until completely aware of environment. Provide assistance in getting home.
Atonic seizures (also called drop attacks)	The legs of students between two to five years of age suddenly collapse. After ten seconds to a minute, can recover, regain consciousness, and stand and walk again.	No first aid needed (unless the child is hurt in the fall), but the student should be given a thorough medical evaluation.
Myoclonic seizures	Sudden brief, massive muscle jerks that may involve the whole body or parts of the body. May cause students to spill what they are holding or fall off a chair.	No first aid needed, but should be given a thorough medical evaluation.
Infantile spasms	Starts between three months and two years. If sitting up, the head will fall forward and the arms will flex forward. If lying down, the knees will be drawn up, with arms and head flexed forward as if reaching for support.	No first aid, but prompt medical evaluation is needed.

From *Seizure Recognition and First Aid*, copyright Epilepsy Foundation of America, 4351 Garden City Drive, Landover, MD 20785 (1-800-EFA-1000).

with the largest increase occurring in the last decade. The health hazards associated with excess weight are considerable, and so it is vital that children form sound nutritional habits in their early years. The primary causes of obesity are poor diet, overeating, and lack of vigorous daily activity. Dysfunction of the endocrine glands, which regulate fat distribution in the body, accounts for a very small percentage of child obesity.

Cardiorespiratory Disorders

The major cardiorespiratory disorders found among elementary school children include cardiovascular impairments (such as rheumatic fever) and respiratory impairments (such as asthma). These impairments, and suggestions for those who teach physical education to children suffering from such disorders, are discussed in the following sections.

Cardiovascular Impairments

The major concern in this area for elementary school teachers is the aftereffects of rheumatic fever, which is the cause of approximately two-thirds of all cardiovascular problems. Rheumatic fever can be dealt with by following these guidelines:

1. The amount and type of physical activity for a child who has had rheumatic fever must be prescribed by a physician.
2. Rheumatic fever flourishes in the northern parts of the United States and in Canada, particularly in winter and spring. Teachers should watch for early and suspicious signs, such as chronic colds, quick fatigue, and serious weight losses.
3. The vast majority of children who have had rheumatic fever can eventually participate in physical activities. Once the family doctor gives the child permission to participate in physical activities, the teacher should allow only moderate and brief participation during the first few weeks. As the child demonstrates the capacity to keep up without showing early signs of fatigue, gradually increase the amount and intensity of exercise. A simple monitoring device can be used to determine the level of exercise tolerance that is appropriate for the child. Take the child's pulse rate before the physical activity is started. The pulse rate should rise during exercise, then return to the resting pulse approximately three minutes after the end of the physical activity. If the pulse rate is still excessively high after three minutes, reduce the amount of exercise.

Respiratory Impairments

Two of the most common respiratory disorders are asthma and cystic fibrosis. This discussion will be limited to asthma, since it is the most common respiratory condition that still permits the child to participate in a wide range of physical activities. Teachers interested in a discussion of cystic fibrosis should consult the selected references at the end of this chapter.

Asthma is a disease of the lungs that is characterized by swelling of the mucus membrane lining, excessive secretion of mucus, and spasms of the bronchial tubes. The general symptoms are coughing, heavy wheezing, and a constriction, or tightening, of the chest. Approximately 3 percent of the population of North America are asthmatic. Between 3 and 10 percent of all school-age children are asthmatic, and boys suffer from asthma almost two times as much as girls. If the following guidelines are followed, most asthmatic children can participate in the regular physical education program.

1. Children with asthmatic conditions should, within the limits of their ability, attempt to increase their level of general fitness and health. Planned developmental programs can help asthmatic children reach this goal.

2. Children with asthma should avoid vigorous and sustained activities, particularly in cold and dry climates.
3. Any causative agent (such as dust on tumbling mats or pollen from flowering trees or plants) should be avoided.
4. A gradual warm-up to vigorous activity may be helpful to some asthmatic children.
5. Teachers should know what to do if a student indicates that an asthmatic attack is starting.

Orthopedic Impairments

The term *orthopedic impairment* denotes any congenital or acquired impairment that has produced a motor disability. This category includes birth defects, amputations, spina bifida, and a variety of crippling conditions caused by trauma (such as acid, fires, or accidents). Each type of physical disability within this broad orthopedic classification must be individually evaluated with respect to the nature and intensity of the activity. If the child is a member of the physical education class, however, the following general guidelines apply:

1. Wherever possible, create tasks that the disabled child is capable of performing; this leads to self-reliance and self-respect.
2. The teacher and children of any class that has a child with an orthopedic disability should treat this child in a normal manner, helping where really necessary, but never pampering her.

Traumatic Brain Injury

Traumatic brain injury is known as the "silent epidemic," because each year hundreds of children suffer such injury through accidents involving motor vehicles, bicycles, falls, and projectiles (such as softballs, baseballs, and bats). Recently, more attention has been given to children returning to school after these injuries. A teacher who has a child who has recently recovered from a traumatic brain injury needs to be aware of the cognitive, psychomotor, social, and emotional challenges facing the child. Quite often, many previously learned motor skills have to be relearned. Basic cognitive skills such as reading, mathematics, and spelling also have to be relearned. Emotional mood swings, paired with episodes of aggressive behavior, are not unusual and are part of the rehabilitation expectancy. What the teacher might not observe, depending on the child's trauma background, are periods of mild aggression, poor memory, lack of coordination, and poor sense of balance. In addition, there is a need to be sensitive to the fact that when a child's participation in an activity must be restricted, the child might feel anger and denial.

Physical Awkwardness

The term *physically awkward* refers to children who do not suffer from a known neurological or physical disability, yet have difficulty learning and performing basic motor skills. The percentage of children who could be classified as physically awkward for their age level is unknown, but it might be alarmingly high. Gubbay (1975) suggested that as many as 6 to 11 percent of school-age children have serious difficulties in learning motor skills. Hence, it is important for teachers to understand the general characteristics of physical awkwardness. Unfortunately, there is very little agreement on how to identify physically awkward children. No single measure of physical awkwardness can be found to identify even one-half of the children in a group of clumsy children. It appears that the children identified as physically awkward are a heterogeneous group. The following descriptors appear in clinical accounts of physically awkward children.

1. Poor school achievement
2. Confusion and delay in hand dominance
3. Illegible handwriting
4. Immature drawing
5. Reading difficulties
6. Low self-esteem and self-concept
7. Failure in complex motor sequences
8. Difficulty in balance and spatial orientation
9. Low physical fitness

In addition, there appear to be other common warning signs of physical awkwardness, including these: late in walking, poor catching skills, avoidance of ball games and playground equipment, awkward running style, difficulty in learning to ride a bicycle, and a dislike of climbing equipment. The child might also have social problems (few friends) and difficulty coping with failure.

Early identification of children with movement problems may allow for remedial help before sensitive periods of development have passed. Consultation with parents, medical practitioners, and other professional groups equipped to offer professional advice on remedial programs is recommended.

C O N C E P T

13.4 *Good Posture Is Correct Alignment of the Body While Moving, Standing, or Holding a Variety of Positions*

Postural Deviations

Parents, teachers, and school officials have always been concerned about children's posture, particularly because there appears to be a strong relationship between posture and such factors as perceptual acuity, emotional health, and general fitness. Slanting desks, adjustable chalkboards, and improved lighting have been installed to enhance and maintain correct posture. However, chronic television viewing and inadequate daily exercise for many children have continued to produce numerous postural problems, which are readily detectable and can be corrected by appropriate exercise programs.

There is no clear definition or standard of "good" posture that can be applied to all children, whether they are standing, sitting, or moving. Standing posture is judged by the alignment of body segments. The child in figures 13.8 and 13.9 has good posture because his body segments are evenly balanced over the base of support. Viewed from the side, the plumb line runs from a little in front of the ankle through the knee, pelvis, shoulders, and ear. In this position, the natural curves of the body are moderate, with the head, shoulders, pelvis, knees, and feet balanced evenly on each side of the line. Viewed from the front, the plumb line runs midway through the head, vertebrae, and hips and equidistant between the feet.

A child with good posture requires a minimum contraction of antigravity muscle groups to keep her body erect and balanced, but when a child slouches, the upper back muscles must contract to shift the body to the correct posture. If she continues to slouch, her muscles gradually adapt to that position and she might develop chronic poor posture if it is not corrected.

Two types of postural deviations are common among elementary school children. The first type—functional postural deviations—are caused by faulty muscular development, as when a child continually slouches, causing the upper back muscles to gradually adapt to this position, or habitually carries a heavy newspaper bag or school books on one side of the body (e.g., on the right shoulder), or consciously pushes the stomach forward, causing an exaggerated low back curvature. The second type of postural deviations—structural postural deviations—can be caused by congenital defects, traumatic injuries, or functional postural deviations that were not corrected by special remedial programs. Structural deviations normally require highly specialized corrective programs involving surgery, bracing, and extensive remedial exercise programs. On the other hand, functional impairments, which are common among elementary school children, are correctable through a regular physical education program and additional special exercises. The following functional postural deviations are most typical and can be observed, measured, and corrected with proper exercise.

Common Posture Problems

The following correctable deviations can be observed when the child is standing beside a plumb line.

Round Upper Back (Kyphosis)   Round back, or kyphosis, is a marked increase in the curve of the back (figure 13.10). The head and shoulders are usually held in a forward position, and the backward curve of the upper body causes the pelvis to tilt forward slightly and the knees

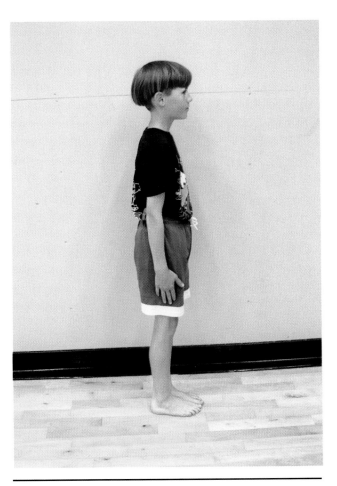

Figure 13.8   Good posture—side view.

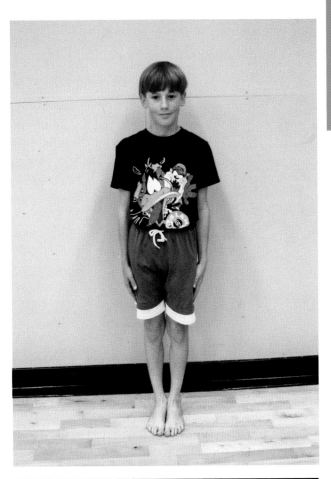

Figure 13.9   Good posture—front view.

to bend somewhat. This condition increases the strain on the upper back muscles and shifts the weight of the body to the front of the foot.

Hollow Back (Lordosis)   Hollow back, or lordosis, is an exaggerated forward curve of the lower back (figure 13.11). The most common signs are a protruding abdomen, a swayback, and hyperextension of the knees.

Lateral Curvature (Scoliosis)   Lateral curvature, or scoliosis, can be C-shaped, extending the length of the spinal column, or S-shaped, with a small curve on the upper back and a compensating curve on the lower back (figure 13.12). The C-shaped curve is normally toward the left, since most children are right-handed and tend to lean to the weaker side. This comes from the constant elevation of the right arm and the tendency to lean toward the left side of the desk while writing and performing other sitting activities.

Methods of Assessing Posture

The classroom teacher is generally in the best position to assess his students' postures. Most teachers are genuinely

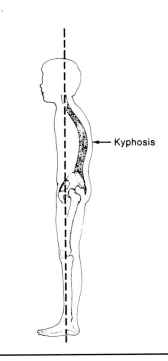

Figure 13.10   Round back (kyphosis).

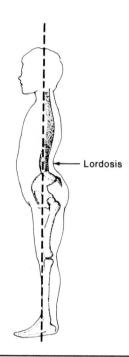

Figure 13.11 Hollow back (lordosis).

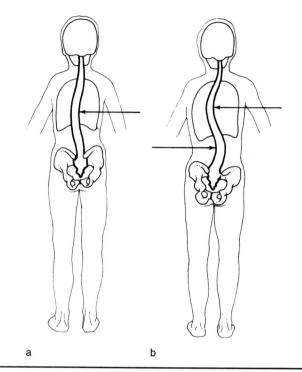

Figure 13.12 Lateral curvature (scoliosis)—(*a*) C-type curve and (*b*) S-type curve.

concerned about the way a child sits at his desk and how he moves in his daily activities. For most teachers, the evaluation of posture is primarily one of continual subjective observation. When he notices a major change in a child's posture, the teacher brings in the school nurse or parent to determine whether the change is due to a muscular weakness or to other factors, such as nutrition, eyesight, or an emotional disturbance.

If a teacher wishes to use a simple screening test, she might consider the side- and rear-view plumb line test and the posture chart shown in figure 13.13. The chart can be used in various ways, depending on the interests of the teacher, the ages of the children, and the time available. Most teachers can complete the test in the classroom.

Methods of Improving Posture

The plumb line test is designed as a basic screening device. It can detect major postural problems and, perhaps more important, make the child more conscious of her posture when standing, sitting, or moving through a variety of movement patterns. The foundation of good posture, however, is the possession of optimum levels of muscular strength, endurance, flexibility, and efficient motor skill patterns. If special programs are warranted, the following exercises will assist in correcting functional postural defects and in enhancing general muscular strength, endurance, and flexibility (see chapter 8).

1. *Exercises for improving head and neck position:*
   Shoulder pull, p. 170
2. *Exercises for improving round shoulders:*
   Rung travel sideways, p. 602
   Pull-ups, p. 173

Push-ups, p. 173
Arm and shoulder stretch, p. 170
3. *Exercises for improving lower back:*
   Side trunk stretch, p. 171
   Trunk twister, p. 171
   Lower back stretch, p. 171
   Knee-to-nose touch, p. 176
4. *Exercises for improving abdominal muscles:*
   Curl-ups, p. 174
   Head and arm raises, p. 175
   Floor bicycle pump, p. 174
   Reverse curl, p. 175
5. *Exercises for improving functional scoliosis:*
   Single-rung traveling, p. 601
   Trunk stretch, p. 175

The importance of maintaining good posture cannot be overemphasized. Helping children develop a positive attitude toward their own posture is the wisest approach. The suggestions listed below help reinforce this basic approach.

1. Teach children to understand the reasons for maintaining good posture.
2. Teach children to alternate shoulders on a regular basis when carrying heavy shoulder bags, knapsacks, etc.
3. Stress the personal and social values of good posture.
4. Avoid nagging children about their posture.
5. Consult with parents and specialists regarding the nature and type of exercise program that would be appropriate for a child with a functional posture impairment.

Name: _____

Date: _____
First evaluation: _____
Second evaluation: _____
Third evaluation: _____

Key to score:
Note: Use figures *a* and *b* as a Normal (0) rating. Children should assume a relaxed, "normal" posture when taking this test.

Normal	0
Slight	1
Moderate	2
Severe	3

a. Side view

Side View	First Evaluation	Second Evaluation	Third Evaluation
A Body Lean: Forward			
Backward			
B Forward Head			
C Round Shoulders			
D Round Dorsal Curve			
E Protruding Abdomen			
F Hyperextended Knees			
Back View			
G Head Tilt: to right			
to left			
H Shoulder: lower on right			
lower on left			
I Bow Legs			
J Knock-knees			
K Feet pointing out			
Feet pointing in			
L Curve of Vertebrae: C-curve			
S-curve			

Plumb line
Through middle of ear
Through shoulder joint
Through middle of hips
Through middle of knee
Slightly in front of anklebone

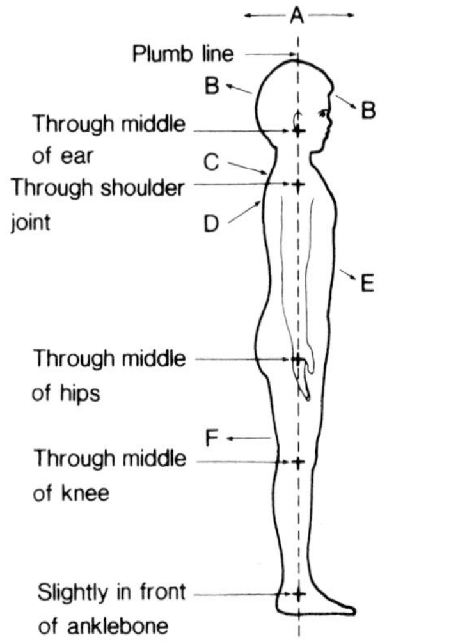

b. Back view

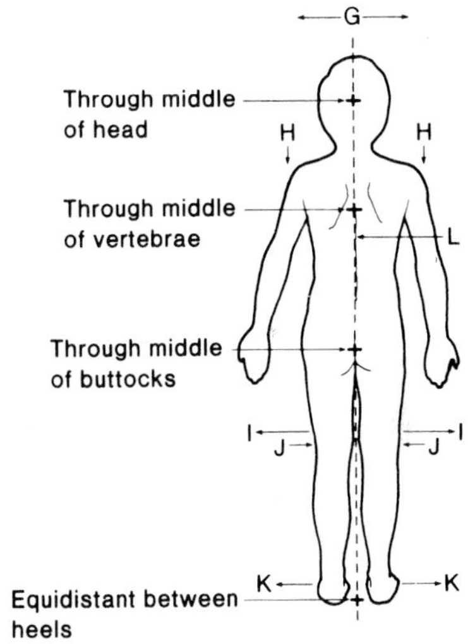

Through middle of head
Through middle of vertebrae
Through middle of buttocks
Equidistant between heels

Figure 13.13　Posture chart using the plumb line test.

INTEGRATING IN THE INTRAMURAL PROGRAM

The intramural program provides an excellent opportunity to integrate children with special needs. This can be accomplished by modifying games to accommodate children with a variety of physical or mental disabilities. For example, change the basketball game by adding a slow lane where only walking is permitted. Or include a rule that baskets scored from a sitting position are worth double point value. The latter rule allows nondisabled children to show off their shooting skill from a seated position. It also permits children in wheelchairs to demonstrate their skill on an equal basis.

A number of other intramural activities are fun and competitive, yet do not require complex motor skills or total body movement. Most children, for example, enjoy chess, checkers, tic-tac-toe, and many other such games. The disabled child needs no special program for these and is treated during such events as an equal competitor who does not receive any special favors. This situation is a healthy example of effective integration of all children regardless of physical abilities.

Another way of accommodating the child with disabilities is through self-directed activities. A child with a paraplegic disability can be given a physical fitness program based on movements he can perform and on projected levels of accomplishment. These challenges can be easily translated into points to allow the child to enhance his own self-image through contributing to his homeroom or house point total.

Sources of additional ideas

A variety of resource centers and associations concerned with exceptional children provide resource materials to the classroom teacher on request. Teachers should write to the appropriate association and indicate the specific type of assistance required. In addition, a number of excellent books dealing with children with special needs are in print. A few examples of the types available are provided in the list of selected readings at the end of this chapter.

Resource Centers

Adapted Physical Activity Academy, AAHPERD, 1900 Association Drive, Reston, VA 22091

National Consortium for Physical Education and Recreation for Individuals with Disabilities (Address changes every two years with the new president). Contact Dr. Claudine Sherrill, 11168 Windjammer Drive, Frisco, TX 75034

The Council for Exceptional Children Information Center, 1920 Association Drive, Reston, VA 22091

National Information Center for Children and Youth with Disabilities, P.O. Box 1492, Washington, DC, toll free 1-800-999-5599

Note: In addition, district and state departments of public instruction normally have special education divisions or departments.

Associations

American Alliance for Health, Physical Education, Recreation and Dance, 1900 Association Drive, Reston, VA 22091

American Federation of the Physically Handicapped Inc., 1376 National Press Building, Washington, DC 20004

American Hearing Society, 817 14th Street, NW, Washington, DC 20005

American Heart Association, Inc., 1790 Broadway, New York, NY 10019

Association for the Aid of Crippled Children, 345 East 46th Street, New York, NY 10017

Children's Bureau, Department of Health, Education, and Welfare, Washington, DC 20014

Learning Disability Association of America, 4156 Library Road, Pittsburg, PA 15234

Muscular Dystrophy Association of America, Inc., 1790 Broadway, New York, NY 10019

National Association for Mental Health, 10 Columbus Circle, New York, NY 10019

National Association for State Directors of Special Education, Suite 320, 1800 Diagonal Road, Alexandria, VA 22314

National Association for the Deaf, 814 Thayer Avenue, Silver Springs, MD 20910

National Down Syndrome Society, 666 Broadway, New York, NY 10012

National Epilepsy League, 208 North Wells Street, Chicago, IL 60606

United Cerebral Palsy Association, 50 West 57th Street, New York, NY 10019

United States Office of Education, Department of Health, Education, and Welfare, Washington, DC 20202

Summary Review

Inclusion means we must integrate children with special needs into the regular physical education instructional program as well as, where feasible, into extraclass activities. The overview of federal laws clearly indicates our responsibilities. Each type of disability has been described along with suggestions and ideas to meet the needs and interests of these children.

INDIVIDUAL *and* **GROUP** **PROJECTS**

1. Select one type of mental or physical disability and prepare a list of modifications that can be made in teaching games to help integrate children with this type of disability into the instructional program. Repeat the same task with gymnastic and dance activities.

2. In groups of three or four, brainstorm ideas that will help other children understand and assist children using wheelchairs or special braces.

3. Prepare a list of special considerations that must be adhered to when teaching children with asthmatic conditions.

4. Students administer the plumb line posture test to each other. Select a few students who have posture deviations and discuss what should be done if these were elementary school children.

5. In groups of two or three students, develop a special "Fitness at Home" program for a child who is classified as obese. Your program should include suggestions relating to exercise, diet, and good health habits.

SELECTED READINGS

Arnheim, D. D., and W. A. Sinclair. 1985. *Physical education for special populations: A developmental, adapted, and remedial approach.* Englewood Cliffs, NJ: Prentice Hall.

Block, M. E. 1994. *A teacher's guide to including students with disabilities in regular physical education.* Baltimore: Paul H. Brookes.

Delacato, C. 1959. *The treatment and prevention of reading problems.* Springfield, IL: Charles C. Thomas.

Dunn, J., and H. Fait. 1989. *Special physical education: Adapted, individualized and developmental.* Dubuque, IA: Wm. C. Brown.

Grossman, H. J., ed. 1984. *Manual on terminology and classification in mental retardation.* Washington, DC: American Association of Mental Deficiency.

Gubbay, F. 1975. Clumsy children in normal schools. *Medical Journal of Australia* 1:233–36.

Horvat, M. 1990. *Physical education and sport for exceptional students.* Dubuque, IA: Wm. C. Brown.

Kasser, S. L. 1995. *Inclusive games.* Champaign, IL: Human Kinetics.

Kavale, K., and P. D. Mattson. 1983. One jumped off the balance beam: Meta-analysis of perceptual motor training. *Journal of learning disabilities* 16:165–73.

Kephart, N. C. 1960. *The slow learner in the classroom.* Columbus, OH: Charles E. Merrill.

Miller, A. G., and J. V. Sullivan. 1982. *Teaching physical activities to impaired youth: An approach to mainstreaming.* New York: Wiley.

Morris, L. R., and L. Schulz. 1989. *Creative play activities for children with disabilities.* Champaign, IL: Human Kinetics.

National Education Steering Committee of Moving to Inclusion Initiative. 1994 *Moving to inclusion.* CAHPER, 1600 Naismith Drive, Gloucester, Ontario, Canada K1B 5N4.

Sherrill, C. 1997. *Adapted physical activity, recreation, and sport.* 5th ed. Dubuque, IA: Brown & Benchmark.

Stainback, S., W. Stainback, and M. Forest. 1989. *Educating all students in the mainstream of regular education.* Baltimore: Paul H. Brookes.

CHAPTER 14

Enhancing Academic Concepts and Skills

KEY CONCEPTS

14.1 Academic concepts and skills can be taught and reinforced through a variety of physical activities

14.2 Movement experiences can stimulate children to express their thoughts through the written word

14.3 Physical education is a rich environment for teaching democratic ideals

14.4 Art, music, and physical education help children communicate their ideas and feelings about themselves and their immediate environment

KEY OBJECTIVES

After completing this chapter you should be able to:

1. Understand the meaning and importance of integrating physical education with other subjects
2. Teach and reinforce academic concepts and skills through the medium of games, dance, and gymnastic activities
3. Adapt inventive and cooperative game challenges to teach academic concepts and skills

One of the fundamental themes throughout this book is that physical education makes unique contributions to the general goals of elementary education. Through a broad-based program of activities and effective teaching strategies, young children progressively increase their physical attributes and learn the knowledge and skills associated with a variety of physical activities. Through the medium of play—both directed and cooperative—a child also learns about self-control and cooperative behavior.

Elementary school teachers fully realize that learning in one area, such as arithmetic, can be strengthened by learning in another area, as when children add up the number of points in a game played in a physical education lesson. Research evidence provided by Humphrey (1990) and Cratty (1971) supports this general point of view. Their studies strongly indicate that children tend to learn certain academic concepts better through the motor activity medium than through the traditional academic medium. Also, teaching academic skills and concepts through a kinesthetic medium seems to be more favorable for children with average or below-average intelligence.

Contemporary education uses the term *integration* to describe this mutual relationship between subject areas. Integration implies a two-way street in which each subject area has a unique place and role in the child's total education. Whenever a concept or skill in one subject area can be fortified or acquired through another subject, the relationship should be consciously planned. This can occur in two ways in the elementary school. The first approach is to use the assigned time for an academic subject, such as math, and use physical activities within this time period to teach or reinforce a particular skill or concept. A simple example of this approach would be a first-grade teacher using a grid, drawn on the floor of the classroom or outside on the blacktop, to teach number recognition or simple addition. The essential point is that the time spent on this grid activity is not considered part of the allocated time for physical education. The second approach is, first, to plan a well-balanced physical education program for a particular grade. Once the program is established, the classroom teacher can modify activities within each unit to reinforce academic skills and concepts concurrently taught in the classroom.

To illustrate: Suppose that a third-grade teacher is teaching the concept of sets in math and a games unit in physical education to emphasize controlling the ball with the hand. Without changing the main emphasis of the games unit, she substitutes Squirrel in the Forest (p. 320), doubles hopscotch (p. 358), and Loose Caboose (p. 332) for three previously selected games. The three new games now emphasize the game skills as well as mathematical sets. In addition, she designs a series of creative game challenges that include sets as part of each game. These changes show how the teacher meets the objectives of her games unit and reinforces learning in another subject area.

With the two approaches in mind, the remaining portion of this chapter will illustrate the potential contributions that physical education can make to other subjects in the elementary curriculum. The resource sections of this book (chapters 16–30) also include examples of how game, dance, and gymnastic activities are used to teach or reinforce a variety of academic concepts and skills.

LANGUAGE ARTS

Language arts in the elementary school is not a single subject. Rather, it is the basis or prerequisite for learning in all areas of education. Through language arts, a child learns to communicate—to listen, speak, read, and write. Although many of these skills are learned in a systematic way during the language arts period, many children learn these skills, or at least reinforce them, in other subject areas. The medium of play, whether imaginary or real, provides a rich, enjoyable, and stimulating environment in which a child can develop these communication skills.

Figure 14.1   Steal the Bacon.

C O N C E P T

14.1 *Academic Concepts and Skills Can Be Taught and Reinforced Through a Variety of Physical Activities*

The following list of traditional and creative games and suggested activities shows the types of language arts skills that can be taught through physical activities. There are numerous advantages to the physical education program when these skills are practiced or expressed through game, dance, or gymnastic activities. Rules and regulations are clarified, keener insights into movements involving game skills or dance patterns can develop, and a deeper appreciation of the art of movement can result as children learn to integrate and communicate their ideas and feelings through speech, writing, and movement.

Traditional Games

Traditional games include simple running games that generally involve one or more taggers, boundaries, and special rules. They also include simple ball games, such as dodgeball and four square, as well as a variety of guessing and manipulative game activities such as marbles and hopscotch. The following sample games illustrate how they can be modified to teach language concepts and skills in an enjoyable and exciting way.

Steal the Bacon

Two teams line up, each behind its own end line. On each team the players assign themselves numbers by counting off. The beanbag is placed in the middle of the playing area. The teacher calls out a number, say four—and player 4 from each team races for the beanbag (figure 14.1). When a player picks up the beanbag, she must run back across her own end line without being tagged by the opposing player. If she is touched by the opposing player before reaching her endline, her opponent receives one point. On the other hand, if she reaches her end line without being tagged, her team is awarded one point.

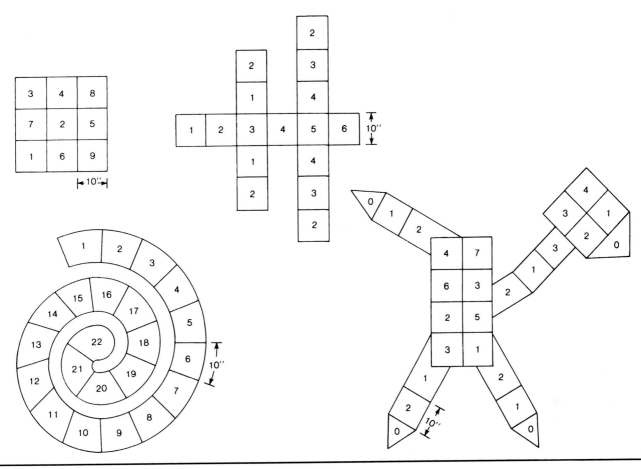

Figure 14.2   Grid patterns.

Language Application   The following suggestions will assist the teacher in adapting Steal the Bacon to a variety of language arts skills.

1. Instead of numbers, use adverbs. The teacher calls out, "He drives safely," and the two players who are designated as "safely" run out to pick up the beanbag.

Team A	Team B
1 carefully	5 safely
2 daily	4 early
3 dangerously	3 dangerously
4 early	2 daily
5 safely	1 carefully

   For a more thought-provoking game, the teacher calls out, "She is a safe driver. She drives _____,"—leaving it to the students to figure out which adverb is correct and to run out to pick up the beanbag.
2. Instead of numbers, use pronouns, vowels, prepositions, and so on and repeat the game.
3. Change numbers to family names (*grandfather, grandmother, son,* etc.) and use in an English as a Second Language program to reinforce word recognition.

My Ship Is Loaded

Arrange the class into groups of three or four players and seat them on the floor. In each small group, one child starts rolling a ball to another and calls, "My ship is loaded with cars" (or another cargo). The player who receives the ball repeats what the first child said and adds a new item, rolling the ball to another player while calling, "My ship is loaded with cars and hats." Each player, in turn, adds a new item. When a child fails to repeat all the "cargo," the ball is given to the player on his right, who starts a new game.

Language Application   The following are suggestions for adapting My Ship Is Loaded to a variety of language skills.

1. Change the cargo to one classification of items, such as clothing, food, household items, or toys.
2. Change the cargo to calling out pronouns, such as *she, me,* etc.
3. Change the cargo to items that all begin with the same letter, such as buttons, bows, and boxes.

Grids

A rectangle, square, or pattern grid can be an effective, enjoyable learning medium for young children (figure 14.2). Grids can be drawn on blacktop or on plastic mats or sheets. Plastic sheets store easily, and they provide a means of designing a series of learning experiences that range from simple to complex challenges. All that is required is to tape the corners of the plastic sheets to any surface.

Figure 14.3 The first player hops, jumps, or uses part of his body.

Language Application   The following suggestions will help the teacher use grids to teach children a variety of language arts skills. First, draw or place on the blacktop three or four grids as shown in figure 14.3.

1. Match letters. The teacher or a child calls out a letter, and the performer hops, jumps, or uses parts of the body to land on or touch the appropriate letter. Repeat with vowels, spelling words, and so on.
2. Have the children select three or four letters in a row (e.g., *C*, *D*, and *E*), then have them hop or jump to each letter in the correct sequence.
3. Have the children cut out a letter, hop with it to the corresponding letter on the grid, then run and write it on the blackboard.
4. Have the children land on a consonant and sound it out with a word, such as "*C* as in *cat*." Repeat with vowel sounds.

Inventive Games

During the past few years, the inventive games approach has become very popular in the elementary school physical education program. This problem-solving method, however, has been used almost exclusively to guide children to create their own running, tag, and simple ball games. The following examples will illustrate how this approach can be adapted to teach a wide variety of language arts skills in exciting and challenging ways.

Before adapting this approach to teaching language arts or other academic concepts and skills, each teacher should learn how to pose simple inventive game challenges as described in the introduction to part 6, "Game and Movement Activities." As soon as you feel confident using this approach, begin to adapt it to teach a variety of language arts, mathematics, science, and other subject areas. The following examples, illustrate how to pose

inventive game challenges that involve a variety of language arts concepts and skills.

Challenge No.1: Word Recognition

Make up sets of cards as shown

Set 1:	apples	pears	grapes
Set 2:	potatoes	carrots	beans

Two players have one set of cards between them. Pose the following challenge.

Challenge   "Can you make up a hopping game with your partner that uses three word cards? You must call out one or more words in your game."

Challenge No.2: Prefixes and Suffixes

Three children draw a word grid on a gymnasium mat or outside on the blacktop. The grid has sixteen squares with prefixes as shown in the illustration. When everyone is ready, pose the following challenge.

Challenge   "See if you can design a game for three players using the prefix grid. You must use a hop, a jump, and a change of direction in your game."

ab-	pro-	pre-	mis-
ex-	sub-	de-	ad-
com-	un-	db-	ob-
in-	non-	re-	trans-

Suggestions and Variations
1. Repeat game with suffixes.
2. Add flash cards with words like *move* and *take*. One child flashes a card, say the one with *move*. The jumper calls out "remove!" and hops onto the prefix *re-*.
3. Design new grids that can be used to emphasize one or more language arts concepts and skills.

Additional Activities

The following games and activities can be used to enhance a variety of language arts concepts and skills.

1. Use the games listed in table 14.1 to teach or reinforce a skill or concept.
2. Listen to and follow the directions of a game, dance, or movement skill.
3. Listen to animal sounds made by the teacher (or a child); then do appropriate animal-like movements.
4. Listen to a story or poem; then act it out.
5. Listen to music and move according to particular noises, such as loud (banging), soft (tapping lightly on a triangle), or quick (fast tempo).
6. Have each child sing a rope-jumping rhyme (chapter 26) or singing game (chapter 29) and act out or interpret the story while singing the verses.

TABLE 14.1 Activities for Enhancing Language-Arts Concepts and Skills

Games	Concept or Skill	Page
Do As I Do	Listening	324
My Ship Is Loaded	Word recognition, remembering	305
Rattlesnake and Bumblebee	Speaking	306
Puzzled Words	Spelling	306
Spell Act	Spelling	306
Charades	Spelling	306
Hopscotch	Letter recognition	329
Alphabet Game	Letter recognition, spelling	342
Modified Musical Chairs	Spelling	361

7. Debate the value of daily physical education, the Olympics, or coed physical education.
8. Use body movements to make letters of the alphabet—individually, with a partner, or with three or more children.
9. Recognize and illustrate these through movement: numbers, letters, shapes, or symbols printed or projected (overhead or on a screen).
10. Spell words with individual parts of the body (e.g., finger or leg tracing letters of words), with whole body, or with a partner or small group. In groups of three, make the letters of the words *cat, Bruce, Mississippi;* choose words according to the appropriate grade level.
11. Write about physical education experiences, such as "How I learned to swim" or "How I climbed to the top of the apple tree."
12. Read sport stories.
13. Describe a movement sequence, such as a throwing skill, a gymnastic sequence, or a folk dance movement.
14. Make up new jingles and accompanying movements (in partners or groups) for contemporary popular commercials.
15. Write out descriptions of creative games.

C O N C E P T

14.2 *Movement Experiences Can Stimulate Children to Express Their Thoughts Through the Written Word*

The previous examples illustrate how physical activities can be used as a medium through which a variety of academic concepts and skills can be taught. The following sample poems illustrate how a child's experiences on large apparatus

can be used as the subject or focus for creative writing. This goes far beyond using physical activities to enhance a single concept or skill. Movement experiences on very exciting and challenging apparatus can stimulate children to express their thoughts and feelings through the written word. These poems also reveal children's understanding and attitudes about themselves and their movement experiences.

Climb Up the Climbing Wall
Then do a swift turn on the box,
Do an interesting roll on a mat
Flip and twirl over the bars,
Even though I'm scared,
I dare to do a flip!
The world is turning upside down,
And then I land perfectly
I climb up the ropes
I put hand over hand,
I am being daring and risky,
But I do it anyway.
　　　　—Tristane (grade 4)

Gymnastics
Risky, daring
outrageous,
I have now accomplished it and I'm done
The dangerous jumps, the freaky flips,
I never gave up,
I tried my best.
Practice practice;
It makes me feel proud,
That since I practiced,
I did it well.
I feel great
I feel secure.
　　　　—Katlie (grade 4)

Going Over
Going under
Going way up to the top,
Going through too.
I don't know about you
But I like traveling.
Do you?
I Like P.E.
Don't you?
Going all around,
Going through the bars,
Slithering up the ropes like a snake,
We climb the ropes so high.
I hope you like climbing,
Because I do.
I jumped way up in the air,
So might you, too.
I hope that when you get there
Nobody gets hurt.
　　　　—Ryan (grade 4)

These poems are examples from a long-term project designed to integrate physical education with writing (Sahli 1993). The results of this study indicate that the children, at both primary and intermediate levels, improved their thinking skills, showed a significant increase in their enjoyment of physical education, and demonstrated improved communication skills. In addition, they became more critical of their own work and more willing to take risks in their writing and physical endeavors. Further, their poetic writing reinforced their movement vocabulary and extended their thinking in the aesthetic domain. The predominant use of poetic writing reinforces the connection between writing and movement experiences. Finally, the integration of writing and physical education provided the children with an intrinsic link to learning in the cognitive, affective, and physical domains.

Mathematics

The contemporary elementary school mathematics curriculum includes the acquisition of skills, principles, and concepts relating to whole numbers, mathematical sentences, sets, the metric system, field properties, geometry, measuring, and graphing. Classroom teachers from kindergarten to grade 6 have used the medium of physical activity, both in the classroom and on the playing field, to teach a variety of these mathematical skills and concepts. For example, a first-grade teacher has been teaching the concept of adding numbers. Time has been spent in the classroom on number recognition, writing numbers, verbal counting, and manipulation of small objects into groupings. Also, during the physical education period the teacher uses the game Red Light (p. 323), involving counting, and Squirrel in the Forest (p. 320), involving grouping into threes, to fortify the concepts of adding and sets. Numerous other mathematical skills and concepts can be taught through the game, dance, and gymnastic activities listed in table 14.2. Teachers should modify or add to each activity as necessary to accommodate the particular concept or skill being emphasized.

Adding and Subtracting

Several additional activities, such as using grids, counting rhythmic beats, and keeping score, can be used to reinforce adding and subtracting skills. A few examples of each follow.

1. Using grids: A rectangle, square, or patterned grid similar to a language arts grid can be a very effective and enjoyable learning medium for young children. The adding, subtracting, and number-recognition challenges can involve hopping, jumping, placing parts of the body on the appropriate number, and so on. (See figure 14.4).
2. Count the number of beats or steps in a dance.
3. Count the number of jumps in rope skipping.

TABLE 14.2 Activities for Teaching Mathematical Skills and Concepts through Movement

Games	Concept or Skill	Page
Mousetrap	Adding	324
Red Light	Adding and subtracting	323
Squirrel in the Forest	Sets	320
Call Ball	Number recognition	329
Dodgeball	Subtraction	327
Loose Caboose	Sets	332
Beanbag Basket	Adding and subtracting	328
Hopscotch	Number recognition, subtracting	329
Marbles	Adding and subtracting	330
Jacks	Adding and subtracting	331
Musical Chairs	One less than	361
Doubles Hopscotch	Sets	358
Juggle a Number	Adding and subtracting	361
Co-op Tag	Adding and subtracting	362
Nine-Person Skip	Adding	362

4. Keep team scores.
5. Determine the number of persons on a team or in a group.
6. Determine how far away one is from being "up to bat" by adding (or subtracting) one's assigned batting number to (or from) the number of the current batter.
7. Compare individual or team scores (for example, blues beat reds 10 to 5; blues won by 5 points—subtracting).

Multiplying and Dividing

The following activities illustrate how various physical activities can help children learn multiplying and dividing concepts and skills.

1. Grids: Another example using figure 14.4 demonstrates the versatility of grids. For example, a challenge such as "9 times 8 equals" requires the child to hop on 9, then on ×, then on 8, then on the equals sign, then to 7 and 2. Challenges involving two players and using parts of the body, or combining the grid with stacks of cards with matching numbers, illustrate the various possibilities of this type of grid.
2. Divide class into halves, quarters, thirds, and so on.
3. Divide playing time into halves, quarters, and thirds.

Numbers and Geometric Forms

1. Make whole numbers with your body (figure 14.5).
2. Make a whole number with a skipping rope on the floor. Jump over the rope that many times.

Figure 14.4   "Equals 9."

Figure 14.5   "Make a zero with your partner."

3. Make different geometric shapes with your body or with a partner.
4. Throw balls or beanbags at targets made of different geometric shapes.
5. Travel on the floor across apparatus in a specific shape or pathway—for example, curved, zigzag, or straight.
6. Make different angles and symmetrical or asymmetrical forms with your body, with a partner, or with a small group.

Measuring and Graphing

1. Measure the length, width, or height of playing field or courts.
2. Measure the number of hours and minutes spent on various physical education or other recreational activities.
3. Make drawings according to scale (e.g., one inch = five feet) of playing courts and field surfaces. Compare linear measurements, perimeters, and areas of two or more play areas as fractions or percentages. These tasks can be presented as questions, such as these:
   "What percentage of the soccer field does the goal area take up?"
   "How many basketball courts will fit into the playing field?"
   "How many times would you have to run around the volleyball court to cover the same distance as once around the track?"

4. Make a circle graph showing time allotments for various physical activities in an intramural program.
5. Construct a bar graph showing changes in heart rate in relation to changes in level of physical activities.

Inventive Games

Because concepts of sets are taught throughout the elementary school grades, two examples are provided to illustrate how to use the inventive game approach with young and older children. In the first example, sets of twos, threes, and fours are taught to a group of eight-year-olds. The second example, for older children, illustrates how a large group can be broken down into subsets on the basis of a variety of features and properties.

Sets for Younger Children

A third-grade class is learning the concepts of sets in a mathematics unit. The teacher has also planned a games unit that will include Snowball (sets of two), Loose Caboose (sets of three), and Numbers (sets of three). When the children begin to understand the concepts of sets and have played the three games, the teacher begins to pose several inventive game challenges described below.

Challenge No. 1: Sets of Two

This first game involves one child, eight beanbags, and a limited space in which to play the game.

Challenge "Can you arrange your equipment in sets of two and make up a game that involves jumping over sets and a change of direction?"

After each child has designed and played the first game, the teacher adds other related challenges described in the next three challenges.

Challenge No. 2: Sets of Three

Repeat challenge no. 1, substituting sets of three or four.

Challenge No. 3: Change Requiring Physical Skill

Repeat challenge no.2 and change the way of moving to running, hopping, leaping, etc.

Challenge No.4: Change Quantity of Equipment

Arrange the class into groups of four children, with twelve pieces of equipment for each group. Pose the challenge:

Challenge "Can your group design a new game in your own space and use twelve pieces of equipment? Your game must arrange the equipment in sets of two, three, or four."

Sets for Older Children

Prior to giving this group of eleven-year-olds a challenge, the teacher noted the gender and eye color of the children. She found there were fifteen boys with brown eyes and nine girls with blue eyes. The teacher assigned six brown-eyed boys and six blue-eyed girls to group A. This composition provided a potential for different arrangements by gender as well as possible subsets by eye color. The second group, composed of nine brown-eyed boys and three blue-eyed girls, held a similar potential if they were grouped in sets of three. The teacher then gave each group twelve pieces of small equipment. The twelve pieces of equipment provided a structure to create sets of six, four, three, or two. These sets could also involve players grouped in similar numbers. The next four challenges illustrate how the teacher used this basic structure to teach sets in a very interesting and challenging way.

Challenge No.1: Sets

Challenge "See if your group of four can make up a game using twelve pieces of equipment and staying in your own space. Somewhere in your game you must use sets of two, three, or four."

Challenge No. 2: Change Quantity of Equipment

Repeat challenge no. 1, but change the number of equipment pieces to twenty-four. This provides for sets of eight or twelve.

Challenge No.3: Increase the Size of the Group

Repeat challenge no. 2 and consolidate the two groups into one group of twenty-four children. Now there is an increased potential for different sets and groupings by eye color.

Challenge No.4: Change in the Method of Moving

Repeat any of challenges No. 1–3 and change the method of moving to running, hopping, or jumping. Mathematics, like every other subject in the elementary school curriculum, should be fun and exciting to learn. The inventive game challenges presented under each age level provide a physical medium to learn mathematical concepts and skills. These games also provide a creative avenue to express ideas and to experience a sense of joy and success while children play their own games.

Cooperative Games

The previous example of sets were provided to illustrate how inventive games are used to teach math skills. The examples that follow represent a simple but important extension of this approach, in that they add one or more cooperative elements to the inventive game challenge.

Involving children in cooperative learning tasks, as described in chapter 17, has academic and social value. For example, it provides an effective medium through which children learn to share in finding the solution to a problem. A collective answer can often be more exciting and enriching than an individual's response to the same task. And when specific cooperative elements, such as cooperation and trust, are added to the challenge, cooperative behavior becomes a mandatory dimension of the game.

The next three challenges illustrate how to gradually progress from a simple inventive game challenge to the addition of one or more elements of cooperative behavior. Similar sets of challenges could be designed to enhance academic concepts and skills in language arts, science, and other academic subjects.

Challenge No.1: Counting, Partners, and No Equipment

This challenge is the first of three tasks involving partners, without any equipment and requiring a fairly structured series of movements. No mention is made of the use of space; hence, partners can decide for themselves whether to stay in one location or to make up a game using all the available space. It should also be noted that this challenge lays the groundwork for the next two tasks, which involve the cooperative elements described in chapter 17.

Challenge "Can you make up a counting game with your partner in which you position yourselves face-to-face, side by side, and in one other position you make up yourself?"

Challenge No.2: Counting, Partners, Equipment, and Trust

In this challenge, the addition of two pieces of equipment has a general influence on the nature of the game the two players will create. For example, the ball was included to help players find a medium for counting. The wand was added to encourage some form of trust to develop between the two

TABLE 14.3 Cooperative Games Stressing Academic Concepts

| Name of Game | Number of Players | Developmental Level | | | Academic Concepts and Skills | Page |
		I	II	III		
Doubles Hopscotch	2	X	X		Sets of two, one less than	358
Juggle A Number	5	—	X	X	Adding, subtracting, dividing	361
Cross-Over Blanket Volleyball	12	—	—	X	Adding	362
Nine-Person Skip	11	—	—	X	Adding, subtracting, dividing	362
Eight-Legged Caterpillar	8	—	X	X	Sets of two or more	361
Modified Musical Chairs	Class	—	X	X	Subtracting	361
Co-op Tag	Class	—	X	X	Sets	362
Tug-o-Peace	Class	—	X	X	Force	361
Geometry Class	Class	—	X	X	Geometry shapes	367

players. This could be one player holding or moving the wand while the other player bounced the ball under, over, or around the wand. The last sentence in the challenge makes the cooperative element of trust a requirement rather than an incidental aspect of the game.

Challenge "Is it possible to invent a counting game with your partner using one ball and one wand? Somewhere in your game you must trust your partner to do something with the wand."

Challenge No.3: Counting, Partners, More Equipment, and Cooperation

There is a subtle attempt in this challenge to guide players to work together. This is accomplished by asking them to exchange balls and to keep one score between them. Partners may decide to throw the ball into the air, and hold and maneuver it in various ways. The choice, however, is theirs.

Challenge "Design a counting game with your partner using two balls and one rope. Somewhere in your game you must exchange balls. Also, just keep one score between the two of you."

The process of teaching cooperative games as outlined in chapter 17 should be considered a flexible guideline. This approach is successful when the challenge begins with two or three players and involves one or two cooperative elements. Gradually increase the size of the group and add more elements as children demonstrate an understanding and acceptance of these elements of cooperative behavior.

The cooperative games listed in table 14.3 are also used to teach a variety of academic concepts and skills. They are used in a similar way to running, tag, and simple team games described in chapter 16. However, since these games also stress one or more elements of cooperative behavior, they provide effective avenues for children to share in finding the solutions to academic problems. They also provide a noncompetitive learning environment in which children with different levels of academic ability or with physical disabilities can be integrated with high achievers and nondisabled children.

14.3 *Physical Education Is a Rich Environment for Teaching Democratic Ideals*

SOCIAL STUDIES

The contemporary social studies program in the elementary school is similar to language arts in many ways. It is no longer a series of individual subjects, such as history, geography, or civics, emphasizing facts and events of past or present cultures. Rather, it is an integrated subject area that attempts to help children, according to their ability, understand and appreciate the similarities and differences of social groups, of customs and morals, and of the values that are held by different people in our own or in other countries.

Physical education has been recognized as a rich environment for teaching and experiencing our own democratic ideals and other people's games, dances, and customs and for simulating events and customs of past cultures. The following examples are representative of ways the physical education program can be used to help a child appreciate the importance of the interrelatedness of the peoples of the world.

Home and Neighborhood

1. Pantomime aspects of a child's immediate environment—items in the home (clocks, dishwashers, etc.), farm animals, and roles of people (mother, father, police officer).
2. Study groups in the immediate community with respect to your relationship to them (relatives, church members, and ethnic groups). Role-play to illustrate family relationships, and integrate ethnic games and dances that neighbors have brought from their countries of origin.

3. Design task cards and creative pantomime activities or games to orient children to various aspects of their community—for example, task cards and games involving emergency situations such as fires or accidents, stop and go, and directional and distance signs, and help and respect for others, such as dialing the phone for someone, giving directions, or opening a door.

State and Nation

1. Design maps or grids for games that involve geographical places (countries, provinces, states, capitals), government (branches, names of leaders), or the location of historical or unique areas of your country (Washington, DC, the Grand Canyon, Ottawa, Hudson Bay).
2. Study native Indian or Eskimo cultures, including hunting, farming, dances, games, and other aspects that can be portrayed through physical education activities.
3. Study and participate in the games and dances of early settlers, including rules, dress, or other cultural aspects of each activity (soccer, folk dances, gymnastic activities).
4. Study the history and development of games and dances created in North America (such as volleyball, basketball, and square dances).
5. List games, dances, and other physical activities for holidays. This list could include the Christmas season, Valentine's Day, Easter, St. Patrick's Day, Thanksgiving, the Fourth of July, Canada Day, and other holidays that are important to the local area.

Other Cultures

1. Study and participate in singing games, folk dances, and games of other countries, including such factors as the historical period and the customs of the people.
2. Write about and discuss different types of physical education programs. Those of the United States, Canada, England, and other European countries will illustrate many differences in the political and social environments of the countries.
3. Discuss amateurism and professionalism, particularly in light of the past two or three Olympic games. This will bring out many important questions that youngsters might seek to answer in their lifetimes.

HEALTH AND SAFETY

There are many close relationships between health and physical education that should be exploited by every classroom teacher. Active health programs that show children how to measure their heart rate and breathing rates or that clarify the relationship between exercise, diet, and health are examples of effective integration (figure 14.6).

Figure 14.6 Measuring heart rate.

The following suggestions illustrate how health and safety can be integrated with a variety of physical education activities.

1. Periodically measure height and weight, with discussions about growth, maturation, and the need for daily physical activities.
2. Discuss the importance of personal cleanliness—showering, nails, hair, and so on.
3. Research information on assessment and maintenance of personal health and physical fitness.
4. Class projects that involve studying the school environments, then designing safety rules and procedures for areas and activities.
5. Learn how to administer basic first aid.
6. Class projects investigating the causes and characteristics of various physical disabilities; projects should include various ways of modifying physical activities in order to mainstream children with these special needs.
7. Administer a plumb line posture test to each other, then discuss and create a program that would contribute to good posture when at home, when watching television, and when sitting at desks.
8. Discuss the importance of regular physical examinations, including what is examined and how often one should be examined.
9. Class projects involving nutrition, including a personal analysis of family eating patterns, types of food eaten, calorie counting, and the relationship between diet and exercise.
10. Learn how to take pulse rate, blood pressure, and other physical assessments.

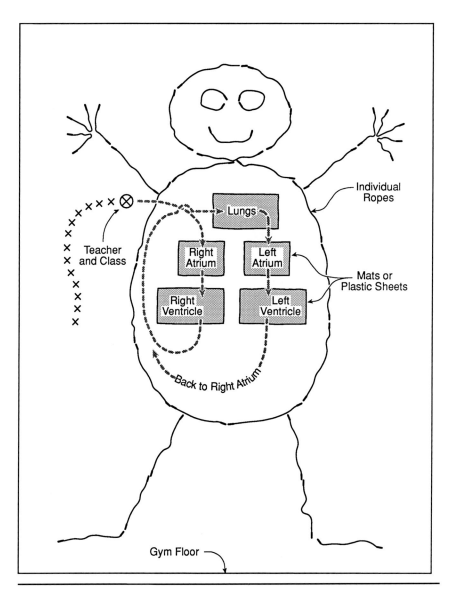

Figure 14.7   Circulation of the blood.

11. Learn how the blood circulates through the body—for instance, by watching a film, using a model of the heart, or drawing the body and tracing the path of the blood through the heart, lungs, and blood vascular system. The following method has been used to teach children how the blood circulates through the body in a physically active, exciting, and enjoyable way. The first thing to do is create a giant lying on his back (figure 14.7). Use individual ropes to form the head, arms, and legs. Lungs and the four chambers of the heart are large mats or plastic sheets. Next, arrange the class in a long line behind you. Explain that the giant is lying on his back, and point to the lungs, heart, arms, and legs. Tell the class to follow you and, as you cross over the right atrium, call out "Right atrium." Each child, in turn, calls out "right atrium" as she or he crosses this part of the body. Continue crossing—the right ventricle, lungs, left atrium, and so on—calling

out each part. After several "journeys" through the body, have one or more children act as leaders and repeat the procedure. Once everyone understands how the blood flows through the body, place a pile of red cards (or beanbags) on the lungs and a pile of blue cards on the right foot. Repeat the running procedure with the children picking up red cards (oxygenated blood) from the lungs, carrying them to the right foot, and exchanging red for blue (deoxygenated) cards. The deoxygenated blood is carried back through the heart to the lungs to be oxygenated.

SCIENCE

Within the elementary school science curriculum, numerous scientific concepts and principles can be illustrated and clarified through a variety of physical education activities. An understanding of how living creatures grow, the wind, temperature, and levers are important concepts that lead to an understanding of the natural and technical environment in which we live. The following examples provide a few illustrations of how scientific principles and concepts can be integrated with a variety of movement activities.

▨ Grouping of Living Creatures

The teacher prepares three or four grids like the one shown in figure 14.8, and a set of flash cards for mammals, fish, reptiles, birds, insects, and amphibians. When the teacher holds up "fish" and calls "three," the first player must hop onto the three different fish. Repeat the game with all the children taking their turns.

Teaching Suggestions
1. Have players move to creatures according to a characteristic, such as "mammals that fly," "a reptile without legs," and "birds that cannot fly."
2. Repeat the original game, but when a player has landed on a square, she must give a characteristic of that species before jumping to the next square.
3. Design similar grids and tasks for prehistoric animals, flowers, plants, etc.

▨ Growth

Pantomime activities to illustrate plant growth, animal movements and behavior, and human growth and developmental stages.

CHAPTER 14

Dog	Horsefly	Ant	Lizard	Seagull	Armadillo
Sparrow	Shark	Toad	Butterfly	Bee	Salmon
Snakes	Duck	Seal	Wasp	Hawk	Alligator
Swordfish	Ostrich	Cod	Frog	Dolphin	Cat
Salamander	Elephant	Fly	Turtles	Trout	Mosquito
Crocodile	Buzzard	Pig	Sea Horse	Bat	Penguin

MAMMALS   REPTILES   FISH
INSECTS   BIRDS   AMPHIBIANS

Figure 14.8   Name that thing.

Matter

Design movement challenges to illustrate the movement of molecules, the solar system, and the expansion and contraction of gases. For example, divide the class in half and have them sit on the floor. Pose a challenge, such as "See if your group can design a series of movements that illustrate how molecules move in solids, liquids, and gases." After a few minutes of planning, let each group perform its series of movements.

Gravity

1. Select a variety of gymnastic stunts, such as a headstand, walking on a balance beam, or balancing on one or two feet. Show how a wide base of support and a low center of gravity provide a stable base of support. (See chapter 3 for a discussion of gravity.)
2. Set up a variety of movements where it is important to have (a) a wide base to maintain a stable resistance to an oncoming object, as in catching a heavy ball and combative activities; (b) an unstable base, as in a racing start or a walking movement; and (c) a center of gravity below the direction of a forceful movement, as in the jump-reach.

Levers

1. Select a series of physical activities to illustrate first-class levers. These could be riding a seesaw or rowing a boat.
2. Repeat activity 1 with second-class levers. These could be pushing a wheelbarrow or opening a door.

3. Repeat activity 1 with third-class levers. This is sometimes called the human lever, since most physical skills involve third-class levers. Examples to study are throwing a ball, lifting a weight, and kicking a ball. (See chapter 3 for examples.)

Motion

1. Show how Newton's laws of motion are important in the performance of such skills as initially starting to move a ball (inertia), serving a volleyball (acceleration), or jumping up from the floor or a soft grass surface (action-reaction).
2. Select a series of movements to illustrate how rotary movements of the human body are transferred to linear movement of the body or objects.

Force

1. Design a series of movement challenges that illustrate the importance of applying muscular force sequentially in the direction of the movement (high jump, standing long jump).
2. Show how the greatest force is generated through the larger muscles, such as leg and hip muscles, rather than by the shoulder or arm muscles (bending down, keeping back straight, and lifting with the legs).
3. Select a series of movements to illustrate how force should be dissipated through the widest surface and the greatest distance (landing and rolling).

C O N C E P T

14.4 *Art, Music, and Physical Education Help Children Communicate Their Ideas and Feelings about Themselves and Their Immediate Environment*

ART AND MUSIC

Art and music can be linked to physical education in a variety of ways. All three areas are used in one way or another to communicate children's ideas and feelings about themselves or about objects in their immediate environment. A teacher who operates in a self-contained classroom can capitalize on the child's interests and abilities in physical activities and relate them to a variety of art forms. Drawing pictures of a gymnastic sequence or painting a picture of a sport hero can motivate children to draw, paint, or express their ideas in a new artistic manner. Music also provides possibilities. The following examples illustrate how art, music, and physical education can all work together to create interesting activities.

Art Activities

1. Draw a movement sequence performed in a previous gymnastic session. A game, event, or dance skill can also be drawn.
2. Construct musical instruments that can be used in creative dance activities (see appendix B).
3. Draw symmetrical and asymmetrical shapes of the body, then include these shapes in movement sequences or creative dance activities.
4. Draw, color, or paint game, dance, or other movement activities. These activities can include sport figures or scenes, court activities, or dancing scenes.
5. Study sculpture, paintings, and other art forms that depict physical movements or activities. For instance, R. T. McKenzie's statues, early Greek friezes, and Egyptian paintings are rich in form and information relating to sport, dance, and gymnastic events.
6. Design bulletin boards and gymnasium murals that illustrate events, movements, or health.
7. Design adventure or creative playgrounds. This activity requires an understanding of children's needs and interests, a knowledge of the structure and strength of materials, and creativity to draw or illustrate ideas using a variety of materials.

Music Activities

1. Teach the basic elements of rhythm, such as underlying beat, measures, tempo, and phrasing as they apply to rhythmic, folk, and creative dance activities (see chapter 28).
2. Use musical accompaniment for warm-up activities and rope jumping, and background music for ball bouncing and some gymnastic sequences.
3. Create songs or musical accompaniments for creative dance activities.
4. Interpret songs, sounds, and musical scores through creative movement.

Summary Review

The examples in this chapter provide a basic idea of the tremendous potential that physical education has to offer other subject areas. The reader will also find many game, dance, and gymnastic activities in the resource sections of this text (chapters 16–30) that can be used to teach numerous academic concepts and skills. Integration, however, is not a one-way street. If integration is to work, academic subject areas should also attempt to fortify principles, concepts, and values inherent in the content areas of physical education.

INDIVIDUAL and GROUP PROJECTS

1. Select textbooks from various elementary school grades and develop lessons that clearly show how concepts and skills from these books can be taught through physical education activities.
2. In groups of two or three, add to the list of suggestions provided under each subject area in this chapter.
3. Prepare a series of inventive game challenges for any mathematical skill that involve bouncing a ball.
4. In groups of three or four, review the format described under "Cooperative Games" and teaching counting. Develop a similar set of challenges to teach another mathematical skill, such as sets, geometrical shapes and multiplication.

Selected Readings

Ashlock, R. B., and J. H. Humphrey. 1976. *Teaching elementary school mathematics through motor learning.* Springfield, IL: Charles C. Thomas.

Blatt G. T., and J. Cunningham. 1981. *It's your move: Expressive movement activities for language arts.* New York: Teachers College Press.

Doray, M. 1982. *J is for jumping: Moving into language arts.* Belmont, CA: Pitman Learning.

Gilbert, A. G. 1977. *Teaching the three R's through movement experiences.* Minneapolis: Burgess.

Hall, T. 1981. *Academic ropes.* Bryon, CA: Front Row Experience.

Humphrey, J. R. 1990. *Integration of physical education in the elementary school curriculum.* Springfield, IL: Charles C. Thomas.

Humphrey, J. R., and J. N. Humphrey. 1990. *Mathematics can be child's play.* Springfield, IL: Charles C. Thomas.

———. 1991. *Developing elementary school science concepts through active games.* Springfield, IL: Charles C. Thomas.

Sahli, J. 1993. *Making a meaningful connection: The integration of physical education with writing.* Thesis, Simon Fraser University, Burnaby, BC.

Werner, P. H., and E. C. Burton. 1979. *Learning through movement: Teaching cognitive content through physical activities.* St. Louis: Mosby.

CHAPTER 15

Adapting Physical Education Activities to the Classroom

KEY CONCEPTS

15.1 Classrooms, hallways, and other academic areas can be used for a variety of physical activities.

15.2 Grid activities can be an effective medium for teaching academic concepts and skills.

KEY OBJECTIVES

After completing this chapter you should be able to:

1. Understand the nature and scope of physical education activities that can take place in the classroom
2. Know how to improvise and modify activities and facilities to cope with a classroom setting
3. Know how to use grid activities to teach academic concepts and skills

In general, physical education activities should be taught in the gymnasium or outdoors on designated instructional areas. However, there are times in many schools when the classroom, hallway, or cafeteria are the only available locations where physical activities can be taught. With a minimum shifting of chairs and desks, and adherence to a few safety rules, numerous physical activities—such as active and quiet games, fitness exercises, and rhythmics—can be taught in these indoor spaces. There is an additional contribution these physical activities can make to the intellectual and social development of children. Many of the game, gymnastic, and rhythmic activities provided in this chapter can also be used as an effective medium through which a wide variety of academic concepts and skills can be taught in an exciting and effective manner.

The information provided in this chapter illustrates how many of the game, gymnastic, and dance activities described in other chapters can be modified and taught in the regular classroom, hallway, or cafeteria. A few additional grid activities, which are particularly adaptable to the classroom, are included.

TEACHING PROCEDURES

With minor adjustments and the establishment of a few basic rules and safety procedures, the classroom can be used for many physical activities. Whenever a large, unobstructed space is required for a physical activity, move the desks and chairs in a safe, quiet, and efficient manner. This procedure can be greatly speeded up by designating teams (by rows or any other type of classroom grouping), then creating a contest to see which group finishes first.

Figure 15.1 Classroom games can be quiet.

CONCEPT

15.1 *Classrooms, Hallways, and Other Academic Areas Can Be Used for a Variety of Physical Activities*

Classrooms, hallways, and cafeterias vary in the amount of free space available, the type of furniture, and acceptable noise levels. The following suggestions, particularly those relating to safety and noise, should be carefully considered before introducing any physical activity to the classroom.

Participation

Provide opportunities for every member of the class to participate in the physical activity. The game activities suggested in the next section present the greatest problem for this. Break the class into as many separate playing groups as possible—three groups, rather than one, playing charades—or modify the game to increase individual and total class participation.

Safety

Remove pencils and other materials from the tops of desks, and keep children away from sharp corners and edges. Other safety procedures, such as permitting running only around alternate rows and only when the noise does not seriously disturb adjacent classrooms, must be translated into simple and clearly understood rules.

Noise

Although classrooms differ with respect to acceptable noise levels, a few basic rules can help keep the noise problem under control (figure 15.1). This applies to the noise within the classroom itself as well as the sound that penetrates the walls and ventilation system to other classrooms. In games and contests, modify verbal commands and require hand clapping instead of team or class yells. A lower volume might be called for in dance activities.

CLASSROOM GAMES

Classroom games, or what are commonly known as "rainy day activities," are simple games, relays, and contests that can be played in the classroom, hallway, or cafeteria (table 15.1). These games usually require little or no adjustment of furniture or elaborate equipment. For classification purposes, these activities are generally designated as either active or quiet, although the dividing line between the two is rather vague. A very enthusiastic class can turn a quiet game into an active one, just as a quiet class can turn an active game into a quiet one. For ease of selection, however, in table 15.1 the more vigorous games are listed as active games and the less vigorous as quiet games.

There is no season or time of day that should be set aside for active or quiet games. Their use depends upon such factors as the basic purpose of the game, the weather, and the amount of time and space available. For example, several games listed in table 15.1 provide an effective medium through which children can acquire academic concepts in an exciting and challenging manner. There are other times during the school day, especially after long periods of mental concentration, when an exciting active classroom game provides the mental relaxation needed by both teacher and students. When selecting classroom games, first decide on the sort of game—active or quiet—you want to use. Second, check table 15.1 to see whether the game involves guessing, relay, imitation, tag, surprise, small manipulation, and/or academic concepts and skills. Finally, check to see if you have the necessary equipment.

Active Classroom Games

Fox and Rabbit (Level I)

Formation   Single circle or children seated
Equipment   Two beanbags
Players   Class
Academic concepts   Language arts—letter and word recognition; science—living creatures; mathematics—number recognition

One beanbag, the "rabbit," is passed around the circle. A second beanbag, the "fox," is started around the circle. When the fox catches the rabbit, the game ends. Start each game with a new player.

TABLE 15.1 Classroom Games

Name of Game	Developmental Level			Guessing	Relay	Imitation	Tag	Surprise	Small Manipulation	Academic Concepts and Skills	Page
	I	II	III								
Active Classroom Games											
Fox and Rabbit	X							X	X	Language arts—letter and word recognition Science—living creatures Mathematics—number recognition	302
Beanbag Basket Relay	X	X			X				X	Mathematics—counting	303
Ringmaster	X	X				X					304
Squirrel and Nut	X	X		X				X	X	Language arts—word recognition	304
Mirror Mirror	X	X					X	X	X	Language arts—letter recognition Mathematics—whole numbers	304
Water Cycle		X	X	X					X	Science—water cycle Language arts—synonyms, antonyms, homonyms, and consonant blends Mathematics—adding, subtracting, multiplying, and fractions	304
Knots		X	X					X	X	Mathematics—counting	304
Beanbag Pile	X	X	X		X				X	Mathematics—subtracting and multiplying	304
Poorhouse		X	X					X			305
Who's Leading?		X	X					X	X		305
Balloon Hit		X	X						X		305
Quiet Classroom Games											
My Ship Is Loaded	X	X						X	X	Language arts—word recognition and memory Social studies—neighborhood and community Health—nutrition	305
Clappers	X	X							X	Language arts—syllables	305
Crambo	X	X		X						Language arts—homonyms	305
Hat Race	X	X	X		X			X	X		305
Rattlesnake and Bumblebee		X	X	X			X	X			306
Human Checkers			X			X			X	Language arts—letter and word recognition	306
Puzzled Words			X		X				X	Language arts—spelling	306
Spell Act		X	X	X			X		X	Social studies—geographical areas	306
Charades			X		X		X		X	Science—species of animals	306

Teaching Suggestions

1. Divide class into two or three groups.
2. Place one child in the center holding a beanbag. The center player calls out "Animal," "Bird," or "Fish," then throws the beanbag to a player. If the word called was "Fish," the player must call out the name of a fish as she catches the beanbag. Players exchange positions if the catcher fails to give a name or did not catch the beanbag.
3. The center player has a set of color cards. Smaller color cards are given to opposite circle players. When the caller shows a color card, the two circle players with this color try to exchange places before the caller reaches one of the spots they have vacated. The caller may show two or more color cards at the same time. When he calls "All colors," everyone must attempt to change positions.
4. Substitute numbers, letters, or words for colors in the above variation.

Beanbag Basket Relay (Levels I–II)

Formation Lines facing baskets about six to eight feet in front of first player
Equipment Beanbags, wastepaper baskets, or hoops
Players Class
Academic concepts Mathematics—counting

Arrange pupils in rows facing the baskets. Draw a line across the front of the rows. On command, the first pupil attempts to throw a beanbag into the basket. One point is awarded for each basket. After shooting, each player retrieves her beanbag, gives it to the next player, and tells the teacher her score.

Continue until the last player has had a turn. The team with the highest score wins.

Teaching Suggestions
1. Divide teams in half. Turn second half around, place baskets at back of room, and play two games.
2. Have children take turns keeping their team's score.

Ringmaster (Levels I–II)

Formation   Single circle with one child in the center
Equipment   None
Players   Class

One child selected as the "ringmaster" stands in the center of the circle. The ringmaster moves about the center of the circle, pretending to crack his whip, and calls out the names of animals. The circle players imitate the animals. If the ringmaster calls out, "All join the parade," the children imitate any animal they wish.

Teaching Suggestions
Call out names of mechanical objects, such as bulldozer, truck, or washing machine.

Squirrel and Nut (Levels I–II)

Formation   Rows
Equipment   Word cards
Players   Class
Academic concepts   Language arts—word recognition

The children sit at their desks with their heads resting on one arm. The other arm is held to the side with the hand in an open position. One child, who is chosen to be the "squirrel," carries a word card and moves quietly around the room. When the squirrel drops the "nut" into the hand of a player, that person jumps up, correctly pronounces the word on the card, then tries to tag the squirrel before the squirrel can reach her own seat.

Teaching Suggestions
1. Prepare sets of word cards for current science, social studies, or other subjects.
2. Have players hop, skip, or travel using other locomotor skills.

Mirror Mirror (Levels I–II)

Formation   Scattered
Equipment   None
Players   Class
Academic concepts   Language arts—letter recognition; mathematics—whole numbers

Arrange the class into pairs with players facing each other. Number players 1 and 2. On signal, player 1 begins to perform a movement, such as winking, moving a finger, or hopping on one foot. Player 2 must copy the actions of player 1 until the teacher calls "Change." When this occurs, the players exchange roles. When the teacher calls "New mirror," everyone must find a new partner and the game continues.

Teaching Suggestions
1. Have players limit movements to making letters or numbers with their bodies.

2. Add other aspects of movement, such as letters that include moving quickly and slowly or numbers that require the use of a small piece of equipment (e.g., ruler, pencil, etc.).

Water Cycle (Levels II–III)

Formation   Rows
Equipment   Chalk and ball
Players   Class
Academic concepts   Science—water cycle; language arts—synonyms, antonyms, homonyms, and consonant blends; mathematics—addition, subtraction, multiplication, and fractions

Arrange players into teams of six players, sitting at their desks and facing the front of the room. The first player is assigned water vapor, with the remaining players assigned rain, land, stream, river, and ocean, respectively. The first player calls out "Water vapor," passes the ball over his head to the next player, who holds it while "Water vapor" runs to the end of the row. The second player calls out "Rain," repeats this action, then everyone moves up one seat. The first team to complete two water cycles wins the game.

Teaching Suggestions
1. The teacher calls out a word, such as, "Cold," and the first player on each team runs up and writes it on the chalkboard. The second player must write the first letter of a synonym, such as *C* for *cool* or *chilly,* just below *cold.* The third player adds the next letter. This procedure continues with the other players until the synonym is written.
2. Repeat game 1 with antonyms, homonyms, and consonant blends.
3. Repeat game 1 with addition, subtraction, multiplication, and fraction problems. For example, in a multiplication challenge such as "7 times table," the first player runs to the chalkboard and writes "$7 \times 1 = 7$." The next player follows with "$7 \times 2 = 14$," and so on until the last player has had their turn.

Knots (Levels II–III)

Formation   Circle
Equipment   None
Players   Six to eight per group

Players begin standing together in a small circle, with their hands at their sides. On signal, all players move their hands forward and grasp other players' hands. Players who are standing next to each other cannot hold hands. When everyone is holding hands, the group, without letting go, begins to untangle itself and return to the original circle formation.

Beanbag Pile (Levels I–III)

Formation   Sitting on the floor in rows
Equipment   One beanbag for each member
Players   Five or six in each row
Academic concepts   Mathematics—counting

Players are seated in a single line formation with beanbags placed in a pile in front of the first player in each line. On the signal "Go," the first player takes a bag and passes it to the second player. The remaining beanbags are passed back one at a time. The last player places the first beanbag on the floor. Each succeeding bag must be placed on top of the other, with only the first beanbag touching the floor. The stack must stand without any assistance from the stacker. If the stack falls, it must be restacked. The first team to pile the bags correctly, and call out the total number of beanbags, wins the relay.

Teaching Suggestions

1. Change position of players, such as kneeling or standing.
2. Require all players to run on the spot or perform other movements while passing the beanbag.

Poorhouse (Levels II–III)

Formation   Semicircle or horseshoe formation
Equipment   None
Players   Class
Academic concepts   Mathematics—subtraction and multiplication

Players choose partners and sit in chairs placed in a horseshoe pattern. Two chairs representing the "poorhouse" are placed at the open end of the horseshoe. Each pair has a number and must keep their hands joined throughout the game. The game begins with the pair in the poorhouse calling out two numbers, such as "two" and "six." The pairs whose numbers are called must change places. During the changeover, the poorhouse pair attempts to reach the chairs of "two" or "six" before the exchanging pairs reach these vacated chairs.

Teaching Suggestions

Integrate math skills with this game. For example, saying "16 ÷ 4" and "8 − 6" would require pairs 4 and 2, respectively, to exchange positions.

Who's Leading? (Levels II–III)

Formation   Circle formation
Equipment   None
Players   Class

One player chosen to be "it" stands outside the circle with his hands over his eyes. The teacher then selects a player in the circle to be the "leader." The leader starts any motion she chooses (blinking her eyes, waving her arms over her head, etc.). "It" opens his eyes and tries to guess who the leader is. As the game progresses, the leader slyly switches to other movements and "it" tries to find this person. Allow two or three guesses, then change the leader and "it."

Balloon Hit (Levels II–III)

Formation   Desks and chairs moved back against the wall
Equipment   Balloons
Players   Scattered

Every player has a balloon. Each child keeps her balloon in the air by hitting it with her "best" hand. Later add "other hand," "elbows," "hit and turn around," "hit and touch the floor," and so on.

Teaching Suggestions

Have half of the class play against the other half. Have them sit or kneel in a scattered formation and use five balloons. Use walls for goals and add other rules as necessary.

Quiet Classroom Games

My Ship Is Loaded (Levels I–II)

Formation   Seated on floor
Equipment   Utility ball (nine or thirteen inches)
Players   Class divided into groups of three or four players
Academic concepts   Language arts—word recognition and memory; social studies—neighborhood and community; health—nutrition

One child starts by rolling a ball to another and saying "My ship is loaded with cars" (or any cargo he wishes). The player who receives the ball repeats what the first child said and adds a new item as she rolls the ball to another player. He would say, "My ship is loaded with cars and hats." Each player in turn adds a new item. When a child fails to repeat all the "cargo," the ball is given to the player on her right, who starts a new game.

Teaching Suggestions

1. Use one classification, such as clothing, food, or neighborhood.
2. Change to opposites—the first player calls "boy," second calls "girl." The third player starts a new word.
3. Have the first player perform a movement, such as scratching his ear. The second player begins scratching her ear, then adds a new movement, such as tapping her knees. This procedure is continued around the circle until someone forgets a movement or performs any movement out of sequence.

Clappers (Levels I–II)

Formation   Circle
Equipment   None
Players   Eight to ten per group
Academic concepts   Language arts—syllables

Arrange groups into small circles around the classroom. The first player in each group claps the number of syllables in her first name, pauses for two seconds, then claps the number again. She continues this action, and any other player with the same number of syllables in his or her name joins in. Allow each group to clap five times, then move to the next player and repeat the game. Repeat for surnames and then for a combination of first and last names.

Crambo (Levels I–II)

Formation   Seated
Equipment   None
Players   Class
Academic concepts   Language arts—homonyms

One child chosen to be "it" starts the game by saying "I am thinking of something [inside or outside the room] that rhymes with rain." Other players ask, "Is it a train?" "Is it a drain?" and so on. The child who guesses correctly becomes "it."

Hat Race (Levels I–III)

Formation   Rows
Equipment   Ruler and hat
Players   Class

Every other row participates. All players stand in the aisles with rulers in their right hands. The first player has a hat, which he places on his ruler. On the signal "Go," he passes the hat over his right shoulder to the next player, who takes the hat with her ruler and passes it over her shoulder to the next player, and so on. The last player in the row walks down the empty aisle to the front of his line. If a player drops the hat, she must pick it up with the ruler; no hands are allowed. Everyone shifts back one position, and the relay continues until all players are back in their original positions.

Teaching Suggestions
Try the game sitting down.

Rattlesnake and Bumblebee (Levels II–III)

Formation Seated at desks or tables
Equipment Two small unlike objects
Players Two equal teams

One player is chosen from each team and sent out of the room. While the two players are out, team captains hide the two articles (team A hides for team B, and vice versa). The two players return and begin looking for their articles. Members of either team "buzz" or "hiss" according to how close each player is to his object. Repeat with two new "finders." One point is awarded for the player, and her team, who finds the object first.

Human Checkers (Level III)

Formation Chairs in a row
Equipment Seven chairs
Players Six on each team

Place seven chairs in a row. Three girls sit on the three chairs at one end, and three boys sit at the other end. The object is to move the girls to the boys' chairs and the boys to the girls' chairs in fifteen moves. Only one move can be made at a time. Moves are made by sliding into an open chair or "jumping" over one person. Players cannot move backward. For example, girl number 3 moves to the spare chair; on the second move, boy number 4 jumps girl number 3, who is now in the spare position, and so on.

Puzzled Words (Level III)

Formation Groups of five to eight players
Equipment Pieces of paper
Players Class
Academic concepts Language arts—letter and word recognition

Organize the class into groups of five to eight children. Give each group a pile of letters that, after reshuffling, will form a word. On signal from the teacher, each group tries to put its word together. The first team to assemble its word wins the game.

Teaching Suggestions
1. After the group puts the word together, allow it to act out the word for the other children to guess.
2. Add three or four piles to each group. When assembled the words would form a phrase or short sentence.

3. Place a set of twenty-six randomly organized cards (one for each letter) in the front of each group. On signal, the first player runs up, finds letter A, and brings it back to his team. Continue game until all cards have been picked up. First team to finish wins the game.

Spell Act (Levels II–III)

Formation Two teams on opposite sides of the room
Equipment None
Players Class
Academic concepts Language arts—spelling

Play this game as a regular spelling match. The letters A and T must not be spoken but must be indicated as follows: *A:* scratch right ear and raise left hand; *T:* scratch left ear and raise right hand.

Teaching Suggestions
1. Change movements for letters *A* and *T*.
2. Use the body to form letters for *A* and *T*.

Charades (Level III)

Formation Small groups
Equipment None
Players Class divided into five or six groups
Academic concepts Social studies—geographical areas; science—species of animals

Each group is allowed sufficient time to work out a charade. A captain is elected from each group. The word or object chosen by a group should have syllables to make it easier to act out. All dramatizations must be in pantomime. One group acts out its charade in front of the class. The captain of the group asks the class to guess the syllable or complete word. If the word is not guessed within a certain time, the captain tells the class and the next group has its turn.

Teaching Suggestions
Ask the class to decide on a specific category from which all words must be chosen, such as books, cities, famous names, songs.

C O N C E P T

15.2 *Grid Activities Can Be an Effective Medium for Teaching Academic Concepts and Skills*

GRID ACTIVITIES

A rectangle, square, or specially designed grid, such as the shape of an animal, can become a vigorous and enjoyable activity as well as an effective learning medium for young children. For classroom use, grids can be drawn on the floor with chalk and easily removed with a rag or brush. However, it is recommended that classroom grids be made on plastic sheets, as this allows the teacher to pre-design a variety of grids suited to different levels of academic and physical ability and available floor space. The

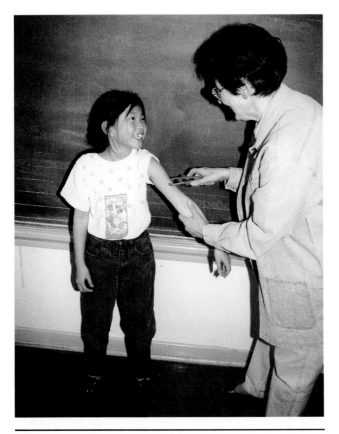

Figure 15.2 Physical fitness testing can be a classroom activity.

Figure 15.3 Simple calisthenics in the classroom.

sheets can be taped to the floor for use, then easily stored away for subsequent lessons.

The grid activities described in chapter 14 (see p. 289 for additional ideas) illustrate how to design and use grids to teach a variety of academic concepts and skills. Each teacher should adapt these grids and accompanying tasks to meet the level of ability and interest of his class. Additional modifications can be made to accommodate children with disabilities—for example, task cards can be attached to strings for children in wheelchairs.

PHYSICAL FITNESS ACTIVITIES

A variety of physical fitness activities can be performed in the classroom. The following examples illustrate how physical fitness tests and circuit training can be performed in the classroom with a minimum amount of furniture adjustment or noise disturbance to adjacent classrooms.

Physical Fitness Testing

Several test items in AAHPERD'S Physical Best fitness test can be easily administered in the classroom (figure 15.2). These items include curl-ups, push-ups, trunk lift,

body composition, and back-saver sit-and-reach. Other cardiovascular activities, such as measuring heart rate and blood pressure or conducting the following cardiovascular experiments (see chapter 8), are easily adapted to the classroom.

Experiment 1: Comparative heart rates
Experiment 2: Heart rate recovery
Experiment 3: Effect of different activities
Experiment 4: Excitement and fear

Calisthenics

Simple calisthenics, with or without musical accompaniment, are some of the easiest activities to perform in the classroom (figure 15.3). Once children appreciate the space limitations, they can do the exercises beside their desks or wherever space is available in the classroom. Brief circuit-type activities, described in chapter 8, also can be designed for the classroom. The advantages are that the teacher can develop a basic circuit that does not require any mats or other equipment and that all children begin and stop after a set number of minutes. In addition, where noise is a problem between adjacent classrooms, circuits can be performed in relative silence and without using a whistle or loud voice to give or change directions.

GYMNASTIC AND MOVEMENT SKILLS

Gymnastic and movement skills include a large number of activities that can be performed in the classroom with a little planning. Such activities as individual stunts and movement skills (chapter 25), small equipment and partner activities (chapter 26), and a few large apparatus skills (chapter 27) can be adapted to the limited space of the regular classroom. The following stunts do not require a mat and thus are more appropriate for classroom use.

Figure 15.4 Performing skills with a beanbag.

Other individual movement skills—shapes, weight bearing, and simple sequences—could also be practiced on the available floor space.

Small Equipment

Classroom use of small equipment, such as beanbags, individual ropes, and hoops, is growing in popularity (figure 15.4). Schools that have adopted daily physical education programs and have limited gymnasium facilities are using the classroom as an alternate exercise area. Since small equipment can be easily transported, it has many classroom applications.

The following activities can be performed in the aisles or in a cleared area at the back of the room.

Beanbag activities, p. 552
Individual rope activities, p. 555
Hoop activities, p. 566
Wand activities, p. 567

Juggling Activities

The basic juggling skills described in chapter 26 can be practiced in a classroom or hallway (figure 15.5). Begin with scarves; as skill improves, gradually introduce bags or balls. If lighting fixtures present a potential hazard, restrict juggling activities to "safe areas" in the classroom or hallway.

Large Apparatus

The use of large apparatus in a typical classroom is limited by the size and weight of the apparatus. However, some

Figure 15.5 Juggling skills can be practiced in the classroom.

companies produce large apparatus that is light, collapsible, and capable of numerous arrangements. Agility apparatus provides several different levels to complement the partner movement challenge. See also chapter 27.

Combining Large and Small Equipment

Figure 15.6 illustrates how station work and a rotation system give every child an opportunity to use a variety of small equipment and large apparatus. Since the area is crowded with equipment, the lesson emphasizes matching balance activities. The task for every station is to develop a matching sequence with one piece of equipment. In this case, movement is limited to the space immediately around each piece of equipment.

RHYTHMIC AND DANCE ACTIVITIES

The classroom setting has numerous advantages when teaching rhythmics, singing games, and folk dance activities. For older children, the familiar environment of the classroom can prove to be a stepping stone for more complex and creative movements in the gymnasium.

Rhythmic Activities

The rhythmic activities described in chapter 28 can easily be performed in the classroom (figure 15.7). It is suggested

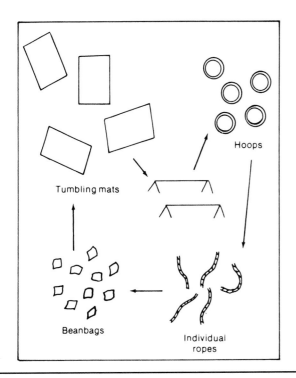

Figure 15.6 Small equipment and large apparatus.

Figure 15.7 Rhythmic activities.

that the same progression—moving from individual to partner to group activities—be followed. Small equipment, such as beanbags, individual ropes, and rhythm sticks, can also be used in the classroom with only minor adjustments. If the noise of a record player or drum is distracting to adja-

cent classrooms, limit the accompaniment to light drumbeats or encourage the children to move in a rhythmic pattern without musical accompaniment. In fact, this will produce some very interesting results.

Singing Games and Folk Dances

Young children, particularly those in kindergarten and first grade, thoroughly enjoy the singing games described in chapter 29. The classroom provides an informal atmosphere in which to learn the words of these games and to practice the basic steps and rhythm patterns. Virtually all singing games can be performed in the space available in a regular classroom.

For older children, folk dance steps, positions, and pathways of movements can be taught in the classroom. If the students have had little exposure to folk dance activities, individual and partner activities involving the basic steps and patterns can be performed in the classroom. This procedure normally breaks the ice for larger group dances that require the larger space of the gymnasium.

Creative Dance

What has been said about the value of an informal classroom atmosphere when teaching folk dance applies even more to creative dance activities. Students can begin with very simple and "directed" follow-the-leader or matching movements and then gradually be introduced to more creative tasks. In time, more creative challenges involving sound, poetry, or other forms of accompaniment can be introduced to the program. The teacher should review the ideas presented in chapter 30 to determine what other creative dance activities can be adapted to the classroom.

Although many interesting and exciting physical activities can be performed in the regular classroom, such activities are inadequate for the child's normal growth and development. Teachers should use the classroom to supplement rather than to replace the gymnasium. There are times, too, when the mood of the class dictates a change of pace before shifting to another subject area.

Summary Review

Many physical activities can be taught in the classroom, hallway, or other indoor areas. However, they should be taught in the classroom only when the gymnasium or outdoor instructional areas are not available. Whenever you are using the classroom for physical activities, make sure the area is free of hazards and consider the potential noise and other disturbances to nearby classrooms.

CHAPTER 15

INDIVIDUAL *and* GROUP PROJECTS

1. Make up a list of safety and noise control rules for classroom physical education activities.
2. In groups of two or three, choose games, dance, or gymnastic activities and describe how they can be adapted to the classroom or hallway.
3. In groups of three or four, design a ten-minute circuit that could be performed by all students at the same time and with the minimum amount of noise.
4. Design two grids that could teach academic concepts and skills. The grids should also involve the use of flash cards or the chalkboard.

SELECTED READINGS

Haseltine, P. 1988. *Games for all children.* Oxford, England: Basil Blackwell.

Humphrey, J. H. 1990. *Integration of physical education in the elementary school curriculum.* Springfield, IL: Charles C. Thomas.

Humphrey, J. H., and J. N. Humphrey. 1990. *Mathematics can be child's play.* Springfield, IL: Charles C. Thomas.

———. 1991. *Developing elementary school science concepts through active games.* Springfield, IL: Charles C. Thomas.

Kamiya, A. 1985. *Elementary teacher's handbook of indoor and outdoor games.* West Nyack, NY: Parker.

Turner, L. F., and S. L. Turner, 1989. *P.E. teacher's skill-by-skill activities program.* West Nyack, NY: Parker.

Wnek, B. 1992. *Holiday games and activities.* Champaign, IL: Human Kinetics.

Game and Movement Activities

Game activities constitute a major portion of the elementary physical education program. As children progress through the elementary grades, game activities are given more time and emphasis, and gymnastics and dance less. Consequently, the teacher should clearly understand the organization of games so that she can select and emphasize the appropriate games, skills, and practice activities without unnecessary repetition. The accompanying introduction to PART 6 is provided to offer a sound basis for the effective teaching of game activities. The introduction translates some of the important motor development and effective teaching information, outlined in chapters 2, 3, and 4, into practical teaching situations, and it provides suggestions relating to the use of instructional space, class management techniques, and a variety of teaching strategies. The introduction also provides practical suggestions for introducing children to "inventive" or "creative" game situations. The reader will find in these sections a sound teaching base for the game and movement activities contained in chapters 16 and 17 and the major games and sport activities introduced in chapters 18 through 24.

Chapter 16 includes simple team games, tag activities, and individual and partner games.

Chapter 17 contains modified traditional games and new cooperative games created by children in the primary and intermediate grades. Chapters 18 through 24 are primarily designed for boys and girls in developmental levels II and III. However, teachers of children in developmental level I should also refer to these chapters for more advanced practice activities and lead-up games that can be modified to meet the skills and abilities of younger children.

Each chapter of this part contains a variety of approaches that can be used to teach game activities. There are situations in every grade when skills, rules, and games should be presented in a more structured and direct way. At other times, however, the application of problem-solving methods through creative or inventive games is appropriate. These chapters show how each approach can be used separately and how the structured and problem-solving methods and techniques can be blended into a single lesson or unit of instruction.

Teaching game activities to elementary school children in large instructional areas, such as the gymnasium or playground, can present unnecessary obstacles. The following suggestions relating to the arrangement of the instructional space and class management and control will help each teacher establish an effective learning environment. The section "Developing Units and Lesson Plans" provides a format for each teacher to develop her own games program.

ARRANGING THE INSTRUCTIONAL SPACE

Most schools have one or more large playground areas that are suitable for running and simple tag games but usually too large to handle a class in a normal conversational manner. To overcome this problem, assign one or two children to mark off the instructional area just before the class is taken outside; traffic cones or milk cartons are excellent markers.

Use a similar technique in a large gymnasium. Do not use equipment, such as metal volleyball posts, that can cause injury if knocked over.

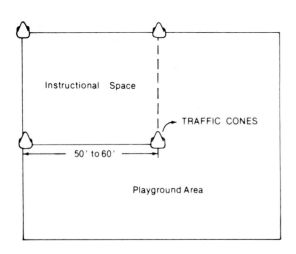

Many of the running and simple team games described in chapter 16 require a lot of beanbags, balls, milk cartons, and other equipment. To ensure maximum use of instructional and playing time, place the equipment in cardboard boxes or nylon sacks and put these in the corners of the instructional area. Team leaders or monitors can do this job extremely well.

CLASSROOM MANAGEMENT AND CONTROL

The following procedures for controlling the class are based on the ideas and practical suggestions for effective classroom management that were presented in chapters 4 and 10, and they can be used by teachers of any grade. Each teacher, of course, will modify the amount of freedom he allows according to his class's maturity and cooperation.

1. Divide the class into four groups. For primary children, use section places 1, 2, 3, and 4. Intermediate children usually prefer to be called *teams* 1, 2, 3, and 4, or to be assigned the names of professional ball teams.
2. Select section leaders or team captains, and be sure to rotate these positions each week to give every child a chance to be a leader.
3. Choose a place for each group to sit whenever you call "Section places"—normally the middle of the instructional area. This is extremely important for good class control. Repeat the procedure until all the children move to their places quickly and efficiently.
4. Follow normal and reasonable safety procedures, paying particular attention to the following:
   a. Tennis shoes should be worn during game activities.
   b. Goal lines should be drawn a reasonable distance from the end or side walls—three to five feet for moderately active games and six to ten feet for vigorous games.
   c. Require that, if possible, glasses and other personal items, such as chains and baggy sweaters, be removed.

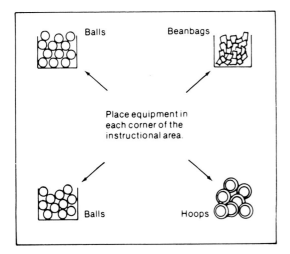

EFFECTIVE USE OF STATION WORK

To illustrate the station work technique, let us assume that a third-grade class knows how to play chair bowling and four square. The teacher wishes to introduce beanbag horseshoes and barnyard golf in the next lesson. During the first few minutes of this lesson, the teacher assigns each team to a station. Brief demonstrations of beanbag horseshoes and barnyard golf are given before each team is allowed to play its assigned game. Each game is played for a few minutes. The teacher then asks the class to stop, return the equipment to its original position, and rotate to the next station. This procedure continues until all the teams

have played the four games. If time does not permit the class to complete the rotation, pick it up in the next lesson.

DEVELOPING UNITS AND LESSON PLANS

A description of how to develop yearly, unit, and daily instructional programs is presented in chapter 9, and comprehensive examples can be found in the accompanying text *Yearly Programs, Units, and Daily Lesson Plans* by Kirchner and Fishburne (1998). Briefly, three basic types of units can be used to organize and teach game activities. Primary teachers often use the multiple unit to cope with the unique characteristics of young children. However, care should be taken to ensure that too much variety does not impede the continuity that is usually needed to ensure effective learning. Intermediate teachers tend to adopt solid or modified units when planning their games program. All teachers, however, should review the advantages and disadvantages of each type of unit before deciding on a particular one. Each unit may also be modified to cope with each local teaching situation.

It is impossible to recommend a standard lesson plan for every teacher to follow rigidly when teaching game activities. However, all lesson plans should follow the "set-body-closure" format. Also, each teacher must adapt to differences in the children's maturity and skill levels, the time allotment, and the supplies available.

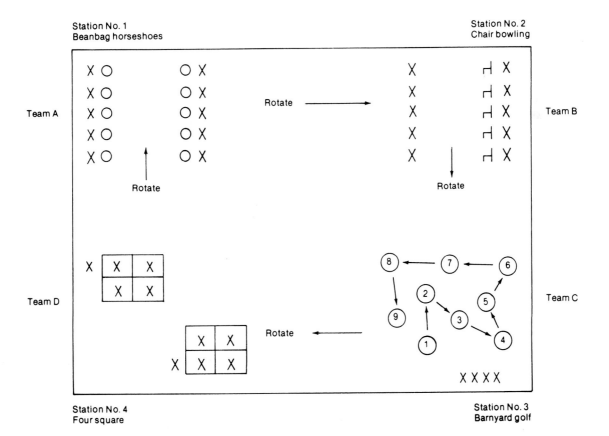

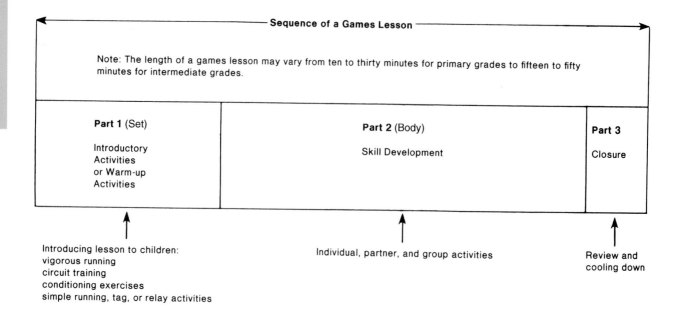

All game lessons begin with stretching and a vigorous warm-up activity such as running, conditioning exercises, or a vigorous tag game (see chapter 16). This is also the time to get the children "set" for the main "body" (skill development) of the lesson. The basic progression for acquiring game skills moves from individual to partner to group activities. This allows a child to practice a skill or movement pattern by herself during the initial phase of part 2 of the lesson, skill development; she then proceeds to partner activities, which is the next step within part 2. With two performers, many more challenges and variations can be introduced; dual activities can also provide important lessons in sharing, give and take, and other forms of cooperative behavior. The latter phase of part 2 is devoted to group activities that stress the skills acquired earlier in the lesson. Finally, closure (part 3) provides an opportunity to review the main concepts or skills of the lesson (evaluation). This time is also used as a cool-down period before children return to the classroom.

If a teacher has only fifteen to twenty minutes to teach a games lesson, there might not be sufficient time to complete all parts of the lesson during one class period. A solution to this is as follows. The first lesson starts with warm-up activities, then proceeds with individual and partner activities. Before finishing partner activities, time runs out. The next lesson then begins with a brief warm-up and goes directly to group activities. A similar procedure can be followed with each succeeding lesson as long as the progression is from individual to partner to group activities for each new skill or movement pattern.

TEACHING MAJOR GAMES

All major games require players to be proficient in a number of specialized skills. The question is, how do children acquire these skills? Chapter 2 differentiated between phy-

logenetic and ontogenetic skills. Phylogenetic skills occur in a predictable sequence and develop somewhat automatically. Examples are walking and running. Ontogenetic skills are learned skills that do not appear automatically through growth and maturation. Examples are the specialized sport skills involved in such games as soccer, basketball, football, and softball. Take, for example, the major game of soccer. A soccer player will require the phylogenetic skill of running, but the skill of running while dribbling a ball is a specialized skill that will not develop automatically due to growth and maturation. This is an ontogenetic skill that must be learned through instruction and practice opportunities (see chapter 3). To acquire specialized sport skills, children need instruction and practice opportunities that develop both declarative and procedural knowledge. For example, if learning the soccer throw-in skill, a child will need to know the correct movement pattern that is permissible for the overhead throw-in according to the laws of the game (declarative knowledge). However, this is insufficient knowledge by itself; the child also needs to physically practice the (ontogenetic) specialized throw-in skill (procedural knowledge).

Further, progression to the third phase of motor learning, known as the automatic stage of skill development (see chapter 3), requires many practices. Unfortunately, in most competitive major game situations children compete for the same ball and do not receive very many practice opportunities. Playing 11-versus-11 full-sided games of soccer, for example, should be minimized during teaching time, since 22 players will be competing for only one ball and most of the children will receive very few practice opportunities in this situation. Although the children will all run and chase the ball (phylogenetic skill), specialized ontogenetic soccer skills (such as dribbling, kicking, and passing) all require manipulative ball skills, and each child requires a ball in order to practice these skills. Without a ball, children will make little progress in developing soccer skills. The same is true for the development of the specialized sport skills associated with most of the major games, where one ball or puck is competed for by many players (e.g., basketball, softball, hockey, football, volleyball).

One further complication is that when a child does receive the ball or puck in a competitive major game situation, she will be under pressure from other players to make quick decisions, and she might have to perform the "whole" skill very quickly. Sound principles of motor learning, such as part-whole learning described in chapter 3, where the child learns a skill in a progression of connected parts, cannot occur in game situations where the child is required to perform the whole skill as quickly as possible. Hence, playing full-sided competitive major games is not a very efficient way of teaching large numbers of children specialized sport skills. Effective teaching requires a variety of instructional strategies that involve individual, partner, and small-group activities, where each child is provided with many developmentally appropriate practice opportunities. Lead-up games and mini-games that can be adjusted (see the environmental variables in chapter 4) to create successful practice opportunities, as well as enjoyable game situations, become the basis for teaching children major sports games. To summarize, the implications for teachers of major sports games are these:

1. All major game activities must be developmentally appropriate, to ensure that all children can achieve success and enjoyment.
2. Effective teaching progressions and strategies that include individual practices and lead-up games need to be provided.
3. Children must be provided with many practice opportunities in order for them to progress toward the automatic stage of skill development.

INCORPORATING THE INVENTIVE GAMES APPROACH

The evolution occurring within the elementary school curriculum is essentially a movement from teacher-directed activities toward a learning environment in which the teacher is an important guide or facilitator of children who learn by example, practice, and the joy of discovery. In gymnastics and dance, we have witnessed the gradual incorporation of the Movement Education approach, which fosters exploration, experimentation, and discovery—key elements in the creative learning process. This approach also allows children to develop according to their own intellectual and physical ability and readiness. In essence, the style of teaching exemplified by Movement Education is parallel to the current practices in other areas of the elementary school curriculum.

Running, tag, and simple team games have traditionally been organized and taught on the premise that skills, rules, and strategies should be learned in an orderly and progressive manner. It would seem imperative that any new approach should still use the common terms, such as *throw, catch,* and *kick,* and that the skills and knowledge of the games should still be acquired. The approach that follows can be incorporated into any primary or intermediate games program to teach basic motor skills, as well as to enhance a child's creative development. This approach can be called an inventive, or creative, games approach, but it is essentially the use of the discovery method of learning in the medium of games.

It was explained in chapter 4 that a teacher can change four elements in the teaching situation to affect the motor behavior of children. These same four elements form the structure within which an inventive game can be played. These four elements are: (1) the number of players—a choice among one player, partners, or a group; (2) the area assigned or available for the game; (3) the equipment that is available or chosen by the players; and (4) the rules and skills. Within this structure, teachers and children can develop an infinite number and variety of games. Some of these games lead to the acquisition of standard sport skills, whereas others contribute to fun and the enhancement of creative abilities, and to physical fitness and general motor development.

Games for developmental level I should be predominantly creative. Beyond level I, however, children are exposed to more formal games. They enjoy learning the proper form of a specific sport skill, practicing drills, or playing lead-up games that increase their proficiency.

A structured program at any level can, and should, incorporate the inventive games approach within a unit or a specific lesson. This blending of methods neither confuses nor restricts the learner. On the contrary, it enriches the learning environment and stimulates the creative process, and it helps the child acquire specific motor skills or more complex strategies involving perceptual, cognitive, and motor abilities. The Structure of Inventive Games chart on the next page provides a basic guideline for teaching individual inventive game lessons.

Developmental Level I

There are several ways to organize and teach inventive games to primary school children. Developmental level I is a time when children start to develop schemas and motor programs and begin to improve their overall motor development (see chapter 3). The approach suggested here begins with simple and fairly structured challenges for this age and developmental level, then gradually allows the children to invent or modify games within the limitations imposed by the teacher.

The procedure should be adapted to the ability, maturity, and interests of the class, and the emphasis that the teacher gives to the inventive games approach obviously depends on his philosophy and the nature of the program. However, a major emphasis on creative activity is suggested for primary games programs.

Structure of Inventive Games

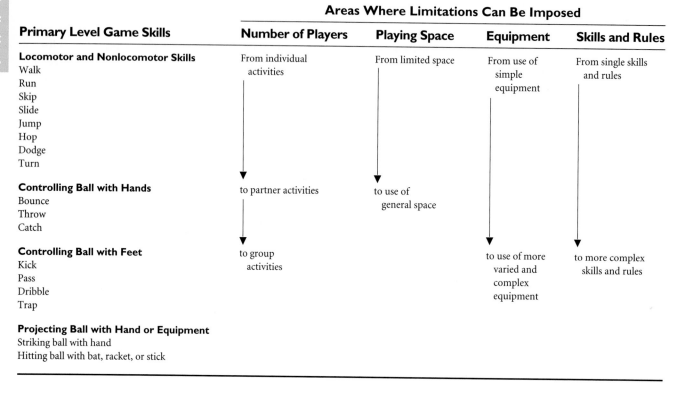

	Areas Where Limitations Can Be Imposed			
Primary Level Game Skills	**Number of Players**	**Playing Space**	**Equipment**	**Skills and Rules**
Locomotor and Nonlocomotor Skills Walk Run Skip Slide Jump Hop Dodge Turn	From individual activities ↓	From limited space ↓	From use of simple equipment ↓	From single skills and rules ↓
Controlling Ball with Hands Bounce Throw Catch	to partner activities ↓	to use of general space		
Controlling Ball with Feet Kick Pass Dribble Trap	to group activities		to use of more varied and complex equipment	to more complex skills and rules
Projecting Ball with Hand or Equipment Striking ball with hand Hitting ball with bat, racket, or stick				

The sample lesson that follows shows how creative games can be incorporated into more formal programs. The lesson plan for creative games has a structure similar to that for plans for other activity areas. The format will vary, of course, according to the children's ages, interests, and prior experiences in creative games.

Example (Developmental Level 1)

Main Emphasis Bouncing a Ball

(This will help develop hand-eye coordination and a motor skill that can be used in formal games such as basketball)

Part 1: Introductory Activity (Set)

If children are accustomed to moving around the floor freely without bumping into each other, have them begin running in different directions. Then have them change speeds, then slide to the right, then to the left. If children are accustomed to warming up by running around the floor and then doing a series of calisthenics, it is not necessary to change the format. After finishing the warm-up, explain what is to follow in the main body of the lesson. A brief question-and-answer session can elicit from the children a need for developing the skill/strategy/knowledge/development that will occur in part 2 of the lesson. Move to the second part of the lesson.

Part 2: Skill Development (Body)

Each child should have a ball; any type of utility ball can be used. Let the children choose their own ball. However, if the balls are different sizes, allocate the bigger ones to children who are less proficient in ball-handling skills. Ask the children to take their balls and find spaces on the floor. When they are properly spaced, pose the following:

1. "Try to stay in your space and bounce the ball very low, then very high." Do not specify one or two hands—let them experiment.
2. "Can you bounce the ball with one hand?" Allow them to practice, then ask, "Can you bounce it with the other hand?"
3. Ask questions that relate to the following skills:
   a. Bounce in different directions (forward, backward, sideways).
   b. Bounce on the floor, then against the wall.
   c. Bounce around small equipment (beanbags, bowling pins, ropes).

Create a game involving the skill that has been practiced. The Structure of Inventive Games chart lists four areas where limitations can be imposed for the games created. As a general guideline, begin at the top and add more complex challenges as the lessons progress. In this first lesson, you could challenge the children to make up a game with a partner, in their own space, using one ball, and requiring a bounce.

Teaching Suggestions

1. Allow sufficient time to practice.
2. Pick out different ways of performing each task and let the other children watch.
3. Praise the children constantly while they are practicing.
4. Ask the children if they can think of another way of bouncing the ball. A child might suggest that they try sitting down or kneeling while bouncing. Have the class try its own challenges.
5. Give the children time to think up a game and practice it.
6. Have a few children demonstrate the games they have created.
7. If time permits, make up a new game and add beanbags, a chair, or a hoop.

Part 3: Closure   Discuss how the groups made up their games and what suggestions they would like to make for the next lesson.

Note: This is a brief ending to the lesson to allow time to make a few comments or to hear one or two suggestions. Avoid too much talking or talking for long periods of time.

General Comments

1. After the children have had time to create and practice their games, select a few for demonstration to the class.
2. Try other variations, such as in partners, in their own space, using two balls and a hoop, and involving a catch.
3. Allow children to make up games with their own imposed limitations.
4. Keep a creative games notebook. Children will create many exciting games that are worth remembering, so record the best ones for posterity. Next year you could use some of these games to illustrate and motivate children to develop similar ones. This project could also be incorporated into the language arts program by having each child or the whole class make up an illustrated creative games notebook.

Developmental Levels II and III

Incorporating the inventive games approach in developmental levels II and III presents some problems for both the teacher and the children. Running, tag, and simple team games are normally selected from a book and taught according to specific rules and regulations. In essence, these are structured activities taught by the direct teaching method. It is possible, however, to add another dimension to these activities by injecting the creative games approach.

The four areas of limitation in the Structure of Inventive Games chart can be used with intermediate children with equal success. Since most children of this age range know and enjoy running, tag, and simple team games, this is the logical place to introduce creative or student-designed games. The first example that follows illustrates how a teacher can begin with a familiar game and transform it into a different and, in most cases, more enjoyable activity. The second example shows how to use the format to develop a framework for more creative student-designed games.

Example 1 (Developmental Level II)

A fourth-grade class appears apathetic in the middle of the afternoon. The teacher decides to take the children outside for a ten-minute game. After a brief discussion, they decide to play dodgeball using two balls. The game is played for a few minutes, then the teacher asks the class to stop and listen.

The teacher has four elements through which she can introduce a change.

1. *Number of players:* Class divided into equal groups
2. *Playing space:* A large circle
3. *Skills and rules:* Throwing and hitting below the waist
4. *Equipment:* Two inflated balls

She decides to pose a challenge by varying the skills and rules. She says, "Start the game over. However, children in the middle must keep both hands on their knees at all times, and the circle players can only roll the ball." After a few minutes of play, she stops the game again and poses another challenge: "In the game you have just played, I changed the rules. Can you think of another rule change that you would like to try?" Several suggestions are made, and the teacher chooses Mary Ann's: "Ms. Brown, since the players inside were put out too quickly, how about all circle players rolling only with their left hand?" (Left-handed players must use their right hands.)

The process of introducing creative, or inventive, games has begun. The main tools are the four elements by which the teacher or the children can impose limitations. As the teacher learns to use the challenge method, she gives more freedom of choice to the children, and with practice, the children appreciate the freedom to modify or create games of their own.

Example 2 (Developmental Level III)

Let us assume that a fifth-grade teacher has experimented with modified tag and simple team games and has noted a positive change in her class's cooperation and enthusiasm. The following suggestions could be tried as part of a regular games lesson or as a ten-minute break:

1. Arrange the class in partners (imposing a limitation on the number of players), give partners a ball and a hoop (limiting the equipment), and tell them to find their own space in the playground area (limiting the playing

space). Pose this question: "Can you make up a game with your partner that includes a bounce, a pass, and your hoop?" (limiting the skills and rules).

2. Join two sets of partners together and pose this question: "With four players, two balls, and two hoops, can you make up a new game that involves all the equipment, a bounce pass, and a dribble?"

3. Now join two groups of four and pose this challenge: "See if you can make up a game using two hoops and one ball."

These examples illustrate how the inventive games approach can be used to modify existing games or to provide a basis for children to invent their own. Children quickly and enthusiastically adapt to this method of teaching. This approach will be used in later chapters, along with more structured methods and techniques, to teach individual skills, rules, and game strategies.

The emphasis that each teacher gives to the structured or inventive games approach will ultimately depend on his own philosophy. Consideration should be given, however, to his own style of teaching—that is, whether he is comfortable with a formal or exploratory approach. An understanding of the type of physical education program the children had in prior grades is another important factor. Finally, the cultural pressures of the community will determine, in no small measure, whether a structured or exploratory approach to teaching game activities will be successful. In the majority of situations, intermediate children have been taught game activities through a structured approach. Hence, it is wise to begin with what the children are familiar with, then gradually inject a few inventive game ideas or challenges to "test the water." Beyond this point, each teacher will emphasize the approach he and his class feel comfortable with.

Locomotor and Manipulative Games

KEY CONCEPTS

16.1 Locomotor and manipulative skills should be taught to children in developmental level I through a generous application of exploratory teaching methods

16.2 Children in developmental level II are in an important transition period in acquiring game skills and strategies

16.3 The major emphasis in a games program for children in developmental level III is on acquiring the knowledge, skills, and strategies of major team and individual sports

16.4 Children from different countries and with different cultural backgrounds play the same games with different names and slight variations in rules

KEY OBJECTIVES

After completing this chapter, you should be able to :

1. Understand the nature and scope of locomotor and manipulative games
2. Apply movement concepts and skills when teaching game activities
3. Teach the basic motor skills of throwing, catching, kicking, and hitting
4. Select and, where necessary, modify game activities to meet appropriate developmental levels of ability and interest
5. Plan and teach a games lesson
6. Incorporate inventive and cooperative game activities into a games lesson

This chapter provides a culturally rich repetoire of locomotor and manipulative games. The purpose and emphasis of these activities vary from level to level. For primary children in developmental level I, particularly those from kindergarten and grade 1, these games provide an important and enjoyable means of acquiring locomotor and manipulative skills. If these activities are taught progressively, with a generous application of exploratory teaching methods, such characteristics as sportsmanship, leadership, and creativity can also be developed naturally.

The purpose of these activities remains the same as children reach developmental level II. This is an important transitional period, however. These children still enjoy running and tag games, but they also are beginning to show a much keener interest in learning the more complex team games such as basketball and volleyball.

By the time children reach developmental level III, the transition is almost complete. The major goal of an upper elementary school games program is to develop knowledge and skills of the major individual and team sports. The running, tag, and simple team games provided in this chapter still have a place in the upper intermediate grades. They are vigorous and enjoyable activities for a classroom break, recess, or warm-up during regular instructional classes.

Numerous suggestions are provided throughout each developmental level to illustrate how locomotor and manipulative games can be used effectively to teach or reinforce academic concepts and skills. These activities can be further adapted or modified to teach other concepts and skills in the elementary school curriculum. The selected readings listed at the end of this chapter provide supporting evidence of the value of these games as a medium through which academic concepts and skills can be acquired. They also are an additional resource for locomotor and manipulative games that can be used to teach a wide variety of academic concepts and skills in language arts, mathematics, science, and social studies.

Also included are a few sample games from an international games project (the best of these games are included in Kirchner [1991]). A few photographs of children playing their traditional games, along with some of their drawings, are provided in each section of this chapter. Teachers and children will note the similarities among children's games, regardless of what country or geographical region they originate in. Several games, such as elastic ropes and marbles, are played in many countries, under different names, but with very similar rules and purposes.

C O N C E P T

16.1 *Locomotor and Manpulative Skills Should Be Taught to Children in Developmental Level I through a Generous Application of Exploratory Teaching Methods*

GAMES FOR DEVELOPMENTAL LEVEL I

The running, tag, and simple team games included in this section contribute to two basic types of game skills. The first, locomotor skills, shown in table 16.1, are extensively emphasized throughout this first developmental level. Manipulative skills relating to rolling, throwing, and catching are also emphasized through individual, partner, and small-group games (figure 16.1). The individualistic

nature of five- and six-year-olds, as well as their motor skill ability, indicates that striking, dribbling, and kicking skills should be taught in small groups and in an exploratory way.

Toward the upper limit of developmental level I, running and tag games are a little more complicated, and simple team games are more structured and require more skill and team play. Because there is such a spread of interests and abilities throughout developmental level I, teachers should try any game from levels I and II that they feel is appropriate. The sample inventive game challenges at the end of this section will illustrate how teachers can design their own challenges to meet the needs, interests, and abilities of their class.

L O C O M O T O R   G A M E S

Squirrel in the Forest

Motor skills Running, dodging, swinging
Movement concepts Personal and general space, traveling
Players Class
Formation Scattered
Playing area Playground, gymnasium, classroom
Equipment None

One-half of the class members are trees and find their personal space in the playing area. The other half of the children are squirrels who run and dodge around the trees without being touched. When a player is touched, he becomes a tree and the tree becomes a squirrel.

Suggestions and Variations
1. Change method of moving to skip, slide, and so on.
2. Change shape and level of trees—sitting, kneeling, and so on.

Figure 16.1 Learning manipulative skills.

TABLE 16.1 Locomotor and Manipulative Games (Developmental Level I)

Name of Game	Type of Game	Players	Motor Concepts and Skills	Movement Concepts and Skills	Academic Concepts and Skills	Page
Locomotor Games						
Squirrel in the Forest	Tag	Half class vs. other half	Run, dodge	Personal and general space, change of direction, change of speed		320
Foxes and Squirrels	Tag	Groups of 3+ taggers	Run, dodge, stop	Personal and general space, change of direction and speed	Mathematics—sets of three	323
Traffic Lights	Run	Class and teacher signals	Walk, run, stop	General space, change of direction, change of speed	Social studies—community safety	323
Fragile Rock	Run	Class and teacher signals	Run, slide	Relationships—sharing		323
Simple Tag	Tag	Class and tagger(s)	Run, dodge	General space, change of direction and speed		323
Automobiles	Run	Class and teacher signals	Run, stop	General space, pathways	Social studies—community safety	323
Red Light	Run	Class and player(s) signals	Run, stop	Change of direction and speed	Mathematics—ordinal numbers and counting	323
Mousetrap	Tag	Circle of players and 5 runners	Run	High and low, change of speed	Mathematics—counting, subtracting, greater and less than	324
Do As I Do	Run	Circle of players and 1 in the middle	Run, jump, hop, etc.	Matching	Language arts—word recognition and following directions	324
Crows and Cranes	Tag	Half class vs. the other half	Run, dodge	Change of direction and speed	Language arts—auditory directions; Mathematics—counting, adding, and subtracting	324
Find Your Letter	Run	Class	Run, slide	General and personal space, change of direction and speed	Language arts—letter and word recognition, vocabulary; Mathematics—whole numbers	324
Hot Spot	Run	Class	Run, stop	Change of direction and speed	Language arts—letter recognition; Mathematics—whole numbers	325
Manipulative Games						
Roll Ball	Roll	1 vs. 1	Roll, catch	Near and far, transfer of weight	Mathematics—adding, cardinal numbers, greater and less than; Language arts—drawing numbers	325
Three Down	Roll	4	Roll	Transfer of weight, strong and light	Mathematics—sets of two, counting, squares and circles	325
Hot Ball	Roll	6–8	Roll, catch	Transfer of weight, change of speed	Mathematics—cardinal numbers and counting	325
Hoop Bounce	Bounce	1 vs. 1	Bounce, catch, slide	Change of direction and speed, transfer of weight	Mathematics—counting; Social studies—social interactions; common goal	325
Two Square	Bounce	1 vs. 1	Bounce, slide	Change of direction and speed	Mathematics—counting; Social studies—taking turns	326
Pirates	Dribble	Class	Run, walk, dribble, dodge	General space, transfer of weight, levels, change of direction and speed		326
Dribble Tag	Dribble	Class	Run, walk, dribble, dodge	General space, transfer of weight, levels, change of direction and speed		326

TABLE 16.1 *Continued*

Name of Game	Type of Game	Players	Motor Concepts and Skills	Movement Concepts and Skills	Academic Concepts and Skills	Page
Butterflies	Throw	1 vs. 1	Throw, catch	Personal space, strong and light, transfer of weight	Mathematics—near and far; Social studies—social interaction; taking turns	326
Throw, Catch, Run	Throw	1 vs. 1	Throw, catch, run	Personal and general space, change of direction and speed		327
Quoit Tennis	Throw	1 vs. 1	Throw, catch, run	Change of direction and speed	Social studies—social interaction; sharing a common goal	327
Simple Dodgeball	Throw	Class	Throw, catch	General space, transfer of weight, change of direction and speed	Mathematics—counting; Social studies—social interaction; working together	327
Steal the Crowns	Retrieve	One-half of class vs. the other half	Run, retrieve	General and personal space, change of direction and speed	Mathematics—subtraction and greater and less than; Language arts—listening; remembering directions	327
Jump the Shot	Jump	5–6	Jump, turn	Levels, strong and light	Mathematics—radius of a circle and quick and slow	327
Snowball	Throw	Class	Throw, run, dodge	General space, transfer of weight, change of direction and speed	Mathematics—subtraction and sets	328
Beanbag Basket	Throw	1 vs. 1	Throw	Transfer of weight, strong and light	Mathematics—counting, adding, greater and less than, and near and far	328
Name It	Hop	5–6	Hop	Personal and general space, pathways	Language arts—letter recognition	328
Queenie I.O.	Throw	5–6	Hop, run, throw, catch	Near and far, change of direction and speed	Social studies—social interaction; working together	328
Call Ball	Throw	6	Throw, catch	Transfer of weight, change of direction	Mathematics—whole numbers; adding and subtracting	329
Soap Box Soccer	Dribble	3	Dribble, run	General and personal space, change of direction and speed	Mathematics—sets	329
Crab Soccer	Kick	Class	Kick	Balance, general space, change of direction and speed		329
American Hopscotch	Throw	1 vs. 1	Throw, hop	Personal space, transfer of weight	Mathematics—counting and greater and less than	329
Marbles	Dribble	2–4	Dribble	Personal space, strong and light, change of direction	Mathematics—adding, subtracting, greater and less than, and diameter and radius of a circle	330
Jacks	Throw	2–4	Throw, catch, balance	Strong and light, personal space, levels	Mathematics—counting and sets	331
Tetherball	Hit	2	Hit	Strong and light, transfer of weight, change of direction and speed		331
Inventive Games	All skills	Individual to group	All skills	All movement concepts		331

Foxes and Squirrels

Motor skills Running
Movement concepts Relationships, personal and general space
Players Class
Formation Scattered in groups of three
Playing area Playground or gymnasium
Equipment None
Academic concepts Mathematics—sets of three

Choose three children to be the foxes. All other children are arranged in groups of three. Numbers 1 and 2 of the group join hands overhead to form a tree. Number 3 is the squirrel and stands under the tree. On signal from the teacher, squirrels run to find a new tree and foxes try to tag a squirrel before she reaches a new tree. Only one squirrel is allowed under a tree. When a fox catches a squirrel, they change positions on the next turn. Repeat game after all squirrels are tagged or under a new tree.

Suggestions and Variations

1. After three turns, have players return to their original positions. Rotate players and continue game.
2. Change method of moving, to skipping, walking, or sliding.

Traffic Lights

Motor skills Run, walk, stop
Movement concepts Traveling, change of direction and speed
Players Class
Formation Scattered
Playing area Playground, gymnasium
Equipment None
Academic concepts Social studies—community safety

Ask children to find their own space. Teach signals. Red means stop, yellow means walk, and green means run. On signal, all children begin to move according to the teacher's signals.

Suggestions and Variations

1. Have children change direction after each signal.
2. Change locomotor skills for yellow and green.

Fragile Rock

Motor skills Run
Movement concepts Relationships—sharing
Players Class
Formation Scattered
Playing area Playground, gymnasium
Equipment Beanbags

Every player places a beanbag on the floor, then places one finger on the beanbag. On signal from the teacher, who is a rock collector, all children begin to run in different directions. While children are running, the rock collector picks up three or four beanbags, then calls out, "Go home!" All children run and place one finger on a beanbag. Two or more players may place one of their fingers on a rock (beanbag). Continue game until only three or four "rocks" are left.

Suggestions and Variations

1. Use hoops instead of beanbags and have players stand inside hoop.
2. Repeat game with different parts touching the rock.

Simple Tag

Motor skills Running, dodging
Movement concepts General space, change of direction
Players Class
Formation Scattered
Playing area Playground, gymnasium
Equipment None

One child is chosen to be "it." All players are scattered within a designated playing area. "It" tries to tag another player. When a player is tagged, he must call out, "I'm it," and the game continues.

Suggestions and Variations

1. Vary the locomotor skill, such as requiring all to hop or skip, or require animal walking movements such as crab walk or bear walk.
2. "It" tags a particular part of the body, such as the side, back, or leg.
3. Any player is safe who assumes a particular position, such as balancing on one foot, crouching, or standing back-to-back with another child.
4. Add one or more taggers.
5. Two or three players are assigned to be "it." They remain "it" for a set period of time (teacher sets time limit). Taggers try to tag other players. When a player is tagged, she forms a bridge with her body. When another "free" player can crawl under the "bridge" without being tagged, the "bridged" player can join the game again.

Automobiles

Motor skills Run, stop
Movement concepts General space, pathways
Players Class
Formation Scattered
Playing area Playground, gymnasium
Equipment None
Academic concepts Social studies—community safety

The teacher stands in the middle of the circle. On "Go!" the children run around the circle, pretending to be automobiles. A child may move out to "pass" another but must then move back into the circle. No one may reverse directions. When the teacher calls "Stop" or blows a whistle, everyone must come to a full stop. A player who fails to stop or who bumps into another player must run and touch the teacher, then return to his place in the circle.

Suggestions and Variations

1. Play the same game moving in a reverse direction.
2. Substitute hand signals or flash cards for "Go" and "Stop."
3. Change game to "animal pass." Children move like crabs, monkeys, and so on, and follow the same rules as automobiles.

Red Light

Motor skills Run, stop
Movement concepts Change of direction and speed
Players Class
Formation Two lines drawn across ends of playing area
Playing area Playground, gymnasium

Equipment None
Academic concepts Mathematics—ordinal numbers, counting

One player chosen to be "it" stands on one line with her back to the opposite line. All other players stand on the opposite line. As "it" begins to count to ten, all players begin running toward her line. At any time before reaching ten, "it" may call out "Red light!" and turn around. If "it" sees anyone moving, she sends him back to the opposite line. The game continues until a player crosses the line. That player becomes "it" and the game starts over.

Suggestions and Variations
1. Use a variety of locomotor movements.
2. Use letters or children's names instead of numbers.
3. Change to counting by twos, fours, tens, etc.

Mousetrap

Motor skills Run, dodge
Movement concepts High and low, change of speed
Players Class
Formation Circle
Playing area Playground, gymnasium
Equipment None
Academic concepts Mathematics—counting, subtracting, greater and less than

Five children are chosen to be "mice," while the remaining children form a large circle called the "trap." The teacher starts the game with the mice outside the circle and the circle players holding hands. When the teacher says, "Open trap," the circle players raise their hands as high as their heads and hold them in this position. The teacher then calls, "Run, little mice, run!" and the mice run freely in and out of the circle. When she says, "Snap," the circle players lower their joined hands. Any mice caught inside the circle must join the circle players. Continue until all mice are caught. Choose new mice and repeat the game.

Suggestions and Variations
1. Always have five "mice" playing; if two are caught, immediately replace with two new "mice" before the next call.
2. Change name to other animals and move in that fashion (crab trap with a crab walk).

Do As I Do

Motor skills Locomotor, inventive movements
Movement concepts Matching
Players Class
Formation Circle
Playing area Playground, gymnasium
Equipment None
Academic concepts Language arts—word recognition, following directions

The teacher stands at the front of the class with two flash cards. One child is chosen to be the first leader and stands in front of the teacher facing the class. The leader begins to perform a movement, such as hopping, running, or walking like a lame puppy. The class does not move until the teacher flashes one of the two cards. If the card "Do This" appears, the class must copy the movements of the leader. When "Do That" is flashed, the class must stop moving while the leader continues to perform his movements. As the game continues, the leader continues to change to other movements and the teacher continues to randomly flash the two cards. Change leaders after two or three different movements.

Suggestions and Variations
1. Have the leader display written directions on flash cards.
2. Limit the game to animal or mechanical movements.

Crows and Cranes

Motor skills Run, dodge
Movement concepts Quick and slow, change of direction
Players Class
Formation Line
Playing area Playground, gymnasium
Equipment None
Academic concepts Language arts—auditory directions; Mathematics—counting, adding, subtracting

Divide class in half and call one group "crows" and the other "cranes." Each team lines up on its center line, facing the other. When the teacher calls, "Crr—ow," the crows turn and run toward their goal line and the cranes try to tag them before they cross it. If a player is tagged, he joins the opposite team. The game continues until the last player is caught.

Suggestions and Variations
1. Draw out the beginning of both words to keep the children in suspense as long as possible.
2. Use other words from the language arts program.
3. Add a third, "neutral" word such as *creep*. If players move when the neutral word is called, they make a funny face or perform a special trick.

Find Your Letter

Motor skills Run, slide
Movement concepts General and personal space, change of direction and speed
Players Class
Playing area Playground, gymnasium
Equipment Letter cards
Academic concepts Language arts—letter and word recognition, vocabulary; Mathematics—whole numbers

Construct a duplicate set of uppercase letter cards. If there are twenty-six children, randomly hand out thirteen pairs of letters, giving one card to each player. On signal, the children begin to run around the playing area. When the teacher calls "Stop," everyone changes to a fast walk, then tries to find the other player with the same letter. As soon as they reach each other, they form the letter with their bodies. When everyone has formed their letter, the teacher calls, "New Letter," signaling partners to separate and begin fast walking until the teacher calls, "Exchange." All children must exchange their cards with the nearest player, and the game continues.

Suggestions and Variations
1. Play same game with words, numbers, colors, or physical objects.
2. Change locomotive skills to hop, jump, etc.
3. Play above games in threes or fours.

Hot Spot

Motor skills Run and stop
Movement concepts Change of direction and speed
Players Class
Formation Scattered
Playing area Playground, gymnasium
Equipment Posters and cardboard cards
Academic concepts Language arts—letter recognition; Mathematics—whole numbers

The teacher scatters three or four cardboard cards for each number from 0 to 9 around the playing area. He holds ten posters with collections of objects, such as four dogs or seven flowers, representing the numbers 0 to 9. When the teacher displays a poster that has five chickens, he asks, "How many?" Each child calls out the name and number of objects and then runs and places one foot on that numeral on the floor. Three or four children may share each card. Continue the game, changing the posters.

Suggestions and Variations
1. Change posters to include sets of objects, such as nine pairs of rabbits, to indicate they must recognize sets of two and run and touch a card displaying a "2."
2. Change cardboard cards to lowercase letters and change posters to display capital letters.

M A N I P U L A T I V E   G A M E S

Roll Ball

Motor skills Roll, catch
Movement concepts Near and far, transfer of weight
Players Class—play in pairs
Formation Scattered
Playing area Playground, gymnasium
Equipment Three balls and one chair for each set of partners
Academic concepts Mathematics—adding, cardinal numbers, greater and less than; Language arts—drawing numbers

Partner 1 stands behind a line with a ball, and partner 2 stands directly opposite, behind a chair. The distance between chair and line is adjusted to create developmentally appropriate challenges. The chair's backrest faces partner 2. The score sheet and a pencil are placed on the seat of the chair. Partner 1 rolls three balls, then changes places with partner 2. Award five points for each ball that rolls through the legs of the chair. The game may be played to any score, selected on the basis of skill and available time.

Suggestions and Variations
1. Hit a milk carton or draw a target on the wall at floor level, rather than using a chair.
2. Substitute beanbags for balls.
3. Bowl backward through outstretched legs.
4. Hit a milk carton placed on other side of chair.

Three Down

Motor skills Rolling
Movement concepts Transfer of weight, strong and light
Players Four per game
Formation Circle
Playing area Playground, gymnasium
Equipment Four clubs, two balls
Academic concepts Mathematics—sets of two, counting, squares, circles

Four clubs are arranged in a square about three feet apart in the middle of an eight-foot circle. Two players are pinsetters. Circle players roll the two balls at the clubs, attempting to knock them down, while the pinsetters keep setting up the clubs. When three clubs are down, the circle players call, "Three down!" Change positions and start a new game.

Suggestions and Variations
1. If pinsetters are too good, reduce to only one pinsetter.
2. Throw or kick the ball.

Hot Ball

Motor skills Roll, catch
Movement concepts Transfer of weight, change of speed
Players Six to eight
Formation Circle
Playing area Playground, gymnasium, classroom
Equipment Ball
Academic concepts Mathematics—cardinal numbers, counting

One child chosen to start the game pretends to set a fire under the ball. She then rolls it and says, "The ball's hot." Circle players try to roll the ball away from them to keep from getting "burned." If the ball goes out of the circle, the person who last touched it becomes "it" and pretends to set the ball on fire again.

Suggestions and Variations
1. Play the same game using feet.
2. Allow circle players to use only the left or right hand to roll the ball.
3. Have children count the number of hits before the ball goes out.

Hoop Bounce

Motor skills Bounce, catch, slide
Movement concepts Change of direction and speed, transfer of weight
Players Two for each game
Formation None
Playing area Playground, gymnasium
Equipment Hoop and ball
Academic concepts Mathematics—counting; Social studies—social interaction, common goal

Two players face each other across the hoop. One player bounces the ball into the hoop so his partner can catch the rebound. Make this a cooperative game by counting one point each time a player catches the rebound. As children become more proficient, have both players move constantly around the hoop as they bounce the ball to each other.

Suggestions and Variations
Have partners add a movement after they have released the ball, such as make a full turn, slide to left and back, and so on.

Two Square

Motor skills Bounce, slide
Movement concepts Change of direction and speed
Players Two per game
Formation Two five-foot squares drawn side-by-side, with one player in each
Playing area Playground, gymnasium
Equipment Ball
Academic concepts Mathematics—counting; Social studies—taking turns

One player stands in each square while the remaining players stand just outside the squares. The player in one square bounce-serves the ball into the other square. (It may be wise to let players throw the ball at first instead of bounce-serving it. As skill increases, require a bounce-serve.) After the ball bounces in the opposing player's square, that player returns it into the server's square by batting it upward with one or both hands. Continue play until one of the following violations occurs:

1. The ball lands out of the square (liners are good).
2. The ball is hit with the fist.
3. The player holds the ball (catches it).
4. The ball is hit downward.

A player committing a violation leaves the game and the next waiting player takes his place.

Suggestions and Variations
1. Play same game with different types and sizes of balls (Nerf, tennis, etc.).
2. Add a trick, such as a bounce hit, then turn around or jump in the air and clap hands.
3. Have waiting players count the number of hits.

Pirates (Germany)

Motor skills Run, walk, dribble, dodge
Movement concepts General space, transfer of weight, levels, change of direction and speed
Players Class
Formation Scattered
Playing area Playground, gymnasium
Equipment Balls

Give about two-thirds of the students a ball and tell them to start bouncing the ball anywhere in the playing area. Scatter the remaining third of the class throughout the playing area. On signal, those without a ball ("pirates") try to steal the ball away from a player who is bouncing a ball. When a player loses her ball, she becomes a pirate.

Suggestions and Variations
Players are safe if they kneel down and dribble.

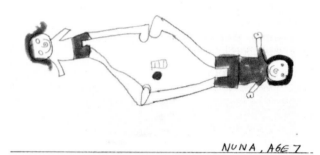

NUNA, AGE 7

Figure 16.2 Butterflies.

Dribble Tag

Motor skills Run, walk, dribble, dodge
Movement concepts General space, transfer of weight, levels, change of direction and speed
Players Class
Formation Scattered
Playing area Playground, gymnasium
Equipment Balls

Players are given their own balls and told to find their own space. Two or three players are designated to be "it." On signal, all players start to dribble their balls with their hands, then "it" attempts, while dribbling, to tag another player. Players exchange positions when tagged.

Suggestions and Variations
1. Players can be safe if they kneel and dribble or are in any other special dribbling position.
2. Play game with series of obstacles (cones, mats, etc.) placed in the playing area.

Butterflies (England)

Motor skills Throw, catch
Movement concepts Personal space, strong and light, transferring weight
Players Two per game
Formation None
Playing area Playground, gymnasium
Equipment One ball and one small container for each set of partners
Academic concepts Mathematics—near and far; Social studies—social interaction, taking turns

Children sit on floor, legs spread (hence the name "Butterflies"). Player 1 throws a ball to player 2. If player 2 catches the ball, she has a chance to throw it into the container and score a point. If player 2 fails to catch the ball, she throws it back to player 1, who has the chance to throw it into the can (figure 16.2). Retake any poor throws.

Suggestions and Variations
1. Move farther apart as skill increases.
2. Use beanbags or different-size balls.

Throw, Catch, Run

Motor skills   Throw, catch, run
Movement concepts   Personal and general space, change of direction and speed
Players   Two per game
Formation   None
Playing area   Playground, gymnasium
Equipment   Post, box, and balls

Arrange post, box, and throwing distance according to the children's level of skill. Player 1 must hold on to the post. Player 2 holds a ball and stands behind the throwing line. Player 2 throws the ball; if it lands and remains in the box, he gets one point and another try. Player 1 must remain at the post until the ball has landed in the box or on the ground. Player 2 throws the ball again; if it does not land and remain in the box, player 2 must fetch it and return it to the box before player 1 can run around the box and back to the post. If player 1 gets back first, they exchange positions. If player 2 gets back first, he gets another turn.

Quoit Tennis

Motor skills   Throw, catch, run
Movement concepts   Change of direction and speed
Players   Two per game
Formation   None
Playing area   Playground, gymnasium
Equipment   Quoit, rope, two chairs
Academic concepts   Social studies—social interaction, sharing a common goal

Place a skipping rope over the backs of two chairs placed about three feet apart. Draw boundary lines on either side of rope. Players throw quoit back and forth over the rope. Emphasize throwing to each other by awarding each player a point each time either player catches a quoit.

Suggestions and Variations
Once skill level is good enough, play competitive game—one tries to throw quoit where opponent cannot catch it.

Simple Dodgeball

Motor skills   Throw, catch
Movement concepts   General space, transfer of weight, change of direction and speed
Players   Class
Formation   Circle
Playing area   Playground, gymnasium
Equipment   Ball
Academic concepts   Mathematics—counting; Social studies—social interaction, working together

Divide class into two teams and place on either side of a line. Players must remain on their side of the line. Players then try to hit each other with a Nerf ball. If a player is hit, she must run to the marker and back before joining the game again.

Suggestions and Variations

Rescue Dodgeball. When a player is hit, he must lie down (or kneel with elbows bent so rescuers can lift and carry him) until another player can pull him to the end line, and both resume playing. However, if a rescuer is hit while trying to rescue her teammate, she must stop and wait to be rescued.

Steal the Crowns

Motor skills   Run, retrieve
Movement concepts   General and personal space, change of direction and speed
Players   Class
Formation   None
Playing area   Playground, gymnasium, classroom
Equipment   Ten to twelve quoits or beanbags
Academic concepts   Mathematics—subtraction, greater and less than; Language arts—listening, remembering directions

Draw two end lines approximately thirty feet apart and divide the play area with a center line and place ten to twelve beanbags or quoits ("crowns") on each end line. Draw a small dungeon on the side of each end line. Divide class in half and place each team behind its own end line. On signal, players from either team try to cross over the center line and steal a "crown." A player cannot be tagged on her own side; however, once she crosses over the line and is tagged, she must go to the dungeon. Players who are tagged while running with a stolen crown must return it before going to the dungeon. Only one prisoner is allowed in a dungeon; hence, when a second prisoner arrives, the "old" prisoner must walk back to her end line before she can enter the game again.

Suggestions and Variations
1. Place one or two hoops on each side as safe houses.
2. Players may stay at a safe house for ten seconds, then must leave.

Jump the Shot

Motor skills   Jump, turn
Movement concepts   Strong and light, levels, quick and slow
Players   Five to six per game
Formation   Circle
Playing area   Playground, gymnasium
Equipment   Rope
Academic concepts   Mathematics—radius of a circle

Center player holds the rope by one end and swings it in a circle, keeping it about one foot off the ground. Circle players try to jump the rope as it approaches. If hit, they are charged with one shot. The game continues for a designated period. The winner, who is the player with the least number of shots charged against him, becomes the "turner" in the next game.

Suggestions and Variations
1. Vary the length and speed of the rope according to level of skill.
2. Have circle players join hands with a partner.
3. Have circle players bounce a ball as the rope is turned; start with a two-hand bounce.

Snowball

Motor skills Throw, run, dodge
Movement concepts General space, transfer of weight, change in direction and speed
Players Class
Formation Two end lines and one center line, with each team scattered on its side of center line
Equipment Balls
Academic concepts Mathematics—subtraction and sets

Divide the class into two equal teams and give each team an equal number of balls (about five or six each). On signal, players attempt to hit opposing players with the balls. Any player who is hit must move to the sideline. Sideline players may retrieve balls and throw them to teammates, but they may not throw them at opponents. The game ends when one player remains.

Suggestions and Variations
Play the same game with both teams grouped in twos or threes.

Beanbag Basket

Motor skills Throw
Movement concepts Transfer of weight, strong and light, near and far
Players Two per game
Formation Line—five feet from basket
Playing area Playground, gymnasium, classroom
Equipment Beanbags and box or basket
Academic concepts Mathematics—counting, adding, greater and less than

Each child is given three consecutive throws at the basket. Award five points if the beanbag goes into the basket, three points if it hits the basket, and one point if it lands within two feet of the basket. After each player completes her throw, she adds up her score, collects the beanbags, gives them to the next player, then waits for her next turn. Add both scores together at the end of the game.

Suggestions and Variations
1. As skill improves, use small baskets or increase the throwing distance.
2. Use Nerf or other soft balls.
3. Change target; for example, to line on floor or square on wall.

Name It

Motor skills Hopping
Movement concepts Personal and general space, pathways
Players Five to six per group
Formation Groups scattered
Equipment Chalk or plastic sheets
Academic concepts Language arts—letter recognition

Draw three or four identical grids on the blacktop or on plastic sheets. (Plastic sheets can easily be stored, and they provide a means of predesigning a series of grids to emphasize a variety of concepts and skills.) Assign five or six children to each grid, and give each child a number. Then call a number and flash a letter. The child whose number is called must hop to the letter, call it out, then hop out of the grid.

Figure 16.3 Queenie I.O.

Suggestions and Variations
The following suggestions will assist teachers in using grids to teach children a variety of academic concepts and skills.

1. Change the size and shape of the grid to suit the ages and interests of the children.
2. Flash word cards and have children hop to each letter of the word.
3. Change grid to pictures and flash words corresponding to the picture on the grid.
4. Change grid to home and neighborhood themes and create games involving the recognition of buildings, people, and places.
5. Change grid to a health theme and create games involving hygiene and safety.

Queenie I.O. (England)

Motor skills Hop, run, throw, catch
Movement concepts Near and far, change of direction and speed
Players Five to six per game
Formation Scattered
Playing area Playground, gymnasium
Equipment Beanbag
Academic concepts Social studies—social interaction, working together

Player throws the beanbag backward over his head in the direction of other players (figure 16.3). After throwing, player 1 remains facing away from them. If the beanbag is caught on the fly without touching the floor, the player who caught it immediately takes the place of player 1 and the game starts again. If the beanbag touches the floor before it is caught, the other players hide it, usually in the hands behind the back, they begin to chant:

Queenie I.O.
Who's got the ball I.O.
It isn't in my pocket

It isn't between my legs
Hop Scotch. (They hop from one foot to the other.)

When chanting begins, player 1 turns around to guess who has the beanbag. To further this aim, player 1 may ask each player in turn to turn around, which they must do, carefully hiding the beanbag if they have it or pretending to hide it if they haven't. Player 1 must also run through the group, and as he passes the other players turn to keep the beanbag concealed. After that, player 1 must make a guess. If he guesses correctly, he takes another turn. If not, the person who has successfully concealed the beanbag takes player 1's place in front.

Call Ball

Motor skills Throw, catch
Movement concepts Transfer of weight, change of direction
Players Six per game
Formation Circle
Playing area Playground, gymnasium
Equipment Ball
Academic concepts Mathematics—whole number recognition, adding, subtracting

Five children form a circle. The center player tosses the ball into the air and calls out a number(s), such as 3, 3 + 2, or 8 − 5 (depending on the age and concepts to be reinforced). The leader then bounces the ball to any player, who must try to catch the ball and give the correct answer before the leader counts to five. Award one point for every correct answer. Keep one group score and change leaders when the group score reaches five.

Suggestions and Variations

1. If skill level is very low, allow one bounce before attempting to catch the ball.
2. Use different types and sizes of balls.
3. Assign each player a consonant blend, such as *bl, cl, gr,* etc. The leader throws the ball and calls out a word that contains an initial consonant blend. Players with consonant blends must call out a word using the consonant, then catch the ball.

Soap Box Soccer

Motor skills Dribble, run
Movement concepts Personal and general space, change of direction and speed
Players Three
Formation None
Playing area Playground, gymnasium
Equipment Ball, traffic cones
Academic concepts Mathematics—sets

A soccer ball is placed on the starting line. Three players hold hands and form a triangle around the ball. They must keep the ball inside the triangle and dribble the ball to the traffic cones and back to starting line.

Suggestions and Variations

Repeat game in groups of two or four.

Crab Soccer

Motor skills Kick
Movement concepts Balance, general space, change of direction and speed
Players Class
Formation Playing area divided into two equal sections, with goals placed on end lines
Playing area Playground, gymnasium
Equipment One ball and two goals

Players from both teams start in a crab walk position and move anywhere in the court area. All players except one goalie for each team remain in a crab walk position. The goalies may use their hands; however, all other players must move the ball with their feet. A foul occurs when a player catches the ball or strikes it with her hands. The teacher should stop the game when a foul occurs and give the ball to the nearest opponent. Award one point for each goal scored.

Suggestions and Variations

1. Practice the crab walk first.
2. After the game is well understood, require striking with hands only or allow a combination of hands and feet.
3. Change to moving on all fours and facing down, and repeat game.
4. Play crab soccer on all "threes."

American Hopscotch

Motor skills Throw, hop
Movement concepts Personal space, transfer of weight
Players Two per game
Formation See Figure 16.4
Playing area Playground, gymnasium
Equipment Buttons, beads, or small objects
Academic concepts Mathematics—counting, greater and less than

The first player stands on his right foot (this is his declared "hopping" foot, and he must use it throughout his turn) outside area 1, holding the "puck" (beanbag, button, etc.) in his hand. He tosses the puck into area 1, hops into this area, picks up the puck while balancing on his right leg, then hops out. He next throws the puck into area 2. He then hops into area 1, straddles ("spread eagle") areas 2 and 3, picks up the puck, hopping and landing with one foot in single spaces and with both feet in adjacent areas. Two hops are permitted in area 10 in order to turn around. A player is out if he steps on a line, tosses the puck onto a line or into the wrong area, changes feet on single hops, or touches his hand or other foot during any hopping or retrieving movement. When a child commits an error, he goes to the back of the line.

Suggestions and Variations

1. French Hopscotch. The game follows the basic rules of American hopscotch, with the player hopping on one foot in single squares and landing with both feet in adjacent squares. However, when a player lands with one foot in area 7 and the other in area 8, she must jump up, turn around in the air, and land in the same areas.

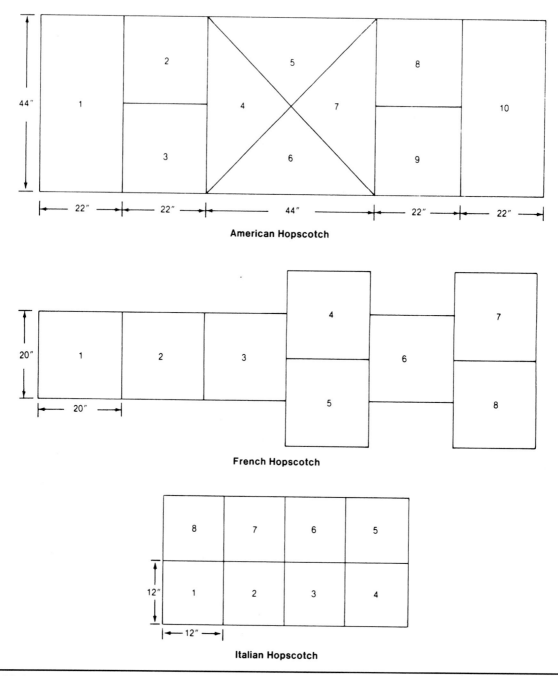

Figure 16.4 Hopscotch.

2. Italian Hopscotch. The first player stands on one foot outside square 1, holding a "puck" (beanbag, etc.) in her hand. She throws the puck into square 1 and then hops into this area. Still standing on one foot, she kicks the puck into square 2, then hops into that square. She continues this pattern to square 8. When she reaches square 8, she places both feet on the ground, picks up the puck, and hops backward through all squares to the starting position. A player is out if she steps on a line, if her puck stops on a line, if she puts both feet down in any square except 8, or if she changes feet. When a child commits an error, she goes to the back of the line.
3. Ask children to design their own pattern (zigzag, circle, etc.) and also make up their own rules.

▨ Marbles (Luxembourg)

Motor skills Throw
Movement concepts Personal space, strong and light, change of direction
Players Two to four
Formation Circle
Playing area Playground, gymnasium
Equipment Marbles
Academic concepts Mathematics—adding, subtracting, greater and less than, diameter and radius of a circle

Each player places one or two marbles in the center of the circle. The playing order is determined by each player throwing his shooting marble (called the taw) toward a line

Figure 16.5   Marbles.

six to ten feet away. The player whose marble is closest to the line shoots first; the player whose marble is next closest shoots second, and so on. A player may shoot from anywhere outside the circle, trying to knock the marbles out of the circle. His taw must remain inside the circle. If successful, he continues from where his taw has stopped (figure 16.5). After all players have had a turn, they remove their taws from the circle. At the end of the game, all marbles should be returned to their owners.

Suggestions and Variations
1. Play doubles. Player 1 of team A shoots until he misses. Player 2 of team A shoots next, followed by player 1 of team B.
2. Exchange taws. Same as marbles except opponents exchange taws.
3. Marble Golf. Sink five or six small cans in a golf course pattern. Use same rules as for Barnyard Golf in the next section.

Jacks

Motor skills   Throw, catch, balance
Movement concepts   Strong and light, personal space, levels
Players   Two to four
Formation   None
Playing area   Playground, gymnasium
Equipment   Jacks and balls
Academic concepts   Mathematics—counting, sets

The first player tosses the jacks on the ground. She then throws the ball into the air. With the same hand, she picks up one jack and tries to catch the ball before it lands. If successful, she places the jack in her other hand and continues playing until she has picked up all the jacks. If unsuccessful, the next player takes a turn. If a player picks up all the jacks, one at a time, she repeats the game, picking up two at a time. Continue with three at a time, and so on.

Suggestions and Variations
1. Pigs in the Pen. Jacks are brushed into the other hand, which is held in a cupped position.
2. Eggs in the Basket. Jacks are picked up and transferred to the opposite hand before the ball is caught.
3. Lazy Susan. The ball is allowed to bounce twice before the jacks are picked up.

Tetherball

Motor skills   Hit
Movement concepts   Strong and light, transfer of weight, change of direction and speed
Players   Two per game
Formation   None
Playing area   Playground, gymnasium
Equipment   See diagram

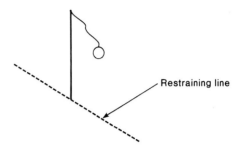

Players stand on opposite sides of the restraining line. One player starts the game by throwing the ball into the air and hitting it in any direction with his hand or fist. The opposing player strikes the ball in the opposite direction only after the ball passes him on the second swing around the pole. The player who winds the ball around the pole first is the winner.

A foul occurs when a player

1. Hits the ball with any part of his body other than his hands.
2. touches the rope or pole.
3. catches the ball.
4. throws the ball.

The penalty for a foul is to forfeit the game to the opponent.

Suggestions and Variations
1. Play "doubles." Players of each team alternate hitting the ball.
2. Play the same game using a paddle.

INVENTIVE GAMES

The following sample challenges illustrate how each of the locomotor and manipulative game skills can be emphasized in small- and large-group games. These challenges are appropriate for children who are closer to the upper end of developmental level I. One of the most important uses of the inventive games approach is to design challenges that emphasize game skills that need extra attention or that help teachers cope with children who have special talents or needs that are not met by the list of games in this chapter.

Locomotor Game

Two players "See if you can make up a game with your partner that must include a run, chasing your partner and using two hoops."

Manipulative Games

Rolling "Can you make up a game for four players where everyone must roll the ball? You can use any four small pieces of equipment in your new game."

CHAPTER 16

Figure 16.6 The transition stage.

Bouncing "Try to invent a new game for three players. You must have a bounce and catch and use one hoop."

Hand dribble "Is it possible to create a game all by yourself where you dribble the ball with one hand and keep your other hand on top of your head?"

Throw and catch "Make up a game for ten players that has a throw and a catch and uses only one goal."

Dribble and kick "Invent a new game for the whole class that includes dribbling the ball with your feet and using ten milk cartons scattered in your playing area."

Hit with small implement "See if you can make up a game with your partner that uses a bat [small paddle or bat made from coat hanger and panty hose—see appendix B] and a small ball."

C O N C E P T

16.2 Children in Developmental Level II are in an Important Transition Period in Acquiring Game Skills and Strategies

GAMES FOR DEVELOPMENTAL LEVEL II

Children in developmental level II are at a transitional stage with regard to game activities (figure 16.6). They still enjoy running, tag, and simple team games. However, during the latter phase of this developmental level, they become markedly more proficient at throwing, catching, dribbling, kicking, and hitting. These changes, along with this age group's psychological and social needs, begin to show a major shift to more organized and challenging team games. Use table 16.2 to select the appropriate games. For low lev-

els of skill and maturity, review the games and suggestions for developmental level I. Conversely, if the skill level and interest are high, do not hesitate to draw from the games listed later in this chapter in table 16.3 or from the lead-up games provided in chapters 18 to 23.

LOCOMOTOR GAMES

■ Loose Caboose

Motor skills   Run, dodge
Movement concepts   General space, change of direction and speed
Players   Class
Formation   Scattered
Playing area   Playground, gymnasium
Equipment   None
Academic concepts   Mathematics—sets

Each group of three forms a line, with each member holding on to the waist of the player in front. The first player is the "engine," the second the "baggage car," and the last the "caboose." Choose two players to be "loose cabooses." On signal, each train tries to prevent a loose caboose from attaching to its own caboose. When a loose caboose does attach, the engine becomes a new loose caboose, and each player moves up one place on the train. If a train pulls apart trying to avoid a loose caboose, this constitutes being caught. Players who have been caught leave the game for one minute.

Suggestions and Variations
1. Change size of groups to four, five, or six.
2. Change method of moving, such as hopping, sliding, or jumping.

■ Back Pass the Beanbag (Australia)

Motor skills   Run, dodge
Movement concepts   Change of direction and speed
Players   Five
Formation   Scattered
Playing area   Playground, gymnasium
Equipment   Beanbag
Academic concepts   Mathematics—counting, multiplying

One person is "it" and stands about twenty feet away from the other four players. She now faces the opposite direction and counts to twenty. The other players stand with their hands behind their backs, passing the beanbag among themselves until "it" calls out "20" (figure 16.7). On that cue, "it" tries to tag one of the players as they all run away, keeping their hands behind their backs, concealing which one of them has the beanbag. "It" must try to catch the player who has the beanbag. Players may secretly pass the beanbag to each other during the game. Once the player with the beanbag is caught, she becomes "it." If a player is caught and doesn't have the beanbag, she can then rejoin the game.

Suggestions and Variations
1. Have players hop or jump or move backward.
2. Have "it" repeat multiplication table instead of counting.

TABLE 16.2 Locomotor and Manipulative Games (Developmental Level II)

Name of Game	Type of Game	Players	Motor Concepts and Skills	Movement Concepts	Academic Concepts and Skills	Page
Locomotor games						
Loose Caboose	Tag	Groups of 3+ taggers	Run, dodge	General space, change of direction and speed	Mathematics—sets	332
Back Pass the Beanbag	Tag	Groups of 5	Run, dodge	Change of direction and speed	Mathematics—counting and multiplying	332
Without Hands	Run	Class	Balance, walk, run	General and personal space, change of direction and speed		335
Stick Touch Tag	Tag	Class + taggers	Run, dodge	General space, change of direction and speed	Mathematics—sets	335
Running Steps	Tag	6–8 players	Run, jump	Personal space, levels, change of speed	Language arts—word recognition and following directions; Mathematics—adding, subtracting, and dividing	335
Numbers	Run	Class	Run, dodge, stop	General space, change of direction and speed, relationships	Mathematics—sets, multiplying, and dividing	336
Steal the Bacon	Tag	12–14 players	Run, dodge, stop	Near and far, change of direction and speed	Language arts—word recognition and parts of speech; Mathematics—whole numbers, adding, subtracting, multiplying, geometrical forms, and dividing; Science—planets, animals, and mechanical objects	336
Red Stop, Green Go	Tag	Class + taggers	Run, stop, dodge	General space, levels, change of direction and speed	Mathematics—sets	336
Crazy Circle	Tag	8–10	Push, pull	Change of direction and speed, strength		337
Mouse and Cheese	Tag	Class	Run, tag, dodge	Change of direction and speed	Language Arts—auditory directions, consonant digraphs, word recognition, prefixes, and suffixes	337
Manipulative games						
Four Square	Bounce	2 to 4	Bounce, catch	Change of direction and speed		337
Progressive Dodgeball	Throw	Class	Throw, catch, dodge	General space, change of direction and speed	Mathematics—counting and subtracting	337
Ricochet	Throw	Half class vs. other half	Throw	Change of direction and speed		338
Bombardment	Throw	Half class vs. other half	Throw, catch, guard	Change of direction and speed		338
Barnyard Golf	Throw	4	Throw	General space, change of direction	Mathematics—adding, subtracting, and averaging	338
Tail of the Rat	Run	Class	Run, manipulative movements	General and personal space, shapes, change of direction and speed		338
Ball Pass	Throw	5–7	Throw, catch, run, dodge	Transfer of weight, change of direction and speed		338

TABLE 16.2 *Continued*

Name of Game	Type of Game	Players	Motor Concepts and Skills	Movement Concepts	Academic Concepts and Skills	Page
Guard Ball	Throw	Class	Throw, catch, guard	Change of direction and speed	Mathematics—adding and subtracting	339
Keep Away	Throw	8–10	Pass, catch, guard	Near and far, change of direction, speed, and levels	Science—electricity	339
Four-Goal Soccer	Kick	Class	Kick, dribble, pass, trap	General and personal space, change of direction and speed	Mathematics—adding and subtracting	339
Goal	Dribble	3	Dribble, shoot, guard	Near and far, change of direction and speed		340
Instant Goal	Dribble	3	Dribble, shoot	Personal and general space, change of direction and speed		340
Trick the Guard	Dribble	2	Dribble, dodge, throw, catch	Change of direction and speed		340
Mimic the Word	Tag	Class	Run, manipulative movements	General and personal space, shapes, change of direction and speed	Language arts—word recognition and suffixes	340
Magic Carpet	Run	Class	Run, dodge	Change of direction and speed	Language arts—word recognition, vocabulary, and sentence structure	340
Place Kickball	Kick	10–20	Run, kick, catch	General space, change of direction and speed	Mathematics—adding, subtracting, averaging, and percentages	341
Boundary Ball	Kick	Half class vs. other half	Kick, trap	General space, change of direction and speed	Mathematics—adding and subtracting	341
Battle Ball	Kick	Half class vs. other half	Kick, trap	General space, change of direction and speed	Mathematics—adding and subtracting	341
Elastic Ropes	Jump	4	Jump	Personal space, change of direction and speed	Mathematics—sets, adding, subtracting, and multiplying	341
Alphabet Game	Jump	1 vs. 1	Jump	Personal space, transfer of weight	Language arts—spelling, prefixes, and suffixes	342
Five-Hole Marbles	Dribble	2–4	Dribble	General and personal space, change of direction, strong and light	Mathematics—counting	342
Softball Croquet	Hit	1 vs. 1	Hit	General space, change of direction, strong and light	Mathematics—counting	342
Long Ball	Hit	10–20	Hit, throw, pitch, catch, run	General space, strong and light, change of direction and speed	Mathematics—counting and averaging	343
Bounce Netball	Volley	12–18	Volley	General space, change of direction, levels		343
Bat Ball	Hit	18–20	Hit, run, throw	General space, change of direction and speed, levels	Mathematics—counting and averaging	343
Inventive Games	All skills	Individual to group	All skills	All movement concepts		344

Figure 16.7 Back passing the beanbag.

Figure 16.8 Running steps.

Without Hands (Zimbabwe)

Motor skills Balancing, walking, running, and sliding
Movement concepts Personal and general space, change of direction and speed
Players Class
Formation Line
Playing area Playground, gymnasium
Equipment Stones

Children stand behind a line with two stones placed on any part of their body. On signal, the children begin to move toward a place designated by the teacher. Once children start moving, they cannot touch the stones with their hands until they reach the designated place. Any player who drops one or both stones must turn around three times, place the stones back on his body, and continue the game. First player to reach the designated place is declared the winner. Repeat game with a new designated place.

Suggestions and Variations

1. Have children hop, skip, or slide while carrying the stone.
2. Have children carry the stone on different parts of their body, such as on their shoulder, elbow, or foot.
3. Play game in twos, with partners holding the two stones between parts of their bodies, such as hips, elbows, or seats.

Stick Touch Tag

Motor skills Run, dodge
Movement concepts General space, change of direction and speed
Players Class
Formation Scattered
Playing area Playground, gymnasium
Equipment Sticks
Academic concepts Mathematics—sets

The game begins with three taggers holding on to a stick. They cannot release their hold as they try to tag another player. When a player is tagged, she holds onto the outside tagger. However, as soon as three players are caught, they pick up the second stick and form a new tagging team. The game continues until the last player is caught.

Suggestions and Variations

1. Substitute a short rope for the stick.
2. As soon as a player is tagged, he must pick up the second stick, hold it over his head, and keep running on the spot until three players are caught.
3. Change the number of taggers to two or four.

Running Steps (South Africa)

Motor skills Run, jump
Movement concepts Personal space, levels, change of direction
Players Six to eight
Formation See diagram
Playing area Playground, gymnasium
Equipment Steps
Academic concepts Language arts—word recognition, following directions; Mathematics—adding, subtracting, dividing

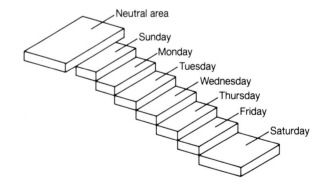

Modify game according to the number of steps that are available. Each step is given a day of the week. The caller stands on the flat surface at the bottom of the stairs and calls out the name of a day. Players must move to the step that was called out (figure 16.8). If they move to the wrong step, they become taggers. If the caller says, "Saturday," all players must touch the bottom step with one foot, then run back to neutral area. The caller tries to tag a player as soon as she touches

CHAPTER 16

Saturday. However, the caller or taggers are not permitted to climb the stairs in pursuit of the player. Change the caller every few minutes.

Suggestions and Variations
Change steps to numbers, verbs, nouns, etc., and repeat game.

Numbers

Motor skills Run, dodge, stop
Movement concepts Change of direction, speed
Players Class
Formation Scattered
Playing area Playground, gymnasium
Equipment None
Academic concepts Mathematics—sets, multiplying, dividing

Class begins in a scattered formation. On "go" signal, players run in different directions. The teacher calls out a number (such as "three"), and all players must form groups of that size. Children who do not make the required group number must make a funny face or sing a rhyme—but no push-ups or the like as punishment.

Suggestions and Variations
1. Have each new group balance on one foot, form a pyramid, or do an additional stunt.
2. Add a ball-bouncing skill to the game—for example, bounce ball at all times, running and forming groups.
3. Change number to a multiplication or division exercise.

Steal the Bacon

Motor skills Run, dodge and stop
Movement concepts Near and far, change of direction and speed
Players Twelve to fourteen
Formation Two lines
Playing area Playground, gymnasium
Equipment Beanbag
Academic concepts Language arts—word recognition, parts of speech; Mathematics—whole numbers, adding, subtracting, multiplying, geometrical forms, dividing; Science—planets, animals, mechanical objects

Two teams line up behind their own end lines. Each player has a number, and the beanbag is placed in the middle of the playing area. The teacher calls out a number, such as four, and player 4 from each team races for the beanbag (figure 16.9). When a player picks up the beanbag, he must run back across his own end line without being tagged by the opposing player 4. If the player is touched by the opposing player before reaching his end line, the opponent receives one point. On the other hand, if the player reaches his end line without being tagged, his team is awarded one point.

Suggestions and Variations
1. Two teams are numbered and stand on a line facing the teacher, who is holding a flag in each hand. The teacher calls a number, such as "five," then the two players with that number race for their flag, run around their own

Figure 16.9 Steal the bacon.

team, return the flag, and go back to their starting position. The player who returns to her own place first wins one point for her team.
2. Change numbers to adverbs. Teacher would call out, "She drives safely," and the two players who are designated as "safely" run out to pick up the beanbag.

1 carefully	5 safely
2 daily	4 early
3 dangerously	3 dangerously
4 early	2 daily
5 safely	1 carefully

3. Change numbers to pronouns, vowels, prepositions, and so on, and repeat the game.
4. In an English as a Second Language Program, change numbers to family names (grandfather, grandmother, son, etc.).
5. Give opposing players on each team a word card with a mathematical definition, such as "four equal sides," "center to circumference," etc. The teacher holds up a word card with the word *radius,* signaling the two opposing players with the cards reading "center to circumference" to run to the teacher.
6. Repeat number 4 with language arts or science words and definitions.
7. Give opposing players opposite words, with the teacher calling out one of these words.

Red Stop, Green Go

Motor skills Run, stop, dodge
Movement concepts General space, levels, change of direction and speed
Players Class
Formation Scattered
Playing area Playground, gymnasium, classroom
Equipment Armbands or chestbands
Academic concepts Mathematics—sets

Three players are designated as "catchers" and wear a red band. Three players are designated as "releasers" and wear a green band. The remaining players scatter in the playing area. On signal, catchers try to tag as many players (other than releasers) as possible. When a player is tagged, he stands still until a releaser can tag him free to move again. The game continues for a few minutes; then change players.

Suggestions and Variations

1. Have tagged players perform a special movement while they are waiting to be released.
2. Play the game in pairs, including the taggers and releasers.

Crazy Circle (Spain)

Motor skills Pushing and pulling
Movement concepts Change of direction, speed, and strength
Players Eight to ten per game
Formation Circle
Playing area Playground, gymnasium
Equipment None

Eight players hold hands and form a circle. One child is chosen to be "it" and stands in the middle of the circle and does not move from this position. On signal, circle players must keep holding hands, then try to maneuver any circle player so the player touches "it." Once a player touches "it," they change positions and the game starts over.

Mouse and Cheese

Motor skills Run, tag, and dodge
Movement concepts Change of direction and speed
Players Class
Formation Circle
Playing area Playground, gymnasium
Equipment Ball and word cards
Academic concepts Language arts—auditory directions, consonant digraphs, word recognition, prefixes, suffixes

Arrange players in a large circle and facing the center. Walk around the circle and assign "ch," "sh," "th," and "ph" successively to the children. Continue assigning digraphs until all children have one. Place a small ball (the "cheese") in the middle of the circle. When the teacher calls out a word such as, "shift," all players who were given the "sh" consonant digraph run around the outside of the circle, then enter the interior through their own space and race toward the cheese. The first player to touch the cheese is the winner. Repeat game with another word and beginning with a new consonant diagram.

Suggestions and Variations

1. Hold up word cards instead of calling out the words.
2. Repeat above game with prefixes. For example: "ad" (advance), "in" (income), "sub" (subtract), and "ob" (observe).

M A N I P U L A T I V E   G A M E S

Four Square

Motor skills Bounce, catch
Movement concepts Change of direction and speed
Players Two to four per game
Formation Sixteen-foot square divided into four 4-foot squares designated as squares A, B, C, and D

Playing area Playground, gymnasium
Equipment Utility ball

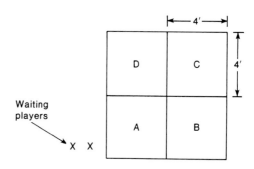

One player stands in each square. The player in square D starts the game by bouncing the ball, then hitting it with one or both hands so that it bounces into one of the other squares. The player receiving the ball hits it after one bounce to any of the other squares. The game proceeds until a player fails to return the ball properly or commits a foul. When this happens, the offending player goes to the end of the waiting line. All players move one square toward D and the waiting player moves to square A.

Basic Rules

1. The ball must arch before landing; it cannot be struck downward.
2. Service always begins from square D.
3. A player may go anywhere to return a fair ball, even out of her own square.
4. The ball may not be held.

Fouls occur when

1. a ball hits any line.
2. a ball is struck with closed fists.
3. a ball hits a player who is standing in his own square.

Suggestions and Variations

1. Two Square. Play same game with two squares, and three or four players.
2. Team Two Square. Same as variation 1, except teammates take alternative turns.

Progressive Dodgeball

Motor skills Throw, catch, dodge
Movement concepts General space, change of direction and speed
Players Class
Formation Three parallel twenty-foot squares designated as A, B, and C
Playing area Playground, gymnasium, classroom
Equipment Ball
Academic concepts Mathematics—counting and subtracting

This game is played in three periods of three to five minutes each. Teams rotate playing areas (A, B, and C) after each period. On signal, a player in one square tries to hit players in either of the other two squares with the ball (below the waist).

No player is eliminated, so a player who is hit should try to get the ball and throw it at an opponent as soon as she is hit. Scores are made by hitting players on another team. The teacher or leader keeps the score for each team, and the team with the highest score after three periods wins. Players may not cross boundary lines.

Suggestions and Variations
Require every player to be constantly on the move.

Ricochet

Motor skills   Throw
Movement concepts   Change of direction and speed
Players   Class
Formation   Two end lines approximately thirty feet from each other, and a center line
Playing area   Playground, gymnasium
Equipment   One large utility ball (twenty-four inches) and approximately twenty small play balls (six inches)

Divide the class in half and arrange students along the end lines, facing each other. Give ten play balls to each team and place the large utility ball in the center of the playing area. On signal, both teams begin throwing the small balls at the large utility ball, attempting to force it over the opponent's goal line. Players may retrieve the play balls from their own half of the playing area; however, they must go back over their own end line before they attempt another throw. The team that forces the ball over its opponent's goal line wins the game.

Suggestions and Variations
1. Have players use different types of throws.
2. Introduce two to four large "throwing" balls.

Bombardment

Motor skills   Throw, catch, guard
Movement concepts   Change of direction and speed
Players   Class
Formation   Players scattered in playing area divided in half, with a four-foot restraining line parallel to and four feet in front of each team's end line
Playing area   Playground, gymnasium
Equipment   Twelve to twenty milk cartons or Indian clubs, ten balls

Place equal numbers of milk cartons or Indian clubs in the two four-feet-deep goal areas. Each team starts with five balls and tries to knock down the cartons or clubs in the opponents' goal area. Players may use their hands or legs to prevent the cartons or clubs from being knocked over. All players must stay on their own half of the playing area. Defending players must also stay in front of the four-foot restraining line. The team that first knocks down all of its opponents' milk cartons or Indian clubs wins. If the game is played in time periods, the team knocking down the most cartons or clubs wins.

Suggestions and Variations
1. Require one or two passes before attempting to score a goal.
2. Use different types of balls.

Barnyard Golf

Motor skills   Throw
Movement concepts   General space, change of direction
Players   Four per game
Formation   Nine hoops or old bicycle tires (or circles drawn on blacktop), scattered and numbered as "holes"
Playing area   Playground, gymnasium
Equipment   One beanbag for each player, nine hoops
Academic concepts   Mathematics—adding, subtracting, averaging

Allow each group of four to arrange its own "golf course," scattering the hoops in the space allocated. Player 1 begins from behind the starting line and attempts to throw her beanbag into the first hoop. If it lands inside or on the rim, she is awarded one point. She then picks up her beanbag and moves to the side of the first hoop and throws her beanbag into the second hoop. As soon as player 1 starts her second throw, player 2 begins his first throw. The game continues until every player has completed the course. The player with the most points wins the game.

Suggestions and Variations
1. This version is more similar to golf. Each player attempts to throw his beanbag into the first hoop. If he fails, he fetches it and tries again. No player can advance to the next "hole" until his beanbag lands in the hoop. This pattern continues around the course. The winner is the player with the lowest score.
2. Tin Can Golf. Sink tin cans into the ground and use old tennis balls and hockey sticks. Play according to the rules of variation 1.
3. Play the above game with partners.

Tail of the Rat (Switzerland)

Motor skills   Locomotor and nonlocomotor
Movement concepts   Personal and general space, shapes, change of direction and speed
Players   Class
Formation   Scattered
Playing area   Playground, gymnasium
Equipment   Tape recorder

This game begins with the players scattered in the playing area. Everyone closes their eyes while the teacher moves through the area and silently touches one of the players to become the "rat." On signal, everyone opens their eyes and begins to move to the rhythm of the music. Suddenly, the "rat" begins to perform a special movement, such as jumping with both hands held overhead. As the "rat" continues to perform this movement, other players who detect that he is the "rat" run behind him and mimic his movements. When the "rat" has six or more players behind him, he stops, spreads his legs, and every player in line must follow his movements. All other players must crawl through their legs. The game starts over with the teacher finding a new "rat" (figures 16.10 and 16.11).

Ball Pass

Motor skills   Throw, run, catch, dodge
Movement concepts   Transfer of weight, change of direction and speed

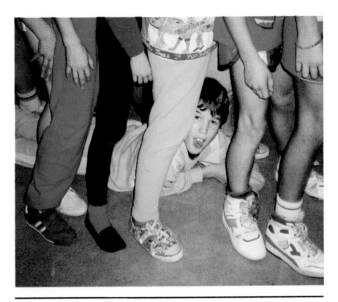

Figure 16.10 Tail of the rat.

Figure 16.11 Children's drawing.

Players Five or six
Formation Circle
Playing area Playground, gymnasium
Equipment Ball

Four players form a circle, and the fifth player stands in the center. One player in the circle has a ball and says "Go." Circle players begin to run counterclockwise and at any time the player with the ball may try to hit the center player below the waist with it. The center player may dodge, jump, or use any other movement to avoid being hit. When the center player is hit, she trades places with the player who hit her.

Suggestions and Variations
1. Vary method of throwing ball.
2. Allow center player to prevent ball from hitting her by using hands.

Guard Ball

Motor skills Throw, catch, guard
Movement concepts Change of direction and speed

Players Class, divided into two teams
Formation A large rectangle (thirty by ninety feet) divided into three equal sections (A, B, and C) with team 1 scattered in center section B and team 2 scattered equally in sections A and C
Playing area Playground, gymnasium
Equipment Ball
Academic concepts Mathematics—adding, subtracting

Players on team 2, using a roll or a bounce pass, try to pass the ball to teammates in the opposite section. The ball must be passed below head level. Players on team 1 attempt to block the passes with their hands. Award one point for each successful pass, and subtract one point when a player on team 1 blocks a pass. Rotate teams every two or three minutes.

Suggestions and Variations
Vary the type of pass.

Keep Away

Motor skills Pass, catch, guard
Movement concepts Near and far, change of direction and speed, levels
Players Eight to ten on each team
Formation Scattered
Playing area Playground, gymnasium, classroom
Equipment Ball
Academic concepts Science—electricity; Mathematics—adding, subtracting

The teacher gives the ball to a player on one team, who then passes it to a teammate. The opposing players attempt to intercept the ball or break up the pass. If successful, they pass the ball to each other. Fouls are called whenever a defensive player grabs or holds onto an offensive player.

Suggestions and Variations
1. Do not let players run with the ball.
2. If adequate space is available, play two games by dividing the class into four teams.
3. If the teams are large and the playing area is limited, rotate in fours or fives every few minutes.
4. For science project, ball becomes "electricity." Players in possession of the ball are "conductors" and opponents are "nonconductors."

Four-Goal Soccer

Motor skills Kick, dribble, pass, trap
Movement concepts Personal and general space, change of direction and speed
Players Class
Formation See figure 16.12
Playing area Playground, gymnasium
Equipment None

The playing area is bounded by four lines. Place four goals (traffic cones or sticks) in the center of each line. Team A's goals are on the north and west side of the field. Team B's are on the east and south side. The game is played without goalies and each team attacks and defends two goals. Soccer rules apply with the exception of the off-side and corner kick rules.

CHAPTER 16

Figure 16.12   Four-goal soccer.

Figure 16.13   Goal.

Goal

Motor skills   Dribble, shoot, guard
Movement concepts   Near and far, change of direction and speed
Players   Three per game
Formation   See figure 16.13
Playing area   Playground, gymnasium
Equipment   Ball

The "goal" is at one end of the playing area, and "home" is at the other end. One player is goalkeeper. The other two players start from "home," dribbling and passing the ball. The player who is in the act of dribbling may not score; however, when he feels his partner is in a good position to score, he shouts "Goal!" just before he passes the ball (figure 16.13). The player receiving the pass must shoot at the goal without any further dribbling. If the ball goes into the goal, each of the two field players gets one point. If the ball misses or if the goalkeeper prevents it from going in, the goalkeeper rushes out and tries to tag one of the players. If the player is tagged before he can reach "home," they exchange positions. If the goalkeeper is unsuccessful, he goes back into goal and the game starts over.

Instant Goal

Motor skills   Dribble, shoot
Movement concepts   Personal and general space, change of direction and speed
Players   Three per game
Formation   None
Playing area   Playground, gymnasium
Equipment   Ball

Three players begin dribbling and passing the ball to each other. Suddenly, player A moves away from the other two and spreads his legs to make a goal. The other two players must dribble and pass the ball at least two times before one of them tries to kick the ball between player A's legs. The game continues, with players B and C taking their turn at making a goal.

Trick the Guard (New Zealand)

Motor skills   Dribble, dodge, throw, catch, guard
Movement concepts   Change of direction and speed
Players   Two per game
Formation   None
Playing area   Playground, gymnasium
Equipment   Ball

One player is the attacker and the other is the defender. The attacker dribbles the ball with her hand within her own half of the playing area until, with a dodge or feinting action to fool the defender, she throws the ball high into the opponent's half. He then runs and tries to catch the ball before it lands on the ground. The defender cannot cross the line but can try to block the throw or intercept it before his opponent can retrieve it. If the attacker catches the ball, she is given a free throw at the goal. Each player has five turns before exchanging positions. The winner is the player with the highest number of points at the end of the game.

Mimic the Word

Motor skills   Locomotor and manipulative skills
Movement concepts   Personal and general space, shapes, change of direction and speed
Players   Class
Playing area   Playground, gymnasium
Equipment   None
Academic concepts   Language arts—word recognition, suffixes

Draw two lines approximately thirty feet apart and place "it" on one line and the remainder of the class on the other line. The group on the line decides on a word, such as *twisting,* and all children mimic this word when they move in this manner as they run toward "it." As soon as "it" guesses the word, he tries to tag as many players as he can before they cross over the opposite end line. Any player who is tagged must stand beside "it" and help him catch players on each successive turn. The last player to be caught wins the game and becomes the new "it."

Suggestions and Variations
1. Use different parts of speech and change word endings.
2. Have the class work in groups of two or three.

Magic Carpet

Motor skills   Run, dodge
Movement concepts   Change of direction and speed
Players   Class in groups of five or six
Formation   Scattered
Playing area   Playground, gymnasium
Equipment   Word cards and wall charts
Academic concepts   Language arts—word recognition, vocabulary, sentence structure

Five one-foot squares are numbered and randomly placed on the playing area. Five charts with corresponding numbers are placed on the wall. Each chart contains new words from current language arts, mathematics, science, social studies, or health units. Charts may include words from separate subjects or a mixture of all subject areas. Five groups of children each form a chain by holding hands. On signal (or with music), the groups run around and through the five squares on the ground. When the teacher calls "Stop," everyone stops. The player in each group who is the closest to the square touches it, then identifies any word from the corresponding number listed on the word chart. After each team has had a turn, the teacher erases each word, if correctly answered, and the game continues. One point is scored for each correct answer. The team with the highest score wins the game.

Suggestions and Variations

1. Have each child make up a sentence with the chosen word.
2. Change the method of moving, such as hopping, sliding, etc.

Place Kickball

Motor skills   Run, kick, catch
Movement concepts   General space, change of direction and speed
Players   Class
Formation   Softball diamond with thirty feet between bases; one team in the field and one in a line formation behind home plate
Playing area   Playground, gymnasium
Equipment   One ball
Academic concepts   Mathematics—adding, subtracting, averaging, percentages

Place the fielding team in the playing area outside the baselines. Each player on the kicking team is given one stationary kick from home plate. If the kick is fair (inside the boundary lines), the kicker tries to run around the bases before a member of the fielding team can get the ball and beat her to home plate. The kicker is out if a fly ball is caught.

Suggestions and Variations

1. After the stationary kick is learned, introduce a "dribble and kick." Draw a line ten to fifteen feet behind home plate and require the kicker to dribble to the plate and then kick the ball.
2. Require that the kick be made with the opposite foot the second time "up to bat."
3. If only a few players make it around the bases, have players run to first base and back.

Boundary Ball

Motor skills   Kick, trap
Movement concepts   General space, change of direction and speed
Players   Class
Formation   Three parallel lines drawn twenty to thirty feet apart, and each team scattered on each side of the center line
Playing area   Playground, gymnasium, classroom
Equipment   One ball
Academic concepts   Mathematics—adding, subtracting

Each team has a ball, which it kicks toward the opponent's goal line. Players on both teams move about freely in their own half of the playing area, trying to prevent the opponent's

ball from crossing the goal line. Players cannot touch the ball with their hands. One point is scored each time the ball crosses the opponent's goal line. One point is deducted each time the ball is touched with the hand.

Suggestions and Variations

1. Once children understand the game, play two games by dividing the class into four teams.
2. Change to a throwing game.

Battle Ball

Motor skills   Kick, trap
Movement concepts   General space, change of direction and speed, levels
Players   Class
Formation   Two parallel lines twenty feet apart, with one team on each line and the players holding hands
Playing area   Playground, gymnasium
Equipment   Ball
Academic concepts   Mathematics—adding, subtracting

Side A tries to kick the soccer ball over side B's goal line. Side B tries to stop the ball and kick it back over side A's line, and so on. The team that kicks the ball over the opponent's line receives two points. The first side to reach a score decided upon by the teacher wins the game. A team loses a point if one of its players touches the ball with his hands, or if the ball is kicked too high—over the heads of the other team.

Suggestions and Variations

1. Have players pass the ball from teammate to teammate before kicking it toward the opponent's line.
2. Allow children to use their hands to prevent the ball from hitting their faces.

Elastic Ropes (Peru)

Motor skills   Jump
Movement concepts   Personal space, change of direction and speed
Players   Four per game
Formation   None
Playing area   Playground, gymnasium
Equipment   Long elastic ropes (pantyhose tied in long strips can be an effective substitute)
Academic concepts   Mathematics—sets, adding, subtracting, multiplying

Players 1 and 2 hold the elastic rope with their legs. Player 3 performs various jumping movements inside the ropes or "in and out of the ropes" (figure 16.14). Player 1 trades places with player 3 and must repeat exactly what player 3 performed. If she makes a mistake or fails to perform a movement, she trades places with player 2. Game continues until player 2 makes a mistake or forgets a movement. Each player has a turn creating her own movements.

Suggestions and Variations

1. Raise the rope and/or change positions of the outside players' feet.
2. Outside players pose movement problems for player number 3. For example, jump in sets of two when inside the ropes and in sets of three when outside the ropes.

Figure 16.14   Elastic ropes.

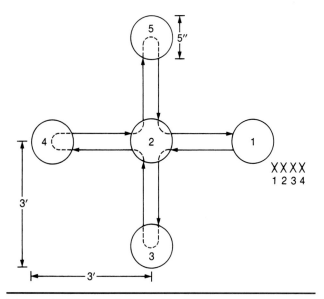

Figure 16.16   Five-hole marbles formation.

	Z		
Y	P	G	O
F	X	R	C
L	J	T	N
S	Q	B	H
W	E	M	D
K	I	V	U
		A	

Figure 16.15   Alphabet game.

Alphabet Game

Motor skills   Jump
Movement concepts   Personal space, transfer of weight
Players   Two per game
Formation   Pattern in figure 16.15 is drawn on dirt, gravel, or blacktop surface, with the size of the squares adjusted according to level of ability
Playing area   Playground, gymnasium
Equipment   None
Academic concepts   Language arts—spelling, prefixes, and suffixes

Player 1 begins in square A and attempts to move from square A to Z, in alphabetical order, without touching any lines. As soon as player 1 touches a line, he is out and player 2 begins. The winner is the player who progresses to the highest letter in the alphabet.

Suggestions and Variations
1. Have each child "touch" a four-letter word (or a longer word) before touching Z.

2. Change letters to numbers, then make up challenges involving adding, subtracting, multiplying, and dividing.
3. Add prefixes and suffixes to the game.

Five-Hole Marbles (Japan)

Motor skills   Throw
Movement concepts   General and personal space, change of direction, strong and light
Players   Three or four per game
Formation   See figure 16.16
Playing area   Playground
Equipment   Marbles
Academic concepts   Mathematics—counting

The playing area has five small holes about three feet apart (see figure 16.16). Player 1 shoots from beside hole 1 and tries to roll her marble into hole 2. If her marble goes into the hole, she leaves it there until her next turn. If her marble does not go into the hole, it remains where it stops. The second player takes his turn. If he hits player 1's marble, player 1 is eliminated from the game. This rule applies to all future plays. If the marble rolls into the hole, player 3 takes her turn. Players keep taking their turns, provided they are not eliminated by being struck by an opponent's marble. The player who returns to hole number 1 first wins the game (figure 16.17).

Softball Croquet

Motor skills   Hit
Movement concepts   General space, change of direction, strong and light
Players   Two per game
Formation   See diagram
Playing area   Playground, gymnasium
Equipment   Stick, block, coat hanger, and ball
Academic concepts   Mathematics—counting

Player A hits the ball from behind the starting line. If the ball goes through both arches, A is given another hit. Player B hits

Figure 16.17 Five-hole marbles.

the ball. Players alternate hitting throughout the game. Whenever a player hits the ball through an arch, he is given another hit. If a player's ball travels and hits his opponent's ball, no infraction occurs. The first person to hit his ball across the starting line wins the game.

Suggestions and Variations

1. Change the pattern of the arches.
2. Play "doubles" croquet and make up your own rotation rules.
3. Play the same game with different-size balls such as field hockey, tennis, or Nerf balls.

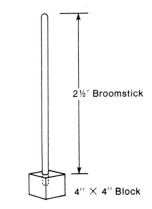

2½' Broomstick

4″ × 4″ Block

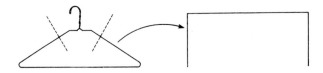

Long Ball

Motor skills Hit, throw, pitch, catch, run
Movement concepts General space, strong and light, change of direction and speed
Players Class
Formation Softball diamond with thirty to thirty-five feet between each base, one team in the field and the other in a file formation behind a restraining line drawn ten feet back and to the right of home plate
Playing area Playground, gymnasium
Equipment Bat, ball, bases
Academic concepts Mathematics—counting, averaging

Divide players into two teams. Each team selects a pitcher and a catcher; other players are fielders or batters. When a ball is hit, the batter runs to first base and, if possible, returns home. The runner may stop on first base, and any number of runners may be on a base at the same time. Runners may not steal home. Any hit is good; there are no fouls in this game. Batter is out when she strikes out, is touched with the ball off base, steals home, or throws the bat or when a fly ball is caught. One point is awarded for each run to the base and back.

Suggestions and Variations

1. Alternate pitchers and catchers.
2. Move pitcher closer as skill indicates.
3. Use a batting tee if skill level is too low.
4. Use a Nerf ball and hit ball with arm.
5. Shorten bases if necessary

Bounce Netball

Motor skills Volley
Movement concepts General space, change of direction, levels
Players Six to nine per team
Formation Drop the volleyball net to a height of about six feet, or string a rope six feet high between two standards. Place one team on each side of the net in rows or in scattered formation.
Playing area Playground, gymnasium
Equipment Net and ball

Play is started by one player hitting the ball over the net. The ball must bounce before being returned. Any number of players can hit the ball any number of times; however, the ball must bounce once between each player. The team that loses the point starts the ball the next time. Fouls occur when the ball is thrown, caught and held, allowed to bounce more than once, or hit out of bounds. When a team commits a foul, the opposite team gets one point.

Suggestions and Variations

1. Instead of requiring one bounce between players, make them hit the ball directly from a volley pass.
2. Change the type of ball; try beach or Nerf balls.

Bat Ball

Motor skills Bat, run, throw
Movement concepts General space, change of direction and speed, levels
Players Nine per team
Formation Softball diamond with thirty to thirty-five feet between each base, one team in the field and the other in a file formation behind a restraining line drawn ten feet back and to the right of home plate
Playing area Playground, gymnasium
Equipment None
Academic concepts Mathematics—counting, averaging

One team is in the field and the other is at bat. Players at bat try to hit the ball into the field and run to first base and back home in one complete trip. The batter may not stop on base. A player who makes a complete trip without being put out scores one run. The batter is out if a fielder catches a fly ball or a fielder touches the runner with the ball before he reaches home. When the team at bat has three outs, it goes into the field and the team in the field comes to bat. The team with the most points at the end of the playing period is the winner. (Teams must have the same number of times at bat.)

Suggestions and Variations

1. Alternate pitchers and catchers.
2. Alternate boys and girls in the batting order. Try two outs if one team stays up too long.
3. Vary the distance between bases according to the level of skill.
4. Use a batting tee if the skill level is too low.

INVENTIVE GAMES

As girls and boys progress through developmental level II, they become increasingly interested in playing in larger group games with more complexity and social interaction. The inventive game challenges can produce more complexity and social interaction. The inventive game challenges presented to children in this age range should reflect these changing characteristics and interests. The following sample challenges are designed for larger groups and emphasize the locomotor and manipulative game skills of developmental level II.

Locomotor Games

Class "Can you design a tag game for the whole class to play? Your game must use five hoops and no player can be eliminated from the game."

Group of eight "See if you can make up a game for eight players that does not involve tagging someone and that also does not use any equipment."

Manipulative Games

Bounce "Invent a game for five players that uses three hoops, a change of direction, and a bounce pass."

Throw and catch "Make up a game for twelve players that includes a throw and catch, a line or wall, and every player always on the move."

Hand dribble "Design a game for the whole class where every player has a basketball (or substitute). Your game must include dribbling the ball with one hand, and four goals."

Foot dribbling "Can you add three new rules to the game Pig in the Middle? Your game will be played with six players."

Hitting "See if you can make up a hitting game for twelve players. You may use a volleyball, beachball, or Nerf ball, and you must hit the ball with your hand."

Figure 16.18 Without hands.

16.3 *The Major Emphasis in a Games Program for Children in Developmental Level III Is on Acquiring the Knowledge, Skills, and Strategies of the Major Team and Individual Sports*

GAMES FOR DEVELOPMENTAL LEVEL III

Running, tag, and simple team games become less important when children reach developmental level III. Their dominant interest, of course, is team sports. Chapters 18 to 24 include skill charts and appropriate lead-up games for each major team sport. However, boys and girls of this age range occasionally enjoy a vigorous running game or a simple team game such as California Kickball or Without Hands (figure 16.18). Listed in table 16.3 are a few of the more popular games these children enjoy playing. Other cooperative games are provided in chapter 17.

Teachers should also review the games listed in the previous developmental level for possible additions to their program of activities. Later in this section, several suggestions will illustrate how the inventive games approach can be applied to children in this age range.

LOCOMOTOR AND MANIPULATIVE GAMES

Dandy Shandy (Jamaica)

Motor skills Throw, dodge

Movement concepts General space, change of direction and speed

TABLE 16.3 Locomotor and Manipulative Skills (Developmental Level III)

Name of Game	Type of Game	Players	Motor Concepts and Skills	Movement Concepts	Academic Concepts and Skills	Page
Locomotor and Manipulative Games						
Dandy Shandy	Throw	Half class vs. other half	Throw, dodge	General space, change of direction and speed		344
King	Tag	Class	Run, throw, dodge	General space, change of direction and speed		346
Tug-of-War	Pull/push	10–12	Push, pull	Strong and light, transfer of weight	Science—inertia	346
California Kickball	Throw/kick	18–20	Run, throw, catch, kick	General space, transfer of weight, change of direction and speed		346
Chain Tag	Tag	Class	Run, tag	General and personal space, change of direction and speed	Mathematics—sets	347
Solids, Liquids, and Gasses	Throw	6–7	Throw, catch	Change of direction and speed	Science—solids, liquids, and gases	347
Borden Ball	Throw	Half class vs. other half	Throw, catch	General space, change of direction and speed		347
Geometrical Shapes	Run	Class	Run	General and personal space; pathways, change of direction	Mathematics—geometrical shapes	347
European Handball	Throw	Half class vs. other half	Throw, run, catch, check	General space, change of direction and speed		348
Open the Window	Tag	7–9	Run, dodge	General and personal space, change of direction and speed	Mathematics—sets	349
Goodminton	Hit	16–18	Hit	Transfer of weight, levels, change of direction and speed		349
Shufflecurl	Shoot	2–4	Shoot	Transfer of weight, strong and light	Mathematics—geometrical forms; science—friction	350
Frisbee	Throw	2	Throw	General space, strong and light, change of direction	Science—force and friction	352
Deck Tennis	Throw	2–4	Throw	Change of direction and speed		350
Paddleball	Hit	2–4	Hit	Change of direction and speed		351
Ultimate	Throw	7 or more	Run, dodge, throw, check	Tranfer of weight, change of direction, speed and levels		352
Inventive Games	All skills	Individual to group	All skills	All movement concepts		353

Players Class
Formation See diagram
Playing area Playground, gymnasium
Equipment Utility or Nerf ball

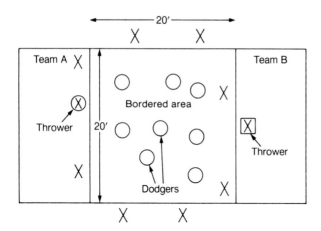

Divide the class into two equal teams and toss a coin to decide which team will be in the bordered area first (the dodgers). The other team spreads around the bordered area to retrieve balls for the two players chosen to be the "throwers." The throwers stand opposite each other and try to hit the players inside the area with the ball(s). The outside players can pick up and pass the ball, but only the two throwers can hit the other team's players. Any player hit with a ball is required to stand outside the bordered area and becomes a member of the thrower's team. After all the players are hit, the other team goes inside the bordered area, and the game is repeated. If the last player from any team dodges ten consecutive balls, her team is allowed to return to the bordered area and dodge the balls again.

King (India)

Motor skills Throw, dodge
Movement concepts General space, change of direction and speed
Players Class
Formation Scattered inside a fifty-foot square
Playing area Playground, gymnasium
Equipment Utility or Nerf ball

One player is chosen to start the game. She throws the ball and tries to hit another player. Players must remain inside the square and use their fists to prevent their bodies from being hit. They also use their fists to hit the ball toward another player. Any player hit must move outside the square. Once a player is outside the square, she continues to play; however, she may not enter the square. If the ball goes out of the square, any player who is on the outside of the square may retrieve it and hit it back into the square (figure 16.19). Game continues until one player, the "king," remains.

Suggestions and Variations
Require players to use their nondominant hand to hit the ball.

Figure 16.19 King.

CONCEPT

16.4 *Children from Different Countries and with Different Cultural Backgrounds Play the Same Games with Different Names and Slight Variations in Rules*

Tug-of-War

Motor skills Pull, push
Movement concepts Strong and light, transfer of weight
Players Ten to twelve per game
Formation Line
Playing area Playground, gymnasium
Equipment None
Academic concepts Science—inertia

Divide class into two equal teams on the basis of the children's weight and strength. Stretch a tug-of-war rope across a center line and place a marker on each side of the rope about five to six feet from the center line. On signal, each team tries to pull the other until the opponent's marker crosses the center line.

Suggestions and Variations
Have players pull from different positions, such as on seat or facing the reverse direction.

California Kickball

Motor skills Run, throw, catch, kick
Movement concepts General space, transfer of weight, change of direction and speed
Players Nine per team
Formation Arrange the playing area the same as in a softball game. Modify the length of bases and other rules according to space and other conditions
Playing area Playground, gymnasium
Equipment Utility ball

The game is played like softball with the following modifications. Use a utility ball or old volleyball. The pitcher rolls the ball and the "batter" kicks it. The batter runs whether

Figure 16.20   Chain tag.

the ball is kicked fair or foul. First base is the only base that the fielding team can touch to get a batter out—on all other bases, the fielder must tag the runner or throw the ball and hit him to get him out. Any number on the batting team may get on a base and stay, and run when they think it is safe to try for another base. On any hit balls, if the fielding team throws the ball to the pitcher, any runner who is between bases must go back to the previous base. Any runner who is between bases on a caught fly ball is automatically out. Change teams after three to six outs, or when everyone on the batting team has had a turn at bat.

Suggestions and Variations
Use a Nerf ball and bat the ball with the arm.

Chain Tag (Czech Republic)

Motor skills   Run, tag
Movement concepts   General and personal space, change of direction and speed
Players   Class
Formation   Scattered
Playing area   Playground, gymnasium
Equipment   None
Academic concepts   Mathematics—sets

Mark off a designated playing area. The teacher selects four players to be "it." On signal, "it" players try to tag the other players. When a player is tagged, he joins hands with "it," then "it" continues to tag other players. The first "it" to tag five players calls out "five caught." When this occurs, the "six-member train" now tries to tag any other train or individual players. The winner is the last train or individual player to be tagged. (See figure 16.20.)

Suggestions and Variations
Split trains when three players are caught. Last individual player wins the game.

Solids, Liquids, and Gases

Motor skills   Passing
Movement concepts   Change of direction and speed
Players   Six to seven per team

Playing area   Playground, gymnasium
Equipment   Basketballs
Academic concepts   Science—solids, liquids, and gases

Divide class into four teams and have each team form a circle with approximately six feet between each player. One player on each team is given a ball. When the teacher calls "solids," players must stretch toward each other to receive and transfer the ball. "Liquids" would require players to bounce-pass the ball, and "gases" would require them to throw the ball. As soon as the class understands the directions, call out each word in random order. If a player drops the ball, she must retrieve it, return to her place in the circle, then continue the game. The first team to move the ball twice around the circle wins the game.

Suggestions and Variations
1. Place a player in the middle and require alternate passes to go to the center player.
2. Have all players moving according to the speed of the molecules—solids move slowly, liquids move fast, and gases move very fast.

Borden Ball

Motor skills   Throw, catch
Movement concepts   General space, change of direction and speed
Players   Class
Formation   Playing areas divided into two equal sections, with each team scattered in each section
Playing area   Playground, gymnasium
Equipment   Football, two posts or traffic cones

Place one goalie from each team in an eight-foot goal area in the center of each end line (use two posts or traffic cones as goalposts). The object is to throw the ball through the opponent's goal. The game begins with a jump ball between two opposing players at the center line. The ball may be thrown in any direction, but it may not be hit or kicked. A player may take a maximum of three steps while holding the ball no longer than three seconds. On penalties, the ball is given to the nearest opponent. Members of the team that do not have possession of the ball may check the player with the ball, but they may not touch, hold, or push him. One point is awarded for each goal. After a point is scored, at halftime, or at any official stopping of play, restart play with a jump ball at the center. If the ball goes over the sidelines, a player on the opposing team throws it into the field of play.

Suggestions and Variations
1. Use different types and sizes of balls.
2. Change the three-second rule or number of steps to meet skill level of the class.

Geometrical Shapes

Motor skills   Running
Movement concepts   General and personal space, pathways, and change of direction
Players   Four equal teams
Playing area   See figure 16.21
Equipment   None
Academic concepts   Mathematics—geometrical shapes

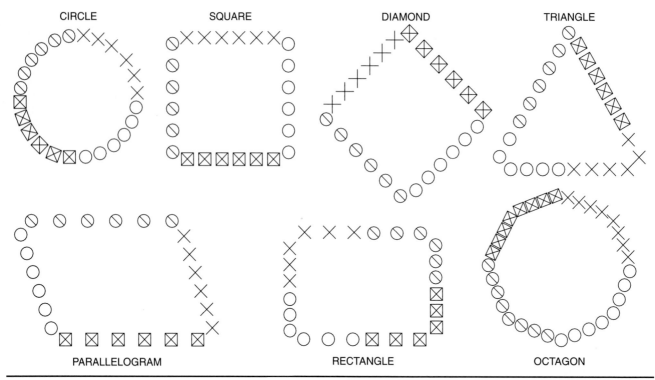

Figure 16.21 Geometrical shapes.

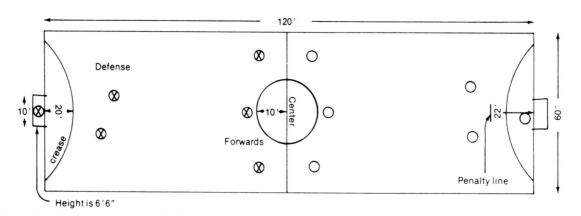

Figure 16.22 European handball.

Divide the class into four equal teams and number each team 1, 2, 3, and 4. Each team forms a line, and the players hold hands and begin to run anywhere within the playing area. When the teacher calls, "Two, diamond, and clockwise," all players must keep moving, and team 2 runs to a place in the playing area where a large diamond could be formed, makes the first part of the diamond and continues to run in place. Since the teacher has called "clockwise," team 3, who is next in this direction, forms the next part of the diamond, followed by teams 4 and 1 (see figure 16.21). When the last player on team 1 is running in place, the teacher calls out "Scatter," signaling each team to return to running through the playing area. If the next call is "Four, octagon, and counterclockwise," team 4 forms the first part of the eight-sided figure, followed by teams 3, 2, and 1. The four groups can also form a triangle or rectangle by placing fewer players on one side of each form, as shown in figure 16.21.

European Handball

Motor skills   Throw, run, catch, check
Movement concepts   General space, change of direction and speed
Players   Six to eight per team
Formation   See figure 16.22
Playing area   Playground, gymnasium, classroom
Equipment   Four goalposts

The object of the game is to throw the ball through the goalposts (see figure 16.22). The game begins with a jump ball between two opposing forward players. Once the ball is tapped out of the center circle, any player may attempt to retrieve it. A player who has possession of the ball may take one to three steps, bounce it, take three more steps, and so on, or attempt to throw it through the goalposts. A player has three seconds to get rid of the ball. A player may check on an opponent in the same way as in basketball. If a defensive player fouls her opponent, the opponent is given a free throw at the point of infraction. All defensive players must stay ten yards away until the throw is made. If the ball goes over the sidelines or end lines, the nonoffending team throws the ball back into play (one- or two-hand throw, according to age and ability). The goalie must stay within the crease (the semicircle around the goalposts); however, no other player may enter this area. One point is awarded for each goal scored from outside the crease area.

Suggestions and Variations
1. Play the game without allowing a bounce.
2. Add "nonscoring" sideline player similar to sideline soccer.
3. Play same game with a Nerf ball, but allow no dribbling or holding.

Open the Window (Denmark)

Motor skills   Running, dodging
Movement concepts   General and personal space, change of direction and speed
Players   Groups of seven
Formation   Line
Playing area   Playground, gymnasium
Equipment   None
Academic concepts   Mathematics—sets

Arrange class into groups of seven within a designated playing area. Three sets of partners line up behind a starting line. One player, the "window," stands ten feet in front of the first set and facing away from the group. When the "window" calls, "Open the window," the two partners at the end of the line run up each side of the line and in front of the "window." Once the runners pass him, the "window" tries to tag one of them before they can join together. If the "window" tags a player, they exchange positions, with the new set of partners returning to the front of the line. The game continues until everyone has had a turn. (See figures 16.23 and 16.24.)

Goodminton

Motor skills   Hit
Movement concepts   Transfer of weight, change of direction and speed, levels
Players   Six or fewer per team
Formation   Two equal teams across a rope or net
Playing area   Playground, gymnasium, classroom
Equipment   Volleyball net (or rope), bats (see diagram of all-purpose game bat in appendix B), badminton bird (used ones are quite suitable) or yarn ball (covered with tape or cloth)

This game is played like volleyball with the following basic rules. The server has only one serve to get the bird over the net, and the bird must clear the net on each serve. The server continues to serve as long as her team wins points. After the first serve has been taken by each team, and after each succeeding "side out," the team receiving the serve rotates one position clockwise. (The front row players move to the right, the back row players to the left, and the left back moves to the left forward position.) Teams change sides after each game.

    The bird may be batted in any direction, but scooping, lifting, and holding are not permitted. The bird, except on

Figure 16.23   Open the window.

Figure 16.24   Children's drawing.

service, may be recovered from the net, provided the player avoids touching the net. The bird may be batted only three times by one team before being returned over the net. A player may not hit the bird twice in succession, but she may give it the first and third hits.

    If any player on the serving team commits any of the following acts, it shall be "side out." If any player on the receiving team commits any of the acts, the serving team is awarded a point. The illegal acts are serving illegally; catching or holding the bird; touching the net with any part

Shufflecurl

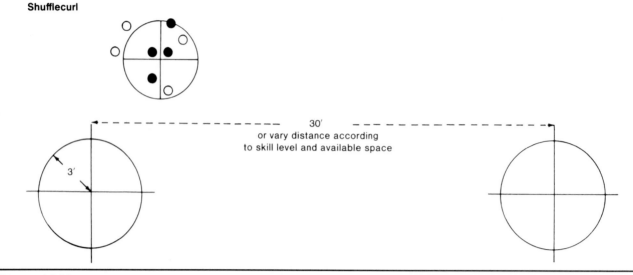

Figure 16.25 Shufflecurl.

of the body or bat (if two opponents touch the net simultaneously, the bird shall be re-served); reaching over the net; playing out of position; touching the floor on the opposite side of the center line; allowing hands or bats over the center line; "spiking" or "killing" the bird when playing a back position.

Suggestions and Variations
1. Play the same game with a Nerf ball. Eliminate the bat and use the flat of the hand.
2. Limit game and use nondominant hand.

Shufflecurl

Motor skills Shooting
Movement concepts Transfer of weight, strong and light
Players Two to four
Formation See figure 16.25
Playing area Playground, gymnasium
Equipment Shuffleboard cues and disks
Academic concepts Science—friction; Mathematics—geometrical forms

The rules are the same as in shuffleboard, but the object is to slide the disks as close to the center of the circle as possible (see figure 16.25). Players in this game also try to knock the opponent's disks out of scoring position. When each player has used his four disks by sliding them to the opposite circle, one "end" has been completed. Two "ends" make one round, and a game may be five, ten, or any other number of rounds. To score, award one point for each disk that a player has placed closer to the center of the circle than the closest disk of his opponent. (In figure 16.25, the player with the black disks would score three points.)

Suggestions and Variations
Play same game with different disks, such as beanbags, quoits, or deflated balls.

Deck Tennis

Motor skills Throw, run
Movement concepts Change of direction and speed
Players Two to four
Formation Court drawn as in figure 16.26, or use any existing volleyball or badminton court
Playing area Playground, gymnasium, classroom
Equipment Deck tennis ring made of rope or plastic tubing, which can be purchased through local sport stores

Singles
The server, standing outside the baseline and on the right half of the court (see figure 16.26), delivers the ring in a forehand fashion. The ring must rise to an arch before it begins to descend into the opponent's right court outside the neutral area. After the serve, the ring may land anywhere in the court. The server must serve into alternate courts each time. The receiver must catch the ring with one hand and immediately return it. The server scores a point if the receiver fails to return the ring or commits one of the following fouls:

1. Catching the ring with both hands
2. Changing the ring to her other hand before returning it
3. Holding the ring too long before returning it (count three seconds)
4. Stepping over the net line
5. Failing to make the ring arc before it begins to descend into the opponent's court

If the server faults or misses the return throw, her opponent then serves. However, no point is scored by the opponent. Game may be played to eleven, fifteen, or twenty-one points.

Doubles
The game is played according to singles rules with some modifications. Each team has two serves in succession. After the receiver has returned the server's toss, any player may return a toss. For example, player A from team 1 serves, and

on
off

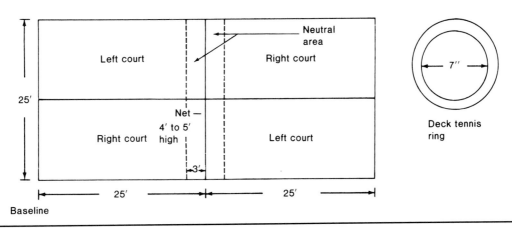

Figure 16.26 Deck tennis.

player C of team 2 catches the ring and returns it to player A. It is legal for player A to catch the ring and return it.

Suggestions and Variations
1. Nerf Ball Deck Tennis. Play the same game with a Nerf ball. Allow one bounce, and hit with an open palm.
2. Paddle Tennis. Play variation 1 with a paddle.

Paddleball

Motor skills Serve, hit, run
Movement concepts Change of direction and speed
Players Two to four
Formation Court drawn as in figure 16.27, using any available wall and floor or ground space. Use chalk or plastic tape to mark court dimensions.
Playing area Playground, gymnasium, classroom
Equipment All-purpose bats, tennis or sponge balls

Singles
The server, standing anywhere between the wall and the serving line, bounces the ball and hits it toward the front wall (see figure 16.27). The ball must hit the wall above the two-foot line and land behind the serving line inside the court. If it does not, the next player serves. After the ball has bounced once, the receiver hits it back to the wall. All returned balls by either player must hit above the two-foot line, but they may land anywhere inside the full court area (sixteen by twenty-six feet). The players alternate hitting the ball. If the server hits the ball above the line and back over the serving line, and the receiver fails to return the ball, the server receives one point. One player continues serving until he faults or misses the ball. Any player may go outside the court to return a ball. Game may be played to eleven, fifteen, or twenty-one points.

Doubles
The game is played according to singles rules with a few modifications. On the serve, the server's teammate stands outside the court to prevent any hindrance to the opponents who are trying to return the service. When the server loses her serve, her teammate takes a turn. Each team, therefore, has two serves in succession. On the serve, either opponent may return the ball. Thereafter, players on each team alternate hitting the ball.

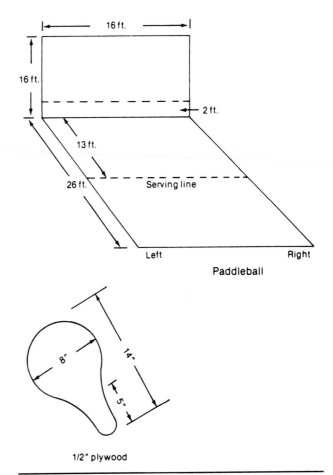

Figure 16.27 Paddleball

Triples
This game is played according to singles rules with the following modifications. The server represents one team and, therefore, is playing against the other two players as a team. When the server loses his service, he moves to the right back court. The right back court player shifts to the left, and the left back court player becomes the new server. After the serve, the server hits every other ball. For example, the server hits, then

Figure 16.28   Throwing a frisbee.

player A of the opposing team, then the server, then player B. Each player keeps his own score.

Suggestions and Variations
1. Handball. Game is played the same as paddleball, except the ball is hit with the hand. Use tennis, sponge, or Nerf balls.
2. Allow two bounces for either paddleball or handball.
3. Adjust serving and restraining line to meet level of ability.

Frisbee

Motor skills   Throw, catch, run
Movement concepts   General space, strong and light, change of direction
Players   Two
Formation   None
Playing area   Playground, gymnasium
Equipment   Frisbee
Academic concepts   Science—force and friction

Frisbee activities, whether throwing the disk for distance, catching it in a variety of unusual ways, or playing new types of Frisbee games, have become very popular with elementary school children. The Frisbee involves a new way of throwing an object and a flight pattern different from that of a thrown or hit ball. More important, Frisbee activities enable children to invent an unlimited repertoire of creative and cooperative game activities.

The backhand throw is the easiest and most popular way of throwing the Frisbee. Stand with feet about shoulder-width apart and weight evenly distributed over both feet. The right foot points toward the target. The disk is held with the thumb on top, index finger on the rim, and the remaining fingers curved under the rim of the disk (figure 16.28a). Shift the weight to the rear foot, then simultaneously twist the trunk toward the target and pull the right arm forward (figure 16.28b). Continue forward and release the disk with a snap of the wrist when the disk is parallel to the ground (figure 16.28c).

Suggestions and Variations
The following activities are simple modifications of partner or team games. Teachers and children are encouraged to invent other variations as well as entirely new Frisbee games.

1. Throw and Catch with Partner. Throw and catch at different levels using a variety of catches. Other variations, such as increasing the distance, using either hand, or performing a trick when catching the Frisbee, can be added to partner activities.
2. Frisbee Golf. Play barnyard golf with a Frisbee, except increase the distance between "holes."
3. Frisbee Tennis. Play deck tennis with a Frisbee, and add or modify any rule to accommodate levels of skill and interest.
4. Frisbee Soccer. Play the same game as soccer and add or modify rules to accommodate levels of skill and interest.
5. Frisbee Softball. Play the same game as softball, and add to or modify the rules to accommodate the level of skill and interest.

Ultimate

Motor skills   Running, dodging, checking, throwing,
Movement concepts   Transfer of weight, change of direction, speed and levels
Players   Seven or more on each team
Formation   Use a full or half soccer field according to the players' level of skill and ability
Playing area   Playground
Equipment   Frisbee

Ultimate is a very active game that combines the throwing skills of Frisbee, the passing and scoring of football, the guarding action of basketball, and the continuous movement of soccer. It can be played with seven or more players on each team and modified to meet the ability level of each class and the size of the playing area.

There are seven players on each team. The game begins with each team standing on their own end line. The object of the game is to catch the disc in the opponent's end zone (beyond the team's end line). To start the game, the disc is thrown by a player on team A toward the receiving team B. As soon as the disc is thrown, all players may move; however, no player on team A may touch the disc until it has been touched by an opponent (figure 16.29). One point is awarded for each fair catch in the end zone. After a goal is scored, teams change ends, and the team that scored throws (called a "throw off") the disc from their end line. The player in possession of the Frisbee is known as the "thrower." The player who is covering an opponent is known as the "marker."

The basic rules of the game are these:

1. No player may run with the disc.
2. The disc may be caught with one or both hands, while the player is stationary or on the move. When the player catches the disc while running, she must immediately stop and establish a pivot foot (as in basketball) before passing the frisbee disc.
3. The disc must be passed from a stationary position and within ten seconds. If it is not passed within ten seconds, the disc is handed to the nearest opponent and the game continues.
4. There are no offsides in this game and the disc may be passed in any direction.
5. If the disc goes over the sideline, it is passed back into play at the point where it crossed and by the nonoffending team.

Figure 16.29   Ultimate.

6. Defending players may guard a thrower in the same way as in basketball. Only one defensive player may guard an opponent, and he must stay at least one frisbee diameter away from that opponent. A guarding player may not touch the disc while it is in the hands of the offensive player. If the defensive player causes the offensive player to drop the disc, the offensive player retains possession and the game continues. All other defensive players must be at least ten feet away from an opponent who has possession of the disc. Defensive players must also allow an opponent who has possession of the disc to pivot in any direction.

7. When a pass is not completed as a result of a bad pass, an incomplete catch, being knocked down by an opponent, or being caught out-of-bounds, the disc is given to the opposing team.

INVENTIVE GAMES

By the time children reach developmental level III, team sports are the order of the day. However, inventive games can be used to complement many lead-up games. If children in developmental level III have not been exposed to the inventive games approach, begin by modifying one or two of their favorite lead-up games. When these children become used to modifying these games, shift to a more exploratory method of posing more open-ended challenges, as illustrated in the following examples.

Throw and dodge The class has played Dandy Shandy in a previous lesson. Arrange the class to play the game in the same way as the previous lesson. After a few minutes, have both teams sit down in opposite areas and pose the following: "Can you add a new rule to your game?" After a few minutes, ask each group to explain its rule, then play the game with two new rules. Repeat the procedure two more times, then move on to another game.

Throw and catch Select Borden Ball and repeat the procedure used to modify Dandy Shandy.

Shooting "Can you invent a shooting game for eight players that uses paddles, one Nerf ball (or sponge ball), and three goals (hoops, wastepaper baskets)?"

Hand dribbling "Create a game for twelve players who have twelve basketballs. Your game must include a dribble, pass, and pivot, and no goals."

Frisbee "Can you invent a Frisbee game for four players, using a volleyball net and court?"

Summary Review

This chapter presents a wide variety of locomotor and manipulative games that are important to all children in the elementary school. Children in level I begin to acquire the basic skills and strategies through an informal and exploratory approach. In level II, girls and boys begin to show more interest and ability to learn more complex skills and movement patterns, yet still enjoy simple running and tag activities. The major emphasis for developmental level III is on acquiring and perfecting skills and strategies of the main individual and team sports.

INDIVIDUAL *and* **GROUP PROJECTS**

1. Select five games from each developmental level, and add one or more additional suggestions or variations.

2. In groups of two or three, prepare a list of creative game challenges that stress the basic locomotor and manipulative skills outlined for children in developmental level I.

3. Interview senior citizens who came to North America as children or young adults, and ask them to describe the games they played as children in their home country.

SELECTED READINGS

Ashlock, R. B., and J. H. Humphrey. 1976. *Teaching elementary school mathematics through motor learning.* Springfield, IL: Charles C. Thomas.

Blatt, G. T., and J. Cunningham. 1981. *It's your move: Expressive movement activities for the language arts class.* New York: Teachers College Press.

CAHPER. 1986. *K–3 games.* Ottawa, Ontario: CAHPER.

Doray, M. (1982). *J is for jumping: Moving into language arts.* Belmont, CA: Pitman Learning.

Draper, M., S. Rosenthel, J. Stillwell, and L. Fahrman. 1989. *The gym dandies series.* Vol. 4. Durham, NC: Great Activities.

Gable, S. 1988. *The gym dandies quarterly: Games games games.* Durham, NC: Great Activities.

Gilbert, A. G. 1977. *Teaching the three R's through movement experiences.* Minneapolis: Burgess.

CHAPTER 16

Hall, T. 1981. *Academic ropes.* Bryon, CA: Front Row Experiences.

Haseltine, P. 1987. *Games for all children.* Oxford: Basil Blackwell.

Humphrey, J. H. 1990. *Integration of physical education in the elementary school curriculum.* Springfield, IL: Charles C. Thomas.

Humphrey, J. H., and J. N. Humphrey. 1990. *Mathematics can be child's play.* Springfield, IL: Charles C. Thomas.

————. 1991. *Developing elementary school science concepts through active games.* Springfield, IL: Charles C. Thomas.

Kamiya, A. 1985. *Elementary teacher's handbook of indoor and outdoor games.* West Nyack, NY: Parker.

Kirchner, G. 1991. *Children's games from around the world.* Dubuque, IA: Wm. C. Brown.

Mauldon, E., and H. B. Redfern. 1981. *Games teaching.* 2d ed. London: Macdonald & Evans.

Morris, B., and J. Stiehl. 1989. *Changing kids' games.* Champaign, IL: Human Kinetics.

Turner, L. F., and S. L. Turner. 1989. *Alternate sports and games for the new physical education.* Needham Heights, MA: Ginn Press.

Werner, P. H., and E. C. Burton. 1979. *Learning through movement: Teaching cognitive content through physical activities.* St. Louis: Mosby.

CHAPTER 17

Cooperative Games and Learning Activities

KEY CONCEPTS

17.1 Cooperative learning methods can teach subject matter and social and collaborative skills at the same time and with equal effectiveness

17.2 Cooperative learning involves children working together in heterogeneous groups toward a common goal, with all children feeling individually responsible for their own efforts as well as the efforts of the group

17.3 Cooperative games are noncompetitive activities that emphasize fun, cooperation, equality, participation, success, and trust

17.4 Children from all cultural backgrounds are capable of inventing cooperative games

KEY OBJECTIVES

After completing this chapter you will understand:

1. The meaning and importance of cooperative learning in the elementary school curriculum
2. The basic elements of a cooperative game
3. How to teach cooperative games
4. How to promote cooperative learning through a variety of instructional techniques

During the latter part of this century the influx of new citizens from every continent has made Canada and the United States culturally very rich societies. However, differences in language, customs, and attitudes within classrooms often cause tensions and misunderstandings. Educators such as Johnson, Holubec, and Kagan (1991) have developed cooperative learning strategies that not only effectively teach academic concepts and skills, but also enhance personal and social relations. The cooperative games and activities described in this chapter are in harmony with these new teaching strategies. As such, they have become an effective medium through which children acquire a variety of game skills as well as a positive approach to learning many social and collaborative skills in an enjoyable and relaxed environment.

The first part of this chapter describes the meaning and importance of cooperative learning and outlines how it is used as an approach to teaching both subject matter and social and collaborative skills. The next section describes the basic elements of a cooperative game. This is followed with a selection of cooperative games that have become very popular with elementary school children, and then by cooperative games invented by children from various parts of the world. The last section describes a few instructional techniques that are used to promote cooperative learning through a variety of physical activities.

Figure 17.2 Everyone receives a measure of enjoyment in cooperative games.

Figure 17.1 Cooperative learning methods help develop social and collaborative skills.

C O N C E P T

17.1 *Cooperative Learning Methods Can Teach Subject Matter and Social and Collaborative Skills at the Same Time and with Equal Effectiveness*

COOPERATIVE LEARNING

Our responsibility as teachers of young children is to help all children develop to their greatest potential. However, intellectual achievement has always been emphasized rather than social and interpersonal skills. In recent years, schools are increasingly being asked to help students develop social and collaborative skills that will prepare them to function effectively in the workplace as well as help them become contributing members of our democratic society. Research studies by Johnson and Johnson (1994), Whistler and Williams (1992) and Slavin (1983) clearly indicate that schools can achieve all the basic subject matter goals and, at the same time, help children develop effective social and collaborative skills through the application of cooperative learning methods (figure 17.1). For example, studies by Johnson, Johnson, and Holubec (1993) have shown that cooperative learning methods, compared to competitive and individualistic learning methods, whether across all grade levels or in different subject areas, achieve significantly better results. Numerous studies have also revealed that children have greater improvement in academic achievement, motivation, positive attitude toward subject matter, self-esteem, and peer relations when cooperative rather than competitive or individualistic methods are used (figure 17.2).

What then is "cooperative learning"? It is an approach, method, or technique that enables and encourages children to work together in heterogeneous groups toward a common goal, while being held individually accountable (Whistler and Williams, 1992). Although there is no single approach or method to implement cooperative learning in the classroom or gymnasium, there are several important elements that must be present in any cooperative learning environment. The first is to organize students into heterogeneous groups that reflect the range of ability and social, racial, and personality characteristics of the class. Groups selected by the teacher or at random work better than student-selected groups.

C O N C E P T

17.2 *Cooperative Learning Involves Children Working Together in Heterogeneous Groups toward a Common Goal, with All Children Feeling Individually Responsible for Their Own Efforts as Well as the Efforts of the Group*

The second and perhaps most important feature of cooperative learning is the establishment of a feeling of positive interdependence within each working group. When students are placed in heterogeneous groups where they might not know or care for each other, the atmosphere is normally tense and threatening to each member. Hence, it is imperative that teachers structure the lesson so students begin to perceive that they are dependent upon each other. Once a group learns that it will "sink or swim" together, the lesson begins to move toward cooperative learning. This is accomplished by helping groups establish a common goal, dividing the work equally among the members, limiting resources so sharing becomes necessary, requiring a single group effort, and providing an individual and a group grade or a reward based on the group's performance.

The third essential component is individual accountability for each student's own learning as well as the learning of all other members of the group. This occurs when the performance of each member of the group is assessed and the results given back to the individual and the group. Such ongoing assessment helps to establish who needs more assistance, additional equipment and supplies, or support from other members of the group. Techniques such as randomly selecting one student in the group to explain the work in progress or having students evaluate each other's contribution to the performance or project, encourages individual accountability and discourages "hitchhiking" on the work of others in the group.

The fourth important element is teaching students how to appreciate and use interpersonal and small-group skills. In a cooperative learning environment, students are required to learn subject matter (task work) and also to learn to use a variety of interpersonal and collaborative skills that are necessary for members to function as part of a team (team work). According to Johnson and Johnson (1994), cooperative learning is inherently more complex than individualistic or competitive learning, because students must simultaneously participate in task work and teamwork. As students begin to work together toward a common goal, they find that social and collaborative skills, such as taking turns, everyone participating, being self-controlled, listening, and encouraging teammates, are vitally important if the group is to realize a common goal. Most teachers have already learned that simply telling children to work together, to share, or to take turns will not work. Children have to be taught the meaning of social and collaborative skills in the same systematic way as any other important academic concept or skill. The process of introducing these social and collaborative skills in a physical education lesson is covered later in the sections "Popular Cooperative Games" and "Techniques for Promoting Cooperative Learning in Physical Education." Cooperative games, particularly those that are invented by children who have learned the meaning of cooperative behavior, are a testimony to the educational value of cooperative learning experiences.

CONCEPT

17.3 Cooperative Games are Noncompetitive Activities that Emphasize Fun, Cooperation, Equality, Participation, Success, and Trust

ELEMENTS OF A COOPERATIVE GAME

Webster's Collegiate Dictionary defines cooperation as an "association of persons for common benefit." Any competitive game, such as volleyball, basketball, or dodgeball, would fit this definition, since a measure of cooperation is required if a team is to win a contest. The contemporary meaning of "cooperative games," however, goes beyond this definition. The cooperative games described in this chapter are essentially noncompetitive activities that emphasize the interaction of people rather than the game or the final score. They normally stress the elements of fun, cooperation, equality, participation, success, and trust. Each of these distinguishing characteristics or elements of cooperative behavior are described below. The game of Cross-Over Blanket Volleyball (p. 362) is used to illustrate how and where each element is emphasized in the rules and the way the game is played. Other games, such as Doubles Hopscotch (p. 358), Modified Musical Chairs (p. 361), and Juggle a Number (p. 361), could serve the same function.

Fun

Everyone must receive a measure of enjoyment from playing the game. The game encourages the players to laugh with, not at, others as they play. And, when finished playing, all players leave the "magic circle" of play with a sense of joy and happiness.

Volleyball has been a favorite game of elementary school children for many years; but it is a competitive game with winners and losers. Cross-Over Blanket Volleyball eliminates the pressure of winning because players are constantly changing sides and scoring is for the total group rather than for individuals. The new rules encourage children to play because the game not only is fun and exciting to play, but also encourages positive social interaction among all players.

Cooperation

Everyone must work together to achieve a common goal. Cooperation involves helping each other and sharing each task as the group moves toward its common goal.

Cross-Over Blanket Volleyball is a very cooperative game. For example, every player must cooperate or the ball cannot be caught or propelled over the net. The new rotation system ensures that each player has a chance to share each task and to learn to help in different group efforts as he or she crosses under the net to join a new group.

Equality

Everyone has an equal role in the game; that is, each player hits the ball roughly the same number of times as any other player, rotates to every other position, and, in part of the game, assumes the leadership role on a rotational basis. The rules of this modified version of volleyball require every player to rotate her or his position on the blanket as well as from one blanket to the other. This ensures equality of all players throughout the game.

Participation

Everyone is actively involved in the game. The rules of the game cannot eliminate any player from playing. Players who are "hit," "touched," or miss a "hit" or "catch" continue to play. Requiring a team effort every time the ball is flipped or caught ensures that everyone has an active and continuous role to play throughout the game. Rotation of players to the opposite side guarantees additional movement on the part of all players. This rule also stresses participating in a total group, rather than on an individual team.

Success

Everyone experiences a sense of accomplishment. Cooperative games have no losers. Success must be personally defined rather than determined by a score or group standard.

Since the score is kept for the whole group, there are no losers in this game. Also, the act of flipping or catching is also a measure of how well the group cooperatively performs. The individual's measure of success centers on how the individual player felt about her contribution as she helped perform each of the collective movements.

Trust

Everyone must be able to place some trust in other players. This means that situations within the game require a player to rely on another player to "miss him," "hold him," "balance him," or perform a movement that considers his safety and well-being. A slight measure of trust is also involved in the part of the game that requires all players to hold the blanket and execute the required movement in unison.

Compared to other games, this game is a relatively weak illustration of the element of trust; but the reader will be able to find games in this chapter that involve much stronger elements of trust.

These six elements of a cooperative game were selected on the basis of a review of articles and books dealing with cooperative games, plus information obtained from field studies with elementary school children. During the past several years, teachers and children from many countries have suggested that other elements, such as "sharing" and "fairness" or "sportsmanship," be added to the list. Each teacher should modify or expand this list of elements to meet the needs, ability, and cultural background of the children in her class.

POPULAR COOPERATIVE GAMES

All of the games described in this section (see table 17.1) are cooperative in nature. Some, such as doubles hopscotch and modified musical chairs, are modified versions of competitive games children have played for years. These modified versions, however, stress the elements of fun, cooperation, equality, participation, success, and trust rather than "winners and losers."

Animals

This game should be played in the gymnasium or outside within a marked area. The teacher selects three animal names, such as *chickens, cats,* and *dogs,* then quietly whispers each name to one-third of the class. On signal from the teacher, the children start to walk and find a place in the playing area and close their eyes. When everyone is standing with their eyes closed, they begin to make a sound of the animal they have been given, then try to find another child who is the same animal and link arms. Players must keep their eyes closed and communicate only by making the sound of their animal.

Suggestions and Variations
1. Play the same game, only require each group to be made up of a chicken, a dog and a cat.
2. Play the same game with eyes open and all players imitating the same animal.

Doubles Hopscotch (Levels I, II)

Partners hold inside hands. Follow the rules of Hopscotch (p. 330), except hop on inside feet in squares 1, 4, 7, and 10, and on outside feet in the other squares. Use one puck between partners and modify any other rule to accommodate Double Hopscotch.

Suggestions and Variations
1. Change methods of holding, moving, and throwing the puck.
2. Adapt Doubles Hopscotch to other games such as marbles and jacks.
3. Change partners after every game.

Ball Balance (Level I)

Begin this game with one utility ball or balloon for every two players. The first challenge should be simple and fun, such as asking each pair of students to balance the ball between their heads. From here, ask them how many different ways they can balance the ball between them (figure 17.3). Once they have discovered three or four ways (between elbows, knees, etc.), try the following suggestions and variations.

Suggestions and Variations
1. How many different ways can you balance the ball between you and your partner and move around the playing area? Try changing your method of moving, such as running, hopping, or crawling on all fours.
2. Join up with another set of partners and repeat some of your movements.
3. Form a circle with three or four sets and try to pass the ball from one set of partners to the next around the circle and without using your hands.

Perpetual Motion Machine (Levels I, II)

This game should start with three or four players. Add more players as their timing and cooperative behavior improves. To begin, the first player starts to move in any way and in any direction. The second player joins on behind and copies the exact movements of the first player. Repeat with each remaining player.

TABLE 17.1　Cooperative Games

Name of Game	Number of Players	Developmental Level	Fun	Cooperation	Equality	Participation	Success	Trust	Page
Animals	Class	I→II	X	X	X	X	X	X	358
Doubles Hopscotch	Class	I→II	X	X				X	358
Ball Balance	Class	I→II	X	X	X	X	X	X	358
Perpetual Motion Machine	3–4	I→II	X	X		X			358
Beanbag Helpers	Class	I→II	X	X	X	X	X		360
Fish Catchers	Class	I→II	X	X	X	X	X	X	360
Recycled Snake Skins	4	III	X	X	X				360
Juggle a Number	5	III	X	X	X			X	361
Twister	5–6	III	X	X	X	X			361
Eight Legged Caterpillar	Class	III		X		X		X	361
Modified Musical Chairs	Class	III	X	X	X	X		X	361
Pass a Person	Class	III		X		X		X	361
Tug-o-Peace	Class	III	X	X	X	X			361
Co-op Tag	Class	III	X	X		X			362
Triangle Tag	Class	III	X	X				X	362
Cross-Over Dodgeball	Class	III	X	X	X	X			363
Airplanes	5	III	X	X			X	X	362
Cross-Over Blanket Volleyball	12–14	III	X	X	X			X	362
Nine-Person Skip	11	III	X	X		X	X	X	362

Figure 17.3 "How many different ways can you balance the ball between you?"

Suggestions and Variations

As soon as the class understands the nature of the game, add the following variations.

1. The first player starts as usual; the second player attaches, copying the movements of the first player, then adds a new movement. Continue with each player adding a new movement.
2. Repeat variation 1, keeping time to a musical accompaniment.
3. Change the leader after each game.
4. Repeat game with a beanbag on every player's head. If any player drops the beanbag, the game starts over.
5. Add small equipment, such as hoops, balls, or wands.

Beanbag Helper (Level I, II)

This game begins with all players balancing a beanbag on their heads. The teacher then says "Walk," signaling everyone to start walking in any direction and, without using their hands, keep the beanbag balanced on their heads. At any moment, the teacher may change the method of moving by calling out "Skip," "Hop," "Move backward," and so on. When a beanbag falls off a child's head, she is frozen. Any child who is nearby, can pick up the beanbag and place it back on the frozen player's head (figure 17.4). The object of the game is to keep everyone moving and to help any player who has dropped the beanbag.

Suggestions and Variations

1. Allow children who are picking up a beanbag to hold their own beanbag on their heads with their free hand.

Figure 17.4 Beanbag Helper.

2. Play the same game with partners holding hands. If either partner drops the beanbag, they must both freeze and another set of partners must come and pick up the beanbag and replace it back on the player's head.

Fish Catcher (Level I, II)

Draw a twenty-foot square playing area and a circle six feet in diameter in the middle. Designate one side of the square to be the "fish" side and the opposite side to be the "shore." One player is chosen to be the "fish catcher." All other players are "fish" and scatter in the playing area. When the fish catcher calls out fish, everyone runs toward the "fish" wall. When the fish catcher calls out "Shore," they run toward the opposite wall. If the Fish Catcher calls out "Fish Catcher," everyone must find one or more players to link arms with and move in any direction. As soon as the fish catcher sees that all of the players are linked and moving, he begins to call out several words. For example, "Sardines" signals everyone to drop contact and run and stand in the center circle. If he calls "Crabs," two players must join together, side by side and upside down, and move like two joined crabs. "Octopus" means three players must sit back to back, elbows linked, feet on the ground, and move around the playing area without breaking contact with each other. When the fish catcher calls "Escape," all players must immediately move back to their original starting positions.

Recycled Snake Skins (Levels II, III)

This modified version of Skin the Snake is played with the following variations. Four players per team stand and place their left hands back through their legs and grasp the right hands of their teammates. Keeping their grip, all players lie down. As soon as all players on a team are lying down, the player at the front of the team releases her grip and runs to find a new group of "threes." Taking the front position, she signals the rear player to stand and move forward. The game continues until the teams have completely changed, or have "a new skin."

Figure 17.5   The group tries to untwist itself.

Juggle a Number (Levels II, III)

Begin with five players in a circle formation. Number players randomly rather than sequentially around the circle. Place five balls behind player 1. Player 1 throws a ball to 2, player 2 throws to 3, and so forth until the ball is returned to player 1. Repeat two or three times, or until all players know the rotation pattern. Members of each group decide how many balls they can keep moving, then player 1 starts throwing the first ball to player 2, and then picks up a second ball and repeats until the selected number of balls are all moving from player to player. If a ball drops, any player may pick it up and try to get it back into the throwing sequence.

Suggestions and Variations

1. Have each group try to keep all five balls moving.
2. Play same game, but with players using only one hand.
3. Play the game with a balloon instead of a ball and have each player keep a beanbag on her head, elbow, or lower back.

Twister (Levels II, III)

Begin with five or six players in a circle formation. All players join hands with two other players, creating a great tangle. When all hands are joined, the group tries to untwist itself without letting go of any handgrip (figure 17.5).

Suggestions and Variations

1. Start with three players, then gradually increase the number.
2. Play same game, but with each player balancing a beanbag on his head.

Eight-Legged Caterpillar (Levels II, III)

This game illustrates how a competitive relay (caterpillar race) can be changed into a cooperative activity. Arrange class into partners. One partner stands behind the other, bends forward, and grasps her partner's ankles. On signal (voice or musical),

all partners move in a caterpillarlike fashion. When the teacher calls "fours," two sets of partners join and keep moving like a caterpillar. Continue to "eight" or "ten," then start over.

Suggestions and Variations

1. Play same game in wicket or crab walk positions.
2. Start with partners of the same sex. When you call fours, sixes, and so on, each new set added must be of the other sex.
3. Before introducing this variation, build a "mountain" by placing one or more mats over a balance beam. Players begin lying facedown on the floor and holding the ankles of the player in front. Without losing their grip, players begin to crawl along the floor then up and over the "mountain."

Modified Musical Chairs (Levels II, III)

This game is played like Musical Chairs, except that no one is eliminated. Start with the whole class and fifteen chairs. When the music stops, players rush to sit down. Instead of eliminating the remaining players, they sit on the knees of seated players, placing their own knees together so that the next players can sit down. Start music again, remove one or more chairs, and continue playing until one chair remains. Allow children to use their hands to help balance other players.

Suggestions and Variations

1. Aerial Musical Hoops. Start with every player in a "hula hoop" position. Say "Go" and everyone runs. When you call "Twos," players join up in twos and keep moving. When you call "Fours," all join up in fours and continue moving. Continue to eight, then start the game over.
2. Floor Musical Hoops. Similar to variation 1, except players place their hoops on the floor. Start music, all run, remove three hoops, and stop music. Everyone runs and stands inside a hoop. Instead of eliminating players, any number of players may stand inside a hoop. Continue playing music and removing hoops. Game gets very exciting and fun when only two or three hoops remain.

Pass-a-Person (Levels II, III)

Divide the class into two groups. The two groups lie on their backs, in two rows, with heads touching and arms extending upward. One player at one end is supported by the upstretched arms and is moved to opposite end of the two rows. As each player finishes, she changes places with a player in the two rows, and the action is repeated.

Suggestions and Variations

Roll a person. All class members lie side by side, in one long line, facedown. One player lies across the backs of the other players, then all players begin to roll toward the opposite end. As each player is rolled "off," she changes places with a player in the "rolling line."

Tug-o-Peace (Levels II, III)

Begin with class members standing equal distance apart along the side of a rope. Class members count off in twos (1-2-1-2 . . .) then turn and face each other. On the signal "Pull," the 1s pull against the 2s, usually with no winner, but a lot of fun.

Suggestions and Variations

1. Arrange class in the same fashion as the first game, except have an extra 1 and an extra 2 player stand next to their own teammates. On signal, extra players tickle the opposing player, who is attempting to pull.
2. Same arrangement as the first game, but sitting down. On signal "Pull," each pulls and stands up.

Co-op Tag (Levels II, III)

The following co-op tag games are similar to other tag activities, except that a player is safe when involved in a designated type of cooperative behavior.

1. Back-to-Back Tag. One person designated as "it" tries to tag the other players, who run to avoid him. A player is safe when in a back-to-back position with another player. Back-to-back players keep moving, and then separate after five seconds.
2. Elbow-Linked Tag. Same as variation 1, except players are safe when they link elbows.
3. Hug Tag. Same as variation 1, except players are safe when they are hugging. Set special rules, such as "partners may hug for a maximum of five seconds," "fours for seven seconds," "sixes for eight seconds," and so forth. Let players keep their own count.
4. Ball Balance Tag. Arrange class into partners. Partners hold a ball (utility or Nerf) between their heads, sides, backs, or any other specified part of their bodies. Designate one set of partners to be "it." All, including "it" partners, move in the designated contact position.

Airplanes (Level III)

Arrange groups of five players behind a starting line. One player in each group lies facedown with arms and legs stretched out to the sides. The four carriers grasp the "airplane's" elbows and ankles and carry her to a turning line then back to the starting line. Repeat for each player on the team.

Suggestions and Variations

1. Since this is not a relay race, team members carry their airplane back and forth at their own speed.
2. Do not play this game on rough gravel or other dangerous surfaces.
3. For safety, have the airplane land first with feet, then hands.

Cross-Over Blanket Volleyball (Level III)

Arrange two teams of six or seven players on each side of a volleyball net (rope will do). Each team holds a blanket, keeping the net side open. One team starts with the ball on the blanket and tries to flip it over the net to the other team. As soon as the ball leaves the blanket, one player from the "sending team" crosses under the net and joins the other team. Receiving team tries to catch the ball in the blanket and return it to the other team. Each time the ball is returned, a player crosses under the net. One "collective" point is awarded to the group each time the ball crosses over the net and is successfully caught (figure 17.6).

Figure 17.6 Cross-Over Blanket Volleyball.

Suggestions and Variations

1. Try same game with two or three players crossing under the net after each toss.
2. Play same game with different types and sizes of balls.
3. Play same game with two or more balls—all balls must be tossed together.

Nine-Person Skip (Level III)

Three to nine players stand next to a rope. On signal, outside players turn the rope and all players jump rope (figure 17.7).

Suggestions and Variations

1. Start game with three or four players, then gradually increase the number.
2. Have jumpers enter one by one.
3. Have jumpers hold or bounce a ball.

Triangle Tag

Arrange the class into groups of four. Three players join hands, with one player designated as the "target." The fourth player is "it" and must stay outside the triangle of players. On signal "it" tries to tag the "target." However, triangle players all cooperate to protect the "target" by moving and shifting to keep "it" away from him (figure 17.8). "It" cannot reach across a triangle player and must tag the "target" on his or her

Figure 17.7 Nine-Person Skip.

Figure 17.8 All cooperate to protect the target.

TABLE 17.2	**Cooperative Activities**			
Name of Activity	**Developmental Level**			**Page**
	I	**II**	**III**	
Partner Balance Stunts	————————→			537
Partner Rope Skipping		——————————→		563
Leap Frog	——————→			516
Rocking Chair	——————→			517
Elephant Walk	——————————→			521
Chinese Get-Up	——————————→			517
Centipede	——————→			524
Pig Walk	——————→			521
Partner and Group Pyramids		————————————→		541
Wand Activities		——————————→		570
Juggling Activities		————————→		575
Rhythmic Activities	——————————————→			611
Creative Folk Dance Activities	——————————→			626

back. When this occurs, a new "it" and "target" are chosen and the game continues.

Suggestions and Variations
1. Form three sets of triangles and designate two "its." The "it" players may try to tag "targets" from any set of three triangle players.
2. Have triangle players place hands around each other's shoulders or waists.

Cross-Over Dodgeball

This game is similar to cross-over volleyball and is played with only five or six players. Instead of forming a circle, arrange the teams on either side of a center line. The game begins with a player on one side throwing the ball and trying to hit an opponent below the waist. A player who is hit immediately crosses over the line and joins the other team. The object of the game is to end up with both teams on one side of the line.

Suggestions and Variations
1. Add two or more balls to the game.
2. Add more players (8–10 per team) and play the game in partners. Partners must hold hands, and if one is hit, both cross over the line.

Numerous cooperative activities are included in the gymnastic and dance sections of this book. The activities in table 17.2 include cooperative movements between partners, small groups, or the whole class. Many of these activities can be incorporated into a variety of cooperative games.

C O N C E P T

17.4 *Children from All Cultural Backgrounds Are Capable of Inventing Cooperative Games*

TABLE 17.3   Elements of a Cooperative Game

Game Elements				Cooperative Elements
Players	**Space**	**Equipment**	**Skills and Rules**	
From two to all class members	From limited to all available space	From no equipment to many types and pieces of equipment	From no required skills and rules to many skills and rules	Fun, cooperation, equality, participation, success, and trust

COOPERATIVE GAMES CREATED BY CHILDREN

The process used in guiding children to create their own cooperative games is a simple extension of the approach used when teaching creative games. To illustrate, the first four columns of table 17.3 are used to set limitations for children to create their own games. Hence, if we pose a challenge, such as "Make up a game with your partner, in your own space, using one ball and two hoops and a dribble," children might or might not create a cooperative game. Their game might become a dribbling contest around the hoops or a cooperative game, such as dribbling and passing as each player dribbles around her own hoop. By adding the fifth column, "cooperative elements," we lead children to develop a creative game that possesses one or more of the elements of fun, cooperation, equality, participation, success, and trust.

There is one general comment we have received from numerous teachers who have used the cooperative games approach. They have consistently found that if children do not understand the meaning of these elements, they almost never produce a cooperative game. Hence, before posing any challenge involving one or more of these elements, teach the children the meaning of these words. This can be accomplished by discussing the elements in class and illustrating them by playing several cooperative games, such as Cross-Over Blanket Volleyball or Modified Musical Chairs.

When children understand these terms, pose a cooperative game challenge that stresses one or more of the cooperative elements listed in the last column. Each game usually stresses nearly all six cooperative elements. The important aspect of the challenge is to get children to think consciously about one or two key cooperative elements and to stress them in their game. The games listed in table 17.4 were invented by children in other countries. They are examples of more than a thousand games one of the authors received as part of an international game exchange project. In the fifty countries that participated in this study, all children, regardless of geographical area or cultural background, were capable of creating cooperative games. Many games arising from the same challenges were remarkably similar from country to country. The only major difference in these games was the type and amount of equipment that was used in each geographical location.

Figure 17.9 "Call out a name and throw the ball up."

■ **Passing in the Square (Israel) (Levels I, II)**

Challenge See if you can make up a game with four players, using two balloons, two nylon balls, and four plastic strips (approximately four feet long). Your game must involve the cooperation of all players.

The children build a square with the four plastic strips. Each player stands on one corner holding a balloon or nylon ball (figure 17.9). Player one calls out the name of another player and throws her ball up into the center of the square. The child whose name was called must quickly call another player's name, throw her balloon into the center, then try to catch player 1's ball. If a ball is dropped or goes out of reach, everyone stops and returns to the starting position. The game continues until all four names are called out. Player 2 begins the next game.

TABLE 17.4 New Cooperative Games Created by Children

Name of Game	Country	Type of Game	Developmental Level (I, II, III)	Fun	Cooperation	Equality	Participation	Success	Trust	Page
Passing in the Square	Israel	Ball	I→II	X	X	X	—	X	—	364
Bomb in the Box	England	Manipulation	I→II	X	X	X	X	X	X	366
Give and Take	Zimbabwe	Manipulation	I→II	—	X	X	X	X	—	366
Stick Exchange	Japan	Manipulation	II→III	X	X	X	—	—	X	366
Blind Flight	Luxembourg	Manipulation	II→III	—	X	X	X	X	X	366
The Worm	Greece	Manipulation	II→III	X	X	X	X	X	X	367
Geometry Class	Argentina	Manipulation	II→III	—	X	X	X	X	X	367
Jump Ball	Botswana	Ball	II→III	X	X	X	X	—	—	367
Clock	Czech Republic	Ball	II→III	X	—	X	X	—	—	367
Paga-Ajuda	Brazil	Tag	II→III	X	X	X	X	X	—	368
Frog, Jump, Slide	South Africa	Manipulation	II→III	X	X	X	X	X	—	368
Ting, Ting, Ting	Mexico	Tag	II→III	X	X	X	X	—	—	368

Figure 17.10 All players pass the objects at the same moment in Give and Take.

Figure 17.11 Bomb in the Box game sketched by a student.

Figure 17.12 Stick exchange.

■ Give and Take (Zimbabwe) (Levels I, II)

Challenge Make up a game that involves ten children per group. Each player must have a ball (or some small object). Players must pass their balls at the same moment so that, at any time, each player is passing and receiving a ball.

Ten players form a circle, kneel, and hold the ball in their right hand. On signal from a player, all players pass the ball along the ground and in front of the player to the right (figure 17.10). As the ball is passed, all players call out "One." Passing and counting continues until the group calls out "Ten." Repeat game in the opposite direction.

■ Bomb in the Box (England) (Levels I, II)

Challenge Make up a game that has six players. You must use a hoop and a skipping rope. Your game must have equal turns, everyone must take part, and you must use trust in your game.

Players line up as shown in figure 17.11. Player 1 places her hoop on her foot. Without using her hands, she passes it "footwise" to player 2. Each player repeats this movement until the hoop reaches player 5. Player 5 must now lift the hoop over the rope (held by player 6)without using her hands, then changes positions with player 6. Player 6 picks up the hoop with his foot, returns to the front of the line, and passes the hoop to player 2. Continue the rotation until everyone has had a turn.

■ Stick Exchange (Japan) (Levels II, III)

Challenge Can you design a cooperative game with your partner using any available equipment? Your game must stress

that each player has an equal role in the game and must, in some way, place trust in the other player.

Two players assume a crawling position and face each other. One player places one end of a stick on his right shoulder, and the other player places the other end on his left shoulder. Without using their hands, they try to help each other move the stick to their other shoulder (figure 17.12) while gradually shifting to a standing position. After reaching a standing position, they try to reverse directions and return the stick to the original position. If either player uses his hands or if the stick drops off either player's shoulder, they must start over from the beginning.

■ Blind Flight (Luxembourg) (Levels II, III)

Challenge See if you can make up a game for ten players, using all the available space and equipment. Your game must stress equality, participation, success, and trust.

The first nine players hold the rope at their side and place paper bags over their heads. The last player (guide) arranges

Figure 17.13   Blind flight.

Figure 17.14   Everyone tries to keep in contact in The Worm.

the four traffic cones, comes back to her group, and teaches it three nonverbal commands. These are (1) "Pull right," meaning front player turns right; (2) "Pull left," meaning front player turns left; and (3) "Pull on both," meaning front player moves straight ahead. The guide then tries to lead the group to the first traffic cone (figure 17.13). When the front player touches the first traffic cone, he places the cone in another spot, then trades places with the guide. The old guide takes the paper bag and moves to the back of the group to become the last player. The group continues to the next cone, changes players, and continues this pattern to the last player.

The Worm (Greece) (Level II, III)

Challenge   Invent a game for the whole class using your group's own space, and stress fun, participation, and equality.

One child is selected to be the leader. All remaining players line up behind the leader and place their hands on the knees of the player in front (figure 17.14). When everyone is ready, the leader begins to move forward, then moves in various directions. Everyone tries to keep in contact until the teacher

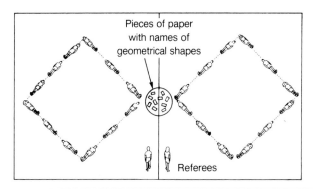

Figure 17.15   Geometry Class.

signals everyone to stop. The last player in the line becomes the new leader and the movement is repeated.

Suggestions and Variations
1. Change position of hands; for instance, place hands on shoulders, head, or ankles.
2. Have the last player in line become the leader—everyone moves backward.

Geometry Class (Argentina) (Levels II, III)

Challenge   See if you can make up a game for the whole class, using all of the available space and no equipment. Your game must stress participation and equality.

Divide the class into two teams. Each team writes the names of five different shapes on separate pieces of paper and places them facedown in the middle of the playing area. By turns, one member from each team selects one piece of paper and whispers to his teammates the geometric shape they have to form. The other team tries to guess the name of the shape before they exchange positions (figure 17.15).

Jump Ball (Botswana) (Levels II, III)

Challenge   Can you make up a game with three players and one ball? Somewhere in your game you must have a bounce and a catch.

Three players stand in a straight line. Player 1 bounces the ball in front of player 2. As soon as the ball leaves player 1's hands, players 1 and 2 exchange positions, while player 3 catches the ball. Player 3 returns to her original position, then bounces the ball in front of player 1, who is now in the middle position. The game continues for five or six rotations.

Clock (Czech Republic) (Levels II, III)

Challenge   Develop a game for the whole class and use four balls. Your game should also stress fun, equality, and cooperation.

Arrange the four groups as shown in figure 17.16. The first player in each group holds the ball in both hands. When the teacher says "Go," the first player in each group passes the ball clockwise, then moves clockwise to the back of the next line. The game continues until all players return to their starting positions.

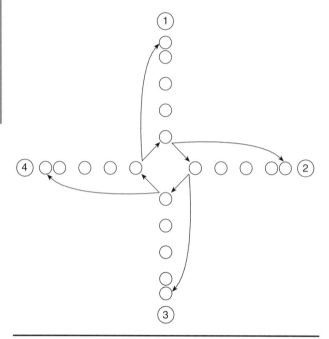

Figure 17.16   Movement of the clock.

Figure 17.17   She holds "it's" hand in Paga-Ajuda.

Figure 17.18   Frog, Jump, Slide.

Paga-Ajuda (Tag and Help) (Brazil) (Levels II, III)

Challenge   Invent a new tag game for the whole class, using all the available space and no equipment. Your game must stress participation and equality.

One player is chosen to be "it," and all other players scatter in the playing area. On signal from the teacher, "it" tries to tag another player. When a player is tagged, she holds "it's" hand (figure 17.17) and both try to tag another player. Each player who is tagged holds hands with the last player until every player is tagged.

Frog, Jump, Slide (South Africa) (Level II, III)

Challenge   See if you can make up a game for six players, using all the available space and no equipment. Your game must stress participation and equality.

The group begins standing in a row with legs apart. The last player starts crawling through the legs (figure 17.18). As soon as she has passed under two players, the next player follows,

and so on until the last player has crawled through the line. Next they spread apart but remain in a row, and each player leapfrogs over every other member of the team. Finally, the front player leads everyone around a full circle and back to the starting position. The last player moves to the front of the line, and the game repeats. Continue the game until all players are back in their original positions.

Ting, Ting, Ting (Mexico) (Level II, III)

Challenge   Can you invent a game of cooperation for four players and use four small pieces of equipment.

Draw a playing square with four X's in the middle. Players may stand or squat in their corners. They take turns throwing or sliding their lids so that they land on all or part of an X (one lid per X). Once each player has had a turn, and provided there are still lids that have not landed on an X, the player that is closest to any remaining lid retrieves it and throws or slides it toward any remaining X. The game continues until the last X is covered.

TECHNIQUES FOR PROMOTING COOPERATIVE LEARNING IN PHYSICAL EDUCATION

The following four techniques can be used in physical education classes to clarify and enhance cooperative learning. Each technique, however, should be modified to suit the differences in age, ability, and cultural background of each class.

Sharing a Goal

The following example illustrates how a teacher can "quietly" require each student to contribute equally to cooperative games challenge by having them share a goal. Arrange the class into partners and give each set one ball, then pose the following challenge:

Challenge See if you can make up a game with your partner, in your own space, using one ball and you must keep one score. As you begin to design your game, player 1 must provide the first idea for the game. Player 2 follows with her idea, and so on until you have made up your game.

In the above challenge, "keeping one score" encourages partners to cooperate and share their successes. In addition, requiring each child to take his turn developing the game means each child is contributing equally to the game. The following are some other applications of this technique:

1. Repeat the above with two players designing a new practice activity for soccer or basketball.
2. Repeat the above with two children developing a gymnastic routine or creative dance sequence.
3. Repeat the above with two or three students creating a new obstacle course in the gymnasium, a new hopscotch pattern, or a new intramural poster.

Corners

Using corners is a cooperative learning technique that enables students to choose and discuss a particular dimension of a topic. The teacher posts signs with different parts of a topic in designated corners of the room. Then each student selects one particular dimension in response to a question asked by the teacher, and moves to the appropriate corner.

Example A: Volleyball Skills
"What skills would you like to develop?"
[Corner #1—Serve]
[Corner #2—Bump]
[Corner #3—Set]
[Corner #4—Spike]

Example B: Cooperative Games
"What elements of cooperative games are you most interested in?"
[Corner #1—Cooperation]
[Corner #2—Equality]
[Corner #3—Participation]
[Corner #4—Trust]

Once in a corner, students discuss reasons for their choice. The teacher randomly selects one or two children from each corner to report their thinking to the class.

Think, Pair, and Share

In this technique, players are first arranged in partners. The teacher then poses a question or problem for each player to privately think about and formulate a tentative answer. As soon as both players have a tentative solution, they begin to share their answers with each other. Once they have shared these, they move to create a new answer, which could be a blending of each other's ideas or a new answer based upon discussion and, hopefully, joint agreement. The process is this:

1. Think—Formulate an answer individually.
2. Pair—Share your answer with a partner.
3. Share—Create a new answer through discussion.

An example of this technique would be to have partners practice a basketball bounce-pass with both players constantly on the move. After a few minutes, the teacher stops the activity and poses the following question: "Can you add two pieces of small equipment to your practice activity?" The process begins with "Think"; that is, each player sits down and thinks of the two pieces of equipment she would select and how it could be used in the practice activity. Next is "Pairs": partners explain to each other how they might use the equipment and the types of movements that would improve their performance. Finally, "Share" involves partners agreeing upon the selection of the two pieces of equipment and using movement patterns suggested by one of the players.

T-Charting

T-Charting is another useful technique for helping children understand the importance and use of a variety of social and collaborative skills. Students can work with the teacher, individually, in partners, or in small groups to develop a T-Chart for a particular skill. In our example, the teacher assigned the skill "Using quiet voices" to small groups. The left column shows one group's list of a variety of things they could do to speak softly or to communicate without using their voices. The righthand column lists various comments children could make to encourage everyone to speak softly or communicate using body language.

Skill: Using Quiet Voices

What Students Can Do	What Students Can Say
Talk with a lower voice	Let's remember to speak softly or whisper.
Sit near each other	Let's sit close together.
Place fingers to lips to indicate to speak with a lower voice	We are doing a great job of talking quietly.
Use hand signals or body gestures instead of talking	Let's try some hand signals.

The following social skills are important, particularly in physical education classes. The teacher in discussions with her class should add other social and collaborative skills they consider to be important. Dividing the class into small groups and assigning one of the following skills to each group helps to clarify their meaning and emphasize their importance.

Other Important Social and Collaborative Skills

Taking turns	Asking questions
Sharing equipment	Being self-controlled
Praising	Clarifying ideas
Everyone participates	Describing feelings
Staying on task	Moving quietly within and
Controlling anger	to groups
Accepting differences in attitudes and abilities	Checking for understanding
Listening	Criticizing ideas and not people
Resolving conflicts	Integrating ideas
Following directions	Negotiating

Summary Review

This chapter's outline of the process of teaching cooperative games should be considered a flexible guideline. This approach is successful when the children understand the meaning of cooperative behavior. Once the children have learned this, begin with two or three players and involve one or two cooperative elements. Gradually increase the size of the group and add more elements as the children demonstrate an understanding and acceptance of the elements of cooperative behavior. Social and collaborative skills can also be taught through the application of instructional techniques such as sharing a goal; corners; think, pair, and share; and T-charting.

INDIVIDUAL *and* **GROUP** **PROJECTS**

1. Select a practice activity in soccer and softball, and describe how you would add to or modify it to stress cooperation.
2. Choose a lead-up game or relay activity, and describe how it could be converted into a cooperative activity.
3. In groups of two, three, or five, select a lead-up game and begin to change it into a cooperative activity.
4. In groups of four or five, design a series of cooperative game challenges that begin with two players and one or two cooperative game elements. Once the challenges are written out, share them with another group. Finally, select one challenge from each group, arrange the class according to the required number of players, then pose the challenge to the class.
5. In small groups of four or five, select a social skill and T-chart it in the manner illustrated in the example "Using a Quiet Voice."

Selected Readings

Abrami, P. C., B. Chambers, C. Poulsen, C. De Simone, S. D'Apollonia, and J. Howden. 1995 *Classroom connections: Understanding and using cooperative learning.* New York: Harcourt Brace.

Fluegelman, A. 1981. *More new games.* New York: Doubleday.

Johnson, D. W., and R. T. Johnson. 1994. *Learning together and alone.* 4th ed. Needham Heights, MA: Allyn & Bacon.

Johnson, D. W., R. T. Johnson, and E. W. Holubec. 1993. *Circles of learning.* 4th ed. Minneapolis: Interaction Book Co.

Kirchner, G. 1991. *Children's games from around the world.* Dubuque, IA: Wm. C. Brown.

Morris, D. 1976. *How to change the games children play.* Minneapolis: Burgess.

Orlick, T. 1982. *The second cooperative games book.* New York: Pantheon Books.

Slavin, R., 1983. *Cooperative learning.* New York: Longman.

Whistler, N., and J. Williams. 1992. *Literature and cooperative learning: Pathway to literacy.* Sacramento, CA: Literature Co-Op.

CHAPTER 18

Soccer Activities

KEY CONCEPTS

18.1 Soccer activities must be developmentally appropriate to ensure that all children can achieve success and enjoyment

18.2 Specialized soccer skills are acquired through instruction and practice opportunities

18.3 Playing a full-sided competitive game of soccer is not a very efficient way of teaching large numbers of children specialized soccer skills

18.4 Effective teaching progressions, that provide all children with individual practices and lead-up games, are required to develop the skills and knowledge associated with soccer

18.5 To develop soccer skills to the automatic stage of skill development requires many practice opportunities (time on-task)

18.6 Inventing soccer-type games stimulates creativity and allows children to adjust the game to their own developmental level

KEY OBJECTIVES

After completing this chapter you will be able to:

1. Design developmentally appropriate soccer activities for elementary school children
2. Plan and organize teaching units and individual lessons in soccer
3. Organize practice activities and lead-up games appropriate for soccer development
4. Plan and organize soccer practice activities and lead-up games that incorporate the inventive games approach
5. Evaluate units, lessons, and individual techniques used in soccer
6. Identify key teaching points associated with the basic skills of soccer
7. Employ teaching progressions that lead to successful development of soccer skills and concepts
8. Understand the rules and basic strategies associated with soccer

Of all the major sports played in the United States and Canada, soccer has shown the most rapid increase in participation in recent years. It requires a great deal of skill in running, dribbling, and kicking. However, it is an inexpensive sport— requiring only a ball and two goalposts—and involves total body movement, making it an excellent activity for upper elementary children. Furthermore, only a few basic skills and rules need to be learned to enjoy the game.

This chapter provides sufficient information to develop a major soccer unit. The central purpose is to give children an opportunity to acquire the basic soccer skills, rules, and playing strategies through as many enjoyable, gamelike situations as possible. Modification of practice activities and lead-up games, coupled with the application of the inventive games approach, should be the rule rather than the exception when teaching soccer.

This chapter provides detailed descriptions of basic soccer skills together with key teaching points. Practice activities and teaching progressions through lead-up and mini-games are described and provided.

C O N C E P T

18.1 *Soccer Activities Must Be Developmentally Appropriate to Ensure That All Children Can Achieve Success and Enjoyment*

EMPHASIS AND PROGRESSION

Children have usually learned to kick a stationary or moving ball by the end of third grade. Their ability to stop the ball is normally limited to a simple foot or leg trap. They understand dribbling but are not very proficient at it, as they tend to use their toes and to "kick and chase."

As outlined in table 18.1, a systematic presentation of the basic soccer skills and rules should begin in fourth grade. These children should learn to kick and pass with either foot, to control the ball with the side of the foot, and to increase their control while dribbling. A few of the basic rules relating to kicking, handling the ball, and checking should also be introduced in this grade. Lead-up games, such as Circle Soccer and Soccer Dodgeball, should be emphasized, rather than playing the official game or a modified version.

C O N C E P T

18.2 *Specialized Soccer Skills are Acquired Through Instruction and Practice Opportunities*

Throughout fifth grade, improved passing, trapping, and dribbling skills should be emphasized. After these basic skills are acquired, the children should be introduced to a few of the more specialized kicking skills, the side-of-leg trap, and heading the ball. More advanced lead-up games, such as Forwards and Backs and Mini- or Seven-Person Soccer with more specific rules and playing positions, are also indicated.

Although children in this age group should be involved in mini-soccer games, and occasionally the full-sided game, their skill level still calls for a lot of individual and small-group practice and lead-up activities. Therefore, balancing the time spent on these two types of activities is very important. Mini-soccer, which uses half the field, is also more desirable for the intramural program than the official eleven-person game, because it allows more children to participate.

C O N C E P T

18.3 *Playing a Full-Sided Competitive Game of Soccer Is Not a Very Efficient Way of Teaching Large Numbers of Children Specialized Soccer Skills*

TEACHING PROCEDURES

The general instructional procedures discussed above and in previous chapters also apply to teaching soccer activities. Of particular importance are the development of a unit of instruction discussed on pages 197–201 and the illustrated lesson on page 203. In addition, the inventive games approach (p. 315) can be applied successfully when teaching soccer activities.

Developing a Soccer Unit

Each teaching situation varies according to the length of the unit and lesson and the available facilities and equipment, so the following approach should be considered as only a basic guideline. Soccer is a relatively new sport to many teachers and children, and this outline should be modified to meet each situation.

Step 1: Determine the length of the unit. Since a class may have from one to five physical education lessons a week, the units should be expressed in terms of the number of lessons.

Step 2: Assess the class's level of ability. The evaluative techniques at the end of this chapter can be used. Having the class play one or two lead-up games also provides an overview of its ability.

Step 3: List sequentially the skills, rules, and playing strategies that will be emphasized.

TABLE 18.1	Suggested Sequence of Presenting Soccer Skills and Rules	
	Developmental Level II	**Developmental Level III**
Kicking		
Instep Kick	Pass with either foot	Increase distance and accuracy
Inside-of-Foot Kick	Pass with either foot	Increase distance and accuracy
Outside-of-Foot Kick	Introduce	Increase distance and accuracy
Punting		Introduce
Volley Kick		Introduce
Rules: Kickoff	Introduce	
Free Kick		Introduce
Corner Kick	Introduce	
Goal Kick	Introduce	
Penalty Kick		Introduce
Trapping		
Foot Trap	Acquired or introduce	Refine
Side-of-Foot Trap	Introduce	Refine
Leg Trap		Introduce
Body Trap		Introduce
Rules: Handling the Ball	Introduce	
Dribbling		
Inside of Feet	Acquired or introduce	Increase accuracy and speed
Outside of Feet	Acquired or introduce	Increase accuracy and speed
Heading		
Stationary Heading		Introduce
Feet Off Ground		Introduce
Throw-In		
From Behind Head	Introduce	Increase distance and accuracy
Rules: Throw-in	Introduce	
Tackling		
With Feet	Introduce	Refine
Rules: Charging	Introduce	
Other Rules		
Team Positions	Introduce	
Goalkeeper Privileges		Introduce
Rules: Offside		Introduce

30-Minute Lesson

10–15%	15–80%	5–10%
3–5 minutes	5–20 minutes	1–3 minutes
Introductory Activities	*Skill Development*	*Closure*
Vigorous running, dodging, and conditioning exercises	Demonstrations Individual practice Partner and practice activities Exploratory activities Lead-up games modified or official game of soccer	Review and cool-down

Step 4: Choose the appropriate practice activities and lead-up games. Later in this chapter, the practice activities, listed by skill, are organized into individual, partner, and group activities. The lead-up games are appropriate for developmental levels II and III.

Structure of a Lesson

The following approach is a basic guideline for planning and teaching a lesson. Each lesson should include a vigorous introductory activity that is related to the general theme of the lesson. The second part of the lesson should be devoted to acquiring and practicing one or more skills and playing a variety of lead-up games. Finally, closure allows time to review the key points of the lesson and to relax.

18.4 *Effective Teaching Progressions, That Provide All Children with Individual Practices and Lead-Up Games, Are Required to Develop the Skills and Knowledge Associated with Soccer*

Adjust shorter or longer lessons on the basis of time allocation. Introductory Activities and Closure should always be included in each lesson. The length of time devoted to part two of the lesson depends on the stage of development of the unit and the ability of the students.

Each soccer lesson should begin with running, dodging, and general conditioning activities to increase the children's cardiorespiratory endurance and to prepare them for the next part of the lesson. During the first few lessons, the demonstration and practice activities should be given a considerable amount of time in order to introduce and practice skills and playing strategies. After a skill is explained and demonstrated, each child should have an opportunity to practice it without excessive pressure and to test and explore other ways of performing a movement pattern. Once the children understand the skill and can perform it, they should practice with partners. Since most classes are coeducational, partner activities are an excellent way to cope with varying levels of ability and to mix boys and girls subtly.

18.5 *To Develop Soccer Skills to the Automatic Stage of Skill Development Requires Many Practice Opportunities (Time On-Task)*

Inventive or Creative Games

Partner activities also provide a springboard for introducing inventive games. For example, in lessons emphasizing passing and trapping, partners can be challenged to "make up a game with your partner that involves a pass and a trap . . . and a hoop" (or any other piece of small equipment). Refer to chapter 16 for more ideas. The more structured practice activities that are used in this part of the lesson can be presented initially in a more formal or direct manner. After the class has practiced the activity, the teacher can introduce variations by presenting simple challenges to each group. For example, if the class is practicing the game Keep Away, a challenge, such as "See if you can play the same game but add a hoop" (or three beanbags), gives each group a chance to create a new version of the game.

18.6 *Inventing Soccer-Type Games Stimulates Creativity and Allows Children to Adjust the Game to Their Own Developmental Level*

During the latter phase of part 2, lead-up games provide a low-key means of practicing skills in a gamelike situation. Playing space should be used to maximum capacity. Divide the playing field into halves or quarters so that two or four games can be played. The inventive games approach also works extremely well with lead-up games. Limit these games in a small way at first; later, challenge each group to design its own game or to choose any equipment it wants. This will open the door to many new and exciting soccer-type games. Use closure to emphasize one or two key points of your lesson and to provide praise and constructive comments.

As the soccer unit progresses, more time should be devoted to lead-up and modified games and less time to practice activities. Group activities should include a wide variety of lead-up games, inventive games, and to a lesser degree mini- or official soccer. The more competitive aspects of soccer and other team games should be reserved for the junior and senior high school physical education program.

The following suggestions can also help in developing a safe and effective program of activities:

1. Limit the playing field to a small, manageable instructional area. Mark off a 100-foot square section of the field with traffic cones or milk cartons (p. 312) for demonstrations and practice activities. Enlarge the area as needed.
2. Soccer requires a great deal of endurance, particularly of the heart and lungs and the leg muscles. Increase running and other endurance activities gradually and systematically. Watch for overfatigued children and switch them to less demanding positions.
3. Although soccer rules do not allow any players except the goalie to use their hands, adjustments should be made for the children's safety. They should be taught to protect their faces against oncoming balls, and, in addition, girls should be instructed to fold their arms across their chests to prevent injury.
4. One of the cardinal principles of good teaching is total participation by all children. Whenever possible, keep each team small and divide the playing area so two or more games can be played.

DESCRIPTION OF SKILLS

Soccer is basically a kicking and running game; however, when played correctly, such skills as dribbling, trapping, heading, and throwing are also necessary for maximum success and enjoyment. Each of these skills will be described, along with the more common faults to observe and correct.

Figure 18.1 Instep kick.

Kicking

In soccer, the ball may be kicked with either foot from a stationary, running, or volley (while in the air) position. Certain fundamentals should be stressed in every practice and game situation. First, players should keep their eye on the ball as it approaches them or as they approach the ball. Second, players should kick the ball with their instep (top side of the foot)—never with their toes. Finally, after the ball has been kicked, players should follow through with their kicking foot for a short distance in the direction of the kick. Each of these fundamentals applies to the following five basic kicking skills.

Instep Kick

The instep kick (figure 18.1), used for passing and for shooting at the goal, is the most common skill in soccer. Just before the ball is kicked, the nonkicking foot is slightly flexed and even with the ball. The head and trunk lean slightly forward, with the arms extended sideways, and the kicking leg is well back, with the knee slightly bent (figure 18.1a). As the kicking leg moves downward and forward, the knee moves forward and over the ball. The ankle extends downward to allow the top of the instep to contact the ball (figure 18.1b). Follow through by continuing the forward movement of the kicking leg (figure 18.1c).

Key Teaching Points

1. Look at the target, then at the ball.
2. Keep toe of kicking foot pointing down.
3. Contact center of ball with instep.
4. Use arms to maintain balance.
5. Follow through with an upward swing of the leg.

Inside-of-Foot Kick

This is a variation of the instep kick and is used for short, accurate passes or for shooting at the goal (figure 18.2). The

Figure 18.2 Kicking with inside of foot.

body is bent slightly forward, with the weight evenly distributed on both feet. The front of the ball should be even with the toes and about six inches to the side of the kicking foot. Shift weight to the nonkicking foot and swing the kicking foot outward, with knee slightly bent (figure 18.2a). Swing the foot down and toward the ball, contacting it with the inside of the foot (figure 18.2b). Follow through with the kicking foot crossing in front of the opposite leg (figure 18.2c).

Key Teaching Points

1. Look at the target, then at the ball.
2. Keep a slight forward body lean throughout the kicking action.
3. Turn the toe of the kicking foot outward to allow inside of foot to contact the ball.
4. Follow through upward and in front of the opposite leg.

CHAPTER 18

Figure 18.3   Kicking with outside of foot.

Figure 18.4   Volley kick.

Outside-of-Foot Kick

This kick requires a pushing or jabbing action with the outer part of the foot. It is used for short passes or dribbling without breaking the running movement. The player stands slightly to the side of the ball. Bend the nonkicking leg and shift weight onto it (figure 18.3a). Bend knee of kicking leg with toe pointing down, then swing leg toward the ball (figure 18.3b). Contact the ball with the outer edge of the foot and follow through in the direction of the kick (figure 18.3c).

Key Teaching Points

1. Begin with the body at a slight angle to the ball.
2. Look at the target, then at the ball.
3. Snap the lower leg quickly to the side contacting the ball with the outside edge of the foot.
4. Follow through in the direction of the ball.

Volley Kick

The volley is performed when the ball is in flight. This is a difficult kick, so elementary school children should not be expected to do it with a high degree of accuracy. However, because this kick is a time-saver and because it generates much force, children will attempt to perform it. The player stands with the nonkicking foot in front and weight evenly distributed on both feet. The head and body face the ball and the body tilts forward slightly (figure 18.4a). As the ball approaches, the player shifts weight to the nonkicking foot and raises the kicking leg, with the knee slightly bent and the toes pointing down (figure 18.4b). The player contacts the ball with the top of the instep and follows through in a forward and upward direction (figure 18.4c).

a. Hold ball chest high. b. Swing kicking leg forward. c. Contact ball with top of foot. d. Follow through to an extended leg position.

Figure 18.5   Punting.

Key Teaching Points

1. Take a quick look at the target, then quickly focus on the oncoming ball.
2. Keep body leaning slightly forward.
3. Contact the ball with instep and toe down.
4. Follow through in the direction of the ball.

Punting

The goalkeeper is the only player allowed to punt. The ball is held about chest high (figure 18.5a). The kicking leg swings forward and upward as the ball is dropped (figure 18.5b). As the leg moves in a forward and upward direction, the ball contacts the instep (figure 18.5c). Follow through into an extended leg position (figure 18.5d).

Key Teaching Points

1. Take a quick look at the target, then look at the ball.
2. Hold the ball with two hands.
3. Drop the ball, rather than throwing it downward.
4. Contact the ball high on the instep.
5. Follow through in the direction of the ball.

Trapping

Trapping is stopping the ball while it is moving through the air or on the ground. Any part of the body except the hands and arms may be used. The type of trap a player uses depends on the flight of the ball, the position of opponents, and the amount of time the trapper has. Upper elementary school children should be able to perform the following four trapping skills.

Front Foot Trap

The front foot trap is used to trap a rolling or bouncing ball. As the ball approaches, the player raises her foot about

a   b

Figure 18.6   Front foot trap.

six inches off the ground, with her toes up, forming a V between the ground and the sole of the foot (figure 18.6a). When the ball contacts the sole, the foot relaxes to let the ball lose its recoil action and remain beneath the foot (figure 18.6b).

Key Teaching Points

1. Keep eyes on the ball.
2. Move into position and directly face the oncoming ball.
3. Raise leg from the hip, keeping knee slightly bent.
4. As the ball is contacted, apply pressure to the top of the ball.

Side-of-Foot Trap

The side-of-foot trap is used in the same manner as the front foot trap; the main difference is the direction from which the ball approaches. The player raises her trapping

Figure 18.7   Side-of-foot trap. The foot gives slightly.

Figure 18.8   Leg trap.

leg four to five inches off the ground, with the inside of the foot toward the ball. As the ball strikes, the foot relaxes to absorb the force of the ball, allowing it to drop rather than to recoil forward (figure 18.7).

Key Teaching Points
1. Keep eyes on the ball.
2. Move into position and directly face the oncoming ball.
3. Lean the body in the direction of the oncoming ball.
4. When the ball contacts the inside of the foot, allow the foot to move slightly backward to slow down the ball.

Leg Trap
The leg trap is used when the ball is approaching from a high volley or a low bounce. As the ball approaches, the player shifts his weight to the nontrapping foot nearest the oncoming ball. His trapping leg bends at almost a right angle and his foot is well off the ground (figure 18.8a). When the ball makes contact, the leg gives a little to prevent the ball from rebounding too far forward (figure 18.8b).

Key Teaching Points
1. Keep eyes on the ball.
2. Move into position and directly face the oncoming ball.
3. Contact the ball halfway between knee and hip.
4. When the ball contacts the thigh, draw the leg back to allow ball to drop to the ground.

Body Trap
The body trap is used when the ball is descending from a high volley or when a player wants to prevent a high-rising ball from getting past him. To perform this type of trap, the player brings arms forward but does not touch the ball with his hands or arms. Legs should be shoulder-width apart, with knees slightly bent. Lean backward, tuck chin in, and contact ball on the chest (figure 18.9a). As the ball contacts the chest, draw slightly back to allow the ball to drop to the

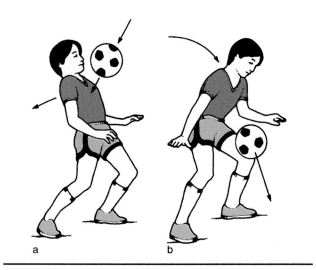

Figure 18.9   Body trap.

ground (figure 18.9b). Girls should fold their arms across the chest and press elbows snugly against the body when attempting this trapping skill (figure 18.10).

Key Teaching Points
1. Keep eyes on the ball.
2. Move into position and directly face the oncoming ball.
3. Give with the ball as it contacts the chest.

Dribbling

Dribbling in soccer is moving the ball with short pushes by the inside or outside of either foot. These pushes permit the player to control the ball, whether dribbling forward or sideward. Although dribbling with the inside of the foot is quite easy, good ball control requires use of the outside of either foot. Dribbling backward is bad practice, as it only helps the opponent.

Figure 18.10 Chest protected body trap.

Figure 18.11 Dribbling. Push, or "persuade," the ball.

The body should be bent forward slightly, with the head over the ball. Gently push or "persuade" the ball, keeping the head up high enough to make an offensive move and to watch oncoming opponents (figure 18.11).

Key Teaching Points
1. Dribble with short, controlled steps.
2. Keep the ball close to the feet when near opponents.
3. Keep looking around while dribbling to know where opponents and teammates are positioned.
4. Push, rather than kick, the ball.

Heading

Heading is hitting or bunting the soccer ball with the front of the forehead. As the ball approaches, the player bends her knees and leans back from the hips. Arms are raised, and slightly to the side (figure 18.12a). She then shifts her body weight forward and upward and brings her head forward to meet the ball (figure 18.12b). The ball must contact the front of the forehead, with a continuous forward movement of the body in the direction of the intended flight of the ball (figure 18.12c). The key to good heading lies in correctly judging the speed and height of the oncoming ball.

Key Teaching Points
1. Keep eyes on the ball.
2. Bend from the hips.
3. Just before contact, thrust the head and trunk forward.
4. Follow through in the direction of the ball.

Figure 18.12 Heading.

Throw-In

Whenever the ball goes over the sidelines, it is put back into play by a throw-in. The ball is thrown from behind the head with both hands. Parts of both feet remain on the ground until the ball leaves the player's hands, although any position of the feet is permissible. Begin with one foot in front of the other or with the feet parallel. Hold the ball with fingers at the side and thumbs behind (figure 18.13a). Simultaneously raise the ball up and behind the head, lean backward, and bend the knees (figure 18.13b). Shift the trunk forward and upward and bring the ball over the head, extending the arms toward the direction of the throw. Release the ball and follow through with hands and arms (figure 18.13c).

Figure 18.13 Throw-in.

Key Teaching Points

1. Keep both hands behind the ball.
2. Keep both feet in contact with the ground.
3. Make one move backward followed by one move forward.
4. Learn to follow through and step into the playing field.

Tackling

In soccer the team in possession of the ball is known as the *offensive,* or *attacking,* team. Any defensive player may legally tackle a player who has possession of the ball, but only from the front or side, with the feet or shoulders. Using the hands or tackling from behind is against the rules. When tackling, the defensive player watches the ball and the opponent's feet for clues to the direction she may take (figure 18.14a). The body weight should also be evenly distributed on both feet in order to shift right or left. The tackle should be made when the opponent is slightly off balance, which is just before she begins to dribble or pass the ball (figure 18.14b).

Key Teaching Points

1. Be quick and decisive when approaching an opponent who has possession of the ball.
2. Tackle the opponent when she is in control of the ball but is slightly off balance, usually when she pushes the ball forward a little.
3. Be ready to pass the ball as soon as you gain possession.

Goalkeeping

The primary responsibility of the goalkeeper is to keep the ball from crossing over the goal line and between the goalposts. To accomplish this task, the goalkeeper can catch or deflect the ball away from the goal.

a. Watch feet for clues

b. Tackle when opponent is off balance

Figure 18.14 Tackling.

Figure 18.15 Get in line with the oncoming ball.

Figure 18.16 Both hands behind the ball, with fingers pointing down.

Figure 18.17 Draw the ball into the chest.

Figure 18.18 Hands behind the ball.

Figure 18.19 Punch shot.

The technique used to catch a ball depends on the location of the oncoming ball. The first move is to get in line with the oncoming ball (figure 18.15). Next, catch it with both hands and pull the ball toward the chest. When a ball is approaching along the ground, slightly flex the knees, bend forward and down, and place both hands behind the ball with fingers pointing down (figure 18.16). Scoop the ball upward into the arms and chest (figure 18.17). A ball approaching from below the waist should be caught with hands down similar to the stance position, then draw ball back into chest. For balls approaching above the waist, the arms are up, elbows sideways, and the ball is caught with the hands behind the ball, fingers pointing up and thumbs close together (figure 18.18).

The technique used to deflect a ball that cannot be caught is a punch or push shot. The punch shot is made with clenched fists (figure 18.19) and players may hit the ball with one or both hands.

Key Teaching Points
1. Keep the body between the goal and the ball.
2. Move out from the goal to cut down the angle of the approaching ball.
3. Watch the ball, not the player.
4. Keep fingers spread and always pull a caught ball toward the chest.

PRACTICE ACTIVITIES AND LEAD-UP GAMES

Table 18.2 includes practice activities and lead-up games for developmental levels II and III. As children move from level II to III, there should be an increase in their level of skill and general playing ability. The majority of practice activities relating to kicking and trapping skills involve two or more players. However, the few individual activities that follow give each child opportunities to get used to the bounce of the ball and to control the ball with the feet. Partner and small-group activities provide more realistic ball-handling situations including one or more skills. The procedure used to teach passing and trapping can also be followed when teaching dribbling skills. Begin with individual activities, add small equipment, move on to partner activities, and then perform group activities. Heading and throw-in skills are normally practiced together in partner or group activities. However, individual activities can be practiced if a wall is available. Tackling is normally practiced in combination with another skill, and two or more players are involved. The lead-up games in table 18.2 allow children to practice the skills learned in each section.

PRACTICE ACTIVITIES

The following practice activities are arranged to allow students to progress from individual, to partner, to group activities.

Throw, Bounce, Trap

Motor skills Throw, bounce, trap
Movement concepts Moving into space, use of space
Players Individual
Formation Scattered

TABLE 18.2   Practice Activities and Lead-Up Games

Name of Activity	Type of Activity	Players	Developmental Level		Soccer Concepts and Skills	Movement Concept	Page
			II	III			
Practice Activities							
Throw, Bounce, Trap	Trap	Individual	———————→		Throw, bounce, trap	Moving ball into space, use of space	381
Wall Kicking	Kick, trap	Individual	———————→		Kick, trap	Use of space, change of direction, strong and light	382
Juggle the Ball	Kick	Individual	———————→		Kick	Strong and light, personal space	383
Individual Dribbling	Dribble, trap	Individual	———————→		Dribble, trap	Moving into space, change of direction	383
Throw and Head	Throw, head	Individual	———————→		Throw, head	Moving into space, change of direction	384
Stop, Go, Turn	Dribble, stop, turn	Individual	———————→		Dribble, stop, turn	Moving into space, change of direction, pathway, and speed	384
Passing and Trapping	Pass, trap	2	———————→		Pass, trap	Moving into space, changing direction and pathway	384
Wall Passing and Trapping	Pass, trap	2	———————→		Pass, trap	Use of space, change of direction	384
Target Shooting	Pass, trap	2	———————→		Pass, trap	Moving into space, change of direction and speed	385
Circle Passing	Pass, trap	2	———————→		Pass, trap	Moving into space, change of direction and speed	385
Follow the Leader	Dribble	2	———————→		Dribble	Moving into space, change of direction and pathway	385
Dribble and Pass	Dribble, pass, offensive play	2	———————→		Dribble, pass	Moving into space, change of direction, pathway, and speed	385
Throw and Head	Throw, head	2	———————→		Throw, head	Moving into space, change of direction, pathway, and speed	386
Partner Keep Away	Dribble, dodge, stop	2	———————→		Dribble, dodge, stop	Moving into space, change of direction, pathway, and speed	386
Triangle Pass	Pass, trap	3	———————————→		Pass, trap	Change of direction	386
Kicking for Distance	Kick	4–5	———————————→		Kick	Moving into space, strong and light	386
Goal Kicking	Kick, trap	4–6	———————————→		Kick, trap	Moving into space	386
Goal Heading	Head, throw	4–6	———————————→		Head, throw	Moving into space, use of space, change of direction and speed	386
Shuttle Dribble and Tackle	Dribble, tackle	4	———————→		Dribble, tackle	Moving through space, change of direction and speed	387
One vs. Two Players	Dribble, pass, tackle	3	———————→		Dribble, pass, tackle	Moving into space, change of direction and speed	387

Playing area   Playground, gymnasium
Equipment   Ball

Each child has a ball (any inflated ball can be used) and finds his own space in the playing area. Have the child throw his ball into the air, allow it to bounce once, and then try to trap it with one foot. Add other limitations, such as trapping with the left foot, the side of the leg, or the chest.

▧ Wall Kicking

Motor skills   Kick, trap
Movement concepts   Use of space, change of direction, strong and light
Players   Individual
Formation   Line
Playing area   Playground, gymnasium
Equipment   Ball

TABLE 18.2 *Continued*

Name of Activity	Type of Activity	Players	Developmental Level		Soccer Concepts and Skills	Movement Concept	Page
			II	III			
Lead-up games							
Circle Soccer	Kick, trap	14 or 5 per team	———————▶		Kick, trap	Personal space, moving into space	387
Soccer Dodgeball	Kick, trap	Class	———————▶		Kick, trap	Moving into space, change of direction and speed	387
Boundary Ball	Kick, trap	20–30	———————▶		Kick, trap	Moving into space, change of direction and speed	387
Change Soccer	All skills	6 per game	———————▶		All soccer skills	Use of available space, change of direction, pathway, and speed	387
Marble Soccer	Shoot, trap	3–4 per game	———————▶		Shoot, trap	Moving into space, strong and light	388
Circle of Fun	Dribble, shoot	6 per game	———————▶		Dribble, pass, shoot, tackle	Moving through space, change of direction and speed	388
Punt Back	Kick, trap	4–20	———————▶		Kick, trap	Use of available space, moving into space	388
Alley Soccer	Pass, trap, kick	20–24	———————▶		Pass, trap, kick	Personal space, moving into space, change of direction and speed	388
Forwards and Backs	Pass, dribble, trap	20–24	———————▶		Pass, dribble, trap	Personal space, moving into space, change of direction and speed	389
Four-Goal Soccer	All skills	8–10	———————▶		All soccer skills	Use of available space, moving into space, change of direction and speed	389
Seven-Person Soccer	All skills	14	———————▶		All soccer skills	Use of available space, moving into space, change of direction, pathway, and speed	389

Arrange children in a line formation along available wall surface. Each player stands about six feet from the wall, kicks the ball to the wall, and retrieves her own rebound with a foot or leg trap.

Suggestions and Variations
1. Allow each child to kick the ball as it rebounds (no trap required).
2. Start several yards back from the ball, run up and kick it, and trap the rebound.
3. Start several yards back, dribble to a line, kick the ball to the wall, and trap the rebound.
4. Place a target on the wall (a circle or square) and repeat previous activities.
5. Repeat previous activities with the opposite foot.

Juggle the Ball

Motor skills   Kick
Movement concepts   Strong and light, personal space
Players   Individual
Formation   Scattered
Playing area   Playground, gymnasium
Equipment   Soccer ball

Juggling a ball is not part of playing soccer; nevertheless, this is an excellent practice activity for a small space and for learning to control the ball. This practice activity should be introduced in steps. First, the player drops the ball toward his instep. Then he softly kicks it back up and catches it. Next, he drops the ball onto the thigh (figure 18.20), rebounds it, and catches it. Then he repeats the drop to the instep, kicks the ball up two times, and catches it on the second kick. He repeats with the thigh. As skill improves, allow players to combine the kick with instep to thigh, to instep to other foot, to head then back to foot, and so on.

Individual Dribbling

Motor skills   Dribble, trap
Movement concepts   Moving into space, change of direction
Players   Individual
Formation   Scattered
Playing area   Playground, gymnasium
Equipment   Soccer ball

Each child has a ball (any inflated ball) and finds her own space in the playing area. Allow children to dribble anywhere within the playing area, as long as they do not bump into other players.

Figure 18.20   Drop ball onto the thigh.

Figure 18.21   Dribble and stop.

Suggestions and Variations

1. Dribble and stop on whistle or voice command (figure 18.21).
2. Dribble in different directions on voice command (right, forward, left, right).
3. Dribble with the outside of the foot.
4. Give each player two or more pieces of small equipment (beanbags, hoops) and have her dribble around them.
5. Add other skills, such as dribbling, stopping, trapping, and then shooting at the wall.

Throw and Head

Motor skills   Throw, head
Movement concepts   Moving into space, change of direction
Players   Individual
Formation   Scattered
Playing area   Playground, gymnasium
Equipment   Soccer ball

Each player has a ball and stands about five or six feet from the wall. Practice the throw-in, then do a throw-in and head the rebound back to the wall. Repeat the throw-in, then turn sideways and attempt to head the ball back to the wall.

Stop, Go, Turn

Motor skills   Dribble, stop, turn
Movement concepts   Moving into space, change of direction, pathway, and speed
Players   Individual
Formation   Scattered
Playing area   Playground, gymnasium
Equipment   Soccer balls

Mark off a square of about twenty by twenty yards. Every player has a ball. On "Go" signal, all players dribble the ball in different directions, avoiding other players as they move

through the playing area. On "Stop" signal, players must stop the ball with their feet and be ready for the next signal. On "Go" signal, they all start dribbling again. As they continue dribbling, the teacher calls "Turn," signaling every player to turn in any direction in which there is space to move.

Suggestions and Variations

1. Change method of signaling by hand signals (hand overhead—"Go," hand forward—"Stop," hands sideways—"Turn"). This requires all players to watch both ball and teacher as they move through space.
2. Add obstacles to the playing space.

Passing and Trapping

Motor skills   Pass, trap
Movement concepts   Moving into space, change of direction and pathway
Players   Two
Formation   Scattered
Playing area   Playground, gymnasium
Equipment   Soccer ball

Partners sharing one ball find a space in the playing area. They stand about ten to fifteen feet apart. One player passes to the other, who traps the ball and returns the pass.

Suggestions and Variations

1. Change the type of pass and trap.
2. Repeat with one player stationary and the receiving players on the move.
3. Repeat above with both players on the move.
4. One player tries to kick the ball through the outstretched legs of his partner.

Wall Passing and Trapping

Motor skills   Pass, trap
Movement concepts   Use of space, change of direction
Players   Two

Formation None
Playing area Playground, gymnasium
Equipment Soccer ball

This drill is essentially the same as wall kicking. One player kicks the ball to the wall and her partner traps it and returns the kick. All other variations can be adapted to partner activities.

Target Shooting

Motor skills Pass, trap
Movement concepts Moving into space, change of direction and speed
Players Two
Formation See diagram
Playing area Playground, gymnasium
Equipment Soccer ball and traffic cones

Partners share one ball and two traffic cones (or milk cartons). Arrange partners and equipment as shown. One partner kicks the ball through the goals (cones) and the other partner traps the ball and repeats the kicking skill.

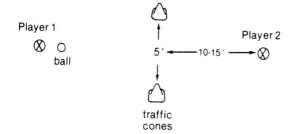

Suggestions and Variations
1. Change the type of kicking and trapping skills.
2. Change the angle of shooting.
3. Change the distance between goals.
4. Change the distance from the goals.

Circle Passing

Motor skills Pass, trap
Movement concepts Moving into space, change of direction and speed
Players Two
Formation Circle
Playing area Playground, gymnasium
Equipment Soccer ball

One player moves around a stationary partner. Stationary partner passes and traps the ball while circling player dribbles and passes.

Suggestions and Variations
1. Change the type of pass and trap.
2. Reverse directions.
3. Repeat activity without involving a trap.
4. This is an opportune time to introduce the problem-solving method. For example, after practicing several variations of the previous activity, pose a question such as "Can you change the position of your traffic cones and make up a drill that involves an inside-of-foot pass and a leg trap?" If children have experienced the inventive games

Figure 18.22 Follow the leader.

approach, a challenge such as "Using two cones and a ball, create your own passing and trapping drill" will produce a wide variety of responses.

Follow the Leader

Motor skills Dribble
Movement concepts Moving into space, change of direction and pathway
Players Two
Formation Line
Playing area Playground, gymnasium
Equipment Balls

This is an excellent activity to teach ball control and keeping an eye on another player. Each player has a ball. One partner dribbles in any direction and her partner follows (figure 18.22).

Suggestions and Variations
1. Partners dribble side by side.
2. Add one or more obstacles to dribble around.

Dribble and Pass

Motor skills Dribble, pass, offensive play
Movement concepts Moving into space, change of direction, pathway, and speed
Players Two
Formation None
Playing area Playground, gymnasium
Equipment Soccer ball

Partners dribble and pass a ball back and forth.

Suggestions and Variations
1. Add two or more obstacles to dribble around.
2. Repeat earlier drills with outside of feet.
3. Add other skills such as dribble, pass, and trap.

Throw and Head

Motor Skills Throw, head
Movement concepts Moving into space, change of direction, pathway, and speed
Players Two
Formation Line
Playing area Playground, gymnasium
Equipment Soccer balls

Partners stand about eight to twelve feet apart, facing each other. One partner, using a throw-in pass, throws the ball high into the air so that it descends just in front of his partner. That partner attempts to head the ball forward and downward toward the first partner's feet. Repeat several times, then change positions.

Suggestions and Variations

1. Tie a rope between two posts; the height may vary from four to six feet. Repeat the original activity but with the throw-in going over the rope and the headed ball returning under the rope.
2. Place a hoop on the floor between the players. Repeat the original drill, requiring the headed ball to hit the center of the hoop.

Partner Keep Away

Motor skills Dribble, dodge, stop
Movement concepts Moving into space, change of direction, pathway, and speed
Players Two
Formation Scattered
Playing area Playground, gymnasium
Equipment Soccer balls

One player is given a ball and tries to keep it by dribbling, dodging, stopping, and pivoting away from her partner. As soon as the defensive partner touches the ball, players exchange positions and repeat the drill.

Suggestions and Variations
Partners stand about twenty feet apart, facing each other. On signal, each approaches the other. The player with the ball tries to dribble past her opponent, while the defensive player attempts to gain possession of the ball.

Triangle Pass

Motor skills Pass, trap
Movement concepts Change of direction
Players Three
Formation Triangle
Playing area Playground, gymnasium
Equipment Ball

Arrange three players in a triangle (eight to ten feet apart). First player passes ball to the right. Second player traps and passes ball to the next player. Continue pattern for a few minutes, then call "Change," signaling players to reverse directions.

Kicking for Distance

Motor skills Kick
Movement concepts Moving into space, strong and light
Players Four to five per group
Formation Scattered
Playing area Playground, gymnasium
Equipment Soccer balls

Divide the class into squads of four or five players. One squad lines up to kick, while the other scatters in the field to retrieve the ball. The field can be marked with lines every five yards or the retrievers can simply mark the kick. Each child on the kicking squad kicks the ball three or four times, depending on the number of balls available. Mark where the ball lands, not where it rolls. After each player on the kicking squad has had a turn, change squad positions.

Suggestions and Variations
The kicking squad may vary the type of kick—a stationary kick, a punt, or a kick while the ball is rolling forward.

Goal Kicking

Motor skills Kick, trap
Movement concepts Moving into space
Players Four to six per group
Formation Semicircle
Playing area Playground, gymnasium
Equipment Soccer balls

Divide the class into squads of four to six players and arrange them in semicircles on each side of the goalposts (traffic cones or milk cartons). Player on team A kicks the ball through the goal, and any player on the opposite team traps the ball and returns the kick. If the ball goes through the retrieving team, allow the player who was closest to the ball as it passed by to retrieve it.

Suggestions and Variations

1. Vary the type of kick—a stationary kick, kicking a moving ball, using the inside and outside of the instep. (Move closer to the goal when practicing this type of kick.)
2. Place a player in the center of the goalpost to practice goaltending (guarding the goal).
3. Practice volley kicking. Players on team A must throw the ball over the goalposts. Any player on team B may attempt to kick the ball through the goalposts before it lands.

Goal Heading

Motor skills Head, throw
Movement concepts Moving into space, use of space, change of direction and speed
Players Four to six per group
Formation Line
Playing area Playground, gymnasium
Equipment Soccer balls

Divide the class into as many squads as you have goals. (Wire backstops or any substitute goal area will work for this drill.) Arrange squads in a line ten feet in front of and parallel to the goal. Player A in each squad moves fifteen feet in front of his team beyond the goal, turns, and faces the second player in the line. Player A throws to B, who attempts to head the ball through the goal. Player B chases his own ball, throws it to A, and then returns to the end of the line.

Suggestions and Variations
Make two lines facing the goal, with A standing on the goal line and the front players of the two lines standing ten feet

away. A throws the ball up between the first two players. Both attempt to head the ball back to A.

Shuttle Dribble and Tackle

Motor skills   Dribble, tackle
Movement concepts   Use of space, moving into space, change of direction and speed
Players   Four per group
Formation   See diagram
Playing area   Playground, gymnasium
Equipment   Soccer balls

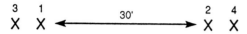

This is a basic shuttle relay formation, with the following modifications. Player 1 dribbles the ball toward the other line, while player 2 moves out to tackle player 1. Player 1 tries to reach the opposite line without being tackled, and player 2 attempts to touch the ball. Allow about twenty seconds of play, then blow the whistle and start the next two players.

One vs. Two Players

Motor skills   Dribble, pass, tackle
Movement concepts   Use of space, moving into space, change of direction and speed
Players   Three per group
Formation   Scattered
Playing area   Playground, gymnasium
Equipment   Soccer balls

Two players attempt to keep the ball away from the third player. If player 3 touches the ball, the opposing player who last touched it changes position with him.

Suggestions and Variations
1. Add a goal behind the defensive player and require the two offensive players to move in and attempt to score.
2. Repeat the previous activities and change the combination to one of the following:
   a. One defensive player vs. three offensive players
   b. Two defensive players vs. two offensive players
   c. Two defensive players vs. three offensive players

LEAD-UP GAMES

The lead-up games described in this section can be used for developmental levels II and III. Numerous suggestions are provided to illustrate how these activities can be modified to cope with facilities, equipment, and levels of playing ability. Teachers are also encouraged to use the inventive games approach to modify these games or to help the children invent their own lead-up games.

Circle Soccer

Motor skills   Kick, trap
Movement concepts   Personal space, moving into space
Players   Four or five per team
Formation   Circle

Playing area   Playground, gymnasium
Equipment   Ball

The captain of one team begins play by kicking the ball toward the opponents. The players on each team attempt to kick the ball past the opposing players, below their waists. They also must try to prevent the ball from going out of the circle on their own side. Every player remains at her place in the circle while the ball is in play. One point is awarded each time the ball is kicked out of the circle.

Suggestions and Variations
1. Introduce a second ball to the game.
2. Restrict kicking to the right foot, then to the left foot.
3. Expand the size of the circle.

Soccer Dodgeball

Motor skills   Kick, trap
Movement concepts   Moving into space, change of direction and speed
Players   Class
Formation   Circle
Playing area   Playground, gymnasium
Equipment   Soccer ball

The circle players attempt to hit the players inside by kicking the ball at them. Inside players cannot use their hands to stop the ball, except for a pass that may strike the face. When a player is hit below the waist, he joins the circle. The winners are the last three players remaining inside the circle.

Suggestions and Variations
1. Introduce a second ball to the game.
2. Add a new rule, such as every player must be constantly moving or inside players must hop while circle players use only a side-of-foot kick.
3. Ask each team to make up a new rule for the opposing side.

Boundary Ball

Motor skills   Kick, trap
Movement concepts   Moving into space, change of direction and speed
Players   Ten to fifteen on each team
Formation   Playing area divided by a centerline, with players scattered on their own side of the centerline
Playing area   Playground, gymnasium
Equipment   Soccer balls

Each team has a ball, which it kicks toward the opponent's goal line. Players may move about freely in their own half of the field to prevent the opponent's ball from crossing the goal. However, they cannot touch the ball with their hands. One point is scored each time a ball crosses a goal line.

Suggestions and Variations
1. Restrict players to one type of kick and one type of trapping skill.
2. Give each team an additional ball.
3. Ask children to suggest a new rule.

Change Soccer

Motor skills   All soccer skills

Movement concepts   Use of available space, change of direction, pathway, and speed
Players   Six per game
Formation   See diagram
Playing area   Playground, gymnasium
Equipment   Ball and four goalposts

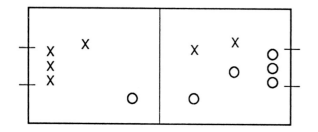

Three players on each team are goalies and cannot use their hands to stop a ball. The remaining three players may move anywhere within the playing area. Game begins with a kickoff in the center of the field. When the teacher calls "Change," everyone must immediately exchange positions with the goalies, then return to playing the game. Use soccer rules as they apply to this game.

Marble Soccer

Motor skills   Shoot, trap
Movement concepts   Moving into space, strong and light
Players   Three or four per game
Formation   Scattered around circle
Playing area   Playground, gymnasium
Equipment   Soccer balls

Draw a circle (six to ten feet in diameter) and place a ball in the center. Three players stand outside the circle and one player is given a ball. The player with the ball kicks it, trying to hit it into the center of the circle. If she hits it, she receives one point; if it is knocked out of the circle, she receives five points. Players may enter the circle to retrieve their own ball but may not kick their ball while in the circle. First player to score 21 points wins the game.

Circle of Fun

Motor skills   Dribble, pass, shoot, tackle
Movement concepts   Moving through space, change of direction and speed
Players   Three per team
Formation   Circle
Playing area   Playground, gymnasium
Equipment   Soccer balls and traffic cones

Draw a large circle in the playing area and place a traffic cone in the center. All players start outside of the circle. The object of the game is to shoot from outside the circle and knock down the traffic cone. Once the game begins, each team tries to keep possession of the ball and score goals. All players are permitted to run through the circle, but no player is allowed to touch the ball while it is in the circle. If the ball remains in the circle without the traffic cone being knocked down, the player who last kicked it may run in, pick it up, run out of the circle, and place it on the ground to continue the game.

Punt Back

Motor skills   Kick, trap
Movement concepts   Use of available space, moving into space
Players   Four to twenty
Formation   Scattered on each side of a playing area
Playing area   Playground, gymnasium
Equipment   Soccer ball

A captain is chosen for each team. The ball is placed in the middle of the field and the captain of the kicking team kicks the ball to start the game. Once the game has started, opposing teams stay at least fifteen feet apart. Any member of the receiving team may trap the ball. The player who traps the ball kicks it toward the opponent's goal. If a player kicks the ball over the opponent's goal, his team receives one point. The team that did not score starts the ball from the center of the field. Any player who contacts another player who is attempting to kick the ball commits a foul. A free kick is then awarded to the other team.

Suggestions and Variations

1. Add two or more balls.
2. Limit kicks to either an instep, side-of-foot, or punt kick.
3. Ask each team to suggest a new rule.

Alley Soccer

Motor skills   Pass, trap, kick
Movement concepts   Personal space, moving into space, change of direction and speed
Players   Ten to twelve per team
Formation   See diagram
Playing area   Playground, gymnasium
Equipment   Soccer ball

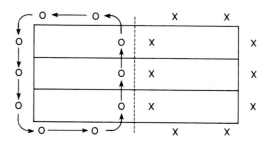

Each team has three forwards, who may move anywhere within their own alley. All remaining players on each team remain on the sideline and goal line of their own half of the field. No player may touch the ball with her hands. The player in the middle alley starts the game by passing the ball to another forward player. Forwards pass the ball back and forth to other forwards or to sideline players as they attempt to move it forward and kick it over the opponent's goal line below the waist of the opposing players. One point is awarded for each goal. If the ball goes over the sideline, it is thrown in by the nearest player on the team that did not allow it to go over the line. Only forwards may score a goal. Rotate players after a set time and according to the rotation pattern shown in the diagram.

Suggestions and Variations
1. Add one free forward, who may roam anywhere.
2. Limit skills to one type of pass and one type of trap.
3. Allow sideline players to score a goal.

Forwards and Backs

Motor skills   Pass, dribble, trap
Movement concepts   Personal space, moving into space, change of direction and speed
Players   Ten to twelve per team
Formation   See diagram
Playing area   Playground, gymnasium
Equipment   Soccer balls

The center forward of team A starts the game with a kickoff. Team A forwards try to kick the ball over the opponent's goal line. Players on team B try to gain possession of the ball and kick it over their opponent's goal line. Forwards may not cross back over their own center zone line, and backs may not cross the center zone line. Only forwards can score a goal. Each goal counts one point. If the ball goes over the endline or sideline, it is thrown in by the nearest player on the opposite team.

Suggestions and Variations
1. Change forwards and backs every few minutes.
2. Add sideline players with rules similar to Sideline Soccer.
3. Vary the type of kick and trap.

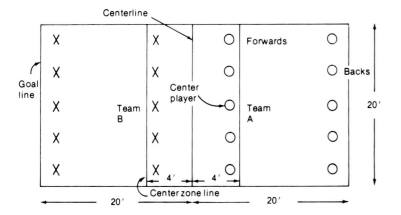

Four-Goal Soccer

Motor skills   All soccer skills
Movement concepts   Use of available space, moving into space, change of direction and speed
Players   Four or five per team
Formation   See figure 18.23
Playing area   Playground, gymnasium
Equipment   Soccer ball and four goals

A field has four goals marked with the flags (figure 18.23). These are located in the center of each line. The game begins with two teams of five players. The number of player, however, an be increased to seven or eight per team. The game is played without goalkeepers and each team attacks and defends two goals (see markers). Soccer rules are applied, with the

exception of using no offside or corner kicks (original description of game).

Seven-Person or Mini-Soccer

Motor skills   All soccer skills
Movement concepts   Use of available space, moving into space, change of direction, pathway, and speed

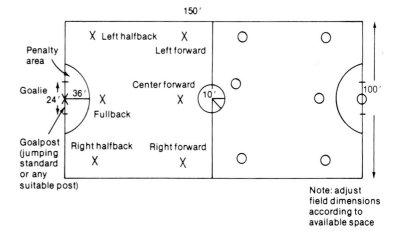

Players   Seven per team
Formation   See diagram
Playing area   Playground, gymnasium
Equipment   Soccer ball

See the official rules of soccer in the following section. Since there are seven players on each team, this is an ideal game to accommodate an average-size physical education class. The playing field is normally divided in half to allow two games to be played at the same time. Modify any rule to cope with local conditions.

Suggestions and Variations
Young players tend to "follow the ball" rather than play their positions. Too often the fullback and halfbacks are "caught" too far in front of their forwards. To prevent this, play seven-person soccer, but after the kickoff, require:
1. Forwards must remain in their opponent's half of the field.
2. Backs must remain in their own half of the playing field.

SOCCER RULES AND REGULATIONS

By the time children reach fifth grade, they should have learned the majority of skills necessary to play soccer. This does not imply, however, that time should not be devoted to practice activities and lead-up games. With some basic modifications, the game of soccer should be played in its entirety periodically during an instructional unit. This will help children understand that practice sessions and lead-up activities are designed to improve the speed and accuracy of the required skills.

    I. Field of play
       A. Length of field—not more than 120 yards and not less than 110 yards

Figure 18.23 Four-goal soccer.

B. Width of field—not more than 75 yards and not less than 65 yards

II. Names of players and line-up positions (positions of players at the start of the game, after a goal is scored, and after half-time): Over the years, soccer's playing positions have evolved to four general positions. The goalie is the first defensive position. Immediately in front are four defenders, who are most often near their own goal. The outside defenders are called wing fullbacks and the inside players fullbacks. The middle line is the midfielders, who play between the defenders and forwards. These players are the workhorses of the team, as they move back to help the defenders when in trouble and forward to help the forward line when on the offense. Forwards or strikers are normally nearest the opponent's goal line. *Playing system* is a term that describes how the players on a team are positioned. The general starting system for elementary school children is the one described. It is known as the 4-3-3 system. A 4-2-4 system would include four defenders, two midfielders and four forwards.

III. Penalty kick: If a defensive player other than the goalie touches the ball with her hands in the eighteen-by-forty-four-yard penalty area, a penalty kick is awarded to the offensive team. This kick is made from the twelve-yard penalty mark by any member of the offensive team. The goalie stands on the line between the goalposts, and all other players stand outside the penalty area until the ball is kicked. After the ball is kicked, any player from either team may enter the penalty area.

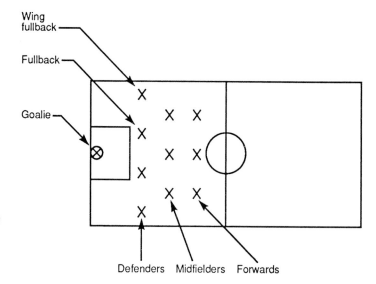

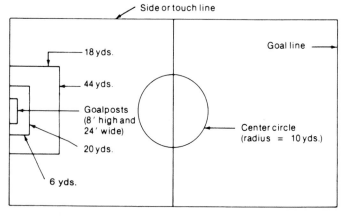

IV. Free kicks: The direct free kick and the indirect free kick

   A. Direct free kick: This is a kick from which a goal may be scored directly. In other words, the ball can be kicked from where an infraction occurred and travel directly through the goal. Defenders must stay ten yards away from the ball until it is kicked. This kick is awarded to a team when any opposing player commits any of the following infractions outside the penalty area (a direct free kick awarded inside the penalty area automatically results in a penalty kick, taken from the penalty mark).

      1. Kicking an opponent.

      2. Charging in a violent and dangerous manner.

      3. Tripping an opponent.

      4. Handling the ball. (The goalkeeper may handle the ball only when he is inside the penalty area. If he handles the ball when he is outside the penalty area, a direct free kick is awarded to the opposing team.)

      5. Pushing with the hands or arms. The ball is placed on the spot where the infraction happened. Any player on the team awarded the kick lines up three or four yards behind the ball and players from both teams stand anywhere in front of him, providing they are at least ten yards away. The whistle sounds, the ball is kicked, and play resumes.

   B. Indirect free kick: This is a kick from which a goal cannot be scored, unless the ball is touched by another player before it enters the goal. This kick is awarded to a team when any opposing player commits any of the following infractions.

      1. A player kicks the ball a second consecutive time after a kickoff, a free kick, a goal kick, or a corner kick.

      2. A ball is not kicked forward from a penalty kick.

      3. The goalie carries the ball more than four steps.

      4. Misconduct—improper language, unnecessary arguing, and so on.

      5. Offside.

      6. Obstruction other than holding.

      7. The ball is passed (by kicking the ball) to the goalkeeper by a player on the goalkeeper's own team. (Note: The ball can be headed, thrown directly from a throw-in, or chest-passed to the goalkeeper.)

V. Throw-in: When the ball is kicked, headed, or legally forced over the sideline by a player, the opposing team is awarded a throw-in. The ball is put back into play from behind the sideline at the point where the ball went out. The player who makes the throw-in must have both hands on the ball and throw it from behind his head. He must also have parts of both feet in contact with the ground until the ball is released. If the ball is not thrown in properly, the opposing team is awarded the second throw-in.

VI. Corner kick: When the ball is kicked, headed, or legally forced over the goal line (but not between the goalposts) by a defensive player, the opposing team is awarded a corner kick. The ball is placed on the corner of the field (where the sideline meets the goal line) on the side the ball went out. Usually a wing player kicks the ball into play. All other players stand anywhere on the field, provided they are at least ten yards from the ball.

VII. Goal kick: When the ball is kicked, headed, or legally forced over the goal line by a player on the attacking team, a goal kick is awarded to the defensive team. The ball is placed anywhere in the goal area. Any defensive player may kick the ball back into play; however, it must leave the penalty area for it to be in play. If it does not, the kick is repeated. The offensive team remains outside the penalty area until the ball crosses over the penalty area boundary.

VIII. Offside: A player is offside if the ball is kicked forward toward a player, by one of her own team players, and she does not have two opponents in front of her at the moment the ball is played. She is not offside, however, if (1) she is in her own half of the field; (2) two opponents are nearer their goal than she is at the moment the ball is played; (3) she receives a ball directly from a corner kick, a throw-in, or a goal kick; or (4) the ball is passed back to the player.

   A. Offside: The right winger is offside because she does not have two defensive players in front of her at the moment the ball is kicked.

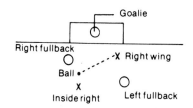

   B. Not offside: In this case, "at the moment" the inside right kicks the ball, the right winger has two defensive players in front of her. Now the right winger may dribble in and attempt a shot at the goal.

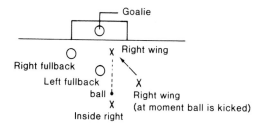

TABLE 18.3 **Evaulation Checklist**

Rating

1	Needs practice	1st evaluation _____
2	Shows progress	2nd evaluation _____
3	Has acquired skill or concept	3rd evaluation _____

Name	Pass	Trap	Dribble	Shoot	Tackle	Use of space	Move through space	Change of direction	Change of pathway	Change of speed

TABLE 18.4 **Soccer Skill Test**

Name	Kick and Trap (Total Pts.)	Dribbling	Shooting	Subjective Evaluation	Total Score	Grade
1						
2						
3		Rank total scores for the class, then convert to letter				
4		grades or ratings (superior, good, etc.).				
5						

IX. Scoring: A goal is awarded to the attacking team if any player kicks, heads, or legally causes the ball to cross over the goal line between the goalposts and under the crossbar. A ball accidentally kicked through the goal by a defensive player, therefore, would count for the attacking team.

EVALUATIVE TECHNIQUES

The evaluative checklist in table 18.3 is an example of a teacher-made formative evaluative tool to assess the general progress of the class. A simple rating of 1, 2, and 3 can be used to provide a quick evaluation of each student's level of soccer ability, as well as how well each child understands and uses the five key movement concepts.

Although a number of standardized tests measure soccer skills, they generally are designed for secondary and college-level students. These tests, however, can be modified to meet the ability of upper elementary children. The following test battery is an example of a "teacher-made" test that can be administered without elaborate equipment and in a short period of time (see table 18.4). Keep scores from year to year in order to develop appropriate norms for your school.

Test 1: Kick and Trap

Draw a line five feet from the wall. The ball is placed on the line. Each player attempts to kick the ball and hit the front wall as many times as possible within thirty seconds. All kicks must be taken from behind the five-foot line. If a player loses

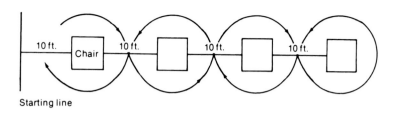

Starting line

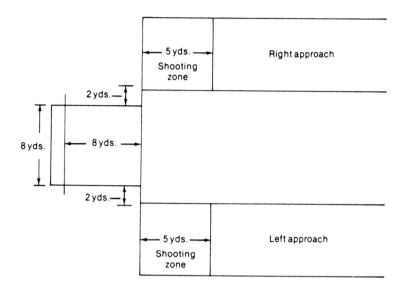

control of the ball, she may retrieve it with her feet and continue kicking. Award one point for each successful hit. Allow two trials and record the highest score.

Test 2: Dribbling

Arrange four chairs as shown in the diagram. Place a ball on the starting line. Each player starts behind the starting line, with both hands resting on their knees. On the signal "Go," she dribbles the ball around the chairs in a zigzag pattern. One point is awarded for each time she passes a chair as she moves forward and as she returns to the starting line. Allow thirty seconds for the test. Allow two trials and record the highest score.

Test 3: Shooting

Arrange the field markings in front of the goalposts as shown. A player may use the right or left approach. The player starts dribbling the ball in the approach area and continues moving into the shooting zone. While in the shooting zone, the player attempts to kick the ball through the goalposts. Ten trials are given, with five points awarded for each successful goal.

Test 4: Subjective Evaluation

Establish criteria that represent the skills and playing ability required in soccer. For example, evaluating a player's use of

such skills as passing, dribbling, team play, and defensive ability, the teacher awards each player a total score from zero to fifty points. Three players can be used as judges, with the average score recorded.

Summary Review

The game of soccer requires players to be knowledgeable about the rules of the game and to understand appropriate game-playing strategies. Players also need to be proficient in a number of specialized soccer skills. These skills must be learned, as they do not develop automatically through growth and maturation. Individual practices, lead-up games, and mini-games that can be adjusted to create successful practice opportunities, as well as enjoyable game situations, become the basis for teaching children soccer. The objective is to increase children's knowledge of soccer and to help develop their soccer skills toward the automatic stage of development. To develop specialized sport skills to the automatic stage requires many individual practices. Hence, children need to be provided with lots of developmentally appropriate practice opportunities. This will lead to successful soccer skill development and enjoyment of the game. If this objective is achieved, then children will possess the knowledge, skills, and desire to continue playing this major game throughout their lives.

INDIVIDUAL *and* GROUP PROJECTS

1. Divide into groups of three. Each group member chooses two different soccer skills. Design lesson plans to teach each basic skill. Then teach your two basic soccer skills to one member of your group while the third member observes the effectiveness of your instruction. Each group member takes a turn at being teacher, student, and observer. Observers might find useful the observational checklist for the evaluation of teaching, provided in Table 11.7 on page 247. When you have all taught your skills, discuss and evaluate your experiences in each role (teacher, student, observer), and suggest possible ways to improve your teaching.

2. In pairs, study the rules and regulations of soccer. Then pose questions to each other on the rules and regulations.

3. In chapter 4, it was suggested that one of the challenges facing teachers is the adjustment of the teaching environment to meet the developmental levels of the children. Four environmental variables under the teachers' control were identified:
   a. Rules
   b. Space
   c. Number of participants
   d. Amount or type of equipment

   One or more of these variables can be adjusted to create success on behalf of students. In small groups, discuss how these four variables can be adjusted when teaching children soccer. Creative ideas and specific recommendations should be formulated and shared with other groups.

4. Chapter 13 identified a number of disabilities that afflict young children. In small groups, choose four disabilities and discuss how children with these disabilities can be integrated into soccer activities. Consider what adjustments will have to be made to accommodate each child's developmental level and to ensure success. Debate possible techniques and methods of evaluation. Share ideas with other groups.

5. A feature of this text is the idea of teaching and enhancing academic skills and concepts through physical education activities. In small groups, discuss and create ideas to teach or enhance academic skills and concepts through soccer activities. Each group is then allocated a small selection of the soccer practice activities and lead-up games. Create ways to teach or enhance academic skills and concepts through these practice activities and lead-up games. Consider ways to evaluate the students. Share ideas with other groups.

SELECTED READINGS

Caerver, W. 1983. *Soccer fundamentals for players and coaches.* Englewood Cliffs, NJ: Prentice Hall.

CAHPER. 1985. *Soccer-type games.* Ottawa, Ontario: CAHPER.

Hooper, C. A., and M. S. Davis. 1985. *Coaching soccer effectively.* Champaign, IL: Human Kinetics.

Simon, J. M., and J. A. Reeves. 1982. *The soccer games book.* Champaign, IL: Leisure Press.

Turner, L. F., and S. L. Turner. 1989. *P.E. teacher's skill-by-skill activities program.* West Nyack, NY: Parker.

Waiters, T., and B. Howe. 1988. *Coaching 6, 7, and 8 year olds.* Vancouver, BC: World of Soccer.

KEY CONCEPTS

19.1 Specialized hockey skills are acquired through instruction and practice opportunities

19.2 Hockey activities must be developmentally appropriate to ensure that all children can achieve success and enjoyment

19.3 Safety considerations must be emphasized when teaching children hockey activities

19.4 To develop hockey skills to the automatic stage of skill development requires many practice opportunities (time on-task)

19.5 Effective teaching progressions, that provide all children with individual practices and lead-up games, are required to develop the skills and knowledge associated with hockey

19.6 Playing a full-sided competitive game is not a very efficient way of teaching large numbers of children specialized hockey skills

KEY OBJECTIVES

After completing this chapter you will be able to:

1. Design developmentally appropriate hockey activities for elementary school children
2. Plan and organize teaching units and individual lessons in hockey
3. Organize pratice activities and lead-up games appropriate for hockey development
4. Plan and organize hockey practice activities and lead-up games that incorporate the inventive games approach
5. Evaluate units, lessons, and individual techniques used in hockey
6. Identify key teaching points associated with the basic skills of hockey
7. Employ teaching progressions that lead to successful development of hockey skills and concepts
8. Understand the rules and basic strategies associated with hockey

Field hockey is a relatively new game to many North Americans. Its origins, however, date back over 2,000 years to ancient Greece and Egypt. During the Middle Ages, field hockey was known as "hurling" in Ireland, as "shinty" in Scotland, and as "hoquet" in France. The modern version of hockey started in England around the middle of the nineteenth century. Today, the game is played in more than one hundred countries and is enjoyed equally by men and women.

Field hockey has also become very popular with elementary school children. Because it is relatively new, it provides an enjoyable medium for boys and girls to learn to play together on an "even skill" basis. Improvised equipment, along with numerous modified lead-up hockey type games has made field hockey one of the fastest growing activities in the elementary physical education program.

EMPHASIS AND PROGRESSION

Many of the basic skills and simple playing strategies of hockey are introduced in developmental level II through street hockey and organized floor hockey during school hours. Although field hockey is similar to these games, it has several unique skills and rules (table 19.1) that should be learned correctly and in an organized manner in level III.

C O N C E P T

19.1 *Specialized Hockey Skills Are Acquired through Instruction and Practice Opportunities*

During level II, the main emphasis is learning the correct way to dribble, pass, and shoot a ball. Children of this age range should also learn how to stop a ball and a few basic rules of the game. The major portion of any unit of instruction should be devoted to practice activities and lead-up games.

The basic dribbling, passing, and shooting skills continue to be emphasized through level III. Teachers should expect a general increase in the accuracy, speed, and control of these skills. New skills, such as the scoop shot, tackling, and dodging, should be introduced in this level. More time should also be devoted to seven-person hockey, and occasionally time should be allowed for playing eleven-person field hockey. The latter is important in order to give each child an opportunity to understand and appreciate the importance of good ball control and positional play in the full-sided game.

C O N C E P T

19.2 *Hockey Activities Must Be Developmentally Appropriate to Ensure That All Children Can Achieve Success and Enjoyment*

TEACHING PROCEDURES

Throughout this chapter, numerous references are made to various sections in chapter 18, "Soccer Activities." The reason for this is that both soccer and field hockey may be relatively new to many elementary school children and the same approach can be used to teach both activities. In addition, many of the practice activities and lead-up games described in chapter 18 can be easily adapted to field hockey skills. Teachers should also adapt the procedures for teaching soccer when organizing and planning a hockey unit.

The following suggestions will assist teachers in coping with several problems that are unique to hockey:

1. Hockey can be a dangerous sport if children are not taught proper stick handling and legal checking methods. Since boys and girls play this activity together, it is especially important that the proper skills be taught and enforced.
2. If sticks are not available for every member of the class, station work (p. 215 and 313) and a rotation system should be used.
3. Hockey, like soccer, requires a high level of strength and endurance. Teachers should plan practice activities and lead-up games so the children gradually build up their cardiorespiratory endurance. Station work can be used for alternating vigorous running drills with less tiring shooting activities.
4. During all hockey type activities, the goalkeeper should wear a protective face mask, chest pads, and leg protectors. Shin guards for field players are also recommended.

C O N C E P T

19.3 *Safety Considerations Must Be Emphasized When Teaching Children Hockey Activities*

DESCRIPTION OF SKILLS

Field hockey skills are classified as dribbling, passing, hitting, and receiving. The following skills should be taught to elementary school children in a systematic and progressive way. Special attention must be given to proper stick handling, reinforcing it throughout every lesson.

C O N C E P T

19.4 *To Develop Hockey Skills to the Automatic Stage of Skill Development Requires Many Practice Opportunities (Time On-Task)*

TABLE 19.1	Suggested Sequence of Presenting Hockey Skills and Rules	
Skills and Rules	**Developmental Level II**	**Developmental Level III**
Dribbling	Introduce	Increase speed and accuracy
Rules: Dribbling with the flat side of the stick	Introduce	
Passing	Introduce	Increase speed, distance, and accuracy
Receiving	Introduce	Increase speed of the ball
Hitting: Forward, Right, Left	Introduce	Increase distance and accuracy
Scoop shot	Introduce	Increase accuracy
Rules: Hit with flat side of stick		Introduce
Tackling		Introduce
Rules		
Fouls		Introduce
Dodging		Introduce
Rules		
Offside		Introduce
Pass Ball	Introduce	
Rules: Player positions		Introduce

C O N C E P T

19.5 Effective Teaching Progressions, That Provide All Children With Individual Practices and Lead-Up Games, Are Required to Develop the Skills and Knowledge Associated with Hockey

Grip

The basic hockey grip is fundamental to all shooting, dribbling, and fielding skills. The left hand stays at the top of the stick while the right hand slides up or down the stick according to how the ball should be moved. To begin, grasp the stick in the middle with the right hand and hold it parallel to the ground. The toe of the blade should be sticking up, with the flat side of the blade facing left. Grasp the top of the stick with the left hand, with the V of the hand pointing down toward the blade. Lower the stick to the ground and turn the blade so that it faces outward. Keeping the same grip with the left hand, reposition the right hand eight to twelve inches below the left hand. The result is that the hands grip the handle from opposite sides (figure 19.1). Players will want to experiment to find the most suitable distance between their hands. Players should carry the stick ahead and to the right of their feet, with the body leaning forward slightly and head over the ball.

Key Teaching Points

1. Keep a firm grip with the left hand and allow the stick to rotate in your right hand.
2. Left hand up, right hand down.
3. Maintain a slight forward body lean.

Figure 19.1 Grip.

Dribbling and Stopping

Dribbling in hockey is a controlled means of propelling the ball along the ground with the hockey stick. The ball is dribbled in the front and slightly to the right of the feet by making short taps with the flat side of the blade (figure 19.2a). The movement is from the shoulder, forearm, and wrist. In open field play and when the opponent is not near, the ball

Figure 19.2 Dribbling and stopping.

may be tapped ten to fifteen feet ahead, followed by short running steps, then another tap of the ball. The flat side of the blade should always be to the ball, and the blade should be close to the ground. To stop the ball, rotate the wrist to bring the flat side of the stick over the ball (figure 19.2b).

Key Teaching Points
1. Keep a firm grip.
2. Rotate from shoulders.
3. Think "tap" . . . "stop" . . . "look."

Controlled Dribbling

For more controlled dribbling, spread the hands farther apart (figure 19.3a). To push the ball right, rotate the stick with the left wrist so that the flat side of the stick taps the left side of the ball (figure 19.3b). Keep the ball and stick in front of the body, then rotate the stick back to the right side of the ball (figure 19.3c).

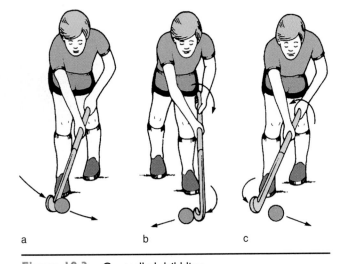

Figure 19.3 Controlled dribbling.

Key Teaching Points
1. Hold arms in front of body.
2. Reach for the ball in front of the body.
3. Push, rather than strike, the ball.
4. Watch where you are going and where teammates and opponents are positioned.

Push Pass

The push pass is used for short passes or to shoot at the goal. Dribble the ball in a forward direction and, when ready, place that side of the stick against the ball, look at the target, then look down (figure 19.4a). Sweep the ball toward the target (figure 19.4b).

Key Teaching Points
1. Keep the ball close to the stick prior to making the pass.
2. Sweep the ball—don't hit it.
3. Follow through in the direction of the pass.

Receiving

Receiving a hockey ball or puck (figure 19.5) is very similar to fielding a grounder in softball. The face of the stick is at a right angle to the direction of the oncoming ball. As the ball contacts the stick, loosen the grip slightly to absorb the impact of the ball. Contact the ball as far away from the body as possible to allow the force to be absorbed over the greatest distance.

Figure 19.4   Push pass.

Figure 19.5   Receiving.

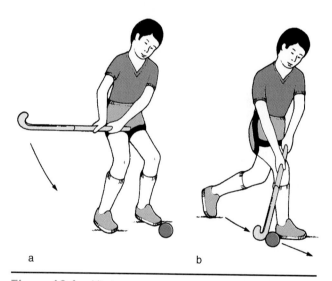

Figure 19.6   Hitting.

Key Teaching Points

1. Meet the ball in front and to the right of the body.
2. As the ball is contacted, give slightly to stop the ball.
3. Move quickly into the next playing position.

Hitting

Hitting is forcefully hitting the ball along the ground. The left drive is the most common driving stroke, used for long and medium passes, shots on goal, and free and corner hits. When moving into position to hit the ball, the right hand shifts next to the left hand. The left shoulder points in the direction of the drive, and the head is over the ball. The arms swing back, keeping the stick below shoulder level (figure 19.6a). Then bring the arms forward and downward and contact the ball just off the lead foot (figure 19.6b). Follow through low and in the direction of the hit.

Key Teaching Points

1. Keep hands close together.
2. Use a short back swing and a quick hit.
3. Follow-through should be low to the ground.

Scoop Shot

The scoop shot is used to lift the ball slightly off the ground in order to dodge an opponent, to pass, or to shoot the ball into the corner of the goal. Contact the ball in front, with the stick tilted back as it is placed under the ball (figure 19.7a). Then make a strong lifting and shovel-like action with the right arm, but using no follow-through (figure 19.7b).

Key Teaching Points

1. The stick should contact and lift the ball without any sound.

Figure 19.7   Scoop shot.

a. Approach with blade close to the ground.

2. The scoop is a controlled lifting action.
3. There is no follow-through action.

Tackling

A tackle is a legal means of taking the ball away from an opponent. Move in toward the opponent with eyes on the ball, body well forward, with weight evenly distributed over both feet. Hold the blade of the stick close to the ground (figure 19.8a). Make the tackle when the ball is farthest from the opponent's stick. At that moment, place the face of the blade on the ball perpendicular to the ground (figure 19.8b). As soon as you have possession of the ball, immediately pass it to another player or quickly dribble it away from the opponent.

b. Blade is on the ball and perpendicular to the ground.

Figure 19.8   Tackling.

Key Teaching Points
1. Keep your eyes on the ball and the opponent's stick.
2. Keep both hands on your stick.
3. When ready to move, make your action quick and direct; do not swing your stick toward the ball.

Dodging

A dodge is an evasive movement that an offensive player uses to move the ball past an opponent. It is essentially a controlled pass to oneself. In figure 19.9, the dribbler pushes the ball to the right, then runs around the other side to pick up her own pass. Timing is the most important part of this movement. The ball must be pushed late enough to prevent the opponent from backing up to gain possession of the ball.

Key Teaching Points
1. Keep the ball close to your stick.
2. Do not give away your move by an early shift or look to where you intend to pass the ball.

3. Move very quickly after your dodge to regain possession of the ball.

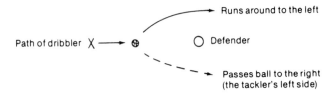

Goalkeeping

In most instances, proper goalkeeping equipment is not available in small enough sizes for elementary school children. If lighter balls such as tennis or perforated plastic balls are used, goalkeepers should wear shin guards and a face mask for protection.

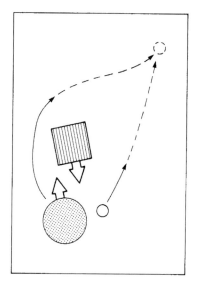

Figure 19.9   Dodging.

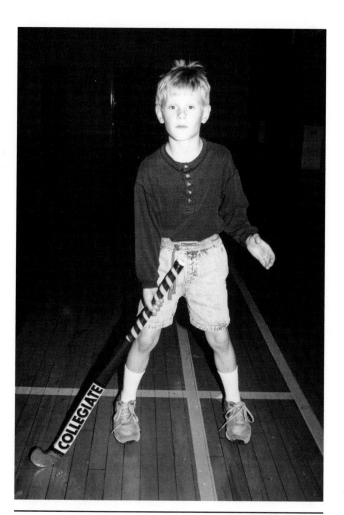

Figure 19.10   Stand in a ready position, with the stick in the right hand.

The goalkeeper should stand about one yard in front of the goal and move in a semicircle from post to post. He should stand in a ready position, with the stick held in the right hand and the flat side of the stick facing forward (figure 19.10). The left hand is positioned with the palm facing forward, body leaning slightly forward, knees partially flexed, and feet in a comfortable stride position.

The goalkeeper is permitted to stop the ball with any part of the body and the ball is permitted to rebound off the body or hand. The goalkeeper is not allowed to hold the ball or throw it into the field of play. He can, however, clear the ball with the stick or kick it clear with his foot.

PRACTICE ACTIVITIES AND LEAD-UP GAMES

The following practice activities are, in many respects, modifications of soccer drills and relay activities. A few hockey type activities are also included in this section (table 19.2). Since field hockey may be a new game to many children, these practice activities are extremely important in developing basic skills. Also, many of the lead-up games are adaptations of soccer lead-up games. Teachers should modify these games to meet the class's general level of ability and the limitations of facilities and equipment.

C O N C E P T

19.6 *Playing a Full-Sided Competitive Game Is Not a Very Efficient Way of Teaching Large Numbers of Children Specialized Hockey Skills*

TABLE 19.2   Practice Activities and Lead-Up Games

Name of Activity	Type of Activity	Players	Developmental Level II	III	Hockey Concepts and Skills	Movement Concepts	Page
Practice Activities (Adapted from Soccer Activities)							
Wall Kicking	Shoot	Individual	——————→		Shoot, receive	Moving ball into space	382
Individual Dribbling	Shoot	Individual	——————→		Dribble	Moving into space, change of direction	383
Stop, Go, Turn	Dribble, stop	Individual	——————→		Dribble, stop	Moving through space, change of direction	384
Passing and Trapping	Dribble, pass, stop	2	——————→		Dribble, pass, receive	Moving into space, change of direction, pathway, and speed	384
Wall Passing and Trapping	Shoot, receive	2	——————→		Pass, trap	Use of space, change of direction	384
Target Shooting	Shoot, receive	2	——————→		Shoot, receive	Moving into space, change of direction and speed	385
Circle Passing	Pass, receive	2	——————→		Pass, receive	Use of available space, change of direction and pathway	385
Follow the Leader	Dribble	2	——————→		Dribble	Moving into space, change of direction, pathway, and speed	385
Dribble and Pass	Dribble, pass	2	——————→		Dribble, offensive play	Moving into space, change of direction, pathway, and speed	385
Partner Keep Away	Dribble, dodge	3	——————→		Dribble, dodge, stop	Moving into space, change of direction, pathway, and speed	386
Triangle Pass	Pass, receive	3	——→		Pass, receive	Moving into space, change of direction	386
Goal Heading	Shoot, receive	4–5	——————→		Shoot, receive	Moving into space, change of direction and speed	386
One vs. Two	Dribble, pass	3	——————→		Dribble, pass, tackle	Moving into space, change of direction, pathway, and speed	387
Push Pass	Pass, receive	3	——————→		Pass, receive	Moving through space, change of direction	403
Lead-Up Games (Adapted from Soccer Activities)							
Circle Hockey	Shoot, receive	8–10	——————→		Shoot, receive	Moving through space, change of direction	387
Change Hockey	All skills	12	——————→		All hockey skills	Moving into space, change of direction, pathway, and speed	387
Zone Field Hockey	All hockey skills	10–12 per team	——————→		All hockey skills	Moving into space, change of direction and speed	403
Line Field Hockey	Pass, receive	6–8 per team	——————→		Shoot, pass, receive	Moving into space, change of direction, pathway, and speed	403
Hockey Golf	Shoot, receive	2 per game	——————→		Shoot, receive	Moving into space, change of direction and speed	403
Circle of Fun	Dribble, shoot	6 per game	——————→ ——————→		Dribble, pass, shoot, tackle	Moving through space, change of direction, pathway, and speed	388
Partner Keep Away	Dribble, dodge	3	——————→		Dribble, pass, dodge, tackle	Moving into space, change of direction and speed	386

Most of the practice activities and lead-up games provided in this section are appropriate for developmental levels II and III. As children move from level II to level III, there should be an increase in their level of skill and general playing ability.

P R A C T I C E A C T I V I T I E S

Push Pass

Motor skills Pass, receive
Movement concepts Moving into space, change of direction
Players Three per activity
Formation See diagram
Playing area Playground, gymnasium
Equipment Sticks and ball

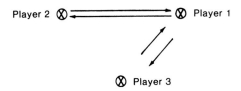

Arrange three players as in diagram. Player 1 passes to player 2. Player 2 returns to player 1, who then passes to player 3. Player 3 returns the ball to 1, and the sequence begins again.

Suggestions and Variations
1. Pass from player 1 to 2 to 3 to 1 and continue in the same pattern.
2. Repeat number 1, with every player moving one position to the left. Player 1 dribbles to 2's position and passes to 2, who has shifted to 3's position.

L E A D - U P G A M E S

Zone Field Hockey

Motor skills All hockey skills
Movement concepts Moving into space, change of direction and speed
Players Ten to twelve per team
Formation See diagram
Playing area Playground, gymnasium
Equipment Hockey sticks and balls

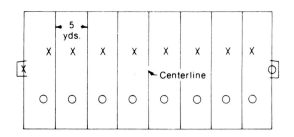

The game starts with a face-off between two opposing players at the center of the field. All players must remain in their own five-yard zone. The game is played like regular field hockey. After each goal is scored, the player in the zone closest to the centerline becomes the new goalie, and all the other players move forward into the next zone.

Line Field Hockey

Motor skills Shoot, pass, receive
Movement concepts Moving into space, change of direction, pathway, and speed
Players Six to eight per team
Formation See diagram
Playing area Playground, gymnasium
Equipment Sticks and ball

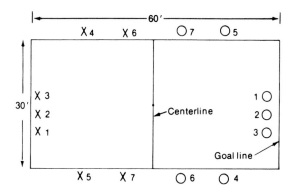

The ball is placed in the middle of the field. On signal, player 1 from each team runs out and tries to gain possession of the ball. Once the ball is in possession, a player may pass to any side player or try to shoot the ball over her opponent's goal line. No other player on her team may enter the field of play or score a goal. After each goal, rotate players and start the game again.

Suggestions and Variations
1. Allow two players to come out each time.
2. Shorten the distance between goals as skill improves.

Hockey Golf

Motor skills Shoot, receive
Movement concepts Moving into space, change of direction and speed
Players Two per game
Formation See diagram
Playing area Playground, gymnasium
Equipment Eight traffic cones, sticks, and ball

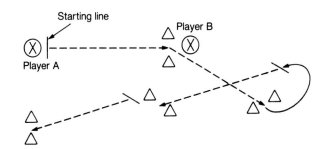

The playing positions for field hockey are shown in the diagram. Also, the same field dimensions for soccer can be used for hockey. Inclusion of the semicircle (or penalty area) is the only difference in the general layout of the field. Player A attempts to drive the ball through the traffic cones. If successful, he is awarded one point. Player B retrieves the ball and changes places with player A. Player B takes his turn, and the game continues around the four sets of traffic cones. Vary the distance and size of the goal according to the ability of players.

Suggestions and Variations
Play same game in teams. Each player on team A takes his turn before changing positions with the other team.

FIELD HOCKEY RULES AND REGULATIONS

The following basic rules of field hockey are essentially a modification of regulation field hockey. By dividing a playing field in half, two games with seven players on a team can be played (one goalie, one fullback, two halfbacks, and three forwards). Since the game is similar to soccer, it is wise to introduce it after the class has been exposed to a unit of soccer.

The playing positions for field hockey are the same as for soccer (chapter 18). Also, the same field dimensions can be used for both games. Inclusion of the semicircle (or penalty area) is the only difference in the general layout of the field.

I. Field of play: Field is 60 by 100 yards. Adjust to available space.

II. Time: Two periods of thirty minutes (divide your available time in two). Teams change ends at halftime.

III. The pass-back is a pass from the center backward to another player. (Bully is no longer used.) This is taken at the center of the field at the start of the game, after each goal, and after halftime. During the pass-back, all other players stand on their own side of the face-off line until the ball is played.

IV. Ball rolls over sideline: When a ball is forced over a sideline, a hit is awarded to the opposing team. A hit must be performed with the stick in contact with the ball throughout the stroke. All other defending players must be five yards away.

V. Ball sent over end line:
A. If by the attacking team, the defending team is awarded a free hit sixteen yards from the end line, opposite the spot where the ball crossed.
B. If by the defending team, the attacking team is awarded a corner hit. The hit must be taken from a point on the end line within 15 feet from the corner of the field.

VI. Fouls committed outside the penalty area (the semicircles in front of goals): A free hit is awarded to the opposing team. All players must be five yards away from the player taking the hit. Fouls are
A. Using any part of the stick except the *flat surface of the blade*
B. Raising the stick above the shoulder
C. Using any part of the body to propel the ball
D. Hitting another player, or hooking, slashing, or interfering with opponent's stick
E. Being offside, which means that an offensive player who is in his opponent's half of the field and does not have possession of the ball must have two opponents between him and the goal line.

VIII. Fouls committed inside the penalty area:
A. If by the attacking team, the defending team is awarded a free hit from anywhere inside the semicircle.
B. If by the defending team, any player on the attacking team is given a free hit on a spot seven yards in front of the center of the goal. All other players, except the goalie, must remain behind the twenty-five-yard line until the penalty hit is taken.

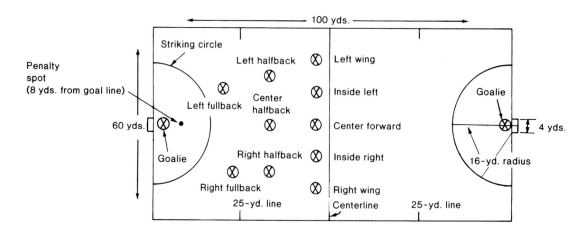

EVALUATIVE TECHNIQUES

Very few standardized hockey tests are available for elementary school children, so the teacher must develop her own. Since hockey is a relatively new activity, several of the basic skills can be easily developed into objective test items, and most classroom teachers can make reasonably accurate subjective ratings of the child's general playing ability.

If a teacher wishes to develop a simple test battery, tests 2, 3, and 4 from the previous chapter on soccer activities can be modified for hockey. Other items should be added at the teacher's discretion.

Summary Review

The game of hockey requires players to be knowledgeable about the rules of the game and to understand appropriate game-playing strategies. Players also need to be proficient in a number of specialized hockey skills. These skills must be learned, as they do not develop automatically through growth and maturation. Individual practices, lead-up games, and mini-games that can be adjusted to create successful practice opportunities, as well as enjoyable game situations, become the basis for teaching children hockey. The objective is to increase children's knowledge of hockey and to help develop their hockey skills toward the automatic stage of development. To develop specialized sport skills to the automatic stage requires many individual practices. Hence, children need to be provided with lots of developmentally appropriate practice opportunities. This will lead to successful hockey skill development and enjoyment of the game. If this objective is achieved, then children will possess the knowledge, skills, and desire to continue playing this major game throughout their lives.

INDIVIDUAL *and* **GROUP** PROJECTS

1. Form groups of three. Each group member chooses two different hockey skills. Design lesson plans to teach your two basic skills. Then teach one group member your two basic hockey skills while the third member observes the effectiveness of your instruction. Each group member takes a turn at being teacher, student, and observer. Observers might find useful the observational checklist for the evaluation of teaching, provided in Table 11.7 on page 247. When you have all taught your skills, discuss and evaluate your experiences in each role (teacher, student, observer) and suggest possible ways to improve your teaching.
2. In pairs, study the rules and regulations of field hockey. Then pose questions on the rules and regulations for each other to answer.
3. In chapter 4, it was suggested that one of the challenges facing teachers is the adjustment of the teaching environment to meet the developmental levels of the children. Four environmental variables under the teachers' control were identified:
    a. Rules
    b. Space
    c. Number of participants
    d. Amount or type of equipment

    One or more of these variables can be adjusted to create success on behalf of students. In small groups, discuss how these four variables can be adjusted when teaching children hockey. Formulate creative ideas and specific recommendations and share these with other groups.
4. Chapter 13 identified a number of disabilities that afflict young children. In small groups, choose four disabilities and discuss how children with these disabilities can be integrated into hockey activites. Consider what adjustments will have to be made to accommodate each child's developmental level and to ensure success. Debate possible techniques and methods of evaluation. Share ideas with other groups.
5. A feature of this text is the idea of teaching and enhancing academic skills and concepts through physical education activities. In small groups, discuss and create ideas to teach or enhance academic skills and concepts through hockey activities. Each group is then allocated a small selection of the hockey practice activities and lead-up games. Create ideas for teaching or enhancing academic skills and concepts through these practice activities and lead-up games. Consider ways to evaluate students. Share ideas with other groups.

SELECTED READINGS

CAHPER. 1985. *Floor hockey type games.* Ottawa, Ontario: CAHPER.

Falla, J. 1987. *Hockey: Learn to play the modern way.* New York: Sports Illustrated Winner's Circle Books.

Field Hockey Canada. 1993. *Level I, II, III coaching manuals.* Ottawa, Ontario: CAHPER.

John, J. 1980. *Field hockey handbook.* North Vancouver, BC: Hancock House.

Wein, H. 1985. *The science of hockey.* 3rd ed. London: Pelham Books.

CHAPTER 20

Flag or Touch Football Activities

KEY CONCEPTS

20.1 Social, historical, and cultural influencess have generally denied girls the opportunity to play football

20.2 Specialized football skills are acquired through instruction and practice opportunities

20.3 Football activities must be developmentally appropriate to ensure that all children can achieve success and enjoyment

20.4 Effective teaching progressions, that provide all children with individual practices and lead-up games, are required to develop the skills and knowledge associated with football

20.5 Safety considerations must be emphasized when teaching children football activities

20.6 Inventive games promote problem solving and creativity, and can help reduce dominance among children in football activities

20.7 To develop football skills toward the automatic stage of skill development requires many practice opportunities (time on-task)

20.8 Playing a full-sided game of football is not a very efficient way of teaching large numbers of children specialized football skills

KEY OBJECTIVES

After completing this chapter you will be able to:

1. Design developmentally appropriate football activities for elementary school children
2. Plan and organize teaching units and individual lessons in football
3. Organize pratice activities and lead-up games appropriate for football
4. Plan and organize football practice activities and lead-up games that incorporate the inventive games approach
5. Evaluate units, lessons, and individual techniques used in football
6. Identify key teaching points associated with the basic skills of football
7. Employ teaching progressions that lead to successful development of football skills and concepts
8. Understand the rules and basic strategies associated with football

When football is suggested as an activity for elementary school children, parents and teachers usually think of it in terms of the competitive game involving expensive equipment, elaborate coaching, and the problems associated with a contact sport. These are valid points that should be taken into consideration. However, this does not mean that modified games involving many of the skills of football should not be taught to children in the upper intermediate grades. Appropriate football skills and rules can be taught through modified games such as field ball, flag football, and touch football. None of the practice activities or lead-up games suggested in this chapter involve tackling or any other form of body contact. Thus, the nature of these activities, coupled with such instructional techniques as station work and inventive games, provides an opportunity for boys and girls to participate in a cooperative and enjoyable way.

This chapter has been arranged to help teachers develop an instructional unit that takes into consideration such factors as coeducational classes, variable levels of instruction, and available equipment. It is strongly suggested that flag rather than touch football be emphasized in the regular instructional period. Flag football is the same as touch football, except two flags attached at the waist of each player are removed. Pulling off these flags avoids disputes over whether a player was actually touched with two hands.

EMPHASIS AND PROGRESSION

The problems of teaching football skills are very similar to those found in teaching basketball and softball. Many boys, even ten- and eleven-year-olds, can throw a spiral pass, punt a ball, and elucidate the advantages of a single- or double-wing formation. Others may not have even thrown or kicked a football. Although girls enjoy throwing and catching a football and playing many of the lead-up games described in this chapter, cultural patterns have generally denied them equal opportunity to play football. Consequently, their understanding and skill are generally much less developed than that of boys.

C O N C E P T

20.1 *Social, Historical, and Cultural Influences Have Generally Denied Girls the Opportunity to Play Football*

Although major differences in skill level appear within each grade, the following suggested sequence of presenting skills provides a basic guideline for most elementary school situations (table 20.1).

Basic throwing and catching skills have normally been learned in the primary grades, so the main task for developmental level II is to learn to throw and catch an oblong ball. These children should also be introduced to punting.

C O N C E P T

20.2 *Specialized Football Skills Are Acquired Through Instruction and Practice Opportunities*

The major skills and playing strategies should be taught at level III. Children in these grades should learn the various stances and how to throw a ball to a moving receiver. They should also learn other ways of passing the ball and a few simple play patterns.

TEACHING PROCEDURES

Teaching flag or touch football activities presents a few major problems for most upper elementary school classes. As stated earlier, football has been mainly an activity for boys. Even with coeducational classes, girls were usually given other games to play while the boys enjoyed touch or flag football. However, most girls enjoy football activities and, therefore, should participate in many practice activities and lead-up games, with a few modifications to cope with differences in skill level and previous football experience. An inadequate number of footballs also is often a major problem for teachers planning partner and small-group practice activities. The following suggestions are intended to assist the teacher in developing an integrated and meaningful football unit.

C O N C E P T

20.3 *Football Activities Must Be Developmentally Appropriate to Ensure That All Children Can Achieve Success and Enjoyment*

Station Work

Station work is basically organizing the field into stations where specific skills are practiced by small groups. Each group practices the skill assigned to a station for several minutes, then rotates to the next station. Boys and girls may be mixed at each station, or they may be separated if their level of skill varies widely or they prefer to work with their own gender. If only a few footballs are available, use them at stations 3 and 5 and use a soccer, Nerf, or utility ball for the other stations.

TABLE 20.1	Suggested Sequence of Presenting Football Skills and Rules	
Skills and Rules	**Developmental Level II**	**Developmental Level III**
Passing		
Forward pass	Introduce	Increase accuracy and distance
Lateral pass		Introduce
Centering	Introduce	Increase accuracy
Rules: Passing and receiving	Introduce	
Scoring	Introduce	
Catching		
Pass receiving	Introduce	Refine
Receiving a kicked ball	Introduce	Refine
Stance		
Three-point stance		Introduce
Four-point stance		Introduce
Rules: Line of scrimmage		Introduce
Punting		Introduce
Rules: Kickoff	Introduce	
Safety		Introduce
Blocking		Introduce
Rules: Use of hands and shoulders		Introduce
Other Rules		
Downs		Introduce
Position and plays		Introduce

20.4 *Effective Teaching Progressions, That Provide All Children with Individual Practices and Lead-Up Games, Are Required to Develop the Skills and Knowledge Associated with Football*

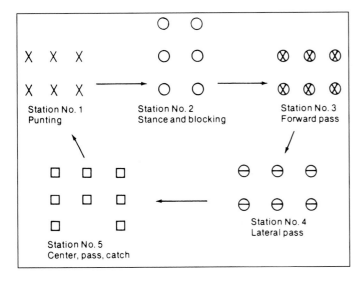

Station No. 1
Punting

Station No. 2
Stance and blocking

Station No. 3
Forward pass

Station No. 4
Lateral pass

Station No. 5
Center, pass, catch

In addition, the following considerations and safety procedures should be included in a football instruction unit.

1. Use junior-size footballs.
2. Play flag rather than touch football. If commercial flags are not available, strips of plastic or cloth may be used.
3. All positions should be rotated frequently to permit each player to experience and enjoy the skills required for each position.

20.5 *Safety Considerations Must Be Emphasized When Teaching Children Football Activities*

Inventive Games Approach

It has been stated in previous chapters that the inventive games approach can be used to teach skills as well as to nurture children's creative abilities. This approach can be applied to football, too. If two boys and two girls are assigned a drill, such as "center, throw, and catch," the boys will normally show more skill and, thus, will dominate the practice session. However, a challenge such as "In groups of four, make up a drill in which the ball must be alternately passed from a boy to a girl" encourages cooperative planning and copes with the problem of one gender dominating.

CONCEPT

20.6 *Inventive Games Promote Problem Solving and Creativity, and Can Help Reduce Dominance among Children in Football Activities*

Adding small equipment, such as milk cartons or traffic cones, can also break down the rigidity of many football drills and make the practice activity less competitive and more enjoyable. The teacher could add "Use four milk cartons in your drill" to the earlier challenge. Passing is still emphasized in the drill, but the additional equipment adds to the challenge and encourages everyone in the group to suggest ways of incorporating it.

DESCRIPTION OF SKILLS

Touch or flag football requires the same skills as the competitive game, with the exception of tackling and blocking. For elementary school children, the emphasis should be on passing, catching, and kicking skills, team positions, and simple play formations.

CONCEPT

20.7 *To Develop Football Skills to The Automatic Stage of Skill Development Requires Many Practice Opportunities (Time On-Task)*

Passing

Three types of passing are used in touch football. The forward pass is similar to the baseball throw; however, it requires a different hand grip and release so that the ball spirals. Lateral passing is a sideward throw of the ball and is an effective technique virtually anywhere in the field of play. Hiking or centering the ball is a throw used solely by the center to start each play from the line of scrimmage.

Forward Pass

When executing a forward pass, the player stands with the foot opposite his throwing arm forward and pointing in the direction of the throw. His weight is evenly distributed on both feet, and he holds the ball with both hands. The fingers of his throwing hand grip the lace behind the center of the ball, and the other hand holds the front and side of the ball. The ball is shifted back past the ear and the body is rotated away from the throw. The elbow of the throwing arm should be kept high (figure 20.1a). Young children with proportionately smaller hands find this difficult and

Figure 20.1   **Forward pass.**

tend to drop the elbow in order to hold the ball in this position. The ball is then rotated toward the target, the forearm and wrist are thrust forward, and the wrist is dropped to allow the ball to roll off the fingers (figure 20.1b and c). This "roll-off" gives the ball the spiral action. Follow through in the direction of the ball.

Key Teaching Points

1. Grip ball with fingers spread over laces.
2. Just prior to throwing, the nonthrowing side should be pointing toward the pass receiver.
3. Keep ball above shoulder as throwing arm moves back.
4. Throw ball from behind the ear with a strong shoulder and wrist snapping action. Follow through with fingers pointing toward receiver.

Lateral Pass

The lateral pass is basically a sideways throw of the ball. The ball is shifted from a one-arm carry to two hands. Once the ball is firmly held in both hands, shift it to the opposite side of the intended throw (figure 20.2). Then bring the ball across the body and release it about waist high.

Key Teaching Points

1. Shift weight and ball to opposite side prior to throwing the ball.
2. Swing the ball across the body.
3. Release and follow through toward the receiver.

Centering the Ball

Once the ball is placed into position for the next play, it cannot be removed from the ground until a pass, or hike, is made by the center player. The center player positions his body in a wide stride position, with his knees bent and his body weight well forward over his shoulders and arms. He then grasps the ball with the fingers of his right hand spread over the lace, and the left hand on the side and near the back of the ball. On signal from the quarterback, the center extends his arms and hands backward through his legs and releases the ball off his fingertips (figure 20.3a and b).

Figure 20.2 Lateral pass.

Key Teaching Points
1. Spread legs and point toes forward.
2. Reach forward and place hands on the ball.
3. Thrust the ball backward with both hands.
4. Immediately after releasing ball, shift forward and upward.

Catching

A ball thrown from a quarterback or a lateral pass is normally caught with an underhand catch. However, a forward pass is usually caught while on the run, requiring balance, timing, and a cradling action of the hands. This skill requires an accurate pass and lots of practice on the part of the receiver.

At the moment the receiver is ready to catch the ball, he turns slightly toward the passer, with his hands held forward and upward (figure 20.4a). His elbows are slightly flexed and his fingers spread. He reaches for the ball (figure 20.4b), immediately pulls it toward his body (figure 20.4c), then shifts it to a carrying position. The ball is carried with one hand under and around the front end of the ball. The other end of the ball is held close to the body by the inside of the forearm and elbow.

Key Teaching Points
1. Keep your eye on the ball.
2. Move into position to reach and receive the ball.
3. Quickly shift ball into proper carrying position.

Carrying the Ball

The ball is carried with the arm farthest away from the opposing player. It is cradled on the inner surface of the arm with the end tucked into the notch formed by the elbow and forearm (figure 20.5).

Key Teaching Points
1. Always keep the body between the ball and the defender.
2. Carry the ball close to the body.
3. Keep a firm grip on the ball.

Handoff

The handoff is an elusive exchange of the ball from one player to another. This skill should be executed in such a way that, at the moment of exchange, the ball may be given to a teammate or faked to allow the ball carrier to run with or pass the ball. When the handoff is executed, the ball carrier shifts the ball to the hand closest to the approaching receiver.

The receiver moves forward with his nearest arm flexed and in front of his chest and palm down (figure 20.6). The lower arm is just below with arm bent and palm facing up. At the moment the two players pass each other, the ball is either handed to the receiver or faked (known as a bootleg) by the ball carrier in order to continue to run or to pass the ball.

Key Teaching Points
1. Stress handing rather than throwing the ball to the oncoming receiver.
2. Practice alternating the handoff and the bootleg maneuvers until both moves appear to be the same.

Stance

The type of starting position a player takes depends on whether she is in an offensive or a defensive situation and whether she is playing on the line or in the backfield. The following stances are typical positions for defensive or offensive playing situations.

Figure 20.3   Centering the ball.

a. Elbows flexed
   and fingers spread

b. Reaches for the ball

c. Cradling action of hands

Figure 20.4   Catching.

Figure 20.5 Carrying the ball.

Figure 20.6 Handoff.

Figure 20.7 Offensive position: three-point stance.

Figure 20.8 Defensive position: four-point stance.

ward and lightly resting on the forward arm and knuckle. The head is up, trunk parallel to the ground, feet even or with one foot slightly in front of the other. If one foot is slightly back, it should be on the same side as the hand that is resting on the ground (figure 20.7).

Key Teaching Points
1. Keep the head up and parallel to the ground.
2. Keep most of the weight over the legs.

Four-Point Stance (Defensive Player)
Assume a crouched position with both hands on the ground. The head is up, back parallel to the ground, and feet about shoulder width apart. The weight is evenly distributed over the balls of both feet (figure 20.8).

Key Teaching Points
1. Keep head up and eyes focused on the play.
2. Keep an even balanced position over both legs.
3. Be ready to shift toward either side.

Three-Point Stance (Offensive Player)
Assume a crouched position, feet approximately shoulder width apart, and the weight of the body shifted slightly for-

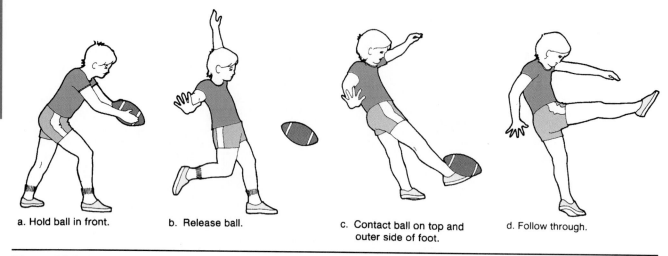

Figure 20.9 Punting.

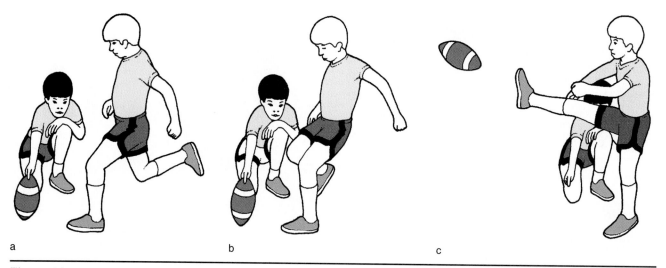

Figure 20.10 Placekick.

Punting

The player stands with his right foot slightly forward and his weight evenly distributed over both feet. He holds the ball with his right hand on the right side near the front of the ball. His left hand holds the left side of the ball (figure 20.9a). He steps right, then left, and simultaneously drops the ball as he brings his kicking leg forward (figure 20.9b). The ball should be contacted with the top and slightly outer side of the foot (figure 20.9c). He then continues the forward and upward movement of his kicking leg (figure 20.9d). His arms should extend sideways to assist balance.

Key Teaching Points

1. Keep eyes on ball until it is kicked.
2. Release rather than throw the ball toward the kicking foot.
3. Straighten the kicking leg forward and upward with a high follow-through.

Placekick

The ball holder should hold the ball for a right-footed player with his right hand and on the opposite side with his left hand for a left-footed kicker. The ball should be held with one or two fingers and slanting slightly backward toward the kicker (figure 20.10a). Laces of the ball face away from the kicker. The kicker runs toward the ball, places the nonkicking foot to the side and slightly behind the ball (figure 20.10b). The kicking leg swings forward, contacting the ball with the top of the foot, and continues forward and upward in the direction of the ball (figure 20.10c).

Key Teaching Points

1. Practice the approach until the nonkicking foot is consistently placed just behind the ball and slightly to the side.
2. Just prior to beginning the downward swing, bend the kicking leg backward (hyperextended) at the hip and flex the knee.

Figure 20.11 Act as an obstruction.

3. Follow through in the direction of the ball.
4. Keep eyes on the ball until it is kicked.

Blocking

A player in flag or touch football may block by simply placing his body in the way of an opponent. When an offensive player blocks, he must have both feet on the ground and his forearms must be held against his chest when he contacts the defensive player. The defensive player may use her hands to protect herself but is limited to touching the shoulders and body of the blocker (figure 20.11). Do not permit players to drop to their knees to improve their blocking stance.

Key Teaching Points
1. Keep a slightly forward body lean.
2. Keep elbows out and forearms close to the chest.

PRACTICE ACTIVITIES AND LEAD-UP GAMES

Football activities normally require two or more players in practice situations. Normally, two or more skills are prac-

ticed in the same drill. The lead-up games described in this section may be played by boys and girls together or separately, depending on the children's ability (table 20.2). If their skill and experience vary widely, girls and boys are normally much happier playing separate games. This is particularly true for children who have reached the middle to upper limits of skill proficiency of developmental level III.

C O N C E P T

20.8 *Playing a Full-Sided Game of Football Is Not a Very Efficient Way of Teaching Large Numbers of Children Specialized Football Skills*

P R A C T I C E   A C T I V I T E S

Partner Passing

Motor skills Pass, catch
Movement concepts Moving into space, change of direction, pathway, and speed
Players Two
Formation None
Playing area Playground, gymnasium
Equipment Football

Players begin fifteen to twenty feet apart. Require them to throw with a spiral pass and catch with an underhand or overhand catch.

Suggestions and Variations
1. One partner runs and tries to catch the other's pass.
2. One partner centers, then runs forward to catch the other's pass.
3. Both run and pass back and forth, using a lateral pass.
4. Partners punt and catch.
5. One partner runs with (or without) the ball and the other partner tries to block the oncoming opponent.
6. Repeat above with one partner trying to tag the other.

Blocking Practice

Motor skills Feint, dodge
Movement concepts Moving into space, change of direction and speed
Players Ten to twelve per group
Formation See diagram
Playing area Playground, gymnasium
Equipment None

```
    X          X Offense  X          X          X
 ├─ 8 ft. ─┤   _____   _____   _____   _____

    O          O Defense  O          O          O
```

Arrange the field and players as shown in the diagram. One player is designated as the offense, the other as defense. Both assume a football stance position. On signal "hike," the offensive player attempts to get past the defensive player. The

TABLE 20.2 Practice Activities and Lead-Up Games

Name of Activity	Type of Activity	Players	Developmental Level		Hockey Concepts and Skills	Movement Concepts	Page
			II	III			
Practice Activities							
Partner Passing	Pass, catch	2	————————➤		Pass, catch	Moving into space, change of direction, pathway, and speed	415
Blocking Practice	Feint, dodge	10–12	————————➤		Feint, dodge	Moving into space, change of direction and speed	415
Pass and Defend	Pass, catch	4	————————➤		Pass, catch, defensive moves	Moving into space, change of direction, pathway, and speed	416
Punt and Catch	Punt, catch	6–10	————————➤		Punt, catch	Moving into space, change of direction and speed	417
Adapted from Soccer Activities							
Circle Passing	Pass, catch	2	————————➤		Pass, catch	Moving into space, change of direction and speed	385
Triangle Pass	Pass, catch	3	————————➤		Pass, catch	Moving into space, change of direction	386
Kicking for Distance	Kick	4–5	————————➤		Kick	Moving into space, strong and light	386
Lead-Up Games							
Football End Ball	Pass, catch	6–8	————————➤		Pass, catch	Moving into space, change of direction and speed	417
Punt Back	Punt, catch	Class	————————➤		Punt, catch	Moving into space, change of direction and speed	417
One-Down Football	Pass, catch	16–20	————————➤		Throw, catch, tag	Moving into space, change of direction and speed	417
Grab It	Run, tag	Class	————————➤		Run, tag	Moving into space, change of direction and speed	418
Keep Away and Score	Pass, catch	8–10 per team	————————➤		Pass, catch	Moving into space, change of direction and speed	418

offensive player must stay within the eight-foot line and may feint, dodge, or do any movement to get around the defensive player.

Suggestions and Variations
Repeat the drill with a ball.

◾ Pass and Defend

Motor skills Pass, catch, defensive move
Movement concepts Moving into space, change of direction, pathway, and speed
Players Four per group
Formation See diagram
Playing area Playground, gymnasium
Equipment Football

Arrange field and players as shown in diagram. The center snaps the ball to the passer. As soon as the passer has the ball, the receiver runs forward and tries to catch the pass. The defender moves at the same time and tries to prevent the receiver from catching the pass or tries to intercept it. If the skill level is high enough, allow the receiver and defender to move at the moment the snap is made.

Punt and Catch

Motor skills   Punt, catch
Movement concepts   Moving into space, change of direction and speed
Players   Six to ten per team
Formation   See diagram
Playing area   Playground, gymnasium
Equipment   Football

A player from one team punts the ball over the neutral zone into the opponent's area. The opponent closest to the ball tries to catch it. If successful, he punts the ball back and the game continues. If an opponent misses a catch (it must be in the air), the kicking side is awarded one point. If the ball does not pass out of the neutral zone, the captain of the opposite team may enter the zone to retrieve it. No score is awarded if the ball lands outside the playing area.

Suggestions and Variations
1. Rotate the lines on each team after a number of points have been scored or at set intervals.
2. Play the same game using a forward pass.

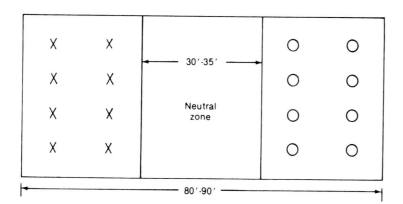

LEAD-UP GAMES

Football End Ball

Motor skills   Pass, catch
Movement concepts   Moving into space, change of speed and direction
Players   Six to eight per group
Formation   See diagram
Playing area   Playground
Equipment   One football per game

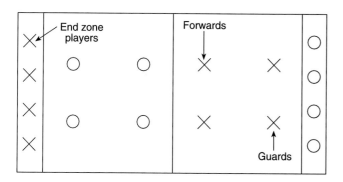

Arrange the field and players as shown in the diagram. The objective of the game is for a forward player to pass the ball to an end zone player. Players must remain in their own zones, and guards can only pass to forwards and forwards to end zone players. The game begins with a jump ball between two opposing forwards. The team that gets the ball tries to throw the ball to an end zone player, who must catch it while in the end zone area. Balls crossing end or side lines are put into play by the nearest player who did not cause the ball to go out of bounds. The ball is put into play by a throw from behind the line and closest to where the ball went out of bounds. Players may not hold the ball longer than five seconds, cross over into an opponent's territory, or push or hold an opponent. If a penalty occurs, the ball is given to the nearest opponent and the game continues. Award one point for each successful catch by an end zone player. Resume play with a jump ball at the center.

Punt Back

Motor skills   Punt, catch
Movement concepts   Moving into space, change of direction and speed
Players   Class
Formation   Half of a regular playing field, with each team scattered on its own side of the field
Playing area   Playground, gymnasium, classroom
Equipment   Football

The object of this game is to punt the ball over the opponent's goal line. One player begins the game by punting the ball from her own twenty-five-yard line. Once the game is started, opposing players must stay at least ten yards apart. If the ball is caught by a player on the opposite team and she calls "mark" and remains motionless for two seconds, she then has two options: (1) she may take five steps and then punt the ball, or (2) she may pass it to any teammate. All players on her team, however, may be checked (as in basketball) as they try to catch the pass. If a player catches the ball, she must kick it from the point of the catch. If the catcher moves her feet while she is catching the ball or fails to call "mark," she is allowed only three steps before kicking the ball. If the ball is not caught, the player who secures the ball must punt it from the point where it was stopped.

A ball that goes over the sideline is punted back from the point where it went over the line. A ball that is caught in the air behind the goal line does not count as a point; it is put back into play by a punt from the goal line. One point is awarded for a successful punt over the goal line, provided it is not caught. The ball is put into play again at the twenty-five-yard line.

Suggestions and Variations
Use a placekick or a forward pass instead of a punt.

One-Down Football

Motor skills   Throw, catch, tag
Movement concepts   Moving into space, change of direction and speed
Players   Eight to ten per team
Formation   See diagram

Playing area   Playground, gymnasium
Equipment   Football

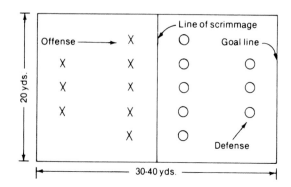

To start the game, both teams line up on opposite sides of the centerline. One team is designated as the offense and is given one down to score a touchdown. After the hike, the ball may be run or passed any number of times in any direction from any position on the field. The defensive team attempts to tag the ball carrier below the waist with two hands. If a player is tagged before he reaches the opponent's goal line, the ball is downed and the other team takes its down at this point. If a ball is intercepted, the game continues, with the defensive team becoming the offensive team.

Suggestions and Variations

1. When introducing this game, have all players play "man-to-man," that is, linemen checking linemen and backs checking backs. Later, variations can be made to meet the wishes of the defensive team.
2. Play same game using only the lateral pass.

Grab It

Motor skills   Run, tag
Movement concepts   Moving into space, change of direction and speed
Players   Class
Formation   Large rectangular field
Playing area   Playground, gymnasium
Equipment   Flag football tags

Place one-half of class on one endline and the other half on the opposite line. Every player has a tag tucked into the back of his shorts. On signal, everyone runs to the appropriate line and tries to protect his own tag from being stolen while stealing as many as he can before reaching the opposite line.

Keep Away and Score

Motor skills   Pass, catch
Movement concepts   Moving into space, change of direction and speed
Players   Eight to ten per team
Formation   Large rectangular field with centerline
Playing area   Playground, gymnasium
Equipment   Football

Each team stands on its own endline. One player is given the ball and his team begins to run, pass, and catch toward the

opposite endline. The opposing team runs out to intercept the ball. When a player is tagged, he must immediately drop the ball, and he and his teammates must wait until an opponent has picked up the ball before anyone can resume running and tagging. Loose balls may be picked up by any player from either team. Score one point for each touchdown.

TOUCH FOOTBALL RULES AND REGULATIONS

It is recommended that upper elementary school children play seven-person touch or flag football. Commercial flags may be purchased from local sports stores, or you may improvise your own. (Flags are sometimes called tags.)

I. Field layout and lineups: See field layout and team positions in the accompanying diagram.

II. Start of game: The game is started with a kickoff (punt or placekick) from the goal line. The ball must be kicked past the centerline and must land within the field of play. If the first ball is kicked out-of-bounds, it is kicked again. If the second kick goes out-of-bounds, the other team starts play at its twenty-yard line. The kickoff team may recover the ball only after the other team touches and fumbles it.

III. Offensive play:
A. Once a player who is returning the kickoff is touched, the ball is placed on the spot where he was tagged. The line drawn through this spot is known as the *scrimmage line*. In all cases, the ball must be placed five paces in from the sideline.
B. The offensive team has four downs to move the ball into the next twenty-yard zone or to score a touchdown. Always start a new series of downs whenever a team crosses a zone line.
C. The offensive team must have at least three players on the scrimmage line when a play begins. The center player must pass the ball backward through his legs. A backfield player who receives the ball may run with it, hand off, or throw a lateral or forward pass from behind the line of scrimmage. Any player except the center may receive the forward pass. The offensive team may punt on any down, providing it calls for a punt formation. When this occurs, neither team may cross the scrimmage line until the punt receiver has caught the ball.

IV. Defensive play:
A. The defending team must remain behind the scrimmage line until the ball has left the opposing center's hands. A special rule applies to a punt, as previously described.
B. A defensive player may stop the ball carrier if she removes the flags from her opponent's waist.

Field layout:

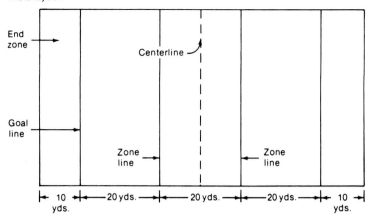

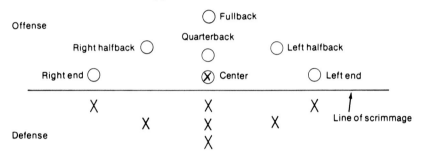

V. Blocking: A player may block only by placing his body in the way of an opponent. Review the description of blocking earlier in this chapter.

VI. Scoring: Points are awarded for the following:
   A. Touchdown: Six points. Following the *touchdown,* one play or down is given to the scoring team from the three-yard line, and one more point is awarded if the team crosses the goal line with the ball.
   B. Safety: Two points. The defensive team is awarded two points if the team in possession of the ball is tagged behind its own goal line. Immediately following the *safety,* the ball is put into play by the team scored against by a kickoff from behind the goal line.

VII. Touchback: A *touchback* occurs when a defensive player intercepts a ball behind her own goal line and does not run it out, or when the ball is kicked over the goal line by the offensive team. The ball is taken to the twenty-yard line and given to the defending team.

VIII. Penalties: Award five yards to the nonoffending team for the following infractions:
   A. Pushing, holding, or tripping
   B. Unsportsmanlike conduct
   C. Interfering with the pass receiver
   D. Offside

IX. Length of game: Two eight-minute periods

EVALUATIVE TECHNIQUES

A few standardized tests are designed to measure the basic football skills. The majority of these tests, however, are designed for high school or college-level players, so they must be modified for elementary school players (table 20.3). This "teacher-made" test battery can be administered without elaborate equipment and in a short period of time. Use students to assist in testing, and keep scores from year to year in order to develop appropriate norms for your school.

Test 1: Accuracy Pass

Place a target on the wall as shown in the diagram. Each player is given ten consecutive throws from behind the starting line. She must use a forward pass. Score six, four, and two points for hits within each respective circle. If the ball hits a line, award the higher score. Record the total score.

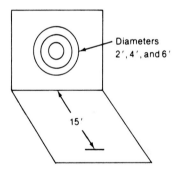

Test 2: Punting

Place lines on the field as shown in the diagram. Stakes can be used as a substitute for gypsum lines. Each player must punt a regulation-size football from behind the starting line. Mark where the ball lands with a stick or small object. Allow a total of three kicks and record the highest score. Yards are equivalent to points.

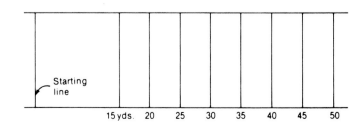

TABLE 20.3   Touch Football Skill Test

Name	Accuracy Pass (Total Pts.)	Punting (Total Pts.)	Ball Carrying (Total Pts.)	Subjective Evaluation (50 Pts.)	Total Score	Grade
1						
2						
3		Rank total scores for the class, then convert to letter grades or ratings (superior, good, etc.).				
4						
5						

Test 3: Ball Carrying

Arrange four chairs as shown in the diagram. Place a ball on the starting line. Each player stands behind the starting line, with both hands resting on his knees. On signal, he picks up the football and runs around the left side of the first chair, and continues the zigzag running pattern around each chair. Allow thirty seconds for the test. One point is awarded for each chair he passes correctly. Two trials are allowed, with the highest score recorded.

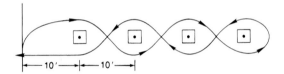

Test 4: Subjective Evaluation

Establish criteria that represent the skills and playing ability required in touch football, such as passing, feinting, kicking, and defensive ability. The teacher or a group of three players awards each player a total score ranging from zero to fifty points. When three players are judging, take an average of their scores.

Summary Review

The game of football requires players to be knowledgeable about the rules of the game and to understand appropriate game playing strategies. Players also need to be proficient in a number of specialized football skills. These skills must be learned, as they do not develop automatically through growth and maturation. Individual practices, lead-up games, and mini-games that can be adjusted to create successful practice opportunities, as well as enjoyable game situations, become the basis for teaching children football. The objective is to increase children's knowledge of football and to help develop their football skills toward the automatic stage of development. To develop specialized sport skills to the automatic stage

requires many individual practices. Hence, children need to be provided with lots of developmentally appropriate practice opportunities. This will lead to successful football skill development and enjoyment of the game. If this objective is achieved, then children will possess the knowledge, skills, and desire to continue playing this major game throughout their lives.

INDIVIDUAL *and* **GROUP** **PROJECTS**

1. Form groups of three. Each group member chooses two different football skills. Design lesson plans to teach your two basic skills. Then teach one group member your two basic football skills while the third member observes the effectiveness of your instruction. Each group member takes a turn at being teacher, student, and observer. Observers might find useful the observational checklist for the evaluation of teaching, provided in Table 11.7 on page 247. When you have all taught your skills, discuss and evaluate your experiences in each role (teacher, student, observer), and suggest ways to improve your teaching.

2. In pairs, study the rules and regulations of touch football. Then pose questions on the rules and regulations for each other to answer.

3. In chapter 4, it was suggested that one of the challenges facing teachers is the adjustment of the teaching environment to meet the developmental levels of the children. Four environmental variables under the teachers' control were identified:
   a. Rules
   b. Space
   c. Number of participants
   d. Amount or type of equipment

One or more of these variables can be adjusted to create success on behalf of students. In small groups, discuss how these four variables can be adjusted when teaching children football. Formulate creative ideas and specific recommendations and share these with other groups.

4. Chapter 13 identified a number of disabilities that afflict young children. In small groups, choose four disabilities and discuss how children with these disabilities can be integrated into football activites. Consider what adjustments will have to be made to accommodate each child's developmental level and to ensure success. Debate possible techniques and methods of evaluation. Share ideas with other groups.

5. A feature of this text is the idea of teaching and enhancing academic skills and concepts through physical education activities. In small groups, discuss and create ideas to teach or enhance academic skills and concepts through football activities. Each group is then allocated a small selection of the football practice activities and lead-up games. Create ideas for teaching or enhancing academic skills and concepts through these practice activities and lead-up games. Consider ways to evaluate students. Share ideas with other groups.

SELECTED READINGS

CAHPER. 1985. *Football type games.* Ottawa, Ontario: CAHPER.

Fooss, D. 1984. *Complete handbook of winning football drills.* Newton, MA: Allyn & Bacon.

Kamiya, D. 1985. *Elementary teacher's handbook of indoor and outdoor games.* West Nyack, NY: Parker.

Phillip, J. A., and J. D. Wilkerson. 1990. *Teaching team sports: A coeducational approach.* Champaign, IL Human Kinetics.

Torba, E. M. 1983. *The Boys Club guide to youth football.* New York: Leisure Press.

Turner, L. F., and L. S. Turner, 1989. *P.E. teacher's skill-by-skill activity program.* West Nyack, NY: Parker.

CHAPTER 21

Volleyball Activities

KEY CONCEPTS

21.1 Specialized volleyball skills are acquired through instruction and practice opportunities

21.2 Playing a regulation full-sided game of volleyball is not a very efficient way of teaching children volleyball skills and concepts

21.3 Volleyball activities must be developmentally appropriate to ensure that all children can achieve success and enjoyment

21.4 Effective teaching progressions, that provide all children with individual practices and lead-up games, are required to develop the skills and knowledge associated with volleyball

21.5 To develop volleyball skills toward the automatic stage of skill development requires many practice opportunities (time on-task)

KEY OBJECTIVES

After completing this chapter you will be able to:

1. Design developmentally appropriate volleyball activities for elementary school children
2. Plan and organize teaching units and individual lessons in volleyball
3. Organize pratice activities and lead-up games appropriate for volleyball
4. Plan and organize volleyball practice activities and lead-up games that incorporate the inventive games approach
5. Evaluate units, lessons, and individual techniques used in volleyball
6. Identify key teaching points associated with the basic skills of volleyball
7. Employ teaching progressions that lead to successful development of volleyball skills and concepts
8. Understand the rules and basic strategies associated with volleyball

Volleyball was originated by William G. Morgan in 1895 while he was teaching at the YMCA in Holyoke, Massachusetts. Although the rules, number of players, and size of the ball have changed since that first game, volleyball can be classified as an American contribution to the world of sports. Today it is played by millions of people in more than sixty countries each year. This phenomenal growth in such a short time is probably due to the game's simplicity, enjoyment, and contributions to physical fitness.

Because volleyball can be adapted to the available facilities and varying levels of proficiency, it is a particularly good activity for the upper elementary physical education program.

EMPHASIS AND PROGRESSION

One of the most difficult tasks in teaching physical education is determining whether the children are familiar with the activity you wish to teach and whether they have the potential to develop the required skills. Volleyball is no exception. Some children already understand the rules of the game and have acquired a few of the basic skills. Others may not have seen a volleyball game or even have hit the ball correctly. With these factors in mind, the following suggested sequence for presenting skills and rules should be considered as a basic guideline.

Prior to the beginning of developmental level II, most children have learned to hit a utility ball from a bounce (two square and four square) or to hit a volleyball with a two-hand overhand hit. The main skills and playing strategies of volleyball are normally taught in the upper elementary grades. In developmental level II, as indicated in table 21.1, the overhand pass and underhand serve should be introduced with a beach ball. Once the skill level is high enough, a volleyball training ball or regular volleyball should be used. Serving distances, as well as the height of the net, should be adjusted to each class's ability.

C O N C E P T

21.1 *Specialized Volleyball Skills Are Acquired through Instruction and Practice Opportunities*

The major emphasis throughout level III should be on refining the underhand serve and overhand pass and to learn the more advanced skills of the game. The latter skills include the forearm or bump pass, overhand serve, set-up, and net recovery. Although children in this age range enjoy playing regulation volleyball, such play should be limited. Such games as modified volleyball and sideline volleyball are more appropriate, as they contribute to skill development yet allow for greater participation and success by every player.

C O N C E P T

21.2 *Playing a Regulation Full-Sided Game of Volleyball Is Not a Very Efficient Way of Teaching Large Numbers of Children Specialized Volleyball Skills and Concepts*

TABLE 21.1   Suggested Sequence of Presenting Volleyball Skills and Rules

Skills and Rules	Developmental Level II	Developmental Level III
Volleying		
Overhand pass	Introduce	Refine
Forearm pass (bumping)		Introduce
Rules: Number of hits	Introduce	
Rotation	Introduce	
Line violations	Introduce	
Personal fouls		Introduce
Serving		
Underhand serve	Introduce	Refine
Overhand serve		Introduce
Rules: Serving positions		Introduce
Side out and points		Introduce
Setup		Introduce
Recovery from Net		Introduce
All Other Official Rules		Introduce

TEACHING PROCEDURES

A general format for planning a unit of instruction has been discussed extensively in previous chapters. Teachers should review the teaching procedures discussed in chapter 18 prior to developing a volleyball unit. In addition, the sample lesson plans in chapter 18 and the suggestions about incorporating the creative games approach can be applied to volleyball activities.

C O N C E P T

21.3 *Volleyball Activities Must be Developmentally Appropriate to Ensure That All Children Can Achieve Success and Enjoyment*

The following suggestions may help the teacher with some of the problems that are unique to teaching volleyball activities.

1. When there is only one instructional area, such as a gymnasium, choose or modify activities to be played on smaller courts (divide the volleyball court in half) and require fewer players (six or fewer) on a team.
2. During the initial stages of a volleyball unit, use beach, foam, or lightweight volleyball training balls. Young children, particularly third graders, normally lack sufficient arm and wrist strength to hit a heavy ball. Lighter balls are also slower, allowing children more time to get into position.
3. Adjust the height of the net to the ability of the class. As a general guideline, the net should be six feet high for level II children and seven feet high for level III children. Ropes with a few ribbons spaced every few feet can be substituted for a net.
4. Require the ball to be rolled to the server in all lead-up games or any type of modified volleyball activity that involves two teams on opposite sides of the net. Experienced teachers can verify the amount of time this simple procedure saves.

C O N C E P T

21.4 *Effective Teaching Progressions, That Provide All Children with Individual Practices and Lead-Up Games, Are Required to Develop the Skills and Knowledge Associated with Volleyball*

DESCRIPTION OF SKILLS

There are two basic skills in volleyball, passing (or volleying) and serving a ball. Each of these skills, however, can be modified such as the two-hand underhand volley, requiring use of the forearms. Basic skills for intermediate grades—passing, serving, the set, and net recovery—are described and illustrated in this section.

C O N C E P T

21.5 *To Develop Volleyball Skills to the Automatic Stage of Skill Development Requires Many Practice Opportunities (Time On-Task)*

Passing, or Volleying

The ball may be passed, or volleyed, to another player or over the net by an underhand or overhand hit. Both hands must be used in the overhand pass, whereas the forearms are normally used in the underhand pass. Children should be taught to watch the ball, not their hands or opponents. Body weight should be evenly distributed on both feet before the ball reaches the player. Finally, stress follow-through with the hands and arms after the ball has been hit.

Two-Hand Overhand Pass

The two-hand overhand pass is the most important volleyball skill for elementary school children to learn. It is virtually the prerequisite to playing volleyball; therefore, it requires a great deal of practice and constant correction by the teacher. The feet are in a forward stride position, with knees bent, back straight, and weight evenly distributed over both feet. Arms are extended upward and forward, with elbows rotated outward. The wrists are hyperextended, thumbs pointing toward each other, fingers relaxed and pointing diagonally upward (figure 21.1a). As the ball approaches, the player should be able to see through the window created by her thumbs and fingers. As the ball drops, the player extends her body upward and slightly forward, flexing the wrist and fingers, and contacts the ball with the fingers (figure 21.1b). After the ball is hit, follow through is in the direction of the ball (figure 21.1c).

Key Teaching Points

1. Move into correct position, with hands and elbows up prior to hitting the ball.
2. Look through the "window" made by thumbs and spread fingers.
3. Contact the ball close to the forehead.
4. Contact the ball with the fingers and thumbs.
5. Snap the wrists forward and upward and follow through in the direction of the ball.

Forearm Pass

The forearm pass, also known as a "bump" or "bounce" pass, is used to receive a serve and to handle a ball that is too low or too far from the midline of the body to use an overhand pass.

As the ball approaches, the player moves into a position in which the midline of the body is in line with the ball. In the ready position (figure 21.2a), feet are in a forward stride position, with the back straight, seat down, knees bent, and weight evenly distributed over both feet. The arms are held at a forty-five-degree angle forward

Figure 21.1 Two-hand overhand pass.

Figure 21.2 Forearm pass.

and away from the body, with elbows straight, palms up, and fingers together. Simultaneously, one hand is placed diagonally onto the fingers of the other hand, and legs are extended to lift body and arms upward. As the ball is contacted just above the waist, the arms are straight and the thumbs are pointing downward (figure 21.2b). Follow-through is a continuation of the upward extension of the legs and a very slight upward movement of the arms (figure 21.2c).

Key Teaching Points
1. Move into correct position prior to executing the pass.
2. The ball should be contacted when it is between the knees and waist.
3. Contact the ball on the forearms between the wrists and elbows.
4. Upon contact, "lift" the body upward by straightening the legs. Do not swing forearms upward to hit the ball.
5. Do not follow-through.

a   b   c

Figure 21.3   Serving.

Serving

It is permissible to serve the ball from either an underhand or overhand position. The hand may be open or closed. Boys and girls in the intermediate grades are capable of developing a high level of skill in both serves. Begin with the underhand serve and, after sufficient skill has been developed, introduce the overhand "float" serve.

Underhand Serve

The underhand serve is performed with the left foot (right foot for left-handed players) slightly in front of the right foot. The weight is on the rear foot and the body is bent forward slightly (figure 21.3a). The ball is held with the palm of the left hand in a "ready" position in front of the right knee. The right arm is extended backward and upward. As the right arm swings down and forward, a small step is taken as the weight shifts to the front foot. The ball is hit with the heel of the right hand (figure 21.3b) or the side of the fist. Immediately before the hand contacts the ball, the ball is released out of the left hand. Continue the follow-through action of the right arm (figure 21.3c).

Key Teaching Points

1. Opposite foot to striking hand should be in forward position.
2. Draw striking hand directly backward with straight arm.
3. Simultaneously, take a short step and swing arm downward and forward.
4. Follow through to about shoulder level.

Overhand Serve

The overhand serve should be learned only after a player has mastered the underhand serve. The advantages of the overhand, or "float," serve are that it can place the ball accurately and it has an element of deception caused by its floating and wobbling action.

The server stands with hips and shoulders square to the net, ball held chest high and in line with the right shoulder. Feet are in a stride position with the left foot pointing toward the net and the right foot pointing diagonally toward the right. Weight is evenly distributed over both feet. The server's right hand is held in a ready position just above the right foot. The ball is tossed up with the left hand two or three feet above the right shoulder (figure 21.4a). As the toss is made, the weight shifts to the back foot. As the ball begins to descend, the weight is shifted to the front foot and the striking arm snaps forward (figure 21.4b). Contact is made near the center of the ball with the heel of the hand and palm and the ball is hit through the midline. The wrist remains rigid as contact is made (figure 21.4c).

Key Teaching Points

1. Opposite foot to striking hand should be in a forward position.
2. Hold the ball about eye level.
3. Simultaneously, shift weight to rear foot as toss is made, then to front foot as striking hand moves forward.
4. Snap the wrist as contact is made and do not follow through with the extended arm.

The Set

The set is a two-hand overhand hit, normally the second hit in the series of three that is allowed each team. This overhand hit is used to pass the ball about fifteen feet above the receiver and approximately one foot away from the net. Since the ball moves in the direction the body is

Figure 21.4   Overhand serve.

facing, it is extremely important for the setter to get into position under the ball and facing the intended receiver just before the pass is made.

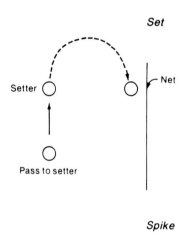

Set

Setter ○ - - - → ○ — Net

↑

○

Pass to setter

Spike

Key Teaching Points

1. Move into correct position just before passing the ball.
2. Watch the ball through the triangle made by fingers and thumb.
3. Pass the ball in a high arc so it floats down to the intended receiver.
4. Quickly move back to playing position.

Net Recovery

The one- or two-hand forearm pass is used to recover a mispassed ball from the net. The player stands with her

Figure 21.5   Two-hand forearm pass.

side to the net in order to move quickly toward or away from the net, or to pass in any direction. Whenever possible, use a two-hand forearm pass (figure 21.5) and contact the ball as low as possible. Normally, the lower the ball, the farther it is away from the net; thus, the easier it is to pass to another player or directly over the net. The one-hand forearm pass (dig) should only be used when poor position or lack of time prevents application of the two-hand pass (figure 21.6).

Key Teaching Points

1. Move quickly into the correct position.
2. Hit the ball upward and slightly away from the net.
3. Quickly move back to playing position.

Figure 21.6 One-hand forearm pass.

PRACTICE ACTIVITIES AND LEAD-UP GAMES

The following activities are designed to allow students to practice one or more volleyball skills in an enjoyable, gamelike situation (table 21.2). Each skill should begin with individual activities so that children develop a basic understanding of the skill and can explore the limits of their ability. Partner activities should follow, stressing ball control and positional play. Finally, group activities involving three or more players provide a gamelike experience while concentrating on one or two basic skills. There is ample opportunity in each type of activity for teachers to inject the inventive games approach by modifying existing drills or creating student-designed practice activities.

The lead-up games described in this section are popular in both developmental levels. However, children in level II require the greatest number of modifications to the rules and court dimensions in order to provide a game that is within their general level of ability. Teachers should modify any of these games to meet the level of ability and interest of each class.

PRACTICE ACTIVITIES

Individual Volleying

Motor skills   Throw, overhand volley
Movement concepts   Personal space, transfer of weight
Players   Individual
Formation   Scattered
Playing area   Playground, gymnasium
Equipment   Volleyballs, Nerf balls, or beach balls

Arrange players in a scattered formation. This drill requires one ball for each child; however, any type of inflated ball can be used. Begin with each player throwing the ball into the air

and catching it close to her forehead after one bounce. She should be in a semicrouched position. Gradually introduce the following individual variations.

1. Throw the ball up, perform an overhand volley on the returning ball, then catch it.
2. Throw . . . set . . . set . . . catch.
3. Throw . . . set . . . set . . . continue.
4. Throw . . . set . . . allow one bounce . . . set . . . catch.
5. Throw . . . kneel and set . . . stand and set . . . catch.
6. Repeat variations 1 to 3 while sitting.
7. Arrange the class in a line formation around the gymnasium approximately six feet from the wall. Have the children
   a. Throw the ball against the wall, set, and catch
   b. Throw against the wall, set, set, and catch
   c. Throw against the wall and continuously set the ball back to the wall
   d. Throw against the wall, allow one bounce, set, and catch

Partner Passing

Motor skills   Passing
Movement concepts   Moving into space, change of direction and speed
Players   Two
Formation   Scattered
Playing area   Playground, gymnasium
Equipment   Volleyball

Partners standing about ten feet apart are arranged in a scattered formation. One partner throws a high pass and the other catches it. Stress moving into position to receive the ball. Player 1 throws to player 2. Player 2 sets back to 1, who catches the ball. Player 1 throws to 2. They continue to set to each other. Player 1 throws to 2. As soon as player 1 has thrown, he moves to a new position. Player 2 then sets to 1, then moves to his new position. Continue pattern.

Suggestions and Variations

1. Partners are arranged around the gymnasium about ten feet from the wall. Player 1 throws against the wall and player 2 sets the ball above player 1. Player 1 catches. Partners change positions and repeat. Player 1 throws against the wall, player 2 sets back to wall. Continue drill, alternating sets. Repeat above variation, but require a bounce before the return set is attempted.
2. Arrange partners on opposite sides of a net or rope. Player 1 throws over the net and player 2 sets back over the net to 1, who catches the ball. Repeat above variation, but continue setting back and forth.

Partner Serving

Motor skills   Serve, volley, set
Movement concepts   Moving into space, change of direction and speed
Players   Two
Formation   Scattered
Playing area   Playground, gymnasium
Equipment   Volleyball

Arrange partners on opposite sides of the net. Adjust the distance to the class's level of ability. Have partners free serve

TABLE 21.2　Practice Activities and Lead-Up Games

Name of Activity	Type of Activity	Players	Developmental Level		Volleyball Concepts and Skills	Movement Concepts	Page
			II	III			
Practice Activities							
Individual Volleying	Throw, volley	Individual	→————————→		Throw, overhead volley	Personal space, transfer of weight	429
Partner Passing	Volley	2	→————————→		Volley, catch	Moving into space, change of direction and speed	429
Partner Serving	Volley, serve	2	→————————→		Serve, volley, set	Moving into space, change of direction and speed	429
Triangle Passing	Pass	3	→————————→		Pass	Moving into space, change of direction	431
Volley and Backset	Volley	3	→————————→		Volley, set	Moving into space, change of direction	431
Hit the Square	Volley	3	→————————→		Throw, volley	Moving into space, change of direction	431
Set Up the Ball	Set	4	→————————→		Volley, set	Moving into space, change of direction and speed	431
Shuttle Volley	Volley	5–6	→————————→		Throw, volley	Moving into space, change of direction and speed	431
Circle Volley	Volley	5–6	→————————→		Throw, volley	Personal space, moving into space	432
Zigzag Volley	Volley	6–8	→————————→		Throw, volley	Personal space, moving into space, change of direction	432
Baseline Serving	Serve	Class	→————————→		Serve	Use of available space, serving into empty space	432
Circuit Volleying	All skills	Class	→————————→		All skills	Use of available space, moving into space, change of direction, speed, and pathway	432
Lead-Up Games							
Nebraska Ball	Serve, volley	9 per team	→————→		Serve, volley	Personal and general space, change of direction	432
							432
Bound Ball	Serve, volley	6–10 per team	→————→		Serve, volley	Moving into space, change of direction	433
Mass Volleyball	Serve, volley	6–9 per team	→————→		Serve, volley	Moving into space, change of direction	433
Newcomb	Serve, volley	6–9 per team	→————→		Serve, volley	Moving into space, change of direction	433
Keep It Up	Volley, bump	6–9 per team	→————————→		Volley, bump	Personal space, levels, change of direction	433
Donkey	Volley, bump	5–6 per team	→————————→		Volley, bump	Moving into space, levels, change of direction and speed	433
Modified Volleyball	Serve, volley	6–9 per team	→————————→		Serve, volley, rotate	Personal space, moving into space, change of direction and speed	433
Volleyball Keep Away	Volley	5–6 per team	→————————→		Volley	Moving into space, change of direction and speed	434
Four-Way Volleyball	Volley, serve	4–5 per team	→————————→		Serve, volley, bump	Change of direction and speed	434
Sideline Volleyball	Ball skills	8–10 per team	→————————→		Serve, volley, bump	Moving into space, change of direction and speed	434
Cross-Over Blanket Volleyball	Running	8–10 per team	→————————→		Running	Moving into space, change of direction	362

back and forth. Move partners closer together. Player 1 serves to player 2, who sets the ball back to player 1. Change positions and repeat. One partner serves to the wall, the other catches the ball and repeats the serve. One partner serves and the other sets back to the wall. Continue setting until one partner misses a return.

Triangle Passing

Motor skills Passing
Movement concepts Moving into space, change of direction
Players Three
Formation Triangle
Playing area Playground, gymnasium
Equipment Volleyball

Arrange groups of three in a triangle pattern with about fifteen feet between players. Player 1 volleys to 2, 2 volleys to 3, and 3 volleys to 1.

Suggestions and Variations
1. Player 1 volleys to 2, then moves forward to take player 2's position. Player 2 volleys to 3 and moves to her position. Continue pattern.
2. Repeat first practice activity and introduce a bump on alternate hits.

Volley and Backset

Motor skills Volley, set
Movement concepts Moving into space, change of direction
Players Three
Formation Line
Playing area Playground, gymnasium
Equipment Volleyball

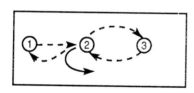

Player 1 volleys to 2, 2 backsets to 3; player 2 turns and faces 3, 3 volleys to 2, and 2 backsets to 1. Repeat movement.

Suggestions and Variations
Player 1 volleys to 2; 2 volleys to 1; 1 volleys to 2; 2 backsets to 3.

Hit the Square

Motor skills Throw, volley
Movement concepts Moving into space, change of direction
Players Three
Formation See diagram
Playing area Playground, gymnasium
Equipment Volleyball

The leader tosses the ball to the first player, who tries to return a high arc set into the square. Each player is given three turns before going to the back of the line. The leader rotates after every player has had a turn.

Suggestions and Variations
The leader throws, the first player returns a set and then goes to the back of the line, and the leader returns a set to the second player in the line.

Set Up the Ball

Motor skills Volley, set
Movement concepts Moving into space, change of direction and speed
Players Four
Formation See diagram
Playing area Playground, gymnasium, classroom
Equipment Volleyball, net

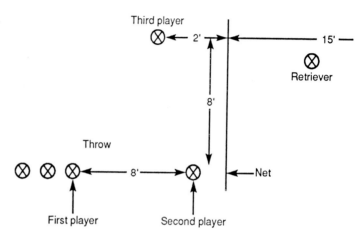

Player 1 throws a high arc pass to player 2, who sets up the ball for player 3. Player 3 attempts to pass the ball over the net to the retriever. After each play, the retriever goes to the back of the line and all other players move up one position.

Suggestions and Variations
1. Player 1 throws the ball up to himself, then volleys it to player 2. The drill continues as previously described.
2. Repeat original drill with retriever attempting to pass the ball to the next thrower.

Shuttle Volley

Motor skills Throw, volley
Movement concepts Moving into space, change of direction and speed
Players Five or six per group
Formation Shuttle
Playing area Playground, gymnasium
Equipment Volleyball

Divide class into squads of five or six players. Arrange squads in a shuttle formation with about six feet between players. Player 1 throws the ball to player 2. Player 2 volleys it to player 3, who has taken player 1's position. Each player goes to the end of the line after volleying the ball. Reverse the direction of the throw after everyone has had a turn.

Suggestions and Variations
1. Same formation with net between lines.
2. Volley with one or two hands.
3. As proficiency develops, increase the distance between the lines.

CHAPTER 21

Circle Volley

Motor skills   Throw, volley
Movement concepts   Personal space, moving into space
Players   Five or six per group
Formation   Circle
Playing area   Playground, gymnasium
Equipment   Volleyball

Divide class into squads of five or six players. Arrange each squad in a circle formation with about five feet between each player. Player 1 throws the ball up and toward player 2, who volleys it to player 1. Player 1 then throws to player 3 and so on until every circle player has volleyed the ball back to player 1.

Suggestions and Variations

1. As proficiency increases, have player 1 throw to player 2, who volleys to player 3. Player 3 volleys to player 4, and so on around the circle.
2. Keep It Up. After the first player has started the drill, allow anyone to hit the ball and see how long the squad can keep it up.

Zigzag Volley

Motor skills   Throw, volley
Movement concepts   Personal space, moving into space, change of direction
Players   Six to eight per group
Formation   Zigzag
Playing area   Playground, gymnasium
Equipment   Volleyball

Divide the class into squads of six to eight players. Arrange squads in a zigzag formation, with about ten feet between each line. Player 1 throws the ball across to player 2, who volleys the ball to player 3. Continue the zigzag volleying pattern.

Baseline Serving

Motor skills   Serve
Movement concepts   Use of available space, serving into empty space
Players   Class
Formation   Line
Playing area   Playground, gymnasium
Equipment   Volleyballs

Divide class into two squads, with each evenly distributed along its baseline. One player from each team is assigned to the retriever position. Use as many balls as you have available. Any child on the baseline may begin by serving the ball over the net. The ball is then served back by the child who retrieves it. No serving order need be kept. The retriever's job is to catch and pass the ball back to anyone on his team.

Suggestions and Variations

1. Raise or lower height of net according to skill level of class.
2. Place one or more large mats on each side of net and near the middle of the court. Direct players to try to hit the mat.

Circuit Volleying

Motor skills   All skills
Movement concepts   Use of available space, moving into space, change of direction, pathway, and speed

Players   Class
Formation   See diagram
Playing area   Playground, gymnasium
Equipment   Volleyballs

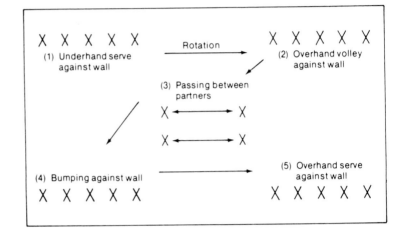

Divide the class into five teams and arrange as in the diagram. On "go," each team practices its respective skill for a set period of time (ranging from one to several minutes). At the end of each practice period, each team places the ball on the floor and rotates to the next station. Continue rotation.

LEAD-UP GAMES

Nebraska Ball

Motor skills   Serve, volley
Movement concepts   Personal and general space, change of direction
Players   Nine on each team
Formation   Scattered on each side of the net (or rope)
Playing area   Playground, gymnasium, classroom
Equipment   Volleyball court, net or rope, beach ball or large utility ball

Establish a serving line approximately ten to fifteen feet from the net. One player serves the ball over the net. Any number of players may hit the ball before it returns over the net. A point is scored when the ball hits the floor. Start play on the side where the ball hits the floor.

Suggestions and Variations

1. Lengthen the distance of the serving line.
2. Limit the number of passes to five, four, then three.
3. Limit passing to forearm passes.

Bound Ball

Motor skills   Serve, volley
Movement concepts   Moving into space, change of direction
Players   Six to ten per team
Formation   Scattered on each side of net
Playing area   Playground, gymnasium
Equipment   Volleyball

The server, standing anywhere behind the endline, bounces the ball once and then hits it over the centerline. The ball must bounce once before an opposing player is allowed to return it over the line. Each team is allowed three hits; however, the ball must bounce between each hit. No player is allowed to hit the ball twice in succession. If the ball hits the centerline, it is considered dead and the play is retaken. Balls hitting boundary lines are still in play. If the nonserving team fails to return the ball within three bounces, the serving team is awarded one point. If the serving team fails to get the serve over the centerline or fails to return a played ball, no point is scored and the ball is given to the other team. Game continues to fifteen points.

Suggestions and Variations
1. Have server begin from behind a fifteen-foot serving line.
2. Add a net or rope and require players to pass the ball over it.

Mass Volleyball

Motor skills   Serve, volley
Movement concepts   Moving into space, change of direction
Players   Six to nine per team
Formation   Players of each team arranged in equal rows on each side of the net
Playing area   Playground, gymnasium
Equipment   Volleyball

Any player may serve the ball from anywhere in her court. Teams volley the ball back and forth across the net. Anyone may hit the ball as many times as she wishes; however, only three players may touch the ball before returning it over the net. Change the serve after a team fails to return the ball. The serving team scores one point whenever the opposing team commits one of the following fouls: (1) failing to return the ball, (2) catching the ball, (3) knocking the ball out-of-bounds, (4) allowing the ball to touch the floor, or (5) touching the net. A game may be played to any number of points (eleven or fifteen is desirable).

Suggestions and Variations
1. Have players serve from behind a serving line.
2. Allow any number of players to hit the ball as many times as they wish before returning it over the net.
3. Limit passing to either overhand or forearm passes.

Newcomb

Motor skills   Serve, volley
Movement concepts   Moving into space, change of direction
Players   Six to nine per team
Formation   Volleyball court with teams arranged in equal rows on each side of net
Playing area   Playground, gymnasium
Equipment   Volleyball court, net, volleyball or large utility ball

Server serves the ball over the net. The other team tries to return the ball after the serve, with any number of players allowed to hit the ball. The server continues until his team loses the ball. Only the serving team scores. A predetermined time limit or score is set. Fouls are (1) hitting the ball out-of-bounds, (2) holding the ball, (3) touching the net, (4) walking with the ball, (5) throwing the ball out-of-bounds, or (6) letting the ball hit the floor.

Suggestions and Variations
1. If skill level is too low, allow the ball to bounce once before it is hit. Also, adjust the position of the serving line to the level of skill.

2. Blind Newcomb. Play the same game with a blanket draped over the net to restrict visibility, which provides an element of fun and excitement.

Keep It Up

Motor skills   Volley, bump
Movement concepts   Personal space, levels, change of direction
Players   Six to nine per team
Formation   Circle
Playing area   Playground, gymnasium
Equipment   Volleyball

Each circle tries to keep its ball in the air by volleying it from player to player. The ball may be hit to any player in the circle. The team that keeps the ball up the longest wins.

Suggestions and Variations
1. Simplify the game by allowing one bounce between each hit.
2. Place a player in the middle of the circle.
3. As skill improves, allow only one type of pass.

Donkey

Motor skills   Volley, bump
Movement concepts   Moving into space, levels, change of direction and speed
Players   Five or six per team
Formation   Groups
Playing area   Playground, gymnasium
Equipment   Volleyball

Arrange class into groups of five players. Players form a line facing a wall, with the first player standing about four feet from the wall and holding a ball. The first player throws the ball up, then volleys it above a line drawn seven feet up the wall. The next player must move forward and volley the ball above the seven-foot line. A player who misses a volley gets the first letter and so on until he reaches D-O-N-K-E-Y. Once a player reaches "Donkey," he continues to play until three players have reached "Donkey." When this happens, change positions of players and begin a new game.

Modified Volleyball

Motor skills   Serve, volley, rotate
Movement concepts   Personal space, moving into space, change of direction and speed
Players   Six to nine per team
Formation   See diagram
Playing area   Playground, gymnasium
Equipment   Volleyball

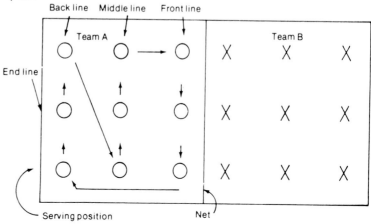

The server stands behind the end line and serves the ball over the net. If the level of skill is too low, allow any player in the front line to assist the ball over the net. The opposing team attempts to get the ball back over the net before it touches the ground. The ball can be volleyed by as many players on either team as is necessary to return the ball over the net. All other volleyball rules and scoring apply to this game.

Suggestions Variations
1. Allow the server two tries to get the ball over the net.
2. Use only one type of pass.
3. Fanny Ball. Play the same game using a beach ball and with all players remaining in a sitting position.

Volleyball Keep Away

Motor skills   Volley
Movement concepts   Moving into space, change of direction and speed
Players   Five or six per team
Formation   Teams scattered with a designated play area
Playing area   Playground, gymnasium
Equipment   Volleyball

By volleying the ball from one team member to another, the team with the ball tries to keep the ball away from the other team. Members of the other team try to intercept the ball. It can be intercepted only when it is dropping (on the downward arc). After the ball has been intercepted, the team in possession volleys the ball. The team volleying the ball the highest number of times wins. A time limit also may be used.

Suggestions and Variations
1. Limit playing area to enhance ball control.
2. Limit game to one type of pass.

Four-Way Volleyball

Motor skills   Serve, volley, bump
Movement concepts   Moving into space, change of direction and speed
Players   Four or six per team
Formation   See diagram
Playing area   Playground, gymnasium
Equipment   Volleyball and two nets or ropes

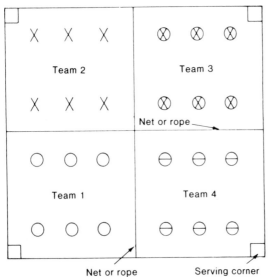

There are four separate teams in this game. Players in courts 1 and 2 may serve only into courts 3 and 4. Similarly, players in courts 3 and 4 may serve only into courts 1 and 2. However, after the serve, a team may hit the ball into any of the other three courts. When a fair serve is made and the ball touches the floor or fails to get out of the receiver's court within the allotted three hits, the serving team scores one point and continues serving as in regular volleyball. However, when a receiving team hits the ball into another court fairly, this team becomes the serving team the moment the ball leaves its court. If the new receiving team fails to pass the ball out of its court, the new serving team is awarded one point. All other regular volleyball rules apply.

Suggestions and Variation
Limit any receiving team to only one pass.

Sideline Volleyball

Motor skills   All volleyball skills
Movement concepts   Moving into space, change of direction and speed
Players   Eight to ten per team
Formation   See diagram
Playing area   Playground, gymnasium
Equipment   Volleyball

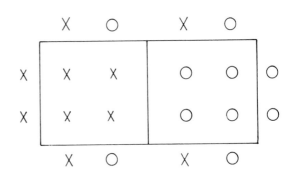

This game is played like regular volleyball, with the addition of active sideline players. Sideline players stay in their assigned positions; they cannot enter the court area, but they are permitted to pass any loose balls from either team, providing the balls have not touched the ground. Sideline players cannot pass to each other. A hit made by a sideline player is a free hit for his team and does not count as one of the team's hits. Rotate the court and sideline players after six points are scored and continue the game to fifteen points.

Suggestions and Variations
1. Count sideline hits.
2. Restrict sideline hits to one type of volley.

VOLLEYBALL RULES AND REGULATIONS

Although there are fewer skills to learn in volleyball than the other major sports, it is one of the more difficult games for boys and girls in developmental levels II and III. The difficulty, in most cases, is the result of inadequate arm and shoulder girdle strength and inaccuracy in serving and volleying. Nevertheless, fifth and sixth graders should be exposed to the complete game of volleyball early in the instructional unit. Modify the rules to meet the level of skill, available facilities, and number of children. Consider modifying the length of the game, the number of players, the height of the net, type and size of ball, and the size of the playing court.

I. Field of play: See the diagram.

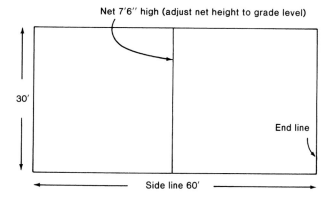

Net 7'6" high (adjust net height to grade level)

30'

End line

Side line 60'

II. Recommended net heights:
Grade 4—six feet
Grade 5—seven feet
Grade 6—seven feet

III. Positions and Rotation Pattern (after opponents lose their serve): See the diagram.

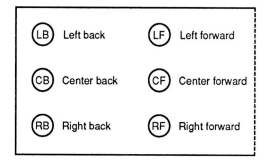

LB Left back LF Left forward

CB Center back CF Center forward

RB Right back RF Right forward

IV. To start the game: The right back player starts the game by serving the ball from behind the endline. She is allowed only one serve.

V. To return the ball: After the ball has been served, players on both sides must abide by the following rules:
A. Any player who receives the ball is allowed one volley (hit) over the net or to another teammate.
B. The ball may not be volleyed (hit) more than three times by a team before it is sent over the net.
C. A ball that hits the net on the return volley and falls into the opponent's court is a fair ball.
D. A ball that hits the net on the return volley and falls back into the court from which it was sent may be played before it hits the ground, provided (1) it is not volleyed by the player who hit it into the net and (2) it was not volleyed by more than two players before it hit the net.

VI. To play: The server hits the ball over the net. If the opposing team fails to return it over the net, one point is awarded to the serving team. However, if the ball is returned to the serving team and it fails to return again, the serving team loses the serve. No point is awarded on the loss of serve. Player rotation should be made only by the team receiving the serve.

VII. Violations: If any of the following violations is committed by the serving team, the serve is lost. This is called side out. If one is committed by the receiving team, the serving team is awarded one point.
A. Failing to make a fair or legal serve
B. Returning the ball in any way other than by hitting it. Balls may not be caught and thrown over the net.
C. Volleying the ball more than three times before it goes over the net
D. Letting the ball touch the floor outside the court lines. Note: A ball may be played from outside the court area if it has not touched the ground.
E. Failing to return the ball over the net
F. Failing to rotate in the proper order

VIII. Scoring:
A. Only the serving team can score.
B. Eleven, fifteen, or twenty-one points constitutes a game. A team must win by two points; thus, if the score is ten-all in an eleven-point game, one team must score two successive points to win.

EVALUATIVE TECHNIQUES

There are numerous methods of measuring volleyball skills and knowledge. The majority of tests used by classroom teachers are of an objective nature and usually are modifications of existing standardized test batteries. Teachers should be encouraged to develop their own test batteries and keep scores of each test in order to develop appropriate norms for their teaching situations. The test battery in table 21.3 is an example of a "teacher-made" test that can be administered to the children in a short period of time.

Test 1: Wall Volley

Draw one line on the wall six feet up from the floor and a second line on the floor three feet from the wall. The player must stand behind this line, toss the ball in the air, and volley it against the wall above the six-foot line. One point is awarded for each hit above the line. Score the number of hits made in twenty seconds. A player who drops the ball within this period may pick it up and continue volleying. Allow two trials and record the highest score.

Test 2: Serving over the Net

Each player is given ten consecutive serves, with each successful serve awarded five points. This test can be modified

TABLE 21.3	Volleyball Skill Test					
Name	Wall Volley (Total Pts.)	Service Over Net (20 Pts.)	Forearm Pass (20 Pts.)	Subjective Evaluation (50 Pts.)	Total Score	Grade
1 2 3 4		Rank total scores for the class, then convert to letter grades or ratings (superior, good, etc.).				

by dividing the opposite court into zones, with each given a different point value. For example, make three equal zones running perpendicular to the net; the zone farthest from the server would equal five points; the next one, three points; and the nearest zone, one point.

Test 3: Forearm Pass

One student, who will throw the ball over the net, stands behind a line drawn six feet away from the net. Adjust the height of the net according to grade level. The student taking the test stands in the opposite court behind a line drawn six feet away from the net. The first student throws the ball in a high arc over the net. The second student (testing) must pass the ball back over the net with a forearm pass. Repeat four times and award five points for each successful pass. If the throw was too low and poorly thrown, allow the player another try.

Test 4: Subjective Evaluation of Playing Ability

Establish criteria that represent the skills and playing ability required in volleyball. For example, using such factors as positional play, alertness, volleying ability, and team play, the teacher awards each player a score from zero to fifty points. Three players can be used as judges, with the average score recorded.

Summary Review

The game of volleyball requires players to be knowledgeable about the rules of the game and to understand appropriate volleyball playing strategies. Players also need to be proficient in a number of specialized volleyball skills. These skills must be learned, as they do not develop automatically through growth and maturation. Individual practices, lead-up games, and mini-games that can be adjusted to create successful practice opportunities, as well as enjoyable game situations, become the basis for teaching children volleyball. The objective is to increase children's knowledge of volleyball and to help develop their volleyball skills toward the

automatic stage of development. To develop specialized sport skills to the automatic stage requires many individual practices. Hence, children need to be provided with lots of developmentally appropriate practice opportunities. This will lead to successful volleyball skill development and enjoyment of the game. If this objective is achieved, then children will possess the knowledge, skills, and desire to continue playing this major game throughout their lives.

INDIVIDUAL *and* **GROUP** **PROJECTS**

1. Form groups of three. Each group member chooses a different volleyball skill. Design a lesson plan to teach your basic skill. Then teach one group member your basic volleyball skill while the third member observes the effectiveness of your instruction. Each group member takes a turn at being teacher, student, and observer. Observers might find useful the observational checklist for the evaluation of teaching, provided in Table 11.7 on page 247. When you have all taught your skills, discuss and evaluate your experiences in each role (teacher, student, observer), and suggest possible ways to improve your teaching.

2. In pairs, study the rules and regulations of volleyball. Then pose questions on the rules and regulations for each other to answer.

3. In chapter 4, it was suggested that one of the challenges facing teachers is the adjustment of the teaching environment to meet the developmental levels of the children. Four environmental variables under the teachers' control were identified:
   a. Rules
   b. Space
   c. Number of participants
   d. Amount or type of equipment

One or more of these variables can be adjusted to create success on behalf of students. In small groups, discuss how these four variables can be adjusted when teaching children volleyball. Formulate creative ideas and specific recommendations and share these with other groups.

4. Chapter 13 identified a number of disabilities that afflict young children. In small groups, choose four disabilities and discuss how children with these disabilities can be integrated into volleyball activites. Consider what adjustments will have to be made to accommodate each child's developmental level and to ensure success. Debate possible techniques and methods of evaluation. Share ideas with other groups.

5. A feature of this text is the idea of teaching and enhancing academic skills and concepts through physical education activities. In small groups, discuss and create ideas to teach or enhance academic skills and concepts through volleyball activities. Each group is then allocated a small selection of the volleyball practice activities and lead-up games. Create ideas for teaching or enhancing academic skills and concepts through these practice activities and lead-up games. Consider ways to evaluate students. Share ideas with other groups.

SELECTED READINGS

CAHPER. 1985. *Volleyball-type games.* Ottawa, Ontario: CAHPER.

Kamiya, A. 1985. *Elementary teacher's handbook of indoor and outdoor games.* West Nyack, NY: Parker.

Kluka, D. A., and P. J. Dunn. 1989. *Volleyball.* Dubuque, IA: Wm. C. Brown.

NAGUS. 1989. *Volleyball guide.* Reston, VA: AAHPERD.

Philipp, J. A., and J. D. Wilkerson. 1990. *Teaching team sports: A coeducational approach.* Champaign, IL: Human Kinetics.

Samula, L., and T. Valeriote. 1984. *Volleyball development model.* Vanier, Ontario: Coaching Association of Canada, Canadian Volleyball Association.

Scates, B. L., and B. J. Ferguson. 1989. *Winning volleyball drills.* Dubuque, IA: Wm. C. Brown.

Turner, L. F., and S. L. Turner. 1989. *P.E. teacher's skill-by-skill activities program.* West Nyack, NY: Parker.

Viera, B. C., and B. J. Ferguson. 1989. *Teaching volleyball: Steps to success.* Champaign, IL: Leisure Press.

CHAPTER 22

Basketball Activities

KEY CONCEPTS

22.1 Basketball skills are acquired through instruction and practice opportunities

22.2 Basketball activities must be developmentally appropriate to ensure that all children can achieve success and enjoyment

22.3 Effective teaching progressions, that provide all children with individual practices and lead-up games, are required to develop the skills and knowledge associated with basketball

22.4 To develop basketball skills to the automatic stage of skill development requires many practice opportunities (time on-task)

22.5 Playing a full-sided competitive game of basketball is not a very efficient way of teaching large numbers of children specialized basketball skills

KEY OBJECTIVES

After completing this chapter you will be able to:

1. Design developmentally appropriate basketball activities for elementary school children

2. Plan and organize teaching units and individual lessons in basketball

3. Organize pratice activities and lead-up games appropriate for basketball

4. Plan and organize basketball practice activities and lead-up games that incorporate the inventive games approach

5. Evaluate units, lessons, and individual techniques used in basketball

6. Identify key teaching points associated with the basic skills of basketball

7. Employ teaching progressions that lead to successful development of basketball skills and concepts

8. Understand the rules and basic strategies associated with basketball

B asketball, like volleyball, originated in the United States and has since become a sport that is played in nearly every country in the world. There is no single reason for its popularity as both a participant and spectator sport. Children, youths, and adults enjoy the game because it is fun and challenging, and it contributes to many important components of physical fitness. Since the game can be modified to meet court size limitations and varying levels of skill, it should be considered a basic activity for the upper elementary physical education program. This chapter has been organized to provide a format for teaching basketball skills and knowledge to these children.

EMPHASIS AND PROGRESSION

Many basketball skills have been learned in earlier grades or out of school. The many backyard basketball courts not only attest to the popularity of the sport, but they also provide the opportunity for elementary school children to learn basketball skills from their older brothers and sisters and parents. Consequently, there is a wide variation in the level of basketball skill in virtually every intermediate grade in the elementary school. With these considerations in mind, the suggested sequence of presenting skills and rules in table 22.1 is provided as a basic guide.

By the time children have reached developmental level II, most of them have learned several of the basic skills involved in passing, catching, dribbling, and shooting. However, the acquisition of these skills prior to developmental level III should not result in a conscious extension of the basketball program down to the primary grades. Rather, developmental levels I and II should continue to emphasize low-organization games, with some of the specialized skills of basketball and other sports being acquired in the process.

The main emphasis throughout developmental level III should be to continue practicing the basic passing, catching, dribbling, and shooting skills to improve accuracy and proficiency. Children should also be introduced to a few new shooting skills and several main rules of basketball. More emphasis is placed on using both hands, pivoting and weaving, and general playing ability. It is a period of refining playing skills and team strategies.

CONCEPT

22.1 *Basketball Skills Are Acquired through Instruction and Practice Opportunities*

TEACHING PROCEDURES

Teaching the skills and team strategies of basketball to children in developmental levels II and III presents several problems. A main one, as stated earlier, is that the skill level and playing ability of these children vary widely. Some children have played on out-of-school teams or have their own backyard hoops, whereas others have not had any experience with the game. The challenge to the teacher is to cope with these major differences in the design and presentation of an instructional unit.

TABLE 22.1 Suggested Sequence of Presenting Basketball Skills and Rules

Skills and Rules	Developmental Level II	Developmental Level III
Passing		
Chest pass	Acquired or introduce	Increase proficiency and accuracy
Bounce pass	Acquired or introduce	Increase proficiency and accuracy
Two-hand overhead pass		Introduce
One-hand bounce pass	Acquired or introduce	Increase proficiency and accuracy
Baseball pass	Acquired or introduce	Increase distance and accuracy
Catching		
From below the waist	Acquired or introduce	Catch while moving
From above the waist	Acquired or introduce	Catch while moving
Rules: Line violations	Introduce	
Out-of-bounds	Introduce	
Dribbling		
While standing and moving	Acquired or introduce	Dribble, weave, and pivot
Rule: Traveling		Introduce
Shooting		
One-hand push	Introduce	Increase distance and accuracy
Lay-up Introduce	With either hand	
Free throw		Introduce
Rules: Scoring	Introduce	
Key positions		Introduce
Related skills		
PivotingIntroduce	Refine	
Feinting	Introduce	
Guarding	Introduce	Refine
Rebounding		Introduce
Rules: Personal fouls		Introduce

22.2 *Basketball Activities Must Be Developmentally Appropriate to Ensure That All Children Can Achieve Success and Enjoyment*

Developing a Basketball Unit

The general instructional procedures discussed in previous chapters also apply to basketball activities. Of particular importance is the process of developing units of instruction in chapter 18 and the structure of a lesson on page 373. In addition, the inventive games approach described on page 315 can be applied to the teaching of basketball activities.

Since the length of the unit and the lesson, as well as the facilities and equipment available, will vary in each teaching situation, the following suggested approach should be considered a basic guideline. Modify it to cope with your individual situation.

Step 1: Determine the length of your basketball unit. Express this in the number of lessons rather than weeks.

Step 2: Assess the general level of ability of your class (see the evaluative techniques at the end of the chapter).

Step 3: Select the skills and rules you wish to emphasize in your unit (see table 22.1).

Step 4: Choose the appropriate practice activities and lead-up games.

Structure of a Lesson

The detailed explanation of how to plan a lesson described in chapter 18, "Soccer Activities," should be followed when preparing and presenting basketball activities. The procedure of moving from individual to partner to group activities can be adapted successfully to each basketball lesson.

22.3 *Effective Teaching Progressions, That Provide All Children with Individual Practices and Lead-Up Games, Are Required to Develop the Skills and Knowledge Associated with Basketball*

DESCRIPTION OF SKILLS

Basketball skills can be broadly classified as passing, catching, dribbling, shooting, guarding, and feinting. Each skill, in turn, can be subdivided, such as the chest pass, two-hand overhead pass, and baseball pass. Each of these skills is described in this section, accompanied by a list of the more common faults.

22.4 *To Develop Basketball Skills to the Automatic Stage of Skill Development Requires Many Practice Opportunities*

Passing

Passing is transferring the ball from one player to another, from a stationary position or while in motion. A player may pass the ball with one or both hands and from a variety of positions. The basic fundamentals of all passes are (1) accuracy—avoiding "wild throws," (2) following through with every pass, and (3) shifting the ball as quickly as possible from a receiving position to a passing position.

Two-Hand Chest Pass

The two-hand chest, or push, pass is one of the most useful and effective passes in basketball. Since its main advantages are ease and speed of delivery, it is the pass used most often, particularly for short distances.

Assume a forward-stride position, with weight evenly distributed over both feet. Grip the ball with both hands, fingers spread around the sides of the ball, with thumbs behind and close together (figure 22.1a). Simultaneously shift weight to rear foot and the ball toward the chest, keeping elbows comfortably at the side of the body, waist high and pointing toward the floor (figure 22.1b). Step forward, extend arms, and turn thumbs downward. Release the ball with a quick wrist snap downward and outward, giving the ball a slight backspin (figure 22.1c).

Key Teaching Points
1. Hold the ball on tips of fingers and thumbs.
2. Keep elbows reasonably close to sides of body and pointing down.
3. Step forward with the dominant foot.
4. Extend arms and push thumbs downward.

Two-Hand Bounce Pass

The two-hand bounce pass is performed by bouncing the ball on the floor before it rebounds to the receiver (figure 22.2). This type of pass provides a deceptive action to get the ball past an opponent to another teammate. In order for a teammate to receive the ball about waist high, the ball should strike the floor two-thirds the distance between the two players and nearer the receiver.

Key Teaching Points
1. Begin with weight distributed evenly over both feet.
2. Keep ball close to chest and elbows reasonably close to sides of body.
3. Take a quick step, extend arms, and release ball with a quick snap of the wrists.
4. Catcher should receive the ball about waist high.

Figure 22.1 Two-hand chest pass.

Figure 22.2 Two-hand bounce pass.

Two-Hand Overhead Pass

The two-hand overhead pass is extremely effective for short passes and when a player wishes to throw the ball to a teammate above the reach of an opponent. In addition, when the ball is held overhead, it is very easy to "fake" or pretend to pass, thus putting the opponent off guard before the ball actually is released. Start the pass with feet apart and weight evenly distributed over both feet. Hold the ball above the head, elbows slightly flexed, hands on the side of the ball, and wrists extended (figure 22.3a). Shift the arms forward, release the ball, and follow through in the direction of the ball (figure 22.3b).

Figure 22.3 Overhead pass.

Passer (2/3 of total distance) Receiver

a   b   c

Figure 22.4   Pass around a defensive player.   **Figure 22.5**   Baseball pass.

Key Teaching Points
1. Begin with one foot in front of the other.
2. Hold the ball just above the head, with wrist cocked.
3. Simultaneously take a short step forward, extend arms, and snap the wrist.
4. Follow through in the direction of the pass.

One-Hand Bounce Pass

This pass is particularly effective when a player is closely guarded. It is used to pass the ball quickly around a defender directly from a dribble (figure 22.4). As the offensive player is bouncing the ball close to a defender, she pivots on her right foot, turns the left side of her body in the direction of the pass, steps on her left foot, then releases a bounce pass with her right hand. The pivot action allows the offensive player to step around the defender and protect her pass with her body.

Key Teaching Points
1. Keep the body low in approaching the defender.
2. Use the body to protect the pass.
3. Release the pass with the hand slightly behind the ball rather than on top of it.

Baseball Pass

The baseball pass is used when a player wishes to throw the ball a long distance. Care must be exercised in using this pass, particularly with beginners, as it may lead to inaccurate passing. Begin the pass with one foot slightly forward and weight evenly distributed over both feet. Hold the ball in front of the body, with elbows bent and fingers spread around the sides of the ball. Bring arms back and transfer the ball to the right hand when it is above the shoulder and behind the ear (figure 22.5a). Shift body weight to the right foot as the hands shift backward. Extend right arm forward, rotate body toward the left, and shift weight to forward foot (figure 22.5b). Release the ball with a final snap of the wrists and fingers (figure 22.5c).

Key Teaching Points
1. Simultaneously shift weight to right foot as the right arm is drawn backward.
2. Simultaneously shift weight to front foot as throwing arm moves forward.
3. Release ball with a snap of the wrist and follow through in the direction of the throw.

Catching

Basic catching skills have been described in an earlier section of this book (see chapter 6). In basketball, the overhand catch (figure 22.6) is used when the ball is caught above the waist. The fingers point up for this catch. The underhand catch (figure 22.7) is used to catch a ball below the waist. The fingers point down. In both types of catches, the receiver reaches out and catches the ball on his fingertips, then gradually relaxes his arms to reduce the speed of the oncoming ball. However, because young children often do not have adequate strength to catch the basketball in this manner, allow them to catch the ball with their palms, then quickly shift to a fingertip grip.

Key Teaching Points
1. Keep your eyes on the ball and quickly move into position to catch it.
2. Catch the ball on the tips of the fingers and thumb.
3. Relax arms as ball is caught.
4. Quickly shift ball into offensive passing position.

Dribbling

Dribbling is controlled bouncing in any direction and at varying speeds. The basic fundamentals to stress in teaching this skill are (1) do not slap the ball downward—push it toward the floor; (2) learn to dribble with either hand; and (3) when not being guarded, bring the ball in front of the body and raise the height of the dribble to increase running speed.

Figure 22.6 Overhand catch.

Figure 22.7 Underhand catch.

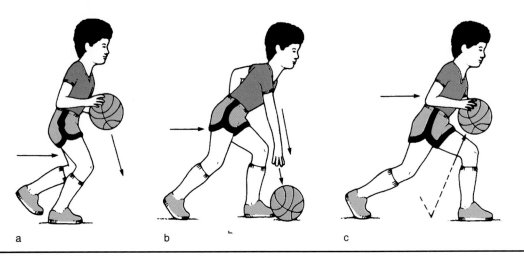

a   b   c

Figure 22.8 Dribbling.

The dribbler's body leans forward slightly, with knees partially flexed, and head up. The wrist of the dribbling hand is relaxed, with fingers cupped and spaced apart (figure 22.8a). "Push" the ball toward the floor off the finger-tips (figure 22.8b). As the ball rebounds, fingers, wrist, and arm "ride" back with the ball (figure 22.8c).

When being checked, place the body between the opponent and the ball. When dribbling, keep an eye on the opponent to watch for sudden moves and to shift the ball to a more advantageous position. Also, when being guarded, keep the ball close to the body and lower the bounce to between the waist and the knees.

a   b   c

Figure 22.9 One-hand set shot.

Key Teaching Points
1. Keep head up and eyes on target.
2. Push the ball toward the floor.
3. Allow fingers, wrist, and arm to ride back with the ball.
4. Keep knees slightly bent and trunk leaning slightly forward.

Shooting

While all the skills of basketball are important, none is as important as shooting. When teaching the following basic shooting skills, stress two fundamental principles: (1) watch the target instead of the ball and (2) follow through after every shot.

If elementary school children are to learn shooting skills correctly and efficiently, the height of the basket rim should be lowered from the official ten feet to a height that allows the children to shoot without undue strain. The appropriate height for upper elementary school children should be between eight and nine feet, depending on the children's age and ability.

One-Hand Set Shot (Push Shot)

The one-hand set shot is performed by placing the same foot as the shooting hand slightly in front of the body. The ball is held with both hands opposite the chin and above the lead foot (figure 22.9a). The back is straight with knees partially bent. In a simultaneous action, straighten the knees, release the nonshooting hand, extend the shooting arm forward and upward, and push the ball toward the basket (figure 22.9b). Release the ball with a slight snap of the wrist and fingers (figure 22.9c).

Key Teaching Points
1. Keep eyes focused on rim of basket.

2. Extend elbow toward basket and release ball with a high arc.
3. Release ball with a slight snap of the wrist.

Lay-Up Shot

The lay-up, which involves dribbling, leaping, and the ability to judge distance, can be learned by boys and girls in the intermediate grades. In fact, most children are more successful at this skill than at the one-hand set shot. The reason is the short distance between the hand and the rim of the basket when the ball is released.

Approach the basket at a forty-five-degree angle (figure 22.10a). Just prior to shooting, shift the weight to the foot opposite the shooting hand, and raise the ball as far as possible with both hands (figure 22.10b). Release the nonshooting hand as the shooting arm carries the ball up. Then release it off the fingertips (figure 22.10c). The ball should bounce against the backboard about eighteen inches above the hoop, then drop into the hoop.

Key Teaching Points
1. Keep eyes focused about eighteen inches above the rim and on the backboard.
2. Take-off foot is opposite the shooting hand.
3. Lay the ball against the backboard.
4. Land on both feet and flex knees to absorb shock.

Free Throw (Two-Hand Underhand)

The one-hand set shot is normally used for free throws. However, some children may not have sufficient strength to throw the ball with one hand from the foul line. Allow them to use this shot.

Stand with the back straight, knees slightly bent, arms straight, and weight equally distributed over both feet. Hold the ball with the fingertips of both hands slightly under the

Figure 22.10   Lay-up shot.

Figure 22.11   Free throw.

ball (figure 22.11a). In a simultaneous action, swing arms forward and upward and straighten the knees (figure 22.11b). It is important to keep the back straight throughout this movement and to release the ball off the tips of the fingers (figure 22.11c).

Key Teaching Points
1. Keep eyes focused on rim of basket.
2. Keep back and arms straight.
3. Release ball off fingertips.
4. Follow through in the direction of the ball.

Pivoting

Footwork in basketball involves stopping, starting, pivoting, and turning in all directions and at varying speeds. When teaching the pivot and turn, stress the importance of gaining body control before attempting the pivot or turn. Also, teach pupils not to change the pivot foot once it is declared; otherwise, traveling will be charged. Finally, emphasize the need to maintain fingertip control of the ball for quick release after the pivot is made.

Prior to performing a pivot, make sure the weight is evenly distributed on both feet (figure 22.12a). Hold the ball firmly with the fingertips of both hands and keep the elbows out to protect the ball. As soon as one foot becomes the pivot foot, it must remain on the floor. The player may turn in any direction on her pivot foot (figures 22.12b and c); however, she may not drag it away from the original pivot spot. The opposite foot is permitted to step in any direction.

a   b   c

Figure 22.12   Pivoting.

Key Teaching Points
1. Make sure weight is evenly distributed on both feet before declaring your pivot foot.
2. Trunk is bent slightly forward with elbows out.
3. Pivot in any direction, but don't drag the pivot foot.

Defensive Skills

It is essential that elementary children first learn to move the ball by dribbling and passing, and then learn the basic skills of defense. It is important to stress the fact that legally stopping an opponent from scoring is just as important as scoring itself. The following basic defense techniques should be emphasized, particularly in the fifth and sixth grades.

Approach an offensive player, keeping body bent slightly forward, and stop with one foot slightly in front of the other. Weight is equally distributed over both feet, seat down, back straight, and arm flexed and slightly away from the body (figure 22.13a). If the opponent is within shooting range, hold the hand that is opposite the opponent's shooting hand high and at face level (figure 22.13b). Move by shuffling the feet—never cross one foot over the other.

Key Teaching Points
1. Never cross the feet when guarding an opponent—use a sliding step.
2. Keep the buttocks low and the back upright.
3. When checking, keep one hand up at all times.
4. Do not reach across for a ball; move the body to a position in front of the offensive player and then attempt to take the ball.
5. Always try to get the body in front of the offensive player.

a. Body bent slightly forward, Knees flexed, and weight evenly distributed over both feet

b. Stance to guard an opponent, who is within shooting range

Figure 22.13   Defensive skills.

6. Guard with one hand toward the ball and the other hand toward the opponent.

PRACTICE ACTIVITIES AND LEAD-UP GAMES

The following practice activities will assist in developing passing, shooting, dribbling, and pivoting skills (table 22.2). Modify any of them to overcome the limitations of the playing area and variations in the children's level of skill and interest.

All activities described in this section are designed to give each student the maximum amount of practice. If there are not enough basketballs, use soccer balls, volleyballs, or utility balls. Also, it is important for the teacher to circulate among the students during practice activities in order to correct errors or to provide encouragement and praise where needed.

Many of the low-organization games and relays described in chapter 16 can be modified and used as passing, catching, and other basketball skills.

The lead-up games described in this section are designed to give children practice in playing games that require one or more basketball skills. Each game can be modified to meet the class's ability and the available facilities and equipment. Whenever possible, divide the playing area into two, three, or four sections to allow two or more games to be played at the same time.

C O N C E P T

22.5 *Playing a Full-Sided Competitive Game of Basketball Is Not a Very Efficient Way of Teaching Large Numbers of Children Specialized Basketball Skills.*

P R A C T I C E   A C T I V I T I E S

One-Knee Dribble

Motor skills   Dribble
Movement concepts   Personal space, levels, change of direction and speed
Players   Individual
Formation   Scattered
Playing area   Playground, gymnasium
Equipment   Basketball or other inflated balls

All players are scattered. They kneel on one knee and begin bouncing the ball with the same hand as the kneeling knee. This drill eliminates unnecessary arm action. Players should keep their eyes on the teacher and "feel" for the ball.

Suggestions and Variations

1. Dribble the ball, with the elbow of the opposite arm at the side.
2. Move the ball backward and forward.
3. Move the ball around the front of the opposite leg and change hands.
4. Move the ball under the leg to the other hand.
5. Bounce the ball in rhythm set by the teacher.

6. Play follow the leader while kneeling. This makes everyone look at the leader and not the ball.
7. Repeat these drills while standing.

Wall Passing

Motor skills   Pass, catch
Movement concepts   Moving into space, change of direction and speed
Players   Individual
Formation   Scattered along wall
Playing area   Playground, gymnasium
Equipment   Basketball

Players should stand approximately five feet from the wall and gradually move back as their skill increases. This wall drill can be used to practice all types of passing and catching skills.

Suggestions and Variations

1. Put lines or targets on the wall to increase accuracy.
2. Add timing contests—for example, the number of hits in ten seconds.

Movement Drill

Motor skills   Dribble
Movement concepts   Moving into space, change of direction and speed
Players   Individual
Formation   Scattered
Playing area   Playground, gymnasium
Equipment   Basketball

The teacher or a leader stands in front of the group, then dribbles to the right, left, forward, or any other direction. All players move in the same direction as the leader but with a mirror image, bouncing the ball with the appropriate hand.

Suggestions and Variations

The leader may use hand directions instead of actually shifting positions.

One on One

Motor skills   Run, dodge, check
Movement concepts   Moving into space, change of direction and speed
Players   Two
Formation   Scattered
Playing area   Playground, gymnasium
Equipment   Basketball

Partners, facing each other, are scattered around the gymnasium. Without a ball, one player attempts to run past the other. The defensive player moves his body into position to stop the offensive player. He may not use his arms and feet to stop the player or lean into him. Players are not allowed to touch each other.

Suggestions and Variations

1. Repeat drill with a ball.
2. Repeat variation 1 and dribble toward a basket.
3. The following combinations can be used in a variety of ways. Begin each with passing only, then add dribbling, and finally add a target. (Improvise according to available backboards.)

Two on one	Three on one
Two on two	Three on three
Two on three	

TABLE 22.2 Practice Activities and Lead-Up Games

Name of Activity	Type of Activity	Player	Developmental Level II	III	Basketball Concepts and Skills	Movement Concept	Page
Practice Activities Adapted from Soccer Activities							
Circle Passing	Pass	2	———→		Dribble	Moving into space, change of direction and speed	385
Follow the Leader	Dribble	2	———→		Dribble	Using available space, moving into space, change of direction and speed	385
Triangle Pass	Pass	3	———→		Pass	Moving into space, change of direction	386
Practice Activities							
One-Knee Dribble	Dribble	Individual	———→		Dribble	Personal space, levels, change of direction and speed	448
Wall Passing	Pass	Individual	———→		Pass, catch	Moving into space, change of direction and speed	448
Movement Drill	Dribble	Individual	———→		Dribble	Moving into space, change of direction and speed	448
One on One	Dodge, check	2	———→		Run, dodge, check	Moving into space, change of direction and speed	448
Partner Passing	Pass, catch	2	———→		Pass, catch	Moving into space, change of direction and speed	450
Pig in the Middle	Pass, check	3	———→		Pass, catch, check	Moving into space, change of direction and speed	450
Circle Passing	Pass, catch	5–6	———→		Pass, catch	Moving into space, change of direction and speed	450
Weave Dribble	Dribble	4–5	———→		Dribble	Moving into space, change of direction and pathway	451
Whistle Dribble	Dribble	3–4	———→		Dribble, stop, pivot	Moving into space, change of direction and speed	451
Basket Shooting	Dribble, shoot	5–6	———→		Shoot, dribble, guard	Moving into space, change of direction and speed	451
Dribble and Shoot	Dribble, shoot	3–4	———→		Dribble, shoot	Moving into space, change of direction, pathway, and levels	451
Set Shot Shooting	Shoot, dribble	6–8		———→	Shoot, Pass	Shooting into space, levels	451
Pass, Post, Shoot	Dribble, pass	3		———→	Dribble, pass, pivot, shoot	Moving into space, change of direction	451
Pivot and Pass	Pivot, pass	6–8		———→	Pivot, pass	Personal space, change of direction	452
Lay-Up Shooting	Shoot, dribble	10 per group		———→	Dribble, shoot, catch	Moving into space, change of direction	452
Modified Lead-Up Games from Other Chapters							
Change Basketball	All skills	6 per team	———→		All basketball skills	Moving into space, change of direction, pathway, and speed	387
Circle of Fun	Dribble, shoot	6 per team	———→		Dribble, pass, shoot, guard	Moving into space, change of direction and speed	388
Alley Basketball	Pass, shoot	20–24	———→		Pass, check, shoot	Personal space, moving into space, change of direction and speed	388
Donkey	Pass	5–6 per team	———→		Pass, catch	Moving into space, change of direction and speed	433

TABLE 22.2   Continued

Name of Activity	Type of Activity	Player	Developmental Level		Basketball Concepts and Skills	Movement Concept	Page
			II	III			
Lead-Up Games							
Bucket Ball	Pass	5–6 per team	←————————→		Pass, catch, dribble, shoot, guard	Moving into space, change of direction and speed	452
Keep Away	Pass	3–4 per team	←————————→		Pass, catch, pivot, dribble	Moving into space, change of direction and speed	452
Basketball Touch	Pass, catch	4–5 per team	←————→		Pass, catch, guard	Moving into space, change of direction and speed	452
Sideline Basketball	All skills	10–12 per team	←————————→		All basketball skills	Moving into space, change of direction and speed	453
Twenty-One	Shoot, catch	3–4 per game	←————————→		Shoot, catch	Shooting into space, levels	453
Basketball Snatch Ball	Dribble, shoot	5–6 per team	←————————→		Dribble, shoot	Moving into space, change of direction	453
In-and-Out Basketball	Shoot	5 per team	←————————→		All basketball skills	Moving into space, change of direction and speed	453
Captain Ball	Dribble, pass	8–10 per team	←————————→		Dribble, pass, guard	Personal space, moving into space, change of direction and speed	453

Partner Passing

Motor skills   Pass, catch
Movement concepts   Moving into space, change of direction and speed
Players   Two
Formation   Circle
Playing area   Playground, gymnasium
Equipment   Basketball

Partners scattered around playing area stand about ten to fifteen feet apart, depending on skill. Each player remains in a stationary position. After a few minutes of practice, have one player remain stationary and the other move around him. After a few more minutes of practice, have both players move, pass, and catch.

Suggestions and Variations
1. Use different types of passes—two-hand bounce, one-hand bounce, baseball.
2. Add obstacles between players.

Pig in the Middle

Motor skills   Pass, catch, check
Movement concepts   Moving into space, change of direction and speed
Players   Three
Formation   Line
Playing area   Playground, gymnasium
Equipment   Basketball

Arrange three players in a line, with approximately six feet between each. The two outside players are the end players, while the middle player is designated as the "pig." Allow the end players to move to the right or left. They attempt to pass the ball to each other without the "pig" touching the ball. If the "pig" touches the ball, he replaces the person who threw it. The ball may not be thrown above the reach of the middle player, who must always advance toward the ball.

Circle Passing

Motor skills   Pass, catch
Movement concepts   Moving into space, change of direction and speed
Players   Five or six
Formation   Circle
Playing area   Playground, gymnasium
Equipment   Basketball

Divide the class into squads of five or six players. Arrange the children in circles, with approximately six feet between them. Player 1 turns toward player 2 and passes the ball to him; player 2 catches the ball, turns toward player 3, and passes to him; and so on. If the ball is dropped, it is retrieved by the receiver, who returns to his place in the circle and continues the drill.

Suggestions and Variations
1. Five Against One. One player goes to the center of the circle. The five outside players pass the ball to each other, always skipping a person, while the center player tries to intercept the pass. When the center player intercepts a pass, he switches positions with the player who threw the ball.
2. One player goes to the center of the circle with the ball and passes to each player in the circle.
3. Double Passing. This is similar to variation 2, with the addition of one more ball. Require the center player to make a bounce pass, while the circle players make direct passes.

Weave Dribble

Motor skills   Dribble

Movement concepts   Moving into space, change of direction and pathway

Players   Four or five

Formation   Line

Playing area   Playground, gymnasium

Equipment   Basketball

Divide the class into squads of about four or five players. Arrange each squad in a straight line formation, with about ten feet between each player. Player 1 dribbles around player 2 and back and around the opposite side of each successive player until he is back in his original position. Everyone moves up one position and player 1 goes to the rear of the line.

Suggestions and Variations

Use chairs or pins instead of players for obstacles.

Whistle Dribble

Motor skills   Dribble, stop, pivot

Movement concepts   Moving into space, change of direction and speed

Players   Three or four per group

Formation   Line

Playing area   Playground, gymnasium

Equipment   Basketballs

Divide class into squads of about three or four players. Line up the squads at one end of the floor. The teacher stands in the center of the playing area. When you blow the whistle, the first player from each squad dribbles forward. When you blow the whistle again, all players stop immediately and hold the ball ready for the next move. As soon as any player reaches a line parallel to you, he turns and dribbles back to his team.

Suggestions and Variations

1. Use hand signals rather than the whistle for stopping and starting; this encourages the "head-up" dribble. A hand over the head means dribble; a hand straight down means stop.
2. Extend arms sideward (right or left) as a signal to pivot right or left. The signals then would be hand over head (dribble forward), hand down (stop), arm out to right (pivot right, then back and ready for the next command).

Basket Shooting

Motor skills   Dribble, shoot, guard

Movement concepts   Moving into space, change of direction and speed

Players   Five or six per group

Formation   Line

Playing area   Playground, gymnasium

Equipment   Basketball

Divide the class into as many squads as you have baskets. Arrange each squad in a file formation behind the free throw line. One player remains on the endline behind the basket. The first player dribbles forward, and the player on the endline comes forward to guard the basket. The player with the ball attempts a shot, and then both players try to recover the rebound. Whoever retrieves it passes it on to the next player. The two rebound players exchange positions; that is, the player who took the shot moves behind the endline and the guarding player goes to the end of the line behind the free throw line.

Suggestions and Variations

1. Have two offensive players team up and try to get by the guard and shoot.
2. Do the same with two guards and two offensive players.
3. Repeat with two guards and three offensive players.

Dribble and Shoot

Motor skills   Dribble, shoot

Movement concepts   Moving into space, change of direction, pathway, and levels

Players   Three or four per group

Formation   Line

Playing area   Playground, gymnasium

Equipment   Basketball and chairs

This drill follows three stages, with the last stage arranged as shown in the diagram.

1. Each player stands three to four feet away from the basket, takes one step with the left foot (if shooting with the right hand), and shoots.
2. Same as stage 1, but begin with the right foot.
3. Place chairs in a line at approximately a forty-five-degree angle. Chairs should be about three to four feet apart. Players dribble around the chairs and shoot.

Set Shot Shooting

Motor skills   Shoot, pass

Movement concepts   Shooting into space, levels

Players   Six to eight per group

Formation   Semicircle

Playing area   Playground, gymnasium

Equipment   Basketball

Arrange six to eight players in a semicircle near a basket. One player, the leader, is stationed under the basket with a ball. The leader passes the ball to the first player in the semicircle, who attempts a set shot. The leader recovers each ball and passes it to each player in sequence. Adjust the distance from the basket according to the group's level of skill.

Suggestions and Variations

Use two or more balls and have the leader return the balls to any player.

Pass, Post, Shoot

Motor skills   Dribble, pass, pivot, shoot

Movement concepts   Moving into space, change of direction

Players   Three per group

Formation   See diagram

Playing area   Playground, gymnasium

Equipment   Basketball

The post player remains stationary throughout the drill. The ball is given to the offensive player, who tries to maneuver past the defensive player and take a shot at the basket. The ball may be passed back and forth between the offensive player and the post player until the offensive player is ready to move toward the basket and attempt a shot. Allow about thirty seconds to complete the drill, then blow the whistle and rotate players to the next position.

X Defensive player

⊗ Post player

◯ Offensive player

Suggestions and Variations

Set up two drills on each side of the key. If facilities and equipment are limited, draw circles on the wall and place traffic cones or other markers on the floor and restrict players to their assigned areas.

Pivot and Pass

Motor skills Pivot, pass
Movement concepts Personal space, change of direction
Players Six to eight per group
Formation Circle
Playing area Playground, gymnasium
Equipment Basketball

Circle formation, with six to eight players standing about ten feet apart. Each player faces the center of the circle. A player on each side of the circle is given a ball. On signal, each player with a ball keeps his left foot on the ground and pivots a quarter-turn away from the center of the circle, then steps forward on his right foot and passes to the next player. Continue the drill around the circle, then repeat reversing directions.

Lay-Up Shooting

Motor skills Shoot, dribble, catch
Movement concepts Moving into space, change of direction
Players Ten per group
Formation Lines
Playing area. Playground, gymnasium
Equipment Basketball

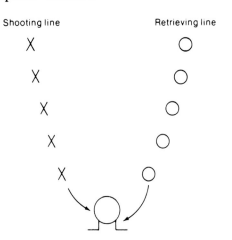

Arrange two lines of players at a forty-five-degree angle to the basket. The first player in each line should be about twenty feet from the basket. The first player in the shooting line dribbles toward the basket and attempts a lay-up shot, then goes to the end of the retrieving line. The first player in the retrieving line leaves his line at the same time as the shooting player to retrieve the ball and pass it to the next player in the shooting line. The retriever then goes to the end of the shooting line. Continue the drill to the last shooting player; then reverse lines and repeat drill.

LEAD-UP GAMES
. . . .

Bucket Ball

Motor skills Pass, catch, dribble, shoot, guard
Movement concepts Moving into space, change of direction and speed
Players Five or six per team
Formation A rectangle drawn approximately thirty by forty feet or the gymnasium divided into two playing courts
Playing area Playground, gymnasium, classroom
Equipment Two wastepaper baskets and one ball for each game

Place wastepaper baskets on the floor at the center of the endlines. If desired, a player may stand on a chair and hold the basket. Players on team A pair off with players on team B, and each checks the other. The game begins with a jump ball between two opposing players. The game continues until one team makes a basket. The general rules of basketball are followed; however, modify any rule as desired.

Suggestions and Variations
1. Play the same game, but use two hoops suspended from the ceiling or walls as goals.
2. Play the same game, but require one type of locomotor movement such as jumping, hopping, or sliding.

Keep Away

Motor skills Pass, catch, pivot, dribble
Movement concepts Moving into space, change of direction and speed
Players Three or four per team
Formation Scattered within a designated playing area
Playing area Playground, gymnasium, classroom
Equipment Basketball

On signal, the teacher gives the ball to one team, which passes it among themselves, trying to keep it away from the other team. Players on the opposing team check as in regular basketball. If teams are large and space is limited, rotate in fours or fives every few minutes.

Suggestions and Variations
1. Limit person in possession of the ball to three steps before passing the ball.
2. Require every player to pivot before passing the ball.

Basketball Touch

Motor skills Pass, catch, guard
Movement concepts Moving into space, change of direction and speed

Players   Four or five per team
Formation   Two teams scattered within a designated playing area, with one goalie standing on the baseline
Playing area   Playground, gymnasium
Equipment   Basketball

Arrange two teams in scattered positions within the court area. Goalies stand on opposite lines and may move up and down their own line. Court players are allowed to pass the ball any number of times as they try to pass it to their goalie. Players may check but are not allowed to dribble the ball. Start game with one player throwing in the ball from the middle of the sideline.

Suggestions and Variations

Add limitations, such as only use an overhand pass or every player must dribble three steps, pivot, then pass the ball.

Sideline Basketball

Motor skills   Pass, catch, shoot, dribble, pivot
Movement concepts   Moving into space, change of direction and speed
Players   Ten to twelve per team
Formation   Five players from each team play in the court area, while the remaining players from both teams are placed alternately along the sidelines and endlines. Leave equal spaces between line players.
Playing area   Playground, gymnasium, classroom
Equipment   Basketballs

Basketball rules are followed, except the ball may be passed to a sideline player. Sideline players cannot enter the court, dribble, or pass to another sideline player. Start the game with a jump ball in the center of the playing area. The team that gains possession is designated as the offensive team. If the defensive team intercepts the ball, it must pass to one of its sideline players before it becomes the offensive team. Stepping over the sideline gives the ball to opponents on their sideline. Players on the sidelines rotate with players on the floor. Field goals score two points and free throws one point.

Suggestions and Variations

1. Require every third pass to go to a sideline player.
2. Limit number of steps court players may travel before passing or shooting the ball.
3. Ask each team to suggest a new rule.

Twenty-One

Motor skills   Shoot, catch
Movement concepts   Shooting into empty space, levels
Players   Three or four per game
Formation   Players of each group scattered around one basket
Playing area   Playground, gymnasium, classroom
Equipment   Basketball

The object of this game is for any player to score twenty-one points by a combination of field shots and free throws. Player 1 shoots from the free throw line, while the other players stand wherever they wish in the playing area. Player 1 continues shooting from the free throw line until he misses, with each successful basket counting one point. When he misses, any player who can get possession of the ball may try for a field goal; if successful, it counts two points. If the try for a field goal fails, any player who can get the ball may try for a field goal. This procedure continues until a field goal is made. After a field goal is made, the ball is given to player 2, who takes his turn at the free throw line. Continue until one player has twenty-one points.

Suggestions and Variations

1. Reduce game point to nine or eleven.
2. Allow field goal attempts to be a lay-up shot from the closest side to the basket.

Basketball Snatch Ball

Motor skills   Dribble, shoot
Movement concepts   Moving into space, change of direction
Players   Five or six per team
Formation   Divide class into two equal groups. Each team on opposite lines. Place two basketballs on a line midway between two opposing teams.
Playing area   Playground, gymnasium
Equipment   Basketballs

Players are numbered consecutively and must stand in this order on the sideline of the playing area. When the teacher or leader calls a number, that player from each team runs to one of the balls, picks it up, dribbles it to the basket, and shoots until he makes a basket. When he succeeds, he dribbles back and replaces the ball. The first player to make a basket and return the ball scores one point for his team.

Suggestions and Variations

1. Players may run by pairs, with two players from each team having the same number. In this case, the ball must be passed between the players three times before and after the shot is made.
2. Require specific types of shooting skills.
3. Add a math challenge for fun, such as "8–5" or "⅓ of 12," instead of the simple number.

In-and-Out Basketball

Motor skills   Shoot, catch, dribble, pivot
Movement concepts   Moving into space, change of direction and speed
Players   Five per team
Formation   Two teams playing in half of the basketball court, and a third "waiting" team on the sideline
Playing area   Playground, gymnasium, classroom
Equipment   Basketball

Regular basketball rules apply, with the following modifications: (1) three teams play in half the court; (2) two teams play, while the third team remains on the side line; (3) when a field goal or free throw is made, the third team takes the loser's place; and (4) each player is allowed only two dribbles.

Suggestions and Variations

1. If goals are not being scored, use a time limit instead.
2. Have waiting team practice passing or dribbling skills.

Captain Ball

Motor skills   Dribble, pass, guard
Movement concepts   Personal space, moving into space, change of direction and speed

Players Eight to ten per team
Formation See diagram (Note: two games can be played in each half of a typical elementary school gymnasium.)
Playing area Playground, gymnasium
Equipment Two basketballs, eight hoops

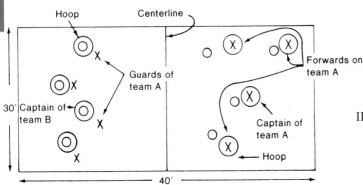

The captain and three forward players of team A must keep one foot inside their hoops. Four guards from team A may roam anywhere in team B's side of the playing area; however, they cannot enter the hoop of any opposing player. The object of this game is for the guards to get the ball to any of their forward players. The forward players, in turn, try to get the ball to their captain. Start the game with a jump ball between two opposing guards. Award two points each time the captain receives the ball from one of his forwards.

Fouls occur when
1. A guard steps into an opposing player's hoop, steps over the centerline or boundary line, or throws the ball directly to the captain (ball is given to the nearest forward player on opposing team).
2. A forward steps out of his circle, holds the ball longer than five seconds, or commits unnecessary rough play (ball is given to the nearest guard on the opposing team).

Suggestions and Variations
1. Add more circle or guard players. Even numbers make the game more difficult.
2. Require only one type of pass.
3. Add any rule or modification as desired.

BASKETBALL RULES AND REGULATIONS

Basketball is probably the most popular team sport in the upper elementary grades. Although skill development, especially ball handling and shooting skills, necessitates that the majority of the time be spent on practice activities and lead-up games, the full game should be played occasionally during a unit of instruction. Modify the rules, such as lowering the height of the basket and limiting the number of dribbles, to encourage the development of specific skills. Care should be taken, however, not to play the full game too often, perhaps neglecting needed skill development.

I. Field of play: Adjust court and key dimensions to available space.

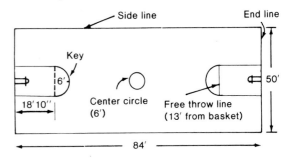

II. Positions:

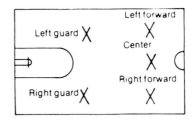

III. To start game: The game is started at the center circle. The referee tosses the ball in the air between the two opposing centers, who attempt to tap it to one of their teammates. This jump ball is also used when the ball goes out of bounds and the referee is uncertain which team caused it to go out and to start the second half of the game.

IV. After a successful free throw: The ball is put into play at the end of the court by the defending team.

V. After a ball goes out of bounds: The ball is put into play from behind the line and immediately in front of the place where it went out. Any player from the team that did not cause it to go out may put it into play.

VI. Game time: The game is divided into four quarters of six minutes each.

VII. Points: Two points are awarded for every field goal and one point for every successful free throw.

VIII. Substitution: One or all substitutes may enter the game whenever the ball is not in play (out of bounds, before a jump ball, etc.).

IX. Violations: A violation is charged against a player if she:
A. Travels—takes more than one step with the ball without dribbling
B. Double dribbles—dribbles the ball, stops, then dribbles again without another player handling the ball or palms the ball (that is, does not clearly dribble or dribbles with two hands)
C. Steps on or over a boundary line while in possession of the ball
D. Kicks the ball

TABLE 22.3 Basketball Skill Test

Name	Passing (Total Pts.)	Dribbling (Total Pts.)	Shooting (50 Pts.)	Subjective Evaluation (50 Pts.)	Total Score	Grade
1 2 3		Rank total scores for the class, then convert to letter grades or ratings (superior, good, etc.).				

E. Stays longer than three seconds in the key area under the offensive basket, in which case play is stopped and the referee awards a throw from the sideline to the other team near the point where the infraction occurred

X. Fouls: A foul is charged against a player if he:
   A. Kicks, trips, or pushes another player
   B. Holds or charges another player
   C. Commits unsportsmanlike conduct

XI. The penalty: Play is stopped and the referee awards one or two free throws to the nonoffending team from the free throw line.
   A. One free throw is awarded to a player who is fouled while participating in an activity other than shooting. If the free throw is successful, the defending team puts the ball into play from behind the end line. If the free throw is unsuccessful, the ball continues in play.
   B. Two free throws are awarded to a player who is fouled when he is shooting. If the second free throw is successful, the defending team puts the ball into play from behind the end line. If the second free throw is unsuccessful, the ball continues in play.

EVALUATIVE TECHNIQUES

Several tests can be used to measure the basic passing, dribbling, and shooting skills. The following test items are reliable and quite easy to administer. Modify any of them to meet your own teaching situation and add additional ones if desired. Also keep scores from each year in order to build appropriate norms for your school (table 22.3).

Test 1: Passing

Place a target on the wall as shown in the following diagram. The player must stand and pass from behind the ten-foot line. He has thirty seconds to hit the target as many times as possible. If a player drops the ball within the time period, he may pick it up, return to the ten-foot line, and continue adding to his cumulative score. One point is

scored for each pass that lands on the target area. Allow two trials and record the highest score.

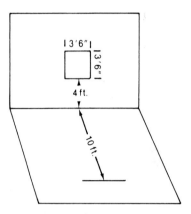

Test 2: Dribbling

Arrange four chairs in a line at ten-foot intervals from the starting line. A ball is placed on the starting line. Each player stands behind the starting line, with both hands resting on her knees. On signal "go," she picks up the ball and dribbles around the chairs in a zigzag pattern. One point is awarded each time she passes a chair. Allow twenty seconds for the test. Two trials are allowed, with the highest score recorded.

Basketball test no. 2

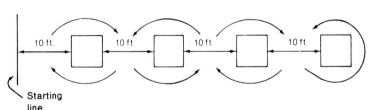

Test 3: Shooting

Draw a line at a 45-degree angle thirty feet from the basket. Each student attempts ten lay-up shots. He must begin dribbling from the thirty-foot line and attempt a shot when he reaches the basket. Award five points for each successful basket. Other shooting tests, such as free throws or one- or two-hand sets, may be substituted for the lay-up test.

Test 4: Subjective Evaluation

Establish criteria that represent the skills and playing ability required in basketball. Using shooting ability, dribbling, defensive skill, and passing, the teacher can award each player a total score from zero to fifty points. Three players can be used as judges, with the average score recorded.

Summary Review

The game of basketball requires players to be knowledgeable of the rules of the game and to understand appropriate basketball playing strategies. Players also need to be proficient in a number of specialized basketball skills. These skills must be learned, as they do not develop automatically through growth and maturation. Individual practices, lead-up games, and mini-games that can be adjusted to create successful practice opportunities, as well as enjoyable game situations, become the basis for teaching children basketball. The objective is to increase children's knowledge of basketball and to help develop their basketball skills toward the automatic stage of development. To develop specialized sport skills to the automatic stage requires many individual practices. Hence, children need to be provided with lots of developmentally appropriate practice opportunities. This will lead to successful basketball skill development and enjoyment of the game. If this objective is achieved, then children will possess the knowledge, skills, and desire to continue playing this major game throughout their lives.

INDIVIDUAL *and* **GROUP** PROJECTS

1. Form groups of three. Each group member chooses two different basketball skills. Design lesson plans to teach your two basic skills. Then teach one group member your two basic basketball skills while the third member observes the effectiveness of your instruction. Each group member takes a turn at being teacher, student, and observer. Observers might find useful the observational checklist for the evaluation of teaching, provided in Table 11.7 on page 247. When you have all taught your skills, discuss and evaluate your experiences in each role (teacher, student, observer), and suggest possible ways to improve your teaching.

2. In pairs, study the rules and regulations of basketball. Then pose questions on the rules and regulations for each other to answer.

3. In chapter 4, it was suggested that one of the challenges facing teachers is the adjustment of the teaching environment to meet the developmental levels of the children.

Four environmental variables under the teachers' control were identified:
   a. Rules
   b. Space
   c. Number of participants
   d. Amount or type of equipment

One or more of these variables can be adjusted to create success on behalf of students. In small groups, discuss how these four variables can be adjusted when teaching children basketball. Formulate creative ideas and specific recommendations and share these with other groups.

4. Chapter 13 identified a number of disabilities that afflict young children. In small groups, choose four disabilities and discuss how children with these disabilities can be integrated into basketball activities. Consider what adjustments will have to be made to accommodate each child's developmental level and to ensure success. Debate possible techniques and methods of evaluation. Share ideas with other groups.

5. A feature of this text is the idea of teaching and enhancing academic skills and concepts through physical education activities. In small groups, discuss and create ideas to teach or enhancing academic skills and concepts through basketball activities. Each group is then allocated a small selection of the basketball practice activities and lead-up games. Create ideas for teaching or enhancing academic skills and concepts through these practice activities and lead-up games. Consider ways to evaluate the students. Share ideas with other groups.

SELECTED READINGS

CAHPER. 1985. *Basketball-type games.* Ottawa, Ontario: CAHPER.

Garchow, K., and A. Dickinson. 1992. *Youth basketball: A complete handbook.* Dubuque, IA: Wm. C. Brown.

Johnson, C. 1989. *Practical basketball for teacher and coach.* Champaign, IL: Stipes.

Kamiya, A. 1985. *Elementary teacher's handbook of indoor and outdoor games.* West Nyack, NY: Parker.

Krause, J. V. 1991. *Basketball skills and drills.* Champaign, IL: Leisure Press.

Philipp, J. A., and J. D. Wilkerson. 1990. *Teaching team sports: A coeducational approach.* Champaign, IL: Human Kinetics.

Turner, L. F., and S. L. Turner. 1989. *P.E. teacher's skill-by-skill activities program.* West Nyack, NY: Parker.

Wilkes, G. 1990. *Basketball.* 5th ed. Dubuque, IA: Wm. C. Brown.

CHAPTER 23

Softball Activities

KEY CONCEPTS

23.1 Specialized softball skills are acquired through instruction and practice opportunities

23.2 Softball activities must be developmentally appropriate to ensure that all children can achieve success and enjoyment

23.3 Inventive games provide opportunities for creativity and help equalize gender and skill-level differences

23.4 Playing a full-sided competitive game of softball is not a very efficient way of teaching children softball skills and concepts

23.5 Safety considerations must be emphasized when teaching children softball activities

23.6 Effective teaching progressions, that provide all children with individual practices and lead-up games, are required to develop the skills and knowledge associated with softball

23.7 To develop softball skills toward the automatic stage of skill development requires many practice opportunities (time on-task)

KEY OBJECTIVES

After completing this chapter you will be able to:

1. Design developmentally appropriate softball activities for elementary school children

2. Plan and organize teaching units and individual lessons in softball

3. Organize practice activities and lead-up games appropriate for softball

4. Plan and organize softball practice activities and lead-up games that incorporate the inventive games approach

5. Evaluate units, lessons, and individual techniques used in softball

6. Identify key teaching points associated with the basic skills of softball

7. Employ teaching progressions that lead to successful development of softball skills and concepts

8. Understand the rules and basic strategies associated with softball

Softball is an extremely popular recreational activity throughout Canada and the United States and in many other countries. Its popularity is probably due in part to the game's relative ease and safety. In addition, softball requires only a minimum amount of protective equipment and a smaller playing field than is required for baseball.

If softball is to be played as a competitive recreational game, every participant must know the rules and be reasonably proficient in the basic throwing, catching, and batting skills. Furthermore, each child should be given an opportunity to play every position. Assigning only the more proficient players to the catcher, pitcher, and first base positions is educationally unsound.

This chapter has been organized to provide a basic approach to teaching softball to upper elementary school children. Although lead-up games should be emphasized more than regulation softball during the instructional period, the official game or a modified version should be played occasionally to provide an opportunity for the class to understand the skills and playing strategies and, of course, for the teacher to test the children's abilities as batters and fielders.

EMPHASIS AND PROGRESSION

The problems of selecting and teaching softball skills and rules are very similar to those found in teaching basketball activities. Through television, organized leagues, and "sand-lot" games, most children of this age level are already acquainted with many of the skills and rules of softball. Thus, there will be a very wide variation in the development of softball skills in virtually every grade and within each class. The suggested sequence of presenting skills and rules in table 23.1, therefore, should be used as a basic guideline.

Table 23.1 indicates that children normally have been introduced to most throwing and catching skills prior to developmental level II. During level II, continued emphasis should be given to improving the throwing, catching, and batting skills, and to acquiring the basic rules and strategies of the game.

Developmental level III should be seen as continuous periods of refining the basic softball skills. More experienced players will also develop a reasonable level of skill in the sidearm throw and bunting. Most of these children should also show major improvement in general positional play. It is not uncommon for these children to be able to steal a base, sacrifice, or make a double play.

23.1 *Specialized Softball Skills Are Acquired through Instruction and Practice Opportunities*

TEACHING PROCEDURES

The approaches used to teach softball and basketball are very similar. Many elementary school children have played modified versions of softball such as scrub and two-person softball; their skill and general understanding of the game are well beyond the beginner stage. However, children who have not had this advantage are far behind in skill development and general playing ability. Since the teaching approach suggested for soccer can apply equally to softball, review chapter 18 to see how a unit of instruction and individual lessons can be developed.

23.2 *Softball Activities Must Be Developmentally Appropriate to Ensure That All Children Can Achieve Success and Enjoyment*

The inventive games approach suggested in previous chapters can also be applied with equal success to softball activities. Presenting such challenges as "Make up a four-person drill emphasizing grounding and a sidearm throw" provides freedom for a group to develop an activity that is challenging and enjoyable yet concentrates on one or two important skills. You can also cope with problems associated with gender and peer performances through this problem-solving approach.

23.3 *Inventive Games Provide Opportunities for Creativity and Help Equalize Gender and Skill-Level Differences*

The following suggestions apply more specifically to problems associated with teaching softball activities.

1. Softball is too inactive for most of the players. To help overcome this problem:
   a. Rotate positions as often as possible.
   b. Use a batting tee if pitching and batting abilities are generally low.
   c. Select lead-up games that require smaller playing areas and fewer players.

TABLE 23.1 Suggested Sequence of Presenting Softball Skills and Rules

Skills and Rules	Developmental Level II	Developmental Level III
Throwing		
Overhand throw	Acquired or introduce	Increase distance and accuracy
Underhand throw	Acquired or introduce	Increase speed and accuracy
Pitching	Acquired or introduce	Increase speed and accuracy
Sidearm throw		Introduce
Rules: Safe and out	Introduce	
Fair and foul ball	Introduce	
Strike zone	Introduce	
Pitching rule	Introduce	
Catching and Fielding		
Catching low and high throws	Acquired or introduce	Increase proficiency
Catching fly balls	Acquired or introduce	Increase proficiency
Fielding grounders	Acquired or introduce	Increase proficiency
Rules: Fielding positions	Acquired or introduce	
Foul tip	Introduce	
Bunt rule		Introduce
Batting		
Batting	Acquired or introduce	Increase distance and accuracy
Fungo hitting	Introduce	Increase distance and accuracy
Bunting		Introduce
Rules: Balls and strikes	Introduce	
Base Running		
To first base	Acquired or introduce	Increase speed
Around bases	Introduce	Increase speed
Rules: Touching base	Introduce	
Off base on caught fly	Introduce	
Related Skills		
Positional play		Introduce
Stealing bases		Introduce
Double play		Introduce
Sacrifice		Introduce

d. Modify the official game, such as two outs before changing positions or all players hitting before changing sides, or shorten the distance between bases.

CONCEPT

23.4 Playing a Full-Sided Competitive Game of Softball Is Not a Very Efficient Way of Teaching Large Numbers of Children Softball Skills and Concepts

2. Several safety precautions should be considered during every instructional and recreational period involving softball activities.
   a. All waiting batters should stay behind a designated safety line located to the rear and on the first base side of the catcher.

b. Every player should be taught how to release the bat after hitting the ball. Stringent enforcement of this rule is extremely important for everyone's safety.
c. Properly-fitting face masks should be provided for the catcher.
d. Sliding should be prohibited, since it can cause unnecessary injury and tear street clothes.
e. All bases should be made of soft material.

CONCEPT

23.5 Safety Considerations Must Be Emphasized When Teaching Children Softball Activities

3. An umpire should be used in the more complex lead-up games and in every modified or regulation softball

game. Establish a procedure for rotating the umpire as the teams change positions.

4. Modify every game to cope with the class's general level of ability and interest.

5. If softball gloves are available, they should be in good condition. Infielders should have priority for use.

6. Some children will ask if they can wear their own gloves during the softball unit. The teacher and her class should discuss this situation and reach a group decision about wearing personally owned gloves.

7. One of the most common complaints by elementary school teachers is the insufficient number of balls and bats for practice activities. This can be overcome by using a station system and rotating groups. The accompanying illustration shows several partner and group activities involving a variety of skills going on simultaneously. Each group rotates to the next station after a set period of time. If the groups do not have time to rotate through all the stations in one lesson, simply continue in the next lesson.

C O N C E P T

23.6 Effective Teaching Progressions, That Provide All Children with Individual Practices and Lead-Up Games, Are Required to Develop the Skills and Knowledge Associated with Softball

Station System for Softball

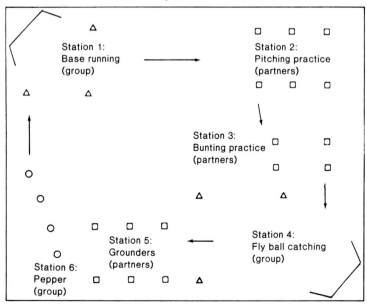

Available field space

DESCRIPTION OF SKILLS

Softball skills for elementary school children can be classified as hitting and fielding skills. All throwing and catching skills are appropriate for this age range. As for batting skills, most children have little difficulty learning to hit a ball with a full swing, although bunting and fungo batting present some problems.

C O N C E P T

23.7 To Develop Softball Skills to the Automatic Stage of Skill Development Requires Many Practice Opportunities

Throwing

The major part of all fielding and defensive play depends on how fast and how accurately a player can throw the ball. Although the skill and style of performance vary from child to child, each is capable of throwing an overhand, sidearm, and underhand toss or pitch with relative ease and accuracy.

Gripping the Ball

The softball can be gripped in two basic ways. If the hand is large enough, the ball can be held between the thumb and first two fingers, with the third and fourth fingers resting against the side of the ball. Elementary school children's smaller hands make it necessary for them to grip the ball with the thumb, and all four fingers spread around the side and bottom of the ball (figure 23.1a). However, only the top surface of the fingers should touch the ball. The grip is correct if the young thrower can see daylight between the ball and his hands (figure 23.1b).

Overhand Throw

This is the basic throw for all players, except the pitcher. Begin in a staggered stride position with the weight on the back foot, throwing arm extended backward, wrist cocked, and ball facing the rear. At this point, the left side faces the direction of the throw and the left arm extends forward (figure 23.2a). In a simultaneous movement, the upper right arm moves upward and forward and the left arm moves down and back as the weight shifts to the front foot (figure 23.2b). With a snap of the wrist, the ball is released off the fingers and toward the target (figure 23.2c). In the follow-through action, the throwing-side shoulder moves forward and downward as the weight shifts to the front foot (figure 23.2d).

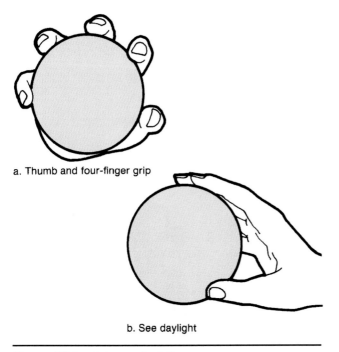

a. Thumb and four-finger grip

b. See daylight

Figure 23.1 Gripping the ball.

Key Teaching Points

1. Keep eyes focused on the target.
2. Begin in a staggered stride position with the weight on the rear foot.
3. Rotate hips and shoulders as throwing arm moves backward.
4. Throwing arm moves forward and upward with the elbow leading.
5. Release ball slightly above and in front of the head.
6. Follow through toward the target and finish with the throwing-side foot even with the opposite foot and weight evenly distributed over both feet.

Sidearm Throw

The sidearm throw is used when the ball is thrown a short distance and in a hurry; thus, it is the most effective throw for infielders. As the ball is received, keep the body low and shift weight to the rear foot (figure 23.3a). Move the throwing arm to a horizontal position with the elbow bent and the ball in a throwing position (figure 23.3b). The opposite elbow should face the target. Simultaneously shift weight to the front foot as the throwing arm moves across and

a   b   c   d

Figure 23.2 Overhand throw.

a   b   c

Figure 23.3 Sidearm throw.

CHAPTER 23

parallel to the ground (figure 23.3c). The ball is released with a snap of the wrist. In the follow-through action, the throwing arm moves horizontally toward the target as the elbow of the opposite arm moves backward.

Key Teaching Points

1. Keep eyes focused on the target.
2. Keep throwing arm below shoulder level.
3. Swing the throwing arm parallel to the ground.
4. Follow through in the direction of the throw.

Underhand Toss

The underhand toss is used for short, quick throws, most often around the infield area. The player extends his upper arm and forearm backward as his weight shifts to his rear foot. On the forward movement, his arm swings down and forward and his weight is shifted to the front foot (figure 23.4). As the ball is released, the player follows through with his upper arm and hand in the direction of the throw.

Key Teaching Points (For Underhand Toss)

1. Keep eyes focused on the target.
2. Grip ball with fingers and thumb.
3. Simultaneously swing arm downward and forward.
4. Release ball off fingers and point in the direction of the throw.

Pitching

The pitcher stands with feet parallel, holding the ball in front with both hands, and facing the batter (figure 23.5a). He moves both hands forward until his arms are extended to about waist high and releases his left hand

Figure 23.4 Forward pendulum action of the arm.

a   b   c

Figure 23.5 Pitching.

from the ball as he brings his throwing arm down and back. At the top of the backswing, his body twists slightly toward his pitching arm and his weight is on his right foot. In a simultaneous action, he swings his left arm forward close to the body, rotates his shoulders toward the right, and steps forward on his left foot (figure 23.5b). As the ball is released off the fingers, he follows through with the pitching arm (figure 23.5c).

Key Teaching Points
1. Keep eyes focused on the target.
2. Keep pivot foot in contact with pitcher plate.
3. Simultaneously step forward as arm rotates forward and downward.
4. Follow through in the direction of the batter.

Catching and Fielding

Good fielding ability requires the player to be able to catch a high fly ball and a variety of throws and to stop a ball hit along the ground. In all types of fielding it is important to be in a ready position, with the feet spread apart comfortably and the weight on both feet. The trunk leans forward slightly and the knees are flexed. The hands are in front of the body about knee high. The eyes are on the ball (figure 23.6).

Key Teaching Points
1. Keep eyes focused on the oncoming ball.
2. Stand with trunk bent slightly forward, knees partially bent, and weight evenly distributed over both feet.
3. Put hands in front of knees, with fingers spread apart.

Catching

If the ball approaches below the waist, the fingers point with the little fingers together or if wearing a glove, palm of glove faces upward (figure 23.7a). When the ball approaches above the waist, the thumbs are together and the fingers point upward (figure 23.7b). As the ball is caught, the hands recoil toward the body to deaden or soften the force of the oncoming ball (figure 23.7c).

Figure 23.6 Fielding—ready position.

a   b   c

Figure 23.7 Catching.

CHAPTER 23

a

b

Figure 23.8 Fielding grounders.

Key Teaching Points

1. Keep eyes focused on the oncoming ball.
2. Move quickly into position to catch the ball.
3. Extend arms toward the ball, then recoil and shift ball to throwing hand.

Fielding Grounders

The first important move in grounding a ball is to shift the body toward the direction of the oncoming ball. As the fielder moves toward the ball, she shifts her weight forward, holding her arms low and in front of her body. Just before grounding the ball, she stops, with her left foot in front of her right foot, her knees bent, and her trunk well forward (figure 23.8a). She contacts the ball just inside her front foot with her left hand, then covers or traps it with her throwing hand (figure 23.8b). The eyes should be kept on the ball until it is firmly held. Once the ball is caught, the fielder begins to straighten up and takes a step in the direction of the throw.

Fielding a ground ball requires good fielding position and split-second timing to catch the ball on a good bounce. Because of these factors, plus the use of poor and uneven playing fields, the "sure-stop" grounding skill should be used, particularly by outfielders. This is similar to the regular grounding skill, except that the fielder makes a half turn toward the direction in which the ball is approaching, then lowers and rests on the back knee. The thigh and lower leg provide a good rebound surface for a ball that is missed (figure 23.9).

Key Teaching Points

1. Keep eyes focused on the oncoming ball.
2. Move quickly into position to field the ball.

Figure 23.9 "Sure-stop" grounding.

3. Stop the ball with the nonthrowing hand and cover it with the throwing hand.
4. Once the ball is caught, quickly shift into a throwing position.

Hitting the Ball

A softball can be hit in three ways. The first, and most important, is hitting a pitched ball with maximum force and follow-through. *Bunting* is a form of hitting a pitched ball; however, it requires a different grip, force, and follow-through. *Fungo batting* is simply throwing the ball up with

a   b   c

Figure 23.10   Gripping the bat.

one hand, regrasping the bat, and hitting the ball before it hits the ground.

The bat may be gripped in one of three positions, depending on the batter's strength and the type of hit desired. In the long grip (figure 23.10a), the hands are placed close to the bottom of the bat. For the medium grip (figure 23.10b), the hands are moved up one to two inches. For the choke grip (figure 23.10c), the hands are three to four inches from the knob of the bat. In each grip, the bat is held with the hands together and the fingers and thumbs wrapped around the handle. For right-handed batters, the right hand grips the handle above the left hand.

Batting

The batter stands with his feet parallel and about shoulder-width apart and weight evenly distributed over both feet. The left side of the body faces the pitcher. The bat is held at the back of the head about shoulder high. The arms are bent at the elbows and held away from the body. As the ball leaves the pitcher's hand, the batter shifts his weight to the rear foot (figure 23.11a). He then swings the bat forward as his weight shifts to the lead foot (figure 23.11b). After the ball is contacted, the batter continues to swing the bat around in a wide arc, ending over the left shoulder (figure 23.11c).

Key Teaching Points
1. Keep eyes focused on the pitched ball.
2. Begin with weight evenly distributed over both feet.
3. Turn head and look at the pitcher's throwing hand.

4. As bat swings downward and forward, rotate hips, trunk, and shoulders toward the pitcher.
5. Contact ball in front of front hip and follow through around the body.

Bunting

In bunting, the bat is placed in the way of the oncoming pitch, then allowed to "give" as the ball contacts the bat. Begin in a normal batting position (figure 23.12a). As the ball moves toward the strike zone, the batter draws her rear foot forward and squares her body to the pitcher. At the same time, she slides her top hand up the bat. The bat is held with the thumb on top and the fingers underneath (figure 23.12b). When the ball is hit, the bat slips back toward the palm of the hand as the arms recoil back toward the chest. The bat is angled in the direction of the intended bunt.

Key Teaching Points
1. Always begin in a normal batting position.
2. Keep in mind that slow pitches are easiest to bunt.
3. Emphasize "giving" or "catching with the bat" as the ball makes contact with the bat.
4. Do not follow through.

Fungo Batting

Fungo batting is useful for hitting the ball during fielding practice and in many lead-up games. Start with the feet parallel and comfortably spread apart, with the weight evenly distributed on both feet. Suspend the bat over the

a   b   c

Figure 23.11 Batting.

a   b

Figure 23.12 Bunting.

Figure 23.13 Fungo batting.

right shoulder while holding the ball in the left hand (figure 23.13a). Simultaneously toss the ball up and swing the bat down and forward, grasping it with the left hand (figure 23.13b). Continue forward, transferring the weight to the front foot and twisting the body toward the left. Hit the ball approximately in front of the left foot (figure 23.13c) and follow through with a swing around the left shoulder.

Key Teaching Points
1. Keep eyes on the ball until it is hit.
2. Grip the bat about ten inches up the grip.
3. Toss the ball about three feet above shoulder.
4. Simultaneously swing from shoulder, regrasp with left hand, contact ball, and continue forward swing around body.

Base Running

As soon as a ball is hit, the batter drops the bat and runs as fast as possible to and through first base. If she decides to try

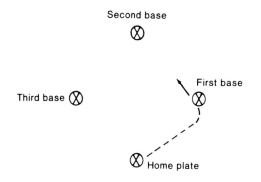

Figure 23.14 Running bases.

to run to second base, she begins curving to the right a few feet before reaching first base, touches the inside corner of the bag, and continues running to second base (figure 23.14).

Key Teaching Points
1. Hold onto the bat until the follow-through is completed.
2. Drop the bat and run as fast as possible toward first base.
3. Keep eyes focused on the base.
4. Touch and run through the base.

TABLE 23.2 Practice Activities and Lead-Up Games

Name of Activity	Type of Activity	Players	Developmental Level II	III	Softball Concepts and Skills	Movement Concepts	Page
Practice Activities							
Throwing and Catching	Throw, catch	2	————————▶		Throw, catch grounders	Moving into space, change of direction and speed	469
Partner Batting	Bat, catch, throw	2	————————▶		Throw, hit, catch	Hitting into empty space, strong and light	469
Overtake the Base	Throw, catch, run	8–10 per squad	————————▶		Throw, catch, run	Moving into space, change of direction, pathway, and speed	469
Fly Ball Catching	Hit, catch, throw	6–8 per squad	————————▶		Hit, catch, run	Hitting into empty space, levels, change of direction	469
Swing at Four	Hit, catch, throw	10–12 per squad	————————▶		Pitch, hit, catch, throw	Moving into space, change of direction and speed, strong and light	469
Pepper	Hit, catch, throw	5–6 per squad	————————▶		Hit, catch, throw	Moving into space, change of direction and speed	470
Lead-Up Games							
Flies and Grounders	Hit, catch	6 per group	————————▶		Throw, hit, field	Hitting into empty space, levels, change of direction and speed	470
One Old Cat	Throw, hit, catch	9 per team	————————▶		Throw, catch, hit	Hitting into empty space, moving into space, change of direction and speed	470
Long Ball	Throw, hit	9 per team	————————▶		Throw, catch, hit	Hitting into empty space, moving into space, change of direction and speed	470
Tee Ball	All skills	9 per team	—————————▶		All softball skills	Moving into space, strong and light, change of direction and speed	471
Twenty-One Softball	Throw, catch	9–10 per team	————————▶		Throw, catch, hit	Moving into space, change of direction and speed, strong and light	471
Overtake the Ball	Catch, throw	5–7 per team	———▶		Throw, catch	Change of direction and speed	471
Roll at the Bat	Hit, catch, throw	4–5 per group	———▶		Fungo hit, catch, throw	Moving into space, hitting into empty space, change of direction and speed	471
Beatball Softball	Hit, catch, throw	9 per team	————————▶		Throw, catch, hit	Moving into space, hitting into empty space, change of direction and speed	471
Scrub	All skills	7–9 per team	—————————▶		All softball skills	Moving into space, hitting into empty space, change of direction and speed	471
Five Hundred	Fungo hit, catch, throw	4–6 per group	———▶		All softball Skills	Moving into space, change of direction and speed	472

PRACTICE ACTIVITIES AND LEAD-UP GAMES

Most practice activities for softball involve partners or small groups. Each of the following drills and practice activities should be modified to cope with the available space, time, and equipment (table 23.2).

The following lead-up games are designed to provide maximum participation and practice in one or more softball skills. As a general guideline, use these games extensively in level II and proportionately less in level III. Playing the official game of softball can be a challenging and enjoyable experience for upper elementary school children, but only when the majority of players have developed adequate throwing, catching, and batting skills. These lead-up games can be played in smaller areas and require fewer players than the regulation game.

PRACTICE ACTIVITIES

▪ Throwing and Catching

Motor skills Throw, catch grounders
Movement concepts Moving into space, change of direction and speed
Players Two
Formation None
Playing area Playground
Equipment Softball

Perhaps the most common type of softball practice activity involves two players. Some of the most useful partner activities are described.

1. Have the partners throw and catch. Have both partners remain stationary, varying the distances; then have one remain stationary while the other moves, practicing grounders.
2. Have the pitcher and catcher alternate positions.
3. Practice hitting a target. Set up a target on a wall or the ground for pitching or accurate throwing practice.
4. Partners throw to each other but make the ball bounce before it reaches the receiver.
5. One partner throws a grounder while the other partner throws ball directly back.

The inventive games approach can be used quite effectively in partner activities to increase skill and to provide an avenue for unique and enjoyable practice activities. The following example should provide a general idea:

Situation: Divide the class into partners. Give the partners a ball and one piece of small equipment (bat, hoop, traffic cone). *Challenge:* "Can you make up a practice activity (or drill) with your partner that includes a sidearm throw, a grounder, and one piece of small equipment?" Allow the class several minutes to make up their games, then select one or two partner groups and have them demonstrate their games.

▪ Partner Batting

Motor skills Throw, hit, catch
Movement concepts Hitting into empty space, strong and light
Players Two
Playing area Playground
Equipment Ball and bat

The success of any softball game centers on each player's ability to hit the ball. Too often, however, batting practice is one player hitting the ball to ten or more very inactive fielders. The following partner activities are very effective in developing batting skills.

1. One player hits the ball off a tee to his partner. Use a traffic cone mounted on a cardboard box as a substitute tee.
2. One player fungo hits to his partner.
3. Add a third player. One player pitches, another bats, and the third player fields the ball. Rotate after three hits.
4. Practice close-range bunting. One player pitches, while the batter attempts to bunt the ball back.

▪ Overtake the Base

Motor skills Throw, catch, run
Movement concepts Moving into space, change of direction, pathway, and speed
Players Eight to ten per squad
Formation Diamond
Playing area Playground
Equipment Ball

Divide the class into squads of eight to ten players. Arrange the squads around the bases, with player A at the pitcher's line, B on home plate, C on first base, D on second, and E on third. The remaining players form a line near home plate. When the whistle blows, player A throws to B, B throws to C, and so on around the diamond to home plate. At the same time A throws the ball, F takes off for first base and continues around the bases, attempting to reach home plate before the ball. Two rules apply: (1) The base runner must touch all bases and (2) the players rotate after each run. A takes B's position, B goes to C's, F takes A's. Everyone shifts one place to the right, with player E on third going to the back of the line.

Suggestions and Variations
1. Make two diamonds, with the smaller one for runners and the larger one for throwers.
2. Add one or more fielders.

▪ Fly Ball Catching

Motor skills Hit, catch, throw
Movement concepts Hitting into empty space, levels, change of direction and speed
Players Six to eight per squad
Formation Scattered
Playing area Playground
Equipment Softball and bat

Place one batter at home plate and scatter the remaining players in the field. The batter, using fungo batting, hits fly balls into the field. When a fielder catches a fly ball, he becomes the batter.

Suggestions and Variations
1. Place all fielders in a large semicircle and require the batter to hit two balls to each player in turn. Rotate after the last player has received his second fly.
2. Add a pitcher and a catcher.

▪ Swing at Four

Motor skills Pitch, hit, throw, catch
Movement concepts Moving into space, change of direction and speed, strong and light
Players Ten to twelve per squad

Formation   Squads
Playing area   Playground
Equipment   Baseballs, bats, bases

Divide the class into two or three squads of ten to twelve players. Arrange squads in infield positions, with spare players in a line behind home plate. The pitcher throws four balls to each batter, who attempts to hit them into the infield. Infield players retrieve the balls and throw them to first base. The first baseman returns the balls to the pitcher. Rotate players after each player has had four hits. The batter takes the third baseman's position and everyone shifts one place to the left. The catcher goes to the back of the "waiting" line, and the pitcher becomes the catcher.

Suggestions and Variations
Add outfielders and allow batters to hit anywhere.

Pepper

Motor skills   Hit, catch, throw
Movement concepts   Moving into space, change of direction and speed
Players   Five or six per squad
Formation   Line
Playing area   Playground
Equipment   Softball, bat

Divide the class into groups of five or six. Place five players in a line, with about ten feet between each player. One player, the "leader," stands about twenty feet in front of the line with her bat. The first player in the line pitches the ball to the leader, who hits it to the next player in line. The second player fields the ball and pitches it back to the leader. Continue the drill to the last player, then rotate the leader.

Suggestions and Variations
If a line player misses the ball, he goes to the end of the line. If a batter misses a fair pitch, he changes places with the player at the end of the line.

LEAD-UP GAMES

Flies and Grounders

Motor skills   Throw, hit, fielding
Movement concepts   Hitting into empty space, levels, change of direction and speed
Players   Six per group
Formation   Scattered
Playing area   Playground
Equipment   Softball and bat

The batter hits the ball into the field off the tee or fungo-style. The player in a position to catch the ball calls "Mine" and attempts to catch it. A player receives five points for catching a fly ball, three points for a ball caught after one bounce, and one point for a grounder. The first player to reach fifteen points becomes the new batter.

Suggestions and Variations
1. Substitute a pitcher for fungo hitting.
2. Require only one type of throw.

One Old Cat

Motor skills   Throw, catch, hit
Movement concepts   Hitting into empty space, moving into space, change of direction and speed
Players   Nine per team
Formation   Players divided into two teams of nine each, with one team in the field and one at bat
Playing area   Playground
Equipment   Softball, bat, bases

The first player on the batting team hits the ball into the field and tries to run to first base and home in one complete trip. She may not stop on the base. If she makes a complete trip without being put out, she scores one run for her team. The runner is out if (a) a fielder catches a fly ball or (b) a fielder touches the runner with the ball before she reaches home. When the team at bat makes three outs, it goes into the field and the team in the field comes to bat. The team with the highest score at the end of the playing period wins. (Teams must have the same number of times at bat.)

Suggestions and Variations
1. Alternate pitchers and catchers. Alternate boy and girl in batting order.
2. Try two outs if one team stays up too long.
3. Vary the distance to the base according to the level of skill.
4. Use batting tee if skill level is too low.

Long Ball

Motor skills   Throw, catch, hit
Movement concepts   Hitting into empty space, moving into space, change of direction and speed
Players   Nine per team
Formation   Class divided into two equal teams. The fielding team consists of a pitcher and a catcher, with the remaining players scattered in the field.
Playing area   Playground
Equipment   Softball, bat, bases

Each team selects a pitcher and a catcher. Other players are fielders or batters. When a batter hits the ball, he runs to the base and, if possible, returns home to score a point. Any hit is good and there are no fouls. The base runner may stop on first base, and any number of runners may be on base at the same time. Runners may not steal home. The batter is out when he strikes out, is touched off base, steals a base, throws the bat, or hits a fly ball that is caught. One point is awarded for each run.

Suggestions and Variations
1. Substitute a batting tee if skill level is too low.
2. Change any rule or add new ones as need or interest dictates.

Tee Ball

Motor skills All softball skills except pitching and stealing bases
Movement concepts Moving into space, strong and light, change of direction and speed
Players Nine per team
Formation Regulation softball field
Playing area Playground
Equipment Softball, tee, bases

This game is played in the same way as softball, with the following modifications.

1. The batter is allowed one hit off the tee.
2. Since there is no pitcher, no one is permitted to steal a base. A runner must stay on base until the ball is hit by a teammate.

Twenty-One Softball

Motor skills Throw, catch, hit
Movement concepts Moving into space, change of direction and speed, strong and light
Players Nine or ten per team
Formation Regulation softball field
Playing area Playground
Equipment Softball, bat, bases

Play according to regular softball rules, with the following exceptions: The batter gets three swings to hit the ball. When she hits the ball, she runs the bases in order until she is put out. A runner safe at first scores one point; at second, two points; at third, three points; and at home, four points. Teams exchange places after three outs. The first team to score twenty-one points wins.

Suggestions and Variations
1. Change pitcher and catcher each time the teams change positions.
2. Use fungo or hit off a tee.
3. Change scoring to eleven or fifteen points rather than twenty-one.

Overtake the Ball

Motor skills Throw, catch
Movement concepts Change of direction and speed
Players Five to seven per team
Formation Circle
Playing area Playground
Equipment Softball

The players stand in a circle and count off by twos. The ones are members of one team and the twos, the other. Each team selects a captain, who stands in the center of the circle. Both captains have a ball. On signal, each captain tosses his ball to any team member, who tosses it back to the captain. The captain tosses it to the next team member (in a clockwise direction), who also tosses it back to the captain. The ball is tossed in this manner clockwise around the circle by both teams until each ball has been thrown to all members of the team and is back in the captain's hands. One team "overtakes" the other when its ball passes that of the other team as the balls are tossed around the circle. The team that tosses the ball completely around the circle first scores one point. When a team overtakes and finishes first, it scores two points. The first team to score five points wins the game.

Suggestions and Variations
1. Play the game with various kinds of balls and different throws and passes.
2. Vary the distance according to the level of skill.

Roll at the Bat

Motor skills Fungo hit, catch, throw
Movement concepts Moving into space, hitting into empty space, change of direction and speed
Players Four or five per group
Formation Outdoor playing area, with fielders scattered, facing the batter
Playing area Playground
Equipment Softball, bat

One player chosen to be the first batter hits the ball anywhere into the field of play. If a player catches a fly ball, she rolls it back and tries to hit the bat, which has been placed on the ground. The length of the bat must face each "roller." If the ball is not caught, it is thrown back to the batter again. A fielder becomes the new batter when (a) she successfully rolls a ball back and hits the bat, (b) she catches two fly balls, or (c) she successfully retrieves three grounders. All players start at zero when a new batter takes a turn.

Beatball Softball

Motor skills Throw, catch, hit
Movement concepts Moving into space, hitting into empty space, change of direction and speed
Players Nine per team
Formation Regular softball field
Playing area Playground
Equipment Softball, bat, bases

Play according to regular softball rules, with the following exceptions: Any fielder who gets the ball must throw it to the first baseman, who must touch the base with the ball in his hand, then throw from first to second, second to third, and third to home. If the ball gets home ahead of the runner, he is out. If the runner beats the ball home, he scores a run for his team. After three outs, the teams exchange places.

Suggestions and Variations
1. Use fungo or tee hitting.
2. Move the bases closer together.
3. Require one type of throw, such as a sidearm or underhand toss.

Scrub

Motor skills All softball skills
Movement concepts Moving into space, hitting into empty space, change of direction and speed

Players Seven to nine on each team
Formation Regular softball field
Playing area Playground
Equipment Softball, bat, bases

One player (the "scrub") stands at bat. All other players are numbered: the catcher is one; pitcher, two; first baseman, three; and fielders, four and up. The batter hits a pitched ball and must run to first base and back. She is out if she is tagged at first or home, strikes out, slings her bat, or hits a fly ball that is caught. If she gets home, she bats again. The batter is allowed only three times at bat; then she becomes the last fielder. If the batter is put out, every player moves up one position.

Suggestions and Variations

1. If a player catches a fly ball, he exchanges positions with the batter.
2. Two players may be up at the same time. In this situation, the first batter is permitted to stop on first base and be hit home by the other batter.
3. Use tee or fungo hitting.

▪ Five Hundred

Motor skills Fungo hit, throw, catch, field
Movement concepts Moving into space, change of direction and speed
Players Four to six per team
Formation Scattered
Playing area Playground
Equipment Softball, bat

One player is chosen to be the first batter. The object of the game is for each fielder to try to be the first to reach 500 points. Points are scored as follows: 100 for catching a ball on the fly, 75 for a ball caught on the first bounce, and 50 for fielding a grounder. The same number of points is deducted from a player's score if he commits an error. As soon as a player has reached 500 or more points, he exchanges positions with the batter.

Suggestions and Variations

1. Use a pitcher.
2. Require only one type of throw.
3. Add a roll at the bat and award another 100 points for hitting it.

SOFTBALL RULES AND REGULATIONS

Although skill development varies for each grade and class, the complete game of softball should be played periodically throughout a softball unit. By playing the game according to the basic rules, children learn to appreciate the value of practice and team play. Modifications might include shortening the length between bases and substituting a batting tee for a pitcher. While children are playing the full game, the teacher should note their major weaknesses so she can select appropriate drills and lead-up games that can be used to improve these deficiencies.

I. Field of play and positions: See illustration.

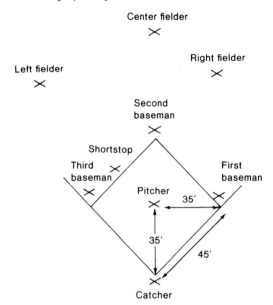

II. Batting order: Players are permitted to hit in any order; however, it is wise to have players bat according to their positions. Once an order is established, it cannot be changed, even if players change their positions.

III. The batter advances to first base when she:
   A. Hits a fair ball and reaches base before the ball does
   B. Is walked (receives four called balls)
   C. Is hit by a pitched ball
   D. Is interfered with by the catcher when batting

IV. The batter is out when he:
   A. Has three strikes
   B. Is thrown out at first
   C. Is tagged before reaching first base
   D. Hits a fair or foul ball that is caught on the fly
   E. Hits the third strike and the catcher catches the ball
   F. Bunts a foul on the third strike
   G. Throws the bat more than ten feet
   H. Steps on home plate when batting
   I. Interferes with the catcher when he is catching a fly or putting out a runner coming home
   J. Fouls any ball to the catcher that rises above the batter's head and is caught

V. When traveling the bases, the base runner:
   A. May advance to the next base after a fly is caught
   B. Must advance to the next base when forced to do so by another base runner
   C. May advance one base on an overthrow at first or third base
   D. May advance two bases when overthrows are in the field of play

TABLE 23.3   Softball Skill Test

Name	Accuracy Throw (total pts.)	Distance Throw (total pts.)	Fielding (total pts.)	Subjective Evaluation (50 pts.)	Total Score	Grade
1 2 3 4		Rank total scores for the class, then convert to letter grades or ratings (superior, good, etc.).				

E. May attempt to steal a base as soon as the ball leaves the pitcher's hand

F. May advance to the next base on a fair hit that is not caught on the fly

VI. The base runner is out when she:

A. Leaves the base before the ball leaves the pitcher's hand

B. Is forced to run to the next base and does not arrive before the fielder touches the base with the ball in his possession

C. Leaves the base before a fly ball is caught and a fielder tags him or that base before he returns

D. Is hit by a batted ball when off base

E. Intentionally interferes with a member of the fielding team

F. Is tagged when off base

G. Fails to touch a base and the fielder tags him or the base before he returns

H. Passes another base runner

I. Touches a base that is occupied by another base runner

VII. The pitcher:

A. Must stand with both feet on the rubber, face the batter, and hold the ball in front with both hands

B. Is allowed one step forward and must deliver the ball while taking that step

C. Must deliver the ball with an underhand throw

D. Cannot fake or make any motion toward the plate without delivering the ball

E. Cannot deliberately roll or bounce the ball

F. Cannot deliver the ball until the batter is ready

VIII. If there is an illegal pitch, the batter is entitled to take a base.

IX. The game is five to seven innings, as agreed by both teams. When there is not sufficient time to complete the game, the score reverts to the even innings score (the score after both squads have been up to bat the same number of times).

X. One point is scored each time a batter touches home base after touching each base sequentially.

E**VALUATIVE TECHNIQUES**

Several tests can be used to measure the basic softball skills. The following tests are quite reliable and can be administered with student help in a short period of time. Modify any test item to meet your own teaching situation and add items if desired. Also, keep scores from year to year in order to build appropriate norms for your school (table 23.3).

Test 1: Accuracy Throw

Place a target on the wall as shown in the diagram. Use a regulation softball. A player is given ten consecutive throws from behind the throwing line. She must use the overhand throw. Score six, four, and two for hits within each respective circle. If a ball hits a line, award the higher value. Allow only one trial and record the total score.

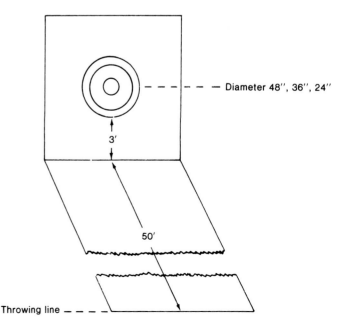

Test 2: Distance Throw

Place lines on the field as shown. Stakes can be used as a substitute for white gypsum lines. Use a regulation softball. Award points according to where the ball lands.

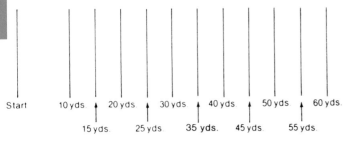

Start   10 yds.   20 yds.   30 yds.   40 yds.   50 yds.   60 yds.
   15 yds.   25 yds.   35 yds.   45 yds.   55 yds.

Test 3: Fielding

Place lines on a field as shown. Stakes or other "corner" markers can be substituted for lines. The teacher (or a student who is proficient at fungo batting) bats a grounder into the field area. As soon as the ball is batted, the player runs from the starting line, picks up the ball inside the field area, and throws it to the catcher. Ten trials are given, with five points awarded for each successfully fielded ball. Since it is difficult to hit grounders with reasonable consistency, use your discretion to allow retrials on any ball you feel was unfair to the contestant. Also, if batting skill is too poor, substitute a throw for the fungo batting.

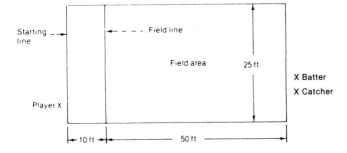

Starting line — Field line — Field area — 25 ft. — X Batter / X Catcher — Player X — 10 ft. — 50 ft.

Test 4: Subjective Evaluation

Establish criteria that represent the skills and playing ability required in softball. Since it is difficult to construct a fair and reliable test for batting, include this skill as part of your subjective evaluation. Consider other skills such as base running, catching, and team play. Award a total point score (zero to fifty points) and use three players as judges. Take an average of the three ratings.

Summary Review

The game of softball requires players to be knowledgeable about the rules of the game and to understand appropriate game-playing strategies. Players also need to be proficient in a number of specialized softball skills. These skills must be learned, as they do not develop automatically through growth and maturation. Individual practices, lead-up games, and mini-games that can be adjusted to create successful practice opportunities, as well as enjoyable game situations, become the basis for teaching children softball. The objective is to increase children's knowledge of softball and to help develop their softball skills toward the automatic stage of development. To develop specialized sport skills to the automatic stage requires many individual practices. Hence, children need to be provided with lots of developmentally appropriate practice opportunities. This will lead to successful softball skill development and enjoyment of the game. If this objective is achieved, then children will possess the knowledge, skills, and desire to continue playing this major game throughout their lives.

INDIVIDUAL and GROUP PROJECTS

1. Form groups of three. Each group member chooses a different softball skill. Design a lesson plan to teach your basic skill. Then teach one group member your softball skill while the third member observes the effectiveness of your instruction. Each group member takes a turn at being teacher, student, and observer. Observers might find useful the observational checklist for the evaluation of teaching, provided in Table 11.7 on page 247. When you have all taught your skills, discuss and evaluate your experiences in each role (teacher, student, observer), and suggest possible ways to improve your teaching.

2. In pairs, study the rules and regulations of softball. Then pose questions on the rules and regulations for each other to answer.

3. In chapter 4, it was suggested that one of the challenges facing teachers is the adjustment of the teaching environment to meet the developmental levels of the children. Four environmental variables under the teachers' control were identified:
   a. Rules
   b. Space
   c. Number of participants
   d. Amount or type of equipment

   One or more of these variables can be adjusted to create success on behalf of students. In small groups, discuss how these four variables can be adjusted when teaching children softball. Formulate creative ideas and specific recommendations and share these with other groups.

4. Chapter 13 identified a number of disabilities that afflict young children. In small groups, choose four disabilities and discuss how children with these disabilities can be integrated into softball activities. Consider what adjustments will have to made to accommodate each child's developmental level and to ensure success. Debate possible techniques and methods of evaluation. Share ideas with other groups.

5. A feature of this text is the idea of teaching and enhancing academic skills and concepts through physical education activities. In small groups, discuss and create ideas to teach and/or enhance academic skills and concepts through softball activities. Each group is then allocated a small selection of the softball practice activities and lead-up games. Create ideas for teaching or enhancing academic skills and concepts through these practice activities and lead-up games. Consider ways to evaluate students. Share ideas with other groups.

SELECTED READINGS

Athletic Institute. 1991. *Youth League baseball: Coaching and planning edition.* North Palm Beach, FL: Athletic Institute.

CAHPER. 1985. *Fastball-type games.* Ottawa, Ontario: CAHPER.

Elliott, J., and M. Ewing. 1991. *Youth softball: A complete handbook.* Dubuque, IA: Brown & Benchmark.

Houseworth, S. D., and F. V. Rivkin. 1985. *Coaching softball effectively.* Champaign, IL: Human Kinetics.

Kneer, M. E., and C. L. McCord. 1987. *Softball: slow and fast pitch.* Dubuque, IA: Wm. C. Brown.

Polter, D. L., and G. A. Breckmeyer. 1989. *Softball: Steps to success.* Champaign, IL: Leisure Press.

CHAPTER 24

Track and Field and Cross-Country Activities

KEY CONCEPTS

24.1 Specialized track and field skills are acquired through instruction and practice opportunities

24.2 Personal goal setting, and not competition between children, should form the basis of track and field and cross-country activities

24.3 Safety considerations must be emphasized when teaching children track and field activities

24.4 Track and field and cross-country activities must be developmentally appropriate to ensure that all children can achieve success and enjoyment

24.5 Effective teaching progressions, that provide all children with individual practices and lead-up activities, are required to develop the skills and knowledge associated with track and field and cross-country activities

24.6 To develop the specialized skills of track and field requires many practice opportunities

KEY OBJECTIVES

After completing this chapter you will be able to:

1. Design developmentally appropriate track and field and cross-country activities for elementary school children
2. Plan and organize teaching units and individual lessons in track and field and cross-country activities
3. Organize practice and lead-up activities that are appropriate for track and field and cross-country activities
4. Evaluate units, lessons, and individual techniques used in track and field and cross-country activities
6. Identify key teaching points associated with the basic skills of track and field and cross-country activities
7. Employ teaching progressions that lead to successful development of the skills and concepts associated with track and field and cross-country activities
8. Understand the rules and regulations of track and field and a variety of cross-country activities

Upper elementary school children have a keen interest in track and field activities. They can participate in these events according to their ability and motivation. Furthermore, track and field activities are relatively easy to teach, require little expense, and provide vigorous competitive experience for all children. The inherent values of this activity, coupled with the feasibility of modifying facilities, make it one that should be considered a basic requirement in the elementary physical education program.

This chapter describes the basic track and field events and cross-country activities, and presents some methods of organizing and teaching these activities. Special attention has been given to developing improvised equipment and planning track meets.

EMPHASIS AND PROGRESSION

Skill development in any of the official track and field events depends on the performer's potential or inherent ability and the amount and type of previous training. Taking these factors into consideration, the suggested sequence of skills shown in table 24.1 provides a rough guideline. In this type of activity, improvement in individual events is not simply the accumulation of new skills; it is the sequential addition of skills plus improvement in form and general conditioning.

CONCEPT

24.1 Specialized Track and Field Skills are Acquired through Instruction and Practice Opportunities

The early phase of developmental level II is an important starting point for many track and field skills. These children should be introduced to correct starting positions, sprints, and distance running. They also should develop reasonable skill in the standing and running long jumps, as well as the high jump using the scissors method.

TABLE 24.1 Suggested Sequence of Presenting Track and Field Skills and Rules

Skills and Rules	Developmental Level II	Developmental Level III
For distance runs	Introduce	Refine
For sprints	Introduce	Refine
Rules: False start	Introduce	
Running		
Sprints	40- to 60-yard dashes	50- to 80-yard dashes
Relay running		Introduce
Hurdling		Introduce
Distance running	500- to 600-yard run	Increase distance and speed
Jogging	1 to 2 miles	1 to 3 miles
Rules: Lane position		Introduce
Passing rule		Introduce
High jumping		
Scissors method	Introduce	Increase height and form
Straddle method		Introduce
Rules: Number of jumps	Introduce	
Long jumping		
Standing long jump	Introduce	Increase distance and form
Long jump	Introduce	Increase distance and form
Rules: Foot fault	Introduce	
Triple jump		
Rules: Foot fault		Introduce
Shot put		
Rules: Foot fault		Introduce
Other rules		
General track meet rules	Introduce	

TABLE 24.2	Proficiency Levels for Track and Field (Combined Scores for Girls and Boys)						

| | **Minimum to Optimum Records** | | | | | | |
| | **Age 9** | | **Age 10** | | **Age 11** | | **Age 12** | |
Events	**Low**	**High**	**Low**	**High**	**Low**	**High**	**Low**	**High**
50-yard dash (sec)	11.0	7.0	10.0	6.0	9.5	6.0	9.0	6.0
220-yard run (sec)	43.0	33.0	42.0	31.0	40.0	32.5	38.0	30.5
150-yard run (sec)	29.0	23.0	27.0	22.0	25.0	19.1	23.0	18.2
High jump	2′7″	3′	2′11″	3′4″	3′0″	3′10″	3′6″	4′2″
Standing long jump	3′7″	6′4″	4′0″	6′4″	4′8″	6′8″	4′10″	6′11″
Running long jump	10′5″	11′8″	11′0″	12′2″	12′0″	13′2″	13′0″	14′2″
Triple Jump	11′6″	14′3″	12′	15′	13′	16′	14′	17′
Softball throw	35′	165′	45′	175′	70′	205′	76′	207′
Shot put	8′6″	13′	9′	15′	10′	16′	12′	17′

Most of the remaining track and field skills are introduced in developmental level III. These youngsters are interested in and capable of learning baton passing, hurdling, high jumping using the straddle method, putting the shot, and triple jumping. They display a major increase in skill and performance levels in track and field events.

EXPECTED PROFICIENCIES

Proficiency in track and field events is measured in time or distance; table 24.2 provides a rough estimate of what can be expected of elementary school children. If teachers are introducing track and field activities similar to those listed, it is wise to establish school records. Use the suggested high and low records as a guide in establishing "expected" performance standards for your school. Personal goal setting should be used to motivate children (see chapter 4) in track and field and cross-country activities. Competing to beat personal standards helps to deemphasize competition between children.

C O N C E P T

24.2 *Personal Goal Setting, and Not Competition between Children, should Form the Basis of Track and Field and Cross-Country Activities*

TEACHING PROCEDURES

Several important factors must be considered when planning a track and field unit. Although it is important for all children to experience the enjoyment and challenge of all the events, they should be allowed to concentrate on a few events that they enjoy and do well. This means the teacher should introduce the children early to as many track and field events as possible. Each child can then select a certain number of events for more extensive practice.

A second major consideration is how to cope with available space and equipment. Because there is never enough equipment for all children to practice the same event at the same time, station work should be used. The track and field circuit provides a basic guideline.

It is important to locate each event in a relatively permanent place on the field. Jumping pits are normally in the corners of the field. A temporary track can be made by placing traffic cones or milk cartons filled with sand or earth in an oval pattern. Placing the shot-put circles inside the oval provides a safe, restricted area for this event. Sprints and hurdles can be located near each other for dual-instruction purposes.

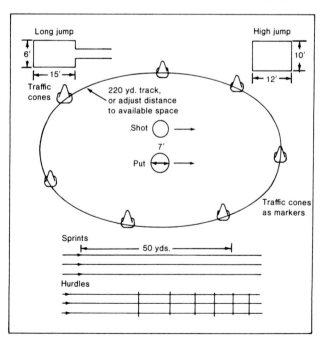

Track and Field Circuit

C O N C E P T

24.3 *Safety Considerations Must Be Emphasized When Teaching Children Track and Field Activities*

Once the general layout is established, the teacher can divide the class into squads and assign each to a station. Give brief demonstrations at each station, then allow time for practice before the squads are rotated to the next station. Rotation should alternate track events and field events.

The following general considerations and safety procedures should be included in every track and field unit of instruction.

1. All facilities and equipment should be checked before the class begins. In particular, look for broken glass or other hazardous materials in jumping pits and field areas.
2. Each lesson should begin with a comprehensive warm-up or conditioning period involving running, jogging, and conditioning exercises designed to increase strength, endurance, and flexibility.
3. Whenever possible, provide instruction to mixed groups rather than separating boys and girls. The difference in performance levels of girls and boys at this age is more often due to motivation and prior experience than to physiological differences.
4. Require all children to wear tennis or running shoes. Do not allow any child to participate in bare feet or with spiked track shoes.
5. Provide special considerations and support for children with weight problems. This includes setting realistic goals and providing ongoing support, especially to children who are excessively overweight.
6. Provide special consideration and events for children with disabilities.

C O N C E P T

24.4 *Track and Field and Cross-Country Activities Must Be Developmentally Appropriate to Ensure that All Children Can Achieve Success and Enjoyment*

DESCRIPTION OF SKILLS

There are two basic types of events in track and field: (1) running events, which include sprints, hurdles, and longer endurance runs, and (2) field events, which include the high jump, long jump, triple jump, and shot put. These skills should be taught to all students regardless of their inherent ability. Once the children have been exposed to these skills, allow them to select and concentrate on the events that are best suited to their potential capabilities.

Figure 24.1 Standing start. Body leans forward slightly.

C O N C E P T

24.5 *Effective Teaching Progressions, that Provide All Children with Individual Practices and Lead-Up Activities, are Required to Develop the Skills and Knowledge Associated with Track and Field and Cross-Country Activities*

Starting

The starting position for running events is determined by the length of the race. For short races, such as twenty- and thirty-yard dashes, the "kneeling start" or "sprint start" is best. For longer races, the "standing start" is more acceptable.

Standing Start

In the standing start (figure 24.1), one foot is close to the starting line and the other foot is slightly to the rear. The head is up, the trunk is bent forward, the knees are slightly flexed, and the weight is on the front foot. The opposite arm to the lead foot is held forward, with the elbow flexed, while the other arm is down and slightly back.

Sprint Start

The sprint start is important to the success of any beginning sprinter. The form and techniques of this skill are quite easy to master, even for fourth graders.

On the "on your mark" command, the runner kneels and places the toe of his front foot six to twelve inches behind the starting line (figure 24.2a). The front foot is normally the opposite foot to the "kicking foot." He extends his arms straight down, with the weight on the fingertips. (If children do not have adequate arm and shoulder girdle strength, allow them to support their weight on their knuckles.) The runner squeezes his fingers together to make a "bridge" with the thumb. On "set" he raises his lower knee and buttocks until his back is straight and parallel to

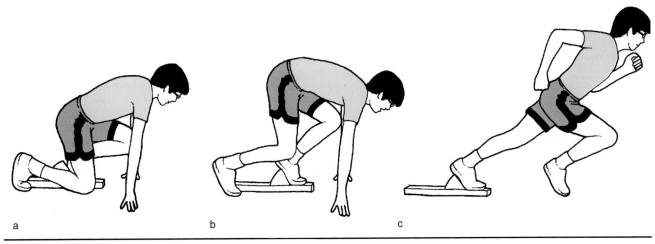

Figure 24.2 Sprint start.

Figure 24.3 Sprinting form.

Figure 24.4 Distance running form.

the ground (figure 24.2b). His weight should be evenly distributed between his hands and his front foot. His head is not raised, as he should be looking at a spot on the ground a few feet in front of the starting line. On "go" he drives forward with his lead leg and, at the same instant, brings his rear leg forward (figure 24.2c).

Key Teaching Points
1. At the starting position, keep head looking at a spot a few feet in front of the hands.
2. Teach children to react to a starting signal rather than trying to anticipate it.
3. Keep body low and exaggerate forward lean during the first steps off the mark.

Running

There are several types of running positions, each with its own body lean, arm action, and foot contact. The elementary school track program, however, involves only two

types, sprinting form and distance running form. In the sprinting form (figure 24.3), the runner's body leans well forward and contact is made with the ball or front of the foot. The arms are bent at the elbows and swing vigorously from the shoulders. In distance running (figure 24.4), the body is more erect and the weight is taken on the heel, then rocked forward. The elbows are bent slightly and the arm action is less vigorous than in sprinting.

Key Teaching Points
Teach runners to run in a straight line—arms straight forward and backward.

Relay Running

There are two types of baton passes. The visual pass allows the receiver to look back at the moment of the pass. The blind pass requires the receiver to keep looking straight ahead as she receives the baton. Although the visual pass is slower, it is recommended for elementary school children.

CHAPTER 24

Figure 24.5 Relay receiver forms a V.

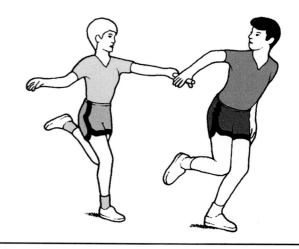

Figure 24.6 Passing the baton upward into the hand.

Visual Pass

The runner who is to receive the baton draws her right hand straight back toward the approaching runner. She holds her fingers together, pointing to the side, while she points her thumb toward her body. This forms a V into which the approaching runner places the baton (figure 24.5). The approaching runner brings the baton up into the receiving runner's hand (figure 24.6). As soon as the front runner receives the baton, she brings it forward into her left hand in preparation for the next pass.

When students are ready to practice baton passing at full speed, it is important that they establish their own check marks—when they should start to run. As a general rule, have the runner place a mark on the ground five yards back of his starting point.

The incoming runner starts fifty yards back of the passing zone and runs as fast as possible. When he passes the check mark, the outgoing runner turns and runs as fast as possible. When the outgoing runner reaches the passing zone, he puts his hand back for the baton. He must be inside the passing zone before he receives the baton or his team is disqualified. If the incoming runner cannot catch up to the outgoing runner, the check mark should be moved closer to the outgoing runner's starting point. If the incoming runner runs past the outgoing runner, the check mark should be moved farther back from the outgoing runner's starting point.

Key Teaching Points

1. As the runner with the baton gets close to the exchange zone, the baton should be in his left hand.
2. Receiver should have his right hand back as he begins to run in the exchange zone.
3. Receiver looks back to make sure the baton is placed in his extended right hand.

Standing Long Jump

The performer stands with his toes just behind the starting line, his feet comfortably spread, his knees bent, and his trunk well forward (figure 24.7a). After several preliminary swings with the arms, he swings his arms forward and upward vigorously and extends his legs. As soon as his feet leave the ground, he begins to flex his knees, keeping his arms forward (figure 24.7b). He lands with his feet parallel and his trunk and arms extended forward (figure 24.7c).

Key Teaching Points

1. In the starting position, the weight is well forward in an almost overbalanced position.
2. Simultaneously push off from both feet and swing arms forward and upward.
3. Flex at the waist as the arms move forward and upward.

Long Jump

A successful long jumper must be able to combine jumping and speed. Elementary school children have sufficient speed for this event and can execute the approach flight and landing relatively well. The performer begins several yards back from the takeoff board, runs forward, and places her takeoff foot on the board

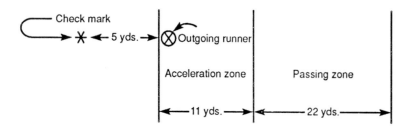

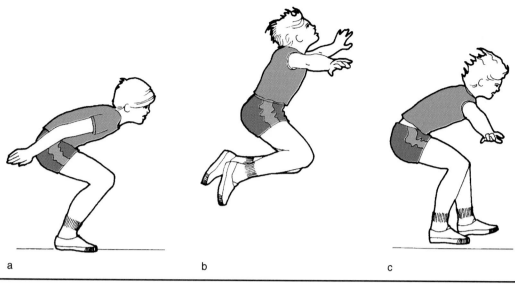

Figure 24.7 Standing long jump.

Figure 24.8 Long jump.

(figure 24.8a). As soon as she leaves the board, she brings her rear leg and both arms forward and upward (figure 24.8b). Her heels contact the ground and she immediately thrusts both arms back (figure 24.8c), forcing her body well forward.

An effective technique to help students gain height in the jump is to suspend a hat from a crossbar or on the end of a rope attached to a stick (figure 24.9). The height of the hat should be adjusted so that the student jumps to maximum height in order to put the hat on his head. The distance from the takeoff point varies, but it should be a little more than half of the total jump.

Key Teaching Points
1. Have each child pace out the correct number of strides, then practice the approach until the takeoff becomes consistent.
2. After the takeoff, keep head up and reach upward and forward.
3. Vigorously thrust arms backward upon landing.

Hurdles

Elementary school children can run the hurdles with speed and efficiency. The main reason they usually do not learn the proper form is because the hurdles are set too high, too far apart, or both.

When the runner is approximately seven feet from the hurdle, she lifts her lead leg and extends it forward (figure 24.10a). The arm opposite to the lead leg should also extend forward (figure 24.10b). She continues moving her lead leg forward and upward until it clears the hurdle. The rear leg then starts forward, with the toes turned up. Note the impor-

tant forward body lean as the runner prepares for the next stage. She draws her lead leg down and thrusts her trailing leg forward (figure 24.10c). Throughout this whole movement, the shoulders should be parallel to the finish line.

The following stages should be followed when introducing hurdles:

1. Begin by having the children sprint about twenty-five yards.
2. Place an obstacle (a cane or an old broom handle) on the ground approximately halfway or between thirty to forty-five feet from the starting line. Again, the children sprint the full length; however, they should make no attempt to hurdle the obstacle.
3. Place a second obstacle on the ground so that it is midway between the third and fourth strides (figure 24.11). The teacher can check whether runners are taking the correct three strides between hurdles by observing if they are taking very short steps (usually five) or if they land on a different foot after each hurdle (usually four steps). In order to assist the runner in developing the three-step sequence between hurdles, set up numerous courses (see diagram) so that each runner can select the one that fits his step pattern.

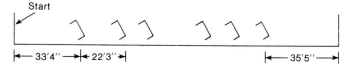

Figure 24.9 Technique for gaining height.

4. The obstacles should now be raised nine to twelve inches. If adjustable hurdles are unavailable, use shoe boxes, bricks, wooden blocks, or small stands. A cane or rope can be placed on top of these materials as the object to hurdle over. Using a rope, secured by beanbags to hold it in place, allows easy adjustment of

a   b   c

Figure 24.10 Jumping hurdles.

| **T**ABLE 24.3 | Recommended Competitive Hurdles (12 and Under)* | | | | |

Height of Hurdles	Number of Hurdles	Start to First Hurdle	Between Hurdles	Last Hurdle to Finish Line	Total Distance
20″ to 30″	6	33′4″	22′3″	35′5″	60 yards

*Adjust the height of the hurdle to meet the performer's level of ability

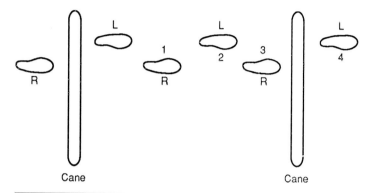

Figure 24.11 Introducing hurdles.

the rope height to raise or lower it to the developmental level of the hurdler. Beanbags allow the rope to easily pull away if the child fails to clear the height. Let the children practice and then gradually raise the hurdle height to thirty inches. When the obstacle approaches twenty-four inches, the children should be taught what to do with the trailing leg. Have them walk down beside the hurdle. As they approach it, have them step in front and slightly to the side of the hurdle with their lead leg and then take the trailing leg over the hurdle. The thigh of the trailing leg should be parallel to the top of the hurdle; then it should be brought through quickly into the next stride. Once the correct technique is acquired, the children should jog down beside the hurdles doing the same drill. Finally, have them run from the starting position and hurdle in the center of each hurdle (table 24.3).

Key Teaching Points
1. The takeoff must be between five and seven feet from the hurdle. The actual distance depends on the child's size and strength. This seems like a long way when standing and looking at it, but it is very easy to negotiate the hurdle from this distance when in motion.
2. Take off from the ball of one foot and land on the opposite foot.
3. Bring the knee of the lead leg up quickly toward the hurdle.

4. Bring the lead leg down quickly. Snap the trailing leg through quickly into the next running stride.
5. Keep shoulders parallel to the finish line throughout the whole movement.
6. Keep the same number of strides between each hurdle and lead with the same foot.

High Jump

Two types of jumping styles are described here. The "scissors style" is the easier of the two and should be learned first. The "straddle roll," although more difficult to learn, is the better of the two in terms of heights that can be reached. Regardless of the method taught, it is imperative that a good landing surface be provided. Children will not learn to jump correctly if they are afraid to land in the pit. Although foam rubber is more acceptable, shavings or an improvised rubber tube pit provide a satisfactory landing surface.

A very inexpensive jumping pit can be constructed by using discarded automobile tire inner tubes. Place tubes on the ground, as shown in appendix B, and tie them together. Then place a tumbling mat on top of the tubes. This provides a safe and comfortable landing surface that can be used both indoors and outdoors.

Scissors Method

The jumper approaches from the left at a slight angle to the bar—15 to 20 degrees (figure 24.12a). He takes a few steps, plants his right ("takeoff") foot, then swings his left foot high into the air. The left leg continues over the bar (figure 24.12b), followed by the right in a scissors action. At the same time, the arms swing forward and upward, assisting the upward lift of the body (figure 24.12c). The left foot lands first, followed by the right, completing the scissors action.

Key Teaching Points
1. Practice the run of the approach until the takeoff foot hits the same spot every time.
2. Stress a vigorous upward thrust of the front leg and both arms.
3. Land on the lead foot.

a   b   c

Figure 24.12 High jump—scissors style.

a   b   c   d

Figure 24.13 Straddle roll.

Straddle Method

Proper technique must be stressed when introducing this method of jumping. Poor technique leads to little or no improvement and a disillusioned jumper. The jumper approaches from the left side approximately 45 degrees to the bar. He takes a few steps, plants his left ("takeoff") foot, swings his right leg forward and upward, and raises his arms (figure 24.13a). He continues the upward and forward movement, extending his body and lifting his leg upward (figure 24.13b). At the height of the jump, his body is parallel to the bar (figure 24.13c). He continues "rolling" over the bar, landing on his hands and right leg (figure 24.13d).

Key Teaching Points

1. Practice the run of the approach until the takeoff foot hits the same spot every time.
2. Make sure the last three steps are fast, with the body leaning slightly backward.
3. At the top of the jump, the jumper should "lay out" and roll across the top of the bar with a twist of the body.

a. Hop right   b. Land right   c. Step left   d. Jump

Figure 24.14 Hop, step, and jump.

Triple Jump: Hop, Step, and Jump

This event is a very popular event among boys and girls alike. The appeal seems to be both the distance that is traveled and the immediate improvement once the proper techniques are learned. The runner starts thirty to forty yards back to gain maximum speed at the takeoff mark. The first stage is a hop on the right foot from the takeoff board (figure 24.14a). To maintain forward speed, the hop is kept low. The left leg drives forward and the jumper lands on her right foot (figure 24.14b). She continues forward with a thrust of the left leg (figure 24.14c), lands on the heel of her left foot, and rocks forward toward the toe. She continues the forward action by pushing off from her left foot (figure 24.14d) and landing on both feet in the pit.

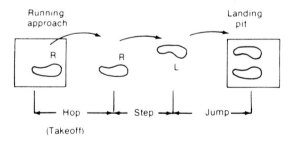

Key Teaching Points
1. Have each child pace out the correct number of steps, then practice the approach until the takeoff foot hits the board every time.
2. Keep the hop low and, upon landing on the right foot, drive the left leg forward.
3. Continue forward thrust of left leg and land on heel of the left foot.
4. Immediately following the step, reach forward and upward.

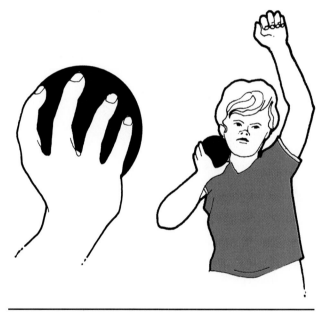

Figure 24.15 Holding the shot.

Shot Put

The six-pound shot put event has proved to be an extremely safe and enjoyable activity for boys and girls in the upper elementary school. The performer stands near the back of the circle, with his weight on his right leg and his left toe touching the ground. He holds the shot in a "cradled" position on the side of his neck (figure 24.15). He extends his left arm upward for balance (figure 24.16a). He then lowers his trunk over his right leg and raises his left leg upward and toward the front of the circle (figure 24.16b). In a simulta-

a. Weight on right foot   b. Lower trunk   c. Shift forward   d. Push shot off fingertips

Figure 24.16 Putting the shot.

neous action, he drives his right leg toward the front of the circle and shifts his left leg in the same direction. Throughout this shifting movement, the body should be kept low (figure 24.16c). At the end of this shifting movement, he begins to extend his right leg upward, rotates his trunk toward the front, and extends his right arm forward and upward. The shot is released with a final push off the fingertips (figure 24.16d). The body continues to move around to the left side.

To construct a throwing area for shot putting, take a piece of rope approximately five feet long and tape the ends. Drive two nails through the rope exactly three and a half feet apart. Hold one nail stationary and scribe an arc with the other end.

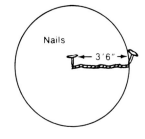

Nails

←— 3'6" —→

Key Teaching Points
1. Learn to push, rather than throw, the shot.
2. Begin near the back of the circle, flex the knee, and lower the body.
3. Once in the lowered position, immediately thrust the left leg forward and upward and shift the right leg in the same direction.
4. Keep low through the shifting movement.
5. Rotate and extend the body, then push the shot off the fingertips toward the landing area.

PRACTICE ACTIVITIES

Track and field skills require a great deal of individual attention by the teacher and extensive practice by the student. The following practice activities should be used throughout the track and field unit to supplement individualized instruction and to encourage a competitive spirit among all members of the class.

CONCEPT

24.6 *To Develop the Specialized Skills of Track and Field Requires Many Practice Opportunities*

■ Continuous Running

A set distance is established. For example, the children could be asked to run one mile on the track or to run from the school to a point one mile away. Each child runs as far as he can, then walks the rest of the mile. With practice, the children should gradually increase the distance they run. Enjoyable courses can be set up on the school ground or in a nearby park or wilderness area.

■ Interval Training

This is the most commonly used training method among track and field athletes. This form of training has three components: (1) the distance covered on each interval, (2) the recovery period between intervals, and (3) the number of repetitions performed. The following example illustrates this form of training.

A group of children are training for a 440-yard race. The best time for the group is seventy seconds. Since the length of the interval is 220 yards, the time is reduced to thirty-five seconds expected for each 220-yard run. Each child attempts to run the first 220 yards within thirty-five seconds, rests or walks for three minutes, then attempts to run the next 220 yards within thirty-five seconds. This procedure continues to the end of the fifth 220-yard run. When a runner can complete the five 220-yard runs in the time allotment, the training can be increased in three different ways: (1) reduce the running time, (2) reduce the recovery period, or (3) require more repetitions (increase to six or seven 220-yard runs).

■ Walk, Jog, Run

Make a small track out of traffic cones or any other type of markers. Teach the children the difference between walking, jogging, and running. A jog is about half speed and a run is full speed. To start, students are allowed to walk at their own speed around the markers. The first blow of the whistle means that everyone jogs. The second blow means that everyone runs at top speed. The third blow means that everyone jogs, and the fourth blow means everyone walks. Continue this sequence.

Teaching Suggestions
At the beginning of the unit, allow more time between the walk and jog phases and short periods at top speed. Gradually increase the time at full speed.

Start and Pass

Arrange class into a line formation, with six to eight on each team. Put half the team behind each of two starting lines twenty-five feet apart. This is essentially a starting drill. The teacher should use the following commands: "Take your marks," "Set," and "Go," or blow a whistle. On the whistle, two runners on each team behind opposite lines make fast starts and run until they pass each other. At the passing point, each player slows to a walk and goes to the rear of the line.

Teaching Suggestions
1. Each player runs all the way over the opposite line, then slows down to a walk back to the rear of the line.
2. Use standing and kneeling starts.

Call Race

Arrange two teams of five to ten runners on a starting line. Draw a turning line thirty feet in front of the starting line. Line up each team along the starting line. Number the players on each team. The teacher calls out any number, such as "four." Both number four players run to the turning line and back across the starting line. Continue calling numbers at random until all runners have had a turn.

Teaching Suggestions
Call out "Take your mark," "Set," and then the number. Only players whose numbers are called should run. The remaining players stand up and wait. This is an excellent starting drill.

Number of Jumps

Arrange class in a long line formation, with the children's toes touching the starting line. Draw a finish line twenty to thirty feet in front of the starting line. Each child begins on the starting line and makes a standing broad jump as far as possible. Her subsequent jumps start from where her heels touched. The object is to see who can make it across the finish line in the fewest number of jumps.

Teaching Suggestions
Use partners to mark landing positions and to count jumps.

Over the Rope

Arrange teams of five to eight in a line formation, facing a mat. This high-jumping activity can be used outside on grass or indoors on mats. Two players hold a long skipping rope at various heights while the remainder of the squad practices the scissors or straddle roll over the rope.

Baton Passing

The class is divided into groups of four to eight runners placed in a single line approximately four feet apart as shown in the diagram. From a stationary position, the children start passing the baton from the end of each line. The first runner passes with his left hand to the runner in front, who takes the baton in his right hand. He immediately brings it forward into his left hand in preparation for the next pass. The baton should be brought up into the receiving runner's right hand. When the baton reaches the front of the line, everyone turns around and the drill is repeated.

After the students have the feel of passing the baton in a stationary position, have them do it in a slow jog. Therefore, the distance between runners will have to be increased. Repeat the drill, gradually increasing the speed and the distance between runners.

TRACK AND FIELD MEET RULES AND REGULATIONS

The organization and general rules and regulations of any elementary school track and field meet will depend on the children's general interest, the available time, and the facilities. The following information, although not complete, will assist in developing the facilities, meet rules, and order of events for most elementary school track meets.

I. Track dimensions: The 220-yard running track illustrated in figure 24.17 can be constructed on most outdoor playing areas.

II. High jump pit: The pit should be twelve feet long and ten feet wide. Sawdust or shavings should be used to fill the pit, which should be boarded with straw bales. (Also see appendix B for an improvised pit constructed of rubber tubes.)

X Baton ──────→	X ──────→	X ──────→	X ──────→	X
Pass with left	Take with right and pass with left			
X Baton	X	X	X	X
X Baton	X	X	X	X
X Baton	X	X	X	X

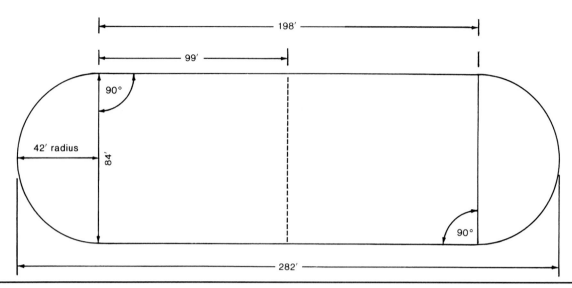

Figure 24.17 Plan for a 220-yard running track.

III. Long jump pit: The runway to the pit should be approximately thirty yards long, with an eight-inch takeoff mark five feet from the pit. The pit should be ten feet wide and twenty feet long. It should be filled with fine sand.

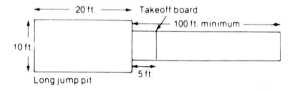

IV. Order and number of events: Each school may vary the length of dashes and include additional events. The following order of events should provide a format for scheduling:

A. 50-yard dash
B. Shot put
C. Standing long jump
D. Long jump
E. 220-yard relay
F. High jump
G. 220-yard run
H. Triple jump
I. Softball throw
J. Hurdles
K. Obstacle race
L. Tug-of-war

V. Track and field officials: The following jobs should be allocated to teachers or dependable students:
A. Meet director
B. Starters, same for all track events
C. Finish judges—head finish judge, first-, second-, and third-place judges, and additional place judges, if desired
D. Field judges—one judge and one helper for the high jump, standing long jump, triple jump, and running long jump
E. Announcer and head recorder with assistants for running messages and obtaining results of the events

VI. Meet requirements: Each school should establish its own eligibility requirements for the following situations:
A. Number of events each participant may enter. For example, perhaps each child could enter two track events and one field event.
B. Classification of participants. Several methods can be used to classify participants such as age, grade, or a classification index.
C. Number of places and point awards. For example, the first four places could be recorded with five, four, three, and two points, respectively.

Many other questions need to be answered if the track meet is to be successful. Give some thought to types of awards, methods of keeping school records, and required practice before a participant is eligible for the track and field meet. Once you and the students agree on the basic rules and regulations of the track meet, take time to explain them to the students and post rules in the classroom and gymnasium.

Novelty Track and Field Meet

A novelty or mock track and field day is composed of a variety of enjoyable novelty events. This type of special day provides an avenue for young and older children to work together, and to emphasize fun and cooperation, rather than competing in traditional track and field events.

In the Novelty Track Meet chart, the meet begins with all children of each house participating in a round robin tug-of-war, followed by each house dividing into four groups of mixed partners (one primary level child with one intermediate level child). This provides an opportunity for young children to participate with older children in a fun-type activity. After this event, boys and girls from each

Novelty Track Meet

Begin: Tug-of-War. Primary and intermediate children of each house all pull on the same rope.

Mixed Partner Activities: One primary and one intermediate child
Partners rotate through: 1. 3-legged race—partners with tied ankles
2. Egg and spoon race—partners hold hands with primary child holding spoon and egg
3. Partner ball toss—partners stand behind a line, hold inside hands and the ball. Five joint throws into the basket.

Primary Children *Individual Activities*	**Intermediate Children** *Individual Activities*
Groups of three children per house rotate through: 1. Sack race—12 per heat 2. Obstacle race—6 courses 3. Chin pass relay—12 per heat 4. Chair ring toss—4 chairs and 12 quoits	Groups of three children per house rotate through: 1. Nerf shot put 2. Frisbee throw 3. Obstacle race 4. Juggle a number

Final Event: Slow-Motion Bicycle Race
1. Primary children's bicycle race
2. Intermediate children's bicycle race

house separate into primary and intermediate groups, then rotate through four individual activities. The final slow motion bicycle race brings all children back to their four houses. Primary children from each house first compete in a slow-motion bicycle race, followed by a similar race among intermediate children.

The events in the novelty track meet are provided as sample events. Since the underlying purpose is fun and cooperation, design a scoring system that will reflect this goal—lots of points for participation and sportsmanship. One final suggestion: station a parent or teacher at four locations in the general playing area. Whenever one of these observers notices something special, such as good sportsmanship or a special effort on the part of an individual or team to cooperate, the observer blows a horn or whistle and awards the player(s) with bonus points for their house. This special award mechanism can also be used, in a subtle way, to keep the running house scores fairly even. It is also an effective means of rewarding disabled children for their efforts as participants or meet helpers.

CROSS-COUNTRY ACTIVITIES

The following cross-country activities may be taught as part of a track and field unit or as separate events throughout the school year.

Hash Running

Hash running is a team race in which markers are located along the route, hidden directions are located near the

markers, and a total team effort is required in order to finish the race in the shortest period of time. The following example provides a basic format that can be used in any rural or urban school.

Before the class arrives for physical education, set up your "hash course." In the sample course, the starting position is in front of the school. Each team (the size is optional) starts here (stagger the starting times) and is told it will find the first marker—a red ribbon placed on a goalpost—within fifty yards of the starting position. As soon as the marker is found by any member of the team, she calls to her teammates and they all come to the marker. They know that the first hidden directions will be somewhere within fifty yards (keep this distance constant) of the marker. The teammates move in different directions until one finds the directions, located on the school wall. This pattern continues throughout the course. The team that returns in the

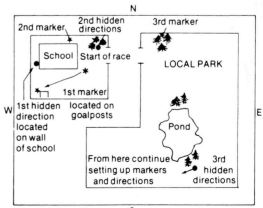

TABLE 24.4   Word Description Chart

Name: John Smith

Time allowed: 10 minutes
Start time:
Finish time:
Penalty points: (at 5 points a minute)

No.	Description of Landmark (Checkpoint)	Value	Insert Code Letter
1	On the east end of softball backstop	15	T
2	On the north side of flower garden	10	B
3	On the south goalpost of field B	5	C
4	On the northwest side of an old stump	10	F
5	On the northeast end of the softball stands	15	R
6	On the bench near three pine trees	15	U
7	On the southwest side of field A	10	A
8	On the west corner of statue	25	Y

Total points _____
Penalty points _____
Final score _____

shortest time wins the race. Following are some considerations in hash running:

1. Since most physical education periods last approximately thirty minutes, begin with three or four markers, then increase the number and difficulty as experience dictates.
2. Make a rule that markers must be located before the directions, because some children may find directions first.
3. Although teams are staggered, one team may catch up to another and "give away" vital information. Encourage teams to make up diversionary signals if this occurs.
4. If you have taught orienteering and compass directions, use these skills in hash running.
5. Since schools in urban areas have problems with traffic and restrictive park areas, take care in planning hash courses to ensure the children's safety and the protection of public gardens.

Score Orienteering

Each player is given a hand-drawn map of the area, including all necessary landmarks—buildings, statues, trees, paths, and so on. Figure 24.18 shows a school and the immediate major landmarks. Each player is also given a "word description chart." Note in table 24.4 that each description is simple, and that the farthest sites are awarded the highest points. Players leave the starting point at a designated time and, with the aid of their maps and charts, try to find the various landmarks or checkpoints.

General Procedure and Instructions

Each student writes her name on her chart and leaves everything else blank. Four or five runners leave the starting

point at the same time; to avoid congestion, allow thirty seconds between groups. The teacher marks the starting time on each chart, and the runners have ten minutes (or whatever time the teacher sets) to go to as many checkpoints as possible before returning to the recorder's desk. The teacher has placed a code letter on each landmark, or checkpoint, before the orienteering lesson and, when a runner arrives at the checkpoint, he places that code letter in the appropriate space on the recording sheet. Runners may choose their own order of reaching checkpoints. A runner is penalized five points for each minute she exceeds the ten-minute time limit.

Teaching Suggestions

Competitions can be developed on the basis of one type of landmark such as trees, flowers, or buildings. If a school is near a park or wilderness area, the possibilities are almost unlimited. Also, the addition of compasses and authentic maps of the area open the door to an enjoyable and constructive recreational pursuit. Finally, if a teacher is not skillful at reading a compass or a geographical map, she can find many people in the community, such as scout leaders and surveyors, more than willing to donate their services.

Cross-Country Running

Cross-country or long-distance running activities for elementary school children must be based on sound medical evidence and good training principles. A brief review of the medical evidence, along with statements made by qualified experts, provides a basis for selecting appropriate long-distance running activities for children in the primary and intermediate grades. Proper jogging form and appropriate cross-country activities are also described for a variety of instructional and extraclass programs.

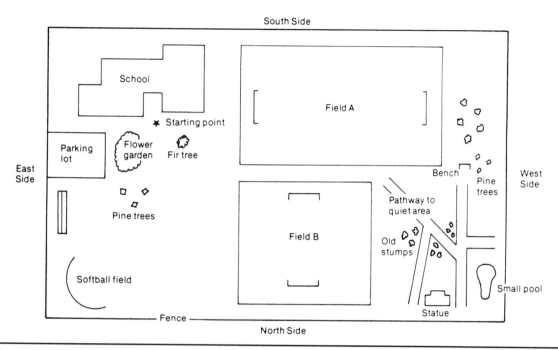

South Side

East Side

West Side

North Side

Figure 24.18 Map of the area.

Physical and Psychological Effects

According to the American Academy of Pediatrics, medical evidence of injury to children running long distances is limited and largely anecdotal (American Academy of Pediatrics 1982). The main concern about long-distance running and children relates to the immediate and long-term physiological and psychological effects of this activity. Physiologically, there is general concern about possible damage to the epiphyseal or growth plates at the ends of long bones. Other considerations relate to overtaxing the heart and respiratory systems and to damaging the tendons of the knees and ankles. Long-distance runs, such as ten to fifteen kilometers, under extreme competitive pressure and high temperatures may cause children to overextend themselves (Olson 1982). With respect to psychological effects, the evidence is still very limited. The main concern expressed by psychologists, parents, and educators is the undue stress to win and the negative aftereffects on the loser. Also, long-distance running or racing is not seen by most children as an inherently enjoyable activity. Children, if given the opportunity, would rather play a game than train for long hours in an activity that is essentially void of fun and social interaction.

The conclusion to be drawn from scientific evidence is that long-distance competitive running events primarily designed for adults are not recommended for children prior to physical maturation (American Academy of Pediatrics 1982). This does not mean that elementary school children do not enjoy or need to participate in recreational running activities such as cross-country running, hash running, or orienteering events. The following activities are

designed to provide fun and variety in a very beneficial form of physical activity.

Running Activities

Cross-country running is a recreational run through a course marked on the school grounds or adjacent park area. The length of the course will depend on the age and condition of the participants and the type of terrain (blacktop, grass, etc.). The following chart provides a rough guideline for upper primary and intermediate grades.

Age	Distance
8–9	1 to 1-1/2 miles
10–11	1 to 2 miles
12–13	1–1/2 to 3 miles

Prior to puberty there are essentially no major physiological reasons boys and girls cannot run, jump, or do any other physical activity with equal ability. Hence, set the same standards for both sexes. If girls are slower, the reasons are attributed to social or cultural factors. With time and equal opportunities, girls perform as well, and at times, better than boys of similar ages.

Cross-country running requires good training methods and lots of variety in the course. The following suggestions and activities help make this activity fun for all participants.

1. Teach children the proper long-distance form of running.

2. Begin this program with such activities as interval training or walk, jog, run.

3. Organize cross-country activities for partners. Children normally pair up on the basis of friendship and ability.

4. Provide variety in cross-country activities by introducing the following tasks while the children are running:

   a. Dribbling and passing a ball
   b. Skipping
   c. Balancing an object
   d. Maneuvering over obstacle courses
   e. Running a certain distance, then hopping, jumping, or performing any other skill for a set number of repetitions, then running again

Guidelines for Long-Distance Running

The following suggestions help establish an enjoyable, beneficial, and educationally sound long-distance running program for elementary school children.

1. Run with arms relaxed—elbows bent—and swinging in a slight arc across the body. The hands should not cross the center line of the body.

2. Tilt hips slightly backward to flatten the curve of the lower back.

3. Land on the heel and rock forward and off the front of the foot. Bouncing is caused by pushing up on the toes and thus should be eliminated.

4. Knees should be bent on landing.

5. Breathing should be relaxed, emphasizing the exhale phase to ensure an adequate exchange of air.

6. Wear proper shoes. Shoes that are too short or too long are damaging to the runner's feet.

7. Cool down after long runs with walking and stretching exercises.

EVALUATIVE TECHNIQUES

Although performance in track and field and cross-country events appears to be easy to evaluate, quite the contrary is true. Each event is scored on the basis of either distance or time. The problem lies in placing a value on improvement rather than merely awarding an arbitrary number of points for the student's ranking in each event. This is further complicated by the philosophy underlying a track and field unit. At this age level, girls and boys should be free from excessive competitive pressure and should not have to judge themselves against the standards set by exceptional athletes.

The solution is to allow students to select a certain number of events and then record their initial and final scores. In this approach, the evaluation of performance and improvement becomes a personal assessment. A child who is a low achiever can set a realistic goal without worrying about who is the best in each event. Similarly, the outstanding performer can set a high standard, which motivates her to work at maximum capacity.

Summary Review

Although track and field activities can be classified under the general headings of run, jump, and throw, success in these events requires specialized skills and knowledge. The development of these specialized skills is influenced by the child's innate abilities and through instruction and practice opportunities. Careful planning and organizational decisions are required to maximize children's time on-task. Station work, rotating children between track and then field activities, is recommended. Facilities, equipment, and teaching strategies also must be adjusted to accommodate the developmental levels of all children. Personal goal setting should be used to motivate children and to deemphasize competition between children. Through correct instruction and practice opportunities, children will learn the correct technique and form for running short distances and for running long distances. There are a number of enjoyable and beneficial cross-country running activities that can be adapted to suit the developmental levels of elementary school children.

Due to the specific nature of both track and field and cross-country activities, and the unique environments in which they occur, safety considerations must be emphasized at all times. If children are provided a safe environment with lots of developmentally appropriate practice opportunities that lead to successful performances and enjoyment, they will develop the specialized skills and knowledge associated with track and field and cross-country activities. If this objective is achieved, then the children will possess the knowledge, skills, and desire to continue these activities throughout their lives.

INDIVIDUAL *and* **GROUP** **PROJECTS**

1. Form groups of three. Each group member chooses two different track skills. Design lesson plans to teach your two basic skills. Then teach one group member your two skills while the third member observes the effectiveness of your instruction. Each group member takes a turn at being teacher, student, and observer. Observers might find useful the observational checklist for the evaluation of teaching, provided in Table 11.7 on page 247. When you have all taught your skills, discuss and evaluate your experiences in each role (teacher, student, observer), and suggest possible ways to improve your teaching.

2. In pairs, study the rules and regulations of a track and field meet. Then, pose questions on the rules and regulations for each other to answer.

3. In chapter 4, it was suggested that one of the challenges facing teachers is the adjustment of the teaching environment to meet the developmental levels of the children. Four environmental variables under the teachers' control were identified:
   a. Rules
   b. Space
   c. Number of participants
   d. Amount or type of equipment

   One or more of these variables can be adjusted to create success on behalf of students. In small groups, discuss how these four variables can be adjusted when teaching children track and field and cross-country activities. Formulate creative ideas and specific recommendations and share these with other groups.
4. Chapter 13 identified a number of disabilities that afflict young children. In small groups, choose four disabilities and discuss how children with these disabilities can be integrated into track and field and cross-country activities. Consider what adjustments will have to be made to accommodate each child's developmental level and to ensure success. Debate possible techniques and methods of evaluation. Share ideas with other groups.
5. A feature of this text is the idea of teaching and enhancing academic skills and concepts through physical education activities. In small groups, discuss and create ideas to teach and/or enhance academic skills and concepts through track and field and cross-country activities. Each group is then allocated a small selection of the track and field practice activities and/or cross-country activities. Create ideas for teaching or enhancing academic skills and concepts through these activities. Consider ways to evaluate students. Share ideas with other groups.
6. In small groups, design a novelty track and field meet appropriate for all elementary school children. Discuss how all developmental levels, including special needs, are to be accommodated.

SELECTED READINGS

American Academy of Pediatrics. 1982. "Risks in long-distance running for children," *Physician and Sportsman* 10:8.

CAHPER. 1985. *Track and field in elementary school.* Ottawa, Ontario: CAHPER.

Foreman, K. 1982. *Coaching track and field techniques.* 4th ed. Dubuque, IA: Wm. C. Brown.

Gambetta, V., ed. 1989. *The Athletic Congress's track and field coaching manual.* Champaign, IL: Leisure Press.

Olson, E. 1982. "Kid stuff," *Runner* (November).

Powell, J. 1987. *Track and field fundamentals for teacher and coach.* Champaign, IL: Stipes.

P A R T 7

Gymnastic and Movement Activities

PART 7 has been organized to meet the conditions existing in the majority of elementary schools. Many classroom teachers are still teaching gymnastic activities through a reasonably structured approach. At the same time, however, they are attempting to apply Movement Education concepts and skills to various parts of their gymnastic programs.

The three chapters in PART 7 attempt to bridge the gap between the structured and the Movement Education approaches to teaching gymnastic activities. Chapter 25 provides the basic stunts and tumbling activities. At the end of this chapter, the concepts and skills of Movement Education are introduced systematically. Numerous examples show how to incorporate these movement ideas into stunt and tumbling lessons or units of instruction. Similarly, chapters 26 and 27 present the structured skills that are performed with small equipment and large apparatus and provide additional suggestions for applying movement concepts and skills.

Each elementary grade presents unique organization and teaching problems. The children's age and maturity dictate the amount of material that can be covered within the allocated time in the gymnasium or activity room. The number of mats available may be the reason for organizing a class in aparticular way, and the teacher's ability and confidence in handling this type of physical activity may be the central reasons for organizing a class in a certain fashion and for selecting particular activities. Regardless of such individual conditions, the following general teaching suggestions apply to all grade levels:

1. Children should be taught to listen to your normal conversational voice for all directions and commands. Once they learn to move and listen to your voice, there is no need to rely on a loud whistle.

2. Teach children standard procedures for (a) changing into their clothes and entering the gymnasium, (b) using their free time before the lesson begins, and (c) lining up in a specific way or place before the lesson begins or at any time you want to speak to all of the class.

3. Try to provide maximum participation and movement for each child during the instructional period. If a limited number of mats and other equipment means that the children must wait in long lines, the program should be changed. Techniques such as station work, task cards, and rotation procedures can be adapted to any grade level.

4. Establish a stunts and tumbling program based on the children's individual abilities and progress. Do not establish a set number of skills for every child to accomplish. Some children simply are physically incapable of performing certain stunts. A wide variety of activities should be presented to each grade level.

5. Establish and consistently maintain a basic list of safety rules and regulations. These should include the following:

   a. If children are permitted to wear street clothes during an activity, do not allow bulky sweaters or jewelry.

   b. Children should not be allowed to practice any stunt or tumbling activity unless the teacher is in the gymnasium.

   c. When a stunt requires a spotter, children should be taught the proper spotting techniques. Once the techniques are learned, children should be permitted to perform stunts with the assistance of the required number of spotters.

PURPOSES AND TECHNIQUES OF SPOTTING

In stunts and tumbling or other gymnastic movements, spotting is defined as providing assistance in the perfor-

mance of a skill. Spotting is both a teaching technique and a safety device. The teaching aspect is accomplished by the teacher or classmate holding the performer or positioning himself to assist the performer. For example, the spotter helps the performer maintain balance while performing a headstand. In an agility move, the spotter gently pushes or lifts at the strategic moment, helping her get the "feel" of the movement before she attempts it on her own. The safety aspect of spotting involves positioning one or two helpers near the performer to provide additional support and to prevent a loss of balance, a fall, or an accident.

It is difficult to say which stunts and gymnastic skills require the use of spotters. Furthermore, the teacher and the child must judge when to remove close spotting so the child can attempt the skill alone. As a general guideline for elementary school children, be overcautious until you are completely sure the performer can execute the skill with relative ease.

The following suggestions may also help you find a safe procedure and environment for teaching the more difficult and challenging stunts and tumbling and gymnastic skills:

1. Analyze each stunt's points of difficulty and teach spotters the correct position and movements.

2. Teach spotters to stay close to the performer but not to hamper movement.

3. Use the strongest and most reliable children for the most difficult stunts.

4. Teach children not to "overspot." Instruct spotters to help only when the performer needs an extra lift or push so he does not come to rely too much on the assistance.

DEVELOPING UNITS AND LESSON PLANS

There are several methods of organizing units and teaching individual or sequential lesson plans involving stunts and tumbling, small equipment, or large apparatus activities. The approach you decide to use will depend on such factors as the children's age, the time and equipment available, and the emphasis the teacher wishes to give to one or more activities or movement skills. Thus, a standard unit or lesson plan suitable for any developmental level would be of little value. The sample lessons in the next three chapters illustrate how teachers can use the structured skills and Movement Education concepts and skills in a variety of lesson formats.

KEY CONCEPTS

25.1 Specialized gymnastic stunts, tumbling, and movement skills are acquired through instruction and practice opportunities

25.2 Safety considerations must be emphasized when teaching children gymnastic stunts, tumbling, and movement skills

25.3 To develop gymnastic stunts, tumbling, and movement skills requires many practice opportunities

25.4 Effective teaching progressions, that provide all children with appropriate lead-up activities, are required to develop gymnastic stunts, tumbling, and movement skills

25.5 Using the analogy between a written sentence and a movement sentence helps children understand the concept of a gymnastic sequence or routine

25.6 Posing gymnastic challenges stimulates creativity and allows children to adjust their gymnastic activities and routines to their own developmental level

25.7 Gymnastic activities must be developmentally appropriate to ensure that all children can achieve success and enjoyment

KEY OBJECTIVES

After completing this chapter you will be able to:

1. Design developmentally appropriate gymnastic activities for elementary school children
2. Understand the nature and scope of gymnastics in the elementary school physical education program
3. Understand the scope and sequence of gymnastic stunts, tumbling, and movement skills in elementary school gymnastics
4. Apply movement concepts and skills when teaching gymnastics to elementary school children
5. Teach gymnastics through a Movement Education approach
6. Plan and organize teaching units and individual lessons in gymnastic activities involving stunts, tumbling, and movement skills
7. Plan a safe environment for teaching children gymnastic stunts, tumbling, and movement skills
8. Identify key teaching points associated with gymnastic stunts, tumbling, and movement skills
9. Employ teaching progressions that lead to the successful development of gymnastic stunts, tumbling, and movement skills

The gymnastic activities most familiar to elementary school children are probably stunts and tumbling. For generations, children have learned to mimic animal walks; to balance on their heads, hands, and other parts of their bodies; and to perform a variety of agile tumbling skills. The purposes of these activities have remained the same. Children learn to move their bodies safely and gracefully. They improve their strength, agility, balance, and other important aspects of physical fitness, and they learn the importance of safety and perseverance when attempting a difficult stunt or tumbling skill.

One of the most exciting additions to this program has been the introduction of movement concepts and skills developed in the Movement Education approach. These unstructured skills and movement concepts, coupled with the use of exploratory teaching methods and techniques, have provided an effective way for every child to experience success and enjoyment, regardless of physical ability or prior gymnastic experience.

This chapter has been organized to help teachers cope with the varying programs and conditions that exist in elementary schools. The main instructional emphasis for the three developmental levels is described to provide a guideline for selecting appropriate skills and movement concepts. The sample lesson plans in the next section illustrate how teachers can select from four skill areas when developing lesson plans. All stunts and tumbling activities have been organized under four general sections for ease of use. Tumbling activities include all movements that involve a rotation of the body, such as a forward roll and cartwheel. These skills are listed in their approximate order of difficulty. The sequential lead-up skills for several key tumbling movements are listed immediately below each skill. The section "Agility Activities" includes skills that involve transferring weight, springing, or moving with a partner in different ways. Balance activities include holding an upright or inverted position while stationary or moving. The section "Movement Education Concepts and Skills" describes the four main elements of Movement Education. Sample lesson plans illustrate how teachers can develop lessons that emphasize movement concepts or a combination of movement concepts with tumbling, agility, or balance skills.

DEVELOPMENTAL LEVEL I

The stunts and tumbling activities contained in this section include numerous animal movements, balance stunts, simple partner activities, and tumbling and safety skills. These activities are the foundations on which the more advanced stunts and tumbling skills are built. As in a later section of this chapter, there is a very close relationship between the activities described and many Movement Education skills. Each naturally complements the other.

CONCEPT

25.1 *Specialized Gymnastic Stunts, Tumbling, and Movement Skills Are Acquired through Instruction and Practice Opportunities*

If an individual or a class's skill level is high, move on to more advanced skills. As children progress into the next developmental level, they become ready for more challenging skills.

DEVELOPMENTAL LEVEL II

As children progress to developmental level II, the tumbling, agility, and balance skills become increasingly more difficult. Also, teachers should begin to place more emphasis on the quality and form of each movement. Boys and girls in this developmental level thoroughly enjoy partner and group agility and balance activities. These children also are capable of developing fairly complex movement sequences individually, in partners, or in small groups.

DEVELOPMENTAL LEVEL III

The stunts and tumbling program for level III is essentially a continuation of the level II program. As children progress to the more advanced tumbling, agility, and balance stunts, more strength, power, and control are required. More spotters are needed because of the difficulty and potential hazards of performing several balance and tumbling movements. Pyramid building, particularly involving two or more students, requires strength, balance, and teamwork. If

Sample Lesson No. I

Developmental level I
Length of lesson   Twenty minutes
Equipment   Gymnasium—no available mats
Emphasis   Balance and agility skills

Part I	Part 2	Part 3
Warm-up (3 to 5 minutes): Run, stop, change direction	Tumbling activities (10 to 15 minutes): Log Roll Agility activities: Lame Puppy Walk Balance activities: Stork Stand Game: Simple Tag	Closure (2 minutes): Sitting and discussing how to balance on different parts of the body

the children in this developmental level have been taught the Movement Education concepts and skills, they will develop complex sequences that show a high level of quality and creativity.

> **C O N C E P T**
>
> **25.2 Safety Considerations Must Be Emphasized When Teaching Children Gymnastic Stunts, Tumbling, and Movement Skills**

SAMPLE LESSON PLANS

There are several methods of organizing individual or sequential lesson plans involving tumbling, agility, and balance activities. The approach you decide to use will depend on such factors as the children's age, the time and equipment available, and the emphasis you wish to give to one or more activities or movement skills. Thus, a standard unit or lesson plan suitable for any grade level would be of little value.

The sample lesson plans in this section can be used as models or basic guidelines to design lessons from the four resource sections in this chapter. As a general rule, begin each lesson with a vigorous warm-up activity, such as running, jumping, and landing, followed by exercises designed to increase general strength and fitness (see chapter 8). Circuit training and vigorous tag and team games are also appropriate warm-up activities. The rest of the lesson should include a mixture of tumbling, agility, balance, and movement concepts and skills.

Sample lesson no. 1 considers lack of equipment, the attention span of five-year-olds, and a need to provide variation in movement skills within the context of a single lesson. The lesson emphasizes tumbling, balance, and agility skills. A chasing game from chapter 16 fulfills cardiorespiratory fitness needs, along with other personal and social needs. This type of lesson is very popular with kindergarten and first-grade teachers.

Sample lesson no. 2 illustrates how to cope with a minimum amount of equipment and how to use station work. The rotation pattern allows the child to practice a balance stunt, then shift to skills involving agility or climbing. Emphasis throughout the lesson, however, is on individual balance and agility skills. The same equipment layout could be used for several lessons, with variations in skills and sequence development.

> **C O N C E P T**
>
> **25.3 To Develop Gymnastic Stunts, Tumbling, and Movement Skills Requires Many Practice Opportunities**

The two sample lessons emphasize the acquisition of individual balance or agility skills. Once children have acquired a repertoire of agility and balance stunts and can practice them independently and safely, a further challenge can be presented. The next task is to encourage children to perform two or more stunts or movement skills in a sequence.

> **C O N C E P T**
>
> **25.4 Effective Teaching Progressions, That Provide All Children with Appropriate Lead-Up Activities, Are Required to Develop Gymnastic Stunts, Tumbling, and Movement Skills**

Gymnastic Sequences and Movement Sentences

Encouraging children to build their own gymnastic sequences is an important learning progression, because this stimulates creativity and problem solving. However, the concept of a sequence is abstract, and some children have difficulty understanding it. To help children have a more concrete

Sample Lesson No. 2

Developmental level II
Length of lesson Thirty minutes
Equipment Three large mats, eight individual ropes, four benches, three climbing ropes
Emphasis Balance and agility skills

Part 1	Part 2	Part 3
Warm-up (3 to 5 minutes): Run, change direction; tag game	Station work (20 to 25 minutes): Rotating to next station every four minutes	Closure (2 minutes): Sitting and discussing how to build a sequence

Tumbling:
Station 1: Forward and Backward Rolls
Station 2: Frog Stand, Knee Dip, Swing Turn
Station 3: Strengthening exercises, making shapes while holding on to rope
Station 4: Walking, Swing Turn
Station 5: Agility skills: Egg Roll, Heel Click

understanding of the term *sequence,* a comparison can be made between a gymnastic movement sequence and a written sentence. A written sentence is a collection of words connected together to convey ideas, meanings, and feelings; a gymnastic sequence is a collection of gymnastic stunts, tumbling, and movement skills connected together to convey ideas, meanings, and feelings. Hence, a gymnastic sequence can be thought of as a "movement sentence." This concept builds on children's existing knowledge (written sentences). As children learn new stunts, tumbling, and movement skills, they can think of these new skills as new "words" to add to their movement vocabulary. As their movement vocabulary builds, they will be able to express their creative ideas through more elaborate sentences. One further advantage of the movement sentence approach is that it provides a clear analogy for the start and finish positions associated with sequence work. A written sentence commences with a capital letter and ends with a full stop. Hence, a movement sentence must start with a capital letter (such as standing straight like a capital letter *I*) and finish with a full stop (such as standing straight like a capital letter *Y*). Challenges can then be made by the teacher in terms of creating movement sentences. For example, children might be asked to create a movement sentence that involves two static balances and one dynamic balance—"and don't forget your capital letter and full stop!" Young children find this approach more appealing and easier to comprehend, compared to a challenge to create a gymnastic sequence or routine. Teachers who wish to use the movement sentence approach will need to substitute the term *movement sentence* for the term *sequence* or *routine* in the gymnastic challenges that occur throughout this text. The following examples illustrate the types of challenges that can be presented to children during a gymnastic lesson. As a basic guideline, begin with simple, structured challenges involving known and previously practiced stunts, and progress to more creative challenges that allow maximum freedom to interpret and create individual or partner routines (movement sentences).

C O N C E P T

25.5 *Using the Analogy between a Written Sentence and a Movement Sentence Helps Children Understand the Concept of a Gymnastic Sequence or Routine*

Example Challenges for Individual Agility Sequences

Developmental Level I

"Can you start with a Log Roll (p. 504), change to a Crab Walk (p. 517), then go back to a Log Roll?"

"You know how to perform a Forward Roll (p. 505), a Side Roll (p. 505), and a Backward Diagonal Roll (p. 507). Can you perform a movement sentence showing all these stunts, one after the other?"

"Select three agility stunts that can be performed on the floor. Arrange your own movement sentence to include these stunts and practice until you can move smoothly from one movement to the other."

Developmental Level II

Partners have one mat to share.

"Make up matching movement sentences (facing each other, side by side, or follow the leader) that includes a balance, a roll, and a new balance stunt."

"In partners, design matching movement sequences on the floor that have a cartwheel and at least three other agility stunts."

Developmental Level III

"Make up a movement sentence beginning with Rolling the Log (p. 518), shift to a Seal Slap (p. 524), and finish with a Jump Through (p. 525)."

"Can you make up a movement sentence that combines a Kip (p. 528), a Forward Drop (p. 523), and a Judo Roll (p. 508)?"

C O N C E P T

25.6 Posing Gymnastic Challenges Stimulates Creativity and Allows Children to Adjust Gymnastic Activities and Routines to Their Developmental Level

---

Example Challenges for Individual Balance Sequences

Developmental Level I

"Remember the Tightrope Walk and how you balanced on one leg? Can you show me how you can start with balancing on one leg, then Tightrope Walk for three steps, then balance on the other leg?"

"Show me a Turk Stand, a One-Leg Balance, and another Turk Stand all in a row."

Developmental Level II

"Using the mat, make up a movement sentence that has a Headstand and two other balance stunts."

Developmental Level III

"Make up a movement sentence using the following stunts: The Bridge (p. 534), V-Sit (p. 534), and Headstand (p. 533)."

"Using a mat, make up a movement sentence that has a Headstand and two other balance stunts."

TUMBLING ACTIVITIES

The tumbling activities listed in this section include skills that involve a rolling action of the body (see figures 25.1 through 25.30). Each rotational skill is listed in table 25.1 according to its level of difficulty. Teachers should recognize that some children will lack the physical maturity or ability needed to perform the more difficult skills. Special considerations should be given to children who have low levels of physical fitness and motor skill ability. Children who are overweight or obese should also be given special care and attention as they perform Forward or Backward Rolls and other skills that require the weight of the body to be taken by the arms.

C O N C E P T

25.7 Gymnastic Activities Must Be Developmentally Appropriate to Ensure that All Children Can Achieve Success and Enjoyment

---

AGILITY ACTIVITIES

Agility activities are movements that involve body action (figures 25.31 through 25.79). The simplest type of agility activity is the animal walk that primary children enjoy performing. Elementary school children also enjoy agility skills involving partners, provided their partners have about the same level of ability. Other types of agility skills are movements that involve a springing action such as a Heel Click or Neckspring. These skills are arranged in table 25.2 according to their approximate order of difficulty.

BALANCE ACTIVITIES AND PYRAMID BUILDING

Balance activities include a wide variety of individual, partner, and group stunts (figures 25.80 through 25.116). The simple individual balance activities, such as One-Foot Balance and Stork Stand, are enjoyed by virtually all children in developmental level I. In developmental level II, balance activities, such as the Headstand and partner balance stunts, require more strength and balance ability. The same challenge is provided to older children in developmental level III, as they attempt to master the Handstand or a difficult Pyramid involving six or seven participants (table 25.3).

CHAPTER 25

TABLE 25.1   Tumbling Skills

Name of Stunt	I	II	III	Movement Concepts	Page
	Developmental Level				
Log Roll	———►			Transfer of weight, change of direction, low level	504
Side Roll	———►			Transfer of weight, curled shape, change of direction, medium level	505
Forward Roll:					
Looking Back Through Legs	———►			Transfer of weight, medium level	505
Back Roller	———►			Transfer of weight, curled shape, change of direction	505
Forward Roll	———►			Transfer of weight, curled shape	505
Forward Roll to One-Leg Stand		———►		Transfer of weight, curled and stretched shape	506
Forward Roll to Jump Tuck		———►		Transfer of weight, curled and stretched shapes, force	506
Consecutive Rolls		———►		Transfer of weight, curled shape	506
Dive Forward Roll			———►	Transfer of weight, curled shape, force, speed	506
Eskimo Roll			———►	Transfer of weight, curled shape, levels	506
Backward Diagonal Roll	———►			Transfer of weight, curled shape, levels, force	507
Egg Roll		———►		Transfer of weight, curled shape	507
Backward Roll:					
Back Rocker	———►			Transfer of weight, curled shape	508
Finger Touch	———►			Transfer of weight, curled shape	508
Back Shoulder Roll		———►		Transfer of weight, curled shape, change of direction	508
Judo Roll		———►		Transfer of weight, curled shape, levels	508
Backward Roll		———►		Transfer of weight, curled shape	509
Backward Roll to Knee Scale		———►		Transfer of weight, curled shape, levels	509
Backward Straddle Roll			———►	Transfer of weight, wide shape	509
Triple Roll		———►		Transfer of weight, force, change of direction, levels	510
Backward Extension			———►	Transfer of weight, stretch and curled shapes	510
Cartwheel:					
Single Mule Kick	———►			Transfer of weight, force, levels	511
Mule Kick	———►			Transfer of weight, force, levels	511
Side Kick	———►			Transfer of weight, force, change of direction, levels	512
Half Cartwheel		———►		Transfer of weight, force, change of direction	512
Cartwheel		———►		Transfer of weight, force, change of direction	512
Round-Off			———►	Transfer of weight, force, change of direction and speed	513

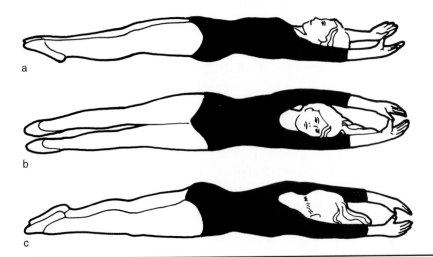

Figure 25.1 Log roll. This is the easiest roll to perform. Lie on the back, with the arms extended over the head and the hands locked together. Keep the body in a straight line and roll to the side and then around to the starting position.

Variations:

1. Children should also learn to roll toward either side, stop halfway through, and change directions.
2. Change position of arms.
3. Combine log rolls with other stunts, such as from a long roll, change to a crab walk, to a long roll, to a bear walk.

Figure 25.2 Side roll. Begin in a back-lying position. Perform the roll with elbows, knees, and nose "hidden" or tucked in. Explain to young children that hiding these parts of the body helps them roll in a ball-like fashion and protects vulnerable parts.

Variations:
1. Roll toward either side.
2. "See if you can roll from a log to a side to a log roll."
3. "See if you can combine a side roll, a log roll, and a balance stunt."

Figure 25.3 Looking back through legs. Begin in a squat position, with hands on the floor. Lean forward, raise hips, and look back through the legs.

Figure 25.4 Back roller. Crouch down at one end of the mat and place fingertips on the floor. Slowly roll backward, tuck chin in, bring knees to chest, and wrap arms around knees. Continue rolling backward until head touches the mat. Roll forward to starting position.

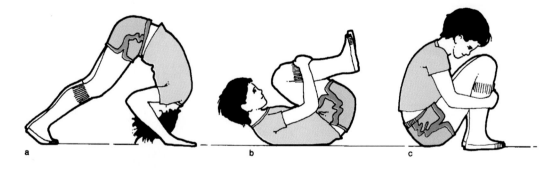

Figure 25.5 Forward roll. Most children have already learned the forward roll before the first grade and can usually demonstrate many variations involving different leg and arm positions. Begin in a squat position, with the head up, the arms extended forward slightly, and the fingers pointing straight ahead. Push off from the toes, raise the seat, and tuck the chin to the chest. Continue forward movement, landing on the base of the neck and the top of the shoulders. Push off with the hands and continue forward motion to a crouching or standing position.

Variations:
1. Start from a standing position and end in a standing position.
2. "Try three different ways to change your leg position as you perform the roll."
3. Try supine and straddle sit.
4. "See if you can perform a forward, log, and side roll in any order you like."

CHAPTER 25

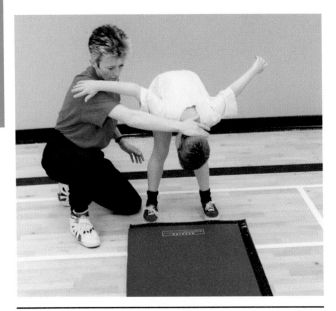

Figure 25.6 Forward roll spotting. Kneel on right side of performer. Place right hand on the back of the performer's head and left hand near the back of the right thigh. As the childs rolls forward, gently lift with the right hand and push forward with the left hand against the right thigh.

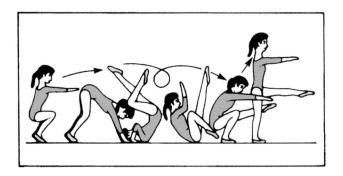

Figure 25.7 Forward roll to one-leg stand. Begin in a partially crouched position. Roll forward and end in a one-leg stand, with arms forward.

Figure 25.8 Forward roll to jump tuck. Begin in a partially crouched position. Roll forward to crouched position. Jump forward and upward to a tucked position, then land.

Figure 25.9 Dive forward roll. Begin in a partially crouched position in front of the mat. Spring forward, slightly arch the back, and push off with both feet. There is a moment when the body is totally off the floor; then the hands touch as the body makes a forward roll.
Variations:
1. Perform movement from a standing start or from a run, jump, and dive roll.
2. Perform a dive roll over partner in a low crouched position.

Figure 25.10 Eskimo roll. One partner lies on his back and the other partner stands, facing forward and near his partner's head. The partner on the floor grasps his partner's ankles and raises his own legs in order to allow his partner to grasp each leg above the ankles. Top partner leans forward, places partner's feet on the floor, and then performs a forward roll. Lower partner follows, and both continue performing a series of forward rolls.

Figure 25.11 Backward diagonal roll. This is one of the most important safety rolls. It is a means of rolling backward with a gradual dissipation of speed, thus preventing injury as well as providing an effective and graceful means of shifting from one movement to another. The roll is performed by rolling backward and bringing both legs to the side of one ear.

This takes the weight off the neck and allows the child to roll off the shoulder. It is an appropriate skill for children who are not strong enough to perform the backward roll.

Variations:

1. Roll to both sides.
2. "Can you combine a log, side, and backward diagonal roll?"

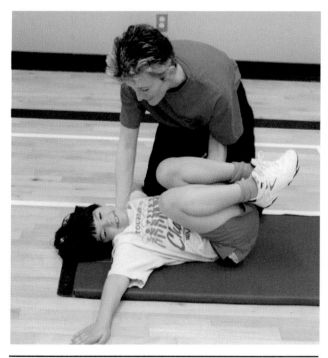

Figure 25.12 Backward diagonal roll spotting. Kneel on the performer's left side and face in the direction of the backward diagonal roll. Place the right hand under the left shoulder with fingers spread and hold the left hand near the performer's seat and ready to assist the performer in the backward movement.

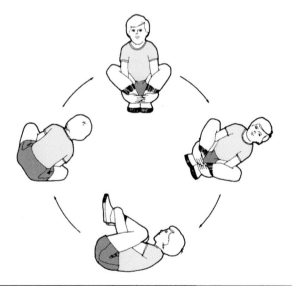

Figure 25.13 Egg roll. Begin in a squat position. Place the arms on the inside of the knees, then stretch the hands around the lower legs and overlap them over the feet. Roll sideways, on the shoulder, to the back, to the shoulder, and then back to a sitting position. Continue the action around the circle to the starting position.

Variations:

1. Roll toward right, then left side.
2. "See if you can vary your leg and hand position and repeat this stunt."

Figure 25.14 Back rocker. Start in a squat position at the edge of the mat, facing away. Grasp the shins with the hands and rock back until the head touches the mat. Then return and repeat movement.

Figure 25.15 Finger touch. Start in a squat position at the edge of the mat, facing away. Raise the hands by the ears, with palms facing forward and chin tucked. Roll back until both hands touch the mat. Then return to starting position.

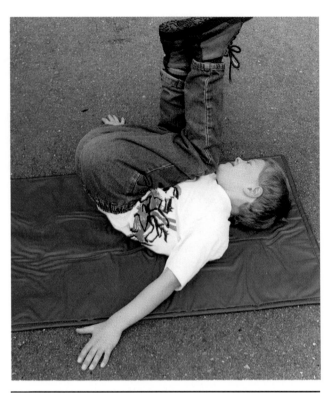

Figure 25.16 Back shoulder roll. Begin in a squat position. Roll back, turn head to right, and roll over right shoulder.

Figure 25.17 Judo roll. Start this roll from a standing position. Bend forward, extend the right arm, and turn the head toward the left side. As the body moves forward and downward, swing the right arm toward the left and contact the mat with the top of the right shoulder. Continue the forward rolling action over the back and side, then move forward and upward.

Variations:

1. Perform roll to opposite side.
2. Run, then perform a judo roll from a one-foot takeoff.

Figure 25.18 Backward roll. This is the most difficult roll to perform because it requires the weight to be taken on the arms during the roll. Begin in a squat position, with the body weight evenly distributed on the fingers and toes. The back should be toward the mat. Push off the hands and roll backward, keeping the knees to the chest and the chin down (a).

Continue backward roll until the body weight is well over the shoulders (b). At this point, push off with the hands, and land on the knees and toes (c).
Variations:
1. Perform backward roll with legs straight.
2. "Change position of legs as you perform a backward roll."

a

b

Figure 25.19 Backward roll spotting. Stand on the right side of the performer (a). As she rolls onto her shoulders (b), gently lift performer upward and backward.

Figure 25.20 Backward roll to knee scale. Start in a standing position, with hands at sides. Roll backward, and end in a knee scale position.

Figure 25.21 Backward straddle roll. Begin in a straddle support position. Keep knees straight and roll backward, ending in a straddle support position.

Figure 25.22 Triple roll. This is a continuous log roll involving three performers. As the center performer (#3) begins to roll to his right, the outside performer (#1) begins to thrust himself upward, over, and toward the center performer's previous position. The new center performer (#1) continues to roll toward the other side. As soon as he starts his roll, performer (#2) thrusts himself up, over, and toward the center position. This action is then continued for several rotations. The important aspects of this triple stunt are the timing of each performer and the quick recovery of the outside performer.

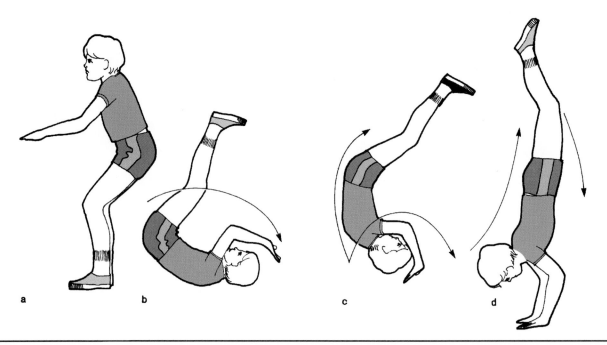

Figure 25.23 Backward extension. This roll starts with the same backward rolling action as the backward roll. As soon as the hands begin to press against the mat, the legs begin to extend upward. At the moment the legs are vertical, vigorously push off from the hands and snap the feet downward toward the mat, landing in a partially crouched position.

Spotting:

Use the same spotting technique described for the backward diagonal roll.

a

b

Figure 25.24 Single mule kick. Begin standing, with arms raised overhead and facing the mat; one foot is slightly in front of the other (a).

Bend forward, head up; place hands on mat, then kick back leg upward (b).

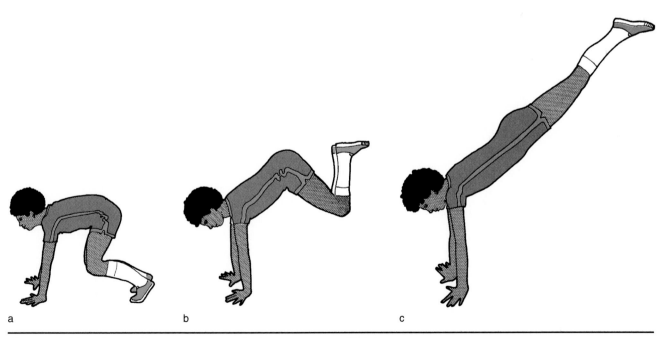

a   b   c

Figure 25.25 Mule kick. Begin in a semicrouched position, with hands about shoulder-width apart, knees bent, and feet together. In a simultaneous movement, shift weight over hands, and vigorously thrust legs upward and backward.

Variations:
1. Thrust backward, upward, and apart.
2. Twist body to side as legs extend backward and upward.
3. "Can you add your own variation to this stunt?"

Figure 25.27 Half cartwheel. Start with the right foot slightly in front of the left and arms overhead. Bend forward and toward the right foot. Place right hand, then left hand on the mat and swing around and land in a partially crouched position.

Figure 25.26 Side kick. Begin standing, with arms raised overhead and facing the mat, with the right foot slightly in front of the left. Bend forward, keeping head up. Place hands on the mat, kick left leg upward, and swing hips toward the left side. Land on both feet, facing the side, and return to starting position.

a

b

c

Figure 25.28 Cartwheel. Begin with the back straight, the arms extended sideward, and the legs approximately shoulder-width apart. Bend toward the left, placing the left hand, then the right, on the mat and, at the same time, raising the side. Note: In the middle of this stunt, the legs and arms should be fully extended and the body in a straight line. Continue sideways, placing right, then left leg on the mat and ending in the starting position.

Figure 25.29 Cartwheel spotting. Stand opposite the spot where the performer's hands will be placed. Cross the right arm over the left, then place both hands on the performer's hips as she pushes off from her lead foot. Aid the performer in her sideward motion and vertical balance position when indicated.

a   b   c

Figure 25.30 Round-off. The first part of the round-off is the same as the cartwheel. As soon as both feet are off the ground, bring them together, then make a half turn toward the left (counterclockwise). Bend at the hips, and land on both feet, facing the opposite direction.

Spotting:
Stand on the left side of the performer and opposite the spot where his hands will be placed. As the performer places his right hand on the mat, place your left hand under his right shoulder. Lift as he pushes off from his hands when indicated.

CHAPTER 25

TABLE 25.2   Agility Skills

Name of Skill	I	II	III	Movement Concepts	Page
	Developmental Level				
Alligator Crawl	→			Transfer of weight	515
Camel Walk	→			Transfer of weight, change of direction	515
Puppy Dog Walk	→			Transfer of weight, change of direction, force	515
Jump Turn	→			Transfer of weight, change of direction	515
Lame Puppy Walk	→			Transfer of weight, change of direction, balance	516
Wring the Dishrag (partner)	→			Transfer of weight, change of direction, relationships	516
Bouncing Ball	→			Change of direction and levels	516
Leap Frog (partner)	→			Transfer of weight, change of direction, relationships	516
Knee Jump	→			Force, levels	517
Rocking Chair (partner)	→			Transfer of weight, change of direction, force, relationships	517
Crab Walk	→			Transfer of weight, change of direction	517
Chinese Get-Up	→			Transfer of weight, force, balance, relationships	517
One-Foot Jump	→			Transfer of weight, force, balance	518
Rabbit Jump	→			Transfer of weight, force, balance	518
Rolling the Log	→			Transfer of weight, change of direction	518
Frog Jump	→			Transfer of weight, force, balance	519
Measuring Worm	→			Transfer of weight, levels, balance	519
Circle Roll (partners)	→			Transfer of weight, change of direction	519
Coffee Grinder	→			Transfer of weight, change of direction	519
Front Support to Stand		→		Transfer of weight, force, change of direction, levels	520
Upside-Down Touch (partner)	→			Transfer of weight, force, change of direction, relationships	520
Carousel (partner)	→			Transfer of weight, force, change of direction, relationships	520
Double Crab Walk		→		Transfer of weight, force, change of direction, relationships	520
Prone Knee Fall	→			Transfer of weight, levels	521
Elephant Walk (partner)	→			Transfer of weight, force, change of direction	521
Pig Walk (partner)		→		Transfer of weight, change of direction, relationships	521
Co-op Hopping	→			Transfer of weight, force, relationships	521
Siamese Twins	→			Transfer of weight, force, relationships	522
Hitchhiker Walk	→			Transfer of weight, force, relationships	522
Horseback Ride	→			Transfer of weight, force, balance, relationships	522
Double Wheelbarrow (triple)		→		Transfer of weight, balance, relationships	522
Upswing		→		Transfer of weight, force, levels	523
Forward Drop		→		Transfer of weight, force	523
Centipede		→		Transfer of weight, force	524
Seal Slap			→	Transfer of weight, force	524
Jackknife			→	Transfer of weight, force	524
Heel Click			→	Transfer of weight, force	524
Jump Through			→	Transfer of weight, force	525
Handspring over Partner (partner)			→	Transfer of weight, force, relationships	525
Knee Handspring (partner)			→	Transfer of weight, force, relationships	525
Handspring			→	Transfer of weight, force, levels, change of speed	526
Neckspring			→	Transfer of weight, force, levels, change of speed	527
Headspring			→	Transfer of weight, force, levels, change of speed	527
Kip			→	Transfer of weight, force, levels, change of speed	528

Figure 25.31 Alligator crawl. Begin lying facedown on the floor, with elbows slightly bent. Move along the floor by moving right arm and right leg. Later, try moving with right arm and left leg, then left arm and right leg, and so on.

Figure 25.32 Camel walk. Place one foot in front of the other, bend over from the waist, and lock hands behind back to represent the camel's hump. Walk slowly, raising the head and chest with each step.

Variations:
1. Walk backwards or sideways.
2. "See if you can keep your arms in the same position and sit down . . . then stand up."
3. "Can a camel run or gallop?"

Figure 25.33 Puppy dog walk. Begin in a crouched position, with weight on hands and feet. Keep head up and move on all fours.

Variations:
1. Move in different directions—backwards, sideways, and so forth.
2. "Can you show me how a pussy cat . . . squirrel . . . or monkey would walk?"

Figure 25.34 Jump turns. Begin with knees slightly bent, feet about twelve inches apart, and arms close to body. Jump up and make a half turn to the left.

Variations:
1. Jump and make a three-quarter or full turn.
2. Jump, turn, and clap hands.
3. "Can you jump, turn, and do something in the air before you land?"
4. "See if you can jump and turn, then land and roll."

Figure 25.35 Lame puppy walk. Begin with both hands and one foot on the floor. Keep the head up and walk or run "on all threes" like a lame puppy.
Variations:
1. Move in different directions—sideways, backward, and so on.
2. Change the position of the hands—farther apart, facing inward like a monkey, and so on.
3. Do a double lame puppy walk, with one hand and one foot on the floor.
4. "Show me how you can lie down, roll over right back to the same lame puppy position."

Figure 25.36 Wring the dishrag. Partners face each other and join hands. With hands joined, each partner raises one arm (right for one partner and left for the other), and they turn back-to-back. Repeat with the other arms to return to the original position.
Variations:
1. When in a back-to-back position, both raise one leg as high as possible.
2. "When in this back-to-back position, can you do something different?" (bend down, twist to one side, etc.)

Figure 25.37 Bouncing ball. Stand erect, with arms at the sides and feet approximately shoulder-width apart. Take short jumps and gradually lower the body. Continue jumping and lowering the body until the hands touch the floor. This should simulate a ball coming to rest. Repeat action upward until the standing position is again reached.
Variations:
1. Repeat stunt, turning body as stunt is performed.
2. "Try to change the position of your hands or feet as you perform your stunt."

Figure 25.38 Leap frog. One partner squats, keeping her head down. The other partner assumes a semicrouched position about two feet behind, with his hands resting on his partner's shoulders. Back partner spreads his legs and leaps over his partner. Continue sequence for several jumps.
Variations:
1. Raise the height of lower performer.
2. After performing a vault, land and roll.
3. Add two or more performers. Last performer in the row leap frogs over all performers before next person begins the sequence.

Figure 25.39 Knee jump. Stand with the feet about shoulder-width apart, the knees slightly bent, and the arms raised forward and sideways. Jump up, pull the knees up to the chest, wrap the hands around the lower legs, release grip, and land on the toes. Landing should be made with the knees bent.
Variations:
1. Jump up, straddle legs.
2. Jump up and slap seat, feet, or other parts.
3. "Invent a new position in the air."

Figure 25.41 Crab walk. Start with the hands and feet on the ground. The back should be fairly straight to keep the seat off the ground. Walk forward by lifting the left hand and right leg up and forward.
Variations:
1. Walk backwards and sideways.
2. Walk with one foot in the air.
3. Balance a ball (or small object) on your tummy and walk.
4. "Can you hold one hand on your head, or tummy, and walk?"

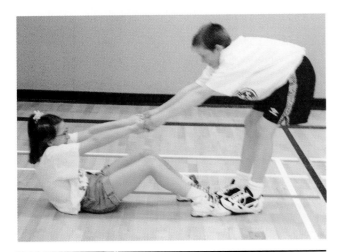

Figure 25.40 Rocking chair. One partner lies on the floor on her back, with her knees bent and her arms extended upward. The other partner stands at her feet, bends forward, and grabs her hands. One partner rocks back, pulling the other up and forward until they have changed positions.
Variation:
"Try the same stunt with both performers keeping one foot off the ground at all times."

Figure 25.42 Chinese get-up. Partners sit back-to-back, with their elbows locked, knees bent and together, and feet flat on the floor. Both rise off the floor by pushing against each other and, if necessary, taking short backward steps.
Variations:
1. Stop when halfway up and walk forward, sideways, and backward.
2. When all the way up, one pulls partner off floor. Repeat to other side.
3. "Can you think of a way to add or change this stunt?" (add a third person, etc.)

Figure 25.43 One-foot jumps. Begin standing on left leg, with arms extended forward and sideways. Keep arms forward, then swing right leg backward, then forward, and push off toe. Land on left toe. Continue movement in a forward direction.

Variations:

1. Change legs.
2. Jump, and perform same movement in a backward direction.
3. "Can you jump and extend your leg in other directions?"

Figure 25.44 Rabbit jump. Begin in a squat position, with the body weight over the toes. Leap forward and land on the hands and then the feet to simulate a rabbit hop.

Variations:

1. Hop backward.
2. "Try to kick your feet high as you land on your hands."
3. "How many different directions can a rabbit hop?" (examples—circle, zigzag)

Figure 25.45 Rolling the log. Begin in a front-leaning position. Keeping the right hand on the floor and the legs, feet, and back straight, swing the left arm up and over the turning body. When the left hand returns to the floor, swing the right arm up and toward the left side, turning the body back to the original position.

Variations:

1. Perform stunt toward right and left sides.
2. "Can you change a part of this stunt to make it more challenging?"

Figure 25.48 Circle roll. Partners join hands, keep legs straight, and turn in a circle.

Figure 25.46 Frog jump. Begin in a squat position, with hands on the floor. Jump forward and land on the hands, followed by the toes touching the floor. Gradually increase height and distance.

Figure 25.47 Measuring worm. Begin in a squat position, with the arms shoulder-width apart and the hands on the ground. Without moving the feet, take short steps with the hands until the legs and the back are straight. Now, without moving the arms, take short steps with the feet until the toes touch the backs of the hands.
Variations:
1. Keep one leg in the air at all times and repeat measuring worm.
2. "Can you perform the measuring worm with a partner or in threes?"

Figure 25.49 Coffee grinder. Begin in a side-leaning rest position, with free hand extended upward. Keep the body straight and slowly walk forward and around to make a full circle.
Variations:
1. Repeat stunt backward.
2. Change position of free arm, and repeat stunt.

Figure 25.50 Front support to stand. Begin in a front support position. Shift body to a squat position, then jump to a standing position.

Figure 25.52. Carousel. Partners stand facing each other with toes touching, arms extended, and holding hands. On signal, partners begin to move in a clockwise direction around and back to the starting position.
Variations:
1. Extend one leg back and repeat the movement.
2. Release one hand and repeat the movement.

Figure 25.51 Upside Down Touch. Partners begin in a back lying position, heads close together, hands grasping each other, and legs on the floor. On signal, raise legs and touch toes.
Variations:
1. Raise legs up, spread apart and touch toes.
2. One partner has a ball between her feet. She raises up and transfers the ball to her partner at the top of the movement.
3. Raise legs up then one partner lowers legs to the right and the other to the left. Both touch the mat and return to the starting position.

Figure 25.53 Double Crab Walk. One partner assumes a crab walk position with hands and feet on the floor and seat off the floor. The other partner assumes the same crab walk position in front and places his hands on his partner's ankles. On signal, partners try to move in a forward direction without losing contact with each other.

Figure 25.56 Pig walk. One partner assumes a partial push-up position, with her legs apart and her seat up. The lower partner faces the opposite direction and shifts backward until her arms are opposite her partner's ankles. The lower partner wraps her legs around her partner's trunk and grasps her partner's ankles. The upper partner takes short, "piglike" steps.

Variations:
1. Keep in pig walk position, lower toward mat, roll sideways, and return to original position.
2. "Try to modify this stunt in any way possible."
3. "Is it possible to design a three-person pig walk?"

Figure 25.54 Prone knee fall. Start on knees, with body erect and arms at side. Fall forward and land on hands, with a gradual bending of the arms to break the fall.

Figure 25.55 Elephant walk. One partner sits on the floor, with her legs extended sideward, while the upper partner bends down and places his hands between her legs (his feet are opposite the sitting partner's shoulders). The lower partner wraps her legs around the upper partner's trunk and places her hands over his seat. The lower partner rises off the floor and the upper partner takes short, "elephantlike" steps while the lower partner holds on.

Variations:
1. Walk backward and sideways.
2. "Can you and your partner make up a new animal walk? Give it a name!"

Figure 25.57 Co-op Hopping. Partners stand facing each other and raise left leg upward and forward to be held above the ankle by each partner's right hand. Players then extend left arm sideways and begin to hop toward one side then toward the other side.

Variations:
1. One partner hops in a forward direction while the other hops backwards.
2. Change position of legs and repeat movements.
3. Vary the position of the left arm, such as, holding it above the head, behind the back, or joining hands with your partner.

Figure 25.58 Siamese Twins. Partners assume a push-up position facing each other and with heads touching. On signal, partners move clockwise, making a complete rotation without losing head contact.

Variations:

1. Perform push-ups without losing head contact.
2. Keep head contact and raise one hand off the floor.
3. Keep contact and raise one leg off the floor.

Figure 25.60 Horseback ride. Lower partner assumes a hand-knee balance position. The top partner places his feet on his partner's seat, bends forward and places his hands on his shoulders. Lower partner raises knees off the floor and starts to walk on all fours.

Variation:

Repeat original movement with top partner facing the opposite direction and with his feet on his partner's shoulders and hands resting on his seat.

Figure 25.59 Hitchhiker Walk. One partner begins with hands, one knee and one foot on the floor. The other partner places her feet on the support's shoulders, leans forward and grasps her partner's lower legs just above the heels. On signal, lower partner starts to move forward on all fours. Top partner maintains her grip and assists her partner as he moves in a forward direction.

Variations:

1. Lower partner does not move his hands then begins to move his feet sideways making a complete circle. Repeat toward the other side.

Figure 25.61 Double wheelbarrow. The first performer gets down on his hands and knees. Second performer places her hands about two feet in front of the first performer, then she places her legs on top of the first performer. The third performer then grasps the first performer's ankles and raises upward. On command from standing performer, "wheelbarrow" moves forward, with right hands, then left hands, moving together.

Figure 25.62 Upswing. Kneel with arms extended sideward and backward. Swing arms forward and upward vigorously; at the same time, push off from the feet. Finish in a partially crouched position.

Variations:

1. Repeat stunt, with a quarter or half turn in the air.
2. "Can you modify this stunt in any way?"

Figure 25.63 Forward drop. Stand with the arms extended downward beside the body. In a simultaneous action, begin to fall forward, allowing the hands and arms to gradually absorb the downward momentum.

Variations:

1. Knee Drop: Begin in a kneeling position, with arms extended over the head. Fall forward in a similar manner as the forward drop.
2. Repeat forward drop but raise one leg and keep it off the ground as you drop.

Figure 25.64 Centipede. This stunt should be performed by three children of equal size and strength. First performer gets down on his hands and knees. Second performer places his hands about two feet in front of the first performer, then his legs and hips on top of the first performer. Third performer repeats the same steps as the second performer. The centipede now walks with the first performer using hands and feet while the other two use only their hands.
Variations:
1. Walk backward and sideways.
2. Try turning around.

Figure 25.65 Seal slap. Begin in a front-lying position, with the toes on the ground and the hands directly under the shoulders. Simultaneously push off from the hands and toes, clap the hands in the air, and return to the starting position.
Variations:
1. Attempt a double clap before returning to the starting position.
2. Instead of pushing off, see how far you can extend arms forward without touching the ground with your stomach (long bridge).
3. "Repeat seal slap and invent a new position of the arms and head when in the air."

Figure 25.66 Jackknife. Begin in a partially crouched position, with arms extended forward and sideways. Jump upward and raise legs, touching toes with hands, and return to starting position.
Variations:
1. Repeat stunt with a run and a two-foot takeoff.
2. Run; jump; perform a tuck, straddle, twisted or other shapes; and land.

Figure 25.67 Heel click. Start in a partially crouched position, with arms sideways and slightly backward. Jump up, click heels together, and return to the starting position.
Variations:
1. Start on one foot, jump up, click heels, and return to starting position.
2. Run, jump, click heels, and land on both feet.
3. Make up a sequence of three heel clicks, each starting from a different position.

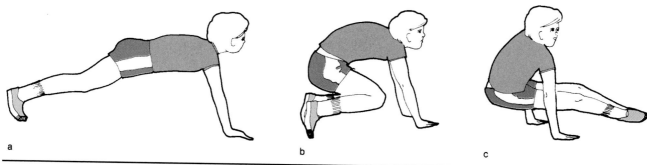

a   b   c

Figure 25.68 Jump through. Begin in a front-leaning support position, with the hands about shoulder-width apart. In one continuous movement, shift the legs forward between the arms to a back-leaning support position.

Variations:
1. Walk Through: Same as above but walk through the movement.
2. Side Shift: Same as the walk through, except that, as the performer moves forward, he tilts slightly to one side, raises the opposite arm off the floor, and brings his legs through.

Figure 25.69 Handspring over partner. This is a lead-up stunt to the handspring. One partner kneels on the mat, places her hands well apart, and tucks her head toward his chest. The standing partner places his hands opposite the trunk of the kneeling partner, keeping his arms straight, and raises one leg off the mat. Still keeping his arms straight, he kicks upward with his free leg, pushes off with his back leg, and rolls over the kneeling partner.

Figure 25.70 Knee handspring. The knee handspring can also serve as a lead-up stunt to the handspring. One partner lies on her back, with her knees bent and together and her arms extended forward. The standing partner places her hands on her partner's knees, lowers her body forward, and raises one leg slightly off the mat. The top partner then swings her top leg up, pushes off her lower leg, and continues the forward movement, placing her shoulders against the lower partner's hands. The lower partner keeps her arms extended to assist the top partner's forward motion.

a   b   c

Figure 25.71 Handspring. Begin in a standing position. Run forward, skip on the left foot, place the right foot on the mat and then the hands, with the arms extended. Continue the upward and forward thrust of the right leg, followed by the left leg. When the body is in front of the head, push off from the hands and land on both feet, with the knees partially bent.

Figure 25.72 Handspring spotting. Stand on the right side of the performer at the spot where his hands will land. Place your left hand on his right upper arm near the shoulder. As the performer shifts forward and upward, lift with the right hand and guide the forward action with your left hand. A second spotter may be required on the other side of the performer.

Figure 25.73 Neckspring. This stunt should be taught from a stationary position over a rolled mat. Once the performer can execute the kipping action, he should be allowed to attempt the skill with a running approach to the rolled mat. Run toward the rolled mat, take off with both feet, place the hands on the mat, bend the arms, and place the back of head on the mat. Roll forward, dropping the legs, then extend the legs forward and upward vigorously and push off the hands.
Spotting:
Use same technique as for the kip.

Figure 25.74 Headspring. This stunt is similar to the neckspring and should also be taught from a stationary position over a rolled mat. Once the performer can execute a kipping action, he should be allowed to attempt the headspring with a running approach. Run toward the rolled mat, take off with both feet, place the hands, then the top of the head, on the rolled mat. Keep the head and hands on the mat and bring the extended legs forward until an "overbalanced" position is reached. Then extend the legs up and forward vigorously and push off with the hands. Land on both feet, swing the arms forward, and bend the knees to regain a forward balanced position.
Spotting:
Use the same spotting technique described for the forward handspring.

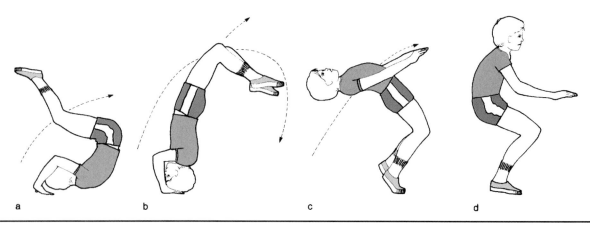

a b c d

Figure 25.75 Kip. Begin in a back-lying position, with arms at sides and legs extended. From this position, raise the legs and rock back until the knees are above the head (a). Note: The fingers should be pointing toward the body. Vigorously thrust the legs forward and upward and push off with both hands (b). Continue raising trunk forward and upward (c), and land in a partially crouched position (d).

Figure 25.76 Kip spotting. Kneel on the right knee at the performer's left side. Place the left hand on the performer's left upper arm and the right hand around the performer's lower arm. As the performer kips, pull with your left hand and lift upward with the right hand.

Figure 25.78 Knee walk. Start with the hands and knees on the mat. Reach back and grasp the feet or ankles. Shift the weight to the left side and take a short step with the right knee. Continue movement with short steps forward.
Variations:
1. Walk backward and sideways.
2. "See if you can balance on one knee for three seconds."

Figure 25.77 Tuck V-sit. Begin in a crouched position, with hands wrapped around knees. Raise feet off floor, and balance on seat.

Figure 25.79 Stork stand. Stand on one leg, with arms extended sideways. Raise left leg and rest bottom of foot against the knee.
Variations:
1. Change position of arms.
2. Repeat stunt and try to bend left leg.

TABLE 25.3 Balance Skills

Name of Skill	Developmental Level			Movement Concepts	Page
	I	**II**	**III**		
Tuck V-Sit	→▶			Balance	528
Knee Walk	→▶			Balance, transfer of weight	528
Stork Stand	→▶			Balance, transfer of weight	529
Thread the Needle	→▶			Balance, transfer of weight	530
Scale Stand (partner)	→▶			Balance, transfer of weight, relationships	530
Turk Stand	→▶			Balance, force	530
Single-Leg Balance	→▶			Balance, wide shape, transfer of weight	530
Hand-Knee Balance	→▶			Balance, transfer of weight	531
Twin Balance (partner)	→▶			Balance, force, relationships	531
Rear Support	→▶			Balance	531
Single-Knee Balance	→▶			Balance, transfer of weight	531
Seat Stand (partners)	→▶			Balance, force, levels, relationships	532
Teddy Bear Stand		→▶		Balance, levels	532
Ankle Stand		→▶		Balance, relationships	532
Push-Up Stand		→▶		Balance, relationships	532
Wheel Stunt		→▶		Balance, levels, relationships	532
Frog Stand		→▶		Balance, force	533
Headstand		→▶		Balance, levels	533
Swing Turn		→▶		Balance, change of direction	534
Walking Down Wall			→▶	Balance, transfer of weight	534
V-Sit			→▶	Balance	534
The Bridge			→▶	Balance	534
Headstand Variations			→▶	Balance	535
Handstand			→▶	Balance, transfer of weight, force	535
Handstand Roll Out to Jump			→▶	Balance, transfer of weight	536
Handstand to Bridge			→▶	Balance, transfer of weight	536
L-Support			→▶	Balance, transfer of weight	536
Side Stand (partner)			→▶	Balance, relationships	537
Table (partner)			→▶	Balance, relationships	537
Back Layout (partner)			→▶	Balance, levels, relationships	537
Flying Dutchman (partner)			→▶	Balance, levels, relationships	538
Knee and Shoulder Stand (partner)			→▶	Balance, levels, relationships	538
Knee Stand (partner)			→▶	Balance, levels, relationships	539
Individual Pyramid			→▶	Balance, levels, relationships	539
Double Pyramid			→▶	Balance, levels	540
Triple Pyramid			→▶	Balance, levels, relationships	541
Quadruple Pyramid			→▶	Balance, levels, relationships	541
Group Pyramid			→▶	Balance, levels, relationships	541

Figure 25.80 Thread the needle. Begin in a standing position, arms straight in front, with hands grasping. Keeping hands touching, bend forward, raise right foot up and through arms. Return to starting position.
Variations:
1. Repeat with opposite foot.
2. Change hand position (interlocking fingers, grasping wrists, etc.) and repeat.
3. "Can you add your own variation to this stunt?"

Figure 25.81 Scale stand. One partner stands with feet together and arms extended forward. The other partner holds the partner's hands, then balances on one leg and extends free leg back to a front scale position.

Figure 25.82 Turk stand. Begin in a cross-legged sitting position, with the arms folded across the chest and the body leaning forward slightly. Without releasing the grip, lean forward and extend the legs to a standing position. Return to the cross-legged sitting position.
Variation:
Lower yourself all the way down; roll onto your back without uncrossing your arms. Return to a standing position.

Figure 25.83 Single leg balance. Stand on one leg, with the knee slightly bent, lower the trunk, and raise the arms and other leg until they are parallel to the floor.
Variations:
1. Extend the elevated leg to the side.
2. Place the arms in different directions—pointing forward or downward or holding against the sides.
3. Place sole of elevated foot against side of other leg (stork stand).
4. "Can you balance on one leg and twist your body?"
5. "See if you can swing your free leg forward and turn around and face the other way."
6. "Can you balance on one leg, jump, and change to balancing on the opposite leg?"

Figure 25.84 Hand-knee balance. Begin with hands and knees on the mat. Simultaneously raise arms and right leg off the mat.
Variations:
1. Try raising the same arm and leg off the mat.
2. "Can you perform the hand-knee balance, then show me a twist in your body?"

Figure 25.86 Rear support. Start in a sitting position. Gradually raise seat off mat until body forms a straight line.
Variations:
1. "Can you balance on one foot and twist your body when you get into the rear support position?"
2. Turn over to a front support position.

Figure 25.85 Twin balance. One partner assumes a hand-knee balance position. The other performer places her knees on the lower partner's seat, with her hands on her shoulders.

Figure 25.87 Single-knee balance. Begin in a partial crouched position, with hands and knees on the mat. Simultaneously raise body up and move arms sideward while right leg gradually extends backward.
Variations:
1. Change position of arms after reaching balance position.
2. Change balance leg.

Figure 25.88 Seat stand. One partner assumes a hand-knee balance position. The other partner stands and balances on the lower partner's seat.

Figure 25.89 Teddy bear stand. Begin this stunt with forehead and hands making a triangle. The feet should be on the mat. Gradually "walk" forward on the toes until the knees are near the elbows. At this point, slowly shift knees to rest on elbows.

Figure 25.90 Ankle stand. Lower partner sits on mat. Upper partner stands with feet on each side of lower partner's knees. Upper partner grasps lower partner's ankles while upper partner raises lower partner's legs above her head.

Figure 25.91 Push-up stand. Back partner assumes a hand-knee balance position. Front partner raises right leg and places it on his partner's right shoulder. Repeat with opposite leg.

Figure 25.92 Wheel stunt. Center performer stands with legs apart and arms extended sideward. Outside performers place feet near center's foot, grasp hands, then lean outward.

Figure 25.93 Frog stand. Squat with the arms straight, hands resting on the floor and knees outside the elbows. The fingers should be pointing forward and spread apart for balance. Lean forward slowly, pressing the inside of the thighs against the elbows. As the feet rise off the ground, lower the head and trunk. Return to the starting position.

Variations:

1. Shift forward and perform a forward roll.
2. Shift forward, place head on mat, and perform a headstand.

Figure 25.95 Headstand spotting. Kneel on the left side of the performer and place left hand under performer's shoulder. As she lifts her legs, grasp the shin of the left leg with right hand. Once she is in the headstand position, gradually release the hands, but keep them a few inches away and ready for support. A second spotter can be added to the other side.

Figure 25.94 Headstand. Form a triangle with the hands and forehead. Push off the mat with the toes of both feet, flex the knees, and raise the body to a halfway position. Once the body is in a stable, balanced position, continue raising the legs until the body forms a straight line. Note: Too much arch in the back tends to cause the body to fall forward.

Suggested progression in learning this stunt:

1. Begin in position (a), walk forward on toes, shift to position (b), and return.
2. Repeat (a) to full headstand.
3. Kick up from position (a).
4. Perform stunt as shown.

Figure 25.96 Swing turn. Begin balancing on left leg, with arms extended sideways. Swing left leg backward, then forward. As leg moves forward, rise up on toes and pivot toward the left side, making a half turn.
Variations:
1. Change balance leg.
2. Reverse direction of free leg.

Figure 25.98 V-sit. Sit with the knees bent, feet flat on the floor, and the hands grasping the sides of the ankles. Still grasping the ankles, extend the knees and balance on the seat.
Variations:
1. Repeat stunt holding toes.
2. When in the V-sit position, release grip and extend arms and legs sideways.
3. "Can you modify this stunt while still emphasizing a balance on the seat?"

Figure 25.97 Walking down wall. Stand facing away from the wall, with the feet about two feet away from the wall, the elbows high, and the palms facing up and toward the wall. Arch the head and shoulders back and place the hands on the wall. Walk the hands down the wall and touch the head to the mat. This movement should be performed without moving the feet; however, most children will have to move their feet a little farther away from the wall as they reach the lower phase of the arched position. Use a spotter when a performer first tries this stunt.
Variations:
1. Keep one foot in the air throughout movement.
2. Walk up the wall. Start in push-up position with heels touching the wall. Gradually move backward to a handstand position, with feet resting on wall.

Figure 25.99 The bridge. Sit on the edge of the mat, holding the elbows high and the palms of hands facing up. Lower the back and place the palms on the mat, then arch the body.
Variations:
1. When in the arched position, raise and extend one leg.
2. Lower body, place head on mat, and extend arms sideways (wrestler's bridge).
3. "Can you perform a bridge with a variation in the arm, leg, or trunk position?"

Figure 25.100 Handstand. Begin this stunt with the arms approximately shoulder-width apart, hands on the mat, and the fingers slightly bent (this aids in maintaining balance). Both feet should also be on the mat in the starting position, with the right knee slightly bent. With the body weight well forward on the arms, kick the right leg up and follow with the left. Continue the upward movement of the legs, ending with the legs, body, and arms in a nearly straight line. The head should be well forward to assist in maintaining balance.
Variations:
1. Handstand against the wall, then bend elbows (about halfway) and straighten to original position.
2. Walk on hands.

Figure 25.101 Headstand variations: Review headstand before attempting the following variations.
Variations:
1. Change the position of the legs, such as straddle, one forward and one backward, and so on.
2. Hold a ball or beanbag between legs.
3. "See if you can balance on your head and change the position of any other part of your body."

Figure 25.102 Handstand spotting. This is similar to the spotting technique described for the headstand. Both spotters stand on either side of the performer and place their hands under her shoulders. As the performer lifts her legs, each spotter grasps the calf of the nearest leg. Once the performer is in the handstand position, the spotter should gradually release the hands but keep them a few inches away and ready to give support.

Figure 25.103 Handstand spotting. Use the same spotting technique described for the headstand. An alternate method is to stand just in front of the spot where the performer's hands will be placed. The spotter's left leg should be extended back to provide a firmly balanced position. As the performer shifts his legs upward, the spotter should brace the performer's right shoulder against her own right leg and catch his legs as they come up.

a

b

Figure 25.104 (a) Handstand roll out to jump. From the handstand position, bend arms, tuck body, roll to a squat, and continue forward and upward to a lunge position. Land with knees bent. (b) Handstand to bridge. From the handstand position, lower and arch body, and land with head up and body in a full arched position.

Figure 25.105 L-support. Sit on the floor, with the legs together and pointing straight ahead. Rest the hands on the floor below the shoulders. Keep the shoulders slightly forward of the hips, press down, and raise the hips and legs off the floor.

Figure 25.107 Table. Base partner assumes a crab-walk position, with his thighs and trunk in a straight line. Top partner straddles base, places her hands on base's shoulders and feet on his knees. Top performer then raises seat until thighs and trunk are in a straight line. Both heads are facing the ceiling.
Variations:
1. When balance is reached, base partner raises right foot and top partner raises left foot into the air.
2. "Try to invent a new double balance stunt, with both facing the ceiling."

Figure 25.106 Side stand. Base partner assumes a wide kneeling position, with his weight evenly distributed on his arms and legs. Top performer stands on the side and curls her arm around his partner's trunk. The palms of both hands face up. The top performer leans across her partner and gradually raises her knees to a partially bent position above her partner's back. Then she extends her legs fully.
Variations:
1. "See how many ways the top performer can change the position of her legs."
2. "Is it possible for one or both performers to add a twist to their balanced position?"

Figure 25.108 Back layout. The base partner lies on her back, extends her arms up, and bends both knees. The soles of her feet should face her partner's back. The top partner rests the small of her back against her partner's feet and slowly extends back as her partner straightens her legs. The base partner can give support to the top partner by holding her arms just above the wrists.
Variation:
Repeat stunt and release hand grip as balance is achieved.

Figure 25.109 Back layout spotting. Stand near the top of the base performer's right shoulder, assist in placing the feet, and maintain balance when indicated.

Figure 25.110 Flying Dutchman. Base performer lies on his back, extends his arms up, and bends both knees. Top performer faces the base performer, grasps his hands, and places his stomach against the support's feet. Base performer extends his legs; then the top performer arches his back, releases his hands, and extends his arms sideways. Note: Begin with a spotter to find balance position and as a standby safety person.

Figure 25.111 Knee and shoulder stand. The base partner lies on his back, with his knees bent and his arms up. The top performer stands facing her partner and places her hands on her partner's knees as she brings her shoulders forward. The base partner places his hands on the top performer's shoulders. As soon as the top performer's shoulders are held in a fixed position, she begins to raise her legs until they are in a vertical position.

Variations:

1. Top performer places one leg forward and one extending backward.
2. "Find a new position for your legs." (sideways, knees flexed, etc.)
3. "What other way can you modify this stunt?"

Figure 25.112 Knee stand. Base partner stands with his legs about shoulder-width apart, bends forward, and places his head between his partner's legs. Top partner places her hands on base partner's shoulders, and base partner grasps upper partner's thighs. Base partner begins to stand up, while top partner places her feet on base partner's thighs, releases her hands from her partner's shoulders, and begins to arch forward.

Variation:

"Can you redesign this stunt so that the final balance position of the top performer is facing the reversed direction?"

Figure 25.113 Individual balance and poses.

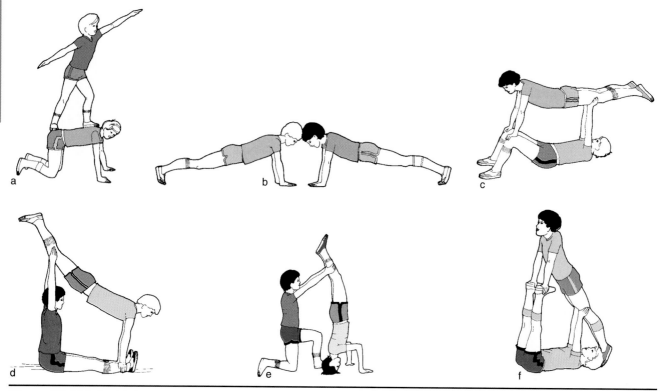

Figure 25.114 Dual balance and poses.

A human pyramid is usually considered to be a group of students forming a pyramidlike structure, with one child at the top and the others gradually tapering to the sides. This is known as a true pyramid; however, other kinds of pyramids have high points somewhere within the pyramid or even at the ends. The block illustrations may be used as basic guides in constructing pyramids with two or more students.

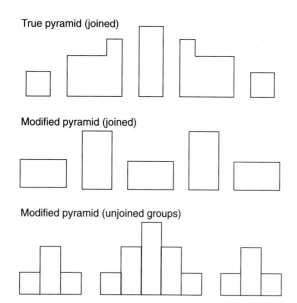

The first stage of pyramid building is to learn to create individual poses that can be used for the center, side, and end position. Many balance stunts, such as the Headstand and the V-Sit, can be used. Other poses can be added (figure 25.113). It is also important to allow the class to design its own individual positions.

The next stage in pyramid building is the development of dual stunts. Again, many dual balance stunts can become the nucleus of a pyramid. Require the heaviest and strongest students to form the base of the pyramid and lighter students to be on top (figure 25.114).

Once the dual stunts are learned, combine these positions. A symmetrical, six-person pyramid can be formed, with two facing base stands and one individual pose, such as the Dog Stand—on each end—facing the center. Beyond this point, the teacher and students can use their imaginations to design and construct an unlimited variety of pyramids. Examples are shown in figures 25.115 and 25.116.

Since pyramid building involves teamwork and timing, the teacher should develop a standard procedure or set of whistle cues. The first cue could mean that all students stand at attention and face one direction. The second cue could signal all participants to move into the ready or primary position. A third blow might be necessary in two- and three-person pyramids for the upper participants to shift into final position. A similar procedure should then be followed when dismounting.

Figure 25.115 Triple and quadruple balance poses.

Figure 25.116 Group pyramids.

MOVEMENT EDUCATION CONCEPTS AND SKILLS

Introducing movement concepts and skills is more difficult for intermediate teachers than for primary teachers. By the time boys and girls reach the fourth or fifth grade, they have learned many stunts and tumbling skills, normally through a process of explanation, demonstration, and practice. It would be difficult and unwise to change this process completely and adopt a new movement vocabulary and a new way of learning. A more profitable approach is for the intermediate teacher to acquire an understanding of the basic movement concepts and skills described in this section, then to introduce them gradually into the regular stunts and tumbling program. If the class is receptive to these ideas and demonstrates the ability to work independently and safely, greater emphasis can be put on the movement concepts and skills.

The four Movement Education elements—body awareness, qualities, space awareness, and relationships—are described on the following pages. Wherever possible, suggestions are offered for teaching the movement skills of each element, along with ideas for relating or incorporating them into the stunts and tumbling activities of the primary or intermediate program. The sample unit and lesson in this section provide a general format for teachers to follow when developing their own themes and lesson plans.

The stunts and tumbling skills described in the previous sections are classified as structured skills or movement patterns. Each skill is performed in a standard way; however, variations are allowed in the position of the hands or legs. In order to overcome the structured limitations of formal stunts and tumbling activities, many of the movement concepts and skills developed in the Movement Education approach are being incorporated into stunts and tumbling and into activities with small equipment and large apparatus. These movement concepts and skills allow children to perform movements according to their own levels of physical and creative ability.

However, the problems encountered when introducing unstructured movement concepts and skills to stunts and tumbling activities are similar to those encountered when introducing the problem-solving method in games programs. Introducing the movement concepts and skills to primary children, particularly those in the first two grades, is relatively easy because primary children do not have a wide background of stunts and tumbling skills. Instead, many of their skills involve imitative movements rather than the complex skills of balance and agility taught in later grades. Also, primary children are normally taught through more informal methods, both in the classroom and in the gymnasium. As a consequence, primary teachers have little difficulty incorporating movement concepts and skills into their stunts and tumbling programs. Once the teacher understands this movement vocabulary, she usually gives more emphasis to movement concepts and skills and less to structured stunt activities.

Body Awareness (What the Body Can Do)

Body awareness describes the ways in which the body or its parts can be controlled, balanced on, or moved from one position to another. Skills involved in body awareness fall into the following three groups.

Balancing, or Weight Bearing

A child is capable of balancing, or taking the weight, on different parts of the body. He can balance on one foot, on his head, or on all "threes" such as in the Lame Puppy Walk. In order to help the child learn what parts of the body he can balance on, it is necessary to present a challenge in the form of a movement problem and then let him answer the challenge in his own way. The question should begin with such phrases as "See if you can . . . ," "How many ways . . . ," "Can you . . . ," or "Try to discover . . ."—rather than a direct command such as "I want you to . . ." The following questions show how to use the problem-solving method to assist the child in

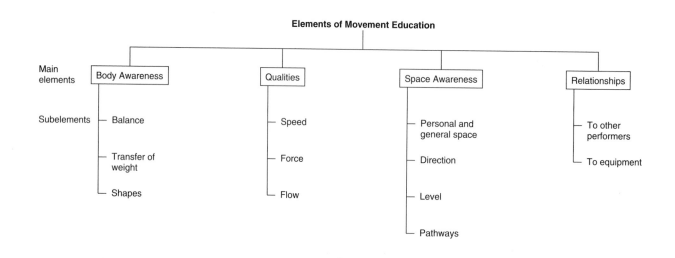

Figure 25.117 "Can you balance on two or three parts?"

finding his own way of balancing on one or more parts of the body.

1. "Can you show me the One-Leg Balance?" Children may have already learned this balance stunt.
2. "See if you can balance on your seat." This is still somewhat structured, yet the question allows each child to put his arms and legs in any position he wishes. A series of similar questions directing the child to balance on other parts—side, back, stomach—could follow.
3. Present a series of questions involving two or more parts of the body (figure 25.117)—"Can you balance on one foot and two other parts of your body?" "Can you balance on three (or four) different parts of your body?" "Can you find another way of balancing on three parts of your body?"

The main task within this subelement of body awareness is to help children become aware of the many different ways in which they can balance their bodies. The movement challenges begin with a familiar stunt (the One-Leg Balance), then shift to specific parts of the body. The final challenge mentions only a certain number of "points of contact," thus providing more freedom for the child to discover other ways that the body or its parts can be balanced.

Transfer of Weight

Transfer of weight, the second subelement of body awareness, is the ability to shift from one balanced position to another. This skill can be developed as a logical extension of balancing on different parts of the body (figure 25.118). The following illustrate how this progression can occur:

1. From one known skill to another: "Can you show me the Measuring Worm Stunt, then change to a Headstand?" (This is shifting from one three-point balance to another three-point balance.)
2. From a known part to three unknown parts: "See if you can balance on your seat, then shift to balancing on three different parts of your body." (This is shifting from a one-point balance to a three-point balance.)
3. From unknown parts to unknown parts: "Can you show me a three-point balance, then shift to a two-point balance?"

Figure 25.118 Transfer of weight.

Figure 25.119 "Can you make a curled shape?"

Shapes

Shapes, the third subelement of body awareness, includes the ways the human body can make stretched, curled, wide, narrow, and twisted shapes. The task is similar to balancing or weight bearing in that questions must be presented to help the children discover what shapes they can perform.

Stretched and curled shapes should involve the whole body first, then progress to individual parts. Questions should encourage the children to make the following shapes from various starting positions.

1. *Curled shapes* (figure 25.119)
   a. From a sitting position
   b. From a standing position
   c. While in flight
   d. From a front, back, or side lying position
   e. From a curled position to another curled position

Figure 25.120 "See if you can show me a stretched shape."

Figure 25.121 Wide shapes.

Figure 25.122 Twisting—body stabilized.

2. *Stretched shapes* (figure 25.120)
   a. From a standing position
   b. While in flight
   c. From a sitting position
   d. From a front, back, or side lying position
   e. From a stretched position to another stretched position

Progression should be from a stationary position into a curled or stretched shape. Begin with questions or statements directed at curled shapes (from a–e), then try the same with stretched shapes (a–e), or switch from one to the other. Following are samples:

"Can you curl up and make a very small, ball-like shape?"

"Can you make a stretched shape from a standing position?"

"See if you can repeat your stretched shape or find a new one and then change into a curled shape."

"See if you can start with the Turk Stand and, when you are low to the ground, roll to a very curled-up shape."

Allow the class sufficient time for experimentation. During this time, look for unusual shapes and provide encouragement and praise wherever necessary. Choose one or two shapes and let the children show them to the rest of the class; don't always choose the same children.

Once the class has a general understanding of stretch and curl, introduce wide and narrow and twisted shapes in a similar way. Wide and narrow shapes, like curled and stretched shapes, are contrasting. A wide shape (figure 25.121) requires the legs, arms, or both to be away from the trunk. In contrast, a narrow shape is characterized by its thinness, which means the arms or legs must be close together or in line with the trunk.

A twisted shape can be performed in two ways. The first is by holding one part of the body in a fixed, or stabilized, position, such as on the floor, and then turning the body or any part of it away from the fixed base. In figure 25.122, the body is stabilized as the feet restrict the degree of twisting. A twisted shape can also be made when the body is in flight. In this case, one part of the body is held in a fixed position while the other part turns away from the *fixed* part, producing a twisted shape. Although it could be argued that the latter is a *turn* (usually defined as rotation of the body and loss of a fixed contact), with younger children the synonymous use of *twist* and *turn* is quite acceptable. The meaning can be refined later.

At this stage in the introduction of movement skills and concepts, children should learn the meaning of balance and shape. They should also be able to develop simple sequences involving a variety of shapes and balance skills.

Qualities (How the Body Moves)

The element of qualities describes how the body moves from one position to another in relation to speed, force,

Figure 25.123 Speed—quick and slow.

Figure 25.124 A strong, forceful movement.

Figure 25.125 Measuring worm stunt.

Figure 25.126 General space.

and flow. Speed is the ability to move quickly or slowly from one position to another (figure 25.123). Force is the effort involved in a single movement or throughout a series of related movements. A child may leap high into the air, demonstrating a strong, forceful movement of the leg muscles (figure 25.124). In contrast, a gentle shift from a high stretch to a low curl illustrates a light or gentle movement. Flow is the smooth transition or linking of one movement pattern to another.

These aspects of qualities can be integrated into previously learned stunts, tumbling and safety skills, and the three components of body awareness. The following examples show a few of the many applications of speed, force, and flow to a single skill or a sequence of skills:

1. *Stunts:* Ask the class to perform the Measuring Worm Stunt. After one or two practices, ask the class to perform part of the stunt very slowly and part very quickly (figure 25.125).

2. *Tumbling skills:* Pose a challenge such as "See if you can move slowly from a Log Roll to a Side Roll, then quickly from a Side Roll back to a Log Roll."

3. *Shapes:* Ask the class to make up a sequence of stretched, curled, and wide shapes. After each child knows his sequence, pose the following suggestion: "As you practice your sequence, try very hard to make each movement link smoothly to the next with no sudden stops or jerky movements between each skill." The stress here is on flow, or the ease and efficiency of moving from one shape or position to another.

Space Awareness (Where the Body Moves)

The third element, space awareness, includes movement skills relating to use of general or limited space, direction, and levels of movement.

All the space in a gymnasium that can be used by a child constitutes his *general space* (figure 25.126). In contrast, *limited,* or *personal, space* is the immediate area a child can use around him to perform a movement or series of movements. When a child is challenged to perform a series of different balance positions while remaining inside his hoop, he

Figure 25.127 Limited space.

a

b

c

Figure 25.128 Matching shapes.

is using his personal, or limited, space (figure 25.127). Direction is the ability to move safely and purposely in a variety of pathways, such as forward, backward, or sideways, and to trace out pathways such as over, under, around, and through. Levels concerns the ability to perform a movement or series of movements that requires the body to be low to the ground, as when performing a series of rolls, at a medium level, as in moving on all fours, or at a high level, as when performing a cartwheel or a leap from the floor.

Many of these aspects of space awareness have been stressed in teaching stunts and tumbling and, to a lesser degree, when teaching the movement skills of body awareness and qualities. For example, when each of the tumbling skills is introduced, each child begins on his own mat. This is his personal, or limited, space. Gradually, his space is expanded to two mats, then to three, and finally to all the mats available in the general space of the gymnasium. Each child is also asked to move to an open space on the mat. His rolling movement may be forward, sideways, or diagonal.

Relationships

The fourth element of Movement Education is the relationship of the individual or group to other performers or objects.

Partner Relationships

Movements with a partner can involve matching shapes (figure 25.128), contrasting shapes (figure 25.129), or one child acting as the leader while the other acts as the follower through a sequence of movements.

Many useful and enjoyable partner activities can be applied to a stunts and tumbling program. All of the partner activities described under the stunts sections for primary and intermediate children are essentially dual balance stunts or tandemtype agility walks. With "matching," "contrasting," and "following" challenges, partner activities can be greatly enriched. Following are examples of the many ways that partners can develop structured and unstructured movement sequences.

1. *Matching movements using structured skills:* "See if you can make up a sequence (or routine) with your partner that begins with a Headstand, includes a Roll, and ends with both in a balancing position" (figure 25.130).

Figure 25.129 Contrasting shapes.

a

b

c

Figure 25.130 Partner relationships—symmetrical shapes.

2. *Contrasting movements using unstructured skills:* "One partner makes a stretched shape and the other partner makes a contrasting curled shape. Next, the first partner makes another stretched shape and his partner makes a contrasting curled shape." Repeat with two new stretched and curled shapes. Allow time to practice the contrasting shapes in a smooth sequence.
3. *Follow the leader:* One partner leads and the other copies each movement. Challenges can be "Make a shape, change direction, make another shape, change direction," and so on. "Develop a sequence of balancing and rolling, with one following the other" or "Make up a sequence with your partner that includes a change of direction and a change in speed."

Equipment Relationships

Equipment relationships involve the ability to perform a movement in a manipulative way, such as balancing or rolling with a hoop (figure 25.131, or in a nonmanipulative manner, such as leaping over a hoop (figure 25.132). Numerous examples of these types of relationships are described in the next two chapters.

This introduction to the four movement elements has simply opened the door to a range of movement skills. Each of the skills within body awareness, qualities, space awareness, and relationships is unstructured and, thus, allows children to perform each movement in their own unique ways. Since these movement skills can be mixed with stunts or tumbling skills, they enrich a child's movement experience.

Figure 25.131 Performing a movement in a manipulative way.

Figure 25.132 Performing a movement in a nonmanipulative way.

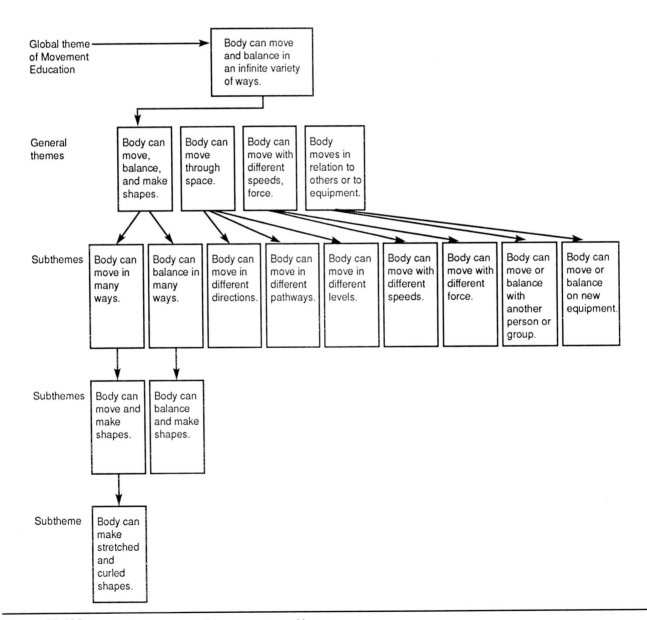

Figure 25.133 Developing Movement Education units and lessons.

DEVELOPING UNITS AND LESSON PLANS

Units and lesson plans in Movement Education are developed from a central theme, or idea. As shown in figure 25.133, the global theme of gymnastics is exploring how the body can move and balance in an infinite variety of ways. At the next level are the general themes, which represent the four elements of Movement Education. These are normally too broad to develop teachable themes or units. The subthemes, such as "Body can balance in many ways," could be developed into a short theme involving four to six lessons. A single lesson theme of balancing on different parts of the body could then be developed for a thirty-minute lesson. An outline of this unit and a sample lesson plan follow, as a format for developing similar units and lessons.

◼ Developmental Level I

Theme Body can balance in many ways
Number of lessons Six
Main theme Balancing in different ways
Subthemes Change of direction and level, change of speed

Main theme content

1. Balance on different parts of the body—seat, knees, elbows, one foot, and so on.
2. Balance on large and small parts of the body.
3. Balance on flat and sharp parts of the body.
4. Balance on upper and lower parts of the body.
5. Combine subthemes, such as change of speed, with balancing on different parts.
6. Design and perform simple sequences with ease, efficiency, and form.

◼ Lesson No. 1: Balancing on Different Parts of the Body

Part 1: Introductory Activity (3–4 minutes)
—Run, change directions.
—Run, change directions, and on signal "stop" touch floor with fingers of both hands.
—Run, "stop" (touch floor), and balance on one foot . . . next time "seat," and so on.

Part 2: Skill Development (10–12 minutes)
This is the part of the lesson where the main theme is developed. The first two or three challenges will normally take up the allotted ten to twelve minutes. If time permits, complete #4 or add one or more similar challenges.

Find a Space—all move to scattered positions.

Challenges:

1. "Show me how you can balance on . . . 'your seat' . . . [wait a few moments] . . . 'your side' . . . 'knees and one elbow,'" and so on.
2. "Can you show me how you can balance on a big 'patch'? . . . Now a 'patch and one point.'" Continue asking for different patches and points.

3. Introduce "take the weight on" for the word "balance." "See if you can take the weight on three parts of your body . . . four parts, 'a new three parts'" and so on.
4. Repeat challenge no. 3, introducing the subtheme "speed." "Can you balance on three parts and move very slowly to four parts? . . . Now, try it again and balance on three, slowly to four parts, then quickly back to three."

Part 3: Closure—Discuss Various Ways of Balancing
During the next lesson, introduce or repeat any of the previous challenges. At the end of the last challenge, ask the children to get a hoop and find a new space. Pose the following challenges involving a hoop.

1. "Place your hoop on the floor. Can you balance on your seat on the inside of the hoop? . . . one part inside the hoop? . . . one part inside and two parts outside?" . . . Continue.
2. "Show me how you can hold onto the hoop with both hands and balance on one foot . . . one foot and the hoop must touch the floor." . . . Continue.
3. Continue adding "quick and slow" to one or more challenges. Subsequent lessons would continue to stress balance but would add subelements, such as change of direction and levels, and using other small equipment.

Teachers and children in developmental levels II and III normally modify this theme approach to cope with the backgrounds and interests of older children. The following suggestions can help these teachers incorporate some of the movement concepts and skills of Movement Education.

1. Continue to organize units and lessons in the same general way.
2. As you teach routines involving balance, tumbling, and agility skills, begin to use some of the movement concepts, for example, "Develop a routine that has one tumbling and two balance skills." After a few minutes add, "Can you move quickly from a balance to the next balance, then slowly back to the first balance?"

Such phrases as "balance on four," "change of direction and level," and "moving quickly and slowly" are understandable and acceptable to older children. As the children demonstrate their ability to create routines, gradually use more movement concepts and skills.

◼ Summary Review

Gymnastic stunts, tumbling, agility, and movement skills contribute to many areas of a child's development. Gymnastic stunts are movement skills that involve controlled body movements, such as the balance stunts of headstand or handstand. Tumbling activities include all movements that involve rotation of the body, such as a forward roll or a cartwheel. Agility skills include skills that involve transferring weight, such as springing forward or moving sideways. These gymnastic stunts, tumbling, and agility skills allow children to communicate and express their ideas, feelings, and thoughts, in an artistic and aesthetic form, through the nonverbal medium of movement. Further, development of such skills contributes to body and spatial awareness, and provides opportunities to develop strength, flexibility, and other components of physical fitness. Combining the traditional gymnastic stunts, tumbling, and movement skills with the Movement Education approach allows all children to achieve success, because they can accomplish challenges at their own unique levels of development.

INDIVIDUAL and GROUP PROJECTS

1. In small groups, discuss safety considerations when teaching gymnastic stunts and tumbling skills. Pay particular attention to children with special needs. Share recommendations between groups.

2. In small groups, discuss the benefits and drawbacks of teaching gymnastics through a Movement Education approach. Share your opinions with other groups.

3. Form groups of three. Each group member chooses two different tumbling skills (see Table 25.1). Design lesson plans to teach your two basic skills. Then teach one group member your two tumbling skills while the third member observes the effectiveness of your instruction. Each group member takes a turn at being teacher, student, and observer. Observers might find useful the observational checklist for the evaluation of teaching, provided in Table 11.7 on page 247. After you have all taught your skills, discuss and evaluate your experiences in each role (teacher, student, observer), and suggest possible ways to improve your teaching.

4. In chapter 4, it was suggested that one of the challenges facing teachers is the adjustment of the teaching environment to meet the developmental levels of the children. Four environmental variables under the teachers' control were identified:
   a. Rules
   b. Space
   c. Number of participants
   d. Amount or type of equipment

   One or more of these variables can be adjusted to create success on behalf of students. In small groups, discuss how these four variables can be adjusted when teaching children gymnastic stunts and tumbling skills. Formulate creative ideas and specific recommendations and share these with other groups.

5. Chapter 13 identified a number of disabilities that afflict young children. In small groups, choose four disabilities and discuss how children with these disabilities can be accommodated in gymnastic activities. Consider what adjustments will have to be made to accommodate each child's developmental level and to ensure success. Debate possible techniques and methods of evaluation. Share ideas with other groups.

6. A feature of this text is the idea of teaching and enhancing academic skills and concepts through physical education activities. In small groups, discuss and create ideas to teach or enhance academic skills and concepts in the areas of science, mathematics, and language arts through the use of tumbling skills, agility skills, and balancing stunts. Also consider how to evaluate students' acquisition of such skills and concepts. Share ideas with other groups.

SELECTED READINGS

Blatt, G. T., J. and J. Cunningham. 1981. *It's your move: Expressive movement activities for the language arts class.* New York: Teachers College Press.

CAHPER. 1985. *Gymnastics: A movement approach.* Ottawa, Ontario: CAHPER.

Graham, G., S. A. Holt-Hale, and M. Parker. 1987. *Children moving.* Mountain View, CA: Mayfield.

Kirchner, G., C. Cunningham, and E. Warrell. 1978. *Introduction to movement education.* 2d ed. Dubuque, IA: Wm. C. Brown.

Ryser, O., and J. Brown. 1990. *A manual for tumbling and apparatus stunts.* Dubuque, IA: Wm. C. Brown.

Wall, J., and N. Murray 1994. *Children and movement.* 2d ed. Dubuque, IA: Wm. C. Brown.

Werner, P. H., and T. C. Burton. 1979. *Learning through movement: Teaching cognitive content through physical activities.* St. Louis: Mosby.

CHAPTER 25

KEY CONCEPTS

26.1 Safety considerations must be emphasized when teaching children gymnastic stunts and manipulative skills using small equipment

26.2 Posing gymnastic challenges stimulates creativity and problem solving

26.3 Gymnastic stunts and manipulative skills involving small equipment must be developmentally appropriate to ensure that all children can achieve success and enjoyment

26.4 Manipulative skills involving small objects are acquired through instruction and practice opportunities

26.5 When teaching gymnastic stunts and manipulative skills using small equipment, effective teaching progressions, involving appropriate lead-up activities, are required

26.6 Using a Movement Education approach, when teaching gymnastic stunts and manipulative skills using small equipment, assists in accommodating children of all developmental levels

KEY OBJECTIVES

After completing this chapter you will be able to:

1. Design developmentally appropriate gymnastic activities using small equipment
2. Understand the scope and sequence of gymnastic stunts and manipulative skills using small equipment
3. Use small equipment to provide movement challenges in gymnastics
4. Apply Movement Education concepts and skills when teaching gymnastic stunts and manipulative skills with small equipment
5. Plan a safe environment for teaching children gymnastic stunts and manipulative skills with small equipment
6. Teach and enhance academic concepts and skills when teaching gymnastic stunts and manipulative skills with small equipment
7. Identify key teaching points associated with gymnastic stunts and manipulative skills when using small equipment
8. Employ teaching progressions that lead to the successful development of gymnastic stunts and manipulative skills with small equipment

The material in this chapter provides two basic services. The first, and perhaps more common, is to teach children how to manipulate small objects with different parts of the body. The second is to provide a logical extension of the Movement Education approach, which was begun in the previous section. For example, small equipment, such as beanbags, individual ropes, and wands, is used to provide more difficult challenges involving one or more of Laban's elements of movement.

The material in this chapter has been organized to provide primary and intermediate teachers with sufficient information to teach a wide variety of manipulative skills, and to expand a child's understanding of movement concepts.

TEACHING PROCEDURES

The addition of small equipment activities to a gymnastic lesson presents several organizational and instructional problems. The following suggestions will assist you in incorporating small equipment into your gymnastic program.

CONCEPT

26.1 *Safety Considerations Must Be Emphasized When Teaching Children Gymnastic Stunts and Manipulative Skills Using Small Equipment*

Routine Procedures

Perhaps the most frustrating aspect of using small equipment is getting it out and putting it away in an orderly manner. One of the most successful and efficient ways of handling equipment is to have each type to be used in a lesson placed in boxes or containers near the instructional area. The teacher can then give instructions about who will be using what type of equipment and where their working areas will be. When the equipment is not being used, it is returned to the appropriate container. Suggestions for carrying and placing such equipment as wands and hoops are given in the sections on each type of equipment.

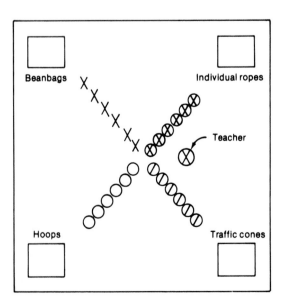

Using Small Equipment

It was stated in the previous chapter that small equipment should be used to provide additional challenges to movement skills. Since each class and grade level varies according to the time and equipment available and the students' background of skill, no standard application of this equipment can be recommended.

CONCEPT

26.2 *Posing Gymnastic Challenges Stimulates Creativity and Problem Solving*

Activities and Developmental Levels

The nature and variety of small equipment makes it difficult to arrange skills in the exact order of difficulty. Table 26.1 provides a basic guideline that teachers can use when selecting and emphasizing small equipment activities.

CONCEPT

26.3 *Gymnastic Stunts and Manipulative Skills Involving Small Equipment Must Be Developmentally Appropriate to Ensure That All Children can Achieve Success and Enjoyment*

BEANBAG ACTIVITIES

Beanbags are the most common type of small equipment and are available to virtually every classroom teacher. Beanbags should be at least six inches square for the activities suggested in this program. Cloth covers, rather than smooth plastic or nylon ones, are preferred for homemade beanbags.

Although beanbags traditionally have been used by primary teachers for simple games and manipulative activities, they have many applications at the intermediate level. The more familiar, structured beanbag activities are presented first to illustrate contemporary beanbag use in the gymnastic program. Following that is a section on how the beanbag can be used as an obstacle or focus point in developing movement concepts and skills.

TABLE 26.1 Small Equipment Activities

Activity	Developmental Level I	II	III	Page
Beanbag Activities				
Individual Activities	→	→		553
Partner Activities	→			554
Movement Skills	→	→	→	554
Rope-Jumping Activities				
Individual Activities	→	→	→	555
Partner Activities		→	→	563
Long Rope Activities	→	→	→	563
Movement Skills	→	→	→	565
Hoop Activities				
Individual Activities	→	→	→	566
Partner Activities	→	→	→	567
Movement Skills	→	→	→	567
Wand Activities				
Individual Activities	→	→	→	568
Partner Activities	→	→	→	568
Movement Skills	→	→	→	568
Parachute Activities				
Exercises	→	→	→	572
Games	→	→	→	572
Dances	→	→	→	573
Movement Skills	→	→	→	573
Indian Clubs, Milk Cartons and Traffic Cones	→	→	→	574
Juggling Activities		→	→	575

CONCEPT

26.4 *Manipulative Skills Involving Small Objects Are Acquired through Instruction and Practice Opportunities*

Individual Activities

The beanbag can be used to increase the difficulty of many previously acquired stunts and tumbling skills, as well as with many new balance and stunt activities. The following examples illustrate the beanbag's versatility:

CONCEPT

26.5 *When Teaching Gymnastic Stunts and Manipulative Skills Using Small Equipment, Effective Teaching Progressions, Involving Appropriate Lead-Up Activities, Are Required*

1. *Stunts and tumbling skills:*
   a. Camel Walk (p. 515), beanbag behind neck

   b. Knee Walk (p. 528), beanbag on head
   c. Bouncing Ball (p. 516), beanbag on head
   d. Single-Knee Balance (p. 531), beanbag on head or arm
   e. Forward Roll (p. 505) and Side Roll (p. 505), beanbag under chin
   f. Turk Stand (p. 530), beanbag on head
   g. L-Support (p. 536), beanbag between knees

2. *Throwing and catching skills:* The wide surface and lack of rebound property make the beanbag a valuable tool in helping young children learn how to throw and catch. Following are a few examples of how primary teachers can use the beanbag to develop hand-eye coordination (figure 26.1):
   a. Toss the beanbag into the air and catch it with both hands, with the left hand, then with the right.
   b. Toss the beanbag into the air, change direction or perform a hand movement (clap hands, touch the floor), and then catch the beanbag.
   c. Place targets on the floor (hoops, milk cartons) and throw the beanbag into the target. Change throwing skill and distance.

Figure 26.1 Balance the beanbag on your hand.

d. Move, throw, and catch. Use a variety of locomotor skills (running, skipping, and so on) and throw and catch beanbags, moving around the instructional area.

3. *Balance the beanbag on different parts of the body.* Designate specific parts of the body—head, elbow, and so on. Change body position and continue. For example, "Put the beanbag on your back and balance on one foot."

4. *Move the beanbag with different parts of the body:* Ask the class to propel the beanbags with their knees and catch them; then designate other parts of the body such as the head, foot, elbow, and shoulder.

Partner Activities

Many of the previous individual skills can be performed with two performers:

1. *Throwing and catching:*
   a. Throw the beanbag back and forth, changing the distance and the type, position, and angle of throw to create variable practices (figure 26.2).
   b. Throw and catch with two beanbags.
   c. Throw and catch with one or both performers on the move.

2. *Pass and catch the beanbag with different parts of the body:* Propel it with the feet and catch it with the hands or feet. Propel it with the head and catch it with the stomach or another part of the body.

Applying Movement Skills

The individual and partner activities previously described indicate the value and potential of beanbag activities in

Figure 26.2 Throw and catch the beanbag.

developing throwing, catching, balancing, and agility skills. If children have been taught through the problem-solving method and understand movement concepts and skills, the next step is to use beanbag activities in a much more creative and challenging way. The following examples illustrate how the beanbag can be used as an obstacle to balance on or with and as an object to maneuver on or over. By posing tasks or challenges using movement skills, children explore and discover the various ways their bodies or body parts can manipulate and control small obstacles.

Although the same challenge can be presented to primary and intermediate children, the movement response should be different. As children progress through the grades, they acquire more skill and movement understanding, which is revealed in the complexity and quality of their movement patterns. Following are examples of the types of questions or instructions that should be given. Each teacher, however, should present challenges according to her class's gymnastic background and receptiveness to this exploratory approach.

C O N C E P T

26.6 *Using a Movement Education Approach, When Teaching Gymnastic Stunts and Manipulative Skills Using Small Equipment, Assists in Accommodating Children of All Developmental Levels*

1. *Balance and transfer of weight:*
   a. "How many different parts of your body can you balance the beanbag on?"
   b. "Place the beanbag on the floor. Can you balance with one part of your body on the beanbag?"
   c. "Place the beanbag on your seat and see how many ways you can balance on three different parts of your body."
   d. "Place a beanbag on the floor. How many different ways can you balance over the beanbag?" (figure 26.3).
   e. "How many different ways can you cross the beanbag?"

Figure 26.3 "How many different ways can you balance over the beanbag?"

Figure 26.4 Jump over a beanbag, change directions, and jump over another beanbag.

2. *Direction and speed:* Scatter beanbags around the floor area and pose these challenge activities illustrating how the beanbag acts as an obstacle or focus point in the development of directional movements and the quality of speed.
   a. "Move around as many beanbags as possible, but do not jump over any."
   b. "Run in any direction and when you come to a beanbag, run completely around it; then move to another beanbag."
   c. "Move in any direction and, as you approach a beanbag, jump over it, land, and then change direction to find another beanbag" (figure 26.4).
   d. "Can you run in different directions, showing a change of speed every time you jump over a beanbag?"
   e. "Run and jump over a beanbag."

3. *Shapes*
   a. "Can you make a stretched shape, with the beanbag on the highest part of your body?"

   b. "See if you can keep the beanbag on one part of your body while you try to make two different curled shapes."

4. *Relationships:* Each partner has a beanbag.
   a. "Place the beanbags on the floor and make up a matching sequence that shows a change of direction and a change of speed."
   b. "Keep the beanbag between your feet and make up a matching sequence that includes moving forward, backward, and sideways."
   c. One child leads and the other must match her movements" (figure 26.5).

ROPE-JUMPING ACTIVITIES

Children perform three basic types of rope-jumping activities in the primary and intermediate grades. One is rope jumping that involves light, graceful leaps over a rope turned by an individual or with a partner. The second is long rope jumping, which involves jumping over a long rope turned by two performers. Finally, ropes are used in a variety of ways to enhance movement concepts and skills.

Children of all ages enjoy performing individual rope-jumping skills with or without musical accompaniment. In the primary grades, the level of interest or skill varies little between boys and girls. For many years, the trend has been for girls to continue this activity through the intermediate grades and for boys to shift their interests to other types of activities. However, recent physical fitness programs, such as "Jump Rope for Heart," have created a very positive change in boys' attitudes toward all types of rope-jumping activities. Today this activity is enjoyed equally by boys and girls and with virtually no difference in skill level.

Individual Activities

Several kinds and thicknesses of rope can be used for individual rope jumping. A ⅜-inch sash cord is probably the best; however, any rope, sash or plastic, up to ½-inch thick is acceptable. It is equally important to have the proper length of rope for each child. To determine the correct length, have the child stand in the center of the rope; it should extend from armpit to armpit (figure 26.6). An incorrect length adversely affects performance.

The correct rope-jumping form is to hold the ends of the rope loosely in the fingers, with the thumbs placed on top of the rope and pointing to the sides. The elbows are held close to the sides, with the forearms and hands pointing slightly forward and away from the body (figure 26.7). To start the rope turning, swing the arms and shoulders in a circular motion; once the rope begins to follow the circular motion, all further action should be initiated from the wrists and fingers. The jumping action should be a slight push off the toes, just high enough to allow the rope to pass under the feet.

a

b

c

Figure 26.5 "Follow your partner." One child leads. The other child must match her movements.

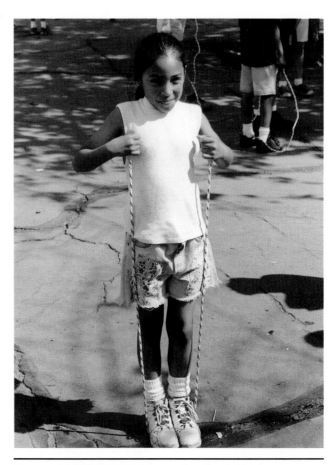

Figure 26.6 Having the correct length of rope is important for the child to jump properly.

Figure 26.7 Correct jumping form.

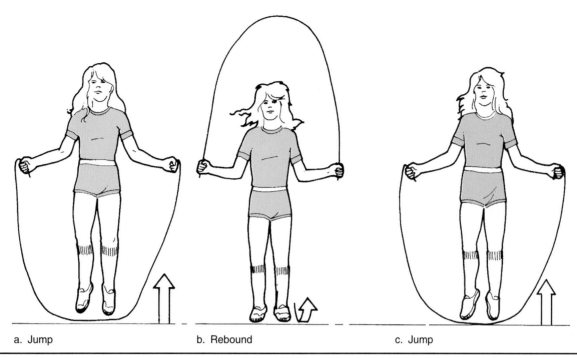

a. Jump   b. Rebound   c. Jump

Figure 26.8 Two-foot basic. The two-foot basic step includes two jumps for each complete turn of the rope. Pull the rope around and jump over it, and take a second "rebound" jump as the rope passes backward and upward.

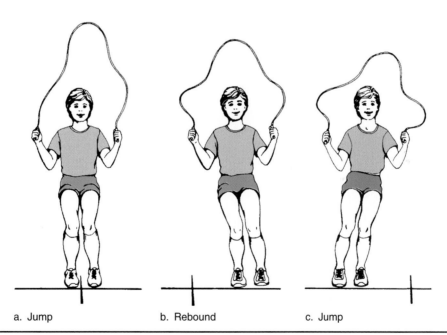

a. Jump   b. Rebound   c. Jump

Figure 26.9 Skier. A double-foot jump represents the leg actions of a skier. (a) Stand with feet together and straddling a line. (b) Use a two-foot basic action, jump over rope, and land about one and one-half feet on the other side of the line. (c) Take a rebound jump, then jump and shift both feet back to the other side of the line. Once the skill is learned, try shifting feet forward and backward.

The following rope-jumping skills are listed in approximate order of difficulty. It is helpful to begin each new step without a rope. Once the child can execute the foot movements, let him try with a rope. At this stage, a musical background helps the child keep up a steady rhythm. Any folk-dance record, with a 4/4 rhythm, such as "Shoo Fly" or "Pop Goes the Weasel," works very well. All popular tunes with a similar beat work as well and, in fact, are enjoyed more than folk-dance records by upper elementary school children.

Many of the basic steps shown in figures 26.8 to 26.19 can be performed in slow or fast time and with the rope turned forward or backward. With slow rhythm, the

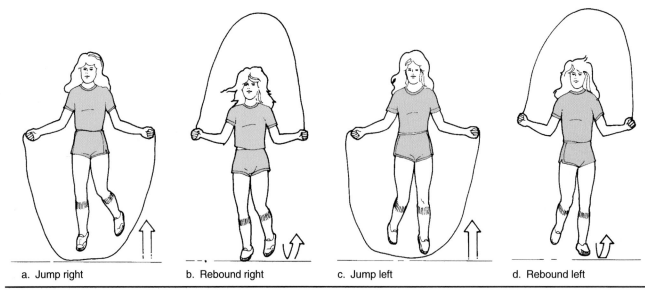

Figure 26.10 Alternate step. Jump over rope with the right foot (jump), hop on same foot (rebound), jump over rope with left foot (jump), and hop on the same foot (rebound). Pass the rope overhead.

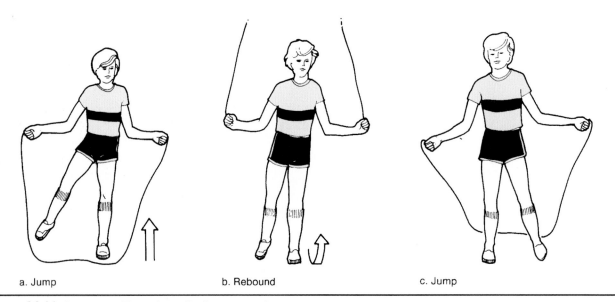

Figure 26.11 Swing step. This is basically the same as the alternate step, except swing the "free leg" forward, backward, or to the side during the rebound step.

performer jumps over the rope, takes a rebound jump in place as the rope passes overhead, and then performs the original step or shifts to a new movement. The pattern is jump-rebound-jump. With slow musical accompaniment, the performer jumps over the rope on every other beat. With a fast rhythm, the rope is turned twice as fast, so the performer executes a step only as the rope passes under her feet. With fast musical accompaniment, the performer jumps over the rope on every beat.

Once the children have learned two or more basic steps, they can begin to create many interesting and enjoyable routines. A few suggestions follow; however, each child should have an opportunity to develop his own routine.

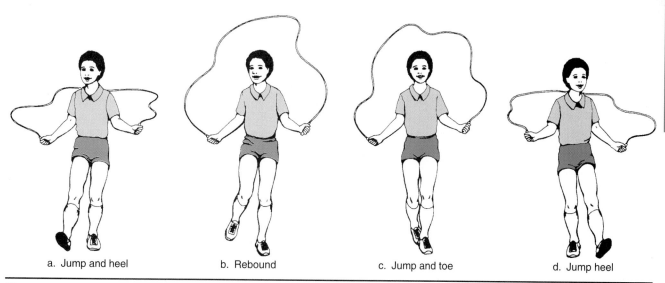

a. Jump and heel   b. Rebound   c. Jump and toe   d. Jump heel

Figure 26.12 Heel toe. This is a combination of the "heel to heel" and "toe to toe" steps. Begin by standing on left foot, then jump on left foot, simultaneously placing heel of right foot forward (a). Take a rebound jump (b) on the left foot. Jump and land on left foot and place right toe to back of left heel (c). Jump and land on right foot and place heel of left foot forward (d). Continue pattern.

a. Jump and knee   b. Rebound left   c. Jump and kick   d. Rebound right

Figure 26.13 Can can. Stand on the left foot. Jump on left foot and bring right knee up, pointing toe down (a). Rebound on left foot (b). Jump on left and kick right leg as high as you can (c). Jump on right foot and bring left knee up (d). Continue pattern.

1. Combine a change of speed with the alternate step.
2. Make up a sequence involving three different steps.
3. Make up a sequence involving a hop, an alternate step, and a change of direction.
4. Perform three different steps in a cross-arm position.
5. Move in different directions, using hopping, jumping, and rocking-step skills.
6. Make up a sequence, with the rope turning backward.

a. Hop left

b. Rebound left

Figure 26.14 One-foot hop. Perform the one-foot hop with each turn of the rope or with a rebound step after each jump over the rope. However, continue hopping on one foot for several rotations of the rope before transferring to hopping on the opposite foot.

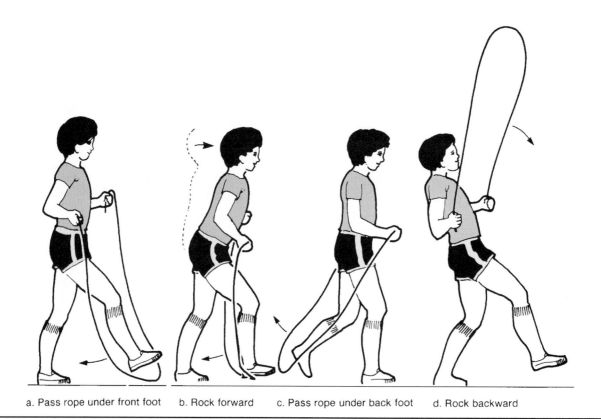

a. Pass rope under front foot   b. Rock forward   c. Pass rope under back foot   d. Rock backward

Figure 26.15 Rocker. When performing the rocker step, one leg is always forward and the weight shifts from the back to the front, or lead, foot. As the rope passes under the front foot, transfer the weight forward, allowing the back foot to raise and the rope to pass under it. After the rope passes under the back foot and begins its upward and forward arch, "rock" back, transferring the weight to the back foot.

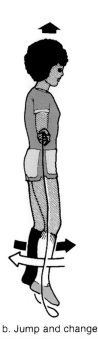

a. Begin in a stride position

b. Jump and change

c. Land in a stride position

Figure 26.16 Spread legs. Begin the spread-legs step in a front stride position, with the weight evenly distributed on both feet. Pull the rope around, jump, and as it passes under change the position of the feet. Continue pattern.

a. Begin in a cross-legged position

b. Jump and cross

c. Left leg over right

Figure 26.17 Crossed legs. Begin the cross-leg step with the right leg crossed in front of the left leg and the weight evenly distributed on both feet. Pull the rope around, jump, and as it passes under cross the left leg over the right. Continue the pattern, alternating the front leg position.

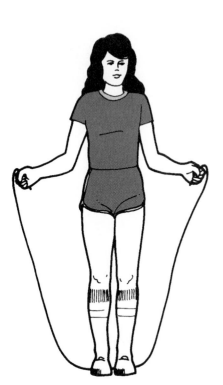
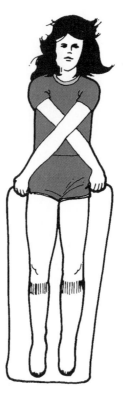

a. From a regular rope-skipping position . . .   b. . . . to cross left over right . . .   c. . . . right hand up under left armpit.

Figure 26.18 Crossed arms. Crossing arms should take place during an ongoing rope-jumping movement. As the rope begins its forward and downward movement, cross the left arm over the right and bring the right hand up and under the left armpit. Make the next jump in this position. Continue in the crossed-arm position or alternate the crossed-arm position on each turn of the rope.

a. Jump   b. Turn—turn   c. Jump

Figure 26.19 Pepper. The pepper step is two full turns of the rope while the performer's feet are off the ground.

a   b   c

Figure 26.20 Partner activities with an individual rope.

Partner Activities

Children can perform several enjoyable partner activities with an individual rope. Many variations and routines can be developed from the following basic starting positions. One partner begins with a two-foot basic step (figure 26.20a). As the rope comes forward and down, the outside partner enters (figure 26.20b) and then turns around and jumps out (figure 26.20c). Some variations follow:

1. Partners perform mirror images, hopping, jumping, or other basic rope-jumping steps.
2. Outside partner turns her back to her partner and they continue jumping.
3. Outside partner keeps the same jumping cadence as her partner but begins to make a quarter or a half turn, then jumps back to her original position.

Partners stand facing each other with the rope held in the same hand. Some variations follow:

1. One partner moves in, then out.
2. One partner moves in, followed by her partner.
3. When both are inside, they make up a sequence of matching steps.

LONG-ROPE-JUMPING ACTIVITIES

Long-rope jumping is performed with one or more children jumping over a rope turned by two other children. The rope can be turned two different ways for jumping activities. Teach the Front Door first, then introduce the Back Door skill (figure 26.21). To assist in teaching both types of jumping skills, use the suggested list of rope-jumping rhymes in the next section.

Figure 26.21 Front door. The children turn the rope toward the jumper (clockwise), and the jumper waits until the rope is moving away from her before she runs in. Back door: The turners turn the rope away from the jumper (counterclockwise), and the jumper waits until the rope has passed its highest peak and is moving downward before she runs in.

The following progression of rope-jumping activities can be performed by entering through either the front or back door.

1. Run under the rope.
2. Run in, jump once, run out.
3. Run in, jump several times, run out.
4. Run in, jump once on one foot, run out.
5. Run in, jump several times on one foot, run out.
6. Run in, jump making quarter, half, three-quarter, or full turns with each jump, run out.
7. Run in, jump on alternate feet, run out.
8. Run in, touch the floor with the hands on every other jump, run out.

9. Run in, squat (on all fours), jump in this position, run out.
10. Run in, jump up and touch toes, land, run out.
11. Run in, turners gradually increase speed to "hot pepper," slow down, run out.
12. Run in, turners gradually raise rope off the ground ("high water").
13. Run in with a ball, bounce the ball several times, run out.
14. Repeat these skills with a partner.
15. Place arm over partner's shoulder, run in, jump several times, run out.
16. With partner, run in, stand back to back, jump several times, run out.
17. With partner, run in, face partner, hold partner's right leg, jump several times, run out.
18. Follow the leader with four or five players and one chosen to be the leader. The leader runs in and performs any skill or stunt, then runs out. Each player follows and repeats the leader's stunt.

Rope-Jumping Rhymes

Rope-jumping rhymes, like singing games, are centuries old and belong to people of many nations. The first four rhymes are perhaps the most popular in North America. Each region may also have slight variations. Encourage children to use their own version.

Down by the Meadow
Down by the meadow where the green grass grows,
There sits (call the name of jumper) sweet as a rose.
She sang, she sang, she sang, she sang so sweet,
And along came (jumper's sweetheart's name), and
Kissed her on the cheek.
How many kisses did she get?
1, 2, 3, 4, etc.
(Child keeps jumping until she misses.)

Teddy Bear, Teddy Bear
Teddy Bear, Teddy Bear, turn around.
Teddy Bear, Teddy Bear, touch the ground.
Teddy Bear, Teddy Bear, shine your shoes.
Teddy Bear, Teddy Bear, that will do.
Teddy Bear, Teddy Bear, go upstairs.
Teddy Bear, Teddy Bear, say your prayers.
Teddy Bear, Teddy Bear, turn out the light.
Teddy Bear, Teddy Bear, say good night.
Teddy Bear, hop on one foot, one foot.
Teddy Bear, hop on two feet, two feet.
Teddy Bear, hop on three feet, three feet.
Teddy Bear, hop right out.

Johnny on the Ocean
Johnny on the ocean,
Johnny on the sea,
Johnny broke a bottle,

And blamed it on me.
I told ma,
Ma told pa.
Johnny got a whipping
And a ha! ha! ha!
How many whippings did he get?
1, 2, 3, etc. (Child keeps jumping until she misses.)

I'm a Little Dutch Girl
Charlie Chaplin went to France
To teach the pretty girls
The hula dance.
First on the heel,
Then the toe,
Do the splits,
And around you go.
Salute to the Captain,
Curtsey the Queen,
Touch the bottom of the submarine.

All in Together
All in together, this fine weather,
January, February, March, etc.
(Jumper runs in on the month of his birthday.)
All out together, this fine weather,
Jaunary, February, March, etc.
(Jumper runs out on the month of his birthday.)

I Love Coffee
I love coffee, I love tea, I love (name).
I dislike coffee, I dislike tea, I dislike (name).
So go away from me.
(Child who is jumping calls the name of another child, who comes in, then goes out.)

Mabel, Mabel
Mabel, Mabel, set the table,
Don't forget the salt, vinegar, pepper. . . .
(Turners turn "pepper" on the last word.)

Fudge, Fudge
Fudge, Fudge, tell the judge,
Mama's got a newborn baby.
Wrap it up in tissue paper,
Send it down the elevator,
Elevator one, splits . . . elevator two . . . splits, (and so on until the jumper misses. Jumper performs the splits on the word "splits.")

Apple, Apple
Apple, Apple, up in the tree,
Tell me who my lover shall be,
A, B, C, D, E, etc. (Jump to each letter until the jumper reaches his sweetheart's first initial.)

Mama, Mama
Mama, Mama, I am sick,
Send for the doctor, quick, quick, quick.
Mama, Mama, turn around,

Figure 26.22 High jumping.

Figure 26.23 Crossing with a cartwheel.

Mama, Mama, touch the ground.
Mama, Mama, are you through?
Mama, Mama, spell your name.
(Child performs actions indicated in the verse.)

Playground Ideas with Long Ropes

Long ropes have traditionally been used for jumping activities. The following examples illustrate other enjoyable uses of one or two long ropes:

1. *Jumping over one rope:* Two performers hold a long rope approximately two feet off the ground (vary the height according to the ability of the group). Activities may include:
   a. High jumping (figure 26.22)
   b. Jumping and making shapes in the air
   c. Jumping and turning in the air
   d. Crossing the rope with a cartwheel movement (figure 26.23)
   e. Follow-the-leader activities

2. *Jumping over two ropes:* Two performers hold two ropes about two feet off the ground. Repeat the same skills (figure 26.24). Then have the rope holders hold one rope low and the other high; repeat the skills.

These few examples should provide the teacher with a starting point. The creative teacher and class will come up with other ideas, such as jumping over one rope, then crawling under the other or hopping, jumping, or performing another locomotor movement from one end to the other.

Applying Movement Skills

Several basic rope-jumping skills that can be performed by an individual or with a partner have been described. A rope can also be used in many other interesting and challenging

Figure 26.24 Jumping over two ropes.

ways. For example, it can become an obstacle to manipulate, as when tying a knot using only the feet. It can also become an obstacle to maneuver around or over, such as finding many ways of crossing a rope.

It is possible to apply the problem-solving method and the movement skills described in the previous chapter to individual rope activities. The rope, thus, becomes a means of further challenging the physical and creative abilities of the child. The four movement concepts and the various movement skills become the framework for developing a series of tasks or challenges. Following are some examples:

1. *Balance or weight bearing:* "See if you can hold the rope with both hands and balance on both knees and one elbow." This is a manipulating activity.

2. *Shapes:* "Can you make a twisted shape with your rope?" This is another manipulating activity.

3. *Direction:* "Place the rope on the floor in any pattern you like and make up a sequence that involves three changes in direction" (figure 26.25). This is a maneuvering activity.

4. *Force and rolling:* "Place the rope on the floor, then move a few steps away from it. See if you can run, leap over the rope, land, and roll."

CHAPTER 26

Figure 26.25 "How many ways can you cross the rope?"

Figure 26.27 Hula hooping.

Figure 26.26 Sequence of matching shapes with a partner.

5. *Relationships and force:* "With your partner and one rope, make up a sequence that has three different pulling actions."
6. *Relationships and shapes:* "Can you make up a sequence of matching shapes with your partner? You may use one or two ropes any way you like" (figure 26.26).

HOOP ACTIVITIES

The introduction of hoop activities adds challenge and variety to any gymnastic program. Hoops are inexpensive, easily stored, and, most important, a very versatile piece of equipment. It is strongly recommended that a class set, plus

six to eight extra hoops, be purchased. A mixture of the standard 42-inch hoops and the smaller 36-inch hoops is adequate for any elementary grade.

Since hoops can be extremely noisy, establish a strict routine for getting them out of the equipment room and carrying them to instructional areas. Require the children to place their hoops on the floor gently and to sit inside them while listening to instructions.

A few of the more common activities will be presented, followed by several suggestions for applying movement skills to hoop activities. The following hoop individual and partner activities can be presented as a direct challenge. However, variations occur in the way the children attempt to perform the skills.

Individual Activities

1. Hula Hooping: This skill is normally performed around the waist; however, other areas of the body, such as the arm, leg, wrist, and ankles, can also be used (figure 26.27).
2. Hula Jumping: The hoop can be used as a jumping rope. This is an effective rope jumping substitute, particularly for primary children.
3. Place the hoop on the floor, then jump over it (figure 26.28), or jump across it.
4. Roll the hoop with a reverse spin and jump over it as it returns.
5. Spin the hoop. While it is spinning, try to run around it or jump over it before it falls.
6. Place the hoop on the floor. Walk around the edge of the hoop or run and jump into the center and then out.

Figure 26.30 "Balance over your hoop."

Figure 26.28 Jump over it.

Figure 26.29 Jump over.

Partner Activities

1. Play catch with one or two hoops.
2. Target throwing with partner: One partner throws the hoop at a designated part of his partner, such as his arm, right leg, or head. Vary the distance according to the level of skill.
3. One partner holds the hoop in a horizontal position while the other tries to run and jump over it or crawl under it or through it (figure 26.29).
4. One partner rolls the hoop while the other partner attempts to crawl through it.

Applying Movement Skills

The hoop has become one of the most popular pieces of small equipment for use with movement skills. The following challenges illustrate the scope and versatility of this piece of equipment.

1. *Balance or weight bearing* (figure 26.30): "Can you balance over the hoop?" "Can you balance with three parts on the hoop?" "See if you can balance on four parts and hold the hoop off the ground." "On how many different parts of your body can you balance the hoop?"
2. *Shapes and flow:* "Make up a sequence of three different shapes while holding your hoop."
3. *Rolling and flow:* "Can you roll while holding onto your hoop?"
4. *Direction:* "Place four hoops on the floor in any pattern you wish, then make up a sequence that shows four changes in direction." After the sequence is developed, "Now add a change of speed or level to your sequence."
5. *Relationships and shapes:* "Make up a sequence with your partner in which one partner holds the hoop and the other moves from shape to shape."

WAND ACTIVITIES

Initially, a lack of commercial equipment in many elementary schools forced teachers to improvise with what was available or to make their own equipment. The wand is an example of the latter. Discarded broom handles or ¾-inch to 1½-inch doweling cut into 36-inch or 42-inch lengths are adequate for elementary school children. Wands present the same noise problem as hoops, so establish a similar handling procedure as suggested for hoops.

Numerous structured stunts can be performed with a wand. In addition, a wide variety of movement tasks or challenges can be designed to use the wand in a manipulative

Figure 26.31 Finger balance. Hold wand with one hand, then place the index finger of the opposite hand under the end of the wand. Release grip and balance the wand on the end of the finger. After practice, try balancing wand while walking forward and backward and then running.

Figure 26.32 Foot balance. Place wand near the big toe, raise the foot off the floor, release grip, and try to balance the wand on the foot.

way or as an obstacle to maneuver around or over. The following activities should begin in the second or third grade. However, movement challenges using the wand can begin in the first grade.

Individual and Partner Activities

The stunts in figures 26.31 to 26.40 are some of the many individual and partner activities children can perform with wands.

Applying Movement Skills

The wand can be as useful as a hoop or rope in developing movement concepts and skills. The following examples illustrate how balance, levels, and relationships can be further enhanced by a wand:

Figure 26.33 Back touch. Begin with the legs straight and the feet approximately shoulder-width apart. Grasp the wand close to one end. Arch back, place the end of the wand on the mat, and continue arching back and down.

Figure 26.34 Double foot balance. Begin in a back-lying position, hold the wand above the head and place the feet under the wand. Release hands and extend the legs upward, keeping the wand balanced across the feet.

1. *Balance or weight bearing:* If the class has had prior experience with a wand, try these: "See how many different parts of your body you can balance the wand on." "Is it possible to balance the wand on your elbow (knee, stomach, and so on)?"

a

b

Figure 26.35 Jump through stick. Stand with the knees partially bent and the feet about twelve inches apart. Hold the wand with the palms face down and the arms spread apart and the fingers grasping it (a). While keeping the arms straight, jump up and over the wand, landing in front, with the knees slightly bent (b).

Figure 26.36 Thread the needle. Begin in a back-lying position, knees bent, and hold the wand in front of the body. Without losing balance or touching the wand, bend the knees, pass the feet up and under the wand, and return to the original position.

Figure 26.37 Twist away. Partners stand with their feet about shoulder-width apart. They grasp the wand with palms facing down. Each partner attempts to twist to her right. As soon as one partner releases her grip, the other is declared the winner.

Figure 26.38 Floor touch. Partners sit on the floor in a cross-legged position. They grasp the wand, with their palms facing down and their arms partially flexed. The wand must be parallel to the floor. On a signal from the teacher, each child tries to touch the wand to the floor on his right side. Change sides after each contest.

2. *Transfer of weight and flow:* "Can you hold the wand with both hands and roll along the floor?" "Place the wand on the floor and see how many ways you can cross it using your hands and feet."
3. *Levels and shapes:* "See if you can show me three stretched shapes—one low, one halfway up, and a high stretch—while holding a wand with both hands." "Can you make a twisted shape over your wand? Now under your wand?"
4. *Relationships:* Each partner has a wand. "Make up a sequence of matching (or contrasting) shapes with your partner" (figure 26.40).

PARACHUTE ACTIVITIES

Parachute activities have become an integral part of many elementary physical education programs. Children from grades two through six enjoy performing a variety of stunts, games, and rhythmic activities while holding a parachute and moving in a variety of ways. The following sections outline the basic teaching procedures and illustrate how parachute activities can contribute to fitness, skill development, and cooperative behavior. This type of activity is one of the most "fun" group experiences for all children—from the highly skilled to the severely disabled.

Figure 26.39 Dishrag. This is similar to Wring the Dishrag. Both partners must maintain their grips throughout the movement.

Figure 26.40 Matching shapes.

Figure 26.41 Circle sitting.

Figure 26.42 Fruit basket.

Figure 26.43 Making waves.

Figure 26.44 Umbrella.

Figure 26.45 Mushroom.

Circle Sitting

During the first lesson, have the children sit in a circle, with each child about two feet from the edge (skirt) of the parachute (canopy) (figure 26.41). Gradually introduce the following positions and turns:

1. *Overhand grip:* Grip the edge of the parachute with the palms facing down.
2. *Underhand grip:* Grip the edge of the parachute with the palms facing up.
3. *Mixed grip:* Grip the edge of the parachute with the palm of one hand facing up and the palm of the opposite hand facing down.
4. *Fruit basket:* This is a resting position. Begin with feet about shoulder-width apart, arms downward, and hands grasping the parachute with an overhand grip (figure 26.42). To coordinate all future group movements, begin with a preparatory signal, such as "ready," then a command such as "go" or "begin."
5. *Making waves:* Begin in the fruit basket position. All children begin to gently shake the parachute (small waves) up and down (figure 26.43). An increase in arm movements and speed increases the wave action. Other variations, such as odd numbers moving up while even numbers move down, or half the class up and the other half down, produce different wave effects.

6. *Umbrella:* Begin in the fruit basket position. On command, lift the chute overhead (figure 26.44). A slow count of 1, 2, 3 is normally needed to lift the chute into an umbrella position.
7. *Mushroom:* Begin in the fruit basket position. On signal, lift the chute to an umbrella position, then quickly take one step in and pull the chute down, holding the edge firmly to the ground (figure 26.45).

CHAPTER 26

Exercise Activities

The ultimate value of the following exercises is derived when the child is required to hold the chute taut and stretch, pull, or twist with an "overload" effort. Repetitions within exercises should be adjusted to the number that is appropriate for each child.

Side Stretcher

All students hold the chute taut with the left hand. The left knee is on the floor, and the right leg extends side-ways, with the right hand resting on the right leg. On command, the chute is pulled toward the right side. Repeat to opposite leg.

Row the Boat

All children sit with legs extended under the chute. The canopy is held with an overhand grip, arms bent, and chute touching the chest. On command, bend forward, extend arms, and touch hands to toes. Return to an upright position. Continue rowing action. Some variations follow:

1. Place right arm backward and repeat exercise.
2. Cross arm in front of chest and repeat exercise.

Curl-Ups

Begin with the body under the parachute in a curl-up position. In this position, the chute is held with an overhand grip and held taut under the chin. Hold this grip and sit up to an upright position, then return to starting position.

Push-Ups

Children first make a mushroom, keeping their hands and knees on the edge of the chute. Extend legs back-ward, perform one or more push-ups, then return to a starting position.

Chest Raiser

Children begin in a front lying position, facing the parachute, arms extended forward, and grasping chute with an overhand grip. Have all move backward until the chute is taut. On signal, raise arm upward, hold for a few seconds, then return to starting position. Some variations follow:

1. Raise arms and legs at the same time.
2. Hold chute with one hand and repeat exercise.
3. Begin lying on your side with a mixed grip and repeat exercise.

V-Sit

Children begin in a back lying position, top of head facing the chute, and palms facing upward, grasping the chute. Keep the chute taut, then raise chest and straighten legs to a V-sit position. Return to starting position.

Figure 26.46 Circus tent. From an umbrella position, all move under, turn around, kneel down, and hold chute to floor, then scramble out before chute falls on them.

Game Activities

Number Exchange

Children are numbered from one to five around the circle. When the parachute is in the umbrella position, the leader calls one or two numbers. Players with these numbers exchange positions.

Snatch Club

Divide class into two groups, then number each player in each group. Place a pin in the middle of the circle. When the chute is in an umbrella position, call a number. Each player then tries to snatch the club and return to his position before the other tags him.

Circus Tent

From an umbrella position, all move under, turn around, kneel down, and hold the chute to the floor; then they scramble out before the chute falls on them (figure 26.46).

Parachute Golf

Place five or six balls on the chute. All players try to get the balls to drop through the hole (figure 26.47).

Dash Under

Begin in the fruit basket position. As the parachute begins to rise up, two players from opposite sides exchange positions before the parachute returns to the fruit basket position (figure 26.48).

Popcorn

Begin in the fruit basket position with five or six balls in the middle of the parachute. All players try to keep all the balls in the air (figure 26.49).

Figure 26.47 Parachute golf.

Figure 26.50 Dance with the parachute.

Dance Activities

The parachute is extremely useful in teaching a variety of dance activities (figure 26.50). All locomotor steps can be taught to children while they are holding the chute in the fruit basket, umbrella, or other position. Changing directions, such as forward, sideways, and backward, as well as position exchanges can also be done while performing movements with the parachute. Rhythmic activities described in chapter 28 can be performed with the parachute. Marches, Dixieland tunes, and many current hits can be used as musical accompaniments for these rhythmic activities. Several folk dances, such as Pop Goes the Weasel, Seven Jumps, and Cshebogar, can also be performed with modification while holding the parachute.

Applying Movement Skills

Several movement skills, creative games, and inventive rhythmic sequences can be performed with a parachute. The following suggested challenges provide a basic starting point:

Movement Skills

1. "Hold the chute in the fruit basket position and make a stretched, curled, and twisted shape." Hold in the same position and balance on two parts, three parts, one knee and one elbow, and so on.
2. Hold chute with one hand and change direction and level.

Creative Games

Divide the class into four working groups. Each group invents a game, then teaches the whole class.

1. "Design a game that starts with the parachute in the fruit basket position and uses one ball and four beanbags."
2. "Can you make up a game for the class that uses the parachute, one ball, and four bowling pins?"

Figure 26.48 Dash under.

Figure 26.49 Popcorn.

Figure 26.51 "Run and jump over a piece of equipment."

Figure 26.52 "How many ways can you balance over your equipment?"

Rhythmic Skills

1. Use same approach as in creative games.
2. "Make up a sequence that has a run, hop, and jump while holding onto the parachute."
3. "Can you design a routine that has a skip, slide, change in direction, and change in level?"

INDIAN CLUB, MILK CARTON, AND TRAFFIC CONE ACTIVITIES

The success of any gymnastic program is very closely related to the number and variety of small equipment available to each child. Since most elementary schools lack sets of the previously described equipment, the following "bits and pieces" can be useful. Discarded bowling pins from local bowling alleys make excellent substitutes for Indian clubs. Plastic-coated milk cartons are also readily available. Traffic cones, which are used extensively in the games program as field markers and goals, are also a valuable addition to the gymnastic program.

These types of small equipment are basically used as obstacles to maneuver around or over. They are also used in combination with other small equipment, such as individual ropes, hoops, and wands, to provide more complex and creative challenges. Following are examples of their use:

1. *Direction, speed, and force:* Scatter all available Indian clubs, milk cartons, and traffic cones around the floor area. The following challenges can be used to develop directional movements and a change of speed:
   a. "Run in different directions around the equipment."
   b. "Repeat with a change in speed."
   c. "Run sideways, diagonally, and backward around the equipment."
   d. "Run, jump over any piece of equipment, land, move to a new piece of equipment, and repeat" (figure 26.51).
   e. "Repeat with a land and roll."

Figure 26.53 "Develop a matching sequence."

2. *Shape and balance:*
   a. "How many ways can you balance over your equipment?" (figure 26.52).
   b. "Can you balance with one part of your body on the equipment and one part on the floor?"
   c. "Make three different shapes over your equipment."
   d. "Run, jump, and make a shape over your equipment."

3. *Relationships:* Each partner has one piece of equipment.
   a. "Make three matching shapes over your equipment."
   b. "Develop a matching sequence that includes a balance, a shape, and a change of direction" (figure 26.53).

Figure 26.54 Juggling.

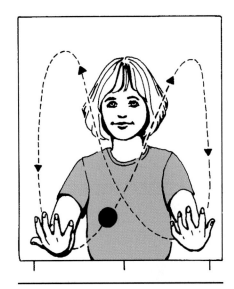

Figure 26.55 Figure eight pattern.

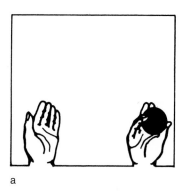
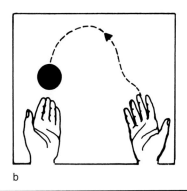
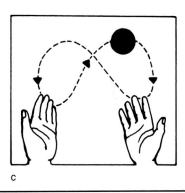

a   b   c

Figure 26.56 Step 1: one-bag throwing.

JUGGLING ACTIVITIES

Juggling with scarves, bags, balls, and clubs has become another very popular activity within the elementary physical education program (figure 26.54). Boys and girls can learn this activity within a short period of time and can become equally adept at it. It is an excellent hand-eye coordination skill, it allows every child to be active, and it is inexpensive. Perhaps its real value lies in its noncompetitive and life-long recreational use. Once the basic cascade, or figure eight, pattern is learned, a child's juggling repertoire can be expanded to include different throwing items and an unlimited number of exciting and challenging routines.

When introducing a juggling program, make sure every child has three items to juggle. Light scarves are extremely useful in demonstrating the basic cascade pattern. Juggling bags, which are easier to use than balls, may be purchased commercially or made by children. Balls of various sizes and weights are the third choice when teaching basic juggling. Once children have acquired the basic juggling skill, they will seek more challenging routines using disks, clubs, or other objects.

The basic juggling skill is performed in a figure eight pattern in an area roughly between the waist and top of the head (figure 26.55). Once proficiency has been acquired in this basic skill, a performer may throw high, to the side, or under one leg, but the basic figure eight movement is always maintained. Follow the next four steps to learn how to juggle with three bags. Master each step before moving on to the next one.

Step 1: One-bag throw. Hold the bag with the fingertips and thumb of your dominant hand (figure 26.56a). Scoop right hand toward the left and release bag at about the middle of your body. Let the bag rise, then catch it as it descends down the left side (figure 26.56b). Scoop left hand toward the middle and throw the bag upward toward the right side (figure 26.56c). Continue practicing this figure eight pattern until it is a smooth wrist and fingerlike action.

Step 2: Hold and throw. Pick up two bags and hold them on the heels of your hands. Pick up the third bag and hold it with fingertips and thumb (figure 26.57a). Throw the third bag from hand to hand in the figure eight pattern (figures 26.57b, c).

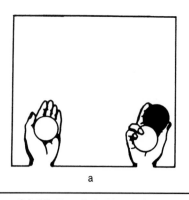
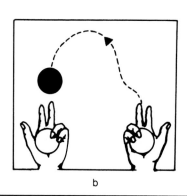
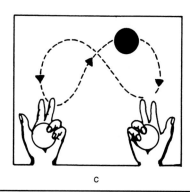

Figure 26.57 Step 2: hold and throw.

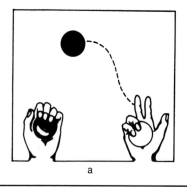

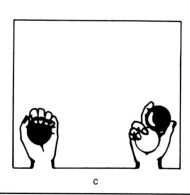

Figure 26.58 Step 3: exchange two bags.

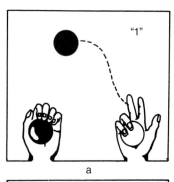
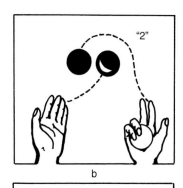
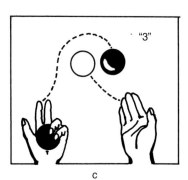

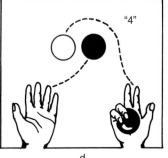

Figure 26.59 Step 4: three-bag juggling.

Step 3: Exchange two bags. Hold two bags in your dominant hand and one in the other hand. Throw the bag from the fingertips of your dominant hand and call "1" (figure 26.58a). When the bag reaches its highest point, call "2," then scoop the bag from your less dominant hand upward and under the other bag (figure 26.58b). The bag coming to the

less dominant hand should land on the palm. The bag coming to the dominant hand should be caught with the fingertips and thumb (figure 26.58c).

Step 4: Three-bag juggling. Throw the bag from your dominant hand and call "1" (figure 26.59a). When bag 1 peaks, scoop the bag from the less dominant hand and call "2" (figure 26.59b). When bag 2 peaks, scoop the bag from your dominant hand and call "3" (figure 26.59c). When bag 3 peaks, throw the bag from your less dominant hand and call "4" (figure 26.59d). When bag 4 peaks, throw the bag from your dominant hand and call "5" (figure 26.59e). Keep throwing and counting in this figure eight pattern.

If children have difficulty, have them repeat to the end of figure 26.59c, ending with two bags in the left hand and one in the right. Repeat figures 26.59a, b, and c several times, then start from the first figure and continue on through figure 26.59e. Once children master to the end of figure 26.59e, they have learned to juggle.

Summary Review

Using small equipment activities leads to the development of fine manipulative abilities and the specific motor skills involved in manipulating small objects with different parts of the body. Further, through the enjoyable medium of gymnastic and movement activities involving small equipment, children can develop movement skills and concepts while enhancing various components of physical fitness. In addition, creativity and problem solving can be facilitated through the use of appropriate challenges and a Movement Education approach.

5. View the video *How the Circulatory System Works* (see appendix A). In small groups, design a series of lessons involving gymnastic activities and small equipment that will enhance or teach the major concepts covered in the video. Share your lesson plans and ideas with other groups.

Selected Readings

American Heart Association. 1984. *Jump for the health of It: Basic skills.* Dallas: American Heart Association.

Doray, M. 1982. *J is for jumping.* Belmont, CA: Pitman Learning.

Melson, B., and V. Wornell. 1986. *Rope skipping for fun and fitness.* Wichita, KS: Woodlawn.

Prentup, F. B. 1980. *Skipping the rope.* Boulder, CO: Pruett.

Skolnik, P. S. 1974. *Jump rope.* New York: Workman.

Solis, K. M. and B. Budris. 1991. *The jump rope primer.* Champaign, IL: Human Kinetics.

Walker, D. A., and J. Haskin. 1986. *Double dutch.* Hillside, NJ: Enslow.

Wasserman, S. 1990. *Serious players in the primary classroom.* New York: Teachers College Press.

INDIVIDUAL *and* **GROUP** PROJECTS

1. In small groups, plan lessons showing how gymnastic activities with small equipment can be used to teach or enhance academic concepts and skills in science and mathematics. Plan how to evaluate the expected learning outcomes. Share lesson plans with other groups.

2. Individually or in small groups, design a series of stations for teaching gymnastic activities with small equipment. Outline the station set-up and produce a set of task cards to indicate the activities that should occur at each station.

3. In small groups, plan a series of problem-solving challenges involving gymnastic activities and small equipment. One of the group acts as the teacher, presenting challenges, while the rest perform the activities. Take turns so that each member of the group has the opportunity to present movement challenges.

4. In small groups, discuss safety considerations when teaching gymnastic stunts and manipulative skills with small equipment. Pay particular attention to children with special needs. Share recommendations between groups.

CHAPTER 27

Large Apparatus Activities

KEY CONCEPTS

27.1 Safety considerations must be emphasized when teaching children gymnastic activities that take place on or next to large apparatus

27.2 Gymnastic stunts and movement skills performed on large apparatus must be developmentally appropriate to ensure that all children can achieve success and enjoyment

27.3 As their muscular strength and endurance improves, together with their proficiency and confidence, children will be capable of more complex and more challenging gymnastic stunts and movement skills on large apparatus

27.4 Effective teaching progressions, providing all children with appropriate lead-up activities, are required when teaching gymnastic stunts and movement skills that take place on large apparatus

27.5 Posing gymnastic challenges stimulates creativity and allows children to adjust their gymnastic activities and routines on large apparatus to their own developmental level

KEY OBJECTIVES

After completing this chapter you will be able to:

1. Design developmentally appropriate gymnastic activities that take place on large apparatus
2. Understand the scope and sequence of gymnastic activities on large apparatus
3. Use large apparatus to provide movement challenges in gymnastics
4. Apply movement concepts and skills when teaching gymnastic activities that take place on large apparatus
5. Plan a safe environment for teaching children gymnastic activities that take place on large apparatus
6. Teach and enhance academic concepts and skills when teaching gymnastic activities that take place on large apparatus
7. Identify key teaching points associated with gymnastic activities that take place on large apparatus
8. Employ teaching progressions that lead to the successful development of gymnastic activities on large apparatus

he fundamental purpose of large apparatus in any gymnastic program is to provide an opportunity for children to test their ability on more challenging equipment and to improve physical fitness. This chapter continues the central theme of the previous chapter. The basic skills that can be performed on such apparatus as the balance beam, vaulting box, and climbing rope are described and illustrated. Then numerous suggestions are given for applying movement skills to this apparatus or integrating them with many of the traditional climbing, balancing, and vaulting movements performed on or over large apparatus.

TEACHING PROCEDURES

The following suggestions will assist the teacher in organizing and teaching both structured and movement skills with a variety of large apparatus:

1. Children of all ages should learn to carry and arrange apparatus—the position of the body when lifting a heavy piece of equipment—with a concern for their own safety and that of the class (figure 27.1).

| C | O | N | C | E | P | T |

27.1 *Safety Considerations Must Be Emphasized when Teaching Children Gymnastic Activities That Take Place On or Next to Large Apparatus*

---

2. The arrangement of individual and multiple pieces of equipment and apparatus should complement the main theme of the lesson. For example, if the theme is "change of direction" and four benches are used, they should be scattered to encourage movements in a variety of directions. If the benches are placed in a row, the children will usually follow one or two classmates around each bench.

3. Since there is never enough large apparatus, adopt station work, using both small and large apparatus, coupled with a rotation system. In the following diagram, the lesson stresses force (jumping and landing) and change of direction. The hoops, benches, traffic cones, and vaulting boxes are arranged to complement this theme. Each group practices at a station for a few minutes and then rotates to the next station. This gives each child an opportunity to use both small and large apparatus during an average lesson.

4. Whenever a stunt or movement pattern requires a spotter or spotters, proper instruction should be given

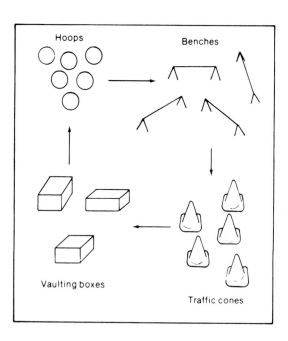

Figure 27.1 Carry the apparatus with safety and concern for all children.

to the children prior to and during the time they act as spotters. This is particularly important with vaulting skills over a box or bench.

5. Task or challenge cards can be used effectively with large apparatus activities.

6. Mats should be used with large apparatus according to school district policy. Several illustrations appear in this chapter of children performing stunts and movement skills without mats under the apparatus. These children have been taught a series of safety skills and only to attempt skills according to their level of skill and ability.

27.2 *Gymnastic Stunts and Movement Skills Performed on Large Apparatus Must Be Developmentally Appropriate to Ensure That All Children Can Achieve Success and Enjoyment*

Developmental Level I

Three types of large apparatus contained in this chapter stress balance, agility, or arm and shoulder strength and endurance. Many of the skills listed for this developmental level have been learned as stunts and tumbling activities or as movement skills and sequences. This is particularly true of balance beam and some vaulting activities. Activities on the climbing rope, horizontal bar, and ladder require a great deal of arm and shoulder girdle strength and endurance. Hence, it is important to begin with simple movements with minimum repetitions, as well as to use movement challenges that stress these key components of fitness. As children gain strength, proficiency, and confidence, they will be ready to attempt more challenging stunts, listed in the next developmental level.

27.3 *As Their Muscular Strength and Endurance Improves, Together with Their Proficiency and Confidence, Children Will Be Capable of More Complex and More Challenging Gymnastic Stunts and Movement Skills on Large Apparatus*

Developmental Level II

Children in developmental level II have gained sufficient strength, endurance, and proficiency to perform many of the more complex apparatus skills and movement patterns. They are also at the stage in development where they feel it is important to test the limits of their physical ability. As a consequence, teachers should make sure children do not attempt skills beyond their capability.

27.4 *Effective Teaching Progressions, Providing All Children with Appropriate Lead-Up Activities, Are Required When Teaching Gymnastic Stunts and Movement Skills That Take Place on Large Apparatus*

Developmental Level III

As children in this developmental level progress to the more complex stunts, more strength, endurance, and control are required. Like the more advanced tumbling stunts, more spotters are needed because of the potential hazards of performing many balance, vaulting, and climbing stunts. Children who have been exposed to movement education will be able to apply movement concepts and skills to large apparatus in very creative and challenging ways.

BALANCE BEAM AND BENCH

The balance beam and bench have been used in gymnastic programs for a number of years. However, they have been used in a very limited way, usually flat on the ground, with children performing stunts on or across the long axis. When the balance beam—fitted with a hook or connector on one end—is placed at different angles or used in combination with other apparatus, the variety of movements and challenges becomes infinitely greater. This applies to teaching structured skills as well as the movement concepts and skills described in the previous two chapters. A wide variety of structured skills is presented in the relative order of difficulty, followed by suggestions for applying movement skills to the balance beam and bench.

Individual Activities

Activities performed on the balance beam and bench require two types of balance skill: (1) static balance and (2) dynamic balance. *Static balance* is the ability to maintain a fixed position, such as in the foot and knee balance. *Dynamic balance* is the ability to maintain correct body position while moving, as when walking forward and backward or when performing the one-foot hop. Most developmental level I balance skills are basically dynamic. As the children's strength and skill increase, the more advanced static balance activities can be introduced. Each of the suggested skills can be made more challenging by narrowing the space, raising the height, or by varying the angle of the beam or bench.

The skills listed in table 27.1 and shown in figures 27.2 through 27.8 can be performed on the broad surface of the bench or on the narrow beam. To assist in learning, have the children practice all the stunts on the floor, then move to the broad surface of the bench, and finally advance to the narrow surface of a beam. Any fixed line on the floor can serve as an imaginary balance beam or bench.

TABLE 27.1   Balance Beam Skills

Name of Stunt	Developmental Level			Movement Concepts	Page
	I	**II**	**III**		
Locomotor Skills (chapter 6)	⟶			Balance, transfer of weight, change of speed	105
Turk Stand (chapter 25)	⟶			Balance, levels	530
Swing Turn	⟶			Balance, transfer of weight	534
Front Dismount	⟶			Balance, transfer of weight	583
Rear Support (chapter 25)	⟶			Balance, transfer of weight	531
Camel Walk (chapter 25)	⟶			Balance, transfer of weight	515
Jump Turn (chapter 25)	⟶			Balance, transfer of weight, force	515
Bouncing Ball (chapter 25)	⟶			Balance, transfer of weight, levels	516
Foot and Knee Balance	⟶			Balance, transfer of weight, levels	583
Side Balance	⟶			Balance, transfer of weight	583
Stork Stand (chapter 25)	⟶			Balance, transfer of weight	529
Squat Mount		⟶		Balance, transfer of weight	583
Foreward Roll (chapter 25)		⟶		Balance, transfer of weight	505
Lame Puppy Walk (chapter 25)		⟶		Balance, transfer of weight	516
Crab Walk (chapter 25)		⟶		Balance, transfer of weight	517
Rabbit Jump (chapter 25)		⟶		Balance, transfer of weight	518
Measuring Worm (chapter 25)		⟶		Balance, transfer of weight, levels	519
One Foot Jump (chapter 25)		⟶		Balance, transfer of weight, force	518
Jackknife			⟶	Balance, transfer of weight	584
Squat On One Leg			⟶	Balance, transfer of weight, levels	584
Backward Roll (chapter 25)			⟶	Balance, transfer of weight	509
Frog Stand (chapter 25)			⟶	Balance, transfer of weight	533
Heel Click (chapter 25)			⟶	Balance, transfer of weight	524
Cartwheel (chapter 25)			⟶	Balance, transfer of weight	512
Bridge (chapter 25)			⟶	Balance, transfer of weight	534
L Support (chapter 25)			⟶	Balance, transfer of weight	536

a   b   c

Figure 27.2 Swing turn. Walk to the center of the beam. Shift weight to the left foot and swing the right leg forward. Continue swinging the right leg forward, lift up on the ball of the left foot, and make a half turn, facing the opposite direction.

Variations:

1. Hop forward and repeat stunt.
2. Combine the swing turn with a side balance and a squat on one leg.
3. Make up your own routine with a swing turn and two other stunts.

Figure 27.3 Front dismount. Begin in a crouched position, with the arms straight and the hands grasping the outside edges of the balance beam. Extend the legs back until the head, trunk, and legs form a straight line. Lift the legs up and sideways, push off with the hands, and land on both feet beside the balance beam.

Figure 27.5 Side balance. Walk to the center of the balance beam and stop, with the left foot in front of the right. Turn the left foot sideways, shift weight to the ball of the foot, and lift the right foot off the beam, arch the back, and raise the right leg.
Variations:
1. Hop to center, then perform the side balance.
2. Repeat stunt, turn sideways, and change the position of your right leg.
3. See if you can perform a front knee balance, shift to a side balance, then back to a front knee balance facing the opposite direction.

Figure 27.4 Foot and knee balance. Begin with the right foot well in front of the left, the knees bent, and the arms extended sideways. Bend the knees until the left knee rests on the beam. Hold this position for a few seconds, then extend and return to the starting position.
Variations:
1. "Can you repeat this stunt with a change in arm position?"
2. "Can you add another variation to the stunt?"

Figure 27.6 Squat mount. Stand with the feet about shoulder-width apart, the body erect, and the hands resting on the balance beam. While keeping the hands on the beam, jump up slightly forward, placing the feet on the beam.
Variations:
1. Straddle Mount: Mount, placing feet outside of hands.
2. Squat Mount: Perform a balance stunt, leap off, and land with flexed knees.
3. Leap off, make a tuck shape, and land with flexed knees.

Figure 27.7 Jackknife. Sit on the beam, with the legs extended, the heels of both feet resting on the beam, and the hands holding the top edge of the beam. Bend the knees and raise the feet off the beam. Continue the upward movement of the feet, lower the trunk backward, and straighten the legs. After practice, raise the legs without bending the knees and touch the feet with the fingertips.
Variations:
1. Repeat stunt, raising right leg and left arm.
2. "Can you repeat this stunt and twist your body in some way?"
3. "See if you can add your own variation to this stunt."

Figure 27.8 Squat on one leg. Stand on the left foot, with the arms extended sideways and the right foot off the beam. Bend the left knee and raise the extended right leg forward and upward. Lower the body until the left knee is fully flexed.
Variations:
1. Repeat on opposite leg.
2. "In how many positions can you place the right leg while balancing on your left foot?"
3. "Can you shift from your balance position to the same position, facing the opposite direction?"
4. "Can you shift from a squat on one leg to a side-balance position?"

Several small equipment activities described in the previous chapter also can be performed on the beam or bench (figure 27.9). It may be wise to require students to perform the skill on the bench before they attempt it on the narrower surface of the balance beam.

1. *Beanbag activities:*
   a. Throw and catch to self.
   b. Balance beanbags on different parts of the body and perform a series of balance stunts.

2. *Rope-skipping activities:* Basic skills, particularly the two-foot basic, one-foot hop, and rocker step

3. *Hoop activities:*
   a. Hula Hooping
   b. Hula Jumping

4. *Wand activities:*
   a. Foot Balance
   b. Thread the Needle

Figure 27.9 Small equipment activities on the balance beam.

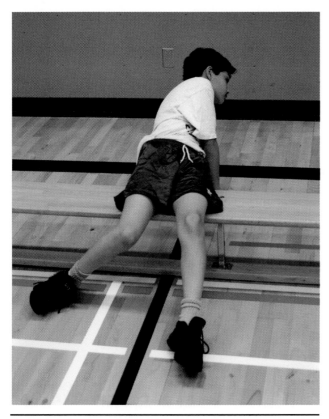

Figure 27.10 Twisted shape on the balance beam.

Figure 27.11 "Can you make a series of twisted shapes?"

C O N C E P T

27.5 Posing Gymnastic Challenges Stimulates Creativity and Allows Children to Adjust Their Gymnastic Activities and Routines on Large Apparatus to Their Own Developmental Level

Applying Movement Skills

One of the teacher's first tasks is to help children use the balance beam or bench in a variety of ways when performing a single movement skill or a sequence of movements. A movement task such as "See if you can make a twisted shape on the balance bench (or beam)" usually produces something like the shape illustrated in figure 27.10. The parallel arrangement of the benches lacks imagination. Also, the use of the word *on* encourages all children to begin their movements from the same starting position. Questions should be presented in such a way that children begin to see the apparatus in a much wider perspective. Rephrasing the question to "Can you make a series of twisted shapes using various parts of the balance bench?" allows for greater scope, as illustrated in figure 27.11. Thus, when applying movement ideas to the balance beam or bench, think of the apparatus as either a point of contact or an obstacle to move around, across, or over (in flight). The following movement challenges illustrate this application:

1. *Direction and speed:* Move around the benches, showing a quick change of direction.
2. *Balance and transfer of weight:* Travel across the benches by changing from two to three to two points of balance.
3. *Balance, shape, and direction:* Develop a sequence traveling across the bench, including a twisted shape, balancing on the side, and a change of direction.
4. *Flight and rolling:* Beginning anywhere on the floor, run, jump onto a bench, leap off, land, and perform a safety roll. The roll may be a sideways, diagonal, or forward roll. Repeat and perform a stretched, twisted, or curled shape before landing.
5. *Relationships:* The balance beam or bench can be one of the most effective and versatile apparatus for developing the concept of relationships. The following examples illustrate how matching and contrasting can be integrated with other concepts and skills such as levels, direction, and speed:
   a. "Develop a sequence of matching shapes with your partner on the top surface of your bench." "Repeat with one partner on the bench and the other on the floor" (figure 27.12). "Repeat with both touching the bench."
   b. "With one partner leading and the other following, make up a sequence of balance positions as you move from one end of the bench to the other."

At this stage in the development of movement concepts and skills, the angle of the bench or its combination with other types of apparatus adds to the challenge. These variations provide a greater opportunity for the children to test and expand their physical and creative abilities. A challenge such as "Make up a sequence that shows a change in level" is complemented by the angle of the bench. Also, adding chairs to the same challenge creates new dimensions for partners as they develop a matching sequence.

a   b   c

Figure 27.12 Patterns on and off the ground. Matching shapes with one on the ground and one on the bench.

CLIMBING ROPE

A variety of climbing, swinging, and movement skills can be performed with a climbing rope. With proper instruction, including strengthening exercises for the arm and shoulder muscles, as well as following a sequential progression of skills, children can develop a high level of skill on the hanging ropes.

Suggestions for safety procedures and conditioning exercises are presented, followed by a description of the basic climbing skills and ideas for applying movement skills to this apparatus.

Safety Procedures

Many school districts require that a mat be placed under the climbing rope when a child is performing a climbing or swinging skill. It must be recognized, however, that the mat has very little resilience and thus may have little value in preventing an injury. The following suggestions and procedures contribute far more to a child's safety than a mat:

1. Teach the proper hand and foot grip techniques for climbing and descending the rope.
2. Set individual goals rather than an arbitrary standard for every child to accomplish.
3. Use spotters for difficult stunts, particularly those involving inverted hangs.
4. Establish safe and sensible rules for children, including the following:
   a. Never use ropes when a teacher is not present.
   b. Always climb down a rope; never slide.
   c. Never leave a rope swinging when you have finished with it.
   d. Never touch other performers on the rope unless you are spotting.
   e. Never climb a swinging rope.

TABLE 27.2   Conditioning Exercises for Rope Climbing Skills

Exercise	Region of Body	Page
Single Mule Kick	Arm and shoulder girdle	511
Mule Kick	Arm and shoulder girdle	511
Cartwheel	Arm and shoulder girdle	512
Crab Walk	Arm and shoulder girdle	517
Rabbit Jump	Arm and shoulder girdle	518
Elephant Walk	Arm and shoulder girdle	521
Measuring Worm	Arm and shoulder girdle	519
Frog Jump	Arm and shoulder girdle	519
Frog Stand	Arm and shoulder girdle	533
Pull-Ups	Arm and shoulder girdle	159
Push-Ups	Arm and shoulder girdle	161
Coffee Grinder	Arm and shoulder girdle	519
Curl-Ups	Abdominals	160
V-Sit	Abdominals	534

Conditioning Exercises

Climbing skills require sufficient arm and shoulder strength to raise and support the full weight of the body. The abdominal muscles also play a very important role in both climbing and descending skills. The exercises listed in table 27.2 help increase the general strength and endurance of these muscle groups:

TABLE 27.3	Rope Climbing Skills				

	Developmental Level				
Exercise	I	II	III	Movement Concepts	Page
Rope Pull-Ups	→——→			Force, level, shapes	587
Reach and Pull	→——→			Force, level, shapes	587
Letters	→——→			Force, shapes	588
Backward Roll	→——→			Force, change of direction, shapes	588
Jump and Tuck		→——→		Force, shapes	588
Hands and Leg Hold		→——→		Force, transfer of weight	588
Skin the Cat		→——→		Force, transfer of weight, change of direction	589
Bench Swing and Drop		→——→		Force, transfer of weight, change of direction, shapes	589
Scissors Climb			→——→	Force, levels, transfer of weight	589
Foot and Leg Lock Climb			→——→	Force, levels, transfer of weight	589
Stirrup Climb			→——→	Force, levels, transfer of weight	590

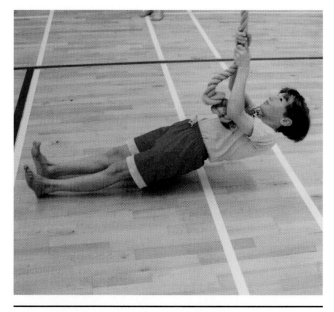

Figure 27.13 Pull-ups. Lie under the rope, with the hands grasping it. Gradually raise the body upward. As strength increases, repeat exercise, but keep the body straight throughout the movement.

Figure 27.14 Reach and pull. Sitting under the rope with the arms extended over the head and grasping the rope, pull body up. As strength increases, keep the legs extended and parallel to the floor.

Individual Activities

The individual skills in table 27.3, some of which are shown in figures 27.13 to 27.23, are listed in their approximate order of difficulty. Since many elementary school children lack sufficient arm and shoulder girdle strength, time should be spent on the preliminary conditioning exercises and the simpler climbing and swinging skills before attempting the more advanced skills. Success leads to success; this is extremely important with rope-climbing activities.

Applying Movement Skills

The hanging rope can be used to develop movement skills in three basic ways: (1) movement challenges relating to shapes and weight bearing with a stationary rope, (2) movement challenges while the rope is swinging, and (3) movement challenges with the rope associated with another type of large apparatus.

Figure 27.15 Letters. Hang between two ropes and make shapes of letters (Y, X, L, etc.).

Figure 27.16 Backward roll. Lie on back and grasp ropes with arms extended. Perform a backward roll with legs tucked, straddled, or in other positions.

Figure 27.17 Jump and tuck. Begin in a standing position facing the rope. Jump up, grasp the rope and draw the knees up to the chest.

Variations:

1. Repeat, but this time draw legs up above the head.
2. Repeat and draw legs up and over the head so that toes point toward the floor.
3. Repeat and draw the legs up, then spread them sideways above the head.

Figure 27.18 Hands and leg hold. Begin in a standing position, jump up, grasp the rope, wrap legs around the rope, and hold for several seconds.

Variations:

1. From hands and leg hold, release right then left hand.
2. From hands and leg hold, release right hand and right leg and hold for several seconds.

Figure 27.19 Skin the cat. Reach up and grasp the rope. Pull legs up and over the head to a back hang position and return to original position.

Figure 27.20 Bench swing and drop. Place a bench several feet away from the rope. Carry the rope back to the bench and hold it with a bent arm position and facing forward. Swing forward and drop off at the upper end of the swing.
Variations:
1. Swing forward and backward and land on the bench.
2. Swing forward and raise the knees to the chest.
3. Swing, make a half or full turn and land.

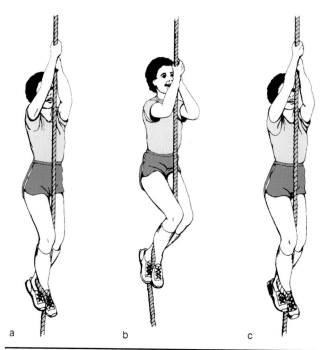

a   b   c

Figure 27.21 Scissors climb. (a) Grasp the rope with one hand slightly above the other. Pull the body up, with the right leg slightly in front of the left. Place rope inside the right knee and around the outside of the left foot. Cross the left leg over the back of the right leg, and press the inside of the left foot against the rope. (b) Release the pressure on the rope with the feet, then raise knees toward the chest. (c) Lock the feet firmly against the rope, straighten legs, and reset hands (moving hand over hand) above the head. (d) To descend, keep pressure against feet and lower body in hand-under-hand position until knees are bent. Hold hands firmly and lower legs to new position, then lock feet again. Continue pattern.

a   b   c

Figure 27.22 Foot and leg lock climbs. (a) Grasp the rope with one hand slightly above the other. Pull the body up and loop the rope over the top of the right foot. Place the left foot on top of the rope, thus "locking" the foot position. (b) Pull the body up to a new position. (c) Repeat upward movement. (d) Descend by maintaining the locked position of the legs, then move the hands down in a "hand-under-hand" fashion until the knees are against the chest. Hold the hand grip and slowly lower the legs to an extended position. Continue action to the floor.

Figure 27.23 Stirrup climb. (a) Grasp the rope with one hand slightly above the other. Pull the body up and let the rope rest against the left side of the body. The rope then passes under the left foot and over the right foot. (b) Release pressure of feet and raise body. (c) Lock grip of feet, raise hand to higher position, and continue action. (d) To descend, move hand under hand and control pressure against the feet.

Figure 27.24 Balance three parts on the rope.

The following movement tasks illustrate each type of challenge: "Can you balance with one part of your body on the floor and three parts on the rope?". "How many different shapes can you make while holding the rope?" (figure 27.24). "Can you make different shapes while holding the rope and with both feet off the ground?" "Repeat previous challenge while the rope is swinging." Place one bench near both ends of the rope swing. "Swing and land on each bench." "Swing, make a half turn, and land on the opposite bench."

SPRINGBOARD, BEATBOARD, AND VAULTING BOX

The springboard and vaulting box are two of the oldest apparatus in the gymnastic program. In this chapter, the term *vaulting box* includes other similar apparatus, such as the vaulting bench, the jumping box, and the long horse, since they are used in much the same way. Teachers who do not have a vaulting box should refer to the diagrams of inexpensive equipment in appendix B.

The majority of vaulting stunts are usually performed from the springboard onto a mat. Once children have developed sufficient skill in using the springboard and controlling their bodies while in flight, the vaulting box can be added to provide greater challenge and versatility of movements. The approach, takeoff, and landing are essentially the same for all vaulting activities, so children should practice these movements until they become automatic (figure 27.25). A well-executed and consistent takeoff allows the child to concentrate on height and the execution of a specific vault.

Individual Activities

The first few stunts listed in table 27.4 help performers develop a consistent takeoff and execute aerial and landing movements with control and efficacy. The remaining vaults listed can be performed over a box or long horse with a takeoff from the floor, or off a springboard. Some of the stunts are shown in figures 27.26 to 27.38.

Applying Movement Skills

The springboard, beatboard, and vaulting box can be used individually or in combination with other apparatus to provide interesting and challenging movement tasks involving body awareness, qualities, space awareness, and relationships. For example, all the individual shapes performed in flight from the floor can be applied to the springboard, or beatboard. These provide additional height and time necessary for executing curled or stretched, wide or narrow, and

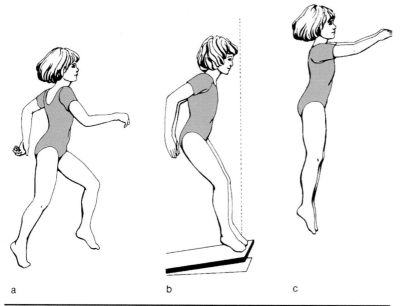

a   b   c

Figure 27.25 Approach and takeoff. The hurdle step is used to change running speed into a two-foot takeoff roll. (a) Begin with a few short running steps, then take off with the right foot and swing the opposite leg and arms forward and upward. (b) Land with arms swinging downward and backward and knees slightly bent. When the performer's toes touch the board, the body should be just behind a vertical line drawn through the performer's toes. This position allows the performer to gain (c) maximum height and control, rather than a rapid and uncontrolled low forward shifting action. Land with knees bent and continue into a forward roll.
Variations:
1. After takeoff, make a tuck, straddle, or twisted shape, land and roll.
2. After takeoff, perform a quarter, half, or full turn, land and roll.

Figure 27.26 Knee mount. Stand on the springboard with hands resting on the box. Jump upward and forward and land on lower legs. Repeat mount with a run and a two-foot takeoff. Stand up, leap off, land, and roll. Use the same spotting as for the squat vault.
Variations:
1. After leaping off, make a tuck, straddle, or twisted shape, land and roll.
2. After leaping off, perform a half turn, land, and execute a backward diagonal roll.

TABLE 27.4   Springboard and Vaulting Box Skills

Name of Stunt	Developmental Level			Movement Concepts	Page
	I	II	III		
Movement Skills	———→			Force, transfer of weight, shapes, levels	590
Approach and Takeoff		———→		Force, transfer of weight, shapes, levels	591
Knee Mount		———→		Force, transfer of weight, shapes, levels	591
Squat Mount		———→		Force, transfer of weight, shapes, levels	592
Flank Mount		———→		Force, transfer of weight, shapes, levels	592
Straddle Mount		———→		Force, transfer of weight, shapes, levels	592
Squat Vault			———→	Force, transfer of weight, shapes, levels	593
Flank Vault			———→	Force, transfer of weight, shapes, levels	593
Straddle Vault			———→	Force, transfer of weight, shapes, levels	594
Headspring			———→	Force, transfer of weight, shapes, levels	594

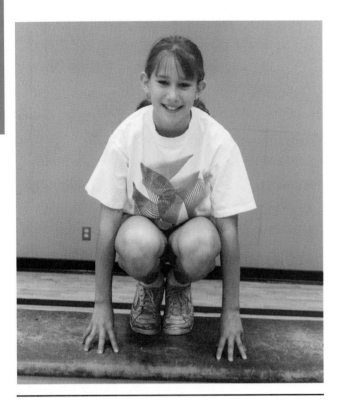

Figure 27.27 Squat mount. Stand on the springboard with hands resting on the box. Jump upward and forward, and land in a squat position. Repeat mount with a run and a two-foot takeoff. Stand up, leap off, land, and roll. Use the same spotting as for the Squat Vault.
Variations:
Repeat variations for the knee mount.

Figure 27.28 Flank mount. Stand on the springboard with hands resting on the box. Jump upward and forward, swing both straight legs to the right side and release the right hand. Land on the top of the box with right leg on top of the left leg and the right hand resting on the right thigh. Repeat mount with a run and a two foot takeoff. Stand up, leap off, land and roll. Use the same spotting as for the squat vault.
Variations:
Repeat variations for the knee mount.

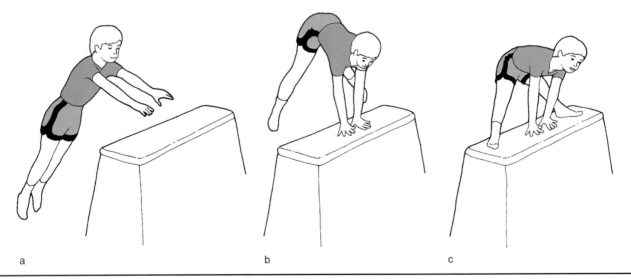

a   b   c

Figure 27.29 Straddle mount. Stand on the springboard with hands resting on the box. Jump upward, spread legs sideways, and land on the top of the move box in a straddle position. Repeat mount with a run and a two foot takeoff. Stand up, leap off, land, and roll. Use the same spotting as for straddle vault.
Variations:
Repeat variations for the knee mount.

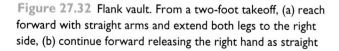

Figure 27.31 Spotting. Stand on the opposite side of the vaulting box and to the right of the oncoming performer. As she moves over the box, grasp her right wrist with your right hand. As she shifts forward, supply additional support to her upper body with your left hand.

Figure 27.30 Squat vault. (a) From a two-foot takeoff (b) reach up, leaning slightly forward, and touch hands on top of the box. (c) Simultaneously tuck the knees close to the chest and continue forward and upward. (d) Land with a gradual bending of the knees.

Figure 27.32 Flank vault. From a two-foot takeoff, (a) reach forward with straight arms and extend both legs to the right side, (b) continue forward releasing the right hand as straight legs pass over box, (c) continue forward and downward, and (d) land with a gradual bending of the knees.

Figure 27.34 Spotting. Stand close to the box directly in front of the oncoming performer. If she catches her toes or has too much forward momentum, place your hands on her shoulders to break the fall. If the performer clears the box and does not have too much forward momentum, step to the side quickly.

Figure 27.33 Straddle vault. (a) From a two-foot takeoff, (b) reach forward with straight arms and extend legs sideward. (c) Continue forward and upward, raising chest upward, bringing legs together, (d) Land with a gradual bending of the knees.

Figure 27.35 Headspring. (a) From a two-foot takeoff, (b) place the hands and then the head on top of the box as the body extends upward and over. (c) When the body is in a forward "overbalanced" position, push off from the fingertips and (d) land with a gradual bending of the knees. *Note:* Most children tend to push off before they reach the overbalanced position, which causes them to "drop" onto the box rather than gradually arch and land.

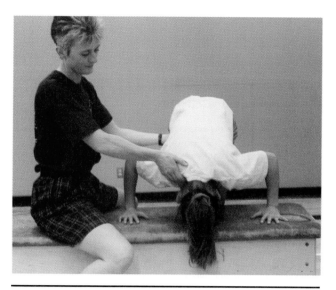

Figure 27.36 Spotting. Use one spotter. As the performer's hands contact the top of the horse, place your hand on the performer's shoulder and support her through the movement to a safe landing position.

Figure 27.37 Make a shape in the air.

Figure 27.38 Move from one side to the other side of the apparatus.

The vaulting box should also be used as an additional challenge for the development of other movement concepts and skills. It is important to present challenges in such a way that all surfaces—particularly the sides and ends—are used when answering movement tasks. The following examples illustrate the variable use of the vaulting box:

1. *Shapes and balance:*
   a. "Make a stretched (or wide or twisted) shape on the side, end, and top of the box."
   b. "Can you balance with one part on the apparatus and two parts off?"
   c. "See if you can balance with part of your body on top of the apparatus and part on the side or end of the apparatus."
   d. "Move from one side of the apparatus to the other" (figure 27.38).

2. *Relationships:*
   a. "Make up a matching (or contrasting) sequence of shapes, with one partner on top of the apparatus and the other on the floor."
   b. "How many different balance positions can you make with your partner on the side or top of the apparatus?"
   c. "Make up a sequence with your partner on the apparatus and show a change in balance."

Sequences involving body awareness, qualities, space awareness, and relationships can be designed to include the springboard and vaulting box individually or in combination with other small and large apparatus. The selection and arrangement of the apparatus should complement the movements of the sequence. Excessive rearrangement of apparatus serves little purpose in the development of movement skills, so teachers should caution children if they tend to waste time in arranging apparatus. One arrangement of apparatus should last for several lessons.

twisted shapes. In addition, since children have learned safety rolls—sideward, backward, and forward—they should be able to land and roll with grace and ease. The movement task shown in figure 27.37 illustrates the additional challenge and increased quality of movements performed from the springboard or beatboard. Similar movements can also be performed from the vaulting box.

TABLE 27.5   Horizontal Bar Skills

Name of Stunt	Developmental Level			Movement Concepts	Page
	I	II	III		
Two Arm Hang	→→→			Force, shapes, relationships	596
Hang Like a Monkey		→→→		Force, shapes, transfer of weight, relationships	597
Arm and Leg Hang		→→→		Force, transfer of weight, relationships	597
Double-Leg Hang		→→→		Force, transfer of weight, relationships	597
Skin the Cat		→→→		Force, transfer of weight, relationships	598
Front Support			→→→	Force, transfer of weight, relationships	598
Scramble over Fence			→→→	Force, transfer of weight, relationships	598
Single-Knee Swing			→→→	Force, transfer of weight, relationships	599
Inverted Hang			→→→	Force, transfer of weight, relationships	599
Knee Circle			→→→	Force, transfer of weight, relationships	599
Bird's Nest			→→→	Force, shape, transfer of weight, relationships	600
Sideways Circle			→→→	Force, transfer of weight, relationships	600

HORIZONTAL BAR

In comparison with stunts on other indoor apparatus, stunts performed on the horizontal bar are extremely difficult for elementary school children. Thus, teachers must give a great deal of encouragement. In most cases, the initial disinterest in this apparatus is the result of insufficient arm and shoulder strength rather than an inherent absence of skill. The following suggestions will help maintain enthusiasm and prevent unnecessary accidents:

1. Check equipment before allowing children to perform any stunt.
2. Make sure you are in the proper position to spot for safety.
3. Begin with simple stunts and progress to more difficult ones.
4. Stress forward grip with fingers over top of bar and facing forward, with thumbs under the bar and facing the fingers.

Individual Activities

The stunts in table 27.5 are listed according to their approximate order of difficulty. Figures 27.39 to 27.50 illustrate some of the stunts.

Applying Movement Skills

Proficiency on this apparatus depends upon a child's level of arm and shoulder girdle strength and endurance. Movement challenges can be designed to allow children with minimal levels of fitness to perform movements within their own level of ability. The same challenge also allows the more fit child to execute movements that involve the highest level of fitness and motor ability. The following

Figure 27.39 Two arm hang. Jump up, grasp bar with forward grip and arm extended. Hold position for several seconds.
Variations:
1. Hang and raise knees up as far as possible.
2. Keep legs straight, then raise them forward and upward.
3. Hang and change position of legs: spread; one forward, one reversed; crossed; aerial walking; etc.
4. Hang and release one hand.

Figure 27.40 Hang like a monkey. Jump up and grasp the bar, with the palms forward and the hands a few inches apart. Swing the right leg up and over the bar, resting the heel on top. Bring the left leg up and over the right leg and rest the back of the left leg on top of the right foot.
Variations:
1. Pull chest to bar.
2. Shift leg to side, pointing to the floor, and so on.
3. Travel forward and backward by sliding hands and feet along the bar.

Figure 27.41 Arm and leg hang. Jump up and grasp the bar with palms facing forward. Draw one leg through arms and around the bar. Hang with the arms straight and the lower leg extended forward.
Variations:
1. Change legs and repeat.
2. Lift one hand off the bar, then regrasp.
3. From this position shift toward each side and return.
4. From the hanging position, raise the chin to the bar and return.

Figure 27.42 Double leg hang. Jump up and grasp the bar with the palms facing forward and the hands about shoulder-width apart. Draw both legs up and over the bar, drop the knees over it, and rest the back of knees firmly against the bar. Keep the knees bent and release grip. Reach up, grasp bar, and return to the starting position.
Variations:
1. Twist the body toward each side.
2. Change position of arms.
3. With a spotter, swing back and forth.

Figure 27.43 Skin the cat. Jump up and grasp the bar with palms facing forward. Draw both legs up and through the arms and over until the legs are extended downward. Return to the starting position.

Variations:

1. From the reverse hang position, release grip and drop to the ground.
2. From the reverse hang position, change position of the legs—straddle, crossed, etc.

Figure 27.44 Front support. Jump up and take a front support position, with the arms straight and hands on top of the bar. Jump down.

Variations:

1. From the front support position, push off with the arms and jump slightly upward and backward.
2. From the front support position, adjust body to balance on the stomach, with arms extended sideways.

Figure 27.45 Scramble over fence. Jump up and take a front support position with arms straight and hands on top of the bar. From this position, bring right, then left, leg over the bar and sit on the top with arms extended sideways.

Variations:

Change position of arms—one forward and one backward, behind the head, etc.

Figure 27.46 Single-knee swing. Jump up and grasp the bar with palms facing forward. Draw one leg through the arms and around the bar. Point opposite leg toward the sky then swing it forward and downward and continue swinging back and forth.

Variations:

1. Change legs and repeat movement.
2. Swing to a sitting position on the bar. (Use a spotter until the performer demonstrates control throughout the movement.)

Figure 27.47 Inverted hang. Jump up and grasp the bar with palms facing forward, and hands about shoulder-width apart. Draw both legs up and under the bar. As the legs pass over the bar they are extended upward, close to the bar, until the body is perpendicular to the mat.

Variation:

Once in an inverted position, extend legs sideways.

Figure 27.48 Knee circle. Begin sitting on the bar with a reverse grip. The right leg is over the bar with the knee bent. The left leg is under the bar extended and pointed down. Shift the weight upward and forward, circle the bar and back to the original position.

Variations:

1. Reverse grip and perform a backward knee circle.
2. Change leg positions and repeat movement.

Figure 27.49 Bird's nest. Jump up and grasp bar, with palms facing forward. Draw both legs up and through arms. Drop legs over the bar, resting back of knees firmly against the bar. Simultaneously shift lower legs backward and fully arch the back until the back of the heels rest against the bar and arms are extended.

Variations:

1. Remove one leg and extend it backward.
2. Bring legs back through the arms, then extend legs upward into an inverted hang.

examples illustrate how movement challenges are applied to this type of apparatus.

1. "How many different ways can you get on and off the bar?"
2. "Can you hold onto the bar and make two different shapes?"
3. "See if you can balance with part of your body on the apparatus and part on the ground."
4. "Discover two different ways of moving across the bar."
5. "Can you balance on the top of the bar and make a curled, stretched, or twisted shape?"
6. "Can you balance with parts of your body above and parts below the bar?"
7. "Is it possible to hold the bar, swing, and jump off?"

HORIZONTAL LADDER

Activities performed on the horizontal ladder are similar to horizontal bar activities. Both require a great deal of strength and endurance of the arm and shoulder girdle muscles. Therefore, follow the progression of skills in

Figure 27.50 Sideways circle. Begin sitting on the bar with one leg on each side and legs locked. The arms are straight with the hands grasping the bar in front and close to the body. Fall sideways and try to complete a full circle.

table 27.6 and do not require *full travels*—that is, all the way across the ladder—until sufficient strength and endurance are developed. As a starting point, require the children to make it one quarter of the distance. Increase the number of rungs each day until the children reach the full distance without undue stress (figures 27.51–27.55).

The following safety hints require continuous reinforcement. Before the children begin to play or practice stunts on the apparatus, take a few minutes to stress the following:

1. Check the apparatus before pupils are allowed to perform stunts.
2. Stand close to performers while they are attempting a difficult stunt in order to help them and to prevent accidents.

TABLE 27.6 Horizontal Ladder

Name of Stunt	Developmental Level		Movement Concepts	Page
	II	III		
Inverted Push-ups	——————▶		Force, transfer of weight, relationships	601
Single-Rung Traveling	——————▶		Force, transfer of weight, relationships	601
Rung Travel Sideways	——————▶		Force, transfer of weight, relationships	602
Side Rail Travel	——————▶		Force, transfer of weight, relationships	602
Double-Rail Travel		——————▶	Force, transfer of weight, relationships	603

Figure 27.51 Inverted push-ups. Grasp rung with palms facing forward, swing legs upward and over the rung. Hook heels over the rung then raise chin to the rung. Repeat movement several times then return to starting position.
Variations:
1. Hook only one leg over the rung and repeat movement.
2. From the inverted hang position, release one hand and twist body toward each side.

3. Require pupils to stand at least five feet from the apparatus while waiting for their turn.
4. Allow only two pupils on the ladder at the same time.
5. Require that the second pupil not begin a stunt until the first child is at least halfway across the ladder.
6. Require pupils to travel in the same direction.
7. Require that two parts of the body be in contact with the apparatus during the performance of all movements.
8. Do not permit children to touch or hinder a child who is performing a stunt.

Figure 27.52 Single-rung traveling. Climb up one end of the ladder, rest feet on the step, and grasp each side pole with one hand. Reach forward and grasp the second rung with one hand, palms facing forward, and the third rung with the other hand. Simultaneously shift the body forward toward the forward hand and release the back hand. Continue forward, grasping the next rung. Repeat the movement with the opposite hand and continue traveling forward to the opposite end.
Variations:
1. Change position of legs as you travel—knees tucked, legs straddled, or one leg in front of the other.
2. Double-Rung Travel: Begin with both hands on one rung. Swing forward and backward and, at end of a forward swing, release both hands and regrasp the next rung with both hands.

Figure 27.53 Rung travel sideways. Begin with hands on separate rungs and body facing sideways. Shift right hand to same rung as left hand, then shift left hand to next rung. Continue pattern to end of ladder.

Individual Activities

The stunts listed in table 27.6 are arranged according to their approximate level of difficulty.

Applying Movement Skills

The horizontal ladder is similar to the horizontal bar in that both require sufficient strength and endurance to perform even the simplest movements. As this apparatus normally has side structures with two or more rungs, all parts should be incorporated into several movement challenges. The sample challenges listed below illustrate how the sides and overhead ladder are used in movement tasks.

1. "Can you balance with part of your body on the side of the apparatus and part on the overhead ladder?"
2. "How many different ways can you hang from the ladder?"
3. "See if you can hold onto a rung and swing." "Can you swing and make different shapes?" "Can you swing and land from a forward or reverse swing?"
4. "Can you 'balance' on top of the ladder?" "Can you balance on three parts?" "Can you balance on three parts and show me a twist in your body?"
5. "Discover three different ways of moving across the apparatus."

Figure 27.54 Side rail traveling. Travel along one side rail, using a hand-over-hand movement.
Variations:
1. Change position of legs as you travel.
2. Repeat movement backward.

CLIMBING FRAME

One of the most significant contributions to the elementary school gymnastic program has been the development of new climbing apparatus. This apparatus has been specifically designed to provide more challenging tasks than the traditional gymnastic apparatus. The climbing frame is mounted on a wall with a variety of supplementary attachments, such as beams, poles, ladders, and planks.

Individual Activities

The stunts listed under balance beam, climbing ropes, horizontal bar, and ladder can be performed on the various parts of this apparatus. This apparatus offers an additional feature in that planks, ladders, and poles can be mounted at different levels and angles from the floor to the apparatus, thus providing an extra challenge for each stunt.

Figure 27.56 Matching sequence.

OUTDOOR APPARATUS

In the past few years, there has been a major change in the type of outdoor apparatus being constructed on elementary school playgrounds. Commercial equipment, such as Big Toys, are replacing the more traditional swings, steel climbing frames, and horizontal ladders. This apparatus has been designed to complement the creative and exploratory nature of young children. The general design provides more levels, angles, and holes for young children to jump off, balance on, and crawl through. Creative playgrounds described in chapter 10 are also part of this trend. Natural materials, such as large tree roots and boulders, and discarded building materials or equipment, such as giant sewer pipes and old trucks, are now seen on numerous playgrounds throughout North America.

Many of the movement challenges suggested under horizontal bar, ladder, and climbing frame can be applied to a variety of commercial and natural outdoor apparatus (figure 27.56).

Teachers who are hesitant to use the indoor and outdoor apparatus suggested in this chapter should recognize one of the basic characteristics of the Movement Education approach: Children taught through this approach will not attempt a movement task on any apparatus until they feel mentally and physically ready. If the teacher follows this approach, accidents should rarely occur.

Summary Review

The use of large apparatus for gymnastic stunts and movement activities provides a unique contribution to the physical education program. However, due to the specific nature of large equipment, which often requires children to work at raised heights, special attention needs to be given to safety considerations. Large apparatus provides children with developmental opportunities that cannot easily be accomplished in other areas of the program. For

Figure 27.55 Double Rail Traveling: Grasp both side rails with the palms of both hands facing in, and swing to a hanging position. Travel forward by sliding one hand forward, then the other. Do not release the grip. Slide the hands the full length of the ladder.
Variation:
Repeat movement backward.

Applying Movement Skills

This apparatus should also be seen as a logical extension of the gymnasium in developing moving concepts and skills. The following examples illustrate how this apparatus can be used as an effective instructional laboratory. The skills learned through the teacher's movement challenges help the children learn to use the apparatus in a constructive, safe, and creative way.

1. "Find a place on the apparatus and show me how many different ways you can balance on your spot."
2. "Can you move across the apparatus using different parts of your body?"
3. "See if you can climb up and down the apparatus using your hands and feet."
4. "Can you move through the apparatus and show a low, medium, and high position?"
5. "One partner leads and the other follows. Make up a sequence involving a transfer of weight and a change of direction."
6. "Find a spot on the apparatus with your partner. Can you develop a matching sequence including a stretch, curl, and twisted shape?"

example, activities involving ropes and bars require upper body strength and endurance that is not easily developed through other physical education activities. Further, when children work at different heights and levels on large apparatus, they receive an opportunity to develop spatial awareness at heights not usually experienced in other areas of the physical education program. Work on large apparatus also offers teaching and learning opportunities similar to those for the floor work and small equipment activities discussed in chapters 25 and 26. As discussed in these chapters, creativity and problem solving can be facilitated through the use of appropriate challenges. When a Movement Education approach is used in conjunction with problem-solving challenges, all children have the opportunity to achieve success, because they can create solutions to challenges regardless of their levels of development.

INDIVIDUAL *and* GROUP PROJECTS

1. In small groups, discuss safety considerations when using large apparatus to teach gymnastic activities. Pay particular attention to children with special needs. Share recommendations between groups.

2. In small groups, plan lessons showing how large apparatus activities in gymnastics can be used to teach or enhance academic concepts and skills in science and mathematics. Plan how to evaluate the expected learning outcomes. Share lesson plans with other groups.

3. Chapter 13 identified a number of disabilities that afflict young children. In small groups, choose four disabilities and discuss how children with these disabilities can be accommodated in gymnastic activities that use large apparatus. Consider what adjustments will have to be made to accommodate each child's developmental level to ensure success. Debate possible techniques and methods of evaluation. Share ideas with other groups.

4. Individually or in small groups, design a series of large apparatus stations for teaching gymnastic activities. Outline the station set-up and produce a set of task cards to indicate the activities that should occur at each station.

5. In small groups, visit local elementary schools to identify the type and amount of large apparatus available for use in the school's physical education program. Focusing on balance and transfer of weight, design two stations using the large apparatus available. With permission, set up the stations in the school to gain experience in setting up and putting away large apparatus. Share school experiences with other groups.

SELECTED READINGS

Cooper, P. 1989. *Teaching basic gymnastics: A coeducational approach.* 2d ed. New York: Macmillan.

Corbin, C. B. 1972. *Inexpensive equipment for games, play, and physical activity.* Dubuque, IA: Wm. C. Brown.

Hall, T. 1984. *Inexpensive movement material.* Byron, CA: Front Race Experience.

Ryser, O. E., and J. R. Brown. 1988. *A manual of tumbling and apparatus stunts.* Dubuque, IA: Wm. C. Brown.

Sahli, J. 1993. *Making a meaningful connection: the integration of physical education and writing.* Unpublished Thesis, Burnady, Simon fraser University.

PART 8

Dance and Movement Activities

PART 8 has been organized in a slightly different way from the game and gymnastic sections. Chapter 28 describes the basic rhythmic skills used in game, gymnastic, and dance activities. Chapter 29 includes the most popular singing games and folk dance activities for developmental levels I, II, and III. Chapter 30 describes several approaches to teaching creative dance activities to children in the primary and intermediate grades. Each of these chapters provides guidance in planning, organizing, and teaching developmentally appropriate dance activities to elementary school children.

CHAPTER 28

Rhythmic and Movement Activities

KEY CONCEPTS

28.1 Rhythmic awareness is a basic component of all coordinated movement

28.2 A child who has a well-developed sense of time can perform movements in a rhythmic, coordinated manner

28.3 Rhythmic activities must be developmentally appropriate to ensure that all children can achieve success and enjoyment

28.4 The teaching progression used to teach the elements of rhythm moves from individual, to partner, to group activities

28.5 Posing problem-solving challenges stimulates creativity

28.6 Effective teaching progressions, providing all children with appropriate rhythmic activities, are required to develop rhythmic awareness

28.7 The development of rhythmic awareness should be facilitated through opportunities to participate in rhythmic activities in games, gymnastics, and dance

KEY OBJECTIVES

After completing this chapter you will be able to:

1. Design developmentally appropriate rhythmic and movement activities for elementary school children
2. Understand the scope and sequence of rhythmic activities
3. Understand the elements of rhythm
4. Apply the elements of rhythm to game, dance, and gymnastic activities
5. Plan and organize teaching units and individual lessons involving rhythmic and movement activities
6. Teach rhythmic activities using small equipment
7. Identify key teaching points associated with rhythmic activities
8. Employ teaching progressions that lead to the successful development of rhythmic awareness in children

Rhythm is the ability to repeat an action or movement with regularity and in time to a particular pattern. It is an essential ingredient of all movement, whether throwing a ball, dodging a player, or dancing a polka. Rhythm can be spontaneous, as when a young child makes up a jumping pattern without any musical background or directions imposed by the teacher. The rhythmic activities described in this chapter, however, are more structured in nature and direction, relating to the performance of a variety of body movements in time to a specific musical accompaniment.

The material in this chapter has been arranged to assist children (latter phase of developmental level I through developmental level III) in acquiring a basic understanding of the elements of rhythm and the ways the elements can be combined with a variety of game, dance, and gymnastic movements. Once children understand the elements of rhythm, they can learn other dance activities with greater speed and usually with a very positive attitude. The basic approach of gradually moving from individual to partner to group activities is used. This gradual process of joining younger children in a relaxed and creative manner provides the necessary stepping-stone to folk and creative dance activities for upper elementary school girls and boys. Once the teacher has read this chapters, she will also be able to incorporate many of the ideas into future folk and creative dance units. In addition, rhythmic activities can also be integrated into numerous game and gymnastic activities.

UNDERSTANDING THE ELEMENTS OF RHYTHM

Music and dance have one basic element in common—both are performed within rhythmic structure. Within this structure, the underlying beat, meter, and tempo provide direction and emphasis to the song or to dance movements. All of the following elements of rhythm are interrelated and affect dance movements. They can be introduced to children in a meaningful way through the rhythmic activities described in this chapter.

C O N C E P T

28.1 *Rhythmic Awareness Is a Basic Component of All Coordinated Movement*

Underlying Beat

Perhaps the simplest and most important element of rhythm is the underlying beat of the musical accompaniment. Children can feel the steady pulsation of their heartbeat. Each beat of the heart has the same strength, or intensity, and recurs with the same amount of time between each beat. The normal heartbeat of a child at rest is about 72 beats per minute, spaced evenly over the one-minute period. After vigorous activity, the child's pulse rate increases to about 120 beats per minute. The heart is still beating with an even rhythm, but faster and with a shorter interval between each underlying beat. Like a person's heartbeat, the underlying beat in music is the steady sound, or pulsation, heard or felt as music is played. The underlying beat may be slow, with long and even intervals between each beat, or very fast, with corresponding shorter intervals.

In dance, we move "in time" with the musical accompaniment when each foot, hand, or body movement synchronizes with each successive beat of the music. For example, when children clap their hands or stamp their feet to each beat in the song "Row, Row, Row Your Boat," they are keeping in time to the rhythm of the song. Moving in time to the underlying beat is perhaps the most important prerequisite to all dance activities.

C O N C E P T

28.2 *A Child Who Has a Well-Developed Sense of Time Can Perform Movements in a Rhythmic, Coordinated Manner*

Measure

A measure is an equal grouping of underlying beats. As illustrated in the figure below, four quarter notes are grouped between two bar lines and repeated for three measures.

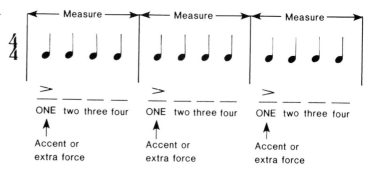

Accent

Accent is the extra force, or stress, given to certain beats in a measure. In the previous figure, the accent is on the first beat in each measure. To children, the accent is heard as a louder beat of the first note or as singing the first word of the measure louder than the other words in the measure.

The purpose of accenting music and movement is to provide variety and excitement to all types of dance activities. Accenting is also used to help children change direction, such as "change direction after every fourth step" or shift to another movement pattern such as "alternately shift from a walk to a run after every fourth beat." In these examples, the emphasis given to the first beat in each measure provides a signal for children to shift to the next movement.

Time Signature

Time signature is the numerical symbol placed in front of written music to explain the underlying rhythm within a measure. The top number of this symbol indicates the number of beats to a measure, whereas the bottom number denotes the kind of note that will receive *one beat*. Four of the most common meters used in the elementary dance program are described here.

4/4 METER: *Denotes four beats in each measure*

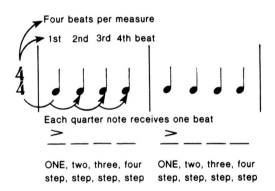

In the 4/4 meter, each quarter note receives *one* beat, producing an even four-count meter rhythm. If a child were walking "in time" to this 4/4 meter, he would *step, step, step, step* evenly within each measure in a moderate walking speed. Since there are four beats, the child would always start each new measure on the same foot. The 4/4 meter is an *even rhythm,* with each underlying beat receiving full note value. This meter can be used with the following steps: walk, run, hop, jump, leap, and schottische.

2/4 METER: *Denotes two beats in each measure*
The accent is on the first and third beats, and quarter notes get one beat.

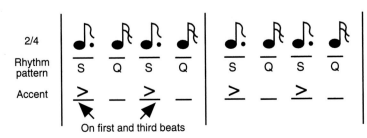

The 2/4 meter is an *uneven rhythm* and is a combination of a *long* and a *short* beat. This meter is used with the following steps: skip, slide, gallop, polka, two-step, and bleking step.

3/4 METER: *Denotes three beats in each measure*
The accent is on the first beat, and quarter notes get one beat.

The 3/4 meter is an *even rhythm,* with each underlying beat receiving full note value. This meter is used for the waltz, mazurka, and varsoviienne.

6/8 METER: *Denotes six beats in each measure*
The accent is on the first and fourth beats, and eighth notes receive one beat.

The 6/8 meter is an *uneven rhythm* and is a combination of a long and a short beat followed by another long and short beat within each measure. This meter is used for the skip and gallop.

Tempo

Tempo is the rate of speed of the music or movement. In musical accompaniment, the tempo can be slow, moderate, or fast, or it may increase gradually from slow to fast.

In folk and creative dance activities, it is important for children to feel and understand the difference among moving slowly, moderately, and very quickly. It is also important for each child to sense different speeds of the same music and to learn to adjust movements to the new tempo of the music.

Rhythmic Pattern

Rhythmic pattern is the grouping of sounds of the song or instrumental music to correspond to the underlying beat of the music. To illustrate, in the song "Ten Little Indians," the sounds of the music are of different durations in order to provide the rhythmic pattern. The words follow the rhythmic pattern, and the rhythmic pattern corresponds to the underlying beat of the 2/4 meter of this music.

Phrase

In music, a phrase is a natural grouping of measures that gives a feeling of a complete musical thought or idea. The rhyme "Baa Baa Black Sheep" extends through the second measure in order to complete a "musical sentence." Musical phrases are used in folk and creative dance activities to complete a series of movements before repeating them or before starting a new series of movements.

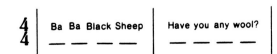

C O N C E P T

28.3 *Rhythmic Activities Must Be Developmentally Appropriate to Ensure That All Children Can Achieve Success and Enjoyment*

Intensity

Intensity refers to the amount of force exerted in a movement or sound. In movement, intensity is recognized as the feeling of heaviness or lightness. In sound, children hear loud and soft sounds in the musical accompaniment.

TEACHING PROCEDURES

The structure of a rhythmics lesson is similar to that of the game or gymnastic lesson described in previous chapters. Each rhythmic lesson normally has an introductory activity, a second skill development activity, and, third, closure. The basic progression used to teach the elements of rhythm is from individual to partner to group activities. The following sample lesson illustrates how to introduce the underlying beat, measure, and accent.

C O N C E P T

28.4 *The Teaching Progression Used to Teach the Elements of Rhythm Moves from Individual, to Partner, to Group Activities*

■ **Sample Lesson: Beat, Measure, and Accent**

Main theme Moving to the underlying beat
Subthemes Measures and accents
Progression Individual to partner to group activities
Music Any fast, popular record with a 4/4 beat

Part I: Introductory Activity

Class members sit in a scattered formation on the floor, with their legs crossed.

1. Have the children clap in the following ways (without music).
   a. Clap knees four times, repeating measure (1, 2, 3, 4; 1, 2, 3, 4; etc.).
   b. Clap hands four times, repeating measure.
   c. Tap the floor four times, repeating measure.
   d. Make up combinations of four claps on knees, then four taps on the floor, and four claps with the hands (figure 28.1).
2. Have the children listen to "music" for the 4/4 meter (four beats per measure) and the accent on the first beat.
3. Repeat 1a through 1d with music.

Figure 28.1   Clap to the beat.

Figure 28.2   Hop to the rhythm.

Additional Ideas   Once the class understands the meaning of the underlying beat and can clap four times within each measure according to the musical accompaniment, other combinations can be attempted in this introductory part of the lesson or at the beginning of a second, third, or fourth lesson, stressing the elements of rhythm:

1. Snap fingers.
2. From a standing position, slap different parts of the body.
3. From a standing position, shake one part of the body. Shake the right hand 1, 2, 3, and 4. Add other parts of the body; shake the right hand and the right leg.
4. Move parts of the body to the rhythm of the music. This could include bending, stretching, swinging, or twisting.
5. Perform locomotor movements to the rhythm of the music—walk, run, hop, or jump (figure 28.2)

Figure 28.3 Clap four times to each other's hands.

Figure 28.4 Then clap four times to own hands.

Part 2: Skill Development

In the initial phase of the second part of the lesson, partners develop simple matching routines with the movements learned earlier.

1. Partners sit on the floor, cross-legged and facing each other. One child begins with four claps on whatever part of his body he chooses; his partner follows. The first performer chooses another part of his body and repeats, with his partner copying him. Continue with two more parts of the body. After the fourth part of the body, ask the partners to work together and perform the four clapping movements simultaneously on the four parts of their bodies.
2. Join partner clapping: Partners sit cross-legged, facing each other, and tap four times on the floor, then four times to each other's hands (figure 28.3), then four times to own hands (figure 28.4).
3. Repeat 2 from a standing position, substituting tapping the floor with tapping or shaking one's own body parts or snapping fingers.

During the various activities of this part of the lesson, consciously stress *accenting* the first beat of each measure. That accent should also be used to signify the start of a new movement or a change in position or direction. If the latter two elements are emphasized, the meaning of a measure also becomes clear to each student.

Additional Ideas   As soon as the class understands the idea of matching clapping movements, the number of combinations becomes almost unlimited. Following are some possibilities to try here or leave until the next lesson:

1. Alternative hand clapping—tap the floor, clap one opposite hand, clap two hands.
2. Alternate a hand clap and a finger snap.

Figure 28.5 Include a twist.

3. Include a turn, twist, or shift of the body after each measure (figure 28.5). This might include four clapping movements, followed by four steps around in a circle, then back to four clapping movements.
4. Develop matching routines facing, clapping, and changing direction (figure 28.6).
5. Combine locomotor movements with clapping, shaking, or snapping fingers.
6. Include a change of direction or level in these routines.

Arrange the class into groups of four. Since this may be the first group experience with this type of rhythmic exercise, it is wise to go slow at the start to allow each child to

CHAPTER 28

a. Facing

b. Clapping

c. Change of direction

Figure 28.6   Develop matching routines.

feel comfortable and to be successful with your challenges. The first challenges should be similar to the ones first presented to individuals, then to partners. These are as follows:

1. In your group of four, sit cross-legged, facing the center of the group. Without music, clap hands four times, tap floor four times, then hands again for four counts.
2. Repeat with music.
3. Make up a routine, with each child tapping the floor, then all clapping hands, then tapping the floor again. "Next time, when you clap hands, place your hands to the side and clap hands with the players on your right and your left." This should be enough to get each group started on its own routine.

If the children are receptive and at ease, allow them to make up their own sitting, standing, or moving routine in their own group of four. If more help is needed pose challenges, keeping them sitting on the floor, then from a standing position, and finally involving locomotor movements.

C O N C E P T

28.5   *Posing Problem-Solving Challenges Stimulates Creativity*

Part 3: Closure

Discuss measure, underlying beat, and accent.

RHYTHMIC ACTIVITIES WITH SMALL EQUIPMENT

Small equipment is used with rhythmic activities in two ways. First, the equipment, such as a rope or hoop, can be used as a focal point or obstacle to move in and out of, around, or over. Second, the equipment, such as a hoop or ball, can be held or manipulated as an extension of the rhythmic movements of the body. Swinging a hoop and bouncing a ball to a rhythm are examples of the latter.

Begin by teaching hand or foot movements without equipment so that the children learn the basic movements and rhythmic patterns. Once these are acquired, introduce equipment to the routine or movement pattern.

C O N C E P T

28.6   *Effective Teaching Progressions, Providing All Children with Appropriate Rhythmic Activities, are Required to Develop Rhythmic Awareness*

Inflated Balls

Ball bouncing is particularly useful in helping children learn to move in time to the underlying beat of music. Any inflated ball can be used. Slow and fast tunes can be used in all of the following individual, partner, and group tasks.

Individual Tasks

Begin bouncing with one hand to the underlying beat of the music. Add the following challenges:

1. Change hands.
2. Bounce to one knee.
3. Bounce the ball around your body.
4. Bounce the ball with another part of your body (elbow, foot, etc.).
5. Bounce the ball and change direction—forward, backward, and sideways.
6. Bounce the ball and change levels—high, medium, and low.
7. Bounce, clap hands, bounce, and turn around.
8. Introduce a skipping rope. Place the rope on the floor in a curved or zigzag pattern. Develop tasks that require a bounce and a change of direction around or across the rope.

Figure 28.7 Move back and forth over the rope.

Partner and Group Tasks

The children can participate in various partner routines such as (1) matching bounces, (2) following the leader, (3) contrasting routines (one high and one low), and (4) bouncing and exchanging the ball on certain beats of the music. Group routines involving four or more players can also be developed by most children in the intermediate grades—for example, "Make up a routine with four players that includes four different bounces, a change of direction, and a change in level."

Individual Ropes

Basic rope-jumping skills and several ideas relating to the development of individual and partner routines were presented in chapter 26, however, no reference was made to musical accompaniment. The following challenges can be performed to musical accompaniment (any current popular tune that has a good beat).

The following examples illustrate the variety of ways a rope can be used in rhythmic activities by an individual or by two or more players.

Individual Tasks

Choose a record with a good 4/4 meter for the following individual tasks:

1. Place the rope on the floor in any pattern desired (straight, curled, or zigzag). Make up a routine of moving back and forth over your rope (figure 28.7). If the children feel the 4/4 even rhythm, they should use a walk, run, jump, hop, or leap step in their routine.
2. Keep the same rope pattern, but change the record or tape to a 2/4 or 6/8 meter. Pose the challenge, "Now make up a new routine, moving back and forth or around your rope." The uneven 2/4 or 6/8 rhythm should encourage children to use a skipping or sliding step in their routine.

Figure 28.8 Develop a two-foot basic step with your partner.

Partner and Group Tasks

1. Develop a routine with your partner, using even rhythm and a two-foot basic step (figure 28.8).
2. Make up a rope-skipping routine, with one partner following the other. (Use uneven rhythm.)
3. Place one rope on the ground and make up a matching routine with your partner, using a 2/4 meter.
4. Have the children place two ropes on the floor and repeat task 1.
5. In groups of four, make up a matching routine in any pattern you like.

Rhythm or Lummi Sticks

Rhythm or lummi sticks* are extremely useful in developing the elements of rhythm. The sticks are approximately ten to twelve inches long and can be made from one-inch doweling or old broomsticks. The sticks are held between the thumb and fingers near the lower third of the stick (figure 28.9).

*Lummi sticks and records can be purchased from Educational Activities, Inc., Box 392, Freeport, NY, 11520.

Figure 28.9 Hold sticks between the thumb and fingers.

Figure 28.10 Make up a routine.

Individual Tasks

The first tasks presented should give each child an opportunity to learn how to tap the sticks to the rhythm of the music and how to shift from one tapping movement to another. Challenges can include the following simple routines:

Sitting Cross-Legged or on Knees

1. Tap the floor four times, tap the sticks together four times, tap the right or left leg four times, and so on.
2. Make up a routine, tapping the floor in front, to the side, and behind you (figure 28.10).
3. Make up a routine that includes tapping, throwing, and catching the sticks and then another tapping movement.
4. Repeat 1, 2, and 3 to a 4/4 musical accompaniment.

Once the children can tap the sticks together, on a part of the body, or on the floor, the sticks can be used to teach accent, intensity, and different meters in a very enjoyable way. Try the following challenges.

5. Repeat 1 and 2, making the first beat in each measure louder than the next three beats.
6. Still sitting cross-legged or kneeling, tap the sticks together on the first beat, then tap the body (thighs, stomach, etc.) the next three times. Continue pattern.
7. Repeat 5 and 6 with the same musical accompaniment as 4.
8. Repeat 5 and 6 with a 2/4 musical accompaniment, tapping the first beat with the two sticks and the second against the body.

Standing

9. Develop a routine of tapping the sticks in front, to the side, behind the back, and against the body. Use a 4/4 and a 2/4 or 6/8 musical accompaniment to emphasize even and uneven rhythms.

10. Develop a routine involving walking, running, hopping, or jumping and tapping the sticks to the 4/4 even rhythm of the musical accompaniment.
11. Develop a routine involving skipping or sliding and tapping the sticks to a 2/4 or 6/8 uneven rhythm of musical accompaniment.

Partner and Group Tasks

The first partner activities should begin with both players sitting about two feet apart in a cross-legged position, facing each other. This position encourages the players to develop routines using the floor for tapping, as well as the partner's sticks. Following are a few sample routines:

1. Without music, hit sticks on the floor, hit both sticks together in front, hit with both arms sideways, hit floor.
2. Without music, partners hit sticks to the floor, hit their own sticks together, exchange right sticks, then exchange left sticks.
3. Repeat 1 and 2 with a 4/4 or 2/4 musical accompaniment.
4. Without music, numerous calistheniclike and other rhythmic routines can be developed with two players standing face to face, side by side, or back to back.
5. Repeat 4 with same musical accompaniment used in 3.
6. Group activities can also be developed with sets of three or more children. Once the children have learned the basic tapping skills and have had rhythmic experience with hoops, balls, and skipping ropes, they will develop creative rhythmic routines with lummi sticks quickly and enthusiastically.

Hoops

Hoops can be used in two ways with rhythmic activities: (1) when placed on the floor, they become an obstacle or focal point to maneuver in and out of, around, or over and (2) when held or manipulated, they can help children move their bodies or parts of them to the rhythm of a drumbeat or music.

Several standardized movement skills described in chapter 26 can be performed in time to musical accompaniment. These skills and the ones provided in the following paragraphs illustrate the versatility of hoops, as well as their effectiveness in teaching the elements of rhythm.

Individual Tasks

Have each child place his hoop flat on the floor. Present challenges, such as the following, that involve locomotor skills and a change of direction.

1. "Make up a jumping routine, moving in and out of your hoop." Later, add other challenges such as "in and out, around, and over." (Use even rhythm, 4/4 or 3/4 music.)
2. Use two or more hoops on the floor and repeat 1.
3. Introduce ball bouncing with a hoop.

Many twirling and movement skills can be done with a hoop. The following provide a basic starting point. Use uneven rhythm—2/4 or 6/8 music.

1. "Can you twirl the hoop on your body to the rhythm of the music "Summer Place'?" Later, substitute back, arm, wrist, leg, or foot.
2. "Can you throw and catch the hoop, keeping in time to the rhythm of the music?"
3. "Develop a routine of swinging, jumping, and twisting."

Partner and Group Tasks

In partners, twirling, throwing, catching, and nonlocomotor skills can be incorporated into a variety of interesting and challenging matching, contrasting, and follow-the-leader routines.

1. Develop a series of challenges involving partners, using one or more hoops and musical accompaniment with an uneven rhythm.
2. Repeat the challenge, using partners, one or more hoops, and locomotor skills performed with an even rhythm accompaniment. (Run, walk, hop, jump, and leap.)
3. Repeat 1 or 2, adding a ball or other small equipment to the original challenge.

Partner activities can be modified easily to add one or more children to each task.

TASK CARDS

Task cards can be applied to individual, partner, or group rhythmic activities with equal success. The following example illustrates the type of information that should be written on the cards.

Six to eight cards with different tasks (but the same music) should be used. Divide the class into small groups. Each child reads the challenge and then develops his own routine. Thus, there are several different types of routines

rather than variations of one task. Various levels of ability can be accommodated by designing cards ranging from very simple tasks to challenges requiring greater skill and creative ability.

When equipment is unavailable for every child to perform a particular activity, use task cards and the station work technique. In the following example, the class is divided into four groups and then subdivided into partners. Each set of partners reads the challenge, then develops a matching routine. Any marching tune can be used for all stations. Allow four to five minutes for the partners to develop their routines, then put on the tune. If time permits, rotate the groups to their next station and repeat the process.

Station 1: Hoops. Make up a matching sequence with your partner that includes three different twirling movements, a pause in your routine, and a change in direction.
Station 2: Individual ropes. Make up a matching routine that includes three different steps.
Station 3: Utility balls. Develop a bouncing routine, with one partner leading and the other following.
Station 4: Lummi sticks. Make up a matching routine that includes a change of direction and a change in level.

The activities presented in this chapter should not be seen as a separate unit of dance. Rather, as was stated earlier, rhythmic activities should be integrated into game, gymnastic, and dance units. This can be done through periodic rhythmic warm-up activities and an occasional complete lesson of rhythmics interspersed within a game or gymnastic unit.

C O N C E P T

28.7 *The Development of Rhythmic Awareness Should Be Facilitated through Opportunities to Participate in Rhythmic Activities in Games, Gymnastics, and Dance*

Summary Review

It is essential that all children develop a strong sense of rhythmic awareness, because this is the basic component of all coordinated movement (see chapter 2). Rhythm is the ability to repeat an action or movement with regularity and in time to a particular pattern; hence, it is the common element in dance and music. Without a sense of timing, a child will be unable to perform rhythmic, coordinated movements and will have difficulty coordinating movement with music. Such a child will experience difficulties performing most dance activities. The physical education program should provide opportunities for children to acquire a basic understanding of the elements of rhythm and the ways the elements can be combined with a variety of game, dance, and gymnastic movements. Rhythmic activities can be integrated into numerous game, dance, and gymnastic

CHAPTER 28

activities. Once children understand the elements of rhythm, they can learn dance activities with greater speed and usually with a very positive attitude. It is recommended that teaching progressions move from individual, to partner, to group activities to enable children to gradually acquire the elements of rhythmic awareness. Creative problem-solving challenges and academic skills and concepts can be integrated into the rhythmical activities to provide a rich learning experience for all children.

SELECTED READINGS

Fleming, G. A. 1990. *Children's dance.* Rev. ed. Reston, VA: AAHPERD.

Harris, J. A., A. M. Pittman, and M. S. Waller. 1988. *Dance awhile.* 6th ed. New York: Macmillan.

Murray, R. L. 1975. *Dance in elementary education.* 3d ed. New York: Harper & Row.

Stinson, S. 1988. *Dance for young children: Finding the magic movement.* Reston, VA: AAHPERD.

INDIVIDUAL *and* GROUP PROJECTS

1. In small groups, design a series of challenge task cards, varying in level of challenge difficulty, for developing rhythmic awareness. One group member acts as the teacher, posing the challenge, while the remaining group members perform the rhythmic activities. Take turns presenting the task card challenges.

2. In small groups, plan lessons showing how rhythmic activities can be used to teach or enhance academic concepts and skills in other curricular subject areas. Plan to evaluate the expected learning outcomes. Share lesson plans with other groups.

3. Prepare lesson plans for developing rhythmic awareness. In pairs, take turns being teacher or learner, using your lesson plans to teach each other rhythmic awareness. Then reflect on your experiences as teacher and learner, and assess the effectiveness of your lesson plans.

Traditional and Contemporary Dances

KEY CONCEPTS

29.1 Basic locomotor skills are used in all traditional and contemporary dances

29.2 Dance activities must be developmentally appropriate to ensure that all children can achieve success and enjoyment

29.3 Singing games promote the performance of basic locomotor skills to musical accompaniment

29.4 When children can move rhythmically to music, they can create their own singing games

29.5 Traditional ways of teaching folk dances involve a sequential part-part-whole instructional approach

29.6 All folk, line, and square dances are made up of five basic elements: steps, direction, pathway, relationship, and formation

29.7 Teaching the five basic elements of a folk, line, or square dance is accomplished through a sequential and progressive part-part-whole process

KEY OBJECTIVES

After completing this chapter you will be able to:

1. Design developmentally appropriate traditional and contemporary dance activities for elementary school children
2. Understand the nature and scope of a traditional and contemporary dance program suitable for an elementary school physical education program
3. Identify the basic elements of all folk, line, and square dances
4. Teach folk, line, and square dances
5. Plan and organize teaching units and daily lessons involving traditional and contemporary dances
6. Apply movement concepts and skills when teaching traditional and contemporary dances
7. Identify key teaching points associated with folk, line, and square dances
8. Employ teaching progressions that lead to the successful development of folk, line, and square dances

All structured dances performed in the elementary school can be broadly classified as traditional or contemporary dances. The classification includes singing games and traditional dances of past cultures, as well as the contemporary dances of this generation. In this chapter, the first two sections have been organized to cope with the unique differences among the three developmental levels. The first section describes the basic steps, dance positions, and movement designs used in the dance program. The next section, "Teaching Dance Activities," provides suggestions for teaching folk, line, and square dance activities using both structured and exploratory methods of instruction. The final section describes traditional and contemporary dances for all three developmental levels. This chapter includes a glossary of terms and a list of sources for obtaining musical records.

DANCE AND EDUCATION

Singing games, American and international folk dances, and other contemporary dances offer a rich contribution to a child's education. Apart from the fitness, coordination, and motor skill development associated with the vigorous activity of dance, there is the tremendous opportunity to focus on the multicultural aspects of dances and to integrate these cultural experiences into other areas of the school curriculum. Dance provides children with an opportunity to gain a greater understanding of their own national heritage and to appreciate and learn the different ethnic backgrounds that contribute to our rich multicultural society. School subjects such as art, music, social studies, and language arts lend themselves easily to integration with dance activities.

The recurring theme throughout this text is the desire to educate children toward the maintainance of active lifestyles. Dance is one of the most popular active pastimes of both youth and adults, yet dance is often given little emphasis in a school physical education program. Clearly, dance education can provide children with skills and knowledge that promote a lifelong pursuit of an active lifestyle. As with other areas of the physical education program, the interest, skills, and knowledge associated with dance must be fostered through careful planning and teaching. Developmentally appropriate dance experiences must occur throughout the elementary school years to ensure correct development of the skills, knowledge, and aesthetic appreciation of dance. Several forms of traditional and contemporary dances make up the elementary school dance curriculum:

Folk dances: Handed down from generation to generation, folk dances are traditional dances of the people. They often portray customs, rituals, and occupations of the country or ethnic group they represent.

Line dances: Line dances are of American origin and have their roots in contemporary country music. These dances are performed without a partner, in lines or scattered formation.

Square dances: Square dances are of American origin and take their name from the fact that they are often performed in a four-couple square. However, some of these dances may also be performed in a large circle or scattered formation. Because square dances, like line dances, are relatively young in origin, they are not considered folk dances.

American dances: These are dances of colonial America. Popular country tunes of the colonial period form the music for these dances.

Native American dances: These dances originated with Native Americans and are often performed during Native American ceremonies and certain other social gatherings.

Singing games (dances): Singing games provide opportunities for young children to perform dance movements to music, poetry, and other forms of creative work.

DANCE STEPS, DANCE POSITIONS, AND MOVEMENT DESIGNS

All traditional and contemporary dance activities use individual locomotor skills, such as walk, run, and jump, or combinations of skills such as slide, skip, two-step, or waltz step. The main individual and combined steps used in most dance programs are described in the section "Dance Steps." The next section, "Dance Positions," describes and illustrates the various ways partners or groups of dancers hold on to each other as they perform a dance. Finally, the various ways dancers move in relation to a partner or other performers, such as meeting and parting, are illustrated in the section "Movement Designs."

C O N C E P T

29.1 *Basic Locomotor Skills Are Used in All Traditional and Contemporary Dances*

Chapter 29 Traditional and Contemporary Dances **619**

Dance Steps

The following seven basic locomotor steps and four combination steps are used in one or more of the three developmental level dance programs.

Walk

A walk may vary from a basic heel-toe walking action to a shuffling movement from ball of foot to ball of foot. In most dances with an even rhythm, the accent, or emphasis, is on the first beat.

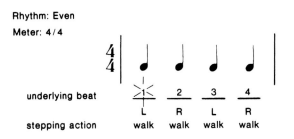

Run

A run may vary from a slow heel-toe run to a fast and vigorous running action from ball or toe of foot to the opposite ball or toe.

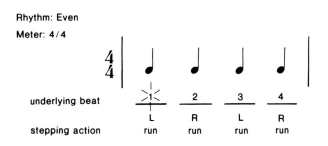

Hop

The hop is a basic springing action from the ball of one foot to the ball of the same foot.

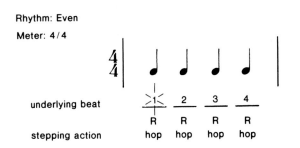

Leap

A leap is a basic springing action from the ball of one foot to a landing on the ball of the opposite foot. A slight or exaggerated knee bend on each landing is followed by a lowering of the heel.

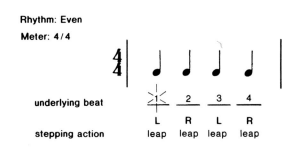

Jump

The jump is a basic springing action from the balls of both feet to the balls of both feet, with a slight overexaggerated knee bend. The heel normally comes down after the ball of the foot has made contact with the floor.

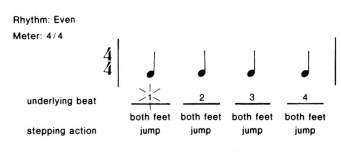

Skip

A skip is a step and a short hop on the same foot, shifting to a step and a hop on the opposite foot. In most dances with an uneven rhythm, the accent is on the first and third beats.

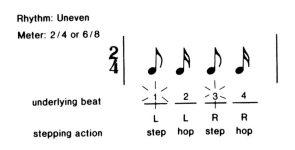

Two-Step

The two-step used in folk and square dances is a combination of a step forward on the ball of the left foot, then a closing action of the right to the left foot (weight is briefly taken on right foot), then a step forward on left foot. Repeat for the next measure, but begin on right foot.

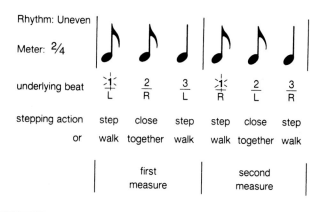

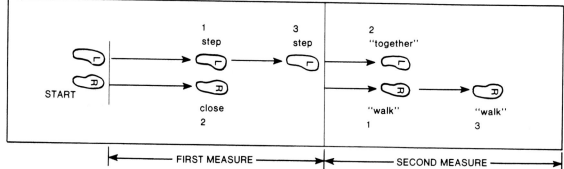

Polka

The polka step is similar to the two-step, with the addition of a hop in the combined sequence of steps. The first measure begins with stepping left, while the next begins with stepping right, alternating this action throughout the dance.

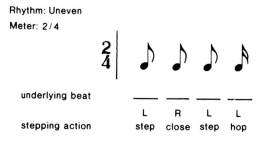

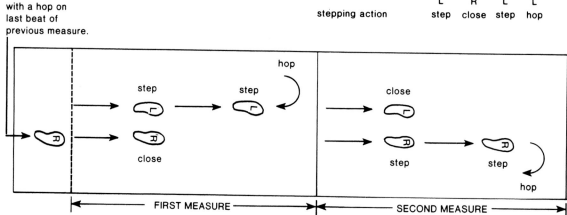

Dance Positions

The various dance positions described and illustrated in figures 29.1 through 29.7 are used in one or more of the three developmental level dance programs.

Movement Designs

The movement designs in figure 29.8–29.13 are the various ways two or more dancers meet, greet, and part. They are used in simple singing games, as well as in folk and square dances.

Figure 29.1 Open position: facing forward, with inside hands joined.

Figure 29.3 Closed position. Stand facing each other, with boy's right arm around girl and his hand resting under her shoulder blade. He holds girl's right hand in his left. Girl's left hand rests on his right shoulder.

Figure 29.2 Schottische, or conversation, position. Stand side-by-side, with girl on boy's right side. Boy's arm is behind girl's back and his hand is on her waist. Girl's left hand rests on boy's right shoulder.

Figure 29.4 Skaters, or promenade, position. Partners stand side-by-side, facing forward. Girl is on boy's right. Both hold right hands and left hands together.

Figure 29.5 Shoulder-waist position. Stand facing each other, with boy's arms outstretched and both hands holding girl's waist. Girl places her hands on boy's shoulders.

Figure 29.7 Varsovienne position. Stand side-by-side and facing forward. Girl is on boy's right. Boy's right arm is behind girl's shoulders and holding her right hand just above her right shoulder. Boy holds girl's left hand in his, about chest high.

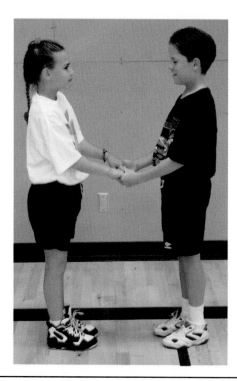

Figure 29.6 Two-hand facing position. Stand facing each other, with elbows bent and holding each other's hands.

Figure 29.8 Meeting.

Figure 29.9 Arching.

Figure 29.11 Weaving.

Figure 29.10 Passing.

Figure 29.12 Starring.

Figure 29.13 Swinging.

TEACHING DANCE ACTIVITIES

Dance activities for an elementary school physical education program begin with the simple singing games enjoyed by early primary children. In the next two developmental levels, children are introduced to a wide variety of contemporary and traditional dances from around the world. These dances can be taught in a systematic manner or through an exploratory or problem-solving approach.

C O N C E P T

29.2 *Dance Activities Must Be Developmentally Appropriate to Ensure That All Children Can Achieve Success and Enjoyment*

Teaching Singing Games

Most primary singing games are individual or partner activities; however, both types are performed in a group situation. Since five-, six-, and seven-year-olds are basically individualistic, the singing games presented in this chapter can be performed individually while the children are in a line, circle, or scattered pattern. With practice and maturity, children progress to more advanced singing games involving intricate patterns and group participation.

Teaching singing games to children in the primary grades, particularly to five- and six-year-olds, should be an enjoyable experience for teachers and a creative experience for children. The children's uninhibited behavior and joy of movement make singing games an appropriate activity. Once they learn the words, they will provide their own accompaniment and an infinite variety of interesting and creative versions of each singing game.

C O N C E P T

29.3 *Singing Games Promote the Performance of Basic Locomotor Skills to Musical Accompaniment*

Early primary children vary widely in maturity, motor ability, and interests, and no single method of teaching will prove successful with this type of activity. Each teacher should experiment with several approaches until she finds the one most suitable to her own style of teaching, usually a combination of techniques. The following suggestions may be helpful:

1. Use a form of musical accompaniment that permits you to work freely with the children, such as commercial records or a tape recording of your own piano accompaniment.
2. Give the name of the singing game and its origin, and mention something about the customs of the people. Illustrate by showing motion pictures, slides, or photographs of the people.
3. Teach the words of the singing game first. Children should practice singing the song until they have nearly memorized it.
4. Teach the basic steps of the singing game after the children have learned the verses.
5. Combine the basic steps with the words and music.
6. Combine the basic steps with the words and music, and begin with a whole-class formation (a large circle). Then progress to smaller groups.
7. Attempt to create a permissive atmosphere in which the children feel free to express their own ideas and movements.

Through singing games, children learn to walk, run, skip, or perform a combination of these basic dance steps to musical accompaniment. When they can move rhythmically to music, they can create their own singing games. Allow them to develop their own dances to favorite nursery rhymes or songs. For example, "Sing a Song of Sixpence" and "I Saw a Ship a-Sailing" have simple phrases and rhythmic melodies that provide the necessary ingredients for new singing games. In addition, children may wish to write their own verses about animals, spaceships, or special events and then try to apply them to musical accompaniment. Finding the appropriate music usually becomes a joint venture for the teacher and class. The table of additional singing games and available records later in this chapter will be of some assistance. Children should also be encouraged to create their own music. Perhaps, too, some children might be fortunate enough to have a teacher with a musical background and the talent to write musical accompaniments to fit the verses they write.

C O N C E P T

29.4 *When Children Can Move Rhythmically to Music, They Can Create Their Own Singing Games*

Teaching Folk Dances

As suggested earlier in this book, there is no one best method of teaching that will work for all occasions. This is particularly true with the problems normally associated with teaching folk dance to children in developmental levels II and III. Often these children lack a strong dance background, and have also been been taught in a more formal or structured way. Differences in physical and social maturity and other important multicultural factors also must be considered when teaching folk dance activities to these older children. With these considerations in mind, the following suggested progression can be used as a starting point for each teacher to develop their own approaches.

1. Acquire a general knowledge of the culture from which the dance originated, and present this to the class, perhaps selecting dances that represent some of the cultures or ethnic backgrounds of the children.
2. Review the music, dance steps, and movements of the dance prior to teaching it. Be confident and at ease so you can show genuine enthusiasm.
3. Start with children sitting near the music. Present the background information about the dance in relation to the class's interest and maturity. Make it meaningful to the children.
4. While children are sitting, play the music and have them tap out the beat, as this helps them become more familiar with the music.
5. While children are sitting, have some students demonstrate the dance, or parts of it. It is also helpful to teach your better students before the class demonstration to ensure they feel comfortable and the movements are correct.
6. Arrange the class into teaching formation for the dance. If it is a single-circle dance, stand two steps inside the circle, demonstrate, move to another part of the circle, and demonstrate. Students tend to mirror what they see, so they will normally forget to reverse the foot movements and direction. When teaching children in front of you, mirror demonstrate: for instance, while facing the class, if you move your right foot, say to the class, "Move your left foot."
7. Have each student walk through the first step (later it may require a partner or group movement) and in a slow tempo. Move to the correct tempo as soon as possible.
8. Have the class repeat this part with music. Call out rhythmic cues.
9. Teach the next part of the dance in the same fashion.
10. Have the class dance the first and second parts consecutively with the music and your cues.
11. Teach each part in a similar way until all parts have been learned.
12. After the last part has been learned, have the class walk through the entire dance in the proper tempo.
13. Repeat the entire dance with music and your rhythmic cues. Gradually reduce your rhythmic cues, increase the volume of the music, and let children enjoy the dance.

C O N C E P T

29.5 *Traditional Ways of Teaching Folk Dances Involve a Sequential Part-Part-Whole Instructional Approach*

Teaching Line Dances

Teaching line dances is very similar to teaching folk dances. Direct methods of teaching involving demonstration and part-part-whole principles of learning, first without the music and then with the music, work particularly well. One teaching technique to consider is to turn your back toward the students when you demonstrate a particular step or movement so they can visualize a movement image they can copy directly. If you demonstrate while facing the students, your right and left visual movements must be cognitively reversed by the students. Providing a direct image of the movement (a view of your back) is easier for students to comprehend and learn from. The following are several other points to consider when teaching line dances:

1. Reinforce heads up, knees slightly bent, and back straight.
2. Hand position: generally on hips, or at waist level as if holding a broomstick horizontally.
3. Keep lines straight. Have students hold right arms out straight so they can just barely touch the next person.
4. Leave out a difficult move if children are experiencing difficulty mastering the movement.
5. With more difficult segments of a line dance, do not demonstrate the complete dance at the beginning. Some students might think the movement is too complex for them to learn and give up early in the learning process.
6. Consider teaching a difficult segment of the line dance first rather than going from beginning to end. The advantage is that each time an easier segment is added, students get to practice the more difficult segment. Hence, by the completion of the line dance, students will have received several practices of the most difficult part of the dance.
7. Have groups of students teach a line dance to the rest of the class.
8. Allow small groups of students to choose their own music and to create their own line dances.
9. Encourage students to create a "school" line dance and to name it.

Teaching Square Dances

American dances include mixers, couples, longways, circles, and square dances that have been developed in North America over the past hundred years. Square dances have become popular with upper elementary school children, perhaps because of the simplicity of the steps and the enjoyment of participation.

Square Dance Calls

Square dances use two types of calls: patter and singing. The patter call is the more traditional form, and involves the caller giving instructions in a rhythmic manner. These calls generally rhyme and fit with the music. Singing calls are considered a modern form of square dance calling. Here the caller gives instructions to the dancers by singing the call to a familiar tune. Other differences between patter and singing calls involve the type of instruction. Patter calls allow the caller to individualize the calls to a particular square dance and group of people. Singing calls tend to provide less freedom or variation for the caller, because the calls are written to fit with a particular dance and tune. Learning to call square dances requires careful planning and practice. Most square dance music is written in 4/4 or 2/4 time, both of which can be broken down into a series of four even beats. Each four beats constitute a phrase for calling. Practice is essential to calling. The caller must provide ample time for the dancers to move through the figures, while at the same time keeping all dancers moving along. Patter calls can be fun and exciting because the caller can adjust the instructions to provide variety and to offer challenges that are at an appropriate developmental level. While teacher calling is preferred, resources are available that provide calling. For example, *Wagon Wheel Fundamentals of Square Dancing, Levels 1, 2, and 3* and *Square Dance Party for the New Dancer, No.1 and No.2* both provide calling. These resources follow different developmental levels and provide sequential progressions for learning square dances. These resources can be obtained through:

Wagon Wheel Records and Books
8459 Edmaru Avenue
Whittier, CA 90605

The following suggestions will help teachers present various types of square dance patterns. A list of terms used in square dancing is provided in the glossary at the end of this chapter.

1. Emphasize fun and enjoyment rather than perfection of every skill.
2. Teach all square dance movements from a circle formation, with each girl standing to the right of her partner.
3. Select square dances that involve simple patterns, and introduce them at a slow speed.
4. Teach the dance by calling the dance patterns first without music and then with it. Once the dance is learned, you may continue calling or use a record that includes the calls.
5. The majority of square dancing is done with a shuffle step rather than a run or hop. Emphasize a smooth and graceful slipping action, landing on the ball of the foot rather than on the heel.

6. The success of square dancing depends, in part, on keeping the square of four couples symmetrical and the partners parallel. Constantly check to see that children maintain the square and partners do not wander away from each other.
7. Encourage children not only to call their own dances, but also to create their own sequences of square dance figures.

Teaching Creative Folk, Line, and Square Dance Activities

The traditional and contemporary dances that are taught to upper elementary school children are rich in cultural heritage. These dances have normally been taught to children formally, with the steps, formations, and gestures of each dance introduced systematically. However, contemporary approaches to teaching elementary school physical education activities use more individualized instructional techniques and more exploratory and problem-solving methods to cope with the characteristics, needs, and interests of this age group. The material that follows is an attempt to introduce a more creative approach to teaching folk, line, and square dance activities. The next section describes the five basic elements of these dances, followed by a suggested approach for teaching each of these elements in a systematic yet creative manner.

Elements of Folk, Line, and Square Dances

Although there are marked differences in the steps, body gestures, and styles between one dance and another, all dances, regardless of age or cultural origin, are made up of five basic elements. The first element, as illustrated, includes the *steps* performed in the dance. Second, dancers move in a specified *direction*. Third, dancers move through a particular *pathway*. Fourth, dancers have a certain *relationship* to each other as they move through the dance. Finally, all dances are performed from a line, square, or circle *formation*. Each element is clarified in the following pages.

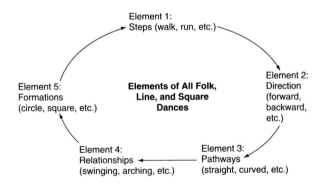

C O N C E P T

29.6 *All Folk, Line, and Square Dances Are Made Up of Five Basic Elements: Steps, Direction, Pathway, Relationship, and Formation*

Element 1: Steps

Seven locomotor steps (walk, run, hop, leap, jump, skip, and slide) represent the basic ways children move in folk, line, and square dance activities. Most of these skills are acquired long before children reach the intermediate grades. Therefore, the emphasis in the dance program is to acquire different styles of performing each locomotor movement; to move gracefully and in time to the rhythm of the music; and to shift tempo, intensity, or other rhythmic skills to meet the challenge and enjoyable subtleties of each dance activity.

Element 2: Direction

All folk, line, and square dance activities require performers to move in either a forward, backward, sideward, or diagonal direction. These are the simplest directions children can move in while performing the basic dance steps.

The "Directions" diagram illustrates how the second element is added to the first element. For example, a child may walk (element 1) forward (element 2) or slide (element 1)

sideways (element 2). The concept of "right-left" can be simplified for young children by placing a colored band on the right or left wrist. The lesson plans in the next section illustrate how elements are added sequentially from one lesson to the next.

Directions

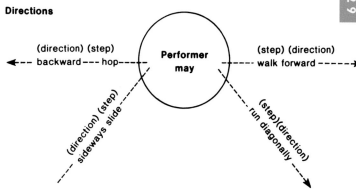

Element 3: Pathway

The third element common to all folk, line, and square dances is the pathway of movement. A pathway can be described as a pattern of movement—such as straight, curved, or zigzag. In the "Pathways" diagram, each pathway is combined with element 1 (steps) and element 2 (direction). Note how directions and pathways relate to each other in dance movements.

Pathways

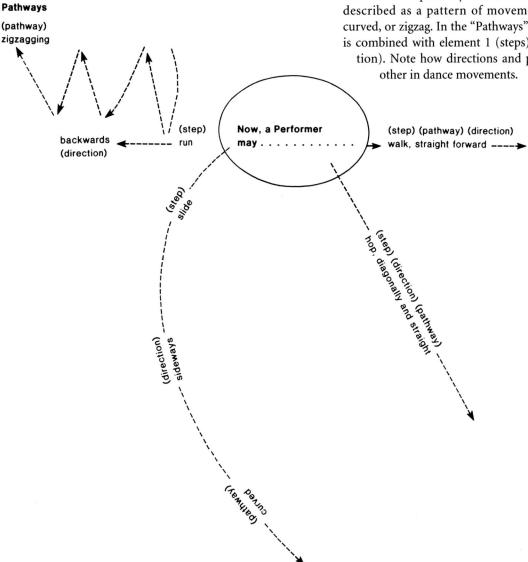

Element 4: Relationship

Element 4 includes two ways dancers relate to each other. The first is the dance position and the way two dancers hold each other throughout the dance. The second type of relationship is the manner in which each performer moves in relation to his or her partner or other performers in the dance. The following is a list of the most common dance positions and movement designs:

Dance positions (review figures 29.1 through 29.7)	Movement designs (review figures 29.8 through 29.13)
Open	Meeting
Closed	Arching
Skaters	Passing
Two-hand facing	Weaving
Shoulder-waist	Starring
Schottische	Swinging
Varsovienne	

Performers may:

in a skater's position (element 4: relationship)
walk eight steps (element 1: steps)
straight forward (element 2: direction, and element 3: pathway)
change to a shoulder-waist position (element 4: relationship) and swing their partners (element 4: relationship).

Element 5: Formation

The fifth element of folk, line, and square dances includes three formations in which folk, line, and square dances are performed: line, circle, and square.

Formations

Line		Circle		Square	
x	x	x x		x x	
x	x	x x		x	x
x	x	x x		x	x
x	x			x x	
x	x				
x	x				

(relationship)
Performers may . . . in promenade position,

(steps) (pathway) (direction)
walk straight forward for eight counts, then promenade

(relationship) (formation)
around the hall.

Teaching the Elements of Folk, Line, and Square Dances

The approach suggested here is a continuation of the rhythmic approach presented in the previous chapter. Hence, it is assumed that children understand the elements of rhythm, such as *even* and *uneven rhythm, accent,* and *underlying beat,*

and can recognize and apply these rhythmic elements to a variety of game, dance, and gymnastic movement skills.

In the previous section, the five elements of dance were described. These elements, illustrated in figure 29.14, can be introduced to children *sequentially* in an informal and relaxed manner through five interrelated stages. To illustrate, in lesson 1, the central theme is to move (walk, run, hop, jump, or leap) in time to an even musical accompaniment. In the introductory activities, children will need to be introduced to the movement activities (central theme) involved in folk, line, or square dance. The introductory activities will need to be adjusted according to the complexity of the movements and the developmental level of the children and their familiarity with the movements. It might be beneficial and necessary to first introduce the children to the movements without music, and to go through the movements with nonlocomotor actions to ensure that the children understand what is required. Once the movement actions are understood, music can be added. Individual, partner, and group activities then focus on the central theme from the beginning to the end of the lesson. Subthemes, such as changes in speed or level, provide some variety and a review of previously acquired movement skills. Although children might change direction within each movement task, specific references to directional movements are deliberately left out of lesson 1.

A combination of direct and indirect teaching styles will be required to teach the elements of folk, line, and square dances. All steps and actions should be taught separately so that children can practice one or two movements at a time, without the worry of coordinating with a partner or group. The part-whole method of instruction progresses to partner and group work, moving the child gently along the learning stages continuum.

C O N C E P T

29.7 *Teaching the Five Basic Elements of a Folk, Line, or Square Dance Is Accomplished through a Sequential and Progressive Part-Part-Whole Process*

Lesson 1: Steps

Main theme Moving to even rhythm
Subtheme Change of speed and level

I. Introductory activities
   A. Individual introduction to walking, running, hopping, jumping, and leaping (may be simulated through nonlocomotor practices to ensure that early cognitive phase of learning is addressed)
   B. Individual walking, running, hopping, jumping, and leaping to 4/4 musical accompaniment
   C. Add change of speed and level to above challenge.

II. Development
   A. In partners: "Make up a matching sequence that includes a run, hop, and jump and two changes in level." Use 4/4 musical accompaniment.

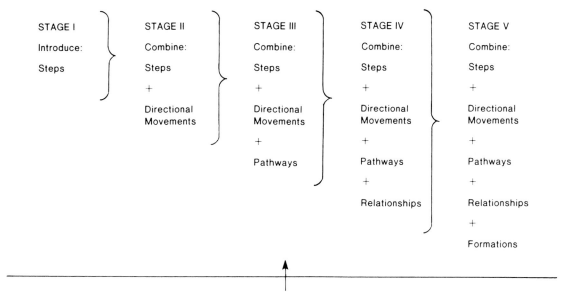

NOTE: Each of the five stages above progresses from:

Individual
to

Partner
to

Group Activities

Figure 29.14 Introducing the elements of folk, line, and square dances.

B. In partners: "Develop a routine that includes clapping, twisting, shaking, running, and hopping steps." Use 4/4 musical accompaniment.

C. In groups of four: Repeat B with four children in each group standing in a line for both challenges.

III. Closure
Discuss meaning of measure, even rhythm, and tempo.

In lesson 2, the central theme of the lesson emphasizes the second element, *direction*. This lesson follows the same pattern established in lesson 1, beginning with individual, shifting to partner, then changing to larger group activities. Subthemes of even and uneven rhythm and changing speed provide variety as well as a review of previously introduced skills.

▨ Lesson 2: Directional Movements

Main theme   Directional movements
Subthemes   Moving to even and uneven rhythm, change of speed

I. Introductory activities
Repeat A and B of lesson 1, adding a change of direction to each respective challenge.

II. Development

A. "Make up a sequence that includes a run and a hop, two changes of direction, and a clapping and shaking movement." Use 4/4 musical accompaniment.

B. In partners: "Begin with one standing behind the other. Create a routine that includes a skip and slide, moving sideways and diagonally, and a change in speed." Use 2/4 musical accompaniment.

C. In groups of three: "See if you can make a routine that includes one locomotor skill performed to an even musical accompaniment and three changes in direction." Use 4/4 musical accompaniment.

D. In groups of four: "Make up a routine that includes uneven rhythm and a change of direction." Use a 2/4 musical accompaniment.

III. Closure
Discuss uneven rhythm and directional movements.

At the completion of lesson 2, each teacher should consider such factors as the tone of the class, segregated or voluntary mixing of boys and girls for partner and group activities, and level of skill, before planning the next few lessons. Some classes might need one or two more lessons that stress directional movements and help develop more positive interpersonal relationships before progressing to stage III in figure 29.14. Hence, the number of lessons required to reach and complete the challenges in stage V depends on these factors and the progress that is made from one lesson to the next. Once children learn the basic elements of folk, line, and square dance through this informal and creative approach, they develop a very positive attitude toward these dance activities.

DANCES FOR THREE DEVELOPMENTAL LEVELS

All traditional and contemporary dances described in this section are grouped according to developmental level. The main dance emphasis for each level is briefly outlined. Because there is such a wide variation in dance backgrounds and local multicultural interests, teachers should use the information in table 29.1 as a general sample of appropriate dances for each level. Other supplementary dances may be more appropriate for some teaching situations. Schools with one or more dominant ethnic groups should attempt to incorporate each group's dance heritage into the program.

Most of the developmental level I dance activities are singing games, and these usually involve a circle formation and simple steps or movement patterns. Singing games are part of the dance heritage of every country. In essence, they are the forerunners of the more complicated traditional and contemporary dances. As such, they provide a foundation on which the more advanced dances can be built.

Because of the cultural and historical significance of these dances, primary teachers should take time to provide interesting materials related to their origin, the customs of the people, and the meanings of various dance movements. This information can be presented in many ways, such as reading stories and poems about the people; displaying pictures, dolls, and other articles; and showing a film about the country.

The dance activities of developmental level II shift toward a variety of folk, line, and square dances performed in various formations and involving more complex dance steps and movement patterns. At this level, children learn to perform many movements, such as swings, arching, heel-toe, and the bleking step, in relatively long and often vigorous dances. Developmental level II is also a time to introduce some of the less complex Native American dances.

The dance program for developmental level III involves everything from more complex line, square, and Native American dances, to folk dances that involve complex steps such as the waltz, polka, schottische, and two-step. These dances require more skill and form than the dances in developmental level II. Introducing students to a greater variety of dance activities gives students the opportunity to develop competency in a wide variety of dances. Such competency will provide the necessary foundation required to successfully participate and enjoy an active lifestyle through involvement in dance activities over the entire life span.

DANCES FOR DEVELOPMENTAL LEVEL I

Baa, Baa, Black Sheep (Level I)
Musical Accompaniment
Childhood Rhythms, Series 7, No. 701
Folkcraft 1191

Measures	Song
1	Baa, baa, black sheep,
2	Have you any wool?
3	Yes sir, yes sir,
4	Three bags full.
5	One for my master,
6	One for my dame,
7	And one for the little boy
8	Who lives in the lane.
9—12	*Chorus:*

Variations
All join hands and take eight slides to the right, then eight slides left. Raise hands and take four steps into the circle and four steps out. Repeat four in and four out. Drop hands and skip sixteen steps counterclockwise.

Formation: Single circle, with girls to right of boys and all facing center
Skills: Stamp, bow and curtsy, turn, and walk

Action
Stamp three times.
Shake fingers.
Nod head twice.
Hold three fingers up.
Turn right and bow or curtsy.
Turn left and bow or curtsy.
Turn around.
Face center and bow or curtsy.

Join inside hands and take sixteen steps counterclockwise.

TABLE 29.1   Singing Games, Folk, Line, and Square Dances

Name of Dance	Type of Dance	Origin	Formation	Dance Skills	Movement Concepts to Stress	Page
Developmental Level I						
Baa, Baa, Black Sheep	Singing game	English	Single circle	Walk, stamp, bow, curtsy, turn	Change of direction, shapes	630
Bludbird	Singing game	American	Single circle	Skip	Change of direction, strong and light	633
Loobie Loo	Singing game	English	Single circle	Walk, skip, slide	Moving into space, change of direction	634
Farmer in the Dell	Singing game	English	Single circle	Walk, clap	Change of direction, relationships	634
Let Your Feet Go Tap, Tap, Tap	Singing game	English	Double circle	Skip, clap	Change of direction, strong and light, relationships	635
Hokey Pokey	Singing game	American	Single circle	Turn, nonlocomotor movements	Moving into space, shapes, strong and light	635
Sally Go Round the Moon	Singing game	English	Single circle	Walk, run, skip, slide	Change of direction, level and speed	636
Danish Dance of Greeting	Folk dance	Danish	Single circle	Clap, stamp, run	Change of direction and speed, strong and light	636
Ring Around the Rosy	Singing game	English	Single circle	Walk, skip	Change of direction and levels	636
The Muffin Man	Singing game	English	Single circle	Walk, clap, skater's position	Moving into space, change of direction	637
Did You Ever See a Lassie	Singing game	Scottish	Single circle	Walk, pantomime	Change of direction, relationships	637
How D'ye Do My Partner	Singing game	Swedish	Double circle	Skip, bow, curtsy	Change of direction, relationships	638
Children's Polka	Folk dance	German	Single circle	Slide, run, hop	Moving into space, strong and light	638
Round and Round the Village	Folk dance	English	Single circle	Skip, bow, curtsy	Change of direction, levels	639
Ach Ja	Folk dance	German	Double circle	Walk, slide, bow, curtsy	Change of direction, relationships	639
Macarena	Line dance	American	Line	Turn, nonlocomotor movements, jump	Change of direction, relationships	640
Oats, Peas, Beans, and Barley	Singing game	English	Single circle	Walk, skip, pantomime	Change of direction, relationships	640
Developmental Level II						
A-Hunting We will Go	Folk dance	English	Two lines	Skip, arch	Moving through space, change of direction, relationships	641
Jolly Is the Miller	Folk dance	English	Double circle	Walk, pantomime	Moving into space, change of direction, relationships	642
Shoo Fly	Folk dance	American	Single circle	Walk, swing, turn	Moving into space, change of direction, relationships	642
Bleking	Folk dance	Swedish	Single circle	Step, hop, bleking step	Moving into space, strong and light, relationships	643
Skip to My Lou	Folk dance	American	Single circle	Walk, skip, swing	Moving into space, change of direction, relationships	643
Paw Paw Patch	Folk dance	American	Double line	Walk, skip, clap	Moving into space, relationships	644
Pop Goes the Weasel	Folk dance	American	Double circle	Walk, skip	Moving into space, levels, relationships	644
Cshebogar	Folk dance	Hungarian	Single circle	Walk, skip, slide	Change of direction, levels, strong and light	645
Greensleeves	Folk dance	English	Double circle	Walk, star, over and under	Change of direction, relationships	645
Glowworm Mixer	Folk dance	American	Double circle	Walk, run, do-si-do	Change of direction and pathways, relationships	646
Little Brown Jug	Folk dance	American	Double circle	Slide, swing	Change of direction, relationships	646

TABLE 29.1 Continued

Name of Dance	Type of Dance	Origin	Formation	Dance Skills	Movement Concepts to Stress	Page
Hora	Folk dance	Israeli	Single circle	Side step, step swing	Change of direction, relationships	646
Troika	Folk dance	Russian	Triple circle	Run, stamp, arch	Change of direction and speed	647
Grand March	Folk dance	American	Line	Walk	Change of direction, relationships	647
Oh Susanna	Folk dance	American	Single circle	Walk, slide, do-si-do	Moving into space, change of direction, relationships	648
Hawaiian Cowboy	Line dance	American	Line	Turn, nonlocomotor movements, slide	Change of direction, relationships	648
Slap Leather	Line dance	American	Line	Slide, clap, stamp, step	Change of direction, relationships	649
Electric Slide	Line dance	American	Line	Slide, clap, stamp, step	Change of direction, relationships	649
Duck for the Oyster	Square dance	American	Square	Turn, step, walk	Change of direction, relationships, pathways	650
Birdie in the Cage	Square dance	American	Square	Swing, turn, step	Change of direction, relationships, pathways	650
Rabbit Dance	Native American	Blackfoot	Circle	Step, hop, turn	Change of direction, relationships, pathways	651
Rain Dance	Native American	Chippewa	Circle	Bend, turn, twist	Change of direction, relationships, pathways	651

Developmental Level III

Name of Dance	Type of Dance	Origin	Formation	Dance Skills	Movement Concepts to Stress	Page
Schottische	Folk dance	Scottish	Double circle	Schottische step	Change of direction, relationships	652
Badger Gavotte	Folk dance	American	Double circle	Slide, two-step	Change of direction, relationships	653
Sicillian Circle	Folk dance	American	Double circle	Walk, chain	Change of direction and pathways	653
Virginia Reel	Folk dance	American	Line	Walk, skip, swing, do-si-do	Change of direction and pathways, relationships	654
Solomon Levi	Square dance	American	Square	Walk, swing	Pathways, relationships	654
Oh Johnny	Square dance	American	Square	Allemande left, walk, swing	Pathways, relationships	655
Ace of Diamonds	Folk dance	Danish	Double circle	Walk, swing	Change of direction, force, relationships	655
Seven Jumps	Folk dance	Danish	Single circle	Step-hop	Change of direction, relationships	656
Norwegian Mountain March	Folk dance	Norwegian	Triple circle	Run, waltz, turn under	Change of direction, relationships	656
Alley Cat	Folk dance	American	Scattered	Touch step, turn, jump	Change of direction, force	657
Korobushka	Folk dance	Russian	Double circle	Schottische step	Change of direction, relationships	657
Klumpakojis	Folk dance	Lithuanian	Double circle	Walk, stamp, polka step	Change of direction and pathways, relationships	658
Red River Valley	Square dance	American	Square	Walk, swing, do-si-do	Change of direction and pathways, relationships	659
Heel and Toe Polka	Folk dance	American	Double circle	Polka step	Change of direction and pathways, relationships	659
Oklahoma Mixer	Folk dance	American	Double circle	Walk, two-step	Change of direction, relationships	660
Rye Waltz	Folk dance	American	Double circle	Slide, waltz step	Change of direction, relationships	660
Tinikling	Folk dance	Phillippine	Line	Tinikling step	Change of direction and speed, relationships	660
Tush Push	Line dance	American	Line	Tap, clap, stamp, step, polka, pivot	Change of direction, relationships	662

TABLE 29.1 *Continued*

Name of Dance	Type of Dance	Origin	Formation	Dance Skills	Movement Concepts to Stress	Page
Flying Ace	Line dance	American	Line	Hop, step, kick, pivot, turn, grapevine	Change of direction, relationships	662
Bad Bad Leroy Brown	Line dance	American	Line	Step, grapevine	Change of direction, relationships	663
Coming Round the Mountain	Square dance	American	Square	Swing, allemande	Change of direction, relationships, pathways	663
Texas Star	Square dance	American	Star	Swing, promenade, step	Change of direction, relationships, pathways	664
Oklahoma Two-Step	Native American	Blackfoot	Line	Bend, turn, twist	Change of direction, relationships, pathways	664
Strawberry Dance	Native American	Chippewa	Circle	Step, turn, twist, hop	Change of direction, relationships, pathways	665

Bluebird (Level I)

Musical Accompaniment
Folkcraft 1180

Formation: Single circle facing center with hands joined forming arches, and one child standing under one arch as the "bluebird"

Skills: Skip

Measures	Song	Action
1–16	Bluebird, bluebird through my window, Bluebird, bluebird through my window, Bluebird, bluebird through my window, Oh Mary,* I am tired. *Chorus:*	The bluebird skips in and out of the arches all around the circle, and at the end of the song, stops behind a circle player.
1–12	Take a little boy (girl) tap him on his shoulder. (Repeat three times)	During chorus, the bluebird taps both hands lightly on the front child's shoulders. Old bluebird keeps hands on new bluebird's shoulders as she repeats the skipping action in a trainlike fashion in and out of the arches.
13–16	Oh Johnny* (Jenny*), I am tired.	Repeat entire song and chorus, adding one child at a time until all are chosen.

*Substitute name of each chosen child.

Loobie Loo (Level I)

Musical Accompaniment
Folkcraft 1184
Childhood Rhythms, Series 7, No. 706
Bowmar Singing Games, Album I, No. 1514

Formation: Single circle facing center with hands joined
Skills: Walk, skip, slide

Measures	Song	Action
	Chorus:	
1–2	Here we go Loobie Loo,	Circle left, using eight walking, skipping, or sliding steps.
3–4	Here we go Loobie Light,	Circle right eight steps.
5–6	Here we go Loobie Loo,	Everyone drops hands and faces the center.
7–8	All on a Saturday night.	
	Verse No. 1:	
1–2	I put my right hand in,	Place right hand toward center of circle.
3–4	I take my right hand out,	Turn, place right hand away from circle.
5–6	I give my hand a shake, shake, shake	Shake hand.
7–8	And turn myself about.	Turn in place.
	Repeat chorus after each verse.	Repeat action of chorus.
	I put my left hand in, etc.	Repeat each verse according to the movement suggested.
	I put my both hands in, etc.	
	I put my right foot in, etc.	
	I put my left foot in, etc.	
	I put my elbows in, etc.	
	I put my shoulder in, etc.	
	I put my big head in, etc.	
	I put my whole self in, etc.	

Farmer in the Dell (Level I)

Musical Accompaniment
Folkcraft 1182
Victor 21618
Bowmar Singing Games, Album II

Formation: Single circle facing center with hands joined, one child, the "farmer," in the center of the circle
Skills: Walk and clap

Measures	Song	Action
1–2	The farmer in the dell,	All walk right around the circle, singing verse while the farmer looks about for a wife.
3–4	The farmer in the dell,	
5–6	Heigh-ho! the cherry-o,*	Continue to walk around the circle as the farmer chooses a wife, who joins him at the center of the circle.
7–8	The farmer in the dell.	
9–10	The farmer takes a wife,	Repeat procedure as directed.
11–12	The farmer takes a wife,	Repeat procedure as directed.
13–14	Heigh-ho! the cherry-o,	Repeat procedure as directed.
15–16	The farmer takes a wife.	Repeat procedure as directed.
	The wife takes a child, etc.	Repeat procedure as directed.
	The child takes a nurse, etc.	Repeat procedure as directed.
	The nurse takes a dog, etc.	Repeat procedure as directed.
	The dog takes a cat, etc.	Repeat procedure as directed.
	The cat takes a rat, etc.	Repeat procedure as directed.
	The rat takes the cheese, etc.	Children in the center crowd around the "cheese" and clap their hands over the cheese's head, while circle players stand still, clap hands, and sing verse.
	The cheese stands alone.	
	The farmer runs away, etc.	Continue walking as the farmer, then wife, and so on, leave the center of the circle.
	(Repeat as each player leaves center of circle.)	

*This song may be sung "derry-o," "dairy-o," or "the dearie-o."

Note: Cheese remains and becomes the new farmer.

Let Your Feet Go Tap, Tap, Tap (Level I)

Musical Accompaniment
Folkcraft 1184
Lloyd Shaw E-7

Formation: Double circle with partners facing each other, boys on the inside and girls on the outside circle
Skills: Skip and clap

Measures	Song	Action
1–2	Let your feet go tap, tap, tap	Tap foot three times on tap, tap, tap.
3–4	Let your hands go tap, tap, tap	Clap hard three times on tap, tap, tap.
5–6	Let your fingers beckon me.	Partners back to each other.
7–8	Come dear partner, dance with me.	Partners join hands and face counterclockwise.
	Chorus:	
1–2	Ta, la, la, la, la, la, la	Children skip around circle singing chorus.
3–4	Ta, la, la, la, la, la, la	
5–6	Ta, la, la, la, la, la, la	
7–8	Ta, la, la, la, la, la, la	

Hokey Pokey (Level I)

Musical Accompaniment
Folkcraft 6026
Capitol 2427
McGregor 6995

Formation: Circle facing center
Skills: Turn and nonlocomotor skills

Measures	Song	Action
1–2	You put your right foot in,	Place right foot in circle.
3–4	You put your right foot out,	Take right foot out of circle.
5–6	You put your right foot in,	Place right foot in circle.
7–8	And, you shake it all about.	Shake right leg.
	Chorus:	
1–2	You do the hokey pokey,	During the first three lines, children raise hands over head and wiggle their bodies as they turn around in place.
3–4	You do the hokey pokey,	
5–6	You do the hokey pokey,	Clap hands three times.
7–8	That's what it's all about.	

Repeat song and action for:

1. Left foot
2. Right arm
3. Left arm
4. Right elbow
5. Left elbow
6. Head
7. Right hip
8. Left hip
9. Whole body
10. Back side
11. Any other part of body

Sally Go Round the Moon (Level I)

Musical Accompaniment
Folkcraft 1198
Victor 45-5064

Formation: Single circle facing center with hands joined
Skills: Walk, run, skip, or slide

Measures	Song
1–2	Sally, go round the moon,
3–4	Sally, go round the stars,
5–6	Sally, go round the chimneypots,
7–8	On a Sunday afternoon—Boom!
	Repeat above.

Action

Walk, run, skip, or slide around the circle. On the word "boom," all jump into the air and clap hands or perform any movement they wish.

Repeat action in opposite direction.

Danish Dance of Greeting (Level I)

Musical Accompaniment
Folkcraft 1187
Merit Audiovisual 1041

Formation: Single circle of couples facing center, the girl on the right side of the boy
Skills: Clap, stamp, bow, curtsy, turn, and run

Measures

Measures	Action
1	Clap hands twice and bow, or curtsy, to child on the other side (neighbor).
2	Clap hands twice, turn and bow, or curtsy, to partner.
3	Stamp on the right foot and then on the left.
4	Turn around in place with four running steps.
5–8	Repeat actions 1–4.
9–12	All join hands and circle to the right with sixteen short running steps.
13–16	Repeat action to the left.

Ring around the Rosy (Level I)

Musical Accompaniment
Folkcraft 1199

Formation: Single circle, girls to right of boys, facing center with hands joined
Skills: Walk and skip

Measures	Song
1–2	Ring around a rosy
3–4	A pocket full of posies,
5–6	At choo, at choo*
7–8	All fall down.
9–10	The cow's in the middle
11–12	Lying down to rest.
13–14	Around the king, around the queen
15–16	We call jump up.

Action

Keeping hands joined, circle left. All stop, face center, sneeze twice, then drop to squatting position on word *down*.

All stay in squat position, sing verse and jump up at end of verse.

*Other words, such as *tish-a, tish-a; hush-a, hush-a; ashes, ashes;* or *one two three* can be substituted.

The Muffin Man (Level I)

Musical Accompaniment
Folkcraft 1188

Formation: Single circle facing center with one child (the "muffin man") in the center
Skills: Walk, clap, skaters' position

Measure	Song
1–2	Oh, have you seen the muffin man,
3–4	The muffin man, the muffin man,
5–6	Oh, have you seen the muffin man,
7–8	Who lives across the way.
9–10	Oh, yes, we've seen the muffin man,
11–12	The muffin man, the muffin man,
13–14	Oh, yes, we've seen the muffin man,
15–16	Who lives across the way.

Pattern

Children join hands and circle to the left using a walk or a slow skip step and singing the first verse.

Children in circle stand facing center and clap hands while singing "The Muffin Man." The child in center chooses a partner from circle and brings him or her back to center (in skaters' position). This child becomes the new muffin man while the old partner returns to circle.

Teaching Suggestions

With large numbers of children start with two muffin men in the center of the circle. Substitute "Drury Lane" as an English version.

Did You Ever See a Lassie (Level I)

Musical Accompaniment
Folkcraft 1183
Lloyd Shaw E-4

Formation: Single circle facing center with hands joined, one child in the center of the circle
Skills: Walk and pantomime

Measures	Song
1–2	Did you ever see a lassie, ("laddie" when boy is in center)
3–4	A lassie, a lassie,
5–6	Did you ever see a lassie
7–8	Go this way and that?
	Chorus:
9–10	Go this way and that way.
11–12	Go this way and that way.
13–14	Did you ever see a lassie
15–16	Go this way and that?

Action

All join hands and walk eight steps to the left, swinging joined hands, then eight steps back.

All stop, release hands, face the child in center and imitate his or her movements. Repeat singing game with a new leader in the center.

Teaching Suggestions

Once the children have learned the basic movements, have them create impressions such as birds, animals, and mechanical toys. And instead of walking, have them walk using swinging and swaying, stamping, and clapping.

How D'ye Do My Partner (Level I)

Musical Accompaniment
Folkcraft 1190
Lloyd Shaw E-3

Formation: Double circle with partners facing, girls on the outside circle
Skills: Bow, curtsy, skip

Measures	Song
1–2	How d'ye do my partner,
3–4	How d'ye do today?
5–6	Will you dance in a circle?
7–8	I will show you the way.
	Chorus:
9–10	Tra, la, la, la, la,
11–12	Tra, la, la, la, la,
13–14	Tra, la, la, la, la,
15–16	Tra, la, la, la, la.
	Repeat song.

Pattern

Boys bow to partners.
Girls curtsy to partners.
Boy offers hand to partner.
Join inside hands and turn counterclockwise.

With joined hands, skip around the circle. At the end of the chorus, girls move one position forward to new partners.

Children's Polka (Kinderpolka) (Level I)

Musical Accompaniment
Folkcraft 1187
Lloyd Shaw E-7

Formation: Single circle with partners facing, both arms extended sideward and hands joined
Skills: Slide, hop, and run

Measures	
1–2	
3–4	
5–8	
9–10	
11–12	
13	
14	
15–16	

Action

Take two slides toward center and step lightly three times.
Take two slides away from center; step lightly three times.
Repeat action of measures 1–4.
Slap own knees once, clap own hands once, and clap partner's hands three times.
Repeat action of measures 9–10.
Hop, placing right heel forward, place right elbow in left hand, and shake finger three times.
Repeat action of measure 13 with left foot.
Turn in place with four running steps and step lightly three times.

Teaching Suggestions

To help children learn the dance pattern, count in this manner:

Step, step, tap, tap, tap. Repeat.
Slap, clap, clap, clap, clap. Repeat.
Hop, one, two, three. Repeat.
Turn around now, tap, tap, tap.

Round and Round the Village
(Go In and Out the Windows) (Level I)

Musical Accompaniment
Folkcraft 1191

Formation: Single circle with all facing center and hands
joined, one or more players are outside the circle
Skills: Skip, bow, and curtsy

Measures	Song	Action
		Circle children join hands and walk clockwise, while outside players skip counterclockwise.
1–2	Go round and round the village,	
3–4	Go round and round the village,	
5–6	Go round and round the village,	
7–8	As we have done before.	
		Children in circle stand and raise arms to form arches (windows) while outside players weave in and out.
1–2	Go in and out the windows,	
3–4	Go in and out the windows,	
5–6	Go in and out the windows,	
7–8	As we have done before.	
		"It" skips around the inside of the circle, stops, and bows or curtsys in front of a partner he or she has chosen.
1–2	Now go and choose a partner,	
3–4	Now go and choose a partner,	
5–6	Now go and choose a partner,	
7–8	As we have done before.	
		"It" skips around inside the circle, followed by the new partner. Circle players skip in the opposite direction.
1–2	Now follow me to London,	
3–4	Now follow me to London,	
5–6	Now follow me to London,	
7–8	As we have done before.	
		The circle players remain in place, clap their hands, and sing while inside players shake hands and bow or curtsy. The chosen player(s) then goes to the outside of the circle while other players return to the circle.
1–2	Shake hands before you leave me,	
3–4	Shake hands before you leave me,	
5–6	Shake hands before you leave me,	
7–8	As we have done before.	

Ach Ja (Oh yes!) (Level I)

Musical Accompaniment
Childhood Rhymes VII
Lloyd Shaw E-2

Formation: Double circle with partners facing
counterclockwise, boys on inside, girls on outside with
inside hand joined
Skills: Walk, slide, bow, and curtsy

Measures	Song	Action
		Walk forward eight steps, then drop hands.
1	When my father and my mother,	
2	Take the children to the fair,	
3	Ach ja,	Partners bow to each other.
4	Ach ja.	Boys bow to girl on right. Girl curtsys.
5	They haven't any money,	Repeat actions 1–4 for 5–8.
6	But it's little that they care.	
7	Ach ja,	
8	Ach ja.	
	Chorus:	
9–16	Tra, la, la, tra, la, la, tra, la, la, La, la, la, la Ach ja, Ach ja. *Repeat song.*	Partners face each other, then take four slide steps counterclockwise, swinging their arms to the side and back on each step. Repeat four slide steps clockwise. Partners bow and curtsy, then the boy steps to the left to meet the next girl. New partners bow and curtsy.
		Repeat dance.

Macarena (Level I)

Musical Accompaniment
"Macarena"
Los del Mar (artist)

Formation: Lines facing front
Skills: Arm actions, turn, jump, clap, step

Measures

1	**Action**
	Right arm straight out in front of body, palms down.
	Repeat with left arm.
2	Repeat with palms up, right arm then left arm.
	Touch right hand to left shoulder.
	Touch left hand to right shoulder.
	Touch right hand to right ear.
3	Touch left hand to left ear.
	Touch right hand to left hip.
	Touch left hand to right hip.
	Touch right hand to right buttock.
4	Touch left hand to left buttock.
	Swing hips three times.
	Clap and jump 1/4 turn counterclockwise.
	Repeat.

Variations

Once the dance is learned, the students can step in place to the underlying beat, starting with their right foot.

A further challenge would be to change the formation to a conga line and walk throughout the gym or classroom while doing the actions.

Oats, Peas, Beans, and Barley (Level I)

Musical Accompaniment
Folkcraft 1182
Folk Dancer MH 1110-A

Formation: Single circle facing center with hands joined, one child in the center of the circle is the "farmer"
Skills: Walk, skip, and pantomime

Measures	Song	Pattern
1–2	Oats, peas, beans, and barley grow,	Farmer in center stands while children in circle walk left, taking small steps. Circle players stop, point to the farmer, shrug, turn right, and stamp their feet.
3–4	Oats, peas, beans, and barley grow,	
5–6	Do you or I or anyone know	
7–8	How oats, peas, beans, and barley grow?	
1–2	First the farmer sows his seed,	Children in circle stop, face the center, and all dramatize the words of the song.
3–4	Then he stands and takes his ease.	
5–6	Stamps his foot and claps his hand.	
7–8	And turns around to view the land.	
1–2	Waiting for a partner,	Children in the circle skip left as the farmer skips around inside the circle and picks a new partner. The farmer and new partner skip around inside the circle.
3–4	Waiting for a partner,	
5–6	Open the ring and choose one in.	
7–8	While we all gladly dance and sing.	
	Chorus:	
1–8	Tra, la, la, la, la, la,	The two farmers continue to skip inside the circle while the others join hands and circle left. "Old farmer" joins the ring and "new farmer" repeats pattern.
	Tra, la, la, la, la, la,	
	Tra, la, la, la, la, la, la,	
	Tra, la, la, la, la, la.	

Additional Singing Games and Folk, Line, and Square Dances for Developmental Level I

Name of Dance	Skills	Formation	Origin	Record Source
Peas, Porridge, Hot	Turn, run	Circle	English	Folkcraft 1190
Popcorn Man	Skip, jump	Circle	American	Folkcraft 1180
Mulberry Bush	Walk, skip, turn, pantomime	Circle	English	Bowman A-1, Folkcraft 1183
Ten Little Indians	Walk	Circle	American	Folkcraft 1197
London Bridge	Walk	Circle	English	Bowmar 36-A(2) RCA 45-5056
Hickory, Dickory, Dock	Run, stamp	Circle	English	Victor 22760
Little Miss Muffet	Walk	Circle	English	Childhood Rhythms Series 7, No. 703
I Should Like to Go to Shetland	Gallop	Circle	English	Folkcraft 1190
Jump Jim Joe	Run, jump	Circle	American	Folkcraft 1193 RCA 45-6182
Chimes of Dunkirk	Skip	Circle	English	Folkcraft 1190
Thread Follows the Needle	Walk	Line	English	RCA 22760 (E-87) Pioneer 3017
Turn the Glass Over	Walk, turn	Circle	English	Folkcraft 1181
Nixie Polka	Polka step	Circle	Swedish	Folkcraft 5785
Rig-a-Jig-Jig	Walk, skip	Circle	American	Folkcraft 1199
Sing a Song of Sixpence	Walk	Circle	English	Folkcraft 1180 RCA Victor 22760
Bingo	Walk, grand	Circle	American	Folkcraft 1189
Carousel	Slide, draw, step, stamp	Circle	Swedish	RCA 45-6179 Pioneer 3044-A
Hansel and Gretel	Heel-toe step, skip	Circle	German	Folkcraft 1 RCA 45-6182
Hinky, Dinky Parlez Vous	Walk, do-si-do, promenade	Square	American	Folkcraft 1059

DANCES FOR DEVELOPMENTAL LEVEL II

A-Hunting We Will Go (Level II)

Musical Accompaniment
Folkcraft 1191
Victor 45-5064
Childhood Rhythms,
Series 7, No. 705

Formation: Two parallel lines (longways set) facing each other, girls on one side and boys on the other
Skills: Skip, arch

Measures	Song	Action
1–2	Oh, a-hunting we will go,	Head couple joins inside hands and skips down between the lines to the foot of the set.
3–4	A-hunting we will go,	
5–6	We'll catch a fox and put him in a box,	Head couple turns around, changes hands, and skips back to the head of the set.
7–8	And then we'll let him go.	
	Chorus:	All other players clap hands while head couple skips down and back.
1–2	Tra, la, la, la, la, la, la,	Head couple skips around the left side of the set, followed by other couples. When the head couple reaches the foot of the line, it forms an arch under which all other couples pass. Head couple remains while the second couple becomes the head couple.
3–4	Tra, la, la, la, la, la,	
5–6	Tra, la, la, la, la, la, la, la, la, la,	
7–8	Tra, la, la, la, la, la.	

Repeat dance with new head couple.

Jolly Is the Miller (Level II)

Musical Accompaniment
Folkcraft 1192
Lloyd Shaw E-10

Formation: Partners form a double circle facing counterclockwise with girls on the inside; one player, the "miller," stands in the center
Skills: Walk and pantomime

Measures	Song	Action
1–2	Jolly is the miller who lives by the mill,	Couples join inside hands and walk counterclockwise while singing the song. During the second line, children in the inner circle extend left arms sideward to form a mill wheel. On the last word of the song ("back"), partners drop hands and the inner circle steps forward while the outer circle steps backward. The extra player tries to secure a partner during this exchange. The child without a partner goes to the center.
3–4	The wheel turns around of its own free will,	
5–6	One hand in the hopper and the other in the sack,	
7–8	The hub steps forward and the rim steps back.	

Repeat dance with new partner.

Shoo Fly (Level II)

Musical Accompaniment
Folkcraft 1185

Formation: Single circle with girls on the boys' right, hands joined, and all facing the center of the circle
Skills: Walk, swing, and turn

Measures	Song	Action
1–2	Shoo, fly, don't bother me,	Walk four steps forward, swinging arms.
3–4	Shoo, fly, don't bother me,	Walk four steps backward.
5–6	Shoo, fly, don't bother me,	Walk four steps forward, swinging arms.
7–8	For I belong to somebody.	Walk four steps backward.
	Chorus:	
1–2	I feel, I feel,	Partners join hands and walk around each other in a clockwise direction. Repeat. On the last "morning star," the boy raises his left hand and turns his partner under his arm. The girl is now on the boy's left. The girl on the boy's right becomes his new partner.
3–4	I feel like a morning star,	
5–6	I feel, I feel,	
7–8	I feel like a morning star.	

Join hands and repeat dance.

Bleking (Level II)

Musical Accompaniment
Folkcraft 1188
Lloyd Shaw E-9

Formation: Single circle with partners facing; boys face counterclockwise, girls face clockwise; partners extend their arms forward at shoulder height and join hands
Skills: Bleking step, step, and hop

Measures	Action
1–8	Hop on left foot, extend the right heel forward, keeping the right leg straight. As this movement takes place, thrust the right arm forward and pull the left arm back (count one). Continue for seven more counts, changing the lead foot on each count.
9–16	Partners face each other, extending arms sideways and joining hands. Boy begins with his right foot, girl with her left foot. Partners begin to turn in place by taking seven step-hops in a clockwise direction and end with a stamp on the last count. As the children turn in place, their arms move in a windmill action up and down with each step-hop. Repeat dance in counterclockwise direction.

Skip to My Lou (Level II)

Musical Accompaniment
Bowmar Singing Games Album 3, No. 1522-A
Folkcraft 1192
Folk Dancers FD 34

Formation: Single circle with partners side by side and the girls on the boys' right
Skills: Walk, skip, swing, and promenade

Measures	Song	Action
	Verse No. 1:	Boys walk four steps forward and four steps backward.
1–2	Boys to the center, Skip to my Lou,	
3–4	Boys to the outside, Skip to my Lou,	
5–6	Boys to the center, Skip to my Lou,	Repeat.
7–8	Skip to my Lou, my darling.	
	Verse No. 2:	
1–2	Girls to the center, Skip to my Lou,	Girls repeat patterns as described above.
3–4	Girls to outside, Skip to my Lou,	
5–6	Girls to the center, Skip to my Lou,	
7–8	Skip to my Lou, my darling.	
	Verse No. 3:	
1–6	Swing your partner, Skip to my Lou, (three times)	Partners join hands and swing or skip in place.
7–8	Skip to my Lou, my darling.	
	Verse No. 4:	
1–6	I've lost my partner now what'll I do, (three times)	Release hands. Girls walk forward, boys turn and walk in the opposite direction.
7–8	Skip to my Lou, my darling.	
	Verse No. 5:	
1–6	I've got another one, prettier too, (three times)	New partners promenade counterclockwise to original position, with the girls on the boys' right.
7–8	Skip to my Lou, my darling.	Repeat dance with new partner.

Paw Paw Patch (Level II)

Musical Accompaniment
Folkcraft 1181
Victor 45-5066

Formation: Columns of four to six couples with partners facing forward (to the head of hall)
Skills: Walk, skip, clap, and cast off

Measures	Song	Action
1–2	Where, O where is sweet little Sally?	First girl turns right, casts off, circles clockwise, and goes once around the set with sixteen skipping steps, and back to place. Everyone else remains in place, clapping and singing the song.
3–4	Where, O where is sweet little Sally?	
5–6	Where, O where is sweet little Sally?	
7–8	Way down yonder in the paw paw patch.	
1–2	Come on, boys, let's go find her,	First girl takes the first boy's left hand and leads line of boys around the set. Boys may join hands. Girls in line clap hands. All finish in place facing the front.
3–4	Come on, boys, let's go find her,	
5–6	Come on, boys, let's go find her,	
7–8	Way down yonder in the paw paw patch.	
1–2	Pickin' up paw paws, putting 'em in her pocket,	Partners join hands and follow first couple once around to the right. First couple turns away from each other, with the boy going left and the girl going right, and skips to the foot of the line. The rest of the line moves one place forward.
3–4	Pickin' up paw paws, putting 'em in her pocket,	
5–6	Pickin' up paw paws, putting 'em in her pocket.	
7–8	Way down yonder in the paw paw patch.	

Repeat entire dance with each new "first" girl leading.

Pop Goes the Weasel (Level II)

Musical Accompaniment
World of Fun, M-104-B
Folkcraft 1329
Victor 45-6180

Formation: Double circle in sets of four children, girl on partner's right; couples facing clockwise are couples number 1, while couples facing counterclockwise are couples number 2
Skills: Walk and skip

Measures	Action
1–4	Join hands in a circle of four and circle left with eight skipping or sliding steps.
5–6	Walk two steps forward, raising joined hands, then walk two steps backward, lowering hands.
7–8	Number one couples raise their joined hands to form an arch as number two couples pass under. Number two couples continue forward to meet new partners.
	Repeat dance.

Variation

Formation: Three children form a set, with two children joining inside hands. The third child stands in front with his back to the other two, extends his hands back, and holds the outside hands of the other two. All three face counterclockwise in a large circle.

Measures	Action
1–6	All sets skip around in a large circle.
7–8	On "pop," the child in front skips backward under the raised inside hands of the back couple and continues backward, meeting the couple behind him.
9–14	Repeat measures 1–6.
15–16	Repeat measures 7–8.

Cshebogar (Level II)

Musical Accompaniment
Folkcraft 1196
Lloyd Shaw E-15

Formation: Single circle of couples with hands joined; couples face the center with the girl on the boy's right side

Skills: Walk, skip, slide, and Hungarian turn

Measures	Action
1–4	Take seven slide steps to the left, and end with a jump on both feet.
5–8	Take seven slide steps to the right, and end with a jump on both feet.
9–12	Take four walking steps to the center, raising your hands high as you go. Take four walking steps backward to place in circle, lowering your hands as you return.
13–16	Face partner and place right hand on his or her waist. Raise left arm, pull away from partner, and skip around him or her. (This is a Hungarian turn.)
17–20	Face partner, join hands with arms held at shoulder height. Slide four steps slowly toward the center of the circle, bending toward the center as you slide. Boys start with left foot and girls with right foot.
21–24	Four step-draw steps outward (step-close-step).
25–28	Two draw steps in and two draw steps out.
29–32	Do the Hungarian turn again, then repeat entire dance.

Greensleeves (Level II)

Musical Accompaniment
Folkcraft 6175
Lloyd Shaw E-11

Formation: Double circle facing counterclockwise. Boys are on inside; girls on outside with inside hands joined. Couples are numbered 1, 2 alternately, around the circle to form sets.

Skills: Walk, star, over and under

Measures	Call	Action
1–8	Walk	Starting with left foot, take sixteen walking steps.
9–12	Right-hand star	Each set of two couples forms a right-hand star and takes eight walking steps clockwise.
13–16	Left-hand star	Form a left-hand star and take eight walking steps counterclockwise. At the end of the star, couple 1 is in front of couple 2 and both are facing counterclockwise.
17–20	Over and under	Couple 1 bends low and takes four steps backward as couple 2 raises joined hands and takes four steps forward ("turning the sleeves inside out"). Repeat with couple 2 moving backward and couple 1 arching and moving forward.
21–24	Over and under	Repeat 17–20.

To change this dance to a mixer, couple 2 moves forward on the last four steps of measures 23–24.

Glowworm Mixer (Level II)

Musical Accompaniment
MacGregor 310-B
Windsor 4613-B

Formation: Players form a double circle and all face counterclockwise, boy on inside circle holding the girl's left hand in his right
Skills: Walk, run, and do-si-do

Measures	Action
1–4	Promenade counterclockwise with eight walking steps.
5–8	Promenade clockwise with eight walking steps.
9–12	Pass right shoulders, back-to-back, then step back to place (do-si-do).
13–16	Turn to the right, face new partner, and do-si-do with eight running steps.

Little Brown Jug (Level II)

Musical Accompaniment
Columbia 52007
Folkcraft 1304A
Imperial 1213

Formation: Double circle with partners facing each other, girls on the outside circle, hands joined and raised to shoulder height
Skills: Slide and swing

Measures	Action
1–8	Boy touches his left heel to side, then his left toe next to his right foot. Repeat movement. Take four slide steps to the left. Girls start with outside foot and do the same.
9–16	Repeat measures 1–8 with four slides to the right.
17–24	Clap own thighs four times, then own hands together four times.
25–32	Partners clap right hands together four times, then left hands together four times.
33–40	Hook right elbows with partner and skip around in a circle with eight skipping steps.
41–56	Repeat clapping sequence of measures 17–24 and 25–32.
57–64	Hook left elbows and repeat turns.

Hora (Level II)

Musical Accompaniment
Folkcraft 1110
Folk Dancers MH 1052

Formation: Single circle with arms straight and hands on shoulders of dancers on either side
Skills: Side step, step swing

Measures	Action
1. Right, cross	Step sideward with the right foot.
	Step sideward with left foot and place behind the right foot.
2. Right, swing	Step sideward with the right foot.
	Hop on the right foot and swing left foot forward across the front.
3. Left, swing	Step sideward with the left foot.
	Hop on the left foot and swing right foot forward and across the front.

Teaching cues: Moving toward the left.

   R   L   R   L   L   R
Right, Cross, Right, Swing, Left, Swing

Troika (Level II)

Musical Accompaniment
World of Fun M105
Folkcraft 1170

Formation: Circle of "threes" (one boy in middle of two girls, one girl in middle of two boys, or all boys and all girls), facing counterclockwise

Skills: Run, stamp, and arch

Measures	Call	Action
1–4	Run forward	Run sixteen steps forward.
5–6	Outside under	Center and inside partner raise joined hands, forming an arch, and run in place while the outside dancer, with eight running steps, moves in front of center dancer, under the arch, back around the center dancer to starting position. Center dancer unwinds by turning under the arch.
7–8	Inside under	Repeat with inside dancer turning under.
9–12	Circle left	Sets of three join hands and take twelve running steps, ending with three stamps in place.
13–16		Repeat twelve running steps to the right, ending in a reformed line and with three stamps in place.

As a Mixer:
During the last figure, the center dancer moves forward while the other dancers stamp three times in place.

Grand March (Level II)

Musical Accompaniment
Any marching record

Formation: Boys line up on one side of the room and girls on the other side; all face the foot of the room; the teacher stands in the center of the end line at the head of the room

Skills: Walk

Call	Action
Come down the center in twos.	March to meet partners at the foot of the room. As the couples meet, they turn, join hands, and march down the center to the head of the room, where the teacher is standing to give directions.
Two right and two left.	The first couple turns to the right, the second to the left, and so on.
Come down the center in fours.	When the two head couples meet at the foot of the room, they hold hands and walk four abreast down the center.
Four right and four left.	When children reach the front of the room, they divide again, with four going to the right and four going to the left, and so on.
Come down the center in eights.	When the lines of four meet at the front of the room, they join hands to form a line of eight abreast. The lines of eight march to the head of the room and halt.

Note: This process may be reversed, with lines of eight dividing into columns of four. The columns of four march back to the other end of the room, where the two columns merge into one column of fours. The fours divide at the head of the room, and so on, until all are back to the original position of one couple.

Variations

From "Come down the center in fours," separate into twos, then call: "Form arches," or "Over and under."

First couple forms an arch and the second couple tunnels under. Third couple forms an arch and the fourth couple tunnels under. Continue this pattern.

First odd couple arches over the last couple in line and then under the next and so on down to the front of the line.

Oh Susanna (Level II)

Musical Accompaniment
Folkcraft 1186
Lloyd Shaw E-14

Formation: Partners standing in a single circle facing center, with hands joined, the girl on the boy's right side
Skills: Walk, slide, do-si-do, promenade

Measures	Call	Action
1–8	Slide to the left and slide to the right.	All take eight sliding steps to the right and eight sliding steps to the left.
9–12	Forward and back.	All take four steps to the center and four steps back.
13–16	Girls forward and back.	Release hands. Girls walk four steps toward the center of the circle and four steps back. Boys stand in place and clap hands.
17–20	Boys forward and back.	Boys go to center while girls clap hands.
21–24		Do-si-do with partners.
25–28		Do-si-do with corner girls.
29–32		Everyone promenades around the circle.

Hawaiian Cowboy (Level II)

Musical Accompaniment
"I Knew the Bride When She Used to Rock and Roll"
Nick Lowe (artist)

Formation: Line facing front
Skills: Arm actions, turn, jump, clap

Measures	Action
1	Swirl right fist, with pinkie finger raised, twice clockwise.
	Swirl left fist, with pinkie finger raised, twice counterclockwise.
2	Swirl right palm facing front twice clockwise.
	Swirl left palm facing front twice counterclockwise.
3	Roll arms leaning to right side.
	Roll arms facing center.
4	Roll arms leaning to left side.
	Roll arms facing center.
5	Tap right elbow with left hand twice.
	Tap left elbow with right hand twice.
6	Slide right hand on right buttock.
	Slide left hand on left buttock.
7	Jump forward on two feet twice.
	Jump 1/4 turn counterclockwise (clap),
	Jump forward (clap).
	Repeat.

Slap Leather (Level II)

Musical Accompaniment
"Cadillac Ranch"
Nitty Gritty Dirt Band (artists)

Formation: Lines facing front
Skills: Pivot, turn, jump, clap, stomp, step, slap

Measures	Action
1	Stand with feet together. Pivot heels out, together (2×).
2	Point right toe to the right side and together (2×).
3	Point left toe to the left side and together (2×).
4	Tap right heel forward (2×). Tap right toe behind (2×).
5	Tap right toe forward, right side, behind, right side.
6	Slap inside of right foot with left hand. Pivot 1/4 turn counterclockwise while slapping outside of right foot with right hand. Side step right, vine behind with left foot.
7	Side step right, stomp left foot together (clap). Side step left, vine behind with right foot.
8	Side step left, stomp right foot together (clap). Step behind with right foot, step behind with left foot.
9	Step behind with right foot, stomp left together (clap).
10	Stomp left foot forward, stomp right foot together. ***Repeat.***

Variations

Try doing the Tush Push to this musical selection.
Use peer teaching groups in centers teaching one part of the dance at a time.

Electric Slide (Level II)

Musical Accompaniment
"Get Ready for This"
U2 or Electric Boogie
Marcia Griffiths (artists)

Formation: Lines facing front
Skills: Slide, clap, stomp, step

Measures	Action
1	Slide to the left (3×), clap.
2	Slide to the right (3×), clap.
3	Step back with right foot, step back with left foot, Step back with right foot, lean back and clap.
4	Lean forward, clap, lean backward, clap.
5	Step 1/4 turn counterclockwise, scuff right foot forward. ***Repeat.***

Variations

Substitute slides with grapevines or full turns.
Have students try creative movements in groups of 3–6.

Duck for the Oyster (Level II)

Musical Accompaniment
Educational Recordings:
Square Dance 2A

Formation: Circle and arch. Four couples form the sides of the square (set).
Skills: circle, arch, turn, step

Patter Call

First couple out to the couple on the right.
Circle four for half the night.

Duck for the oyster.

Now dive for the clam, dive.

And duck on through and on to the next.

Action

Couple 1 goes to couple 2, all join hands, and circle to the left going halfway round so that couple 1 faces in toward the set and couple two faces outward.

Couple 1 with hands joined moves under the arch formed by couple 2 and then move backward to face the set again.

Couple 1 forms an arch, and couple 2 with hands joined moves under the arch and then moves back to face the set again.

Couple 2 forms an arch, couple 1 moves under the arch, and on to couple 3.

Repeat the actions with couple 1 going on to do the dance with couples 3 and 4. This sequence is repeated with couples 2, 3, and 4 becoming the visiting couples in turn.

Birdie in the Cage (Level II)

Musical Accompaniment
Educational Recordings:
Square Dance 3

Formation: Visiting couple. Four couples make up the sides of the square. Circle and swing.
Skills: Circle, swing, turn, step

Patter Call

First couple out to the couple on the right. Circle four for half the night.

Now birdie in the cage, three hands round.

Birdie fly out, the crow hop in.

Now the crow hop out, swing your own. Both couples swing.

Action

Couples 1 and 2 join hands and circle half a circle. Couple 1 now faces in toward the set. Couple 2 is now facing toward the outside of the set.

The girl of couple 1 drops hands and steps into the circle made by the three other dancers. The three dancers circle around the "birdie."

The girl backs out of the circle to join hands with the other dancers, while her partner steps into the circle. The three dancers are now circling the "crow."

The dance is repeated with couple 1 moving to couple 3 and then on to couple 4. The entire sequence is then repeated for couples 2, 3, and 4.

Rabbit Dance (Level II)
(Plains Indians: Blackfeet)
Musical Accompaniment
Powwow music to a slow beat

Formation: Couples in a double circle, with boys on the outside. Couples face clockwise and stand side by side with hands clasped behind their backs, right hands joined, and left hands joined.
Skills: Step, hop, turn

Basic Step

Step-close. Beginning with the outside feet, take a step forward, slide the inside feet up close.

Action

Moving clockwise, the dancers take two step-close steps forward, beginning with the outside feet. They then take a step backward with the outside feet. As the drum beat accentuates, couples turn in unison, turning toward the center of the circle and continuing around to face clockwise once again.

Rain Dance (Level II)
(Chippewa)
Musical Accompaniment
Kimbo Educational LKLP-9070-A

Formation: Circle. Four "braves" represent the "four winds," with the "medicine man" in the center of the circle.
Skills: Bend, turn, twist.

Basic Step

Two-heel step: Beginning with the left foot, the dancers place their left toe on the ground lifting the heel high. Heel is dropped and then repeated with the right foot. This basic step is used throughout the dance.

Action

The four winds dance to the center of the circle and back out to its rim. They then move on the inside of the circle to the next wind position. As they move, they begin with both arms up overhead, moving their arms, hands, and fingers to represent the rain coming down. Arms and hands continue to move downward as the winds move to the center (until they are down close to the floor). This action is repeated over and over. They may also rotate in their own circles as they move around the large circle. The dance continues until the dancers have represented all four winds and have returned to their original starting positions. The medicine man dances the "basic step" in the center of the circle throughout the dance.

Variation

Let the children create their own movements as they move around the circle. What movements should the medicine man make What other movements could represent the rain?

Additional Folk Dances for Developmental Level II

Name of Dance	Skills	Formation	Origin	Record Source
Irish Washerwoman	Walk, swing	Circle	Irish	Folkcraft 1135
Teton Mountain Stomp	Walk	Circle	American	Windsor 4615
Kalvelis	Polka, stamp, skip	Circle	Lithuanian	Folkcraft 1418
Bingo	Walk, R, grand	Circle	American	Folkcraft 1189
Crested Hen	Step, hop	Threes	Danish	Victor 6176
Bridge of Avignon	Skip	Double circle	French	Folkcraft 1191
Teddy Bear Mixer	Walk	Double circle	American	Lloyd Shaw E-3
La Raspa	Bleking step	Scattered	Mexican	Folkcraft 1119
Crested Hen	Step-hop	Triple circle	Danish	Folkcraft 1134

DANCES FOR DEVELOPMENTAL LEVEL III

Schottische (Level III)

Musical Accompaniment
MacGregor 4005
Folkcraft 1101
Imperial 1046

Formation: Double circle with partners facing counterclockwise, boys are on the inside circle and holding partners in an open dance position

Skills: Schottische step

Measures	Action
1–2	Partners start with outside feet (boy's left, girl's right), run forward three steps, and hop on outside foot and extend inside foot forward.
3–4	Begin with inside foot and repeat action.
5–6	All perform four step-hops in place.
	Repeat the first six measures as often as desired or substitute the following variations for measures 5 and 6.

Variation 1: Ladies Turn

Boys take four step-hops in place and girls turn under their arms. On the next turn, reverse movements, with the boys turning under the girls' raised arms.

Variation 2: Both Turn

Partners drop hands and dance four skip-hops in place, turning away from each other (boy turns left, girl turns right) on the first step, and ending in the starting position on the fourth step-hop.

Variation 3: Wring the Dishrag

Partners join hands about waist high and both turn under raised arms and continue around and back to the starting position.

Badger Gavotte (Level III)

Musical Accompaniment
MacGregor 610B
Folkcraft 1094

Formation: Double circle with couples facing counterclockwise; partners join hands, girl on the boy's right side

Skills: Slide, two-step, and closed dance position

Measures	Action
1–2	Begin with the outside foot (boy's left, girl's right), walk forward four steps, face partner, join hands, take three sliding steps to the boy's left, and touch the right toe behind the left foot.
3–4	Repeat measures 1 and 2 in the opposite direction.
5–8	Change to a closed dance position and take eight two-steps progressing counterclockwise, with the boys starting with the left foot and the girls with the right foot.
	Repeat dance until music ends.

Sicilian Circle (Level III)

Musical Accompaniment
Windsor A7S4A
Folkcraft 1115, 1242 (with calls)
Methodist 104

Formation: Circle of "sets of four" with couple facing couple, girl on the boy's right side

Skills: Walk, ladies chain, right and left through

Measures	Call	Action
1–4	Now everybody forward and back.	Join inside hands with partner. Take four steps forward toward the opposite couple and four steps backward to place.
5–8	Circle four hands around.	Join hands and circle left with eight walking steps and finish in original places.
1–4	Ladies chain.	Ladies chain across and back with the two girls changing places. The boy takes the approaching girl's left hand in his left, places his right arm around her waist, and pivots backward to reface the opposite couple.
5–8	Chain the ladies back again.	The girls return to their original positions with the same movement.
1–4	Right and left through.	Right and left with opposite couple, over and back. Walk forward to opposite couple's place, passing right shoulders, then, keeping side by side as though inside hands were joined, turn half around as a couple (man turns backward while lady turns forward), and reface opposite.
5–8	Right and left back.	Repeat the same movement, returning to original place.
1–4	Forward and back.	Forward and back.
5–8	Forward again, pass through.	All walk forward eight steps, passing opposite by right shoulder, to meet new couple.
		Repeat dance with new couple.

Virginia Reel (Level III)

Musical Accompaniment
Burns, Album J. No. 558
Lloyd Shaw E-12
Folkcraft 1249

Formation: Six couples in file formation with partners
facing each other, boys on the caller's right
Skills: Walk, skip, swing, do-si-do, cast off

Measures	Call	Action
1–8	Bow to your partner, go forward and back. Go forward and back again.	Players take three skips forward, curtsy or bow, then skip back. Repeat.
9–12	Now forward again with right hand swing, and all the way back.	Partners hold right hands, turn once around, and then back.
13–16	Now forward again with left hand swing, and all the way back.	Partners join left hands, turn once around, then back.
1–4	Now forward again with a two-hand swing, and all the way back.	Partners join both hands and turn clockwise and back.
5–8	Forward again with a do-si-do.	All partners do a do-si-do.
9–16	The head two sashay down the middle and all the way back to the head of the set.	Head couple joins hands and slides down the center of the set and back.
17–24	Cast off, with boys going left and girls going right.	All face the caller, with the boys' line skipping left and the girls' line skipping right, ending at the foot of the set.
25–32	Form an arch and all pass through.	The head couple meets at the foot of the set, joins hands, and raises them to form an arch. The second couple leads the other couples through the arch and moves to the head of the line to become the new head couple.

Repeat dance with each new head couple.

Solomon Levi (Level III)

Musical Accompaniment
MacGregor 007-4A (with calls)

Formation: Square of four couples numbered
counterclockwise, girl on the boy's right side
Skills: Walk, swing, and allemande left

Measures	Call	Action
1–4	Everyone swing your honey; swing her high and low.	Swing partner.
5–16	Allemande left with left hand, and around the ring you go. A grand old right and left. Walk on your heel and toe and meet your honey, give her a twirl, and around the ring you go.	Left hand to corner, walk around corner back to partner. Extend right hand to partner, left to next girl, alternating right and left hands until partners meet. Give partner a swing and promenade.
	Sing chorus.	Promenade around set.
1–8	Oh Solomon Levi, tra la la la la la Oh Solomon Levi, tra la la la la la.	Repeat dance with couples two, three, and four leading. After couple number four completes its turn, have all four couples separate and repeat dance.

Oh Johnny (Level III)

Musical Accompaniment
MacGregor 652A (with calls)
Folkcraft 1037

Formation: Square dance set with girls on boys' right; all
join hands
Skills: Walk, swing, allemande left, do-si-do

Measures	Call	Action
1–4	All join hands and circle the ring.	All couples move to the right in walking steps.
5–8	Stop where you are and give your honey a swing.	In closed dance position, swing partners.
9–12	Swing that little gal behind you.	Boy swings girl on his left.
13–16	Now swing your own.	Boy swings girl on his right.
1–4	Allemande left with the corner gal.	Turn to corners, give left hand to corner girl, walk around her, and return to partner.
5–8	Do-si-do your own.	Fold arms and pass right shoulder to right shoulder around partner and back to corner girl, who becomes new partner.
9–16	Now you all promenade with your sweet corner maid, Singing, "Oh, Johnny, oh, Johnny, oh."	Everyone promenade.
		Repeat dance.

Ace of Diamonds (Level III)

Musical Accompaniment
Folkcraft 1176
Methodist M-102

Formation: Double circle with partners facing
Skills: Walk and swing

Measures	Action
1–4	Clap hands once, stamp on left foot, then hook right elbows with three polka or six skipping steps.
5–8	Clap hands once, stamp on right foot, hook left elbows, and repeat swing.
9–12	Partners face each other with hands on hips. Inside dancers start backward with left foot; outside dancers move forward with right foot. Both take four steps.
13–16	Partners reverse directions for four steps.
17–24	Join inside hands, hop on inside foot, and polka counterclockwise around the circle.

Seven Jumps (Level III)

Musical Accompaniment
Merit Audio Visual: 1043
Methodist M-108

Formation: Single circle with hands joined
Skills: Step-hop

Measures	Action
1–8	Beginning with left foot, take seven step-hops, then jump and land with feet together on the eighth beat.
9–16	Face clockwise, start with right foot and take seven step-hops, then jump and land on both feet, facing the center.
17–18	Drop hand, place hands on hips and raise right knee high, then stamp foot on floor and join hands.
1–18	Repeat measures 1 to 18; however, do not join hands.
19	Raise left knee, stamp foot, and join hands.
1–19	Repeat measures 1 to 19, but do not join hands.
20	Kneel on right knee, stand, and join hands.
1–20	Repeat measures 1 to 20, but do not join hands.
21	Kneel on left knee, stand, and join hands.
1–21	Repeat measures 1 to 21, but do not join hands.
22	Place right elbow on floor and cheek on right fist, then stand and join hands.
1–22	Repeat measures 1 to 22, but do not join hands.
23	Place left elbow on floor and cheek on left fist, then stand and join hands.
1–23	Repeat measures 1 to 23, but do not join hands.
24	Place forehead on floor, stand, and join hands.
1–16	Repeat measures 1 to 16.

Norwegian Mountain March (Level III)

Musical Accompaniment
Folkcraft 1177
Victor 45-6173

Formation: Circle in sets of three children, all facing counterclockwise; the "set" is composed of one boy in the center and slightly in front of two side girls; the boy holds the girls' inside hands and the girls join outside hands, forming a triangle
Skills: Waltz and turn under

Measures	Call	Action
1–8	Waltz run.	Start on the right foot and take eight running waltz steps (twenty-four steps). All should accent the first step of each measure, and the leader should occasionally glance over his right and left shoulders at his partners.
9–10	Boys under.	Boy moves backward with six running steps under the arch formed by the girls' raised arms.
11–12	Left girl under.	Girl on the boy's left takes six steps to cross in front of and under the boy's raised right arm.
13–14	Right girl turns.	Girl on the boy's right takes six steps to turn under the boy's right arm.
15–16	Boy turns.	Boy turns under his own right arm to original position. Repeat dance.

Alley Cat (Level III)

Musical Accompaniment
ATCO 45-6226
Columbia CL-2500

Formation: Scattered with all facing the same direction
Skills: Touch step, turn, jump

Measures	Action
1	Shift right foot to right and touch toe to floor.
2	Close right toe to left foot.
3	Shift right foot to right and touch toe to floor.
4	Close right foot to left and shift weight to right foot.
5–8	Repeat 1 to 4 with left foot.
9–12	Repeat 1 to 4 with right foot being extended back and returning to side of left foot.
13–16	Repeat 1 to 4 with left foot extending back.
17–18	Raise right knee up in front of left knee; repeat.
19–20	Raise left knee up in front of right knee; repeat.
21	Raise right arm in front of left knee.
22	Raise left knee up in front of right knee.
23–24	Clap hands and jump a quarter turn to the right.
	Repeat dance, making a quarter turn toward the right during the last measures of each dance.

Korobushka (Peddler's Pack) (Level III)

Musical Accompaniment
Folkdancer MH 1059
World of Fun M108
Folkcraft 1170

Formation: Double circle, boys on outside with both hands joined
Skills: Schottische step

Measures	Action (Schottische)
Part I:	Directions are for boys. Girls begin on opposite foot.
1–2	Beginning with left foot, boy takes one schottische step away from center; girl moves backward starting on her right foot.
3–4	Repeat action toward center with boy beginning with his right foot and moving backward while girl starts on her left foot and moves forward.
5–6	Repeat 1–2.
7–8	Both hop three times on support foot (boy's left, girl's right). On the first hop, point toe forward; on second, point toe sideward; and on third, close to support foot. Boy clicks heels together on last movement.

Measures	Action
Part II:	
1–2	Release hands and each partner, beginning with the right foot, does a schottische step toward the right.
3–4	Start with left foot and return with one schottische step to face partner.
5–6	Join hands and step-hop forward to partner (balance together), then step-hop backward (balance back).
7–8	With hands still joined, both start on right foot and change places with three walking steps.
9–16	Repeat 1–8.

Klumpakojis (Clumsy Footed) (Level III)

Musical Accompaniment
Folkcraft 1419
RCA Victor EPA 4142

Formation: Double circle, facing counterclockwise, boys on inside, girls on outside with inside hands joined
Skills: Walk, stamp, polka

Measures

Part I:

	Action (Walk)
1–4	Directions are for boys. Girls begin on opposite foot.
	With inside hands joined and free hand on hip, take eight brisk walking steps counterclockwise.
5–8	Release grip, turn left, reverse directions, change hands, and take eight walking steps clockwise.
9–16	Face partner, join right hands, right elbow bent and left hand on hip. Partners walk eight steps around each other in a clockwise direction. Join left hands, left elbow bent, right hand on hip and take eight steps around each other in a counterclockwise direction.

Part II:

	Action (Stamps, claps)
1–4	No action for counts 1, 2, 1, 2, then stamp three times for second measure. No action for counts 1, 2, 1, 2, then clap own hands three times for fourth measure.
5–8	Shake right finger at partner for counts 1, 2, and 3, and hold on count 4. Shake left finger at partner for counts 1, 2, and 3, and hold on 4. Clap right hand of partner, then turn solo counterclockwise in place with two steps. Face partner and stamp three times in place.
9–16	Repeat 1–8.

Part III:

	Action (Polka)
1–8	Take Varsovienne position. Starting with left foot, take sixteen polka steps counterclockwise. On the last two steps, release hands and boy moves forward to meet new partner.

CHAPTER 29

Red River Valley (Level III)

Musical Accompaniment
Imperial 1096
MacGregor Album 8 (with calls)
Folkcraft 1056

Formation: Square of four couples numbered counterclockwise, girl on the boy's right
Skills: Walk, swing, and do-si-do

Measures	Call	Action
1–4	All join hands in the valley.	Everyone joins hands.
5–8	And circle to the left and to the right.	With joined hands, walk four steps left and back four steps to the right.
1–4	And you swing the girl in the valley.	Boys swing corner girls (girl on the boy's left).
5–8	Now swing the Red River Gal.	Boys return to their own partners and swing them.
1–4	Now you lead right down the valley.	Number one and number three couples walk to couples on their right and join hands in a circle.
5–8	And you circle to the left, then to the right.	Walk four steps to the left and back four steps to the right.
9–12	Two ladies star in the valley.	Girls star with right hands (join right hands) in the center of the set and walk once around clockwise.
13–16	Now swing with the Red River Gal.	Boys swing partners.
1–4	Same couples to the left down the valley.	Couples number one and three walk to their left and join hands with new couples.
5–8	And you circle to the left and to the right.	Walk four steps to the left and back four steps to the right.
9–12	Now two gents star in the valley.	Boys star with their right hands and turn once around clockwise.
13–16	And you swing that Red River Gal.	Everyone swings with his partner. Repeat entire dance with two side couples taking the active part. Instead of a star, do-si-do the second time, elbow swing the third, and so on.

Heel and Toe Polka (Level III)

Musical Accompaniment
Burns, Evans, and Wheeler
Album 2, No. 225
Folkcraft 1166
MacGregor 400B

Formation: Double circle, with partners facing counterclockwise; open dance position with girl on boy's right side
Skills: Polka step

Measures	Call	Action
1–2	Heel and toe.	Partners touch outside heels forward and bend backward slightly. Touch toes of outside feet backward, bend forward slightly, and take three running steps forward (heel and toe, and step, step, step).
3–4	Heel and toe.	Repeat 1–2 with inside foot.
5–8	Heel and toe.	Repeat measures 1–4.
9–16		Partners face each other, the boy places his hands at the girl's waist and the girl places her hands on the boy's shoulders. All polka around the circle in a counterclockwise direction.

Oklahoma Mixer (Level III)

Musical Accompaniment
Folkcraft 1035
Methodist World of Fun 102
MacGregor 400

Formation: Double circle of couples, with girl on boy's right; take the Varsovienne position, with the left foot free
Skills: Walk, heel-toe, and two-step

Measures	Action
1–2	Begin with the left foot and take two, two-steps.
3–4	Begin with the left foot and take four walking steps forward.
5–8	Repeat measures 1–4.
9–12	Place the left heel forward and to the left, then the left toe opposite the right foot. Hold left hand, release right. Girls walk to the center of the circle in front of the boys as the boys move to the outside of the circle. The girls finish facing clockwise; the boys, counterclockwise.
13–16	The boy does a right heel and toe and takes three steps in place. The girl does a right heel and toe and walks to the boy behind.
	Repeat dance with new partner.

Rye Waltz (Level III)

Musical Accompaniment
Folkcraft 1103
Imperial 1044

Formation: Double circle with boys in the center facing girls; partners take an open dance position
Skills: Slide and waltz step

Measures	Action
1–4	Boys extend left toe to the side and return to inside of right foot. Repeat point and close. Girls perform the same movement with the right foot. Girls take three slide steps to the boys' left and touch right toe behind left foot.
5–8	Repeat in opposite direction.
9–16	Waltz around the room, with boys using their right shoulders to lead.

Tinikling (Level III)

Tinikling is a very exciting Philippine folk dance depicting the movements of the long-legged, long-necked tinikling bird, which is similar in appearance to the crane, heron, and flamingo. In the tinikling dance, the "bird" moves around two persons, who sit on the floor and manipulate two nine-foot-long bamboo poles in an attempt to trap the bird's legs. The poles are placed about two feet apart on two blocks of wood. The players holding the bamboo poles slide them across the boards and strike them together on count one. On counts two and three, they lift the poles about an inch off the boards, open them about one foot apart and tap them twice against the boards. The musical accompaniment is a 3/4 waltz meter with a distinct "strike, tap, tap" rhythm throughout the dance.

Several basic tinikling steps can be performed individually or in combination. Once children learn to perform the following stepping movements, they soon will develop combinations and routines.

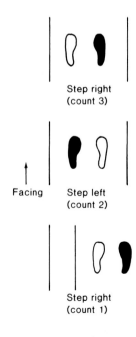

Step right (count 3)

Facing

Step left (count 2)

Step right (count 1)

Figure 29.15 Basic step.

Figure 29.17 Straddle step.

Figure 29.16 Basic step-partner routine.

brought together, the dancer takes a step forward on the right foot to the opposite side. The pattern is reversed on the next measure, with a step back on the left foot, a step back on the right foot, and a step back to the original position on the left foot.

When the class has learned the basic steps and pole movements, the poles can be arranged in a variety of patterns to allow the children to move in different directions. A few examples are shown in the following diagrams.

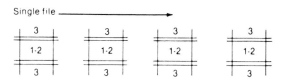

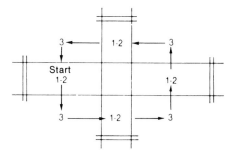

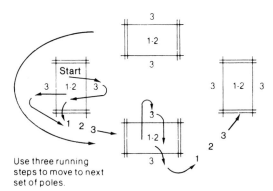

Basic Step

The dancer begins outside of the poles with her right side closest to the pole. With the 3/4 rhythm, one step is performed outside the poles as they are hit together and two steps inside the poles as they are tapped twice on the blocks. The rhythm pattern is step left (outside poles), step right (inside poles), step left (inside poles), step right (outside the rightside), and continue back. The basic step can be performed alone (figure 29.15) or with a partner (figure 29.16). After the basic step is learned, the following variations can be attempted.

Straddle Step

The dancer performs two jumps with feet together inside the poles and a straddle jump when the poles are brought together (figure 29.17). The rhythm pattern is out-in-in.

Forward and Back

The dancer stands facing the poles. The movement consists of a step forward with the right foot inside the poles, followed by a step forward on the left foot. As the poles are

Tush Push (Level III)

Musical Accompaniment
"Trouble"
Travis Tritt (artist)

Formation: Lines facing front
Skills: Tap, clap, stomp, step, polka, pivot

Measures	Action
1	Tap right heel forward, move right heel towards left knee, tap right heel forward (2×).
2	Switch. Tap left heel forward, move left heel towards right knee, tap left heel forward (2×).
3	Jump right forward, left forward, right forward, clap.
4	Bounce right hip forward (2×), left hip backward (2×).
5	Swing hips clockwise (2×).
6	Polka forward: R, L, R, rock step (step forward on left foot, shift weight to right foot).
7	Polka backward: L, R, L, rock step (step backward on right foot, shift weight to left foot).
8	Polka forward: R, L, R, step forward on left foot, pivot 1/2 turn clockwise.
9	Polka forward: L, R, L, step forward on right foot, Pivot 1/4 turn counterclockwise.
10	Pivot 1/4 turn counterclockwise, Pivot 1/4 turn counterclockwise, stomp right foot, clap.
	Repeat.

Variations

Try this to "Cadillac Ranch" by the Nitty Gritty Dirt Band

Flying Ace (Level III)

Musical Accompaniment
"Snake Oil"
Steve Earle (artist)

Formation: Lines facing front.
Skills: Hop, step, kick, pivot turn, grapevine.

Measures	Action
1–2	Kick left forward, kick right, kick left, step left to side, grapevine right behind, step left to side.
3–4	Kick right, step right to side, grapevine left behind, step right to side. Pivot 1/2 turn clockwise, Rock, step, rock. (Step forward on left foot, shift weight back to right foot, step forward on left foot.)
5	Pivot 3/4 turn counterclockwise, Rock, step, rock. (Step forward on right foot, shift weight back to left foot, step forward on right foot.)
	Repeat.

Variations

Replace kicks with hops.

Another version of this dance is called Four Corners. This version is dance in a large circle that moves counterclockwise around a group of dancers doing the Hawaiian Cowboy. Larger steps are taken in order to travel and the 3/4 turn is substituted with a 1/2 turn.

Bad Bad Leroy Brown (Level III)

Musical Accompaniment
"Bad Bad Leroy Brown"
Jim Croce (Artist)
Lifelong Records, A135571

Formation: Lines facing front
Skills: Grapevine, scissors step

Measures	Action
1	Two step-close-step forward, leading with right foot.
2	Begin on right foot, three steps forward and close left foot to the right.
3	Grapevine: Moving to the right step on the right, cross the left behind the right, step right to the right, and kick or swing the left foot in front of the right.
4	Grapevine: Repeat moving to the left, finish with a swing or kick of the right leg in front of the left.
5	Beginning with the right foot, step backward with two slow strutting steps.
6	Beginning with the right, take four steps backward.
7	Step sideways to the right with the right foot and close the left foot to the right. Cross the right foot in front of the left and pause.
8	Step left to the left side. Close the right foot to the left, cross the left foot in front of the right (scissors), turning one quarter turn to the right.
	Repeat.

Variation

Working in small groups, get students to create their own movements.

Coming Round the Mountain (Level III)

Musical Accompaniment
Educational Recordings:
Square Dance 4

Formation: Symmetrical square set, four couples; ladies chain swing, allemande left and right, and promenade
Skills: Chain, swing, allemande left and right, promenade

Singing Call

The head two couples chain, side couple swing. Chain them around the mountain, chain them home. The side two couples ladies chain, head two couples swing again. Chain them round the mountain, chain them home. Allemande left your corners, allemande right your partners. Come all the way around your partner to the next girl on the right.

Swing this lady up and down, swing her round and round and round. And promenade that pretty mountain gal.

Action

Follow the singing call instructions. All dancers walk around their partner, and continue moving forward to the next dancer.

Promenade with new partner to the boy's home position. The dance is repeated until dancers are with their original partners. The second time the action begins with the head couples chain. The third and fourth times the dance begins with the side couples chain.

Texas Star (Level III)

Musical Accompaniment
Educational Recordings;
Square Dance 4

Formation: Star, four couples
Skills: Swing, promenade, step

Patter Call

Now ladies to the center and back to the bar. And gents to the center with a right hand star. Take the right hand out, put the left hand in, come back again.

Now meet your partner, gonna pass her by. Pick up the next one on the sly with the arm around her waist. Now keep your arm around her waist.

The men back out and the ladies come in with a turn and a half. And ladies star with a right hand cross. And everybody swing and everybody whirl.

Swing with the lady round you go, and the ace is high and the deuce is low.

Put her on the right, let's promenade, Walk around that hall.

Action

Boys reverse directions, changing to a left hand star.

Continue moving the star counterclockwise with the girl by the boy's side.

Boys break the star, couples turn moving counterclockwise one and a half turns. The girls form a right hand star in the center.

Girls break the star and swing with their new partners.

The dance is repeated until the girls are returned to their original partners.

Oklahoma Two-Step (Level III)
Plains Indians (Blackfeet)

Musical Accompaniment
Powwow music with a medium beat

Formation: Lead couple has couples in a line behind, hands are joined by crossing the arms in front, right hand to right hand, and left to left
Skills: Bend, turn, twist, arch, etc.

Basic Step

Step-close: The dancers step forward with the outside feet and step to close with the inside feet. Repeat with the same foot leading. This step is used throughout the dance.

Action

The dancers follow the path of the lead couple, who have a choice of moves. They may choose to move:
a. In circles
b. Forward or backward
c. Like a snake
d. Forming an arch, with couples moving under the arch and then forming additional arches. The arching continues until the head couple is once again at the head of the line
e. Splitting with partners, moving in different pathways and then rejoining with same partner
f. In a spiral
g. In and out of circles
h. With creative moves chosen by the lead couple

Variations

Change the lead couple to give all children the chance to create their own movements

Strawberry Dance (Level III)
(Chippewa)
Musical Accompaniment
Kimbo Educational: KLP 9070-A

Formation: Single circle of dancers, some representing the chief, medicine man, and other members of the tribe
Skills: Step, turn, twist, bend, hop

Basic Step
Touch step: With knees slightly bent, dancers take a step forward on the left foot (beat 1). They touch the right foot forward (beat 2), then to the side (beat 3), and then back (beat 4). Repeat stepping forward on the right foot and touching with the left.

Action
The chief dances to the center of the circle and places a decorated blanket of a dead warrior on the ground. The medicine man dances around the blanket to chase away the evil spirits and bless the ground. The other members of the tribe move into the circle one by one to present their gifts to the dead warrior. They dance to the edge of the circle and continue to move clockwise until all have been to the blanket.

Variation
Perform the dance to celebrate spring and the strawberry season rather than to the memory of a dead warrior.

Additional Folk, Line, and Square Dances for Developmental Level III

Name of Dance	Skills	Formation	Origin	Record Source
Mayim	Walk, hop, grapevine	Circle	Israeli	Folkcraft 1108
Hop Morr Anika		Circle	Swedish	Victor 4162
Road to the Isles	Walk, schottische	Couples	Scottish	Imperial 1105A
Hinkey Dinkey	Swing, promenade	Square	French	Folkcraft 1012 (with call)
Let's Square Dance	Walk	Square	American	Victor 3001
Hohsey Square Dance	Walk	Square	American	MacGregor (Album 4618)
Chester Schottische	Schottische	Circle	American	Folkcraft 1101
Miserlou	Walk, grapevine	Circle	Greek	Merit Audio Visual 1046
Jessie Polka	Two-step, polka step	Couples	American	Folkcraft 1071
Put Your Little Foot	Varsovienne	Couples	American	Folkcraft 1165
Varsovienne	Varsovienne	Circle	American	Folkcraft 1034
Hot Time	Walk, swing, allemande	Square	American	Folkcraft 1037
Ten Pretty Girls	Walk	Circle	American	World of Fun 113
Cotton Eye Joe	Polka	Free	American	World of Fun 118
Brown Eye Mary	Walk, skip, promenade, allemande	Circle	American	Folkcraft 1186
Five Foot Two	Two-step	Double circle	American	Folkcraft 1420

RESOURCE INFORMATION

1. *Suggested records*
   a. "Special Folk Dances" (Tinikling, Carinosa, Czardas, Vengorka and Tarantella in 3/4 meter), RCA Victor, EPA-126
   b. "Alley Cat," ATCA 45-6226
   c. "No Matter What Shape," Liberty Records, 55836

2. *Film*
   Tinikling—the Bamboo Dance (16 mm), Martin Moyer Productions, 900 Federal Avenue East, Seattle, WA

GLOSSARY OF TERMS

The following words and phrases occur frequently in folk, line, and square dances for children in the intermediate grades.

Active couple(s)
The couple(s) designated to start a dance or to whom a part of the dance is addressed.

Advance
To move forward, usually with walking steps.

Allemande left
From a circle or square formation with all dancers facing the center, the boy joins his left hand with the girl on his left and walks around counterclockwise and back to his starting position.

Allemande right
Same as allemande left but in the opposite direction.

Arch
Two dancers join inside hands and raise arms to form an arch.

Balance
In square dancing, the usual movement following a "swing your partner." Partners face each other, join right hands, and step back with weight on the left foot and the right heel touching in front. Both partners may also bow slightly.

Banjo (right parallel) position
Variation of closed position in which boy and girl make a one-eighth turn counterclockwise to a diagonal position.

Bow and curtsy
The bow, performed by the boys, may be a simple nod of the head or an elaborate and pronounced deep bend of the trunk. The curtsy, performed by the girls, may be a simple nod of the head or an elaborate and pronounced deep bend of the knees and a graceful sideward extension of the dancing costume.

Break
Release hands.

Chain (ladies chain)
In square dancing, the girls move across to the opposite couple, extending their right hands to each other as they pass, then their left hands to the opposite boy. The boy places his right hand behind the girl's back, grasping her right hand, and turns her one full turn counterclockwise.

Circle
Dancers join hands and move toward the right or left.

Clockwise
The same direction as the hands of a clock.

Closed position
Partners face each other, with shoulders parallel and toes pointing forward, the boy's right arm around the girl, with his hand on her lower back. The girl's left hand and arm rest on the boy's upper arm and shoulder. The boy holds the girl's right hand in his left.

Corner
When facing the center, the boy's corner is the girl on his left and the girl's corner is the boy on her right.

Counterclockwise
The opposite direction as the hands of a clock.

Divide or split the ring
Active couples pass through the opposite couples.

Do-si-do
These words mean "back to back" and usually involve two persons who are facing each other. The two dancers walk forward; pass right shoulders; without turning move to the right, passing back to back; and then walk backward to the starting position.

Elbow swing
Partners face each other, hook elbows (left or right), and turn with small steps.

Even rhythm
The beats in a rhythm pattern are given the same value.

Forward and back
This figure involves dancers facing each other. Both sides advance four steps forward (or three steps and a bow) and take four steps backward.

Grand right and left
This is a weaving pattern and usually follows an allemande left. Face partner and join right hands, pass and give left hand to the next dancer, and continue weaving around set.

Grapevine
A step toward the left side (count 1), step right behind left foot (count 2), step left to side (count 3), then step right foot in front of left (count 4).

Head couple
In square dancing, the couple nearest the music or caller.

Home
The starting place at the beginning of a dance.

Honor
Salute or bow to partner or other dancers.

Open position
Partners stand side-by-side, facing the same direction, with inside hands joined.

Opposite
The person or couple directly across the square.

Polka
A hop on right foot, step forward on left, close right to left, then step forward on left.

Promenade
This is the skaters' position in which partners stand side-by-side and face the same direction. The girl stands on the boy's right. Partners join left hands about waist high, then join right hands above the left arms.

Sashay
The American term for the French "chassé." These are sliding steps sideward.

Separate
Partners leave each other and move in opposite directions.

Square
Four couples, with each forming one side of a square.

Star or wheel
Two or more dancers join right hands in the center of the set and walk forward or backward as directed.

Swing
This is a rhythmic rotation of a couple with a walking step, buzz step, two-step, or skip. The swing may be a one-hand, two-hand, elbow, or waist swing.

Tempo
Rate of speed at which music is played.

RECORD SOURCES

The following list of record companies covers musical accompaniment for all singing games and folk, line, and square dances taught in the elementary school program. Teachers can order company catalogs and be placed on company mailing lists.

Bob Ruff Records
8459 Edmarce Ave.
Whittier, CA 90605

Dance Record
Distributers
(Folkcraft Records)
12 Fenwick St.
Newark, NJ 07114

Educational Activities
Inc.
P.O. Box 382
Freeport, NY 11528

Educational Record
Sales
157 Chambers St.
New York, NY 10007

Folk Dances Record
Service
P.O. Box 201
Flushing, NY 11520

Hoctor Products for
Education
159 Franklin Turnpike
Waldwich, NJ 07463

Kimbo Records
P.O. Box 477
Long Beach, NJ 07740

Lloyd Shaw Foundation,
Sales Division
12225 Saddle Strap Row
Hudson, FL 33567

Summary Review

All traditional and contemporary dances use individual locomotor skills. Basic steps, positions, and movement designs provide the foundation for these dances. Teaching dance activities is best accomplished through a sequential part-part-whole teaching progression. Further, all dances, regardless of age or culture of origin, are made up of five basic elements: steps, direction, pathway, relationship, and formation. Teaching these five basic elements is accomplished through a progressive parts teaching approach. Although more direct methods of teaching are most effective for teaching folk, line, and square dances, creative folk dance, creative line dance, and creative square dance can be achieved through exploratory and problem-solving instructional techniques.

SELECTED READINGS

CAHPER. 1983. *Folk dance in the elementary school.* Ottawa, Ontario: CAHPER.

Evans, J. 1981. *Let's dance.* Toronto, Ontario: Can-Ed Media.

Harris, J. A., A. M. Pittman, and M. S. Waller. 1988. *Dance awhile.* 6th ed. New York: Macmillan.

Mynatt, C. V., and B. D. Kaiman. 1975. *Folk dancing for students and teachers.* Dubuque, IA: Wm. C. Brown.

Snider, M. 1980. *Folk dance handbook.* North Vancouver, BC: Hancock House.

INDIVIDUAL *and* GROUP PROJECTS

1. Videotape no. 3, on teaching folk dances (see appendix A), introduces a seven-step teaching process that is based on the principle of part-whole learning (see chapter 3). View this videotape, then form groups. Each group develops a lesson plan for a folk dance, based on the principle of part-whole learning. Then teach the other groups your folk dance.

2. Chapter 13 identified a number of disabilities that afflict young children. In small groups, choose four disabilities and discuss how children with these disabilities can be integrated into folk dance activities. Consider what adjustments will have to be made to accommodate each child's developmental level to ensure success. Debate possible techniques and methods of evaluation. Share ideas with other groups.

3. A feature of this text is the idea of teaching and enhancing academic skills and concepts through physical education activities. In small groups, discuss and create ideas to teach or enhance academic skills and concepts in social studies, language arts, and mathematics through traditional and contemporary dance activities. Consider methods of evaluation. Share ideas with other groups.

4. Based on the evaluation techniques and methods discussed in chapter 11, design a selection of assessment methods and techniques suitable for evaluating folk and square dancing activities.

5. Form three groups. Each group is assigned a different developmental level dance or singing game from table 29.1. Plan and teach your dance or singing game to the other two groups. Then discuss and reflect on the effectiveness of your teaching.

6. In small groups, students design a series of lessons to teach primary aged children basic steps, dance positions, and movement designs. Students are to visit a local elementary school and use the lesson plans to teach a group of primary aged children. In small groups, students reflect on the effectiveness of their lesson plans, methods of evaluation, and effectiveness of the teaching.

CHAPTER 30

Creative Dance Activities

KEY CONCEPTS

30.1 The four elements of Laban's classification of movement can be used as the basic structure for developing a creative dance program

30.2 An appropriate choice of creative dance themes can stimulate interest and excitement, and can facilitate creativity

30.3 In creative dance, the emphasis is on self-expression demonstrated through movement

30.4 Creative dance activities must be developmentally appropriate to ensure that all children can achieve success and enjoyment

30.5 Creative ideas can be facilitated through the introduction of various stimuli

30.6 The appropriate choice of sound accompaniment is critical to the success of creative dance activities

30.7 The teacher's voice can be an effective stimulus in a creative dance lesson

KEY OBJECTIVES

After completing this chapter you will be able to:

1. Design developmentally appropriate creative dance activities for elementary school children
2. Understand the nature and scope of a creative dance program suitable for an elementary school physical education program
3. Use themes and a variety of stimuli and sound accompaniment when teaching creative dance
4. Plan and organize teaching units and daily lessons involving creative dance activities
5. Apply movement concepts and skills when teaching creative dance
6. Plan a safe environment for teaching children creative dance
7. Identify key teaching points associated with creative dance activities
8. Employ teaching progressions that lead to the successful development of creative dance activities

C reativity cannot exist in the abstract, and neither can creative teaching. As teachers, we want children to be able to feel and express their ideas through movement; we want them to be creative. However, no child can be imaginative or creative without a vocabulary of words, concepts, and ideas. Neither can a child express a creative movement without a vocabulary of movement skills and an awareness of various forms of internal and external stimuli.

Our task in enhancing the child's creative process is twofold. First, we must recognize the level of cognitive and motor development of the age group we are teaching. Primary children, for example, have a limited vocabulary and a limited capacity for abstract thinking. Their world of ideas is very small; they normally demonstrate "being like" or "imitation of" in their first attempts at creative movements. However, boys and girls in the intermediate grades have a rich vocabulary, as well as interest in exploring abstract ideas and the capacity to carry out these ideas. Their movement vocabulary has also expanded far beyond the basic locomotor skills to personal reservoirs of complex movement skills and motor patterns.

Our second task in enhancing the creative process is to develop an approach or format that can be used to encourage children to develop their own creative ideas and to express them through movement. In parts 6 and 7, Laban's four movement elements of body awareness, space awareness, qualities, and relationships were used as a framework to teach movement concepts and skills. This chapter will use these four elements of movement as the basic structure for developing a creative dance program for all three developmental levels.

STRUCTURE FOR DEVELOPING A CREATIVE DANCE PROGRAM

All movements performed by a child can be analyzed according to the specific body actions that are involved (body awareness), the effort (qualities), the space (space awareness) within which a movement takes place, and the position (relationships) of the body to equipment or other performers (figure 30.1). This is illustrated in figure 30.3. In gymnastics, as described in chapters 25, 26, and 27, all movements can be taught according to this classification system. However, since the emphasis in gymnastics is primarily the efficiency and utility of movement, descriptive terminology, such as *swirl*, *hasty*, and *retreating*, are not used. In creative dance, the emphasis is on self-expression demonstrated through movement. This requires additional expressive words to explain and stimulate creative movements.

C O N C E P T

30.1 *The Four Elements of Laban's Classification of Movement Can Be Used as the Basic Structure for Developing a Creative Dance Program*

Choose a Theme

The theme a teacher chooses for a creative dance program should be based on several important considerations. The starting idea should be exciting and meaningful to the children. For example, the theme of "spaceships" would appeal to the imaginations of seven-year-olds. Another reason for this choice is that outer space and astronauts offer unlimited possibilities for young children to develop their creative talent in planning and expressing their ideas through movement. In short, from the child's point of view, the theme must be meaningful and stimulating; from the teacher's point of view, it must be practical as a vehicle to increase the child's creative expression through movement (figure 30.2).

Figure 30.1 Relationship to the ground or other performers.

Figure 30.2 Choosing a theme.

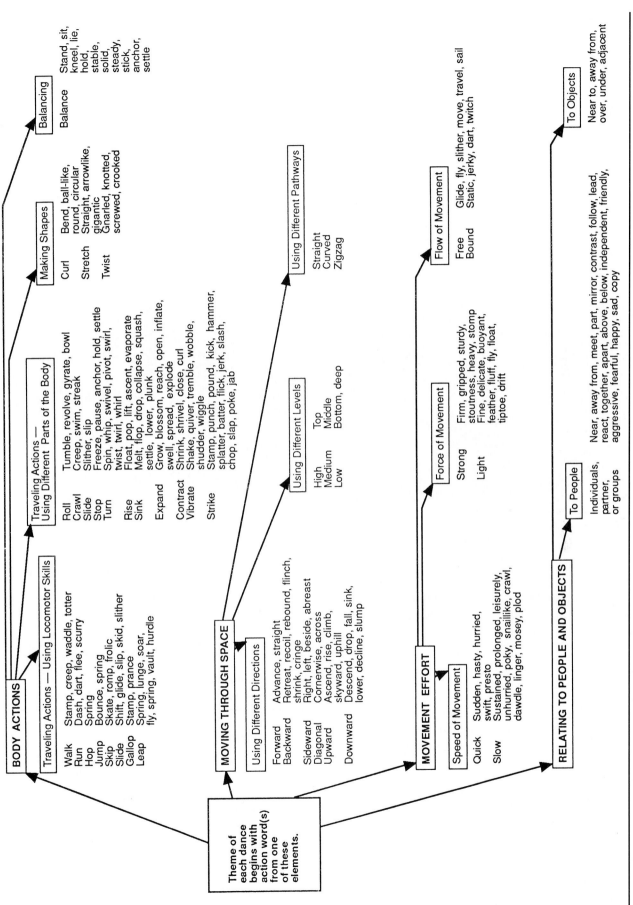

Figure 30.3 Structure of a creative dance program.

CHAPTER 30

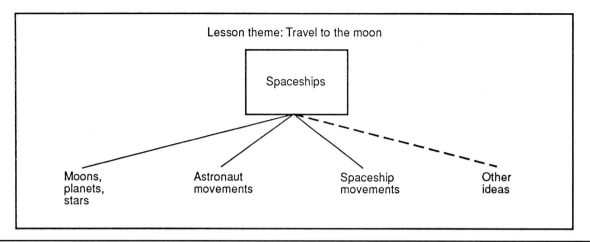

Lesson theme: Travel to the moon

Spaceships

Moons, planets, stars   Astronaut movements   Spaceship movements   Other ideas

Figure 30.4   Ideas for themes.

Figure 30.5   Brainstorming.

Figure 30.6   Simulate the takeoff.

C O N C E P T

30.2 *An Appropriate Choice of Creative Dance Themes Can Stimulate Interest and Excitement, and Can Facilitate Creativity*

Brainstorm

The next step in the process is to decide what elements of the chosen theme should be included in the program. Carrying through with the previous example, ideas that could be developed are shown in figure 30.4. Each of these ideas, such as "astronaut movements" or "spaceship movements," could be covered in a single lesson or over many lessons. The length and scope depend on how the idea is developed by the teacher and her class (figure 30.5). In this example, spaceship movements are selected as a general idea, then reduced to a shorter theme of "travel to the moon," as illustrated in the lesson plan for Travel to the Moon.

C O N C E P T

30.3 *In Creative Dance, the Emphasis Is on Self-Expression Demonstrated Through Movement*

Select Movement Actions

Since the theme of the accompanying lesson is travel to the moon, it involves a takeoff (figure 30.6), movement through space, and a landing. The main theme of the lesson is pathways and a subtheme is speed. Many words can be used to stimulate the takeoff, flight through space, and landing on the moon (table 30.1). These ideas are developed in the second part of the lesson.

Lesson Plan for Travel to the Moon

Things to Emphasize	Sample Lesson	Teaching Points
Part I: Introductory Activity Stress general vigorous activity.	Listen to the drum beat (show, slow, quick, and stop).	See if children can keep in time to drum beat.
Stress one or more movement concepts of lesson. Introduce musical accompaniment.	Travel through space in time to the drum beat. Stop when the drum beat stops. Travel and stop while moving "in straight lines" . . . "now curved pathways."	See if children change speed and stop with control. Repeat activities with musical accompaniment.
Part II: Skill Development Begin to develop main theme of lesson. Begin to expand movement vocabulary. Encourage children to select and repeat movement. Encourage children to develop simple sequences.	Show how rocket develops burst of speed (vibrate, shake). Show how rocket takes off after countdown (slow, sustained, strong, swift). Show how spaceship moves and stays in orbit around earth. Leave orbit to new destination heading for the moon. When reach new destination, orbit the moon and slow down. Land on the moon.	Play tape recording of a spaceship launch. Discuss ways to show motor warming up, weightlessness, re-entry, how spaceship speeds up and slows down. Look for and encourage early signs of selecting and repeating movement.
Part III: Dance Composition Apply concepts and skills from part II to a dance sequence. Add relationship to a partner. Allow time for practice and refinement. Allow time to perform for class.	Practice takeoff, orbit the earth, travel to the moon, orbit the moon, and land on the moon. Work with partner and develop a twin launch.	Help students who find difficulty in developing their own sequence. Encourage children to share each other's ideas.
Part IV: Closure Cover main theme.	Discuss elements of dance.	Allow children to decide what theme(s) might be possible for the next two or three lessons.
Discuss future lessons derived from this theme.	Discuss other possible lessons with another space theme.	

TABLE 30.1 Movement Possibilities

Body Actions	Moving through Space	Movement Effort	Relation to People and Objects
Walk	Forward—advance	Quick—sudden, swift	People: near, far, meet, part, together, apart, above, below
Run	Backward—recoil	Slow—sustained	Objects: near, away, inside, outside, over, under
Leap—soar, fly	Upward—ascend, rise, climb	Strong—heavy	
Slide—glide	Skyward	Light—fly, float, drift	
Stop—anchor, hold	Downward—descent, fall, lower, decline	Flow—glide, fly	
Turn—spin, swirl, twirl	High—top		
Rise—float, lift	Medium—middle		
Sink—drop, settle, lower	Low—bottom		
Expand—reach, open, inflate, explode	Straight, curved, zigzag		
Vibrate—shake, quiver, tremble, shudder			
Strike—flick, jerk, slash, poke, jab			

Figure 30.7　Sharing ideas.

Plan the Structure of the Dance

During the third part of the lesson, children begin to integrate the concepts and skills learned in part 2 into a creative dance. The structure of their dance should include a beginning (takeoff), a story or adventure (moving through space), and an ending (landing). For young children, a form of accompaniment, such as a percussion instrument, a poem, or taped music, is used to move the dance through each stage of development.

CONCEPT

30.4 *Creative Dance Activities Must Be Developmentally Appropriate to Ensure That All Children Can Achieve Success and Enjoyment*

A teacher cannot anticipate the success of any creative dance lesson. If the class has not had experience in this type of activity and the teacher is trying this type of lesson for the first time, at first each lesson may seem isolated. Gradually, however, as children build a repertoire of movements and learn to think and move in creative patterns, each lesson will appear to be too short. The teacher will also develop greater powers of observation and more effective uses of her voice, percussion instruments, and all other forms of musical accompaniment. The consequence will likely be a central theme, beginning with the first lesson and carried throughout subsequent lessons. When this occurs, the format will emphasize the last portion of the lesson to allow the children maximum freedom to create, refine, and express their feelings and ideas through creative dance movements. Finally, provide time at the end of the lesson for children to perform their dances and to share their ideas with other members of the class (figure 30.7).

TABLE 30.2　Stimuli for Creative Movements

Stimuli	Developmental Level		
	I	II	III
Balloons	X		
Fairy tales	X		
Animals	X	X	
Pictures	X	X	
Witches	X	X	
Fire		X	
Thanksgiving		X	
Weather (snow, wind, etc.)	X	X	X
Trees and plants	X	X	X
Stories and poems	X	X	X
Journeys	X	X	X
Marionettes	X	X	X
Mechanical objects (robots)	X	X	X
Rubber bands	X	X	X
Clay	X	X	X
Wire	X	X	X
Sports		X	X
Astronauts	X	X	X
Halloween	X	X	X
Fall (leaves, rain, frost)	X	X	X
Winter (cold, snow, wind)	X	X	X
Christmas	X	X	X
Spring (growing, unfolding)	X	X	X
Easter (searching, drawing, painting)	X	X	X
Water (solid, liquid, gas, flowing)	X	X	X
Insects	X	X	X
Space (planets, stars, travel)	X	X	X

STIMULI

The previous section provided one way to teach a creative dance program using Laban's basic elements of body awareness (actions), body effort (qualities), space, and relationships. These aspects of movement are the paints of the painter or the notes of the musician. The ways in which body movements are joined together by individuals, partners, or groups should result both from the teacher's guidance and the children's creativity. Creative movements can be further enhanced by the effective use of a wide variety of meaningful stimuli, such as objects, stories, and paintings. Whatever external stimulus a teacher uses should be both within the bounds of the children's understanding and potentially rich in forms of expression. The examples in table 30.2 have proved appropriate for elementary school children. The following sample lesson also illustrates how a teacher can approach the class and build several creative dance lessons from one central idea.

Sample Lesson Plan: Clouds and Nature

Suggested Teaching Procedure	Possible Responses from Children

1. Movement introduction
Have children sit in a scattered formation on the floor. The following questions and discussion will provide the stimulus for the interpretive movements:
  a. Think of coming to school on a nice, warm day, when the sky is filled with pretty white clouds. What do the clouds look like?
  b. If you could touch a cloud, what do you think it would feel like?
  c. If you were a big cloud, what would you do on a nice, warm day?
2. Interpretive movements
  a. Let's all move about the room as if we were clouds in the sky.
  b. To indicate light movements: Can you run very lightly on your tiptoes?
  c. What else is soft and light and makes you feel like moving as you did?
  Introduce musical accompaniment: tambourine, triangle, or song bells.
  d. Can you move your arms and your whole body very softly and lightly while I play the triangle? (Vary the speed, but always keep the intensity very soft.)
  e. Seated in scattered formation: We have talked about light and soft things and moved so we felt that way. What is very different from softness?
  f. What can you think of that is the opposite of soft, fluffy clouds?
  g. Move around the room again, but this time we will be heavy and hard. (Use drum or blocks for accompaniment.)
	1. Movement introduction
	The responses to your questions will be tangible objects that are familiar to this age group.
	  a. Mashed potatoes, cotton candy, or cotton balls
	
	  b. Soft and fluffy like whipped cream or Daddy's shaving cream
	
	  c. Sleep, fly around and look at everyone, ride with the wind
	2. Interpretive movements
	  a. Running; romping; moving on tiptoes; or making heavy, pronounced steps
	  b. Running lightly, swinging or swaying, and so on
	
	  c. Kitten, bunny, feathers
	
	  d. Children may remain in the same spot or shift about the room, with light, expressive movements.
	
	  e. Stones, big and fat, heavy, rough
	
	  f. Giants, elephants, sledgehammer
	
	  g. Heavy pounding with feet and clenched fists, dragging arms to imitate elephant walk

C O N C E P T

30.5 *Creative Ideas Can be Facilitated through the Introduction of Various Stimuli*

Primary Program Sample Lesson (Level II)

Lesson Clouds and nature
Basic theme Interpretive movements
Formation Multiple (scattered, line, and circle)

The purpose of this lesson is to stimulate light and heavy movements, with emphasis on the quality rather than the direction of the response. A short discussion should precede this lesson to familiarize children with new words and the concept of clouds as part of nature. This can be done through class discussion or stories and poems about clouds.

Additional Suggestions Reorganize the class into partners or small groups and pose questions that require a group effort to express the movement. For example, ask partners to interpret two thunderclouds moving toward each other. Continue the lesson, emphasizing soft and heavy movements. For the conclusion, discuss the movements, or play a record and allow the children to interpret the music.

Additional Resource Material

The sample lesson can assist in developing a basic approach to teaching creative or interpretive movements. Numerous other methods and techniques can be used with equal success. Table 30.3 contains possible animal, mechanical, and nature movements that can be used as an additional source.

TABLE 30.3 Resources for Developing Creative Movements

	Types of Movement	Musical Accompaniment
Animal Movements		
Bear	Heavy, slow walk; run; climb	Drum (slow), woodblock, claves
Camel	Slow, bouncy walk; carry object	Drum (uneven)
Elephant	Heavy, slow, rocking walk; lift object	Drum (slow, heavy)
Frog	Hop, jump, bounce, bend	Drum (short, quick)
Worm	Curl, bend, stretch	Scraper
Monkey	Fast crawl, bent-knee jumps	Woodblock
Rabbit	Jump, bend, run, sniff	Woodblock
Soldier	Crawl, run, march	Drum, drum rolls
Tall person/short person	Bend and stretch, bent-knee walk, tiptoe walk	Drum (fast and light, heavy and slow)
Cat	Cautious walk, run, play, stretch	Woodblock, sticks
Chicken	Choppy, quick walk; scratch; peck; flap arms	Woodblock (short, quick)
Raggedy Ann/Andy	Loose, floppy walk; swing; bend	Drum, tambourine
Giant	Slow, heavy walk and run; exaggerated movements	Drum (heavy and slow), cymbals
Horse	Gallop, prance (knees high), walk, carry rider	Woodblock
Butterfly	Light, sustained movements; use of arms; soft runs; skips	Gong, cymbals
Mechanical Movements		
Bulldozer	Push, bend, walk, show effort	Drum, scrapers
Dump truck	Bend and stretch, lift, locomotion, show effort	Drum
Lumber loader	Bend and stretch, lift, slow and sustained, show effort	Drum
Washing machine	Twist, roll, bounce	Scraper, drum
Ditchdigger	Bend and stretch, push and lift, show effort	Drum
Lawn sprinkler	Twist, turn, bend, stretch	Shakers, maracas
Top	Twist, turn, run, skip, walk, fall	Scraper, cymbals, gong
Clock	Locomotion (percussive), swing and sway (stiff)	Woodblock
Percolator	Rise and fall, jiggle and bob (loose and floppy)	Woodblock (accelerating beat)
Pop-up toaster	Rise and fall, bend and stretch, hop, jump	Woodblock, drum
Airplane	Rise and fall, sustain arm movements with running	Drum (vibratory beats)
Typewriter	Walk, hop, jump (short, quick), bend, stretch	Woodblock, triangle, bell
Nature Movements		
Wind	Use of arms, turn and smooth run, bend and stretch while running	Drum, tambourine
Rain	Rise and fall, bend and stretch, shake	Drum, maracas
Flower	Bend and stretch, swing and sway	Drum, tambourine
Bee	Swing and sway, whip and slash with arms and trunk	Drum, tambourine
Sun	Rise and fall, bend and stretch, big and small movements	Gong, cymbals
Cloud	Sustained, smooth movements; tiptoe walks and runs; swing and sway	Cymbals, drum
Shadow	Darting walks and runs, bend and stretch, strike and dodge	Drum, woodblock
Moon	Rise and fall, bend and stretch, sustained locomotion	Drum
Wave	Rise and fall, skip, swing and sway, dynamic falls	Drum (loud and soft), cymbals
Fire	Strike and dodge, jump, turn, hop, stretch	Drum (first slow, loud, and soft)
Smoke	Rise, turn, swing, sway, run, skip, stretch	Cymbals, tambourine

The movements can be performed with the musical accompaniment listed.

The following list of recordings have been recommended by leading dance specialists as appropriate accompaniment for many of the creative dance activities listed in table 30.3.

Bowmar Records, 622 Rodier Dr., Glendale, CA 91201.

1. *Children's Rhythms in Symphony.* Music of great composers for creative and interpretative movement.

2. *Rhythm Time,* No. 1 (023) and No. 2 (024). Music for basic movement.

Educational Activities Inc., Box 392, Freeport, NY 11520.

1. *Authentic Afro-Rhythms: Early Elementary through College.* Selection of rhythms from Africa, Cuba, Haiti, Brazil, Trinidad, and Puerto Rico.

2. *Rain Dance and Canoe Dance.* Selection of drums and chants.

Folkways Scholastic Records, 907 Sylvan Ave.,
Englewood Cliffs, NJ 07632.

1. *Sounds, Rhythms, Rhyme, and Mime for Children,*
   FC 14504. Music and rhymes related to African
   culture.
2. *Sounds of New Music,* FX 6160. Orchestra sounds
   associated with farmyard scenes, factory, and
   space.

RCA Records, 1132 Avenue of Americas, New York,
NY 10036.

1. *Adventures in Music.* A twelve-album series for
   grades 1 to 6. Excellent music resource for all types
   of creative dance activities.

The Dimension 5 Records, Box 185 Kingsbridge
Station, Bronx, NY 10463.

1. *Electronic Records for Children.* A selection of
   exciting and interesting electronic musical
   recordings.

The following companies, in addition to those mentioned above, provide catalogs and listings of musical selections appropriate for elementary school creative dance activities.

Educational Record Sales, 157 Chambers St., New
York, NY 10007.
Phoebe James Products, Box 134, Pacific Palisades, CA
90272.
Kimbo Education Record Co., Box 477, Long Branch,
NJ 07740.
Hoctor Educational Records Inc., Waldwick, NJ 07463.
S and R Records, 1609 Broadway, New York, NY
10017.
Children's Music Center, 5373 West Pico Blvd., Los
Angeles, CA 90019.

SOUND ACCOMPANIMENT

The value of a sound accompaniment to a creative movement is judged on its ability to stimulate and enhance a child's imagination and creative movements. The proper selection and application of sound accompaniment are critical to the success of a creative dance program. Some of the more important considerations relating to the teacher's voice, percussion instruments, recorded music, and class-made instruments follow.

C O N C E P T

30.6 *The Appropriate Choice of Sound Accompaniment Is Critical to the Success of Creative Dance Activities*

Teacher's Voice

All teachers are aware of the effect of their voices in the classroom, activity room, and gymnasium. In creative dance, however, the manner and tone of a teacher's speaking voice can become important stimuli in evoking creative movements. Simply speaking softly to children can encourage slower, lighter movements. Similarly, speaking sharply in a loud voice or drawing out the words provides sufficient stimulus for another type of movement response. When a teacher adds other characteristics to her voice, such as hissing, clicking, or humming sounds, the mood and action of the dance is directed in a variety of ways. The reservoir of sounds a young performer can make should also be exploited to the fullest, since such sounds provide an equally important stimulus.

C O N C E P T

30.7 *The Teacher's Voice Can Be an Effective Stimulus in a Creative Dance Lesson*

Percussion Instruments

Various percussion instruments are useful in a creative dance program. The drum, tambourine, and cymbals are ideal when teaching children to move in time to the beat and tempo of a musical accompaniment. Perhaps the drum is the most useful in the initial stages of teaching creative dance; however, the following percussion instruments are also valuable:

1. Banjo drums
2. Improvised drums—large and small containers such as coffee tins and plastic containers with plastic or cloth covers
3. Tambourine
4. Woodblocks—solid or hollow
5. Rhythm sticks—varying in size from ½ inch by 6 inches to ½ inch by 12 inches
6. Castanets
7. Coconut shells
8. Cymbals
9. Triangle
10. Bells—assorted sizes, individual and on a strip of cloth
11. Shakers—may be made with gravel, beans, or sand

Recorded Music

The use of recorded music in any creative dance program needs little elaboration. What a teacher and class select depends on the availability of records or tapes. The general availability of tape recorders suggests another inexpensive and flexible way of adding musical accompaniment to the dance program. If tape recorders are used, a format should be established for recording music and for classifying and storing school tapes.

CHAPTER 30

Classmade Instruments

When a teacher or class makes inexpensive equipment, it is normally due to financial reasons. The suggestions that follow are based, to a very minor degree, on available finances and, to a major degree, on the positive effects of making one's own musical instrument.

Getting children interested in creative dance is a difficult task for many classroom teachers. No simple list of teaching suggestions will work for every teacher. However, when children make their own musical instruments, a very positive attitude develops, both toward the instruments and toward using them to accompany their creative dance movements.

The instruments shown in appendix B can be made by children from grades 2 to 6. In the process of making their own instruments, children learn to use a variety of tools and materials. Each child's instrument must make a sound that pleases him, his peers, and the teacher. The enjoyment children receive from creating their own percussion instruments varies; some enjoy making and decorating the instruments, whereas others simply like to hear their own musical accompaniment. Whatever the reasons, the classmade instruments shown in appendix B are easy and fun to construct and provide a reservoir of enjoyable and useful instruments.

Summary Review

Creative dance activities offer opportunities for self-expression through movement and serve as an effective medium for nonverbal communication. Creative dance activities emanate from a starting "theme," which is developed in conjunction with Laban's four elements of movement. Using the theme, action words are developed from Laban's four elements (body awareness, space awareness, effort, and relationships). The action words form the basic structure around which movements are created. That is, movement actions are created to represent the action words, and this forms the basis of the creative dance. To facilitate creativity, and to stimulate active participation among children, you can use a variety of stimuli when teaching creative dance. In a similar way, sound accompaniment, in the form of music, percussion instruments, or the teacher's voice, can catalyze creativity and active participation.

INDIVIDUAL *and* **GROUP** PROJECTS

1. Form small groups. Each group is assigned a theme and then plans a series of creative dance lessons around their theme. Each group uses their lesson plans to teach the other groups their creative dance activities.

2. View Videotape no. 4 (see appendix A) on teaching creative dance activities

and then debate, in small groups, the advantage of using Laban's four movement elements when teaching creative dance activities. Compare your views with those of the other groups.

3. Form small groups. Design assessment techniques and methods suitable for evaluating creative dance experiences. Share ideas between groups.

4. A feature of this text is the idea of teaching and enhancing academic skills and concepts through physical education activities. In small groups, discuss and create ideas to teach or enhance academic skills and concepts in language arts, social studies, mathematics, and science through creative dance activities. Consider evaluation methods. Share your ideas with the other groups.

5. Form small groups. Each group is assigned one of the following creative dance themes: (1) machines, (2) dinosaurs, (3) undersea creatures, (4) space monsters, (5) robots, (6) insects. Develop your allocated theme into a creative dance activity. Each group performs their creative dance and demonstrates how it involves academic concepts or skills that can be taught to children through the dance.

SELECTED READINGS

Benzwie, T. 1991. *A moving experience: Dance for lovers of children and the child within.* Reston, VA: AAHPERD.

Boorman, J. 1969. *Creative dance in the first three grades.* Don Mills, Ontario: Longmans Canada.

———. 1971. *Creative dance in grades four to six.* Don Mills, Ontario: Longmans Canada.

CAHPER. 1988. *Creative dance.* Ottawa, Ontario: CAHPER.

Fleming, G. A. 1976. *Creative rhythmic movement: Boys and girls dancing.* Englewood Cliffs, NJ: Prentice Hall.

———. 1990. *Children's dance.* Rev. ed. Reston, VA: AAHPERD.

Joyce, M. 1980. *First steps in teaching creative dance to children.* Palo Alto, CA: Mayfield.

Lewte, G. 1982. *No handicap to dance: Creative improvisation for people with and without disabilities.* London: Souvenir Press.

National Dance Association. 1990. *Guide to creative dance for young children.* Reston, VA: AAHPERD.

———. 1988. *Dance curricula guidelines.* Reston, VA: AAHPERD.

———. 1990. *Dance resource guide.* Reston, VA: AAHPERD.

Stinson, S. 1988. *Dance for young children: Finding the magic in movement.* Reston, VA: AAHPERD.

Wall, J., and N. Murray. 1994. *Children and movement.* 2d ed. Dubuque, IA: Wm. C. Brown.

Zurulnik, A., and J. Abeles. 1985. *Resource list for children's dance.* Michigan Dance Association, 300 Bailey St., Room 201, East Lansing, MI 48823.

APPENDIXES

APPENDIX A Videotape Series D: Teaching Elementary School Physical Education

Series D consists of five videotapes designed for use in preservice and in-service physical education programs for elementary school teachers. The first four videotapes describe class management techniques, organization of content, and teaching strategies. The fifth provides a comprehensive and graphic display of how the heart and circulatory system work.

Videotape No. 1: *Teaching Game Activities*

This videotape describes how game activities are organized and taught to children who fall within three developmental levels of motor ability. Suggestions relating to class organization, lesson plans, and the use of various direct and problem-solving teaching strategies are provided for each developmental level.

Videotape No. 2: *Teaching Gymnastic Activities*

Two contemporary types of gymnastic activities are currently being taught to elementary school children. *Teaching Gymnastic Activities* describes the similarities and differences in content and teaching strategies used to teach Educational and Olympic gymnastics. Ideas and suggestions are also provided on how to integrate these two approaches according to the interest and background of the children in each developmental level.

Videotape No. 3: *Teaching Folk Dance Activities*

Folk dance activities have traditionally been taught through a series of stages to allow children to learn each dance in an orderly and progressive manner. This videotape illustrates how children in the primary and intermediate grades first learn how to keep time to a music accompaniment, as well as the meaning of a measure, an accent, tempo, and a musical phrase. From here, scenes illustrate how children learn singing games, folk dances, and square dances through a progressive series of steps. The latter part of this videotape illustrates how young and older children learn to modify the dances they have learned by adding new steps, directions, and movement patterns.

Videotape No. 4: *Teaching Creative Dance Activities*

Creative dance activities can be taught through direct and problem-solving methods and by using a variety of stimuli such as photographs, stories, poems, and visual presentations. This videotape discusses the value and importance of a creative dance program and describes the basic steps that are followed when guiding young children to interpret ideas and feelings through creative dance activities. Laban's elements of movement are stressed throughout this videotape, as are the limitation, or problem-solving, methods of teaching.

Videotape No. 5: *How Your Heart and Circulatory System Work*

This videotape is designed for upper elementary school children. It describes how the heart and circulation work, explains the function of blood, describes how to monitor heart rate and blood pressure. The videotape also illustrates how various factors such as exercise, fear, and excitement affect the heart rate. The latter section of the tape briefly explains various diseases and disorders of the heart.

1. **Skipping Ropes**
2. **Horizontal Bar**
3. **Wands**
4. **Vaulting Box**
5. **Jumping Boxes**
6. **Plastic Hurdles**
7. **Jumping Pit**
8. **All-Purpose Game Bat**
9. **Sand Blocks**
10. **Tambourines**
11. **Wooden Nail Keg Drum**
12. **Metal Drum**
13. **Plastic Plant Pot Drum**
14. **Rattlers**
15. **Jingle Bats, Bands, Pin-Ons, and Sticks**
16. **Coat Hanger Racquets**
17. **Beanbags**
18. **Markers and Scoops**
19. **Hoops**
20. **Bowling Pins**

1. Skipping Ropes

To Cut Ropes

1. Measure the desired length of rope.
2. Wrap tape around the rope 5 inches above and below the cut mark (plastic tape) preferred, adhesive acceptable).
3. Place rope on small wooden block and cut rope in middle of taped area.

To Store Ropes

1. Since there may be three or four different lengths of rope, dip the ends of the ropes in different colors of paint to represent short, medium, and long lengths. (Dip about 6 inches.)
2. A simple way to store ropes is across or over a bar as shown. The standard can be of any design, with the top bar about 4 feet off the floor.

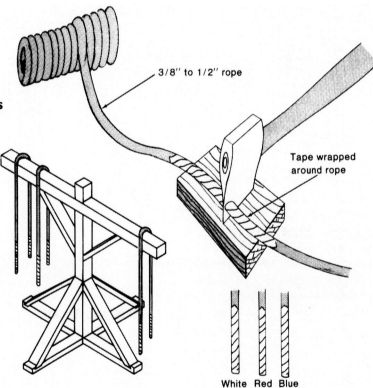

3/8″ to 1/2″ rope

Tape wrapped around rope

White Red Blue

2. Horizontal Bar

General Features

The horizontal bar can be made for an approximate cost of fifteen to twenty dollars. It is designed for efficient assemblage and storage. The bolt, as shown in detail B, prevents the bar from rotating while stunts are being performed. The bar is held firmly to the upright standard with a fixed 2 3/4-inch washer on the inside and a washer and bolt as shown in detail D. For efficient storage, the side support shown in detail A may be drawn upward.

Designed by Bill Bressler
Drawn by Gary Sciuchetti

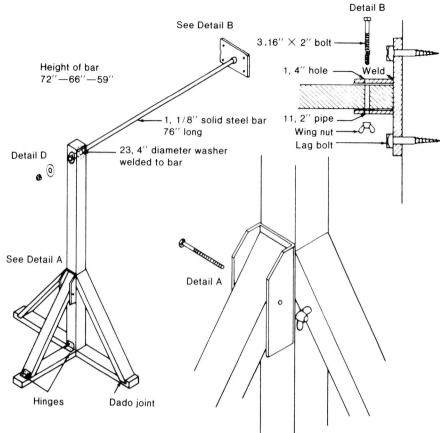

See Detail B

Height of bar
72″—66″—59″

Detail D

1, 1/8″ solid steel bar
76″ long

23, 4″ diameter washer
welded to bar

See Detail A

Hinges   Dado joint

Detail B

3,16″ × 2″ bolt

1, 4″ hole   Weld

11, 2″ pipe
Wing nut
Lag bolt

Detail A

3. Wands

General Information

A set of wands (see chapter 26 for appropriate lengths) may be made from old broomsticks. Cut off each broomstick at the desired length and round both ends. Dip the end of each set of wands in different colors of paint to facilitate each selection.

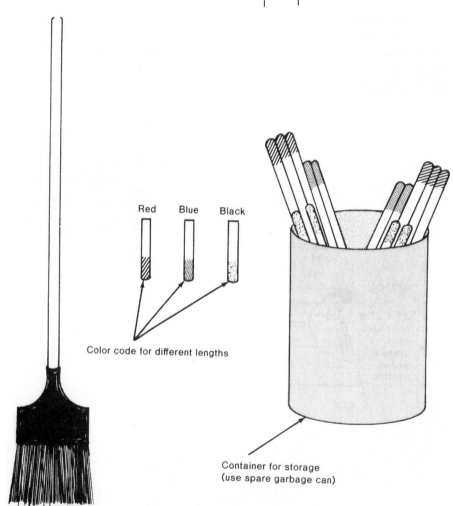

Red   Blue   Black

Color code for different lengths

Container for storage
(use spare garbage can)

4. Vaulting Box

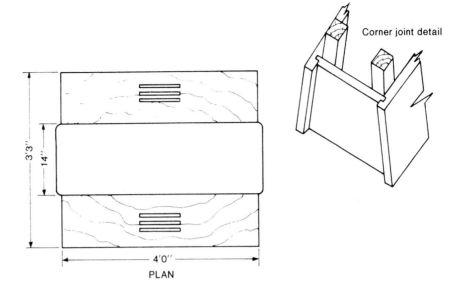

Corner joint detail

3'3"
14"
4'0"

PLAN

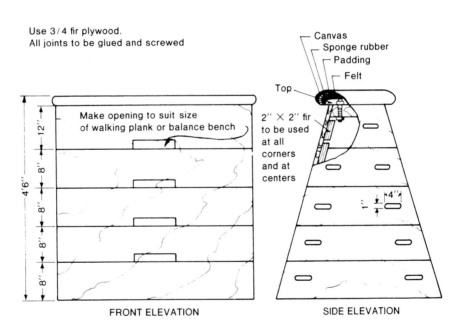

Use 3/4 fir plywood.
All joints to be glued and screwed

Canvas
Sponge rubber
Padding
Felt

Top

Make opening to suit size
of walking plank or balance bench

2" × 2" fir
to be used
at all
corners
and at
centers

4'6"
12"
8"
8"
8"
8"

1"   4"

FRONT ELEVATION

SIDE ELEVATION

Finish: Wiped white rez stain-shellacked and varnished

5. Jumping Boxes

General Features

The jumping boxes shown here can be made for approximately fifty dollars, depending on the number of boxes and the size of each. A minimum of three for each set is recommended. *Do not* cover top with rubber matting or cloth material. Sand all corners and, if desired, paint or varnish.

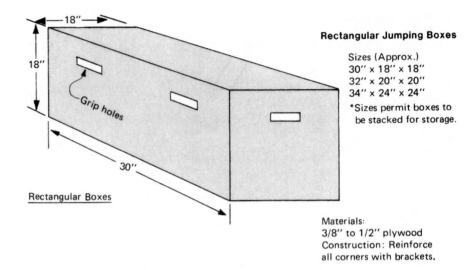

18"

18"

Grip holes

30"

Rectangular Boxes

Rectangular Jumping Boxes

Sizes (Approx.)
30" x 18" x 18"
32" x 20" x 20"
34" x 24" x 24"
*Sizes permit boxes to be stacked for storage.

Materials:
3/8" to 1/2" plywood
Construction: Reinforce all corners with brackets.

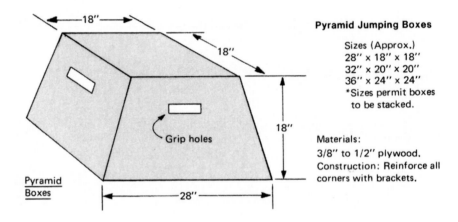

18"

18"

18"

Grip holes

18"

Pyramid Boxes

28"

Pyramid Jumping Boxes

Sizes (Approx.)
28" x 18" x 18"
32" x 20" x 20"
36" x 24" x 24"
*Sizes permit boxes to be stacked.

Materials:
3/8" to 1/2" plywood.
Construction: Reinforce all corners with brackets.

6. Plastic Hurdles

Materials

1. 1-inch plastic pipe
2. 90-degree elbow fittings
3. Velcro strips
4. Wood or webbed crossbar

How to Make

1. Cut two 29-inch, two 14-inch, and one 28-inch pieces of plastic hose.
2. Insert glue in ends of elbows, then insert pieces of plastic hose as shown in the diagram.
3. Attach velcro strips on crossbar and at different heights on the vertical posts.

Velcro

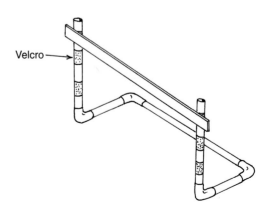

7. Jumping Pit

How to Make

Rubber tubes are placed on the ground, as shown in the diagram, and tied together. A tumbling mat is then placed on top of the tubes. This provides a safe and comfortable landing surface. The jumping pit can be used indoors or outdoors.

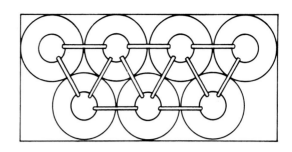

8. All-Purpose Game Bat

Materials

1. ¼-inch good quality plywood
2. ½-inch fir strips
3. Sandpaper and glue

How to Make

1. Cut out circular bat and paddle handles.
2. Sand surfaces and round edges.
3. Glue handles.
4. Varnish or paint surfaces.
5. Tape handles for extra strength and better gripping surface.

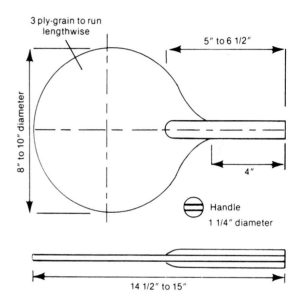

9. Sand Blocks

Materials

1. Two blocks of wood (approx. 4 inches by 6 inches by 1 inch)
2. Sandpaper or emery paper (different grades)
3. Thumbtacks, glue, or screws
4. Thread spools or knobs

How to Make

1. Cut blocks of wood.
2. Sand surfaces and round edges.
3. Glue or screw on handle.
4. Cover bottom surface with sandpaper and tack each end. Use different grades of sandpaper or emery paper to make different sounds.
5. Decorate as desired.

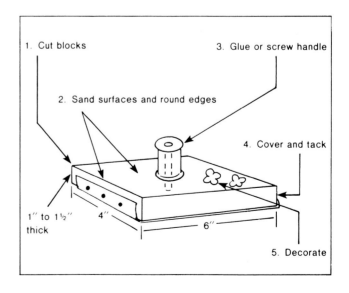

10. Tambourines

Materials

1. *Pie plate tambourine:* Old pie plate, safety pins, bells or strings, and bottle caps or roofing discs
2. *Ping-pong bat tambourine:* Old table tennis bat, nails and bottle caps, or roofing discs
3. *Stick tambourine:* Stick (6 inches by 1½ inches by ¾ inch) and bottle caps or roofing discs

How to Make a Pie Plate Tambourine

1. Make nail holes around outer edge of pie plate. Sand rough side of nail hole.
2. Attach safety pin and bell to each hole, or attach string and bottle caps (two per string) to teach hole.
3. Decorate as desired.

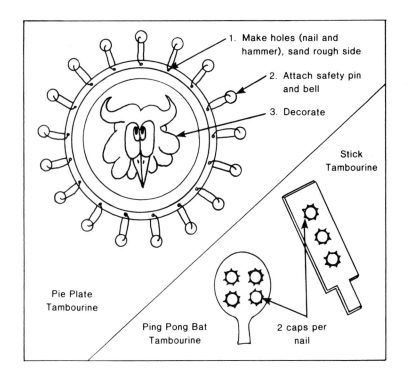

1. Make holes (nail and hammer), sand rough side
2. Attach safety pin and bell
3. Decorate

Stick Tambourine

Pie Plate Tambourine

Ping Pong Bat Tambourine

2 caps per nail

11. Wooden Nail Keg Drum

Materials

1. Nail keg (or any wooden container that has not been waterproofed or sealed)
2. Medium and fine sandpaper
3. Tacks (upholstery tacks)
4. Paints
5. Floor seal
6. Muslin, nitrate solution

How to Make

1. Sand with medium, then fine sandpaper.
2. Paint outside surface of keg with floor seal. Add a second coat after twenty-four hours.
3. Apply one coat of flat white paint. (If still darkish, add another coat after twenty-four hours.)
4. Decorate keg with bright enamel paints.
5. Cut muslin (or sailcloth) about 2 inches larger than top of nail keg.
6. Place muslin on top, drawing evenly down sides, and place thumbtacks 1 inch below top rim.
7. Start above tacks and wind colored yarn around keg and work down to cover ends of muslin. Tuck yarn under last row and tie.
8. Apply five or six coats of nitrate solution to muslin and yarn. Allow each coat to dry thoroughly.

NOTE: *Drum beaters:* A drum stick can be made by wrapping a soft cloth (cotton, wool) around end of dowel. Cover with leather, muslin, or sailcloth, and wrap with heavy cord.

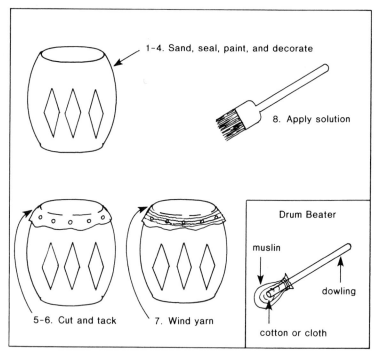

1-4. Sand, seal, paint, and decorate

8. Apply solution

5-6. Cut and tack

7. Wind yarn

Drum Beater

muslin

dowling

cotton or cloth

12. Metal Drum

Materials

1. Metal can (paint, coffee, etc.)
2. Inner tubing or rubber sheeting
3. Wire and yarn
4. Paints

How to Make

1. Remove top and bottom lids; remove any paper and soak to dissolve dirt and/or glue.
2. Apply one or two coats of flat white paint, then decorate with bright enamel paint (keep decoration toward the middle, as the outside 2 inches will be covered with tubing).
3. Cut two rubber sheets 2 inches larger than opening. Puncture holes 1 inch in from outer edge and about 2 inches apart. Lace twine through holes.
4. Place first sheet over top end and wrap twine 1 inch below top of rim. Repeat on bottom.
5. Pull top and bottom laces tight and tie.
6. Tie a twine to top lace, then to bottom, and zigzag lace around drum. This will hold both ends tight.

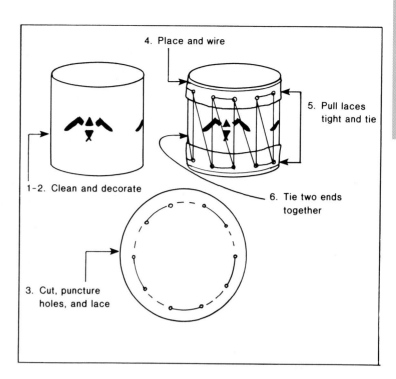

13. Plastic Plant Pot Drum

Materials

1. Plastic plant pots of various sizes
2. Masking tape
3. Muslin or sailcloth
4. Paint and yarn

How to Make

1. Seal drain holes with masking tape. Apply two or three strips over each hole.
2. Apply one or two coats of flat white paint.
3. Cut a circle of muslin to cover top plus sides and 1 inch under bottom edge.
4. Cut out triangles evenly spaced around circumference of cloth circle. Fold remaining ends down ½ inch and sew to form ½-inch hem open at both ends.
5. Lay cloth over top, down sides, and under bottom edge. Lace heavy twine through hems of the ends, pull, secure, and tie.
6. Wrap yarn around upper edge and just below vertical lines.
7. Apply five or six coats of nitrate solution to all muslin and yarn. Allow each coat to dry thoroughly.
8. Decorate as desired with enamel paint.

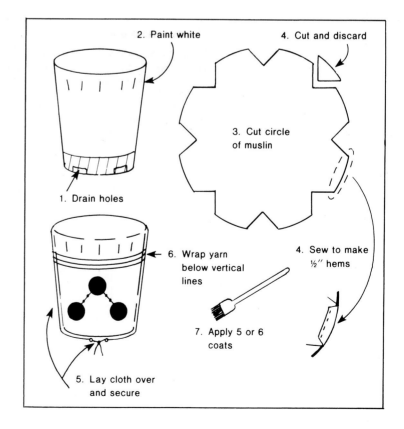

14. Rattlers

Materials

A rattler can be made from any container that can be easily sealed and that permits a variety of material to move freely inside the container:

1. A tennis ball container with rice or dried peas
2. A wooden matchbox with peas, rice, or sand
3. A plastic vinegar bottle with marbles or nuts with shells on
4. Plastic tubing (1½-inch) with seeds

NOTE: The rattling sound of any container is determined by a combination of the size, shape, and material of the container combined with the nature of the rattling material. Experiment with different materials in each container to find the most appealing sound.

How to Make

1. Where necessary, clean container and remove all labels.
2. Place materials inside and seal opening. For tubes, cover ends with plastic or cloth and wrap with masking tape.
3. Decorate with paper, string, or paint.

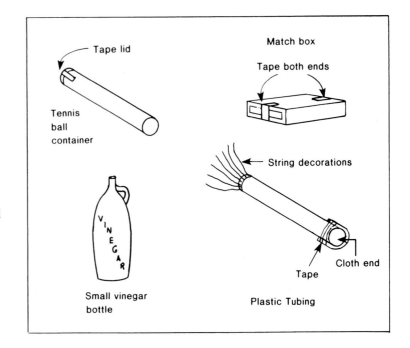

15. Jingle Bats, Bands, Pin-Ons, and Sticks

Materials

1. *Jingle bats:* Coat hanger, tongue depressors masking tape, six to eight bells, string
2. *Jingle bands:* 6- to 8-inch cloth bands, four or five bells, string
3. *Jingle pins:* Bells in sets of three or four, string, safety pin
4. *Jingle sticks:* 8-inch stick, two circle-head screws, six bells, string

How to Make

See diagrams and modify each type of jingle instrument to the available materials and creative abilities of the children.

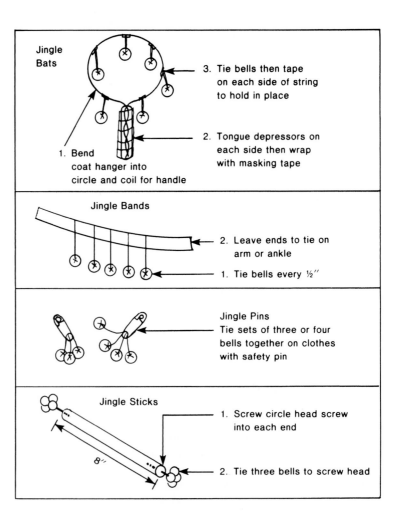

16. Coat Hanger Racquets

Materials
1. Coat hangers
2. Nylon hose
3. Masking tape

How to Make
1. Straighten the hanger hook.
2. Bend hanger into a diamond shape.
3. Slide hanger into the hose, pull tightly, and twist loose ends around the handle.
4. Tape handle, bend half of the handle back, and retape whole handle.

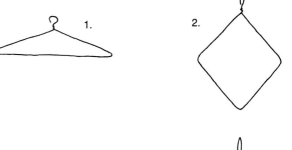

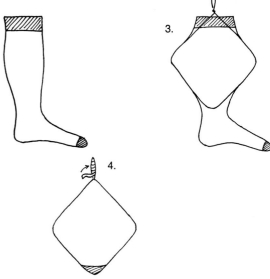

17. Beanbags

Materials
1. Scrap cloth, such as denim or canvas
2. Beans

How to Make
1. Cut 6 ½-inch squares.
2. Sew up three sides.
3. Fill beanbag with beans (use a commercial beanbag to determine the amount to put into each bag).
4. Sew up fourth side.

Beanbag

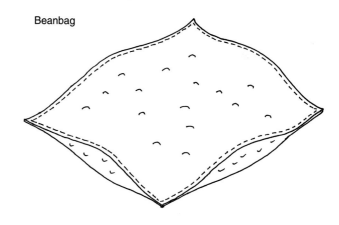

18. Markers and Scoops

Materials

1. One-gallon plastic jugs
2. Scissors or carpet knife
3. Sandpaper

How to Make

1. *For field markers*
   a. Fill one-third of jug with sand.
   b. Place different color tapes on markers or paint for use as field or goal markers.
2. *For scoops*
   a. Trace cutting line with marking pencil or pen.
   b. Cut off lower section and sandpaper edges.

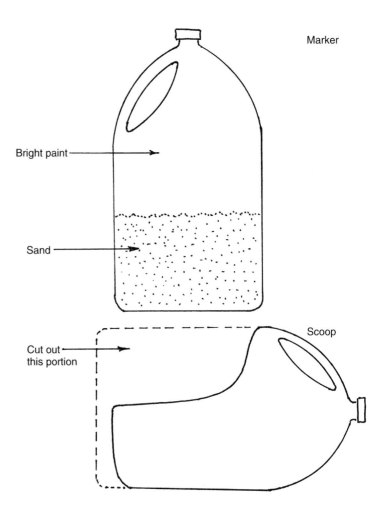

19. Hoops

Materials

1. ½-inch plastic water pipe
2. ½-inch doweling
3. Tacks or staples
4. Glue

How to Make

Cut hose into 7-foot, 10-inch sections (makes 30-inch hoops).
2. Cut 3″ pieces of doweling.
3. Place glue inside both ends of the hose.
4. Insert 3-inch doweling and staple or tack each end to the doweling.
5. Tape over doweling area of the hose.

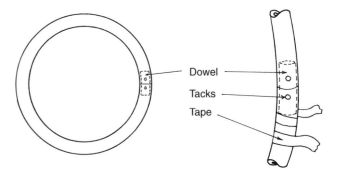

20. Bowling Pins

Materials
1. Discarded tenpin bowling pins (contact your local bowling alley for used pins)
2. Saw and sandpaper
3. Paint

How to Make
1. Cut off lower two inches of the pin and sandpaper rough edges.
2. Paint and/or number each pin.

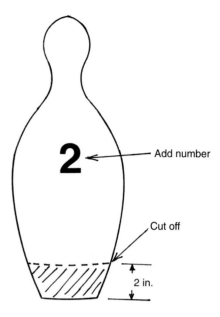

Add number

Cut off

2 in.

A PPENDIX C

Apparatus, Equipment, and Supply Companies

A buyers guide is published annually by the American Alliance for Health, Physical Education, Recreation and Dance (AAHPERD). The buyers guide includes an alphabetical listing of the latest products and services available in health, fitness, leisure, sport, dance, and physical education. This is one of the most comprehensive listings of North American companies and corporations that manufacture and produce apparatus, equipment, and supplies for physical education use. The buyers guide and further information can be obtained from:

AAHPERD
1900 Association Drive
Reston, VA 22091
1–800–213–7193
Internet address: http://www.aahperd.org
The following manufacturers provide a variety of equipment and supplies appropriate for elementary school physical education:

Bill Fritz Sports Corporation
PO Box 860
Cary, NC 27512
1–919–362–1748
Fax 1–919–362–1750
Physical education and sports supply and equipment company

Cambridge Educational
PO Box 2153
Charleston, WV 25328–2153
1–800–468–4227
Fax 1–304–744–9351
Videos, posters, books, CD-ROMs, and software for physical education, health, nutrition, and substance abuse

Centaur Products Inc.
6855 Antrim Avenue
Burnaby, BC, Canada V5J 4M5
1–604–430–3088
General apparatus and equipment (climbing frames, etc.)

Fisher
PO Box 1985
Salisbury, NC 28145
1–800–438–6028
Fax 1–704–637–7941
Exercise mats, folding mats, landing mats, track and field equipment

Flaghouse Inc
150 North MacQuesten Parkway
Mt. Vernon, NY 10550
1–800–793–7900
Fax 1–914–699–2961
Distributer of athletic, physical education, and recreation products for ages 8 to adult and supplier of products for special populations

Gerstung Gym-Thing Inc.
1400 Coppermine Terrace
Baltimore, MD 21209–2012
1–800–922–3575
Fax 1–410–337–0471
Inovative Movement Education and rhythmic gymnastic equipment

JAY Distributors
PO Box 191332
Dallas, TX 75219
1–800–793–6843
CDs, records, tapes, videos, and variable-speed CD players

Northern Athletic
4289–95 Street
Edmonton, Alberta, Canada T6E 5R6
1–403–450–0976
Fax 1–406–450–0982
Full range of equipment (large and small apparatus) and sporting goods

Porter Athletic Equipment Co.
2500 S. 25th Avenue
PO Box 2500
Broadview, IL 60153
1–708–338–2000
Fax 1–708–338–2060
Gymnastic and major games apparatus

Rhythms Productions/Tom Thumb Music
PO Box 34485
Los Angeles, CA 90034–0485
1–310–836–4678
Fax 1–310–837–1534
Learning-through-movement records and cassettes for multicultural, fitness, folk, rhythms, and dance—all ages

Sportime
One Sportime Way
Atlanta, GA 30340–1402
1–800–444–5700
1–404–449–5700
Fax 1–800–845–1535
General apparatus and equipment

The Lloyd Shaw Foundation
2924 Hickory Court
Manhattan, KS 66503
1–913–539–6306
Music and instructions for folk and square dances, K–6

US Games Inc.
PO Box 117028
Carrollton, TX 75011–7028
1–800–327–0484
Fax 1–800–899–0149
Small equipment and parachutes

Wolverine Sports
745 State Circle
Ann Arbor, MI 48108
1–313–761–5690
Fax 1–313–761–8711
General apparatus and equipment

APPENDIX **D** Using Technology to Enhance Your Physical Education Program

Advances in technology have created a variety of opportunities for teachers to enhance and expand their physical education programs. Computer programs, ideas shared on the "information highway" (Internet), electronic mail connections (e-mail), compact discs (CD-ROM), and inexpensive heart-rate monitors are just a few of the technological advances that impact on physical education. However, due to the rapid advances being made in the electronics and computer area, it is not possible to consider here all areas of technology that currently exist or that might exist in the near future. The purpose of this short review is to provide ideas and suggestions, user-friendly information, and resource information that will help teachers become involved with and more confident about technological opportunities in the area of physical education.

The first section provides a brief overview of the "information highway," or the Internet, and explains basic terms. A glossary of terms appears at the end of this appendix. Technological opportunities are then discussed with regard to specific chapters in the text.

Information Highway

Schools across North America have computers that are interconnected through a network (the Internet) that allows students and staff to openly share information with other connected users of this computer network (who are from all over the world). This open information network has come to be known as the "information highway." The internetwork of connections that link this giant network of computers together can be viewed as a giant spider web. Hence, the term *World Wide Web* is used to describe the Internet's construction. The Internet provides access to a vast array of information on a vast array of topics. To help identify and locate a specific area or topic of information on the web, a "web browser" program is used. One method of identifying and sharing information on a common topic is by means of a "newsgroup." To locate and access a newsgroup, an Internet user can use a web browser such as Netscape Navigator, Newswatcher, or Microsoft Explorer and do a search for, for example, "newsgroups K–12 physical education." This will locate newsgroups (people and information). The teacher can subscribe to these, post questions, respond to questions, share ideas, conduct surveys, or simply read about what is current or what concerns teachers of physical education.

Electronic Mail (E-Mail)

Electronic mail allows teachers to be contacted through their computer's electronic mail address. Teachers can also contact others via their e-mail addresses. Anyone with an e-mail address can subscribe through the Internet to "Listserv." Listserv provides a means of sharing ideas and discussing issues related to specific topics. Again, a search for listservs related to physical education can be conducted from a web browser, and then the listservs can be subscribed to through e-mail. However, it is advisable that you find out how much mail the listserv delivers on a daily basis. Some listservs deliver up to a hundred messages a day.

Shareware and Freeware

Most computer software programs are purchased for personal use. However, a large number of programs are available as "shareware" and "freeware." Shareware is software that the user tries out for a specified period of time; if you decide to keep the software, you send a small payment to its creator. Freeware is software that is free. Shareware and freeware can be downloaded from many sites on the Internet.

Ideas to Incorporate Technology into the Physical Education Program

Once teachers become familiar with the Internet and the use of other modern technologies, they soon see that the number of possible ways to incorporate technology into the physical education program is limitless. The ideas presented here are merely intended to stimulate teachers' creativity in enriching their physical education programs.

Chapter 1: Elementary School Physical Education

The latest textbooks, resources, position statements, curriculum materials, etc., can easily be learned about through newsgroups on the Internet. Curriculum resources and other information can be accessed from professional associations such as AAHPERD and CAHPERD.

Students might want to start their own newsgroup and share ideas and physical education experiences with other students around the world. A student-centered physical education newsgroup can be a very valuable experience. However, newsgroup postings are not edited, so student participation on an adult newsgroup should be carefully monitored.

Chapter 2: Children and Activity

There is a software program available to measure body mass index. Refer to the resource section at the end of this appendix for the program *Body Mass Index,* available as shareware.

Logs of anecdotal records could be kept on the computer to help determine whether students are operating at the appropriate developmental level. The computer log can be included in the student's portfolio or used in other reporting methods.

Chapter 3: Learning Motor Skills

Computerized technology can be very useful in illustrating mechanical principles of movement to children. For instance, the program Life Forms can be used to demonstrate that the amount of force exerted affects the speed of an object. It also can illustrate the importance of control when using implements to strike an object, and it can demonstrate the corresponding level of difficulty associated with the length of the implement. This approach provides declarative knowledge that will be combined with procedural knowledge gained through physical practices.

Chapter 4: Using Teaching Strategies and Techniques

The latest physical education textbooks, resource materials, etc., can easily be learned about through newsgroups and web sites on the Internet. Teaching materials and other information can be accessed from professional associations such as AAHPERD and CAHPERD.

Chapter 5: Movement Concepts and Skills

Laban's movement concepts are used as a basis for identifying themes in physical education lessons and units of study. The use of a thesaurus in a word-processing program can provide teachers and students with limitless options for theme-based work. For example, a theme such as "strong and light" might become "forceful and fine-touch" or "robust and delicate," not only expanding the children's vocabulary but also providing opportunities to enrich their movement quality.

Chapter 6: Locomotor, Nonlocomotor, and Manipulative Skills

Videotapes of appropriate movement patterns can be made available to students and set up as a learning center or used for teaching in the classroom. Students who view the proper form for running, for instance, have a greater chance of self-correcting than students who have not had proper instruction and models. Inappropriate techniques can be carried into adulthood, increasing the risk of injury and other adverse affects. Correct demonstrations can be achieved through these videotaped movements.

Chapter 7: Learning about the Human Body and Wellness

There is now a wide selection of devices available for measuring and recording heart rate. Unfortunately, student reliability in measuring a heart rate is very low, so it might be helpful to use specialized equipment when measuring resting and active heart rates, given the considerable accuracy required. Parent volunteers might also be helpful for the purpose. Further information on measuring devices such as heart rate monitors can be obtained through AAHPERD and CAHPERD.

Chapter 8: Assessing and Improving Physical Fitness

A variety of available software programs demonstrate the efficiency of the cardiovascular system. This will help the students understand how their bodies work and how exercise helps the system become more efficient. See, for example, the CD-ROM entitled *The Heart: A Virtual Exploration,* which is referenced below under CD-Rom resources.

There are many devices available for testing and recording physical fitness. Several are discussed in chapter 8, and further references can be found in the resource section. Laser and infrared technology have altered the way body fat is measured. A field trip to a local fitness facility or a college or university fitness center might provide children with an opportunity to view such technology.

Chapter 9: Planning the Instructional Program

In planning lessons and units, the teacher can be greatly aided through the use of a word-processing program. Unit plans can be outlined and then saved as a "stationary pad" so the basic format is there for each unit that is planned. The same format could be used in lesson planning where the teacher has a basic outline to work from (see the example on the next page).

Planning lessons with the use of a word processor allows for easy modification when necessary and provides a quick way for the teacher to monitor what was taught and when the lesson or unit took place.

Chapter 10: Organizing Personnel, Facilities, and Equipment

Scheduling can be done with ease with a variety of software programs. Many of these are available as shareware or freeware and can be downloaded from the Internet (refer to the resources section for more information). However, URLs (Uniform Resource Locations—Internet addresses) change frequently, so if these are unavailable you might find what you are looking for by conducting a search using any of the available Internet "search engines."

Inventory can be taken very logically with the use of a computer-based log. The numbers and condition of supplies can be tracked, which will aid in the ordering process. A computer log is also very easy to modify as the inventory changes from year to year.

Chapter 11: Selecting Evaluative Methods and Techniques

Criterion-referenced tests can be developed on the computer and individualized for each student. A spreadsheet can be used to develop checklists and rating scales. Remember that evaluation should always relate to the objectives of the program, unit, and individual lessons, so the development of checklists and rating scales would correspond with those objectives. A variety of checklists are provided in chapter 6 and throughout the text.

Lesson Plan

Grade Level and Unit No.:

Unit Objectives:

Lesson No.:

Lesson Objectives:

Academic Concepts and Skills:

(Teach or Reinforce)

Equipment:

Theme and Subtheme:

Content	Teaching Strategy/Organization
Entry Activity:	
(3 mins)	
Part 1: (Set)	
Introductory Activity:	
(3–5 mins)	
Part 2: (Body)	
Skill/Concept Development:	
(10–15 mins)	
Part 3: (Closure)	
Culminating Activity:	
(5 mins)	
Evaluation:	
Student/Lesson/Unit:	
Self-Reflection:	

Computerized personal activity logs (PALs) can be kept by students who have easy access to computers. The advantage of recording this information on computer rather than on paper is that it provides continuous records that can accompany children throughout their school years. If goal setting has resulted in quantitative data, then averages can be calculated and personal bests can be highlighted and printed out. Many programs allow children to easily chart their progress with graphs, and they can save these on their personal disks. Bar graphs display levels of progress at a glance. When students log their own results, they develop their computer and math skills and learn to take responsibility for their own psychomotor achievement. This also provides the teacher with important evaluative information, as it provides accurate data on a student's progress.

The teacher may want to use a database system for maintaining anecdotal records of the students' work. The database can be used to identify developmentally appropriate activities and for assessment and evaluation purposes.

Videotaping student performance and activity is a very useful tool for providing concrete information to parents and students as to their level of competence and achievements.

Chapter 12: Designing Extraclass Programs

The school's database can be very useful in planning the intramural or extracurricular program. With each student's name on file, heterogeneous groupings can be made quickly and efficiently by the school's office personnel or other knowledgeable staff members.

A word-processing program can be used to make score sheets, keep track of team scores and attendance, and supply information sheets and rules for referees and teacher supervisors.

These items can be stored on disk and would require only minor changes from year to year.

Chapter 13: Integrating Children with Special Needs

Children with special needs can be included in computer centers to gain important declarative knowledge (strategies, rules, etc.). Metal coverplates are available for computer keyboards to assist students who do not have the dexterity to hit only one key at a time.

Motorized wheelchairs have allowed many children to become more independent. This also allows the teacher to be more inclusive in the instructional approach. Children in wheelchairs can fully participate in physical education activities when the teacher sets out clear guidelines and sensitizes the other students to the special considerations involved in moving near a wheelchair.

Chapters 14 and 15: Academic Concepts and Skills/Classroom Activities

Through newsgroups on the Internet, teachers can share resources and ideas on successful lessons and topics that relate to academic concepts and skills, and classroom activities. Computers can be used in conjunction with classroom physical activity in a variety of ways. For example, the spelling relay and exercise activity can be accommodated in the classroom while academic concepts and skills are taught.

Spelling Relays (Levels II–III)

Formation Six or seven teams of 3 or 4
Equipment One computer per team
Players Class
Academic concepts Language arts—Spelling,
Physical education outcomes Team building, calisthenic exercising

Teams gather at the front of the room. Each team is allocated a computer at the back of the room. The teams are provided with a topic, theme, or beginning letter. Team members must then relay-race to the computer and correctly spell as many words as they can in a given time. Then they return to their team and join the others in performing calisthenics while awaiting their turns. Students can correct and formulate spelling lists following the relay race. This activity combines speed, fitness, academic competence, keyboarding skills, and team building.

Chapter 16: Locomotor and Manipulative Games

Technology can be used to expand the visual schema and declarative knowledge base associated with locomotor and manipulative game skills. A variety of available software programs can assist in this area (e.g., Life Forms). Illustrations of the different types of lever systems, the effects of the length of a lever, the effects of gravity, throwing trajectory angle, and other biomechanical principles can all be viewed on computer. Students' skill acquisition and performance will improve if they can see and visualize the skills and desired outcomes.

Chapter 17: Cooperative Games and Learning Activities

The Internet can be an excellent resource for building a repertoire of cooperative games from around the world. Contacts made through a newsgroup or e-mail might provide the most up-to-date sources of games that are being played by children around the world.

Chapters 18–23: Major Games

A variety of CD-ROM discs relate to major games played in North America and around the world. Also, there are a number of web sites on the Internet that deal with major sports. For example, through the Sport Information Resource Centre (SIRC), the BASEBALL file is available. This covers published material on all aspects of the game from popular literature to scientific studies.

Chapter 24: Track and Field and Cross-Country Activities

Students might want to track their progress by means of a spreadsheet on which they enter their individual performances in a variety of events. This will also enable them to calculate their averages and track their personal best for each event. Appropriate goal setting can also take place.

Planning the school track and field, sports, or activity day is a highly organizational endeavor, for which the school's database can be very useful. Each student's name is on file, so heterogeneous groupings can be made by the school's office personnel or other knowledgeable staff members. This system might also be useful for individual or team scorecards, name tags, and progress logs. Results can be tallied by means of a computer or laptop kept outside during the event.

Videotaping the students in action is an excellent way of providing coaching tips and pointing out techniques that require modification or correction. Understanding the benefit of a forward lean while running might become more embodied by a child who can visually detect the difference between incorrect and proper form.

Chapters 25–27: Gymnastic Activities

The latest gymnastics textbooks, resource materials, etc., can easily be discussed and learned about through newsgroups and web sites on the Internet. Teaching materials and other information can also be accessed at the web sites of professional associations such as AAHPERD and CAHPERD. Information on the latest gymnastic equipment and apparatus is also available on the Internet.

Chapter 28: Rhythmic and Movement Activities

A tape or CD player with adjustable speed is a very useful tool for teaching dance. Rhythm activities can be made progressively more difficult by beginning at a slower tempo (largo) and increasing to a faster tempo (presto). The tempo of a musical selection can be measured with a metronome or by counting the number of beats per second with the use of a stopwatch or a watch with a second hand.

Chapter 29: Traditional and Contemporary Dances

Again the tape or CD player with adjustable speed is an asset to the teacher of dance. Being able to adjust the speed as students master the steps of a folk dance will provide the students with feelings of success as they progress through the dance. If however, this advanced technology is unavailable in the school, the teacher might also provide varied selections of music that gradually increase in tempo. Keep in mind that the tempo is the number of beats per second.

Chapter 30: Creative Dance Activities

Technology can provide interesting stimuli for creative dance. Something as basic as an overhead projector can provide the basis for shadow dancing. Colored tissue paper placed on top will create a variety of moods. Water, oil, food coloring, etc., can be added to a glass pie or cake plate placed on top of the overhead to create various effects. Simply use eye droppers to add food coloring, shampoo, oil, and so on to create a moving image on the screen or wall. Homemade slides also can provide an interesting atmosphere.

Where an overhead computer palette or projector is available, slide shows can be prepared on computer disks by the students and compiled as a backdrop for their dance sequence. Story can be integrated in the process of developing the dance.

Lighting can be very effective in setting the mood in many dance explorations. Strobe lights and black lights provide effective means of dramatic intonations. Handheld neon or glow-in-the-dark items can also provide interesting effects in a creative dance.

With the use of a computer drawing program, students at developmental level III would be able to create movement patterns and action emphasis cards for use in their dance creations. These could be stored on their disks and could be used in different combinations for other creative dance units.

Shareware Physical Education Resources

This section contains downloadable shareware physical education resources. The shareware is available on various platforms and can be accessed through the web site http://search.shareware.com.

Aerosoft Fitness Log 3.0

May 06, 1995—184 K DOS
Keeps track of your aerobic activity.

Body Mass Index

March 21, 1993—7 K MAC
Calculates body mass index given a person's height and weight.

ErgoMinder Demo

August 08, 1995—335 K MAC
Fully functional demo but with only four ergonomic exercises (full version has sixteen); gives friendly reminders with exercises (demonstrated by the Ergo-Dudes) for your ergonomic comfort and health.

Exercise Font Size 24

March 27, 1991—82 K MAC
Based on the very old photographs (late 1800s) by Muxbridge of human body studies. This font has human figures jumping, walking, flipping, and so on.

Exercise Log

April 22, 1995—297 K MAC
Stores information about each workout you do in an unlimited number of sports or activities.

Sport Specific Fitness Cards

January 03, 1996—1 K
Handy exercise cards.

CD-ROM Resources

This section is designed to point students and teachers to information about fitness, lifestyle, and health that is available on CD-ROM.

The Heart: A Virtual Exploration

http://sln.fi.edu/biosci/heart.html
Explore the makings of the heart and learn how to take care of it through exercise.

Life Forms

ftp://fas.sfu.ca/pub/cs/graphics/lifeforms/
Life Forms allows you to create movement for multiple articulated figures, particularly realistic movement for human figures. Movement sequences can be used in animations, dance choreography, games, multimedia titles, sports, movement education, space visualization, and human motion studies. Designed to be easy to use, Life Forms is also powerful enough to produce sophisticated results in a minimum amount of time compared to other animation systems.

CD-ROM Outlet
(http://www.shoplet.com/cdrom/health.html)

Following are some of the programs that can be ordered from this site.

3D Body Adventure by Knowledge Adventure Inc.;

$35.95 (Prod # EDT44779). Take an adventurous travel through the human body and all its parts. Students learn anatomy, medicine, nutrition, diseases, biology, and reproduction. Windows 95, 3.1, and Mac compatible. 3D body adventure CD-ROM hybrid knowledge adventure. (MAC/WIN CD-ROM)

Active Trainer by Lasermedia Inc.; $45.95

(Prod # SHP47050). An interactive personal trainer on a Mac/Windows CD-ROM, sold as a complete fitness kit with a tape measure and skinfold caliper. Starts with a video-guided fitness test using the items in the kit. Based on the user's test results and personal goals, Active Trainer develops a customized fitness program and gives personal advice from a database of over 300 videos. (MAC/WIN CD-ROM)

Health Powerpak by Softkey Budget; $19.95

(Prod # MED44015). Explore the wonders of the human body with Bodyworks Voyager. Learn the specifics of the human heart with Smart Heart. Also serves as a medical and health reference tool. (IBM CD-ROM)

Mayo Clinic Health Encyclopedia by IVI Publishing;

$63.95 (Prod # MED46706). Mayo Clinic Health Encyclopedia has valuable health care information with features that make it easy to use. This personal health library includes: Mayo Clinic: Family Health Book CD-ROM; Mayo Clinic: The Total Heart CD-ROM; Mayo Clinic: Family Pharmacist CD-ROM; and Mayo Clinic:

Sports, Health & Fitness CD-ROM. Features include easy-to-use format, videos, and CD-ROM. (IBM CD-ROM)

Mayo Clinic Sport Health by IVI Publishing; $42.95

(Prod # MED40044). A very comprehensive fitness resource. Includes information on general fitness, anatomy and physiology, nutrition, exercise, injury prevention and management, choosing equipment, sports psychology, and personal trainers. Requires: PC, 486/33 MHz or better, 8MB ram, double-speed CD-ROM drive, VGA 640 × 480 monitor displaying 256 colors, MS-DOS. (IBM CD-ROM)

Physical Education Links on the Internet

Some helpful sites on the World Wide Web. Keep in mind that URLs (Internet addresses) do change and there is no way to assure the currency of these locations.

http://www.mhhe.com/socscience/hper
McGraw-Hill's physical education page

news: k12.ed.health-pe
Physical education newsgroup
physed-l-request@@ciao.trail.bc.ca
E-mail to subscribe to k–12 listserv

http://cs1.mum.edu/exss_dept/iahperd
Iowa AHPERD, with links to physical education related Listservs

http://espnet.sportszone.com
ESTNet SportsZone

www.sportsline.com
CBS Sportsline

The Sport Information Resource Centre (SIRC)

SIRC is the largest resource center in the world collecting and disseminating information in the areas of sport, physical education, physical fitness, health, wellness, and sports medicine. The SPORT Database is available on CompuServe (http://www.compuserve.com) or through SPORT Discus (CD-ROM) (http://www.silverplatter.com).

Glossary of Terms

Internet
A collection of computer networks connected throughout the world.

WWW
World Wide Web. The Internet construction that allows users to travel through the network via graphical displays of text and pictures. Uses documents written with HTML.

HTML

Hypertext markup language. The language that is used to create the World Wide Web documents.

HTTP

Hypertext transport protocol. The usual prefix for World Wide Web addresses.

URL

Universal resource locator. The address of an Internet resource.

Browser

An application program that allows the Internet user to navigate through the World Wide Web. Also called a web browser.

Web Site

A collection of HTML documents on the World Wide Web—found by pointing a web browser at the web site's URL.

GLOSSARY

The following words and phrases occur frequently in the instructional and extraclass physical education program. (A separate glossary for folk, line, and square dance terms is provided in chapter 29, and a glossary of computer technology terms is provided in appendix D.)

A

Accent
The emphasis given to a beat in a series of beats in a measure.

Accident
An unforeseen event occurring without the will or design of the person whose act causes it.

Active lifestyle
A lifestyle that includes physical activity as a regular part of daily routines.

Activity independence
To be physically active at one's own desire and not reliant on another person.

Act of God
A situation due to forces beyond the control of the defendant.

Advance
Move forward, usually with walking steps.

Advance organizer
Introductory information given to increase the ease with which new material, given at a later date, can be understood and learned.

Aerobic exercise
Exercise performed with an adequate supply of oxygen.

Agility
The ability to shift the body in different directions quickly and efficiently.

Agility apparatus
All types of indoor and outdoor climbing apparatus.

Anaerobic exercise
Exercise performed in the absence of oxygen.

Anorexia nervosa
An eating disorder characterized by loss of at least 25 percent of body weight, due to a preoccupation with body image and weight loss.

Apparatus work
The second part of a gymnastic lesson. Also, the second part of a Movement Education lesson, concerned with the application of movement ideas to large and small apparatus.

Arch
Two dancers join inside hands and raise their arms.

Asthma
A condition of the lungs that causes labored breathing and wheezing.

Asymmetry
A position or movement characterized by the unevenness of opposite parts of the body. Using a line drawn through the vertebral column, all twisting, curling, or held positions in which greater stress is given to the limbs on one side are asymmetrical positions.

Atrophy
A reduction in size.

Attack
Players who are designated as forward line players.

Attacking team
The team that has possession of the ball; also known as the offensive team.

B

Backcourt
The half of the basketball court farthest from the offensive basket.

Balance
The ability to maintain a stationary position or to perform purposeful movements while resisting the force of gravity. Also, the ability to hold the body in a fixed position. (The common expression is "weight bearing.")

Baseline
The end line of a basketball court.

Bases loaded
Runners on every base.

Basket
Circular goal located on the backboard.

Baton
A short, round stick passed between members of a relay team.

Beat
The constant, steady pulsation in a movement or musical accompaniment.

Benchmark
A term used to describe behavior that indicates performance toward a standard.

Block
One or two defensive players jump up at the same time as the spiker, with their hands raised and facing the oncoming ball.

Blocking
A legal method of stopping an opponent.

Boarding
Holding a player against the wall.

Body awareness
The way in which the body or parts of it can move (stretch, bend, twist, and turn).

Body composition
The relative percentage of fat, compared to other tissues of the body.

Body mechanics
The efficient and effective use of the body in maintaining good alignment and performing daily tasks.

Body of a lesson
The major part of a lesson where the skill or concept to be learned is emphasized.

Bound flow
A momentary pause in a sequence of movement.

Box
The specific area marked and designated as the catcher's area, the batter's area, or the coach's area.

Brainstorming
Dance ideas developed by a teacher and his class.

Breach of duty
A teacher's failure to fulfill her required duties to her students.

Bulimia
An eating disorder characterized by binge eating followed by self-induced vomiting or purging.

Buzz
Holding wieght on one foot while pushing with the other foot.

C

Calisthenics
Conditioning exercises designed to improve physical fitness.

Cardiac output
The volume of blood the heart pumps out each minute.

Cardiorespiratory endurance
The ability of the heart and lungs to sustain activity.

Cardiovascular fitness
The efficiency of the heart, lungs, and blood vessels.

Center
The middle position on the forward line, usually played by the tallest player on the team.

Center of gravity
The point on the body around which the weight of the body is equally distributed.

Cerebral palsy
Neurological impairment caused by damage to the motor areas of the brain.

Circuit training
Repeating one or more exercises as many times as possible within a time limit.

Clockwise
In the same direction as the movement of hands of a clock.

Closure
A short review session at the end of the lesson.

Command
A teaching method in which the teacher controls the subject to be learned and how it is to be learned.

Concept
The degree of meaning a person possesses about an experience.

Continuity
Movements following each other in succession.

Contra or longways
In dance, couples standing in a long line, with boys on one side and girls on the other.

Contributory negligence
Failure of an injured party to exercise due care and concern for her own welfare.

Cooperative game
A game stressing one or more elements of cooperative behavior.

Cooperative learning
An arrangement where students work together to help each other learn and achieve a common goal.

Corner
When the defending team causes the ball to go over the endline, the attacking team is awarded a free hit from the nearest corner of the field.

Corner kick
A placekick awarded to the attacking team after the defending team has sent the ball over its own goal line.

Counterclockwise
In the opposite direction as the movement of the hands of a clock.

Crease
The semicircular area around the goal area.

Creative dance
The expression of ideas and feelings through unstructured movement.

Creative games
Games invented by children.

Creative playground
A unique arrangement of outdoor apparatus (commercial or locally constructed).

Creativity
The degree of inventiveness.

Criterion-referenced test
A measure of a person's performance evaluated against a qualitative standard.

Cumulative record
A method of plotting a child's performance (skill or physical fitness items) at the beginning and end of each year.

Curl
An action that flexes or bends the body or its parts.

Curriculum
The total experience within the physical education program that is provided for all children.

D

Dance position
The relative body and hand position of one dancer to another.

Declarative knowledge
Theoretical knowledge associated with knowing what to do in order to perform a motor skill.

Defensive team (defense, defending team)
The team that does not have possession of the ball.

Development
The systematic and progressive acquisition of concepts and skills.

Diamond
The area inside the four bases.

Diaphysis
The center of bone growth located in the middle of the long bones.

Dink
A deception drop volley executed from a spiked position.

Direct free kick
A free kick from which a goal may be scored directly.

Direct method
A teaching method in which the choice of the activity and how it is performed is entirely the teacher's.

Discipline
A form of control imposed internally by an individual or externally by another person in control of the learning environment.

Dodge
A means of evading an oncoming tackler.

Double elimination tournament
A consolation bracket added to a single elimination tournament to assure that each team plays at least two games.

Double play
A defensive play by the fielding team, resulting in two outs.

Down
A method of starting play after the ball has been stopped. In football, each team is given four downs to advance the ball ten yards.

Down syndrome
Moderate retardation caused by a genetic factor.

Dribble
A means of advancing the ball or puck with a series of short taps.

Drive
Hitting the ball from a moderate to a long distance. Also, a quick dribbling movement toward the opponent's basket.

Duration recording
Recording the amount of time an event takes place.

E

Earned run
A run scored as a result of an offensive play and not as a result of an error committed by the defensive team.

Endurance
The ability to continue a muscular effort or movement over a prolonged period of time.

Entry activity
Free practice time prior to the beginning of a lesson.

Epilepsy
A condition of the nervous system characterized by seizures and convulsions.

Epiphysis
The center of growth located near the ends of the long bones.

Error
A mistake committed by the defensive team.

Established duty
A duty a teacher has to his pupils.

Evaluation
The subjective and objective assessment of program effectiveness and student progress.

Event recording
Recording the number of times an event takes place.

Exceptional child
A child who deviates from the normal intelligence, physical health, motor ability, or behavioral characteristics of the average or typical child.

Extraclass program
A cooperative and competitive program that occurs outside of normal curriculum time.

Extrinsic motivation
The desire to complete a task in order to gain an external reward.

F

Fair ball
Any legally batted ball that is touched, or lands, in fair territory.

Fan
A player who misses the third strike.

Fast break
A situation in which the defensive team gains possession of the ball and moves it into a scoring position before the opposing team can recover into a defensive position.

Feedback
Information about one's performance.

Feint
A deceptive movement to mislead an opponent.

Fielding
Gaining possession of the ball or puck.

Flexibility
The range of movement of a joint.

Flick
A method of putting the ball or puck into the air.

Flight
The ability to propel the body into the air.

Flow
The ability to link one movement to another with control and harmony.

Folk dance
Dance patterns of past cultures.

Force
The degree of effort or tension involved in a movement.

Forced out
A defensive player in possession of the ball touches a base before a runner who is forced to move to that base.

Forward and back
This figure may involve one or more dancers facing each other. Both advance four steps forward (or three steps and a bow) and four steps backward.

Foul
An illegal act, such as tripping or holding an opponent, that results in a direct free kick being awarded to the nonoffending team.

Foul ball
A hit ball that lands outside of fair territory.

Free hit
A hit awarded to the opposing team after a breach of the rules.

Free throw
An unguarded shot taken from the free throw line. If the shot is successful, the shooting team scores one point.

Frontcourt
The part of the basketball court nearest each team's goal.

Fundamental motor skills
Locomotor, nonlocomotor, and manipulative skills and movement patterns.

G

Gallop
A sliding movement performed in a forward direction.

Games of low organization
Activities such as relays, tag, and simple team games that involve one or more basic skills and a minimum of roles and playing strategies.

General space
The physical area in which a movement takes place.

Growth
An increase in size.

Guided discovery
A teaching method in which the teacher guides the learner through a series of activities.

H

Hash running
A team race, with markers and hidden directions located along the route.

Heading
Playing the ball by striking it with the head.

Health-related physical fitness
The ability to perform activities without undue fatigue and to show resistance to the development of disorders that limit one's functional capacity.

Heart rate
The number of times a person's heart beats in one minute.

Heats
Preliminary track-and-field events to determine who will compete in the final events.

High sticking
Raising the stick above shoulder level.

Hike
The movement of the ball from the center player to the quarterback.

Home
The original starting place of a dance.

Honor
Salute or bow to one's partner or to other dancers.

Hop
Transfer weight from one foot to the same foot.

Humanism
A philosophy that asserts the dignity and worth of human beings and their capacity for self-realization through reason.

Hyperopia
Farsightedness; distant objects can be seen clearly but nearby objects appear blurred.

I

IEP (individualized educational plan)
A systematic plan to meet the needs of children with special needs.

Illegal contact
Any contact of the ball in which it comes to a visible resting position.

Indirect free kick
A free kick from which a goal may not be scored directly.

Indirect method
A teaching method that allows the children to choose the activity, as well as how and what they will perform within the activity.

Individual games
Low-organization games played by one person with or without small equipment.

Individualized learning
A system of teaching that adapts to each learner's abilities, needs, and interests.

Infield
The playing area within and immediately adjacent to the diamond.

Infringement
An illegal act, such as being offside, that results in an indirect free kick being awarded to the nonoffending team.

In loco parentis
Acting in the place of the parent.

Inning
A division of the game in which both teams play until each has three players out.

Instructional unit
The organization of material around a central activity or theme of instruction.

Instructional variety
Refers to the variability or flexibility of instructional delivery during a lesson.

Intensity
The quality or force of music or movement.

Interschool athletics
Competition between schools in team and individual sports.

Interval recording
The systematic observation of events, conducted at various intervals of time.

Intramural program
Competitive or club activities offered during nonclass time, on a voluntary basis, and within the jurisdiction of one school.

Intrinsic motivation
An internal desire to achieve a given standard or goal.

Introductory activity
The first part of a lesson, which involves a general warm-up and lasts for approximately three to five minutes.

Isometric exercise
Contraction of muscles involving a push, pull, or twist against an object that does not move.

Isotonic exercise
Contraction of muscles that involves both shortening and lengthening the muscle fibers.

J

Jog
A slow, easy run.

Journal
A personal written record of a child's lived experiences.

Jump
A light transfer of weight from one foot or both feet to both feet.

Jump ball
A situation in which two opposing players simultaneously gain possession of the ball, and the referee tosses it up between the two players.

Jump shot
A shot taken while the player has both feet off the floor.

K

Kickoff
A short kick taken by the center forward at the center of the field. The kickoff is used to start the game, at halftime, and after each goal is scored.

Kyphosis
A marked curve of the upper back.

L

Ladder tournament
A tournament that uses a ladder to advance positions; players on lower rungs may challenge players on one or two rungs above them.

Lap
One complete circuit around the track.

Lateral
A sideways pass of the ball.

Lay-up
A shot taken close to the backboard. The ball is released off one hand and gently placed over the rim or against the backboard to allow it to rebound into the basket.

Lead-up game
A game that involves one or more concepts and skills of a major team sport.

Leap
A light transfer of weight from one foot to the other foot.

Learning disabilities
Inherited conditions that cause mild or moderate learning difficulties.

Lesson plan
A flexible daily plan that includes objectives, content, organizational procedures, teaching cues, evaluation, and references.

Level
The relative position of the body or any of its parts to the floor or apparatus. Level may be applied to either stationary activity or position.

Liability
A violation of an obligation to perform a duty.

Limitation method
A teaching method in which the choice of the activity or the way it is performed is limited by the teacher.

Linear motion
A movement in which the body or an object as a whole moves in a straight line.

Locomotor skills
Basic motor skills involving a change of position of the feet and/or a change of direction of the body (e.g., walking).

Lordosis
An exaggerated forward curve of the lower back.

M

Mainstreaming
Placing students with disabilities into the regular physical education program.

Malfeasance
An unlawful act resulting in injury or an adverse effect on a person.

Manipulative skills
Motor skills that involve the control of objects primarily with the hands and feet (e.g., bouncing a ball).
Maturation
The general progress from one stage of development to a higher, more complex stage. Maturation occurs as a function of time and is independent of experience.

Measure
A repetitive grouping of underlying beats.

Method
A general way of guiding and controlling the learning experiences of children.

Misfeasance
Improperly performing a lawful act.

Modified teaching unit
A unit of instruction that emphasizes one type of activity and provides a minor focus on one or more other activities.

Movement design
The way two or more dancers meet, greet, and part during a dance.

Movement Education
An approach to teaching physical education, that uses Laban's four elements of movement as the content and stresses exploratory teaching strategies.

Movement ideas
A movement concept related to one or more of Laban's basic movement elements—qualities, body awareness, space awareness, and relationships.

Movement training
The second part of a Movement Education lesson, which is concerned with the development of movement themes and activities.

Multiple teaching unit
A unit of instruction that includes two or more activities.

Muscular endurance
The ability of the muscular system to sustain performance.

Muscular strength
The ability of the muscles to overcome resistance.

Myopia
Nearsightedness; distant objects appear blurred, but nearby objects are seen clearly.

N

Negligence
An act, or the absence of one, that falls below the legal standard for the protection of others against unreasonable risk or harm.

Net recovery
A fair move to play the volleyball after it has been hit into the net by a teammate.

Neuromuscular skills
Motor skills under the voluntary control of the brain.

Nonfeasance
Failure to perform a required act.

Nonlocomotor skills
Movements of the body performed from a relatively stable base (e.g., twisting).

Norm-referenced tests
A test battery that uses quantitative data to serve as a standard by which individual performances are measured.

Novelty track meet
A track and field day in which children participate in a variety of novelty events.

Nutrients
The constituents of food that sustain human physiology (i.e., proteins, carbohydrates, fats, vitamins, minerals, and water).

Nutrition
The relationship between physiological functioning and the essential elements of the food we eat.

O

Obesity
A condition characterized by excessive bodily fat tissue.

Obstacle course
An arrangement of small and large equipment designed to improve physical fitness and skill development.

Obstruction
When a player runs between an opponent and the ball.

Offense (offensive team)
The team that has possession of the ball.

Offside
When a player is illegally in the opponent's half of the field and there are fewer than two opposing players in front of the player at the moment a teammate plays the ball in a forward direction.

Olympic meet
A tournament that includes a number of individual, dual, and team events.

One-on-one
A situation in which one offensive player tries to outmaneuver one defensive player.

Ontogenetic skills
Motor skills that are dependent upon learning and the environment for development (e.g., roller skating).

Open
Partners stand side-by-side, with their inside hands joined. Girls stand to the boys' right.

Opposite
The person or couple directly across the square.

Out
The retirement of a batter after three strikes. Also, a base runner who is caught or forced out.

Outfield
The fair territory located beyond the infield.

Overload
A performance of an exercise or activity that requires the individual to exert more than a normal effort.

P

Pace
The rate of speed the runner sets for a particular distance run.

Passing zone
An area on the track within which the baton must be passed.

Pathways
Directional routes that are straight, curved, or zigzag.

Pattern
The arrangement of a series of movements in relation to shape, level, and pathway.

Penalty kick
If a foul is committed by the defending team within the penalty area, the attacking team is given a direct free kick from the twelve-yard mark, directly in front of the goal. All other players must be outside the penalty area until the kick is taken.

Perceptual-motor response
The process of perceiving a stimulus and translating it into a motor response.

Personal activity log (PAL)
A personal journal to record a child's activity patterns and to establish future goals.

Personal space
The area around an individual that can be used while keeping one part of the body in a fixed position on the floor or apparatus; also known as limited space.

Phrase
A group of measures that fit together into a meaningful whole.

Phylogenetic skills
Movement behaviors that develop in a predictable and somewhat automatic sequence (e.g., walking).

Physical awkwardness
A term used to describe children who do not suffer from any known neuromuscular disorder, yet exhibit poor motor coordination and fitness.

Physical disability
Suffering from a disease or physical disability.

Physical education,
The part of the educational process that contributes to the physical, emotional, social, and mental development of each child through the medium of physical activity.

Physical fitness
The degree to which a person is physically able to function.

Physically gifted
Possessing a unique talent or ability in physical fitness.

Pinch hitter
A substitute hitter.

Pivot
A player who has possession of the ball may move one foot while keeping the other foot in contact with the floor.

Play day
An interschool event in which children from two or more schools play on the same team.

Pop-up
A high fly ball that lands in or near the infield.

Portfolio
A purposeful collection of children's work that shows both progress and achievement.

Post
The post player is normally a pivot player positioned near the key with his or her back toward the basket.

Posture
The relative alignment of the body segments.

Power
The ability of the body to apply a maximum muscular contraction with the quickest possible speed.

Probing
Encouraging students to elaborate upon a given answer.

Procedural knowledge
The knowledge required to physically perform a motor skill.

Proximate cause
A situation in which the teacher's behavior is the main factor causing injury to a student.

Punt
A kick performed by dropping the ball and contacting it with the top of the foot before it touches the ground.

Pyramid tournament
A form of competition in which participants are arranged in a pyramid structure. Players are permitted to challenge others in the row above.

Qualities
How the body can move. It is the ability to move quickly or slowly, the ability to perform light or heavy movements, and the flow with which one movement is linked to another.

RBI
Runs batted in by a player.

Rebound
A shot attempted at the basket that falls back into the court area.

Reflection
A process of personal self-evaluation used for the purpose of improvement.

Relationship
The position of the body in relation to the floor, apparatus, or other performers.

Relay activities
Activities that involve a race between two or more participants or teams.

Respiratory rate
The number of times an individual inhales in one minute.

Resting heart rate
The number of times a person's heart beats per minute while in a quiet state of resting.

Rhythmic
Performing a variety of body movements in time to a specific rhythmic accompaniment.

Rotary motion
A movement that traces out an arc or circle around an axis or fixed point.

Round-robin tournament
A tournament in which every player plays every other player in the tournament.

Run
A transfer of weight from one foot to the other, with a momentary loss of contact with the floor by both feet.

S

Safety
When a defensive player in possession of the ball is trapped behind his or her own goal line. The attacking team is awarded two points.

Safety training
Teaching children to move and land safely and efficiently. In a broader context, it refers to the individual's safety on or around apparatus and to the individual's concern for the safety of other participants.

Scoliosis
A lateral curvature of the spinal column.

Scoop
A method of raising the ball into the air.

Scratch
A foul committed by stepping over the scratch line.

Scrimmage line
The line on which each down begins. The defending team must remain behind this line until the ball has left the center's hands.

Self-image
The feeling and/or opinion a child has about himself or herself.

Sequence
A series of movements performed in succession.

Set shot
A shot taken from a stationary position.

Setup
This is normally the second hit by a team and is directed to a forward player, who then may attempt a spike or a volley over the net.

Shape
The image presented by the position of the body when traveling or stationary.

Side out
A violation committed by the serving team.

Singing games
A form of folk dance considered to be a forerunner of the more complicated traditional dances.

Single elimination tournament
A tournament in which a player or team is eliminated from further competition after one loss.

Skill development
The second part of a lesson.

Skinfold calipers
An instrument used to measure amount of body fat.

Skip
A combination of a long step and a short hop, with the lead foot alternating after each hop.

Slide
A combination of a step and a short leap, which can be performed forward, sideways, or backward.

Sociogram
A technique used to study the relationships within groups.

Solid teaching unit
An extensive period of instruction devoted exclusively to one type of activity.

Space
The area in which a movement takes place.

Spatial awareness
The ability to move the body or its parts in specific directions.

Speed
The ability to perform successive movements of the same pattern in the shortest period of time.

Spike
A volleyball hit downward into the opponent's court.

Spiral
A forward pass in which the football moves with a spiral action, with the point of the ball leading.

Sports day
An interschool competitive event in which teams represent their own schools.

Square
Four couples, each forming one side of a square.

Square dance
A type of American folk dance.

Stance
The starting position of a football player.

Star or wheel
Two or more dancers join right hands in the center of the set and walk forward or backward as directed.

Station work
A technique of organizing the class into small working units.

Steal
A player advances to another base after the ball leaves the pitcher's hand and before the infield player can tag the advancing player with the ball.

Stimuli
Objects, stories, or paintings used in a creative dance lesson to stimulate movement ideas.

Strength
The amount of force a muscle or group of muscles can exert.

Stretch
Move the body or parts of it from a flexed to an extended position.

Stride
The distance between the right and left foot imprints on a track. The measurement is made from the toe of the back foot to the heel imprint of the lead foot.

Structure
Structuring refers to helping children organize where lesson content fits into their own learning experiences.

Success rate
The rate at which a child understands and correctly completes tasks.

Supplies
Materials that are expendable within one or two years.

Swing
A rhythmic rotation of a couple with a walking step, buzz step, two-step, or skip. The swing may be a one-hand, two-hand, elbow, or waist swing.

Symmetry
In Movement Education, symmetry describes a movement or balance position in which both sides of the body would look identical if an imaginary line were drawn through the middle of the body.

T

Tackle
A method of getting the ball away from an opponent.

Task cards
A technique in which instructions or challenges are written on cards.

Teaching formation
A specific way of organizing the class such as line, circle, or shuttle patterns.

Team teaching
The organization of teachers and students into instructional groups that permits maximum utilization of staff abilities.

Technique
Part of a method.

Tempo
The rate of speed of music or movement.

Theme
A central movement idea.

Throw-in
A two-hand overhand free throw awarded to the team that did not cause the ball to cross over the sideline.

Time
The speed with which a movement takes place (quick, slow, sudden, or sustained).

Time on-task
The amount of learning time devoted to the task by a student.

Tort
A legal wrong.

Touchback
When a defensive player intercepts the ball behind his or her own goal line and places it on the ground rather than attempting to run it out over the goal line. One point is awarded to the attacking team.

Touchdown
When a member of the attacking team carries the ball over the goal line or a teammate catches a ball while in the end zone. The attacking team is awarded six points.

Tournament
A method of organizing small and large groups for competition.

Trapping
Stopping the ball using any part of the body except the hands.

Traveling
Moving in various directions by transferring weight from one part of the body to another. Also, a player who takes more than one step with the ball without dribbling it.

Turn
A rotation of the body and loss of the initial fixed point of contact (e.g., turning in a full arc).

Twist
One part of the body is held in a fixed position on the floor or apparatus and the rest of the body is turned away from the fixed position (e.g., twisting the trunk to the side and back).

Underlying beat
The steady pulse of a musical accompaniment.

Varsovienne position
The boy stands slightly behind and to the left of his partner. While both are facing the same direction, the girl raises both hands to about shoulder height and the boy joins his right hand with the girl's right hand and his left hand with the girl's left hand.

Volley
A type of kick in which the ball is contacted while it is in the air.

Walk
A rhythmic transfer of weight from one foot to the other. One foot is always in contact with the ground. Also, this occurs

when four balls are called on the batter, who advances to first base.

Weight
The degree of muscle tension involved in the production of a movement, or the maintenance of a static position involving tension.

Wellness
A positive way of life that involves seeking and maintaining the highest level of health and well-being.

Wide
An action that moves the arm or legs away from the trunk.

Zone defense
A type of defense in which the defensive players are assigned specific areas of the court to guard.

INDEX

GAME ACTIVITIES

Classroom Games

Balloon Hit, 305
Beanbag Basket Relay, 303
Beanbag Pile, 304
Charades, 306
Clappers, 305
Crambo, 305
Fox and Rabbit, 302
Hat Race, 305
Human Checkers, 306
Knots, 304
Mirror Mirror, 304
My Ship is Loaded, 305
Poorhouse, 305
Puzzled Words, 306
Rattlesnake and Bumblebee, 306
Ringmaster, 304
Spell Act, 306
Squirrel and Nut, 304
Water Cycle, 304
Who's Leading?, 305

Cooperative Games

Airplanes, 362
Animals, 358
Ball Balance, 358
Beanbag Helper, 360
Blind Flight, 366
Bomb in the Box, 366
Clock, 367
Co-op Tag, 362
Cross-Over Blanket Volleyball, 362
Cross-Over Dodgeball, 363
Doubles Hopscotch, 358
Eight-Legged Caterpillar, 361
Frog, Jump, Slide, 368
Fish Catchers, 360
Geometry Class, 367
Give and Take, 366
Juggle a Number, 361
Jump Ball, 367
Modified Musical Chairs, 361
Nine-Person Skip, 362
Paga-Ajuda, 368
Pass a Person, 361
Passing in the Square, 364
Perpetual Motion Machine, 358
Recycled Snakeskins, 360
Stick Exchange, 366
The Worm, 367

Ting, Ting, Ting, 368
Triangle Tag, 362
Tug-o-Peace, 361
Twister, 361

Locomotor Games

Automobiles, 323
Back Pass the Beanbag, 332
Chain Tag, 347
Crazy Circle, 337
Crows and Cranes, 324
Do As I Do, 324
Find Your Letter, 324
Foxes and Squirrels, 323
Fragile Rock, 323
Geometrical Shapes, 347
Hot Spot, 325
King, 346
Loose Caboose, 332
Mouse and Cheese, 337
Mousetrap, 324
Numbers, 336
Open the Window, 349
Parachute Games, 570
    circle sitting, 571
    circus tent, 572
    dance activities, 573
    dash under, 572
    number exchange, 572
    parachute golf, 572
    popcorn, 572
    snatch club, 572
Red Light, 323
Red Stop, Green Go, 336
Running Steps, 335
Simple Tag, 323
Squirrel in the Forest, 320
Steal the Bacon, 336
Stick Touch Tag, 335
Traffic Lights, 323
Without Hands, 335

Manipulative Games

Alphabet Game, 342
American Hopscotch, 329
Ball Pass, 338
Barnyard Golf, 338
Bat Ball, 343
Battle Ball, 341

Beanbag Basket, 328
Bombardment, 338
Borden Ball, 347
Bounce Netball, 343
Boundary Ball, 341
Butterflies, 326
California Kickball, 346
Call Ball, 329
Crab Soccer, 329
Dandy Shandy, 344
Dribble Tag, 326
Elastic Ropes, 341
European Handball, 348
Five-Hole Marbles, 342
Four Goal Soccer, 339, 389
Four Square, 337
Goal, 340
Goodminton, 349
Guard Ball, 339
Hoop Bounce, 325
Hot Ball, 325
Instant Goal, 340
Inventive Games, 344
Developmental Level 1, 315, 331
Developmental Level 2, 317, 353
Developmental Level 3, 317, 353
Jump the Shot, 327
Keep Away, 339
Long Ball, 343
Magic Carpet, 340
Mimic the Word, 340
Name It, 328
Pirates, 326
Place Kickball, 341
Progressive Dodgeball, 337
Queenie I.O., 328
Quoit Tennis, 327
Ricochet, 338
Roll Ball, 325
Simple Dodgeball, 327
Snowball, 328
Soap Box Soccer, 329
Softball Croquet, 342
Solid, Liquid, Gases, 347
Steal the Crowns, 327
Tail of the Rat, 338
Three Down, 325
Throw, Catch, Run, 327
Trick the Guard, 340
Tug-of-War, 346
Two Square, 325
Ultimate, 352

DANCE ACTIVITIES

GYMNASTIC ACTIVITIES

Stunts and Tumbling

Alligator Crawl, 515
Ankle Stand, 532
Back Layout, 537
Back Rocker, 508
Back Roller, 505
Backward Diagonal Roll, 507
Backward Extension, 510
Backward Roll, 509
Backward Roll to Knee Scale, 509
Backward Shoulder Roll, 508
Backward Straddle Roll, 509
Bouncing Ball, 516
Camel Walk, 515
Carousel, 520
Cartwheel, 512
Centipede, 524
Chinese Get-Up, 517
Circle Roll, 519
Coffee Grinder, 519
Consecutive Rolls, 506
Co-op Hopping, 521
Crab Walk, 517
Dive Forward Roll, 506
Double Crab Walk, 520
Double Wheelbarrow, 522
Egg Roll, 507
Elephant Walk, 521
Eskimo Roll, 506
Finger Touch, 508
Flying Dutchman, 538
Forward Drop, 523
Forward Roll, 505
Forward Roll Looking Back Through Legs, 505
Forward Roll to Jump Tuck, 506
Forward Roll to One-Leg Stand, 506
Frog Jump, 519
Frog Stand, 533
Front Support to Stand, 520
Half Cartwheel, 512
Hand-Knee Balance, 531
Handspring, 526
Handspring Over Partner, 525
Handstand, 535
Handstand Roll Out to Jump, 536
Handstand to Bridge, 536
Headspring, 527
Headstand, 533
Headstand Variations, 535
Heel Click, 524
Hitchhiker Walk, 522
Horseback Ride, 522
Jackknife, 524
Judo Roll, 508

Jump Through, 525
Jump Turn, 515
Kip, 528
Knee and Shoulder Stand, 538
Knee Handspring, 525
Knee Jump, 517
Knee Stand, 539
Knee Walk, 528
Lame Puppy Walk, 516
Leap Frog, 516
Log Roll, 504
L-Support, 536
Measuring Worm, 519
Mule Kick, 511
Neckspring, 527
One-Foot Jump, 518
Pig Walk, 521
Prone Knee Fall, 521
Puppy Dog Walk, 515
Push-Up Stand, 532
Pyramids
    double, 540
    group, 541
    individual, 539
    quadruple, 541
    triple, 541
Rabbit Jump, 518
Rear Support, 531
Rocking Chair, 517
Rolling the Log, 518
Round-Off, 513
Scale Stand, 530
Seal Slap, 524
Seat Stand, 532
Siamese Twins, 522
Side Kick, 512
Side Roll, 505
Side Stand, 537
Single Knee Balance, 531
Single Leg Balance, 530
Single Mule Kick, 511
Stork Stand, 529
Swing Turn, 534
Table, 537
Teddy Bear Stand, 532
The Bridge, 534
Thread the Needle, 530
Triple Roll, 510
Tuck V-Sit, 528
Turk Stand, 530
Twin Balance, 531
Upside-Down Touch, 520
Upswing, 523
V-Sit, 534
Walking Down the Wall, 534

Wheel Stunt, 532
Wring the Dishrag, 516

Small Equipment

Beanbag activities, 552
    applying movement skills, 554
    partner activities, 554
    stunts, 553
Hoop activities, 566
    applying movement skills, 567
    individual activities, 566
    partner activities, 567
Indian clubs, milk cartons, and traffic cone
    activities, 574
Juggling activities, 575
Parachute activities, 570
    chest raiser, 572
    curl-ups, 572
    fruit basket, 571
    making waves, 571
    mushroom, 571
    push-ups, 572
    row the boat, 572
    side stretcher, 572
    umbrella, 571
    V-sit, 572
Rope-jumping activities, 555
    alternative step, 558
    applying movement skills, 565
    can can, 559
    crossed arms, 562
    crossed legs, 561
    heel toe, 559
    long rope jumping skills, 563
    one-foot hop, 560
    partner activities, 563
    pepper, 562
    rocker step, 560
    skier, 557
    spread legs step, 561
    swing step, 558
    two-foot basic step, 557
Wand activities, 567
    back touch, 568
    dishrag, 570
    double foot balance, 568
    finger balance, 568
    floor touch, 570
    foot balance, 568
    jump through stick, 569
    matching shapes, 570
    thread the needle, 569
    twist away, 569

INDEX